WORD BIBLICAL COMMENTARY

General Editors
David A. Hubbard
Glenn W. Barker †

Old Testament Editor
John D. W. Watts

New Testament Editor
Ralph P. Martin

WORD BIBLICAL COMMENTARY

VOLUME 42

Ephesians

ANDREW T. LINCOLN

WORD BOOKS, PUBLISHER • DALLAS, TEXAS

Word Biblical Commentary
EPHESIANS
Copyright © 1990 by Word, Incorporated

All rights reserved. No portion of this book may be reproduced in any form without the written permission of the publisher.

Library of Congress Cataloging-in-Publication Data
Main entry under title:

Word biblical commentary.

  Includes bibliographies.
  1. Bible—Commentaries—Collected works.
BS491.2.W67   220.7′7   81-71768
ISBN 0–8499–0241–X (vol. 42)   AACR2

Printed in the United States of America

The author's own translation of the text appears in italic type under the heading "Translation," as well as in brief Scripture quotations in the body of the commentary, except where otherwise indicated.

8 9 9 QBP 11 10 9 8

FOR DAVID AND PAUL
εἰς ἄνδρα τέλειον (Eph 4:13)

Contents

Editorial Preface   ix
Author's Preface   x
Abbreviations   xiii
Main Bibliography   xxix

INTRODUCTION   xxxv
1. Content/Structure/Genre/Style   xxxv
2. Relation to Colossians and the Rest of the Pauline Corpus   xlvii
3. Authorship/Pseudonymity/Canon   lix
4. Setting and Purposes   lxxiii
5. The Thought of Ephesians   lxxxvii

COMMENTARY   1
Prescript (1:1, 2)   1
Blessing of God for His Salvation in Christ (1:3–14)   8
Thanksgiving with Prayer for Believers' Knowledge of God and Their Awareness of the Church's Significance (1:15–23)   45
God's Gracious Salvation as Resurrection and Exaltation with Christ (2:1–10)   83
The Gaining of the Gentiles' Privileges of Participation in God's New Temple Through Christ's Reconciliation (2:11–22)   122
Paul as Minister of the Mystery to the Gentiles (3:1–13)   166
Further Prayer—for the Completeness of the Readers' Experience of God—with Doxology (3:14–21)   196
The Church's Calling to Maintenance of the Unity It Already Possesses (4:1–16)   222
Exhortation to Live According to the New Humanity Rather than the Old (4:17–24)   270
Practical Injunctions About the Old and New Life (4:25–5:2)   292
From Darkness to Light (5:3–14)   316
Wise and Spirit-Filled Living (5:15–20)   337
Household Relationships—Wives and Husbands (5:21–33)   350
Household Relationships—Children and Parents (6:1–4)   395
Household Relationships—Slaves and Masters (6:5–9)   411
Concluding Appeal to Stand Firm in the Battle against Spiritual Powers (6:10–20)   429
Postscript (6:21–24)   461

Indexes   469

Editorial Preface

The launching of the *Word Biblical Commentary* brings to fulfillment an enterprise of several years' planning. The publishers and the members of the editorial board met in 1977 to explore the possibility of a new commentary on the books of the Bible that would incorporate several distinctive features. Prospective readers of these volumes are entitled to know what such features were intended to be; whether the aims of the commentary have been fully achieved time alone will tell.

First, we have tried to cast a wide net to include as contributors a number of scholars from around the world who not only share our aims, but are in the main engaged in the ministry of teaching in university, college, and seminary. They represent a rich diversity of denominational allegiance. The broad stance of our contributors can rightly be called evangelical, and this term is to be understood in its positive, historic sense of a commitment to Scripture as divine revelation, and to the truth and power of the Christian gospel.

Then, the commentaries in our series are all commissioned and written for the purpose of inclusion in the *Word Biblical Commentary*. Unlike several of our distinguished counterparts in the field of commentary writing, there are no translated works, originally written in a non-English language. Also, our commentators were asked to prepare their own rendering of the original biblical text and to use those languages as the basis of their own comments and exegesis. What may be claimed as distinctive with this series is that it is based on the biblical languages, yet it seeks to make the technical and scholarly approach to a theological understanding of Scripture understandable by—and useful to—the fledgling student, the working minister, and colleagues in the guild of professional scholars and teachers as well.

Finally, a word must be said about the format of the series. The layout, in clearly defined sections, has been consciously devised to assist readers at different levels. Those wishing to learn about the textual witnesses on which the translation is offered are invited to consult the section headed *Notes*. If the readers' concern is with the state of modern scholarship on any given portion of Scripture, they should turn to the sections on *Bibliography* and *Form/Structure/Setting*. For a clear exposition of the passage's meaning and its relevance to the ongoing biblical revelation, the *Comment* and concluding *Explanation* are designed expressly to meet that need. There is therefore something for everyone who may pick up and use these volumes.

If these aims come anywhere near realization, the intention of the editors will have been met, and the labor of our team of contributors rewarded.

General Editors: *David A. Hubbard*
Glenn W. Barker †
Old Testament: *John D. W. Watts*
New Testament: *Ralph P. Martin*

Author's Preface

The letter to the Ephesians, with its lofty themes and lofty language, has evoked equally lofty praise. While few would indulge in the extravagance of praising it as "the divinest composition of man" (cf. S. T. Coleridge, *Table Talk*, May 25, 1830, in *Specimens of the Table Talk of the Late Samuel Taylor Coleridge*, ed. H. N. Coleridge [London, 1835] 88), many more would be prepared to agree that it is "the crown of Paulinism" (cf. C. H. Dodd, "Ephesians," *The Abingdon Bible Commentary*, ed. F. C. Eiselen, E. Lewis, and D. G. Downey [New York: Abingdon, 1928] 1224–25). Others, however, have not found Ephesians so congenial. Some, though sympathetic to its message, struggle with its apparently turgid style and abstract truths (cf., e.g., W. Sanday and A. Headlam, *Romans* [Edinburgh: T. & T. Clark, 1895] lv); others see its emphasis on the Church as a distortion of Paul's thought which, they believe, may well need reversing rather than ratifying (cf., e.g., E. Käsemann, *Perspectives on Paul* [ET; London: SCM, 1971] 120–21), while one scholar, because of the difficulties surrounding the purpose of the letter, depicts it as "the Waterloo of commentators" (cf. E. J. Goodspeed, *The Meaning of Ephesians* [Chicago: University of Chicago Press, 1933] 15).

My own theologically oriented assessment of the letter's impact will be found in the final brief comments of the *Introduction*. But commentators' feelings about and assessments of the text on which they have worked are inevitably colored by their own circumstances. I have experienced both the attractions and the difficulties of Ephesians, and at the same time the process of writing about them has had its peaks and troughs. The commission to write this commentary has accompanied me through a transatlantic move from an American seminary to the quite different demands of an English theological college, and through a further move to a British university. It has also accompanied me through an extended period of domestic trauma. To take up the language of the epistle, the work on the commentary has had its times of being exhilarated by the exposure to "the heavenlies" and its times of battling it out "in the evil days." During the latter I have indeed wondered whether I had met my Waterloo!

I am grateful, therefore, to the editor, Professor R. P. Martin, for his trust in and encouragement of my contribution to the series, and for his patience with my "mismanagement of career moves," each of which meant missing out on extended sabbatical leaves which could have been devoted to the completion of this project. The pleasure of having the editor as a colleague in Sheffield during the last eighteen months has also acted as a spur to finishing the writing. Ephesians' style of writing can be contagious. I am grateful, therefore, also to J. Christopher Thomas, whose reading of the rough draft of the commentary has, in particular, spared readers from having too many lengthy sentences inflicted on them.

My completion of the latter stages of the work owes much to the friendship and love of Carol, to whom and for whom I am thankful.

Of the many writings on Ephesians which have contributed to this commentary, I am indebted most to three other commentaries—to the older English commentary by J. A. Robinson for its lucid syntactical and exegetical insights, and to the more recent commentaries by two German Catholic scholars, J. Gnilka and R. Schnackenburg, for their thorough discussions of the concepts of the letter in their first-century setting. As far as my own contribution is concerned, I shall be pleased if, as well as helping the reader to think the writer's thoughts after him, and thereby to be in a better position to interact with those thoughts, this commentary is able to demonstrate the value of keeping an eye on the rhetorical purpose of the flow of thought. I hope, too, that for some readers it will become evident that a decision in favor of a post-Pauline setting in no way diminishes and may well, in fact, enhance the value of the letter's message for the Church.

In comparison with those in some of the other volumes in this series, the *Explanation* sections in this commentary are longer. In them I have attempted to provide the reader with the fruit of the more detailed earlier sections and to pick out the particular theological emphases of each passage. I trust that the ability to read through the *Explanations* in order to gain relatively quickly an understanding of the thrust of particular passages and a sense of the overall flow of thought in the letter will compensate for the small degree of repetition that is involved.

Sheffield, England.
February, 1990.

ANDREW T. LINCOLN

Abbreviations

A. General Abbreviations

A	Codex Alexandrinus	infra	below
ad	comment on	in loc.	*in loco*, in the place cited
Akkad.	Akkadian	Jos.	Josephus
א	Codex Sinaiticus	lat	Latin
Ap. Lit.	Apocalyptic Literature	loc. cit.	the place cited
Apoc.	Apocrypha	LXX	Septuagint
Aq.	Aquila's Greek Translation of the OT	M	Mishnah
		masc.	masculine
Arab.	Arabic	mg.	margin
Aram.	Aramaic	MS(S)	manuscript(s)
B	Codex Vaticanus	MT	Masoretic text (of the Old Testament)
C	Codex Ephraemi Syri		
c.	*circa*, about	n.	note
cent.	century	n.d.	no date
cf.	*confer*, compare	Nestle	Nestle (ed.), *Novum Testamentum Graece*[26] rev. by K. and B. Aland
chap(s).	chapter(s)		
cod., codd.	codex, codices		
contra	in contrast to	no.	number
CUP	Cambridge University Press	n.s.	new series
		NT	New Testament
D	Codex Bezae	obs.	obsolete
DSS	Dead Sea Scrolls	o.s.	old series
ed.	edited by, editor(s)	OT	Old Testament
e.g.	*exempli gratia*, for example	p., pp.	page, pages
et al.	*et alii*, and others	*pace*	with due respect to, but differing from
ET	English translation		
EV	English Versions of the Bible	// , par(s).	parallel(s)
		par.	paragraph
f., ff.	following (verse or verses, pages, etc.)	passim	elsewhere
		pl.	plural
fem.	feminine	Pseudep.	Pseudepigrapha
frag.	fragments	Q	Quelle ("Sayings" source for the Gospels)
FS	*Festschrift*, volume written in honor of		
		q.v.	*quod vide*, which see
ft.	foot, feet	rev.	revised, reviser, revision
gen.	genitive	Rom.	Roman
Gr.	Greek	RVmg	Revised Version margin
hap. leg.	*hapax legomenon*, sole occurrence	Sam.	Samaritan recension
		sc.	*scilicet*, that is to say
Heb.	Hebrew	Sem.	Semitic
Hitt.	Hittite	sing.	singular
ibid.	*ibidem*, in the same place	Sumer.	Sumerian
id.	*idem*, the same	s.v.	*sub verbo*, under the word
i.e.	*id est*, that is	sy	Syriac
impf.	imperfect	Symm.	Symmachus

Tg.	Targum	v, vv	verse, verses
Theod.	Theodotion	viz.	*videlicet,* namely
TR	Textus Receptus	vg	Vulgate
tr.	translator, translated by	v.l.	*varia lectio,* alternative reading
UBSGT	The United Bible Societies Greek Text	vol.	volume
Ugar.	Ugaritic	x	times (2x = two times, etc.)
UP	University Press		
u.s.	*ut supra,* as above		

Note: The textual notes and numbers used to indicate individual manuscripts are those found in the apparatus criticus of *Novum Testamentum Graece,* ed. E. Nestle and K. Aland et al. (Stuttgart: Deutsche Bibelgesellschaft, 1979[26]). This edition of the Greek New Testament is the basis for the *Translation* sections.

B. Abbreviations for Translations and Paraphrases

ASV	American Standard Version, American Revised Version (1901)	Moffatt	J. Moffatt, *A New Translation of the Bible* (NT 1913)
		NAB	The New American Bible
AV	Authorized Version = KJV	NEB	The New English Bible
GNB	Good News Bible = Today's English Version	NIV	The New International Version (1978)
JB	Jerusalem Bible	NJB	New Jerusalem Bible (1985)
JPS	Jewish Publication Society, *The Holy Scriptures*	Phillips	J. B. Phillips, *The New Testament in Modern English*
KJV	King James Version (1611) = AV	RSV	Revised Standard Version (NT 1946, OT 1952, Apoc. 1957)
Knox	R. A. Knox, *The Holy Bible: A Translation from the Latin Vulgate in the Light of the Hebrew and Greek Original*	RV	Revised Version, 1881–85
		TEV	Today's English Version

C. Abbreviations of Commonly Used Periodicals, Reference Works, and Serials

AAS	*Acta apostolicae sedis*		antiken Judentums und des Urchristentums
AARSR	American Academy of Religion Studies in Religion	AGSU	Arbeiten zur Geschichte des Spätjudentums und Urchristentums
AASOR	Annual of the American Schools of Oriental Research	AH	F. Rosenthal, *An Aramaic Handbook*
AB	Anchor Bible		
ABR	*Australian Biblical Review*	AHR	*American Historical Review*
AbrN	*Abr-Nahrain*	AHW	W. von Soden, *Akkadisches Handwörterbuch*
ACNT	Augsburg Commentary on the New Testament	AION	*Annali dell'istituto orientale di Napoli*
AcOr	*Acta orientalia*		
ACW	Ancient Christian Writers	AJA	*American Journal of Archaeology*
ADAJ	Annual of the Department of Antiquities of Jordan	AJAS	*American Journal of Arabic Studies*
AER	*American Ecclesiastical Review*		
AfO	*Archiv für Orientforschung*	AJBA	*Australian Journal of Biblical Archaeology*
AGJU	Arbeiten zur Geschichte des		

Abbreviations

AJBI	*Annual of the Japanese Biblical Institute*	*ASS*	*Acta sanctae sedis*
AJP	*American Journal of Philology*	*AsSeign*	*Assemblées du Seigneur*
AJSL	*American Journal of Semitic Languages and Literature*	*ASSR*	*Archives des sciences sociales des religions*
AJT	*American Journal of Theology*	*ASTI*	*Annual of the Swedish Theological Institute*
ALBO	Analecta lovaniensia biblica et orientalia	ATAbh	Alttestamentliche Abhandlungen
ALGHJ	Arbeiten zur Literatur und Geschichte des hellenistischen Judentums	ATANT	Abhandlungen zur Theologie des Alten und Neuen Testaments
ALUOS	Annual of Leeds University Oriental Society	ATD	Das Alte Testament Deutsch
AnBib	Analecta biblica	ATDan	*Acta Theologica Danica*
AnBoll	Analecta Bollandiana	*ATJ*	*African Theological Journal*
ANEP	J. B. Pritchard (ed.), *Ancient Near East in Pictures*	*ATR*	*Anglican Theological Review*
ANESTP	J. B. Pritchard (ed.), *Ancient Near East Supplementary Texts and Pictures*	*AUSS*	*Andrews University Seminary Studies*
ANET	J. B. Pritchard (ed.), *Ancient Near Eastern Texts*	BA	*Biblical Archaeologist*
ANF	The Ante-Nicene Fathers	BAC	Biblioteca de autores cristianos
Ang	*Anglicum*	BAGD	W. Bauer, *A Greek-English Lexicon of the New Testament and Other Early Christian Literature*, ET, ed. W. F. Arndt and F. W. Gingrich; 2d ed. rev. F. W. Gingrich and F. W. Danker (University of Chicago, 1979)
AnOr	Analecta orientalia		
ANQ	*Andover Newton Quarterly*		
ANRW	*Aufstieg und Niedergang der römischen Welt*, ed. H. Temporini and W. Haase, Berlin		
ANT	Arbeiten zur Neutestamentlichen Textforschung	BAH	Bibliothèque archéologique et historique
Anton	*Antonianum*	*BangTF*	*Bangalore Theological Forum*
AOAT	Alter Orient und Altes Testament	*BAR*	*Biblical Archaeology Review*
AOS	American Oriental Series	BASOR	*Bulletin of the American Schools of Oriental Research*
AP	J. Marouzeau (ed.), *L'année philologique*	BASP	*Bulletin of the American Society of Papyrologists*
APOT	R. H. Charles (ed.), *Apocrypha and Pseudepigrapha of the Old Testament*	BBB	Bonner biblische Beiträge
		BCSR	*Bulletin of the Council on the Study of Religion*
ARG	*Archiv für Reformationsgeschichte*	BDB	F. Brown, S. R. Driver, and C. A. Briggs, *Hebrew and English Lexicon of the Old Testament* (Oxford: Clarendon, 1907)
ARM	Archives royales de Mari		
ArOr	*Archiv orientální*		
ARSHLL	Acta Reg. Societatis Humaniorum Litterarum Lundensis	BDF	F. Blass, A. Debrunner, and R. W. Funk, *A Greek Grammar of the New Testament* (University of Chicago/University of Cambridge, 1961)
ARW	*Archiv für Religionswissenschaft*		
ASNU	Acta seminarii neotestamentici upsaliensis		

BDR	F. Blass, A. Debrunner, and F. Rehkopf, *Grammatik des neutestamentlichen Griechisch*	*BRev*	*Bible Review*
		BS	Biblische Studien
		BSac	*Biblica Sacra*
BeO	*Bibbia e oriente*	*BSO(A)S*	*Bulletin of the School of Oriental (and African) Studies*
BET	Beiträge zur biblischen Exegese und Theologie		
		BSR	Bibliothèque de sciences religieuses
BETL	Bibliotheca ephemeridum theologicarum lovaniensium		
		BT	*The Bible Translator*
BEvT	Beiträge zur evangelischen Theologie	*BTB*	*Biblical Theology Bulletin*
		BU	Biblische Untersuchungen
BFCT	Beiträge zur Förderung christlicher Theologie	*BulCPE*	*Bulletin du Centre Protestant d'Études* (Geneva)
BGBE	Beiträge zur Geschichte der biblischen Exegese	*BVC*	*Bible et vie chrétienne*
		BW	*Biblical World*
BHH	*Biblisch-Historisches Handwörterbuch*	BWANT	Beiträge zur Wissenschaft vom Alten und Neuen Testament
BHK	R. Kittel, *Biblia hebraica*		
BHS	*Biblia hebraica stuttgartensia*	*BZ*	*Biblische Zeitschrift*
BHT	Beiträge zur historischen Theologie	BZAW	Beihefte zur ZAW
		BZET	Beihefte zur Evangelische Theologie
Bib	*Biblica*		
BibB	Biblische Beiträge	BZNW	Beihefte zur ZNW
BibLeb	*Bibel und Leben*	BZRGG	Beihefte zur ZRGG
BibNot	*Biblische Notizen*		
BibOr	Biblica et orientalia		
BibS(F)	Biblische Studien (Freiburg, 1895-)	*CAD*	*The Assyrian Dictionary of the Oriental Institute of the University of Chicago*
BibS(N)	Biblische Studien (Neukirchen, 1951-)		
		CAH	*Cambridge Ancient History*
BiTod	*The Bible Today*	CAT	Commentaire de l'Ancien Testament
BIES	*Bulletin of the Israel Exploration Society* (= *Yediot*)		
		CB	*Cultura biblica*
BIFAO	*Bulletin de l'institut français d'archéologie orientale*	*CBG*	*Collationes Brugenses et Gandavenses*
BILL	Bibliothèque des cahiers de l'Institut de Linguistique de Louvain	*CBQ*	*Catholic Biblical Quarterly*
		CBQMS	CBQ Monograph Series
		CBVE	*Comenius Blätter für Volkserziehung*
BJRL	*Bulletin of the John Rylands University Library of Manchester*		
		CCath	Corpus Catholicorum
		CChr	Corpus Christianorum
BJS	Brown Judaic Studies	CGTC	Cambridge Greek Testament Commentary
BK	Bibel und Kirche		
BKAT	Biblischer Kommentar: Altes Testament	CGTSC	Cambridge Greek Testament for Schools and Colleges
BL	*Book List*		
BLE	*Bulletin de littérature ecclésiastique*	*CH*	*Church History*
		CHR	*Catholic Historical Review*
BLit	*Bibel und Liturgie*	*CIG*	*Corpus inscriptionum graecarum*
BLS	Bible and Literature Series		
BNTC	Black's New Testament Commentaries	*CII*	*Corpus inscriptionum iudaicarum*
BO	*Bibliotheca orientalis*	*CIL*	*Corpus inscriptionum latinarum*
BR	*Biblical Research*		

CIS	*Corpus inscriptionum semiticarum*
CJT	*Canadian Journal of Theology*
ClerRev	*Clergy Review*
CLit	*Christianity and Literature*
CM	*Cahiers marials*
CNT	Commentaire du Nouveau Testament
ComLit	*Communautes et liturgies*
ConB	Coniectanea biblica
Concil	*Concilium*
ConNT	*Coniectanea neotestamentica*
CQ	*Church Quarterly*
CQR	*Church Quarterly Review*
CRAIBL	*Comptes rendus de l'Académie des inscriptions et belles-lettres*
CrQ	*Crozier Quarterly*
CSCO	Corpus scriptorum christianorum orientalium
CSEL	Corpus scriptorum ecclesiasticorum latinorum
CTA	A. Herdner, *Corpus des tablettes en cunéiformes alphabétiques*
CTJ	*Calvin Theological Journal*
CTQ	*Concordia Theological Quarterly*
CurTM	*Currents in Theology and Mission*
CV	*Communio viatorum*
DACL	*Dictionnaire d'archéologie chrétienne et de liturgie*
DBSup	*Dictionnaire de la Bible, Supplément*
Diak	*Diakonia*
DISO	C.-F. Jean and J. Hoftijzer, *Dictionnaire des inscriptions sémitiques de l'ouest*
DJD	Discoveries in the Judean Desert
DL	*Doctrine and Life*
DOTT	D. W. Thomas (ed.), *Documents from Old Testament Times*
DR	*Downside Review*
DS	Denzinger-Schönmetzer, *Enchiridion symbolorum*
DT	*Deutsche Theologie*
DTC	*Dictionnaire de théologie catholique*
DTT	*Dansk teologisk tidsskrift*
DunRev	*Dunwoodie Review*
EBib	*Etudes bibliques*
EBT	*Encyclopedia of Biblical Theology*
EcR	*Ecclesiastical Review*
ED	*Euntes Docete* (Rome)
EE	*Estudios Eclesiásticos*
EglT	*Église et théologie*
EHAT	Exegetisches Handbuch zum Alten Testament
EKKNT	Evangelisch-katholischer Kommentar zum Neuen Testament
EKL	*Evangelisches Kirchenlexikon*
Emman	*Emmanuel*
EncJud	*Encyclopedia judaica* (1971)
EnchBib	*Enchiridion biblicum*
EpR	*Epworth Review*
ER	*Ecumenical Review*
ErJb	*Eranos Jahrbuch*
EstBib	*Estudios biblicos*
ETL	*Ephemerides theologicae lovanienses*
ETR	*Etudes théologiques et religieuses*
ETS	Erfurter Theologische Studien
EvK	Evangelische Kommentar
EvQ	*Evangelical Quarterly*
EvT	*Evangelische Theologie*
EW	*Exegetisches Wörterbuch zum Neuen Testament (EWNT)*, ed. H. Balz and G. Schneider, 3 vols. (Stuttgart: Kohlhammer, 1980–83)
Exp	*Expositor*
ExpTim	*The Expository Times*
FB	*Forschung zur Bibel*
FBBS	*Facet Books, Biblical Series*
FC	Fathers of the Church
FM	*Faith and Mission*
FRLANT	Forschungen zur Religion und Literatur des Alten und Neuen Testaments
FTS	Frankfurter Theologische Studien
GAG	W. von Soden, *Grundriss der akkadischen Grammatik*
GCS	Griechischen christlichen Schriftsteller
GKB	Gesenius-Kautzsch-Bergsträsser, *Hebräische Grammatik*

Abbreviations

GKC	*Gesenius' Hebrew Grammar*, ed. E. Kautzsch, tr. A. E. Cowley	ICC	International Critical Commentary
GNT	Grundrisse zum Neuen Testament	IDB	G. A. Buttrick (ed.), *Interpreter's Dictionary of the Bible*
GOTR	Greek Orthodox Theological Review	IDBSup	Supplementary volume to *IDB*
GRBS	*Greek, Roman, and Byzantine Studies*	IEJ	*Israel Exploration Journal*
Greg	*Gregorianum*	IER	*Irish Ecclesiastical Record*
GThT	*Geformelet Theologisch Tijdschrift*	ILS	H. Dessau (ed.), *Inscriptiones Latinae Selectae* (Berlin, 1892)
GTJ	*Grace Theological Journal*	Int	*Interpretation*
GuL	*Geist und Leben*	ISBE	*International Standard Bible Encyclopedia*, ed. G. W. Bromiley
HALAT	W. Baumgartner et al., *Hebräisches und aramäisches Lexikon zum Alten Testament*	ITQ	*Irish Theological Quarterly*
		ITS	*Indian Theological Studies*
HAT	Handbuch zum Alten Testament	JA	*Journal asiatique*
HB	*Homiletica en Biblica*	JAAR	*Journal of the American Academy of Religion*
HBT	*Horizons in Biblical Theology*		
HDR	Harvard Dissertations in Religion	JAC	Jahrbuch für Antike und Christentum
HeyJ	*Heythrop Journal*	JAMA	*Journal of the American Medical Association*
HibJ	*Hibbert Journal*		
HKAT	Handkommentar zum Alten Testament	JANESCU	*Journal of the Ancient Near Eastern Society of Columbia University*
HKNT	Handkommentar zum Neuen Testament	JAOS	*Journal of the American Oriental Society*
HL	*Das heilige Land*		
HNT	Handbuch zum Neuen Testament	JAS	*Journal of Asian Studies*
		JBC	R. E. Brown et al. (eds.), *The Jerome Biblical Commentary*
HNTC	Harper's NT Commentaries		
HR	*History of Religions*		
HSM	Harvard Semitic Monographs	JBL	*Journal of Biblical Literature*
		JBR	*Journal of Bible and Religion*
HTKNT	Herders theologischer Kommentar zum Neuen Testament	JCS	*Journal of Cuneiform Studies*
		JDS	Judean Desert Studies
		JEA	*Journal of Egyptian Archaeology*
HTR	*Harvard Theological Review*		
HTS	Harvard Theological Studies	JEH	*Journal of Ecclesiastical History*
HUCA	*Hebrew Union College Annual*	JES	*Journal of Ecumenical Studies*
HUTh	Hermeneutische Untersuchungen zur Theologie	JETS	*Journal of the Evangelical Theological Society*
		JHS	*Journal of Hellenic Studies*
		JIBS	*Journal of Indian and Buddhist Studies*
IB	*Interpreter's Bible*		
IBD	*Illustrated Bible Dictionary*, ed. J. D. Douglas and N. Hillyer	JIPh	*Journal of Indian Philosophy*
		JJS	*Journal of Jewish Studies*
		JMES	*Journal of Middle Eastern Studies*
IBS	*Irish Biblical Studies*		

Abbreviations

JMS	Journal of Mithraic Studies	LJ	Liturgisches Jahrbuch
JNES	Journal of Near Eastern Studies	LLAVT	E. Vogt, Lexicon linguae aramaicae Veteris Testamenti
JPOS	Journal of the Palestine Oriental Society	LouvStud	Louvain Studies
		LPGL	G. W. H. Lampe, Patristic Greek Lexicon
JQR	Jewish Quarterly Review	LQ	Lutheran Quarterly
JQRMS	Jewish Quarterly Review Monograph Series	LR	Lutherische Rundschau
JR	Journal of Religion	LSJ	Liddell-Scott-Jones, Greek-English Lexicon
JRAS	Journal of the Royal Asiatic Society	LTK	Lexikon für Theologie und Kirche
JRE	Journal of Religious Ethics		
JRelS	Journal of Religious Studies	LTSB	Lutheran Theological Seminary Bulletin
JRH	Journal of Religious History		
JRomH	Journal of Roman History	LUÅ	Lunds universitets årsskrift
JRT	Journal of Religious Thought	LumVie	Lumière et Vie
JSJ	Journal for the Study of Judaism	LVit	Lumen Vitae
		LW	Lutheran World
JSNT	Journal for the Study of the New Testament	MC	Modern Churchman
		McCQ	McCormick Quarterly
JSOT	Journal for the Study of the Old Testament	MDOG	Mitteilungen der deutschen Orient-Gesellschaft
JSOTSup	JSOT Supplement Series	MelT	Melita Theologica
JSS	Journal of Semitic Studies	MeyerK	H. A. W. Meyer, Kritisch-exegetischer Kommentar über das Neue Testament
JSSR	Journal for the Scientific Study of Religion		
JTC	Journal for Theology and the Church	MM	J. H. Moulton and G. Milligan, The Vocabulary of the Greek Testament (London: Hodder, 1930)
JTS	Journal of Theological Studies		
JTSA	Journal of Theology for South Africa		
		MNTC	Moffatt NT Commentary
Jud	Judaica	MPAIBL	Mémoires présentés à l'Académie des inscriptions et belles-lettres
KAI	H. Donner and W. Röllig, Kanaanäische und aramäische Inschriften		
		MPG	Patrologia Graeca, ed. J. P. Migne, 1844ff.
KAT	E. Sellin (ed.), Kommentar zum Alten Testament		
		MScRel	Mélanges de science religieuse
KB	L. Koehler and W. Baumgartner, Lexicon in Veteris Testamenti libros	MTS	Marburger theologische Studien
		MTZ	Münchener theologische Zeitschrift
KD	Kerygma und Dogma		
KEK	Kritisch-exegetischer Kommentar über das Neue Testament	MUSJ	Mélanges de l'université Saint-Joseph
		MVAG	Mitteilungen der vorder-asiatisch-ägyptischen Gesellschaft
KlT	Kleine Texte		
KTR	King's Theological Review (London)		
		NAG	Nachrichten von der Akademie der Wissenschaften in Göttingen
LCC	Library of Christian Classics		
LCL	Loeb Classical Library		
LD	Lectio divina	NB	New Blackfriars
Leš	Lešonénu	NCB	New Century Bible (new ed.)
LingBib	Linguistica Biblica		

NCCHS	R. C. Fuller et al. (eds.), *New Catholic Commentary on Holy Scripture*
NCE	M. R. P. McGuire et al. (eds.), *New Catholic Encyclopedia*
NClB	New Clarendon Bible
NedTTs	*Nederlands theologisch tijdschrift*
Neot	*Neotestamentica*
NESTR	*Near East School of Theology Review*
NewDocs	*New Documents Illustrating Early Christianity, A Review of Greek Inscriptions, etc.*, ed. G. H. R. Horsley, North Ryde, NSW, Australia
NFT	New Frontiers in Theology
NGS	New Gospel Studies
NHS	Nag Hammadi Studies
NICNT	New International Commentary on the New Testament
NIDNTT	C. Brown, ed., *The New International Dictionary of New Testament Theology*, 3 vols. (Grand Rapids: Zondervan, 1975–78)
NiewTT	*Niew theologisch tijdschrift*
NIGTC	New International Greek Testament Commentary
NJDT	*Neue Jahrbücher für deutsche Theologie*
NKZ	*Neue kirchliche Zeitschrift*
NorTT	*Norsk Teologisk Tijdsskrift*
NovT	*Novum Testamentum*
NovTSup	Supplement to *NovT*
NPNF	Nicene and Post-Nicene Fathers
NRT	*La nouvelle revue théologique*
NTA	*New Testament Abstracts*
NTAbh	Neutestamentliche Abhandlungen
NTD	Das Neue Testament Deutsch
NTF	Neutestamentliche Forschungen
NTL	New Testament Library
NTS	*New Testament Studies*
NTSR	The New Testament for Spiritual Reading
NTTS	New Testament Tools and Studies
Numen	*Numen: International Review for the History of Religions*
NZM	*Neue Zeitschrift für Missionswissenschaft*
OBO	Orbis biblicus et orientalis
ÖBS	Österreichische Biblische Studien
OCD	*Oxford Classical Dictionary*
OGI	W. Dittenberger (ed.), *Orientis graeci inscriptiones selectae* (Leipzig: Hirzel, 1903-5)
OIP	Oriental Institute Publications
OLP	*Orientalia lovaniensia periodica*
OLZ	*Orientalische Literaturzeitung*
Or	*Orientalia* (Rome)
OrAnt	*Oriens antiquus*
OrChr	*Oriens christianus*
OrSyr	*L'orient syrien*
ÖTKNT	Ökumenischer Taschenbuch-Kommentar zum NT
OTM	Oxford Theological Monographs
OTS	*Oudtestamentische Studiën*
PAAJR	*Proceedings of the American Academy of Jewish Research*
PC	Proclamation Commentaries
PCB	M. Black and H. H. Rowley (eds.), *Peake's Commentary on the Bible*
PEFQS	*Palestine Exploration Fund, Quarterly Statement*
PEQ	*Palestine Exploration Quarterly*
PFay	Fayûm Papyri
PG	*Patrologia graeca*, ed. J. P. Migne
PGM	K. Preisendanz (ed.), *Papyri graecae magicae*
PhEW	*Philosophy East and West*
PhRev	*Philosophical Review*
PJ	*Palästina-Jahrbuch*
PNTC	Pelican New Testament Commentaries
PO	Patrologia orientalis
POxy	Oxyrhynchus Papyri
ProcIBA	*Proceedings of the Irish Biblical Association*

PRS	Perspectives in Religious Studies	RHPR	Revue d'histoire et de philosophie religieuses
PRU	Le Palais royal d'Ugarit	RHR	Revue de l'histoire des religions
PSTJ	Perkins (School of Theology) Journal	RivB	Rivista biblica
PTMS	Pittsburgh Theological Monograph Series	RM	Rheinisches Museum für Philologie
PTR	Princeton Theological Review	RNT	Regensburger Neues Testament
PVTG	Pseudepigrapha Veteris Testamenti graece	RR	Review of Religion
		RSLR	Rivista di Storiae Letteratura Religiosa (Turin)
PW	Pauly-Wissowa, Real-Encyklopädie der klassischen Altertumswissenschaft	RSO	Rivista degli studi orientali
		RSPT	Revue des sciences philosophiques et théologiques
PWSup	Supplement to PW	RSR	Recherches de science religieuse
		RTL	Revue théologique de Louvain
QDAP	Quarterly of the Department of Antiquities in Palestine	RTP	Revue de théologie et de philosophie
		RTR	Reformed Theological Review
RA	Revue d'assyriologie et d'archéologie orientale	RUV	La Revue de l'Université Laval
RAC	Reallexikon für Antike und Christentum	RUO	Revue de l'université Ottawa
RArch	Revue archéologique		
RB	Revue biblique	SacPag	Sacra Pagina
RBén	Revue Bénédictine	SAH	Sitzungberichte der Heidelberger Akademie der Wissenschaften (phil.-hist. Klasse)
RCB	Revista de cultura biblica		
RE	Realencyklopädie für protestantische Theologie und Kirche		
		Sal	Salmanticensis
REA	Revue des Études Augustiniennes	SANT	Studien zum Alten und Neuen Testament
RechBib	Recherches bibliques	SAQ	Sammlung ausgewählter kirchen- und dogmengeschichtlicher Quellenschriften
REg	Revue d'égyptologie		
REJ	Revue des études juives		
RelArts	Religion and the Arts		
RelS	Religious Studies	SAWB	Sitzungsberichte der (königlich preussischen) Akademie der Wissenschaften zu Berlin (phil.-hist. Klasse)
RelSoc	Religion and Society		
RelSRev	Religious Studies Review		
RES	Répertoire d'épigraphie sémitique		
		SB	Sources bibliques
RestQ	Restoration Quarterly	SBB	Stuttgarter biblische Monographien
RevExp	Review and Expositor		
RevistB	Revista biblica	SBFLA	Studii biblici franciscani liber annuus
RevQ	Revue de Qumrân		
RevRel	Review for Religious	SBJ	La sainte bible de Jérusalem
RevScRel	Revue des sciences religieuses	SBLASP	Society of Biblical Literature Abstracts and Seminar Papers
RevSém	Revue sémitique		
RevThom	Revue thomiste		
RGG	Religion in Geschichte und Gegenwart	SBLDS	SBL Dissertation Series
		SBLMasS	SBL Masoretic Studies
RHE	Revue d'histoire ecclésiastique	SBLMS	SBL Monograph Series

SBLSBS	SBL Sources for Biblical Study		preussischen Akademie der Wissenschaften
SBLSCS	SBL Septuagint and Cognate Studies	SPB	Studia postbiblica
		SR	*Studies in Religion / Sciences Religieuses*
SBLTT	SBL Texts and Translations		
SBM	Stuttgarter biblische Monographien	SSS	Semitic Study Series
		ST	*Studia theologica*
SBS	Stuttgarter Bibelstudien	STÅ	*Svensk teologisk årsskrift*
SBT	Studies in Biblical Theology	StBibT	*Studia biblica et theologica*
		STDJ	Studies on the Texts of the Desert of Judah
SC	Source chrétiennes		
ScEccl	*Sciences ecclésiastiques*	STK	*Svensk teologisk kvartalskrift*
ScEs	*Science et esprit*	Str-B	H. Strack and P. Billerbeck, *Kommentar zum Neuen Testament*, 4 vols. (Munich: Beck'sche, 1926–28)
SCR	Studies in Comparative Religion		
Scr	Scripture		
ScrB	*Scripture Bulletin*	StudBib	*Studia biblica*
SD	Studies and Documents	StudNeot	Studia neotestamentica
SE	*Studia Evangelica* 1, 2, 3, 4, 5, 6 (= TU 73 [1959], 87 [1964], 88 [1964], 102 [1968], 103 [1968], 112 [1973]	SUNT	Studien zur Umwelt des Neuen Testaments
		SVTP	*Studia in Veteris Testamenti pseudepigrapha*
		SWJT	*Southwestern Journal of Theology*
SEÅ	*Svensk exegetisk årsbok*		
Sef	*Sefarad*	SymBU	Symbolae biblicae upsalienses
SeinSend	*Sein Sendung*		
Sem	*Semitica*		
SémiotBib	*Sémiotique et Bible*		
SHAW	Sitzungsberichte heidelbergen Akademie der Wissenschaften	TantY	*Tantur Yearbook*
		TAPA	*Transactions of the American Philological Association*
SHT	Studies in Historical Theology	TB	*Theologische Beiträge*
		TBC	Torch Bible Commentaries
SHVL	Skrifter Utgivna Av Kungl. Humanistika Vetenskapssamfundet i Lund	TBl	*Theologische Blätter*
		TBT	*The Bible Today*
		TBü	Theologische Bücherei
		TC	Theological Collection (SPCK)
SJLA	Studies in Judaism in Late Antiquity		
		TD	*Theology Digest*
SJT	*Scottish Journal of Theology*	TDNT	G. Kittel and G. Friedrich, eds., *Theological Dictionary of the New Testament*, 10 vols., ET (Grand Rapids: Eerdmans, 1964–76)
SMSR	*Studi e materiali di storia delle religioni*		
SNT	Studien zum Neuen Testament		
SNTSMS	Society for New Testament Studies Monograph Series	TextsS	Texts and Studies
		TF	*Theologische Forschung*
SNTU	*Studien zum Neuen Testament und seiner Umwelt*	TGl	*Theologie und Glaube*
		Th	*Theology*
SO	Symbolae osloenses	ThA	*Theologische Arbeiten*
SOTSMS	Society for Old Testament Study Monograph Series	ThBer	*Theologische Berichte*
		THKNT	Theologischer Handkommentar zum Neuen Testament
SPap	*Studia papyrologica*		
SPAW	Sitzungsberichte der		

Abbreviations

ThViat	Theologia Viatorum	VC	Vigiliae christianae
TJ	Trinity Journal	VCaro	Verbum caro
TJT	Toronto Journal of Theology	VD	Verbum domini
TLZ	Theologische Literaturzeitung	VetC	Vetera Christianorum
TNTC	Tyndale New Testament Commentaries	VF	Verkündigung und Forschung
TP	Theologie und Philosophie (ThPh)	VKGNT	K. Aland (ed.), Vollständige Konkordanz zum griechischen Neuen Testament
TPQ	Theologisch-Praktische Quartalschrift	VoxEv	Vox Evangelica (London)
TQ	Theologische Quartalschrift	VS	Verbum salutis
TRev	Theologische Revue	VSpir	Vie spirituelle
TRu	Theologische Rundschau	VT	Vetus Testamentum
TS	Theological Studies	VTSup	Vetus Testamentum, Supplements
TSAJ	Texte und Studien zum Antiken Judentum	WA	M. Luther, Kritische Gesamtausgabe (= "Weimar" edition)
TSFB	Theological Students Fellowship Bulletin	WBC	Word Biblical Commentary
TSK	Theologische Studien und Kritiken	WC	Westminster Commentary
TT	Teologisk Tidsskrift	WD	Wort und Dienst
TTKi	Tidsskrift for Teologi og Kirke	WDB	Westminster Dictionary of the Bible
TToday	Theology Today	WF	Wege der Forschung
TTS	Trier theologische Studien	WHAB	Westminster Historical Atlas of the Bible
TTZ	Trierer theologische Zeitschrift	WMANT	Wissenschaftliche Monographien zum Alten und Neuen Testament
TU	Texte und Untersuchungen	WO	Die Welt des Orients
TWAT	G. J. Botterweck and H. Ringgren (eds.), Theologisches Wörterbuch zum Alten Testament	WTJ	Westminster Theological Journal
TWNT	G. Kittel and G. Friedrich (eds.), Theologisches Wörterbuch zum Neuen Testament	WUNT	Wissenschaftliche Untersuchungen zum Neuen Testament
TynB	Tyndale Bulletin	WW	Word and World
TZ	Theologische Zeitschrift	WZKM	Wiener Zeitschrift für die Kunde des Morgenlandes
UBSGNT	United Bible Societies Greek New Testament	WZKSO	Wiener Zeitschrift für die Kunde Süd- und Ostasiens
UCL	Universitas Catholica Lovaniensis		
UF	Ugaritische Forschungen	ZA	Zeitschrift für Assyriologie
UFHM	University of Florida Humanities Monograph	ZAW	Zeitschrift für die alttestamentliche Wissenschaft
UNT	Untersuchungen zum Neuen Testament	ZDMG	Zeitschrift der deutschen morgenländischen Gesellschaft
US	Una Sancta	ZDPV	Zeitschrift des deutschen Palästina-Vereins
USQR	Union Seminary Quarterly Review	ZEE	Zeitschrift für evangelische Ethik
UT	C. H. Gordon, Ugaritic Textbook	ZHT	Zeitschrift für historische Theologie
UUÅ	Uppsala universitetsårsskrift		

ZKG	*Zeitschrift für Kirchengeschichte*
ZKNT	*Zahn's Kommentar zum NT*
ZKT	*Zeitschrift für katholische Theologie*
ZMR	*Zeitschrift für Missionskunde und Religionswissenschaft*
ZNW	*Zeitschrift für die neutestamentliche Wissenschaft*
ZRGG	*Zeitschrift für Religions- und Geistesgeschichte*
ZST	*Zeitschrift für systematische Theologie*
ZTK	*Zeitschrift für Theologie und Kirche*
ZWT	*Zeitschrift für wissenschaftliche Theologie*

D. Abbreviations for Books of the Bible, the Apocrypha, and the Pseudepigrapha

OLD TESTAMENT

Gen	2 Chr	Dan
Exod	Ezra	Hos
Lev	Neh	Joel
Num	Esth	Amos
Deut	Job	Obad
Josh	Ps(Pss)	Jonah
Judg	Prov	Mic
Ruth	Eccl	Nah
1 Sam	Cant	Hab
2 Sam	Isa	Zeph
1 Kgs	Jer	Hag
2 Kgs	Lam	Zech
1 Chr	Ezek	Mal

NEW TESTAMENT

Matt	1 Tim
Mark	2 Tim
Luke	Titus
John	Philem
Acts	Heb
Rom	Jas
1 Cor	1 Pet
2 Cor	2 Pet
Gal	1 John
Eph	2 John
Phil	3 John
Col	Jude
1 Thess	Rev
2 Thess	

APOCRYPHA

1 Kgdms	1 Kingdoms
2 Kgdms	2 Kingdoms
3 Kgdms	3 Kingdoms
4 Kgdms	4 Kingdoms
1 Esd	1 Esdras
2 Esd	2 Esdras
Tob	Tobit
Jdt	Judith
Add Esth	Additions to Esther
4 Ezra	4 Ezra
Wis	Wisdom of Solomon
Sir	Ecclesiasticus (Wisdom of Jesus the son of Sirach)
Bar	Baruch
Ep Jer	Epistle of Jeremy
S Th Ch	Song of the Three Children (or Young Men)
Sus	Susanna
Bel	Bel and the Dragon
Pr Man	Prayer of Manasseh
1 Macc	1 Maccabees
2 Macc	2 Maccabees
3 Macc	3 Maccabees
4 Macc	4 Maccabees

E. Abbreviations of the Names of Pseudepigraphical and Early Patristic Books

Adam and Eve	Life of Adam and Eve
Apoc. Abr.	Apocalypse of Abraham (1st to 2nd cent. A.D.)
2-3 Apoc. Bar.	Syriac, Greek *Apocalypse of Baruch*
Asc. Isa.	Ascension of Isaiah
Apoc. Mos.	Apocalypse of Moses
As. Mos.	(See *T. Mos.*)
Apoc. Elijah	Apocalypse of Elijah
1-2-3 Enoch	Ethiopic, Slavonic, Hebrew *Enoch*
Ep. Arist.	Epistle of Aristeas
Ep. Diognetus	Epistle to Diognetus
Jub.	Jubilees
Mart. Isa.	Martyrdom of Isaiah
Odes Sol.	Odes of Solomon
Pss. Sol.	Psalms of Solomon
Sib. Or.	Sibylline Oracles
T. 12 Patr.	Testaments of the Twelve Patriarchs
T. Abr.	Testament of Abraham
T. Judah	Testament of Judah

T. Levi	Testament of Levi, etc.	Magn.	Ignatius, Letter to the Magnesians
Apoc. Pet.	Apocalypse of Peter	Phil.	Ignatius, Letter to the Philadelphians
Gos. Eb.	Gospel of the Ebionites		
Gos. Eg.	Gospel of the Egyptians	Pol.	Ignatius, Letter to Polycarp
Gos. Heb.	Gospel of the Hebrews		
Gos. Naass.	Gospel of the Naassenes	Rom.	Ignatius, Letter to the Romans
Gos. Pet.	Gospel of Peter		
Gos. Thom.	Gospel of Thomas	Smyrn.	Ignatius, Letter to the Smyrnaeans
Prot. Jas.	Protevangelium of James		
Barn.	Barnabas	Trall.	Ignatius, Letter to the Trallians
1–2 Clem.	1–2 Clement		
Did.	Didache	Mart. Pol.	Martyrdom of Polycarp
Diogn.	Diognetus	Pol. Phil.	Polycarp, Letter to the Philippians
Herm. Man.	Hermas, Mandates		
Sim.	Similitudes	Iren. Adv. Haer.	Irenaeus, Against All Heresies
Vis.	Visions		
Ign. Eph.	Ignatius, Letter to the Ephesians	Tert. De Praesc. Haer.	Tertullian, On the Proscribing of Heretics

F. Abbreviations of Names of Dead Sea Scrolls and Related Texts

CD	Cairo (Genizah text of the) Damascus (Document)	1QM	Milḥāmāh (War Scroll)
		1QS	Serek hayyaḥad (Rule of the Community, Manual of Discipline)
Hev	Nahal Hever texts		
Mas	Masada texts	1QSa	Appendix A (Rule of the Congregation) to 1QS
Mird	Khirbet Mird texts		
Mur	Wadi Murabbaʿat texts	1QSb	Appendix B (Blessings) to 1QS
p	Pesher (commentary)		
Q	Qumran	3Q15	Copper Scroll from Qumran Cave 3
1Q, 2Q, 3Q, etc.	Numbered caves of Qumran, yielding written material; followed by abbreviation of biblical or apocryphal book	4QFlor	Florilegium (or Eschatological Midrashim) from Qumran Cave 4
		4QMess ar	Aramaic "Messianic" text from Qumran Cave 4
		4QPrNab	Prayer of Nabonidus from Qumran Cave 4
QL	Qumran literature		
1QapGen	Genesis Apocryphon of Qumran Cave 1	4QTestim	Testimonia text from Qumran Cave 4
1QH	Hôdāyôt (Thanksgiving Hymns) from Qumran Cave 1	4QTLevi	Testament of Levi from Qumran Cave 4
		4QPhyl	Phylacteries from Qumran Cave 4
1QIsa^{a,b}	First or second copy of Isaiah from Qumran Cave 1	11QMelch	Melchizedek text from Qumran Cave 11
1QpHab	Pesher on Habakkuk from Qumran Cave 1	11QtgJob	Targum of Job from Qumran Cave 11

G. Abbreviations of Targumic Material

Tg. Onq.	Targum Onqelos	Tg. Ket.	Targum of the Writings
Tg. Neb.	Targum of the Prophets	Frg. Tg.	Fragmentary Targum

Sam. Tg.	Samaritan Targum	Tg. Yer. II	Targum Yerušalmi II*
Tg. Isa.	Targum of Isaiah	Yem. Tg.	Yemenite Targum
Pal. Tgs.	Palestinian Targums	Tg. Esth I, II	First or Second Targum of Esther
Tg. Neof.	Targum Neofiti I		
Tg. Ps.-J.	Targum Pseudo-Jonathan		
Tg. Yer. I	Targum Yerušalmi I*	*optional title	

H. Abbreviations of Other Rabbinic Works

ʾAbot R. Nat.	ʾAbot de Rabbi Nathan	Pesiq. Rab Kah.	Pesiqta de Rab Kahana
ʾAg. Ber.	ʾAggadat Berešit	Pirqe R. El.	Pirqe Rabbi Eliezer
Bab.	Babylonian	Rab.	Rabbah (following abbreviation for biblical book: Gen. Rab. [with periods] = Genesis Rabbah)
Bar.	Baraita		
Der. Er. Rab.	Derek Ereṣ Rabba		
Der. Er. Zuṭ.	Derek Ereṣ Zuṭa		
Gem.	Gemara		
Kalla	Kalla	Sem.	Semaḥot
Mek.	Mekilta	Sipra	Sipra
Midr.	Midraš; cited with usual abbreviation for biblical book; but Midr. Qoh. = Midraš Qohelet	Sipre	Sipre
		Sop.	Soperim
		S. ʿOlam Rab.	Seder ʿOlam Rabbah
		Talm.	Talmud
Pal.	Palestinian	Yal.	Yalquṭ
Pesiq. R.	Pesiqta Rabbati		

I. Abbreviations of Orders and Tractates in Mishnaic and Related Literature

ʾAbot	ʾAbot	Mid.	Middot
ʿArak.	ʿArakin	Miqw.	Miqwaʾot
ʿAbod. Zar.	ʿAboda Zara	Moʿed	Moʿed
B. Bat.	Baba Batra	Moʿed Qaṭ.	Moʿed Qaṭan
Bek.	Bekorot	Maʿas. Š.	Maʿaśer Šeni
Ber.	Berakot	Našim	Našim
Beṣa	Beṣa (= Yom Ṭob)	Nazir	Nazir
Bik.	Bikkurim	Ned.	Nedarim
B. Meṣ.	Baba Meṣiʿa	Neg.	Negaʿim
B. Qam.	Baba Qamma	Nez.	Neziqin
Dem.	Demai	Nid.	Niddah
ʿEd.	ʿEduyyot	Ohol.	Oholot
ʿErub.	ʿErubin	ʿOr.	ʿOrla
Giṭ.	Giṭṭin	Para	Para
Ḥag.	Ḥagiga	Peʾa	Peʾa
Ḥal.	Ḥalla	Pesaḥ.	Pesaḥim
Hor.	Horayot	Qinnim	Qinnim
Ḥul.	Ḥullin	Qidd.	Qidduš in
Kelim	Kelim	Qod.	Qodašin
Ker.	Keritot	Roš. Haš.	Roš Haššana
Ketub.	Ketubot	Sanh.	Sanhedrin
Kil.	Kilʾayim	Šabb.	Šabbat
Maʿaś.	Maʿaśerot	Šeb.	Šebiʿit
Mak.	Makkot	Šebu.	Šebuʿot
Makš.	Makširin (= Mašqin)	Šeqal.	Šeqalim
Meg.	Megilla	Soṭa	Soṭa
Meʿil.	Meʿila	Sukk.	Sukka
Menaḥ.	Menaḥot	Taʿan.	Taʿanit

Tamid	Tamid	Yad.	Yadayim
Tem.	Temura	Yebam.	Yebamot
Ter.	Terumot	Yoma	Yoma (= Kippurim)
Ṭohar.	Ṭoharot	Zabim	Zabim
T. Yom	Tebul Yom	Zebaḥ	Zebaḥim
ʿUq.	ʿUqṣin	Zer.	Zeraʿim

J. Abbreviations of Nag Hammadi Tractates

Acts Pet. 12 Apost.	Acts of Peter and the Twelve Apostles	Melch.	Melchizedek
		Norea	Thought of Norea
Allogenes	Allogenes	On Bap. A	On Baptism A
Ap. Jas.	Apocryphon of James	On Bap. B	On Baptism B
Ap. John	Apocryphon of John	On Bap. C	On Baptism C
Apoc. Adam	Apocalypse of Adam	On Euch. A	On the Eucharist A
1 Apoc. Jas.	First Apocalypse of James	On Euch. B	On the Eucharist B
2 Apoc. Jas.	Second Apocalypse of James	Orig. World	On the Origin of the World
Apoc. Paul	Apocalypse of Paul	Paraph. Shem	Paraphrase of Shem
Apoc. Pet.	Apocalypse of Peter	Pr. Paul	Prayer of the Apostle Paul
Asclepius	Asclepius 21–29	Pr. Thanks	Prayer of Thanksgiving
Auth. Teach.	Authoritative Teaching	Prot. Jas.	Protevangelium of James
Dial. Sav.	Dialogue of the Savior	Sent. Sextus	Sentences of Sextus
Disc. 8–9	Discourse on the Eighth and Ninth	Soph. Jes. Chr.	Sophia of Jesus Christ
		Steles Seth	Three Steles of Seth
		Teach. Silv.	Teachings of Silvanus
Ep. Pet. Phil.	Letter of Peter to Philip	Testim. Truth	Testimony of Truth
Eugnostos	Eugnostos the Blessed	Thom. Cont.	Book of Thomas the Contender
Exeg. Soul	Exegesis on the Soul		
Gos. Eg.	Gospel of the Egyptians	Thund.	Thunder, Perfect Mind
Gos. Phil.	Gospel of Philip	Treat. Res.	Treatise on Resurrection
Gos. Thom.	Gospel of Thomas	Treat. Seth	Second Treatise of the Great Seth
Gos. Truth	Gospel of Truth		
Great Pow.	Concept of our Great Power	Tri. Trac.	Triparite Tractate
Hyp. Arch.	Hypostasis of the Archons	Trim. Prot.	Trimorphic Protennoia
Hypsiph.	Hypsiphrone	Val. Exp.	A Valentinian Exposition
Interp. Know.	Interpretation of Knowledge	Zost.	Zostrianos
Marsanes	Marsanes		

Main Bibliography

Commentaries

Abbott, T. K. *A Critical and Exegetical Commentary on the Epistles to the Ephesians and to the Colossians.* Edinburgh: T. & T. Clark, 1897. **Allan, J. A.** *The Epistle to the Ephesians.* London: SCM, 1959. **Barth, M.** *Ephesians.* 2 vols. New York: Doubleday, 1974. **Beare, F. W.** "Ephesians." In *The Interpreter's Bible,* Vol. 10. Nashville: Abingdon, 1953, 597–749. **Beet, J. A.** *A Commentary on St. Paul's Epistles to the Ephesians, Philippians, and Colossians.* 3rd ed. London: Hodder & Stoughton, 1902. **Bengel, J. A.** "Ephesians." In *Bengel's New Testament Commentaries.* Vol. 2. Tr. C. T. Lewis and M. R. Vincent. Reprint Grand Rapids: Kregel, 1981. **Benoit, P.** *Les Épîtres de Saint Paul aux Philippiens, à Philemon, aux Colossiens, aux Éphésiens.* Paris: du Cerf, 1959. **Bruce, F. F.** *The Epistle to the Ephesians.* London: Pickering and Inglis, 1961. ———. *The Epistles to the Colossians, to Philemon, and to the Ephesians.* Grand Rapids: Eerdmans, 1984. **Caird, G. B.** *Paul's Letters from Prison.* Oxford: Oxford University Press, 1976. **Calvin J.** *Commentaries on the Epistles of Paul to the Galatians and Ephesians.* Tr. W. Pringle. Edinburgh: T. & T. Clark, 1854. **Chadwick, H.** "Ephesians." In *Peake's Commentary on the Bible,* ed. M. Black and H. H. Rowley. London: Nelson, 1962, 980–84. **Chrysostom, J.** *Commentary on the Epistle to the Galatians, and Homilies on the Epistle to the Ephesians.* Oxford: J. H. Parker, 1845. **Conzelmann, H.** "Der Brief an die Epheser." In *Die Briefe an die Galater, Epheser, Philipper, Kolosser, Thessalonicher und Philemon,* ed. J. Becker, H. Conzelmann, and G. Friedrich. Göttingen: Vandenhoeck & Ruprecht, 1976, 86–124. **Dahl, N. A.** "Ephesians." *Harper's Bible Commentary,* ed. J. L. Mays. San Francisco: Harper and Row, 1988, 1212–19. ———. et al. *Kurze Auslegung des Epheserbriefes.* Göttingen: Vandenhoeck & Ruprecht, 1965. **Dale, R. W.** *The Epistle to the Ephesians.* London: Hodder & Stoughton, 1901. **Dibelius, M.,** and **Greeven, H.** *An die Kolosser, Epheser, an Philemon.* Tübingen: Mohr, 1953. **Eadie, J. A.** *A Commentary on the Greek Text of the Epistle of Paul to the Ephesians.* 3rd ed. Edinburgh: T. & T. Clark, 1883. **Ernst, J.** *Die Briefe an die Philipper, an Philemon, an die Kolosser, an die Epheser.* Regensburg: F. Pustet, 1974. **Ewald, P.** *Die Briefe des Paulus an die Epheser, Kolosser und Philemon.* 2nd ed. Leipzig: Deichert, 1910. **Foulkes, F.** *The Epistle of Paul to the Ephesians.* London: Tyndale Press, 1963. **Gaugler, E.** *Der Epheserbrief.* Zürich: EVZ, 1966. **Gnilka, J.** *Der Epheserbrief.* Freiburg: Herder, 1971. ———. *Der Kolosserbrief.* Freiburg: Herder, 1980. **Haupt, E.** *Die Gefangenschaftsbriefe.* Göttingen: Vandenhoeck & Ruprecht, 1902. **Hendriksen, W.** *Ephesians.* Grand Rapids: Baker, 1967. **Henle, F. A.** *Der Epheserbrief des heiligen Apostels Paulus.* Augsburg, 1908. **Hodge, C.** *Commentary on the Epistle to the Ephesians.* London: James Nisbet, 1876. **Houlden, J. L.** *Paul's Letters from Prison.* Harmondsworth: Penguin, 1970. **Hugedé, N.** *L'Épître aux Éphésiens.* Geneva: Labor et Fides, 1973. **Johnston, G.** *Ephesians, Philippians, Colossians, and Philemon.* London: Nelson, 1967. **Lightfoot, J. B.** *St. Paul's Epistles to the Colossians and to Philemon.* London: Macmillan, 1879. **Lindemann, A.** *Der Epheserbrief.* Zürich: Theologischer Verlag, 1985. **Lock, W.** *The Epistle to the Ephesians.* London: Methuen, 1929. **Lohse, E.** *Colossians and Philemon.* Tr. W. R. Poehlmann and R. J. Karris. Philadelphia: Fortress, 1971. **Martin, R. P.** *Colossians and Philemon.* London: Oliphants, 1974. ———. "Ephesians." In *Broadman Bible Commentary.* Vol. 11. Nashville: Broadman, 1971, 125–77. **Masson, C.** *L'Épître de Paul aux Éphésiens.* Neuchâtel: Delachaux et Niestlé, 1953. **Meinertz, M.,** and **Tillmann, F.** *Die Gefangenschaftsbriefe.* Bonn: Hanstein, 1931. **Meyer, H. A. W.** *Critical and Exegetical Handbook to the Epistle to the Ephesians and the Epistle to Philemon.* Tr. W. P. Dickson. Edinburgh: T. & T. Clark, 1880. **Mitton, C. L.** *Ephesians.* London: Oliphants, 1976. **Moule, C. F. D.** *The Epistles of Paul the Apostle to the Colossians and to Philemon.* Cambridge: Cambridge University Press, 1968. **Moulton,**

H. K. *Colossians, Philemon and Ephesians.* London: Epworth, 1963. **Mussner, F.** *Der Brief an die Epheser.* Gütersloh: Gerd Mohn, 1982. **O'Brien, P. T.** *Colossians, Philemon.* WBC 44. Waco, TX: Word Books, 1982. **Olshausen, H.** *Biblical Commentary on St. Paul's Epistles to the Galatians, Ephesians, Colossians, and Thessalonians.* Edinburgh: T. & T. Clark, 1851. **Patzia, A. G.** *Colossians, Philemon, Ephesians.* New York: Harper and Row, 1984. **Pfammatter, J.** *Epheserbrief, Kolosserbrief.* Würzburg: Echter Verlag, 1987. **Robinson, J. A.** *St. Paul's Epistle to the Ephesians.* 2nd ed. London: Macmillan, 1904. **Roon, A. van.** *De Brief van Paulus aan de Epheziers.* Nijkerk: Callenbach, 1976. **Salmond, S. D. F.** "The Epistle of Paul to the Ephesians." In *Expositor's Greek Testament.* Vol. 3. London: Hodder and Stoughton, 1903. **Schlatter, A.** *Die Briefe an die Galater, Epheser, Kolosser und Philemon.* Stuttgart: Calver, 1963. **Schlier, H.** *Der Brief an die Epheser.* Dusseldorf: Patmos, 1957. **Schnackenburg, R.** *Der Brief an die Epheser.* Zürich: Benzinger, 1982. **Schweizer, E.** *The Letter to the Colossians.* Tr. A. Chester. London: S.P.C.K., 1982. **Scott, E. F.** *The Epistles to the Colossians, to Philemon, and to the Ephesians.* London: Hodder and Stoughton, 1930. **Simpson, E. K.,** and **Bruce, F. F.** *The Epistles of Paul to the Ephesians and to the Colossians.* Grand Rapids: Eerdmans, 1957. **Soden, H. von.** *Die Briefe an die Kolosser, Epheser, Philemon; die Pastoralbriefe.* Freiburg: Mohr, 1893. **Staab, K.** *Die Gefangenschaftsbriefe.* Regensburg: Pustet, 1959. **Swain, L.** *Ephesians.* Wilmington, DE: M. Glazier, 1980. **Synge, F. C.** *St. Paul's Epistle to the Ephesians.* London: S.P.C.K., 1941. **Taylor, W. F.,** and **Reumann, J. H. P.** *Ephesians, Colossians.* Minneapolis: Augsburg, 1975. **Thompson, G. H. P.** *The Letters of Paul to the Ephesians, to the Colossians, and to Philemon.* Cambridge: Cambridge University Press, 1967. **Westcott, B. F.** *St. Paul's Epistle to the Ephesians.* London: Macmillan, 1906. **Wette, W. M. L. de.** *Kurze Erklärung der Briefe an die Colosser, an Philemon, an die Epheser und an die Philipper.* Leipzig: Weidmann, 1843. **Zerwick, M.** *Der Brief an die Epheser.* Düsseldorf: Patmos, 1962.

Monographs and Articles

Adai, J. *Der Heilige Geist als Gegenwart Gottes in den einzelnen Christen, in der Kirche und in der Welt.* Frankfurt: Peter Lang, 1985. **Albani, J.** "Die Metaphern des Epheserbriefes." *ZWT* 45 (1902) 420–40. **Alexander, N.** "The Epistle for Today." FS W. Barclay, *Biblical Studies,* ed. J. R. McKay and J. F. Miller. London: Collins, 1976, 99–118. **Allan, J. A.** "The 'In Christ' Formula in Ephesians." *NTS* 5 (1958–59) 54–62. **Arnold, C. E.** *Ephesians: Power and Magic.* Cambridge: CUP, 1989. **Baker, N. L.** "Living the Dream: Ethics in Ephesians." *SWJT* 22 (1979) 39–55. **Barth, M.** *The Broken Wall.* London: Collins, 1960. ———. "Conversion and Conversation: Israel and the Church in Paul's Epistle to the Ephesians." *Int* 17 (1963) 3–24. ———. "Die Einheit des Galater- und Epheserbriefs." *TZ* 32 (1976) 78–91. ———. *Israel und die Kirche im Brief des Paulus an die Epheser.* Munich: Kaiser, 1959. ———. "Traditions in Ephesians." *NTS* 30 (1984) 3–25. **Benoit, P.** "Body, Head, and *Pleroma* in the Epistles of the Captivity." In *Jesus and the Gospel.* Vol. 2. Tr. B. Weatherhead. London: Darton, Longman and Todd, 1974, 51–92. ———. "L'Horizon paulinien de l'Épître aux Éphésiens." *RB* 46 (1937) 342–61, 506–25. ———. "Rapports littéraires entre les épîtres aux Colossiens et aux Éphésiens." In *Neutestamentliche Aufsätze.* FS J. Schmid, ed. J. Blinzler, O. Kuss, and F. Mussner. Regensburg: Pustet, 1963, 11–22. **Best, E.** *One Body in Christ.* London: S.P.C.K., 1955. ———. "Recipients and Title of the Letter to the Ephesians: Why and When the Designation 'Ephesians'?" *ANRW* 2.25.4 (1987) 3247–79. **Bieder, W.** "Das Geheimnis des Christus nach dem Epheserbrief." *TZ* 11 (1955) 329–43. **Bogdasovich, M.** "The Idea of *Pleroma* in the Epistles to the Colossians and Ephesians." *Downside Review* 83 (1965) 118–30. **Borland, A.** "God's Eternal Purpose." *EvQ* 34 (1962) 29–35. **Bouttier, M.** "L'horizon catholique de l'épître aux Éphésiens." In *L'Évangile, hier et aujourd'hui.* FS F. J. Leenhardt. Geneva: Labor et Fides, 1968, 25–37. **Bowman, J. W.** "The Epistle to the Ephesians."

Int 8 (1954) 188–205. **Bratcher, R. G.**, and **Nida, E. A.** *A Translator's Handbook on Paul's Letter to the Ephesians.* London: United Bible Societies, 1982. **Bruce, F. F.** "St. Paul in Rome: 4. The Epistle to the Ephesians." *BJRL* 49 (1967) 303–22. **Burger, C.** *Schöpfung und Versöhnung: Studien zum liturgischen Gut im Kolosser- und Epheserbrief.* Neukirchen-Vluyn: Neukirchener Verlag, 1975. **Cadbury, H. J.** "The Dilemma of Ephesians." *NTS* 5 (1959) 91–102. **Caldwell, E. C.** "The Purpose of the Ages." *PTR* 16 (1918) 374–89. **Cambier, J.** *Vie Chrétienne en Église: L'Épître aux Éphésiens lue aux chrétiens d'aujourd'hui.* Paris: Desclée, 1966. **Caragounis, C. C.** *The Ephesian Mysterion.* Lund: Gleerup, 1977. **Carr, W.** *Angels and Principalities.* Cambridge: CUP, 1981. **Cerfaux, L.** "En faveur de l'authenticité des épîtres de la captivité." In *Littérature et Théologie Pauliniennes.* Bruges: Desclée de Brouwer, 1960, 60–71. **Chadwick, H.** "Die Absicht des Epheserbriefes." *ZNW* 51 (1960) 145–53. **Colpe, C.** "Zur Leib-Christi-Vorstellung im Epheserbrief." In *Judentum, Urchristentum, Kirche,* ed. W. Eltester. Berlin: de Gruyter, 1964, 172–87. **Corley, B.** "The Theology of Ephesians." *SWJT* 22 (1979) 24–38. **Coutts, J.** "The Relationship of Ephesians and Colossians." *NTS* 4 (1958) 201–7. **Cross, F. L.**, ed. *Studies in Ephesians.* London: Mowbray, 1956. **Dahl, N. A.** "Der Epheserbrief und der verlorene erste Brief des Paulus an die Korinther." In *Abraham unser Vater.* FS O. Michel, ed. O. Betz, M. Hengel, and P. Schmidt. Leiden: Brill, 1963, 65–77. ———. "Ephesians, Letter to the." *IDBSup* (1976) 268–69. ———. "Gentiles, Christians, and Israelites in the Epistle to the Ephesians."In *Christians among Jews and Gentiles,* ed. G. W. E. Nickelsburg, and G. MacRae. Philadelphia: Fortress, 1986, 31–39; also *HTR* 79 (1986) 31–39. ———. "Interpreting Ephesians: Then and Now." *CurTM* 5 (1978) 133–43. **Danker, F. W.** "Ephesians, Epistle to the." *ISBE* 2 (1982) 109–14. **Dautzenberg, G.** "Theologie und Seelsorge aus paulinischer Tradition: Einführung in 2 Thess, Kol, Eph." In *Gestalt und Anspruch des Neuen Testaments,* ed. J. Schreiner. Würzburg: Echter, 1969, 96–119. **Davies, W. D.** *Paul and Rabbinic Judaism.* 2nd ed. New York: Harper and Row, 1967. **Deichgräber, R.** *Gotteshymnus und Christushymnus in der frühen Christenheit.* Göttingen: Vandenhoeck & Ruprecht, 1967. **Efird, J. M.** *Christ, the Church, and the End: Studies in Colossians and Ephesians.* Valley Forge, PA: Judson, 1980. **Ernst, J.** *Pleroma und Pleroma Christi.* Regensburg: F. Pustet, 1970. ———. "Von der Ortsgemeinde zur Grosskirche—dargestellt an den Kirchenmodellen des Philipper- und Epheserbriefs." In *Kirche im Werden,* ed. J. Hainz. Munich: F. Schoningh, 1976, 123–42. **Fendt, L.** "Die Kirche des Epheserbriefs." *TLZ* 77 (1952) 147–50. **Findeis, H.-J.** *Versöhnung—Apostolat—Kirche.* Würzburg: Echter Verlag, 1983. **Fischer, K. M.** *Tendenz und Absicht des Epheserbriefs.* Göttingen: Vandenhoeck & Ruprecht, 1973. **Fung, R.** "The Doctrine of Baptism in Ephesians." *StBibT* 1 (1971) 6–14. **Gewiess, J.** "Die Begriffe πληροῦν und πλήρωμα in Kolosser- und Epheserbrief." In *Vom Wort des Lebens.* FS M. Meinertz. Münster: Aschendorff, 1951, 128–41. **Gnilka, J.** "Das Akkulturationsproblem nach dem Epheser- und Kolosserbrief." In *Fede e cultura alla luce della Bibbia.* Turin: Editrice Elle Di Ci, 1981, 235–47. ———. "Das Kirchenmodell des Epheserbriefes." *BZ* 15 (1971) 161–84. ———. "Das Paulusbild im Kolosser- und Epheserbrief." In *Kontinuität und Einheit,* ed. P. G. Müller and W. Stenger. Freiburg: Herder, 1981, 179–93. ———. "Paränetische Traditionen im Epheserbrief." In *Mélanges Bibliques.* FS B. Rigaux, ed. A. Descamps and A. de Halleux. Gembloux: Duculot, 1970, 397–410. **Goguel, M.** "Esquisse d'une solution nouvelle du problème de l'épître aux Éphésiens." *RHR* 111 (1935) 254–84; 112 (1935) 73–99. **Goodspeed, E. J.** "Ephesians and the First Edition of Paul." *JBL* 70 (1951) 285–91. ———. "Ephesians, the Introduction to the Pauline Collection." In *New Solutions of New Testament Problems.* Chicago: University of Chicago Press, 1927, 11–20. ———. *The Key to Ephesians.* Chicago: University of Chicago Press, 1956. ———. *The Meaning of Ephesians.* Chicago: University of Chicago Press, 1933. **Gore, C.** *St. Paul's Epistle to the Ephesians.* London: John Murray, 1898. **Gregg, J. A. F.** "The Commentary of Origen upon the Epistle to the Ephesians." *JTS* 3 (1902) 233–44, 398–420, 551–76. **Grob, F.** "L'image du corps et de la tête dans l'Épître aux Éphésiens." *ETR* 58 (1983) 491–500. **Halter, H.** *Taufe und Ethos: Paulinische Kriterien für das Proprium christlicher Moral.* Freiburg: Herder, 1977. **Hanson, S.** *The Unity of the Church in the New Testament: Colossians and Ephesians.* Uppsala: Almquist & Wiksells, 1946. **Holtzmann, H. J.** *Kritik der Epheser- und Kolosserbriefe auf Grund einer Analyse ihres Verwandtschaftsverhältnisses.* Leipzig: Engelmann, 1872. **Hort, F. J. A.** *Prolegomena to St. Paul's Epistles to the Romans and the Ephesians.* London: Macmillan, 1895. **Houlden, J. L.** "Christ and Church in Ephesians." *SE* 6 (1973) 267–73. **Howard, G.** "The Head/Body Metaphors of Ephesians." *NTS* 20 (1974) 350–56. **Jeal, R. R.** "The Relationship between Theology and Ethics in the Letter to the Ephesians." Ph.D. diss., University of Sheffield, 1990. **Käsemann, E.** "Epheserbrief." *RGG* 2:517–20. ———. "Ephesians and Acts." In *Studies in Luke-Acts,* ed. L. E. Keck and J. L. Martyn. London: S.P.C.K., 1968, 288–97. ———. "Das Interpretationsproblem des Epheserbriefes." In *Exegetische Versuche und Besinnungen.* Vol. 2. 3rd ed. Göttingen: Vandenhoeck & Ruprecht, 1970, 253–61. ———. *Leib und Leib Christi.* Tübingen: Mohr, 1933. ———. "Paulus und der Frühkatholizismus." *ZTK* 60 (1963) 75–89. **King, A. C.** "Ephesians in the Light of Form Criticism." *ExpTim* 63 (1952) 273–76. **Kirby, J. C.** *Ephesians, Baptism and Pentecost.* London: S.P.C.K., 1968. **Knoch, O.** "Die Botschaft des Epheserbriefes." In *"Durch die Gnade Gottes bin ich, was ich bin."* Ostfildern: Schwabenverlag, 1984, 74–89. **Kuhn, K. G.** "The Epistle to the Ephesians in the Light of the Qumran Texts." In *Paul and Qumran,* ed. J. Murphy-O'Connor. London: Geoffrey Chapman, 1968, 115–131. **Lightfoot, J. B.** "The Destination of the Epistle to the Ephesians." In *Biblical Essays.* London: Macmillan, 1893, 375–96. ———. *Notes on Epistles of St. Paul.* London: Macmillan, 1895. **Lincoln, A. T.** *Paradise Now and Not Yet.* Cambridge: CUP, 1981. ———. "A Re-examination of 'The Heavenlies' in Ephesians." *NTS* 19 (1973) 468–83. ———. "The Use of the OT in Ephesians." *JSNT* 14 (1982) 16–57. **Lindemann, A.** *Die Aufhebung der Zeit: Geschichtsverständnis und Eschatologie im Epheserbrief.* Gütersloh: Gerd Mohn, 1975. ———. "Bemerkungen zu den Adressaten und zum Anlass des Epheserbriefes." *ZNW* 67 (1976) 235–51. ———. *Paulus im ältesten Christentum: Das Bild des Apostels und die Rezeption der paulinischen Theologie in der frühchristlichen Literatur bis Marcion.* Tübingen: Mohr, 1979. **Lona, H. E.** *Die Eschatologie im Kolosser- und Epheserbrief.* Würzburg: Echter Verlag, 1984. **MacDonald, M. Y.** *The Pauline Churches.* Cambridge: CUP, 1988. **Mackay, J. A.** *God's Order: The Ephesian Letter and This Present Time.* London: Nisbet and Macmillan, 1953. **MacPhail, J. R.** "Ephesians and the Church of South India." *SJT* 10 (1957) 57–75. **Martin, R. P.** "An Epistle in Search of a Life-Setting." *ExpTim* 79 (1968) 296–302. ———. *Reconciliation: A Study of Paul's Theology.* London: Marshall, 1981. **Meeks, W. A.** "In One Body: The Unity of Humankind in Colossians and Ephesians." In *God's Christ and His People,* ed. J. Jervell and W. A. Meeks. Oslo: Universitetsforlaget, 1977, 209–21. **Meritan, J.** "L'ecclésiologie de l'épître aux Éphésiens." *RB* 7 (1898) 343–69. **Merkel, H.** "Der Epheserbrief in der neueren exegetischen Diskussion." *ANRW* 2.25.4 (1987) 3156–3246. **Merklein, H.** *Das kirchliche Amt nach dem Epheserbrief.* Munich: Kösel, 1973. ———. "Paulinische Theologie in der Rezeption des Kolosser- und Epheserbriefes." In *Paulus in den neutestamentlichen Spätschriften,* ed. K. Kertelge. Freiburg: Herder, 1981, 25–69. **Metzger, B. M.** *A Textual Commentary on the Greek New Testament.* London: United Bible Societies, 1971. **Meyer, R. P.** *Kirche und Mission im Epheserbrief.* Stuttgart: Katholisches Bibelwerk, 1977. **Mitton, C. L.** "The Authorship of the Epistle to the Ephesians." *ExpTim* 67 (1955–56) 195–98. ———. *The Epistle to the Ephesians.* Oxford: Clarendon Press, 1951. ———. "The Relationship between 1 Peter and Ephesians." *JTS* 1 (1950) 67–73. **Moir, I. A.** "The Text of Ephesians Exhibited by Minuscule Manuscripts Housed in Great Britain—Some Preliminary Comments." In *Studies in New Testament Language and Text,* ed. J. K. Elliott. Leiden: Brill, 1976, 313–18. **Moody, D.** *Christ and the Church.* Grand Rapids: Eerdmans, 1963. **Mooney, C. F.** "Paul's Vision of the Church in 'Ephesians.'" *Scr* 15 (1963) 33–43. **Moule, C. F. D.** *An Idiom-Book of New Testament Greek.* 2nd ed. Cambridge: C.U.P., 1971. **Moule, H. C. G.** *Ephesian Studies.*

London: Hodder and Stoughton, 1900. **Murphy-O'Connor, J.** "Truth: Paul and Qumran." *Paul and Qumran*, ed. J. Murphy-O'Connor. London: Geoffrey Chapman, 1968, 179–230. ———. "Who Wrote Ephesians?" *TBT* 18 (1965) 1201–9. **Mussner, F.** *Christus, das All und die Kirche.* 2nd ed. Trier: Paulinus, 1968. ———. "Contributions Made by Qumran to the Understanding of the Epistle to the Ephesians." In *Paul and Qumran*, ed. J. Murphy-O'Connor. London: Geoffrey Chapman, 1968, 159–78. ———. "Die Geschichtstheologie des Epheserbriefes." *BibLeb* 5 (1964) 8–12. **Ochel, W.** *Die Annahme einer Bearbeitung des Kolosser-Briefes im Epheser-Brief.* Würzburg: Konrad Triltsch, 1934. **Odeberg, H.** *The View of the Universe in the Epistle to the Ephesians.* Lund: Lund Universitets Arsskrift, 1934. **Percy, E.** *Der Leib Christi in den paulinischen Homologoumena und Antilegomena.* Lund: Gleerup, 1942. ———. *Die Probleme der Kolosser- und Epheserbriefe.* Lund: Gleerup, 1946. ———. "Zu den Problemen des Kolosser- und Epheserbriefes." *ZNW* 43 (1950–51) 178–94. **Perels, O.** "Kirche und Welt nach dem Epheser- und Kolosserbrief." *TLZ* 76 (1951) 391–400. **Pokorny, P.** *Der Epheserbrief und die Gnosis.* Berlin: Evangelische Verlagsanstalt, 1965. ———. "Epheserbrief und gnostische Mysterien." *ZNW* 53 (1962) 160–94. ———. "Soma Christou im Epheserbrief." *EvT* 20 (1960) 456–64. **Polhill, J. B.** "The Relationship between Ephesians and Colossians." *RevExp* 70 (1973) 439–50. **Reuss, J.** "Die Kirche als 'Leib Christi' und die Herkunft dieser Vorstellung bei dem Apostel Paulus." *BZ* 2 (1958) 103–27. **Ridderbos, H.** *Paul: An Outline of His Theology.* Tr. J. R. de Witt. Grand Rapids: Eerdmans, 1975. **Roels, E.** *God's Mission: The Epistle to the Ephesians in Mission Perspective.* Franeker: Wever, 1962. **Roon, A. van.** *The Authenticity of Ephesians.* Leiden: Brill, 1974. **Rowston, D. J.** "Changes in Biblical Interpretation: Ephesians." *BTB* 9 (1979) 121–25. **Sampley, J. P.**, et al. *Ephesians, Colossians, 2 Thessalonians, The Pastoral Epistles.* Philadelphia: Fortress, 1978. **Sanders, E. P.** *Paul and Palestinian Judaism.* London: SCM, 1977. **Sanders, J. T.** "Hymnic Elements in Ephesians 1–3." *ZNW* 56 (1965) 214–32. **Schille, G.** "Der Autor des Epheserbriefes." *TLZ* 82 (1957) 325–34. ———. *Frühchristliche Hymnen.* Berlin: Evangelische Verlagsanstalt, 1965. **Schlier, H.** *Christus und die Kirche im Epheserbrief.* Tübingen: Mohr, 1930. **Schmid, J.** *Der Epheserbrief des Apostels Paulus.* Freiburg: Herder, 1928. **Schnackenburg, R.** "Der Epheserbrief im heutigen Horizont." In *Massstab des Glaubens.* Freiburg: Herder, 1978, 155–75. ———. "Er hat uns mitauferweckt: Zur Tauflehre des Epheserbriefes." *LJ* 2 (1952) 159–83. ———. "Gestalt und Wesen der Kirche nach dem Epheserbrief." In *Schriften zum Neuen Testament.* Munich: Kösel, 1971, 268–87. ———. "L'Idée de 'Corps du Christ' dans la lettre aux Éphésiens: Perspective pour nôtre temps." In *Paul de Tarse. Apôtre du nôtre Temps*, ed. L. de Lorenzi. Rome: Abbaye de St. Paul, 1979, 665–85. **Schweizer, E.** "Zur Frage der Echtheit des Kolosser- und des Epheserbriefes." *ZNW* 47 (1956) 287. **Smalley, S. S.** "The Eschatology of Ephesians." *EvQ* 28 (1956) 152–57. **Smith, D. C.** "The Ephesian Heresy and the Origin of the Epistle to the Ephesians." *Ohio Journal of Religious Studies* 5 (1977) 78–103. **Steinmetz, F.-J.** "Jenseits der Mauern und Zäune: Somatisches Verständnis der kirchlichen Einheit im Epheserbrief." *Geist und Leben* 59 (1986) 202–14. ———. "Parusie-Erwartung im Epheserbrief? Ein Vergleich." *Bib* 50 (1969) 328–36. ———. *Protologische Heilszuversicht: Die Strukturen des soteriologischen und christologischen Denkens in Kolosser- und Epheserbrief.* Frankfurt: Josef Knecht, 1969. **Stott, J. R. W.** *God's New Society: The Message of Ephesians.* Leicester: Inter-Varsity, 1979. **Summers, R.** *Ephesians: Pattern for Christian Living.* Nashville: Broadman, 1960. **Tachau, P.** *"Einst" und "Jetzt" im Neuen Testament.* Göttingen: Vandenhoeck & Ruprecht, 1972. **Usami, K.** *Somatic Comprehension of Unity: The Church in Ephesus.* Rome: Biblical Institute Press, 1983. **Vanhoye, A.** "L'épître aux Éphésiens et l'épître aux Hébreux." *Bib* 59 (1978) 198–230. **Warnach, V.** "Taufwirklichkeit und Taufbewusstsein nach dem Epheserbrief." *Liturgie und Mönchtum* 33/34 (1963–64) 36–51. **Weiss, H.-F.** "Gnostische Motive und antignostische Polemik im Kolosser- und im Epheserbrief." In *Gnosis und Neues Testament*, ed. K.-W. Tröger. Berlin: Evangelische Verlagsanstalt, 1973, 311–24. **Wild, R. A.** " 'Be Imitators of God': Discipleship in the

Letter to the Ephesians." In *Discipleship in the New Testament,* ed. F. Segovia. Philadelphia: Fortress, 1985, 127–43. **Williamson, L.** *God's Work of Art.* Richmond, VA: CLC Press, 1971. **Wilson, R. A.** " 'We' and 'You' in the Epistle to the Ephesians." *SE* 2. (1964), 676–80. **Wink, W.,** *Naming the Powers.* Philadelphia: Fortress, 1984. **Yates, R.** "Principalities and Powers in Ephesians." *NB* 58 (1977) 516–21. **Zwaan, J. de.** "Le 'rythme logique' dans l'épître aux Éphésiens." *RHPR* 6 (1927) 554–65.

Introduction

Select Bibliography

Barker, G. W.; Lane, W. L.; and **Michaels, J. R.** *The New Testament Speaks.* New York: Harper and Row, 1969. **Childs, B. S.** *The New Testament as Canon: An Introduction.* London: SCM, 1984. **Fuller, R. H.** *A Critical Introduction to the New Testament.* London: Duckworth, 1966. **Guthrie, D.** *New Testament Introduction.* 3rd ed. London: Tyndale Press, 1970. **Johnson, L. T.** *The Writings of the New Testament.* London: SCM, 1986. **Keck, L. E.,** and **Furnish, V. P.** *The Pauline Letters.* Atlanta: John Knox, 1975. **Koester, H.** *Introduction to the New Testament.* 2 vols. Philadelphia: Fortress, 1982. **Kümmel, W. G.** *Introduction to the New Testament.* Rev. ed. Tr. H. C. Kee. Nashville: Abingdon, 1975. **Martin, R. P.** *New Testament Foundations.* Vol. 2. Grand Rapids: Eerdmans; Exeter: Paternoster, 1978. **Marxsen, W.** *Introduction to the New Testament.* Tr. G. Buswell. Philadelphia: Fortress, 1968. **Moffatt, J.** *An Introduction to the Literature of the New Testament.* 2nd ed. Edinburgh: T. & T. Clark, 1912. **Perrin, N.,** and **Duling, D. C.** *The New Testament: An Introduction.* 2nd ed. New York: Harcourt Brace Jovanovich, 1982. **Roetzel, C. J.** *The Letters of Paul.* Atlanta: John Knox, 1975. **Schenke, H.-M.,** and **Fischer, K. M.** *Einleitung in die Schriften des Neuen Testaments.* 2 vols. Gütersloh: Gerd Mohn, 1978. **Wikenhauser, A.** *New Testament Introduction.* Tr. J. Cunningham. New York: Herder & Herder, 1958.

1. Content/Structure/Genre/Style

Bibliography

Alexander, P. S. "Epistolary Literature." In *Compendia Rerum Judaicarum ad Novum Testamentum.* Vol. 2, ed. M. E. Stone. Assen: van Gorcum, 1984, 579–96. **Audet, J. P.** "Literary Forms and Contents of a Normal Εὐχαριστία in the First Century." *SE* 1. (1959) 643–62. **Aune, D. E.** *The New Testament in Its Literary Environment.* Philadelphia: Westminster Press, 1987. **Berger, K.** "Hellenistische Gattungen im Neuen Testament." *ANRW* 2.25.2 (1984) 1031–1432, 1831–85. ———. *Formgeschichte des Neuen Testaments.* Heidelberg: Quelle & Meyer, 1984. **Bjerkelund, C. J.** *Parakalô.* Oslo: Universitetsforlaget, 1967. **Burgess, T. C.** "Epideictic Literature." *Studies in Classical Philology* 3 (1902) 89–261. **Dahl, N. A.** "Interpreting Ephesians: Then and Now." *CurTM* 5 (1978) 133–43. **Doty, W.** *Letters in Primitive Christianity.* Philadelphia: Fortress, 1973. **Jewett, R.** *The Thessalonian Correspondence.* Philadelphia: Fortress, 1986. **Johanson, B. C.** *To All the Brethren.* Stockholm: Almquist & Wiksell, 1987. **Kennedy, G. A.** *New Testament Interpretation through Rhetorical Criticism.* Chapel Hill: University of North Carolina Press, 1984. **Lausberg, H.** *Handbuch der literarischen Rhetorik.* 2nd ed. Munich: Max Hueber, 1973. **Malherbe, A. J.** "Ancient Epistolary Theorists." *Ohio Journal of Religious Studies* 5 (1977) 3–77. **O'Brien, P. T.** *Introductory Thanksgivings in the Letters of Paul.* Leiden: Brill, 1977. **Perelman, Ch.** *The Realm of Rhetoric.* Notre Dame: University of Notre Dame Press, 1982. **Perelman, Ch.,** and **Olbrechts-Tyteca, L.** *The New Rhetoric.* Notre Dame: University of Notre Dame Press, 1969. **Roberts, J. H.** "Pauline Transitions to the Letter Body." In *L'Apôtre Paul,* ed. A. Vanhoye. Leuven: Leuven University Press, 1986, 93–99. **Sanders, J. T.** "The Transition from Opening Epistolary Thanksgiving to Body in the Letters of the Pauline Corpus." *JBL* 81 (1962) 348–62. ———. "Hymnic Elements in Ephesians 1–3." *ZNW* 56 (1965) 214–32. **Schubert, P.** *Form and Function of the Pauline Thanksgivings.* Berlin: A. Töpelmann, 1939. **Stowers, S. K.** *Letter Writing in Greco-Roman Antiquity.*

Philadelphia: Westminster Press, 1986. **Thyen, H.** *Der Stil der jüdisch-hellenistischen Homilie.* Göttingen: Vandenhoeck & Ruprecht, 1955. **White, J. L.** *The Form and Function of the Body of the Greek Letter.* Missoula, MT: Scholars Press, 1972. ———. "Saint Paul and the Apostolic Letter Tradition." *CBQ* 45 (1983) 433–44. ———. "New Testament Epistolary Literature." *ANRW* 2.25.2 (1984) 1730–56. **Zwaan, J. de.** "Le 'rythme logique' dans l'épître aux Éphésiens." *RHPR* 6 (1927) 554–65.

The letter to the Ephesians falls into two distinct, though not totally separate, parts—chaps. 1–3 and chaps. 4–6—with the "Amen" at the end of chap. 3 and the change to direct exhortation at the beginning of chap. 4 as clear division markers. Recognition of these two parts is determinative for discussion of each of the areas of content, structure, genre, and style.

The two parts reflect the writer's two major concerns, often described loosely as theological or doctrinal and ethical. But particularly the former label of "theological" or "doctrinal" does not do enough justice to either the form or content of chaps. 1–3. Within the framework of an extended thanksgiving these chapters contain a reminder to the Gentile Christian readers of the privileges and status they enjoy as believers in Christ and members of the Church, reinforcing for them their significance in God's plan for history and the cosmos. The second part of the letter then constitutes an appeal to live in the Church and in the world in the light of these realities and not simply to become merged into the ethos of the surrounding culture. There is an explicit link between the two parts through the notion of calling. If chaps. 1–3 are a reminder of the readers' calling (cf. 1:18, "that you may know what is the hope of his calling"), then chaps. 4–6 are an exhortation to live in a manner appropriate to that distinctive calling (cf. 4:1, "I . . . exhort you therefore to lead a life worthy of the calling with which you were called"). Simply to see Ephesians in terms of the discourse on the unity of the Church which begins at 2:1 (cf. Keck and Furnish, *The Pauline Letters*, 127; Patzia, 113–18) does not do enough justice either to the content and thrust of 2:1–10, 3:1–13, and 3:14–21 or to the bulk of the paraenesis. Similarly, to entitle 1:3–3:21 "The Mystery of the Inclusion of the Gentiles" is to read this theme into 1:3–2:10 and 3:14–21 in an unwarranted fashion, and to describe 4:1–6:20 as "Exhortation to Unity of Spirit in Peace" is not to take sufficient account of the varying emphases of the different sections of paraenesis (*pace* Roetzel, *The Letters of Paul*, 105–6).

The first three chaps. have the overall framework of a long thanksgiving (cf. also J. T. Sanders, *JBL* 81 [1962] 348–62; Gaugler, 124–25). They open with a eulogy or blessing of God for all the privileges of salvation enjoyed by the readers (1:3–14) and move into a thanksgiving period with its intercessory prayer-report for the addressees' knowledge of God and his power and of the Church's significance in his purposes (1:15–23). The intercessory prayer-report is picked up again later, focusing this time on the readers' experience of power, love, and fullness (3:1, 14–19), before the first half is rounded off with a doxology (3:20, 21). The remainder of this first part of the letter pursues the writer's aim in a form less explicitly related to liturgy. The initial intercession (1:15–23) blends into a reminder of the greatness of the salvation God has accomplished for the readers. This reminder is expressed by means of the twofold contrast between their past and their present: first, in terms of the change from spiritual death to new life in Christ (2:1–10) and, second, in terms of the change from being deprived Gentiles in comparison with Israel to being part of the one new humanity with access to the Father and a place in the new temple of the Church (2:11–22). This anamnesis (cf. 2:11, *"remember, therefore . . ."*) is a recalling of the heritage of the past in a way that is formative for present attitudes and actions. It is continued when the return to intercession (3:1, 14–19) is interrupted by a further reminder, this time of what the readers, as part of the one Church with its significant role, owe to the ministry of the apostle Paul (3:2–13). There are also, of course, aspects of anamnesis, the remembering of God's graciousness and power at work on behalf of believers, in the *berakah* and thanksgiving (cf. also Audet, *SE* 1 [1959] 646, 655 n. 1, 659 n. 1).

If the first half of the letter is distinguished by its epistolary use of liturgical forms and its elements of anamnesis, the second half is distinguished by the extent of its concern with paraenesis. From its opening direct appeal in the *parakalō* clause taken over from the Pauline letter ("I . . . exhort you therefore," 4:1), the latter half is almost totally given over to ethical exhortation, the major sections of which employ the writer's favorite term for believers' conduct, the verb περιπατεῖν, "to walk" (cf. 4:1; 4:17; 5:2; 5:8; 5:15). The readers are urged first to play their part in maintaining the unity of the Church, which is on its way to maturity through its ministers of the word and the love of all its members (4:1–16), and then to live as those who have been taught the Christian tradition and are members of the new humanity rather than the old (4:17–24). The distinctive conduct required of Christian believers is given more specificity in the two sections which follow. Their words and deeds are to reflect the contrast between their new life and their old (4:25–5:2) and the contrast between what is appropriate for the believing community and what is characteristic of sinful outsiders. By preserving such a contrast the readers will in fact have an effect on the darkness of the surrounding moral climate (5:3–14). The readers are then enjoined to live wisely and to appropriate the power of the Spirit, which will result in corporate edification and worship (5:15–20). Such living will also result in mutual submission in the specific relationships between husband and wife, parent and child, master and slave, set out in this writer's version of the household code with its distinctive elaboration of the marriage relationship in the light of the relationship between Christ and the Church (5:21–6:9). The paraenesis culminates in a call to the readers to be strong and stand firm in the spiritual battle against the powers of evil that are arrayed against them and to engage in constant prayer (6:10–20).

Like a number of other early Christian compositions, Ephesians resists clear-cut classification in terms of ancient epistolary and rhetorical categories (cf. also Aune, *The New Testament in Its Literary Environment*, 199, 203, for the general point about NT letters). More work is needed on this important aspect of the letter, and what follows is simply an outline of some of the considerations involved. Ephesians appears to be an adaptation of the Pauline letter form. It does have the usual prescript with its mention of writer and addressees and its Christian greetings (1:1, 2) and ends with some typical closing features, e.g., a reference to an apostolic representative (employing the same wording as Col 4:7, 8), a wish of peace, and a grace-benediction (6:21–24). Are the prescript and the postscript simply a framing device for a letter-essay or philosophical letter (cf. Aune, *The New Testament in Its Literary Environment*, 167–68; Berger, *ANRW* 2.25.2 [1984] 1132–38)? Ephesians does have some features in common with such letters in that it provides teaching which leads to advice about how to live, but it is distinguished by the liturgical elements in the first part, some of which are also epistolary characteristics of the Pauline letter. It is therefore more than just a theological tract barely disguised as a letter (*pace* Käsemann, *RGG* 2:518; Fuller, *A Critical Introduction to the New Testament*, 66; Conzelmann, 86; Lindemann, *ZNW* 67 [1976] 240; Schenke and Fischer, *Einleitung* 1:174). In addition to its beginning and end, it makes use of such elements of Paul's letters as an introductory eulogy, a thanksgiving period and intercessory prayer-report, and paraenesis, though it is the only letter in the Pauline corpus with both a eulogy and a thanksgiving period (cf. also van Roon, *Authenticity*, 45–56).

But does Ephesians have a letter body? There are difficulties in determining where the body begins and ends in Paul's letters (cf. Doty, *Letters in Primitive Christianity*, 34; Aune, *The New Testament in Its Literary Environment*, 183, "the analysis of the central section of early Christian letters remains problematical"). But it can be said that Ephesians has few of the usual features of the Pauline letter's body—its own formal opening, its transitional formulae, and its concluding "eschatological climax" or mention of an apostolic parousia or travel plans. In regard to the prominence of the features of the thanksgiving period and the absence of a normal body, Ephesians is perhaps closest to 1 Thessalonians (cf. also Bjerkelund, *Parakalô*, 184–85, who holds that in terms of structure Ephesians should be compared with 1 Thessalonians; Kümmel, *Introduction*, 351–52). Schubert (*Form and Function of the Pauline Thanksgivings*, 16–27; cf. also O'Brien, *Introductory Thanksgivings in the Letters of Paul*, 141–46) suggested that 1 Thessalonians had no main body because the thanksgiving of 1:2–3:13 itself constitutes the body. However, White (*The Form and Function of the Body of the Greek Letter*, 70–72) argues that the body is a structural element, though to be sure, taken up into, shaped by, and logically dependent on the thanksgiving. Jewett (*The Thessalonian Correspondence*, 71–78, 216–21) provides a sketch of the various views and suggests, in a combination of epistolary and rhetorical analysis, that 1:2–5 is to be seen as the thanksgiving proper with 1:6–3:13 as the *narratio* of the grounds for thanksgiving. In Ephesians the material immediately after the initial thanksgiving period proper does not have a disclosure formula or a formula of request, which frequently introduces the body. Roberts ("Pauline Transitions," 93–99) argues that creedal statements can also function as transitions to the letter body, but it is very doubtful whether Eph 1:22, 23 is best described as a discrete period containing a creedal statement, as he claims. Instead 2:1 continues the train of thought already begun in the intercessory prayer-report about the display of God's power on behalf of believers but now gives this more direct application to the readers.

Yet if it is the case that the body of the Pauline letter has as a major characteristic two parts to its argumentation—first, a more tightly organized theological part and, second, a less tightly constructed appeal for the concretization of the principles espoused earlier (cf. White, *The Form and Function of the Body of the Greek Letter,* 159; *ANRW* 2.25.2, 1746–48; Aune, *The New Testament in Its Literary Environment,* 188, 191)—then 1:3–3:21 and 4:1–6:20 correspond to those parts. Other scholars (cf. Doty, *Letters in Primitive Christianity,* 27, 37; Roetzel, *The Letters of Paul,* 22–24), however, see paraenesis as a separate section after the body in the Pauline letter, so that its three main sections are thanksgiving, body, and paraenesis. In this case Ephesians could be seen as replacing the body by extending both the thanksgiving and the paraenesis. We suggest, therefore, that 1:3–3:21 functions as the equivalent to the first part of the body, which here has the overall shape of an extended thanksgiving period (cf. also Dibelius-Greeven 78), and that the *parakalō* clause in 4:1 acts as the transition to the paraenesis, which can be taken as the equivalent of the body's second major part. In fact, thanksgiving and paraenesis make good companions. Bringing them together in the central section of the letter in this way can be seen to be a natural development from the Pauline letter. As we have seen, among Paul's own letters, 1 Thessalonians constitutes a move in this direction. In any case, thanksgivings in Paul's letters already begin to argue that a particular course of action is required by the situation (cf. Doty, *Letters in Primitive Christianity,* 32). As Schubert (*Form and Function of the Pauline Thanksgivings,* 89) puts it, "All Pauline thanksgivings have either explicitly or implicitly paraenetic function."

Noticeably, however, Ephesians in its body and as a whole lacks the marks of the typical Pauline letter's addressing of particular and immediate issues. It contains no list of personal greetings, and its themes and their treatment are more general than specific. Thyen (*Der Stil der jüdisch-hellenistischen Homilie,* 63, 119–20) proposed that the body of the letters of Paul, with their teaching and paraenesis, reflected the manner in which Paul preached to his congregations and may therefore have been influenced by the synagogue homily. The body of Ephesians seems even more like the written equivalent of the oral presentation the writer would have delivered to a congregation at its assembly for worship. It is the written equivalent of a sermon or homily (cf. Alexander, "Epistolary Literature," 584, who claims that the Jewish literary letter may have grown out of the sermon and been regarded as "the written analogue of the sermon"; he cites *2 Apoc. Bar.* and Romans as examples). Certainly its liturgical forms would have enabled the reading of the letter to fit appropriately into a liturgical setting. Its opening sequence of eulogy, thanksgiving, intercession, and doxology was widespread in Jewish and early Christian worship. As J. T. Sanders (*ZNW* 56 [1965] 214) asserts, "the doxology at the end of ch. 3 is a *closing* liturgical element, just as the blessing and thanksgiving in ch. 1 are opening liturgical elements" (cf. also Gnilka, 27; Kirby, *Ephesians,* 84–89; 126–38). Of course, the concluding "Amen" in 3:21 also signals the liturgical setting of the letter (cf. O. Cullmann, *Early Christian Worship* [London: SCM, 1953] 23–24, "The liturgical Amen, likewise taken over from Judaism, is said by the congregation, as we see from 1 Cor 14:16"; cf. also Kirby, *Ephesians,* 88, on the importance of this congregational response). Indeed Ephesians has been described as a liturgical homily (cf. Gnilka, 33, and on liturgical elements in homilies cf. also Thyen, *Der Stil,* 28–31). No certainty can be attached to such a classification, however, since there is no clearcut evidence from this period of any fixed forms for either early Christian or Jewish synagogue homilies (cf. Aune, *The New Testament in Its Literary Environment*, 197, 202).

The two basic parts of this written discourse and their functions may nevertheless reflect general patterns familiar from Jewish tradition. One example is the "covenant speech" pattern in which a reminder of what God had done on behalf of his people was followed by a call to keep his commandments. Sections of Deuteronomy have this sequence, and the book also includes a song of praise (cf. L. Hartman, "Bundesideologie in und hinter einigen paulinischen Texten," in *Die paulinische Literatur und Theologie,* ed. S. Petersen [Göttingen: Vandenhoeck & Ruprecht, 1980] 103–18, for the influence of this sort of material on Paul's letters and thought). It is possible that Jewish proselyte baptism exerted some influence, since much later sources (cf. *b. Yebam.* 47; *Gerim* 1.5) indicate that an address of congratulation and exhortation accompanies the rite (cf. also F. Gavin, *The Jewish Antecedents of the Christian Sacraments* [London: S.P.C.K., 1928] 31–32, 35, 56). But the adoption of the rite and its interpretation was still evolving during the last part of the first century C.E., so uncertainty must still surround its influence on early Christian ceremonial. It is easy to see, however, why the sort of sermon the body of Ephesians reflects has been related to a Christian baptismal setting (cf. esp. Kirby, *Ephesians,* 150–61; also R. R. Williams, "The Pauline Catechism," 89–96; Dahl, *TZ* 7 [1951] 241–64; Coutts, *NTS* 3 [1956–57] 115–27; Pokorný, *ZNW* 53 [1962] 160–94), in which the preacher recalled the activity of God in the change from believers' past to their present and then appealed to them to live out the significance of their baptism. But, although the letter contains some strong baptismal motifs, its content is not simply to be reduced to an exposition of the significance of this rite. Its subject is much broader—Christian existence as a whole.

Ephesians is sometimes classed as a general letter (cf., e.g., Aune, *The New Testament in Its Literary Environment,* 218), but, despite its more general nature in comparison with the undisputed Pauline letters, the letter's content is not solely determined by the situation of its writer. The content shows clear signs that the writer does have a pastoral concern for a particular group of recipients, certain churches in western Asia Minor, and has shaped his material to meet their needs (cf. also Schnackenburg, 19; see further Section 4). In terms of ancient epistolary theory there is nothing to disqualify it as a letter. It is a real communication, speaking in the written medium to those absent as though they were present, and is adapted to the circumstances and mood of its addressees as far as these can be ascertained (cf. also Dahl, *IDBSup* [1976] 268; *contra,* e.g., Kümmel, *Introduction,* 356; Mussner, 17). Its style is a mixture of the graceful and ornamentative with the plain and direct (cf. Malherbe, *Ohio Journal of Religious Studies* 5 [1977] 15–27). Its letter form should not therefore be dismissed as nonreal but should be seen as a natural extension of the Pauline letter in the direction of an epistolary sermon or homily.

Dahl has called Ephesians "a letter of reminder and of congratulation" (*CurTM* 5 [1978] 141). Although its first part does have a congratulatory tone, its reminder of what the readers have become as the Church is not, of course, in the form of a direct congratulation of the readers. This would not in any case be in line with the writer's perspective on the grace of God, to which, he holds, believers owe everything. The reminder, therefore, takes the shape of a celebration before God of all that he has accomplished for these believers, and it takes place in the context of praise and thanksgiving. So, is the first part of Ephesians more like an ancient letter of congratulation or more like one of thanksgiving (though not to the readers but to God for what he has done for the readers)? Ancient epistolary theorists determined the type of a letter in the light of the action its writer intended to perform through it. In terms of its overall intended effect on the readers, the first part, with its thanksgiving and reminders, serves primarily to bolster their sense of their calling, their awareness of their status as those who belong to the Church. In that sense it is probably best seen as a Christian version of the letter of congratulation. But in any case the letter's two parts mean that its genre is a mixed one. The second part is a variation on the Greek letter of advice—the *logos protreptikos* or *logos parainetikos* (cf. Aune, *The New Testament in Its Literary Environment*, 161; Berger, *ANRW* 2.25.2 [1984] 1138–45). The letter as a whole then brings together what Pseudo-Demetrius (*Epistolary Types* 11, 19) would call the congratulatory and the advisory, and Pseudo-Libanius (*Epistolary Styles* 4, 5, 20, 45, 52, 67, 92) the congratulatory and the paraenetic types of letter (cf. Malherbe, *Ohio Journal of Religious Studies* 5 [1977] 28–39, 62–77).

Ephesians, as we have it, is in the form of a letter, but since the letter would have been meant to be read aloud to its recipients, and since, as we have suggested, the bulk of it is equivalent to a sermon, a rhetorical analysis of it is also appropriate (cf. also Johanson, *To All the Brethren*, 42–43, on the relationship of rhetorical analysis to letters; for a more detailed discussion of the rhetoric of Ephesians as it affects the relationship of the two halves of the letter, see also R. R. Jeal, "The Relationship between Theology and Ethics in the Letter to the Ephesians," Ph.D. diss., University of Sheffield, 1990). The congratulatory and the paraenetic, the reminder of the readers' calling and the appeal to live out that calling, combine the epideictic and the deliberative rhetorical genres (cf. Lausberg, *Handbuch der literarischen Rhetorik*, 53–61, for a discussion of the three main genres and their possible combinations; cf. also Berger, *Formgeschichte*, 17–19; as G. Lyons [*Pauline Autobiography: Toward a New Understanding* (Atlanta: Scholars Press, 1985) 64] points out, "The freedom ancient writers exercised in the mixing of genres and in the organization of a discourse complicates rhetorical analysis making a measure of subjectivity unavoidable.") Perelman's and Olbrechts-Tyteca's description of epideictic rhetoric serves to illumine the intended effect of the first part of Ephesians: "The argumentation in epideictic discourse sets out to increase the intensity of adherence to certain values, which might not be contested when considered on their own but may nevertheless not prevail against other values that might come into conflict with them. The speaker tries to establish a sense of communion centered around particular values recognized by the audience and to this end he uses the whole range of means available to the rhetorician for purposes of amplification and enhancement" (*The New Rhetoric*, 51; cf. also

Kennedy, *New Testament Interpretation through Rhetorical Criticism,* 74–75). They also point out that this kind of oratory is a showpiece for artistic virtuosity and is most in danger of becoming rhetoric in the pejorative sense of the word. The ornamentative thanksgiving and prayer of Eph 1–3 is an effective rhetorical strategy. It is one thing for a writer to argue a case with his readers, which may or may not be persuasive, but it is another thing to give thanks and pray for them. This sets up a different relationship in which the readers are affirmed, in which their sympathies are gained, and in which a common relationship to God and to Christ and common values grounded in this relationship are consolidated. It avoids focusing on any differences between the writer and the readers, it eschews confrontation, and it goes beyond linear argumentation to touch the readers' religious emotions and Christian commitment.

In the deliberative genre a speaker or writer seeks to persuade an audience to take certain actions. Paraenesis is not necessarily deliberative. It can function in both deliberative and epideictic rhetoric, depending on whether it is calling for a change of behavior or simply reiterating common values (Aune, *The New Testament in Its Literary Environment,* 191, 208; Berger, *ANRW* 2.25.2, 1139). Though some of the paraenesis in Ephesians is a reminder of common values (cf., e.g., 4:20, 21) and calls for a preservation of what is already the case (cf. 4:3; 6:10–17, which returns to the epideictic genre, see below), for the most part the writer is seeking an adjustment in the readers' behavior so that, where necessary, it will become more distinctly Christian, that is, more in line with what he deems to be appropriate for those who belong to the Church. Paraenesis frequently functioned, as it does in places here, to remind those addressed of what they should already know, but it did this in order to exhort them to take action on the basis of this knowledge. This second part of the letter attempts by persuasive (protreptic) and dissuasive (apotreptic) means to encourage the readers to take certain actions in the future and is therefore primarily deliberative. In fact, the epideictic first part of the letter leads well into the deliberative second part, for the role of the epideictic "is to intensify adherence to values, adherence without which discourses that aim at provoking action cannot find the lever to move or inspire their listeners. . . . The goal is always to strengthen a consensus around certain values which one wants to see prevail and which should orient actions in the future. It is in this way that all practical philosophy arises from the epideictic genre" (Perelman, *The Realm of Rhetoric,* 19–20; cf. also Burgess, "Epideictic Literature," 96, 101–2, 229–34, on the close links between the epideictic and the deliberative). In Ephesians the combination of the two rhetorical genres makes for a more powerful overall impact. The celebration, worship, and prayer that precede the paraenesis are likely to move and inspire the readers to the action called for more effectively than if the letter had consisted primarily of a string of exhortations. It is significant that the *peroratio* of 6:10–20, which sums up the concerns of the whole letter, combines both epideictic and deliberative elements. However, it returns primarily to the epideictic with its call to stand firm in the battle and thus to preserve the values the writer has attempted to instill in his readers.

An epistolary analysis of the letter in the light of the above discussion would result in the following:

1:1,2	I. Prescript
1:1a	A. Sender
1:1b	B. Addressees
1:2	C. Greeting
1:3–6:20	II. Body
1:3–3:21	A. Extended Thanksgiving
1:3–14	1. Eulogy
1:15–23	2. Initial Thanksgiving Period and Intercessory Prayer-Report
2:1–10	3. Reminder of Readers' Experience of Salvation
2:11–22	4. Reminder of Readers' Privileges as Gentile Participants in the New Creation and New Temple
3:(1)2–13	5. Reminder of Readers' Debt to Paul and His Ministry
3:14–21	6. Intercessory Prayer-Report and Doxology
4:1–6:20	B. Paraenesis
4:1–16	1. Exhortation to Maintenance of the Church's Unity
4:17–24	2. Exhortation to Live According to the New Humanity Rather Than the Old
4:25–5:2	3. Practical Injunctions about the Old and New Life
5:3–14	4. Exhortations about Speech, Sexual Morality, and Living as Children of Light
5:15–6:9	5. Exhortation to Wise and Spirit-Filled Living in Worship and in Household Relationships
6:10–20	6. Exhortation to Stand Firm in the Spiritual Battle and to Constant Prayer
6:21–24	III. Postscript
6:21, 22	A. Reference to Apostolic Representative, Tychicus
6:23	B. Wish of Peace
6:24	C. Grace-Benediction

A brief rhetorical outline of the letter on the other hand might be as follows:

1:1–23	I. Exordium
1:1, 2	A. Prescript
1:3–14	B. Eulogy
1:15–23	C. Thanksgiving and Prayer
2:1–3:21	II. *Narratio* of Grounds for Thanksgiving
2:1–10	A. Reminder of Readers' Salvation in Christ
2:11–22	B. Reminder of Readers' Privileges as Gentile Participants in the New Creation and New Temple
3:(1)2–13	C. *Digressio*: Reminder of Readers' Debt to Paul and His Ministry
3:1, 14–21	D. *Transitus* of Intercessory Prayer and Doxology
4:1–6:9	III. *Exhortatio*
4:1–16	A. Exhortation to Maintenance of the Church's Unity
4:17–24	B. Exhortation to Live as the New Humanity

4:25–5:2		C. Seven Specific Exhortations about the Old and New Life
5:3–14		D. Exhortations about Speech, Sexual Morality, and Living as Children of Light
5:15–6:9		E. Exhortation to Wise and Spirit-Filled Living in Worship and in Household Relationships
6:10–24	IV.	*Peroratio*
6:10–20		A. Final Exhortation to Stand Firm in the Spiritual Battle
6:21–24		B. Postscript

Through its eulogy about their salvation and its thanksgiving and intercessory prayer on their behalf, the exordium leads the readers into this epistolary discourse in such a way as to make them receptive to its message (cf. Quintilian 3.8.7; 4.1.5, on the exordium's function of gaining the audience's favorable disposition and sympathy toward the discourse). The *narratio* functioned as a report of the circumstances on which the audience was to base its perspective or actions (cf. Aristotle, *Rhet.* 3.6.1–11; Quintilian 4.2.1). Here there is a skillful transition from the exordium into the *narratio* with its recalling of the readers' past experience. This continues the flow of thought, as what has previously been said about Christ is now applied to the readers (cf. Lausberg, *Handbuch der literarischen Rhetorik*, 163). The *narratio* often contains an excursus or *digressio*, found here in 3:2–13 (cf. Lausberg, *Handbuch der literarischen Rhetorik*, 187–88), Quintilian (4.3.1) suggests that a digression in the *narratio* enables speakers to move to "some pleasant and attractive topic with a view to securing the utmost amount of favor from their audience." Certainly someone writing in Paul's name is calculated to increase his readers' favor and trust by digressing about the suffering apostle's ministry on their behalf. Together with the *transitus* such a digression helps the readers to be well disposed toward the ethical admonitions in Paul's name that are about to follow (cf. also Quintilian 4.3.9). The return to intercessory prayer and the doxology of 3:14–21 are harder to classify rhetorically but are probably best seen as having the role of a *transitus*, which frequently concludes a *narratio* in a powerful affective manner and can function as a new exordium (cf. Lausberg, *Handbuch der literarischen Rhetorik*, 188–89). Just as on an epistolary analysis Ephesians does not contain a normal letter-body, so on a rhetorical analysis it does not contain the usual argumentatio that was at the center of most discourses. Instead, this is replaced by the extended *exhortatio* (cf. Quintilian 3.6.47; 9.2.103), which begins at 4:1. In rhetorical terms the exhortation of 6:10–20 is to be thought of as the main part of the *peroratio*, providing a striking final appeal to the readers, which sums up the need to guard all that belongs to their calling in the battle against hostile opposing forces and attempts to arouse them to the appropriate action by the threefold use of the verb "to stand."

The style of Ephesians matches the contents of its two parts. In the first part what may be called the language of worship is dominant. This is appropriate to its epideictic genre, in which "the style is the most distinctive feature. . . . A tendency to ornament of every kind is fostered. . . . 'A pomp and prodigality of words,' well-balanced periods, a style half poetic, half oratorical, are the qualities most desired" (Burgess, "Epideictic Literature," 94). Hymns and other forms of praise to the gods were considered a standard type of this genre (cf. Burgess, "Epideictic Literature," 110–14, 130, 174–80, 191–94). To put across his thoughts and give them a presence that acts upon the readers' sensibilities, the writer uses a number of stylistic techniques such as repetition, synonymy, and amplification. As Perelman puts it, "Without doubt, to create presence it is useful to insist at length upon certain elements; in prolonging the attention given them, their presence in the consciousness of the audience is increased. Only by dwelling upon a subject does one create the desired emotions" (*The Realm of Rhetoric*, 37). Characteristic of the style of Ephesians are the repetition and parallelism of its many long, and in some cases, exceedingly long sentences. In the latter category are 1:3–14; 1:15–23; 2:1–7; 3:1–7; 4:11–16; 6:14–20. These long sentences extend themselves by means of relative clauses, clauses with ὅτι or another conjunction and participial constructions. K. G. Kuhn points out that these tapeworm-like sentences, which drag on with loosely strung together clauses, also occur with frequency in the Qumran literature, especially in the Hymns of Thanksgiving, and suggests that their presence in Ephesians is to be explained on the basis of a continuity of tradition (*Paul and Qumran*, 116–20). Again and again words which are either synonymous or related in meaning are linked by means of a genitive construction. In this way, for example, the writer dwells on the notion of divine power—ἡ ἐνέργεια τοῦ κράτους τῆς ἰσχύος αὐτοῦ, lit., "the working of the strength of his might" (1:19), ἡ ἐνέργεια τῆς δυνάμεως αὐτοῦ, "the working of his power" (3:7), or τὸ κράτος τῆς ἰσχύος αὐτοῦ, "the strength of his might" (6:10)—or the divine will—ἡ εὐδοκία τοῦ θελήματος αὐτοῦ, "the good pleasure of his will" (1:5), or ἡ βουλὴ τοῦ θελήματος αὐτοῦ, "the purpose of his will" (1:11). A similar effect is achieved by various sorts of parallelism. Synonyms and words connected in meaning are placed side by side, e.g., σοφία καὶ φρόνησις, "wisdom and insight" (1:8), or τὰ παραπτώματα καὶ αἱ ἁμαρτίαι, "trespasses and sins" (2:1). Elaborative phrases are added, e.g., the addition of "the forgiveness of trespasses" to "redemption through his blood" (1:7). Participles adjacent in meaning are linked or juxtaposed (e.g., περιζωσάμενοι . . . καὶ ἐνδυσάμενοι . . . καὶ ὑποδησάμενοι . . . ἀναλαβόντες, "having girded . . . and having put on . . . and having shod . . . taking up" [6:14–16]), as are infinitive constructions (e.g., καταλαβέσθαι . . . γνῶναι, "to grasp . . . to know" [3:18, 19]). There is also a parallelism of content, what van Roon calls a "rhyming of thoughts" (*Authenticity*, 135–58; cf. also de Zwaan, *RHPR* 6 [1927] 554–65). In 2:14–18, for instance, there are three different statements about peace in vv 14a, 15c, 17, four about unity in vv 14b, 15b, 16a, 18, and two about the destruction of enmity in vv 14c–15a, 16b.

The simple repetition of key words or cognates or synonyms is another feature of Ephesians' distinctive style. So, for example, there is a piling up of terms associated with God's choice, purpose, or good pleasure in 1:3–11 (ἐξελέξατο, προορίσας, εὐδοκία [2x], θέλημα [3x], προέθετο, οἰκονομία, ἐκληρώθημεν, προορισθέντες, πρόθεσις, βουλή), with knowledge in 1:17, 18 (σοφία, ἀποκάλυψις, ἐπίγνωσις, πεφωτισμένους, εἰδέναι), with power in 1:19, 20 (δύναμις, ἐνέργεια, κράτος, ἰσχύς, ἐνήργησεν), and with God's grace, mercy, and love in 2:4–8 (ἔλεος, ἀγάπη, ἠγάπησεν, χάρις [3x], χρηστότης). On occasions there is also the use of paronomasia and the repetition of sounds for particular rhetorical effect (e.g., τὸ πλήρωμα τοῦ τὰ πάντα ἐν πᾶσιν πληρουμένου in 1:23; cf. also Lausberg, *Handbuch der literarischen Rhetorik*, 322–25). The stringing together of prepositional phrases is another device which adds to the repetitive nature of the style (e.g., εἰς υἱοθεσίαν διὰ Ἰησοῦ Χριστοῦ εἰς αὐτόν, κατὰ τὴν εὐδοκίαν τοῦ θελήματος αὐτοῦ, εἰς ἔπαινον . . . [1:5, 6], or πρὸς τὸν καταρτισμὸν τῶν ἁγίων εἰς ἔργον διακονίας εἰς οἰκοδομὴν τοῦ σώματος τοῦ Χριστοῦ [4:12]). There are also numerous prepositional phrases with ἐν, many of which round off clauses. The prepositions provide temporary pauses in the chantlike rhythm of some of the long sentences, and the series of long syllables at the end of a number of groups of words also have a slowing down effect.

The writer shows in other places in the letter that he is capable of producing more succinct, lively, and direct discourse, so it should be assumed that where he adopts a profuse and effusive style it is done deliberately in order to achieve particular results. He speaks repeatedly of "riches" (τὸ πλοῦτος)—"the riches of grace" (1:7; 2:7), "the riches of glory" (1:18; 3:16), "the riches of Christ" (3:8)—and through the constant recurrence of πᾶς (48x), the wealth of words, and the exalted formulations attempts to convey in appropriate language something of the riches which he is expounding. Van Roon (*Authenticity*, 182–90) suggests that such a style is on the frontier between two worlds. On the one hand, its repetitions and parallels are reminiscent of Hebrew poetry, and, on the other, it is in line with Greek epideictic rhetoric such as would be used in ceremonial orations of praise. The explanation for this, he claims, is that the psalms and wisdom literature inspired Hebrew- and/or Aramaic-speaking Jews to a devotional and moralizing style of speech, the sort of style that is to be found in the Qumran writings, especially 1QH. Then, within a sphere, where, besides Hebrew and Aramaic, Greek was also spoken, this style of speech became translated into an equivalent Greek style. It is this Hellenistic Jewish style that influenced early Christian liturgy and that the writer of Ephesians is employing. In order to evoke thankfulness and worship among his readers, the writer employs the forms and language of thanksgiving and worship with which they would have been familiar. Ornamental, flowery language was normal in worship. Parts of Ephesians' style may seem ponderous or ostentatious to the modern reader, but what must be borne in mind is its likely affective connotations for its original readers. Since paraenesis for the most part involves discrete thoughts rather than continuity of argumentation, the style of the latter part of Ephesians is more direct, with shorter sentences and the use of imperatives, participles with imperatival force, and expressions of exhortation followed by an infinitive. But there are places where something of the style of the first half of the letter flows over into the second, particularly in 4:1–16; 5:21–33; 6:10–20. It is noticeable that these are places where the writer's distinctive concerns are added to the traditional material. (For more detailed discussion of the style of Ephesians, see the discussion under *Form/Structure/Setting* of the various sections of the commentary and Schmid, *Epheserbrief*, 130–331; Percy, *Probleme*, 179–252; van Roon, *Authenticity*, 100–212.)

The style is enhanced by the writer's use of traditions, which are also effective in reinforcing common values. The two different parts of the letter for the most part make use of two different types of traditional material—liturgical in the first part and paraenetic in the second. In the first half there are not only traditional liturgical forms of eulogy, intercessory prayer, and doxology but also traditional liturgical language within 1:3–14, creedal formulations in 1:20–23, and hymnic material in 2:14–16. The "once . . . now" contrast schema from early Christian preaching has also been woven into the structure of 2:1–10 and 2:11–22, while Scripture is employed directly in 2:17 and indirectly in 1:20, 22. Traditional material to be found in the second half includes early Christian catechetical material (e.g., 4:22–24), *topoi* or sentences (cf. 4:25–5:20), lists of virtues and vices (cf. 4:31–32; 5:3, 4; 5:9), and the household code (cf. 5:21–6:9). Jewish Scripture is put to paraenetical use also (cf. its direct use in 5:31, 32; 6:2, 3; 6:14–17; cf. also 4:8; and its indirect use in 4:25, 26; 5:18), and liturgical or hymnic fragments (5:14), confessional formulae (4:4–6), and traditional formulations (e.g., 5:2, 25) are not missing from this part of the letter (cf. the more detailed discussion under *Form/Structure/Setting* of the various sections; also Barth, *NTS* 30 [1984] 3–25; Fischer, *Tendenz und Absicht*, 136–208; Gnilka, "Paränetische Traditionen," 397–410; King, *ExpTim* 63 [1952] 273–76; Lincoln, *JSNT* 14 [1982] 16–57; J. T. Sanders, *ZNW* 56[1965] 214–32). Colossians and a number of passages from Pauline letters function as traditional material also, but the relation of Ephesians to these will be discussed in the following section.

2. Relation to Colossians and the Rest of the Pauline Corpus

Bibliography

Benoit, P. "Rapports littéraires entre les épîtres aux Colossiens et aux Éphésiens." In *Neutestamentliche Aufsätze*. FS J. Schmid, ed. J. Blinzler, O. Kuss, and F. Mussner. Regensburg: Pustet, 1963, 11–22. **Coutts, J.** "The Relationship of Ephesians and Colossians." *NTS* 4 (1958) 201–7. **Dahl, N. A.** "Der Epheserbrief und der verlorene erste Brief des Paulus an die Korinther." In *Abraham unser Vater*. FS O. Michel, ed. O. Betz, M. Hengel, and P. Schmidt. Leiden: Brill, 1963, 65–77. **Merklein, H.** "Eph 4, 1–5, 20 als Rezeption von Kol 3, 1–17." In *Kontinuität und Einheit*. FS F. Mussner, ed. P. G. Müller and W. Stenger. Freiburg: Herder, 1981, 194–210. ———. "Paulinische Theologie in der Rezeption des Kolosser- und Epheserbriefes." In *Paulus in den neutestamentlichen Spätschriften*, ed. K. Kertelge. Freiburg: Herder, 1981, 25–69. ———. *Das kirchliche Amt*, 28–44. **Mitton, C. L.** *Epistle*, 55–158, 280–338. **Ochel, W.** *Die Annahme einer Bearbeitung des Kolosser-Briefes im Epheserbrief*. Würzburg: Konrad Triltsch, 1934. **Percy, E.** *Probleme*, 360–433. **Polhill, J. B.** "The Relationship between Ephesians and Colossians." *RevExp* 70 (1973) 439–50. **Roon, A. van.** *Authenticity*, 413–37. **Schmid, J.** *Epheserbrief*, 384–457.

One of the most fascinating of the various enigmas that surround the letter to the Ephesians is the nature of its relationship to another letter in the Pauline corpus, namely, Colossians. The relationship between these two letters is by far the closest within the Pauline corpus, and within the NT as a whole is rivaled only by that among the synoptic Gospels and that between 2 Peter and Jude. Not only is this issue an intriguing one in its own right, but the stance one adopts on it is also a decisive factor in attempts to resolve the problem of the authenticity of Ephesians. In fact Dibelius-Greeven go so far as to claim that it is *the* decisive factor ("Das Verhältnis von Eph zu Col bietet den Punkt dar, von dem aus die Echtheitsfrage zu entscheiden ist" [83]). For reasons of space, only a sketch of the issues and not a detailed argumentation can be presented here.

The bare statistics are these. Of the 1,570 words in Colossians, 34 percent reappear in Ephesians, and conversely 26.5 percent of the 2,411 words in Ephesians are paralleled in Colossians (cf. Mitton, *Epistle*, 57). Yet, strangely, this remarkable interdependence is not produced by extended passages occurring in the same form in each letter. In only one passage, the recommendation of Tychicus (Eph 6:21, 22 // Col 4:7, 8), is there an extended verbatim agreement of twenty-nine consecutive words. Elsewhere there are three places where seven consecutive words show exact correspondence (Eph 1:1, 2 // Col 1:1, 2; Eph 3:2 // Col 1:25; Eph 3:9 // Col 1:26) and two places where five consecutive words have an exact parallel (Eph 1:7 // Col 1:14; Eph 4:16 // Col 2:19).

Such statistics, however, do little to reveal the great extent of the similarity between the two letters. It is Colossians, of all the other letters, that comes closest to the distinctive style of Ephesians. It too has some long sentences, frequent relative clauses, genitive constructions, and prepositional phrases with ἐν (cf. the detailed discussion of its style by W. Bujard, *Stilanalytische Untersuchungen zum Kolosserbrief als Beitrag zur Methodik von Sprachvergleichen* [Göttingen: Vandenhoeck & Ruprecht, 1973]). What is more, the overall structure and sequence of the letters is similar.

As the chart on p. xlviii shows (cf. other attempts to chart the overall relationship by Schmid, *Epheserbrief*, 412; Ernst, 254–55), in both parts of the letter Ephesians has much of its thematic material in common with Colossians, and in its main blocks this material is in the same sequence. In the first parts of the letters, the prescript, the thanksgiving period with its intercessory prayer-report, the reminder of the readers' previous experience of alienation and present experience of reconciliation, and the discussion of Paul as the suffering apostle with his special ministry of the mystery of the gospel are all parallel. Of course, each letter treats these forms and subjects in a slightly different fashion, so that, for example, Ephesians, in distinction from Colossians, places its discussion of past alienation and present reconciliation in the context of the Gentiles' alienation from Israel and their present privileges as members of the new creation and new temple. Even sections of the letters which appear distinctive when viewed in sequence do in fact have their counterparts elsewhere in the other letter. The additional statement in Colossians' intercessory prayer-report (1:13, 14) about believers' experience of salvation as a transference from the old dominion to the new can be seen to have its more developed counterpart in Eph 2:1–10 (*contra* Merklein, *Das kirchliche Amt*, 43–44, who attempts to make a case that Eph 2:1–10 is part of a commentary in 2:1–22 on Col 1:21–23, suggesting links between 2:1–10 and Col 1:21 and between 2:19–22 and Col 1:23 that are too tenuous to be convincing). Similarly, the hymnic material about the cosmic Christ in Col 1:15–20 has some striking parallels with the additional statement in Ephesians' intercessory prayer-report (1:20–23) about the cosmic Christ and his relationship with the Church. In terms of the structuring of material, what is primarily unique to the first half

Comparison of Ephesians and Colossians

Col	Unique to Col	Parallel Material	Unique to Eph	Eph
1:1,2		Prescript		1:1,2
			Eulogy	1:3–14
1:3–14		Thanksgiving Intercessory prayer report		1:15–23
	(Additional statement about believers' experience of salvation)		(Additional statement about cosmic Christ and his relationship to the Church)	
1:15–20	Hymnic material about supremacy of cosmic Christ in creation and reconciliation			
			Reminder of readers' experience of salvation	2:1–10
1:21–23		Reminder of readers' experience of alienation then but reconciliation now		2:11–22
	(additional statement about necessity of continuing and Paul's ministry)		(context of alienation from Israel then but Gentile privileges now)	
1:24–29		Paul as suffering apostle and his ministry of the mystery		3:1–13
2:1–3:4	Interaction with false teaching			
			Intercessory prayer-report and doxology	3:14–21
		(head-body relation Col 2:19 // Eph 4:15,16)	Exhortation to maintenance of Church's unity	4:1–16
3:5–17		Injunctions about old and new humanity—sexual morality, anger, truth, love, thankfulness, and worship		4:17–5:20
			(Light/darkness contrast 5:8–14)	
3:18–4:1		Household code	(Christ and the Church 5:22–32)	5:21–6:9
			Spiritual warfare	6:10–17
4:2–4		Exhortation to prayer		6:18–20
4:5,6	Conduct toward outsiders			
4:7–9		Commendation of Tychicus		6:21,22
4:10–17	Greetings			
4:18	(Autograph)	Grace-benediction	(Peace wish)	6:23,24

of Colossians is the section which counters the false teaching, and what is unique to the same part of Ephesians is its liturgical framework of a eulogy and a second intercessory prayer-report followed by a doxology. Even here, however, though the main topics of these sections are distinctive, there are verbal parallels, which, in the case of Eph 3:14–21, show that its writer works sequentially with the Colossians material, for in 3:1–13 he had employed Col

1:23c–28 and now in 3:14–21 he takes up language from the last part of that passage and from what follows after in Col 1:29–2:10.

In the second half of the letters the bulk of the paraenesis has parallel material in the same broad sequence. There are injunctions about putting off the old and putting on the new humanity. When these injunctions become more specific, they involve in both cases exhortations about sexual morality, anger, speech, truthfulness, love, forgiveness, thankfulness, and worship. There then follows the instruction about relationships within the household in the sequence of wife-husband, child-parent, and slave-master. What is particularly striking about this agreement is that, although household codes appear elsewhere, there is no parallel in non-Christian and other early Christian literature to the specific order of injunctions followed in Colossians and Ephesians. Both letters close with a similar exhortation to prayer, the commendation of Tychicus, and a grace-benediction. Again there are distinctives in the way the same subject matter is treated. In comparison with the similar material in Col 3:5–17, Eph 4:17–5:20 has an additional contrast between light and darkness in 5:8–14, and the household code in Ephesians is expanded by the sustained analogy between the relationship of husband and wife and that of Christ and the Church. In Colossians the grace-benediction is preceded by a signature statement, and in Ephesians it is combined with a wish of peace.

Unique to Colossians are the paraenesis about conduct in relation to outsiders in 4:5, 6 and the list of personal greetings in 4:10–17. In Ephesians the opening exhortation about the maintenance of the Church's unity and its growth toward maturity in 4:1–16 and the peroration about believers' warfare against spiritual powers in 6:10–17 are unique. Yet even here, as will be seen below, both Col 4:5, 6 and Eph 4:1–16 have strong verbal links with material elsewhere in the other letter. There is no reason to speculate about an original letter or outline which simply contained what we have reconstructed in the column of parallel material (*pace* van Roon, *Authenticity*, 413–37, who argues for an original common blueprint of this sort). Nor is it adequate to hold that the two letters simply reproduce common traditions (*pace* Greeven in his postscript in Dibelius-Greeven, 113; Ernst, 257, who sees this as the primary, though not the only, explanation; Dahl, "Der Epheserbrief," 71–72). Even if there was some use of common traditions, it looks far more likely that the primary explanation must be that one letter served as the model for the other (cf. also Merklein, *Das kirchliche Amt*, 39; for a survey of the various solutions which have been proposed by recent writers, including theories about interpolation put back into an original Colossians by the writer of Ephesians from his composition modeled on the original Colossians, first proposed by H. J. Holtzmann [*Kritik der Epheser- und Kolosserbriefe auf Grund einer Analyse ihres Verwandtschaftsverhältnisses* (Leipzig: Engelmann, 1872)], see Polhill, *RevExp* 70 [1973] 439–50, and for a listing of the positions taken by earlier scholars, see Schmid, *Epheserbrief*, 393–408). If Ephesians provided the model for Colossians, then Colossians would have abbreviated sections with important content, reducing Eph 2:11–22 to Col 1:21–23 and Eph 5:21–33 to Col 3:18, 19, for example, and would have expanded the section with personal greetings from Eph 6:21, 22 to Col 4:7–17. The far more obvious hypothesis is that Colossians served as the basis for Ephesians, which omits the interaction with a specific false teaching and the greetings from and to particular individuals and expands the rest of the material to make it more general and to adapt it to its own purposes (*contra* Coutts, *NTS* 4 [1958] 201–7; van Roon, *Authenticity*, 414–26, who suggest unconvincingly that much of the evidence points to the priority of Ephesians).

But it is not simply that Ephesians builds on the overall structure and thematic sequence of Colossians. There are also very close verbal links, as has been noted earlier, and an examination of some of these will reveal more of the nature of the relation between the two letters (cf. the synoptic arrangement of the Greek of both letters in Mitton, *Epistle*, 279–315, which is most useful for such an examination). A more detailed discussion can be found under *Form/Structure/Setting* of the relevant sections of the commentary. Here we shall look first at the sort of links found between material within the parallel sections outlined above. In the prescript the similarities between the description of the sender and the wording of the greeting are not surprising. What is striking is that, in the description of the addressees, only Colossians and Ephesians, among the letters of the Pauline corpus, call them both "saints" and "faithful in Christ (Jesus)." At the beginning of the thanksgiving period in Eph 1:15–17, there is the phenomenon of "conflation" (cf. Mitton, *Epistle*, 65), which is found in a number of other places also. The writer here combines wording from two parts of the parallel section in Colossians: 1:4 and 1:9. Similarly, Eph 2:11–16 clearly takes up Col 1:21, 22 (cf. especially ἀπηλλοτριωμένος, ἀποκαταλλάσσειν, σῶμα, σάρξ) but also has links through its use of tradition with the hymnic material in Col 1:15–20 (cf. the notions of making peace between two entities, the blood of Christ, and "through the cross") and brings in terminology from Col 2:11, 14 (cf. circumcision made with or without hands and "regulations"). The section on Paul's apostolic sufferings on behalf of the Gentiles in Eph 3:1–13 contains numerous verbal links with Col 1:24–29, on which it is based: θλῖψις, ὑπὲρ ὑμῶν, διάκονος, οἰκονομία, "given to me for you," the revelation schema with its "mystery" previously "hidden" but now disclosed, τοῖς ἁγίοις, τὸ πλοῦτος, ἐνέργεια, and δύναμις. As well as differences in the content of the mystery and the naming of its recipients (discussed later in this section), there are as usual the slight verbal differences so often found in the writer's use of Colossians. So, for example, Eph 3:2, in taking up Col 1:25, adds τῆς χάριτος after τὴν οἰκονομίαν, making the description "given to me for you" now qualify "the grace," rather than immediately qualify "the stewardship."

In the paraenesis of the second half, Eph 4:17–24 is dependent on Col 3:5–11 for its talk of a previous way of living, for its terminology of putting off the old humanity and putting on the new, for the vices it mentions, and for the notions of renewal and the new humanity's relation to God's creative activity. Yet again such material is rearranged by the writer of Ephesians to suit his own purposes, and such variations are introduced as changing participial constructions to infinitive constructions for the language of putting on and putting off and changing Colossians' description of the new person from νέος to καινός and its verb for "to renew" from ἀνακαινοῦν to ἀνανεοῦν. The next sections of paraenesis in Eph 4:25–5:14 also take up elements from Col 3:5–11 and the following verses in 3:12–14a, including the vices and virtues listed in Eph 4:31, 32 which are an adaptation of those found in Col 3:8, 12, 13, the vices of Eph 5:3–5 from Col 3:5, 8, the mention of the coming wrath of God in Eph 5:6 from Col 3:6, and the "then . . . now" contrast in Eph 5:8 from Col 3:7, 8. Eph 5:15–20 are dependent on Col 3:16, 17, employing their mention of mutual edification through psalms, hymns, and spiritual songs and of singing in the heart, and conflate this with Col 4:5 and its notions of walking wisely and redeeming the time. Mitton (*Epistle*, 246) designates the use of Col 3:17 in Eph 5:20 as "a curious instance of the merely accidental association of words prevailing over the meaning which they were originally used to convey." This is because Eph 5:20 takes the participle εὐχαριστοῦντες, "giving thanks," from the second half of Col 3:17 and adds to this the phrase "in the name of our Lord Jesus Christ," which is its version of "in the name of the Lord Jesus," from the first half of Col 3:17. In Colossians this phrase had been associated not with giving thanks but with doing all things, while the "all things" from Colossians has been transferred to the clause in Ephesians about giving thanks. With the household code, almost all the words from Col 3:18–4:1 have been taken over in the same sequence in Eph 5:21–6:9. Ephesians not only retains Colossians' Christianizing of the code by bringing believers' relationship to their Lord to bear on its exhortations but also provides its own more developed Christian interpretation. Both exhortations to prayer in Eph 6:18–20 and Col 4:2–4 have the participle προσευχόμενοι and are concerned about being alert or watchful (Eph, ἀγρυπνοῦντες; Col, γρηγοροῦντες) and about perseverance (προσκαρτερήσει; προσκαρτερεῖτε). The content of the prayer has to do with the apostolic word (λόγος; λόγου), with the apostle's proclaiming of the mystery (γνωρίσαι τὸ μυστήριον τοῦ εὐαγγελίου; λαλῆσαι τὸ μυστήριον τοῦ Χριστοῦ), for which he is imprisoned (ὑπὲρ οὗ πρεσβεύω ἐν ἁλύσει; δι' ὃ καὶ δέδεμαι), and with his doing this in the manner that he ought to (ἵνα . . . ὡς δεῖ με λαλῆσαι). Finally, as noted in the statistics provided earlier, the letters' postscripts in Eph 6:21, 22 and Col 4:7, 8 have twenty-nine consecutive words that are exactly the same and in the same order. Ephesians has made no additions; it has simply omitted the two words καὶ σύνδουλος, "and fellow servant," from the description of Tychicus, which has the effect of heightening the significance of Paul's own distinctive role.

As has been noted, Ephesians is not only dependent on Colossians in the major sections that they have in parallel, but there are also terminological links outside these sections. Again, similar phrases are placed in quite different contexts. The eulogy of 1:3–14 is found only in Ephesians, but it has a large number of parallels with Colossians. The turn of phrase in 1:4, ἁγίους καὶ ἀμώμους κατενώπιον αὐτοῦ, is taken from Col 1:22 but omits its additional καὶ ἀνεγκλήτους. 1:6, 7 incorporates Col 1:13, 14, ἐν ᾧ ἔχομεν τὴν ἀπολύτρωσιν . . . τὴν ἄφεσιν, but substitutes "in the beloved" for "in the Son of his love" and "transgressions" for "sins," and adds "through his blood" in an apparent conflation with Col 1:20. "In all wisdom and insight" is the Eph 1:8 version of "in all wisdom and understanding" from Col 1:9. In Eph 1:10 the language of "all things," "things in heaven and things on earth," being related to Christ, echoes that of Col 1:20, and "having heard the word of truth, the gospel" in Eph 1:13 has its origin in Col 1:5. The thanksgiving and intercessory prayer-report not only have parallels with the same material in Colossians but also have links with other parts of that letter. 1:18, with its mention of hope and the riches of glory, employs the same vocabulary as Col 1:27. 1:19, 20 use the same terminology about God's work in raising Christ from the dead that can be found in Col 2:12. 1:21 has the names of the powers that can be found in Col 1:16, and 1:22 takes up the designation of Christ as the head of the Church that occurs in Col 1:18. The statement of Eph 2:5 that God "made us alive even when we were dead in trespasses" has its equivalent in Col 2:13, although Ephesians changes the order of the first four words in the Greek and after συνεζωοποίησεν, "made alive," has a simple dative instead of σύν with the dative. The second intercessory prayer-report and the doxology in 3:14–21 have no parallel with Colossians in terms of overall form but do have terminological links with the earlier letter, especially 1:27–2:10. "The riches of glory" in 3:16, for example, corresponds to the same phrase in Col 1:27. The formulation "rooted and grounded in love" in 3:17 conflates participles from Col 2:7 and Col 1:23. The thought of "being filled up to all the fullness of God" in 3:19 takes up the terminology of Col 2:9, 10, and the wording of 3:20, "in accordance with the power which is at work within us," echoes that of Col 1:29. The first section of its paraenesis, 4:1–16, is distinctive to the structure of Ephesians, but here again there are clear parallels with Colossians. In particular, 4:2–4 condenses Col 3:12–15 and employs its key words—humility, gentleness, patience, bearing with one another, love, bond, peace, called, and one body. 4:15–16, "the head, Christ, from whom the whole body, joined and brought together by every ligament which gives supply, makes bodily growth," is also dependent upon Col 2:19. The characteristic minor variations are again there. Ephesians has added the explanatory "Christ" before the relative clause, substituted συναρμολογούμενον for ἐπιχορηγούμενον, using the latter's cognate noun with the phrase about ligaments, which it has modified by its usual preference for πᾶς with the singular form of the noun, and changed "grows with a growth" to "makes growth."

This last example brings us to another aspect of the relationship between Ephesians and Colossians—the use of the same term but with different connotations. Some (e.g., Dibelius-Greeven, 84; Ochel, *Annahme*, 3; Mitton, *Epistle*, 84; Gnilka, 12; Ernst, 256–57) claim that this phenomenon is found in Col 2:19 and Eph 4:15–16, the former using σῶμα to mean the cosmos (cf. Col 2:10) and the latter using it to mean the Church. But, in fact, this particular example is not at all convincing. Colossians has already reinterpreted "body" in its original cosmic sense to mean the Church in Col 1:18, and Col 2:19 almost certainly takes it in this same sense (cf. Lohse, *Colossians*, 122; Schweizer, *Colossians*, 163; O'Brien, *Colossians*, 147–48; cf. also Percy, *Probleme*, 382–84; Guthrie, *New Testament Introduction*, 395). Ephesians simply takes this reinterpretation for granted, so that this parallel may underline the priority of Colossians but does not substantiate any change in the meaning of terms (cf. also Merklein, *Das kirchliche Amt*, 30–31). The same applies to the use of the term οἰκονομία in the two letters (Col 1:25; Eph 1:10; 3:2, 9). As opposed to a number of interpreters, who claim that there is a wholesale change of meaning in Ephesians (cf. Mitton, *Epistle*, 91–94; Merklein, *Das kirchliche Amt*, 33, 173–74; Gnilka, 12; Ernst, 257), we argue in the commentary that, although, in

Eph 1:10 and 3:9 in relation to God's activity, the term refers to his act of administrating, in 3:2 in relation to Paul's activity and under the influence of the similar context of Col 1:25, it may well refer to the office of administrating, i.e., the apostle's stewardship. The addition of the genitive τῆς χάριτος is not a decisive argument against this, since it can be seen as a genitive of apposition, grace often being the functional equivalent for Paul's apostolic office in his own writings (cf. Rom 1:5; 12:3; 1 Cor 3:10; 15:10; Phil 1:7). This would indicate what one should expect—that a term can be used differently in different contexts—but it also suggests that where there is the same context the writer of Ephesians is dependent on the prior use in Colossians.

Are the various uses of πλήρωμα any more significant? In comparison with the way the term is employed in other letters in the Pauline corpus, it is its use in Colossians that is decisive for its force in Ephesians. In Col 1:19; 2:9, it stands for the divine fullness which has taken up residence in Christ, though according to Col 2:10 believers have access to this fullness and by means of the cognate verb can be said to be filled in Christ. Ephesians can also talk about believers' relationship to the fullness of God (3:19) and the fullness of Christ (4:13), but it goes further than Colossians in actually using the noun πλήρωμα to refer to the Church (1:23). So whereas in the theologically pregnant uses of the term the focus in Colossians is primarily Christological, in Ephesians the focus is primarily ecclesiological. Mitton (*Epistle*, 97) overstates the case when he claims that there is a major break and that "one would expect to find in Ephesians that when the word πλήρωμα is used it would bear some of the new significance attached to it in its two occurrences in Colossians; but this we do not find." Instead, there has been a development between the two letters, and it is one that corresponds to the shift in emphasis between their perspectives. Something similar occurs with the term μυστήριον. In Col 1:26, 27 the specific content of the mystery is Christ, though it is related to the Gentiles: the mystery among the Gentiles is Christ. In Eph 3:3–6, however, the Gentiles are now part of the mystery; the mystery of Christ involves "the Gentiles being joint heirs and joint members of the body and sharers in Christ Jesus through the gospel." While the emphasis in Colossians is still on the Christological aspect (cf. also 2:2; 4:3), Eph 3 has put far more emphasis on the Gentile element and developed this in an ecclesiological direction. Elsewhere in Ephesians the mystery has to do with the summing up of all things in Christ (1:9, 10), the Church as the means of disclosure of God's wisdom to the powers (3:9, 10), and the relation between Christ and the Church (5:32). Again Mitton (*Epistle*, 90), operating with too rigid a notion of *the* meaning of a term, instead of seeing that a word can take on different connotations in different contexts, exaggerates when he speaks of "the great difference in the significance attached to this word in the two letters." Without repudiating that the mystery centers in Christ, Ephesians can develop the significance of the mystery within a new frame of reference by highlighting different implications of what has happened in Christ, particularly the one Church out of Jews and Gentiles that has resulted (cf. also Merklein, *Das kirchliche Amt*, 31, 32). What is a much greater change is the modification Ephesians makes in the designation of the recipients of the mystery. Whereas in Col 1:26 the mystery is disclosed to τοῖς ἁγίοις, "the saints," God's people as a whole, in Eph 3:5 ἁγίοις becomes an adjective, "holy," which qualifies a much narrower group of recipients, namely apostles and prophets. This reflects a different ecclesiastical perspective also found elsewhere in the change from believers' being built up in Christ in Col 2:7 to their being built up on the foundation of the apostles and prophets in Eph 2:20 (cf. also Mitton, *Epistle,* 85–86; Gnilka, 12; Merklein, *Das kirchliche Amt,* 33).

What has emerged from this overview is the dependence of Ephesians on a prior Colossians in terms of its overall structure and sequence, its themes, and its wording. Yet what is also absolutely clear is that this is a free and creative dependence, not a slavish imitation or copying. As far as the wording goes, as well as repetition of brief snatches, there are nearly always modifications through a change of word order, omissions, additions, and conflations. This phenomenon suggests a writer who has immersed himself in his source material to such an extent that it has become part of his way of thinking. It also suggests that, through an association of the source's words or ideas in his mind, he is able to combine phrases from its different parts. The similarities and yet the development in the use of terms and themes indicate a stage of further reflection since the time of Colossians. During it the writer has been able to employ the earlier material by way of inspiration for his own fresh interpretation of the same Pauline tradition in a new situation. Whether the nature of the dependence should be designated as literary is almost academic. Certainly the writer has at some stage had access to a copy of Colossians, but whether he actually has referred to it during the composition of this letter, so that it is there before him as he writes, or whether his memorization of its contents is so good that this is unnecessary, is difficult to determine. In any case these are not exclusive alternatives. The twenty-nine consecutive words from Colossians that appear in Eph 6:21, 22 in all probability indicate that the writer consulted his copy of the earlier letter at this point, though it is possible that they could be explained on the basis of memory if the writer had a particular personal reason for knowing this passage so exactly (cf. also Mitton, *Epistle,* 59, but cf. 244, 248; also *Ephesians,* 11, where he concludes more firmly for the former alternative; and cf. even van Roon, *Authenticity,* 416, who declares, "There can be no solution but that this should be attributed to a literary dependence of some kind"). It is highly likely then that the dependence of Ephesians on Colossians should be seen as in some sense a literary one (cf. also Ochel, *Annahme,* esp. 6, 71–72; Merklein, *Das kirchliche Amt,* 39; "Paulinische Theologie," 26–27; "Eph 4, 1–5, 20," 195–96). In fact, Ephesians' redaction of Colossians is similar to that which can be shown to have taken place in the case of Josephus' use of the *Letter of Aristeas* in his *Jewish Antiquities* (12.2.1–15 §§ 12–118). There is literary dependence as Josephus paraphrases his source, but there are only two places where there is a sequence of identical words—one broken sequence of twelve words and another sequence of ten words. For the most part, it is only short phrases or individual words that are identical in the two works, and Josephus has omitted, conflated, and embellished material from his source in order to make his own particular points (for a detailed study, see A. Pelletier, *Flavius Josèphe: Adapteur de la Lettre d'Aristée* [Paris: Cerf, 1962]).

When the two letters are taken as a whole, the main lines of Ephesians' reinterpretation of the material in Colossians can be seen clearly. Colossians had been aimed specifically at a situation where false teaching was becoming a threat and had responded by stressing the supremacy of Christ in relation to the heavenly dimension and believers' interest in it and by setting its ethical exhortation in the framework of a contrast between heaven and earth (cf. Lincoln, *Paradise,* 110–34). Ephesians assumes the cosmic Christology of Colossians but is more general and places more emphasis on the Church in its reminder to its readers of their identity as believers. They are part of a new humanity made up of Jews and Gentiles, part of the body of Christ, the fullness of Christ, the new temple, the mature person, and the bride of Christ. The framework for the ethical exhortation is no longer the contrast between the heavenly and the earthly but one between insiders and outsiders, the Church and the surrounding world (cf. also Merklein, "Eph 4, 1–5, 20 als Rezeption von Kol 3, 1–17," 194–210). A study of such redaction of the Colossian material by the writer obviously makes a major contribution to the discussion of the distinctive interests and purposes of Ephesians. At the same time the specific fruits of such an approach in the detailed remarks in the commentary serve to reinforce our conclusions about Ephesians' dependence on and adaptation of Colossians (cf. also Ochel, *Annahme,* 15–71, for an attempt at a thorough, though not always persuasive, analysis of Ephesians' editing of individual passages from Colossians; this analysis does not, however, support his conclusion that Ephesians was originally meant to replace Colossians [73]).

But Ephesians is not only dependent on Colossians; it also makes use of other letters in the Pauline corpus. The Pastoral Epistles are not included in this consideration, since the minor correspondences that exist between them and Ephesians suggest a knowledge of Ephesians by their author rather than vice versa (cf. Mitton, *Epistle,* 173–75). The following discussion attempts to show something of the extent of Ephesians' use of the Pauline letters. Only some of the clearer and more substantial parallels are mentioned. The appropriate *Form/Structure/Setting* and *Comment* sections in the commentary deal further with these and other possible parallels. Mitton's discussion and appendices (*Epistle,* 98–158, 280–315, 322–38; cf. also Goodspeed, *The Key to Ephesians,* 2–75, for the English text of possible parallels) are helpful in providing a wealth of data, although some of the examples he gives are by no means convincing. On some occasions the parallels from other letters are conflated in their use by Ephesians and in other cases wording from elsewhere in the Pauline corpus is conflated with wording from Colossians.

We begin with the eulogy of 1:3–14, which takes over wording and ideas from other letters. The opening words echo the blessing of 2 Cor 1:3, "Blessed be the God and Father of our Lord Jesus Christ"; v 5 with its notion of predestination and adoption as sons takes up Rom 8:29 (cf. Rom 8:15, 23); v 10 has the idea of "the fullness of time" as does Gal 4:4; and vv 13, 14 (cf. also 4:30), which talk of being sealed with the Spirit as a guarantee and link the Spirit with the promise, combine notions from 2 Cor 1:22 and Gal 3:14. The beginning of the thanksgiving period and intercessory prayer-report in 1:15, 16 seems to be dependent on Philem 4, 5 for its language of "making mention of you in my prayers" and "faith in the Lord Jesus" and "love for all the saints." 1:21, 22 with the list of powers who have been put under Christ's feet may well take up 1 Cor 15:24, 27 and conflate it with Col 1:16. In chap. 2 the phrase "like the rest" in v 3 and the clause "having no hope" in v 12 are both drawn from 1 Thess 4:13. Verses 8, 9, with their treatment of salvation as by grace, a gift, by faith, with no works and no boasting, draw on Rom 3:24–28; 4:2. The notion of access through Christ in v 18 (cf. also 3:12) comes from Rom 5:2, and the "holy temple" imagery of vv 20–22, with its language of growth, building on a foundation, and the dwelling of the Spirit, takes up 1 Cor 3:6, 9–12, 16. The depiction of Paul and his ministry in 3:1–13 talks of "Paul, the prisoner of Jesus Christ" in v 1, as does Philem 1; of joint heirs in v 6, as does Rom 8:17; of "the grace given to me" in v 7, as does Rom 12:3; and in v 8 employs the language of "riches" and "unsearchable" from Rom 11:33 and "the least" and "grace" from 1 Cor 15:9, 10. There are no significant parallels in 3:14–21.

In the second half of the letter the opening appeal of 4:1 combines wording from Rom 12:1, "I exhort you therefore," and 1 Thess 2:12, "walk worthily" and "call." Verse 4, with its notion of one body, is reminiscent of Rom 12:5, and v 11, with its listing of apostles, prophets, and teachers, echoes 1 Cor 12:28. The depiction of Gentile living in 4:17–19 is dependent on Rom 1:21, 24 for its terminology of futility of mind, darkened thinking, and giving themselves up to impurity, and conflates this with the terminology of alienation from Col 1:21. In the more specific injunctions of 4:25–5:2, the motivation of being members of one another in v 25 derives from Rom 12:5, the language of "working hard . . . with one's own hands" comes from 1 Cor 4:12, the wording of 5:1, "as beloved children" and "become imitators," takes up that of 1 Cor 4:14, 16, and v 2 combines "Christ loved us and gave himself for us" from Gal 2:20 (cf. also Eph 5:25) with "fragrant offering" and "sacrifice to God" from Phil 4:18. In 5:3–14, v 5, with its mention of the fornicator, the covetous person, the idolater, and inheritance in the kingdom of God, has a parallel in 1 Cor 6:9, 10. In defining the covetous person as an idolater, the verse shows that it is at the same time dependent on Col 3:5. Verse 8, with its contrast between the children of light and those who belong to the darkness, takes up the theme of 1 Thess 5:5–7. Verse 10, with its talk of "discovering" and "what is pleasing," harks back to Rom 12:2, and v 11, with the phrase "works of darkness," draws on Rom 13:12. The use of Pauline letters continues in 5:15–6:9. Verse 17 and its notion of "knowing what is the will of the Lord" is another passage (cf. 5:10) that harks back to Rom 12:2. Verse 23, with its discussion of Christ as head and then of the husband as the head of the wife, takes up ideas from 1 Cor 11:3 in order to conflate them with Col 3:18, while vv 30, 31, with their use of the phrase "members of Christ" in conjunction with the quotation of Gen 2:24, "the two shall become one flesh," recalls 1 Cor 6:15, 16. The exhortation to slaves in 6:5, 6 is dependent on the similar exhortation in Col 3:22, which it combines with the contrast between pleasing men and serving Christ already found in Gal 1:10. The command to masters in 6:9 weaves together the similar command in Col 3:25 and the wording of Rom 2:11 that "there is no partiality with him." The peroration of 6:10–20 takes up in its battle imagery of vv 14–16 terminology from 1 Thess 5:8 about "putting on the breastplate" and "the helmet of . . . salvation." In its call to prayer in vv 18–20, it conflates Col 4:2–4 with wording from Phil 4:6, "with all prayer and supplication," while the idea of an imprisoned ambassador for the gospel is inspired by 2 Cor 5:20 and Philem 9.

This sampling of typical parallels between Ephesians and other letters in the Pauline corpus indicates that the dependence of the former on the latter is fairly extensive. Ephesians makes greater use of Romans than any other letter, even when the latter's length is taken into consideration (*pace* van Roon, *Authenticity,* 432–37, who claims that the greatest correspondence is with 1 Corinthians). Interestingly, there are no significant parallels with 2 Thessalonians, whose authenticity is disputed by a number of modern scholars. That its dependence on the other letters is much more extensive than the usual similarities one might expect to find among writings by the same author is shown by Mitton, who illustrates the point by a specific comparison between Philippians and the other letters and concludes that "the parallels in Ephesians are twice the number of those in Philippians even when full allowance is made for the greater length of Ephesians" (*Epistle,* 109). The use of the other letters is, however, not so extensive or systematic as to indicate that Ephesians is simply a mosaic of the other Pauline letters or that it was designed in this way to be an introduction to the Pauline corpus (*contra* Goodspeed, *The Meaning of Ephesians*). The way in which the other letters are employed in Ephesians suggests that its writer knew them so well that, although Colossians is his primary model and source, he was able to draw on their wording and ideas. His knowledge of them is such that he is also able to make occasional verbal and thematic associations between a passage in one letter and a passage in another, or between a passage in another Pauline letter and a passage in Colossians, and to weave this material creatively into his own fresh interpretation of the Pauline gospel (*pace* van Roon, *Authenticity,* 432–37, and Dahl, "Der Epheserbrief," 75, who attempt to argue that the correspondences all derive from knowledge of common traditional material, not from knowledge of the letters). In this way Ephesians is an updating of Paul's gospel. It has Colossians as its model but further "paulinizes" its fresh interpretation by taking up phrases and themes from the Pauline letters, in which its writer is steeped. If Colossians is non-Pauline, then the material from the other letters functions also as a "paulinization" of liturgical and paraenetic community traditions which are taken up in both the letters (cf. also Merklein, "Paulinische Theologie," 38–40, 63).

The writer has worked on Colossians and the Pauline tradition in a fashion similar to that in which Jewish exegetes often worked on Scripture; he himself provides an explicit midrash on Scripture in 4:8–10. It may well be that he treats Pauline material as authoritative tradition that needs reformulating for a new situation. His method is certainly not the same as pesher (*pace* Merklein, *Das kirchliche Amt,* 43, who claims that parts of Ephesians are "almost a type of pesher" on Colossians), but it might be seen as a loose form of implicit midrash. One form of midrashic interpretation was the "anthological style" which reemployed phrases or catchwords from familiar texts, sometimes conflating these texts, in order to formulate new instruction (cf. R. Bloch, "Midrash," *DBSup* 5 [1957] cols. 1263–81). It is probably better, however, to talk more generally of the writer's actualization of authoritative tradition (cf. also Meade, *Pseudonymity and Canon,* 153–54) and to realize that such an actualization of earlier texts could take place by means of a variety of methods (cf. also the observations above about the similarities to Josephus' use of the *Letter of Aristeas*).

3. Authorship/Pseudonymity/Canon

Bibliography

Aland, K. "Falsche Verfasserangaben? Zur Pseudonymität im frühchristlichen Schrifttum." *TRev* 75 (1979) 1–10. ———. "The Problem of Anonymity and Pseudonymity in Christian Literature of the First Two Centuries." *JTS* 12 (1961) 39–49. ———. "Noch einmal: Das Problem der Anonymität und Pseudonymität in der christlichen Literatur der ersten beiden Jahrhunderte." In *Pietas*. FS B. Kötting, ed. E. Dassmann. Münster: Aschendorff, 1980, 121–39. **Balz, H. R.** "Anonymität und Pseudepigraphie im Urchristentum: Überlegungen zum literarischen und theologischen Problem der urchristlichen und gemeinantiken Pseudepigraphie." *ZTK* 66 (1969) 403–36. **Bauckham, R.** "Pseudo-Apostolic Letters." *JBL* 107 (1988) 469–94. **Baur, F. C.** *Paulus der Apostel Jesu Christi.* Stuttgart: Becker & Müller, 1845, 449–55. **Brox, N.** *Falsche Verfasserangaben: Zur Erklärung der frühchristlichen Pseudepigraphie.* Stuttgart: Katholisches Bibelwerk, 1975. **Brox, N.**, ed. *Pseudepigraphie in der heidnischen und jüdisch-christlichen Antike.* Darmstadt: Wissenschaftliche Buchgesellschaft, 1977. **Cadbury, H. J.** "The Dilemma of Ephesians." *NTS* 5 (1958–59) 91–102. **Conzelmann, H.** "Paulus und die Weisheit." *NTS* 12 (1965–66) 231–44. ———. "Die Schule des Paulus." In *Theologia Crucis—Signum Crucis.* FS E. Dinkler, ed. C. Andresen, and G. Klein. Tübingen: Mohr, 1979, 85–96. **Donelson, L. R.** *Pseudepigraphy and Ethical Argument in the Pastoral Epistles.* Tübingen: Mohr, 1986, 7–66. **Dunn, J. D. G.** "The Problem of Pseudonymity." In *The Living Word.* London: SCM, 1987, 65–85. **Erasmus, D.** *Novum Testamentum Annotationes.* Basel: Froben, 1519, 413. **Evanson, E.** *The Dissonance of the Four Generally Received Evangelists and the Evidence of Their Respective Authenticity Examined.* Ipswich, 1792. **Fenton, J. C.** "Pseudonymity in the New Testament." *Theology* 58 (1955) 51–56. **Fischer, K. M.** "Anmerkungen zur Pseudepigraphie im Neuen Testament." *NTS* 23 (1976) 76–81. **Goodspeed, E. J.** "Pseudonymity and Pseudepigrapha in Early Christian Literature." In *New Chapters in New Testament Study.* New York: Macmillan, 1937, 169–88. ———. *The Meaning of Ephesians.* **Guthrie, D.** "The Development of the Idea of Canonical Pseudepigraphs in New Testament Criticism." In *The Authorship and Integrity of the New Testament*, ed. K. Aland. London: S.P.C.K., 1965, 14–39. **Harrison, P. N.** "The Author of Ephesians." *SE* 2 (1964) 595–604. **Hengel, M.** "Anonymität, Pseudepigraphie und 'Literarische Fälschung' in der jüdisch-hellenistischen Literatur." In *Pseudepigrapha*, Vol. 1, ed. K. von Fritz. Vandoeuvres-Genève: Fondation Hardt, 1972, 231–308, 309–29. **Laub, F.** "Falsche Verfasserangaben in neutestamentlichen Schriften." *TTZ* 89 (1980) 228–42. **Meade, D. G.** *Pseudonymity and Canon.* Tübingen: Mohr, 1986, esp. 139–57. **Merklein, H.** *Das kirchliche Amt,* 19–54. **Metzger, B. M.** "Literary Forgeries and Canonical Pseudepigrapha." *JBL* 91 (1972) 3–24. **Mitton, C. L.** "The Authorship of the Epistle to the Ephesians." *ExpTim* 67 (1955–56) 195–98. ———. *Epistle.* **Nineham, D. E.** "The Case against the Pauline Authorship." In *Studies in Ephesians*, ed. F. L. Cross. London: Mowbray, 1956, 21–35. **Patzia, A. G.** "The Deutero-Pauline Hypothesis: An Attempt at Clarification." *EvQ* 52 (1980) 27–42. **Percy, E.** *Probleme,* 179–98. **Rist, M.** "Pseudepigraphy and the Early Christians." In *Studies in New Testament and Early Christian Literature.* FS A. P. Wikgren, ed. D. E. Aune. Leiden: Brill, 1972, 75–91. **Roon, A. van.** *Authenticity.* **Sanders, J. N.** "The Case for the Pauline Authorship." In *Studies in Ephesians*, ed. F. L. Cross. London: Mowbray, 1956, 9–20. **Schenke, H.-M.** "Das Weiterwirken des Paulus und die Pflege seines Erbes durch die Paulus-Schule." *NTS* 21 (1974–75) 505–18. **Schille, G.** "Der Autor des Epheserbriefes." *TLZ* 82 (1957) 325–34. **Schweizer, E.** "Zur Frage der Echtheit des Kolosser- und Epheserbriefes." *ZNW* 47 (1956) 287. **Sint, J. A.** *Pseudonymität im Altertum: Ihre Formen und ihre Gründe.* Innsbruck: Universitätsverlag Wagner, 1960. **Speyer, W.** *Die literarische Fälschung im Altertum.* Munich: Beck, 1971. ———. "Religiöse

Pseudepigraphie und literarische Fälschung im Altertum." *JAC* 8/9 (1965–66) 82–125.
Usteri, L. *Die Entwicklung des paulinischen Lehrbegriffs.* Zürich: Orell Füssli, 1824, 2–8.
Wette, W. M. L. de. *Lehrbuch des Neuen Testaments.* Berlin: Reimer, 1826, 254–65.

It will already have become clear from the first two sections of the *Introduction* that authorship of Ephesians by a follower of Paul is being presupposed. An autobiographical note may be appropriate at this point. In my early work and writing on Ephesians, I operated on the assumption that the letter came from Paul himself (cf. "A Re-examination of 'the Heavenlies' in Ephesians," *NTS* 19 [1973] 468–83; *Paradise Now and Not Yet,* 8, 135–39, but see 197 n. 29). This was primarily because at the time I held that one should opt for its authenticity if a plausible case for its setting in the life of Paul could be made and unless there were weighty reasons against this. The argument that the letter's predominantly realized eschatology was non-Pauline, taken in itself, did not seem to be weighty enough. However, the more I have worked on the text as a whole, the more persuaded I have become that seeing the letter as the work of a later follower of Paul makes better sense of its contents. Detailed probes of particular aspects of the letter have served to reinforce this conviction (cf. "The Use of the OT in Ephesians," *JSNT* 14 [1982] 16–57, and "Ephesians 2:8–10: A Summary of Paul's Gospel?" *CBQ* 45 [1983] 617–30). A similar change of perspective on authorship can be traced between the earlier and the later work on Ephesians of Nils A. Dahl (cf. his "Adresse und Proömium des Epheserbriefs," *TZ* 7 [1951] 241–64, with his "Ephesians," *IDBSup* [1976] 268–69), Franz Mussner (cf. his *Christus, das All und die Kirche,* with *Epheser,* 33–34) and Rudolf Schackenburg (cf. his *Baptism in the Thought of St. Paul,* tr. G. R. Beasley-Murray [Oxford: Blackwell, 1964], in which Ephesians is treated as a source of Paul's theology, with *Epheser,* 20–25). I am aware that Heinrich Schlier provides a notable precedent for a move in the opposite direction on this issue. His change of mind and embracing of Pauline authorship may not have been unconnected with his conversion to Roman Catholicism. Apparently, however, he intimated yet another change of mind since the writing of his commentary and expressed doubts about attributing the letter to Paul (cf. Schnackenburg, 21 n. 16).

I shall attempt to summarize some of the major arguments in support of my position, but first it is worth reminding ourselves that the text does not give the reader immediate access to its author. Instead, as literary approaches to the Bible have made us aware, the reader first of all meets the "implied author." The implied author is a construct evoked by the text and inferred and assembled by the reader from all the components of the text. It is a further question what the relationship is between this implied author and the actual author. We shall pursue this after sketching some of the salient features of the implied author.

This author is singular and calls himself Paul (1:1; 3:1). He claims apostolic authority (1:1) and describes himself as a suffering prisoner for Christ, the gospel, and the Gentiles (3:1, 13; 4:1; 6:19, 20), yet gives no concrete details of his suffering or imprisonment. He has only a general knowledge of his addressees (1:13, 15,16) and has to spell out his assumption that they will have heard of his ministry (3:2). The lack of personal greetings reinforces this picture of the author as having no intimate connection with his readers. Nevertheless, he asks for their prayers for his bold proclamation of the gospel (6:19, 20) and recommends Tychicus as his representative who will pass on personal news (6:21, 22).

By the use of the first person plural pronoun the author frequently identifies himself with all believers (cf. 1:3–12, 14; 1:19; 2:3–7, 10; 2:14–16, 18; 3:12, 20; 4:7, 13–15; 5:2; 6:12). At one point he even goes so far as to call himself "the very least of all the saints" (3:8).

He uses the OT as one major authoritative tradition among other liturgical and paraenetic traditions with which he is familiar (see the way in which the same introductory formula is employed for the OT citation in 4:8 as for the early Christian baptismal fragment in 5:14). In his use he is in control of a variety of exegetical methods available to contemporary Judaism, such as midrash pesher and typology, which he makes subservient to his Christian perspective. When this feature is put together with depicting his readers as at one time "Gentiles in the flesh" and "the uncircumcision" (2:11) and with calling outsiders "Gentiles" (4:17), our implied author, "Paul," emerges as a Jewish Christian.

He is eager to tell his readers that he has been given a distinctive revelation about the place of the Gentiles in the Church. In fact, he asks them to recognize, in what he has just written in the letter, his special insights into this mystery (3:2–6). Through his ministry this implied author is the agent of an already-achieved unity of Jew and Gentile. His apostolic mission in bringing the Church into being is part of God's cosmic purpose, and his suffering mediates salvation, eschatological glory, to the Gentiles (3:7–13). Though having this unique ministry, the implied author can at the same time set himself among other holy apostles and prophets as a recipient of the revelation of the mystery (3:5). Along with them he is part of the foundation of the Church (2:20).

The implied author has an appreciation of the greatness of the salvation God has provided in Christ and a profound awareness that every part of Christian existence is pure gift and must be attributed to God's initiative (cf. esp. 1:3–14; 2:1–22). As part of this theocentric perspective he holds that God's purpose of harmony for the whole cosmos is accomplished through Christ. He has a vision of a greater spiritual quality for his readers' lives and believes in the power of God to bring this about (cf. esp. 1:15–23; 3:14–21). He considers the law to be abolished, the unity of Jew and Gentile to have been achieved through Christ's work of reconciliation, and the Church to be a new creation replacing the old order with its divisive categories of Jew and Gentile (2:11–18). He is particularly concerned to stress the significance of this Church for his readers (cf. 1:22, 23; 2:19–22; 3:10, 21; 4:1–16). He takes seriously the Church's future in history, emphasizing the need for its unity and the place of apostles, prophets, evangelists, pastors, and teachers in producing unity and maturity (4:1–16). Finally, it is clear that he wants his readers to lead a distinctive life in the world. He is concerned about their speech and sexual morality, and wants their lives to be characterized by thanksgiving, love, Spirit-filled worship, and an awareness of their place in a battle against the powers of evil. He sees the need for Christian motivations to be brought to bear within the traditional structures of the household. In attempting to provide such motivations he sets out an exalted view of marriage, whereby it is to be modeled on the relationship between Christ and the Church, and quotes an OT text promising long life on earth as a reward to obedient children.

If these are some of the characteristics, views, and concerns of the implied author intrinsic to the text, can we move from this figure to positing the actual author who adopted such features for this particular work? There are three options: (*i*) the apostle Paul himself, (*ii*) a secretary who was given a free hand by Paul during his lifetime, and (*iii*) a later follower of Paul writing in his name. Although the secretary hypothesis might be of some value in regard to issues of language and style, it does nothing to solve the problems of differences in theology, of the letter's apparent later perspective, and, as we shall see, of its relationship to Colossians (for arguments against this hypothesis from both proponents of Pauline authorship and of pseudonymity, see Percy, *Probleme*, 421–22; Barth, 40–41; Mitton, *Epistle*, 249–50). The first and the third should therefore be seen as the major contending options. Of course, in order to decide between them, factors extrinsic to the text of Ephesians itself must also be brought into play, and, because of the nature of the case, judgments can only be in terms of probabilities. I shall not attempt here to lay out and then seek to refute the arguments that can be advanced in favor of Pauline authorship. This sort of discussion can be found in the standard New Testament introductions. Instead, I shall concentrate on providing briefly the positive arguments for the third option.

In all probability, it is submitted, a later follower of Paul writing in his name is responsible for the portrait of Paul that can be constructed from the letter by the reader and for its other features. Erasmus (1519) had doubts about the letter's authenticity because of its style, while Evanson (1792), Usteri (1824), and de Wette (1826 and 1843) were all early representatives of the view that the letter was not by Paul but by a later disciple. This opinion was also promulgated by F. C. Baur (1845) and his pupils. For what it is worth, this is now the consensus view in NT scholarship, though a sizable minority continues to uphold Pauline authorship (cf., e.g., Percy, *Probleme*, 448; Schlier, 22–28; Guthrie, *New Testament Introduction*, 479–508; Barth, 36–50; Caird, *Paul's Letters*, 11–29; Bruce, *Epistles*, 229–40; however, van Roon, *Authenticity*, 438–39, and Johnson, *The Writings of the New Testament*, 367–72, have versions of Pauline authorship which overlap with the secretary hypothesis, since they appeal to the influence of a scribe or fellow workers to account for some differences). It should be noted in passing that although Ephesians appears to have been an uncontested part of the canon of Paul's letters since the time of Marcion and it was clearly accepted as being by Paul since the time of Irenaeus and Tertullian, we know nothing about how this situation came about. Therefore, this cannot be a decisive factor in discussion of the original authorship (for further discussion, see below on the dating of the letter).

Apart from the fact that the undisputed letters of Paul (including Romans) are addressed to specific concrete needs of his churches, whereas Ephesians is far more general, there are some other major reasons for thinking that the case for pseudonymity is the stronger one.

(a) *The point of view* of the implied author is later than that of the apostle

Paul. 3:1–13 in particular reads far more like the estimate of Paul's apostleship on the part of someone looking back than like Paul talking about himself. Paul was certainly capable of stressing the significance of his apostleship when this was under attack, but the need to tell the readers that they will have heard of his ministry and then to recommend his own insights in 3:4 in an unqualified fashion and under no provocation is best explained as the device of someone who wishes to boost claims for the authority of the apostle's teachings for a later time. Similarly, 3:5, with its willingness to attribute to other apostles the reception of the special revelation about the Gentiles which the historical Paul regarded as part of his distinctive calling and its use of the term "holy" in a particular, limited way for this group of apostles, suggests a post-apostolic setting for this apostolic self-portrait. The humility of 3:8, "the very least of all the saints," is also exaggerated, lacking the spontaneity of 1 Cor 15:9, with Paul's reference to himself as "the least of the apostles."

Elsewhere in the letter, too, though Paul is supposed to be speaking, it is as if he is being treated as a revered figure, a dignitary. Missing is his personal presence of the undisputed letters with its passion, urgency, joy, and anger (cf. also Ernst, 260). The tensions and struggles of Paul's ministry are no longer apparent. The admission of the Gentiles and with it Paul's controversial teaching on justification are no longer issues. Had such a state of affairs been reached in the lifetime of Paul? 2:11–22 looks back on an achieved unity, has no need to qualify its assertion of the abrogation of the law, and can regard Paul along with the other apostles and prophets as part of the Church's foundation. This writer appears not to feel the same problems as the Paul of Romans about the Church's relation to Israel. There is no wrestling with the question of Israel's future. Instead Israel is an entity from the past, and the focus is all on the new "third race," the one Church out of Jews and Gentiles (cf. also 3:6). The implied author's thoroughgoing emphasis on the universal Church and the significance he assigns to its ministers in 4:11, 12 are also better explained, because of the development they suggest, by a perspective later than that reflected in the undisputed Pauline letters.

(b) *The theological emphases* of the implied author are different from those of the apostle Paul. No doubt a few of these emphases could be accounted for by the historical Paul having to address a different situation than the situations encountered in the undisputed letters. However, the number of differences that have to be accounted for are too many for this to be a convincing explanation for the whole phenomenon. Some of the points that will be mentioned here overlap with the previous discussion of a later perspective, since such a perspective is obviously one explanation for a number of the differences.

The historical Paul's stress on the death of Christ and his theology of the cross have faded into the background. The cross is only mentioned in 2:16 as the agency of reconciliation, and then it is in dependence on Col 1:20, while the death of Christ is touched on in the traditional formulations of 1:7; 5:2; and 5:25. Instead, all the weight of the letter is on Christ's resurrection, exaltation, and cosmic lordship. Similarly, when it comes to the believer's relationship to Christ, there is no mention of dying with Christ but only of being raised and seated with Christ. While the historical Paul of Romans is at pains to point out that his gospel does not abolish the law (3:31), Ephesians claims that this is precisely what Christ had done (2:15), and the same verb, καταργεῖν, is used in each case. No longer do we find the typical discussion of Galatians and Romans about justification by grace through faith set over against works of the law. Instead Ephesians in 2:8–10 talks more broadly of salvation by grace through faith, which it sets over against works in general, human effort. The same passage speaks of "good works" (plural), a phrase avoided in the undisputed Paulines. What is more, this passage does away with the typical distinction for Paul between present justification and future salvation and in its place depicts salvation as already completed for believers, using the perfect tense of the verb σῴζειν.

This perspective of realized eschatology is characteristic of the letter as a whole. The Church is a community with a future in the world, and the talk is not of its awaiting the Parousia with eager expectation but rather of its growing up toward its head (4:15). The expectation of the Parousia has receded even more than in Colossians, which at least refers in 3:4 to Christ's appearance in glory. In Ephesians there is no reference to the Parousia as such, though there are general references to a future consummation in 1:14; 4:30; 5:5; and 6:13. The focus is more on believers' present relationship to the exalted Christ in the heavenly realm (cf., e.g., 1:3; 1:20–23; 2:6). There are other consequences of these differing perspectives. In 1 Cor 7, because of his perception of the urgency of the times, Paul is able only to make concessions about marriage. In Eph 5, however, a high value is now placed on marriage as it is compared to the relationship between Christ and the Church. Similarly, the household code of Ephesians reflects a more long-term perspective on life in this world in its instructions about the Christian training of children and its use of LXX Exod 20:12 to promise long life on earth to those children who honor their parents (6:1–4).

The historical Paul can talk of the Church of God as a comprehensive entity in 1 Cor 15:9 and Gal 1:13 in connection with his previous persecuting activity (cf. also 1 Cor 12:28) but most frequently reserves the term ἐκκλησία for local assemblies of believers. In contrast, Ephesians employs ἐκκλησία exclusively of the universal Church (cf. 1:22; 3:10, 21; 5:23–25, 27, 29, 32). The term "fullness," which in Colossians was ascribed to Christ, is now in Ephesians applied to this universal Church (1:23). The concentration on this sort of ecclesiology with its vision of the universal Church as one (4:4), holy (5:26, 27), catholic (1:22, 23), and apostolic (2:20) in all probability reflects a stage beyond that of the ministry of Paul. Indeed, seeing the apostles and prophets as the foundation of the Church is a different perspective from that of Col 2:7, let alone from that of the exclusive imagery of 1 Cor 3:11.

The writer of Ephesians in his broad vision of the Church's role in God's purposes for the world sees it, not in continuity with an Israel which still has its own part in God's plan, but rather as a replacement for Israel, a new creation (2:11–22). One can agree with Barth (47–48) that the undisputed Paul is not just an existentialist theologian of individual justification but is concerned about the unity of Jews and Gentiles in the one people of God. Yet this observation does nothing to lessen the gap between the perspective of the irenic Paul of Romans, with his reflections on the continuing significance of ethnic Israel, and the writer of Eph 2, for whom the significance of Israel lies in the past.

Introduction

Finally, a few of this letter's minor theological peculiarities and differences from the undisputed Paulines can be mentioned. Ephesians depicts the evil powers as a close threat to Christian existence and at work "in the air" (2:2; 6:12). It is unique in its concept of believers actively exposing the darkness that surrounds them (5:11, 13). Despite its theocentric perspective, in some places Christ is given a more prominent role than in the undisputed letters. So, for example, Christ is the subject of the verb "to reconcile" in 2:16 and not simply the one through whom God reconciles, as in 2 Cor 5:18, 19; Rom 5:11; and Col 1:20. In 4:11 it is Christ who gives apostles, prophets, and the other ministers, not God who appoints them, as in 1 Cor 12:28.

(c) Ephesians exhibits *significant differences of language and style* from the undisputed Pauline letters. It contains 40 *hapax legomena* for the NT and 51 further words not found in the undisputed Pauline letters (cf. Percy, *Probleme,* 179–80). This statistic is not particularly significant in comparison with those for other NT writings. What is more important in regard to the letter's distinctive vocabulary is to note that there are words unique to Ephesians that have greater affinity with post-apostolic literature (e.g., ἄθεος [2:12], ἄσοφος [5:15], ἑνότης [4:3], εὔνοια [6:7], εὔσπλαγχνος [4:32], κληροῦν [1:11], μέγεθος [1:19], ὁσιότης [4:24], συνοικοδομεῖν [2:22]; cf. also Schnackenburg, 22 n. 19). More important than individual words unique to Ephesians are the combinations of words, the phrases, which are unique within the Pauline corpus and reflect this letter's distinctive mode of expression. These include εὐλογία πνευματική, "spiritual blessing" (1:3), καταβολὴ κόσμου, "foundation of the world" (1:4), ἡ ἄφεσις τῶν παραπτωμάτων, "forgiveness of trespasses" (1:7), τὸ μυστήριον τοῦ θελήματος αὐτοῦ, "mystery of his will" (1:9), οἰκονομία τοῦ πληρώματος τῶν καιρῶν, "administration of the fullness of time" (1:10), ὁ λόγος τῆς ἀληθείας, "the word of truth" (1:13), ὁ πατὴρ τῆς δόξης, "the Father of glory" (1:17), παραπτώματα καὶ ἁμαρτίαι, "trespasses and sins" (2:1), ὁ αἰὼν τοῦ κόσμου τούτου, "this world-age" (2:2), τὰ θελήματα τῆς σαρκός, "the wishes of the flesh" (2:3), ἡ πρόθεσις τῶν αἰώνων, "the eternal purpose" (3:11), μανθάνειν τὸν Χριστόν, "to learn Christ" (4:20), τὸ πνεῦμα τοῦ νοός, "the spirit of the mind" (4:23), μιμηταὶ τοῦ θεοῦ, "imitators of God" (5:1), τὰ πνευματικὰ τῆς πονηρίας, "the spirit-forces of evil" (6:12) (cf. also Gnilka, 16). Other unique stylistic features are this letter's use of the phrase ἐν τοῖς ἐπουρανίοις (1:3, 20; 2:6; 3:10; 6:12) with reference to the heavenly realm instead of ἐν τοῖς οὐρανοῖς (2 Cor 5:1; cf. Col 1:5, 16, 20) and of the term διάβολος, "devil" (4:27; 6:11), instead of σατανᾶς, "Satan" (Rom 16:20; 1 Cor 5:5; 7:5; 2 Cor 2:11; 11:14; 12:7; 1 Thess 2:18; 2 Thess 2:9). It also employs διὸ λέγει (4:8; 5:14), which does not appear in the undisputed Paulines, as an introductory formula for citations. The prepositions ἐν and κατά are found far more frequently in Ephesians than in the undisputed letters, and, in contrast to Colossians, there are several formulae with ἐν that do not occur in those letters: ἐν τῷ κυρίῳ Ἰησοῦ, "in the Lord Jesus" (1:15), ἐν τῷ Χριστῷ Ἰησοῦ, "in Christ Jesus" (3:11), ἐν τῷ Ἰησοῦ, "in Jesus" (4:21).

We have already discussed the style of Ephesians in our first main section, but what needs to be underlined in this context is the way in which its characteristic features distinguish it from other letters in the Pauline corpus. Gone is the direct, incisive argumentation of the earlier letters. This is replaced by a heavier, pleonastic style. As Sanday and Headlam (*The Epistle to the Romans*

[Edinburgh: T. & T. Clark, 1902⁵] lv) write, "We shut up the epistle to the Romans, and we open that to the Ephesians; how great is the contrast! We cannot speak here of vivacity, hardly of energy. . . . In its place we have a slowly moving, onwards advancing mass, like a glacier working its way inch by inch down the valley." Moffatt (*Introduction*, 389) puts it somewhat more positively, "In Paul's letters there is always something of a cascade; in Ephesians we have a slow, bright stream which brims its high banks." The frequent piling up of synonyms, the genitival combinations, the long sentences, the repetition of certain phrases, and the lack of conjunctions and particles are striking, even in comparison to Colossians (on which see W. Bujard, *Stilanalytische Untersuchungen zum Kolosserbrief* [Göttingen: Vandenhoeck & Ruprecht, 1973]). The long sentences are not simply to be explained by liturgical influence in the first part of the letter. It is not only the sentences of 1:3–14; 1:15–23; 2:1–7; 3:14–19 that need to be considered, but also 3:1–7 and, in the second paraenetical part of the letter, 4:11–16; 5:7–13; 6:14–20. There are one or two comparable sentences in terms of length in the undisputed Paulines, but not nearly this many and not all in one letter. This feature of Ephesians pushes van Roon (*Authenticity*, 105–11, 206) to opt for someone in the Pauline circle as the writer. It does suggest as the actual author someone more heavily influenced than Paul appears to be by the impact on Hellenistic Jewish writing of the style characteristic of the Qumran hymns (cf. also Schnackenburg, 23). Indeed K. G. Kuhn claims that "Semitic syntactical occurrences appear four times more frequently in the Epistle to the Ephesians than in all the remaining letters of the corpus Paulinum" (*Paul and Qumran*, 116).

(d) *The relationship of Ephesians to Colossians* points decisively away from Pauline authorship of Ephesians. If what we have suggested about the relationship between Ephesians and Colossians is correct, there are a number of clear implications about the authorship of Ephesians. Since the authorship of Colossians itself is still disputed, this discussion of the implications will not presuppose any clearcut position on that issue. Amongst recent commentators on Colossians, Lohse and Gnilka argue for its pseudonymity, while Martin and O'Brien defend its authenticity. But so far defenders of authenticity have not dealt adequately with the detailed case against it on the grounds of style made by W. Bujard, *Stilanalytische Untersuchungen zum Kolosserbrief*. Schweizer attempts a mediating position, holding that the letter is neither Pauline nor post-Pauline and suggesting that it was written by Timothy while Paul was still alive but imprisoned and unable to write or dictate. What is clear is that *if* both Colossians and Ephesians are non-Pauline, Colossians stands closer to Paul in terms of its content and its time of composition than does Ephesians. What is also clear is that if Colossians is regarded as non-Pauline, then, because of its relation to Colossians, Ephesians must also be seen as non-Pauline (cf. also Mitton, *Epistle*, 56).

Defenders of the authenticity of Ephesians, however, invariably assume or are prepared to argue for the authenticity of Colossians. According to such a view, it is then argued that the relationship between the two letters can be accounted for by their both having come from the same person, Paul. He addressed Colossians to a specific situation, then at roughly the same time wrote the more general Ephesians as a circular to a group of churches in the same area as Colossians, and sent both of them by the hand of Tychicus (cf.

Schmid, *Epheserbrief*, 392–455, and Percy, *Probleme*, 360–433, who attempt to show that the parallels and divergences between the letters are best explained in this way, and are followed by Schlier, 24–25). But the nature of the similarities and divergences, with wording rearranged and phrases conflated such as we have described above, makes such a hypothesis highly unlikely. To underline one example, if the same writer had written Eph 5:20 almost immediately after Col 3:17, is he really likely to have changed the thought while keeping substantially the same wording, to have tinkered with the phrasing without regard to the earlier context which had provided its meaning? One might expect the same writer to make use of some of the thoughts and wording of his first composition but not to do so in the particular way in which the writer of Ephesians has employed Colossians as his model. It is one thing for a writer to reproduce the same ideas in the same words or even in different words, but it is quite another for a writer within a short period of time to reproduce the same words and phrases to express different ideas (cf. also Nineham, "The Case against . . . ," 27–28). And of course there is no similar correspondence between any other Pauline letters. Galatians and Romans provide one illustration of what might be expected from the same writer reflecting on some similar themes but addressing his thoughts to different situations, but their relationship is very different from that between Colossians and Ephesians (*pace,* e.g., J. B. Lightfoot, "The Destination of the Epistle to the Ephesians," in *Biblical Essays* [London: Macmillan, 1893] 395, who claims, "The Epistle to the Ephesians stands to the Epistle to the Colossians in very much the same relation as the Romans to the Galatians. The one is the general and systematic exposition of the same truths which appear in a special bearing in the other"; also J. N. Sanders, "The Case for. . . ," 17). There is another major factor in the case of Galatians and Romans which does not make it a helpful analogy, and that is the period of time that elapsed between the two. This is precisely what cannot have occurred on the supposition of Pauline authorship of Ephesians. Otherwise one would have to entertain the extraordinarily difficult picture of Paul at a later stage looking up a copy of his earlier letter to the Colossians and studying it for inspiration for ideas and wording and also just happening to have Tychicus on hand to deliver this letter also (cf. also Mitton, *Epistle,* 76–77, 254–55).

So if Paul was the author of both letters, he must have written Ephesians almost immediately after Colossians. But the almost insurmountable difficulty with this is that, as we have seen, some of the theological divergences in the use of key terms and themes have to be explained not simply by their having been placed in a different context but by that new context having come about through a process of further reflection producing a changed perspective. This changed perspective, while in continuity with that of Colossians, at a number of points requires for its explanation a lapse of time (cf. also Mitton, *Epistle,* 254; Merklein, *Das kirchliche Amt,* 32, 35; Schnackenburg, 29). The argument then is not, as some suggest, that key terms from Colossians have a totally different meaning in Ephesians, but that the changed perspective in which those terms are employed means that the letters could not have been written at the same time, which is what must be supposed if Pauline authorship of Ephesians is claimed (cf. also Ochel, *Annahme,* 4).

As we have already asserted, to resort to the hypothesis of Paul's use of a secretary to explain the relationship between the letters is of little help. It is unlikely that a secretary authorized by Paul would retain the style and language of the earlier Colossians but then subordinate it and his master's thought to his own theological ideas (for further arguments against this hypothesis, see Percy, *Probleme,* 421–22; Guthrie, *New Testament Introduction,* 508 n. 1; Merklein, *Das kirchliche Amt,* 38; Schnackenburg, 29). Everything points instead to a later follower of Paul who used Colossians as the basis for his own reinterpretation of the Pauline gospel (cf. also, e.g., Moffatt, *Introduction,* 375–81; Kümmel, *Introduction,* 358–61; Mitton, *Epistle,* esp. 254–55, 261; Schnackenburg, 29; Mussner, 18, 34). Defenders of the authenticity of Ephesians sometimes object to this conclusion on the grounds that a conscious imitator would have kept far more closely to his model and that "the spiritual and intellectual power of Ephesians, together with its freedom from a slavish reproduction of Colossians, is extremely improbable in an imitator" (Guthrie, *New Testament Introduction,* 494; cf. also Caird, *Paul's Letters,* 25). But such an objection only has force because it presupposes a model of the later Paulinist as an imitator who has to copy slavishly for fear of being found out. As Meade (*Pseudonymity and Canon,* 142) points out, not only is this "denied by certain brilliant figures in Jewish pseudepigraphy (2 Isaiah, Qoheleth), it is denied by the very basis of Jewish pseudepigraphy itself. It was precisely the purpose of the author to be in touch with the thoughts of his pseudonym: not just to 'imitate' him, but to think his thoughts after him." As soon as one grants a Pauline disciple any creativity and fresh pastoral insight in his adaptation of material from Colossians, as one surely must, the counterargument loses its effectiveness. And as Moffatt (*Introduction,* 375) reminds us, "the synoptic problem is enough to show that the deliberate employment of a source was not incompatible with original work on the part of an early Christian writer."

It is difficult to determine whether both the writer of Colossians and the writer of Ephesians were disciples of Paul, or whether only the writer of Ephesians was a later disciple and was employing what he considered to be a genuine Pauline letter, i.e., Colossians, in his reinterpretation of the Pauline tradition (cf. also Ernst, 257). The writer of Ephesians may have considered Colossians to have come from the hand of Paul himself, and he may or may not have been right in this supposition. On the other hand he may have believed Colossians to be Pauline in the sense of being the product of another follower of Paul, possibly while Paul was still alive (cf. the view of Schweizer, *Colossians,* 23–24), and therefore treated Colossians as the model of the sort of writing that could be done in the apostle's name (cf. Merklein, *Das kirchliche Amt,* 41).

Four main types of argument have been presented for the view that the real author of Ephesians is not Paul himself but a follower of his, and particular weight has been given to the fourth type. In addition, each of these main categories has included several specific supporting arguments based on evidence from the text. The case can therefore be seen as involving a cumulative argument. Caird (*Paul's Letters,* 24; cf. also Guthrie, *New Testament Introduction,* 504) believes the cumulative nature of the argument to be a problem for advocates of non-Pauline authorship. But there are two ways of looking at the issue. On the one hand, it is true that if the cumulative argument is framed in terms of basing one probable case upon another, the probability of the overall case becomes smaller rather than greater. On the other hand, if the various arguments are taken as separate strands, then these arguments and the amount of evidence in their favor produce an impressive case (cf. also Mitton, *Epistle,* 17; Nineham, "The Case against . . . ," 23). It is one thing for the defender of Pauline authorship, in the face of awkward evidence that suggests the probable author was someone other than Paul, to invoke the burden-of-proof argument and to respond once or twice by saying, "Yes, but it is still *possible* that Paul could have written that for this particular reason. . . ." But when such a defense has to be produced again and again, doubts must begin to be raised about the tenability of the position being defended. The question in each case is not "Is it possible that Paul could have done this?" but "Is it *probable?*" In particular, is it probable that in one letter Paul would show such strong peculiarities in such significant areas? Sometimes the proponents of Pauline authorship concede the difficulty of their position. Caird (*Paul's Letters,* 29), for example, admits that Ephesians "is curiously unlike the other Pauline letters" and has to hold that this is the result of Paul's mind becoming more expansive and taking in unparalleled concepts in a reflective mood at the end of his life. Is it not more probable that the letter was written by someone other than Paul? Barth (49) responds to such a question by attempting to turn the arguments about linguistic and theological differences on their head and claiming that "*because* some typically Pauline words have a slightly different, perhaps unique, meaning in Ephesians, and *because* deviations from a straight party-line Paulinism are indisputable, Ephesians may have to be considered authentic. Only a foolish plagiarist or editor would have been unaware of the changes, additions, corrections he made." But, as in the case of arguments about the use of Colossians, the anachronistic assumption in such a claim must be exposed. In first-century pseudonymity, as we shall see, we are not dealing with plagiarism or with the necessity of slavish imitation lest one be found out but with a device for passing on authoritative tradition in a creative way.

One further major argument is used against the view that Ephesians is deutero-Pauline. Both Jülicher (*Einleitung in das Neue Testament* [Tübingen: Mohr, 1931⁷] 141–42) and Percy (*Probleme,* 443) give as their main reason for not being able to accept the deutero-Pauline hypothesis that they can discern no purpose for producing such a letter in the name of Paul. It is our contention, however, that the letter's purpose, though general, emerges clearly from an analysis of its contents and that its message is entirely appropriate for bolstering the self-understanding and thereby guiding the behavior of the churches of the Pauline mission in Asia Minor after the death of the apostle (see Section 4 on "Purposes"). The persuasiveness of this view of the overall purpose will of course depend on whether the detailed commentary on the text, on which it depends, is found to be convincing.

There has been speculation about the exact identity of the real author. Amongst the candidates who have been proposed are Onesimus (cf. Goodspeed, *Meaning*), Tychicus (cf. Mitton, 230; *Epistle,* 27, 268), and Luke (cf. Martin, *ExpTim* 79 [1968] 296–302; *New Testament Foundations,* 2:230–32; Adai, *Der heilige Geist,* 22–24, who believes this to be a strong possibility; but cf.

Mitton, 17). But each proposal involves guesswork to a greater or lesser extent, and in any case the enterprise stands little chance of success, given that a major purpose of the writer's choosing to express himself in the way he has was to divert attention from his own identity and focus it on that of the apostle in whose name he writes. Perhaps the most that can be said is that because of his way of speaking about Israel and the Gentiles in 2:11, 12, his particular use of the OT, his familiarity with other Jewish traditions, including those of the Hellenistic synagogue, and his style with its Hebraisms, the real author was in all probability a Jewish Christian admirer of Paul. He may well have been a member of a Pauline "school" in the loose sense of that term, a circle of those who began as his fellow workers in the Pauline mission and from which there later emerged some who consciously and deliberately worked with the heritage of Paul's thought in order to preserve it and pass it on in a form adapted for their own times (cf. also Gnilka, 21; Conzelmann, "Die Schule," 88–95; Schenke, *NTS* 21 [1974–75] 505–18; K. Berger, *Exegese des Neuen Testaments* [Heidelberg: Quelle & Meyer, 1977] 226–34; cf. also E. E. Ellis, "Paul and His Co-Workers," *NTS* 17 [1970–71] 437–52; W.-H. Ollrog, *Paulus und seine Mitarbeiter* [Neukirchen: Neukirchener, 1979]). Conzelmann (*NTS* 12 [1965–66] 233) and Merklein (*Das kirchliche Amt*, 40–41) suggest that such a Pauline school tradition is to be located in Ephesus (cf. also Patzia, *EvQ* 52 [1980] 33–34; for a survey of ancient schools which were more clearly defined communities than any Pauline "school" appears to have been, see R. A. Culpepper, *The Johannine School* [Missoula, MT: Scholars Press, 1975] 39–260).

To claim that, although the implied author of the letter is the apostle Paul, the actual author of Ephesians is a later follower of Paul is obviously also to maintain that this author has used the literary device of pseudonymity. This was a widespread and accepted literary practice in both Jewish and Greco-Roman cultures. In the Hebrew Bible, writings are attributed to great names such as Moses, David, Solomon, and Isaiah. Such writings must have been produced after these figures had died, and in them earlier authoritative traditions were elaborated and contemporized but attributed to the figures at their source (cf. Meade, *Pseudonymity and Canon*, esp. 103–5, for a summary of the significance of this material). It would have been clear to all that such figures could not have been the actual authors. Pseudonymity was, as Dunn ("Problem," 68) suggests, "a means of affirming the continuity of God's purpose between the circumstances of the named author and the circumstances of the actual author." As is well known, there are also numerous pseudepigrapha in early Judaism—writings (apocalypses, testaments, prayers, collections of sayings) attributed to ideal or authoritative figures from the past. It was also a convention in Hellenistic rhetoric for a speaker to give proof of his authority by adopting the persona of an authoritative figure. This was known as *sermocinatio* or *prosopopeia* (cf. Quintilian 9.2.29–31), speaking in character to produce presence, a sense of dramatic and psychological immediacy (cf. Lausberg, *Handbuch der literarischen Rhetorik*, 129, 155, 407–11, 543, 548). Pseudepigraphical letters, like authentic letters, also attempted to convey the presence of the sender to their recipients (cf. Donelson, *Pseudepigraphy*, 64–65).

In regard to the letter form in particular, the pseudonymous didactic letters of the philosophical schools (e.g., the Pythagorean, Cynic, Neo-Platonist school productions) offer some analogies from the Greco-Roman world (cf. Donelson, *Pseudepigraphy*, 7–66; Sint, *Pseudonymität*, 114, 157–59). Similarly, the *Epistle of Jeremiah*, the *Epistle of Enoch* (*1 Enoch* 92–105), the *Epistle of Baruch* (*2 Apoc. Bar.* 78–87), the correspondence between Solomon, Hiram, and Pharaoh in Eupolemos and Josephus (*Ant.* 8.2.6–7 §§ 50–54), the letters contained in 1 and 2 Maccabees, the *Epistle of Barnabas*, the *Epistle to the Laodiceans*, *3 Corinthians*, and the *Second Epistle of Clement* provide examples from Jewish and early Christian literature. The *Letter of Aristeas*, though pseudonymous, is not itself in epistolary form, and the earliest writers who mention it do not describe it as a letter (cf. also Alexander, "Epistolary Literature," 580). In addition, the consensus of scholarship holds that within the NT at least 2 Peter (cf. especially R. J. Bauckham, *Jude, 2 Peter*, WBC 50 [Waco: Word Books, 1983] 131–35, 158–62) and the Pastoral Epistles (cf. most recently Donelson, *Pseudepigraphy*, 54–66) are further instances of the use of pseudonymity. So within particular intellectual or religious traditions it was common for the names of revered leaders or teachers from the past to be attached to a community's important literature. Within early Christianity toward the end of the first century, Peter and Paul especially had become identified as revered apostolic figures in various parts of the church. So, when it became necessary to appeal to the original apostolic message as the norm for the present, their names could be invoked to represent the apostolic tradition as a whole. Clement of Rome (c. 96 C.E.) referred to them as "the greatest and most virtuous pillars of our church" (*1 Clem.* 5.2) and regarded them as the guarantors of the particular tradition he wished to commend to his readers (e.g., *1 Clem.* 42.1–5; 44.1, 2).

The earliest Christian writers of pseudepigrapha remained under the influence of Jewish notions of authorship and revelation whereby pseudonymity involved the assertion of authoritative tradition, but, in regard to *form*, employed the pseudepigraphical letter, which was an especially Greco-Roman literary device. Pseudepigraphical letters in the Greco-Roman world frequently invent extraneous mundane details and personal references for the sake of verisimilitude and in order to provide the occasion for the promulgation of philosophical teaching and the portrayal of a particular philosopher as a model for the readers (cf. the numerous examples in Donelson, *Pseudepigraphy*, 23–42). There is no reason to think of the device of pseudonymity in negative terms and to associate it necessarily with such notions as forgery and deception (*pace* Schmid, *Epheserbrief*, 391, who, in a confusion of literary and moral categories, claims that pseudonymity cannot be squared with the writer's own exhortation in 4:25, "put off falsehood and let each one speak the truth with his neighbour"). The idea of "intellectual property," basic to modern discussion of legitimate claims to authorship, plagiarism, and copyright laws, played little or no role in ancient literary production.

In regard to deception, the situation is somewhat more complex. Undoubtedly some pseudepigrapha were intended to deceive (cf. Donelson, *Pseudepigraphy*, 11), and there is a need to investigate each proposed example of pseudepigraphy, including canonical ones, to see whether this was likely in a given case. Though some recent writers on the phenomenon believe that NT pseudepigrapha were composed and promoted openly as a transparent fiction (cf., e.g., Aland, "Noch einmal," 193–94; Dunn, "Problem," 84, "almost certainly the final readers were not in fact deceived"), others hold that the situation was more ambiguous, to say the least (cf., e.g., Donelson, *Pseudepigraphy,* 49–55; Meade, *Pseudonymity and Canon,* 198). Meade (*Pseudonymity and Canon,* 198) allows that if a document had its origin in a "school," "then within the school the work would most likely have been openly known and acknowledged to be pseudonymous (though no less authoritative)."

Questions also need to be asked about the recipients of a pseudepigraphical letter (cf. esp. Bauckham, *JBL* 107 [1988] 475–92). Were there intended specific recipients, to whom the letter was sent, and would they have been deceived? Or was the letter simply slipped into a collection of letters with the hope that some later general readers would take it for one of Paul's or Peter's original letters? Unfortunately, there is often not enough evidence to answer such questions. In the case of Ephesians, however, it remains likely that the letter was intended for churches of the Pauline mission in Asia Minor in the generation after the apostle's death, and, as we have seen, that its writer was in fact a member of a Pauline "school." If Ephesians was written after the death of Paul, it is hard to believe that these churches of the Pauline mission in Asia Minor would not have known of such an important event as his martyrdom. Rather they would have recognized this product of one of their trusted teachers as in harmony with the Pauline tradition that he and others had continued to mediate to them. Therefore both writer and original readers would have been knowing participants in this particular mode of communication, in which the writer wishes to present his teaching not simply as his own but as in the apostolic tradition which has Paul as its source.

Tertullian (*Adv. Marcion.* 4.5) could later write, "it is allowable that that which pupils publish should be regarded as their masters' work." Paul is the guarantor of the true tradition and his authority is brought into play in order to establish the apostolic as the norm (cf. also Balz, *ZTK* 66 [1970] esp. 420–31; Laub, *TTZ* 89 [1980] 228–42). In this letter's pseudepigraphic framework the author identifies himself with the suffering, imprisoned apostle (cf. 3:1, 13; 4:1; 6:20), and thus presumably with the last stage of Paul's ministry, in an attempt to pass on the Pauline heritage. In this way the writer becomes the mouthpiece for the Pauline tradition as he both creates a hearing for it and reinterprets it for a new situation. As Meade (*Pseudonymity and Canon,* 153–54, 157) concludes, "Ephesians can be seen as a creative attempt to secure the Pauline heritage . . . and to relate it to the church at large, by the actualization of the apostolic doctrine and lifestyle. . . . Therefore . . . literary attribution in Ephesians is primarily an assertion of authoritative Pauline tradition, not of literary origin." The writer's activity in updating the message of Paul can be compared with the process of updating the words of Jesus that is commonly recognized to have occurred in the Synoptics and particularly in the Fourth Gospel (cf. also Laub, *TTZ* 89 [1980] 234–35; Meade, *Pseudonymity and Canon,* 106–15; Dunn, "Problem," 78–81).

When did the writer produce this letter? When the attempt is made to determine the *terminus ad quem,* claims that Clement of Rome was dependent on Ephesians cannot be substantiated (cf. also Gnilka, 18; *pace* Guthrie, *New Testament Introduction,* 480, 516). Probably the first early church father to show clear knowledge of Ephesians is Ignatius (e.g., Ign. *Pol.* 5.1; *Smyrn.* 1.1), although any literary dependence of Ignatius on Ephesians is disputed by some scholars (cf., e.g., Lindemann, *Paulus,* 199–221). A date between 80 and 90 C.E. (cf. also Kümmel, *Introduction,* 366; Merklein, *Das kirchliche Amt,* 48) would allow both for the writer's post-apostolic perspective and knowledge of Paul's letters and for the letter to have become associated with the collection of Paul's letters and thus have become known to Ignatius by the first decade of the second century. It is worth noting that explicit attribution of the letter to Paul is first found in Tertullian, though he also makes it clear that he holds that the letter to the Laodiceans, which Marcion earlier included among the Pauline epistles, is in fact the letter to the Ephesians.

There should be no suggestion that to decide that Ephesians is pseudonymous is somehow to detract from the validity or authority of its message as part of the NT canon. This could be said to be committing the "authorial fallacy," that is, to set more store by who wrote a document than by what it says. Van Roon (*Authenticity,* 2) does this, and operates with assumptions that he fails to spell out about what is truly canonical within the canon, when he says, "If the final verdict is that the work is not authentic, the fact will be that although the Christian church has always invested the epistle with canonical authority, it will nevertheless have to be relegated to the periphery of the New Testament." At least Barth (50), though he defends Pauline authorship, is clear that the issue does not affect the letter's authority: "a concession to those questioning the authenticity is necessary: Inspiration, highest authority, and imperishable value can be ascribed to Ephesians even when the epistle is 'bereft of its apostolic authorship' " (cf. also J. N. Sanders, "The Case for . . . ," 9). Whether written by Paul or by a follower, Ephesians is now canonical; it has the same authoritative and foundational status for the Church's teaching and life as, for example, one of the gospels or Paul's letter to the Romans. As Meade (*Pseudonymity and Canon,* 215–16) argues, "the discovery of pseudonymous origins or anonymous redaction in no way prejudices either the inspiration or the canonicity of the work. Attribution, in the context of canon, must be primarily regarded as a statement (or assertion) of authoritative tradition." By its inclusion within the Pauline corpus, Ephesians is already part of the "canonical" Paul, whatever its relation to the "historical" Paul. The significance of this for an appreciation of the letter's message and impact will be reflected on further in the final section of this *Introduction.*

4. SETTING AND PURPOSES

Bibliography

Arnold, C. E. *Ephesians: Power and Magic.* Cambridge: CUP, 1989, 5–40, 123–24, 165–72. **Best, E.** "Recipients and Title of the Letter to the Ephesians: Why and When the Designation 'Ephesians'?" *ANRW* 2.25.4 (1987) 3247–79. **Chadwick, H.** "Die Absicht des Epheserbriefes." *ZNW* 51 (1960) 145–53. **Dahl, N. A.** "Gentiles, Christians, and Israelites in the Epistle to the Ephesians." *HTR* 79 (1986) 31–39. **Fischer, K. M.** *Tendenz und Absicht des Epheserbriefes.* Göttingen: Vandenhoeck & Ruprecht, 1973. **Lindemann, A.** "Bemerkungen zu den Adressaten und zum Anlass des Epheserbriefes." *ZNW* 67 (1976) 235–51. **Lona, H. E.** *Die Eschatologie im Kolosser- und Epheserbrief.* Würzburg: Echter Verlag, 1984, 428–48. **MacDonald, M. Y.** *The Pauline Churches.* Cambridge:

CUP, 1988, 85–158. **Martin, R. P.** "An Epistle in Search of a Life-Setting." *ExpTim* 79 (1968) 296–302. **Meade, D. G.** *Pseudonymity and Canon.* Tübingen: Mohr, 1986, 142–48. **Meeks, W. A.** "In One Body: The Unity of Humankind in Colossians and Ephesians." In *God's Christ and His People,* ed. J. Jervell and W. A. Meeks. Oslo: Universitetsforlaget, 1977, 209–21. **Schnackenburg, R.** "Der Epheserbrief im heutigen Horizont." In *Massstab des Glaubens.* Freiburg: Herder, 1978, 155–75. **Smith, D. C.** "The Ephesian Heresy and the Origin of the Epistle to the Ephesians." *Ohio Journal of Religious Studies* 5 (1977) 78–103.

The issues of the setting and purposes of a letter are closely related. In the case of most of the letters in the Pauline corpus, scholars have usually set about reconstructing the setting of the recipients by taking the explicit statements about and references to the situation being addressed, associating these with implications that can be drawn from the particular concerns and problems that are treated in the letter, and correlating this material with other available relevant historical, geographical, and social data about the place of the letter's destination. In a somewhat circular fashion this reconstruction is then employed to give sharper definition to an analysis of the letter's message and the purposes it was meant to achieve in the setting to which it was addressed. Scholars are accustomed to employing this method on 1 Corinthians to discuss, for example, the views of the Corinthians on the resurrection or the social setting of the dispute over food offered to idols, or on Romans to investigate the relations between Gentile Christians and Jewish Christians in the various congregations in Rome, or on Colossians to talk about the false teaching and its inroads into the church in Colossae, in order then in each case to elucidate the letter's response. For such scholars, Ephesians, however, proves a source of frustration. It simply does not contain references to a specific setting or problems, and therefore other external data cannot be brought to bear in the same way as with other letters to build up a more detailed picture of the particular situation being addressed. Some interpreters, as we shall see, are determined nevertheless, despite the lack of evidence, to discover a specific setting. It seems more appropriate, however, to respect the distinctiveness of this letter's lack of specificity by concentrating on the general implications of the letter itself and by being content with the correspondingly general contours of the setting that may be cautiously reconstructed.

Focusing on the rhetorical situation of the letter helps to avoid some of the pressures and frustrations imposed by the demand to discover immediately a specific historical life-setting. The rhetorical situation can be defined in terms of the rhetorical occasion to which the text is understood as a fitting response, and in terms of the rhetorical problem or problems that the author has to overcome in order to win the recipients over to his or her point of view. Investigation of the rhetorical situation will not ignore the historical life-setting but directs attention first and foremost to what can be inferred both from the picture of the implied writer and recipients that emerges from a text and from the text's rhetorical genre and strategies. Such an investigation of the communicative function of a text, by asking what responses are called for, can elucidate the author's purposes. It can then ask what must have been the situation that the author thought such responses would affect, before finally making the move of suggesting what must have been the actual historical situation to which such a rhetorical situation corresponds (cf. also, e.g., E. Schüssler Fiorenza, "Rhetorical Situation and Historical Reconstruction in 1 Corinthians," *NTS* 33 [1987] 386–403).

Some of the work for such an investigation of Ephesians has already been done in the preceding sections. It has been noted that the mixture of rhetorical genres—epideictic in the first half of the letter and deliberative in the second half—reflects the writer's twofold strategy. He wishes both to intensify the readers' adherence to the Christian convictions, values, and concepts that he and they have in common and to persuade them to take action that will bring their lives into greater conformity to what he deems to be appropriate to their shared perspective. The first part reinforces their sense of Christian identity, the privileges and status they enjoy as believers who are part of the Church. The second part appeals to them to demonstrate that identity as they live in the Church and in the world. The first part has a congratulatory tone and attempts to secure the goodwill of the recipients through its language of blessing, thanksgiving, intercessory prayer, and doxology. It does not, however, simply repeat what they already know adequately but, particularly through its anamnesis in chap. 2, with the sharp contrasts between the readers' past and present, and through its digression in 3:1–13 bringing to their attention their relation to the apostle's ministry, indicates that the readers are not as aware as they should be of some of the dimensions of their Christian identity. In addition, through its intercessory prayer-reports, it suggests knowledge, love, and the experience of God's power as areas for the readers' growth. The ethical exhortations of the second part build on the rapport established with the readers in the first part and set out the sort of conduct to which the writer wishes them to attain. The final rhetorical strategy, the *peroratio* of 6:10–20, combines the emphases of both parts of the letter by stressing the identity of believers—Christian soldiers clad in God's armor and dependent on Christ's power—and by spelling out again the virtues they are to demonstrate—truthfulness, righteousness, peace, and faith. The main concluding exhortation—to stand in the cosmic battle—also sums up the two emphases, appealing to the readers to maintain and appropriate their identity and position of strength as they practice distinctively Christian living. This exhortation is not so much a call to changed behavior as a call to firm resolve in preserving the values the writer hopes will by now have been instilled in his readers.

A sketch of the implied author has been provided in Section 3. Among the characteristics delineated, the following should be recalled at this point. He is a Jewish Christian who appears to have a general but not intimate knowledge of his readers. He claims Paul's name and authority and special insight into God's purposes for Gentile Christians in the Church. He desires an improved quality of living for his readers, in their relation to God and Christ, in their relationships within the Church, and in their conduct in the world. He stresses the significance of the Church as one body created out of Jews and Gentiles, God's power, Christ's exaltation, Paul's mission, maintaining unity, reaching maturity, tradition and the teachers who pass it on, speech, sexual morality, worship, household relationships, and the cosmic powers.

As regards the implied readers of the original letter, we cannot be sure whether they were linked in the address with a particular church or churches in a specific city or cities. Not surprisingly, what is made clear from the outset, however, is that they are to be seen as Christians. A host of images and descriptions underline such an identity. They are designated as "saints" (1:1, 15, 18; 3:18; 5:3; 6:18) and as "believing" (e.g., 1:1, 13, 15; 2:18; 3:12). They are among "all who love our Lord Jesus Christ" (6:24). They are children of light and God's work of new creation (cf. 5:8; 2:10). As such, they are those who have experienced the grace of God (e.g., 1:6, 8; 2:5, 8) and the love of God and Christ (e.g., 2:4; 5:2, 25), together with the redemption (1:7), forgiveness (1:7; 4:32), life (2:5), salvation (1:13; 2:5, 8), reconciliation (2:14–18), and sealing with the Spirit (1:13; 4:30) that flow from this love and grace. They are also those who are incorporated into Christ and have been united with him in his resurrection and exaltation (e.g., 1:1, 3–14, 15; 2:5, 6); yet at the same time they are still in a battle against hostile cosmic powers (6:12).

A number of the images and descriptions used of the implied readers are corporate ones and make clear that they belong to a larger grouping of Christian believers, to the universal Church. They have links with all saints (2:19; 3:18; 6:18). They belong to "the brothers and sisters," have been adopted as sons and daughters into God's family, are his dearly loved children and members of his household (cf. 6:23; 1:5; 5:1; 2:19). They are part of the Church, which is related to the exalted Christ (1:22; 3:10; 3:21; 5:23, 25, 27, 29, 32). They are members of Christ's body (1:23; 2:16; 3:6; 4:4, 16; 5:23; cf. also 4:25), part of God's temple, which has Christ as its keystone and the apostles and prophets as its foundation (2:19–22). They belong to one new humanity which was created out of Jews and Gentiles (2:14–16; 3:6) and is characterized by its unity (4:1–6).

Somewhat more specifically, in terms of their ethnic background, these Christian readers who are part of the universal Church are Gentiles. This identification is made explicit in the way they are addressed in 2:11 and 3:1, in the depiction of their past as religiously deprived in comparison with that of Israel (2:11–13), and in the reference to their past Gentile lifestyle in 4:17. It is also implicit in the way that past is described in 2:1–3 and in the view of their relationship to Paul's ministry to the Gentiles which underlies the digression of 3:2–13.

The implied readers are assumed to know of Paul (1:1; 3:1; 6:21, 22), of his special proclamation of the gospel and ministry to the Gentiles (3:2, 3, 7, 8; 6:19), and of his suffering and imprisonment (3:13; 4:1; 6:20).

The readers envisaged by the author, although they are Gentiles, are also assumed to know the Jewish Scriptures, to accept their authority, to be conversant with the author's method of interpreting them and persuaded by the results of that interpretation (cf. 2:17; 4:8–10; 5:31, 32; 6:2, 3). In addition they accept the authority of Christian liturgical traditions (e.g., 5:14) and have received Christian instruction which included paraenetical material (cf. 4:20–24).

Despite their identification as Gentile Christian members of the Church and despite all that they already know and have experienced of the gospel as mediated by Paul, the implied readers are those who need to grow and make progress in a number of areas. In fact, they need a greater awareness of the blessings and privileges that are attached to their identity as believers in Christ and members of the Church. The rehearsing of the blessings of salvation in the opening eulogy (1:3–14) serves this purpose, as do the reminders of their past death and disobedience and religious deprivation in contrast to their present life and salvation and participation in the one new humanity and the new temple (2:1–22). They also need reminding of Paul's unique ministry to the Gentiles and of the debt they owe to this (3:1–13). Although the writer is thankful for the faith the readers exercise as those in Christ and for the loving concern they demonstrate for all believers (1:15), at the same time through his prayer-reports they are seen as in need of further insight, further knowledge of the hope to which their salvation leads, of the wealth of glory involved in God's dealings with his people, and in particular of the great power available on their behalf (1:17–19). What is more, they need to be energized by the presence of the Spirit and of Christ within them, they need to know more of the all-embracing love of Christ, and they need to have a more complete experience of the fullness of the life and power of God (3:14–19).

The extended paraenesis of the second part of the letter indicates that, although the implied readers have already received ethical instruction (4:20–24), they need to be reminded of some major implications of the righteousness, holiness, and truth involved in living out the life of the new humanity. Because they are in danger of accommodating to the values of the surrounding world (cf. also Lona, *Eschatologie*, 435), they need to give special attention to such areas as dealing with anger, cultivating edifying speech, forgiving and loving others, living lives of purity that will expose and transform the lives of sexual impurity around them, worshiping, and giving thanks. They need to demonstrate distinctively Christian attitudes and behavior in their household arrangements. Both the beginning and the end of the paraenesis are particularly significant for our picture of the implied readers. These readers are to devote their energies to maintaining the Church's unity and living in harmony. They are to play their part in helping the whole Church to attain to maturity in the face of false teaching and are to recognize the special role of pastors and teachers in that process (cf. 4:1–16). In the face of the opposition of cosmic powers the implied readers are those who will see themselves as Christian soldiers and will avail themselves of the resources of Christ's strength and God's full armor. They need determined resolve to stand firm, and they will demonstrate such resolve by living lives of truthfulness, righteousness, peace, and faith, by appropriating salvation and proclaiming the gospel, and by maintaining a constant state of prayerfulness and alertness (cf. 6:10–20).

If "rhetoric is that quality in discourse by which a speaker or writer seeks to accomplish his purposes," and if "the ultimate goal of rhetorical analysis, briefly put, is the discovery of the author's intent and how that is transmitted through a text to an audience" (Kennedy, *New Testament Interpretation through Rhetorical Criticism*, 3, 12), then the above sketch of the elements in the rhetorical situation has already uncovered, by implication, some of this writer's purposes. Before we gather these together, it is worth pausing in order to say a little more about those passages in which the writer of Ephesians makes his purposes explicit by expressing directly his concerns for his readers. Not surprisingly, these occur primarily in the intercessory prayer-reports of the thanksgiving period, the place in the Pauline letter in which the main thrust of the writer's concerns is most frequently anticipated.

Since the first half of the letter can be seen as an extended thanksgiving, there are two prayer-reports in Ephesians, one near the beginning in 1:16b–19 and one near the end in 3:14–19, in which the writer airs his concerns for his readers more directly. In 1:16b–19 he tells them that he prays for their growth in knowledge, that they will be given through the Spirit wisdom and revelation to enable them to understand God and his purposes for their lives. Inner enlightenment should lead to their greater awareness of three matters in particular: the hope of the consummation of salvation, which they have as the result of God's calling, the glorious benefits which are theirs because of God's possession of his people, and the great power of God, his redemptive energy displayed in the resurrection and exaltation of Christ, which is available to them. In 3:14–19, the prayer for the readers' growth involves their inner strengthening through the Spirit and through Christ's indwelling, their being rooted and grounded in love, their knowing something of the all-embracing love of Christ, and their experiencing to the fullest extent the life and power of God. Again, no specific concern nor actual set of problems emerges from these prayer-reports. Instead, the writer sees his readers' needs in general terms. They need an improvement in the quality of their lives before God. They need growth in their relationship to God in Christ through the Spirit. The need for further knowledge and the need for a greater experience of divine power or strength are common to both prayer-reports. That these needs have to do first of all with the readers' inner orientation and motivation is clear from the emphasis on the heart in both passages and on the inner person in the second. The writer therefore perceives his readers to be lacking in appreciation for or awareness of the significance of central aspects of the gospel, which relate to their identity and security, and to be beset by a sense of powerlessness and a lack of resolve. In addition, the prayer of the second report suggests that instability and a sense of insufficiency are among these perceived needs. Two important parts of the second half of the letter—the pericopes which frame the paraenesis—reinforce that these are the kinds of needs the writer is intending to meet. 4:1–16, which makes clear that the writer's call will be for more distinctively Christian living as well as greater knowledge, immediately focuses on the need for unity and talks about replacing immaturity and instability by corporate growth in love toward Christ, which is at the same time growth toward unity of faith and knowledge, toward maturity and completeness. The final appeal of 6:10–20 to be strong, to stand firm against evil powers, and to put on the divine armor underlines once more that the author wishes to address what he considers to be weakness, vacillation, lack of resolve, and insufficient appropriation of the resources for living given by God.

A brief summary of what has been discovered about the rhetorical situation would include the following factors. Someone writes in the name of Paul, who is to be seen as part of the Church's foundation. He has special insights into God's purposes for the cosmos and the place of the one Church out of Jews and Gentiles in those purposes. He attempts both to reinforce the common values which establish his readers' identity as Gentile Christians who belong

Introduction

to the Church and to persuade them to change their behavior to that which is more appropriate to such an identity. He makes this attempt because he perceives the readers to be lacking in strength, resolve, stability, and maturity, and to need greater knowledge, inner renewal, corporate growth in love, and more distinctively Christian behavior in a variety of areas of their lives.

Such a summary may appear not to amount to very much, hardly to have been worth the effort, or not to have advanced the discussion. Of course, one major factor about the setting has been resolved. It is not in the lifetime of Paul. It has already been argued that, although the implied author is Paul, the actual author is a later Jewish Christian follower of Paul who employs the device of pseudonymity in order to pass on the Pauline tradition in a situation after the apostle's death. Therefore, the actual readers are likely to be Gentile Christian members of churches of the Pauline mission, who, in the generation after his death, need to be reminded of the debt they owe to Paul as the prominent preacher to the Gentiles among the holy apostles and prophets (cf. 3:1–13). In fact, our summary takes us still further. It points us in a significantly different direction from a number of recent scholarly proposals about the letter's occasion and purposes, which are either purely general, treating the letter as a theological treatise, or quite specific, suggesting very particular problems which gave rise to the letter.

Among the former is the designation of the letter by Schlier (21–22) as a wisdom speech. This designation is endorsed by Bruce (*Epistles*, 246), who also sees it as "the quintessence of Paulinism" (*Epistles*, 229). Conzelmann (86) holds Ephesians to be a theoretical theological essay, and Lindemann (*Paulus im ältesten Christentum*, 41) considers it to be a sort of dogmatics in draft form, which sets out the ontology of a timeless church withdrawn from the problems of its own day (*Aufhebung*, 7, 248). But these proposals do not explain the letter's selection of topics, nor its mode of presenting them, nor the impact they were meant to have on the readers.

Only slightly more specific are the hypotheses which treat the letter as a homily for a baptismal occasion (cf., e.g., Dahl, *TZ* 7 [1951] 263–64; Coutts, *NTS* 3 [1956–57] 125–27) or as a reminder to "young Gentile Christians of the implications of their faith and baptism" (Dahl, *HTR* 79 [1986] 38). The same objections apply. In addition, the single mention of the term "baptism" (4:5) in a context devoted not to baptism but to unity, and a few metaphors, behind which a baptismal reference may lie, make it unlikely that baptism itself was a major concern in the writing of the letter (cf. also Arnold, *Ephesians*, 135–36). Kirby (*Ephesians*, 144–61), who does become more specific by claiming that the letter was intended for renewing baptismal vows probably on the Feast of Pentecost, can only do so by moving into further unfounded speculation.

Our own discussion of the purposes which emerge from the letter also suggests the inappropriateness of other more specific proposals. The well-known hypothesis of Goodspeed (*Meaning*, 1–75, followed with some qualifications by Mitton, *Epistle*, 45–51) is that Ephesians was intended as an introduction to a newly formed collection of Paul's letters, which had been provoked by a reading of Acts. But, as is often pointed out, the letter does not read like such an introduction, the priority of Acts to Ephesians and its influence on the author are problematic, and there is no evidence that Ephesians ever stood at the head of a Pauline canon. There are no signs from the letter itself that a main purpose was to combat opponents (*pace*, e.g., Pokorný, *Der Epheserbrief und die Gnosis*, 21, who sees the opposition as Judaistic Gnosticism, and Smith, *Ohio Journal of Religious Studies* 5 [1977] 78–103, who believes the opponents to be former pagans who had adopted speculative Judaism before they became Christians and who are arrogant about more mainstream Judaism). Chadwick (*ZNW* 51 [1960] 145–53) suggested that the letter was written to demonstrate the antiquity of the Christian message in the face of embarrassment on the part of its readers over the seeming late arrival of the Church on the scene. Hence, the writer shows the Church's continuity with ancient Judaism, its universality, and its links with heaven so that it can be seen as a metaphysical entity encompassing all generations. This proposal highlights some elements that are there in the letter but misinterprets the needs of the readers that they are designed to meet. If the letter does not read like a polemic, it also does not read like this sort of extended apologetic, and its concern with the past is not with antiquity per se but with God's dealings with Israel, which is treated in such a way as to enable the readers to appreciate their present privileges in contrast to their past deprivation. Others, in order to explain the occasion of the letter, latch on to a supposed crisis in which unity between Jewish Christians and Gentile Christians is threatened. Käsemann ("Ephesians and Acts," 291; cf. also Fischer, *Tendenz und Absicht*, 79–94) claims, "The letter betrays its historical setting precisely here. What Paul mentioned hypothetically in Romans 11:17ff. has happened here: Jewish Christianity is pushed aside and despised by the steadily growing Gentile Christianity." But this is to misinterpret the letter's treatment of the themes of unity and the Church's relationship to Israel and to misconstrue the force of its rhetoric (see *Commentary* on 2:11–22). Fischer (*Tendenz und Absicht*, 21–39), in his reconstruction of the letter's occasion, adds to a crisis in regard to unity between Jewish and Gentile Christians a crisis in ecclesiastical development. He argues that the letter was written at a time when the new order of episcopacy was being promoted in Gentile Christian congregations in Asia Minor. The writer attempts to combat this innovation by supporting the more charismatic structure that prevailed in the period of the Pauline mission and by stressing apostles and prophets as foundational. But this reconstruction involves a highly speculative argument from the letter's silence about bishops, presbyters, or deacons.

Moving in a rather different direction from his assessment described above, Lindemann (*ZNW* 67 [1976] 242–43) has also proposed that a different sort of crisis gave rise to the writing of Ephesians—a situation of persecution in the reign of Domitian, for which the readers needed comfort and strengthening. He believes the battle imagery in 6:10–20 points in this direction. But this reference is a slender basis on which to build such a view. Although it could be claimed that Ephesians and Revelation respond to such a perceived threat to Christians in Asia Minor in quite different ways, one would surely expect to find more evidence in Ephesians that the writer had this threat in mind. Besides, the imagery of "the evil day" and "the burning arrows of the evil one" requires no such external persecution for it to make sense in the context of believers' spiritual battle against hostile cosmic powers (cf. also

Schnackenburg, 30). One further example of a more specific proposal about the letter's setting is that of Arnold (*Ephesians: Power and Magic*, esp. 123–24). He holds that the emphasis on the cosmic powers and the theme of power in the letter suggests that it was written to those who had come from a background in magical practices and involvement in the cult of the Ephesian Artemis, who were oppressed by the demonic realm, and who were tempted to combine their Christian faith with magical practices. Again, this suggestion does not take sufficient account of the variety of the readers' needs that has emerged from our analysis. It isolates one particular theme, making the cosmic powers too much the foreground rather than the background of the writer's concerns, it moves too far beyond the evidence of the letter itself, and in the end, despite Arnold's disclaimers, it links the setting too closely to Ephesus itself.

The general aspects of the purposes of the letter which emerged from the analysis of its rhetorical situation indicate why Ephesians so easily transcends its original setting and has had such a broad and universal appeal. There will always be Christians in a variety of settings of whom it could be said that they were in need of inner strength, further knowledge of their salvation, greater appreciation of their identity as believers and as members of the Church, increased concern for the Church's unity, and more consistent living in such areas as speech, sexuality, and household relationships. These general purposes do not mean, of course, that the letter was not addressed to a particular group of recipients, but they make all the clearer the hazardous nature of attempts to propose specific settings for the letter and the caution that should be exercised in any discussion of an actual setting.

But what then can be said about the actual setting and recipients of the letter? The geographical location of such recipients cannot be identified with any great certainty. It is usually assumed that they were situated in Asia Minor or, more particularly, western Asia Minor. But what is the evidence to support this assumption? It is true that there were churches founded on Paul's Gentile mission in this area and therefore a continuing influence of the Pauline mission could be expected here, but the apostle also founded churches and had a continuing influence elsewhere in the Roman Empire. The later association of the letter with Ephesus is of little help. Hypotheses about the letter being linked with Ephesus because it was originally written from this city, or because a copy of it was left there, or because on the basis of similarities with Ignatius' letter to the Ephesians it was believed this letter was also to the Ephesians, are unconvincing (cf. the extended discussion by Best, *ANRW* 2.25.4 [1987] 3247–79). If, as Best considers most likely, the designation "Ephesians" was not given to the letter until a collection of a reasonably large number of Pauline letters had come into being, then this consideration makes the association with Ephesus late. Best also suggests that at this late date, when memory of Paul's long stay in Ephesus had faded and there was not wide knowledge of Acts, a text of the letter which had no geographical location was assigned this one. This designation was given after deducing from the other letters a place in which Paul had worked and which ought to have been the recipient of such a letter. 1 Cor 15:32; 16:8 would have made Ephesus a strong candidate (cf. Best, *ANRW* 2.25.4 [1987] 3278–79). But this whole suggestion means that the later ascription is likely to have very little actual connection with the original recipients.

The commentary on 1:1 will suggest the possibility that the letter was originally addressed to the churches of Hierapolis and Laodicea in the Lycus Valley. The choice of these two names is supported somewhat by Marcion's familiarity with the tradition of a connection between this letter and Laodicea, but more by Ephesians' use of Colossians, in which Hierapolis and Laodicea are the churches linked with Colossae because all three are served by Epaphras (cf. Col 4:13). In theory, simply because the writer has employed the thoughts and wording of Colossians as his starting point, this need not mean that his own letter is addressed to recipients in the same vicinity as Colossians. In this case, however, the fact that the writer of Ephesians chooses to keep the extended recommendation of Tychicus found at the end of Colossians may well suggest that this is not only part of his device of pseudonymity, but that Tychicus would have been known to the recipients as one of the leading representatives of the Pauline mission. Elsewhere he is associated with Asia Minor (cf. Col 4:7, 8; Acts 20:4; 2 Tim 4:12), and so it could well be that the recipients are expected to know him because they are in Asia Minor.

One further possible corroborating strand of evidence taken from the letter's use of Colossians is worth mentioning. In Colossians the writer's combat with the syncretistic philosophy is very much to the fore. He employs some of its terminology, addresses its concern with cosmic powers and the heavenly realm, and attempts to deal with the sense of inadequacy these had engendered among some of the Colossian Christians. Ephesians retains similar language and concepts, but uses them as the backdrop against which it develops its own distinctive interests. This may suggest that some of the local concerns which provoked the letter to the Colossians are assumed to be still around in the recipients' setting, although no longer seen as part of a pressing problem to be addressed directly. If the writer of Ephesians has one eye on the sort of cosmological concerns which are reflected in Colossians (and there is a general warning against false teaching in 4:14), they may have been characteristic of this area as a whole. If any of the readers are being made to feel inferior and are tempted to seek enhanced knowledge through the means offered by mystery cults, it is made clear where true knowledge of the mystery and genuine access to the heavenly realm are available. In any case, Colossians acted as the catalyst for Ephesians' own development of the cosmic implications of salvation and for its own treatment of the heavenly dimension as a major focus of its realized eschatology. But both this distinctive treatment of cosmic issues and the closely related area of the history-of-religions background to the letter are perhaps even more directly related to the influences on the writer's thought than they are to the setting of the recipients. The history-of-religions background for Ephesians will not be dealt with separately in the *Introduction*. Instead interaction and parallels with other strands of thought are handled in the commentary in those places where they are relevant to the discussion of particular texts. (For an excellent overview of how the recent history of interpretation has sought the key to the letter in either an OT or Essene or Hellenistic Jewish or Gnostic background, see H. Merkel, "Der Epheserbrief in der neueren Dis-

Introduction

kussion," *ANRW* 2.25.4 [1987] esp. 3176–212, and for a good brief exposition of why Hellenistic Judaism provides most illumination for some of the main concepts in the letter, see Gnilka, 33–45.)

The strands of evidence, some of them slender, that link Ephesians to western Asia Minor have now been seen, and given the lack of further data in the letter, this does seem the most plausible geographical setting. There is a growing bibliography of works about Asia Minor and about early Christianity in that area, some of which follows, but how useful it is in illuminating a document which has so little specificity must be a matter of some debate.

Arnold, C. E. *Ephesians: Power and Magic.* Cambridge: CUP, 1989, 5–40. **Bauer, W.** *Orthodoxy and Heresy in Earliest Christianity.* Trans. and ed. R. A. Kraft and G. Krodel. Philadelphia: Fortress, 1971, 61–94. **Bean, G. E.** *Aegean Turkey.* New York: Praeger, 1966. ———. *Turkey beyond the Maeander.* London: Ernest Benn, 1971. ———. *Turkey's Southern Shore.* New York: Praeger, 1968. **Dickey, S.** "Some Economic and Social Conditions of Asia Minor Affecting the Expansion of Christianity." In *Studies in Early Christianity,* ed. S. J. Case. New York: Century, 1928, 393–416. **Elliger, W.** *Ephesos: Geschichte einer antiken Weltstadt.* Stuttgart: Kohlhammer, 1985. **Elliott, J. H.** *A Home for the Homeless.* Philadelphia: Fortress, 1981, 59–100. **Hemer, C. J.** *The Letters to the Seven Churches of Asia in their Local Setting.* Sheffield: JSOT, 1986. **Johnson, S. E.** "Asia Minor and Early Christianity." In *Christianity, Judaism, and Other Greco-Roman Cults.* Part 2. Ed. J. Neusner. Leiden: Brill, 1975, 77–145. ———. "Early Christianity in Asia Minor." *JBL* 77 (1958) 1–19. ———. "Unsolved Questions about Early Christianity in Anatolia." In *Studies in New Testament and Early Christian Literature,* ed. D. E. Aune. Leiden: Brill, 1972, 181–93. **Jones, A. H. M.** *The Cities of the Eastern Roman Provinces.* 2nd ed. Oxford: Clarendon, 1971, 28–94. **Koester, H.** *Introduction to the New Testament.* Vol. 2. Philadelphia: Fortress, 1982, 241–347. ———. "The Origin and Nature of Diversification in the History of Early Christianity." *HTR* 58 (1965) 279–318. **Lindemann, A.** *Paulus im ältesten Christentum.* Tübingen: Mohr, 1979. **Magie, D.** *Roman Rule in Asia Minor to the End of the Third Century after Christ.* 2 vols. Reprint. New York: Arno, 1975. **Meeks, W. A.** *The First Urban Christians.* New Haven: Yale University Press, 1983, 42–45. **Meinardus, O. F. A.** *St. John of Patmos and the Seven Churches of the Apocalypse.* Athens: Lycabettus, 1974. **Miltner, F.** *Ephesos: Stadt der Artemis und des Johannes.* Vienna: Franz Deuticke, 1958. **Norris, F. W.** "Asia Minor before Ignatius: Walter Bauer Reconsidered." *SE* 7. Berlin: Akademie-Verlag, 1982, 365–77. **Oster, R. E.** *A Bibliography of Ancient Ephesus.* Metuchen, NJ: ATLA and Scarecrow, 1987. **Ramsay, W. M.** *The Cities and Bishoprics of Phrygia.* 2 vols. Oxford: Clarendon, 1895, 1897. ———. *The Historical Geography of Asia Minor.* Reprint. Amsterdam: A. M. Hakkert, 1962. ———. *The Social Basis of Roman Power in Asia Minor.* Reprint. Amsterdam: A. M. Hakkert, 1967. **Robinson, T. A.** *The Bauer Thesis Examined: The Geography of Heresy in the Early Christian Church.* New York: Edwin Mellen Press, 1988, 93–205. **Yamauchi, E.** *New Testament Cities in Western Asia Minor.* Grand Rapids: Baker, 1980.

These writings indicate that there is little agreement about the development of early Christianity in western Asia Minor toward the end of the first century C.E. and also that more work will have to be done on how the picture of the recipients which emerges from Ephesians fits into the overall history of the early Christian movement in Asia Minor. What were the fortunes of Pauline Christianity in Asia Minor after the death of the apostle? Bauer's view that Pauline Christianity never gained much influence in Asia Minor is increasingly questioned, and so the proposal that Ephesians was "a last ditch stand by a well-known representative of Paul in his final attempt to regain Asia for the Pauline gospel by publishing an assemblage of Pauline teaching" (R. P. Martin, *New Testament Foundations,* 2:233) has to be seen as equally open to question. How do the Fourth Gospel, Revelation, 1 Peter, the Pastorals, Cerinthus, Papias, and Ignatius contribute to our knowledge of the competing and coalescing strands of early Christianity in Asia Minor? Only two minor points connected with this larger question can be noted here. First, if Laodicea was one of the churches meant to receive Ephesians, then the diagnosis of its spiritual state in this letter is somewhat different from that provided by the seer in Rev 3, who indicts it for its ostentatious self-sufficiency yet ineffectiveness and spiritual blindness (cf. Hemer, *Letters,* 178–209). Second, the similarities between Ephesians and 1 Peter may be of such a nature as to suggest a literary relationship between these documents and a relationship in which 1 Peter is dependent on Ephesians (cf. esp. Mitton, *Epistle,* 176–97; but cf. also Lindemann, *Paulus,* 252–61, who disputes literary dependence).

A further question that arises is why the writer apparently only addresses Gentile Christians. Were there only Gentile Christians in the churches addressed? Or could it be that the writer is not addressing whole churches in a particular locality but only Gentile Christian members of them or perhaps Gentile Christian house churches? What was the relationship of the recipients to Jewish Christians? Again, the letter itself gives the contemporary reader no help in answering such questions. One can only agree with Dahl's assessment (*HTR* 79 [1986] 36–37) that "if there were Christians of Jewish origins among the addressees, the author takes no account of them" and that "the author of Ephesians had a keen interest in the Jewish roots and origin of the church but failed to show any concern for the relationship of his audience to contemporary Jews in or outside the church."

Some scholars move away from direct deductions from the text of Ephesians and forgo hypotheses about a specific setting in order to sketch the spiritual and intellectual milieu of Asia Minor as part of the general crisis affecting the Hellenistic world. There is some justification for such a move, and these scholars can provide a general background that correlates indirectly with a number of the emphases of the letter and the needs of the readers that have emerged from our analysis (cf. esp. Gnilka, 47–49; Lona, *Eschatologie,* 435–41; cf. also Lincoln, *Paradise,* 116–18, 138–39; Arnold, *Ephesians,* 146–47). Despite the external political and economic unity brought about by the consolidation of Roman power, individuals felt little sense of social integration or of belonging. Instead, in a cosmopolitan environment, old traditions and allegiances, including religious ones, were seen as inadequate, and many people felt uprooted and alienated. The cosmos, once seen as ordered, was now perceived to be hostile and to be inhabited by demonic powers opposed to human well-being. In such a setting religious syncretism gained ground. It was informed by monotheistic convictions—there was one God in heaven, just as there was one emperor on earth—but this universal God was viewed as removed from interest in and contact with this world. Accordingly, the way of salvation was seen in terms of the individual's attempt to escape from this world and to ascend to the upper realms of the cosmos. Mystery religions and magical rites offered this sort of salvation through deliverance from the world and protection from demonic powers, while fostering speculation about the cosmos. Such concerns shed light on the syncretistic teaching which is combated in Colossians. It could well be also that this general religious milieu contributed to the confusion about their identity and the disorientation that appears to characterize the readers of Ephesians. It would also help to explain the way in which the writer of Ephesians transforms cosmic concerns by emphasizing the salvation God has provided in history through Christ, the corporate nature of Christian existence, and the responsibility of the Church in the world.

But in the end, the letter's temporal setting within the development of early Christianity may well be more important than its geographical location or the crisis in the Hellenistic religious world for attempting to identify the sort of recipients who might have had the needs to which the letter attests. If the writer was a disciple of Paul writing in his name after the apostle's death, then of course the recipients are also situated in this post-apostolic period. One should not, however, simply speak in passing of the apostle's death, for this would have been an extremely significant factor in the situation of the letter's recipients (cf. also Meade, *Pseudonymity*, 148, who goes so far as to claim that "all of the problems of Ephesians stem from one fundamental problem: the loss of Paul as a unifying source of authority"). Not only does it explain the fact that they need to be reminded of their debt to the apostle (cf. 3:1–13), but it would also account for the lack of a sense of cohesion and communal identity that might well be felt by Pauline churches once the presence of the apostle and his coordination of the activities of his team of coworkers had disappeared from the scene. There was not the same sense of what it meant to be part of a unified Church, part of an entity that was more than a local group. Hence, the call for maintenance of unity and the emphasis on the recipients' being part of the universal Church. Hence also, the need for the Pauline tradition to be continued and the prominence given to teachers in passing it on.

For second-generation Pauline Christians, other major elements that gave shape and meaning to the earlier generation's perspectives had also been displaced. Jerusalem had fallen and yet the expected end of history had not come. Nor had the salvation of all Israel, hoped for by the Paul of Romans, materialized. Hopes of an imminent parousia were fading and among Pauline Christians reassessment of Gentile Christians' relationship to Israel needed to be made. For some Gentile Christians not only was there a deficient sense of all that they already had in the salvation they had experienced, but there was also a decreasing awareness of that Church's origins and its place in the history of God's purposes that included his dealings with Israel. Pauline churches were now also having to adjust to the prospect of a more extended co-existence with their surrounding society.

It would not be surprising if these factors led to a loss of a clear sense of their identity on the part of these Gentile Christians in Pauline mission churches and if, along with this, there was an insufficient concern about distinctively Christian behavior. Laxity in ethical matters could have resulted both from natural tendencies for Gentile Christians to draw wrong conclusions from Paul's law-free gospel and also, in the process of accommodation to the surrounding society, from the pressures simply to adopt its ethical values. Hence the large amount of the letter given over to paraenesis.

It was into this sort of setting, then, that the message of Ephesians was directed. As we have seen, broadly speaking, the letter was intended to reinforce its readers' identity as participants in the Church and to underline their distinctive role and conduct in the world. In reminding the readers of their identity and roots, the writer tells them that they are part of a universal Church, one new humanity out of Jew and Gentile. They owe this status, in large part, to Paul and his insight into the gospel. But the movement of which they are a part is not just another new cult. It is linked with God's previous working within Israel and is a decisive stage in the completion of his purposes in Christ. Indeed, ultimately it is rooted in his electing purposes from before the foundation of the world. The Church of which the readers are members is not just one among a number of competing movements. Through their relationship with Christ they are in touch with the God who is the Creator of the whole cosmos and whose plan of salvation includes that cosmos and its harmony in Christ. In fact, the salvation they have already experienced is an essential part of the outworking of that plan, and what has been accomplished in the Church's unity is an anticipation and pledge of final cosmic unity.

The readers are to be proud of such an identity and such a calling and are to live them out. They are to have an awareness of God's global or cosmic purposes, but are then to act locally in a way that is appropriate to this unique community's role in the world. They should not, therefore, simply accommodate themselves to surrounding values. Instead, the writer sets out some of the ethical distinguishing marks of the new humanity God has created in Christ and indicates that, as his readers embody these, they will discover that their life in their community illuminates some of the surrounding darkness.

But the writer's efforts to persuade his readers to realize their true identity and behave accordingly are not carried out purely on an intellectual level and only by didactic means. He is wise enough to know that it cannot simply be assumed that if people have a right understanding they will do what is right. The rhetoric of the letter shows that he knows that it is not enough to hold before his readers the vision of their vocation, of the kind of people they are called to be. He also appeals to the deep springs of their experience, their emotions, the common values they celebrate in their worship. He constantly communicates his vision of their identity through the language and forms of worship and prayer. He also helps them to define more clearly who they are by inviting them to remember what God has done for them in Christ. In this way also, they are reminded that they are part of a worshiping community with a distinctive tradition and a distinctive corporate life. The writer is concerned to motivate his readers, and he knows that a deeper sense of their corporate Christian identity and a greater desire to please God in wise and holy living will flow out of the sort of remembering of God's activities on their behalf that is accompanied by thanksgiving. At the same time, he assures them that in living out their calling they are not on their own. The power which God has displayed in acting in Christ and in changing the readers' status he has also made available to them to enable them to be the sort of people he wants them to be.

In attempting to motivate his readers, the writer is concerned both about their apparent disorientation on account of an insufficient sense of hope and a loss of clear goals and purpose, and about their accompanying flagging resolve. He stresses the importance of hope, spells out what this hope involves for the whole cosmos, and gives the readers some sense of destiny by indicating the Church's relationship to God's purposes. In addition, he sets before them the goal of growth toward maturity and toward the appropriation of the unity God has given, a growth in understanding, mutual edification, and love. He knows that the readers' future goals will not be achieved by neglecting the past but by recalling their individual and corporate narratives and building on tradition. He claims that Christ has provided all that is necessary for reaching the goals through ministers of the word who will pass on and apply the Pauline tradition. That tradition is not just doctrinal but also ethical—"learning Christ," being "taught in him, as the truth is in Jesus." The way into the future is by appropriating, building on, creatively adapting past tradition. What the writer advocates for others, he practices himself. Not surprisingly, Ephesians is full of Pauline traditions, especially Colossians, but also reminiscences of other letters and liturgical, doctrinal, and paraenetical traditions, which the writer now employs for his own purposes. Again, his rhetorical strategy makes this more effective. Instead of simply saying that he is passing on Pauline traditions, he makes it more personal, direct, and forceful by adopting the device of Paul himself appealing to the churches.

In particular his concluding appeal reinforces his purpose in the letter as a whole. In the face of flagging enthusiasm, lack of spiritual energy, and deficient sense of purpose, he calls on the readers to be strong and to stand firm. He gives them a new image by which to think of themselves—Christian soldiers engaged in a battle. The pieces of armor which they are to put on or use—truth, righteousness, peace, faith, salvation, and the word of God—involve conscious appropriation of key elements of their identity. He reminds them that living out the vision of the calling he has set before them will not just take place automatically. It will meet with resistance, the chief source of which is the cosmic powers of evil that can still affect negatively the way in which they demonstrate their calling. His forceful rhetoric makes clear to the readers that they are in a battle, but his positive reinforcement of their self-image is maintained—they are on the winning side. What they need to do is to appropriate the resources that have been made available—God's armor, Christ's power, the Spirit—and prayer is emphasized as the crucial means of tapping such resources. As the readers stand firm, both by maintaining their identity and by living it out, the result will be that the Pauline gospel will continue to be proclaimed and to triumph despite adversity.

5. THE THOUGHT OF EPHESIANS

Bibliography

Adai, J. *Der Heilige Geist als Gegenwart Gottes in den einzelnen Christen, in der Kirche und in der Welt.* Frankfurt: Peter Lang, 1985. **Arnold, C. E.** *Ephesians: Power and Magic.* Cambridge: CUP, 1989, 123–60. **Barth, M.** "Conversion and Conversation: Israel and the Church in Paul's Epistle to the Ephesians." *Int* 17 (1963) 3–24. **Benoit, P.** "Body, Head, and *Pleroma* in the Epistles of the Captivity." In *Jesus and the Gospel*, Vol. 2. Tr. B. Weatherhead. London: Darton, Longman and Todd, 1974, 51–92. **Bouttier, M.** "L'horizon catholique de l'épître aux Éphésiens." In *L'Évangile, hier et aujourd'hui*. FS F. J. Leenhardt. Geneva: Labor et Fides, 1968, 25–37. **Brown, R. E.** *The Churches the Apostles Left Behind*. New York: Paulist Press, 1984, 47–60. **Corley, B.** "The Theology of Ephesians." *SWJT* 22 (1979) 24–38. **Dahl, N. A.** "Interpreting Ephesians: Then and Now." *CurTM* 5 (1978) 133–43. **Dautzenberg, G.** "Theologie und Seelsorge aus paulinischer Tradition: Einführung in 2 Thess, Kol, Eph." In *Gestalt und Anspruch des Neuen Testaments*, ed. J. Schreiner. Würzburg: Echter, 1969, 96–119. **Fendt, L.** "Die Kirche des Epheserbriefs." *TLZ* 77 (1952) 147–50. **Gnilka, J.** "Das Kirchenmodell des Epheserbriefes." *BZ* 15 (1971) 161–84. **Halter, H.** *Taufe und Ethos: Paulinische Kriterien für das Proprium christlicher Moral*. Freiburg: Herder, 1977. **Hanson, S.** *The Unity of the Church in the New Testament: Colossians and Ephesians*. Uppsala: Almquist & Wiksells, 1946. **Houlden, J. L.** "Christ and Church in Ephesians." *SE* 6 (1973) 267–73. **Käsemann, E.** "Ephesians and Acts." In *Studies in Luke-Acts*, ed. L. E. Keck and J. L. Martyn. London: S.P.C.K., 1968, 288–97. **Knoch, O.** "Die Botschaft des Epheserbriefes." In *"Durch die Gnade Gottes bin ich, was ich bin."* Ostfildern: Schwabenverlag, 1984, 74–89. **Lincoln, A. T.** *Paradise Now and Not Yet*. Cambridge: CUP, 1981. ———. "The Use of the OT in Ephesians." *JSNT* 14 (1982) 16–57. **Lindemann, A.** *Die Aufhebung der Zeit: Geschichtsverständnis und Eschatologie im Epheserbrief*. Gütersloh: Gerd Mohn, 1975. **Lona, H. E.** *Die Eschatologie im Kolosser- und Epheserbrief*. Würzburg: Echter Verlag, 1984. **MacDonald, M. Y.** *The Pauline Churches*. Cambridge: CUP, 1988, 85–158. **Martin, R. P.** *Reconciliation: A Study of Paul's Theology*. London: Marshall, 1981. **Meeks, W. A.** "In One Body: The Unity of Humankind in Colossians and Ephesians." In *God's Christ and His People*, ed. J. Jervell and W. A. Meeks. Oslo: Universitetsforlaget, 1977, 209–21. **Merkel, H.** "Der Epheserbrief in der neueren exegetischen Diskussion." *ANRW* 2.25.4 (1987) 3156–246. **Merklein, H.** *Das kirchliche Amt nach dem Epheserbrief*. Munich: Kösel, 1973. ———. "Paulinische Theologie in der Rezeption des Kolosser- und Epheserbriefes." In *Paulus in den neutestamentlichen Spätschriften*, ed. K. Kertelge. Freiburg: Herder, 1981, 25–69. **Meyer, R. P.** *Kirche und Mission im Epheserbrief*. Stuttgart: Katholisches Bibelwerk, 1977. **Mussner, F.** *Christus, das All und die Kirche*. 2nd ed. Trier: Paulinus, 1968. ———. "Die Geschichtstheologie des Epheserbriefes." *BibLeb* 5 (1964) 8–12. **Odeberg, H.** *The View of the Universe in the Epistle to the Ephesians*. Lund: Lund Universitets Arsskrift, 1934. **Percy, E.** *Die Probleme der Kolosser- und Epheserbriefe*. Lund: Gleerup, 1946. **Perels, O.** "Kirche und Welt nach dem Epheser- und Kolosserbrief." *TLZ* 76 (1951) 391–400. **Ridderbos, H.** *Paul: An Outline of His Theology*. Tr. J. R. de Witt. Grand Rapids: Eerdmans, 1975. **Roels, E.** *God's Mission: The Epistle to the Ephesians in Mission Perspective*. Franeker: Wever, 1962. **Schlier, H.** *Christus und die Kirche im Epheserbrief*. Tübingen: Mohr, 1930. **Schmid, J.** *Der Epheserbrief des Apostels Paulus*. Freiburg: Herder, 1928. **Schnackenburg, R.** "Der Epheserbrief im heutigen Horizont." In *Massstab des Glaubens*. Freiburg: Herder, 1978, 155–75. ———. "Er hat uns mitauferweckt: Zur Tauflehre des Epheserbriefes." *LJ* 2 (1952) 159–83. ———. "Gestalt und Wesen der Kirche nach dem Epheserbrief." In *Schriften zum Neuen Testament*. Munich: Kösel, 1971, 268–87. **Steinmetz, F.-J.** *Protologische Heilszuversicht: Die Strukturen des soteriologischen und christologischen Denkens im Kolosser- und Epheserbrief*. Frankfurt: Josef Knecht, 1969. **Usami, K.** *Somatic Comprehension of Unity: The Church in Ephesus*. Rome: Biblical Institute Press, 1983. **Wild, R. A.** "'Be Imitators of God': Discipleship in the Letter to the Ephesians." In *Discipleship in the New Testament*, ed. F. Segovia. Philadelphia: Fortress, 1985, 127–43.

Any adequate discussion of the thought of Ephesians would draw out clearly the relation of the letter's symbols and concepts to its setting and purposes.

It would show the function of its symbolic universe in supporting the sense of identity and role the writer attempts to give his readers with their specific needs. It would analyze the way in which the theology and ethics of the letter are part of the writer's explanation to the readers of who they are as a social entity and the way in which they help to plot the readers' place in time and space, in history, society, and the cosmos. Such a discussion would also interact with the wealth of scholarly treatments both of the thought of the letter as a whole and of its major individual themes. It would also make some attempt to appropriate critically the theology of Ephesians for present-day concerns. The limits of this volume forbid such a full-scale treatment at this point in the *Introduction,* and the writer will attempt a fuller discussion in a future publication. It has been thought worthwhile, however, to provide a brief summary in sketch form of some of the main elements of the letter's thought and an even briefer concluding reflection on its overall impact.

(a) Eschatology

If Ephesians is to be seen as a reinterpretation of Paul for the particular needs of Gentile Christians in a later generation, it makes sense to begin this survey of its thought in the area that was so determinative for the apostle himself. With other interpreters, I hold that the coherent core of Paul's thought, which comes to different expression in a variety of settings, is his eschatology which centers in Christ, and that this is fundamental for the rest of his thinking, including his thinking about justification (cf., e.g., Ridderbos, E. P. Sanders, Beker, for various recent formulations of this approach to Paul). As is well known, one main strand in Paul's eschatological framework is the concept of the two ages found in some Jewish apocalypses. Paul modifies this in various ways because of what he believes to have happened in Christ. He sees the time between the resurrection and the parousia as the overlap of the ages in which there is a tension between present and future aspects of the blessing of the end-times. Ephesians shares this eschatological framework. In fact, it contains the only explicit reference in the Pauline corpus to both ages: "above every name that is named, not only in this age but also in that which is to come" (1:21). But as compared with the rest of the Pauline corpus, Ephesians has a much greater emphasis on the present or realized aspect of eschatology. This emphasis becomes clear from the beginning of the letter. In the opening lines of the opening eulogy God is blessed, because he "has blessed us with every spiritual blessing in the heavenly realms in Christ" (1:3). The benefits of the age to come are seen as having already become a present spiritual and heavenly reality for believers. This perspective is also expressed in striking fashion in the contrast that is made between the readers' previous situation, in which their conduct was "in accordance with this world-age" (2:2), and their present situation, in which God "raised us up with him and seated us with him in the heavenly realms in Christ Jesus" (2:6). The latter part of this statement, in particular, spells out boldly and explicitly what is only implicit in Col 3:1–3, on which it is dependent. Believers' union with Christ is such that they share in the triumph of his exaltation to heaven (cf. 1:20). Elsewhere in the NT, believers' rule with Christ is referred to only as a promise for the future (cf., e.g., Rev 3:21, "He who conquers, I will grant him to sit with me on my throne, as I myself conquered and sat down with my Father on his throne"), but here in Ephesians this rule has already been accomplished. Christ's exaltation involved his triumph and rule over hostile cosmic powers, as 1:20–22 made clear, and, because of their relationship with Christ, believers are now seen as part of the new dominion's superiority over the old, participating in its liberation from the powers.

The distinctive emphasis of Ephesians is on realized eschatology, but it does retain some future elements (cf. 1:14; 2:7; 4:30; 5:5; 6:8, 13). It is noticeable that these references to the future emerge more obviously in the second half of the letter, where the writer makes use of more traditional paraenetical material. In his attempt to assure his readers of what God has accomplished for them and to reinforce their identity as Christian believers, the writer does not lose all realism about Christian existence. He is under no illusion that sharing in Christ's victory brings removal from the sphere of conflict. Those who have been *seated* with Christ in the heavenly realms are at the same time those who must *walk* in the world (cf. 2:10; 4:1, 17; 5:2, 8, 15) and who must *stand* in the midst of the continuing battle with the powers (cf. 6:11–16).

(b) Christology

What is distinctive about Ephesians' view of Christ is in keeping with what is distinctive about its eschatology. Although there are a few brief references to Christ's death (cf. 1:7; 2:13, 16; 5:2, 25), the emphasis is on Christ's exaltation, as elements of the cosmic Christology of Colossians, which emerged in the encounter with syncretism and its cosmic concerns, are taken further.

This cosmic lordship of Christ is elaborated at the end of the thanksgiving section, which speaks of the working of God's "mighty strength which he accomplished in Christ when he raised him from the dead, and seated him at his right hand in the heavenly realms far above every principality and authority and power and dominion and every name that is named. . . . And he placed all things under his feet and gave him as head over all things to the Church, which is his body, the fullness of him [Christ] who fills all things in every way" (1:20–23). Christ's resurrection and exaltation mean that the center of gravity in God's cosmic drama of salvation has moved from the realm of earth to that of heaven and that a change in the power structures of this world has been brought about. Ps 110:1 and Ps 8:6, which Paul had used in 1 Cor 15:25–27 to speak of Christ's rule at the end of history, are adapted by the writer of Ephesians and applied to Christ's present status, as he is depicted as the last Adam who is already Lord with dominion over the cosmos. As head over the cosmos Christ fills it with his sovereign rule. This same note is struck later when Christ is said to have "ascended far above all the heavens in order that he might fill the cosmos" (4:10).

Since Christ is depicted as head over all things, it is not surprising that he is also described as head of the Church. He is both its beginning and its end, the source and the goal of its growth (cf. 4:15, 16; cf. also 5:23). He is the one who is the keystone of the temple structure, the top stone in whom the whole structure coheres (cf. 2:20). It can be seen that in Ephesians it is not so much that Christology is swallowed up by ecclesiology as that the ecclesiology is thoroughly Christological. What is said about the Church depends on what has been said about what God has done in Christ, but at the same time what is said about Christ is always related to believers and the Church.

The relationship between Christ's cosmic lordship and his lordship over the Church is an intriguing one. The two are not simply set in parallel, but the former is subordinated to the latter, as, in both Eph 1 and Eph 4, cosmic Christology is made to serve the needs of the readers. The portrayal of Christ's cosmic lordship in the thanksgiving section assures the readers that this world is not simply a continual chaotic battleground in which dominant hostile forces need to be placated. Instead, in Christ's resurrection and exaltation God has shown that the world is his creation over which he has put Christ in control so that life can be lived in trust in his power. What is more, the writer stresses that God has given Christ as head over the cosmos *to the Church* (1:22). All the rule and authority God has given to Christ is to be used on behalf of the Church since God has also given this exalted Christ to the Church. In the light of such an assertion the readers are to see themselves not as a numerically and sociologically insignificant group but as part of the universal Church which can only be truly understood in relation to its Lord in the heavenly realm who exercises all power on its behalf. Similarly, in Eph 4 the point of the application of Ps 68 to Christ's ascent to be cosmic Lord is that his triumphant exaltation results in his giving of gifts, the gifts of ministers of the word necessary to equip the Church for its task in the world. In other words, the writer's vision of the Church's calling is not to be thought of as a totally unrealizable ideal, because the cosmic Christ has given the Church the resources it needs to be able to demonstrate its unity, to proclaim the truth in love, and to attain to maturity.

The letter's cosmic Christology and its eschatology come together in the eulogy's description of the mystery which has been disclosed to believers. The readers are shown that the divine election which has grasped them also involves God's purpose for history: "to sum up all things in Christ, things in heaven, and things on earth in him" (1:10). This unifying of the cosmos and restoration of its harmony were achieved in principle when God exalted Christ to heaven as cosmic Lord, thereby ensuring the inseparable connection between heaven and earth that enables both heavenly things and earthly things to be summed up in him. This part of the opening blessing is meant to help the readers to see that to be in Christ is to be part of a program which is as broad as the universe, a movement which is rolling on toward a renewed cosmos where all is in harmony.

(c) Salvation

Already it has been seen that salvation in Ephesians is predominantly realized, has its center in Christ, and is cosmic in scope. These features and others are underlined in the reminder of the readers' salvation in the first half of Eph 2 (vv 1–10). There, salvation is presented as a rescue act accomplished on behalf of believers, which involves a movement from death to life, from conduct characterized by trespasses, sins, sensual indulgence, and disobedience to that characterized by good works, from this present world-age to the heavenly realms, from bondage to the forces which rule this world to victory with Christ over hostile powers, and from liability to God's wrath to experience of his mercy, love, and kindness. All of this is "by grace . . . not from yourselves," "through faith . . . not by works" (2:8, 9). Paul had used this language of grace, faith, and works in association with justification terminology (cf. esp. Rom 3:24–28). It appears that the writer of Ephesians deems the use of righteousness terminology in its distinctive Pauline sense no longer appropriate for Gentile Christians, for whom polemics with Jewish Christians about admission to the community was a matter of the past. So he has taken the essentials of the justification discussion, set them in this context of a realized eschatology through participation in Christ, and subsumed them under the inclusive category of salvation to give them a more general reference. In this process of reinterpretation the perfect passive participle σεσῳσμένοι, "have been saved," is employed (2:5, 8). So in Ephesians even the broad general notion of salvation can be spoken of as a completed event. Also, what in Paul is always clearly "works of the law" and belongs firmly to the contexts of Galatians and Romans has now become in Ephesians simply "works." Removed from its original polemical context it now has a far broader reference and stands for human effort in general. Most readers of Paul after 70 C.E. have found one of the primary contexts of his work—the battle for admission of Gentiles to the new community with its debate about circumcision and the law—no longer immediately relevant. Here, the writer of Ephesians takes the first steps in showing how the main elements of that debate can be reinterpreted and given more general scope.

The second half of Eph 2 (vv 11–22) provides another key passage in Ephesians' distinctive treatment of salvation, particularly with its imagery of reconciliation. The change from the readers' pre-Christian past to their present in the Church is this time said to have been produced by Christ's reconciliation (2:16). In the only extended reflection on Christ's death in the letter, his death on the cross is seen as effecting peace both on a horizontal and a vertical level. By dealing with the law as the source of hostility, Christ's death overcame the alienating divide between Jews and Gentiles and was the creative power which produced a unified new humanity from these two groups. It is this emphasis on the horizontal social dimension that Ephesians contributes to the notion of reconciliation which it takes up from Paul. The major division within humanity in the first-century world is reckoned to have been overcome, as Jews and Gentiles with their ethnic and religious differences are seen to have been reconciled in the one body of the Church. But the vertical element of Pauline reconciliation, restoration to God's acceptance and favor, is not missing, for Christ's death effected this restoration at the same time for both groups, who now enjoy the privilege of access to God's fatherly presence (2:17, 18).

(d) Relation to Judaism

In the latest epistles of Paul, he was still engaged in a life-and-death struggle with rival Jewish Christian groups, but Ephesians looks back on an achieved unity between Jew and Gentile in the Church as the one body (cf. 2:11–22). Gone are the heated struggles with rival groups about the terms of Gentile admission and about the law and gone also is the apostle's personal agony, expressed in Romans, about the relation of believers to ethnic Israel. Ephesians exhibits a detachment from such issues, reflecting its setting toward the end of the first century C.E. when Paul's position on admission of Gentiles had been firmly established, Jerusalem had fallen, and Gentile Christians in terms of influence and numbers were dominant in the churches of Asia Minor. Such Gentile Christians were liable to be ignorant of their roots and needed to be reminded of the privilege of their salvation and the greatness of what had been accomplished in order for them to take their place in the Church. But unlike the Gentile Christians in Rom 11, they are not told that they have been added to a given Jewish base. The Gentiles' former disadvantages have been reversed, not by their being incorporated into Israel nor even by their joining a renewed Israel of Jewish Christians, but by their being made members of a new community which transcends the categories of Jew and Gentile, an entity which is a new creation. The two former groupings have not simply merged, but one new person has been created in place of the two (2:15). In Ephesians, then, the emphasis is on discontinuity with Israel, and the concept of the Church is in fact, if not in name, that of the "third race." This stance toward Israel goes hand in hand with the writer's treatment of the law, for he asserts that in order to deal with the divisiveness produced by the law, Christ had to abolish the law (2:14, 15). For Paul, too, the period of the law had come to an end, but in Romans he is more careful and dialectical in expressing himself than elsewhere (cf. Rom 3:31). The writer of Ephesians presents the apostle's basic position in an unqualified fashion, though, again like Paul, he is not averse to calling on the law for secondary support for his ethical admonitions when that suits him (cf. 6:2, 3).

The writer's use of the Jewish Scriptures also fits the general perspective on Judaism suggested above. OT traditions are one source among a number of authoritative traditions which he employs to further his purposes. Whereas in the discussions of Gal 3 and 4 and Rom 4, 9–11, and 15, where unity between Jewish Christians and Gentile Christians is a live issue, the OT plays a key role and is cited as part of a fulfillment-of-promise approach to Scripture, in Ephesians the OT is used only somewhat incidentally in connection with this topic in 2:17. Ephesians lacks this promise-and-fulfillment use of Scripture. Indeed it would be quite inappropriate, given the perspective expressed in 3:5—that the mystery of the inclusion of the Gentiles "was not made known to the sons of men in other generations as it has now been revealed to his holy apostles and to prophets by the Spirit." According to Ephesians, the OT writers were ignorant of the sort of blessing that was to come to the Gentiles.

(e) Church and World

As is well known, the concept of the Church is very much to the fore in Ephesians. The term ἐκκλησία occurs nine times. In Paul this term is used most frequently for the actual gathering of a group of local Christians or for the local group which gathered regularly, although in a few places the apostle appears to have in view an entity which is broader than the local gathering (cf. Gal 1:13; 1 Cor 10:32; 12:28; 15:9; Phil 3:6). Colossians certainly refers to a Church which consists of all believers (1:18, 24) in addition to local gatherings (4:15, 16). But in Ephesians all nine references are to the universal Church, the Christian community seen in its totality.

The writer uses a variety of images for this new people of God. It is God's family (2:19), the new temple (2:20–22), Christ's fullness (1:23; 4:13), and Christ's bride (5:23–33). The dominant image, however, is that of the body of Christ, which occurs ten times in the letter. Again, via Colossians, it has become a depiction of the universal Church as distinct from the more local application of the image in 1 Cor 12 or Rom 12. Only 4:15, 16 explicitly retain the original comparison involving the interdependence of the parts of an organism. Elsewhere, it is used for viewing the Church as a compact whole. While in 1 Corinthians the use of the image is colored by the eucharistic tradition with its focus on the crucified body of Christ, here in Ephesians the concentration on Christ's exaltation colors the use of the image, as the Church as body is seen in relation to Christ as its head (though the juxtaposition of these images should not be taken as part of one physiological model: see the commentary's discussion of 1:22b, 23). When the body metaphor is elaborated in 4:1–16, it is in order to depict the Church as a dynamic corporate entity, which grows as its individual members are involved in a continual process of mutual adjustment, and which is on the move toward unity and maturity. The body of Christ is a structured unity that can contain the diversity of the essential contributions of each individual member (4:7, 16) and the especially significant role of certain people—the apostles, prophets, evangelists, pastors, and teachers (4:11–16). The writer underlines the role and authority of such ministers of the word as they preserve and apply the apostolic tradition. He looks back on the apostles and prophets themselves as the foundation of the Church (2:20). These revered leaders of the first generation can, in fact, be described as "holy apostles and prophets" (3:5), from whom Paul is singled out in particular as the one entrusted with the revelation of the "mystery" of God's purposes for the Gentiles (3:1–13).

Ephesians is supremely concerned about the unity of the Church. The writer exhorts the Church to maintain the unity it already possesses and stresses that the essential ingredient for achieving the harmony of unity in diversity is love (4:1–16). For him, the quality of the Church's corporate life has everything to do with fulfilling its role in the world. As it embodies the unity it already possesses, the Church fulfills its calling to be the paradigm of the cosmic unity which is the goal of the salvation God provides in Christ (cf. 1:10). This role of the Church is outlined in 3:9, 10, where its existence is seen as God's announcement to the principalities and authorities in the heavenly realms that he is going to make good on his multifaceted and wise plan for cosmic unity. Because the Church is the one new humanity in place of two (2:15), the one body (2:16; 4:4), it can be depicted as providing the powers with a tangible reminder that their authority has been decisively broken and that everything is going to be united in Christ.

Not only is this letter concerned about the unity of the Church; it also stresses the holiness of the Church. Believers have been chosen to be holy and blameless (1:4). They are growing into a holy temple in the Lord (2:21). They have put on the new humanity, which is characterized by holiness (4:24). All kinds of impurity belong to their past life (4:17–19) and are so inappropriate to the lives of "saints" or holy ones that they should not even be named among them (5:3–14). How could anything else be the case for those who have come to realize that the goal of Christ's sacrificial death was the sanctification of his Bride, the Church, whom he has cleansed by washing in water through the word in order to present her to himself in splendor, without spot or wrinkle, but rather holy and blameless (5:25–27)?

But the perspective of Ephesians is not one in which the Church and the rest of creation are fixed in a state of permanent opposition and alienation. Rather, the Church as Christ's fullness provides the present focus for and demonstration of that presence, which now fills the cosmos in a hidden way but which will do so openly and completely (cf. 1:22, 23). The second half of the letter does, however, underline the Church's holiness and draws a sharp distinction between the conduct of believers and that of those in the sinful surrounding society (4:17–24; 5:3–14). Yet the distinctive behavior required of the new humanity, of the children of light, is not achieved by flight from the world but by living responsibly in the world, in the ordinary structures of human life—husband-wife, parent-children, and master-slave relationships (cf. 5:21–6:9). In contrast to the attitude to marriage in 1 Cor 7, where it, along with the other structures of this world, is seen as passing away, the exalted view of marriage in Eph 5 as reflecting the heavenly reality of the union between Christ and his Church and the use of the household code as a whole provide evidence that the writer believes the Church to have a future in this world with which it needs to come to terms. In contrast to the earlier baptismal vision of equality of Gal 3:28, Ephesians accepts and even reinforces the basic structures of patriarchal marriage and the institution of slavery and then within them brings to bear Christian motivations of love and service.

(f) Impact

How do Gentile Christians removed from the original context in which Paul expressed his gospel, removed from the urgency of its pervasive eschatological perspective and from the particularities of its Jew-Gentile concerns, appropriate the apostle's message? As he attempts, toward the end of the first century, to inspire a Gentile audience which has little awareness of any Jewish heritage and different expectations about the future of the Church in the world, the writer to the Ephesians provides us with one answer. His model for reinterpreting Paul has of course joined the genuine Paul and become part of the canonical image of Paul.

Its impact will inevitably be different for different readers at different times and any attempt to evaluate it a somewhat personal enterprise. Certainly the letter's vision of the Church is bold and impressive. Difficult as it frequently is to reconcile the vision of a unified universal Church with the empirical reality of a myriad of traditions, denominations, factions, and petty politics and personality disputes even within those factions, such a vision needs to be appropriated, if contemporary Christians are not to give up on their ecumenical endeavors. The scandal of present ecclesiastical divisions is not in the variety of the theological convictions, preferences for forms of worship, or cultural distinctives that they express. It lies in Christians allowing these to prevent them from providing a visible demonstration that in Christ God has united them in *one* body and *one* Spirit. A central challenge of the letter's picture of the Church's calling is that Christians should spare no effort to find ways and structures for maintaining the unity of the Spirit in visible demonstrations of cooperation and unity in worship, witness, and social action. Catching the vision of Ephesians about the Church will mean that, from within their own traditions, Christians will increasingly reach out to worship and work with other believers, so that they can embody what Hans Küng has called an "evangelical catholicity," which centers on the gospel, and a "catholic evangelicity," which has the breadth of perspective to take in the continuity in time of the faith and its community and the universality in space of the faith and its community (cf. *On Being a Christian* [New York: Pocket Books, 1978] 503). Ephesians does not, however, allow unity to be seen as simply an in-house issue for the Church. It sees the unity of the Church as providing the principalities and powers, and, by extension, all hostile alienating forces at work in this world, with a tangible reminder that their dominion has been decisively broken and that God is going to make good on his purposes in Christ for *cosmic* unity (cf. 3:9, 10). When Christians become discouraged, feel weak and insignificant, succumb to an individualistic piety, or lose their sense of identity and purpose, Ephesians can provide the necessary reminder of the important part they have to play in God's cosmic plan, of the fact that the quality of their life together in the Church has everything to do with the Church's carrying out its task in the world, and of the power that has been made available in Christ to move them on toward the fulfillment of such a calling.

Ephesians' reinterpretation of Paul has been criticized both for its tendency to a triumphalistic portrait of the Church and for a view of Christian existence which fails to embrace the dark side of life and therefore lacks the profundity of a theology of the cross with its note of God's identification with human suffering. The former criticism applies more to a misuse of the letter's imagery and forgets both that the confidence of the original readers needed to be boosted and that its message was intended to produce not arrogance but humble gratitude for God's grace (cf. also Schnackenburg, "Der Epheserbrief," 172). The latter criticism is, however, more telling. For a more compelling perspective on life with its ambiguities and anguish within the NT one would turn to parts of the genuine Paul or to the Gospel of Mark. Yet no single NT document can be expected to contain all the truth, and the optimistic vision which characterizes Ephesians, with its theological grasp of and doxological response to God's grace in the gospel of Christ, its depiction of God's purposes in Christ in terms of peace and reconciliation on a universal and cosmic scale, and its view of the Church's role in the advancing of those purposes of cosmic harmony through a life of holiness and love, can still be immensely attractive and provides a powerful incentive for hope. The genuine Paul, for a variety of reasons, found it necessary in his letters to put his primary stress on the cross, though it is always seen in the light of the resurrection. Ephesians places its emphasis on the resurrection and exaltation. By drawing out the implications for the Church of this dimension, which was certainly there in the genuine Paul, Ephesians can be seen to be making its complementary contribution to the canonical Paul's gospel of the crucified and risen Christ.

Prescript (1:1, 2)

Bibliography

Batey, R. "The Destination of Ephesians." *JBL* 82 (1963) 101. **Best, E.** "Ephesians i.1." *Text and Interpretation,* ed. E. Best and R. McL. Wilson. Cambridge: Cambridge University Press, 1979, 29–41. ———. "Ephesians 1.1 Again." *Paul and Paulinism,* ed. M. D. Hooker and S. G. Wilson. London: S.P.C.K., 1982, 273–79. ———. "Recipients and Title of the Letter to the Ephesians: Why and When the Designation 'Ephesians'?" *ANRW* 2.25.4 (1987) 3247–79. **Dahl, N. A.** "Adresse und Proömium des Epheserbriefes." *TZ* 7 (1951) 241–64. ———. "The Particularity of the Pauline Epistles as a Problem in the Ancient Church." *Neotestamentica et Patristica,* FS Cullmann, Leiden: Brill, 1962, 261–71. **Harnack, A.** "Die Adresse des Epheserbriefes des Paulus." *SPAW* 37 (1910) 696–709. **Lightfoot, J. B.** "The Destination of the Epistle to the Ephesians." *Biblical Essays.* London: Macmillan, 1893, 375–96. **Lindemann, A.** "Bemerkungen zu den Adressaten und zum Anlass des Epheserbriefes." *ZNW* 67 (1976) 235–51. **Percy, E.** *Die Probleme der Kolosser- und Epheserbriefe,* 449–66. **Roon, A. van.** *The Authenticity of Ephesians,* 72–85. **Santer, M.** "The Text of Ephesians i.1." *NTS* 15 (1969) 247–48. **Schenk, W.** "Zur Entstehung und zum Verständnis der Adresse des Epheserbriefes." *Theologische Versuche* 6 (1975) 73–78. **Schmid, J.** *Der Epheserbrief des Apostels Paulus,* 37–129. **Zuntz, G.** *The Text of the Epistles.* London: Oxford, 1953.

Translation

¹*Paul, an apostle of Christ Jesus by the will of God, to the saints who are*[a] *also faithful in Christ Jesus:* ²*Grace to you and peace from God our Father and the Lord Jesus Christ.*

Notes

[a] The words "in Ephesus" are not included in this translation and are omitted in the Greek in a number of early manuscripts. Since this textual question affects not only one's view of the addressees but also decisions about the authorship and purpose of the letter and since there is no clear consensus on it in NT scholarship, it requires extended discussion. Schmid offers a comprehensive review of earlier discussion and Best ("Ephesians i.1") gives an overview of more recent proposals.

The manuscript evidence is as follows. ἐν Ἐφέσῳ is omitted by P⁴⁶ ℵ* B* 424c 1739. In addition, Origen and Basil, and, in all probability Marcion and Tertullian, did not have the phrase in their texts. P⁴⁶ differs slightly from the other evidence in also omitting the definite article τοῖς before οὖσιν. The vast majority of manuscripts do have ἐν Ἐφέσῳ, including ℵc A B³ D G K, although D (Codex Claromontanus) also differs from the others by the omission of the definite article before οὖσιν.

The combination of the original scripts of codices Sinaiticus and Vaticanus with the earliest manuscript evidence for Ephesians, P⁴⁶, is strong external evidence for the omission of the geographical location in the earliest text. There are also good internal reasons that can be adduced against the originality of "in Ephesus." According to the account in Acts, Paul had not only founded the church at Ephesus but had had an extensive ministry there (cf. Acts 18:19–21; 19:1–20:1; 20:17–38). Yet in this letter there are clear indications that Paul does not know the addressees personally (cf. 1:15; 3:2; 4:21) and there is a complete absence of any personal greetings. Certainly this makes an Ephesian address highly unlikely on the assumption of Pauline authorship. Even Meyer, 18, who upholds the traditional view of Pauline authorship and an Ephesian address, has to confess, "Nevertheless, this epistle, as an apostolical letter to the Ephesians . . . remains an enigma awaiting further solution." Against the suggestion of Barth, 11, 67 (made earlier by Neudecker, *Einleitung ins NT* [Leipzig, 1840] 502), there is no real indication in the letter itself that only one group in the congregation, namely, Gentiles baptized after Paul had left the area, is being addressed. An Ephesian address is equally unlikely on the assumption of authorship by a skillful admirer or disciple of Paul who had any knowledge of the apostle's ministry. Lindemann, *ZNW* 67 (1976) 238, believes that the Paulinist addressed the letter to Ephesus because of his knowledge of Paul's close links with that church. But this view has to ignore the fact that the writer would then contradict this in 1:15; 3:2; and 4:21. Gnilka, 6, also in support of an Ephesian address as original, claims that the Paulinist, removed in time from the period of Paul's ministry, would not be concerned with the verisimilitude, yet this appears to be exactly his concern in including 6:21, 22.

The earliest extant text then is likely to have read τοῖς ἁγίοις τοῖς οὖσιν καὶ πιστοῖς. It is comparatively easy to see how the other variants could have developed from this original. Because of the three successive -οις endings, the scribe of P46 may have been guilty of haplography and missed the second τοῖς. Then, once the superscription "To the Ephesians" became attached to the letter, and because οὖσιν in other Pauline addresses is followed by ἐν and a geographical location, it would only seem natural to supply ἐν Ἐφέσῳ to this particular address.

The earliest reading also satisfies the criterion of being the more difficult reading. The English translation above hides the fact that the Greek syntax is extraordinarily difficult to construe. Indeed Blass-Debrunner-Funk, para. 413(3), consider this use of the participle οὖσιν to be impossible without a further adjunct to the predicate, which evidently in their judgment ἐν Χριστῷ Ἰησοῦ does not supply, whereas ἐν Ἐφέσῳ would do so. Schnackenburg, 38, believes τοῖς ἁγίοις τοῖς οὖσιν to be comprehensible as a single phrase meaning simply "to the local saints" (cf. also F. J. Foakes Jackson and K. Lake, ed., *The Beginnings of Christianity* I, Vol. 4 [London: Macmillan, 1933] 56; J. H. Moulton and N. Turner, *A Grammar of New Testament Greek*, Vol. 3 [Edinburgh: T. & T. Clark, 1963] 151–52). He argues that although such a use of the participle is out of line with Paul's usage, the pseudonymous writer could well have proceeded differently. Against this, it must be said that it is unlikely that a writer wanting to remain faithful to the Pauline tradition by taking up the letter form would deliberately introduce this alteration at the beginning of his writing. Also, none of the examples Schnackenburg adduces for his suggested meaning from Acts (5:17; 13:1; 14:13) or that others cite from the papyri are clear parallels because in them the participle is used with or closely accompanied by some explanatory phrase (cf. also the criticism of this view by Best, "Ephesians i.1," 33). But in any case discussions of the participle by itself still ignore the very important fact that the καί is extremely awkward. Although the translation above, "to the saints who are also faithful in Christ Jesus," is the most obvious, as Best, "Ephesians i.1," 32, has most recently pointed out, it is doubtful whether the Greek can easily be made to have this meaning (*contra* Abbott, viii). It is also difficult to see what it means, since what appears to be intended as a qualifying description simply repeats what by definition the saints should already be, that is, faithful in Christ Jesus.

The main attempts to interpret the text as it stands have not been convincing. This applies particularly to Origen's early attempt which takes τοῖς οὖσιν to refer to those called out of non-existence into real existence through participation in the one who is Being itself (cf. Exod 3:14 and J. A. F. Gregg, "The Commentary of Origen upon the Epistle to the Ephesians," *JTS* 3 [1902] 235). Since Paul elsewhere can refer to the Jerusalem church as "the saints" (e.g., Rom 15:25–31), some take the address to designate two groups, Jewish Christians and Gentile Christians who are also faithful in Christ Jesus, claiming that in 2:19 also "saints" refers to Jewish Christians and that in other parts of the letter "we" and "you" also convey a distinction between Jewish Christians and Gentile Christians (cf. Kirby, *Ephesians: Baptism and Pentecost*, 170 and n. 86; Caird, 31). But, as we shall see, neither of these claims can be substantiated and in none of the other addresses of the Pauline letters does "saints" have this restricted meaning. It is unlikely that a follower of Paul, taking up the usual Pauline form of address in order to preserve continuity with the apostolic tradition, would introduce such a change of meaning. The same objection tells against those who would take οἱ ἅγιοι to be simply a reference to the people of God in the OT tradition, the Jews, a term which then has to be qualified by a specifically Christian description (for differing versions of such a view cf. Beare, 602, 611; Kümmel, *Introduction*, 355; Schenk, *Theologische Versuche* 6 [1975] 76).

Another, more popular approach to the text as it stands is to suggest that there was an intentional gap left after τοῖς οὖσιν because this was a circular letter and as it, or copies of it, circulated to the various churches, the messenger or the church itself would supply the appropriate place name.

This was first proposed by J. Ussher, *Annales Veteris et Novi Testamenti* (London: Crook, 1650–54), taking up hints made by Beza and Grotius, and is supported by such scholars as Lightfoot, "Destination," 392; Robinson, 11–13; Percy, *Probleme,* 461–64; Zuntz, *The Text of the Epistles,* 228 n. 1; and Houlden, 250. But there are a number of considerations that tell decisively against this suggestion. There are no texts of Ephesians that actually contain such a lacuna. Furthermore, O. Roller, *Das Formular der paulinischen Briefe* (Stuttgart: Kohlhammer, 1933) 199–212, 520–25, has shown that there are no other examples of letters in the ancient world with such lacunae. Also, would not such a circular have included ἐν, which after all would remain a constant in the address? If the gap in the original was to be filled in by each church, why would copies without a place name continue to exist? Finally, this suggestion offers no explanation for the καί, which remains awkward and inconsistent with other Pauline addresses.

These difficulties in construing the reading τοῖς ἁγίοις τοῖς οὖσιν καὶ πιστοῖς may well indicate that, although it is our earliest extant reading, it is not what was originally written. There are two main hypotheses about the original text which can provide convincing explanations for the earliest reading we have. Schmid, *Epheserbrief,* 125–29 (followed by Best, "Ephesians 1.1 Again," 276–78), conjectured that the author wrote τοῖς ἁγίοις καὶ πιστοῖς ἐν Χριστῷ Ἰησοῦ. This has the advantage of being very similar to the address in Colossians, the letter which in many ways serves as a model for Ephesians. The suggestion is that the general letter which had this address became associated with Ephesus and the ensuing superscription "to the saints who are in Ephesus" eventually entered the text. The insertion of this geographical element was, however, made very awkwardly before καὶ πιστοῖς. On this view, at a later stage, a scribe either remembered that the original had no geographical reference or noted the inconsistency between the letter's contents and an Ephesian address, and omitted the reference to Ephesus, thus producing our earliest extant reading. As Best, "Ephesians 1.1 Again," 278, admits, the weakness of this hypothesis is that it requires a considerable amount of textual development and therefore necessitates a substantial lapse of time.

Since, instead of such a long and complicated process, the following suggestion necessitates only one stage prior to our earliest reading, it is to be preferred. In setting out this solution, which, given the limitations of the evidence, provides the best available explanation for the earliest reading, we take up and modify the proposal made by van Roon, *Authenticity,* 72–85. When the address of Ephesians is compared to those in other Pauline letters, it becomes evident that the use of the present participle of "to be" demands a subsequent geographical location (and not the phrase "in Christ Jesus," which Santer, *NTS* 15 [1969] 247–48, conjectures as originally following the participle). Cf. for example 2 Cor 1:1 (τῇ ἐκκλησίᾳ τοῦ θεοῦ τῇ οὔσῃ ἐν Κορίνθῳ, σὺν τοῖς ἁγίοις πᾶσιν τοῖς οὖσιν ἐν ὅλῃ τῇ Ἀχαΐᾳ) or Phil 1:1 (πᾶσιν τοῖς ἁγίοις ἐν Χριστῷ Ἰησοῦ τοῖς οὖσιν ἐν Φιλίπποις). Yet, as we have seen in the case of Ephesians, adding a place name still leaves us with an awkward address that involves a syllepsis or zeugma (linking two words or phrases with a word that is in a different relation to each of them) and that is out of line with other Pauline addresses on account of the καί. This same objection also tells against the view that the original location was simply Laodicea, which Marcion attested and which Harnack (*SPAW* 37 [1910] especially 700, 706–8) supported, in the belief that the place name was omitted later because of the negative reference to Laodicea in Rev 3:14–17.

But if there were two place names in the address—τοῖς ἁγίοις τοῖς οὖσιν ἐν . . . καὶ ἐν . . . πιστοῖς ἐν Χριστῷ Ἰησοῦ—this would not only help to explain the καί but also bring this address into harmony with the syntax of other Pauline addresses where we find a dative construction simply followed by an attributive phrase. 1 Cor 1:2 has τῇ ἐκκλησίᾳ τοῦ θεοῦ τῇ οὔσῃ ἐν Κορίνθῳ, ἡγιασμένοις ἐν Χριστῷ Ἰησοῦ κλητοῖς ἁγίοις, and similarly Rom 1:7 has πᾶσιν τοῖς οὖσιν ἐν Ῥώμῃ ἀγαπητοῖς θεοῦ, κλητοῖς ἁγίοις. Which, then, were the two place names originally mentioned? Connected with his argument for the letter's authenticity, van Roon suggested that the intended readers would be in an area which the messenger, Tychicus, visited on his journey to Colossae and in which Paul himself had not worked. He opted for the towns mentioned in Col 4:13, Hierapolis and Laodicea, believing that this would also fit Paul's concern, expressed in Col 2:1–3, for the other churches in the Lycus Valley. Many who hold the letter to be a circular also consider these towns to have been the primary locations on its circuit (cf. Percy, *Probleme,* 457; Dahl, *TZ* 7 [1951] 245–48; Schlier, 31, 32). However, van Roon's suggestion would be equally appropriate if the letter were by a follower of Paul, who writes to churches in Asia Minor around Ephesus and makes use particularly of Colossians. Colossians is the only other Pauline letter to describe its recipients as "faithful . . . in Christ" in its prescript. Later, in the postscript, Eph 6:21, 22 will also take up Col 4:7, 8. Consistent with his overall use of Colossians, the writer continues in the

Pauline tradition by addressing the letter to particular churches mentioned in Colossians which were not known personally by Paul and which Tychicus could have visited. The original address would therefore have been τοῖς ἁγίοις τοῖς οὖσιν ἐν Ἱεραπόλει καὶ ἐν Λαοδικείᾳ, πιστοῖς ἐν Χριστῷ Ἰησοῦ. Such an original would also account for the tradition of a connection of this letter with Laodicea with which Marcion was familiar (cf. Tertullian, *Adv. Marc.* 5.11).

The earliest textual reading known to us came about through the desire of a scribe to universalize the sphere of the letter's influence by omitting the place names originally attached. We know that there was this tendency on the part of some in the ancient world through the textual history of Romans and the remark of Tertullian in *Adv. Marc.* 5.17 that "the title is of no interest, since in writing to a certain church the apostle is writing to all." A well-known statement to this effect can also be found in the Muratorian canon: ". . . the blessed Paul himself, imitating the example of his predecessor, John, wrote to seven churches only by name. . . . But although he wrote twice to the Corinthians and Thessalonians, for reproof, it is nevertheless obvious that one church is known to be dispersed throughout the whole globe of the earth. For John also, while he wrote in the Apocalypse to seven churches, nevertheless speaks to all" (cf. the text in A. Souter, *The Text and Canon of the New Testament*, rev. C. S. C. Williams, 2nd ed. [London: Duckworth, 1954] 191–94). In regard to Romans, the best explanation for a version of the letter ending at 14:23, as for a version ending at 15:33, as for versions with the reference to Rome omitted from 1:7 and 1:15, is that they were produced to give the letter more general significance and more ecumenical impact (cf. H. Gamble, *The Textual History of the Letter to the Romans* [Grand Rapids: Eerdmans, 1977], and N. A. Dahl, "Particularity," 266–67, 270, who also provides a similar argument about the textual tradition at 1 Cor 1:2). It can be argued that in view of the more general nature of the body of these letters, Romans and Ephesians especially lent themselves to this catholicizing treatment. In the case of Ephesians the scribe simply deleted the two geographical locations but left the connective καί. On any view the awkwardness of the καί is hard to explain, but it is far more probably explained by the clumsiness of a scribe in making the omission than by an original author deliberately writing the text we have. Once the superscription "To the Ephesians" became attached to the letter (see under *Setting and Purposes* in the *Introduction* and the extensive discussion in Best, *ANRW* 2.25.4 [1987] 3247–79), it is easy to see how ἐν Ἐφέσῳ would be inserted into the earlier form of the text and thereby to account for the unusual position of this geographical reference in the readings which have it. Against Best, "Ephesians i.1," 40, it is scarcely an objection to this hypothesis that the scribe who later added "in Ephesus" on these grounds was not consistent with the earlier scribe who on different grounds had deleted "in Hierapolis" and "in Laodicea."

Form/Structure/Setting

Ephesians opens in the fashion of the typical Pauline letter. As is well known, Paul had adapted the basic pattern of the Hellenistic letter to suit his own purposes (for an introduction to the issues cf. W. G. Doty, *Letters in Primitive Christianity* [Philadelphia: Fortress Press, 1973]). In Greco-Roman letters the prescript took the standard form of "writer to addressee, greetings!" Paul's version of this opening frequently expanded its elements by providing a description of his own relation to Christ and of the status of the recipients of the letters as believers in Christ and by giving the greeting a Christian content. Here in Ephesians too the name of Christ is mentioned in connection with all three elements of the prescript. The writer, as a follower of Paul who wishes to claim the authority of the apostle behind his elaboration of Paul's teaching, naturally takes up the form of communication on which Paul had placed his stamp and continues in the tradition of the Pauline epistolary prescript.

The only unusual feature of the form in comparison with the other Pauline letters is that Paul alone is named as sender. Elsewhere, with the exception of Romans, the letters generally considered to be authentically Pauline all mention co-senders. It is sometimes argued in support of the authenticity of

Ephesians that the reason no associates or co-workers of Paul are mentioned here is that, like Romans, this letter was written to those not known personally to Paul. However, this argument cannot stand, since Colossians was also written to a congregation not known personally by Paul (cf. Col 1:4; 2:1) and yet in its prescript Timothy is mentioned alongside Paul. Against van Roon, *Authenticity*, 85–87, Colossae is in no different position in regard to its relationship to Paul than the other churches of the Lycus Valley (cf. Col 4:13). In addition, if Rom 16 is integral to the original letter and was sent to Rome, Paul certainly had a number of personal acquaintances in the Roman congregation (cf. K. P. Donfried, "A Short Note on Romans 16," *JBL* 89 [1970] 441–49; C. E. B. Cranfield, *A Critical and Exegetical Commentary on the Epistle to the Romans*, 2 vols. [Edinburgh: T. & T. Clark, 1975–79] 1:9–11; Gamble, *Textual History*, esp. 36–55, 84–95). Romans is distinctive in this aspect of its address, not primarily because Paul was not known personally to its recipients but because the apostle is writing to a congregation that does not owe its origin directly or indirectly to the Pauline mission and so the letter has to serve in a number of ways as a self-introduction in which Paul attempts to show the relevance of his own apostleship to the situation of the Roman Christians (cf. Rom 1:1–15). This consideration does not apply to any other of Paul's letters, and certainly any congregations addressed in the Lycus Valley or in the area of Asia Minor around Ephesus would have come into being through the ministry of Paul or his associates. If anything, then, this deviation in Ephesians from the customary Pauline practice of mentioning co-senders, who are associates in his work on the gentile mission, could well be an indication that a Paulinist is writing in the name of Paul alone in order to focus on the authority of the apostle himself behind the traditions that are being transmitted (cf. also ἐγὼ Παῦλος in 3:1 and ἐγὼ ὁ δέσμιος ἐν κυρίῳ in 4:1).

Comment

1 Παῦλος ἀπόστολος Χριστοῦ Ἰησοῦ διὰ θελήματος θεοῦ, "Paul, an apostle of Christ Jesus by the will of God." This Pauline self-designation is in the same words as those of Col 1:1 and 2 Cor 1:1 (cf. also 1 Cor 1:1). It signaled the official character of Paul's communication to his churches, since he wrote as the authorized representative of the exalted Christ and as one whose authority came not from his self-appointment to this office but from God's election of him to it—"by the will of God." We have already given reasons for thinking that here this authority is being claimed for his message by a follower of Paul conscious of standing in his apostolic tradition. On Paul as *the* apostle to the Gentiles, see under 3:1–13 where this explicit focus of the text is discussed.

τοῖς ἁγίοις . . . πιστοῖς ἐν Χριστῷ Ἰησοῦ, "to the saints . . . faithful in Christ Jesus." As in 1 Cor 1:1, 2 Cor 1:1, Rom 1:1, Phil 1:1, and Col 1:2, the recipients of the letter are addressed as "saints," the holy people whom God has set apart for himself. In these other places the term is synonymous with the whole group of believers being addressed, and its scope is therefore likely to be no different here. Further consideration of interpretations that would give the term a restricted reference here has been given in the discussion of the text under *Notes*. The readers, then, are described in the light of their relationship to God, not primarily, of course, in terms of their actual moral condition, but as his holy people in continuity with the OT designation of Israel (cf. LXX Exod 19:6). The writer will expand on the implications of this term ἅγιοι in 1:4 where he sees holiness as the result of God's election and in 5:26, 27 where he views it as an effect of Christ's death on behalf of the Church. The saints are further designated as "faithful," which is to be seen as in apposition to "saints" and as having reference to the same group (cf. Col 1:2, which is also the only other Pauline address to employ this term for the recipients and so could well have influenced its use here). "Faithful" is to be understood in the sense of having faith or exercising belief rather than of being trustworthy or reliable. As an adjective, πιστός means "believing" in Gal 3:9. Used as a substantive, it began to take on the semitechnical sense of "believer"; in 2 Cor 6:15 the believer (πιστός) is contrasted with the unbeliever (ἄπιστος), and by the time of the Pastorals this usage seems to have become fixed (cf. 1 Tim 4:10, 12; 5:16; 6:2; Titus 1:6). At the time of the writing of Ephesians perhaps this final stage has not yet been reached because the term here is qualified by the addition of the phrase ἐν Χριστῷ Ἰησοῦ. This is to be taken as a separate attributive phrase. It is not that ἐν plus the dative is here serving to denote the object of belief (cf. 1:15, *contra* Schenk, *Theologische Versuche* 6 [1975] 76). Instead the phrase "in Christ Jesus" refers to the relationship of union with Christ which results from having been incorporated into him (cf. Col 1:2, "faithful brothers in Christ," and for further discussion of the significance of "in Christ" in Paul and in Ephesians see below on 1:3). Through their relationship to Christ the addressees of this letter are marked out not only in terms of God's choice of them as his holy people but also in terms of their believing response, though, as the writer will go on to assert, they owe even this to God's gracious initiative (cf. 2:8).

2 χάρις ὑμῖν καὶ εἰρήνη ἀπὸ θεοῦ πατρὸς ἡμῶν καὶ ἡυἁίου Ἰησοῦ Χριστοῦ, "Grace to you and peace from God our Father and the Lord Jesus Christ." The actual salutation part of the prescript is worded in exactly the same way here as in Rom 1:7; 1 Cor 1:3; 2 Cor 1:2; Phil 1:2; and Philem 3. The other salutations in the Pauline letters involve a variation in the possessive adjectives (Gal 1:3; 2 Thess 1:2) or in the naming of the sources of grace and peace (1Thess 1:1; Col 1:2). It is usually agreed that Paul replaced the standard Hellenistic greeting χαίρειν with the similar-sounding but theologically more profound term χάρις, "grace," and combined this with the Greek version of the normal Jewish greeting "Shalom"—εἰρήνη. The closest parallel to this is the combination "mercy and peace" in some Jewish salutations (cf. *2 Apoc. Bar.* 78:2). Paul gave the benefits of grace and peace a distinctly Christian framework by specifying God our Father and the Lord Jesus Christ as their origin and made his salutation serve as a form of prayer-wish. Here also the writer desires for his readers the experience of the undeserved favor and deep well-being which flow from Christ and from the God who through Christ is known as Father. The two elements, grace and peace, recur, though not linked so immediately, in the epistle's closing blessing of 6:23, 24, and before that, in the body of the letter, they represent two of its major themes, χάρις occurring ten times (1:6, 7; 2:5, 7, 8; 3:2, 7, 8; 4:7, 29) and εἰρήνη six times (2:14, 15, 17; 4:3; 6:15).

Explanation

Possibly addressing his letter to the churches of Hierapolis and Laodicea to preserve a Pauline flavor, a disciple of Paul writes in the name of the apostle to the churches of the Pauline mission in Asia Minor in the area around Ephesus. His earnest wish is for Paul to continue to speak to a situation in the churches which arose after the apostle's death. So, following the ancient literary device of pseudonymity, he makes use not only of Paul's name, but also of the Pauline letter form and the typical features of the Pauline prescript as he adapts the liturgical traditions of Paul's churches and Paul's own teaching in order to bring them to bear on the new historical and ecclesiastical circumstances. In this way, Paul's authority is claimed for the magnificent interpretation of his message which follows in the rest of the epistle. Yet its opening greetings, despite their stereotyped form, would have been intended by the writer to be received by his readers in the same way as, at an earlier date, those of the apostle himself would have been received by his original churches.

Blessing of God for His Salvation in Christ (1:3–14)

Bibliography

Ahern, B. "The Indwelling Spirit, Pledge of Our Inheritance—Eph 1.14." *CBQ* 9 (1947) 179–89. **Allan, J. A.** "The 'In Christ' Formula in Ephesians." *NTS* 5 (1958–59) 54–62. **Best, E.** "Fashions in Exegesis: Ephesians 1:3." *Scripture: Meaning and Method.* FS A. T. Hanson, ed. B. P. Thompson. Hull: Hull University Press, 1987, 79–91. **Cambier, J.** "La Bénédiction d'Eph. 1, 3–14." *ZNW* 54 (1963) 58–104. **Caragounis, C. C.** *The Ephesian Mysterion,* 39–52; 78–96; 143–57. **Coune, M.** "A la louange de sa gloire. Eph 1, 3–14." *AsSeign* 46 (1974) 37–42. **Coutts, J.** "Ephesians 1.3–14 and 1 Peter 1.3–12." *NTS* 3 (1956–57) 115–27. **Dahl, N. A.** "Adresse und Proömium des Epheserbriefes." *TZ* 7 (1951) 241–64. **Debrunner, A.** "Grundsätzliches über Kolometrie im NT." *TBl* 5 (1926) 231–33. **Deichgräber, R.** *Gotteshymnus und Christushymnus,* 40–43; 64–76. **Denton, D. R.** "Inheritance in Paul and Ephesians." *EvQ* 54 (1982) 157–62. **Drago, A.** "La nostra adozione a figli di Dio in Ef 1,5." *RivB* 19 (1971) 203–19. **Dreyfus, F.** "Pour la louange de sa gloire (Ep 1,12.14): L'origine vétéro-testamentaire de la formule." *Paul de Tarse. Apôtre du nôtre Temps,* ed. L. de Lorenzi. Rome: Abbaye de S. Paul, 1979, 233–48. **Fischer, K. M.** *Tendenz und Absicht,* 111–18. **Gibbs, J. G.** *Creation and Redemption: A Study in Pauline Theology.* Leiden: Brill, 1971, 114–34. **Hammer, P. L.** "A Comparison of κληρονομία in Paul and Ephesians." *JBL* 79 (1960) 267–72. **Hartin, P. J.** "ΑΝΑΚΕΦΑΛΑΙΩΣΑΣΘΑΙ ΤΑ ΠΑΝΤΑ ΕΝ ΤΩ ΧΡΙΣΤΩ (Eph. 1:10)." *A South African Perspective on the New Testament,* ed. J. H. Petzer and P. J. Hartin. Leiden: Brill, 1986, 228–37. **Hofius, O.** "'Erwählt vor Grundlegung der Welt' (Eph. 1.4)." *ZNW* 62 (1971) 123–28. **Innitzer, T.** "Der 'Hymnus' im Epheserbrief (1,3–14)." *ZKT* 28 (1904) 612–21. **Jayne, D.** "'We' and 'You' in Eph. 1:3–14." *ExpTim* 85 (1974) 151–52. **Jankowski, A.** "L'espérance messianique d'Israël selon la pensée paulinienne, en partant de Proelpizein (Ep 1, 12)." *De la Tôrah au Messie,* ed. M. Carrez, J. Doré, and P. Grelot. Paris: Desclée, 1981, 475–81. **Kessler, P. D.** "Unsere Berufung zum göttlichen Leben. Betrachtung über den Prolog des Epheserbriefes." *BLit* 40 (1967) 110–22. **Krämer, H.** "Zur sprachlichen Form der Eulogie Eph. 1.3–14." *Wort und Dienst* 9 (1967) 34–46. **Kruse, C.** "Il significato di περιποίησις in Eph. 1.14." *RivB* 16 (1968) 465–93. **Lang, F.** "Die Eulogie in Epheser 1, 3–14." *Studien zur Geschichte und Theologie der Reformation,* ed. L. Abramowski and J. F. G. Goeters. Neukirchen-Vluyn: Neukirchener Verlag, 1969, 7–20. **Lemmer, H. R.** "Reciprocity between Eschatology and Pneuma in Ephesians 1:3–14," *Neot* 21 (1987) 159–82. **Lightfoot, J. B.** *Notes on Epistles of St. Paul.* London: Macmillan, 1895, 307–24. **Lincoln, A. T.** "A Re-Examination of 'The Heavenlies' in Ephesians." *NTS* 19 (1973) 468–83. **Lohmeyer, E.** "Das Proömium des Epheserbriefes." *TBl* 5 (1926) 120–25. **Lyonnet, S.** "La bénédiction de Eph.1, 3–14 et son arrière-plan judaique." *A la Rencontre de Dieu,* FS A. Gelin. Le Puy: Éditions Xavier Mappus, 1961, 341–52. **Maurer, C.** "Der Hymnus von Epheser 1 als Schlüssel zum ganzen Briefe." *EvT* 11 (1951–52) 151–72. **McHugh, J.** "A Reconsideration of Ephesians 1.10b in the Light of Irenaeus." *Paul and Paulinism,* ed. M. D. Hooker and S. G. Wilson. London: S.P.C.K., 1982, 302–9. **McNicol, J.** "The Spiritual Blessings of the Epistle to the Ephesians." *EvQ* 9 (1937) 64–73. **Montagnini, F.** "Christological Features in Eph 1:3–14." *Paul de Tarse: Apôtre du nôtre Temps,* ed. L. de Lorenzi. Rome: Abbaye de S. Paul, 1979, 529–39. **Mussner, F.** "Das Volk Gottes nach Eph 1, 3–14." *Concilium* 1 (1965) 842–47. **O'Brien, P. T.** "Ephesians 1: An Unusual Introduction to a New Testament Letter." *NTS* 25 (1979) 504–16. **Odeberg, H.** *The View of the Universe in the Epistle to the Ephesians.*

Robbins, C. J. "The Composition of Eph 1:3–14." *JBL* 105 (1986) 677–87. **Sanders, J. T.** "Hymnic Elements in Ephesians 1–3." *ZNW* 56 (1965) 214–32. **Schattenmann, J.** *Studien zum neutestamentlichen Prosahymnus.* Munich: C. H. Beck, 1965, 1–10. **Schille, G.** *Frühchristliche Hymnen,* 65–73. **Schnackenburg, R.** "Die grosse Eulogie Eph 1, 3–14." *BZ* 21 (1977) 67–87. **Trinidad, J. T.** "The Mystery Hidden in God: A Study of Eph. 1, 3–14." *Bib* 31 (1950) 1–26. **Wilson, R. A.** "'We' and 'You' in the Epistle to the Ephesians." *Studia Evangelica* 2, ed. F. L. Cross. TU 87. Berlin: Akademie-Verlag, 1964, 676–80.

Translation

³ *Blessed be the God and Father of our Lord Jesus Christ, who has blessed us with every spiritual blessing in the heavenly realms in Christ,* ⁴ *even as he chose us in him before the foundation of the world to be holy and blameless before him in love.* [a] ⁵ *He has predestined us for adoption as his own sons through Jesus Christ,* [b] *in accordance with his good pleasure and will,* ⁶ *to the praise of the glory of his grace with which he has highly favored us in the Beloved,* ⁷ *in whom we have redemption through his blood, the forgiveness of trespasses, in accordance with the richness of his grace* ⁸ *which he lavished upon us with all wisdom and insight.* [a] ⁹ *He has made known to us the mystery of his will, in accordance with his good pleasure which he purposed in Christ* ¹⁰ *for the administration of the fullness of time, to sum up all things in Christ, things in heaven and things on earth in him;* ¹¹ *in whom we were also appointed, having been predestined in accordance with the plan of him who carries out all things according to the purpose of his will,* ¹² *in order that we, who have already hoped in Christ, might be for the praise of his glory.* ¹³ *You also are in him,* [c] *having heard the word of truth, the good news of your salvation; in him also, when you believed, you were sealed with the promised Holy Spirit,* ¹⁴ *which* [d] *is the guarantee of our inheritance vouching for God's redemption of his possession, to the praise of his glory.*

Notes

[a] In the original Greek text 1:3–14 constitutes one sentence. For the sake of intelligibility the translation has not attempted to convey this stylistic feature. Instead, its sentence divisions have followed what appear to be the main structural dividers in this passage. For discussion of this and of the relation of the last part of v 4 to v 5 and the last part of v 8 to v 9 see *Form/Structure/Setting* below.

[b] The Greek text has εἰς αὐτόν after διὰ Ἰησοῦ Χριστοῦ. This has been interpreted as a reference to God (cf. Lightfoot, 314; Abbott, 9; Westcott, 10; Cambier, *ZNW* 54 [1963] 75–76; Krämer, *Wort und Dienst* 9 [1967] 42; Schnackenburg, *BZ* 21 [1977] 81; Caragounis, *Mysterion,* 87; Barth, 80) rather than Christ (cf. Schlier, 54; Gnilka, 73; Ernst, 272). The αὐτόν most naturally refers back to the subject of προορίσας, and αὐτοῦ, which then occurs twice in this same clause, clearly has this reference. In this way εἰς αὐτόν would stand in parallel to κατενώπιον αὐτοῦ of the previous clause and διὰ Ἰησοῦ Χριστοῦ εἰς αὐτόν would follow the Pauline pattern of *per Christum in Deum* (cf. W. Thüsing, *Per Christum in Deum* [Münster: Aschendorff, 1965]). The sonship therefore has God as its goal, "toward him," and this emphasis is suggested in the translation by adding "his own" to the notion of adoption as sons.

[c] The translation for the sake of greater smoothness hides an anacoluthon at this point in the original. A literal translation would be "in him you also . . . ," which is not in fact completed until the second part of the verse with "you were sealed," but by then the writer has started the thought again with "in him also. . ."

[d] Some manuscripts, including ℵ D gr K, have the masculine relative pronoun ὅς, while others,

including p⁴⁶ A B G, have the neuter ὅ, which agrees with the gender of the preceding noun πνεῦμα. The United Bible Societies' second edition of the Greek NT opted for the former as original, while the third edition opted for the latter. This indicates the difficulty of a decision. Although the neuter appears to have somewhat stronger external support, it is easier to see how ὅς would have been changed to ὅ than vice versa, and in the end this factor should probably be given greater weight. There would be no clear reason for a scribe to alter the grammatically correct ὅ, but if ὅς were original it might well be changed by a scribe who failed to realize that the author had assimilated the gender of the relative pronoun to that of the following noun ἀρραβών.

Form/Structure/Setting

This opening passage with its outburst of praise has the form of an extended blessing or *berakah* ("Blessed be God, who has . . ."); the OT and Jewish worship provide the background for this form. εὐλογητός, "blessed," is frequently used in the LXX to render the Hebrew *bārûk*. C. Westermann (*The Praise of God in the Psalms,* tr. K. R. Crim [London: Epworth Press, 1966] 87–89) has shown that in the OT the earliest form of *berakah* occurred when an individual responded simply to an act of God's deliverance or provision (e.g., Gen 14:20; 24:27), that later it became associated with the cult and was used in Israel's corporate worship (e.g., Solomon's prayer at the dedication of the temple begins and ends with the *berakah* formula in 1 Kgs 8:15, 56), and that a further stage of development is evidenced by the use of the *berakah* to conclude the books of the Psalter (Pss 41:13; 72:18, 19; 89:52; 106:48). Such eulogies remained dominant in Jewish worship and can be found in the Qumran literature (e.g., 1QS 11.15; 1QH 5.20; 10.14; 11.27, 29, 32, 33; 16.8), in Zechariah's prayer of Luke 1:68–75, and in rabbinic Judaism where they were the most characteristic formulae for prayer, as prayers such as the *'Ahăbâ Rabbâ* and the *Šĕmônēh ʿEśrēh* show. The form of the latter, the Eighteen Benedictions of the synagogue service, can be seen from the first benediction:

> Blessed art thou, O Lord our God and God of our fathers, God of Abraham, God of Isaac, and God of Jacob, the great, mighty and revered God, the most high God, who bestowest loving-kindnesses, and possessest all things; who rememberest the pious deeds of the patriarchs and in love will bring a redeemer to their children's children for thy name's sake. (*The Authorized Daily Prayer Book of the United Hebrew Congregations of the British Commonwealth of Nations,* tr. S. Singer [London: Eyre and Spottiswoode Ltd., 1962] 46).

S. Lyonnet, "La bénédiction," in fact draws heavily on the second benediction in the liturgy before the *Shema* to shed light on issues in Eph 1:3–14. Its language forms part of the broad Jewish background of the eulogy, but the details are much less closely related than Lyonnet supposes. In these Jewish blessings God is usually praised for some action on his part already performed, such as creation or redemption, or praised for some action desired for the future such as the provision of food or the coming of his kingdom. While in the OT the predicate was almost always in the third person, in the later Jewish blessings, as the above example shows, the address is frequently in the second person. In this regard the eulogy in Ephesians corresponds with the third person form of the OT *berakah.* In terms of Westermann's categories of "declarative" and "descriptive" praise (*Praise of God*, 81–142), it is declarative in that it is a response to definite actions of God on behalf of his people.

Though anchored firmly in Jewish worship, the liturgical form used by the author of Ephesians has a specifically Christian flavor in that the God of Israel, to whom praise is ascribed, is now known as "the Father of our Lord Jesus Christ." This formulation appears to have been a fixed pattern for Christian eulogies, since this is also the way the predicate is phrased in the other two major eulogies in the NT—those in 2 Cor 1:3, 4 and 1 Pet 1:3–12. The Christian focus of this particular blessing is hard to miss, since "in Christ" or "in him" is repeated in nearly every verse. Such repetition emphasizes that all that God has done for his people, which issues in their praise, has been done in Christ (cf. also Montagnini, "Christological Features," 529–39). In addition there appears to be no precedent outside the NT for the particular form of an introductory eulogy in a letter. One example is sometimes cited from the letter of Hiram to Solomon in 2 Chron 2:11, 12. But the place of the blessing in this passage is clearly secondary. Originally it was an independent blessing before the letter, as 1 Kgs 5:21 (Hebrew, 5:7 Eng.) indicates, and the citation of the 2 Chronicles passage by Eupolemos (Eusebius, *Praep. evang.* 9.34) and Josephus (*Ant.* 8.53) by no means constitutes evidence that an introductory blessing in a letter had become a fixed practice (cf. Deichgräber, *Gotteshymnus*, 64; Lang, "Die Eulogie," 19; *contra* Dahl, *TZ* 7 [1951] 250–51). This feature of the letter form then is a specifically early Christian one with 2 Cor 1:3, 4 providing the first example.

In regard to its language and style this sentence, the length of which (26 lines in the United Bible Societies' text) is unparalleled in the NT, has produced quite diverse reactions among scholars. Frequently cited is E. Norden's comment that it is "das monströseste Satzkonglomerat . . . das mir in griechischer Sprache begegnet ist" (ET: "the most monstrous sentence conglomeration . . . that I have encountered in Greek"; *Agnostos Theos*, Berlin: Teubner, 1913, 253). Danker (*ISBE* 2 [1982] 110) asserts, "As a syntactical salmagundi, the marvelous spiral of Eph 1:3–14 is probably without rival in Greek literature," while Masson (149) could write, "On est frappé de la plénitude de son verbe, de sa majesté liturgique, de son rythme perceptible du commencement à la fin" (ET: "one is struck by the fullness of the language, its liturgical majesty, its perceptible rhythm from beginning to end").

The long sentence stretches itself out by means of relative clauses, participial constructions, and the piling up of prepositional phrases and synonyms. Typical of this style of *oratio perpetua* are the three prepositional phrases of v 3, which are all introduced by the preposition ἐν—ἐν πάσῃ εὐλογίᾳ πνευματικῇ, "with every spiritual blessing"; ἐν τοῖς ἐπουρανίοις, "in the heavenly realms"; and ἐν Χριστῷ, "in Christ"—and the heaping up of prepositions in the clause in vv 5, 6—εἰς υἱοθεσίαν διὰ Ἰησοῦ Χριστοῦ εἰς αὐτόν, κατὰ τὴν εὐδοκίαν τοῦ θελήματος αὐτοῦ εἰς ἔπαινον δόξης . . . , "*for* adoption *through* Jesus Christ *to* himself *in accordance with* his good pleasure and will *to* the praise of the glory. . . ." Synonyms are sometimes linked in a genitive construction (cf. ἡ εὐδοκία τοῦ θελήματος αὐτοῦ, "the good pleasure of his will" [v 5], ἡ βουλὴ τοῦ θελήματος αὐτοῦ, "the purpose of his will" [v 11]) or combined in other ways (cf. ἐν πάσῃ σοφίᾳ καὶ φρονήσει, "with all wisdom and insight" [v 8], and τοῦ θελήματος αὐτοῦ, κατὰ τὴν εὐδοκίαν αὐτοῦ, "of his will, in accordance with his good pleasure" [v 9]). Other stylistic features of the sentence are paronomasia, the use of cognate verbs and nouns together (cf. εὐλογητός . . . εὐλογήσας . . . εὐλογίᾳ [v 3] and χάριτος . . . ἐχαρίτωσεν [v 6]), and the parallelism produced by the threefold use of εἰς ἔπαινον (τῆς) δόξης . . . αὐτοῦ in vv 6, 12, and 14. The writer speaks of the wealth and abundance of God's grace (τὸ πλοῦτος, v 7; ἐπερίσσευσεν, v 8), and the recurrence of πᾶς (vv 3, 8, 10, 11) and the heaping up of words and phrases in this profuse and effusive style are a deliberate attempt to express the riches of which he speaks in an appropriate way. This is the language of prayer and worship, and not surprisingly many of the stylistic features noted above are the result of Semitic influence (cf. Deichgräber, *Gotteshymnus*, 72–75) and have some of their closest parallels in the Qumran literature. K. G. Kuhn has pointed out that they are characteristic of the Hebraic style of the liturgical and hymnic language of the Qumran writings where "we come across these long-drawn-out, loosely connected tape-worm sentences which cause difficulties to the translator as regards punctuation" and "cannot fail to notice the striking similarity between a sentence such as the one we find in Eph 1:3–14 and the typical Hebrew sentence structure of the Qumran texts" ("The Epistle to the Ephesians in the Light of the Qumran Texts," *Paul and Qumran* [1968] 117).

Repetition and redundance are of the essence of liturgy and here the repetition of certain words and phrases, the repeated genitives, and the collection of synonyms not only have the effect of intensifying the force of the concepts involved but also serve to provide the sentence with a certain rhythm. In addition the succession of long syllables in a number of places periodically slows down the flow of words so that a chantlike effect is produced as the eulogy is spoken (cf. van Roon, *Authenticity*, 158–62). The one major feature of this liturgical prose which is typically Hellenistic rather than Semitic is its hypotaxis. Its clauses are syntactically subordinated to each other rather than arranged in parataxis or *parallelismus membrorum* (couplets) as in Hebrew poetic and liturgical texts (cf. also Deichgräber, *Gotteshymnus*, 75; Gnilka, 57). It is likely then that the language and style of the eulogy reflect a Hellenistic Judaism where the devotional tone and style of the Hebrew psalms and the Qumran hymns has had a profound impact and has been translated into an equivalent Greek style (cf. van Roon, *Authenticity*, 188–89). As Caragounis (*Mysterion*, 45) remarks, "In the case of the *Eighteen Benedictions* the word *bārûk* is repeated in each Benediction. In Eph. on the other hand, the author declares God εὐλογητός and then tries in one sweep to enumerate all his reasons for eulogising him. The result may be somewhat clumsy, but it is quite effective in another way, in presenting, in a torrential manner, all that constitutes God's blessings."

Numerous attempts have been made to lay bare the structure of this sentence with its hymnic qualities. In the process some scholars believe they have been able to isolate a hymn which the author has taken up and used, while others consider the entire passage itself to constitute a hymn which can be divided into clear strophes and lines. Some have based their structural division on syntactical features such as the three main verbs ἐξελέξατο, "chose," ἐχαρίτωσεν, "favored," and ἐπερίσσευσεν, "lavished," or the three aorist participles εὐλογήσας, "blessed," προορίσας, "predestined," and γνωρίσας, "made known," or the repetition of εἰς ἔπαινον τῆς δόξης αὐτοῦ, "to the praise of his glory," or the position of ἐν Χριστῷ, ἐν ᾧ, and ἐν αὐτῷ. Others have divided the eulogy on the basis of its content according to a trinitarian pattern where in the first part God the Father is central, in the second Christ, and in the third the Spirit, or according to a temporal schema where at the beginning God's blessing of believers in the past is the focus, then the present, and finally the future. Some of the more important proposals should be mentioned briefly.

Innitzer appears to have been the first to divide the passage into strophes according to the rules of classical Greek meter. He found three strophes (vv 3–6; 7–12; and 13, 14) which treated God, Christ, and the Spirit respectively and the whole was to be considered "einen verhüllten Hymnus, einen Lobgesang im schlichten Gewande der Kunstprosa" (ET: "a disguised hymn, a song of praise in the simple clothing of artistic prose"; *ZKT* 28 [1904] 619). Lohmeyer (*TBl*; 5 [1926] 20–25) on the basis of meter and also of the prominent place of the aorist participles, produced a four strophe structure (vv 3, 4; 5–8; 9–12; and 13, 14 as the fourth strophe, the application, which was of a slightly different length than the others). Both Innitzer and Lohmeyer used colometry in their analyses, but its use, with particular reference to Lohmeyer's work, was thoroughly criticized by Debrunner (*TBl* 5 [1926] 231–33; cf. also van Roon's criticism of Innitzer and Lohmeyer on similar grounds, *Authenticity*, 158–59). This sort of criticism did not deter Masson's later attempt to detect a hymn which the author used. On the grounds of parallelism of the number of syllables and assonance of the first and last syllables he grouped the passage into six strophes, each of which had two stanzas, each of which in turn had four lines, except that the first stanzas of the first two strophes had five lines each. In Masson's reconstruction each line ends with the syllable -ου or -ω (cf. 148–51). A similar analysis on the basis of syllable count and rhyming of last syllables in the line has been provided by Schattenmann (*Studien*, 1–10) but his effort resulted in four strophes (vv 3–6a; 6b–10a; 10b–12; 13, 14). Both analyses are open to Debrunner's original charge of forcing normal grammar and syntax unnaturally and of arbitrariness in their writing and arranging of lines and syllables (cf. also Cambier, *ZNW* 54 [1963] 60 n. 7, and Deichgräber, *Gotteshymnus*, 69, in regard to Masson, and Deichgräber, *Gotteshymnus*, 71–72, and Krämer, *Wort und Dienst* 9 [1967] 36–37, for a more detailed substantiation of this criticism in regard to Schattenmann).

Even more speculative in their attempts to find an original hymn are Coutts, Schille, and Fischer. Coutts (*NTS* 3 [1956–57] 115–27) believes the passage to be a homily based on a liturgical prayer. This liturgical form is discovered by omitting 76 of the eulogy's 202 words in order to arrive at three strophes of six lines, each ending with the refrain "to the praise of his glory." Deichgräber (*Gotteshymnus*, 70) is particularly severe in his discussion of this suggestion, calling it both false and fantastic. Schille (*Hymnen*, 65–73) holds that the passage contains an *Initiationslied*, "song of initiation," with two strophes, vv 5–8 and 9–12a, preceded by an introit in vv 3, 4. Verses 13 and 14 are then supposed to provide a corrective of eschatological reserve to the theology of realized eschatology in the original hymn which the author does not share. This reconstruction contains a number of improbabilities (cf. Deichgräber, *Gotteshymnus*,

70) and its presupposition about the writer's eschatology is unfounded (cf. Lincoln, *Paradise Now and Not Yet,* 166–68). Fischer (*Tendenz,* 111–18) also considers that the original hymn behind the passage has been extensively reworked. His reconstruction omits 87 of the 202 words in vv 3–14 and transposes others in order to arrive at three strophes, each ending with "to the praise of his glory" (vv 4–6a; 7, 8, 12a; 13b, 14), and in this way the cosmic Christology is held to be the author's addition to the hymn. Fischer himself (114) realizes that this reconstruction is "sehr unsicher," "very uncertain," and Schnackenburg (*BZ* 21 [1977] 70) has pointed out some of its problems.

In general it has to be said that these proposals that the passage is a hymn which is being quoted or a reworking of an original hymn are unlikely. Its language and style are too similar to the rest of the first three chapters for it to be possible to isolate an entity which is clearly different. In its present form it reads very much as an integrated whole. No two reconstructions are able to agree on the original and its divisions. In addition, these attempts all fail to take account of the several connections between the language of this passage and that of Colossians, which suggest that the author drew on that letter and weigh strongly against the eulogy or its core having had some independent existence (see the comments on the individual verses below, section 2 of the *Introduction,* and also Sanders, *ZNW* 56 [1965] 227–29; Mitton, 43, 65). The consensus among most recent writers is that the eulogy is an ad hoc composition on the part of the author in elevated liturgical language (cf. Maurer, *EvT* 11 [1951–52] 154; Schlier, 41; Sanders, *ZNW* 56 [1965] 229; Deichgräber, *Gotteshymnus,* 65–66; Gnilka, 60; Ernst, 268; Mitton, 44; O'Brien, *NTS* 25 [1979] 509). It is likely that woven into his composition are both some traditional liturgical language and some Pauline phrases. The nature and amount of the traditional material is not such as to warrant the proposal of Lang ("Die Eulogie," 16) that a preformed eulogy lies behind the passage.

Though abandoning any recourse to an original hymn, some scholars still hold that the writer's composition has a clear strophic structure. Schlier (39–40) holds that an analysis must do justice to the close connection between form and content and sees a benediction formula in v 3 which is developed in the first major part of the eulogy (vv 4–10). This is divided into three strophes (vv 4–6a; 6b, 7; 8–10) based on the main verbs (ἐξελέξατο, ἐχαρίτωσεν, ἐπερίσσευσεν). The formal features become looser toward the end of the eulogy, and vv 11–14 are then treated as a "double strophe" in which the "in Christ" phrases are determinative of the structure. Cambier (*ZNW* 54 [1963] 58–104) works first on the sequence of thought in the passage and then ties in his investigation of structure which concludes that there is an introduction (v 3) and three strophes (vv 4–6; 7–12; 13, 14) each ending with "to the praise of his glory." The first strophe has two couplets (v 4; vv 5, 6), the second three couplets (vv 7, 8a; 8b–10; 11, 12) and the third two (v 13; v 14). These couplets are in turn made up of lines arranged in an a b a sequence. A major problem with Schlier's attempt to make the three main verbs determinative can be seen when the strophes have to divide v 6 unnaturally and break the relative clause's close connection with its antecedent (cf. also the criticism of Krämer, *Wort and Dienst* 9 [1967] 36, and Schnackenburg, *BZ* 21 [1977] 71). For Cambier's analysis to agree with the shift in content of the eulogy, there should be a major division at v 9, as the subject moves from the benefit of forgiveness to that of being included in the cosmic dimensions of God's purpose in Christ (cf. Sanders, *ZNW* 56 [1965] 225, and the further criticism of Deichgräber, *Gotteshymnus*, 71).

Robbins (*JBL* 105 [1986] 677–87) has suggested that the sentence length and method of composition of the eulogy accord with certain principles of Greek rhetoric. He argues that the structure is determined by the amount of speech that can be fitted between breaths, and by the unity and completeness of thought of what fits between the breaths. This seems a plausible suggestion, but analysis according to these criteria is no less subjective than most of the other structural analyses. Robbins' own reconstruction appears forced, and he confesses that there is "some opaqueness of thought" in it. His division into rhetorical periods also does not do enough justice to the continuous flow of this *one* long sentence.

Probably the two most useful discussions of structure are the two most recent longer syntactical analyses of the eulogy, those by Krämer and Schnackenburg. Krämer considers "in Christ" and its equivalents to be central to both the content and the form of the passage and considers that the endings of clauses are especially important for structural divisions. He sees three major parts—the benediction formula of v 3, then vv 4–12, and finally vv 13, 14. The major middle section has three strophes (vv 4–6; 7–10; 11, 12), each of which ends with an ἐν Χριστῷ or equivalent expression, just as does the benediction formula itself. Schnackenburg's treatment (followed by Mussner, 40) is different in that after the opening formula he has six divisions. These consist of vv 3–4, then vv 5–6 beginning with ἐν ἀγάπῃ, vv 7–8, vv 9–10, vv 11–12 beginning with ἐν αὐτῷ, and then vv 13–14. It seems better to allow differences from these two treatments to emerge in interaction with them in the following analysis of the passage than to provide detailed criticism at this point. It should be said, however, that it is the wisest course of action to agree with Sanders (*ZNW* 56 [1965] 227) that "every attempt to provide a strophic structure for Eph 1: 3–14 fails" and therefore to avoid talking about fixed strophes of a hymn. Instead our analysis will deal simply with the major divisions in the flow of the eulogy's syntax (cf. also Gnilka, 59; Schnackenburg, *BZ* 21 [1977] 75). Of course, decisions about syntax and decisions about content and meaning are inevitably interrelated. Our analysis of the flow of the syntax is set out below and a discussion of its salient features follows.

Berakah	Εὐλογητὸς ὁ θεὸς καὶ πατὴρ τοῦ κυρίου ἡμῶν
Formula (v 3a)	Ἰησοῦ Χριστοῦ
I a (v 3b)	ὁ εὐλογήσας ἡμᾶς ἐν πάσῃ εὐλογίᾳ πνευματικῇ
	ἐν τοῖς ἐπουρανίοις ἐν Χριστῷ
b (v 4)	καθὼς ἐξελέξατο ἡμᾶς ἐν αὐτῷ πρὸ καταβολῆς κόσμου
	εἶναι ἡμᾶς ἁγίους καὶ ἀμώμους κατενώπιον
	αὐτοῦ ἐν ἀγάπῃ
II a (vv 5, 6)	προορίσας ἡμᾶς εἰς υἱοθεσίαν διὰ Ἰησοῦ Χριστοῦ εἰς αὐτόν
	κατὰ τὴν εὐδοκίαν τοῦ θελήματος αὐτοῦ
	εἰς ἔπαινον δόξης τῆς χάριτος αὐτοῦ
	ἧς ἐχαρίτωσεν ἡμᾶς ἐν τῷ ἠγαπημένῳ

b (vv 7, 8) ἐν ᾧ ἔχομεν τὴν ἀπολύτρωσιν διὰ τοῦ αἵματος αὐτοῦ
τὴν ἄφεσιν τῶν παραπτωμάτων
κατὰ τὸ πλοῦτος τῆς χάριτος αὐτοῦ
ἧς ἐπερίσσευσεν εἰς ἡμᾶς ἐν πάσῃ σοφίᾳ καὶ φρονήσει
III a (vv 9, 10) γνωρίσας ἡμῖν τὸ μυστήριον τοῦ θελήματος αὐτοῦ
κατὰ τὴν εὐδοκίαν αὐτοῦ ἣν προέθετο ἐν αὐτῷ
εἰς οἰκονομίαν τοῦ πληρώματος τῶν καιρῶν
ἀνακεφαλαιώσασθαι τὰ πάντα ἐν τῷ Χριστῷ
τὰ ἐπὶ τοῖς οὐρανοῖς καὶ τὰ ἐπὶ τῆς γῆς ἐν αὐτῷ
b (vv 11, 12) ἐν ᾧ καὶ ἐκληρώθημεν
προορισθέντες κατὰ πρόθεσιν τοῦ τὰ πάντα ἐνεργοῦντος
κατὰ τὴν βουλὴν τοῦ θελήματος αὐτοῦ
εἰς τὸ εἶναι ἡμᾶς εἰς ἔπαινον δόξης αὐτοῦ
τοὺς προηλπικότας ἐν τῷ Χριστῷ
IV additional ἐν ᾧ καὶ ὑμεῖς ἀκούσαντες τὸν λόγον τῆς ἀληθείας
ἐν ᾧ statement τὸ εὐαγγέλιον τῆς σωτηρίας ὑμῶν
addressing ἐν ᾧ καὶ πιστεύσαντες ἐσφραγίσθητε τῷ πνεύματι
recipients τῆς ἐπαγγελίας τῷ ἁγίῳ
(vv 13, 14) ὅς ἐστιν ἀρραβὼν τῆς κληρονομίας ἡμῶν
εἰς ἀπολύτρωσιν τῆς περιποιήσεως
εἰς ἔπαινον τῆς δόξης αὐτοῦ

Interestingly, this analysis of syntax turns out to be closest in overall terms to Lohmeyer's early division, though of course unlike his attempt it does not appeal to meter for support or treat the divisions as strophes of a hymn. The aorist participles are determinative in the flow of the syntax (with Lohmeyer; also Gnilka, 59: *pace* Krämer, whose concern with ἐν Χριστῷ phrases is too exclusive), but since the latter two are subordinated to ὁ εὐλογήσας they cannot be said to mark separate strophes. The analysis above in fact indicates the subordination of each major clause in the eulogy to the preceding one by the increasing indentation. Each of the first three major divisions also has two parts. The καθώς clause of v 4 marks the beginning of the second part of the first section, while the ἐν ᾧ clauses of vv 7, 11 mark this point in the second and third sections. (Schnackenburg underplays the καθώς clause and overplays the ἐν ᾧ clauses by making them of equal importance to the aorist participles.) The last section, vv 13, 14, with its anacoluthon, can then be seen as an additional ἐν ᾧ statement addressing, and thereby specifically drawing into the eulogy, the recipients of the letter, and concluding appropriately by taking up the doxological phrase εἰς ἔπαινον τῆς δόξης αὐτοῦ. All the preceding parts of the eulogy can be seen to conclude with a prepositional phrase with ἐν.

Other important features for the flow of the syntax which stand out in the analysis provided above (and which are also noted by Krämer and Schnackenburg) are the κατά phrases (vv 5, 7, 9, 11) and the expressions with εἰς (vv 6, 10, 12, 14; cf. also εἰς υἱοθεσίαν and εἰς αὐτόν in v 5 and εἰς ἡμᾶς in v 8). Verse 3a provided the *berakah* formula. Verse 3b, the first part of the first section, is a thematic statement for the rest of the eulogy, setting out in general terms God's blessing of believers in Christ, for which he is worthy of blessing. καθώς, which begins the second part, has both a comparative and causal force and in this way v 4 starts to elaborate on and to ground the previous thematic statement (cf. BDF §453 (2); Percy, *Probleme*, 243–45; Schlier, 49; Lang, "Die Eulogie," 10; Gnilka, 69 n. 3; *contra* Barth, 79, who holds that it indicates the introduction of a quotation). Literally it could be translated "in accordance with the fact that," and it has a similar function in the thanksgiving of 1 Cor 1:4–9 where in v 6 it introduces the grounds for the Corinthians' rich spiritual endowment. ἐν ἀγάπῃ, "in love," is to be placed at the end of this first section rather than related to προορίσας, "he has predestined," at the beginning of the next (cf. AV, RV, NEB; Caird, 35; J. A. Robinson, 143; Lightfoot, *Notes*, 313; Caragounis, *Mysterion*, 84 n. 24, admits the arguments for this construction are the strongest, but then rules it out as not fitting his semantic analysis; *contra* Abbott, 8; Percy, *Probleme*, 268; Dahl, *TZ* 7 [1951] 255; Schlier, 52; Maurer, *EvT* 11 [1951–52] 155; Gnilka, 59, 72 n. 6; Schnackenburg, *BZ* 21 [1977] 77; Ernst [271] and Mitton [50, 51] allow for a connection with both v 4 and v 5). Election grounded in the love of God is of course fine theology. Indeed, some who associated ἐν ἀγάπῃ with v 4 link it to ἐξελέξατο, "he chose" (cf. Lyonnet, "La bénédiction," 348; Krämer, *Wort und Dienst* 9 [1967] 42; and Barth, who holds ἀγάπη has both divine and human associations in v 4), though it is too far removed from the main verb in the syntax for this to be plausible. But "in love" should rather be seen as part of the goal election is intended to achieve in those it embraces—a life before God which is holy and blameless and lived in love. Elsewhere in the letter, with reference to love, its human associations predominate (cf. 1:15; 3:17; 4:2, 15, 16; 5:2, 25, 28, 33; 6:23, 24). More decisively, when ἀγάπη occurs in the introductory section of Pauline letters in intercession or thanksgiving it has a human reference (cf. Col 1:4, 8 and Phil 1:9, 10 where it is associated with being pure and blameless), and in Paul's prayer of 1 Thess 3:12, 13 the three qualities asked for believers are love, blamelessness, and holiness. In addition, construing ἐν ἀγάπῃ in this way fits the pattern of the rest of the eulogy where the various sections conclude with a prepositional phrase with ἐν.

Such a pattern is sometimes disputed at two other points—the end of v 8 and the end of v 10. In the first case the issue is whether the phrase ἐν πάσῃ σοφίᾳ καὶ φρονήσει, "with all wisdom and insight," qualifies the following aorist participle and refers to God's own wisdom and insight (cf. Gnilka, 77; Percy, *Probleme*, 309 n. 66, and Dahl, *TZ* 7 [1951] 259 n. 23, link it with v 9 but refer it to what God gives humans) or whether it belongs to the preceding relative clause and refers to God's gifts of grace (cf. Abbott, 15; Robinson, 30; Schlier, 59; Krämer, *Wort und Dienst* 9 [1967] 43; R. E. Brown, *The Semitic Background of the Term "Mystery" in the New Testament* [Philadelphia: Fortress, 1968] 57 n. 168; Barth, 84, 85, but attempting to include a variety of meanings; Ernst, 274; Schnackenburg, *BZ* 21 [1977] 77). The latter is far more likely, since similar gifts are requested for the readers in the prayer report in 1:17, and since, in the introductory section of Colossians, to which this letter is closely related, the very similar phrase in 1:9—"in all spiritual wisdom and understanding"—clearly refers to what is desired for humans. In the other point of dispute at the end of v 10 some hold that the ἐν αὐτῷ provides a new start and should be associated with v 11 (cf. Schlier, 66; Schnackenburg, *BZ* 21 [1977] 76); but it seems to do more justice to the syntax to take it as part of a whole phrase "things in heaven and things on earth in him," which is in apposition to and epexegetic of the preceding phrase, τὰ πάντα ἐν Χριστῷ (cf. Dahl, *TZ* 7 [1951] 257; Maurer, *EvT* 11 [1951–52] 166 n. 40; Krämer, *Wort und Dienst* 9 [1967] 40; Gnilka, 82). "Things in heaven and things on earth" elaborates on the "all things," and "in him" completes the apposition and with its place of emphasis at the end underlines Christ's mediation of God's cosmic purpose. In this way the pattern of the syntax holds whereby ἐν phrases conclude sections and relative clauses with ἐν ᾧ alternate with aorist participles in beginning new stretches of syntax (here vv 11, 12).

Our analysis of the syntactical structure of the eulogy reinforces our earlier observations on its meditative style. Its structure emerges as each thought builds on the previous one, sometimes explaining, sometimes elaborating, sometimes supplementing, sometimes contributing something new, and sometimes picking up again what has already been said.

Viewed rhetorically, the style and structure of the eulogy enhance its function as an exordium designed to make the recipients of the letter favorable to its content. It encourages assent to and participation in its thanksgiving and praise, as the readers are carried along by its rhythms and flow. Vv 13, 14, in particular, with their change to second person plural address, explicitly involve the readers, appealing to their experience of the great blessings of salvation and thereby enabling them to identify with the writer's thoughts and sympathize with his concerns (cf. Aristotle, *Rhet.* 3.14.11; Quintilian 3.8.7; 4.1.5).

Two questions about the setting of the eulogy need to be addressed briefly. One concerns the eulogy's connection with a baptismal setting and the other its epistolary setting. Dahl (*TZ* 7 [1951] 263–64) held that the eulogy was modeled on eulogies said before baptism, while Coutts (*NTS* 3 [1956–57] 120–27) went further and considered it to be a homily based on a baptismal prayer which can be reconstructed from it. Reasons have already been given for the unlikelihood of this latter, more specific proposal, but there is no reason to deny that eulogies used in Christian worship would be something like this one which contains some motifs that may well be closely connected with baptism. The terminology of vv 5, 6—"sonship," "good pleasure," and "the beloved"— echoes the language of the divine voice at Jesus' baptism (Mark 1:11 cf. also Col 1:13), "forgiveness of sins" (v 7) has close baptismal ties elsewhere in the NT (cf. Acts 2:38; also Col 1:14), and the "sealing of the Spirit" (v 13) could have associations with baptism. The aorist εὐλογήσας in v 3 cannot however be used to argue that the blessing took place in the once-for-all act of baptism (*pace* Dahl, *TZ* 7 [1951] 260; Deichgräber, *Gotteshymnus,* 76; Lang, "Die Eulogie," 15; cf. F. Stagg, "The Abused Aorist," *JBL* 91 [1972] 222–31). It seems best to conclude that some of the traditional material taken up in the eulogy originally had a close connection with baptism but that, since baptismal blessings can be and should be appropriated by the believer again and again in a variety of circumstances, it would be rash to claim any exclusive relationship to baptism for the eulogy as a whole (cf. also Deichgräber, *Gotteshymnus,* 76; O'Brien, *NTS* 25 [1979] 510).

Maurer (*EvT* 11 [1951–52] 168) has entitled 1:3–14 "the key to the whole letter." He means by this that it is a hermeneutical key, since it provides the model for the interplay of OT and what he believes to be Gnostic motifs which characterizes the letter as a whole. Such a title is, however, more appropriate to 1:3–14 in terms of its epistolary function, for the eulogy introduces a number of significant words and themes, upon which the rest of the letter will elaborate. In addition, it introduces them in such a way as to draw the recipients into appreciation of a perspective which is to be basic for the letter's teaching. So, for example, the groundwork is laid for the letter's cosmic perspective with the use of ἐν τοῖς ἐπουρανίοις, "in the heavenly realms," in v 3 for the sphere in which the blessings of salvation are found, and this phrase is taken up again in 1:20; 2:6; 3:10; and 6:12. Likewise τὰ πάντα, "all things," in 1:10 recurs in 1:22, 23; 3:9; 4:6; and 4:10. God's cosmic plan is a mystery which has to be disclosed (1:9), and this language reappears in 3:3–5; 3:9, 10; and 6:19; it also centers in Christ (1:9, 10), and the ἐν Χριστῷ formulation or equivalents which predominate in the eulogy are found again in the letter, particularly in chaps. 2 and 3. The grace of God in the bestowal of salvation is highlighted in vv 6, 7, and grace is a concept also emphasized later in the letter in 2:5, 7, 8; 3:2, 7, 8; 4:7, 29; and 6:24. Some themes found in the eulogy are taken up later in the paraenesis (cf. also O'Brien, *NTS* 25 [1979] 511–12). In fact, the language of election, predestination, God's will and plan in the *berakah* can be seen as a functional equivalent to that of "the calling to which you have been called" (4:1), which the paraenesis exhorts believers to live out. In addition, those who have been sealed by the Holy Spirit (1:13) are exhorted not to grieve the Holy Spirit (4:30), to keep the unity of the Spirit (4:3), to be filled with the Spirit (5:18), to take the sword of the Spirit (6:17) and to pray in the Spirit (6:18). Those who through the Spirit experience the guarantee of their eschatological inheritance (1:14) are later reminded in 5:5 that certain behavior is not compatible with that inheritance. Those who have been predestined for adoption according to God's will (1:5) and given insight into the working of that will (1:9, 11) also need to live in accord with the ethical demands of that will (5:17; 6:6), while those who have heard the word of truth (1:13) are to speak and do the truth (4:15, 21, 25; 6:14). It can be seen that in this way the eulogy fulfills the function which an introductory thanksgiving normally has in a Pauline letter, signaling or announcing in summary form much of the subject matter of the body of the letter (cf. P. Schubert, *Form and Function of the Pauline Thanksgivings* [Berlin: A. Töpelmann, 1939] 24; P. T. O'Brien, *Introductory Thanksgivings in the Letters of Paul* [Leiden: E. J. Brill, 1977] 262). This raises the issue of the relationship of the eulogy to the following thanksgiving and the discussion of why Ephesians contains both, but this will be addressed under *Form/Structure/Setting* on 1:15–23.

Comment

3 For discussion of v 3a (the *berakah* formula) see *Form/Structure/Setting*.
ἐν πάσῃ εὐλογίᾳ πνευματικῇ, "with every spiritual blessing." The three ἐν phrases in v 3 combine to sum up in a general way the content of God's blessing of believers for which he is to be blessed and which will be elaborated in the rest of the eulogy. The blessing consists of God's saving activity in Christ and this fullness of divine blessing can be described as "spiritual," not because it belongs to a person's inner, hidden life (*pace* Caird, 33) but because it is bound up with the Holy Spirit. This sense of "spiritual," as resulting from the presence

and work of the Spirit, is to be found in 5:19 (cf. also Col 1:9; 3:16), and the last two verses of the eulogy, vv 13, 14, indicate that present appropriation of the blessing of the inheritance occurs through participation in the Spirit. Elsewhere in the Pauline corpus the promised blessing to Abraham is seen by Paul to find its fulfillment in terms of the Spirit (Gal 3:14) and "spiritual" can be closely linked, as here, with the heavenly world (cf. 1 Cor 15:44–49 where to have a spiritual body is to bear the image of the heavenly one).

ἐν τοῖς ἐπουρανίοις, "in the heavenly realms," designates the sphere of the spiritual blessings as the heavenly realms. ἐπουράνιος is synonymous with οὐράνιος, and it is not clear whether the nominative of this phrase would have been οἱ ἐπουράνιοι (to be completed by τόποι, "places") or more likely τὰ ἐπουράνια (Abbott, 5; Odeberg, *View*, 7; Schlier, 45; van Roon, *Authenticity*, 215; Barth, 78; Caragounis, *Mysterion*, 147). The most appropriate meaning for this phrase in each of its five usages in Ephesians is a local one. An extensive examination of the interpretation of this phrase and its relationship to Pauline eschatology can be found in my earlier article (*NTS* 19 [1973] 468–83). The origin of the expression is uncertain, though it may well have been a traditional formulation from the worship of the early church on analogy with such expressions as ἐν τοῖς ὑψίστοις (Mark 11:10) or ἐν ὑψηλοῖς (Heb 1:3). Odeberg (*View*, 12, 13), in an influential treatment of the formula, argued that the heavenlies are not the equivalent of heaven in its denotation as the celestial regions in distinction from other parts of the universe but represent the whole of spiritual reality in which the Church participates, and so can be taken as the realm of the Church in Christ. This hypothesis, however, does not do enough justice to the presence of evil powers in the heavenlies (cf. 3:10; 6:12).

Käsemann ("Epheserbrief," 518) and Conzelmann (57) hold that the phrase has links with Gnostic thought, as does Schlier (45–48), for whom it also takes on existential significance as the transcendental dimension of human existence which challenges a person to decision. In its possible liturgical origins and in its use here in the eulogy the phrase is far more likely to have its background in Jewish views of heaven. ἐν τοῖς ἐπουρανίοις is closely related to ἐν τοῖς οὐρανοῖς, and though the writer is speaking predominantly to Gentiles and against a setting of Hellenistic cosmological interests, his use of the formula derives from his own framework, which can be most adequately understood in the light of the OT and Jewish conception of heaven. This cosmological picture was one in which heaven was depicted as the upper part of the cosmos but at the same time stood analogically for the spiritual world above, which the firmament concealed, and beyond that referred also to the realm of divine transcendence. The Hebrew term for heaven is in the plural and this plural is often reflected in the Greek terminology of the NT, ἐν τοῖς οὐρανοῖς, so that this need not indicate any dependence on specific apocalyptic or rabbinic speculations about the number of heavens, but maintains the general reference of the relatively unsophisticated OT perspective. The same applies to ἐν τοῖς ἐπουρανίοις. In this perspective heaven in its created aspect was involved in God's plan for the ages. The heavens as well as the earth are to be shaken and removed in the judgment of the end-time (cf. Isa 51:6; Hag 2:6), while Isa 65:17 and 66:22 speak of the creation of a new heaven and a new earth.

In apocalyptic Judaism also the evil powers in heaven are judged (cf. *1 Enoch* 16.1–4; 21.1–16; 89.59, 60) before the commencement of the coming new age with its new heaven (cf. *1 Enoch* 91.16).

A similar eschatological framework can be found in Paul's thinking and is shared by the author of Ephesians (cf. 1:21). In it both heaven and earth are incorporated in each age, but now heaven and earth take on new significance as they are related to God's acts in Christ. In particular, the heavenly realms in Ephesians are to be seen in the perspective of the age to come, which has been inaugurated by God raising Christ from the dead and exalting him to his right hand (1:20; cf. also Percy, *Probleme,* 181; Caragounis, *Mysterion,* 152, who asserts that the term is "bound up with the salvation events, and has . . . a *heilsgeschichtlich* import"; W. Carr, *Angels and Principalities* [Cambridge: Cambridge University Press, 1981] 93–98). Yet, since heaven is also still involved in the present evil age, there remain hostile powers in the heavenly realms (cf. 3:10; 6:12) until the consummation of the age to come. Here in 1:3, against a background of cosmological concerns on the part of the letter's recipients, there is the indication that the blessings of salvation they have received from God link the recipients to the heavenly realm. The blessings can be said to be in the heavenly realms, yet they are not viewed as treasure stored up for future appropriation, but as benefits belonging to believers now. In apocalyptic writings, aspects of future salvation were sometimes seen as present in heaven (cf. 4 Ezra 7:14, 83; 13:18; *2 Apoc. Bar.* 21.12; 48.49; 52.7). In Ephesians, through what God has done in Christ, the benefits of the age to come have become a present heavenly reality for believers, and for this reason can also be closely linked with the Spirit of that age.

ἐν Χριστῷ, "in Christ." The repetition of this phrase or a variation of it throughout the passage, where it occurs eleven times, highlights the distinctive Christian content of this *berakah* in comparison with its Jewish counterparts. But what is the force of this expression, and is its use in Ephesians different from that in the undisputed Paulines? Whether ἐν Χριστῷ has a set meaning in Paul himself is a highly controverted issue. A. Deissmann in his pioneering study of 1892 (*Die neutestamentliche Formel "in Christo Jesu"* [Marburg: N. G. Elwert]) argued that it was a formula with a local and mystical meaning whereby Christ, as universal Spirit, was the atmosphere which believers occupied. But the work of F. Büchsel (" 'In Christus' bei Paulus," *ZNW* 42 [1949] 141–58), F. Neugebauer ("Das paulinische 'in Christo,'" *NTS* 4 [1957–58] 124–38), and M. Bouttier (*En Christ: Étude d'exégèse et de théologie pauliniennes* [Paris: Presses Universitaires, 1962]) has in fact shown that the phrase has a great variety of force, which must be derived from the context in which it is found. Most frequently its use is instrumental, so that it means "through Christ's agency." But there are a number of references where it does appear to have a local sense in which "Christ is the 'place' in whom believers are and in whom salvation is" (Best, *One Body in Christ,* 8). Such references involve the notion of the incorporation of believers into Christ, and this concept of the incorporation of many in one representative head, together with the use of ἐν, can be seen in the LXX in regard to other figures, such as Abraham (Gen 12:3) and Isaac (Gen 21:12), and in Paul in regard to Adam (1 Cor 15:22). It seems to be used in this sense in regard to Christ in passages such as 2 Cor 5:17, Rom 8:1, or Phil 3:9 (cf. also C. F. D. Moule, *The Origin of Christology* [Cambridge: Cambridge University Press, 1977] 54–62).

Allan (*NTS* 5 [1958–59] 54–62) has argued that the use of ἐν Χριστῷ in Ephesians, where it occurs almost twice as many times as the average for a Pauline letter, differs in that this letter completely lacks any local or incorporative instances of the phrase. He believes that "the writer is not sensitive to the Pauline conceptions of the corporate Christ" (61) and that " 'in Christ' is no longer for this writer the formula of incorporation into Christ, but has become the formula of God's activity through Christ" (59). However his thesis both overestimates the extent to which "in Christ" is a formula of incorporation in Paul and underestimates the extent to which its use in Ephesians involves incorporation. It cannot be denied that in Ephesians with its liturgical style the phrase is used with an almost formal quality and a predominantly instrumental force and refers primarily to Christ's mediation of God's activity toward his people (cf. Gnilka, 66–69). But it is particularly hard to avoid the more intensive incorporative connotation in 2:6 where believers are said to have been raised and seated in the heavenly realms together with Christ "in Christ Jesus." To say with Allan (*NTS* 5 [1958–59] 58) that there "the writer regards Christ not as the inclusive representative but as the mighty companion of the upward way, the one through whom God's uplifting power is brought to bear on us" is to ignore that the wording of this verse takes up that of 1:20. The more straightforward and convincing explanation of the fact that what was said of Christ can now be said of believers is that they are regarded as included in him (cf. also Percy, *Probleme,* 290).

If this is the case, it makes it more likely that here in 1:3 also the writer's thought is that believers experience the blessings of the heavenly realms not only through Christ's agency but also because they are incorporated into the exalted Christ as their representative, who is himself in the heavenly realms (cf. also Schlier, 48; Ernst, 270). Further, if the "in him" of 1:4 is not taken simply to mean that God chose believers before the foundation of the world through Christ's agency but that they can be viewed as united to the preexistent Christ before the foundation of the world and thus chosen by God in him (cf. R. G. Hamerton-Kelly, *Pre-existence, Wisdom, and the Son of Man* [Cambridge: Cambridge University Press, 1973] 180–82; Ernst, 282–83; Caragounis, *Mysterion,* 157), then so far from the incorporative sense of "in Christ" being entirely absent from Ephesians, it could be argued that the author has in fact extended the scope of Pauline usage, both backwards to embrace inclusion in some sense in Christ's preexistence and forwards to make explicit what is only implicit in Col 3:1, namely, inclusion in Christ's exaltation (cf. also Caragounis, *Mysterion,* 158).

4 καθὼς ἐξελέξατο ἡμᾶς ἐν αὐτῷ πρὸ καταβολῆς κόσμου, "even as he chose us in him before the foundation of the world." For the force of καθώς see the comments under *Form/Structure/Setting.* In elaborating on and grounding the thematic statement of v 3 the great theme of God's electing purpose is introduced. The writer asserts that God has blessed believers both because and to the extent that he elected them. The number and variety of words used in this passage to describe God's purpose is impressive: ἐξελέξατο, "chose" (v 4);

προορίσας, "predestined," εὐδοκία, "good pleasure," θέλημα, "will" (v 5); θέλημα, εὐδοκία, προέθετο, "purposed" (v 9); ἐκληρώθημεν, "appointed," προορισθέντες, "predestined," πρόθεσις, "plan," βουλή, "purpose," θέλημα (v 11). God's sovereign purpose in choosing out a people for himself is of course a familiar idea in the OT (e.g., Deut 7:6–8; 14:2), which witnesses to Israel's consciousness of God's choice of her in the midst of the twists and turns in her historical fortunes. God had chosen Abraham so that in him the nations of the earth would be blessed, and Israel's election was not for her own self-indulgence but for the blessing of the nations: it was a privilege but also a summons to service. Christian believers also had this consciousness of being chosen to be the people of God. The new element is signaled by the ἐν αὐτῷ phrase. Their sense of God's gracious choice of them was inextricably interwoven with their sense of belonging to Christ. God's design for them to be his people had been effected in and through Christ. They saw him as God's Chosen One (see below on "in the Beloved," 1:6). Indeed, Paul in Gal 3 treats Christ as in a sense fulfilling Israel's election. Christ is the offspring of Abraham *par excellence* (3:16), and in Christ the blessing of Abraham has come to the Gentiles (3:14) so that they too, because they are Christ's, are Abraham's offspring (3:29). The notion of being chosen in Christ here in Ephesians is likely then to include the idea of incorporation into Christ as the representative on whom God's gracious decision was focused. In respect to that merciful decision of love, which governs God's plan for his creation, the believing community is aware of its solidarity with Christ. It is by explicitly linking the notion of election to that of being "in Christ" that Ephesians takes further the discussion of election found in the undisputed Pauline letters.

God's choice of his people in Christ is said to have taken place "before the foundation of the world." This phrase indicates an element in the thinking about election which cannot be found in the OT and occurs only later in Jewish literature, e.g., *Joseph and Asenath* 8.9 (A); *Midr. Ps.* 74.1; *Midr. Ps.* 93.3; *Gen. Rab.* 1.5 (cf. also Hofius, ZNW 61 [1971] 125–27). Elsewhere in the NT the phrase "before the foundation of the world" is used of God's love for Christ (John 17:24) and his purpose for Christ (1 Pet 1:20), but in regard to believers passages elsewhere in the Pauline corpus provide the closest parallels. In 2 Thess 2:13 the best reading is probably "from the beginning" and its best interpretation is probably as a reference to God's choice from the beginning of time. In 2 Tim 1:9 grace is said to have been given to believers before eternal times, while in Rom 8:29 the prefix in προγινώσκειν, "to foreknow," is usually held to indicate that God's electing knowledge of believers precedes not simply their knowledge of him but the creation of the world. In comparison with Rom 8:28–30 and its eschatological focus, the language of Eph 1:4, by making the pretemporal aspect of election explicit, sets salvation in protological perspective.

Such language functions to give believers assurance of God's purposes for them. Its force is that God's choice of them was a free decision not dependent on temporal circumstances but rooted in the depth of his nature. To say that election in Christ took place before the foundation of the world is to underline that it was provoked not by historical contingency or human merit, but solely by God's sovereign grace. It is the notion of preexistence which makes this formulation possible. If God's election of believers took place before the foundation of the world *in Christ*, this could well presuppose the existence of Christ before the foundation of the world (cf. Col 1:15, 16). Schlier (49) speaks of the Christian adaptation of the Jewish theologoumenon of the preexistence not only of the Messiah but also of the people of salvation, but there are grave difficulties with dating the evidence for either concept in Jewish writings before 70 C.E. (cf. J. D. G. Dunn, *Christology in the Making* [London: SCM, 1980] 70–82; Hofius, *ZNW* 62 [1971] 123–28). Probably then the notion of the election of believers in Christ has been combined with that of the preexistence of Christ. This does not imply the preexistence of the Church, an idea which can be found later in early Christian writings (cf. *2 Clem.* 14.1; Herm. *Vis.* 1.1.6; 2.4.1). It is not the Church but the choice of the Church which precedes the foundation of the world. So if there is to be any talk of the preexistence of the Church, it can only be of "ideal" preexistence, i.e., in the mind or counsel of God (cf. Barth, 112; Gnilka, 70, 71; Hamerton-Kelly, *Preexistence, Wisdom, and the Son of Man* [Cambridge: Cambridge University Press, 1973] 180–82).

It is significant that the language of election before the foundation of the world occurs here in the context of thanksgiving (cf. also 1 Thess 1:4; 2:13). It is part of an expression of gratitude for God's inexplicable grace, not a logical deduction about the destiny of individuals based on the immutability of God's decrees. And, unlike the language of Rom 9:13, 18, 22, Eph 1:4 provokes absolutely no speculation about the negative side of election, reprobation. Overwhelmed by the blessing of being chosen in Christ, the writer does not attempt to find explanations but can only praise the God who is the source of such blessing.

εἶναι ἡμᾶς ἁγίους καὶ ἀμώμους κατενώπιον αὐτοῦ ἐν ἀγάπῃ, "to be holy and blameless before him in love." God's choice of a people in Christ has a goal—that they should exhibit a particular quality of life, described here in terms of holiness and love. For the reasons for connecting "in love" with the goal of election, see the discussion under *Form/Structure/Setting* above. In Phil 1:9, 10 and 1 Thess 3:12, 13 Paul prays for these same features to characterize believers' lives—love in the present and holiness and blamelessness in view of the Parousia. The actual wording of the latter qualities in Ephesians, ἁγίους καὶ ἀμώμους κατενώπιον αὐτοῦ, is taken from Col 1:22, where, as here, there is no clear connection with the Parousia and the words describe believers' present lives. If ἅγιος in 1:1 denoted primarily status, here in 1:4 it indicates the moral condition that belongs to such a status. It is closely connected with ἄμωμος and both have a cultic background. That which is separated to God, such as a sacrificial animal (cf. LXX Exod 29:37, 38; Num 6:14; 19:2) must be without defect. Already in the OT such terminology is also used for ethical purity (e.g., LXX Ps 14:2; 17:24). In Eph 1:4 holiness, blamelessness, and love are complementary terms. On its negative side, holiness is the absence of moral defect or sin, i.e., blamelessness, while, on its positive side, as moral perfection, it displays itself in love which is the fulfillment of God's will. Moral separation from the sinful world and active love are qualities which, in fact, provide a good summary of the ethical exhortation to follow in the second part of this letter. In this reference a theocentric perspective predominates, for a life of holiness, blamelessness, and love has its source in and is a response to the gracious election of God and is lived "before him," that is, conscious that God's presence and God's approval are one's ultimate environment.

5, 6 προορίσας ἡμᾶς εἰς υἱοθεσίαν διὰ Ἰησοῦ Χριστοῦ εἰς αὐτόν, "he has predestined us for adoption as his own sons through Jesus Christ." For the way in which εἰς αὐτόν continues the theocentric viewpoint of v 4 see the discussion under *Notes* above. The sonship to which believers are predestined has God as its goal. Believers bless God the Father, because his choice of them is intended to bring them into a relationship with himself. This theocentric emphasis is maintained throughout vv 5, 6. προορίσας, "predestined," also reemphasizes God's initiative in salvation and develops the notion of God's choice from v 4. It focuses on the divine decision which makes sonship the goal for those who are elect. God's foreordination is celebrated in a hymnic context in the Qumran writings (cf. 1QH 15.13–22). In Paul προορίζειν is used in 1 Cor 2:7 and in Rom 8:29, 30 where it is also connected with the theme of sonship.

The term υἱοθεσία, "adoption as sons," is a Pauline one found also in Rom 8:15, 23; 9:4; and Gal 4:5. It is a term taken from Greco-Roman law where it referred to the adoption as sons of those who were not so by birth. The word can be found in second century B.C.E. inscriptions and in the first century B.C.E. writings of Diodorus Siculus and Nicolaus Damascenus. A well-to-do but childless adult who wanted an heir would adopt a male, usually at an age other than in infancy and frequently a slave, to be his son. In Paul this is applied to the privileged new relationship believers have with God, but must also be seen against the OT background of Israel's relationship with God. Indeed in Rom 9:4 adoption as sons is listed among Israel's privileges by Paul. It becomes a corresponding privilege of the Church also (cf. Rom 9:26; also 2 Cor 6:18). The relationship awaits completion (Rom 8:23) but has the present witness of the Spirit in the meantime (Rom 8:14, 15). Ephesians emphasizes that by God's free predestining choice he adopts believers, taking them into his family and intimate fellowship, establishing them as his children and heirs. It stresses that this privileged relationship of knowing God as Father for those who at one time were "sons of disobedience," "children of wrath" (cf. 2:2, 3) is through the agency of Christ (διὰ Ἰησοῦ Χριστοῦ). Such an assertion sums up the thought of passages such as Gal 3:26; 4:4, 5; and Rom 8:29 that link believers' reception of adoption as sons with the life and work of Christ as God's Son. Sonship is a benefit of the salvation of the end-time and it comes to those included in the Son through whom that salvation has been inaugurated—cf. also "in the Beloved" (1:6). (On adoption, see further T. Whaling, "Adoption," *PTR* 21 [1923] 223–35; H. J. Flowers, "Adoption and Redemption in the Beloved," *ExpTim* 39 [1927–28] 16–21; W. H. Russell, "NT Adoption—Graeco-Roman or Semitic," *JBL* 71 [1952] 233–34; D. J. Theron, "Adoption in the Pauline Corpus," *EvQ* 28 [1956] 6–14; M. W. Schoenberg, "The Adoptive Sonship of Israel," *AER* 143 [1960] 261–73; "υἱοθεσία: The Word and the Institution," *Scr* 15 [1963] 115–23; "St. Paul's Notion of the Adoptive Sonship of Christians," *Thomist* 28 [1964] 51–75; F. Lyall, "Roman Law in the Writings of Paul: Adoption," *JBL* 88 [1969] 458–66; E. Schweizer, "υἱός, υἱοθεσία," *TDNT* 8 [1972] 334–99).

κατὰ τὴν εὐδοκίαν τοῦ θελήματος αὐτοῦ, "in accordance with his good pleasure and will." This is one of the instances of the redundancy of concepts in this writer's style. εὐδοκία, "good pleasure," corresponds to the Hebrew רצון, rāṣôn, and highlights God's will as his good pleasure or favor, while θέλημα, "will," in the LXX most frequently translates חפץ ḥēpeṣ, and in this context can be seen as stressing God's will as his active resolve, his redemptive purpose. The two terms are in close proximity again in 1:9. A similar redundancy can be found in the language of the Qumran writings: cf. CD 3.15 וחפצי רצונו (wḥpṣy rṣwnw), "and the desires of his will." Here in Eph 1:5 it serves the function of reemphasizing that Christian existence as sonship not only has God as its goal but has him as its source, for it is grounded in him and is in accordance with his sovereign good pleasure and gracious resolution to redeem men and women.

εἰς ἔπαινον δόξης τῆς χάριτος αὐτοῦ, "to the praise of the glory of his grace." This phrase is similar to those in vv 12 and 14, but here the emphasis is not simply on God's glory as the object of praise but on his grace. The addition of this concept provides an instance of the combination of genitives which is characteristic of the liturgical style of the letter. Neither this expression nor the closely related ones in vv 12 and 14 can be found in the undisputed Paulines, where the closest parallel is the phrase in Phil 1:11 εἰς δόξαν καὶ ἔπαινον θεοῦ. Here the phrase takes up again the theocentric note of the *berakah*. The goal of believers' predestination as sons and daughters has already been said to be εἰς αὐτόν but now it is also εἰς ἔπαινον δόξης τῆς χάριτος αὐτοῦ. The redemption, which originated with God, has his own glorification as its end. The predestination, which is the product of God's grace, resounds to the praise of the glory of that grace.

τῆς χάριτος αὐτοῦ ἧς ἐχαρίτωσεν ἡμᾶς, "his grace with which he has highly favored us." The genitive case of the relative in this clause is to be explained by the fact that the relative can often be attracted to the case of its antecedent (cf. *BDF* para. 294 [2]). That the noun is followed by its cognate verb (literally "his grace with which he has graced us") obviously serves to emphasize the concept involved and is a phenomenon which occurs again in this letter in 1:19, 20; 2:4; and 4:1. χαριτοῦν, the cognate verb used here, occurs elsewhere in the NT only in Luke 1:28. The blessing of salvation which is the subject of the whole *berakah* can be equated with the notion of grace highlighted in this verse. As in Eph 2:5, 8, grace is seen as the principle of God's redemptive activity which permeates it through and through. And so intensively does God favor believers with his grace that both their existence and their worship become a paean of praise to the splendor of that grace.

ἐν τῷ ἠγαπημένῳ, "in the Beloved," expresses how this grace has come to believers and continues the idea already found in ἐν Χριστῷ (1:3), ἐν αὐτῷ (1:4), and διὰ Ἰησοῦ Χριστοῦ (1:5). This variation uses a term which seems to have been understood as a title for Christ. J. A. Robinson (229–33) and Schlier (56) believe it was a messianic title current among the Jews during the first century C.E., though neither can offer any hard evidence for its pre-Christian usage in such a way. It is safe to say that it became a messianic title among early Christians (cf. also Ign., *Smyrn.* inscr.; *Barn.* 3.6; 4.3, 8). In the LXX it was used of Israel where it translates the hypocoristicon or "pet name" ישרון, yĕšurûn (Deut 32:15; 33:5, 26; Isa 44:2), and more generally designates Israel as God's beloved people (Deut 33:12; Isa 5:1, 7; Jer 11:15; 12:7). In the Pauline corpus this designation for Israel can be transferred to believers, frequently in close association with the concept of election, cf. 1 Thess 1:4; 2 Thess 2:13; Rom 9:25; Col 3:12. Ephesians reflects a transference of the title to Christ as well as to Christians, a transference no doubt facilitated by the closeness of this title to the designation of Jesus as the beloved Son prominent in early Christian tradition—cf. Mark 1:11 par.; Mark 9:7 par., ὁ υἱός μου ὁ ἀγαπητός; also Mark 12:6; Luke 20:13. Ephesians appears to be in indirect contact with this tradition through Col 1:13—τοῦ υἱοῦ τῆς ἀγάπης αὐτοῦ, on which it is a variation. In any case the title makes clear Christ's status as God's specially chosen one, his beloved Son. Verse 6 then confirms the thought found earlier, that God's predestining choice of believers to be his sons and daughters is inextricably tied to Christ's being his chosen one and that their experience of this grace is through their being included in the one who is the beloved Son *par excellence*. Being highly favored with grace means, for the believing community, participation in that divine love with which the Father favored the Son, though the community's participation in this relationship is through adoption (cf. v 5).

7, 8 ἐν ᾧ ἔχομεν τὴν ἀπολύτρωσιν διὰ τοῦ αἵματος αὐτοῦ, τὴν ἄφεσιν τῶν παραπτωμάτων, "in whom we have redemption through his blood, the forgiveness of trespasses." With these words the grace with which believers have been highly favored in the Beloved is elaborated on in terms of some of the present benefits of salvation which they have in him. In fact these words, together with the last phrase of the preceding verse, stand in very close relation to Col 1:13, 14. Against Mitton (52) it is not true to say that "the whole sentence is taken word for word" from that passage. In taking up the language of Colossians the author of Ephesians makes his own variations. We have already noted this in regard to the Christological title. To the notion of redemption is added the phrase "through his blood." This is not found in Col 1:14, although "through the blood of his cross" does occur in Col 1:20 where it appears to be a Pauline addition to the Christological hymn. Finally, whereas Col 1:14 speaks of τὴν ἄφεσιν τῶν ἁμαρτιῶν, Eph 1:7 substitutes a different word for sins, having τὴν ἄφεσιν τῶν παραπτωμάτων. The liturgical language from Colossians, with its baptismal connotations (cf. Lohse, *Colossians*, 40), is therefore taken up in a modified form in the Ephesian *berakah*.

ἀπολύτρωσις, "redemption," is a rare word in nonbiblical Greek and appears only once in the LXX, in Dan 4:34, yet it occurs ten times in the NT, seven of these in the Pauline corpus. The Pauline concept of redemption has its roots in the OT, where in particular the divine act of deliverance from Egypt was often described in terms of redemption (cf. Deut 7:8; 9:26; 13:5; 15:15; 24:18; 1 Chr 17:21). The term's general significance as "deliverance, liberation" is clear. There is a dispute among scholars, however, whether it also has the more specific connotation of the payment of a ransom. In regard to Eph 1:7 some insist this connotation is present (e.g., L. Morris, *The Apostolic Preaching of the Cross*, 3rd ed. [London: Tyndale Press, 1965] 42; Bruce, 31; I. H. Marshall, "The Development of the Concept of Redemption in the New Testament," *Reconciliation and Hope*, FS L. Morris, ed. R. J. Banks [Exeter: Paternoster Press; Grand Rapids: Eerdmans, 1974] 165), while others hold that the term simply signifies deliverance (e.g., Abbott, 11–13; J. A. Robinson, 148; F. Büchsel, "λύω κτλ.," *TDNT* 4 [1967] 354–55; D. Hill, *Greek Words and Hebrew Meanings* [Cambridge: Cambridge University Press, 1967] 73–74; Caird, 36–37; Gnilka, 75). It is true that often in their LXX usage λυτροῦσθαι and its cognates retain the sense of release through paying back. This sense is also frequently clear in the nonbiblical usages of ἀπολύτρωσις, among which are references to the manumission of slaves which involved payment. In addition, Paul does speak of believers as having been bought with a price in 1 Cor 6:20; 7:23; and he uses the verb ἐξαγοράζειν in Gal 3:13; 4:5, in which this idea is also present. On the other hand, many of the LXX usages of the redemption word-group are references to deliverance from danger and especially deliverance from Egyptian bondage and Babylonian exile where no notion of a ransom price is involved. The use of ἀπολύτρωσις in LXX Dan 4:34 does not contain this idea, and it would be natural for Paul to see parallels between God's acts of liberation in the OT and his act of liberation in Christ and use this term in that sense. Certainly some of the uses of ἀπολύτρωσις in the NT refer to God's final eschatological deliverance in Christ where notions of a ransom payment are not present and have to be read into the text (cf. Luke 21:28; Rom 8:23; and the other two occurrences in Eph 1:14; 4:30). It is hard to decide this issue, but it appears to be overdogmatic to insist on ransom connotations for all uses of ἀπολύτρωσις in the NT. It is safer to see these only where they are explicit in the context. They do not appear to be explicit in Col 1:14, which lies behind the Ephesian reference. As we have noted, in taking this up, the writer has added a reference to Christ's blood, and some see this as making the ransom price connotations of redemption clear. As elsewhere in the NT, the blood of Christ signifies his violently taken life and stands for his atoning death (cf. J. Behm, "αἷμα," *TDNT* 1 [1964] 172–76; L. Morris, *The Apostolic Preaching of the Cross*, 3rd ed. [London: Tyndale Press, 1965] 112–28). Strictly speaking, however, διὰ τοῦ αἵματος αὐτοῦ introduces a new metaphor from sacrifice, and διά with the genitive is not used to express cost but has instrumental force. The author of Ephesians has tied down God's deliverance of his people to Christ's work in history by making clear that the means of redemption was Christ's sacrificial death. To be sure, the addition of this sacrificial imagery shows the costly nature of redemption, but this is not the same as insisting that it was actually intended to signify the ransom price.

The forgiveness of trespasses is in apposition to "redemption through his blood" and so depicts the primary way in which believers experience their liberation at present. They can be assured of the cancellation of their offenses against God and thereby of a restored relationship with him. ἄφεσις, "forgiveness," is a term not found in the undisputed Paulines, and indeed Paul does not speak of forgiveness as such (for an attempted explanation of this cf. E. P. Sanders, *Paul and Palestinian Judaism*, 499–501). Too much should not be made of this, however, since forgiveness is implicit in two of Paul's major themes, justification and reconciliation, and the phenomenon should, therefore, certainly not be made a basis for driving a wedge between Colossians and Ephesians, where the concept does occur, and the genuine Paul. Connected with this discussion is the frequent assertion that while the genuine Paul speaks of sin as a power in the singular, Ephesians speaks of sinful deeds in the plural (e.g., Ernst, 274). The dictum is only partially true, however. It is significant that the notion of sin as a power or force is missing from Ephesians, but mention of sins in the plural is not lacking in the genuine letters of Paul. It can be found not only in his use of traditional Christian material (cf. 1 Cor 15:3; Gal 1:4; Rom 4:25) but also in his own formulations (cf. Gal 3:19; Rom 5:16; 7:5; 1 Cor 15:7; 2 Cor 5:19). Here in 1:7 the plural is παραπτώματα rather than ἁμαρτίαι, which is used in every other NT reference to the forgiveness of sins, and this term has the connotation of trespass, transgression, and act of disobedience (*contra* Barth, 83–84, it makes no difference that Gentiles would not themselves have defined their actions with reference to God's law).

κατὰ τὸ πλοῦτος τῆς χάριτος αὐτοῦ ἧς ἐπερίσσευσεν εἰς ἡμᾶς, "in accordance with the richness of his grace which he lavished upon us." The reference in v 7a to the present benefit of redemption which believers experience is framed by the mention of grace. We have seen the way in which grace was highlighted in v 6, and now again the recipients of the letter are not allowed to forget that their redemption is in accord with the full scope of God's grace. The terms τὸ πλοῦτος and ἐπερίσσευσεν with their connotations of abundance and extravagance help to make this notion of grace emphatic, while at the same time leaving the impression that words fail in attempting to describe the inexhaustible resources of God's giving (cf. also 2:7—τὸ ὑπερβάλλον πλοῦτος τῆς χάριτος αὐτοῦ). For the use of περισσεύειν with the concept of grace in Paul, cf. 2 Cor 9:8; Rom 5:15, 20.

ἐν πάσῃ σοφίᾳ καὶ φρονήσει, "with all wisdom and insight." God's lavish grace not only provides redemption but also supplies, along with this, all necessary wisdom and insight to understand and live in the light of what he has done in Christ and its implications (elaborated in vv 9, 10). Reasons for taking this phrase with what precedes rather than as qualifying the following participle have been given above under *Form/Structure/Setting*. The phrase is a variation on the language of Col 1:9, ἐν πάσῃ σοφίᾳ καὶ συνέσει πνευματικῇ, which uses a common LXX combination (cf. Exod 31:3; 35:31; 1 Chr 22:12; 2 Chr 1:10–12; Isa 11:2). Here φρόνησις substitutes for the second part and is itself a term which can be found in close association with σοφία in the LXX (cf. Prov 1:2; 3:19; 8:1; 10:23; Jer 10:12; Dan 2:21; 4 Macc 1:18). Aristotle (*Eth. Nic.* 6.6.7) distinguishes σοφία as more general intellectual understanding and φρόνησις as related to more practical application, but in biblical Greek such a distinction cannot be maintained and the terms function synonymously. Here in Ephesians we have noted that it is characteristic of the writer's style to use two or more words of similar meaning when one would do, and so it is likely that "wisdom and insight" constitute a hendiadys. πάσῃ in this phrase is part of the profuseness of the writer's style (cf. 1:3) but also, as did the ἐν πάσῃ σοφίᾳ of Col 1:9, 28; 3:16, speaks to the background of syncretistic religious interests current in Asia Minor. Paul had reminded the Colossians that, in contrast to the teaching infiltrating the community, which only had the "appearance of wisdom" (2:23), all the treasures of wisdom and knowledge were hidden in Christ (2:3). The force of Eph 1:8 is similar. Whatever wisdom or insight might be sought or might be on offer, there is no genuine wisdom or insight that is not included among God's gifts of grace. Again, rather than having to be achieved through human effort, mystical technique, or ascetic rigor, such wisdom and insight are available simply through the generosity of God's grace.

9, 10 These verses, with the third major aorist participle at their head and with their statement about the mystery of God's will, constitute an important and much discussed part of the eulogy. To see their meaning it is essential to recognize the overall flow of the syntax before analyzing their individual components. In particular it should be recognized that the long prepositional expression κατὰ τὴν εὐδοκίαν . . . τῶν καιρῶν qualifies the aorist participle with its notion of making known the mystery and that the formulation beginning with the aorist middle infinitive ἀνακεφαλαιώσασθαι, which then follows, is appositional to and explanatory of the earlier τὸ μυστήριον τοῦ θελήματος αὐτοῦ. In other words, it is not until v 10b, with the thought of the summing up of all things in Christ, that the content of the mystery of God's will mentioned in v 9a is expressed (cf. also Schlier, 62; Gnilka, 79; Caragounis, *Mysterion,* 95).

γνωρίσας ἡμῖν τὸ μυστήριον τοῦ θελήματος αὐτοῦ, "he has made known to us the mystery of his will." There is a clear link with the last part of v 8 in that the wisdom and insight believers have been given have to do in large part with the ability to understand the mystery of God's will and this has been made possible from God's side because he has chosen to make it known. Against its Semitic background the terminology of "making known a mystery" refers to the disclosure of a formerly hidden secret. However, even in its usage in apocalyptic contexts, μυστήριον need not always be reduced to the notion of a mere secret, but can also carry with it an echo of its original force in connection with the Greek mystery cults—the connotation of the mysterious, that which is beyond ordinary human comprehension (cf. Caragounis, *Mysterion,* 1–34) or of esoteric religious knowledge (cf. A. E. Harvey, "The Use of Mystery Language in the Bible," *JTS* 81 [1980] 320–36). The usage of μυστήριον in LXX Daniel, where it translates the Aramaic רז, *rāz,* forms a major aspect of its Semitic background (cf. Dan 2:18, 19, 27–30, 47) and provides some parallels with its use in Ephesians, since in Daniel it refers to God's purpose, which is a unified plan with eschatological and cosmic dimensions (cf. also Caragounis, *Mysterion,* 134–35). "Mystery" occurs frequently in other apocalyptic writings (e.g., *2. Apoc. Bar.* 81.4; *4 Ezra* 14:5; *1 Enoch* 51.3; 103.2; 104.10) and in the Qumran literature with the terms רז (*rz*), "mystery," and סוד (*swd*), "marvel," (e.g., 1QpHab 7.4, 8, 13; 1QM 3.8; 16.9; 1QS 3.21–23; 4.18; 11.34; 1QH 7.27; 10.4; 11.9, 16). In one place there is a phrase which comes close to Ephesians' "mystery of his will"—לרזי חפצו (*lrzy ḥpṣw*) "the mysteries of his good pleasure" (1QH Frag 3.7). In apocalyptic writings "mystery" usually refers to an event which will only be revealed at the end of history, although since it is already prepared in heaven the seer can have knowledge of it at present (e.g. *4 Ezra* 14:5; *1 Enoch* 9.6; 103.2). At Qumran, however, as here in Ephesians, "mystery" can refer to an event which has already been realized in the community. In 1QS 11.5–8, for example, the community's participation in the angelic assembly is seen as one of God's marvelous mysteries (cf. also R. E. Brown, *The Semitic Background of the Term "Mystery" in the New Testament* [Philadelphia: Fortress Press, 1968] 22–29; H. W. Kuhn, *Enderwartung und gegenwärtiges Heil* [Göttingen: Vandenhoeck & Ruprecht, 1966] 166–75; Gnilka, 78).

Paul uses μυστήριον in a variety of ways. It is found in the plural in 1 Cor

4:1; 13:2; 14:2, and in the singular, but with differing references, in 2 Thess 2:7; 1 Cor 2:1 (where the manuscript evidence is disputed); 2:7; 15:51; Rom 11:25; 16:25 (in all probability a later addition). In Colossians the use of μυστήριον to refer to the heart of Paul's message, God's activity in Christ (cf. 1 Cor 2:7), becomes constant (cf. 1:26, 27; 2:2; 4:3), and it is this reference to the eschatological fulfillment of God's plan of salvation in Christ that has influenced the way the writer to the Ephesians speaks of "mystery" here and in 3:3, 4, 9; 5:32 and 6:19. 1:9, 10; 3:3–10; and 5:32 all unfold different aspects of the one mystery of what God has done in Christ. In the various "mystery" cults, which would have been familiar to the recipients of this letter, the common characteristic was possession of a secret or of secrets, which were made known only to initiates, giving them great spiritual privileges unavailable to others without this knowledge. In the *berakah* of Ephesians the writer sees the Christian community as a highly privileged group also. Believers can bless God that he has disclosed his secret to them and that they have been given wisdom and insight, and yet this secret is one that can be proclaimed openly (6:19) and one that has a scope that goes far beyond the community or any exclusive claims it might be tempted to make for itself, as 1:10b will indicate. (For further discussion of μυστήριον and its background see J. A. Robinson, 234–40; G. Bornkamm, "μυστήριον," *TDNT* 4 [1967] 802–28; K. G. Kuhn, "The Epistle to the Ephesians," 118–19; J. Coppens, "'Mystery' in the Theology of St. Paul and Its Parallels at Qumran," *Paul and Qumran*, ed. J. Murphy-O'Connor [London: Chapman, 1968] 132–58; F. Mussner, "Contributions," 159–63; R. E. Brown, *The Semitic Background of the Term "Mystery" in the New Testament* [Philadelphia: Fortress Press, 1968]; Caragounis, *Mysterion*, esp. 1–34, 117–35; A. E. Harvey, "The Use of Mystery Language in the Bible," *JTS* 81 [1980] 320–36.)

κατὰ τὴν εὐδοκίαν αὐτοῦ ἣν προέθετο ἐν αὐτῷ, "in accordance with his good pleasure which he purposed in him (Christ)." This reaffirms for God's activity of disclosing the mystery of his will what v 5 had asserted of his activity of predestinating believers to adoption as sons and daughters, namely, that such activities are in line with God's sovereign and eternal purpose. θέλημα from the previous clause in v 9 and εὐδοκία in this expression, in fact, repeat the terminology of v 5, while προέθετο further reinforces the notion of God's plan or purpose. Some (e.g., Schlier, 62; Gnilka, 78) believe the προ- prefix to have temporal force and therefore the verb to refer to God's pretemporal resolve as in 1:4. No doubt προέθετο does refer to God's eternal intent, but such a meaning has to be derived from contextual considerations rather than the form of the verb, as its use in Rom 1:13 indicates. God's carefully designed strategy to make known the mystery, like that mystery itself, has always had its focus in Christ—ἐν αὐτῷ.

εἰς οἰκονομίαν τοῦ πληρώματος τῶν καιρῶν, "for the administration of the fullness of time." The purpose of God to make known the mystery of his will embraces history and its ordering. οἰκονομία can refer to (1) the act of administering, (2) that which is administered, an arrangement or plan, and (3) the office or role of an administrator, a person's stewardship; it is often difficult to decide which nuance is in view with a particular usage. In the Greek world οἰκονομία was regularly used for God's ordering and administration of the universe.

Here in 1:10 it also appears to have that active force (cf. also 3:9), while elsewhere (cf. 3:2; 1 Cor 4:1; 9:17; Col 1:25) it refers to Paul's apostolic role and office. In the Pauline corpus it is frequently used in close connection with μυστήριον (cf. 1 Cor 4:1; Col 1:25–27; Eph 3:2–4, 9). Later in patristic writings οἰκονομία was used to refer to the divine plan or economy of salvation and had close associations with covenant terminology (cf. J. Reumann, "*Oikonomia* = 'Covenant': Terms for *Heilsgeschichte* in Early Christian Usage," *NovT* 3 [1959] 282–92), but in regard to Eph 1:10 "one must be cautious here not to read into οἰκονομία too much emphasis on *Heilsplan* or some patristic plan of salvation sense" and to stay with the active meaning of administration or ordering (J. Reumann, "Οἰκονομία-Terms in Paul in Comparison with Lucan *Heilsgeschichte*," *NTS* 13 [1966–67] 164; cf. also Abbott, 17; Robinson, 32; Schlier, 63; Gnilka, 79 n. 4; Barth, 86–88; *contra* W. Tooley, "Stewards of God: An Examination of the Terms ΟΙΚΟΝΟΜΟΣ and ΟΙΚΟΝΟΜΙΑ in the New Testament," *SJT* 19 [1966] 81, who sees οἰκονομία in Eph 1:10 as God's master plan and simply synonymous with μυστήριον).

That which is being administered is, literally, the fullness of the times (plural). οἱ καιροί refers to periods of time and the whole expression τὸ πλήρωμα τῶν καιρῶν reflects the view, found in some apocalypses, of a sequence of periods of time under God's direction (cf. LXX Dan 2:21; 4:37; Tob 14:5; 4 Ezra 4:37; *2 Apoc. Bar.* 40.3; cf. also 1QS 4.18; 1QM 14.14; 1QpHab 7.2, 13). τὸ πλήρωμα in particular reflects the notion that this sequence of time will come to its climax, to its full measure. In this way the expression can be seen to belong to the Christian eschatological terminology found elsewhere in the NT (e.g., Mark 1:15; John 7:8; Acts 1:7; Gal 4:4; 1 Thess 5:1; 1 Tim 6:15). Barth's paraphrase "days of fulfillment" (88–89) conveys something of this flavor. God has ordered history in such a way that it culminates in the achievement of his purpose, as the various eras of history are crowned and completed by a climactic point at which the disclosure of the mystery of his will takes place. This interpretation is in sharp contrast to the highly unlikely view of Lindemann (*Aufhebung*, 95–96), who claims that τὸ πλήρωμα τῶν καιρῶν refers not to the climax of history but to the suspension of temporal categories, the cessation of time (see the title of his monograph *Die Aufhebung der Zeit*). He asserts, without providing evidence, that πλήρωμα refers to a point beyond time, and, operating with a sharp distinction between χρόνος as "duration of time" and καιρός as "point of time" (a distinction which J. Barr, *Biblical Words for Time* [London: SCM, 1969] 44 has clearly shown not to hold), claims that the concept of time and its duration is of no importance for Ephesians. This is to ignore completely the apocalyptic background of the terminology of this verse, its context in early Christian eschatology, and the continuity between Ephesians and Paul's gospel.

ἀνακεφαλαιώσασθαι τὰ πάντα ἐν τῷ Χριστῷ, τὰ ἐπὶ τοῖς οὐρανοῖς καὶ τὰ ἐπὶ τῆς γῆς ἐν αὐτῷ, "to sum up all things in Christ, things in heaven and things on earth in him." We now reach the main point of the clause which begins with γνωρίσας. The mystery which has been disclosed to believers in accordance with God's purpose for history is his summing up of all things in Christ. It must be remembered that ἀνακεφαλαιώσασθαι is derived from κεφάλαιον, not from κεφαλή. κεφάλαιον refers to the main point, the sum or summary (cf. Acts 22:28; Heb 8:1), and ἀνακεφαλαιοῦσθαι has as its basic meaning "to sum up" or "to summarize." It was often used in a rhetorical context to refer to summing up or recapitulating an argument (cf. Quintilian 6.1; Aristotle, *Fragments* 123). Paul uses it with the sense of "to sum up" in Rom 13:9 where love is thought of as the comprehensive command which integrates the others, bringing them together under one focal point. In Eph 1:10 by analogy Christ exercises a similar function with respect to the cosmos. Since later in the letter Christ's role in relation to the cosmos is seen in terms of headship (1:22), many have used this imagery for their exegesis of 1:10 and elucidation of ἀνακεφαλαιώσασθαι. For Schlier (65; idem, "κεφαλή, ἀνακεφαλαιόομαι," *TDNT* 3 [1965] 681–82) the meaning of 1:10 involves the subjection of the cosmos to Christ as its head, while Barth (89–92) translates the verb as "to be comprehended under one head." This procedure has rightly been criticized by J. Barr, *The Semantics of Biblical Language* [Oxford: University Press, 1961] 237–38 and by Mussner, *Christus*, 65. It is both legitimate and illuminating to place the thought of 1:10 in the context of the whole letter and link it with other passages in which a relation between the cosmos and Christ is posited, but this should be done after 1:10 has been exegeted on its own terms. 1:10 then refers to the summing up and bringing together of the diverse elements of the cosmos in Christ as the focal point.

The concept of "summing up" involves recapitulation, as points already made are drawn together in a conclusion, and it is likely that this is something of the force of the prefix ἀνα-, indicating a restoration of harmony with Christ as the point of reintegration (cf. also Mussner, *Christus*, 66). The summing up of all things in Christ means the unifying of the cosmos or its direction toward a common goal. In line with this letter's close links with Colossians, a similar thought about Christ and the cosmos had been expressed in the Colossians hymn in terms of reconciliation and with explicit soteriological connotations (Col 1:20). Both passages appear to presuppose that the cosmos had been plunged into disintegration on account of sin and that it is God's purpose to restore its original harmony in Christ (cf. also Mussner, *Christus*, 66–67; Gnilka, 80; *pace* Caird, 38). The notion of recapitulation which ἀνακεφαλαιώσασθαι involves was developed further by the church fathers: cf. Irenaeus, *Adv. Haer.* 3.18.1; 5.29.2 (cf. also McHugh, "Reconsideration," 304–7) and Origen, *De Principiis* 2.8.4–8; 3.6.6. For a listing of a variety of the interpretations this verb has received in the commentaries, see S. Hanson, *Unity*, 123–25. Once again our own interpretation is in complete disagreement with that of Lindemann (*Aufhebung*, 96–97), who sees ἀνακεφαλαιώσασθαι as related to the Gnostic view of entry into the *pleroma*, and thus as a reference to the dissolution of the cosmos and an equivalent in cosmic terms to the cessation of time he believes is in view in the earlier part of the verse. Such an interpretation does not take seriously the letter's close associations with Colossians, lacks clear supporting lexical evidence, and posits a total break with Paul's gospel with its hope of the redemption, not the dissolution, of the created order (cf. Rom 8:18–23).

The divine purpose is to sum up all things ἐν Χριστῷ. The ἐν αὐτῷ phrase at the end of the verse after the elaboration of τὰ πάντα repeats this thought. Reasons for taking ἐν αὐτῷ with this verse rather than the next have been discussed under *Form/Structure/Setting* above. This thought could be taken in a general instrumental sense as "by means of the Christ event," or it could be that, as with the use of this phrase or its equivalent in 1:3, 4, 5, the more specific notion of representation is in view. Christ sums up the cosmos as its representative. God achieves his purpose for all things through what he accomplishes in the one person, Christ (*pace* Gnilka, 80, it is precisely because Christ is not identical with the cosmos that it could be said that it is summed up in him or that he represents it; cf. also S. Hanson, *Unity*, 125; Lindemann, *Aufhebung*, 98). Christ is the one in whom God chooses to sum up the universe, in whom he restores the harmony of the cosmos. Earlier, "in Christ" has functioned to indicate Christ's being the elect representative in whom believers are included, but now it can be seen that God's comprehensive purpose goes beyond simply humanity to embrace the whole created order. This part of the *berakah* helps believers to recognize that to be incorporated into God's gracious decision about Christ is also to be caught up in God's gracious purpose for a universe centered and reunited in Christ.

The elaboration τὰ ἐπὶ τοῖς οὐρανοῖς καὶ τὰ ἐπὶ τῆς γῆς indicates that we are right to take τὰ πάντα in its widest sense of all things and all beings, that is, the cosmos as a whole and not just humanity (*pace* Davies, *Paul*, 57; Mitton, *Ephesians*, 56–57). This twofold division of the universe was common in Jewish thought where created reality was seen as having two major parts (cf. Gen 1:1) and where heaven as the upper part of the cosmos was regarded as concealing a presently invisible created spiritual order (e.g., 2 Kgs 6:17; Job 1:6; Zech 3:1). For further discussion see the comments above on "in the heavenly realms" (1:3). Here τὰ ἐπὶ τοῖς οὐρανοῖς is a somewhat unusual phrase, since normally one expects ἐν rather than ἐπί when it is used (cf. Col 1:16, 20). Percy (*Probleme*, 181 n. 7) holds that the phrase has been influenced by the formula ἐν τοῖς ἐπουρανίοις, but it is more likely that C. F. D. Moule (*Idiom-Book*, 49) is correct in thinking that this "looks like a merely stylistic variation" on the part of this writer. The "things in heaven" include the spiritual forces, both good and evil, which compete for the allegiance of humanity, and their mention here particularly emphasizes the point, which will be made explicitly in 1:21, 22, that no hostile heavenly power can thwart God's purpose in Christ.

When, according to these verses, is the summing up of all things said to take place? The aorist tense of the infinitive cannot provide a definite answer at this point (*contra* Lindemann, *Aufhebung*, 96). That the mystery has already been disclosed to believers is also not in itself decisive (*contra* Lindemann, *Aufhebung*, 99), for what has been disclosed could be God's purpose for the future (cf. the future content of the mystery disclosed in Rom 11:25–27). Yet elsewhere in Colossians and Ephesians the content of the mystery does refer to a present reality (cf. Col 1:26, 27; 2:2; 4:3; Eph 3:3–6; 3:9, 10; 5:32; 6:19). This factor and the general emphasis on "realized eschatology" in the letter make it likely that from the writer's perspective the "summing up in Christ" has already taken place (cf. also Schnackenburg, 59–60). Certainly he sees believers as living in the climactic period when God is administrating the fullness of time (*contra* Mussner, *Christus*, 68, who sees this as still future and as a reference to the Parousia). Elsewhere in the letter it is Christ's exaltation in particular which is the focus for what God has already done as it affects the cosmos (cf. 1:20–23; 2:6; 4:8–10). S. Hanson (*Unity*, 126) sees the unity of the cosmos achieved through Christ's atoning work on the cross. This may be the emphasis of Colossians, but not of Ephesians. In Ephesians, as a result of Christ's exaltation, God has placed all things under Christ's feet and made him the head over all things (1:22) and Christ fills all things (1:23; 4:10), and these are notions which help one to understand more of what is involved in his summing up of all things. Thus, in the period of fulfillment, God has exalted Christ to heaven as cosmic Lord, thereby ensuring the inseparable connection between heaven and earth that enables both things in heaven and things on earth to be summed up in him. Against Caragounis (*Mysterion*, 144) there is no need to play this down and assert that ἀνακεφαλαιώσασθαι "is essentially a future concept." It is true that there is a tension between "already" and "not yet" in Ephesians in regard to Christ's rule over the powers (cf. 1:21 with 2:2 and 6:12, and cf. Caragounis, *Mysterion*, 145; Lincoln, *Paradise*, 166–68), yet here in the eulogy, in the context of worship, the perspective is one of realized eschatology as the total completion of God's purpose is anticipated. The references to the content of the mystery later in the letter in 3:3–10 also bear on the writer's thought at this point. They indicate, as we shall see, that in his view this cosmic summing up has a proleptic realization in the Church which unites Jews and Gentiles (cf. also Schlier, 65; Gnilka, 81; R. E. Brown, *The Semitic Background of the Term "Mystery" in the New Testament* [Philadelphia: Fortress Press, 1968] 60).

These important verses show clearly that for the writer to the Ephesians God's purpose, focused in Christ, embraces history and the cosmos and that in this way his message is in essential continuity with the core of Paul's gospel and its Christian eschatology (cf. J. C. Beker, *Paul the Apostle* [Philadelphia: Fortress Press, 1980] 11–19; 135–81; Ridderbos, *Paul*, 44–57; Lincoln, *Paradise*, 169–84). At the same time it is highly likely that the concerns of the letter's recipients have influenced the writer's formulation of the particular blessings of salvation mentioned in vv 9, 10. In the related letter to the Colossians false teachers had evidently offered esoteric knowledge gained through ascetic techniques and visionary experiences. Any among the readers of this letter who are tempted to believe that fullness of salvation will mean insight into mysteries are shown that the mystery of God's will has already been made known. It is not discovered by special techniques but is in accordance with God's good pleasure. Instead of presupposing a cosmological dualism where heaven and earth are two separated realms and where the heavenly powers dominate those in the lower evil realm of matter, it involves the bringing together and summing up of heaven and earth in Christ. Those who can see that there is therefore no aspect of this universe which is outside the scope of God's redemptive purpose, in which they too have been included, are thereby given grounds for overcoming any sense of weakness and insecurity in the face of hostile cosmic powers.

11, 12   ἐν ᾧ καὶ ἐκληρώθημεν, "in whom we were also appointed." Believers are now explicitly related to the cosmic Christ in whom all things are summed up. It is through being in this Christ that God's choice has fallen on them. κληροῦν is a *hapax legomenon* in the NT and literally means "to appoint or choose by lot," and so the passive has the force of "to be appointed by lot." In the papyri the passive can simply mean "to be destined, chosen" (cf. BAG 435). The cognate noun κλῆρος is used in Col 1:12 where God is said to have qualified believers for a share in the lot of the holy ones in light. In the LXX κλῆρος was employed in the context of the division of the land by lot for inheritance (e.g., Num 26:55, 56) and also for the individual Israelite's lot or portion in general (cf. Prov 1:14; Wis 2:9; 5:5). This latter notion is a frequent one in Qumran literature (e.g., 1QS 4.26; 11.7; 1QH 3.22). Also in the LXX Israel can be referred to as God's lot or portion (e.g., Deut 9:29 with κλῆρος; also Deut 32:8, 9 with μερίς). Because of such associations of the cognate noun, it has been suggested that the verb here in Eph 1:11 should be rendered "we have been chosen as God's portion," i.e., assigned by God himself as his own lot (cf. J. A. Robinson, 34). The use of κλῆρος in Colossians may well lie behind this use of κληροῦν in Ephesians, but if so, it is the more general reference of κλῆρος as a person's lot or destiny that carries over. In Colossians God qualifies believers for a certain lot or destiny; in Ephesians they have been allotted a destiny or appointed by God. What that destiny is to be is expressed in v 12, but before that another participial clause elaborates on ἐκληρώθημεν.

προορισθέντες κατὰ πρόθεσιν τοῦ τὰ πάντα ἐνεργοῦντος κατὰ τὴν βουλὴν τοῦ θελήματος αὐτοῦ, "having been predestined in accordance with the plan of him who carries out all things according to the purpose of his will." With the use of two prepositional phrases beginning with κατά and a genitive construction linking two synonymous nouns, this clause heavily underlines that believers' appointment in Christ to their destiny is part of God's sovereign purpose. It repeats the earlier emphasis on predestination and the divine will (cf. v 5 and the comments above on προορίζειν and θέλημα). Here this notion is reinforced with the additional nouns πρόθεσις (cf. προέθετο v 9 and Rom 8:28; 9:11 where πρόθεσις is also used in the context of election) and βουλή (signifying "purpose" in the sense of "decisive resolve") and with the description of God as the one who carries out or works all things according to his own will (cf. 1 Cor 12:6; Rom 8:28). God's unconditional freedom is affirmed, for whatever he has purposed is sure to be fulfilled.

εἰς τὸ εἶναι ἡμᾶς εἰς ἔπαινον δόξης αὐτοῦ, "in order that we might be for the praise of his glory," expresses what God has purposed for believers, and is to be linked with ἐκληρώθημεν rather than with the participle προορισθέντες. As in v 4 the purpose of God's choice is that believers be holy and blameless before him in love, and as in vv 5, 6 the purpose of his predestination is that believers be in relationship with himself and to the praise of the glory of his grace, so in vv 11, 12 the purpose of his appointing is that they be to the praise of his glory. God's purpose in choosing Israel had been expressed in similar terms, and the notion of God's acting for the sake of his name and his glory was an integral part of OT thinking (e.g., Isa 43:7, 21; 48:9–11; Jer 13:11; cf. also Dreyfus, "Pour la louange. . . ," 233–48). Now this is said with regard to the purpose and destiny of the Church. In the final analysis God's working out of his purpose serves his own glorification and the believing community exists to further that end. The praise of God's glory is the goal of its whole existence, not merely of its cultic worship.

τοὺς προηλπικότας ἐν τῷ Χριστῷ, "who have already hoped in Christ." As the full translation indicates, this phrase is to be taken in apposition to ἡμᾶς earlier in the verse, so that those whose goal is the praise of God's glory are now further described as those who have already hoped in Christ. ἐν τῷ Χριστῷ denotes the object of their hope (cf. also 1 Cor 15:19) rather than that Christ is the one in whom those who hope exist (*contra* Schlier, 68, followed by Jankowski, "L'espérance," 478–79). Many argue that this elaboration on ἡμᾶς introduces a narrowing of its scope and is a reference to Jewish Christians (cf. Abbott, 21; J. A. Robinson, 34–35; Maurer, *EvT* 11 [1951–52] 166–67; Schlier, 66–68; Coutts, *NTS* 3 [1956–57] 120; Lyonnet, "La bénédiction," 349; Barth, 92, 130–33; Ernst, 279; Caird, 40; Mitton, 57; Mussner, 49–50; Jankowski, "L'espérance," 475–81). On this interpretation the prefix προ- in προηλπικότας is said to indicate either that as Jews they hoped in the Messiah before his coming or that as Jewish Christians they hoped in Christ before the Gentiles. But up to this point the *berakah* has been concerned with the whole community; "we" and "us" refer to all believers. It is unlikely either that at this point there is a sudden change of perspective back to a pre-Christian period with a reference to Israel's messianic expectations or that there is a sudden change of reference so that the first person plural pronoun is now restricted to only one particular group of believers, Jewish Christians. Everything said in vv 11, 12 about believers' appointment to be for the praise of God's glory and about their predestination is equally appropriate for Jewish and Gentile believers (cf. also Dahl, *TZ* 7 [1951] 259–60; Percy, *Probleme*, 266 n. 16; Cambier, *ZNW* 54 [1936] 91–95; Krämer, *Wort and Dienst* 9 [1967] 41, 45; Gnilka; 82; Lindemann, *Aufhebung*, 99; Schnackenburg, 63). So it is believers in general who are said to have hoped in Christ.

προελπίζειν is a *hapax legomenon* in the NT. In compound verbs the προ- prefix usually stresses the notion of "ahead of time" or "beforehand," but when joined to ἐλπίζειν it can simply reinforce the idea already present in the meaning of the simple form of the verb (cf. Posidippus 27.8; Dexippus *Hist.* 32; *Gal.* 16.822). In our translation the "already" is meant to convey something of this strengthening of the idea of hope. Halter (*Taufe und Ethos*, 229, 623 n. 13) relates the προ- prefix to the preexistence of the Church. In that the Church was preexistent it hoped ahead of time. But this interpretation stretches almost to breaking point a notion which we have already seen to be highly disputed (see comments on v 4). The perfect tense of the participle suggests a completed action, the results of which still continue. This would add to the case against any reference to Jewish hope in the Messiah before his coming.

It may well be that a comparison with Colossians sheds light on the writer's formulation here, since Eph 1:12, 13 look very much like a reworking of Col 1:5. As in the case of κλῆρος, where Colossians has the noun (ἐλπίς), Ephesians has the verbal form, and instead of the προ- prefix going with ἀκούειν (cf. Col 1:5 with Eph 1:13) it has been shifted to go with this verbal form. Instead of the community being said, as in Colossians, to have already heard about the hope, here it is said to have already hoped. The use of this verb is significant for the writer's eschatological perspective. For, by definition, "hope" (cf. also 1:18; 4:4) indicates some eschatological reserve despite other expressions of realized eschatology in the *berakah* (cf. Gnilka, 84, *contra* Lindemann, *Aufhebung*, 100–101, who by a tendentious exegesis argues that those who *have* hoped are no longer those who hope and thus ignores the force of the perfect tense of the participle).

13, 14 ἐν ᾧ καὶ ὑμεῖς, "you also are in him." Literally the Greek should be translated "in him you also . . ." and be completed by "were sealed" at the end of v 13. On this anacoluthon in the Greek see *Notes* above. With the ὑμεῖς v 13 introduces a change in the personal pronoun. Those who interpret "we" in v 12 as Jewish Christians take "you" here as a contrasting reference to Gentile Christians. However, the Jew/Gentile theme does not become part of the writer's discussion until 2:11 and even then in 2:11–3:21 "we" is used of all believers, Jews and Gentiles, not just of Jewish Christians. The proposed distinction between "we" as Jewish Christians and "you" as Gentile Christians is one that simply does not hold for the rest of the letter. In fact the return to the first person plural in v 14 tells overwhelmingly against such a proposal. "Our inheritance" is that of all believers, not least of those who have just been described as having been sealed with the Holy Spirit, and is not just the inheritance of Jewish believers. Again, in 1:15–23 the second person plural in vv 15–18 shifts to the first person plural in v 19 but it would be extremely hard to see any Jew/Gentile distinction as remotely envisaged in such a variation. These variations in usage also make it unlikely that the distinction between "we" in v 12 and "you" in v 13 is one between first- and second-generation believers (*contra* Mitton, 57). It is far more likely that the "you" in v 13 marks the point at which the letter's recipients are addressed and explicitly drawn into the blessing offered by believers in general as they are reminded of their reception of the gospel (cf. also Dahl, *TZ* 7 [1951] 259–60; Gnilka, 62, 84; Lindemann, *Aufhebung*, 101; Halter, *Taufe und Ethos*, 229, Jayne, *ExpTim* 85 [1974] 151–52). The writer makes a distinction between believers in general and his present audience, and yet is saying that the same blessings have come upon both groups. This does not necessitate the hypothesis that his present readers are newly baptized (*contra* Wilson, " 'We' and 'You,' " 676–80). What has happened is simply that the more general liturgical style has shaded over into address to the readers. The same phenomenon with a change in the person of the pronoun can be found in the blessing in 1 Pet 1:3–9.

ἀκούσαντες τὸν λόγον τῆς ἀληθείας, τὸ εὐαγγέλιον τῆς σωτηρίας ὑμῶν, "having heard the word of truth, the good news of your salvation." The language of this clause is very similar to that of Col 1:5. There the Colossians are said to have heard about their hope in the word of truth, the gospel. Here "the word of truth" has become the direct object of ἀκούειν, from which the προ- prefix has been dropped, and to εὐαγγέλιον, which is in apposition in both verses, has been added τῆς σωτηρίας ὑμῶν. This formulation takes up the natural terminology of the early Christian mission in regard to "hearing the word" (cf. Rom 10:14–17; Acts 2:37; 13:7, 44; 19:10). Here the message is designated as "the word of truth," a term which continues Paul's emphasis on his apostolic gospel as truth (e.g., Gal 2:5, 14; 5:7; 2 Cor 4:2; 6:7; Col 1:5). In Paul the gospel can also be called "word of the Lord" (1 Thess 1:8; 2 Thess 3:1), "word of God" (1 Thess 2:13; 1 Cor 14:36), "word of Christ" (Col 3:16), "word of life" (Phil 2:16), or "word of reconciliation" (2 Cor 5:19). "Word of truth" focuses on the apostolic gospel as revealing the reality of God's saving purpose and humanity's place in it, as providing access to the truth, and as having truth as its content (cf. also 4:14, 15, 21; for parallels to the Qumran literature where truth is seen as divine revelation and correct teaching, see J. Murphy-O'Connor, "Truth: Paul and Qumran," *Paul and Qumran*, 179–230). The truth of this apostolic message is shown in what it accomplishes, for it is the message which has effected the reader's salvation—"the good news of your salvation" (cf. the reference to their having been saved in 2:5, 8 and to Christ as Savior in 5:23; cf. also Rom 1:16; 1 Cor 1:18). The good news effects a rescue operation, a deliverance from spiritual death, from God's wrath, from bondage to evil powers, sin and the flesh (cf. 2:1–3).

ἐν ᾧ καὶ πιστεύσαντες ἐσφραγίσθητε τῷ πνεύματι τῆς ἐπαγγελίας τῷ ἁγίῳ, "in him also, when you believed, you were sealed with the promised Holy Spirit." One is dependent on context in determining the temporal relationship of the action of an aorist participle to that of the main verb. Here the aorist participle πιστεύσαντες refers to an action coincident in time with that of the main verb ἐσφραγίσθητε (cf. also Acts 19:2: "Did you receive the Holy Spirit when you believed [πιστεύσαντες]?"; cf. Bruce, 36; J. D. G. Dunn, *Baptism in the Holy Spirit* [London: SCM, 1970] 158–59). As regards acceptance of the Christian gospel, believing can be seen to be the vital link between hearing the word and receiving the Spirit. When they believed, the readers of this epistle were sealed with the Spirit. Cattle and slaves were branded with their owner's seal, and so the seal was a mark of ownership and of preservation as the owner's property. In the OT God can be said to set a sign on his elect to distinguish them as his own and protect them from destruction (cf. Ezek 9:4–6). The seal also has this significance in 4 Ezra 6:5 and Rev 7:1–8; 9:4. So believers' reception of the Spirit is the sign that they belong to God in a special sense and have been stamped with the character of their owner. They belong to him now, but they are also protected until he takes complete possession of them (cf. v 14). The Spirit is an eschatological seal who marks believers out as a people who will be protected through the testings, the battles, and the sufferings of the end-time, which are already upon them (cf. 6:10–18). As 4:30 will assert, in the Spirit believers "were sealed for the day of redemption." The terminology of "sealing" (v 13) and "guarantee" (v 14) in connection with the Spirit has been taken from Paul in 2 Cor 1:22.

But to what precise aspect of the readers' experience does the imagery of "sealing" correspond? Some writers argue that it is a reference to the readers' baptism (cf. Kirby, *Ephesians*, 153–54; Houlden, 270; Gnilka, 85; Ernst, 280–81; Schille, *Hymnen*, 69; Halter, *Taufe und Ethos*, 230) but others dispute any reference to this sacrament (cf. Abbott, 22; J. D. G. Dunn, *Baptism in the Holy Spirit*, 160). Schlier (69–70) holds that the "sealing" is specifically the laying on of hands at baptism for the giving of the Spirit, and older writers sometimes saw a reference to the laying on of hands in the rite of confirmation; but for a convincing refutation of this identification, see G. W. H. Lampe, *The Seal of the Spirit* (London: Longmans, Green and Co., 1951) 3–18, 64–94. More can be said in favor of the baptismal reference. It is argued that reception of the Spirit was normally associated with water baptism in the early Christian mission (cf. Acts 2:37–39; 8:12–17; 19:5, 6), and in addition that the term "seal" was used both of circumcision and its Christian counterpart, baptism. In Rom 4:11 Paul links Abraham's circumcision with the function of a seal and in *Barn.* 9.6 the term "seal" is used of circumcision, as it is in some later rabbinic writings (e.g., *Ber.* 7.13, cf. Str-B 3:495; 4:31–33). In the post-apostolic writings baptism is also called a "seal" (cf. *2 Clem.* 7.6; 8.6; Herm. *Sim.* 8.6.3;

9.16.3–6; 9.17.4; *Acts of Thomas* 131). From this evidence it is a short step to the assertion that, since baptism replaces circumcision for the Christian community (cf. Col 2:11), it is likely that already in the NT the language of "sealing" would be taken as a reference to baptism. But there are weaknesses in such a line of argument. It is true that reception of the Spirit was associated with baptism, but it does not follow from this that the two can be identified. The evidence for explicit identification of circumcision in general with a seal and of baptism with a seal comes from the second century and has to be read back into the NT. Finally, the assumption on which the evidence is often read back, namely, that in the analogy between circumcision and baptism in Col 2:11 the meaning of the two rites is identical so that the latter replaces the former, is a dubious one. Some correlation is made between the two, but they are by no means equated (cf. Lohse, *Colossians,* 102; Martin, *Colossians,* 81–83). It seems more likely that "sealing" in this verse is a reference to the actual reception of the Spirit on the part of the readers, a distinguishable event for the early Christians, since it was usually accompanied by observable phenomena (e.g., Acts 8:17, 18; 10:44–46; 19:6). To be sure, this was closely associated with water baptism, but as Caird (41) observes, "we must not confuse the occasion with the event." The "seal of the Spirit" is therefore baptism of the Spirit, to which in the conversion-initiation process baptism in water was the reverse side of the coin, an expression of the faith to which God gives the Spirit (cf. also Barth, 143; G. W. H. Lampe, *The Seal of the Spirit* [London: Longmans, Green and Co., 1951] 5; G. R. Beasley-Murray, *Baptism in the New Testament* [London: Macmillan, 1962] 174).

The Spirit by whom believers are sealed is called, literally, "the Holy Spirit of promise." This could mean, in line with v 14, that he is the Spirit who is full of the promise of things to come. It is more likely, however, to be a Semitism (cf. Moule, *Idiom-Book,* 175) designating the Spirit as the Spirit promised in the Scriptures (cf. Gal 3:14 where the Spirit is seen as the fulfillment of the promise to Abraham, also Acts 2:17 which takes up the promise of Joel 2:28–32). This constitutes the first explicit mention of the Spirit in the letter. Being sealed by the Spirit is a specific blessing for which God is to be blessed, yet at the same time, as v 3 has indicated, there is a sense in which all the blessings of the eulogy can be attributed to the Spirit, since they are "spiritual" blessings.

ὅς ἐστιν ἀρραβὼν τῆς κληρονομίας ἡμῶν, "which is the guarantee of our inheritance." ἀρραβών is a loanword from the Hebrew עֵרָבוֹן, *ʿērābôn* (cf. Gen 38:17–20 where it occurs three times and is usually translated as a "pledge"), and in Hellenistic Greek became the ordinary commercial term for a down payment or first installment. Paul uses the term as a metaphor to show what takes place in God's giving of the Spirit in 2 Cor 1:22; 5:5. In a down payment, that which is given is part of a greater whole, is of the same kind as that whole, and functions as a guarantee that the whole payment will be forthcoming. The Spirit then is the first installment and guarantee of the salvation of the age to come with its mode of existence totally determined by the Spirit. In the context of 2 Cor 5:5 the complete inheritance guaranteed for the believer by his or her present experience of the Spirit is the spiritual resurrection body (cf. also 1 Cor 15:44). The use of the metaphor by the writer to the

Ephesians indicates a maintenance of the Pauline "already/not yet" eschatological tension. The Spirit is seen as the power of the age to come given ahead of time in history, but as still only the beginning and guarantee of the full salvation of that age which is yet to come. In v 14 it is the notion of "inheritance" which conveys the completion of salvation in the future. "Inheritance" terminology is familiar from the undisputed Paulines (cf. Gal 3:18, 29; 4:1, 7, 30; 5:21; 1 Cor 6:9, 10; 15:50; Rom 4:13, 14; 8:17; also J. D. Hester, *Paul's Concept of Inheritance* [Edinburgh: Oliver and Boyd, 1961]). Furthermore, in Galatians it is linked with the Spirit as believers are seen as the offspring of Abraham, those who have come into his inheritance by promise, and this is witnessed by their experience of the Spirit (3:14, 18). Here in Ephesians the Spirit is the guarantee of the inheritance that awaits believers as members of God's family, as his sons and daughters (cf. v 5). Some have claimed that the use of the term κληρονομία in this way constitutes a major difference between the author of Ephesians and Paul, and that whereas in Paul the inheritance is something promised in the past which is fulfilled in the present, in Ephesians it remains future (cf. also 1:18, 5:5; Hammer, *JBL* 79 [1960] 267–72; Gnilka, 86). There appears to be little value to such a claim. It bases too much on the use of a single term, the actual noun κληρονομία, and depends on Colossians also being non-Pauline, since Col 3:24 uses the term with a future reference. But as soon as one broadens the semantic field to include cognate words such as the verb κληρονομεῖν and the noun κληρονόμος, a different picture emerges with both present and future aspects of inheritance being found in Paul. Gal 5:21 and 1 Cor 6:9, 10 are clearly future references and not to be discounted simply because Paul makes use of traditional formulations (cf. also Denton, *EvQ* 54 [1982] 157–62). It appears also to be a contradictory use of eschatological material to claim, on the one hand, that Ephesians is non-Pauline because it uses this term with a future reference, while in Paul it has a present one, and, on the other hand, that it is non-Pauline because of its stress elsewhere on the present aspect of eschatology, while Paul is oriented to the future (e.g., the use of "resurrection" terminology in 2:6). As vv 13, 14 clearly show, both sides of the eschatological tension are present in Ephesians as they are in Paul.

εἰς ἀπολύτρωσιν τῆς περιποιήσεως, "vouching for God's redemption of his possession." This interpretative translation depends on decisions which have to be taken about the meaning of the Greek, which literally rendered would be "for redemption of the possession." RSV ("until we acquire possession of it") and NEB ("until God has redeemed what is his own") both take εἰς in a temporal sense, but illustrate the major alternatives. Does περιποίησις, "possession," refer to believers' possession of promised blessings (Abbott, 23–24; Schlier, 72) or to God's possession of believers (Robinson, 147–49; Cambier, *ZNW* 54 [1963] 96–97; D. Hill, *Greek Words and Hebrew Meanings* [Cambridge: Cambridge University Press, 1967] 74–75; Houlden, 271; Gnilka, 86–87; I. H. Marshall, "The Development of the Concept of Redemption in the New Testament," *Reconciliation and Hope,* ed. R. J. Banks [Exeter: Paternoster Press, 1974] 161–62)? The latter is more likely. Elsewhere in the NT ἀπολύτρωσις is always an act of God. Here too he is the most likely agent of redemption and therefore also the subject of "possession." God's people as the object of his possession is a common OT theme (cf. Exod 19:5; Deut 14:2; 26:18; Mal 3:17) and is found elsewhere in the NT in Acts 20:28 and 1 Pet 2:9. For discussion of the concept of "redemption" see the comments on v 7. Here in 1:14 and in 4:30 redemption has a future reference, while in 1:7 it was treated as a present possession of believers. In relation to the rest of the sentence εἰς in this phrase should be seen as indicating the goal rather than as having a purely temporal sense. The Spirit functions as the guarantee of believers' inheritance, looking toward or vouching for God's full redemption of that for which he has made this down payment. Final deliverance by God means his taking full and complete possession of those who have already become his.

εἰς ἔπαινον τῆς δόξης αὐτοῦ, "to the praise of his glory." The writer has specifically drawn the recipients of the letter into his blessing of God in vv 13, 14 but in doing so has not totally digressed from his *berakah*. This final phrase, a variation on those preceding in 1:6, 12, reaffirms the liturgical character of 1:3–14 as a whole. It is loosely connected to what has gone before in v 14, suggesting both that in completing redemption, by taking possession of his people, God's glory is praised, and that the prospect of such a consummation of his purpose should call forth a response of praise on the part of his creatures now.

Explanation

Using a form of praise rooted in Jewish worship (the *berakah*) and a language and style which suggest the impact of the Hebrew psalms and Qumran hymns on Hellenistic Judaism, the writer introduces his theme in the letter with a eulogy. In one long sentence of liturgical prose he blesses God for all the blessings God has showered upon his people.

The sentence begins with a general thematic statement (v 3), which links these blessings to the presence and work of the Spirit and to the heavenly dimension, and indicates that they come to believers through their incorporation into Christ. The blessings of salvation are then elaborated (vv 4–14) and immediately tied closely to God's electing purpose for and gracious choice of his people. This is a choice which, because it was made before the foundation of the world, provides assurance that salvation is not dependent on temporal contingencies. It is also a choice which has as its goal the formation of a people characterized by holiness and love. God is to be blessed because in his choice of a people he predestined them for an intimate relationship with himself as his sons and daughters and because in his beloved Son he has highly favored them with his grace. Through the generosity of that grace believers now experience in Christ deliverance and forgiveness, and receive the wisdom and insight that they need. They are privileged, because God has revealed to them that his ordering of history focuses in Christ and involves the bringing together of everything in the universe into a state of harmony in Christ. The eulogy then again relates believers, as those who have hoped ahead of time, to this cosmic Christ and to God's sovereign purpose, which issues in the praise of his own glory. Finally it draws the addressees more explicitly into its blessing by reminding them of both their reception of the gospel message and their reception of the Spirit as the guarantee of the final deliverance in which God will take complete possession of his people.

Explanation

Such a bare summary of the contents does not begin to indicate the impact of the language of this passage or the intricate interweaving of its themes. In one sense the language is exalted and extravagant and yet, in another, the very repetition of phrases reveals its poverty and inadequacy to do justice to its subject—salvation on the grandest scale and broadest canvas. The flow of thought spans past, present, and future, and its reflection on God's activity can be seen to have a trinitarian content. The blessings of salvation are related to the pretemporal ("before the foundation of the world," v 4), to the past (what God has done in Christ, v 3, 7; and the believer's past appropriation of this, vv 13, 14), to the present (the current enjoyment of redemption and forgiveness, v 7), to the future (the believer's inheritance which coincides with God's complete possession of his people, v 14), and to the overlap between the present and the future (as this is reflected in the summing up of all things in Christ, v 10, and the experience of the Spirit as a guarantee, v 14). The trinitarian pattern of thought is reflected in God the Father, as the origin of every blessing and the one who chooses his people, Christ, as the beloved Son in and through whom the blessings are mediated and the one to whom redemption both on the personal and on the cosmic level is most closely related, and the Spirit, as stamping his character on the blessings (they are "spiritual," v 3) and as being the one who marks God's ownership and serves as the guarantee of the fulfillment of his purpose.

Although a "trinitarian" element can be discerned, what emerges more clearly from the concentration of the language in the passage is an emphasis on God's purpose or will (vv 4, 5, 9, 11), on the praise of his glory (vv 6, 12, 14), on "in Christ" (vv 3, 4, 6, 7, 9, 10 [twice], 11, 12, 13 [twice]), and on "us"/"we" (vv 3, 4, 5, 6, 7, 8, 9, 11, 12, 14). God as the origin or goal of salvation, Christ as its mediator, and believers as its recipients—these themes give the passage a threefold theocentric, Christological, and ecclesiological focus. God's sovereign will, initiating and working out salvation for his people and for all things in the person and through the agency of Christ and to the praise of his own glory, captures the major thrust of that which fills the writer's thoughts and causes him to bless God. The Christological focus marks off this *berakah* from its Jewish counterparts. Christ's central place means that God's pretemporal purpose focused in him and that he spans the outworkings of that purpose in history. In him God's blessings for his people and for the cosmos have already been realized; in him these blessings provide a present salvation; and in him they contain the assurance of future consummation. Yet for all the centrality of Christ's mediation, his work has God and his purpose as its source and God's glory as its object. The theocentric perspective remains dominant. God's gracious electing purpose shapes past, present, and future. Salvation comes from him, and its object is not simply that human needs may be met, though it accomplishes that, but that God himself may be glorified; hence the variously worded refrain—"to the praise of his glory."

An important part of the eulogy is the middle section which blesses God for revealing that his gracious purpose in history is all-embracing (vv 9, 10). As believers are reminded of the revelation of this mystery, they are brought to realize that the salvation with which they have been blessed centers in the same comprehensive Christ in whom God is working to restore all things.

The divine election which has grasped them is shown to be God's decision to sum up all things in Christ. To be in Christ, therefore, is to be part of a program which is as broad as the universe, a movement which is rolling on toward a renewed cosmos where all is in harmony. Counteracting insecurity and insignificance in the face of the claims of syncretistic mystery religions or cosmic forces, the effect of this part of the blessing is to produce confidence in the God whose gracious decision embraces everything in heaven and on earth, and to inspire those who echo it to play their part in God's administration of the fullness of the times in Christ.

This introductory *berakah* makes use of a liturgical style, but not simply to address God in a hymn; it takes up traditional formulations, but not simply to instruct. Rather, in reminder of God's blessings of salvation in Christ and in praise of God, it functions in such a way as to appeal to the recipients' experience of these blessings and to stimulate them to participate in the grateful praise of God it has inaugurated. Recalling God's blessings in Christ is meant to lead to gratitude and praise. In fact, the whole long sentence functions as a paean of praise into which its readers are invited. For this writer the purpose of the existence of the eschatological people of God is the praise of his grace and glory. As they confess with abandon that to God belongs all the glory, God's people find their fulfillment. It is of the essence of grace to culminate in thanksgiving and of the essence of their relationship as God's sons and daughters to bless their Father constantly for having blessed them so richly in Christ.

At the same time as it stimulates the addressees to give God the glory due to him, the eulogy draws them into the perspective that will be basic to the letter's teaching and exhortation. It helps to open the eyes of the recipients to what has been graciously conferred on them in Christ and, therefore, to the fact that they already have all and more than all that any syncretism can offer. In this way the eulogy has an epistolary function as a prelude and a rhetorical function as an exordium. Its theocentric character, its Christological focus, its cosmic perspective on the mystery, its stress on God's grace, and its notion of the calling of God's people are all significant for the letter as a whole. Using a *berakah* to introduce the concerns of the letter reveals something of the writer's own convictions and priorities. Evidently he has a pervasive sense that "the chief end of man is to glorify God and enjoy him for ever," and this means that the vision of the Church's life and task which he presents in the letter is one that is deeply rooted in that Church's worship, firmly located "in Christ," and profoundly aware of the splendor of God. All of these features will help him to strengthen the recipients' sense of their own identity vis-à-vis their surrounding society. Finally, the writer's praise of God on account of the blessings his addressees have received backs up the assurance that follows immediately in v 16 that he constantly gives thanks to God in his prayers for them.

Thanksgiving with Prayer for Believers' Knowledge of God and Their Awareness of the Church's Significance (1:15–23)

Bibliography

Allen, T. G. "Exaltation and Solidarity with Christ: Ephesians 1.20 and 2.6." *JSNT* 28 (1986) 103–20. ———. "God the Namer. A Note on Ephesians 1.21b." *NTS* 32 (1986) 470–75. **Bedale, S.** "The Meaning of κεφαλή in the Pauline Epistles." *JTS* 5 (1954) 211–15. **Benoit, P.** "Body, Head and *Pleroma* in the Epistles of the Captivity." *Jesus and the Gospel*, Vol. 2. Tr. B. Weatherhead. London: Darton, Longman and Todd, 1974, 51–92. **Best, E.** *One Body in Christ*, 139–59. **Black, M.** "πᾶσαι ἐξουσίαι αὐτῷ ὑποταγήσονται." *Paul and Paulinism*, ed. M. D. Hooker and S. G. Wilson. London: S.P.C.K., 1982, 74–82. **Bogdasovich, M.** "The Idea of Pleroma in the Epistles to the Colossians and Ephesians." *Downside Review* 83 (1965) 118–30. **Carr, W.** *Angels and Principalities*. Cambridge: Cambridge University Press, 1981, 93–111. **Colpe, C.** "Zur Leib-Christi-Vorstellung im Epheserbrief." *Judentum, Urchristentum, Kirche*, ed. W. Eltester. Berlin: de Gruyter, 1964, 172–87. **Deichgräber, R.** *Gotteshymnus*, 161–65. **Delling, G.** "πλήρης κτλ." *TDNT* 6 (1968) 283–311. **Dupont, J.** *Gnosis: La connaissance religieuse dans les Épîtres de Saint Paul*. Paris: J. Gabalda, 1949, 419–93. **Ernst, J.** *Pleroma und Pleroma Christi*. Regensburg: Pustet, 1970. **Feuillet, A.** "L'Église plérôme du Christ d'après Éphés., 1, 23." *NRT* 78 (1956) 449–72, 593–610. **Fischer, K. M.** *Tendenz und Absicht*, 118–20. **Flowers, H. J.** "Paul's Prayer for the Ephesians: A Study of Eph. 1:15–23." *ExpTim* 38 (1926–27) 227–33. **Fowler, R.** "Ephesians 1:23." *ExpTim* 76 (1965) 294. **Gewiess, J.** "Die Begriffe πληροῦν und πλήρωμα im Kolosser- und Epheserbrief." *Vom Wort des Lebens*. FS M. Meinertz. Münster: Aschendorff, 1951, 128–41. **Gundry, R. H.** *Sōma in Biblical Theology*. Cambridge: Cambridge University Press, 1976, 223–44. **Hanson, S.** *The Unity of the Church*, 112–17, 127–29. **Hegermann, H.** *Die Vorstellung vom Schöpfungsmittler im hellenistischen Judentum und Urchristentum*. Berlin: Akademie-Verlag, 1961. ———. "Zur Ableitung der Leib-Christi-Vorstellung." *TLZ* 85 (1960) 839–42. **Hitchcock, A. E. M.** "Ephesians 1:23." *ExpTim* 22 (1910–11) 91. **Howard, G.** "Head/Body Metaphors of Ephesians." *NTS* 20 (1974) 350–56. **Käsemann, E.** *Leib und Leib Christi*. Tübingen: Mohr, 1933. ———. "The Theological Problem Presented by the Motif of the Body of Christ." *Perspectives on Paul*. Tr. M. Kohl. London: SCM, 1971, 102–21. **Lightfoot, J. B.** *Colossians*, 255–71. **Lindemann, A.** *Die Aufhebung der Zeit*, 59–63, 204–17. **McGlashan, A. R.** "Ephesians 1:23." *ExpTim* 76 (1965) 132–33. **Meuzelaar, J. J.** *Der Leib des Messias*. Assen: Van Gorcum, 1961. **Meyer, R. P.** *Kirche und Mission im Epheserbrief*. Stuttgart: Katholisches Bibelwerk, 1977. **Moule, C. F. D.** *Colossians*, 164–69. ———. "'Fulness' and 'Fill' in the New Testament." *SJT* 4 (1951) 79–86. ———. "A Note on Ephesians i, 22, 23." *ExpTim* 60 (1948) 53. ———. *The Origin of Christology*. Cambridge: Cambridge University Press, 1977, 69–89. ———. "Pleroma." *Interpreter's Dictionary of the Bible*, Vol. 3. New York: Abingdon, 1962, 826–28. **Mussner, F.** *Christus, das All und die Kirche*, 29–64, 118–74. **O'Brien, P. T.** "Ephesians 1: An Unusual Introduction to a New Testament Letter." *NTS* 25 (1979) 504–16. **Overfield, P. D.** "*Pleroma*: A Study in Content and Context." *NTS* 25 (1979) 384–96. **Percy, E.** *Der Leib Christi in den paulinischen Homologoumena und Antilegomena*. UUÅ. Lund: Gleerup, 1942. **Pokorný, P.** *Der Epheserbrief und die Gnosis. Die Bedeutung des Haupt-Glieder-Gedankens in der entstehenden Kirche*. Berlin: Evangelische Verlagsanstalt, 1965. ———. "Soma Christou im Epheserbrief." *EvT* 20 (1960) 456–64. **Potterie, I. de la.** "Le Christ, Plérôme de l'Église

(Eph 1.22-23)." *Bib* 58 (1977) 500-524. **Ramaroson, L.** "Une lecture de Éphésiens 1, 15-2, 10." *Bib* 58 (1977) 388-410. **Ridderbos, H.** *Paul: An Outline of His Theology.* Tr. J. R. de Witt, Grand Rapids: Eerdmans, 1975, 362-95. **Robinson, J. A. T.** *The Body.* London: SCM, 1952, 49-83. **Roels, E.** *God's Mission,* 84-139, 229-48. **Sanders, J. T.** "Hymnic Elements in Ephesians 1-3." *ZNW* 56 (1965) 214-32. ———. "The Transition from Opening Epistolary Thanksgiving to Body in the Letters of the Pauline Corpus." *JBL* 81 (1962) 348-62. **Schenke, H.-M.** *Der Gott "Mensch" in der Gnosis: Ein religionsgeschichtlicher Beitrag zur Diskussion über die paulinische Anschauung von der Kirche als Leib Christi.* Göttingen: Vandenhoeck & Ruprecht, 1962. **Schlier, H.** *Christus und die Kirche im Epheserbrief.* Tübingen: Mohr, 1930. ———. "κεφαλή." *TDNT* 3 (1965) 673-82. **Schnackenburg, R.** "L'Idée de 'Corps du Christ' dans la lettre aux Éphésiens: Perspective pour nôtre temps." *Paul de Tarse: Apôtre du nôtre temps,* ed. L. de Lorenzi. Rome: Abbaye de St. Paul, 1979, 665-85. **Schubert, P.** *Form and Function of the Pauline Thanksgivings.* Berlin: A. Töpelmann, 1939. **Schweizer, E.** *The Church as the Body of Christ.* Richmond: John Knox Press, 1964. ———. "The Church as the Missionary Body of Christ." *Neotestamentica.* Zürich: Zwingli Verlag, 1963, 317-29. ———. "Die Kirche als Leib Christi in den paulinischen Antilegomena." *Neotestamentica.* Zürich: Zwingli Verlag, 1963, 293-316. ———. "Die Kirche als Leib Christi in den paulinischen Homologumena." *Neotestamentica.* Zürich: Zwingli Verlag, 1963, 272-92. ———. "σῶμα." *TDNT* 7 (1971) 1024-94. **Wedderburn, A. J. M.** "The Body of Christ and Related Concepts in 1 Corinthians." *SJT* 24 (1971) 74-96. **Wikenhauser, A.** *Die Kirche als der mystische Leib des Christus nach dem Apostel Paulus.* Münster: Aschendorff, 1940. **Wink, W.** *Naming the Powers.* Philadelphia: Fortress, 1984, 3-35, 60-64, 151-63. **Yates, R.** "A Re-examination of Ephesians 1:23." *ExpTim* 83 (1972) 146-51.

Translation

[15] *For this reason, having heard of your faith in the Lord Jesus and your love for all the saints,*[a] [16] *I do not cease giving thanks for you, remembering you in my prayers* [17] *that the God of our Lord Jesus Christ, the Father of glory, may give you the Spirit of wisdom and revelation in the knowledge of him.*[b] [18] *I pray that, the eyes of your heart having been enlightened,*[c] *you may know what is the hope of his calling, what are the riches of his glorious inheritance among the saints,* [19] *and what is the surpassing greatness of his power toward us who believe, according to the working of his mighty strength,* [20] *which he accomplished*[d] *in Christ when he raised him from the dead, and seated him at his right hand in the heavenly realms* [21] *far above every principality and authority and power and dominion and every name that is named not only in this age but also in that which is to come.* [22] *And he placed all things under his feet and gave him as head over all things to the Church,* [23] *which is his body, the fullness of him who fills all things in every way.*

Notes

[a]There is a difficult textual question at the end of v 15. Did the original text read καὶ τὴν ἀγάπην τὴν εἰς πάντας τοὺς ἁγίους, "and your love for all the saints," which is supported by ℵc Dc K Ψ 88 330 451? Or was the second τὴν omitted, as in D* G? Or was τὴν ἀγάπην included at all, because P46 ℵ* A B P 33 Origen all read καὶ τὴν εἰς πάντας τοὺς ἁγίους, "and toward all the saints"? This last option is clearly the best attested. It would mean that the recipients' faith or faithfulness is either found in the sphere of the Lord Jesus or placed in him but at the same time is directed toward all the saints. This would also make it the most difficult reading and the others could be explained as attempts to conform it more to the wording of Col. 1:4, ἀκούσαντες τὴν πίστιν ὑμῶν ἐν Χριστῷ Ἰησοῦ καὶ τὴν ἀγάπην ἣν ἔχετε εἰς πάντας τοὺς ἁγίους. However, with the exception of

Beare (626), Bruce (38), and Barth (146–47), most commentators have decided that the shortest reading is too difficult. Nowhere else in the NT is there a failure to distinguish between faith directed to Christ and to one's fellow believers. Philem 5 is sometimes cited as an example— ἀκούων σου τὴν ἀγάπην καὶ τὴν πίστιν ἣν ἔχεις πρὸς τὸν κύριον Ἰησοῦν καὶ εἰς πάντας τοὺς ἁγίους—but it does not count, since it involves a chiastic construction (cf. Moule, *Colossians and Philemon*, 141; Lohse, *Colossians and Philemon*, 193; Martin, *Colossians and Philemon*, 160–61). It is possible that the writer was influenced by the last part of Philem 5 and did not realize it was part of a chiasmus, but this is unlikely since it would have to assume a much more wooden and insensitive use of Paul's letters than is the case elsewhere in Ephesians. A further objection to the shortest reading as original and the one that best explains the others is that if there was a later assimilation to Col 1:4, this would surely have involved the ἣν ἔχετε of Colossians instead of either the second τήν or simply the absence of any relative expression. It is more likely then that the reading καὶ τὴν ἀγάπην τὴν εἰς πάντας τοὺς ἁγίους is original and that an early scribal error has affected the chief manuscripts. It would certainly be easy for the eye to skip from the first τήν to the second— homoeoarcton (cf. Metzger, *Textual Commentary*, 602). The reading found in D* G can then be explained as an attempt to deal with the awkward second τήν (*pace* Robinson, 295–97, who believes this reading to be original), as can both the rearrangement of the words in 81 104 eth Cyril and the addition in 181.

ᵇThe original Greek text of 1:15–23 forms one sentence. Again, for the sake of English style and intelligibility, the translation has been broken down into a number of sentences and here the words "I pray" have been added in order to begin a new sentence.

ᶜThe place of the participial clause πεφωτισμένους τοὺς ὀφθαλμοὺς τῆς καρδίας in the syntax is not clear. And why are the noun and the perfect passive participle in the accusative case? There are two major explanations. One is to treat the clause as the second direct object of the verb δώῃ in the previous verse so that the petition is that God might give the Spirit of wisdom and revelation and eyes of the heart that have been enlightened (cf. Abbott, 28; Gaugler, 63; Gnilka, 90 n.6). The other is to connect the clause with the indirect object of the preceding verb, with ὑμῖν, and to suggest that, although one might have expected the clause to involve the dative case, its case has been influenced by the following accusative and infinitive construction with which it is also closely linked, εἰς τὸ εἰδέναι ὑμᾶς (cf. Robinson, 149; Westcott, 23–24). On the former explanation one is left without any explicit connective between the two objects, which makes a very awkward construction where "enlightened eyes" appears to be in apposition to "the Spirit of wisdom and revelation." The latter explanation, which connects "eyes that have been enlightened" more clearly with the state of the recipients of the Spirit, is to be preferred.

ᵈThe Greek text at this point should read ἐνήργηκεν rather than the ἐνήργησεν of the UBSGT and Nestle text. The perfect is witnessed by A B Cyril, while the aorist is supported by P⁴⁶ ℵ D G K L P. P⁴⁶, though ancient, often has secondary variants which, as here, attempt to make the text smoother. An original perfect has probably been changed to conform to the following aorist forms. It is much harder to account for a change in the reverse direction (cf. also Abbott, 31; Gaugler, 72; Gnilka, 50, 94).

Form/Structure/Setting

Eph 1:15–23 constitutes an extended thanksgiving which, like the preceding *berakah*, forms one long sentence. In terms of its overall structure this pericope can be divided into three major elements: (1) the thanksgiving proper in vv 15, 16a, followed by (2) an intercessory prayer-report in vv 16b–19, which shades into (3) confessional material in praise of God's power in Christ's resurrection and exaltation and the use of this material to highlight the role of the Church in God's purposes in vv 20–23.

In his work on Pauline thanksgivings Schubert classified these sections of the letter into two general types, those characterized by participial constructions modifying εὐχαριστέω, "I give thanks," and followed by a final clause subordinate to them, and those characterized by a causal ὅτι clause following the principal εὐχαριστέω clause and followed in turn by a consecutive clause introduced by ὥστε. In the first category he placed the thanksgivings found in 1 Thessalonians, Philippians, Colossians, Philemon, and Ephesians and in the second those found in 2 Thessalonians, 1 Corinthians, and Romans (cf. *Form*, 35). The Ephesian thanksgiving has six of the seven formal elements often found in the first category. (*i*) A principal verb of thanksgiving: (οὐ παύομαι) εὐχαριστῶν, 1:16; cf. 1 Thess 1:2; 2:13; Phil 1:3; Col 1:3; Phlm 4. In Ephesians this element does not begin the thanksgiving but is preceded by the opening link with the *berakah* διὰ τοῦτο κἀγώ, "for this reason, I," and by the participial clause expressing the cause for thanksgiving. (*ii*) A temporal expression indicating the frequency with which thanksgiving is offered: οὐ παύομαι, "I do not cease" (1:16; cf. 1 Thess 1:2; 2:13; Phil 1:4; Col 1:3; Philem 4. (*iii*) A pronominal object phrase: ὑπὲρ ὑμῶν, "for you" (1:16; cf. 1 Thess 1:2; Phil 1:4; Col 1:3; P. T. O'Brien, *Introductory Thanksgivings in the Letters of Paul* [Leiden: E. J. Brill, 1977] 78, argues that περὶ ὑμῶν in Col 1:3 is to be taken with εὐχαριστοῦμεν). (*iv*) A participial clause indicating the cause of thanksgiving: ἀκούσας τὴν καθ' ὑμᾶς πίστιν. . . , "having heard of your faith. . . ," (1:15; cf. 1 Thess 1:3, 4; Phil 1:6; Col 1:4; Philem 5. In Eph 1:15, unlike the other references where such a clause follows the verb of thanksgiving, this element precedes the principal verb. (*v*) A participial clause indicating the time of thanksgiving: μνείαν ποιούμενος ἐπὶ τῶν προσευχῶν μου, "when I remember you in my prayers," 1:16; cf. 1 Thess 1:2; Phil 1:4; Col 1:3; Philem 4. (*vi*) A final clause indicating the content of the intercessory prayer: ἵνα ὁ θεός . . . δώῃ . . . , "that the God . . . may give. . . ," 1:17; cf. Phil 1:9; Col 1:9; Philem 6. The one element to be found in other thanksgivings of this type which does not occur in Ephesians is a personal object for the verb of thanksgiving. In fact, God is named as the recipient of the thanksgiving in all the other thanksgivings. However, the naming of God in the intercessory prayer-report here in 1:17 makes clear to whom the thanksgiving is rendered.

Thanksgiving sections in the Pauline letters can be seen as modifications of the Hellenistic letter form which often stated that the writer "gives thanks to the gods" or "makes continual mention of you before the gods" and then provided reasons for the writer's gratitude (cf. Schubert, *Form*, 158–79). But Paul's opening thanksgivings do not simply reflect Hellenistic epistolary style (*pace* Schubert, *Form*, 184; Barth, 161); they reflect also early Christian liturgical style which in turn had its roots in Jewish worship. J. M. Robinson has shown that in Jewish prayers the *berakah* and *hôdāyâ* ("thanksgiving") forms were interchangeable. Even though they used variant formulae, their motif and function were similar. The *hôdāyâ* form was popular at Qumran, as the Hymns of Thanksgiving (1QH) indicate, and in early Christianity there gradually came to be a preference for the thanksgiving formula ("The Historicality of Biblical Language," *The Old Testament and Christian Faith*, ed. B. W. Anderson [New York: Harper and Row, 1963] 124–58; "Die Hodajot-Formel in Gebet und Hymnus des Frühchristentums," *Apophoreta*, FS E. Haenchen, ed. W. Eltester and F. H. Kettler [Berlin: Töpelmann, 1964] 194–235; cf. also J. P. Audet, "Literary Forms and Contents of a Normal Εὐχαριστία in the First Century," *Studia Evangelica* 1, ed. F. L. Cross, TU 86 [Berlin: Akademie-Verlag, 1959] 643–62). The epistolary thanksgivings, therefore, provide a further example of the interaction between Hellenistic and Jewish elements in Paul's cultural climate. In their form and function they are primarily influenced by current letter style, while their content shows the influence of Jewish liturgy. The same observations hold for the Ephesian thanksgiving section which, as we have seen, continues the pattern set by the undisputed Pauline letters, and details of the influence of Jewish liturgical material on the content will be pointed out in the comments on individual verses.

In terms of the elements in its basic formal structure the Ephesian thanksgiving resembles most closely that of Philemon. In the principal thanksgiving clause there are the same two participial constructions—ἀκούσας . . . μνείαν ποιούμενος, "having heard . . . remembering," in Ephesians and μνείαν σου ποιούμενος . . . ἀκούων, "remembering you . . . hearing," in Philemon—and these are immediately followed by a final clause, beginning with ἵνα in Ephesians and ὅπως in Philemon. However, as in the case of the rest of the letter, the closest correspondence in the wording of the Ephesian thanksgiving is with that in Colossians. The introductory link with the *berakah* in 1:15 takes up the wording of Col 1:9; and the way the cause of thanksgiving is expressed is very close indeed to Col 1:4. The intercession introduced by the final clause with ἵνα in 1:17 takes up elements of the intercession in Col 1:9, also introduced by ἵνα; and, as will be noted in *Comment,* other features of the content of the intercession draw on notions prominent in Colossians.

In comparison with other thanksgiving sections, the actual element of thanksgiving for the recipients is relatively brief in Ephesians and betrays no personal knowledge of their specific situation. This supports the view that the writer has intended to write a letter of general interest to a number of churches.

The second structural element in the passage, the intercessory prayer-report of vv 16b–19 with its threefold petition, shares the same characteristic of generality. O'Brien (*NTS* 25 [1979] 516) concludes, "Of all the introductory prayers in the thanksgiving periods this tells us least about a specific situation. It therefore contains petitions that are valid under many sets of circumstances and at various times." In common with other intercessory prayer-reports in thanksgiving sections Eph 1:16b–19 has a verb for praying in participial form, μνείαν ποιούμενος ἐπὶ τῶν προσευχῶν μου, "remembering in my prayers" (cf. Rom 1:9, 10 and Philem 4 for the same terminology). As we have already indicated, the content of the intercessory prayer is often expressed in a final clause. One formal element missing in Ephesians as compared with most of the other intercessory prayer-reports is a prepositional phrase or pronoun indicating those in whose behalf the prayer has been made (cf. ὑμῶν in Rom 1:9, ὑπὲρ πάντων ὑμῶν in Phil 1:4, ὑπὲρ ὑμῶν in Col 1:9, and σου in Philem 4). In 1:16a ὑπὲρ ὑμῶν, "for you," has already been included in the thanksgiving proper, however, and so can be understood to apply also to the intercession clause in the second half of the verse. Intercessory prayer-reports can be found in the letter of 1 Macc 12:6–18 in v 11 and in that of 2 Macc 1:1–10a in v 6. The link in the Pauline letters between thanksgiving and intercessory prayer has parallels in a small number of extant papyrus letters, where thanksgiving and assurances of prayers for the health of the reader are combined (cf. Schubert, *Form,* 160–68). But again, liturgical as well as epistolary factors may well have influenced the combination, since in Jewish prayers thanksgiving or praise was often mixed with petition, though not so much specifically intercession (cf. Pss 9, 29, [59, 69; 1QH 16–18; *Šĕmônēh ʿEśrēh;* cf. also G. P. Wiles, *Paul's Intercessory Prayers* [Cambridge: Cambridge University Press, 1974] 160–62). Certainly with the intercessory prayer-report in Ephesians the writer returns to the liturgical style of his earlier *berakah* with its sequence of relative clauses and genitive constructions, and it is here that parallels with the Qumran thanksgiving hymns predominate. As well as picking up the style of the *berakah*, the intercessory prayer-report takes up some of its themes. The request for "the Spirit of wisdom and revelation in the knowledge of him" (v 17) recalls the terminology of vv 8, 9. The notions of "hope," "riches," and "inheritance" (v 18) recall terms in vv 12, 7, and 14 respectively. "The working of his mighty strength" (v 19) reflects the terminology of "the one who works all things according to the purpose of his will" in v 11. In turn, some of the language of this intercessory prayer-report will be taken up later in 3:1, 14–19 as the writer returns to intercession for his reader.

Where does the thanksgiving end? Both Schubert (*Form*, 34) and O'Brien (*NTS* 25 [1979] 505) see the basic thanksgiving as ending with the intercessory prayer of vv 17–19, though Schubert holds that the overall thanksgiving period extends to v 21 and O'Brien admits the ending is not clear-cut. Sanders (*JBL* 81 [1962] 348–62) attempts to show that the end of a thanksgiving period is to be seen in an eschatological climax in which the present time of thanksgiving is linked with the final days of the supreme rule of God, followed by a form characteristic of Pauline paragraph openings such as παρακαλῶ δὲ ὑμᾶς, ἀδελφοί, "I appeal to you, brothers (and sisters)." On this basis he believes the thanksgiving in Ephesians runs at least as far as 2:10 and that it could well extend to 3:21, pointing out that a doxology also ends the thanksgiving period in 1 Tim 1:17. Wiles (*Paul's Intercessory Prayers*, 158 n. 5; 164 n. 1) considers the limit of the thanksgiving to be 1:23, with 1:21b, "not only in this age but also in that which is to come," providing the eschatological climax, but claims that, as in Col 1, the transition is doubtful since prayer material gradually shades into statements. On the other hand, the whole of 1:20–23 may provide the eschatological climax. It is simply that, in keeping with the predominantly realized eschatology of the first part of the letter, the thanksgiving is linked with the present rule of Christ. As the discussion of the structure of the letter in the *Introduction* to the commentary suggests, Sanders may well be right in his proposal that there is a sense in which the whole of 1:3–3:21 can be viewed as an introductory thanksgiving. Yet within that larger unit a separate *berakah* and a separate thanksgiving can still be distinguished, and 1:15–23 constitutes the latter. The closing portion of Pauline thanksgivings often consists of liturgical material which reflects or substitutes for the *berakah* with which it was the Jewish custom to end a prayer as well as to begin it (cf. J. T. Sanders, *JBL* 81 [1962] 355–62). Here in Eph 1 this phenomenon is present. The intercessory prayer-report passes almost imperceptibly into liturgical material in praise of the exalted Christ, including the eschatological formulation of 1:21b, since the words of the prayer have carried the writer "so far that the prayer had lost itself in the wonder of the blessing prayed for" (Robinson, 73).

We have called the contents of vv 20–23 "liturgical material," but the exact nature of this material has been disputed by scholars. Some hold that it incorporates a hymn (cf. Gaugler, 71; Schille, *Frühchristliche Hymnen*, 103 n. 4; Sanders,

ZNW 56 [1965] 220–23, thinks this a possibility; Fischer, *Tendenz*, 118–20; Deichgräber, *Gotteshymnus*, 161–65, though admitting to many uncertainties about his attempted reconstruction of the hymn). Certainly its subject matter contains elements found in what are generally acknowledged as Christological hymns elsewhere in the NT: Christ's resurrection from the dead, his exaltation, his session at God's right hand, and his supremacy over the powers (cf. Phil 2:6–11; Col 1:15–20; 1 Tim 3:16). Both Deichgräber (*Gotteshymnus*, 163–64) and Fischer (*Tendenz*, 120 n. 5) concede that if a hymn does originally lie behind vv 20–23, it is more likely to have begun with statements about Christ's incarnation and his death in common with other NT Christological hymns than with a reference to the resurrection, so that in fact any reconstruction will be of a fragment of a hymn rather than a complete hymn. In the nature of the case this makes any convincing demonstration of the original much more difficult.

J. T. Sanders (*ZNW* 56 [1965] 220) and Deichgräber (*Gotteshymnus*, 165), however, make a better case for the original fragment's having been composed of much of vv 20 and 22 than Fischer (*Tendenz*, 120) does for the inclusion of v 21a in such material. The lines would then be:

ἐγείρας αὐτὸν ἐκ νεκρῶν
καὶ καθίσας ἐν δεξιᾷ αὐτοῦ
καὶ πάντα ὑπέταξεν ὑπὸ τοὺς πόδας αὐτοῦ
καὶ αὐτὸν ἔδωκεν κεφαλὴν ὑπὲρ πάντα.

Such a reconstruction could be seen to contain *parallelismus membrorum*, the first time with participles and the second time with finite verbs; also, the verbal forms come near the beginning of each line, and there is the repetition of καί. ἐν τοῖς ἐπουρανίοις, "in the heavenly realms," in v 20 could then be seen as a gloss by the writer, using a phrase distinctive to his letter. Verse 21 would be an addition in prose style elaborating on the completeness of Christ's victory over the powers. τῇ ἐκκλησίᾳ at the end of v 22 would be a further gloss, like that in Col 1:18, intended to focus the Christological statement in terms of its significance for the Church, a theme which the author develops further by his descriptive statement in v 23. This hypothesis has its attractions.

On the other hand, the statements in the fragment could equally well have been creedal statements not taken from one particular hymn but woven together by the writer in the liturgical and hymnic style of which he has already shown himself to be capable in 1:3–14 (cf. Gnilka, 94, 96; Barth, 154; Lindemann, *Aufhebung*, 205; Schnackenburg, 70–71). The similarity of the wording of 1:20 with Col 2:12b and especially the similarities between 1:20–22 and 1 Cor 15:24–27 (where both passages involve a combination of the use of Ps 110:1 and the use of Ps 8:6, agree in their wording of the latter as against the LXX and its citation in Heb 2:8, and have the same order and terminology for the three powers ἀρχή, ἐξουσία, and δύναμις) also make one wonder whether it is not more likely that the author has been influenced by earlier Pauline material than that he has made use of a hymn. But against this it can be countered (cf. Sanders, *ZNW* 56 [1965] 222) that 1 Cor 15:24–28 itself reflects elements of early Christian preaching, elements which also found a place in the church's liturgy, so that Eph 1:20–23 can be seen as drawing on material in that liturgical tradition rather than directly on 1 Cor 15. None of the arguments is decisive, and it remains an open question whether vv 20–23 incorporate the fragment of a hymn or make use of creedal formulations phrased in exalted poetic language. However, the absence of decisive arguments for the former position means that the latter is the safer option if one is forced to choose. In either case, as we shall see, the writer shapes such material for his own particular purposes.

It is a striking and much discussed feature of the formal structure of Ephesians that an epistolary thanksgiving is present at all in a composition which has already begun with an introductory *berakah*. This is a feature which makes Ephesians unique in the Pauline corpus. Much of the debate about it has focused on its implications for the question of authorship. Schubert (*Form*, 44, followed by Kirby, *Ephesians*, 131) held that the inclusion of the Ephesian thanksgiving indicated "a highly conscious effort on the part of the author to omit nothing which he considered formally essential in Pauline epistolography." Kirby (*Ephesians*, 132) believed that the thanksgiving was in fact inserted into a liturgical composition which the author already had before him, in order to give it the appearance of a personal letter from Paul. This latter suggestion has little in its favor, however, for in terms of its style and composition the thanksgiving cannot be distinguished from its context, containing liturgical elements and verbal similarities with Colossians to the same extent as does the preceding material in 1:2–14 and that which follows in chap. 2. Whatever its inclusion suggests about authorship, there is no reason to believe it was not composed at the same time and by the same procedures as the rest of the first three chapters (cf. also Mitton, 65). The most telling point that Schubert and Kirby make is that the thanksgiving appears to be redundant, in that an opening *berakah* and an introductory thanksgiving both perform the same function. They are two ways of doing the same thing. O'Brien (*NTS* 25 [1979] 512–13) claims that such arguments about authorship are "a two-edged sword." He holds that Paul in his introductions employed εὐχαριστέω consistently of thanksgivings for God's work in the lives of others and εὐλογητός for blessings in which he participated himself. O'Brien goes on to conclude that the writer who would preserve this distinction while boldly including both a *berakah* and thanksgiving, thereby making this letter different from any other, is most likely to have been Paul. To this it must be said that it is questionable how consistently the alleged distinction holds for the other letters (cf. 1 Thess 3:9; Col 1:12, 13). Even if it did hold, it would only show that there are some formal distinctions between a *berakah* and a thanksgiving, and this would still not meet the point that the two perform the same epistolary function as an introduction.

Instead of becoming entangled in questions of authorship almost immediately, it may well be a more fruitful approach to ask whether the twofold introduction is as distinctive as it is often assumed to be. If the eulogy and thanksgiving forms were interchangeable, then perhaps the structure of Ephesians is not so different from that of 1 Thessalonians, where there is more than one thanksgiving period (cf. 1:2; 2:13; 3:9), or 2 Thessalonians (cf. 1:3; 2:13), or even Colossians with its double thanksgiving statement (cf. 1:3, 4 and 1:9–12). F. O. Francis ("The Form and Function of the Opening and Closing Paragraphs of James and 1 John," *ZNW* 61 [1970] 110–26) has in fact investigated the phenomenon of double opening statements in letters. He shows how in Josephus' version of the exchange of letters between Solomon and Hiram the second letter replaces a thanksgiving by a twofold statement anticipating important thematic material under the rubrics of "blessing" and then "rejoicing" (*Ant.* 8.50–54; cf. also Eupolemus' version of the same letters in Eusebius, *Praep. evang.* 9.33, 34, where the second letter has a blessing followed by a statement which links rejoicing and blessing, although it has no formal thanksgiving). Within the NT itself Francis points to a variety of epistolary double formulae, including thanksgivings, which play a vital role in the structure of the entire body of a letter, as in 1 and 2 Thessalonians; the blessing and reverse thanksgiving which frame the opening statement of 2 Cor 1:3–11 (cf. also M. E. Thrall's argument that 2:14–17 constitutes a second thanksgiving period in the letter in "A Second Thanksgiving Period in II Corinthians," *JSNT* 16 [1982] 101–24); and opening statements which are initiated and carried forward by a pair of thanksgivings, as in Colossians, a pair of rejoicing formulae, as in 3 John, or a combination of blessing and thanksgiving, as in Ephesians. To Francis' list could also be added the second letter found at the beginning of 2 Maccabees (1:10b–2:18), which contains a thanksgiving accompanied by a eulogy. In addition to these observations about epistolary introductions, it must also be said that in terms of Jewish liturgical background a sequence of eulogy followed by thanksgiving can often be found (e.g., Dan 2:20–23; *Jub.* 22.6–9). So, as with the use of thanksgiving periods themselves in the Pauline letters, both epistolary patterns and liturgical factors can help to explain this combination of *berakah* and thanksgiving in Ephesians. Seen in this light the phenomenon has no special implications for authorship. Either Paul or a follower, writing his own version of a Pauline letter, could have produced this variation on double opening statements which perform a similar function.

What functions does the thanksgiving section of 1:15–23 perform? Is it identical to that of the *berakah* in 1:3–14 and therefore totally redundant? We have already pointed out that redundancy of style is a characteristic of the first part of Ephesians, so some redundancy in regard to its formal elements would not be surprising. It is true that the thanksgiving does not introduce any totally new themes. However, it does explicitly mention Christ's resurrection and exaltation for the first time and makes clear the relation between Christ's universal rule and the Church, also introduced as a specific entity for the first time. In this way the thanksgiving has a complementary introductory role to the *berakah*, giving sharper focus to themes already introduced or only implicit. In other Pauline letters the thanksgiving period with its prayer-report not only announces the central message but also anticipates the letter's main paraenetic thrust. Here in Ephesians also, the thanksgiving not only continues the announcement of the central themes, but makes clear, in a way the *berakah* does not, why these themes have been introduced. It is in order that the readers might have a greater knowledge of the God of our Lord Jesus Christ, and of the hope, the privileges, and the power that are available to them through him. The blessings described earlier are to be part of the believers' awareness and increasingly appropriated by them. It is in the thanksgiving section, therefore, that the didactic and paraenetic thrust of the letter is more clearly introduced.

The rhetorical function of the thanksgiving period and prayer-report is as a continuation of the exordium begun by the eulogy. The passage serves as a *captatio benevolentiae,* a statement which secures the goodwill of the recipients. It achieves this through its thankfulness for the readers' faith and love and through its concern for their growth in knowledge and appreciation of God and of the benefits he has made available to them in Christ. As with 1:3–14, the *oratio perpetua* of 1:15–23 means that the readers will also be carried along with the writer's contemplation of God's power in raising Christ and making him sovereign over the cosmos. Both at the beginning and at the end of this contemplation their sympathies for what the writer is saying are maintained through his making clear that all that has happened in Christ is to their advantage: God's power in Christ is for those who believe (v 19) and Christ's sovereignty over the cosmos is exercised on behalf of the Church (v 22).

Comment

15, 16a Διὰ τοῦτο κἀγώ, "for this reason . . . I." The phrase "for this reason" probably points back to the whole *berakah* of vv 3–14, to which the thanksgiving period introduced by these words is complementary. More particularly, it provides a link with vv 13, 14, in which the writer has already drawn the recipients of the letter into his blessing of God as he focused on their experience of the gospel. A number of Pauline thanksgivings have the actual expression of thanksgiving in the singular form (cf. 1 Cor 1:4; Rom 1:8; Philem 4; Phil 1:3, contrast 1 Thess 1:3, 2 Thess 1:3; Col 1:3), but this is the only reference with the emphatic first person pronoun κἀγώ. This feature is consistent with the way in which ἐγώ lays stress on the apostle himself in 3:1 and 4:1 and with the omission of the mention of any co-senders in 1:1. Both factors suggest a disciple writing in the name of Paul alone in order to focus on the apostolic authority behind the message of the letter.

ἀκούσας τὴν καθ' ὑμᾶς πίστιν ἐν τῷ κυρίῳ Ἰησοῦ καὶ τὴν ἀγάπην τὴν εἰς πάντας τοὺς ἁγίους, "having heard of your faith in the Lord Jesus and your love for all the saints." See the discussion under *Notes* for reasons for taking this as the original text. Some hold that the wording suggests hearsay acquaintance with the readers' faith and love, and that this tells against Pauline authorship. If hearsay acquaintance is the force of the wording, it should be clear that this tells only against Pauline authorship of a letter *to Ephesus,* where he had spent a lot of time, but not against Pauline authorship of a circular letter. Col 1:4 uses similar language about those with whom the apostle was not personally acquainted. Philem 5 uses similar language with reference to Philemon, whom Paul clearly did know. But the participle there is in the present tense, and this may make a difference (cf. also Abbott, 25), indicating that Epaphras had brought him news of his co-worker. If the writer is a Pauline disciple, then the wording amounts to a general statement of his knowledge of those to whom he is writing, which echoes Pauline thanksgivings.

The writer has already made reference to his readers' act of belief in v 13. But is "in the Lord Jesus" here the object of the readers' faith (cf. Abbott, 25; Gnilka, 88), or does it denote the sphere in which their faith is exercised (Schlier, 76; Gaugler, 57; Ernst, 284)? Paul usually has the object of faith in the genitive (cf. Gal 2:16, 20; 3:22; Rom 3:22, 25; Phil 3:9) or else uses πρός (Philem 5) or εἰς (Col 2:5). In favor of the former interpretation are the apparent parallelism with τὴν ἀγάπην τὴν εἰς πάντας τοὺς ἁγίους, "love for all the saints," where the prepositional phrase does indicate the object of the readers' love, the LXX background in which ἐν, "in," can be used with πίστις, "faith," and πιστεύειν, "to believe," to denote the object (cf. Jer 12:6; Ps 77:22), and the interchangeability of ἐν, "in," and εἰς, "toward," in popular Greek. On the other hand, when ἐν is used with πίστις elsewhere in the Pauline corpus, it appears to refer to the realm in which faith operates (cf. Gal 3:26; 5:6; Col 1:4; 1 Tim 1:15; 3:13; 2 Tim 1:13; 3:15). The closest verbal correspondence of the thanksgiving here in Ephesians is to that in Colossians, and Col 1:4, τὴν πίστιν ὑμῶν ἐν Χριστῷ Ἰησοῦ, "your faith in Christ Jesus," is a reference to the faith the Colossians exercise as those who are in Christ (cf. Lohse, *Colossians,* 16; Moule, *Colossians,* 49; O'Brien, *Colossians,* 11). This reference, together with normal Pauline usage, tips the weight of the argument in favor of the same meaning in Eph 1:15 (cf. also 1:1 and the comments on "faithful in Christ Jesus"). The readers' "love for all the saints" has been interpreted as proof of the breaking down of barriers between Gentiles and Jews (cf. Caird, 43), but "the saints" here is a reference to believers in general rather than to the Jerusalem church or to Jewish Christians. The same phrase is used in Col 1:4 and Philem 5 where the general, rather than any narrow, reference is in view. The recipients of this letter have an attitude of solidarity with, and concern for, the welfare of other believers. The importance of their relationship with "all the saints" is expressed also in 3:18 and 6:18 (cf. also 6:24). Faith and love are mentioned together in 1:15, as they are in the thanksgivings of 1 Thess 1:3 and 2 Thess 1:3. The other member of the triad which appears frequently in early Christian writings—hope—has already been mentioned in v 12 and will be stressed in the intercessory prayer-report in v 18. Faith, hope, and love are found together in Pauline thanksgiving periods in 1 Thess 1:3 and Col 1:4, 5.

οὐ παύομαι εὐχαριστῶν ὑπὲρ ὑμῶν, "I do not cease giving thanks for you." As in Pauline thanksgivings, there is mention of the constancy of the writer's thanksgiving for his addressees (cf. πάντοτε in 1 Thess 1:2; 2 Thess 1:3; 2:13; 1 Cor 1:4; Phil 1:4; Col 1:3; Philem 4), and this is to be taken in connection with the following reference to prayers. The clause is not a claim to having given over his whole life to thanksgiving, but means that the writer does not forget in his regular times of prayer to give thanks for those to whom he is writing. Such expressions of thanksgiving were, as we have seen, a convention in letter writing, but there is no reason why this one should not reflect the actual prayer life of the writer as much as other letters did that of Paul himself (cf. O'Brien, *Introductory Thanksgivings,* 266). His gratitude to God for those whose faith and love are known to him and of whom his previous description in vv 13, 14 is true is based ultimately on God's own work in Christ, as that *berakah* so clearly indicates.

16b, 17 Just as the wording of the thanksgiving in vv 15, 16a had a close relation to that of Col 1:3, 4, so some of the key words at the beginning of the intercessory prayer-report in vv 16b, 17 can be found in that of Col 1:9, 10.

μνείαν ποιούμενος ἐπὶ τῶν προσευχῶν μου, "remembering you in my prayers," literally, "making remembrance in my prayers." As we noted under *Form/Structure/Setting,* assurances of a writer's constant prayers for the health and welfare of the addressee can be found in Greek papyrus letters. 1 Macc 12:11 also provides an example of this stylistic feature. The same expression "making remembrance" occurs in 1 Thess 1:2; Rom 1:9; Philem 4. Here the unexpressed object, "you," clearly needs to be supplied from the previous clause in v 16a. The writer is indicating that he makes use of what he knows of his readers and their situation to intercede on their behalf before God. His intercession amounts to a prayer for their growth in Christian maturity. In praying for wisdom he is asking for something which, according to v 8, has already been lavishly given. Yet this prayer indicates his realism about the state of his readers— there will always be room for further growth and sanctification—and his appreciation of the object of his request—God's wisdom can never be totally possessed, since it is inexhaustible.

ὁ θεὸς τοῦ κυρίου ἡμῶν Ἰησοῦ Χριστοῦ, ὁ πατὴρ τῆς δόξης, "the God of our Lord Jesus Christ, the Father of glory." The liturgical style of the prayer-report is immediately indicated in this designation of the one to whom the prayer is addressed. The first phrase is reminiscent of the way in which God is described at the beginning of the *berakah* (1:3). It maintains a distinction between God and Christ in which the latter is subordinate, and at the same time it characterizes God as the Christian God, the one uniquely associated with Christ. "The Father of glory" (cf. Acts 7:2, "the God of glory") is a Semitic genitival phrase where frequently the second noun can have adjectival force. To translate it as "the glorious Father," however, probably does not capture sufficiently the force of the OT notion of *kābôd* as the mode of God's being and activity, which lies behind the designation here. "Glory" denotes the splendor of the divine presence and power. In fact, in Paul "glory" and "power" can be synonymous in terms of God's activity (cf. Rom 6:4 and 1 Cor 6:14 with reference to his activity in raising Christ). Here in 1:17, as well as focusing on the radiance of God's being, glory may also be linked with the notion of enlightenment in 1:18 as the power to illuminate (cf. the connection between the glory of God and the light of knowledge in 2 Cor 4:4, 6).

ἵνα . . . δώῃ ὑμῖν πνεῦμα σοφίας καὶ ἀποκαλύψεως ἐν ἐπιγνώσει αὐτοῦ, "that . . . (he) may give you the Spirit of wisdom and revelation in the knowledge of him." In v 8 of the eulogy God has been blessed for supplying in his grace all wisdom and insight. Now this language is taken up in the request that what is already theirs might continue to be communicated to God's people by the Spirit. πνεῦμα σοφίας καὶ ἀποκαλύψεως is a variation on ἐν πάσῃ σοφίᾳ καὶ συνέσει πνευματικῇ, "in all wisdom and insight worked by the Spirit" (Col 1:9). The addition of the notion of revelation corresponds to the writer's emphasis on this theme later (esp. 3:3, 5). πνεῦμα σοφίας occurs a number of times in the LXX, where it refers to the inspiration of the makers of Aaron's garments (Exod 28:3), Bezalel, the craftsman (Exod 31:3; 35:31), Joshua (Deut 34:9, πνεῦμα συνέσεως), and God's Messiah (Isa 11:2). Later the Qumran community claimed for itself, as the pure remnant, the Spirit of understanding, insight, wisdom, and knowledge (1QS 4.3–5) and *1 Enoch* 49.3 could say of the Elect One that "in him dwells the spirit of wisdom, and the spirit which gives insight, and the spirit of understanding and of might." In the OT, wisdom often involves practical knowledge, the ability to choose right conduct, while in Paul it often involves understanding God's activity in Christ and the benefits it brings to believers. Both of these dimensions surface in Ephesians' interest in the notion of wisdom (1:8, 17; 3:10; 5:15) and in its ethical exhortations which make use of elements of wisdom teaching.

The term πνεῦμα ἀποκαλύψεως does not occur in the LXX. 1 Cor 2:10–13 speaks of the revelation that takes place through the Spirit, and in 1 Cor 14:6, 26, 30 ἀποκάλυψις refers to the spiritual gift of receiving and passing on a revealed message. In Ephesians, when the noun ἀποκάλυψις is used again in 3:3 or the verb ἀποκαλύπτειν in 3:5, or its synonym γνωρίζειν in 1:9; 3:3, 5, 10; 6:19, it is in connection with various aspects of the mystery of what God has done in Christ. In 3:5 it is especially stated that such revelation takes place through the Spirit. Whereas in 3:3 the revelation is said to be for Paul himself, and in 3:5 it comes to the holy apostles and prophets, the intercessory prayer-report requests revelation for all believers. It is interesting that the writer does not view revelation as restricted solely to the apostles and prophets, although the revelation that came to them appears to have foundational priority and authority (cf. 2:20; 3:5). Instead, revelation continues to be given by God through the Spirit to all believers to enable them to understand the disclosure of God's secret and to show them how to live in the light of it. Certainly the experience of the Spirit's illumination, which was restricted to a select few in Israel and is granted particularly to apostles and prophets in the Church, can also be seen as belonging to the Church as a whole (cf. Col 1:26; also Barth, 164). The content of this revelation to all believers is suggested by the petition for the threefold enlightenment which follows in vv 18, 19.

There is discussion among the commentators whether πνεῦμα without the definite article refers to the human spirit as the possessor of a spiritual gift (Abbott, 28, Beare, 628, Mitton, 67) or to the holy Spirit as the giver of wisdom and revelation (Flowers, *ExpTim* 38 [1926–27] 227; Gaugler, 62; Caird, 45). It is difficult to make a sharp distinction between the Spirit of God and the human spirit, which is precisely that part of the personality open to the influence of the divine Spirit, and so some see the reference here as being to both equally (Gnilka, 90; Barth, 162). Paul was able to make some distinction, however, and was in fact capable of using πνεῦμα with the two different senses in one sentence (Rom 8:16). In favor of the human spirit as the receiver of spiritual gifts in 1:17 are the reference in 4:23, where it is the human spirit which is renewed, the reference in Gal 6:1, where "spirit of gentleness" appears to denote a human quality, and the fact that ἀποκάλυψις in 1 Cor 14 refers to a spiritual gift possessed by a believer. But the factors which favor an emphasis here on the divine Spirit as giver are weightier. They include the explicit mention of the divine Spirit in connection with revelation in 3:5 (cf. also 1 Cor 2:6–16), the apparent dependence on Col 1:9 where "spiritual" refers to the Spirit, and the close verbal parallel to Rom 8:15 where πνεῦμα υἱοθεσίας, "Spirit of adoption," is to be taken as a reference to God's Spirit. So this is a petition for the Spirit himself to be at work, giving insights into and unveiling aspects of the purpose of God in Christ, an activity which could take place privately, to individuals, or in the corporate assembly gathered for worship.

It is in this way that the writer envisages growth in knowledge of God coming about—ἐν ἐπιγνώσει αὐτοῦ. This phrase picks up on the language of the intercessory prayer-report in Col 1:9, "knowledge of his will," and Col

1:10, "knowledge of God." ἐπίγνωσις occurs several times in Colossians (cf. also 2:2; 3:10) and Ephesians (cf. also 4:13). Its synonym γνῶσις is found in Col 2:3 and Eph 3:19. These are terms which would have been congenial to Hellenistic syncretistic religion with its concern for the communication of esoteric knowledge. It could well be that their use in these letters suggests a contrast with this emphasis in the syncretistic philosophy, indicating that this is a prayer for the genuine article, real knowledge of God (cf. also Barth, 149). For a follower of Paul ἐπίγνωσις has moral, as well as simply intellectual, overtones from the OT background. The living, obedient relationship with God that it involves is dependent on God's prior knowledge of humanity (cf. Gal 4:9; 1 Cor 13:12). In its context, the genuine knowledge of God requested in 1:17 is grounded in a life of faith and love, is produced by the Spirit, and is explained further in the rest of the prayer in vv 18, 19.

18, 19 The rest of the prayer is a petition for a threefold enlightenment. The three clauses beginning with τίς, τίς, and τί ask for knowledge of the hope God's calling brings, knowledge of the wealth of glory laid up in his inheritance in the saints, and knowledge of the immensity of his power. These are three different aspects of the salvation believers should be experiencing, each of which should be given its own weight, rather than the inheritance and the power being subordinated to hope as an expansion on what this hope involves (*pace* Schlier, 81–82).

πεφωτισμένους τοὺς ὀφθαλμοὺς τῆς καρδίας, "the eyes of your heart having been enlightened." On the place of this clause in the syntax see under *Notes*. Is the choice of the image of "light" for knowledge related to the contrast between light and darkness in the Colossian thanksgiving period (Col 1:12, 13), with which this Ephesian thanksgiving period has so much in common? Just as the transference from darkness to light of Col 1:12, 13 has been associated with baptism (cf. Lohse, *Colossians*, 38), so some commentators have suggested that the reference to enlightenment here in 1:18 could be a reference to baptism (cf. Schlier, 79; Houlden, 275). Although certainly at a later date enlightenment is equated with baptism (cf. *Odes Sol.* 15; Justin Martyr, *Apol.* 1.61.12; 1.65.1; *Dial.* 39.2; 122.1, 2, 6), and here in Ephesians the hymn with the line "and Christ will shine upon you" (5:14) is usually connected with baptism, the reference in 1:18 is to an inner enlightenment, affecting "the eyes of your heart." The perfect tense, with its sense of a completed action which has continuing force, must then refer to the illumination of conversion. The readers' state prior to this is indicated by 4:18, "darkened in their understanding," and 5:8, "for once you were darkness." But the writer believes that a decisive transformation has taken place and saving illumination has been brought by the Spirit through the gospel. This has affected the heart, which in OT and Jewish writings was seen as the seat of thought, the organ of practical knowledge and wisdom. A parallel to the language of this clause and its context can be found in the Qumran literature in the blessing of 1QS 2.3, "May He lighten your heart with life-giving wisdom and grant you eternal knowledge!" (cf. also 1QS 11.3–6). The actual phrase "the eyes of the heart" is not found in OT or Jewish writings but occurs in the *Corpus Hermeticum* (cf. 4.11; 7.1) and can also be found later in *1 Clem.* 36.2; 59.3, which may be dependent on Ephesians. This has suggested to some the possibility that the phrase was current in gnosticizing thought but was put to his own use by the writer to the Ephesians (cf. Gaugler, 64).

εἰς τὶ εἰδέναι ὑμᾶς τίς ἐστιν ἡ ἐλπὶς τῆς κλήσεως αὐτοῦ, "that you may know what is the hope of his calling." The writer believes it is essential that the addressees be aware of the hope they can enjoy as a result of the fact that God has called them. The language of "calling" brings to mind that of "choice," "predestination," and "appointment" in the eulogy (1:4, 5, 11), and it will occur again at the beginning of the paraenesis (4:1, 4). The call of God is the actualization in history of his electing purpose and involves God's initiative in bringing a person into relationship with himself (cf. Schlier, 82–84, for a summary of Paul's treatment of the notion of calling). It is powerful and effective in opening up for them that hope which is the content of the gospel. "It is a certain hope: for it rests on the very fact that the calling is God's calling and no weak wish of ours for better things" (J. A. Robinson, 40). Whereas in 1:12 believers' activity in hoping has been stressed, here it is the object of hope, that which is hoped for, which is in view, rather than the disposition itself. That which believers hope for is the consummation of their salvation, the summing up of all things in Christ (1:10). This notion of hope as that which is hoped for accords with the usage of the term in Colossians, where it is said to be already laid up in heaven (1:5), where it is seen as the content of the gospel (1:23), and where Christ among the Gentiles is viewed as the hope of glory (1:27). In line with the thought of Colossians, although hope here has an inevitable future connotation, its reference is not restricted entirely to the future (*contra* Houlden, 275; Mitton, 68). Since hope is so closely tied up to Christ as the content of salvation, it is already present in heaven and there can be awareness of it in the Church. Once the readers were separated from Christ and had no hope (2:12), but now through the work of the Spirit they can have an increasing knowledge of the hope into which God has brought them by his call.

τίς ὁ πλοῦτος τῆς δόξης τῆς κληρονομίας αὐτοῦ ἐν τοῖς ἁγίοις, "what are the riches of his glorious inheritance among the saints." The phrase ὁ πλοῦτος τῆς δόξης occurs elsewhere in Rom 9:23, 24 where it is also connected with God's calling of his people from both Jews and Gentiles. Here the riches of glory are linked particularly to God's inheritance among his people. Many commentators have assumed that the writer is thinking of the believers' inheritance. But whereas 1:14 talked about that—τῆς κληρονομίας ἡμῶν, "our inheritance"— and believers' obtaining their inheritance coincided with God's taking complete possession of his people and thereby his glory being praised, here in 1:18 the talk is of τῆς κληρονομίας αὐτοῦ, "his inheritance," God's inheritance, which focuses not so much on what he gives his people as on the other side of the thought of 1:14, his possession of his people. In the OT God's inheritance is frequently used as a synonym for his people, Israel (cf. Deut 4:20; 9:26, 29; 2 Sam 21:3; 1 Kgs 8:51, 53; 2 Kgs 21:14; Pss 28:9; 33:12; 68:9; 78:62, 71; 94:14; 106:5, 40; Isa 19:25; 47:6; 63:17; Jer 10:16; 51:19). Here his inheritance involves the people of God from both Jews and Gentiles, for it is ἐν τοῖς ἁγίοις, "among the saints." The meaning of ἅγιοι here has been much disputed, however. Several commentators believe the reference is to the angels (cf. Schlier, 84; Gnilka, 91; Schnackenburg, 74; Mussner, 53–54; cf. also my earlier view,

Lincoln, *Paradise*, 144). In the OT the angels can be called "holy ones" (ἅγιοι: LXX Job 15:15; Ps 88:6, 8; Isa 57:15; Amos 4:2; Dan 8:13), and the language of inheritance is used in connection with them at Qumran—"God has given them to his chosen ones as an everlasting possession, and has caused them to inherit the lot of the Holy Ones" (1QS 11.7, 8; cf. also 1QH 11.7, 8)—so that the elect community on earth is seen as joined with the angels in heaven. In Paul ἅγιοι does appear to refer to angels in 1 Thess 3:13 and 2 Thess 1:7, 10, and this may well be the significance of the term in Col 1:12, τῷ ἱκανώσαντι ὑμᾶς εἰς τὴν μερίδα τοῦ κλήρου τῶν ἁγίων ἐν τῷ φωτί, "who qualified us to share in the inheritance of the holy ones in light" (cf. Lohse, *Colossians,* 35, 36; Martin, *Colossians,* 54; Lincoln, *Paradise,* 119). This makes sense in the context of Colossians for designating what is involved in the believers' inheritance. But elsewhere in the NT that inheritance involves a place among the saints, the people of God (cf. Acts 20:32, δοῦναι τὴν κληρονομίαν ἐν τοῖς ἡγιασμένοις πᾶσιν, "to give you the inheritance among all those who have been sanctified"; Acts 26:18, κλῆρον ἐν τοῖς ἡγιασμένοις πίστει τῇ εἰς ἐμέ, "a place among those sanctified by faith in me"; cf. also Wis 5:5). Ephesians uses similar words to those in Col 1:12 but with a different relationship among them and in a difficult context. Here it is *God's* inheritance which is in view and his inheritance consists of the believers who now constitute his people (cf. also Abbott, 30; Gaugler, 69; Houlden, 275; Ernst, 288; Mitton, 68–69). A narrower reference to Israel (Barth, 151) or Jewish Christians (Caird, 45) is not in view in this context. Those who opt for a reference to angels allow the Qumran parallels to be too decisive. A reference to believers as a whole does best justice to the inheritance in 1:18 being God's and not believers', to the emphasis in the eulogy on the people of God as his possession, to the other ἅγιοι references in Ephesians (in 1:1, just previously in 1:15, and then later in 2:19 and 3:8), and to the focus in this letter on the Church and glory in the Church (cf. 3:21; 5:27). This part of the writer's petition, then, is that the readers might appreciate the wonder, the glory of what God has done in entering into possession of his people, the Church from Jews and Gentiles, and the immense privilege it is to be among these saints.

καὶ τί τὸ ὑπερβάλλον μέγεθος τῆς δυνάμεως αὐτοῦ εἰς ἡμᾶς τοὺς πιστεύοντας κατὰ τὴν ἐνέργειαν τοῦ κράτους τῆς ἰσχύος αὐτοῦ, "and what is the surpassing greatness of his power toward us who believe, according to the working of his mighty strength." The writer also desires believers to know the greatness of God's power and attempts to exhaust the resources of the Greek language by piling up four synonyms for power in order to convey an impression of something of the divine might. Three of the terms are in a double genitive construction at the end of v 19 (cf. other genitive constructions with words for power in 3:7 and 6:10). Some commentators have suggested that if there is any distinction of nuance, then δύναμις denotes ability to accomplish something, ἐνέργεια inherent strength or power, κράτος the power to overcome what stands in the way, and ἰσχύς the exercise of power (cf. Schlier, 85; Barth, 152 n. 39). However, the point in the writer's heaping up of these expressions is not their distinctiveness but their similarity. Again, the language of the Colossian thanksgiving period appears to lie behind that of Ephesians, this time from the intercessory prayer-report in Col 1:11, ἐν πάσῃ δυνάμει δυναμούμενοι κατὰ τὸ κράτος τῆς δόξης αὐτοῦ, "may you be strengthened with all power according to his glorious might." The accumulation in terms in Ephesians, however, outdoes that in Colossians. The immense power of God is exercised "toward us who believe." Here there is a change to the first person plural from the second person plural which has dominated the prayer apart from the earlier description of God as "the God of our Lord Jesus Christ." This appears to be simply a stylistic variation. εἰς, "toward," can probably be understood to include the sense of ἐν, "in" (cf. 3:20 where God's power is said to be at work within believers). This life-giving power of the new age was the power which raised Christ from the dead (1:20), was the revelatory power at work in Paul's gospel (3:7), and is the power available now for the people of God in the continuing communication of God's grace. The prayer is that believers should know and appropriate such power.

20, 21 ἣν ἐνήργηκεν ἐν τῷ Χριστῷ ἐγείρας αὐτὸν ἐκ νεκρῶν, "which he accomplished in Christ when he raised him from the dead." The extent of the power available to believers has been demonstrated in what God has already done in Christ, particularly in raising him from the dead and exalting him. ἐνήργηκεν picks up on the cognate noun ἐνέργεια at the end of v 19 and as a perfect signifies a completed action with a continuing effect. That this act of God in Christ does have a determinative effect on believers' understanding of their own existence will be made clear in 2:5, 6. In delineating what God accomplished in Christ there is no mention of Christ's death on the cross. Clearly this is because the focus of the writer's attention is on the power displayed in God's activity, and in Paul's thought the cross is primarily connected with weakness but the resurrection with power (cf. 2 Cor 13:4). Other places in Paul's writings which link the resurrection of Christ with the power of God are 1 Cor 6:14, Rom 1:4, and Phil 3:10. Col 2:12 is particularly significant because it also employs the term ἐνέργεια in connection with God raising Christ from the dead. The creedal-sounding formulation of 1:20 reflects the dominant conviction of early Christianity that Christ was alive, and here, as nearly everywhere else in the NT, his resurrection is seen as an act of God rather than his own act. Yet the emphasis in the writer's thought is not on the resurrection itself but more on the exaltation which receives attention in the rest of vv 20, 21 and which has such importance for the perspective of this letter.

καὶ καθίσας ἐν δεξιᾷ αὐτοῦ ἐν τοῖς ἐπουρανίοις, "and seated him at his right hand in the heavenly realms." Two aspects of Christ's victory over death are featured in the NT—his resurrection and his exaltation to a position of power and authority. Sometimes only the resurrection is mentioned, as in 1 Thess 1:10; Gal 1:1; 1 Cor 15:3; Rom 1:4. Sometimes it is the exaltation alone which is stressed, as in Phil 2:9. At other times, as here in 1:20, both are mentioned (cf. Rom 8:34; Col 3:1; Acts 2:32, 33), but mention of both need not imply that the writer had two separate episodes of resurrection and then ascension in view as in Luke-Acts (*pace* Houlden, 273). The language of exaltation used here is that of the common early Christian tradition of Christ's session at the right hand of God, which takes up Ps 110:1, one of the portions of the OT most frequently referred to in the NT. Ps 110 may well originally have been employed as an enthronement psalm for the king. Its terminology of a session at the right hand had parallels in the ancient Near Eastern world where the king was often represented as seated next to the tutelary deity of a particular city or nation. Occupying a place on the god's right hand meant that the ruler exercised power on behalf of the god and held a position of supreme honor. In the OT itself Yahweh's right hand is represented as the position of favor (Ps 80:18; Jer 22:24), of victory (Ps 20:6; 44:3; 48:10; Isa 41:10), and of power (Exod 15:6; Ps 89:13; Isa 48:13). There is no firm evidence that before the time of the NT the imagery of the psalm was given a messianic interpretation. The earliest definite messianic use in Judaism is to be found in rabbinic traditions dating from the second half of the third century C.E. (cf. D. M. Hay, *Glory at the Right Hand: Psalm 110 in Early Christianity* [Nashville: Abingdon, 1973] 19–153, on the use and meaning of the psalm in Judaism). Whether these traditions have a long history and predate the NT or whether Christians were the first to use the psalm messianically is therefore difficult to say, though a number of studies incline to the former view (cf. Hay, *Glory at the Right Hand*, 30; W. R. G. Loader, "Christ at the Right Hand—Ps. cx.1 in the New Testament," *NTS* 24 [1978] 199). In any case Ps 110:1 came to be applied frequently to Jesus in the early church. Paul had taken up this Christological interpretation in 1 Cor 15:25; Rom 8:34; and Col 3:1. Here the writer continues this tradition in order to evoke Christ's position of supreme favor and honor, his place of victory and power associated with his exaltation to heaven.

With reference to Christ's place of exaltation the writer sets a symbolic phrase, "at his right hand," next to a spatial one, "in the heavenly realms." (See the discussion of the significance of this latter phrase under 1:3 above.) The functions of the two phrases are not to be equated, for the former as a symbol of sovereignty is posited only of Christ, not of believers (cf. 2:6 where despite the other parallels with 1:20 "at his right hand" is omitted). Here, as in other places in the NT (cf. Acts 2:34; Heb 8:1), a reference to Ps 110:1 is juxtaposed with a local setting of heaven, so that while, on the one hand, the writer speaks of Christ in spatial terms, on the other, his use of an expression such as "at his right hand" indicates that he viewed Christ as also breaking through the bounds of such categories (cf. also 4:10). Yet for the early Christians Christ had not simply disappeared nor had he evaporated into a universal spirit, but he had departed to a new sphere, that of heaven, which would be appropriate to his transformed body's mode of existence. In the view of the history of salvation as a cosmic drama, which this writer shares with Paul, Christ's exaltation to heaven means that a shift in the center of gravity from the realm of earth to that of heaven has taken place, for the central figure in the drama of salvation has been moved from the setting of earth to that of heaven, where he now is (cf. 6:9). This is crucial for understanding the writer's perspective in this letter. It is not that Christology has been swallowed up by ecclesiology, but rather that what has happened to Christ becomes determinative for the Church in its relationship to the heavenly realm.

ὑπεράνω πάσης ἀρχῆς καὶ ἐξουσίας καὶ δυνάμεως καὶ κυριότητος, "far above every principality and authority and power and dominion." The scope of the victory God has secured by exalting Christ is made clear by the enumeration of the defeated cosmic powers. This verse does not use the characteristic terms of Valentinian Gnosticism, which spoke of such cosmic beings as "aeons" and "archons" (rulers). Rather, those who trace the language about the powers back to OT and early Jewish beliefs in angelic powers are likely to be right. In fact all four names found here are listed in *2 Enoch* 20–22, where in the seventh heaven ten classes of angels are placed on ten steps according to their rank (cf. also *1 Enoch* 61.10; *T. Levi* 3; 2 Macc 3:24). In Judaism there was the belief that God had delegated authority over the nations to angelic beings. The notion that what happens among these beings in heaven affects what happens among the nations on earth is reflected in Dan 10:13, 20. Monotheistic Jews denied the deity of pagan gods but not their existence and influence, which were linked to the existence of rebellious, fallen angels or demonic powers (cf. Deut 32:17). Their beliefs about such supernatural powers also linked them to the various heavenly bodies and saw them as affecting all aspects of life (cf. *Jub.* 2.2; *1 Enoch* 60.11, 12). It is significant that the term δύναμις is used frequently in the LXX translation of the phrase "Lord of hosts." (For a summary of the place of angelic powers in Jewish thought, cf. Carr, *Angels and Principalities*, 25–40; but cf. also Wink, *Naming the Powers*, 13–35, for an important corrective to Carr.) Paul mentions these same powers in 1 Cor 15:24 but does not include the last term mentioned here in 1:21, "dominion." In Rom 8:38 "principalities" and "powers" appear in a list of possible obstacles between the believer and the love of God in Christ, which also includes "angels."

But these principalities and powers feature most prominently in Colossians, with which Ephesians is so closely connected. In Col 1:16 four powers are named in a different order from Eph 1:21 and θρόνοι "thrones," replaces the term "power," while Col 2:10, 15 both refer to "principalities" and "authorities." It is likely that in the syncretistic teaching being advocated in Colossae these angelic powers were associated with the "elemental spirits" (Col 2:8, 20) and were seen as controlling the heavenly realm and with it a person's access to the presence of God. One way of placating them was the rigorous subduing of the flesh in order to gain visionary experience of the heavenly dimension and participate in their angelic liturgy. This in turn was a means of gaining fullness of salvation, reaching the divine presence and obtaining the esoteric knowledge that accompanied such visions. All this would have been in addition to what the Colossians had heard about Christ, so that in effect he became just another intermediary between humans and God, just one more way of penetrating the heavenly dimension to reach God. The writer in that setting would allow no ultimate dualism in regard to the powers. They were to be seen as subordinate to Christ both in terms of creation and redemption, the latter involving their reconciliation or pacification (cf. 1:20, also Lincoln, *Paradise*, 114–22). This background still has its echoes in Ephesians, as Paul's disciple writes to the churches of the Pauline mission in Asia Minor. In addition to 1:21, 3:10 and 6:12 pick up the language of "principalities" and "authorities." Here in 1:21 the writer makes clear that Christ cannot be viewed as on the same level as other angelic powers in the cosmic hierarchy. His exaltation has placed him above them all.

There has been discussion as to whether the powers listed here are benign or hostile. Carr (*Angels and Principalities*, 98–99) believes the terms here may only apply to abstract notions but asserts that if the reference is to personal spiritual powers, then the list contributes to the Christology, not by pointing to Christ's victory over hostile powers, but simply by associating him with

God as the one who receives the recognition of the heavenly host. Yet when the powers are listed by Paul in 1 Cor 15:24–26, they are among the enemies who are to be put under Christ's feet, and the combination of allusions to Ps 110:1 and Ps 8:6 in connection with these enemies in 1 Corinthians is repeated here in Ephesians (*pace* Carr, *Angels and Principalities*, 90–92, who fails to deal convincingly with this point). 6:12 makes explicit that the principalities and authorities are evil forces (cf. also 2:2) so that in this letter as a whole the powers are to be conceived as hostile beings (cf. also Schlier, 88; Barth, 180; Caird, 46; Gnilka, 95; Wink, *Naming the Powers*, 50–55, 60–61; *pace* Carr, *Angels and Principalities*, 93–111, who has to attempt to argue that Eph 6:12 is an interpolation into the text dating from the middle of the second century).

There is also discussion as to whether the powers, which we have claimed to be supernatural beings, might in fact be human rulers or political structures. The popular demythologizing of these powers in current theology, whereby they represent the structures of human society which oppress people, may well be a valid reinterpretation of a NT concept but it is a reinterpretation. The writer himself believes the powers to be spiritual agencies in the heavenly realm standing behind any earthly or human institutions (cf. 6:12: "for our combat is *not* against flesh and blood, *but* against the principalities, against the authorities, against the world-rulers of this dark domain, against the spiritual forces of evil in the heavenly realms"; *pace*, for example, Barth, 175, who holds that in Ephesians "both visible specific governors and the invisible authority exerted by them; concrete conditions and manifestations of life and the invisible mystery of the psyche" are in view, and Wink, *Naming the Powers*, 60–64). Wink (*Naming the Powers*, 9) is clearly right to assert that the terms for the powers can be employed in the NT for different sorts of powers, sometimes human or earthly, sometimes spiritual or heavenly, and that it will depend on the context as to which is in view in a particular passage. But he too quickly reads a comprehensive meaning, which embraces all these types of powers, into certain passages, especially in Colossians and Ephesians. He also misconstrues Col 1:16, which he makes his paradigm (cf. *Naming the Powers*, 11, 64–67), where the terms for the powers are best understood not as including both things visible and things invisible, but as an elaboration of things invisible, for the benefit of those so concerned with the heavenly realm. πάντα and τὰ πάντα in Eph 1:22, 23 indicate that all things are in subjection to Christ's present rule; but in line with Colossians, on which he is dependent, this writer's use of the specific terminology of "principalities" and "authorities," following on his focus on Christ's exaltation to the heavenly realms, has reference to heavenly spiritual powers, and the "all" that precedes denotes all such powers. Wink's view (104–5) that the cosmic powers do not have a separate spiritual existence but are the inner or spiritual essence, or gestalt, of an institution or state or system may well be a helpful way of appropriating first-century mythology, but it can hardly claim the support of the text of Ephesians. His version of Eph 6:12, "we wrestle not just against flesh and blood but also against principalities, against powers. . . ," (117–18) reflects the type of change in what the writer actually said that is necessary in such a move. (For further support for our view that the powers in Colossians and Ephesians are spiritual agencies cf. also P. T. O'Brien, "Principalities and Powers," in D. A. Carson [ed.], *Biblical*

Interpretation and the Church [Exeter: Paternoster, 1984] 110–50, esp. 133–36; Arnold, *Ephesians*, 41–56).

καὶ παντὸς ὀνόματος ὀνομαζομένου οὐ μόνον ἐν τῷ αἰῶνι τούτῳ ἀλλὰ καὶ ἐν τῷ μέλλοντι, "and every name that is named not only in this age but also in that which is to come." This rhetorical flourish at the end of v 21 underlines the universality of Christ's rule over any imaginable cosmic forces and brings home to believers that they have no possible justification for considering themselves under the control of such powers. The phrase "every name that is named" indicates that the preceding list of names was not meant to be exhaustive and suggests that the powers of which the writer speaks include beings whom many in Asia Minor might regard as deities. "To call on the name" of a deity is a familiar OT expression for worship of that deity, e.g., 1 Kgs 18:24. Arnold (*Ephesians*, 54–55) has drawn attention to the fact that the calling of the names of deities and supernatural powers was fundamental to the practice of magic, and therefore the term ὄνομα itself is pervasive in the magical papyri. It is significant for this writer's view of Christ's supremacy over the names that in Phil 2:9–11 Paul could say that through his exaltation Christ had been given the name above every name.

The explicit mention in 1:21 of the two ages, a notion found in some Jewish apocalypses, provides the only reference in the Pauline corpus to both ages (cf. Matt 12:32). Paul himself saw Christian believers as those "upon whom the end of the ages has come" (1 Cor 10:11) and in a number of places sets believers over against "this age" (cf. Gal 1:4; 1 Cor 1:20; 2:6, 8; 3:18; 2 Cor 4:4; Rom 12:2). When speaking of a present experience of the benefits of the age to come he will often do so in terms of the Spirit or, as in the eschatology of the apocalypses, with reference to the heavenly dimension (cf. Lincoln, *Paradise*, 170–80). It is striking that here in Ephesians where "realized" eschatology is so much to the fore, this reference to "the age to come" treats it as still future (cf. also 2:7). The writer is not here concerned with the Pauline overlap of the ages, but the two ages represent the present and the future in conventional Jewish manner (cf. also Houlden, 276–77; Barth, 155; Mitton, 73; *pace* Schlier, 88; Caird, 47). It is true that the writer's emphasis on Christ's exaltation to heaven and its benefits for the Church indicates clearly that he believes the age to come has already been inaugurated. His view in 1:10 also is that the administration of the fullness of times is already under way. But his use of language in 1:21 remains traditional and has not been coordinated with that perspective (cf. also Schnackenburg, 78, 84). It is also true, however, that the future age will bring nothing new, for the victory of Christ's exaltation above every name in this age continues into the coming age (cf. also Lindemann, *Aufhebung*, 211). This need not imply that temporal categories are of no significance for the writer. The very fact that he still uses traditional two-age terminology is part of the evidence that in Ephesians realized eschatology has not obliterated all futurist eschatology (cf. also 1:14; 2:7; 4:30; 5:5, 27; 6:8, 13).

22a καὶ πάντα ὑπέταξεν ὑπὸ τοὺς πόδας αὐτοῦ, "and he placed all things under his feet." So concerned is the writer to emphasize the supremacy of Christ's heavenly status that he continues to heap up further clauses underlining it. This assertion in v 22a sums up what has preceded with a citation of Ps 8:6 [7 LXX]. It differs from the LXX in that a finite form of the verb replaces a participle and ὑπὸ τοὺς πόδας is preferred to ὑποκάτω τῶν ποδῶν. The wording thereby corresponds to the version of the citation used by Paul in 1 Cor 15:27. Ps 8:6 itself recalls Gen 1:26–28 and honors humanity as created in God's image to exercise dominion over the rest of the created order. In typological fashion Paul has applied this to Christ as the last Adam to whom, by virtue of his resurrection, had been restored dominion over the cosmos (cf. also Phil 3:21). This interpretation has been continued by his follower. πάντα, which in the original psalm referred to that part of the creation below humanity in the hierarchy, now has the same scope as τὰ πάντα in 1:10, 23 so that the whole universe, heaven and earth, cosmic powers and human beings, is seen as subordinated to the exalted Christ. The juxtaposition of the use of Ps 8:6 with the use of Ps 110:1 reminds one of 1 Cor 15:25, 27. But in 1 Cor 15:25, as opposed to Eph 1:20, it is the second part of Ps 110:1, and not the session at the right hand of the first part, to which reference is made. It is likely that Eph 1:20, 22 are dependent on 1 Cor 15, which in turn draws on a common exegetical tradition in the early church whereby Ps 8:6 had become linked to Ps 110:1 in drawing out the implications of Christ's resurrection and exaltation (cf. Heb 1:3, 13; 2:5–8; 1 Pet 3:22). The mediation of this use of the OT via 1 Cor 15:24–28 is suggested by the fact that the wording of Ps 8:6 is the same in both cases and the terminology for the subjugated powers is the same, except that Ephesians has added "dominion" to the end of the list. (For further discussion of this indirect use of the OT cf. Lincoln, *JSNT* 14 [1982] 40–42.) Whereas in 1 Cor 15 the use of Ps 8:6 supports a view of Christ's cosmic lordship which focuses on its full realization at the end of history, here in Ephesians it supports a perspective of realized eschatology, as the ὑπέταξεν is to be taken in a straightforward sense, indicating that the act of subjection has already occurred. This difference is a striking one, though not in itself decisive in regard to the question of authorship, for elsewhere in Paul Christ's rule over the cosmos is seen as having already taken place (cf. Phil 2:10, 11; 3:21b; Col 2:15). But certainly in Eph 1, in the context of prayer, the language of worship of the exalted Lord anticipates the consummation of history.

22b, 23 The final three clauses of the first chapter are some of the most difficult of the whole epistle for the commentator. Not only do they contain major problems of syntax and translation, but they also introduce key terms (head, church, body, and fullness), to which an immense amount of secondary literature has been devoted. The limits of this commentary forbid any full-scale review of and interaction with the literature, but an attempt will be made to sketch the broad outlines of such scholarly discussion.

καὶ αὐτὸν ἔδωκεν κεφαλὴν ὑπὲρ πάντα τῇ ἐκκλησίᾳ, "and gave him as head over all things to the Church." ἔδωκεν has been translated in line with its normal meaning as "gave" rather than as a Semitism reflecting the Hebrew נתן. *nātan*, which can have the sense of "to appoint" (cf. also Abbott, 34; Gnilka, 97; Howard, *NTS* 20 [1974] 353; *pace* Barth, 158). This is how δίδωμι is used throughout Ephesians with an indirect object in the dative case (cf. 1:17; 3:2, 7, 8, 16; 4:7, 8, 11, 27, 29; 6:19). The indirect object here in v 22b is τῇ ἐκκλησίᾳ, and the use of the verb in its more usual sense brings out the characteristic emphasis of Ephesians on God's grace toward the Church.

In fact this last part of the thanksgiving and its use of confessional material is dominated by the concept of the Church. Here is its first explicit mention, but it is immediately given an exalted status, for Christ as cosmic Lord has been given to the Church. The writer has elaborated on the supremacy God has given to Christ in relation to the cosmos in vv 20–22a, but now all these statements about his lordship over the cosmos are subordinated to a statement about God's purpose for Christ in regard to the Church. Syntactically, the weight of this clause falls on τῇ ἐκκλησίᾳ at the end, and the emphasis on the Church continues in the two descriptive clauses which follow. The notion of believers as the people of God has been present both in the eulogy and earlier in this thanksgiving but now comes to explicit focus. This direction in the writer's thought has already been set in v 19 where he has said that the greatness of God's power, which was effective in Christ's exaltation, is "toward us who believe."

Now this is taken further, as the result of that power, and Christ's supremacy over the cosmos is seen to be for the benefit of believers, here described as "the Church." Paul had inherited the term ἐκκλησία from the Christian community, probably from hellenistic Jewish Christian circles (cf. K. Berger, "Volksversammlung und Gemeinde Gottes: Zu den Anfängen der christlichen Verwendung von 'ekklesia,' " ZTK 73 [1976] 167–207). In ordinary Greek usage it meant an assembly or gathering, but in the LXX it was the predominant term for translating קהל, qāhāl, and its usage for the covenant assembly of Israel before Yahweh. In Paul it is used most frequently for the actual gathering of a group of local Christians or for the local group which gathered regularly. But in a number of places he appears to have in view an entity which is broader than the merely local congregation (cf. Gal 1:13; 1 Cor 10:32; 12:28; 15:9; Phil 3:6). Colossians certainly refers to a Church which consists of all believers (1:18, 24), as well as containing references to local gatherings (4:15, 16). Here in Eph 1:22, following Col 1:18, 24 where ἐκκλησία is used in apposition to σῶμα as a designation for the new community in Christ, the reference is to the universal Church, the Christian community in its totality. This is also the case in the other eight uses of the term in Eph 3:10, 21; 5:23, 24, 25, 27, 29, 32 (pace R. Banks, Paul's Idea of Community [Grand Rapids: Eerdmans, 1980] 44–47, who claims that the references in Ephesians are to a heavenly assembly permanently in session).

To the Church in general Christ has been given as head over all. The absence of the article before πάντα in the phrase κεφαλὴν ὑπὲρ πάντα does not mean that this is not a reference to the cosmos (pace Mussner, Christus, 30, 31, who takes the phrase to indicate supreme headship), but is to be explained by the fact that the writer is taking up the language of the psalm citation in v 22a in order to develop his argument in this ecclesiological direction. If πάντα refers to the cosmos, what is the force of κεφαλή in this phrase? In its LXX usage κεφαλή often translates the Hebrew ראש, rō'š, in the sense of "ruler" or "leader" (e.g., Deut 28:13; Judg 10:18 A; 11:11; 2 Sam 22:44; Isa 7:8, 9), the notion of authority being connected with that of priority in the use of the Hebrew term (cf. Bedale, JTS 5 [1954] 211–15). Paul had used "head" with this sense in 1 Cor 11:3, and it is so used in Col 2:10, "the head of all rule and authority," which most clearly stands behind "head over all things" here in Eph 1:22. It should be noted that the writer's point in this verse is not to make an explicit assertion about Christ's headship over the Church, his body. However, a clear implication of the thought that the one who is head over all is given to the Church is that he is also head of the Church. Strictly speaking, the images of "head" and "body" are kept separate here; Christ's headship refers to his relation to the cosmos and then "body" is brought in as a description of the Church to which Christ is given (cf. also Meuzelaar, *Der Leib des Messias*, 122; Howard, *NTS* 20 [1974] 353; *pace* Best, *One Body*, 146–47; J. A. T. Robinson, *Body*, 66).

Nevertheless, because the two images are in close juxtaposition here, because they have been brought very closely together in the influential letter to the Colossians (cf. 1:18; 2:19), and because later in Ephesians they will also be brought more closely together (cf. 4:15; 5:23), something more needs to be said about the relationship between them. Some have been tempted to see them simply as part of one physiological model, in which the head contains the brain which directs the nervous system of the rest of the body and on which the body is dependent (e.g., J. A. Robinson, 43, 103). Bedale (*JTS* 5 [1954] 212; cf. also Ridderbos, *Paul*, 379–82) holds that "this is to be guilty of serious anachronism: for this metaphor, which is 'natural' to us, would be unintelligible to St. Paul or his readers, who had no idea of the real function of the central nervous system." Barth (186–92; cf. also Benoit, *Jesus and the Gospel*, 74) is less inclined to dismiss the physiological model and shows from his investigation of the neurological knowledge of the time that Hippocrates (c. 460–380 B.C.E.) and Galen (c. 130–200 C.E.) did see the brain as the strongest force in a person, ruling the nerves and coordinating what went on in the body. However, another strand in Greek thought, represented by Aristotle and the Stoics, ascribed priority to the heart, and this, of course, was the view found in OT and Jewish thinking where the heart was the center of the personality and its reason and will. In comparison to the terminology of Hippocrates and Galen, Colossians and Ephesians speak of the head and the body, not the brain and the nerves, and there are no clear parallels in Hippocrates or Galen to the notion of the body's growth from the head (Col 2:19; Eph 4:15, 16). Although he toys with it as an explanation, Barth eventually has to concede that the physiology of Paul's time cannot be considered the key to the head-body imagery of this letter.

Others have sought the key in Gnostic thought about the Primal Man-Redeemer who constitutes one huge body (e.g., H. Schlier, *TDNT* 3 [1965] 673–82; idem, *Christus und die Kirche im Epheserbrief*, 37–60; Käsemann, *Leib*, 56–94, 168–71; Pokorný, *Epheserbrief*, 33–81). The Primal Man, the head, bears the cosmos, the body, within himself. The souls of humans are part of the one body, but this has fallen away into matter and become scattered, so that the Redeemer as head has to gather all again into one body. It is not claimed by scholars who suggest this as a key that the myth is found in Ephesians, but that the writer of the letter has been influenced by or interacted with it. Yet the major differences between the dualistic cosmology of the myth and the worldview of Ephesians, and between the uses of the terminology "head" and "body" in the two contexts, make it hard to see the Gnostic myth as the major source of the use of this imagery in Ephesians. Expanding the physiological model to cosmic proportions does not remove its difficulties. Elements of the Gnostic myth do not provide obvious parallels to the notion of the body growing from the head in Eph 4:15, 16. Moreover, in Ephesians, the head, although in intimate relationship with the body, is never made identical to it, as at certain points in the Gnostic schema. Again, although Ephesians sees Christ and the Church as in union (cf. 5:32), it does not see the head plus the body as constituting the one figure of the heavenly Christ (*pace* Schlier, 91, 92). Above all, there are crucial questions about the legitimacy of talking about a uniform Primal Man-Redeemer myth which uses the concept of "body" in this way, given the fragmentary nature and variety of the sources used in its scholarly reconstruction. Even with the discovery of the Nag Hammadi texts there remains no clear literary evidence that such a myth was pre-Christian, but rather much dispute about reading back into the first century the views of texts which are much later (cf. Schenke, *Der Gott "Mensch" in der Gnosis*, esp. 1–5; 155–56; Colpe, *Die religionsgeschichtliche Schule* [Göttingen: Vandenhoeck & Ruprecht, 1961] 171–93, 203–8; for differing views on the validity of reconstructing a pre-Christian Gnosticism from the Nag Hammadi texts cf. E. Yamauchi, "Pre-Christian Gnosticism in the Nag Hammadi Texts?" *CH* 48 [1979] 129–41; G. W. MacRae, "Nag Hammadi and the New Testament," *Gnosis*, FS H. Jonas, ed. B. Aland [Göttingen: Vandenhoeck & Ruprecht, 1978] 144–57).

Earlier Hellenistic views about the cosmos which may have contributed to later Gnostic thought are more likely candidates for influence on the combination of "head" and "body" imagery in Colossians and Ephesians. The LXX does not provide any instances of such a combination. Elsewhere in Greek thought where the city or state was depicted as a body, the ruler could be seen as "head" of the body (cf. Tacitus, *Ann.* 1.12, 13; Plutarch, *Galba* 4.3; Curtius Rufus, *Historiae Alexandri Magni Macedonensis* 10.9.1; Philo, *De Praem. et Poen.* 114, 125). In addition, the body was used as an image for the cosmos and in that context "head" sometimes occured with it. In an Orphic fragment (Fragment 168) Zeus is depicted as head of the cosmos, pervading it with his power as it lies in his mighty body. In Philo, the Logos is seen as the leading principle of the cosmos as the body, and κεφαλή is used for this relationship (*Quaest. in Exod.* 2.117), although other parts of this work in which the term occurs appear to be the work of a Christian interpolator (cf. also *De Somn.* 1.128). It is generally thought that the earlier form of the Colossian hymn contained the assertion in 1:18 that Christ is the head of the body and meant by "the body" the cosmos, and that the author of Colossians by adding "the Church" after "the body" gave the thought of the original line his own direction (cf. Lohse, *Colossians*, 54–55; Schweizer, *Neotestamentica*, 293–301; *Colossians*, 58–59, 82–83; Hegermann, *Schöpfungsmittler*, 138–57). This is the first instance of "head" and "body" coming together in the Pauline corpus. So, it is likely that the relation between "head" and "body" entered Pauline thought in this way via Hellenistic ideas about the cosmos. Earlier letters of Paul use the imagery of "head" for authoritative leader and "body" for the organic interdependence of believers in the church, but do not combine them. The Colossian situation and the Christological emphasis needed to meet it appear to have provided the catalyst for the combination of two originally independent images. The connotations of the Hebrew ראש, *rō'š*, lie behind κεφαλή and mean that in some places κεφαλή is synonymous with ἀρχή and has the force of determinative source or origin; this allows for the development of thought whereby the body is not only in subjection to the head as its authoritative "overlord" but also derives its growth and development from its head (cf. also Bedale, *JTS* 5 [1954] 214).

To return to Eph 1:22b: κεφαλή is used here to denote Christ's position of rule and authority over all things, and as the one given to the Church, the head is an entity distinct from the body. In the juxtaposition of cosmic and ecclesiological perspectives found in this clause, the writer has taken a confessional formulation about Christ's cosmic lordship and subordinated it to his interest in the Church's welfare. All the supremacy and power God has given to Christ he has given to be used on behalf of the Church. In this way the Church is seen to have a special role in God's purposes for the cosmos.

ἥτις ἐστὶν τὸ σῶμα αὐτοῦ, "which is his body." The writer continues his emphasis on the Church in order to spell out its significance further. Since what has been given to the Church is Christ as head over all things, it is not surprising that the Church is now described as Christ's body, particularly since on the two occasions ἐκκλησία is used of the universal church in Colossians, it is also identified as the body of Christ (cf. 1:18, 24). This image is used of the local church in the earlier Paulines, but questions relating to the origin of, and the influences on, Paul's use are disputed ones. Because of the connection of the image with that of "head" in Colossians and Ephesians, our discussion of these questions will inevitably overlap at some points with the preceding discussion of that term.

The notion of the universe as a gigantic cosmic body was fairly widespread. In Iranian thought, the God Aion was depicted as pregnant with the creation and giving birth to all things. This supreme god was conceived of as a huge human figure whose body consisted of the cosmos (cf. Hegermann, *Schöpfungsmittler*, 59–61). In the Greco-Roman world it was also common to compare the cosmos to a body. An important source for this notion is Plato (cf. *Tim.* 30B–34B, 47C–48B). It was developed by the Stoics who emphasized how each element in the universe was part of an organic whole just as each member of the body was (cf. Diog. Laert. 7.138, 142, 143, 147; Cicero, *Nat. Deor.* 1.35; 3.9; Seneca, *Nat. Quaest.* 6.14.1; *Ep.* 95.52; *De Ira* 2.31. 7, 8). The same imagery can be found later in the *Corpus Hermeticum* (cf. 1:2, 3; 4:2; 10:12). It also became part of the thinking of Hellenistic Judaism as evidenced by Philo (cf. *De Plant.* 7; *De Op. Mundi* 82; *De Migr. Abr.* 220; *De Spec. Leg.* 1.210), who combined such a notion with his teaching about the Logos (cf. *De Spec. Leg.* 1.96; *De Vit. Mos.* 2.127, 133, 134).

Another common application of the image of the body was to the social entity of the state in which the individual members have responsibility for each other and for the whole (cf. Plato, *Resp.* 5.464B; Aristotle, *Pol.* 1.1, 2; Cicero, *Phil.* 8.5, 16; *De Off.* 1.25, 85; Seneca, *De Clem.* 1.5.1; Livy, 26.16.19). Well known in this regard was Menenius Agrippa's allegory about the belly and the limbs (cf. Livy, 2.32.8–12). Philo, too, talks of all the parts of the nation being welded into one and the same fellowship as though it were a single body (*De Spec. Leg.* 3.131).

As we have already seen, others believe "body" imagery in Gnostic thought to be decisive for NT usage, since the Primal Man was held to constitute one huge body with the head being the deity and the rest of the body the world.

The reasons given above for doubting that Gnosticism holds the key to the combination of "head" and "body" images also apply in large measure to the latter image alone (cf. also Meuzelaar, *Der Leib des Messias*, 8–10; Schenke, *Der Gott "Mensch,"* 155–56; Mussner, *Christus*, 160–74; Colpe, "Zur Leib-Christi-Vorstellung," 178–82; Wedderburn, *SJT* 24 [1971] 82–85).

Jewish speculations about the physical body of Adam which included all humanity have been suggested as a further possible source for Paul's view of the body of Christ which incorporated the new humanity (cf. W. D. Davies, *Paul and Rabbinic Judaism* [New York: Harper, 1965] 53–57). In certain rabbinic traditions different individuals could be conceived as being derived from or attached to different parts of Adam's body, e.g., *Exod. Rab.* 40.3. Paul was certainly familiar with Jewish ideas about Adam as the representative of humanity, the one who stands for all who are included in him (cf. 1 Cor 15:20–22, 44b–49; Rom 5:12–21). But there is no evidence that in this he was dependent on speculations specifically about Adam's physical body. Rather, it is likely that the overall notion of corporate or representative solidarity has affected his thinking about the incorporation of the new humanity into Christ, although OT and apocalyptic writings in which it is found did not use the "body" image for this notion. Paul's use of "body" imagery in 1 Cor 12:12–27 and Rom 12:4, 5, in its emphasis on the interdependence of diversity in unity, does have some parallels with the use of the image in Greco-Roman thought for the functioning of the state. Yet, in addition, 1 Cor 12 (vv 12, 13, 27) makes a comparison of the body with Christ, talks of baptism into one body, and calls believers the body of Christ, while Rom 12:5 speaks of this body as being in Christ, so that the notion of incorporation into Christ, with its background in Jewish ideas of representative solidarity, is also required for an explanation of Paul's usage (cf. Best, *One Body*, 93–95, 111–12; Schweizer, *Neotestamentica*, 280–90; Wedderburn, *SJT* 24 [1971] 83–96). This is again clear in the earlier reference to the body of Christ in 1 Cor 10:16, 17, which, in addition to the theme of the one and the many, mentions participation in the body of Christ. It is also dependent on the eucharistic tradition about the body of the crucified Christ (cf. 1 Cor 11:23–32), which thus appears to have been a further formative influence in Paul's development of this concept.

By the time of Colossians and Ephesians the term "the body" has become an explicit description of the universal Church as distinct from the more local application of the image in 1 Cor 12 or Rom 12. In fact, of the many references to the "body" in Colossians and Ephesians only two explicitly retain the original comparison involving the interdependence of the parts of a social organism (cf. Col 2:19; Eph 4:15, 16). Elsewhere the term occurs in Col 1:18, 24; 3:15; and Eph 1:23; 2:16; 3:6; 4:4, 12, 16; 5:23, 29. In the majority of these instances it is used for viewing the Church as a compact whole, in relation to Christ as its head. The change in emphasis is introduced by Colossians, as the Pauline gospel interacts with a syncretistic teaching with cosmological interests. The writer found the hymn to Christ (Col 1:15–20), with its cosmic emphases, appropriate for his purposes in instructing the Colossians but changed its conception of the cosmos as Christ's body, similar to that in Hellenistic Judaism of the cosmos as the body penetrated by the Logos, to show that the true body of Christ is the Church, and the permeation of the cosmos by his rule is a present reality in it. The transfer of "body" imagery from the cosmos to the Church was a natural enough move, since Paul had already used this imagery in connection with believers in 1 Corinthians and Romans. The writer of Ephesians continues this emphasis. Here in 1:23 the use of "body of Christ" terminology after ἐκκλησία underlines that the existence of the eschatological people of God has a Christological focus. This writer is just as concerned as was the writer of Colossians to show that, although Christ is head over the cosmos, it is the Church which is his body.

Such an assertion does not lose the essentially metaphorical force of the body language as it was applied to believers in the earlier letters, despite the wish of some interpreters to treat the expression "body of Christ" realistically and see the Church as literally an extension of the incarnation (cf. also Best, *One Body*, 95–101; Gundry, *Sōma*, 223–44; *pace* J. A. T. Robinson, *The Body*, 51, 58; Benoit, *Jesus and the Gospel*, 53–58; Percy, *Leib Christi*, 44). Failure to use simile is no more decisive against the use of metaphor here than, for instance, in 1 Cor 3:9 where Paul says the Corinthian believers *are* God's field, God's building. The approach which presses for a mystical identification of Christ and the Church on the basis of the expression "body of Christ" seizes on a single metaphor and builds on it a whole ecclesiology, which does not do enough justice to the distinction Paul himself was able to make between the continued existence of the individual glorified body of Christ (e.g., Phil 3:21) and the ecclesiological body of Christ. Whereas in 1 Corinthians the use of the ecclesiological metaphor is colored by the eucharistic tradition with its focus on the crucified body of Christ, here in Ephesians the writer's focus on Christ as the exalted head colors his use of the metaphor and paves the way for the remarkable declaration of the glory of the Church as his body: it is his fullness. This depiction must be balanced by the fact that the preceding stress on Christ's headship also implies the total dependence of his Church on Christ and its subordination to him.

τὸ πλήρωμα τοῦ τὰ πάντα ἐν πᾶσιν πληρουμένου, "the fullness of him who fills all things in every way." One scholar has said that this clause contains "an unsolved enigma" (Mitton, *Epistle*, 96) and that in it "the writer intends to say something very important, but precisely what that is cannot be determined with any degree of certainty" (Mitton, 76). The words do seem to have been intended to produce an impressive effect as the stylistic feature of paronomasia, the combination of a cognate noun and verb (already used in 1:3, 6, 19b, 20a), and the further alliteration produced by πάντα and πᾶσιν indicate. The writer's fondness for this effect is evidenced by its repetition in 3:19, ἵνα πληρωθῆτε εἰς πᾶν τὸ πλήρωμα τοῦ θεοῦ, "that you might be filled with all the fullness of God." While remaining aware of the uncertainties of interpretation, we shall set out the problems associated with the clause and make some attempt to suggest the most likely meaning of this sonorous language. There are three major problematic issues.

(1) Is τὸ πλήρωμα in apposition to τὸ σῶμα αὐτοῦ or to αὐτόν (v 22b)? In other words, is the term "fullness" a description of the Church or of Christ? Some scholars prefer the latter option, believing that it has fewer theological difficulties than does a reference to the Church and that it has the advantage of being in line with the use of πλήρωμα in Colossians where it refers to Christ

(cf. 1:19; 2:9). In this way the clause "which is his body" is to be treated as an aside with no integral position in the syntax.

The overall thought would be that God has given Christ as head over all to the Church and as the fullness of him who fills all in all (i.e., God) (cf. Hitchcock, *ExpTim* 12 [1910–11] 91; Caird, 49; Moule, *Colossians,* 164–69; *IDB* 3 [1962] 826–28; McGlashan, *ExpTim* 76 [1965] 133). A variation on this interpretation sees Christ as the fullness of that which is being completely filled (i.e., the Church) (cf. de la Potterie, *Bib* 58 [1977] 513–21). Telling against this view, however, is the syntactical point that πλήρωμα is more naturally read as in apposition to σῶμα, which immediately precedes it, than as referring to αὐτόν, which is twelve words earlier and would involve a very awkward grammatical construction. In addition, the weight of the clause in v 22b is on the end, on τῇ ἐκκλησίᾳ, on the status of the Church in God's purposes, so that in terms of the sequence of thought the two clauses in v 23 would most naturally be expected to enlarge on how the writer views the Church. As Barth (158) says, "Eph 1:23 contains, in the form of appositions, two definitions of the Church: she is Christ's body and she is his fullness" (cf. also Gaugler, 80; Gnilka, 97; Schlier, 99; Ernst, 291; Lindemann, *Aufhebung,* 214; Benoit, *Jesus and the Gospel,* 89; Mussner, *Christus,* 59–60; Schnackenburg, 79–80; Bratcher and Nida, *Handbook,* 37–38). Taking πλήρωμα as a reference to the Church is in line with Eph 3:19, where the prayer is that believers might be filled with all the fullness of God. This shift of reference from Colossians, where the term referred to Christ, has been prepared for by Col 2:9, 10 where, because of their relation to Christ in whom the fullness of deity dwells, believers can also be said to have been filled.

(2) The second problematic area is that surrounding the term πλήρωμα itself. What is the background for its use in Ephesians and is it active or passive in force?

In LXX Jer 23:23, 24 God can be said to fill heaven and earth; in Isa 6:3 and Ps 72:19 the glory of God is said to fill the whole earth; and in Wis 1:7 the Spirit of the Lord, who holds all things together, is also said to fill the world. Such assertions about God's dynamic presence in the world may provide important background, but they do not actually contain the noun πλήρωμα (Feuillet, *NRT* 78 [1956] 462–71, however, sees this as the major direct influence on the usage in Colossians and Ephesians).

Stoic reflection about the cosmos may also have contributed to the currency of the term πλήρωμα in Paul's time, for in it the notion of filling, though again not the noun πλήρωμα, is used in connection with a unified cosmos permeated by the divine Spirit who fills it with his presence and is filled by it (cf. Seneca, *De Benefic.* 4.8.2; Aristides, *Or.* 45.21, 24). For the Stoics nothing in the world is empty, everything is full (cf. Hippolytus, *Ref.* 1.21.5; cf. also Benoit, *Jesus and the Gospel,* 82–83; Ernst, *Pleroma,* 8–11). Stoic thought and terms were probably mediated to the Christian community through the Hellenistic synagogue where they were associated with Wisdom speculation. The popularity of the notion of God as permeating and filling the universe with his power is evidenced by Philo (e.g., *Leg. Alleg.* 3.4; *De Vit. Mos.* 2.238; *De Sacrif.* 67), though he does not use the actual noun πλήρωμα. The noun does occur in later syncretistic literature which reflects gnosticizing tendencies. In the

Corpus Hermeticum God is described as the *pleroma* of all things (16.3) and the *pleroma* of good (6.4), and the cosmos, which is intimately united with God, is termed a *pleroma* of life (12.15). In the *Odes of Solomon* the reference of πλήρωμα is not always clear, but in 26.7 it appears to refer to the sphere of God (cf. also 19.5, 36.6), though in 7.11 the Savior is also the *pleroma,* and the two are linked in 41.13 where it is said that the Son of the Highest has appeared in the *pleroma* of his Father. The expression πᾶν τὸ πλήρωμα is used in 7.13 and 17.7, and the goal of the heavenly journey is to find rest in the *pleroma* in 35.6; 36.1, 2.

The term πλήρωμα plays an important role in the more fully developed Gnosticism of the second century. It stands for the fullness, the totality of the emanations which come from God. As such, it represents the highest spiritual realm, the sphere of perfection and salvation in closest proximity to God and opposed to the lower realm of matter (cf. Nag Hammadi texts such as *Gospel of Truth* 16, 34–36, 41; *Treatise on Resurrection* 44, 46, 49; *Tripartite Tractate* 70, 75, 77, 78, 80, 81, 86, 90, 93–95, 97, 122–25, 136, in *The Nag Hammadi Library in English,* ed. J. M. Robinson [New York: Harper and Row, 1977], where *pleroma* is used with the same sort of sense as Irenaeus and Hippolytus report of the Valentinian system; cf. Irenaeus, *Adv. Haer.* 1.1–5; 1.11.1, 3, 5; 3.11.1; Hippolytus, *Ref.* 6.29–34. On the use of πλήρωμα in Valentinianism cf. Lightfoot, *Colossians,* 263–69; Overfield, *NTS* 25 [1979] 384–88).

Paul had used the term πλήρωμα in 1 Cor 10:26; Rom 11:12, 25; 13:10; 15:29, but not with the sense that predominates in Ephesians (though cf. 1:10). As in the case of "head" and "body" terminology, it is the development of the term in Colossians that is decisive for its use in Ephesians. It appears in the hymn to Christ in 1:19 and is then taken up again in 2:9. This suggests that the Stoic idea of *pleroma* as the divine Spirit pervading the cosmos had been taken up by Hellenistic Jews to depict God's immanence in his creation and was being used by Christians to speak of the fullness of God which decided to dwell in Christ. Wisdom speculation, which is reflected clearly elsewhere in the hymn, may also have been influential in the adoption of this term, since Wisdom was already thought of as pervading and permeating all things (Wis 7:24; cf. 1:7; also Lohse, *Colossians,* 58; Schweizer, *Neotestamentica,* 294; *Colossians,* 77–78). It could be that the author picks up on this term in Colossians and insists that the fullness of deity dwells in Christ bodily, because the term also played a part in the "philosophy" against which he is warning (cf. 2:8) and had a significance somewhere on the trajectory between Stoic and Gnostic usage. The teaching in Colossae appears to have advocated ascetic techniques and knowledge gained by visionary experience as a means of experiencing liberation from hostile cosmic powers, entering the heavenly realm, and participating in the divine fullness. But for the author the *pleroma* is not opposed to the physical realm. As the divine fullness in its totality it has taken up residence in Christ, and believers have access to it in Christ (2:9, 10). Interaction with the syncretistic teaching in Colossae prepares the way for the use of πλήρωμα in Ephesians. Like Col 2:10, Eph 4:13 speaks of believers corporately attaining to the fullness of Christ, and Eph 3:19 contains the prayer that they may be filled with all the fullness of God. Here in Eph 1:23 the writer develops the thought a little further so that, as the Church, believers can actually be called

Christ's fullness. All of this presupposes, with Colossians, that Christ is the one filled by God and able to extend the divine life and power to others. In the OT God's glorious presence could be seen as permeating not only the creation but also the temple (cf. Isa 6:1; Ezek 43:5; 44:4; Hag 2:7), so it should not be surprising that in an epistle which calls the Church "a holy temple in the Lord . . . a dwelling place of God in the Spirit" (2:21, 22) it should also be seen as the place of the dynamic fullness of God in Christ.

It is the passive force of πλήρωμα which best fits this interpretation of the development of the use of the term. The Church is that which is filled or completed by Christ (cf. Lightfoot, *Colossians,* 261; S. Hanson, *Unity,* 127–29; Delling, *TDNT* 6 [1968] 304, J. A. T. Robinson, *Body,* 68–69; Gewiess, "Die Begriffe," 134–35; Feuillet, *NRT* 78 [1956] 456; Ridderbos, *Paul,* 390; Mussner, 57; *Christus,* 60; Best, *One Body,* 141–43; Gaugler, 80; Schlier, 98–99; Gnilka, 97; Barth, 205, 209; Schnackenburg, 80) rather than that which fills or completes Christ (cf. Abbott, 37; J. A. Robinson, 43–44, 255–59; Beare, 637; Overfield, *NTS* 25 [1979] 393; Yates, *ExpTim* 83 [1972] 146–51). In favor of the latter it can be argued that the active meaning covers most of the biblical uses (cf. LXX Ps 23:1; Mark 8:20; Matt 9:16; 1 Cor 10:26; Rom 11:25) and that elsewhere in Greek the term is most frequently used with this sense of "that which fills." It is also argued that the notion of Christ as being completed by the Church need not be thought theologically strange either in the light of Col 1:24, where Paul is said to complete what is lacking in Christ's afflictions, or if it is interpreted as the many, the Church, representing the one, Christ (Yates, *ExpTim* 83 [1972] 149–51; Overfield, *NTS* 25 [1979] 393). Against this, it must be said that everywhere else Christ is portrayed as actively filling believers rather than being filled by them; that Col 1:24 is probably about Christ's sufferings as part of the messianic woes, but here a deficiency in his person would be implied; and that if the writer is simply talking about representation, he has chosen a strange way of doing so with a term which does not have this meaning elsewhere. Above all, this interpretation of the Church as the complement of Christ fails because there is no evidence of πλήρωμα being used of two mutually supplementary things (cf. J. A. T. Robinson, *Body,* 67 n. 2).

Then πλήρωμα with a passive sense can be found elsewhere. The references given above from the *Corpus Hermeticum* are most plausibly taken in a passive sense, e.g., 6.4—ὁ γὰρ κόσμος πλήρωμά ἐστιν τῆς κακίας, ὁ δὲ θεὸς τοῦ ἀγαθοῦ, "for the world is full of evil [that is, filled by evil], while God is full of goodness [that is, filled by goodness]" (cf. also Ernst, *Pleroma,* 12–21). The context of the use of the term by Philo in *De Praem. et Poen.* 65 leaves little doubt that a passive meaning is intended, for there the soul is spoken of as becoming a fullness of virtues "leaving no empty room within itself where other things can enter," and *De Praem. et Poen.* 109 also makes most sense taken in this way (cf. also πλήρωμα καλοκἀγαθίας, "fullness of nobility," *De Spec. Leg.* 1.272; *Quod. Omn. Prob. Lib.* 41). Where a follower of Paul is making his own use of a syncretistic term already exploited in Colossians, it is enough to be able to show that the distinctive use claimed for him was capable of being understood. This is the case, since other uses of πλήρωμα in the passive sense can be evidenced, although its use in the active sense is more common. Ernst (292; idem, *Pleroma,* 120), who has investigated the concept thoroughly in his monograph, concludes that the writer's use of the term is deliberately ambiguous and that it contains several paradoxical nuances, so that here it involves both the Church's being filled by Christ and the Church's completing him. Granted that words can carry a variety of connotations, it seems unlikely that the writer is being deliberately ambiguous at this stage as he develops his thought about the Church or that he would make two quite different theological assertions at the same time. It is preferable to attempt to establish a particular meaning of the original. In this regard, in addition to the specific points already made, the decisive issue must be that of the theological context of the writer's use of this term. Compelling reasons have already been given for believing that he has developed its use to refer to the Church as being filled by Christ. As Christ is filled with God (Col 1:19; 2:9), so his body is filled with Christ. This interpretation is very much in line also with the thought of believers' being filled with all the fullness of God expressed later in 3:19.

(3) The last major area of contention surrounds the final six words of the clause, τοῦ τὰ πάντα ἐν πᾶσιν πληρουμένου. In particular what voice has the present participle πληρουμένου? Is it passive, middle, or middle with an active sense? Again, Ernst (292; idem, *Pleroma,* 120) wishes to treat the meaning as ambivalent and containing both an active and passive sense—Christ fills all but is also completely filled (by the Church). But for reasons similar to those given in the case of πλήρωμα, it is necessary to make a choice. Those who treat the participle as having a passive voice consider the meaning to be that the Church is the fullness of Christ, who is being totally filled—i.e., by God (cf. Feuillet, *NRT* 78 [1956] 458; J. A. T. Robinson, *Body,* 68–69; Best, *One Body,* 143 n. 2) or by the Church (J. A. Robinson, 42–44, 152; Benoit, *Jesus and the Gospel,* 90; Yates, *ExpTim* 83 [1972] 149–51; Overfield, *NTS* 25 [1979] 393). They take the phrase τὰ πάντα ἐν πᾶσιν adverbially. A strong point in favor of this interpretation is that πληροῦσθαι occurs nowhere else in the NT and very rarely elsewhere with an active sense (cf. Xenophon, *Hellenica* 5.4.56; 6.2.14, 35; Plutarch, *Alcibiades* 35.6; Isaeus, *Orat.* 11.48; Plato, *Gorgias* 493e; Thucydides 7.142). Yet against this position it must be said that elsewhere Christ already is the fullness of God, the whole fullness of deity already dwells in him (Col 1:19; 2:9), and that the filling of Christ with God's presence is not seen as a continuing process. It would seem particularly strange for the writer to depict the Church as already "the fullness" but Christ as still being filled. Nowhere else is the passive πληροῦσθαι applied to Christ. Objections have already been raised in the discussion of πλήρωμα to the notion that Christ is being filled by the Church. Finally, it is far from clear that τὰ πάντα ἐν πᾶσιν is best taken adverbially. τὰ πάντα is used in that sense in Eph 4:15, but that is quite different from the whole phrase τὰ πάντα ἐν πᾶσιν. When that phrase occurs in 1 Cor 12:6 it clearly stands for two separate ideas. 1 Cor 15:28 and Col 3:11 are sometimes advanced as parallels, but their earliest texts probably do not include the article before πάντα, and they also are best interpreted as involving two ideas. There is no clear evidence in the NT that the phrase should be taken as the equivalent to the classical Greek παντάπασιν.

Those who opt for the middle voice frequently leave open the question of whether the middle is a true middle, emphasizing the subject's own interest in the action, "fills for himself," or simply an example of the middle with an active sense (cf. Abbott, 38, and S. Hanson, *Unity*, 129, who are unable to decide on this issue, though Howard, *NTS* 20 [1974] 35, does hold out for a true middle where "the action is done for the benefit of something vitally concerned with the subject"). But there appears to be no clear reason for drawing particular attention to the subject and stressing that Christ fills all things for himself in this context, where God is the subject of the main clause in v 22b. It seems preferable, therefore, to treat πληρουμένου as middle with active force, of which there are a number of examples in the NT (cf. also BDF para. 316 [1]; Moule, *Idiom-Book*, 25, though as part of a different overall interpretation; BAGD 581; Roels, *God's Mission*, 245–48; Gewiess, "Die Begriffe," 133–34; Mussner, *Christus*, 59; Gnilka, 99; Gaugler, 80–81; Schlier, 99; Barth, 209; Lindemann, *Aufhebung*, 215; Ridderbos, *Paul*, 390 n. 97; Schnackenburg, 80–81; Bratcher and Nida, *Handbook*, 38). On this interpretation Christ is the one who completely fills all things, that is, fills the cosmos in every respect. This has the advantage of taking τὰ πάντα in its natural sense as the object of the clause and as meaning the cosmos (cf. vv 10, 22), and ἐν πᾶσιν in its straightforward meaning of "in all respects," "in every way" (cf. BAGD 633) and as added for rhetorical effect. It is also in line with the later statement in Eph 4:10 about Christ filling all things. It does not count against the interpretation of πληρουμένου as middle with active force that in the parallel thought of Eph 4:10 the verb is in the active voice. In the NT the active and middle of the same verb can be closely juxtaposed with no apparent distinction of meaning (e.g., καρποφορέω and καρποφορέομαι in Col 1:6, 10).

There is no indication that the writer thought of this filling in a physical sense in the way that the Primal Man of the Gnostic schema is said to fill the universe. Rather the most illuminating parallels remain LXX Jer 23:24, where God is said to fill heaven and earth, and the terminology of Philo, in which on many occasions God can be said to fill τὰ πάντα (e.g., *De Post. Caini* 30; *De Sacrif.* 67–68; *Leg. Alleg.* 1.4; *De Gig.* 47; *De Vit. Mos.* 2.238). By analogy Christ pervades all things with his sovereign rule as he directs them to their divinely appointed goal, the restoration of their meaning and harmony (cf. 4:10; 1:10). It could well be that just as 1:20, 22 draw on 1 Cor 15:24–28 but place Paul's thought in a context of realized eschatology, so this phrase in 1:23 recalls the notion of 1 Cor 15:28 that God will be all in all, πάντα ἐν πᾶσιν, but transfers it to Christ and makes it a present reality.

Our decisions in regard to the three major areas of contention surrounding the last clause of the first chapter mean, then, that the writer's overall thought is that the church is Christ's fullness and that Christ is the one who is completely filling the cosmos. Here, as in 1:22b, ecclesiological and cosmic perspectives are juxtaposed in a way that underlines the Church's special status, for although Christ is in the process of filling the cosmos, at present it is only the Church which can actually be called his fullness. The Church appears, then, to be the focus for and medium of Christ's presence and rule in the cosmos. This entails neither that the Church is the exclusive medium of Christ's presence and rule nor that it will eventually fill the world. Schlier (99) and Benoit (*Jesus and the Gospel*, 90) talk of the cosmos being drawn into the Church. Schweizer (*Neotestamentica*, 314–16, 327–29) thinks in terms of missionary expansion, as does Meyer (*Kirche und Mission*, esp. 28–29, 45–48), who treats τὰ πάντα primarily as the world of human beings and gives πλήρωμα a missionary dimension. To be sure, the writer sees the Church consisting of Jews and Gentiles as a witness to God's purposes for the world, but he does not choose to emphasize the Church's active missionary efforts. Roels (*God's Mission*, 231–32), who investigates the epistle for this theme, finds in 1:22, 23 "not the slightest suggestion either in the context or in the words themselves which points to" a mission perspective. The writer does not make clear exactly how the Church participates in the process of Christ's cosmic rule, but he does see it as the community which manifests Christ's presence and as the community in which the consummation of Christ's rule is anticipated (cf. *Comment* on 3:10).

Explanation

1:3–14 constituted a blessing of God for the great salvation he had accomplished in Christ. Now in another long sentence, which takes the form of a thanksgiving period and has much of the liturgical style of the earlier *berakah*, 1:15–23 in essence reflects a prayer that the letter's recipients might progress to maturity of knowledge and appreciate just how great this salvation is and what is their own place within it.

The sentence begins with a thanksgiving proper (vv 15, 16a) in which the writer claims to express regularly his gratitude to God for the addressees. In a general statement he selects as Christian qualities which are known to him and for which he is thankful the faith they exercise as those who are in Christ and the love they have for their fellow believers. The writer then makes use of his knowledge of their situation to intercede for his readers, again in fairly general terms. To be more accurate, he in fact gives them a report of his intercession (vv 16b–19). The prayer-report contains references back to the preceding blessing, indicating that part of the purpose of the prayer is to ask that the blessings enumerated in the *berakah* may be fully appropriated by the letter's recipients. In 1:8, 9 God had been praised for the spiritual wisdom and insight and the knowledge of his mystery he had granted his people. Now in 1:17 the request is for "the spirit of wisdom and revelation in the knowledge of him." Similarly, "hope," "riches," "inheritance," and "the working of his mighty strength," as topics in the prayer, recall themes from the eulogy in 1:12, 7, 14, 11 respectively. The relationship in this chapter between the eulogy and thanksgiving on the one hand and the intercessory prayer-report on the other, like that between thanksgiving and intercession in Paul's thanksgiving periods, reflects two fundamental aspects of Christian prayer—the acknowledgment of grace received and the request for grace still needed. These, in turn, reflect the present situation of Christian believers with its glory, because of what has already been accomplished, and yet its incompleteness, because the consummation is still outstanding. The writer is not merely satisfied with the past and the present, but rather his contemplation of, and thankfulness for what God has done for his readers make him aware of remaining needs and of new possibilities for knowledge and appropriation of the salvation God has provided.

The writer's report of his intercession commences with his prayer for the Spirit to be at work in all the addressees, giving wisdom—practical understanding of what God has accomplished in Christ—and revelation—disclosure of God's plan for history and the world and how to live in the light of it. In this way there will be growth in these believers' relationship to God, and in their knowledge of him. The saving illumination of the gospel, which has already radically affected their lives, needs to be continued with a threefold growth in knowledge. The writer desires for them to gain an increasing knowledge of the hope of the consummation of salvation, that is, the hope into which God has brought them by calling them into relationship with himself, an increasing knowledge of the wealth of glory that is bound up with God's possession of his people, and, with four different words for power accumulated to drive this home, an increasing knowledge of the immensity of God's power which is operative for his people. The writer's own faith appears to be anchored in a knowledge of God's power so that he is not afraid of asking God for too much as he prays for his fellow believers. In fact, nothing short of God's immense power available on their behalf will enable them to realize the vision this writer has for their lives.

For the writer, the supreme demonstration of the extent of God's power took place in his raising Christ from the dead and exalting him to a position of power and authority in the heavenly realm above all hostile cosmic powers. At this point, the intercessory prayer-report shades over into the magnificent statement which rounds off this thanksgiving period (vv 20–23). It takes up confessional material about God's power in the resurrection, the exaltation, and the cosmic rule of Christ, and also employs some of the imagery used in Colossians in order to elaborate on Christ's supremacy over the powers and highlight the role of the Church in God's purposes. Adapting Paul's use of Ps 110:1 and Ps 8:6 from 1 Cor 15 and applying them to Christ's present status, the writer depicts Christ as the last Adam who is already lord with dominion over the cosmos and any power in it. His readers in Asia Minor still needed to be assured that this world was not simply a continual battleground of warring forces where the hostile powers were in control and needed to be placated. The writer therefore makes clear that there can be no justification for believers considering themselves as in any way in bondage or debt to such powers. Instead, God had shown in Christ's resurrection and exaltation that this world was his creation over which he had put Christ in control and that life could be lived by trust in the Creator's power, which was there for his people.

That God's power is available for his people is underlined in the assertion that God has given Christ as head over all things to the Church. The writer does not simply set Christ's rule and authority over the cosmos in parallel to his relation to the Church but subordinates the former to the latter. In this way, the Church's privileged place in God's purpose for the cosmos becomes clear. Yet that privileged place is due solely to the Church's relation to Christ. All the rule and authority God has given to Christ can be used on behalf of the Church, since God has also given this exalted Christ to the Church. In the Christ, who is head over all, the Church has one who is greater than all the powers ranged against it. The force of this for Christian readers, who, numerically and sociologically, would have been an insignificant grouping in Asia Minor, is that they should not succumb to the temptation to defeatism and think of themselves as an insignificant new cult among many other religious groups. Rather, they are to see themselves as part of the universal Church, which can only be truly understood when seen in relation to its exalted Lord in the heavenly realm, who exercises all power on its behalf. Because of the identity of its head, the Church is a body which is able to confront the powers and which has the whole cosmos as its sphere of witness (cf. 3:10).

In placing both Christ and the Church in a cosmic context the writer employs the terms "head," "body," and "fullness." These terms had taken on special force in Pauline thought through interaction with the syncretistic teaching, with its cosmological concerns, which had threatened the welfare of the Colossian church. While the use of "head" and "body" imagery is similar to that in Colossians, the term "fullness" undergoes an important development here in Eph 1, as it shifts from the reference to Christ in Colossians to an application to the Church. The brief characterization of the Church at the end of the thanksgiving period reinforces that it is constantly to be seen in its relation to Christ. It is his body, the community of believers as an organic whole, which belongs to him and over which he rules. It is his fullness, the community which he fills supremely with his presence and dynamic rule. This depiction of the Church is in the context of the cosmic extent of Christ's activity. Yet such a context only serves to set in sharper relief the significance of the Church's role. For, yes, Christ is the head over all things, but as head over all he has been given to the Church, and only the Church *is* his body. And yes, Christ is filling all things in terms of his sovereign rule, but he fills the Church in a special sense with his Spirit, grace, and gifts (cf. 4:7–11), so that only the Church *is* his fullness. This writer's consistent approach, like that of Paul, is that humanity is to be viewed from the vantage point of what has happened to Christ. Because God has exalted Christ to heaven, believers can enjoy all the benefits of being related to their heavenly Lord. "Body" and "fullness" as descriptions of the Church underline the privileges of that relationship and assert the Church's significance. Yet, at the same time, they clearly presuppose a dependency in the relationship. The Church is nothing in itself. It is a special community only because Christ is its head and his presence fills it.

Any who might be attracted by syncretism's claims to provide access by various means to the fullness of the divine presence are being reminded first that that presence is mediated by Christ, who through his exaltation and rule fills heaven and earth, and then, that it is in the fellowship of the Church that the fullness of Christ's presence is to be experienced. The importance of the Church, for the writer, is that as Christ's fullness it provides the present focus for and demonstration of that presence which now fills the cosmos in a hidden way but which will do so openly and completely. Although the paraenesis in particular draws a clear ethical distinction between believers and surrounding society (e.g., 4:17–24; 5:7–14), the perspective here is not one in which the Church and the rest of creation are two entities fixed in a state of permanent opposition and alienation. Rather, because the Church's head is head over all, and because the one who fills the Church is filling all things, there is now a continuity between the realm of salvation and the realm of creation (cf. the last Adam imagery of v 22), between the Church and the world. The whole of created reality becomes the Church's legitimate concern, and the Church symbolizes the realization of the possibilities inherent in God's purposes in Christ for all creation. As God calls men and women into the new community of the Church, he is in the process of completing his purpose of filling all things with Christ's sovereign presence, of which the essential quality is love (cf. 3:17–19).

Just as the preceding eulogy attempted to treat salvation on a grand scale, so this thanksgiving period opens up broad vistas on God's purposes for his people. Again, its pattern of thought encompasses past, present, and future and can be seen to have trinitarian content. The past element is the activity of God in Christ's resurrection and exaltation and his calling of believers; the present takes in the privileges of being God's people, who have his power made available to them, and also embraces Christ's cosmic rule and the Church's relation to him; and the future is in view with the mention of the hope of believers and of the age to come. The Father of glory is addressed in the intercession and is at work on behalf of people who are his inheritance; Christ is the focus of the Father's activity; and the Spirit is the agent of revelation, who interprets God's activity and enables believers to appropriate what has been accomplished for them. Yet, as in the *berakah,* the inherent pattern of thought in the thanksgiving period is neither a temporal nor a trinitarian one but rather theocentric, Christological, and ecclesiological. In his prayer the writer turns to God. It is knowledge of God that he desires for his readers and thus thoughts of God's calling, God's inheritance, God's power, and God's working in Christ fill the prayer. But Christ is at the center of God's relationship to his people and as a result his resurrection, exaltation, and cosmic rule soon become the focus of attention. "Fullness" language, as applied to God in the OT, and Hellenistic Jewish notions of God filling the world, which to a large extent lie behind the usage of this terminology in Colossians and Ephesians, were a way of expressing God's all-encompassing presence, his all-pervading sovereignty; the same realities were conveyed by Jesus' teaching about God and his kingdom. For this follower of Paul, those realities can now be seen as realized in and mediated by the exalted Christ. Yet, significant as it is that the writer finds himself describing the Church's experience of Christ in terms traditionally used of experience of God, it is the ecclesiological aspect of the thanksgiving period, more than either the theocentric or Christological, which is primarily to the fore. The flow of thought begins and ends with the Church. It commences with thanksgiving and prayer for believers, which lead to contemplation of God's purposes for them in Christ. The thanksgiving and intercession are integrally related to the stress on the role of the Church in a cosmic context at the end of the section. This relationship comes to the fore through the writer's third petition for an increasing knowledge of the power of God effective for his people, which is itself linked with the notion that Christ's rule over all is for the benefit of the Church.

As the overall weight of the thanksgiving period falls on its stress on the Church, it fulfills its epistolary function and complements the *berakah* by introducing more specifically the concerns of the letter as a whole. The writer is concerned for Gentile Christian communities whose members may have been attracted by the claims of others to knowledge of cosmic mysteries or may be in danger of succumbing to the morality of the surrounding world (cf. 4:17–

24) or tempted to think of themselves as belonging to insignificant religious groups or simply confused about the implications of their Christian confession. For this reason he wants to brace them and give them a sense of the identity and role in the world of the community of which they have become a part. His intercessory prayer-report reveals that he believes this can be achieved through a revitalizing of their relationship with God, an increase in their knowledge of him. The Church will be what it ought to be when it becomes more aware of and appropriates the privileges and power God gives his people and the benefits of its relation to the Christ who rules the cosmos.

God's Gracious Salvation as Resurrection and Exaltation with Christ (2:1–10)

Bibliography

Allen, T. G. "Exaltation and Solidarity with Christ: Ephesians 1.20 and 2.6." *JSNT* 28 (1986) 103–20. **Benoit, P.** "Rapports littéraires entre les Épîtres aux Colossiens et aux Éphésiens." *Neutestamentliche Aufsätze,* ed. J. Blinzler, O. Kuss, and F. Mussner. Regensburg: F. Pustet, 1963, 11–22. **Best, E.** "Dead in Trespasses and Sins (Eph. 2.1)." *JSNT* 13 (1981) 9–25. **Carr, W.** *Angels and Principalities.* Cambridge: Cambridge University Press, 1981, 100–104. **Countess, R. H.** "Thank God for the Genitive (Eph. 2:8–10)." *BETS* 12 (1969) 117–22. **Crowther, C.** "Works, Work and Good Works." *ExpTim* 81 (1970) 66–71. **Fischer, K. M.** *Tendenz und Absicht,* 121–31. **Halter, H.** *Taufe und Ethos,* 233–41, 625–29. **Larsson, E.** *Christus als Vorbild.* Uppsala: Almquist & Wiksells, 1962, 105–9. **Lincoln, A. T.** "Ephesians 2:8–10—A Summary of Paul's Gospel?" *CBQ* 45 (1983) 617–30. **Lindemann, A.** *Die Aufhebung der Zeit,* 106–40. **Luz, U.** "Rechtfertigung bei den Paulusschülern." *Rechtfertigung,* ed. J. Friedrich, W. Pöhlmann, and P. Stuhlmacher. Tübingen: Mohr, 1976, 365–83. **Mehlmann, J.** *Natura filii Irae: Historia interpretationis Eph 2, 3 ejusque cum doctrina de Peccato Originali nexus.* Rome: Pontifical Biblical Institute, 1957. **Merklein, H.** "Paulinische Theologie in der Rezeption des Kolosser- und Epheserbriefes." *Paulus in den neutestamentlichen Spätschriften,* ed. K. Kertelge. Freiburg: Herder, 1981, esp. 37–51. **Mussner, F.** *Christus, das All und die Kirche,* 16–20, 24–27, 91–94. **Ramaroson, L.** "Une lecture de Éphésiens 1, 15–2, 10." *Bib* 58 (1977) 388–410. **Riensche, R. H.** "Exegesis of Ephesians 2:1–7." *LQ* 2 (1950) 70–74. **Romaniuk, K.** *L'Amour du Père et du Fils dans la sotériologie de Saint Paul.* Rome: Pontifical Biblical Institute, 1961, 212–16, 247–49. **Sanders, J. T.** "Hymnic Elements in Ephesians 1–3." *ZNW* 56 (1965) 218–23, 232. **Schille, G.** *Frühchristliche Hymnen,* 53–60. **Schnackenburg, R.** *Baptism in the Thought of St. Paul.* Tr. G. R. Beasley-Murray. Oxford: Basil Blackwell, 1964, 73–78. **Steinmetz, F.-J.** *Protologische Heilszuversicht.* Frankfurt am Main: Josef Knecht, 1969, 37–44, 51–67. **Tachau, P.** *"Einst" und "Jetzt" im Neuen Testament.* Göttingen: Vandenhoeck & Ruprecht, 1972.

Translation

> [1] And you were dead through your trespasses and sins[a] [2] in which you once lived in accordance with this world-age, in accordance with the ruler of the realm of the air, of the spirit that is now at work in those who are disobedient.[b] [3] Among them we all also once lived in the passions of our flesh, carrying out the wishes of the flesh and the thoughts, and we were by nature children of wrath like the rest. [4] But God, being rich in mercy, out of his great love with which he loved us,[c] [5] made us alive with Christ[d] even when we were dead through trespasses—by grace you have been saved—[6] and raised us up with him and seated us with him in the heavenly realms in Christ Jesus, [7] so that he might show in the ages to come the surpassing richness of his grace in his kindness to us in Christ Jesus. [8] For by grace you have been saved through faith; and this is not from yourselves, it is the gift of God; [9] it is not by works, lest anyone should boast. [10] For we are his work, created in Christ Jesus for good works, which God prepared in advance in order that we might live in them.

Notes

a The Greek text here does not have a finite verb but rather a participial clause, ὑμᾶς ὄντας νεκρούς . . . , lit. "you being dead. . . ." In fact there is an anacoluthon in the Greek syntax, for this clause is the object of a verb whose subject is introduced in v 4 but which itself does not appear until after the opening clause has been repeated in the first person plural in v 5, ὄντας ἡμᾶς νεκρούς, lit. "we being dead," and can then be seen to be συνεζωοποίησεν, "made alive with." In translating v 1, one can either supply the main verb from v 5—"And you he made alive, when you were dead"—and repeat this when one comes to v 5 (cf. RSV) or simply translate the participle as a finite verb (cf. NIV). Though it perhaps has the disadvantage of not showing immediately the close connection between 1:19–23 and 2:1–7, we have chosen the latter option, since it does convey better the sequence of the Greek text with its delay in introducing a resolution of the sinful situation on which the writer at first dwells.

b The Greek phrase is literally "sons of disobedience." Again the sentence divisions of the first part of this pericope are our own. In Greek vv 1–7 form a single sentence. The translation of vv 8–10 follows the Greek text in its divisions.

c p46 it d.g Ambrosiaster Victorinus-Rome read ἦν ἠλέησεν, "with which he had mercy," instead of ἦν ἠγάπησεν, "with which he loved," and, with D* G, omit the preceding αὐτοῦ, "his." Ramaroson (*Bib* 58 [1977] 389–90) opts for this reading, but as is often the case when p46 varies from most other major witnesses, this is likely to be secondary. The reading could be said to be in line with the style of Ephesians in its combination of cognate noun and verb—ἐλέει, "mercy," and ἠλέησεν, "had mercy"—but it achieves this conformity only by changing the combination of cognate noun and verb already in the text—ἀγάπην, "love," and ἠγάπησεν, "loved." Apart from the wealth of external evidence in its favor, the latter combination is more natural because its noun and verb are in closer proximity.

d p46 B 33 vg cl Ambrosiaster Victorinus-Rome Ephraem Ambrose Chrysostom, amongst other witnesses, support the reading ἐν τῷ Χριστῷ, "in Christ," instead of the straightforward dative τῷ Χριστῷ (ℵ A vid D G gr K P Ψ Hilary Pelagius Jerome al.). However, the ἐν may well have been added through dittography, the unintentional repetition of the last two letters of the preceding word συνεζωοποίησεν (cf. J. A. Robinson, 156), or through assimilation to the phrase ἐν Χριστῷ Ἰησοῦ found after the συν- compounds in v 6. In the latter case this could reflect an interpretation of the συν- prefix in v 5 which does not relate it directly to Christ but sees it as a reference to Jews and Gentiles being united in their participation in God's redemptive activity in Christ.

Form/Structure/Setting

Eph 2:1 begins a new sentence. With the Nestle-Aland and UBS texts we should assume a period and not a comma at the end of 1:23 (*contra* Ramaroson, *Bib* 58 [1977] 392–96). 2:1–10 consists of two sentences in the Greek text, vv 1–7 and vv 8–10. The first part of 2:1–7 is anacoluthic. The subject and the verb of which ὑμᾶς, "you," in v 1 is the object are not introduced until vv 4, 5 and only then in connection with the repetition in a slightly different form in v 5 of the notion first expressed in v 1. In this way 2:1–7 falls into two parts, the anacoluthon in vv 1–3 and the contrasting statement of vv 4–7. This syntactical division of the pericope reflects a threefold division in terms of its content. Verses 1–3 depict the sinful condition of the readers' past existence and indeed that of all humanity. Verses 4–7 express the change occasioned for believers in Christ by God's mercy and grace. Verses 8–10 provide a summary of the nature of the salvation achieved by God. The sections are linked and the progress of the writer's argument is marked by repetitions. "Dead through trespasses" forms the link between vv 1–3 and vv 4–7 when it is repeated in v 5. "By grace you have been saved" is repeated from the middle section to provide the transition in v 8 to the summarizing conclusion about the relationship of grace and works. Verse 5, with its introduction of the first main verb, συνεζωοποίησεν, "made alive with," its repetition in the first person plural of the participial clause from v 1, and its anticipation of the last section through "by grace you have been saved," can be seen to be pivotal for the whole pericope. The use of περιπατεῖν, "to live/walk," at the beginning of v 2 to describe the pre-Christian way of life and again at the end of v 10 to portray Christian living forms an inclusion which demonstrates that vv 1–10 constitute a compact unit.

How does this unit fit into the surrounding flow of thought? The writer has already left the specific intercessory prayer-report of the thanksgiving period and will not return to this until 3:1, 14. That prayer-report had led him into the major theme on which he is now launched—the power of God's actions in Christ and the relevance of this for believers. If the *berakah* and thanksgiving period in chap. 1 set out God's work of salvation and its bearing on the lives of believers in general terms, chap. 2 as a whole makes clearer that bearing by reminding the mainly Gentile Christian readers of their past and pointing out in contrast the privileges of their present situation as those who have experienced God's salvation. The first half of this reminder (vv 1–10) depicts the readers' past as a condition of death, sinfulness, and bondage to evil forces and the flesh, and contrasts it with the present as an experience of God's mercy, of new life, and of the heavenly realms through their relationship with Christ. The second half (vv 11–22) rehearses the past more in terms of alienation from Israel, and describes the present, by contrast, as a belonging to the new people of God, the Church, consisting of both Jews and Gentiles and created by God's reconciling work in Christ. It would be wrong (*contra* Mitton, 79, 80) to see the point of vv 1–10 as stressing individual salvation in order to guard against an overemphasis on the Church, as arguing that "one becomes part of the Church by first becoming a believer; one does not become a Christian by joining the Church." It is doubtful whether such a distinction between individual and corporate categories was in the mind of the writer. He is simply portraying his readers' experience of salvation from two different perspectives. The former is more general and lends itself to personal application, while the latter is more specifically ecclesiological, but, as becomes apparent in v 2 with its mention of conformity to this world and its structures, the former, as well as the latter, contains a more than purely individual dimension.

The καί at the beginning of 2:1, whatever its origins (see the discussion below on the relationship with Col. 2:13) and as it now stands, signals a continuity of theme between vv 1–10 and the thanksgiving period. What God has done in Christ for the Church, which was the focus of the use of the confessional material in the immediately preceding verses, is taken up afresh. The writer asserts that the power of God which was manifested supremely in Christ's resurrection and exaltation is the same power which his readers have themselves experienced. His point is effectively made by the parallels he builds between 2:5–7 and the creedal material in 1:20, 21. Both Christ and believers have been raised from the dead (1:19; 2:5, 6), both Christ and believers have been seated in the heavenly realms (1:20, 2:6), and "in the coming age" (1:21) balances "in the coming ages" (2:7). The actual phrase ἐν τοῖς ἐπουρανίοις, "in the heavenly realms," is employed in both contexts and the compound verbs συνήγειρεν, "raised with," and συνεκάθισεν, "seated with," in 2:6 deliberately recall the simple forms ἐγείρας, "raised," and καθίσας, "seated," in 1:20. Yet the parallel is by no means exact. The death from which Christ was raised was according to 1:20 a physical death, while that from which believers have been raised is the death of an existence characterized by their sinful action. One reason for the anacoluthon of vv 1–3 may well be that before he completes his comparison, the writer wishes to clarify in what sense he speaks of his readers as dead (cf. also J. A. Robinson, 48). At the same time, this elaboration of their past condition functions as a backdrop setting in sharper relief the salvation God has now provided for them.

Less directly, 2:1–10 can also be seen to have connections with the opening *berakah*. God's mercy and love for those dead in trespasses (vv 4, 5) corresponds to the forgiveness of trespasses in 1:7. The richness of God's grace (v 7) takes up the phrase introduced in 1:7. Being seated with Christ in the heavenly realms (v 6) recalls "every spiritual blessing in the heavenly realms in Christ" from 1:3. Finally, the notion of God's having prepared good works for believers to live out (v 10) is similar to the thoughts in 1:4, 11, 12 of God's having chosen believers to be holy and blameless before him in love and having predestined them to live for the praise of his glory.

As has already become apparent, one of the major features of Eph 2 is its twofold contrast between believers' past unredeemed situation and their present privileged experience of salvation. Such a contrast is perhaps more dominant in Eph 2 than elsewhere, but it is not at all uncommon in the NT epistles and is often signaled by a formal contrast involving the terms ποτέ, "once," and νῦν, "now." This formal contrast is clear in 2:11–13. Tachau's monograph, *"Einst" und "Jetzt"*, investigates such material and finds that it reflects a schema whose content is a contrast between the pre-Christian past and the Christian present, and one which is usually, but not always, expressed by the use of ποτέ and νῦν. Such a description of the schema allows him to claim the following passages for it: Rom 5:8–11; 6:15–23; 7:5, 6; 11:30–32; 1 Cor 6:9–11; Gal 1:23; 4:3–7; 4:8–10; Eph 2:1–22; 5:8; Col 1:21, 22; 2:13; 3:7, 8; Phlm 11; 1 Tim 1:13, 14; Titus 3:3–7; 1 Pet 2:10; 2:25 (*"Einst" und "Jetzt"*, 12, 79–85). Tachau's investigation concludes that this schema has no clear antecedent in the OT or intertestamental Judaism (21–70) and that only in *Joseph and Asenath* can any strong formal contrast between ποτέ or sometimes τὸ πρότερον, "formerly," and νῦν be found (52–58). The ποτέ-νῦν contrast is used in Greek rhetoric as a stylistic device (71–78), but Tachau holds that NT usage is far more than rhetorical and involves the substantial element of the contrast between pre-Christian past and Christian present (94). He believes it likely that the original setting for the NT schema was early Christian preaching, and that such preaching may well have been in connection with baptism or recent conversion. Those original connections are, however, no longer accessible because the schema is now found in a variety of different contexts in the NT (80, 133–34). When he comes specifically to deal with Eph 2 (134–43), Tachau argues that vv 1–3 with their ποτέ call for a naming of the present with νῦν, and yet only vv 11–13 bring a resolution of this tension. He claims that vv 1–10 are to be considered incomplete in their contrast, and that the form of chap. 2 as a whole is a contrast between past and present (vv 1–3, 11–13), echoed in the

Form / Structure / Setting

closing section (vv 19–22), but interrupted by two excursuses (vv 4–10, 14–18; cf. also Schille, *Frühchristliche Hymnen*, 54).

Tachau's research into the schema as a whole is helpful, but his analysis of Eph 2 is unconvincing. The initial contrast, which deals with salvation in general terms, is completed in vv 1–10. "Dead through trespasses and sins" (v 1) has as its contrast "made alive" (v 5). Following this world-age and being under the domination of the ruler of the realm of the air (v 2) is in antithesis to being in relationship to Christ (cf. the συν- compounds and ἐν Χριστῷ Ἰησοῦ) and seated in the heavenly realms (vv 5, 6). God's wrath (v 3) is balanced against his mercy, love, grace, and kindness (vv 4, 5, 7), and being by nature children of wrath (v 3) can be paralleled with being saved by grace (vv 5, 8). All the necessary elements of a clear contrast between the past and the present are in fact found in vv 1–7. ὁ δὲ θεός, "but God," of v 4 and then the three aorists and the perfect of the verb forms of vv 5, 6 underline the break between the past and the present which has taken place. The concluding section (vv 8–10) adds further to the contrast not only by the repetition of "by grace you have been saved" (v 8), but also by the final note of "walking" in good works (v 10), which is the converse of the "walking" in trespasses and sins with which the passage began (vv 1, 2). These features indicate a real contrast within vv 1–10 and suggest that it is much better to see vv 1–7, in particular, as an example of the schema where ποτέ is present (v 2) while νῦν is implicit in vv 4, 5 (cf. also Halter, *Taufe und Ethos*, 626 n. 9). Tachau himself (*"Einst" und "Jetzt"*, 81) includes in the schema passages where ποτέ is implicit (Rom 5:8–11; 7:5, 6; 1 Pet 2:25), passages where νῦν is implicit (1 Tim 1:13, 14; Titus 3:3–5) and passages where both ποτέ and νῦν are implicit (1 Cor 6:9–11; Gal 4:3–7; Col 2:13). Eph 2:1–7 then is to be considered an example of the contrast schema where only ποτέ is explicit.

When one compares this example of the schema with others, a number of parallels may be noted. On the pre-Christian side of the contrast, the being dead in 2:1 can be compared, of course, to the same notion in Col 2:13, but also to the death, both physical and spiritual, mentioned in Rom 6:16, 21, 23; 7:5. The "trespasses and sins" of 2:1 recall the trespasses of Col 2:13 and the sins of Rom 7:6, but also "sinners" in Rom 5:8 and "sin" in Rom 6:16–18, 20, 23. Being under the control of the spiritual force of the ruler of the realm of the air in 2:2 is similar to being under the control of the elemental spirits in Gal 4:3, 8. "Disobedience" in 2:2 is found also in Rom 11:30–32 and Titus 3:3. "Passions" (ἐπιθυμίαι) in 2:3 is paralleled in Col 3:7 (cf. 3:5) and Titus 3:3, and has its equivalent in παθήματα in Rom 7:5. Rom 7:5 also speaks of the past as being lived in the flesh, just as 2:3 does here. Finally, "wrath" in 2:3 corresponds to the same notion in Rom 5:9 and Col 3:7 (cf. 3:6). On the positive side of the contrast, present Christian experience involves having been made alive (2:5), which can be compared with Col 2:13 and also with the mention of eternal life in Rom 6:22, 23 and Titus 3:7. It is an experience of salvation (2:5), as in the present aspect of the contrast in Rom 5:9, 10 and Titus 3:5. It is also an experience of God's love (2:4), as in Rom 5:8 (cf. also 1 Tim 1:14); of mercy (2:4), as in Rom 11:30–32; 1 Tim 1:14; Titus 3:5 and 1 Pet 2:10; of grace (2:5, 7), as in 1 Tim 1:14 and Titus 3:7; and of kindness (2:7), as in Titus 3:4. As can be seen from these references, the example of the schema with which Ephesians has most in common is Titus 3:3–7, where there are several parallels in vocabulary, though the terms are found in different sequence. This suggests the possibility of a common tradition which Ephesians and the Pastorals have reworked in their own way. (On the links between Eph 2:1–10 and Titus 3:3–7 cf. Luz, "Rechtfertigung," 370.)

The ποτέ-νῦν schema is generally used in the NT epistles to help in the instruction of believers. Here in Eph 2:1–7 the contrast furthers the application of the more general statements of chap. 1 (cf. also Tachau, *"Einst" und Jetzt"*, 135, 142). It aids the writer in assuring his readers of God's saving activity on their behalf and thereby increases their knowledge of the significance of that activity. This knowledge, in turn, lays the basis for the paraenesis which will come later. If the readers have experienced this contrast between their past and their present, then it must affect the way they live (cf. 4:17–24; 5:7–10). It should also be noted about the particular use of the schema in Eph 2:1–7 that, while temporal categories are to the fore in the contrast, spatial categories have been intermingled. The past is at the same time depicted in terms of this world and the realm of the air, and the present in terms of experience of the heavenly realms (cf. also Steinmetz, *Protologische Heilszuversicht*, 53–54).

Throughout 2:1–10 there is variation in style between first person and second person plural forms. Particularly in regard to vv 1–3, a number of commentators hold that "you" refers exclusively to Gentile Christians, while "we" has in view Jewish Christians (cf. J. A. Robinson, 48; Schlier, 105–6; Barth, 211–12; Ernst, 303). Such a distinction is more plausible here, where it is closer to the explicit discussion of Jews and Gentiles in the second half of the chapter, than it was back in 1:11–13, but it is still unconvincing. It is true that the writer thinks of his readers as predominantly Gentile Christians (cf. 2:11) and that the writer himself could well be a Jewish Christian. But the distinction between "you" and "we" is not intended to be one between Gentile and Jew so much as one between the readers in particular and Christians in general, including the writer (cf. the comment above on 1:13). What is said about those referred to as "we all" in v 3 is not something distinctive to Jews rather than Gentiles, and it becomes clear from the rest of the pericope that the Gentile-Jew distinction cannot be maintained consistently. The "we" who were dead through trespasses in v 5a are not Jews as opposed to the Gentiles who were dead through trespasses in v 1 or as opposed to Gentiles who have been saved by grace in 5b. Similarly the "you" who have been saved by grace in v 8 are not Gentile Christians as opposed to the Jewish Christians who are God's handiwork in v 10. Instead the "you" of vv 1, 2, 5, 8 is the style of addressing the recipients of the letter, which the writer had taken up in 1:13 and used most recently in 1:15–18. What was true of the readers' former sinful state (v 1) was true of the past of all believers, including the writer, as the "we all" of v 3 makes clear. The continuation of the first person plural in vv 4, 5a, 7, 10 is the style of confessional material, which allows for a broad reference to all believers (cf. also Gnilka, 112; Lindemann, *Aufhebung*, 108; Halter, *Taufe und Ethos*, 626 n. 4), and the interchange between the "you" and the "we" style has the force of making the readers feel included in the Church as a whole (cf. also Schnackenburg, 89).

We have referred to the style of confessional material in vv 4–10. Schille would go much further and claim to have isolated an early Christian "initiation hymn" which is cited in vv 4–7, 10 and interrupted by an interpretative prose comment in vv 8, 9 (*Frühchristliche Hymnen*, 53–60, followed to a large extent by Barth 211, 217–218, who thinks, however, that such a liturgical composition could be Paul's own; Fischer, *Tendenz und Absicht*, 121–22, also claims that vv 4–7 involve a citation from a baptismal liturgy with the phrase "in the ages to come" in v 7 to be taken as the writer's gloss to retain an eschatological reserve). Schille later qualifies this by stating that the text cited is not so much an actual hymn as a piece of baptismal liturgy (59). He does, however, think that this liturgical piece contains four stanzas, each of which consists of three lines. He asserts that the first stanza, vv 4, 5a, which talks of God's mercy to those dead through trespasses, constitutes a confession of guilt. The second stanza, vv 5b, 6, which deals with being united with Christ in God's saving acts, he calls a Christological credo. The third stanza, v 7, treats the topic of the demonstration of God's salvation before the powers (a judgment dependent on his doubtful interpretation of the aeons as personal powers), and the fourth, v 10, which mentions the ethical obligations of the new life, is deemed to involve a statement of self-commitment (59). Verse 5c, "by grace you have been saved," on Schille's analysis, is held to be a choral response within the original liturgy, which is then taken up and interpreted in the light of Pauline theology in v 8a (56–57).

The following considerations tell fairly decisively against such a proposal, however. It is not at all clear that Schille's descriptions of each stanza really fit the material to be found in each and therefore that the material as a whole takes us through the stages of the initiation liturgy that he suggests. Verses 4 and 7 show the writer's own typical style. Verse 10, with its discussion of works, has appropriate links with the preceding material in vv 8, 9 and, with its repetition of περιπατεῖν, seems to offer a final deliberate contrast to vv 1–3. Both these factors indicate that it is likely to be basically the writer's own conclusion. The most decisive objection to Schille's construction is that v 6 provides the writer's deliberate parallel to the creedal material he has previously used in 1:20. Of the material in vv 4–7, 10, the clearest candidate for designation as preformulated material is v 5a, on which v 5b "by grace you have been saved" appears to be the writer's inserted comment.

About v 5a, "made us alive with Christ even when we were dead through trespasses," there are questions of relationship with Colossians. In the light of the similarities between 2:1, 5a and Col 2:13, as well as between 1:20 and Col 2:13, J. T. Sanders (*ZNW* 56 [1965] 218–23) has argued that it is a question of the relationship between Eph 1:20–2:7 and Col 2:10–13. Either the writer of Ephesians expanded and reinterpreted the Colossians passage, while preserving its liturgical and hymnic character, or Ephesians and Colossians draw independently on the same or a highly similar liturgical background, as Sanders maintains (cf. also Schille, *Frühchristliche Hymnen*, 33, 55–56; K. Wengst, *Christologische Formeln und Lieder des Urchristentums* [Gütersloh: G. Mohn, 1972] 187–88, who also argue for the dependence of Eph 2:5 and Col 2:13 on a common liturgical source). Both options, however, overestimate both the liturgical character of Eph 2:3–7 (see the preceding discussion) and the liturgical character of Col 2:10–13. There is certainly no unanimity among scholars in regard to the existence of an original liturgical piece underlying this part of Col 2 (Schweizer, *Colossians*, 135, believes its existence to be improbable; Lohse, *Colossians*, 106–7, holds that such traditional material exists only in 2:13c–15; Deichgräber, *Gotteshymnus*, 167–68, claims that if there was such material 2:13a was not part of it; Best, *JSNT* 13 [1981] 10, asserts the necessity of skepticism about such material). The break in thought between Col 2:12 and 2:13 (with their different uses of the reference to death, the alternation between first and second person plural, the change of the subject for the verbs, and the sudden shift from the notion of forgiveness to that of victory over the powers), while explicable in terms of the concerns and the style of Colossians as a whole, seems unlikely in a unified preformed liturgical piece involving Col 2:12–15. Sanders' second option of the independent use of a common liturgical source involves, therefore, the building of a further hypothesis on what are already very unstable foundations. He himself appears to recognize (*ZNW* 56 [1965] 223, 232) that it is much more likely that Eph 2 is dependent on Col 2:10–13, which it has used and expanded in line with its own concerns (cf. also Halter, *Taufe und Ethos*, 234; Best, *JSNT* 13 [1981] 11). Eph 2:1, καὶ ὑμᾶς ὄντας νεκροὺς τοῖς παραπτώμασιν, "and you being dead through trespasses," and Eph 2:5, καὶ ὄντας ἡμᾶς νεκροὺς τοῖς παραπτώμασιν, "and we being dead through trespasses," are dependent on Col 2:13, καὶ ὑμᾶς νεκροὺς ὄντας τοῖς παραπτώμασιν, "and you being dead through trespasses." This relationship with Colossians accounts best for the difficult καί, "and," in both Eph 2:1 and 2:5. Only in Eph 2:1 does the second person pronoun agree with Col 2:13 and in all three references the word order is slightly different. Eph 2:5, συνεζωοποίησεν τῷ Χριστῷ, "made alive with Christ," is dependent on Col 2:13, συνεζωοποίησεν ὑμᾶς σὺν αὐτῷ, "made you alive with him"; Eph 2:6, καὶ συνήγειρεν, "and raised up with," recalls Col 2:12, καὶ συνηγέρθητε, "and you were raised with"; and the notion of being seated with Christ in the heavenly realms in Eph 2:6 is a drawing out of the implications of Col 3:1, 2. Similarly, Eph 2:2, ἐν αἷς ποτε περιεπατήσατε, "in which you once lived," takes up the language of Col 3:7, ἐν οἷς καὶ ὑμεῖς περιεπατήσατέ ποτε, "in which also you once lived," and the reference to God's wrath in Eph 2:3 recalls that in Col 3:6. In many of these cases, the surrounding context in Ephesians is different from that in Colossians, but this feature is characteristic of the overall relationship between the two letters. In this way it can be seen that, rather than having its source in an already formed liturgical tradition, Eph. 2:1–10, like much of the letter as a whole, has Colossians as a major source, while also reflecting the thought and language of the major Pauline letters and, in particular, Romans (cf. especially vv 8, 9).

Negative conclusions about a hymn or liturgical unit lying behind 2:1–10 mean that discussion about the baptismal setting of such traditional material becomes superfluous. But the question remains whether Eph 2:1–10 as it stands has baptismal connections. Certainly the depiction of the change God has accomplished for the readers and of the new life he has provided could be seen as an exposition of the significance of their baptism. The language of 2:1, 5 about being dead through trespasses had been used in its source in Col 2:13 in the context of a reference to baptism (Col 2:12), and this notion of pre-Christian existence as a spiritual death occurs again in Eph 5:14 in what is widely held to be a part of a baptismal hymn. Although it is not possible to claim it as an exclusively baptismal motif, the contrast between past and present, involving the use of ποτέ and νῦν, most probably originated as part of preaching or instruction associated with baptism (cf. Tachau, *"Einst" und "Jetzt"*, 80, 133–34). In addition, Titus 3:3–7, the example with which Eph 2 has most in common, is linked with baptism (cf. Luz, "Rechtfertigung," 370). In particular, the language of 2:5, 6 about being made alive with Christ and being raised with Christ has associations with baptism. Both expressions follow on immediately from the notion of being buried with Christ in baptism in Col 2:12, and in Rom 6:1–4 the notion of participation in Christ's resurrection life comes immediately after the link between baptism and participation in Christ's death and burial. Some writers (e.g., J. D. G. Dunn, *Baptism in the Holy Spirit* [London: SCM, 1970] 160–61; Barth, 234) deny an association of 2:5, 6 with baptism. It is true that the primary reference of these verses is likely to be to the spiritual transformation brought about through believers' union with Christ. But conversion and initiation were seen as one complex, in which baptism expressed this faith-union with Christ, and therefore it is unnecessary to attempt to divorce completely the expression from the spiritual reality expressed. Most scholars therefore relate the notions of 2:5, 6 to baptism (cf. Schlier, 109–11; Schnackenburg, *Baptism,* 73–78; G. R. Beasley-Murray, *Baptism in the New Testament* [London: Macmillan, 1962] 203 n. 3; Kirby, *Ephesians,* 154–56; Steinmetz, *Protologische Heilszuversicht,* 41; Gnilka, 117, 126; Ernst, 305; Halter, *Taufe und Ethos,* 236–37). There is no direct or explicit reference to baptism in 2:1–10, but there is also no reason to deny that the way in which the writer talks about the contrast between pre-Christian past and Christian present, about the change wrought by God's mercy, and about believers' participation in what happened to Christ, would have recalled to his readers the significance of their baptism.

In the persuasive strategy of the writer's discourse, this pericope and the following one, 2:11–22, function together as the *narratio*. The *narratio* reports that which has been done in the past in such a way as to persuade the audience to base their thinking or action upon it. By means of the dramatic contrast in this passage between the readers' past and their present, a contrast addressed directly to the readers and appealing to both their minds and emotions, the writer impresses on them how much they owe to what God has done in Christ. As they recall God's intervention on their behalf and the full salvation they now enjoy in contrast with their previous spiritual death, they are inevitably made aware of the radical reorientation their whole identity has undergone. Such an awareness, together with the mention of good works as part of their complete salvation, prepares them for the ethical implications of the second half of the letter, which the writer will go on to draw from their status as a new creation.

Comment

1 καὶ ὑμᾶς ὄντας νεκροὺς τοῖς παραπτώμασιν καὶ ταῖς ἁμαρτίαις ὑμῶν, "and you were dead through your trespasses and sins." The writer addresses his readers directly again. The readers are primarily Gentile Christians (cf. 2:11)

but this is not deducible either from the force of the καί or the use of the second person plural as over against the first person plural (*contra* Barth, 211–12; cf. the discussion under *Form/Structure/Setting* above on the alternation between "you" and "we" in this passage). What is said about the addressees' past condition is certainly not exclusively true of Gentiles as opposed to Jews. The καί at the beginning is probably dependent, as is the rest of the clause, on Col 2:13a. As it now stands, it functions as a connective with the whole of the preceding pericope rather than with 1:23 specifically. As the rest of this passage will show, the same power that was at work in raising and exalting Christ from physical death has raised and exalted believers from spiritual death.

How is it that the readers' pre-Christian past can be described as a condition of death? Such a description was a natural implication of the way of thinking in which the death and resurrection of Christ was the turning point of history. If Christ's resurrection introduced the life of the age to come ahead of time, then one's state prior to participation in that resurrection life must, comparatively speaking, be viewed as death. In addition, the notion of participation in the events of the end ahead of time can be seen to have a reverse, negative side. The death which comes to all as the wages of sin (cf. Rom 6:23) and which in its final form involves physical death and the judgment of exclusion from the life of God is experienced partially in this life. Best (*JSNT* 13 [1981] 16) has called this "a realized eschatological conception of death." The depiction of this life in terms of an experience of spiritual and moral death, while it took on special force in the light of Christ's resurrection, was not unique to the early Christians. Already in the OT, particularly in the Psalms, a life in disease, sin, alienation, captivity, or under the rule of one's enemies was seen as a life in Sheol or in the realm of death (e.g., Pss 13:1–3; 30:3; 31:12; 88:3–6; 143:3; Hos 13:14; Jonah 2:6; cf. C. Barth, *Die Errettung vom Tode* [Zürich: EVZ, 1947] 91–122). This way of thinking is found also in the Qumran writings in 1QH 3.19, "I thank Thee, O Lord, for Thou hast redeemed my soul from the Pit, and from the Hell (Sheol) of Abaddon Thou hast raised me up to everlasting height," and 1QH 11.10–14, "For the sake of Thy glory Thou hast purified man of sin . . . that bodies gnawed by worms may be raised from the dust . . . that he may stand before Thee with the everlasting host . . . to be renewed together with all the living. . . ." These texts refer not to physical death and future resurrection but to the community member's present experience of salvation. They provide a remarkable parallel to the thought of Ephesians with their notion that entrance into the community is a passing from death to life and to participation in the heavenly realm (cf. Mussner, "Contributions," 174–76; H.-W. Kuhn, *Enderwartung und gegenwärtiges Heil* [Göttingen: Vandenhoeck & Ruprecht, 1966] 78–90). Later, the rabbis could describe the Gentiles or the godless as dead (cf. *m. ʿEd.* 5.2; *y. Ber.* 2.4; *b. Ber.* 18a; *Midr. Qoh.* 9.5; *Gen. Rab.* 39.7). Outside Judaism Stoic writers used the term "dead" in a figurative sense, since they considered that what did not belong to the highest in a person, to the mind or the spirit, was not worthy of being described as alive (cf. *M. Ant.* 2.12.1; 12.33.2). That which a person had in common with the animal world and which separated him or her from the divine was deemed to be dead (cf. Epictetus, *Diss.* 1.3.3; 2.19.27).

In the NT itself "dead" is used metaphorically in the saying found in Matt

8:22 and Luke 9:60 and in the parable in Luke 15:24, 32. In 1 Tim 5:6 and Rev 3:1 it is used of members of the Christian community who are not living the new life as they ought. Outside the Pauline corpus the greatest similarity to the usage in Eph 2:1, 5 is found in the Johannine literature where there is a strong realized eschatology of life and death (cf. John 5:24, 25; 1 John 3:14). Later, Hermas employs the term "dead" of the state of people before their baptism (*Sim.* 9.16.3, 4), and in Gnostic writings the non-initiate could be called dead (cf. *Gos. Phil.* 70.10–17; Hippolytus, *Ref.* 6.35.6).

Obviously the most immediate influence on the usage of the writer to the Ephesians is Col 2:13. But lying behind this are other references in Paul which depict death as a power of the old age and connect it closely with sin (e.g., Rom 5:12–21; 6:23; 1 Cor 15:56). In such references the physical aspect of death's power is very much to the fore, but there are also places where the spiritual aspect of death's reign is in view. In Rom 6:13 believers are as those who have been brought from death to life, and in Rom 7:9, 10, 13 the person under the law is in a state of death. The realized eschatological view of death in Col 2:13 and Eph 2:1 is a natural continuation of such thinking, as the past is contrasted with the present experience of resurrection life. The same concept occurs later in Ephesians when the baptismal hymn is quoted in 5:14, "Awake, O sleeper, and arise from the dead," and 4:18 with its description of Gentile existence as "alienated from the life of God" provides a further comment on what the writer means when he says his readers were dead. It is a theological assessment on the part of the writer, for whom reality is determined by one's relationship to God and who therefore sees the tragic situation of those who are not in a living relationship to God through Christ as one of death.

The readers were dead through their trespasses and sins. In distinction from the statement in Col 2:13 on which it is dependent, Eph 2:1 adds "sins" to "trespasses" instead of the phrase "the uncircumcision of your flesh." On παραπτώματα, "trespasses," and the question of the singular and plural of words for sin in Paul and Ephesians, see the discussion of 1:7. Whereas in Rom 5–7 it is sin, personified as a power in the singular, that predominates in the close association with death (but cf. 5:16; 7:5), here it is acts of sin in the plural. ἁμαρτίαι, "sins," simply adds a synonym to "trespasses," forming a hendiadys (the use of two words coupled by "and" to express one concept). The singulars of both nouns are used interchangeably in Rom 5:12–21, as are the plurals in talking about "forgiveness of sins" in Col 1:14 and 2:13. The use of the two synonyms here provides another example of the redundancy of style of Ephesians and helps to convey an impression of the immensity and variety of the sinfulness of the readers' past. "Trespasses and sins" is in the dative and has been translated "through your trespasses and sins." This dative should be seen as expressing both the cause and the manifestation of death (cf. also Barth, 212; Gnilka, 114; Best, *JSNT* 13 [1981] 19–20). Trespasses and sins both bring about the condition of death and characterize the existence of those who are spiritually dead.

2 ἐν αἷς ποτε περιεπατήσατε, "in which you once lived." This part of the verse recalls the wording of Col 3:7, ἐν οἷς καὶ ὑμεῖς περιεπατήσατέ ποτε . . . , "in which you also once lived. . . ." On the part ποτέ plays in the contrast in this passage, see *Form/Structure/Setting* above. The relative pronoun is a feminine plural because it has been attracted to its most immediate antecedent, ταῖς ἁμαρτίαις, though it should be seen as referring back to the whole phrase "your trespasses and sins." περιπατεῖν, literally, "to walk" (cf. also v 10), is a Hebraism common in the LXX in translating הלך, *hālak*, in its use for ethical conduct or a way of living. The rabbis, of course, used this terminology in speaking of teaching about ethical conduct—*hālākâ*. The use of περιπατεῖν in this sense in the NT is most characteristic of Paul's writings but also occurs in the Johannine literature. Here in Ephesians it will become prominent again later in the paraenetical section of the letter (cf. 4:1, 17; 5:2, 8, 15).

κατὰ τὸν αἰῶνα τοῦ κόσμου τούτου, "in accordance with this world-age." In conjunction with περιπατεῖν, κατά plus the accusative designates the norm of conduct. But should αἰών be taken in its usual sense of "age" or "time span" or as the name of a personal power or deity, Aion? Those who see Ephesians as in some way in interaction with Gnostic thought, in which αἰών was a technical term, often opt for the personal reference here. But this latter interpretation is not dependent on the later Gnostic myth for its support, for the name Aion for a god of endless time is found in several Hellenistic religious and magical contexts, and it is known that there was a cult for this deity in Alexandria around 200 B.C.E. (cf. M. Zepf, "Der Gott Aion in der hellenistischen Theologie," *ARW* 25 [1927] 225–44; H. Sasse, "αἰών," *TDNT* 1 [1964] 198; and the detailed assessment of the evidence by A. D. Nock, "A Vision of Mandulis Aion," *HTR* 27 [1934] 53–104, especially 78–99). It is argued that the triple parallelism of v 2 requires a reference to a personal power alongside the ruler and the spirit who are mentioned. Elsewhere, Paul did associate such a personal power with this age, and in 2 Cor 4:4 talked about the god of this age (cf. also 1 Cor 2:6, 8 where "rulers of this age" may well be a reference to supernatural powers). Here in Eph 2:2 such a figure would be equivalent to the ruler of the realm of the air, to the devil (6:11) or the evil one (6:16). Elsewhere in the NT he is associated with "this world," as in our verse (cf. "the ruler of this world" in John 12:31; 16:11). The singular αἰών is not here qualified by an adjective such as "this" or "coming" and is therefore unlikely to have a temporal force. By the time Ignatius wrote his *Epistle to the Ephesians* (19.1, 2) αἰών appears to have been understood as having a personal reference. This interpretation has a number of adherents among recent writers (cf. A. D. Nock, "A Vision of Mandulis Aion," *HTR* 27 [1934] 89; Schlier, 101; Steinmetz, *Protologische Heilszuversicht*, 61; Gnilka, 114; Barth, 214; Lindemann, *Aufhebung*, 56–59, 109; Halter, *Taufe und Ethos*, 235; Schnackenburg, 91; H. Sasse, "αἰών," *TDNT* 1 [1964] 207, thinks that Eph 2:2 is perhaps the one instance where this mythological conception from syncretism, which later came to play an important part in Gnosticism, has penetrated into the NT).

Against this interpretation it must first be said that the triple parallelism claimed for Eph 2:2 is by no means clear. There is no κατά, "in accordance with," before the reference to "spirit," and "spirit" is probably not to be interpreted as a reference to the same figure as the ruler (see the discussion below). This would be the only place in the NT where αἰών refers to a personal power. The plural in Eph 2:7 and 3:9, which some suggest as supporting references, is extremely unlikely to refer to personal forces. It is also unlikely that the writer would switch from the temporal force of αἰών in 1:21 to a personal reference in 2:2 and then back again to a temporal one in 2:7 without giving some clearer indication of an intended change of meaning. To be sure, Paul does talk about personal powers connected with this age, but he never uses αἰών itself for such powers. Instead he employs ἄρχοντες (1 Cor 2:6, 8) or θεός (2 Cor 4:4) to make his point. In Eph 2:2 good sense can be made of αἰών with a temporal force without having to resort to a reference to the god Aion. The expression "the age of this world" would be just one more example of the piling up of synonyms in genitive constructions in the style characteristic of Ephesians. The following examples are also preceded by κατά: 1:5, κατὰ τὴν εὐδοκίαν τοῦ θελήματος αὐτοῦ; 1:11, κατὰ τὴν βουλὴν τοῦ θελήματος αὐτοῦ; 1:19, κατὰ τὴν ἐνέργειαν τοῦ κράτους τῆς ἰσχύος αὐτοῦ. It should not be surprising that αἰών and κόσμος can also be treated as synonyms, since αἰών had not only temporal but also spatial connotations. In the LXX αἰών appears as a translation of the Hebrew עולם, ʿōlām, which had a dual reference either to "age" or "world," and as the Greek equivalent it was correspondingly pressed into double service. In its sense of "time or duration of the world" it could easily pass over into the sense of "world" itself and become a synonym for κόσμος. Paul in 1 Cor 1:20; 2:6; 3:18, 19, for example, employs αἰών and κόσμος virtually interchangeably (cf. also H. Sasse, "αἰών," *TDNT* 1 [1964] 202–4). It is more likely then that, in line with its other usage in this letter and with this writer's redundancy of style, αἰών is being used in 2:2 with a temporal meaning than that this verse provides the only NT instance of its reference to a deity (cf. also J. A. Robinson, 48, 153; Abbott, 40; Percy, *Probleme,* 259; Gaugler, 85; Mussner, 59; *Christus,* 24–27; Caird, 51; Mitton, 83; Ernst, 203; Carr, *Angels and Principalities,* 100–101). The phrase "this world-age" thus becomes a way of talking about both spatial and temporal aspects of fallen human existence. Instead of being oriented to the life of the age to come and the heavenly realm, the past lives of the readers had been dominated by this present evil age and this world. Their sinful activities were simply in line with the norms and values of a spatio-temporal complex wholly hostile to God.

κατὰ τὸν ἄρχοντα τῆς ἐξουσίας τοῦ ἀέρος, "in accordance with the ruler of the realm of the air." Only now is the solidarity of evil, of which the recipients of the letter were once a part, given a personal connotation. Their lives were under the control of a ruler. Supernatural powers hostile to human welfare and to God's redemptive purposes have already figured in 1:21 and will do so again in 3:10 and 6:11, 12. In Ephesians, however, not only do such principalities and powers appear, but equally prominent is an ultimate personal power of evil behind them, designated here as the ruler of the realm of the air, but in 4:27 and 6:11 as the devil, and in 6:16 as the evil one. For Paul too this age had its god (cf. 2 Cor 4:4), and there was a personal center to the power of evil. But in the undisputed Pauline letters the designations found in Ephesians do not appear, and the name Satan is preferred instead. ἐξουσία is used in this verse for the realm or the sphere of the ruler's authority rather than for that authority itself. This is the way it had been used in Col 1:13, which talks of deliverance from the dominion of darkness and transference to the kingdom of God's beloved Son. Here the realm of the ruler's authority is said to be the air. Elsewhere in Ephesians, hostile powers inhabit the heavenly realms (cf. 3:10; 6:12). This notion has its background in OT and Jewish thought where angels and spirit powers were often represented as in heaven (e.g., Job 1:6; Dan 10:13, 21; 2 Macc 5:2; *1 Enoch* 61.10; 90.21, 24); it was also developed in Philo (cf. *De Spec. Leg.* 1.66; *De Plant.* 14; *De Gig.* 6, 7). What is the relationship of "the air" to "the heavenly realms"? It may be that the writer is using terminology from different cosmological schemes, but it is fairly certain that he intends the two terms to indicate the same realm inhabited by malevolent agencies (*pace* W. Wink, *Naming the Powers* [Philadelphia: Fortress, 1984] 84, who by asserting that the "power of the air" is not the locale of demons but the world atmosphere, the spiritual matrix of inauthentic living, confuses the force of this expression with that of the next phrase; his later discussion of "air" [91] also contradicts this assertion). If there is any distinct connotation, it could be that the "air" indicates the lower reaches of that realm and therefore emphasizes the proximity of this evil power and his influence over the world. In later Judaism the air is in fact thought of as the region under the firmament as in *2 Enoch* 29.4, 5, "And I threw him out from the height with his angels, and he was flying in the air continuously above the abyss." (Cf. also *T. Benj.* 3.4; *Targum of Job* 5.7; and *Asc. Isa.* 7.9; 10.29; 11.23 where the firmament is called the air and the ruler of this world and his angels are said to live in it. Wink, *Naming the Powers,* 83 and n. 96, argues that there is no evidence for the idea of evil spirits in the air prior to Paul, but he has himself already refuted such an assertion earlier [25 n. 38].)

τοῦ πνεύματος τοῦ νῦν ἐνεργοῦντος ἐν τοῖς υἱοῖς τῆς ἀπειθείας, "of the spirit that is now at work in those who are disobedient." There is much discussion about the syntactical place and the meaning of τοῦ πνεύματος, "of the spirit." Some take it as in apposition to τὸν ἄρχοντα, "the ruler," giving another name for the ruler and making clear that he is a spirit power (cf. Gnilka, 115 n. 5; Ernst, 303). But why then the genitive case rather than the accusative which would be expected in agreement with τὸν ἄρχοντα? It could be explained as a genitive of apposition (cf. BDF § 167) or as an unconscious assimilation to the two immediately preceding genitives, but it remains an awkward construction. Others take τοῦ πνεύματος as in apposition to its most immediate antecedent τοῦ ἀέρος, "of the air" (cf. Schlier, 104; Caird, 51). This interpretation can account for the genitive and appeals to a connection between spirit and air on the basis of the fact that in Hebrew and Greek one word could do service for spirit, breath, wind, air, and atmosphere. τοῦ πνεύματος, on this view, would be a further explanation of the air as the spiritual atmosphere which pervades those who are disobedient. There is one more syntactical option. τοῦ πνεύματος could be parallel to τῆς ἐξουσίας, "of the realm," and governed by τὸν ἄρχοντα, "the ruler" (cf. Meyer, 98–99; J. A. Robinson, 154; Abbott, 42). This option again accounts adequately for the genitive and should be preferred as making better sense of the verse. On this interpretation, the personal power of evil is the ruler of the realm of the air, the ruler of the spirit that is now at work in the disobedient.

In references to the Spirit of God πνεῦμα often hovers between personal and impersonal connotations. Here also spirit may be more a reference to a spiritual force or influence than to a personal power. When the writer speaks of evil spirit beings later in 6:12, he uses πνευματικά not πνεύματα. It is worth noting some similarity to Qumran teaching about the two spirits in which people walk (1QS 3.13–4.26), in which the spirit of falsehood is ruled by Belial, the Angel of Darkness. Paul, in 1 Cor 2:12, had recognized that there is a spirit at work in the world which is in antithesis to the Spirit of God. Here in Ephesians, that spiritual force is said to be under the rule of the same evil being who rules the air. The writer makes clear that this ruler's evil influence has both a cosmic and a human sphere. His spiritual influence is now at work in those who are disobedient. This assertion reinforces the observation that the terminology used of the sinful opposition is similar to that used of God's activity in salvation. Not only is πνεῦμα employed, but so also is ἐνεργεῖν, which has just featured in the depiction of the divine activity in 1:20. The mention that this spirit is *now* at work makes clear that although the writer has attributed bondage to the ruler of this world to his Christian readers' past, this does not mean that the ruler's power no longer exists. It is at work in the present in those who have not benefited from God's deliverance in Christ. In fact, the later paraenesis will remind believers that it still poses a threat to them (cf. 4:27; 6:10–20). Here we see something of the "already/not yet" tension so characteristic of Paul's eschatological thought.

Although the ruler of this world has been defeated (cf. 1:20–22), he is not surrendering without a struggle and without still making his powerful influence felt. The expression "sons of disobedience" for those in whom that influence is operative is a Hebraism denoting men and women whose lives are characterized by disobedience. The rebellion against God's will which this term implies includes rejection of the Christian gospel, since the writer states that it is occurring in the present. But the disobedience is not to be limited to this and involves general disregard for God's will (*pace* Schlier, 104; Barth, 216; Caird, 51). Together with the notion of God's wrath (cf. 2:3), this expression "sons of disobedience" will be taken up again in the paraenesis in 5:6.

3 ἐν οἷς καὶ ἡμεῖς πάντες ἀνεστράφημέν ποτε, "among them we all also once lived." ἐν οἷς, "among them," has reference to the immediate antecedent "those who are disobedient" and not to the trespasses and sins of v 1 (*contra* J. A. Robinson, 155; Ramaroson, *Bib* 58 [1977] 397). Not only the readers were to be reckoned among disobedient humanity at one time, but the same goes for all believers, including the writer, who is identifying with his readers—"we all also." In this depiction of the past style of life ποτέ is repeated from v 2, and ἀναστρέφειν, "to live," is used this time as a synonym for περιπατεῖν to denote ethical conduct. The noun ἀναστροφή occurs again in the paraenesis of 4:22 to refer to the past way of life. In that context it is also associated with the notion of "desires."

ἐν ταῖς ἐπιθυμίαις τῆς σαρκὸς ἡμῶν, ποιοῦντες τὰ θελήματα τῆς σαρκὸς καὶ τῶν διανοιῶν, "in the passions of our flesh, carrying out the wishes of the flesh and the thoughts." The major characteristic of the past sinful way of life that is now taken up is its orientation to the flesh. The term "flesh" occurs elsewhere in this letter in 2:11, 14; 5:29, 31; 6:5, 12. But only here, where it occurs twice in the same verse, does it have the negative ethical connotations distinctive of a large number of its uses in Paul. It should not be surprising that such connotations pertain here, since the expression "the passions of the flesh" echoes the language of Gal 5:16, 24, in the context of which Paul contrasted life in the Spirit and its fruit with life in the flesh and its works (cf. also Rom 7:5; 13:14).

Flesh, in such a context, stands not simply for a person's physical existence, but for the sphere of humanity in its sinfulness and opposition to God. It is the sphere in which a person not only displeases God but is also in fact incapable of pleasing God (cf. Rom 8:8). It is the sphere in which life is lived in pursuit of one's own ends and in independence of God. As such, it is not limited to indulgence in sensuality but can take on various forms, including allegiance to the law (cf. Gal 3:3). (On "flesh" in Paul cf. especially R. Bultmann, *Theology of the New Testament* 1 [New York: Charles Scribner's Sons, 1951] 232–46; E. Schweizer, "σάρξ," *TDNT* 7 [1971] 98–151; R. Jewett, *Paul's Anthropological Terms* [Leiden: E. J. Brill, 1971] 49–166; Ridderbos, *Paul*, 93–104; H. Seebass and A. C. Thiselton, "Flesh," *NIDNTT* 1 [1975] 671–82; A. Sand, *Der Begriff "Fleisch" in den paulinischen Hauptbriefen* [Regensburg: F. Pustet, 1967].)

As those whose lives were characterized by disobedience, the readers of this letter were once under the control of the sphere of the flesh. Its desires dominated their lives and had to be fulfilled. Sin pervaded their whole person so that there were no inner recesses untainted by it. Even their thoughts (τῶν διανοιῶν) were corrupt and controlled their actions. It has been suggested that the plural of διάνοια means senses or impulses, with LXX Num 15:39 cited in support (cf. BAGD 187). But there appear to be no grounds for such an interpretation. The plural of the noun should be translated, as one might expect, as "thoughts, dispositions, imaginations." The context will indicate whether such thoughts are seen as good or evil. This holds true of LXX Num 15:39. By making "thoughts" a separate category parallel to "flesh" in the clause "carrying out the wishes of the flesh and the thoughts," however, the writer may well be moving away slightly from Pauline usage, where the sphere of the flesh embraces the thoughts as well as the senses (cf. the mind-set of the flesh in Rom 8:5–7 or the mind of the flesh in Col 2:18), and beginning to confine "flesh" to the sensual (cf. also Lindemann, *Aufhebung*, 113; Percy [*Probleme*, 261–62] attempts to explain this as a stylistic variation but does not really meet the point that such a variation still leaves the reader with the distinction between flesh and thought).

καὶ ἤμεθα τέκνα φύσει ὀργῆς ὡς καὶ οἱ λοιποί, "and we were by nature children of wrath like the rest." When they once lived their lives in such total absorption with the flesh, the writer and all believers were τέκνα . . . ὀργῆς, "children of wrath." This is a Hebraism, like "sons of disobedience" in v 2, which means they were deserving of and liable to wrath. This wrath is clearly God's wrath (cf. Eph 5:6; also Col 3:5, 6) rather than merely an impersonal process of cause and effect or a principle of retribution in a moral universe. The wrath of God is a concept which occurs frequently in Paul's letter to the Romans. It refers to God's active judgment going forth against all forms of sin and evil and is evidence of his absolute holiness (cf. Rom 1:18; 2:5, 8; 3:5; 4:15; 5:9; 9:22; 12:19; 13:4, 5). The Hebraistic expression used here in Eph 2:3 reminds one of the way in which in the OT a person deserving of punishment is spoken of as a "son of stripes" (Deut 25:2) or a person doomed to die is spoken of as a "son of death" (cf. 1 Sam 26:16; 2 Sam 12:5; Ps 102:20). It is also reminiscent of the way in which in apocalyptic literature Cain, in being marked out for judgment, is described as a "son of wrath" (*Apoc. Mos.* 3). In the NT also, Jesus is represented as condemning the proselytizing of the Pharisees, declaring that when they made a convert he was twice as much a "son of Gehenna" as they themselves (Matt 23:15). The children of wrath, then, are those who are doomed to God's wrath because through their condition of sinful rebellion, they deserve his righteous judgment.

As does Paul in Rom 1:18–3:20, the writer makes this category cover all humanity outside Christ. ὡς καὶ οἱ λοιποί means "like the rest of humanity," and in this way the sinful condition and its consequences, which the writer has been describing, become all-embracing in their extent. What was once true of the readers (vv 1, 2) was also once true of all believers (v 3a), and what was once true of all believers is also true of the rest of humanity (v 3b).

The human condition of being destined to judgment in the day of God's wrath is a condition that is "by nature." What is the force of the term φύσει here? Elsewhere the noun φύσις can refer to the natural order of things (cf. Rom 1:26; 1 Cor 11:14), but the actual expression φύσει in the dative, "by nature," occurs elsewhere in the NT in Gal 2:15, "we who are Jews by nature," where it refers to that which comes through birth rather than that which is acquired later (cf. also ἐκ φύσεως in Rom 2:27), in Gal 4:8, where it means "in reality," and in Rom 2:14, 15, where it means "of one's own free will, voluntarily, independently." φύσει in Eph 2:3 belongs with the first of these uses (cf. also A. Bonhöffer, *Epiktet und das NT* [Giessen: Töpelmann, 1911] 146–54; BAGD 869; Barth, 231; *contra* Gnilka, 117). So, in their natural condition, through birth, men and women are "children of wrath."

Some commentators (e.g., J. A. Robinson, 50–51; Gnilka, 117; Barth, 231) wish to dissociate the thought expressed in this verse from any notion of original sin. (On the history of interpretation of this verse in connection with that doctrine, as seen mainly from a Catholic perspective, see Mehlmann's Latin monograph, *Natura filii Irae*.) But if original sin refers to the innate sinfulness of human nature inherited from Adam in consequence of the fall, then such a notion is not entirely alien to the thought of this verse when it speaks of the impossibility of humanity of itself, in its natural condition, escaping God's wrath. To be sure, the verse does not explicitly teach original sin by making a statement about how this tragic plight came to be humanity's natural condition. Yet the idea of the natural condition in which one finds oneself by birth being a sinful state deserving of God's judgment surely presupposes some such view of original sin as is found in Rom 5:12–21, where Paul recognizes that, as well as sinning themselves, men and women, in solidarity with Adam, inherit a sinful situation by sharing in the one sin of the one man (cf. also Schlier, 107; BAGD 869, where Eph 2:3 is translated "we were, in our natural condition [as descendants of Adam], children of wrath.") "By nature" should not of course be taken to mean that sinfulness is of the essence of human nature. In Pauline thought sin is always abnormal, a disorder, but in a fallen world the natural condition of human beings involves experience of that abnormality and disorder. In this sense, Eph 2:1–10 contains a contrast between nature and grace, between fallen human existence in and of itself and the divine initiative required if human life is to be restored to what it was meant to be.

4 ὁ δὲ θεὸς πλούσιος ὢν ἐν ἐλέει, διὰ τὴν πολλὴν ἀγάπην αὐτοῦ ἣν ἠγάπησεν ἡμᾶς, "But God, being rich in mercy, out of his great love with which he loved us." Here the writer begins to return to the thought begun in v 1 but interrupted by his expansion on what it means to be dead through trespasses and sins in vv 2, 3. He has seen clearly the hopeless condition of humanity in sin and painted it in dark colors. Yet the explanation for the overall mood of the first part of the letter being one of praise and thanksgiving to God rather than despair is summed up by the eloquent little phrase at the start of v 4, ὁ δὲ θεός . . . , "but God. . . ." The adversative δέ introduces a contrasting situation brought about because of who God is and what he has done. An implicit νῦν, "now," can be seen as part of this contrast with the ποτέ, "once," of vv 2, 3. There is now in existence a whole new situation because of God's initiative.

This initiative is launched because God is a God not only of righteous wrath (v 3) but also of mercy. ὤν here is a circumstantial participle rather than an attributive one—"being rich in mercy" or "because he is rich in mercy." For no other reason than his mercy, God has rescued men and women from death and given them life. In fact he is "rich in mercy." An equivalent Hebrew description is used of Yahweh in, for example, Exod 34:6 and Ps 145:8. In the LXX ἔλεος, "mercy," normally represents the term חסד, ḥesed, which frequently denotes Yahweh's steadfast covenant loyalty and love, including the mercy of forgiveness when Israel is unfaithful to the covenant. God's mercy is his overflowing active compassion and is freely exercised, excluding all ideas of merit on the part of its object. It is noticeable that the notion of God's mercy is a prominent present element in several examples of the contrast between the pre-Christian past and the Christian present (cf. Rom 11:30–32; 1 Tim 1:13; Titus 3:3–5; 1 Pet 2:10). It plays an important part in the apostle Paul's thinking about God's relationship to humanity in Rom 9–11 in particular (cf. 9:15, 16, 18, 23; 11:30, 31, 32). The idea that believers' experience of salvation is totally unmerited on their part and due solely to God's generosity will be expressed again in the mention of his love, and particularly through the term "grace," which is synonymous with "mercy" and provides the keynote for the latter part of the passage in vv 5, 7, 8.

The other major motive cited for God's initiative in saving his people is his attitude of love. διά plus the accusative of words for emotion indicates motivation. The writer also uses a cognate accusative expression to reinforce his thought—"the great love with which he loved us" (cf. 1:6; 1:19, 20; 4:1, which also employ cognate nouns and verbs). Just as the richness of God's mercy has been stressed, so here is the greatness of his love. Again it is Romans among Paul's letters which provides examples of his reflection on God's love for his people demonstrated in Christ (cf. 5:5, 8; 8:39). As in Romans 5:8, so here in Ephesians the love of God will be shown to have its focus in the love of Christ, which led to his death on behalf of his people (cf. 5:2, 25). Against the background of vv 1–3, it is at once apparent that God's love is not conditional on the suitability of the objects of that love.

5, 6 καὶ ὄντας ἡμᾶς νεκροὺς τοῖς παραπτώμασιν συνεζωοποίησεν τῷ Χριστῷ, "made us alive with Christ even when we were dead through trespasses." As we have already noted, it is only here that the main verb, which governs the thought of the passage to this point, is introduced. To remind his readers of the thought with which he had begun, the writer repeats his words from v 1, omitting "and sins" and changing the person from the second to the first person plural. In line with the progress of thought in vv 1–3, not only the readers but all believers are included in the assertion. The awkward καί at the beginning of this verse is probably best explained on the basis of this repetition of v 1, where its occurrence is in turn to be explained as being in dependence on Col 2:13 (cf. also Best, *JSNT* 13 [1981] 15). As it now stands, it could be a simple connective between two elements, which side by side set what God has done in full perspective: out of his great love and when we were dead through trespasses, he made us alive with Christ (cf. Meyer, 109). Alternatively, the καί might well have the force of intensifying the participial clause which it introduces in the light of what has preceded it: "even when we were dead through trespasses" (cf. also Abbott, 47). God's mercy and love caused him to act on behalf of men and women and to do what was necessary for them, even when they were in such a condition (cf. the similar thought in Rom 5:8, where God is said to show his love for us in Christ's death "while we were yet sinners").

Salvation for those whose plight is spiritual death must involve a raising to life. This is in fact what God has accomplished for believers. He made them alive with Christ. At this point also, Ephesians is reminiscent of Colossians. After the statement in Col 2:13 about the readers being dead through trespasses and the mention of the uncircumcision of their flesh (not taken up by Ephesians until 2:11), there follows the assertion that God made them alive together with Christ, phrased only slightly differently from Ephesians with the preposition σύν before a pronoun in addition to the συν- prefix to the verb— συνεζωοποίησεν ὑμᾶς σὺν αὐτῷ, "made you alive together with him." συζωοποιεῖν is used in the NT only in these two places. The thought in both instances is that new life comes to believers because they share in what has happened to Christ. Although the simple verb ζωοποιεῖν, "to make alive," is used in a number of places in connection with the resurrection of believers from the dead, it is used directly of God's activity on behalf of Christ only in 1 Pet 3:18, "put to death in the flesh but made alive in the Spirit." The closest one comes to such usage in the Pauline corpus is 1 Cor 15:22, 23 where, after Paul's statement that in Christ all shall be made alive, he explains the stages of this event of being made alive, starting with Christ as the firstfruits. Clearly, Christ's being made alive meant also for the writer of Ephesians the resurrection and exaltation, as the next two verbs in v 6 confirm.

Believers' participation in the event of Christ's being made alive is expressed in v 5 through the συν- compound and the dative phrase τῷ Χριστῷ. The συν- prefix does not contain a reference to Jews and Gentiles sharing in a common resurrection (*pace* Barth, 220; Ramaroson, *Bib* 58 [1977] 402). This is not in view in vv 5, 6, where the parallels with 1:20 show that the relationship between the believer and Christ is the writer's intended focus. The idea of participation "with Christ" is in continuity with the thought of Colossians, as we have seen, but also with that of other places in Paul. συν- compounds or expressions using the preposition σύν are frequently found in eschatological contexts referring to living with Christ at the Parousia or after death and to sharing his glory (cf. 1 Thess 4:14, 17; 5:10; Rom 6:8; 8:17; 2 Cor 4:14; Phil 1:23; Col 3:4). A relationship with Christ is in view which affects believers' future destinies because it involves sharing in Christ's destiny. Yet, characteristic of Paul's thought is that a sharing in Christ's glory and resurrection life is conditional on a sharing in the other aspect of his destiny, his death. "With Christ" language is found in connection with two aspects of sharing that death—sharing in it as an event of the past, a death to the old order and its powers, sometimes with explicitly baptismal overtones (cf. Rom 6:4, 5, 6, 8; Gal 2:19; Col 2:12, 20; 3:1), and sharing in its aspect of present suffering (cf. Rom 8:17; Phil 3:10). As we shall see in discussion of συνήγειρεν in v 6, there is some debate about how far "with Christ" language was extended by Paul to refer to a past or present sharing in Christ's resurrection; but, apart from Col 2:12; 3:1, it can be argued that the notion of a present experience of this relationship is in view in 2 Cor 13:4, and the notion of a past experience is implicit in Rom 6. The "with Christ" relationship is closely linked in Paul's thought with his other ways of expressing solidarity with Christ, such as "in Christ" or the notion, developed in Rom 5:12–21, of Christ as the inclusive representative of the new humanity. (On "with Christ" in Paul, cf. E. Lohmeyer, "ΣΥΝ ΧΡΙΣΤΩΙ," *Festgabe für A. Deissmann* [Tübingen: Mohr, 1927] 218–57; J. Dupont, ΣΥΝ ΧΡΙΣΤΩΙ: *L'Union avec le Christ suivant saint Paul* [Bruges: Abbaye de Saint-André, 1952]; W. Grundmann, "σύν-μετά," *TDNT* 7 [1971] 766–97; E. Schweizer, "Dying and Rising with Christ," *NTS* 14 [1967–68] 1–14; R. C. Tannehill, *Dying and Rising with Christ* [Berlin: A. Töpelmann, 1967]; P. Siber, *Mit Christus leben* [Zürich: Theologischer Verlag, 1971].)

Passages such as Rom 4:17 and 8:11, where ζωοποιεῖν is used of future bodily resurrection, remind us that, with the use of the compound in the aorist tense here, the writer is talking about an experience of the resurrection life of the end-time ahead of time. This should not be thought of as totally foreign to Paul's use of ζωοποιεῖν, however. In 1 Cor 15:45 it can be said that Christ has already become creatively life-giving Spirit at his resurrection, and according to 2 Cor 3:6 this Spirit is already at work giving life. In distinction from the reference to having been made alive with Christ in Col 2:13, in Ephesians there are no preceding references to participation in Christ's death (cf. the circumcision of Christ, Col 2:11) or his burial (Col 2:12). But, in Colossians, having been made alive with Christ is closely associated with the following notions of forgiveness of sins and liberation from cosmic powers. Since sins and bondage to an evil supernatural power are present in the depiction of death in Eph 2:1–3, it could well be that forgiveness and liberation are implicit here also in the rescue act of making alive.

χάριτί ἐστε σεσῳσμένοι, "by grace you have been saved." No sooner has the writer at last reached the main verb than he immediately breaks off the flow of thought with a parenthesis addressing the readers. It is an impassioned underlining of what the confessional statements he is making should mean for his readers. It draws their attention to the divine initiative, the definite accomplishment and the continuing reality involved in having been made alive together with Christ. Their new situation has been brought about by grace. In line with Paul's theologically rich use of the term χάρις, "grace," the writer asserts that salvation has been freely given by God to the readers as undeserving sinners.

In the OT, God's gracious approach to his people is often expressed through the verb חנן, *ḥānan*, which is used particularly in the Psalms in the context of Yahweh's rescuing his people from disease, distress, death, or Sheol, and forgiving their sins. How essentially such activity is characteristic of Yahweh and his sovereign freedom is indicated by a reference such as Exod 33:19, "I will make all my goodness pass before you, and will proclaim before you my name, 'The Lord'; and I will be gracious to whom I will be gracious, and will show mercy on whom I will show mercy." The cognate noun חן, *ḥēn*, however, is seldom used of God's gracious action. Instead, it most frequently refers to the favor one person finds in the eyes of another. The noun which corresponds most closely to the semantic range of the verb חנן is in fact חסד, *ḥesed*, denoting overwhelming and unexpected kindness, which when used in the context of the relationship of Yahweh and Israel refers to God's abundant love, a major expression of which is his covenant with his people (e.g., Deut 5:10; 7:9, 12; Ps 89:28; Isa 54:8–10). In the LXX χάρις, with one or two late exceptions, does not normally translate חסד but rather חן. Instead חסד is translated by ἔλεος (cf. v 4 above) and חנן by ἐλεεῖν. Presumably the LXX translators did not consider the use which χάρις had in classical Greek as appropriate enough for the contexts in which חן and חסד appear. In classical Greek the term had three basic meanings: (i) a charming quality that wins favor, (ii) a quality of benevolence that gives favor to inferiors, and (iii) a response of gratitude for a favor given. The second of these meanings had potential for use in contexts of Yahweh's care for his people, but in classical Greek χάρις was not a major philosophical or religious term and had strong aesthetic connotations.

Yet χάρις is the term especially characteristic of the Pauline corpus, where it occurs about one hundred times (most frequently in Romans—twenty-four times), and where more often than not it points to the special nature of God's saving action as one of gratuitous generosity to an undeserving sinful humanity. It is found in contexts where it stands in antithesis to the law (e.g., Gal 2:21; 5:4; Rom 6:14) or sin (e.g., Rom 5:20, 21; 6:1), or where it is associated with Paul's own call to become apostle to the Gentiles (e.g., Gal 1:15; 2:9; 1 Cor 3:10; 15:10). The reason Paul could use this term is that χάρις became popular in the religious sense among Greek-speaking Jews around the time of the completion of the LXX. In Wisdom and Apocalyptic literature χάρις was increasingly used for the eschatological reward of the elect (e.g., Wis 3:9; 4:14, 15; *1 Enoch* 99.13), as a major term for the blessings of the salvation of the end-time (cf. *1 Enoch* 5.4–8), and in association with the revealed wisdom to be found in the Torah. Later Greek translations of the OT (e.g., Symmachus) often render חסד by χάρις. It appears, then, that Pauline terminology represents a stage in the trajectory of the usage of χάρις where its religious connotations have increased and it can be seen as synonymous with ἔλεος or even be preferred to it. (On the background of χάρις and its use in Paul cf. H. Conzelmann and W. Zimmerli, "χάρις," *TDNT* 9 [1974] 372–402; G. P. Wetter, *Charis: Ein Beitrag zur Geschichte des ältesten Christentums* [Leipzig: J. C. Hinrichs, 1913]; J. Wobbe, *Der Charisgedanke bei Paulus* [Münster: Aschendorff, 1932]; R. Bultmann, *Theology of the New Testament* 1 [New York: Charles Scribner's Sons, 1951] 281–91; D. J. Doughty, "The Priority of Charis: An Investigation of the Theological Language of Paul," *NTS* 18 [1972] 163–80; K. Berger, " 'Gnade' im frühen Christentum," *NedTTs* 27 [1973] 1–25; and on the general concept of grace in Judaism and Paul rather than the actual term χάρις cf. E. P. Sanders, *Paul and Palestinian Judaism* [Philadelphia: Fortress, 1977] passim.)

Here in Eph 2:5 the emphasis on grace takes up that already found in the *berakah* in 1:6, 7, and it will occur again and be amplified in 2:7–9. It is given added force by contrasts suggested by the context. As in Paul (e.g., Rom 5:12–21), the abundance and effectiveness of grace is highlighted against a backdrop of sin and death (vv 1, 5). The reality and generosity of grace is appreciated all the more after a statement which shows how seriously God takes human sinfulness, deeming it to be deserving of his wrath (v 3). And from the human standpoint, the necessity of an intervention of grace is underlined when set in contrast to the bankruptcy and doom of a humanity left to itself, left to what it is "by nature" (v 3). "By grace you have been saved" draws the readers' attention to God's sovereign freedom from obligation in saving them.

σεσῳσμένοι, "having been saved," is a perfect passive participle. Apart from the repetition of this term in v 8, the only other places where σῴζειν is used in the perfect tense in the NT are in the Synoptics, where individuals are told by Jesus, "your faith has saved you" (cf. Mark 5:34 par.; 10:52 par.; Luke 17:19). The one instance where such a statement refers not to a healing but to the forgiveness of sins is Luke 7:50. In Paul the verb σῴζειν is normally found in the future tense and the noun σωτηρία in a future context (e.g., Rom 5:9, 10; 10:9, 13; 13:11; 1 Cor 3:15; 5:5), but there are also several references to salvation as a present experience (cf. 1 Cor 1:18; 15:2; 2 Cor 2:15; 6:2; Phil 2:12). In two places salvation is described with an aorist tense. In 1 Cor 1:21 an aorist infinitive is used in a past context, but this is in regard to God's decision and cannot stand as evidence for a completed salvation (cf. 1:18). In Rom 8:24 the aorist passive is employed, but with the significant qualifying phrase "in hope." The difference between Eph 2:5 and the undisputed Pauline letters should, then, be carefully noted, but not exaggerated (*contra*, e.g., Houlden, 283, who claims that it provides one of the best indications that the writer is not Paul; Lindemann, *Aufhebung*, 137: "totally un-Pauline"). For Paul salvation does have past, present, and future aspects. It would not be totally out of place for him to use the perfect of σῴζειν with its normal force of emphasizing the continuing present effect of a past action, as he does with the perfect of other aspects of salvation in Rom 5:2; 6:7. Paul does not use "by grace" or "by faith" with "to save" or "salvation" but with "to justify" or "justification." It appears then that Ephesians takes up Pauline thought, but uses the more general terminology. Similar combinations of the notions of grace and salvation can be found in Acts 15:11 and 2 Tim 1:9. Yet it must also be said that in Paul salvation can be a virtual synonym for justification (in Rom 10:10), and "to justify" is used in the future (Rom 2:13; cf. also Gal 5:5), present (Rom 3:24), and aorist (Rom 4:2; 5:1, 9) tenses, but is also found in the perfect (Rom 6:7). Nevertheless, it is probably fair to say that Rom 5:9 is most characteristic of Paul's use of justification and salvation terminology, where the aorist of the former and the future of the latter are used. By using the more inclusive term and indicating its completion, Ephesians constitutes a break with characteristic Pauline usage.

The perfect tense of "to save" in 2:5 should come as no surprise after the eulogy of 1:3–14, which blesses God for all the blessings of salvation with which he has already graciously blessed believers (cf. also the use of σωτηρία in 1:13). "To save" here is an inclusive term characterizing God's acts of making alive, raising up, and seating with Christ as a deliverance from the plight of the old situation to all the benefits of the new. The perfect tense draws attention to the continuing effects of that rescue act for the present, is in line with the surrounding aorists and the realized eschatology of vv 5, 6, and will be balanced by the future perspective of v 7.

καὶ συνήγειρεν καὶ συνεκάθισεν ἐν τοῖς ἐπουρανίοις ἐν Χριστῷ Ἰησοῦ, "and raised us up with him and seated us with him in the heavenly realms in Christ Jesus." The συν- compounds recall the simple forms ἐγείρας, "raised," and καθίσας, "seated," of 1:20. In contrast to the συν- compound in v 5 there is no accompanying dative; the τῷ Χριστῷ of v 5 is to be understood. The notion of a relationship with Christ is reinforced this time by the accompanying phrase ἐν Χριστῷ Ἰησοῦ. For a discussion of the use of ἐν Χριστῷ in Paul and Ephesians, see *Comment* on 1:3. It is possible that the phrase here means simply "through the agency of Christ Jesus" (cf. J. A. Allan, "The 'In Christ' Formula in Ephesians," *NTS* 5 [1958–59] 58; Gnilka, 120), but it is more likely that this is an instance where it has the stronger sense of "having been incorporated into Christ." The phrase, therefore, provides further explanation of how it can be said that what God did for Christ he did at the same time for believers (cf. also J. A. Robinson, 156; Abbott, 50; Schnackenburg, *Baptism*, 76–77; Schlier, 111; Lindemann, *Aufhebung*, 122). Believers are seen as included in Christ, so what God accomplished for Christ he accomplished for him as the representative, the head of a new humanity. Since "with Christ," which is the force of the συν- prefix, and "in Christ Jesus" both suggest a relationship of solidarity, the combination of the two in v 6 is again characteristic of Ephesians' redundancy of style for the sake of emphasis. Certainly the intimate union between Christ and believers is given heavy stress in v 6. The statement that God has both raised up believers with Christ and seated them with him in the heavenly realms spells out the implications of the relationship of incorporation in Christ in their most developed form in the Pauline corpus.

The notion of resurrection with Christ is not, of course, unique to Ephesians and is found in Col 2:12 and 3:1. There, however, it is expressed in a passive form; believers have been raised with Christ. Here the form is active; God has raised believers with Christ. This suggests that the predominant influence on the writer's formulation has been the earlier statement of 1:20 about God raising Christ; he desires to provide a parallel in the case of believers. However, the thought of Col 2:12 and 3:1 provided the background and opened up the possibility of thinking of this parallel to Christ's resurrection.

How far is such a parallel in line with the thought of the undisputed Pauline letters? Some claim that in Rom 6:1–11 Paul views resurrection with Christ as an event that remains wholly future, so that the assertion of Colossians and Ephesians that believers have already been raised with Christ contradicts Paul's eschatological reserve (e.g., E. Käsemann, *Leib und Leib Christi* [Tübingen: Mohr, 1933] 143; Lohse, *Colossians*, 104, 134 n. 13, 180; Gnilka, 119, 122–23; Lindemann, *Aufhebung*, 125). The claim in this form cannot stand. It is true that in Rom 6:5, 8 the future tense is used, whereas in Col 2:12; 3:1; and Eph 2:6 the aorist is to be found. But in Rom 6 there are two poles to Paul's thinking about resurrection life—it has been entered on by the believer in union with Christ, yet its consummation still lies in the future. Paul's main emphasis in that context is on having died with Christ to the dominion of sin. But this is a precondition which finds its intended completion in the sharing of the new resurrection life of Christ, "so that as Christ was raised from the dead by the glory of the Father, we too might walk in newness of life" (6:4). This present aspect of sharing in Christ's resurrection is seen also in 6:10, 11. Through his resurrection Christ now lives to God, and since they are ἐν Χριστῷ Ἰησοῦ and identified with Christ in both his death and his resurrection life, believers are also to consider themselves alive to God. Unless the apostle thought of believers as already having been identified with Christ in his resurrection, this would simply be make-believe. The "already" pole of Paul's thought about being raised with Christ is clearly there in Rom 6 (cf. also G. R. Beasley-Murray, *Baptism in the New Testament* [London: Macmillan, 1962] 126–46; C. E. B. Cranfield, *Romans* [Edinburgh: T. & T. Clark, 1975] 1:299–316, who in the light of such considerations takes the future tenses of 6:5, 8 as referring to the present moral life of believers). Paul's reference to living with Christ in 2 Cor 13:4, though expressed in the future tense, has clear reference to this life and his relationship with the Corinthians, εἰς ὑμᾶς, "toward you."

When such thought becomes explicit in Col 2:12; 3:1, it is difficult to see why it should be considered un-Pauline. The variation in tense and terminology between Romans and Colossians remains significant not so much for authorship as for an indication of the different emphases of these two letters in response to different situations (cf. Lincoln, *Paradise*, 122–23, 131–34, for a fuller discussion). The thought in Eph 2:6 of God's having raised believers with Christ cannot then in itself be held to be out of line with Paul. Aside from the change from passive to active form in the formulation, two contextual differences between its occurrence here and in Colossians should, however, be noted. Whereas in Colossians having been raised with Christ remains in close association with having died or been buried with Christ (cf. 2:11, 12; 2:20; 3:3), these aspects of union with Christ are absent from Ephesians. In Colossians, also, the eschatological reserve is retained in explicit reference to sharing Christ's resurrection life, as a present hiddenness and a future consummation of this relationship are asserted in 3:3, 4, while in Eph 2 there is no mention of the future aspect of the resurrection life for believers (though there is a more general future reference in 2:7). These differences suggest a development in Ephesians from Colossians in its even sharper realized eschatological focus on the present status of believers.

Nowhere is this more clearly seen than in the statement that God has seated believers with Christ in the heavenly realms. This is a making explicit of what in Col 3:1–3 had only been implicit. There the believer is exhorted to seek τὰ ἄνω, "the things above," because Christ is above and the believer's life is hidden with Christ in God. In Col 3:1 the realm above is closely related to the sphere of resurrection existence, for those whose whole concern is to be the things above, where Christ is, are those who already share his resurrection life. Since resurrection life is heavenly life, by being united with Christ in his resurrection believers participate in the life of the realm above, and the imperatives in 3:1, 2 can be seen to be based on indicatives. The writer of Ephesians has grasped this thought clearly and here spells out its significance boldly. If believers have been given a share in Christ's resurrection life, they can also be said to share in the triumph of its heavenly aspect. Again the desire to complete the parallel with 1:20 dictates the formulation, "and seated us with Christ in the heavenly realms," and the Colossians background opens the way for the thought behind it. For the force of the phrase "in the heavenly realms," see *Comment* on 1:3. It should be observed that along with the parallel between believers and Christ there remains also a distinction. The phrase ἐν δεξιᾷ αὐτοῦ, "at his right hand," in 1:20 is reserved for Christ and not repeated in the case of believers in 2:6. Although believers share in Christ's exaltation, his position in the heavenly realm and his relationship to God are unique.

The most direct influence on the writer at this point appears to be Colossians, but are there any other sources for or parallels to his striking language in 2:6? We do find such language echoed and ascribed to Paul in the Christian Gnostic text of the *Treatise on Resurrection 45*, "Then, indeed, as the Apostle said, 'We suffered with him, and we arose with him, and we went to heaven with him'" (cf. *The Nag Hammadi Library*, ed. J. M. Robinson [New York: Harper and Row, 1977] 51). This later Gnostic use of a combination of Rom 8:17 and Eph 2:6 cannot, however, shed much light on the background of Ephesians. Nor is the gnosticizing thought of the *Corpus Hermeticum*, whereby a heavenly journey liberates the initiate's soul from the material world so that he perceives he is in heaven (cf. 10.25; 13.11), likely to have influenced this notion of God's having seated believers with Christ in the heavenly realms. Greater light is shed on this notion by the motif, which was fairly widespread in apocalyptic writings, of the righteous entering into eschatological life and dominion and sitting on heavenly thrones (cf. Dan 7:22, 27; Wis 3:8; 5:15, 16; *1 Enoch* 108.12; *Apoc. Elijah* 37.3, 4; *T. Job* 33.3–5; *Asc. Isa.* 9:18). In the NT itself this tradition is reflected in passages such as Matt 19:28, 1 Cor 6:2, or especially Rev 3:21, "He who conquers, I will grant him to sit with me on my throne, as I myself conquered and sat down with my Father on his throne" (cf. also 20:4). This tradition of a future role for the righteous and particularly the Rev 3:21 reference, where this is expressed in terms of being seated with Christ, only serve to highlight by contrast the fact that Eph 2:6 claims that this has already been accomplished for believers. Closer to the realized eschatology of Ephesians, while remaining within the developing tradition of Jewish apocalyptic, is the self-understanding of the Qumran community that as an elect group on earth, it already experienced the heavenly realm and formed a liturgical community with the inhabitants of heaven. 1QH 3.19–22 reads, "I thank Thee, O Lord, for Thou hast redeemed my soul from the Pit, and from the Hell of Abaddon Thou hast raised me up to everlasting height. . . . Thou hast cleansed a perverse spirit of great sin that it may stand with the host of the Holy Ones, and that it may enter into community with the congregation of the Sons of Heaven" (cf. also 1QH 11.10–12; H.-W. Kuhn, *Enderwartung und gegenwärtiges Heil* [Göttingen: Vandenhoeck & Ruprecht, 1966] 44–188; Mussner, "Contributions," 164–167; Gnilka, 123–24).

Such ideas current in Judaism had already been adapted by Pauline thought and brought into contact with the cosmological concerns of Hellenistic syncretism in dealing with the situation in Colossae. In Colossians, where the claim of the false teaching threatening the church was that certain regulations had to be observed and certain techniques had to be practiced to achieve access to the heavenly realm, the author had replied with a stress on the realized aspect of his eschatology with its spatial element, showing that believers already participate in heavenly life in Christ (cf. Lincoln, *Paradise,* 110–34). The writer to the Ephesians can continue this emphasis. What is, of course, distinctive about the present experience of the heavenly realm highlighted in Eph 2:6, as opposed to that of Qumran, is that here it is totally dependent on Christ's prior exaltation. The believer's experience is a participation in Christ's life and reign in the heavenly realms. Though more pronounced in Ephesians, this focus on a present experience of heaven, on the spatial aspect of realized eschatology, is not a new departure. Not only is it in continuity with Colossians but also with several passages in the earlier Pauline letters (cf. Gal 4:26; 1 Cor 15:47–49; 2 Cor 12:2–4; Phil 3:20; cf. also Lincoln, *Paradise,* passim). If, as seems likely, Ephesians was addressed to churches of Asia Minor, where syncretism with cosmological concerns similar to those which took specific form in the Colossian philosophy was still prevalent, then this spatial emphasis continued to be appropriate as a means of underlining that God had through Christ done all that was necessary for believers' salvation. The writer is under no illusion, however, that there is no more of significance to happen as regards salvation, and the realized emphasis of 2:6 has to be balanced against the future element in 2:7 (cf. also 1:14; 4:30; 5:5, 27; 6:8, 13).

It still needs to be asked what is meant when it is said of believers who are still in their mortal bodies and still on earth that God has raised them up with Christ and seated them with Christ in the heavenly realms. When Paul used the language of dying and rising with Christ in Rom 6 and Col 2 and 3, he had in view not primarily some subjective religious experience on the part of believers but rather thought of believers as having been Christ's partners in the events of past redemptive history. For him, Christ's death was a death to the old order, to the powers of this age, including sin, and his resurrection was a coming alive to a new order, in which he functioned as Lord with the power of God. Christ's death and resurrection changed the power structures in history. For believers to have died and been raised with Christ was the equivalent of having been transferred from the old dominion to the new, because in God's sight they had been included in what had happened to Christ. The fact of temporal distance created no major problem for Paul because he did not think of individuals as isolated from the power sphere in which they existed, but rather viewed present existence as continuing to be determined by the events on which it was founded. He saw the new dominion as a whole as participating in those events of Christ's death and resurrection through its representative head. Similarly, when the writer to the Ephesians says God has raised believers up with Christ, he too means they have been assigned to the new reality introduced by Christ's resurrection. He extends the range of events in the history of salvation in which believers are to see themselves included, by the reference to having been seated with Christ in the heavenly realms. As 1:20–22 make clear, Christ's exaltation involved his triumph and rule over hostile cosmic powers. A new situation in regard to these powers was inaugurated in history by Christ's victory. That God has seated believers with Christ means therefore that they are part of the new dominion's superiority over the old, participating in its liberation from the powers and its restoration said not to come from a human source but from God as his gift. But the parallelism of the two clauses of v 8b and v 9 suggests, rather, that both are comments about the introductory clause of v 8a. τοῦτο is probably best taken, therefore, as referring to the preceding clause as a whole, and thus to the whole process of salvation it describes, which of course includes faith as its means (cf. also Abbott, 51; Gaugler, 98; Bruce, 51; Schlier, 115; Gnilka, 129; Mitton, 97; Schnackenburg, 98). "Not from yourselves, it is the gift of God" can be seen as a further explanation of the grace aspect of salvation. The precise wording has no antecedent in Paul, but the thought reflects his belief accurately. ἐκ here denotes origin, cause, or source, so οὐκ ἐξ ὑμῶν excludes the readers' causation or authorship of their salvation. The equivalent thought in Paul is his setting the righteousness that comes from God over against people's own righteousness based on law (cf. Rom 10:3; Phil 3:9; cf. also Rom 9:16). A literal rendering of the second part of v 8b would be "God's is the gift." θεοῦ has been placed first in the word order for the sake of an emphatic contrast with the ὑμῶν. Salvation has its source not in the readers but in God, and it comes from him as a gift. τὸ δῶρον is used only here in the Pauline corpus. Elsewhere in Ephesians ἡ δωρεά is the term employed for gift (cf. 3:7; 4:7), and it is this term which was, in fact, used by Paul to refer to the generosity of God's activity in Christ on behalf of men and women (cf. Rom 3:24; 5:15, 17; 2 Cor 9:15).

οὐκ ἐξ ἔργων, ἵνα μή τις καυχήσηται, "it is not by works, lest anyone should boast." This clause of v 9 can be seen as a second comment on v 8a, which in particular provides a further explanation of the faith aspect of salvation. In Paul, as we noted above, works of the law are most frequently set in contrast to faith and regarded as excluding faith (cf. Gal 2:16; 3:2–5, 9, 10; Rom 3:27, 28; 4:2, 3, 5; 9:32), though in one passage, Rom 11:6, the contrast is between works and grace. It should also be observed that the phrase Paul uses is "works of the law," and in the few places where he simply uses the more general term "works" the context makes clear that he still has the law in view, even though he may be discussing the patriarchs (cf. Rom 4:2, 6; 9:11, 32; 11:6). In other words, "not by works" in Paul belongs firmly to the contexts of Galatians and Romans and thus to the apostle's conflict with Judaizers over the relation of Gentile converts to the law and to his assessment of the role of the law in the history of salvation. But here in Ephesians, it is simply the term "works," not "works of the law," that is employed. It is extremely unlikely, in a letter to predominantly Gentile readers, in which the only reference to νόμος, "law" (2:15), occurs in a passage reminding Gentiles of what God did in the past to allow them access to the God of Israel, that "works of the law" are still in view (*contra* Schlier, 116; Mussner, 67). Instead, the writer has again taken up what he believes to be a characteristically Pauline theme in such a way that, removed from its original specifically polemical context, it now has a more general reference (cf. also 2 Tim 1:9; Titus 3:5; *1 Clem.* 32.3). "Works" now stands for human effort in general. Salvation is not achieved by human performance or any attempt to earn God's approval. It is not that, in the writer's mind, works of natural law have replaced works of the Mosaic law (*pace* Meyer, 115), nor that he believes that his Gentile readers are attempting to secure their salvation on the basis of their new holiness of life (*pace* Abbott, simply to coming generations of Christians). The writer's thought is that God has accomplished the resurrection and heavenly session of believers with Christ in order to show the immensity of his grace in a future in which age succeeds age.

The significance of this assertion is threefold. First, the new order which has begun has a future. The writer knows himself to be in the decisive period of God's redemptive activity, which was inaugurated by Christ's resurrection and exaltation, but which is yet to reach its consummation in the coming ages. Second, the divine activity on behalf of believers was of such finality that it will continue as the display of his grace into those coming ages. Third, what God has done is now a reality for believers, but only in the coming ages will it be fully shown for what it is. Only then will it become evident to all what an abundance of grace and kindness God has bestowed on his people through Christ. This third point suggests that just as Eph 2:6 draws out the implications of Col 3:1–3, so Eph 2:7 invites comparison with Col 3:3, 4, where believers' lives are said to be at present hidden with Christ in heaven and to be revealed in glory only at the Parousia.

8, 9 τῇ γὰρ χάριτί ἐστε σεσῳσμένοι διὰ πίστεως, "for by grace you have been saved through faith." The connective γάρ has the force of providing support for the writer's stress on the surpassing richness of God's grace to believers in v 7. He has been right to focus on the display of such grace as central to God's purpose, for, as he had said earlier, it is by grace that believers have been saved. The repetition of the great truth with which he had already interrupted the flow of thought in v 5b serves as a lead into a statement about the nature of salvation in terms of the relationship between grace and works. It is a repetition which has two variations from v 5b. The first is that this time a definite article accompanies the noun "grace," helping to underline that this is the same grace of which the writer has been speaking in v 7. The second is the addition of διὰ πίστεως, "by faith." The more frequently used phrase in the undisputed Paulines is ἐκ πίστεως, but that the two phrases were synonymous for Paul is indicated by their interchangeability in Gal 2:16; Rom 3:25, 26; 3:30. Ephesians prefers διὰ πίστεως (cf. 3:12, 17). As in Rom 3:22–25, a passage central to Paul's view of justification, for this writer also "by grace" and "by faith" are inseparable companions which together provide the antithesis to any suggestion of human merit. God's act of grace is the ground of salvation and faith is the means by which it becomes effective in a person's life. In Paul's thinking faith can never be viewed as a meritorious work because in connection with justification he always contrasts faith with works of the law (cf. Gal 2:16; 3:2–5, 9, 10; Rom 3:27, 28). Faith involves the abandonment of any attempt to justify oneself and an openness to God which is willing to accept what he has done in Christ. The same applies here in regard to salvation. Faith is a human activity but a specific kind of activity, a response which allows salvation to become operative, which receives what has already been accomplished by God in Christ.

καὶ τοῦτο οὐκ ἐξ ὑμῶν, θεοῦ τὸ δῶρον, "and this is not from yourselves, it is the gift of God." In the history of interpretation τοῦτο has been taken by some to refer specifically to the last word in the preceding clause, "faith" (among recent commentators cf. Caird, 53), so that even faith itself is explicitly

God in 2 Cor 9:14, and is found elsewhere in Ephesians in connection with the love of Christ (3:19) and the power of God (1:19). In relation to this last reference and in the light of the parallels between 1:19–21 and 2:4–7 already underlined, it can be said that if the raising of Christ from death to sit in the heavenly realms was the supreme demonstration of God's surpassing power, then the raising of believers from spiritual death to sit with Christ in the heavenly realms is the supreme demonstration of God's surpassing grace (cf. also Bruce, 51). To the terms already used for God's favorable disposition toward his people, "mercy" and "love" (v 4) and "grace" (vv 5, 7), is now added χρηστότης, "kindness," denoting God's sympathetic concern for the welfare of humanity, his goodness active on its behalf (cf. also Rom 2:4, 11:22; Titus 3:4). The demonstration of God's grace took place in his kindness to believers in all that he accomplished for them in and through Christ Jesus. It is worth noting how in 2:4–7 the statement of the goal of salvation corresponds to the statement of its motivation and origin, since "his kindness to us" (v 7) can be compared with "rich in mercy" (v 4) and "that he might show . . . the surpassing richness of his grace" (v 7) clearly matches "by grace you have been saved" (v 5).

The setting for the manifestation of God's grace has been disputed. What is the force of the phrase ἐν τοῖς αἰῶσιν τοῖς ἐπερχομένοις? Some take αἰῶνες as a reference to personal powers (cf. the discussion on 2:2). This requires taking ἐπέρχεσθαι in the sense of "to attack," a sense which it has in Luke 11:22 (cf. also Josephus, *Ant.* 5.195; 6.23). The thought would then be that God's grace toward believers is a disclosure to the hostile aeons that their rule has been set aside and that believers now occupy a privileged position in the cosmos (cf. Conzelmann, 97; H. Hegermann, *Die Vorstellung vom Schöpfungsmittler im hellenistischen Judentum und Urchristentum* [Berlin: Akademie-Verlag, 1961] 150–53; Lindemann, *Aufhebung*, 121–29; Schlier [112–14] and Barth [223] wish to combine both personal and temporal connotations). This interpretation has the virtue of being in line with the thought of 3:10, which speaks of a disclosure being made to the principalities and powers, and can claim that a revelation to the aeons is a familiar theme in Christian Gnostic thought (e.g., *Gos. Truth* I, 22.38–23.1; 27.5–7). The majority of scholars, however, reject this interpretation and agree that the more natural sense of the phrase is the temporal one, "in the ages to come" (cf. H. Sasse, "αἰών," *TDNT* 1 [1964] 206–7; Gaugler, 95; Schnackenburg, 97; *LJ* 2 [1952] 169–70; Mussner, *Christus*, 25 n. 103; Gnilka, 121; Ernst, 308; Halter, *Taufe und Ethos*, 239; Luz, "Rechtfertigung," 370). The phrase begins with the preposition ἐν and is not simply a dative of indirect object which one would expect in the case of the notion of disclosure to the aeons, which one finds in 3:10, and which is the most common construction when ἐνδείκνυμι is used of showing something to someone. ἐπερχόμενος is found elsewhere with αἰών only in *Herm. Vis.* 4.3, 5, where it has temporal force. It is equivalent to ἐρχόμενος in ὁ αἰὼν ὁ ἐρχόμενος, "the age to come" (cf. Mark 10:30; Luke 18:30; Herm. *Sim* 4.8), and to μέλλων in ὁ μέλλων αἰών, "the age to come" (cf. Matt 12:32; Eph 1:21; Heb 6:5). The future is seen, then, in Eph 2:7 in terms of a plurality of coming ages, though the plural may stand under the liturgical influence of the formulae for eternity (cf. 3:21; also H. Sasse, "αἰών," *TDNT* 1 [1964] 206–7; *contra* Mitton, 91, the reference is not of harmony to the cosmos. The imagery of being seated with Christ is not associated with sharing a meal, and thereby a reference to enjoying fellowship with God (*contra* Mitton, 90). Both the parallel with 1:20 and the depiction of the past in 2:2 as being under the control of the ruler of the realm of the air make clear that this picture of the present involves sharing Christ's victory over such powers. In continuity with categories drawn from apocalyptic writings, the past is seen as under the dominance of this age, this world, and its ruler, while present salvation involves enjoying the life and the rule of the age to come made available already in heaven where Christ now is.

Being raised up and seated with Christ has as its basic meaning being viewed by God as included in the events of Christ's resurrection and exaltation determinative for the new dominion, but believers are initiated into the new movement within history and appropriate its reality in their own time through faith and baptism. Since faith represents the believer's commitment and baptism is its expression, there is no reason to deny the suggestion of many commentators that the readers are likely to have associated the language of being raised and seated with Christ with the significance of baptism in their own experience (see the further discussion of a baptismal setting under *Form/Structure/Setting* above). The new dominion into which believers have been initiated is firmly anchored within history. The writer is under no illusion that sharing in Christ's victory brings removal from the sphere of conflict. The rest of the letter provides ample evidence that those who have been seated with Christ in the heavenlies are at the same time those who must walk in the world (cf. 2:10; 4:1, 17; 5:2, 8, 15) and stand in the midst of the continuing battle with the powers (cf. 6:11–16).

7 ἵνα ἐνδείξηται ἐν τοῖς αἰῶσιν τοῖς ἐπερχομένοις τὸ ὑπερβάλλον πλοῦτος τῆς χάριτος αὐτοῦ ἐν χρηστότητι ἐφ' ἡμᾶς ἐν Χριστῷ Ἰησοῦ, "so that he might show in the ages to come the surpassing richness of his grace in his kindness to us in Christ Jesus." Through the ἵνα, this clause concludes the flow of thought begun in v 4 by indicating the purpose of the divine activity that has been depicted. What God has done in making believers alive with Christ, raising them up with him and seating them with him in the heavenly realms, he has done not only for their sake but also as part of the larger purpose of displaying the richness of his grace. Such a thought is familiar from the *berakah* of 1:3–14, where the ultimate goal of salvation was seen as the glory of God (cf. 1:6, 12, 14). In particular, 1:6 expressed the goal of believers' predestination to be sons and daughters of God as "the praise of the glory of his grace." The verb used in the formulation of the goal of salvation here in 2:7 is ἐνδείκνυμι. It goes far beyond the evidence to claim, as does Barth (222, 238–42), that this is a technical juridical term being employed here to indicate that God puts forward believers as "proof" in a cosmic lawsuit. It should be taken in its general sense of "to show, demonstrate." While in Rom 9:22 Paul can speak of God as showing his wrath, here the writer has God showing his grace. As the writer's thought and style attempt to capture something of the extravagance of God's display of grace, it becomes not just grace but "the richness of his grace" (cf. also 1:7), and not just the richness of his grace but "the surpassing richness of his grace."

The present participle of ὑπερβάλλειν is also used to describe the grace of

52). In regard to the latter point, as the paraenetical section of the letter clearly indicates, the danger the writer sees is not that his readers are relying on their outstanding ethical qualities for salvation, but that their lives are being conformed to the surrounding mores and are not holy enough. It is simply that he wants them to have an absolutely clear understanding of their privileged position as recipients of a salvation that is totally God's gracious work. The false teaching attacked in Colossians had already provided an example of how easily this principle can become obscured, as human effort took the form of ascetic regulations and mystical techniques meant to ensure fullness of salvation, though, again, this would not have been specifically in view in the writer's use of the general term "works" here.

God's purpose in providing a salvation that is not based on human effort or performance is to exclude boasting. With this assertion the writer again takes up a typically Pauline theme. Paul had claimed in Rom 3:27 that his gospel of justification by faith left no room for boasting. Boasting accompanies works because they become the ground for self-congratulation and pride in the presence of God (Rom 3:27; 4:2), and drag in the notion of merit, or earning one's reward (Rom 4:4). It was vital to Paul's perspective on salvation that men and women should not be in the position to claim even the least degree of credit for their acceptance by God. Instead, the common denominator in Paul's objection to righteousness by law in Romans and his objection to human wisdom in 1 Corinthians (cf. 1:28–31) is that both involve "boasting." His gospel with its focus on the cross effectively deals with both the predominantly Jewish and the predominantly Greek forms of self-assertion. To boast is to glory in, to put one's confidence in, the flesh (cf. Gal 6:13; Phil 3:3). Boasting perverts human autonomy by making it the object of trust. Paul's gospel brings a new orientation which enables one instead to boast in the Lord (cf. 1 Cor 1:31; 2 Cor 10:17; Rom 5:11; Phil 3:3), particularly in the cross of Christ (cf. Gal 6:14), to recognize that whatever one possesses one has received as a gift (cf. 1 Cor 4:7), and to glory in one's weakness and suffering as the opportunity for the display of God's power (cf. 2 Cor 11:30; 12:9; Rom 5:2, 3). (On "boasting" in Paul, cf. especially R. Bultmann, "καυχάομαι," *TDNT* 3 [1965] 645–54; *Theology of the New Testament* 1 [New York: Charles Scribner's Sons, 1951] 240–46, 264, 281, 315–16.) The writer to the Ephesians also clearly sees that salvation by grace through faith destroys boasting; it leaves people no contribution of their own which they can bring to God. He knows that what is at stake in salvation is God's glory, particularly the glory of his grace, but that works would lead only to human glorying.

10 αὐτοῦ γάρ ἐσμεν ποίημα, κτισθέντες ἐν Χριστῷ Ἰησοῦ ἐπὶ ἔργοις ἀγαθοῖς, "for we are his work, created in Christ Jesus for good works." As in v 8 the flow of thought is continued through the connective γάρ. A further reason is now given why salvation can be said to be a divine gift, not of human origin or by human works, and therefore leaving no room for boasting. Since salvation is seen as a creation in Christ for good works, such works cannot be the cause of their salvation. Likewise, since salvation is *God's* creation, there could be no human works prior to that creation to which it could be attributed. ποίημα is often used in the LXX as a synonym for ἔργον, the other term for "work" used here in v 9 and in the second clause of v 10. In the LXX ποίημα frequently refers to the creation as God's work (e.g., LXX Ps 91:4; 142:5), as it does in its only other use in the NT in Rom 1:20. Here, however, as the context and particularly the following clause make clear, the reference is to believers as God's new creation. In Paul's letters believers are regarded as God's work (cf. Rom 14:20 and Phil 1:6). In Ephesians the writer has been talking of God's power at work for believers (1:19). He can now say that his readers not only benefit from that work but as new creatures are themselves the product of that work. The stress in the Greek is on the first word in the clause, αὐτοῦ, "his." The force is that it is God, not the readers themselves, who has made them what they are as believers. For a similar thought in regard to humanity's place in creation in general see Ps 100:3 (LXX 99:3). Just as humans contributed nothing to their own creation so also they contributed nothing to their new creation; both are God's work.

As God's work, believers have been created in Christ Jesus for good works. "In Christ Jesus" here is shorthand for "through God's activity in Christ." Christ is seen as the mediator of the new creation just as much as he was of the original one (cf. Col 1:16). Paul himself saw the salvation God had inaugurated through Christ as a new creation (cf. Gal 6:15; 2 Cor 5:17), and that perspective is reflected in Ephesians not only here but also in 2:15 and 4:24. God's action of making believers alive with Christ, of raising them up and exalting them with Christ, provided a new start within the world's history. It was more than simply a restoration of conditions before the fall; it involved, rather, the creation of a new humanity as men and women were brought to that destiny God had purposed but which before Christ had not been reached (cf. also N. A. Dahl, "Christ, Creation, and the Church," in *The Background to the New Testament and Its Eschatology*, ed. W. D. Davies and D. Daube [Cambridge: Cambridge University Press, 1956] 422–43). The new creation, which in its widest sense includes the summing up of all things in Christ (cf. 1:9, 10), has already begun as a movement in history in the lives of men and women. These lives are to be characterized by good works. ἐπί with the dative case should be taken as signifying purpose, goal, or result. So good works are not the source but the goal of the new relationship between humanity and God. Salvation is not "by works" but "for works." The notion of being created for a life of obedience for which God alone is credited can be found in various forms in Judaism. 1QH 4.30–32 declares, "Righteousness, I know, is not of men, nor is perfection of way of the son of man; to the Most High God belong all righteous deeds. The way of man is not established except by the spirit which God created for him to make perfect a way for the children of men." There is also the saying found in *m. 'Abot* 2.9, "If thou hast practiced much Torah, take no credit to thyself; for thereunto thou wast created." K. G. Kuhn ("The Epistle to the Ephesians," 128 n. 11) can claim, " 'Created for good works' is a traditional Jewish idea, and 'in Christ Jesus' is its new Christian garb." What is also distinctive about its new garb is that the idea is no longer simply synonymous with obedience to the Torah.

How does the positive attitude to works in v 10, following on the negative attitude of v 9, relate to the teaching of Paul? Clearly, in Paul also, grace always stands in antithesis to a life of sin and involves obedience and moral righteousness, as Rom 6 demonstrates. Faith is only authentic when it is working through love (Gal 5:6). Believers can be urged to do good (1 Thess 5:15; Gal

6:10; 2 Cor 5:10; Rom 13:3) and such conduct can be called good work (Rom 2:7; 13:3). The expression "every good work" is used in 2 Cor 9:8 (cf. also Col 1:10; 2 Thess 2:17), so the idea but not the actual expression "good works" can be found in Paul. The plural ἔργα ἀγαθά or καλά appears to be a formulation characteristic of post-Pauline writings (cf. 1 Tim 2:10; 5:10, 25; 6:18; Titus 2:7, 14; 3:8, 14; Acts 9:36; Heb 10:24). The Titus 3:8 reference, in fact, has a similar context to Eph 2:10, for there also God is said to have saved believers according to his mercy, not by works which they did in righteousness (3:5), yet those who have believed are to be careful to apply themselves to good works (3:8). In relation to the undisputed Pauline letters, Eph 2:10 is distinctive in its use of the precise phrase "good works" and in its assertion that such good works are the goal of the new creation.

οἷς προητοίμασεν ὁ θεὸς ἵνα ἐν αὐτοῖς περιπατήσωμεν, "which God prepared in advance in order that we might live in them." This relative clause, which concludes the verse, underlines both the importance and the divine origin of these good works. The dative οἷς is employed instead of the expected ἅ because it has been attracted to the case of its antecedent. But how can good works be said to exist in advance of their being done? To avoid the difficulty of such an assertion some have suggested that οἷς be taken as a dative of reference and that an implicit ἡμᾶς, "us," is the object of the verb (cf. Abbott, 54–55; NEB, "the good deeds, for which God has designed us"), so that humans rather than their works are the objects of God's advance preparation. But neither this nor the idea that God has simply ordained the circumstances which make good works possible does justice to the writer's thought; it is the good works themselves that God has prepared beforehand. Others suggest that the προ- prefix to the verb is simply a "before" in regard to walking in the good deeds and so has in view the moment of baptism, since with their baptism believers are provided with the potential for practicing the good works that are in a sense already theirs (cf. Schlier, 117; R. G. Hamerton-Kelly, *Pre-existence, Wisdom, and the Son of Man* [Cambridge: Cambridge University Press, 1973] 184; Halter, *Taufe und Ethos*, 241, 629 n. 22). It is far more likely, as the majority of commentators hold (e.g., Meyer, 116; Houlden, 285; Barth, 227, 249; Ernst, 310; Schnackenburg, 99–100), that the prefix indicates that God's preparation precedes not simply the believer's work but also the foundation of the world. In its only other use in the Pauline corpus προετοιμάζειν is employed of God's predestination (Rom 9:23 cf. also LXX Wis 9:8), and we have already seen in the *berakah* that the writer to the Ephesians puts the origins of believers' experience of God's blessing back into preexistence (1:4, 5, 11, 12). What God has purposed can be thought of as already existing with him (cf. *Apoc. Abr.* 22, "whatever I had determined to be, was already planned beforehand, and it stood before me ere it was created, as thou hast seen"). If believers are God's work, then their ethical activity must also proceed from God and so can be thought of as already prepared in God's counsel. Not just their initial reception of salvation, but the whole of believers' lives, including their practical ethical activity, is to be seen as part of God's purpose. The thought of 2:10 is that the good works were already there, and when, through his grace, God made believers alive, raised them up, and seated them with Christ, he created them for these works.

This formulation is an emphatic way of underlining the ethical dimension already present in the assertion of 1:4 that God chose believers before the foundation of the world, in order that they might be holy and blameless before him in love. To say that God has prepared the good works in advance in his sovereign purpose is also to stress in the strongest possible way that believers' good deeds cannot be chalked up to their own resolve, but are due solely to divine grace. It is grace all the way. Even the living out of salvation in good works is completely by grace. But this is not a total determinism. God has prepared the good works in advance "in order that we might live in them." The human activity of "walking" is still necessary; the actual living out of God's purpose in the world has to take place. Karl Barth's dictum that "the distinctive thing about Christian or theological ethics is that we do not have to do any carrying without remembering that we *are* carried" comes close to the perspective of Ephesians (cf. *Ethics,* tr. G. W. Bromiley [Edinburgh: T. & T. Clark, 1981] 516). An inclusion on περιπατεῖν rounds off the contrast which the pericope contains. In contrast to the walking in trespasses and sins of vv 1, 2, the new situation brings a walking in good works. God's saving power reaches its intended goal when there is a changed lifestyle. Only in the actual practice of good works is the contrast between then and now, between death and life, completed. Such a thought has implicit paraenetic force, but the writer does not exploit this until the second half of his letter.

Explanation

In the thanksgiving period the writer had told his readers that his prayer for them was that they might know the surpassing greatness of God's power toward them as believers. Now he plays his own part in helping them to gain such knowledge by reminding them how God's power has affected their lives and what an immense change it has wrought. His reminder takes much of its force from the parallel he draws between the supreme demonstration of God's power in the resurrection and exaltation of Christ (1:19–21) and his activity on behalf of believers. He wants them to realize that just as Christ was physically dead but God raised and exalted him, so they were spiritually dead but God raised and exalted them with Christ. The dramatic change that such an action produced is set out by means of a contrast schema which can be found elsewhere in the NT. It compares the pre-Christian past ("then") with the Christian present ("now") and could well have recalled for the readers much of what their baptism signified. The writer's statement of the significance of what God has done for his readers employs and elaborates on language from Col 2:10–13, and takes up characteristic Pauline themes from elsewhere, particularly from Rom 3:24–28 in vv 8, 9. His statement falls into three parts: a description of the readers', and in fact of all humanity's, sinful past in vv 1–3, which syntactically do not form a complete sentence; an assertion in vv 4–7 of God's loving initiative in delivering humans from their plight through their relationship with Christ; and an elaboration on the gracious nature of the salvation that has been accomplished in vv 8–10.

Throughout the pericope it is primarily from the vantage point of what God has done in Christ that the writer views humanity. This applies not only to the new humanity, whose destiny is seen as incorporated in that of Christ, but also to the old humanity. By contrast to their present enjoyment of resurrection life, the pre-Christian existence of his readers can only be regarded as death. As one who has experienced deliverance from it, the writer has the ability to recognize and describe the pre-Christian situation in all its tragic seriousness. He reminds the readers, therefore, that at one time they were already experiencing in this life that exclusion from a living relationship to God through Christ that will eventually involve physical death and final judgment. This living death was characterized by trespasses and sins, which also brought it about, and tied up with the trespasses and sins are the forces of the world, the devil, and the flesh. The readers' sinful deeds were dictated by the norms of "this world-age," human activity in this age and this world organized in opposition to the will of the Creator. In more mythological language, behind these sins was "the ruler of the realm of the air." An ultimate personal center of evil (the devil; cf. 4:27; 6:11) is seen as influencing this age, particularly through the rebellious spirit still at work in disobedient humanity. This explanation of sin does not, however, do away with human responsibility, for in the next breath the writer can say that not only the readers, but all believers, were at one time those who chose not to obey, who instead gave their consent to the inclinations of the flesh, and who therefore fully deserved God's wrath. Their existence was dominated by the flesh, life lived in pursuit of one's own ends, and controlled by their corrupt thoughts. Left to their fallen natural condition, they were, just like all humanity, deserving of and liable to God's righteous judgment.

Having depicted the readers' past as characterized by death, bondage, and condemnation, the writer now turns to God's decisive action which reversed that condition. The mood changes from one laden with doom to one of exultation. The mention of God's wrath has shown how seriously he takes human sinfulness. But against the background of the real possibility of God's wrath, his mercy and his love shine out in all their radiance. God's initiative to deal with the human plight was launched, not on the basis of some potential within the condition of humanity, but on the basis of his rich mercy and great love. The divine reversal involved making men and women alive with Christ, raising them up and seating them with Christ in the heavenly realms. What God did for Christ, therefore, he has also done for believers. This rescue act is not simply parallel to the events of Christ's triumph, however. It takes place *through* them. For what God accomplished for Christ in those events, he accomplished for him as representative of a new humanity, seen as included in him. The writer's perspective on what has been achieved for humanity is in line with Pauline thought about union with Christ in his death and resurrection, but here the death aspect of that relationship has been omitted, and there is a stronger emphasis on the present status of believers resulting from the relationship. Union with Christ is extended to a union with him in his exaltation to heaven, sharing his triumph over the cosmic powers, and such a notion is the most developed formulation of realized eschatology in the Pauline corpus. It serves to remind the readers that they have been transferred to a new dominion inaugurated by Christ's resurrection and exaltation, in which they can experience new life and liberation from the powers which previously held them enslaved. This whole rescue procedure was designed to show God's grace.

The writer senses that what has happened to believers is the supreme demonstration of the overwhelming richness of that grace, a demonstration which will continue to be effective into the coming ages, and which in the limitless future will be recognized by all for the marvel that it is.

Already this statement about God's decisive action on behalf of believers has been interrupted in v 5b by the writer's impassioned assertion that the salvation which God had provided for the readers, and which had a continuing effect in their lives, was brought about by grace. Now, in the last section of the pericope, this assertion is expanded in a summary of the nature of salvation. By this grace the readers have been saved through faith. What God has done in Christ is seen as a still-effective deliverance, liberation, or rescue from their previous state and one that is provided freely, as a gift, for undeserving rebel subjects. With grace as its ground and faith as its means, this salvation can have nothing to do with any notion of merit. That it is "by grace" means that it has not originated from a human source but comes from God as a gift. That it is "by faith" means the exclusion of human effort and, therefore, of any pride or boasting in the presence of God. The writer wants his readers to be absolutely clear that it is God, and not humans, who is to be given the credit for salvation, and that means the whole of salvation, including believers' good works. The notion of "the self-made man" is totally out of place in such a perspective on Christian existence. In fact, believers can be said to be made by God, his work, his new creation, the goal of which is the life of goodness which was the Creator's original design for humanity. This new way of walking completes the contrast with the walk in trespasses and sins mentioned at the beginning of the pericope. The powerful and gracious activity of God operative on behalf of believers finds its completion, as regards human lives, in a goodness that is expressed in specific works. The writer attempts to make doubly sure that even these do not become the ground for boasting by describing them as objects of God's advance preparation. They were already prepared as part of God's sovereign purpose and therefore must be attributed solely to grace.

It is worth standing back from the flow of thought and underlining the completeness of the contrast between pre-Christian past and Christian present which shapes the major part of the pericope. The movement from then to now is a movement from death to resurrection life, from a lifestyle characterized by trespasses, sins, sensual indulgence, and disobedience to one characterized by good works, from this present world-age to the heavenly realms, and from bondage to the forces which rule this world to victory with Christ above hostile powers. It is a movement from the sphere of selfish autonomy to union with Christ, from domination by the devil to a life controlled from start to finish by God, from what humanity is by nature to what it becomes by grace, and from liability to God's wrath to experience of his mercy, love, kindness, and grace.

In the process of developing these powerful contrasts the writer summarizes a number of characteristic Pauline themes. The depiction of the sinful human condition under the wrath of God is reminiscent of Rom 1:18–3:20. Individual elements in it have their counterpart in the major Pauline letters: bondage to this age in Gal 1:4 and Rom 12:2, domination by a personal power of evil in 2 Cor 4:4, and the rule of the flesh in Gal 5:16–21 and Rom 7:5–21. The notion of a union with Christ which effects a transfer of dominion, which figures prominently in vv 4–7, has points of contact with Rom 6:1–11 and Col 2:12, 13; 3:1, 2. That salvation is by grace and by faith with no works and no boasting involved (vv 8, 9) recalls Rom 3:24–28; Gal 2:16; and 1 Cor 1:29–31, among other passages, while the attempt to relate ethical activity to this salvation has some links with passages such as Phil 2:12, 13 and Gal 5:6. But the Pauline disciple has not only provided a brilliant summary of some of his master's thought on salvation, he has also creatively shaped it for his own purposes with some significant shifts of emphasis. "Flesh" in its negative sense becomes a category distinct from "thoughts." Union with Christ can be extended to embrace union with him in his exaltation. Salvation can be seen as a completed event. The discussion of salvation and works is generalized by removal from its original Jewish or Jewish Christian context, so that the key concepts of justification and the law found in Rom 3:24–28 are missing here. And, as compared with the general stress in Paul on the necessity of the believer's responding to grace by love and obedience in the light of the last judgment, "good works" are specifically mentioned here and attributed solely to God's grace, because he has prepared them in advance.

As in the preceding eulogy and thanksgiving period, the major foci of the writer's thought in this pericope remain God, Christ, and believers. He begins with a grim look at the human scene as he depicts the past plight of believers, but moves to an exalted view of a humanity that shares Christ's destiny and triumph and already experiences the life of heaven—a new humanity that is God's work, created anew to live the life of goodness he has designed for it. Christ is clearly the mediator through whom this change for humanity has been accomplished. God's kindness has been shown to believers "in Christ Jesus" (v 7), and it is "in Christ Jesus" that the new creation has taken place (v 10). Not only so, but believers' solidarity "*with* Christ" in his being made alive, raised up, and exalted (vv 5, 6) can also be said to be "*in* Christ Jesus" (v 6). But it is the theocentric element in the writer's thought which is most to the fore. It is God's decisive initiative which launches salvation ("But God . . . ," v 4), and his mercy and love are the motivating factors behind it. It is God's grace which is the ground of salvation, and it is the display of that grace which is its purpose. Everything about believers' new lives, including their good works, is God's work so that he, and not they, will receive the glory.

Within this theocentric perspective the focus is particularly on God's grace, as the repetition of the assertion "by grace you have been saved" (vv 5b, 8) makes clear. Because of the statements with which the preceding thanksgiving period culminated, asserting the significance of the Church's status and role, and because of the statement here in v 6 that believers have been seated with Christ in the heavenly realms, some have accused the writer of a proud triumphalism in his view of the Church. Yet, this passage suggests that the writer had done his utmost to prevent such a misinterpretation of his formulations. He is at pains to stress again and again, and in a variety of ways, that believers' salvation and resulting situation is nothing at all about which they can boast. Left to themselves they had been deserving only of wrath (v 3). Only through their relationship to Christ has their fate changed (vv 5–7, 10). The new life and link with heaven that have resulted from this relationship are theirs only because of God's mercy and love (v 4), because of his kindness (v 7), because of his grace (vv 5, 7, 8). Their salvation is a pure gift (v 8), and their Christian existence, with anything good which it produces, they owe entirely to God's work. The overall effect of the pericope is to leave its readers wondering not at their own exalted position but at the immensity of God's grace which produced it. And they are left no room to pervert grace in an antinomian way, because the final word is that this grace achieves its end in the good works that have been prepared for them to live in. It could not be clearer that salvation comes to sinful humanity freely, generously, and undeservedly. All that believers have received and hope to receive, they receive not as a reward for services rendered, but as a gift, whose source is the God who has graciously acted in Christ.

This central focus on what God has achieved for the readers by his grace has several effects. It adds to the knowledge of God and of his power at work on their behalf that the writer wishes for his readers (cf. 1:17–19). Together with 2:11–22, it is at the heart of the reminder about believers' privileged relationship to God which the first part of the letter is meant to provide. As a reminder of what God has done for them and of the continuing results of his saving action, the pericope assures the readers of the reality of the present aspect of their salvation. It could well be that this assurance comes because the writer perceives the need to reinforce the identity of his readers as Christian believers. Their vision of what it means to be part of the Christian community was not as strong as it should have been, and they may have been inclined to think of themselves as simply belonging to one among the many religious groupings in Asia Minor. Apparently, along with the fading of a clear sense of their calling had come the temptation to conform to the surrounding world, to the values of "this world-age" and of "those who are disobedient" (cf. 4:17–24). In the writer's attempt to deepen the awareness of their calling by reminding them of the change God has brought about and by using language which would recall the significance of their baptism there lies an implicit exhortation to them to live out their calling in a way that is appropriate to the distinctive work of God on their behalf (cf. also 4:1). After all, they are now part of the new dominion; they are a new creation that has been designed to have the distinctive quality of goodness (v 10).

As one who has been grasped by Paul's gospel and is sensitive to its diagnosis of the human condition, the writer recognizes that there is always the temptation for humans to fall back on their own resources and to delude themselves that they can contribute something to their own standing before God. Colossians, which has influenced him so much, has reinforced for him the need to stress grace, because it has shown that the religious syncretism of Asia Minor could become just as much of a threat to Paul's gospel of grace as Judaizing had been in Galatia. Believers had been made to think that what they had in Christ was not enough and that observance of ascetic regulations and visionary experiences of the heavenly realm were needed for fullness of salvation. This writer wishes, therefore, to make very clear that all that is necessary has been accomplished in Christ ("you have been saved") and accomplished in such a way as to allow God to have the glory ("by grace"). But, as with most of the first half of Ephesians, the didactic function of the pericope does not stand by itself. It is interwoven with the doxological mood carried over from the eulogy and thanksgiving period, so that this reminder of the great salvation that has been accomplished for the readers is also designed to evoke wonder, gratitude, and praise in the face of God's marvelous grace. The writer knows too that such attitudes are often the most powerful motivations for living differently. In this way his stress on grace becomes a major part of the foundation he is laying for the practical ethical exhortation of the second half of the letter. It is grace that enables people to play their roles in the Church's life (cf. 4:7), and grace that is the only adequate resource for a life of good works in this world, as v 10 already indicates so plainly.

The Gaining of the Gentiles' Privileges of Participation in God's New Temple Through Christ's Reconciliation (2:11–22)

Bibliography

Barclay, W. "The One, New Man." In *Unity and Diversity in New Testament Theology.* FS G. E. Ladd, ed. R. A. Guelich. Grand Rapids: Eerdmans, 1978, 73–81. **Barth, M.** "Conversion and Conversation: Israel and the Church in Paul's Epistle to the Ephesians." *Int* 17 (1963) 3–24. **Burger, C.** *Schöpfung und Versöhnung: Studien zum liturgischen Gut im Kolosser- und Epheserbrief.* Neukirchen-Vluyn: Neukirchener, 1975, 117–57. **Coggan, F. D.** "A Note on Ephesians 2:14." *ExpTim* 53 (1941–42) 242. **Deichgräber, R.** *Gotteshymnus und Christushymnus,* 165–67. **Fischer, K. M.** *Tendenz und Absicht,* 79–94, 131–37. **Gärtner, B.** *The Temple and the Community in Qumran and the New Testament.* Cambridge: Cambridge University Press, 1965. **Giavini, G.** "La structure littéraire d'Eph 2:11–22." *NTS* 16 (1969–70) 209–11. **Gnilka, J.** "Christus unser Friede—ein Friedens-Erlöserlied in Eph 2, 14–17: Erwägungen zu einer neutestamentlichen Friedenstheologie." In *Die Zeit Jesu,* ed. G. Bornkamm and K. Rahner. Freiburg: Herder, 1970, 190–207. **Hanson, S.** *The Unity of the Church,* 141–48. **Howard, J. E.** "The Wall Broken: An Interpretation of Ephesians 2:11–22." In *Biblical Interpretation: Principles and Practices,* ed. F. F. Kearley, E. P. Myers, and T. D. Hadley. Grand Rapids: Baker, 1986, 296–306. **Jeremias, J.** "Der Eckstein." *Angelos* 1 (1925) 65–70. ———. "Eckstein-Schlussstein." *ZNW* 36 (1937) 154–57. ———. "γωνία." *TDNT* 1 (1964) 791–93. ———. "κεφαλὴ γωνίας— Ἀκρογωνιαῖος." *ZNW* 29 (1930) 264–80. ———. "λίθος." *TDNT* 4 (1967) 119–59. **Käsemann, E.** "Epheser 2, 17–22." *Exegetische Versuche und Besinnungen,* Vol. 1. Göttingen: Vandenhoeck & Ruprecht, 1960, 280–83. **Klinzing, G.** *Die Umdeutung des Kultus in der Qumrangemeinde und im Neuen Testament.* Göttingen: Vandenhoeck & Ruprecht, 1971. **Lincoln, A. T.** "The Church and Israel in Ephesians 2." *CBQ* 49 (1987) 605–24; also in *The Best in Theology,* Vol. 3, ed. J. I. Packer. Carol Stream, IL: C.T.I., 1989, 61–79. ———. "The Use of the OT in Ephesians." *JSNT* 14 (1982) 25–30. **Lindemann, A.** *Die Aufhebung der Zeit,* 152–81. **Lyall, F.** "Roman Law in the Writings of Paul—Aliens and Citizens." *EvQ* 48 (1976) 3–14. **Martin, R. P.** *Reconciliation: A Study of Paul's Theology.* Atlanta: John Knox Press, 1981; Grand Rapids: Zondervan, 1990, 157–98. **McEleney, N. J.** "Conversion, Circumcision, and the Law." *NTS* 20 (1974) 319–41. **McKelvey, R. J.** "Christ the Cornerstone." *NTS* 8 (1962) 352–59. ———. *The New Temple.* Oxford: Oxford University Press, 1969. **Meeks, W. A.** "In One Body: The Unity of Humankind in Colossians and Ephesians." In *God's Christ and His People,* ed. J. Jervell and W. A. Meeks. Oslo: Universitetsforlaget, 1977, 209–21. **Merklein, H.** *Christus und die Kirche. Die theologische Grundstruktur des Epheserbriefes nach Eph 2, 11–18.* Stuttgart: Katholisches Bibelwerk, 1973. ———. *Das kirchliche Amt nach dem Epheserbrief.* Munich: Kösel, 1973, 118–58. ———. "Paulinische Theologie in der Rezeption des Kolosser- und Epheserbriefes." In *Paulus in den neutestamentlichen Spätschriften,* ed. K. Kertelge. Freiburg: Herder, 1981, 25–69. ———. "Zur Tradition und Komposition von Eph 2, 14–18." *BZ* 17 (1973) 79–102. **Meuzelaar, J. J.** *Der Leib des Messias.* Assen: Van Gorcum, 1961, 59–101. **Michel, O.** "οἶκος κτλ." *TDNT* 5 (1967) 119–59. **Moore, M. S.** "Ephesians 2:14–16: A History of Recent Interpretation." *EvQ* 54 (1982) 163–68. **Mussner, F.** *Christus, das All und die Kirche,* 76–118. ———. "Eph 2 als ökumenisches Modell." In *Neues Testament und Kirche,* ed. J. Gnilka. Freiburg: Herder, 1974, 325–36. **Nauck, W.** "Eph

2, 19–22—ein Tauflied?" *EvT* 13 (1953) 362–71. **Pfammatter, J.** *Die Kirche als Bau.* Rome: Pontificiae Universitatis Gregorianae, 1960. **Rader, W.** *The Church and Racial Hostility.* Tübingen: Mohr, 1978. **Ramaroson, L.** " 'Le Christ, nôtre paix' (Ep. 2, 14–18)." *ScEs* 31 (1979) 373–82. **Rese, M.** "Die Vorzüge Israels in Rom 9,4f. und Eph 2,12." *TZ* 31 (1975) 211–22. **Roetzel, C. J.** "Jewish Christian–Gentile Christian Relations: A Discussion of Ephesians 2, 15a." *ZNW* 4 (1983) 81–89. **Sahlin, H.** " 'Die Beschneidung Christi': Eine Interpretation von Eph 2, 11–22." *SymBU* 12 (1950) 5–22. **Sanders, J. T.** "Hymnic Elements in Ephesians 1–3." *ZNW* 56 (1965) 216–18. ———. *The New Testament Christological Hymns.* Cambridge: Cambridge University Press, 1971, 14–15, 88–92. **Schäfer, K. T.** "Zur Deutung von ἀκρογωνιαῖος Eph 2,20." In *Neutestamentliche Aufsätze*, ed. J. Blinzler, O. Kuss, and F. Mussner. Regensburg: F. Pustet, 1963, 218–24. **Schille, G.** *Frühchristliche Hymnen*, 24–31. **Schnackenburg, R.** "Die Kirche als Bau: Epheser 2:19–22 unter ökumenischem Aspekt." In *Paul and Paulinism*, ed. M. D. Hooker and S. G. Wilson. London: S.P.C.K., 1982, 258–70. ———. "Die Politeia Israels in Eph 2, 12." In *De la Tôrah au Messie*, ed. M. Carrez et al. Paris: Desclée, 1981, 467–74. ———. "Zur Exegese von Eph 2, 11–22 in Hinblick auf der Verhältnis von Kirche und Israel." In *The New Testament Age.* Vol. 2. Ed. W. C. Weinrich. Macon, GA: Mercer University Press, 468–75. **Smith, D. C.** "The Ephesian Heresy." In *Society of Biblical Literature: 1974 Proceedings.* Missoula: Scholars Press, 1974, 45–54. ———. "The Two Made One: Some Observations on Eph 2:14–18." *Ohio Journal of Religious Studies* 1 (1973) 34–54. **Stegemann, E.** "Alt und Neu bei Paulus und in den Deuteropaulinen (Kol-Eph)." *EvT* 37 (1977) 508–36. **Stuhlmacher, P.** " 'Er ist unser Friede' (Eph 2,14): Zur Exegese und Bedeutung von Eph 2,14–18." In *Neues Testament und Kirche.* FS R. Schnackenburg, ed. J. Gnilka. Freiburg: Herder, 1974, 337–58 (ET in idem, *Reconciliation, Law, and Righteousness* [Philadelphia: Fortress, 1986] 182–200). **Tachau, P.** *"Einst" und "Jetzt" im Neuen Testament, Aufsätze zum Neuen Testament.* Vol. 2, ed. G. Klein. 134–43. **Vielhauer, P.** *Oikodome.* Munich: Kaiser, 1979. **Wengst, K.** *Christologische Formeln und Lieder des Urchristentums.* Gütersloh: G. Mohn, 1972, 181–86. **Wilhelmi, G.** "Der Versöhner-Hymnus in Eph. 2:14 ff." *ZNW* 78 (1987) 145–52. **Wolter, M.** *Rechtfertigung und zukünftiges Heil.* Berlin: de Gruyter, 1978, 62–73.

Translation

[11] *Therefore remember that at one time you Gentiles in the flesh, who are called the uncircumcision by what is called the circumcision in the flesh, made by hands,* [12] *remember*[a] *that you were at that time apart from Christ, separated from the commonwealth of Israel and aliens in regard to the covenants of promise, having no hope and without God in the world.* [13] *But now in Christ Jesus you who at one time were far off have come near through the blood of Christ.* [14] *For he is our peace, who has made both one and has broken down the dividing wall,* [15] *having abolished in his flesh the hostility,*[b] *the law of commandments and regulations, in order that he might create the two in himself*[c] *into one new person, thus making peace,* [16] *and might reconcile both to God in one body through the cross, having put the hostility to death in himself.* [17] *And he came and preached the good news of peace to you who were far off and of peace*[d] *to those who were near;* [18] *for through him we both have access in the one Spirit to the Father.* [19] *So then you are no longer aliens and strangers, but you are fellow citizens with the saints and members of the household of God,* [20] *having been built on the foundation of the apostles and prophets, the keystone being Christ Jesus himself,* [21] *in whom the whole building*[e] *being joined together grows into a holy temple in the Lord,* [22] *in whom you also are built together into a dwelling place of God in the Spirit.*

Notes

a ὅτι, "that," in v 12 takes up again the ὅτι of v 11, so in translation the verb from v 11 has been repeated in line with the writer's resumption of the thought with which the pericope begins.

b Texts and translations vary in their decision about whether τὴν ἔχθραν ἐν τῇ σαρκὶ αὐτοῦ, "the hostility in his flesh," belongs to the end of v 14 or the beginning of v 15. On the one hand, the phrase can be taken as connected with the preceding participle λύσας in v 14, and as an elaboration on the breaking down of the dividing wall. On the other hand, it can be seen as connected with the following participle καταργήσας in v 15, and therefore with the notion of abolishing the law of commandments and regulations. Some of the difficulty in the syntax may well be caused by the writer's reworking of original material (see the discussion in *Form/Structure/Setting*). But as regards the final form of his work, syntactical considerations favor the second option. It would be very awkward to have the objects of λύσας on either side of it. It is more natural for phrases which are in apposition to follow one another than to be interrupted by the participle. It is better, therefore, to regard both participles as occurring at the end of the clauses they govern and the phrase "the law of commandments and regulations" as explanatory of the hostility which Christ has abolished in his flesh (cf. also the comments on v 15; J. A. Robinson, 161; *pace* Percy, *Probleme*, 280; Gaugler, 109).

c The second edition of the UBS text has ἐν αὑτῷ, accented with the rough breathing mark, while the third edition has ἐν αὐτῷ. This reflects a debate about the generally accepted conventions of Greek orthography (cf. Metzger, *Textual Commentary*, 602, 616). The unaspirated form should probably be preferred, since in Hellenistic usage it could function as a reflexive in addition to its normal usage (cf. also BDF para. 564[1]). The variant ἐν ἑαυτῷ found in D G Marcion is an interpretation designed to make the reflexive sense clear.

d The second occurrence of εἰρήνην, "peace," in this verse is omitted in the Textus Receptus in line with K L many minuscules syr p,h Marcion Origen al. But the external evidence for its inclusion is strong, including p46 ℵ A B D F G P it d,g vg cop sa,boh goth arm eth. On internal grounds also, it is likely that the writer has reproduced the twofold reference to peace in the underlying OT text (LXX Isa 57:19) but given it a different sequence.

e Should the text read πᾶσα οἰκοδομή with ℵ* B D E F G K Ψ many minuscules Clement Origen Basil Chrysostom Theodoret or πᾶσα ἡ οἰκοδομή with ℵa A C P some minuscules Origen Chrysostom Theophylact? The support for the former anarthrous reading is stronger. On internal grounds it also constitutes the more difficult reading, since it might well be expected to mean "every building," which does not fit the writer's emphasis on the unity of the Church. It is likely, then, that the article was added by copyists because it appeared to be needed by the sense. Justification for interpreting the original anarthrous form in the sense normally associated with the arthrous is found in *Comment* on v 21.

Form/Structure/Setting

In order to arrive at some conclusions about how the writer's thought has been structured, it will be necessary first to evaluate some of the questions of form that have arisen in connection with this pericope.

One of the prominent formal elements in 2:11–22 is the ποτέ . . . νῦν contrast schema, which we have already observed in 2:1–10, where it served to remind the Gentile readers of their past in terms of spiritual death with its various aspects of bondage to the world, the devil, and the flesh, and of the change God had accomplished on their behalf through Christ. The earlier discussion of the background of this schema and its use elsewhere in the NT will be assumed as we analyze its place in this passage. Whereas in the earlier version of the schema the νῦν element was implicit, here both temporal elements are explicit. The pre-Christian past is designated by ποτέ, "then," in vv 11, 13 and by its equivalent τῷ καιρῷ ἐκείνῳ, "at that time," in v 12; it is set over against the Christian present, described as νυνί, "now," in v 13, and in an equivalent as οὐκέτι, "no longer," in v 19. This contrast reminds the readers of their past in terms of the implications of having been deprived Gentiles, as opposed to Jews, in order to show again what has been done on their behalf to change this situation and in order to make them aware of the privileges they now enjoy. Some aspects of the contrast are completed in vv 11–13, but vv 14–18 intervene before other aspects of the pre-Christian past mentioned in v 12 are shown to have been reversed in v 19. The past was a time without Christ (v 12), but the changed present has been brought about "in Christ Jesus" (v 13), i.e., because of their relationship to Christ (though, *contra* Tachau, *"Einst" und "Jetzt"*, 140, this should not be claimed as an absolute use of "in Christ" language). At one time the readers were excluded from the commonwealth of Israel (v 12), but now they are fellow citizens with the "saints" (v 19). Once they were seen as aliens in regard to the covenants of promise (v 12), yet they are no longer aliens and strangers (v 19). Previously they had no hope and were without God in the world (v 12), but currently they are members of the household of God (v 19; though "having no hope," strictly speaking, has no direct parallel, and οἰκεῖοι τοῦ θεοῦ, "members of the household of God," also contrasts with πάροικοι, "strangers," in the previous part of v 19). Once they were far off (v 13), but now they have come near (v 13). This last element of the contrast indicates that it is not a purely temporal one, but, as we saw also in 2:1–10, spatial categories—here "far" and "near"—can be interwoven (cf. also Tachau, *"Einst" und "Jetzt"*, 141). As we shall see below in the discussion of traditional material behind the passage, this particular instance of the contrast schema may well have that found in Col 1:21–23 as its point of departure.

Like other instances of the schema in the NT, this one is characterized by its address to the reader. This feature is particularly noticeable here, for the second person plural found in vv 11–13, 19 contrasts with the first person plural, which begins and ends the material in vv 14–18 (cf. Tachau, *"Einst" und "Jetzt"*, 141). What this use of the schema involves, then, is not a general depiction of the place of the Gentiles in the history of salvation nor a general contrast between Gentiles and Jews, but, more specifically, a contrast between the pre-Christian past in its relation to Israel's privileges and the Christian present of these particular Gentile addressees. The schema had already been used in the context of Gentiles' relationship to Israel in Rom 11:30–32, but perhaps the one other example in the NT of its use in such a context provides a closer parallel. In 1 Pet 2:10 the readers are told, "Once you were no people but now you are God's people."

It can be seen that the ποτέ . . . νῦν schema provides a major structural element in the thought of Eph 2:11–22, particularly since it shapes the key summarizing verse (v 19: ἄρα οὖν . . . , "so then . . ."), yet it is also clear that it is supplemented by other material. Verses 14–18 provide an excursus on how the readers' change of situation was accomplished by Christ, the bringer of peace, and vv 20–22 expand on the imagery for the new community of the Church introduced in v 19. It should also be pointed out that the summary of v 19 takes up the contrast after it has been established in v 15 that Christ has created a totally new entity, the "one new man." Thereby the reversal of the pre-Christian situation which is set out is no longer only a simple direct reversal, but a reversal which transcends the old categories and introduces a new element (cf. the observations in *Comment* on "fellow citizens with the saints" and the way in which Jew-Gentile categories have largely faded from view in the depiction of the new community in vv 20–22). As in 2:1–10, the purpose for which the contrast schema is employed is to serve as a reminder (cf. μνημονεύετε, "remember," v 11) of the privileges the Gentile readers now enjoy. The past lack of privilege in comparison with Israel is not depicted for its own sake, but to assure the readers of the greatness and reality of their salvation by highlighting their highly privileged present situation as members of such a community as the Church is shown to be. This primary purpose of the schema, and therefore of the pericope, must be kept in view.

The stance already taken on the role of the contrast schema means also that decisions have been made about the structure which tell against the alternative view which sees the passage as forming an elaborate chiasmus. Kirby (*Ephesians: Baptism and Pentecost*, 156–57) claims that the whole passage is a chiasmus divided between v 15a and v 15b. There are a number of elements A-K which develop inwardly to a climax and then a series of antithetical parallel elements K^1-A^1 which move outwards from this (cf. also K. E. Bailey, *Poet and Peasant* [Grand Rapids: Eerdmans, 1976] 63, who makes a similar suggestion which has v 15 at the center but six divisions on either side of the chiasmus). Giavini (*NTS* 16 [1969–70] 209–11) holds that vv 11–14a and vv 17–22 are a chiasmus surrounding vv 14b–16, which in turn consist of parallel sets of four elements surrounding the central element in v 15a. Both these arrangements are somewhat contrived. Sometimes the proposed parallel elements are in terms of the wording and sometimes in terms of the ideas involved, and in a number of cases neither kind of parallel is convincing. In addition, the last part of the pericope poses problems for both analyses. In regard to Kirby's proposal, it should be clear that there are no substantial antithetical parallels between a number of the elements at the beginning and at the end, and Giavini has to treat vv 19–22 as one element, making the elements of his chiasmus quite uneven. The element of truth on which these analyses have been built is that the passage does make use of some words and ideas more than once, but at very best it is only loosely chiastic, and these "parallel" features have a more obvious explanation. Verse 19 clearly takes up aspects of v 12, but, as we have seen, this is as a summarizing conclusion to a contrast schema, not as a deliberate attempt at chiasmus. Elements of v 13 recur in v 17, but this is because the terminology of v 13 and of what follows in vv 14–16 is associated in the writer's mind with a Scripture citation which incorporates this language. Finally, vv 15, 16 contain words found in v 14, but this is because they provide an elaboration on the same topic. Parallel elements in these verses could well be there as *parallelismus membrorum* (couplets) from original hymnic material, not because the writer has carefully arranged them as part of a chiastic literary device.

This last point brings us to another major area of discussion in regard to 2:11–22. Does it incorporate traditional material which the writer has molded for his own purposes? Debate has revolved primarily around whether hymnic material lies behind vv 14–18 or vv 19–22. The writer's use of the OT text Isa 57:19 falls of course into the category of use of traditional material, but this will be discussed more fully in the *Comment* on v 17. Discussion cannot

Form/Structure/Setting

be postponed altogether, however, for there are some scholars who wish to deny any redaction of traditional liturgical material in vv 14–18 by proposing rather that vv 13–18 should be seen as a Christian midrash on or exegesis of Isa 57:19 (cf. Stuhlmacher, " 'Er ist unser Friede,' " 347–58; Deichgräber, *Gotteshymnus*, 167 n. 1; Wolter, *Rechtfertigung*, 62–70; Schnackenburg, 112). A number of objections tell against such a proposal. Verse 13 does not quote Isa 57:19 (*contra* Stuhlmacher, " 'Er ist unser Friede,' " 347; Barth, 278). Instead, it speaks of those who were far off having now come near, a notion not expressed in Isa 57:19 itself but common in Jewish discussions of proselytism, and a notion whose language of "far" and "near" then prompts the reference to the different use of these terms in Isa 57:19, which does not, however, come until v 17 (cf. also Lindemann, *Aufhebung*, 84, 177). Nor can αὐτὸς γάρ ἐστιν ἡ εἰρήνη ἡμῶν, "for he is our peace," in v 14 be held to be a reference to Isa 9:5, 6 (*contra* Stuhlmacher, " 'Er ist unser Friede,' " 345; Barth, 261 n. 36; Wolter, *Rechtfertigung*, 72; Schnackenburg, 112–13). There is a strand in rabbinic exegesis in which Isa 9:5, 6 and 52:7 were linked together in a messianic interpretation (cf. Str-B 3:587), and it is certainly the case that the wording of v 17 combines Isa 52:7 with Isa 57:19. But it does not follow from either of these assertions that Isa 9:5, 6 is being referred to here in v 14 or that that text provides the link between a reference to Isa 57:19 in v 13 and its combination with Isa 52:7 in v 17. The gulf between the wording of Isa 9:5, 6 about the prince of peace, which in the LXX is to be found only in Codex Alexandrinus, or between the general LXX rendering of ἐγὼ γὰρ ἄξω εἰρήνην ἐπὶ τοὺς ἄρχοντας, "for I will bring peace upon the princes," followed up by καὶ τῆς εἰρήνης αὐτοῦ οὐκ ἔστιν ὅριον, "and of his peace there is no end," and the wording of v 14 is too wide for even the claim of a definite allusion to be substantiated (*contra* Stuhlmacher, " 'Er ist unser Friede,' " 358). The most that can be said is that Isa 9:5, 6 and Jewish interpretations of it may have paved the way for the sort of attribution of peace to a person that is made here. Finally, the passage simply does not read like a continuous exegesis. In fact, the flow of thought, as we have seen, is such that v 19 follows on most naturally from v 13, and vv 14–18 clearly introduce new material before there is a return to the pattern of thinking of vv 11–13. Rather than introducing a midrash, v 13 is part of the contrast schema of vv 11–13. It is the beginning of v 14, αὐτὸς γάρ ἐστιν . . . , "for he is . . . ," which signals a break; then a further subsidiary break in the flow is signaled by καὶ ἐλθών, "and he came," in v 17, which introduces the OT citation.

The way is now clear for some discussion on its own terms of the question of the use of hymnic material in vv 14–18. Some of the indications that hymnic material could lie behind this section are the break with the surrounding context of the contrast schema, the "we" style that interrupts the "you" style of address to the readers in vv 11–13 and vv 19–22, the opening emphatic predication ("he is our peace"), the pointedly Christological content of the material, the heavy use of participles, the apparent *parallelismus membrorum*, the piling up of a number of *hapax legomena*, and awkward syntax which suggests interpretation. Such features, in the light of the analysis which follows, have made it seem more probable that we are dealing with hymnic material that has been reworked (cf. also Schlier, 122–23; Schille, *Frühchristliche Hymnen*, 24–31;

J. T. Sanders, *ZNW* 56 [1965] 216–18; Fischer, *Tendenz*, 131–37; Gnilka, 147–52; idem, "Christus unser Friede," 190–207; Barth, 261–62; Burger, *Schöpfung*, 117–33; Wengst, *Christologische Formeln*, 181–86; Lindemann, *Aufhebung*, 156–59; Martin, *Reconciliation*, 168—71) than with a straightforward argument (*pace* Mussner, *Christus*, 100–101; Merklein, *BZ* 17 [1973] 79–102; Ernst, 314–21; Schnackenburg, 106–7, 112).

But what is the extent of such hymnic material? Against those who would include v 17 or v 18 (cf. Schlier, 123; Schille, *Frühchristliche Hymnen*, 24–31; Gnilka, 147–52; idem, "Christus unser Friede," 197–200; Barth, 276; Fisher, *Tendenz*, 132; Burger, *Schöpfung*, 128–33), it must be said that the language and concepts of v 17 come from the OT passage Isa 57:19, clearly take up v 13, and are formulated as an address to the readers (cf. the introduction of the second person plural ὑμῖν), and that v 18 reads more like the writer's own summary of the significance of the preceding verses in language reminiscent of Rom 5:2. In addition, neither v 17 or v 18 easily provides reconstructed lines which would be of an appropriate length for the original hymnic material (cf. also Wengst, *Christologische Formeln*, 182–83). It is behind vv 14–16 that there may well be traditional material which spoke of Christ as the one who provides cosmic peace and reconciliation (cf. also J. T. Sanders, *ZNW* 56 [1965] 216–18; Wengst, *Christologische Formeln*, 181–86; Lindemann, *Aufhebung*, 156–59; Martin, *Reconciliation*, 172). An attempted reconstruction of this material follows, with the lines numbered for ease of reference, the position of the writer's glosses indicated by a raised letter above the text, and the glosses themselves placed in square brackets at the end of the appropriate lines:

(1) Αὐτός ἐστιν ἡ εἰρήνη ἡμῶν
(2) ὁ ποιήσας τὰ ἀμφότερα ἓν
(3) καὶ τὸ μεσότοιχον[a] λύσας [[a] τοῦ φραγμοῦ]
(4) τὴν ἔχθραν[b] καταργήσας [[b] ἐν τῇ σαρκὶ τὸν νόμον τῶν ἐντολῶν ἐν δόγμασιν]
(5) ἵνα τοὺς δύο κτίσῃ ἐν αὐτῷ εἰς ἕνα καινὸν ἄνθρωπον
(6) ποιῶν εἰρήνην
(7) καὶ ἀποκαταλλάξῃ τοὺς ἀμφοτέρους ἐν ἑνὶ σώματι τῷ θεῷ[c] [[c] διὰ τοῦ σταυροῦ]
(8) ἀποκτείνας τὴν ἔχθραν ἐν αὐτῷ.

Ephesians' links with Colossians and its thought world become relevant at this point. This reconstructed material has striking points of contact with the hymn to the cosmic Christ which, it is generally agreed, lies behind Col 1:15–20, the last part of which also deals with cosmic reconciliation. ἀποκαταλλάσσειν, "to reconcile," is found in Col 1:20 in connection with the cosmos and here in line 7 in connection with two unspecified entities. Also in Col 1:20 Christ is said to make peace between elements on earth and in heaven (εἰρηνοποιήσας) and here in line 6 it is said that he makes peace between the two entities (ποιῶν εἰρήνην). In Col 1:18 σῶμα, "body," had originally been a reference to the cosmos, but the Pauline gloss interpreted it of the Church (cf. also our discussion of this point and of σῶμα in general at its occurrence in 1:23), and here also in line 7 it refers to the cosmos now seen as united, as does the notion of the one new person in line 5. It is likely, then, that the original hymnic material behind Eph 2:14–16 also has a cosmic context, and that the two entities mentioned (τὰ ἀμφότερα, "both" in line 2; τοὺς δύο, "the two" in line 5; τοὺς ἀμφοτέρους, "both" in line 7) are the two parts of the cosmos, heaven and earth. The neuter formulation τὰ ἀμφότερα is not easy to explain if the passage is treated purely on one level as a straightforward discussion of the relation between Jewish Christians and Gentile Christians. The upper and lower realms of the cosmos were often thought of as in antithesis, with humans in the lower realm of matter experiencing the upper realm and the powers that inhabit it as hostile and threatening. According to the hymn, in order to bring about unity (lines 2, 5) and to achieve reconciliation in the cosmos (lines 6, 7), Christ had to break down the wall dividing the two realms (line 3) and overcome the hostility between them (lines 4, 8). The notion of a cosmic wall between heaven and earth can be found not only in later Gnosticism (cf. Schlier, 129–30; Fischer, *Tendenz*, 133) but also in earlier Judaism (cf. *1 Enoch* 14.9; *3 Apoc. Bar.* 2.1, 2; *T. Levi* 2.7).

The writer of Ephesians finds this notion of Christ as the bringer of cosmic peace and reconciliation appropriate for adaptation to his theme of how Christ has brought Gentiles near and has overcome the barrier that had existed between them and Israel. But before this material from the hymn could be assimilated to the new context it did require some adaptation (*contra* Schlier, 123–40, and Burger, *Schöpfung*, 133–39, who see the Jew-Gentile reference as part of the original hymn). The additions made have left their mark by producing some rather cumbersome syntax, particularly at the beginning of what we have taken to be v 15 in the material's present form. Just as in Col 1 the Christological hymn's notion of cosmic reconciliation was immediately applied to the reconciliation the readers of the letter had experienced (cf. Col 1:21, 22), so here in Ephesians cosmic reconciliation is made to apply to reconciliation on the human level between Gentiles and Jews, but this time by means of glosses on the hymnic material itself. There are in fact two categories of glosses used. The first category is that which applies the material to Jews and Gentiles by explaining the dividing wall as τοῦ φραγμοῦ, the fence or barrier, a term which has associations with Torah (cf. the comments on v 14), and by interpreting the hostility or enmity as that caused by the law with its commandments and regulations, τὸν νόμον τῶν ἐντολῶν ἐν δόγμασιν. The wall that has to be abolished, the enmity that has to be overcome, in Christ's reconciliation of Gentiles and Jews is now seen to involve the law. The second category of gloss is that which ensures that in its new application Christ's work is given the context it requires in the history of salvation. To this end, the writer emphasizes that Christ dealt with the law ἐν τῇ σαρκί, "in his flesh," that is, through his physical death. The same stress is achieved by the addition of the penultimate line of διὰ τοῦ σταυροῦ, "through the cross." This final gloss is reminiscent of Colossians' concern to anchor the cosmic hymn behind Col 1:15–20 in Christ's saving work in history by adding "through the blood of his cross" (cf. Col 1:20). The meaning of the final form of the traditional material in its new context will of course be discussed in *Comment*, but a word about the probable background of the original hymnic material should be said before we conclude our discussion of the tradition history of 2:14–16. Some take its cosmic themes to come from a Gnostic background (cf. Schlier, 123–40; Schille, *Frühchristliche Hymnen*, 24–31; Fischer, *Tendenz*, 132; Wengst, *Christologische Formeln*, 185–86; Lindemann, *Aufhebung*, 157–70), but the objections to the existence of a full-fledged Gnostic Heavenly Man myth which were raised in connection with the background of 1:22, 23 are relevant here also. Since the material has so much in common with the hymn of Col 1:15–20, it is likely that its background will be similar. Many take the background of the Colossian hymn to be the cosmological concerns of Hellenistic Judaism (cf. Lohse, *Colossians*, 46–55; Schweizer, *Colossians*, 63–81), and it seems probable that such concerns have shaped the thought of the traditional material here also (cf. Gnilka, 150–51; Burger, *Schöpfung*, 133–39; cf. also our discussion of the cosmic background of the "head," "body," and "fullness" language of 1:22, 23; for a survey of the discussion of the history-of-religions background cf. Rader, *Church and Racial Hostility*, 177–96).

It has been argued by some that, instead of hymnic material, what lies behind Eph 2:14–18, and indeed behind 2:11–22 as a whole, is Col 1:21–23, and that there are close verbal similarities between the passages (cf. Merklein, *BZ* 17 [1973] 79–102; idem, "Paulinische Theologie," 52–62). We have already indicated some similarities between the original hymn behind Eph 2:14–16 and its interpretation in the passage as it now stands and the hymn of Col 1:15–20 and its interpretation in Col 1:21–23. It should not be thought that it is a case of the tradition on which Eph 2:14–18 is dependent being either hymnic material or Col 1:21–23. The influence of the latter would not make the use of the former superfluous. The terms that Eph 2:14–18 and Col 1:21–23 have in common are ἀποκαταλλάσσειν, "to reconcile," σῶμα, "body," and σάρξ, "flesh." But Ephesians has ἀποκαταλλάσσειν in common with the hymn of Col 1:15–20 along with the notion of peacemaking. σῶμα is used with a different sense in Col 1:21–23 than in Eph 2:14–18, and Ephesians' use of σῶμα is parallel instead to that of the hymn in Colossians. This leaves only σάρξ as an exclusive verbal parallel between the two passages, and we have argued that this is part of Ephesians' gloss on the traditional material, and this may well have been under the influence of Col 1:21–23.

More than actual verbal links between Eph 2:14–18 and Col 1:21–23, it is the parallels in the sequence of thought between Eph 2:11–22 as a whole and Col 1:21–23 that are striking. Col 1:21–23 has a "then . . . now" schema involving the sequence alienation, reconciliation, and concern for believers' holiness and their being founded on the apostolic gospel. Ephesians has taken up the schema and followed the sequence, as it continues to follow the sequence of Colossians in the next pericope, 3:1–13, but it fills out the concepts it takes up and makes them part of larger concerns. Eph 2 uses the term ἀπηλλοτριωμένοι, "separated," but applies it to the Gentiles' relationship to the Jews. To the notion of reconciliation it adds cosmic hymn material similar to that of Col 1:15–20, which was also related to this notion. The concern for holiness and for a relation to the norm of the apostolic gospel is incorporated in its new temple imagery.

The proposal that the material in 2:19–22 constitutes a baptismal hymn (cf. Nauck, *EvT* 13 [1953] 362–71) can be dealt with more briefly. Nauck holds that these verses can be divided into three strophes, that the change of status mentioned in v 19 is a reference to reception into the people of God, which takes place in baptism, and that a number of terms used in vv 20–22 belong to the language of baptismal liturgy (e.g., "to grow," "to be built"). But there are no really clear allusions to baptism in this use of imagery for the Church and the Gentile Christian readers' part in it in vv 19–22. At very best, some of the terms used may have been employed elsewhere with baptismal associations (though the baptismal connections of most of the parallel references Nauck provides would be disputed), but this would not mean that such associations must pertain here also. The style of these verses with their relative clauses in vv 21, 22 is characteristic of the writer himself elsewhere in the letter. Above all, v 19 is far more adequately explained by seeing it as integral to the writer's use of the contrast schema from vv 11–13 and as summarizing its conclusions in the light of his excursus in vv 14–18 (cf. also Merklein, *Das kirchliche Amt*, 119–20).

We are now in a position to see that the overall structure of thought in 2:11–22 falls into three parts. Verses 11–13 lay the foundation, as the writer uses the contrast between their pre-Christian past in relation to Israel and their Christian present to remind his Gentile readers of the privilege of having come near through Christ's death. Verses 14–18 provide further explanation of how this coming near was made possible through Christ's work. The terms "far" and "near" in v 13 remind the writer of Isa 57:19, which speaks of peace for two such groups. However, before he introduces this citation, he prepares the way for its notion of peace. He does this through the traditional material he has to hand, which speaks of Christ as the embodiment of peace and agent of reconciliation for the divided cosmos. This material is reworked in vv 14–16 in terms of the overcoming of the division between Jew and Gentile so that v 17 can then introduce the Isa 57:19 quotation in combination with a further reference to the proclamation of peace from Isa 52:7. Verse 18 rounds off this middle section by encapsulating the results of Christ's peacemaking in terms of access to the Father for both Jews and Gentiles. Verses 19–22 form the last part of the passage; they take up again, in a summarizing fashion and in the light of the middle section, the contrast between the readers' past and present. It is taken up in order to elaborate on the readers' privileged new situation in terms of a series of what are primarily building images for the Church and for the readers' place in this new community, which transcends the division of Jew and Gentile.

2:11–22 in its context in the letter as a whole stands parallel to 2:1–10. There the contrast between the readers' pre-Christian past and Christian present was stated in more general terms. Here it is expressed in more specific terms of their relation to Israel's previous privileged position in God's purposes for salvation. Both passages, with their reminders of the readers' changed situation as a result of what has happened in Christ, can be seen as connected with the desire expressed in the thanksgiving period of 1:15–23 that the readers should have an increased appreciation of the power of God that has been operative on their behalf. In addition, the last part of the thanksgiving period has shown that God's power was effective for his people as the Church, described as Christ's body and his fullness. Here in 2:11–22 this theme is taken up again as the Church is seen as the product of the creative power of Christ's reconciling work and then described as God's household, a building in which Christ is the keystone, a holy temple in the Lord, and God's dwelling place.

As has been noted in the *Introduction* and under *Form/Structure/Setting* on 2:1–10, the present pericope functions together with the previous one as a *narratio*, which reports the past in such a way as to attempt to influence its audience to base their values and their actions upon it. This second dramatic contrast between the readers' past and their present, which calls on them to reflect on their experience, has a powerful rhetorical effect. As they recall God's actions in Christ on their behalf and the privileges they now enjoy in comparison with their past deprivation, and as they see themselves as now part of a community that is growing into a holy temple in the Lord, this is meant to produce an attitude of profound thankfulness and a mind-set that will be ready to accept the ethical implications of being a new holy community, when these are spelled out in the exhortations of the latter part of the letter.

The passage can also be seen to have two major links with the opening *berakah*. First, the blessings of salvation set out there are often described in ways which had been associated with Jewish hopes of salvation, and yet these are the blessings into which the readers are said to have entered (1:13, 14). Similarly here in 2:11–22 the readers' previous deficiencies over against Israel have been more than compensated by the new situation produced by Christ's reconciling work. Second, the uniting of elements in heaven and on earth in a cosmic harmony has been seen as the goal of God's plan in 1:10. The move from cosmic unity to human unity, in the use of traditional material in 2:14–16, shows that the two notions were associated in the writer's mind, and it will become apparent in his discussion in 3:9, 10 that he regards the unity accomplished in the Church as an anticipation of final cosmic unity. The themes of 2:11–22 are taken up in two more ways in 3:1–13. In 3:5, 6 the membership of Gentiles in the same body as Jewish Christians is said to be the mystery that has only now been revealed, and the notion of access to God through Christ is repeated in 3:12. The issue of Gentiles' relationship to Israel or to Jewish Christians is not, however, mentioned in the paraenesis of the second part of the letter. 4:17–24 does speak of the readers' pre-Christian Gentile past and repeat the participle ἀπηλλοτριωμένοι, "separated" (cf. 2:12), but in neither instance in connection with Israel. Instead, the paraenesis exploits in more general terms the notions of unity in the one body (cf. 2:15, 16) in 4:3–5, of peace (cf. 2:14, 15, 17) in 4:3 and 6:15, of growth together (cf. 2:21) in 4:15, 16, and of building (cf. 2:20–22) in 4:12.

The discussion in *Comment* will show that, as elsewhere in the letter, the writer, in addition to his use of the OT, traditional material and Colossians, again makes use of themes from the other Pauline letters. But to what use does he put such material? What is the function of this part of his composition? In line with the subject matter in each of the three main preceding sections of the letter, the purpose here is first of all a reminder of blessing in an attempt to deepen the readers' appreciation of yet another aspect of their great salvation. The predominant contrast schema and particularly the summarizing v 19 make it clear that this is the main point. The readers are to be congratulated on the fact that through Christ's reconciling work they no longer have deprived status as compared with Israel in the outworking of God's plan of salvation, but have become fellow citizens with the saints and members of God's household. In fact, they should realize that they are now part of the new temple. The passage is not therefore meant to be "an argument for corporate unity" (*pace* Mitton, 101; Roetzel, ZNW 74 [1983] 88) or primarily to be an answer to the question "How can Jews *and* Gentiles be the eschatological people of God?"—however important that question might be (*pace* Merklein,

Christus, 28, 71–72, 76). The attempt to discover some setting where there were problems between Jewish Christians and Gentile Christians which would have called forth this pericope in response is also misguided (*pace* Pokorný, *Epheserbrief,* 12, 13). Verses 14–18 do show that through Christ's work both Jews and Gentiles have been able to become part of the new person which has replaced the old entities. But this is something which has been completed, an event which has taken place in the past, and is introduced into the discussion only to elaborate for the Gentile Christians what produced the drastic change in their status. Given that old divisions were overcome in order to achieve the new situation, an obvious implication would be that any present divisions between the two groups are totally incongruous. But this is not an implication that the writer makes any effort to draw. The admission of Gentiles into the Church on equal footing with Jewish Christians, over which there had been so much struggle and over which Paul had expended so much energy, is taken for granted by this writer. It is not an issue for which he has to argue.

It is no clearer from the text itself that the writer is addressing a problem at the other end of the spectrum, that of Gentile Christian arrogance toward Jews and a superiority which looked down on Jewish Christians. This was a problem addressed by Paul in Rom 11:13–32, and one which a number of scholars have suggested as the setting for this passage (e.g., Käsemann, "Ephesians and Acts," 291; Fischer, *Tendenz und Absicht,* 79–94; Martin, *Reconciliation,* 160–61, 166–67). Again, an implication of vv 14–18 could be that there is no room for superiority since both Jewish Christians and Gentile Christians have access to God on an equal footing. But that is not the point of these verses in their context and such an implication is not drawn. In this proposed setting the reminder to Gentile Christians of the reversal of their situation and of the tremendous privileges they now enjoy as part of the new community, which transcends Israel's previous place in the outworking of God's purpose, might well aggravate rather than alleviate the problems. A response similar to Paul's in Rom 11, with its warnings and its exposition of God's continuing purpose for Israel in an effort to deflate Gentile pride, would be far more appropriate.

It is significant, however, that the writer chooses to help his Gentile readers appreciate the greatness of their salvation by setting it in the context of Israel's former privileges and their own former deficiencies. He does this not only because he is in all probability a Jewish Christian, but also because he wants his readers to be aware that their salvation has not taken place in a vacuum. Salvation has a history, they have a place in that history, and there is a sense in which in experiencing salvation they have entered into the heritage of Israel. If one wishes to speak of a problem to which this is the answer, then that problem is not one of Gentile Christian arrogance, but of ignorance of roots and therefore a deficient sense of identity (cf. the similar view of Merklein, *Das kirchliche Amt,* 46–47).

Having recognized in this passage an element of continuity between Gentile Christians and Israel (and the very fact that the Jewish Scriptures can be used to address the readers in v 17 is part of this feature), we must return to its main thrust and observe that the greater emphasis is on the element of discontinuity. The new community of which the Gentiles have become a part is not simply a development out of Israel, according to this writer. Instead, it took a new creation to produce it (v 15). The resulting one new person replaces the two old entities—Israel and the Gentiles (v 15). The privileges the Gentiles now enjoy not only match those which Israel experienced previously, but go beyond them (cf. vv 19–22). This opens up a different perspective on the relation between the Church and Israel from that found in Rom 9–11. In Romans, Paul's position is more dialectical than it had been in the heat of battle in Galatians. Throughout his argument, he shows how both Jew and Gentile are one under the power of sin and the wrath of God and one in being justified by faith, and how they are interlocked in God's purposes for history in such a way that both receive mercy. Yet at the same time, as a Jew, he struggles with the question of whether God still has a distinctive purpose for ethnic Israel. He is utterly convinced of the new thing God has done in Christ whereby Gentiles now inherit Israel's promises; but as he makes clear in the face of Gentile arrogance, Gentile Christians have been added to a given Jewish base, God's election of Israel still holds, and there will be a future salvation for her. In Ephesians, however, Paul's personal agony has disappeared, and Gentiles in becoming Christians are not simply being added to a Jewish base, but they are joining a new community in which the question of Israel's privileged position has been transcended. The concept of the Church here is, in fact if not in name, that of the "third race," neither Jewish nor Gentile (*contra* Barth, 310; on the dangers for the relationship between Christians and Jews which arose from later abuse of the concept, cf. Rader, *Church and Racial Hostility*, 156, 171–73, 228–34). Interestingly, the position of Ephesians turns out to be more like that produced by the sharp logic of Paul's polemic in Galatians, with its stress on the discontinuity in the history of salvation and its assertions that in Christ there is neither Jew nor Greek (3:28), that the heavenly Jerusalem has replaced the present Jerusalem in God's purposes (4:25–27), that neither circumcision nor uncircumcision count for anything, but a new creation (6:15), and that both Jewish Christians and Gentile Christians constitute the Israel of God (6:16). Perhaps, then, the wheel has turned full circle in the development of Pauline thought—from an emphasis on discontinuity between Israel and the new thing God has done for Christian believers in Galatians, to a greater stress on continuity and the future role of Israel in the context of a crucial stage of Paul's own mission and of Jewish Christian/ Gentile Christian questions in Romans, back again to more emphasis on discontinuity in the perspective of Paul's disciple in Ephesians. The difference between the starting point and the finish is not one of basic theological stance but of mood and setting. Galatians is heated polemic at a relatively early stage of conflict between Paul and Judaizing opponents, when Jewish Christians still had the greater weight in terms of influence and probably also of numbers. Ephesians has a cool detachment from Jewish Christian/Gentile Christian conflict, and reflects a setting toward the end of the first century when Paul's position on admission of Gentiles had been established, Jerusalem had fallen, and Gentile Christians in terms of influence and numbers very much overshadowed any Jewish Christians in the churches of Asia Minor.

Comment

11 διὸ μνημονεύετε ὅτι ποτὲ ὑμεῖς τὰ ἔθνη ἐν σαρκί, οἱ λεγόμενοι ἀκροβυστία ὑπὸ τῆς λεγομένης περιτομῆς ἐν σαρκὶ χειροποιήτου, "therefore remember that at one time you Gentiles in the flesh, who are called the uncircumcision by what is called the circumcision in the flesh, made by hands." διό, "therefore," links this pericope with the preceding one. In the light of what has been said in 2:1–10 about the change God has wrought, the readers are now to remember their pre-Christian state from another perspective. What the readers have already heard becomes in this way the point of departure for further reflection. In the biblical tradition, remembering can often involve the attitude (sometimes expressed in cultic action, e.g., Exod 12:14; 1 Cor 11:25) of looking to the past for its implications for the present and future. Here, too, the remembering the readers are called upon to do is meant not only to include mental recall, but also, in the process, to lead to greater appreciation of—and gratitude for—what God has done to change the past and for the present consequences of that reversal.

Most of the terms the writer uses in his designation of the addressees can be found clustered together in Col 2:11, 13 ("circumcision," "uncircumcision," "flesh," "made without hands" as compared to "made with hands" here). We have already seen that the first part of the description of spiritual death in Col 2:13 provided the writer of Ephesians with the formulation with which he began the preceding pericope, 2:1–10. It looks very much as if the second part of that description about "the uncircumcision of your flesh" has provided him with the initial idea for the beginning of this pericope. But there is a striking difference. In the passage in Colossians the language of circumcision and uncircumcision is used metaphorically. His reflection on the text of Colossians has prompted this writer to give its terms a different direction and to use them in their literal sense. He calls his readers "Gentiles in the flesh." Romans or Greeks would not call themselves "Gentiles," so this designation is made from a Jewish standpoint, as is the distinction between the "uncircumcision" (literally, "the foreskin"), standing for the Gentiles, and "the circumcision," representing Jews, since circumcision was viewed as the distinguishing mark of belonging to God's elect people. The additional qualification "in the flesh" underlines that the writer is making an ethnic distinction. In the context and in the light of the further qualification of "the circumcision" as "made by hands," "in the flesh" appears to indicate not only that the distinction is based on a real physical difference, but also that from the Christian perspective of the writer this no longer counts as religiously significant. So from the context "flesh" here takes on some overtones of inferiority, but it does not have the same strong negative ethical sense as in 2:3 (*contra* Barth, 254). It is not the case that elsewhere in Ephesians ἔθνη, "Gentiles," simply means non-Christians and that when he is intending it to mean "non-Jews" as in Paul's writings this writer finds it necessary to add "in the flesh" (*contra* Beare, 599; Martin, *Reconciliation*, 159–60). The writer's use of the term ἔθνη in 3:1, 6, 8 is clearly meant as a reference to non-Jews in the same way that Paul had used the term; 4:17 provides the one instance where a somewhat broader reference appears to be in view.

Gentiles are called by the name "the uncircumcision," which for a Jew often announced the inferiority or even shame of those so branded. They are called this, the writer points out, by those who are called "the circumcision." λεγομένης used adjectivally with περιτομῆς could mean, as some (e.g., Abbott, 56; Ernst, 312) interpret it, "so-called" and indicate that for the writer the title "circumcision" for the Jews is of no account. But such a meaning may be too derogatory (cf. J. A. Robinson, 56; Barth, 254), and it could be that λεγομένης is simply a variation on the more straightforward οἱ λεγόμενοι, "who are called," which has been used in connection with "the uncircumcision." But, in any case, the formulation "what is called the circumcision" does serve to put some distance between the writer and this sort of distinction, suggesting that he is using it to make a point rather than because it was natural to his own outlook. A more negative evaluation of the title "the circumcision" is, however, to be found in the term χειροποίητος, "made by hands." This term and its opposite are frequently used in the NT for the contrast between external material aspects of the old order of Judaism and the spiritual efficacy of the new order (cf. Col 2:11; also, for example, Mark 14:58; Acts 7:48; Heb 9:11, 24). To talk of circumcision in the flesh made by hands is therefore to reflect the Pauline view that this is no longer the real circumcision (cf. Rom 2:28, 29; Phil 3:2, 3; Col 2:11).

Three implications may be drawn from the writer's addressing his readers in the way he does in v 11. These readers in churches of Asia Minor toward the last part of the first century are to be thought of as predominantly, if not exclusively, Gentile Christian. The person who writes from this perspective, who ascribes to Gentiles in the following verse deficiencies they would not themselves have recognized, and yet who at the same time distances himself from these distinctions, is likely to have been a Jewish Christian disciple of Paul. The point to be made in the writer's discussion has to do not so much with present relationships between Jewish Christians and Gentile Christians in Asia Minor, or between the churches and the synagogue, as with Gentile Christians being asked to see their past in terms of categories which were valid at an earlier stage in the history of salvation, when God's purpose was centered in Israel.

12 ὅτι ἦτε τῷ καιρῷ ἐκείνῳ χωρὶς Χριστοῦ, "(remember) that you were at that time apart from Christ." ὅτι picks up the ὅτι of the previous verse and resumes the train of thought interrupted by the lengthy way of describing the readers. The writer is asking his Gentile Christian readers to understand in retrospect the deficiencies of their former pre-Christian state, although at the time they would not have appreciated the privileges of which Israel could boast in relation to the Gentiles. He wishes the readers to reflect on their former condition in this way in order to appreciate all the more the privileges of their own present situation. By detailing Gentile deficiencies of an earlier time in such a fashion, the writer makes clear that he holds that Israel's advantages *at that time* were real ones. Israel's history did have validity, and as Gentile Christians think about their relationship to the salvation God has provided, they should be aware of a significant heritage in Israel.

Our translation takes χωρὶς Χριστοῦ predicatively as the first of the Gentile Christians' former disadvantages, not adverbially in connection with "at that time," i.e., "remember that you were, at that time, apart from Christ," not "remember that you were, at that time when you were apart from Christ, separated . . ." (*contra* J. A. Robinson, 158). It would be a striking thought for Gentile Christians to have to entertain that having been apart from Christ can be set in parallel to having been separated from Israel. Yet the writer can make this point because he conceives of Christ as the Messiah belonging to Israel. His thought here, and later in this verse, appears to be dependent on Rom 9:4, 5, where Paul could say "and of their race, according to the flesh, is the Christ." (Yet, as has been discussed in *Form/Structure/Setting*, the different perspective from the Paul of Rom 9–11 should be noted. For Rom 9:4, 5 the advantages of Israel still play a role in the time after Christ; in contrast, for Ephesians such advantages pertained only for the time prior to Christ [cf. also Rese, *TZ* 31 (1975) 211–22].) That he should make this point is indicative of the writer's Jewish viewpoint; that the matter of messianic expectation should occur to him first is indicative of his Christian perspective on Israel's former advantages. Christ could be thought of in retrospect as present to Israel through the promise (cf. also 1 Cor 10:4, though, however one understands that verse, the wording here in Ephesians does not imply "the preexistence of the Messiah in Israel," *contra* Barth, 256).

ἀπηλλοτριωμένοι τῆς πολιτείας τοῦ Ἰσραὴλ καὶ ξένοι τῶν διαθηκῶν τῆς ἐπαγγελίας, "separated from the commonwealth of Israel and aliens in regard to the covenants of promise." πολιτεία can mean right of citizenship (e.g., Josephus, *Ant.* 12.3.1; Acts 22:28), but it is more likely that it has here the meaning, which πόλις and πολίτευμα can also have, of constitutive government, state, or commonwealth (e.g., Thucydides 1.127.3; Plato, *Rep.* 10.619c; Aristotle, *Pol.* 3.6.1278b, 1279a, where πολιτεία and πολίτευμα are said to have the same force; Aeschines 3.150; 2 Macc 4:11; 8:17). Israel is, therefore, being viewed as a theocratically constituted nation. ἀπαλλοτριοῦν occurs in the NT only in Colossians and Ephesians, but in its other uses refers to estrangement from God (cf. Col 1:21; Eph 4:18). Elsewhere it is usually used of estrangement from that with which one had previously been in relationship. But that cannot be the usage here, where it has the general sense of "not in relationship to, separated from." This separation can be posited of Gentiles in regard to the commonwealth of Israel because God had restricted his electing purposes to Israel. Being separated from the commonwealth of Israel is to be considered a grave disadvantage, not because Israel is already seen as representing the heavenly commonwealth in view in v 19 (*contra* Gnilka, 135), but because of all that is involved in being outside God's election, his covenant relationship, and his line of promise, in short, in being "aliens in regard to the covenants of promise." The only other place in the NT where the plural form "the covenants" is found is Rom 9:4 where Paul states, "to them belong . . . the covenants . . . and the promises." The writer probably has in mind a series of covenants—with Abraham (Gen 15:7–21; 17:1–21), with Isaac (Gen 26:2–5), with Jacob (Gen 28:13–15), with Israel (Exod 24:1–8), and with David (2 Sam 7). All can be seen as based on promise: the promises of God's presence, of descendants, and of the land, which were so essential to Israel's existence. Paul's distinction between the Abrahamic covenant as one of promise and the Sinaitic covenant as one of law (cf. Gal 3:16–22) is not in view here. Previously, then, the Gentiles were outside the line of promise, but, as the writer will point out in 3:6, they now participate in the promise through Christ (cf. also 1:13).

ἐλπίδα μὴ ἔχοντες καὶ ἄθεοι ἐν τῷ κόσμῳ, "having no hope and without God in the world." The first part of this statement is reminiscent of 1 Thess 4:13. There it refers to lack of belief in the resurrection of the dead. That is unlikely to be its force here (*contra* Mitton, 103). Nor is it a statement that Gentiles had no hopes for the future because their golden age was in the past (*contra* J. A. Robinson, 57). A variety of hopes for the future could be found among Gentiles, and this is an evaluation of such hopes. They could be seen as no hope because they were not the true hope, based on the promise to Israel of the Messiah and the salvation of the end-time. It is only Christ among the Gentiles that can produce hope (cf. Col 1:27), and being reminded that in reality in the past they had no hope should cause the readers to appreciate all the more that hope which they now enjoy (cf. 1:18; 4:4). The term ἄθεος, "without God," occurs nowhere else in the NT or LXX. Where it is used in Greek writings, it can denote either a person who does not believe in a deity, an impious person, or a person forsaken by God or the gods. Again the writer's language here is not that of a straightforward description in either of the first two senses, for Gentiles could have a pantheon of gods and be devoted to their religion. The term is used as an evaluation. The Gentile readers may have believed in a god or gods, but they did not have the true God, Israel's God. This evaluation is similar to that of Paul in 1 Cor 8:5, 6; Gal 4:8; 1 Thess 4:5. Perhaps this comes close to the third usage mentioned above, since in comparison to Israel, with her relationship to the true God, Gentiles could be considered as God-forsaken (cf. also Meyer, 124; Gnilka, 136; Barth, 260). They lived in a world without true hope and without the true God, which means that their world can be said to fall into the category of what Paul described as "this world," or of what this writer in his earlier depiction of the Gentiles' past called "this world-age" (2:2).

13 νυνὶ δὲ ἐν Χριστῷ Ἰησοῦ ὑμεῖς οἱ ποτε ὄντες μακρὰν ἐγενήθητε ἐγγὺς ἐν τῷ αἵματι τοῦ Χριστοῦ, "But now in Christ Jesus you who at one time were far off have come near through the blood of Christ." At this point, we find the second part of the contrast schema: νυνί, "now," denoting the Christian present after the ποτέ, "then," and τῷ καιρῷ ἐκείνῳ, "at that time," of vv 11, 12, but also set over against another ποτέ in this verse, as the past is summarized in different terminology and the contrast completed. νυνὶ δὲ ἐν Χριστῷ Ἰησοῦ, "but now in Christ Jesus," has a similar effect to ὁ δὲ θεός, "but God," in 2:4, in announcing the dramatic change in the Gentiles' situation. ἐν Χριστῷ Ἰησοῦ, "in Christ Jesus," does indicate a reversal of the condition of being "apart from Christ," but it is not formulated in direct antithetical parallelism as a predicate (*contra* Tachau, "*Einst*" *und* "*Jetzt*", 140; Mussner, 73). It qualifies the verb "to come near," making clear that the change has taken place on the basis of what God has done in Christ and of believers' being included in him.

γίνεσθαι ἐγγύς, "to come near," is found only here in the NT, though it occurs frequently elsewhere (e.g., Xenophon, *Anab.* 4.7.23; 5.4.16; Thucydides 3.40.6). The use of the language of "near" and "far" here does not constitute a quotation of Isa 57:19 (*contra* Barth, 278; Stuhlmacher, "'Er ist unser Friede,'" 347), or even necessarily an allusion to it. The writer speaks of those far off having come near, a notion not found in Isa 57:19, but one which uses terminology common in Jewish discussions of proselytism. The terminology from proselytism does prompt a reference to Isa 57:19 later, in v 17, but that OT text is not yet in view in v 13. Often in the OT, the Gentile nations can be described as "far off" (רָחוֹק, *rāḥôq*; e.g., Deut 28:49; 29:22; 1 Kgs 8:41; Isa 5:26; Jer

5:15), while Israel is thought of as "near" (קרוב, *qārôb*) to God (cf. Ps 148:14). These terms, "far" and "near," later occur frequently in discussions about proselytes. The related verbs קרב, *qārēb*, and רחק, *rāḥaq*, could mean respectively "to bring a non-Israelite near to God," that is, to accept him as a proselyte, and "to hold a non-Israelite at a distance," that is, to reject him as a proselyte. One example can be found in the *Mekilta* on Exod 18:5—"R. Eliezer says: This was said to Moses by God: 'I, I who said the word by which the world came into being, I am One who welcomes (קרב), not One who repels (רחק)'. As it is said, 'Behold, I am a God that brings near (קרב), saith the Lord, and not a God that repels (רחק)' (Jer 23:23). 'I am He that brought Jethro near (קרב), not keeping him at a distance (רחק). So also thou, when a man comes to you wishing to become a convert to Judaism, as long as he comes in the name of God for the sake of heaven, do thou likewise, befriend him (קרב) and do not repel him (רחק)'" (cf. also *Num. Rab.* 8.4). Proselytes then were those who "came near" the blessing and community of Israel. The noun "proselyte" is, of course, derived ultimately from the Greek verb προσέρχεσθαι, "to approach, come near" (cf. J. A. Loader, "An Explanation of the Term 'prosēlutos,'" *NovT* 15 [1973] 270–77). קרב is also used in the Qumran literature in connection with the notion of entrance into the community (cf. 1QH 14.14; 1QS 6.16, 22; 8.18; 9.15, 16). Given what has been said about the relation of Gentiles to Israel in vv 11, 12, it is surely along the lines of traditional proselyte terminology that the writer of Ephesians has formulated his statement of the change that has taken place. In this context, "far off" also sums up the previously mentioned deficiencies of the Gentile readers' past as being far off from Christ, from the commonwealth of Israel, from the covenants of promise, and from Israel's true hope and true God.

But the language of coming near undergoes a transformation. Because of Christ's work, it can be used of Gentiles in general, not simply of proselytes to Judaism. As the rest of the passage will show, it does not mean that these Gentile Christians, like proselytes, have now become members of the commonwealth of Israel, but rather that they have become members of a newly created community whose privileges transcend those of Israel, as vv 19–22 in particular make apparent. In addition, in the coming near of which this writer speaks, there are of course no special conditions to be fulfilled, since all that is necessary has already been accomplished through Christ's sacrificial death—ἐν τῷ αἵματι τοῦ Χριστοῦ, "through the blood of Christ." For comments on the significance of "the blood of Christ," see the discussion of 1:7. The proselyte background does not mean, however, that the blood of Christ is to be associated with the sacrifice the proselyte had to bring to the temple (*contra* Kirby, *Ephesians*, 157–58; Meuzelaar, *Leib des Messias*, 99), or with Christ's circumcision (cf. Col 2:11; *contra* Sahlin, *SymBU* 12 [1950] 12; G. Vermes, *Scripture and Tradition* [Leiden: E. J. Brill, 1961] 178–92; Martin, *Reconciliation*, 192). The expression "the blood of Christ" is a frequent one in early Christian and especially Pauline usage (cf. Rom 3:25; 5:9; 1 Cor 10:16; 11:25; Col 1:20), and it retains its usual force here.

14–16 A number of the terms in these verses appear to have a dual significance—an original cosmic reference in the hymnic material and a reference to the Jew-Gentile division in the context in which the writer is now using that material. The comments which follow will concentrate on the force of the language in its present context. A brief discussion of its original force has been provided in *Form/Structure/Setting*.

Αὐτὸς γάρ ἐστιν ἡ εἰρήνη ἡμῶν, ὁ ποιήσας τὰ ἀμφότερα ἕν, "for he is our peace, who has made both one." For the far to come near, peace needed to be made between both groups. That peace has its source in, or, even stronger, is embodied in Christ. As becomes clear from vv 16–18, αὐτός, "he," is to be seen as a reference to Christ and introduces a train of thought in which Christ is the central actor. This is different from the pattern of thought of each of the three preceding sections of the letter, where God himself has been the major actor with Christ as his agent. Again, it appears likely that the use of a Christological hymn has prompted the change in pattern here. As is well known, in the OT the notion of peace (שלום, *šālôm*) involves more than the absence of war or cessation of hostilities. It denotes also positive well-being and salvation, and it is frequently seen as God's gift and as a major element of eschatological expectation. In this context in Eph 2, peace does, however, stand primarily for the cessation of hostilities and the resulting situation of unity. It is a relational concept which presupposes the overcoming of alienation (cf. vv 12, 13) and hostility (cf. v 15) between Gentiles and Jews. It is possible that for a Jew such a notion would recall the vision of eschatological peace which would prevail when the Gentiles joined Israel in worship in the temple in Zion, a vision found in Isa 2:2–4 and Micah 4:1–4, although there is no conscious effort to invoke such prophecies here. It is neither peace with God (Rom 5:1) nor cosmic peace (Col 1:20) that is the focus of attention in v 14, although it becomes clear in vv 16–18 that the former is foundational for this writer also. Peace, in v 14, is not merely a concept nor even a new state of affairs, it is bound up with a person. Christ can be said to be not only a peacemaker or a bringer of peace but peace in person. The title "prince of peace" in Isa 9:6 may have prepared the way for such an attribution of peace to a person, but the language here is hardly an allusion to that verse (*contra* Stuhlmacher, "'Er ist unser Friede,'" 345). Later rabbinic thought could call the name of God and of the Messiah "peace" (cf. Str-B 3:587) but not, of course, in specific connection with Jews and Gentiles. That Christ himself is seen as the peace between the two groups here in v 14 is in line with the thought of v 15 that the making of peace, by creating one new person in place of two, occurred "in himself." This identification of Christ with the blessings of salvation that he brings can be found in other places in the Pauline corpus (cf. 1 Cor 1:30; Col 1:27; 3:4).

In the clause "who has made both one," "both" and "one" are in the neuter, denoting entities. The neuter can be used of general categories of people (cf. 1 Cor 1:27, 28), but this is strange here after the masculine plural relative pronouns and participial endings in v 11–13. It is best explained as a remnant of the traditional material which originally referred to heaven and earth (*pace* Merklein, *Christus*, 30, 44, who claims that the writer thinks in terms of the realm of the Jews and the realm of the Gentiles, and that this is the reference here). In this context, however, the reference is clearly to the two groups of people previously discussed, the Gentiles and the Jews. They have not just been brought into a mutual relationship, but have been made one in a unity where both are no longer what they previously were (cf. vv 15, 16, 18). In accomplishing this, Christ has transcended one of the fundamental divisions of the first-century world.

καὶ τὸ μεσότοιχον τοῦ φραγμοῦ λύσας, τὴν ἔχθραν ἐν τῇ σαρκὶ αὐτοῦ τὸν νόμον τῶν ἐντολῶν ἐν δόγμασιν καταργήσας, "and has broken down the dividing wall, the fence, having abolished in his flesh the hostility, the law of commandments and regulations." A justification for taking the syntax of the Greek in this way has been offered in the observations on the text in *Notes*. Such an arrangement means that the second clause can be taken as a further explanation of the first. τὸ μεσότοιχον, "the dividing wall," occurs only here in the NT. τοῦ φραγμοῦ, "the fence," is a genitive of apposition—"the dividing wall, that is, the fence" (cf. also, e.g., Meyer, 127; Abbott, 61; Schlier, 124). We have already suggested that originally the dividing wall had reference to a cosmic wall. The explanation that it is a fence is the writer's gloss in order to adapt the concept to this new context. In making the two groups one, Christ demolished the fence between them.

There are two main options as to what the writer intended by the fence between Jews and Gentiles. Some take it as a reference to the temple balustrade separating the Court of Gentiles from the inner courts and the sanctuary in the Jerusalem temple (cf. Josephus, *Ant.* 15.11.5; *J. W.* 5.5.2). In 1871 one of its pillars was found and on it was the warning inscription: "No man of another race is to enter within the fence and enclosure around the Temple. Whoever is caught will have only himself to thank for the death which follows." Such a reference would powerfully symbolize the alienation of Gentiles from Israel, and temple imagery is used when the writer comes to speak of their new situation in vv 20–22 (cf. J. A. Robinson, 59–60, 158; Abbott, 51; Hanson, *Unity*, 143; McKelvey, *The New Temple*, 108; Mussner, *Christus*, 82–84; Houlden, 290; Mitton, 106). But how likely is it that Gentile Christians in Asia Minor would have understood such an allusion (cf. Dibelius, 69)? How likely is it that knowledge of it would have been commonplace after the destruction of the temple in 70 C.E.? And why does the writer use the term φραγμός for the balustrade when the term found both in the inscription and in the references in Josephus is δρύφακτος? If "having broken down the dividing wall, the fence" is paralleled by "having abolished . . . the hostility, the law. . . ," then it seems more likely that the fence is a reference to the law. The notion of the oral tradition as providing a fence for Torah was a familiar one (cf. *m. 'Abot* 1.1, 2; 3.18), but Torah itself could be seen as providing a fence around Israel. In the second century B.C.E. the *Epistle of Aristeas* declared: "our lawgiver . . . fenced us about [περιφράσσειν] with impenetrable palisades and with walls of iron to the end that we should mingle in no way with any of the other nations, remaining pure in body and in spirit" (139) and "so that we should be polluted by none nor be infected with perversions by associating with worthless persons, he has fenced us about [περιφράσσειν] on all sides with prescribed purifications in matters of food and drink and touch and hearing and sight" (142). It can easily be seen that in functioning as a fence to protect Israel from the impurity of the Gentiles, the law became such a sign of Jewish particularism that it also alienated Gentiles and became a cause of hostility (cf. also Gnilka, 140; Caird, 58–59; Martin, *Reconciliation*, 185–87).

Christ removed or abolished this hostility. ἔχθρα, "hostility," which in the traditional material would have referred originally to the enmity caused by the hostile powers in the cosmos, now refers to the hostility between Jews and Gentiles that is bound up with the law, as τὸν νόμον, "the law," which stands in apposition to τὴν ἔχθραν, makes clear. The objective situation of hostility because of the law's exclusiveness engendered personal and social antagonisms. The laws which forbade eating or intermarrying with Gentiles often led Jews to have a contempt for Gentiles which could regard Gentiles as less than human. In response, Gentiles would often regard Jews with great suspicion, considering them inhospitable and hateful to non-Jews, and indulge in anti-Jewish prejudice (for a collection of material reflecting the hostility from the Jewish side of the divide cf. Str-B 1:359–63; 3:588–91, and for an example from the Gentile side cf. Tacitus, *Hist.* 5.1–13). This lively mutual animosity was one of the uglier elements in the Greco-Roman world.

Christ neutralized these negative effects of the law by doing away with the law. A number of commentators shrink back from such a forthright assertion. Some provide the dogmatic gloss that it was only the ceremonial and not the moral law that was abolished (cf. Hendriksen, 135). Others suggest that it is simply the legalistic, casuistic use of the law that is done away with (cf. Schlier, 126). Still others hold that only one aspect of the law, the law in its divisiveness, but not the law itself, has been annulled (cf. Barth, 287–91). But these efforts to absolve the writer from an alleged antinomianism or supposed contradiction of the major Paulines will not do as an interpretation of τὸν νόμον τῶν ἐντολῶν ἐν δόγμασιν καταργήσας. This lengthy formulation—literally, "the law consisting of commandments which are expressed in regulations"—is characteristic of the style of Ephesians and, at the same time, conveys a sense of the oppressiveness of all the law's commandments. But it is clearly the law itself and all its regulations, not just some of them, which are in view. The formulation may be under the influence of Col 2:14, which is the only other instance of the use of the term δόγματα in the Pauline corpus. There it refers not so much to the Torah as to ascetic regulations (cf. also Col 2:20: δογματίζεσθε), with which Christ dealt in his death. But in discussing how Christ dealt with the law in his death here in Ephesians, the writer may have transferred this term with its pejorative overtones. Given the overall dependence of Ephesians on Colossians, such a transference is likely to have been the work of the writer himself, rather than the gloss of a later redactor, despite the variant reading in P[46] which omits ἐν δόγμασιν (*contra* Roetzel, *ZNW* 74 [1983] 86). Barth (287–91) is, of course, correct to make a close link between the law and its divisiveness; this is demanded by the context. But to make divisiveness one aspect of the law, and the only aspect which is abolished, misses the thrust of v 15. The divisiveness was produced by the law as such, by the very fact that Israel possessed the Torah, and so in order to remove the divisiveness Christ has to deal with its cause—the law itself. He does this "in his flesh." Ephesians nowhere else speaks of Christ's flesh. The analogy with Col 1:22, "in the body of his flesh," suggests that by this phrase the writer intends a reference to Christ's death. In his death Christ abolished the law (cf. Gal 3:13 and Rom 7:4, which associate Christ's death with breaking the law's condemnation and power) and terminated the old order dominated by that law, which had prevented the Gentiles from having access to salvation.

How does this relate to Paul's view of the law? The nature of Paul's view is a highly disputed issue and the limits of space allow us only a brief and therefore oversimplified response. For Paul too the period of the law had come to an end (cf. Gal 2:19; 3:24, 25; Rom 6:14; 7:4–6; 10:4). But, just as we have had cause to observe in regard to his attitude to Israel, in Romans, in particular, he is somewhat more dialectical than this. He can say that believers have been discharged (κατηργήθημεν) from the law in Rom 7:6, but this is different from saying that the law itself has been annulled. Indeed in Rom 3:31 he is at pains to rebut that interpretation of his teaching—"Do we then abolish [καταργοῦμεν] the law by faith? By no means! We establish the law." It is important to understand what Paul means by this last assertion in its context. He does not mean that the law still retains its validity for the new people of God made up of Jews and Gentiles. His point is a narrower one. The law is established by faith, because, as he goes on to show in the immediately following passage (Rom 4:1–25), the law in Gen 15:6 and in its depiction of Abraham, already contains an exposition of his gospel of justification by faith. Though he establishes the law only in the sense of showing that it supports his teaching, it remains significant that Paul feels it necessary to deny the charge of completely abolishing it, and that later in Rom 7 he provides some sort of defense of the law in itself, and in Rom 13:8–10 insists that love involves the fulfilling of the law. We can say that at this point Ephesians is in line with the clear stress on discontinuity in regard to the law's validity that can be found in Paul. But, living in a period when the strong influence of the Jerusalem church and of Jewish Christianity is past, and when Paul's basic perspective on the law is taken for granted by the churches of the Gentile mission in Asia Minor, its writer finds no need to tread as delicately as the Paul of Romans and can present the logic of his master's position in an unqualified fashion. It is, by the way, not without significance that, having made the assertion about the law and its commandments having been abolished, the writer can later draw on one of those commandments (ἐντολὴ πρώτη ἐν ἐπαγγελίᾳ, "the first commandment with a promise," 6:2) for secondary support for his own paraenesis.

ἵνα τοὺς δύο κτίσῃ ἐν αὐτῷ εἰς ἕνα καινὸν ἄνθρωπον ποιῶν εἰρήνην, "in order that he might create the two in himself into one new person, thus making peace." Removing the enmity by abolishing the law has cleared the ground for something new. In fact, Christ's purpose was nothing less than a new creation. We have already encountered this motif in 2:10 where believers were seen as God's creation. Here Christ, particularly through his death (cf. ἐν τῇ σαρκὶ αὐτοῦ earlier in the verse), is seen as the creator of a new humanity. Again, whatever the original force of such language in relation to the cosmic Christ, in this context the one new person stands for the new humanity seen as a corporate entity. Christ has created this corporate new person in himself; the new humanity is embraced in his own person. This notion is dependent on Paul's Adamic Christology, with its associated ideas of Christ as inclusive representative of the new order and of believers being incorporated into him (cf. 1 Cor 12:12, 13; 15:22, 45–49; Gal 3:27, 28; Rom 12:5; Col 3:10, 11). Already, in Paul, such a concept was employed to argue that divisions of race and religion were a thing of the past (cf. Gal 3:28; Col 3:11). Now here in Ephesians it is said that Christ has taken the two divisive elements—Jews and

Gentiles—and created one new person which transcends the two. This is a new creation (cf. Gal 6:15; 2 Cor 5:17) which embodies, on a human level, that summing up of all things in unity which is part of this writer's perspective (cf. 1:10). In common with Paul's view of this new creation in Gal 6:15, in it neither circumcision nor uncircumcision counts for anything. It needs to be underlined that according to Eph 2:15 the nature of Christ's work was a creation, and its product was something new. The separation of the Gentiles from Israel and her election was a cleft so deep that it took the creative act of Christ's death to fill it. Yet Christ has done more than simply to bring Gentiles into Israel's election. The "new person" he has created transcends those categories. In its newness, it is not merely an amalgam of the old in which the best of Judaism and the best of Gentile aspirations have been combined. The two elements which were used in the creation have become totally transformed in the process. This is "the third race" which is different from both Jews and Gentiles (cf. Paul's language in 1 Cor 10:32; cf. Gaugler, 111–12; *contra* Barth, 310). It is possible that in this context "new creation" language could provide a further association with the background of proselyte terminology. In *Joseph and Asenath* 61.4, 5 the proselyte Asenath is said to be "made anew, freshly created, and brought to new life" from the day of her conversion, while in *Gen. Rab.* 39.14 it is said that if anyone brings a Gentile near and makes him a proselyte it is as if he had created him. As in v 13, the language of proselyte conversion would find wider application, here to both Gentiles and Jews as they became part of the new humanity in Christ (cf. also N. A. Dahl, "Christ, Creation, and the Church," in *The Background to the New Testament and Its Eschatology*, ed. W. D. Davies and D. Daube [Cambridge: Cambridge University Press, 1956] 437). A new creation has neutralized the old hostility and thereby peace has been made. The peace in view at this point is between the two old enemies, not with God, and making peace here, as in Col 1:20, is a synonym for reconciling, the notion which follows immediately.

καὶ ἀποκαταλλάξῃ τοὺς ἀμφοτέρους ἐν ἑνὶ σώματι τῷ θεῷ διὰ τοῦ σταυροῦ, ἀποκτείνας τὴν ἔχθραν ἐν αὐτῷ, "and might reconcile both to God in one body through the cross, having put the hostility to death in himself." Up to this point the focus has been on peace on the horizontal level, between Jews and Gentiles, but now this is combined with a vertical perspective as the notion of a reconciliation of both Jews and Gentiles to God is introduced. It is making too much of the fact that reconciliation between Jews and Gentiles is mentioned before reconciliation with God to argue that this reflects a major theological distinctive of Ephesians, whereby ecclesiology absorbs soteriology (*pace* Merklein, *Christus*, 62–71). This claim ignores both the influence of the traditional material on the writer's sequence of thought and the fact that the argument has been set up by the writer in vv 11–13 primarily in terms of the contrast between Gentile and Jew, so that one would naturally expect that issue to be treated first. The previous horizontal perspective does not fade out of the picture in v 16, for the two groups are said to be reconciled in one body. The writer has taken what may well have been originally a reference to the cosmos as applying to the Church in this context. The qualifying adjective "one" makes clear that he has the Church in mind (cf. Eph 4:4; also Col 1:18; cf. also Meyer, 135–36; Best, *One Body*, 153; Gnilka, 143; Merklein, *Christus*, 45–54; Caird, 59; Mitton, 108; Schnackenburg, 117) and not the physical crucified body of Christ (*contra* Percy, *Probleme*, 281; Barth, 298) or both (*contra* Hanson, *Unity*, 145–46; Schlier, 135).

The compound verb ἀποκαταλλάσσειν, "to reconcile," occurs elsewhere only in Col 1:20, 22. There the author had taken the term from the hymn, where it involved the overcoming of cosmic hostility and restoration of harmony between heaven and earth (1:20), and applied it, instead of the simpler form καταλλάσσειν used in Rom 5:10 and 2 Cor 5:18 (cf. also καταλλαγή, "reconciliation," in Rom 5:11; 11:15; 2 Cor 5:18, 19), to the restoration of sinful humanity to God's acceptance and favor. This provided a precedent for the writer to the Ephesians in making a similar transition from the use of the term in the cosmic context of the traditional material to its application here to Jews and Gentiles. It is the emphasis on this horizontal, social dimension that Ephesians contributes to the notion of reconciliation which it takes up from Paul. Such a dimension is not entirely absent from Paul, for, in its context, his appeal to be reconciled to God in 2 Cor 5:20 is at the same time an appeal for reconciliation within the community of faith, and specifically for a reconciliation between the Corinthians and himself. (On reconciliation in Paul, see J. Dupont, *La réconciliation dans la théologie de saint Paul* [Paris: Desclée de Brouwer, 1953]; J. A. Fitzmyer, "Reconciliation in Pauline Theology," in *No Famine in the Land*, ed. J. W. Flanagan and A. W. Robinson [Missoula, MT: Scholars Press, 1975] 155–77; O. Hofius, "Erwägungen zur Gestalt und Herkunft des paulinischen Versöhnungsgedankens," *ZTK* 77 [1980] 186–99; E. Käsemann, "Some Thoughts on the Theme 'The Doctrine of Reconciliation in the New Testament,'" in *The Future of Our Religious Past*, ed. J. M. Robinson [New York: Harper and Row, 1971] 49–64; D. Lührmann, "Rechtfertigung und Versöhnung. Zur Geschichte der paulinischen Tradition," *ZTK* 67 [1970] 437–52; I. H. Marshall, "The Meaning of 'Reconciliation,'" in *Unity and Diversity in New Testament Theology*, ed. R. A. Guelich [Grand Rapids: Eerdmans, 1978] 117–32; R. P. Martin, *Reconciliation: A Study of Paul's Theology;* H. Ridderbos, "The Biblical Message of Reconciliation," in *Studies in Scripture and Its Authority* [Grand Rapids: Eerdmans, 1978] 72–90; P. Stuhlmacher and H. Class, *Das Evangelium von der Versöhnung in Christus* [Stuttgart: Calwer Verlag, 1979] (ET of Stuhlmacher's essay: "The Gospel of Reconciliation in Christ—Basic Features and Issues of a Biblical Theology of the New Testament," *HBT* 1 [1979] 161–90); V. Taylor, *Forgiveness and Reconciliation* [London: Macmillan, 1946].)

Reconciliation of Gentiles and Jews in one body is a parallel thought to that of the creation of the two groups into one new person, and what one would expect as a resolution to the situation of hostility mentioned in v 15. Reconciliation of both groups to God, however, adds an element which does not fit quite as smoothly into the previous context. It is clear from that context that the Gentiles' alienation from Israel involved alienation from God (v 12). But what about Israel? Is not the impression given by vv 12, 13 that Israel's election means that, as distinct from the Gentiles, she is not alienated from God, but rather she is near? But now v 16 speaks of both Jews and Gentiles being reconciled to God. This somewhat conflicting perspective is another indication that vv 14–18 introduce a new element into the discussion, so that v 19 does not simply take up where v 13 left off with a straightforward reversal of the Gentiles' previous relationship to Israel. Verses 14–18 show that what produced the reversal in the Gentiles' status was of such a nature as to relativize the earlier categories and even shed a different light on what had appeared to be Israel's status. Though he obviously does not spell it out, if he were pressed to explain why Jews are now said to be reconciled to God, the writer would presumably respond that the law which separated Gentiles from Israel, and from Israel's God, can now be seen to have also separated Israel from God, and would point to Paul's teaching to this effect in Gal 3:10–22; 2 Cor 3:7–11; Rom 3:19, 20; 7:7–25; 9:30–10:4. The writer has himself already made clear that not only his Gentile readers, but all humanity, were under God's wrath (2:3). Both Jews and Gentiles, then, were in a ruptured relationship with God, at enmity not only between themselves but with God. Yet Christ has now reconciled both groups to God through the cross. This emphasis on the cross may well be, as we suggested earlier, the writer's addition to the traditional material, and as such it would be in line with the editorial additions which mention the cross in Phil 2:8 and Col 1:20. Christ's death is linked with reconciliation in Paul's thought in Rom 5:10; 2 Cor 5:18–21; and Col 1:22. The focus on Christ's death, through the mention of the cross here in v 16, his flesh in v 15, and his blood in v 13, is an important indication that although the writer draws attention in the main to the risen and exalted Christ (cf. 1:19–23; 2:5, 6), he is a faithful enough follower of Paul to insist on Christ's sacrificial death on the cross as the grounds of reconciliation (cf. also the mention of Christ's death in 1:7; 5:2, 25). As the rest of the chapter shows, the reconciliation to God that Christ's death has achieved for both Jews and Gentiles involves access to God (v 18), membership in his family (v 19), and being part of the new temple in which he dwells (v 22).

The last clause, "having put the hostility to death in himself," stands as a parallel to "having abolished the hostility in his flesh" in v 15. Some take ἐν αὐτῷ in its present context as a reference to the cross as the most immediate antecedent (e.g., Gnilka, 144; idem, "Christus unser Friede," 205). But in the light of the force of αὐτός in its various forms throughout vv 14–16 it is better to take this use as a reference to Christ himself, though it will be his death which is particularly in view (cf. ἐν τῇ σαρκὶ αὐτοῦ, "in his flesh," v 15). In his own person given over to death, Christ put to death the hostility bound up with the law. It has been claimed that the hostility mentioned here, in contrast to its earlier reference in v 15, is now hostility between humanity and God, since reconciliation to God has just been discussed (cf. Barth, 264, 291; Gaugler, 117–18, believes both kinds of hostility are in view). This claim, however, ignores the fact that the last clause with its aorist participle involves a backward reference to Christ's action preceding the reconciliation in one body and to God (cf. also Meyer, 136). It rounds off the thought at this point by reminding of the situation of hostility described earlier in vv 11–13 and reemphasizing that Christ's death has changed that past situation.

17 καὶ ἐλθὼν εὐηγγελίσατο εἰρήνην ὑμῖν τοῖς μακρὰν καὶ εἰρήνην τοῖς ἐγγύς, "and he came and preached the good news of peace to you who were far off and of peace to those who were near." Having dwelt on Christ's work of reconciliation, the writer can now take up again the proselyte terminology of "far" and "near" and introduce the OT citation such language had recalled. Of course, the original reference of "far" and "near" in Isa 57:19 was not to Gentiles and Jews but to two groups of Jews, those in exile and those who remained in the land. In later Jewish interpretations of the text, however, 'far' and 'near' could refer to other divisions within Israel—those who through sin have fallen away from God and the righteous (*b. Ber.* 34b) or repentant sinners and the righteous (*Num. Rab.* 11.7; *Mek. Exod.* 20.25). But there was also a tradition which interpreted the "far" of Isa 57:19 as Gentiles—Gentile proselytes (*contra* Martin, *Reconciliation,* 191, who denies any application of the text to proselytes). *Num. Rab.* 8 has an extended discussion of proselytes, in which in one place on the basis of the word order in Isa 57:19 a certain advantage can even be attributed to proselytes: "Why all this? To inform you that the Holy One, blessed be He, brings nigh those that are distant and supports the distant just as the nigh. Nay more, He gives peace to the distant sooner than to the nigh, as it says, 'Peace, peace to him that is far off and to him that is near' (Isa 57:19)" (*Num. Rab.* 8.4 cf. also *Midr. Sam.* 28.6). Just as the writer to the Ephesians had earlier, in v 13, broadened the reference of the far who have come near from proselytes to all Gentile Christians, so here, reading his text in the light of Christ's peacemaking work, he broadens its application so that it is no longer simply a reference to Israelites, as in the OT and parts of rabbinic tradition, nor to proselytes and Israelites, as in other parts of rabbinic tradition, but to his Gentile readers and Jews. (This is far more likely than the speculative notion of D. C. Smith, "Ephesian Heresy," 45–54, followed by Martin, *Reconciliation,* 191–92, that the writer cites Isa 57:19 because it was being exploited by Gentile Christian opponents, former proselytes to Judaism, who reasoned along the lines of *Num. Rab.* 8.4 in order to support their claims of superiority to ethnic Jews).

The LXX wording of Isa 57:19, which reflects the Hebrew construction of the MT, is εἰρήνην ἐπ' εἰρήνῃ τοῖς μακρὰν καὶ τοῖς ἐγγὺς οὖσιν, "peace upon peace to those who are far off and to those who are near." The most significant modification of this text in its appearance in Eph 2:17 is the creative combination that has been made with the notion of preaching peace from Isa 52:7, whereby εἰρήνην, "peace," becomes the object of εὐηγγελίσατο, "he proclaimed." The LXX wording of this part of Isa 52:7 is εὐαγγελιζομένου ἀκοὴν εἰρήνης, "preaching the good news of peace," but in Eph 2:17 the construction of the MT is apparently preferred to that of the LXX. There is evidence of the messianic interpretation of this text in *Pesiq. R.* 35 (cf. also Str-B 3:9–11), but there are questions about how early and widespread this tradition is likely to have been. Certainly this aspect of the servant passages lent itself to Christological interpretation by the early Christians, and here such an interpretation clearly enables the writer to link what he has said about Christ as the embodiment of peace and about his work of reconciliation in vv 14–16 to the "peace to the far and near" language of the Isa 57:19 citation. He also makes use of the langauge of Isa 52:7 in a different context in Eph 6:15.

Other significant differences appear when the wording of Eph 2:17 is compared to Isa 57:19. The twofold reference to peace at the beginning (εἰρήνην ἐπ' εἰρήνῃ, the LXX "peace upon peace") has been broken up so that the rewording, with the second εἰρήνην immediately before "to those who were near," now emphasizes that Christ's peace is proclaimed to the two distnct groups, Gentiles and Jews. But what is the nature of the peace which is proclaimed? Is it peace between the two groups or is it peace with God, which v 16 has brought into the picture? If the wording were "preached peace to the far and near," it could be taken to mean primarily an announcement of peace between the two groups. However, the wording of the verse, which in fact has peace preached to the two groups separately, tips the scales against a horizontal reference for peace as the primary one. The force of the rewording is that a vertical reference for peace now becomes the primary one. Since v 16 has made clear that both groups, "the near" as well as "the far," require reconciliation with God, it is likely that v 17, by talking of a proclamation of peace by Christ to each of the groups, has this vertical dimension primarily in view (cf. also Mussner, *Christus,* 101–2; Merklein, *Christus,* 59–60; Burger, *Schöpfung,* 155; Wolter, *Rechtfertigung,* 71; *contra* Barth, 278). That the vertical reference for peace becomes dominant in v 17 is reinforced by the elaboration of v 18 with its assertion that through Christ the two groups now have access "to the Father." So Christ proclaims a peace with God to each of the groups. But as the preceding context makes inescapably clear, this has inevitable repercussions on the horizontal level for peace between Jews and Gentiles (Lindemann, *Aufhebung,* 84, 177–78, correctly sees this vertical emphasis, but is not to be followed in his attempt to rid the passage of any salvation-history perspective, nor in his beliefs that the author misunderstood the LXX wording he has changed and that the citation does not fit its context in 2:14–18).

A further addition to Isa 57:19 by the writer is the ὑμῖν, "to you," before τοῖς μακράν, "who were far off." This aspect of address to Gentile Christian readers was clear in vv 11–13, and now v 17 takes up again the second person plural pronoun from v 13, a further indication that the material in vv 14–16 provides a parenthetical preparation for the citation in v 17. It is also an indication that the OT citation in this verse does not stand in its own right as a prediction or prophecy which is then said to be fulfilled, but rather provides the wording used in address to the readers. The writer has not lost sight of the fact that his reflection on the message about peace to Jews and Gentiles is part of his specific address to his Gentile readers, reminding them of the new situation into which they have entered through their Christian confession.

The lead into the combined citation at the beginning of v 17, "and he came," still needs comment. If we are correct that vv 14–16 prepare the ground for the Christological interpretation of Isa 52:7 and 57:19, then the καὶ ἐλθών clause provides a transition which summarizes this preparatory material. Such a perspective on the flow of thought in the passage renders redundant much of the discussion about which specific aspect of Christ's ministry the clause has in view. Some take it as a reference to the proclamation of the earthly Jesus (cf. Fischer, *Tendenz,* 131–32; Mitton, 109), others as a reference to the proclamation of the exalted Christ through the apostles (cf. Abbott, 66; Schille, *Frühchristliche Hymnen,* 30; Gnilka, 146; Caird, 60; Bratcher and Nida, *Handbook,* 59), and others as a telescoping together of the Redeemer's ascent, his manifestation to the powers, and his manifestation to the world (cf. Schlier, 137–39). Still others have taken it as a general reference to the whole of Christ's work (cf. Mussner, 84–85; *Christus,* 101; Stuhlmacher, "'Er ist unser Friede,'" 353 n. 59; Burger, *Schöpfung, 156;* Lindemann, *Aufhebung,* 176–77). But it can now be seen a little more specifically as a retrospective reference to vv 14–16, i.e., to that coming of Christ which climaxed in his reconciling death. It is the effect of that accomplishment on the cross (v 16) which can be identified as a preaching of the good news of peace to the far off, the Gentiles, and a preaching of that same good news to the near, the Jews.

18 ὅτι δι' αὐτοῦ ἔχομεν τὴν προσαγωγὴν οἱ ἀμφότεροι ἐν ἑνὶ πνεύματι πρὸς τὸν πατέρα, "for through him we both have access in the one Spirit to the Father." ὅτι, "for," introduces this statement as one which provides the grounds for the assertion of the previous verse that Christ has proclaimed peace to the far off and peace to the near. This reinforces our interpretation of the nature of the peace announced to the two groups. Since both have access to the Father through Christ in the one Spirit, the same good news of peace with God can be brought to both. The language of Rom 5:1, 2 appears to have influenced the writer, for there also having peace with God and having access to grace go together. The term προσαγωγή is taken up again in Ephesians in 3:12, and in all three instances of its use in the NT it is best taken with the intransitive sense of "access" rather than with the transitive sense of "introduction." For Caird (60) the imagery of the term προσαγωγή is political rather than cultic. He claims that "formerly the Jews alone had the rights of citizenship, including the right of audience with the King, while Gentiles lived in the distant provinces of God's empire; but now Jewish privilege has been abolished, and for both Jew and Gentile access to God is available through Christ." It is true that the term can be used for audience with a king (cf. Xenophon, *Cyr.* 1.3.8; 7.5.45), and in this context both v 12 and v 19 contain political imagery. Yet, the notion of approach to God has obvious religious and cultic connotations from the OT, where in the LXX προσάγειν is used of bringing offerings in order to come before God (e.g., LXX Lev 1:3; 3:3; 4:14). Here in Eph 2, where v 13 contains sacrificial imagery and vv 20–22 contain temple imagery, the cultic associations of προσαγωγή as unhindered access to the sanctuary as the place of God's presence must be just as strong as, if not stronger than, the political. It is worth recalling some of the passages in the OT which envisage Gentiles acquiring access to God in the temple in order to pray and worship. Solomon's prayer of dedication in 1 Kgs 8:41–43 speaks of the foreigner who "comes and prays toward this house" and asks God "hear thou in heaven thy dwelling place," while prophecies such as Isa 56:6–8 and Zech 8:20–23 see foreigners coming to Zion to offer sacrifices, to seek the Lord and entreat his favor in the temple which is a house of prayer for all peoples. The writer of Ephesians asserts that the privilege of access, previously known only to one of the parties, the Jews, has now been provided for both parties. Yet again it is not simply that the Gentiles can enjoy what the Jews have enjoyed all the time and continue to enjoy. The old categories are transcended. The access of which the writer speaks is through Christ and is not confined to a specific locality such as the temple.

It is also access to a new relationship to God as Father through the one Spirit. Through Christ, God is experienced as the Father of believers (cf. 1:5), and the Spirit plays his part in mediating a consciousness of that relationship (cf. Gal 4:6; Rom 8:15, 16). The sphere of the flesh (cf. v 11) produced only division between Gentile and Jew, but now in the sphere of the Spirit both have access (cf. also Merklein, *Christus*, 60–61). The emphasis on "the one

Spirit" is parallel to that on "the one body" in v 16, and the two notions occur together again in 4:4, "there is one body and one Spirit." In the one body lives and works the one Spirit. This is a theme which Paul had developed in 1 Cor 12:4–13, especially in v 13, "For by one Spirit we were all baptized into one body—Jews or Greeks, slaves or free—and all were made to drink of one Spirit." The writer has taken up this theme in his own discussion of the uniting of Jews and Gentiles, and it is interesting to note how naturally his thought expresses itself in the "trinitarian" pattern of "through Christ in the Spirit to the Father" (cf. also 1:3, 17; 4:4–6). Access to God as Father through Christ and in the Spirit is the ground of the peace proclaimed to both Jews and Gentiles, but it is also true that the exercise of this new privilege by both groups in the one Spirit is the sign of the peace between them (on the latter cf. also Barth, 312).

19 ἄρα οὖν οὐκέτι ἐστὲ ξένοι καὶ πάροικοι, ἀλλὰ ἐστὲ συμπολῖται τῶν ἁγίων καὶ οἰκεῖοι τοῦ θεοῦ, "so then you are no longer aliens and strangers, but you are fellow citizens with the holy ones and members of the household of God." ἄρα οὖν, "so then," announces a summarizing statement of the main point the writer has been attempting to make. The statement is made in such a way as to provide at the same time a transition to a further development of the argument, as the writer elaborates on the imagery he has introduced. It is formulated in terms of the contrast between the pre-Christian past and the Christian present of the readers, which the writer had left in v 13 in order to explain in vv 14–18 how this contrast had been made possible by Christ's work of reconciliation. His Gentile readers' former status as ξένοι, "aliens," and πάροικοι, "strangers," in relation to Israel (cf. v 12) has been left behind. It is possible that there is a distinction between these terms and that ξένος represents the foreigner, while πάροικος has in view the stranger in the land or the resident alien. But there is no clear difference between the two words in the LXX, where either can be used to translate the Hebrew גֵּר, gēr, and where πάροικος also translates both גּוֹי, gôy, "Gentile," and תּוֹשָׁב, tôšāb, "resident alien," and so it could well be that here in Ephesians also they are not meant to be sharply distinguished and that, in line with the style of this letter, two terms are used, where one would have sufficed, in order to emphasize the Gentiles' previous "outsider" status.

But the readers are no longer completely without a homeland; they are no longer even second-class citizens in someone else's homeland. They now have full citizenship in and belong firmly to a commonwealth, for they are fellow citizens with the holy ones. But who are the ἅγιοι in this reference? Five different interpretations have been put forward: (*i*) Israel or the Jews (cf. Meuzelaar, *Leib des Messias*, 63–64; Barth, 269–70), (*ii*) Jewish Christians (cf. O. Proksch, "αγιος," *TDNT* 1 [1964] 106; Roels, *God's Mission*, 145; Vielhauer, *Oikodome*, 123; Caird, 60), (*iii*) the first Christians seen as a golden generation (cf. Houlden, 292), (*iv*) all believers (cf. Meyer, 141; J. A. Robinson, 67; Abbott, 69; S. Hanson, *Unity*, 147; Gaugler, 120; Mussner, *Christus*, 105–6; Pfammatter, *Die Kirche als Bau*, 76–77; Merklein, *Das kirchliche Amt*, 132; Mitton, 110; Ernst, 322; Bratcher and Nida, *Handbook*, 60–61), and (*v*) the angels (cf. Gärtner, *Temple*, 63–64; Schlier, 140–41; Mussner, 89–91; idem, "Contributions," 166, reversing his previous view in *Christus*, 105–6; Steinmetz, *Protologische Heilszuversicht*, 48 n. 63; Klinzing, *Umdeutung*, 185; Gnilka, 154; Lindemann, *Aufhebung*,

183). In support of the first two interpretations it is argued that this phrase in v 19 stands in contrast to "separated from the commonwealth of Israel" in v 12. But neither of these interpretations, and particularly the first, does enough justice to the fact that in the contrast the writer presents, his Gentile readers' new status transcends the old categories, and that in the creation of the one new person Jew-Gentile distinctions have been overcome. In addition, the second interpretation claims that ἅγιοι is used elsewhere in the Pauline corpus as a reference to Jewish Christians (cf. Rom 15:25, 26, 31; 1 Cor 16:1; 2 Cor 8:4; 9:1, 12). But, in fact, none of these instances, which occur in the context of Paul's discussion of the collection, refer to Jewish Christians in general, but all refer to the Jerusalem church in particular. The third interpretation can appeal to the use of ἅγιος to describe the apostles and prophets in Eph 3:5, but this seems to be too narrow a focus for the phrase in 2:19, and in any case the readers' relation to the apostles and prophets is specifically dealt with in the different imagery of 2:20.

The fourth and fifth interpretations both recognize that in the contrast with v 12 a simple reversal is not in view, and it is difficult to decide between them. In favor of the reference to all believers are the facts that in this writer's view they now constitute the people of God as Israel did in the past, that elsewhere in the letter ἅγιοι is used of Christians in general (cf. 1:1, 15, 18; 3:8; 4:12; 5:3; 6:18), and that the συν- compounds in vv 21, 22 and in 3:6 have in view unity with the rest of the Church. In support of the reference to angels it can be argued that the OT describes angels as "the holy ones" (e.g., Job 15:15; Ps 89:5, 6), that ἅγιοι is used of angels elsewhere in the Pauline corpus (cf. 1 Thess 3:13; 2 Thess 1:7, 10), and that its occurrence in Col 1:12 may well be a reference to angels. In addition, there appear to be strong parallels in the Qumran writings, where "the holy ones" are the angels in heaven with whom the elect community on earth is joined (cf. 1QS 11.7, 8, where the concept of fellowship with the angels is closely linked to that of the community as the temple, also 1QH 3.21–23; 6.10–14; 1QM 12.1, 2). Paul had made use of the concept of believers' attachment to a heavenly commonwealth (πολίτευμα) in Phil 3:20 and the notion of citizenship of heaven is a familiar one in Philo (e.g., *Confus.* 78: πατρίδα μὲν τὸν οὐράνιον χῶρον ἐν ᾧ πολιτεύἀ ονται, "the heavenly region, where their citizenship lies, is their native land") and in early Christian writings (e.g., *Diogn.* 5.9 where believers on earth have their citizenship in heaven: ἐν οὐρανῷ πολιτεύονται). Paul had also made use of the concept of believers' relationship to a heavenly city, the Jerusalem above, in Gal 4:26. The writer to the Hebrews combines this concept with that of fellowship with the angels in Heb 12:22, "you have come to Mount Zion and to the city of the living God, the heavenly Jerusalem, and to innumerable angels in festal gathering." Believers' participation in the heavenly realm has already been featured in 2:6, and it may just be that the idea of a heavenly citizenship with the angels was widespread enough for this to have been understood by the readers as the meaning of συμπολῖται τῶν ἁγίων. But the consistency of meaning for ἅγιοι in its other appearances in Ephesians must give one pause before proposing a different reference in 2:19, and so it may well be more prudent to opt for the fourth alternative. The readers are to see themselves as fellow citizens with the rest of believers.

Not only so, but they are now also οἰκεῖοι τοῦ θεοῦ, "members of God's household." There is a move here from the political imagery of the state of commonwealth to the more intimate picture of a family. οἰκεῖος appears elsewhere in the NT in Gal 6:10 and 1 Tim 5:8. Here its use can be seen as part of a double contrast—both with v 12, where Gentiles were said to be without God, God-forsaken, while here they are depicted as in the bosom of his family, and with the term used earlier in this verse, which also has associations with οἶκος, namely πάροικοι, "those who are away from home," while now Gentiles are to see themselves as at home in God's household. In this way v 19 can be regarded as a restatement of the far and near contrast of v 13. The Gentile readers are no longer far off from Israel and from God as foreigners and outsiders. Their proximity to God now is such that they are fellow citizens with the saints and members of God's own family (*pace* Merklein, *Das kirchliche Amt*, 133–34, and Mussner, 92, who draw attention to the cultic associations of οἶκος τοῦ θεοῦ and see here already a reference to the temple, the term οἰκεῖος itself is most naturally understood as a member of a household rather than as a dweller in the temple).

20–22 ἐποικοδομηθέντες ἐπὶ τῷ θεμελίῳ τῶν ἀποστόλων καὶ προφητῶν, "having been built on the foundation of the apostles and prophets." In these verses the writer introduces building and temple imagery for the new community of the Church, of which his Gentile Christian readers had now become a part. This transition in his thought is facilitated by the ability of οἶκος (cf. οἰκεῖοι in v 19) to refer to household, house, or temple. The imagery at the beginning of v 20 involves the readers' being depicted as bricks which have been built up in a building on top of a foundation (cf. also v 22). The aorist passive participle ἐποικοδομηθέντες, "having been built," indicates both that this being placed on a foundation has already occurred for the readers, presumably in their conversion-initiation, and that God is to be understood now as the one who has brought this about (the "divine passive"; cf. also Gnilka, 155; Barth, 271). Variations on the two terms used in this imagery occur in Colossians. ἐποικοδομούμενοι is found in Col 2:7, and the cognate verbal form from the noun θεμέλιος, "foundation," τεθεμελιωμένοι, "having been founded," is used in Col 1:23 (cf. also Eph 3:17); the contexts call on the readers to continue in the faith they have received through the apostolic gospel. The writer to the Ephesians may well have a similar purpose in view, but his language is even more influenced by that of 1 Cor 3:9–17 than by that of Colossians. There Paul had used the images of a building (οἰκοδομή, 1 Cor 3:9) and a holy temple (ναὸς τοῦ θεοῦ ἅγιος, 1 Cor 3:17) of the Corinthian believers (cf. Eph 2:21) and had talked of God's Spirit dwelling in the temple (1 Cor 3:16 cf. Eph 2:22). There also can be found the language of building on a foundation (ἐποικοδομέω, 1 Cor 3:10, 12, 14; θεμέλιος, 1 Cor 3:10, 11). In that context, Paul had seen himself as the master builder who had laid the foundation—Christ himself—on which Paul, Apollos, Cephas, and other teachers and prophets were continuing to build. But here in Eph 2:20 the language of 1 Cor 3 is put to a different use as the writer makes a significant change in the imagery. The apostles and prophets are no longer seen as those who lay the foundation of Christ or who build upon it but as the foundation itself. Some have taken the genitive as a subjective genitive, "the foundation laid by the apostles and prophets" (e.g., Meyer, 142; NEB; GNB), but such an interpretation, which is sometimes motivated by the desire to harmonize Eph 2:20 with 1 Cor 3:11, introduces total confusion into the writer's use of metaphor, because it makes Christ both the foundation and the keystone. With the vast majority of commentators we should take the genitive as appositional, i.e., the foundation which the apostles and prophets constitute.

The prophets are NT prophets (*pace* Mussner, *Christus*, 108, and K. Rengstorf, "ἀπόστολος," *TDNT* 1 [1964] 441, who are among the few recent writers to support a reference to OT prophets; but see now Mussner, 93). This identification is confirmed by the order of the wording (it is difficult to suppose OT prophets would be placed second) and particularly by the other references to apostles and prophets in 3:5 and 4:11, where NT prophets are unambiguously in view. Some (e.g., Pfammatter, *Kirche als Bau*, 78–97; Sahlin, *SymBU* 12 [1950] 18; D. Hill, *New Testament Prophecy* [London: Marshall, Morgan and Scott, 1979] 139) have claimed that the use of one definite article to cover the two words "apostles" and "prophets" indicates that the same group of people is being referred to under two guises, the select group of apostles who are also prophets, the former term highlighting their mission and the latter their ministry of the word. But in Eph 4:11 apostles and prophets are quite clearly two separate groups (τοὺς μὲν ἀποστόλους, τοὺς δὲ προφήτας, cf. also 1 Cor 12:28; Rev 18:20), and it is unlikely that the writer is indulging in a special usage of the terms here in 2:20. The NT prophets in view then are presumably the men and women who exercise the gift of prophecy under discussion in 1 Cor 11 and 14 and whose activities are mentioned elsewhere in Rom 12:6; 1 Thess 5:20; Acts 11:27; 13:1, 2; 15:32; 19:6; 21:9, 10; Rev 1:3; 10:11; 16:6; 18:20, 24; 19:10; 22:6–10, 18, 19. The apostles and prophets are foundational in the sense of being primary and authoritative recipients and proclaimers of revelation. The apostles were those with special authority from their commissioning by the risen Lord, while the prophets were those with charismatic authority. Some apostles, like Paul, were also prophets, but not all apostles were prophets, and certainly not all prophets were apostles. The apostles provided a foundational link with the risen Christ and, together with the prophets, gave foundational interpretation of what God had done in Christ for the edification of the Church. The reference in *Did.* 11–13 to traveling apostles and prophets, whose teaching and conduct have to be tested, clearly has in view a much broader category of apostles, missionaries or delegates from local churches, and neither group can be said to be considered as foundational for the universal Church. The writer to the Ephesians has a narrower view of apostles, though not as narrow as only the Twelve, and, as becomes clear from 3:5, sees the first generation of prophets as also crucial in establishing the basic outlines of the meaning of what God had done in Christ, particularly in the admission of Gentiles into God's people (cf. Acts 13:1–3 where Luke appears to depict prophets as having a role in the missionary outreach of the Antioch church). He believes the apostles and prophets (3:5), and especially Paul (3:3), to have had a foundational role as those to whom the mystery of Christ was made known in order that it might be proclaimed to the Gentiles.

Although it is not impossible that the imagery of the opening clause of 2:20 was used by Paul himself, it is more likely that it represents the perspective of a follower looking back at the first generation of recipients of revelation.

Whereas in 1 Cor 3:10, 11 Paul saw himself as the master builder laying Christ as the foundation, his disciple now sees Paul himself as part of the foundational generation with the other apostles and prophets. The notion of apostolic foundations for the Church has affinities with other NT texts such as Matt 16:18; Rev 21:14, and with the role of the twelve apostles in the narrative of Luke–Acts. Here in Ephesians, the notion of the foundation of the apostles and prophets is an important part of the writer's attempt to give his Gentile Christian readers a stronger sense of their identity as part of the Church. It points them to their roots and to the source of the normative teaching that is necessary if they are not to be confused and shaken by erroneous ideas (cf. 4:14).

ὄντος ἀκρογωνιαίου αὐτοῦ Χριστοῦ Ἰησοῦ, "the keystone being Christ Jesus himself." This clause, with its present participle in the genitive absolute and its emphatic αὐτοῦ, "himself," in reference to Christ Jesus, serves to set off Christ both from the foundation of the apostles and prophets and from those who have been placed on that foundation. It focuses attention on his present status and function. The following clauses in vv 21, 22 will show how the one who holds a distinctive position relates to the building as a whole. But what is this distinctive position? Since Jeremias proposed that the cornerstone is in fact the final stone of the building, which was probably set over the gate, recent scholarship has been divided over whether ἀκρογωνιαῖος is to be taken as the foundation stone in the building (cf. Percy, *Probleme*, 328–32; Pfammatter, *Kirche als Bau*, 143–51; McKelvey, *NTS* 8 [1961–62] 352–59; idem, *The New Temple*, 195–204; Mussner, 93–95; idem, *Christus*, 108–11; idem, "Contributions," 172 n. 59; Schäfer, "Zur Deutung," 218–24; Merklein, *Das kirchliche Amt*, 144–52; Mitton, 113–14; Schnackenburg, 124–25; idem, "Die Kirche als Bau," 263–64) or as the crowning stone or top stone of the edifice (cf. Jeremias, *Angelos* 1 [1925] 65–70; idem, *ZNW* 29 [1930] 264–80; idem, *ZNW* 36 [1937] 154–57; idem, *TDNT* 1 [1964] 791–93; idem, *TDNT* 4 [1967] 268–80; Vielhauer, *Oikodome*, 125–28; Dibelius-Greeven, 72; Best, *One Body*, 165–66; S. Hanson, *Unity*, 131; Schlier, 142; Gnilka, 158; Conzelmann, 101; Houlden, 293; F. F. Bruce, "New Wine in Old Wineskins: The Corner Stone," *ExpTim* 84 [1972–73] 232; Caird, 61; Barth, 271, 317–19; Lindemann, *Aufhebung*, 185–86 n. 213; cf. also the definition offered in *LPGL* 66, "(stone) as top-most angle or point of pyramid, obelisk etc. . . .").

The evidence that can be adduced for the latter meaning is to be found in Ps 118:22 in Symmachus; LXX 2 Kgs 25:17, where it is used for the head of a pillar; Hippolytus, *Elenchos* 5.7, 35; Tertullian, *Adv. Marc.* 3.7; Aphraates, *Hom.* 1.6, 7; the Peshitta description of the stone of Isa 28:16 as the "head of the wall," and the *Testament of Solomon* 22.7–23.3, from the second or third century C.E., which depicts the completion of Solomon's temple as follows: "Now the temple was being completed, and there was a great corner stone [λίθος ἀκρογωνιαῖος μέγας] which I wished to set as head of the corner [εἰς κεφαλὴν γωνίας] by way of completing the temple of God . . . and he went up the ladder carrying the stone and set it on the summit of the entrance to the temple." The exalted position ascribed to Christ elsewhere in Ephesians (cf. 1:20–23; 2:6; 4:8–10) and the special emphasis on Christ's position as over against the rest of the structure in 2:20 favor this interpretation. As S. Hanson (*Unity*, 131) puts it, "He is not one of the stones of the foundation in common with the Apostles, even if He is a cornerstone, but He is the top stone of the pinnacle of the building. . . . As Christ is the κεφαλή of the σῶμα, He is the ἀκρογωνιαῖος of the οἰκοδομή."

Against such an interpretation a number of objections can be made. This usage is not found in LXX Isa 28:16 or quotations of it which identify ἀκρογωνιαῖος with the foundation stone, and in the Qumran writings there is a close assocation between the cornerstone and the foundation as Isa 28:16 is quoted (cf. 1QS 5.6; 8.4, 5). For this reason McKelvey (*The New Temple,* 201) asserts, "ἀκρογωνιαῖος stands in the same close relation to θεμέλιος in Ephesians 2:20 as it does in Isaiah 28:16." Some of the evidence adduced for the top stone interpretation is of quite late date. It is also argued that the notion of Christ as the top stone is inconsistent with the dynamic imagery of a growing and unfinished building, and that it leaves the relation of Christ to the apostles and prophets unclear. Further, since the writer remains close to 1 Cor 3:10, 11 and Christ has a foundational role there, a similar position for him should be expected here. The cornerstone was placed first in the foundation and all the other stones in the foundation were lined up in accordance with it. Such an interpretation would make clear that the apostles and prophets have Christ as their norm.

The arguments are finely balanced. But some of these objections to the interpretation of Christ as the top stone can be rebutted. For the writer of Ephesians, the notion of a finished structure with Christ as its head is not at all incompatible with the dynamic imagery of growth. He views the Church as already Christ's fullness (1:23) and yet at the same time as having to attain that fullness (4:13; cf. also 3:19). In 4:15, 16, the passage which repeats a number of the expressions found here in 2:20–22, the imagery is precisely that of a body growing up into Christ as the head. So here, on the one hand, the Church is pictured as a finished structure with Christ as the top stone, and yet, on the other hand, it must grow into a temple in him. On such a view, the relation of Christ to the apostles and prophets is not unclear. As in 4:7–16, they are in at the beginning of the Church, but Christ is the exalted Lord over all. They are foundational, but he is the keystone which crowns the whole building.

The crucial question in coming to an exegetical decision is whether we allow the LXX usage in Isa 28:16 and the Christological imagery of 1 Cor 3:11 or the writer's own perspective from elsewhere in this letter to be determinative. The use of ἀκρογωνιαῖος here is probably not a direct allusion to Isa 28:16 anyway, but an appropriation of the "stone" *testimonia,* which were in fairly common use in the early church. In particular, Ps 118:22, "The stone which the builders rejected has become the head of the corner,"—had been seen as an appropriate expression of what God had done in exalting the crucified Jesus to be Lord of all. The rejected stone had become the keystone of the whole structure (cf. Mark 12:10; Acts 4:11). In Rom 9:32, 33 Paul employs a conflation of Isa 28:16 (which omits any reference to the cornerstone) and Isa 8:14, and elsewhere this conflation of Isaiah texts is combined with Ps 118:22 (cf. Luke 20:17, 18), and all three texts are linked in 1 Pet 2:6–8. Isa 28:16 had already, then, been combined with Ps 118:22 and thus with the notion of Christ's elevation to the crowning stone of the building. It would not be surprising, therefore, if the writer of Ephesians has put elements from such a composite *testimonium* to his own use and if ἀκρογωνιαῖος has similar force to κεφαλὴ γωνίας from Ps 118:22. We have already noted that, while employing language from 1 Cor 3, the writer gives it his own distinctive twist, and once "foundation" terminology is applied to the apostles and prophets instead of Christ, it would be natural for him to give Christ the exalted position attributed throughout the rest of his letter. The writer's view of Christ as heavenly Lord and of the Church as growing toward him elsewhere in Ephesians should, therefore, be judged determinative for the use to which he has put traditional material here in 2:20.

ἐν ᾧ πᾶσα οἰκοδομὴ συναρμολογουμένη αὔξει εἰς ναὸν ἅγιον ἐν κυρίῳ, "in whom the whole building being joined together grows into a holy temple in the Lord." We have already argued in *Notes* that the original text read πᾶσα οἰκοδομή and not πᾶσα ἡ οἰκοδομή. This does not mean, however, that the writer now has in view every building in the sense of every local congregation (*contra* Meyer, 146–47; Abbott, 74; Mitton, 115). Rather, in all probability, πᾶσα οἰκοδομή should be taken as a Hebraism which has affected Koine usage and be understood as "all the building" or "the whole building" (cf. LXX 1 Chron 28:8; LXX Amos 3:1; Acts 2:36; 17:26; Rom 3:20; 11:26; cf. also Moule, *Idiom-Book*, 94–95). Here, as in the rest of the letter, the writer has the universal Church in mind. This is the difference, as the building and temple imagery for the Church become explicit, from the use of this imagery in 1 Cor 3, where it referred to the local Corinthian community. οἰκοδομή occurred in 1 Cor 3:9 and is found elsewhere in Ephesians in its more abstract sense of "upbuilding" or "edification" in 4:12, 16, 29. ναός occurred in conjunction with ἅγιος in 1 Cor 3:16, 17 (cf. also its use in 2 Cor 6:16) with reference to the Corinthian congregation, and was used of the individual believer's body in 1 Cor 6:19. Ephesians represents a further stage in the appropriation of temple imagery by the early Christians. Not only the individual believer or the local church, but also all believers, the universal Church, can be held to be the focus of God's presence. This transformation in the understanding of God's temple had been prepared not only by Paul and other early Christians, but also earlier by the Qumran community, which had seen itself as the true spiritual temple in contrast to the corrupt cultus in Jerusalem (e.g., 1QS 8.4–10; 9.5, 6; 4QFlor 1.6, 7). Earlier still, elements in OT prophecy (e.g., Isa 56:6, 7) could envisage the temple in Jerusalem as the universal temple, to which in the end-time all nations would come to worship and pray. Whether or not the writer actually had such prophecies in mind, in this context in Ephesians, where Gentiles are being reminded of the heritage into which they have entered, the temple imagery would certainly lend itself to an eschatological understanding. The readers should perceive that they are living in the time when through Christ they, as Gentiles, have been brought near, given access, and in fact have become part of the temple of the Church. But, again, it can be seen that what has taken place through Christ cannot simply be depicted in categories which are in straightforward continuity with OT expectations. The notion of a pilgrimage by Gentiles to a literal temple in Jerusalem has been completely transformed.

Another strand of reflection on the temple gave it cosmic associations. One does not have to turn only to Gnostic literature for such associations (cf. Schlier,

Christus und die Kirche, 49–60; Vielhauer, *Oikodome*, 125). In the OT and in apocalyptic literature Yahweh's earthly abode in the temple was seen as the counterpart of his heavenly abode, and after the exile the hope of the divine presence in the eschatological temple was increasingly transferred to the heavenly Jerusalem and its heavenly temple (cf. Wis 9:8; *1 Enoch* 90.29; *2 Apoc. Bar.* 4.2–6; *T. Dan* 5.12, 13; *Asc. Isa.* 7.10). In rabbinic thought, via the concept of the sacred stone, which was connected with Gen 28:17, the temple was considered as the gate from earth to heaven and as inhabited by heavenly beings (cf. *b. Yoma* 54b; *Gen. Rab.* 4.2; 68.12 on Gen 28:12; *Yal. Gen.* 120 on Gen 28:22; *Pirqe R. El.* 32.35; *Num. Rab.* 12.4). At Qumran the link between the elect community on earth and the inhabitants of heaven was an intrinsic part of the temple symbolism (e.g., 1QS 11.7, 8). Particularly if 2:20 sees Christ as the top stone of the temple, the writer's use of temple imagery in a letter which frequently links the Church with the heavenly realm may well also carry heavenly connotations (cf. also S. Hanson, *Unity*, 130; Schlier, 140; Gärtner, *The Temple*, 64; Mussner, 95–96; idem, "Contributions," 173; Gnilka, 155; McKelvey, *The New Temple*, 119, 120, is ambivalent on this issue).

The major emphasis in the use of the temple imagery in v 21 is, however, on the relationship of the building to Christ. The Church is constituted and functions only in relation to Christ. ἐν ᾧ, "in whom," draws attention to this at the beginning of the clause, and ἐν κυρίῳ, "in the Lord," does so at the end (*pace* Mitton, 116, who takes the latter as a reference to God). ἐν ᾧ may refer simply to Christ himself as the immediate antecedent rather than to his function as the keystone, but the keystone bore the pressure of the stones forming the arch and its removal could cause the collapse of the whole (cf. Barth, 318 n. 260). ἐν κυρίῳ at the end of the clause seems superfluous. Schnackenburg ("Die Kirche als Bau," 265) suggests that "holy temple in the Lord" may have been a fixed phrase for the Church, but it appears more likely that ἐν κυρίῳ governs the whole notion of growing into a holy temple (cf. also Schlier, 144) and is another example of Ephesians' redundancy of style. If so, this variation may be seen to conform to an overall tendency in the Pauline corpus for what believers are in relationship to Christ to be stated as "in Christ," and for what they are to become or to do in relation to Christ to be stated as "in the Lord" (cf. J. A. Robinson, 72; Barth, 273; C. F. D. Moule, *The Origin of Christology* [Cambridge: Cambridge University Press, 1977] 58–60).

The participle συναρμολογουμένη, "being joined together," is met with again in the NT only in 4:16, and the verb αὔξει, "grows," also occurs again together with its cognate noun in 4:15, 16. Both terms introduce the notion of the Church as an organism, which is more fully developed in 4:15, 16 and which has Col 2:19 as its most immediate inspiration. Gnostic ideas of the primal man's cosmic body as a heavenly building provide some parallels for the mixture of the images of building and organic growth (cf. Schlier, 143–44; *Christus und die Kirche*, 49–58), but both they and Ephesians are anticipated by Philo's combination of the images (cf. Hegermann, *Schöpfungsmittler*, 189–91), and the Qumran writings juxtapose images of planting and building (cf. 1QS 8.5, 6; 1QH 6.7). Both terms also introduce a temporal element into the writer's perspective on the Church. The joining together of all the elements that make up the total structure of the Church is a continuous present activity. As the adjusting and fitting together take place, the Church can be seen as in the process of growth toward its ultimate condition of holiness (cf. also 5:27). Growth and holiness, here, are not simply matters for individual initiates pursuing their own ends, but notions which have a clearly corporate context. It is the growth of the community, the whole Church, which is decisive, and the growth is in this context a qualitative rather than a quantitative concept. The notion of a growing Church inevitably implies both that history and the future are important for this writer, and not totally swallowed up in his realized eschatology, and that the Church is as yet imperfect.

ἐν ᾧ καὶ ὑμεῖς συνοικοδομεῖσθε εἰς κατοικητήριον τοῦ θεοῦ ἐν πνεύματι, "in whom you also are built together into a dwelling place of God in the Spirit." ἐν ᾧ in this last clause in the pericope could refer back to either "the Lord" or "a holy temple" in the preceding clause, but it is more likely that it stands parallel with the ἐν ᾧ of that clause and thus refers back to "Christ Jesus" in v 20. In this way, v 22 can be seen as providing a general parallel to v 21: συνοικοδομεῖσθε, "you are built together," corresponds to συναρμολογουμένη, "being joined together"; the goal of the building process is now termed a dwelling of God rather than a holy temple; and ἐν πνεύματι, "in the Spirit," performs a similar function to that of ἐν κυρίῳ, "in the Lord." The major difference between the last two clauses is that in v 22 the readers are directly addressed. The writer does not allow his picture of the Church to remain in general terms, but applies it to the Gentile Christian recipients of his letter as a reminder of what they have become through their relationship to Christ. They need to be aware of the immensely privileged nature of their new situation. In Christ they are being built into the dwelling place of God himself. They are the bricks that are being built into God's new temple (cf. also 1 Pet 2:5). Again, there is the need for a corporate awareness. The συν- compound here indicates that this is more than an individual experience; the process of being formed into the Church has to take place in the company of fellow believers.

The noun τὸ κατοικητήριον, which occurs elsewhere in the NT only in Rev 18:2, is used in the LXX both of God's abode in the temple in Jerusalem (cf. 1 Kgs 8:13) and of his heavenly dwelling place (cf. 1 Kgs 8:39, 43, 49). Now his dwelling place can be said to be neither a literal temple in Jerusalem nor simply heaven, but the Church, of which the Gentile Christian readers in Asia Minor were a part. ἐν πνεύματι may well color the whole preceding clause so that the Gentile believers are thought of as being built together into a whole structure by the agency of the Spirit (cf. 4:3, 4). More particularly, the Spirit is seen as the means by which God dwells in the Church (cf. 1 Cor 3:16). There are obvious similarities with the description of the Church as a spiritual house in 1 Pet 2:5. The emphasis on God's presence in the Spirit can provide a reminder that when we talk of the "spiritualization" of the concept of the temple, we are not talking of invisibility or immateriality but of the reality of men and women forming the eschatological people of God, dominated by his living power and presence in the Spirit. As elsewhere in the letter (cf. 1:3, 13, 14), it is the Spirit who provides the link between believers on earth and the heavenly realm and makes the Church the place where the heavenly and earthly dwelling places of God merge. The readers' experience as part of the Church is described in this verse by means of a "trinitarian" pattern of thought—"in Christ," "dwelling place of God," and "in the Spirit" (cf. also 2:18). It could be that as well as completing such a pattern of thought, the reference to the Spirit should be seen as completing the pericope by a contrast to the emphasis on the flesh at its beginning in v 11, and as emphasizing that for the Gentile readers in their new situation in the Spirit previous distinctions based on physical and ethnic categories—"in the flesh"—no longer count (cf. also J. A. Robinson, 72, 166). Certainly by the end of the pericope Israel's privileges in proximity to God, which were tied up with the Jerusalem temple, have completely faded from view as the focus of attention has become Gentile Christians' role in the new temple of God in the Spirit.

Explanation

In the previous section, 2:1–10, the writer had reminded his Gentile Christian readers of the dramatic change God had brought about in raising them from spiritual death to new life in Christ. This is now followed by a further reminder of the change in their situation, the reversal of their former status as deprived Gentiles in comparison to Israel in favor of the privileges they now enjoy in their relationship to God and as members of his people. Again, the contrast of the pre-Christian past ("then") with the Christian present ("now") helps to shape the passage, which falls into three main parts. Verses 11–13 set out the reminder in terms of an initial contrast between the Gentiles' former alienation from Israel and her God and their now having come near. Verses 14–18 then adapt a hymn to Christ as bringer of cosmic peace and make use of a combination of Isa 57:19 and Isa 52:7 in order to explain how Christ, through his work of reconciliation, accomplished this change for the Gentiles. Verses 19–22 complete the section, as v 19 summarizes and elaborates on the earlier contrast and leads into a depiction of the Church and the Gentiles' part in it in terms of building and temple imagery in vv 20–22.

As the passage begins, the readers, here explicitly described for the first time as Gentiles, are reminded by this Jewish Christian follower of Paul that their pre-Christian state was one of serious religious deprivation. They are asked to reflect on their former condition in terms of categories valid at a prior stage in the history of salvation in order to appreciate all the more their present privileges. It is obviously the writer's view that at one time Israel had real advantages and that Gentiles, in comparison, had at that time no share in Israel's Messiah. Being excluded from God's electing purpose for the commonwealth of Israel, from the covenant relationship and the promise, they were therefore destitute of the true hope and true God. The dramatic reversal that has taken place for the Gentile readers through their relationship to Christ and through his sacrificial death is described in the language of Jewish proselytism as "having come near." But as the rest of the passage makes clear, this terminology is transformed to mean not membership within Israel, but access to God himself and membership in his newly created community.

The middle section of the pericope elaborates on how Christ's work made this possible. The proselyte terminology of "far" and "near" reminds the writer of an OT passage, Isa 57:19, which speaks of peace for two such groups. Yet before he draws on this, he prepares the ground for its emphasis on peace by applying hymnic material depicting Christ as the embodiment of peace and bringer of reconciliation for a divided cosmos to the situation of a divided humanity. Christ is now said to have made Jews and Gentiles one by demolishing the dividing wall and source of hostility between them, that is, by abolishing the law and all its regulations, and to have accomplished this through his death. That death not only terminated the old order dominated by the law but introduced in its place a new creation, a corporate new humanity ("one new person") which is embraced in his own person. Two aspects of Christ's reconciling work are now set forth. On the horizontal level, he has made peace between the two old enemies, Jews and Gentiles, and reconciled them in the one body of the Church. At the same time, on the vertical level, he has reconciled both groups to God through his death on the cross, indicating, in a way which the opening verses did not, that there is a fundamental sense in which Israel too was alienated from God. The writer is now able to introduce the OT citation which the earlier proselyte terminology recalled; he combines it creatively with Isa 52:7 to give a Christological interpretation, as Christ's work on the cross is seen as his proclamation of peace with God to both the Gentile readers and the Jews. The elaboration on Christ's work concludes with a statement encapsulating the results of Christ's peacemaking in terms of the access he has provided to the Father for both Jews and Gentiles through the one Spirit.

In the light of what has been said about Christ's achievement, the contrast between the readers' past and present is restated in v 19 in terms which transcend the old Jew-Gentile division and which lead into a description of the new community of the Church and the readers' place in it. These Gentile Christians are no longer without a homeland or commonwealth; they can now be said to be fellow citizens in the heavenly commonwealth with the saints and members of the family of God himself. They have been built into God's temple as bricks placed on the foundation of the Church's apostles and prophets, and they are part of a structure which has the exalted Christ as its crowning stone. Joined together with one another, these bricks form a structure which is in the process of growth toward holiness. The writer then completes his reminder to the readers by underlining that they are to see themselves as being built in Christ into the very place in which God himself is present in the Spirit.

In two places in the writer's flow of thought a "trinitarian" pattern to his reflections emerges. In v 18, Jews' and Gentiles' access to God is through Christ and in the Spirit, and in v 22, as part of the Church, the Gentile readers in Christ form the dwelling place of God in the Spirit. Despite these two references to the Spirit, the dominant foci for the writer's thought remain, as in the earlier pericopes, God, Christ, and humanity. But whereas in 2:1–10 the theocentric perspective was most to the fore, here in 2:11–22 Christ's role is given more attention. At the beginning, the contrast between the readers' past and present can be formulated in terms of "apart from Christ" and "in Christ," and at the end, the distinctive place of Christ as the keystone of the temple structure is stressed. But Christ is the focus of attention primarily because the writer has taken up the hymn to Christ in vv 14–16, in which Christ was the central actor rather than simply the agent, and because the wording of the OT citation in v 17 was also appropriate to having Christ as the subject.

Explanation 161

The writer's more usual formulation of God acting on behalf of humanity through Christ does not emerge again until vv 20–22, with their passive participles which have God as the implied subject, and their repetition of "in whom" in reference to Christ as agent. Though Christ is the keystone and the one in whom the structure holds together, it is clear that the building as a whole is God's, his dwelling place. The section begins with the human situation, however, and the contrast of vv 11–13, 19, because it forms part of the address to Gentile Christians, has the readers as the subject of the verbs. The humanity on behalf of which Christ acts is seen first of all in terms of Jews and Gentiles; then, as a result of his activity, the one new person of the Church is created; and by the end of the section the humanity which experiences the working of God is seen exclusively in terms of this Church.

The change from pre-Christian past to Christian present in the Church is produced not by God's salvation as resurrection and exaltation with Christ, as in 2:1–10, but by Christ's reconciliation. Christ as peacemaker is the one who has made the difference. The writer sets this out by changing the notion of Christ's cosmic peacemaking in the traditional material and giving it a historical setting, as he applies it to the Jew-Gentile situation and roots it in what was accomplished on the cross. In retrospect, Christ's death on the cross can be seen as effecting peace both on a horizontal and a vertical level. First of all, by dealing with the law as the source of hostility, his death overcame the alienating divide between Jews and Gentiles and was the creative power which produced a unified new humanity from these two groups. The judgment that in Ephesians Christology has been swallowed up by ecclesiology surely misses the emphasis of this passage, where it is Christ's reconciling death on the cross on which the very existence of the Church depends. The Pauline notion of reconciliation has been applied, then, to the social sphere, as Jews and Gentiles with their ethnic and religious differences are said to be reconciled in the one body of the Church. But the vertical element of Pauline reconciliation, restoration to God's acceptance and favor, is not missing, and Christ's death effected this at the same time for both groups. Not only Gentiles but also Jews required reconciliation to God, and through Christ both now enjoy the privilege of access to his fatherly presence. Christ's whole ministry climaxing in his sacrificial death (cf. "the blood of Christ" in v 13) amounts to a proclamation of the good news of peace with God to both Gentiles and Jews. In fact, Christ is so closely linked to what he has achieved that the whole notion of peace takes on a personal quality and is identified with Christ: "he is our peace" (v 14). The Church is the arena where the results of Christ's peacemaking are to be seen—the one new person (v 15) and the one body (v 16). The peace gained at the cost of Christ's death and realized in the Church is to be preserved and demonstrated (cf. 4:3) and to be proclaimed (cf. 6:15) by the Church in the world. As the rest of the letter indicates, what has been achieved in the Church in the overcoming of the major division within humanity in the first century is an anticipation of God's purpose for the still-divided cosmos (cf. 1:10; 3:10). That major division can be seen as a prototype of all divisions (cf. Gal 3:28; Col 3:11). If the Church in Eph 2 stands for the overcoming of that fundamental division of humanity into either Jew or Gentile, it stands for the overcoming of all divisions caused by tradition, class, color, nation, or groups of nations. Anything less would be a denial of that nature of the Church which this writer takes as axiomatic.

Soteriology in terms of reconciliation, which is the content of 2:14–18, leads to ecclesiology, which is the content of 2:19–22, but which has already been introduced in the earlier section. Indeed, the pericope as a whole contains a rich variety of images of the Church, embracing the categories of people of God, body of Christ, and temple of the Spirit, and setting forth the Church as one, holy, catholic, and apostolic.

The Church is a new creation which replaces the older order with its divided humanity. It forms instead the "new person," a new humanity included in Christ as the representative human being, thereby constituting his "body." This new community is, as we have seen, characterized above all by its unity ("one" in v 14, "one new man" in v 15, and "one body" in v 16). It is the sphere in which hostility has been overcome, reconciliation has been achieved, and peace bears its fruits, and, as such, forms a visible sign of unity for the world. The Church is not only the place of reconciliation between Jews and Gentiles, it is also the place where reconciliation between humanity and God is experienced, where harmony between heaven and earth has been restored, and where access to the Father is enjoyed. The high God of heaven has chosen to make it his dwelling place on earth, and the Christ who has been exalted to heaven forms the crowning stone in its structure. The Church is where men and women experience a sense of being at home, of belonging, not only to one another in a unified humanity as fellow citizens, but also to God himself as part of his household or family. This new society is also a building, a temple, where humans are the building material which God the builder has already made into his dwelling place. No longer the literal temple in Jerusalem but the community of the Church is the focus for God's presence in the world. The Church is already the temple in which God dwells. Yet, it is at the same time a building under construction, where, through their relationship to Christ and to one another, believers are still being shaped into a fit sanctuary for God. It is to be characterized by growth and holiness as it becomes what it already is. None of these elements contributing to the writer's vision of the Church are there as part of an abstract description. They are instead taken up into his address to his readers. They are to see themselves as the building material God has chosen to utilize for his temple of the end-time pervaded by the Spirit (v 22), and thereby to gain a greater sense of their identity as those with a privileged role to play in the working out of God's purposes in this world.

Their new privileged position in the Church owes everything to Christ. He is the one who made access possible, the one who is the keystone of the temple structure, the one in whom the whole structure coheres and into whom they are being fitted, and the one who enables them to grow into what they are meant to be. Their position also owes much to the apostles and prophets. They are the foundation on which Gentiles could be built into the Church, for their proclamation and interpretation of the significance of what God had done in Christ mediated the good news of peace. They serve now as the norm for traditions about that good news.

The passage which finishes with such lofty assertions about the place of

Gentile believers in the new community of the Church had begun by stating the hopeless deficiencies of their former state in comparison with the advantages enjoyed by Israel as God's people. What then is the relationship between Israel as God's people and the Church as God's new people according to this writer? To do justice to the writer's thought we must stress a basic discontinuity between the Church and Israel, and yet note at the same time an element of continuity. From the contrast with which the passage begins as it speaks of the alienation of Gentiles from Israel, her Messiah, and her God, we might have expected a changed situation in which Gentiles now enter into the covenant relationship, which continues with Israel, or at least Israel as represented by Jewish Christians, much as Paul in Rom 11 sees the Gentiles as wild olive branches who are grafted into the olive tree. But these expectations are not fulfilled. It might be held that incorporation of the traditional material with its language of creation and a new person complicated the writer's argument, but he continues its emphasis on discontinuity in the rest of the passage, and even in v 11, with its terminology of "in the flesh" and "made by hands," had already distanced himself from the validity of the distinctions he used. As the text stands, the Gentiles' former disadvantages have been reversed, not by their being incorporated into Israel, even into a renewed Israel of Jewish Christians, but by their being made members of a new community which transcends the categories of Jew and Gentile, an entity which is a new creation, not simply a merging of the former groupings. When it appears that the earlier contrast of vv 11–13 will be taken up again in v 19, we discover that it has been reformulated so that in the depiction of the Gentiles' present privileges the comparison with Israel has been transcended. Gentiles no longer lack a commonwealth. Yet this is not because they are now part of the commonwealth of Israel, but because they are fellow citizens with all the saints in the Church. In the imagery which follows, describing the Church of which they are now a part as God's family, building and temple, the explicit comparison with Israel has dropped from view. Whatever the dangers for the relationship between Christians and Jews which arose from later abuse of the concept, there is no escaping the conclusion that Eph 2 depicts the Church in terms of a new third entity, one which transcends the old ethnic and religious identities of Jew and Gentile. This is a perspective different from that of Rom 9–11, but with strong affinities to the sharp logic of Paul's polemic in Galatians (e.g., Gal 3:28; 6:15, 16).

The discontinuity between Israel, as the people of God, and the Church is evidenced also by vv 16, 17, where Jews as well as Gentiles are said to be reconciled to God by Christ, and where "the near" need peace with God proclaimed to them as well as "the far." Despite what he believed to have been their real advantages, this writer holds also that Israel too was alienated from her God. This perspective of a discontinuity with Israel is associated with the attitude of discontinuity with the law found in v 15. That which was the distinguishing mark of Israel under the old order, the Torah, has been abolished. As the symbol of the particularity and exclusiveness of Israel's election, and thereby the source of hostility and alienation between Jews and Gentiles, it was quite unable to produce peace, but with its removal through Christ's death reconciliation was able to take place on a new basis. The writer does not spell out how Israel too was alienated from God and needed reconciliation; but we should probably assume that, as a good disciple of Paul, he believed that the law which separated Israel from the Gentiles had also come to separate Israel from God and to hold her in a state of slavery and condemnation (cf. Gal 3:10–22; 2 Cor 3:7–11; Rom 3:19, 20; 7:7–25; 9:30–10:4).

Why, then, does he choose to begin this part of his reminder to Gentile Christians in terms of their previous deficiencies as over against Israel? It is not simply that Israel serves as a convenient symbol for the sphere of salvation from which Gentiles were formerly excluded. As a Jewish Christian this writer actually believes that at one time Israel did have real advantages in the history of salvation as God's chosen people, although she had forfeited them. Yet even here his Christian perspective is evident, for most of the advantages he lists look toward the future (cf. "Messiah," "promise," "hope"). There had been a potential continuity because Israel stood under the promise. This is where the focus of continuity lies. The hope of the promised Messiah has been realized, and it is through him that the Gentile Christian readers now have a place in the history of salvation that has its roots back in God's covenants with Israel. Yet, because Israel was unprepared for the way in which the hope was realized, there is no straightforward continuity between her and God's new people. Those who were near and who receive the peace proclaimed to them enter, along with those who were far off and received the same proclamation, into God's new community. In this community, though the law has been abolished, the Scriptures, interpreted in the light of the realization of the hope in Christ, still speak (cf. v 17). About the destiny of those Jews who do not accept Christ and about the future of Israel, this writer has nothing to say. Unlike the Paul of Rom 9–11, who speaks of the continuing election and future salvation of Israel, he appears to view God's purposes as now centered exclusively in the Church. Certainly this passage cannot be treated as providing the basis for conversation between Church and synagogue on the grounds of their common election. The unity of which the passage speaks is not one between Church and synagogue, but one between Gentile Christians and Jewish Christians within the one body of the Church, though, as we have seen, within the context of the whole letter this can be seen as the first visible step toward the bringing of the whole cosmos into unity in Christ (cf. 1:10).

It is often assumed that the whole of Eph 2:11–22 is simply about unity between Gentile Christians and Jewish Christians. On this assumption a life-setting for the letter is sought which will explain this concern with unity either in terms of a continuing struggle about the status of Gentile Christians or in terms of a situation of Gentile arrogance toward Jewish Christians. But vv 14–18 with their exposition of the unity Christ has produced through his reconciling death must not be isolated from their overall context. The writer sees the unity of which they speak as already achieved by Christ and as a fundamental datum of the Church's existence, upon which he can build his main point—the reminder to Gentile Christians of the privileges they enjoy as members of this universal Church. Verses 14–18 are framed by the contrast between past and present, formulated so as to address directly the Gentile Christian readers, and the passage ends with a depiction of God's new temple, which also addresses the readers, reminding them that this is the nature of the community of which they have become a part. The setting which best

Explanation

corresponds to the thrust of the passage is that of predominantly Gentile churches in Asia Minor toward the end of the first century, when Jewish Christian/Gentile Christian struggles were past and when there was a diminishing awareness of the Church's roots and therefore a deficient sense of their identity on the part of Gentile Christians. A Jewish Christian Paulinist is in a good position to speak to this lack and wants to do so in such a way as to build up his readers' assurance of their salvation. This is in accord with his desire reflected in the thanksgiving period of 1:15–23 that the addressees' knowledge of the greatness of God's power toward them as believers should be increased. They are to remember their own history in terms of the history of salvation, not in order to dwell on their old identity in distinction from Israel or on any continuing distinction from Jewish Christians, but in order to appreciate their new identity as part of the one new humanity. As in the preceding pericope, 2:1–10, this reminder of the immense change brought about in their situation is intended to deepen the readers' awareness of both the privilege of their calling as part of God's new temple and the responsibility to live up to that calling through their corporate growth in holiness. In this way, Eph 2:11–22 functions, and can continue to function, as a reminder to a predominantly Gentile Church not to take its blessings for granted. Its relation to the Christ who is Israel's Messiah, its listening to the Hebrew Scriptures as its own Scriptures (cf. v 17), its access to the Father, its links with all believers, and its participation in the spiritual temple which has replaced the Jerusalem temple are only possible because the creative dynamic of Christ's death has enabled those who were far off to come near. Such reflections are designed to lead the readers to a renewed appreciation of, and gratitude for, the powerful nature of Christ's reconciling work, but for which they would have remained without God and without hope in the world. They are designed to give them an incentive to become what they already are as the community where divisions have been healed and God's presence is made known in the world.

This exposition of the privileged situation into which Gentiles have entered can be seen as preparation for what follows in chap. 3, both for the prayer that believers may be empowered to fulfill their role in God's purposes (cf. vv 14–21) and for the parenthetical depiction of Paul's special role in receiving and making known the mystery of Gentile inclusion in the people of God (cf. vv 1–13). It serves particularly as a demonstration of the insight into this mystery which the writer claims to possess (cf. v 4).

Paul as Minister of the Mystery to the Gentiles (3:1–13)

Bibliography

Best, E. "The Revelation to Evangelize the Gentiles." *JTS* 35 (1984) 1–31. **Brown, R. E.** *The Semitic Background of the Term "Mystery" in the New Testament.* Philadelphia: Fortress, 1968, 56–66. **Caragounis, C. C.** *The Ephesian Mysterion,* 52–56, 72–74, 96–112. **Coppens, J.** " 'Mystery' in the Theology of St. Paul and Its Parallels at Qumran." In *Paul and Qumran,* ed. J. Murphy-O'Connor. London: Chapman, 1968, 132–58. **Dahl, N. A.** "Das Geheimnis der Kirche nach Eph 3:8–10." In *Zur Auferbauung des Leibes Christi,* ed. E. Schlink and A. Peters. Kassel: Johannes Stauda, 1965, 63–75. **Davies, L.** "I Wrote Afore in Few Words (Eph 3, 3)." *ExpTim* 46 (1934–35) 568. **Fischer, K. M.** *Tendenz und Absicht,* 95–108. **Gnilka, J.** "Das Paulusbild im Kolosser- und Epheserbrief." In *Kontinuität und Einheit,* 179–93. **Kim, S.** *The Origin of Paul's Gospel.* Tübingen: Mohr, 1981, 20–25. **Klein, G.** *Die Zwölf Apostel.* Göttingen: Vandenhoeck & Ruprecht, 1961, 69–72. **Lincoln, A. T.,** *Paradise Now and Not Yet,* 154–55. **Lindemann, A.** *Die Aufhebung der Zeit,* 221–30. **Lührmann, D.** *Das Offenbarungsverständnis bei Paulus und in den paulinischen Gemeinden.* Neukirchen-Vluyn: Neukirchener Verlag, 1965, 119–33. **Mare, W. H.** "Paul's Mystery in Ephesians 3." *BETS* 8 (1965) 77–84. **Merklein, H.** *Das kirchliche Amt nach dem Epheserbrief,* 159–224. ———. "Paulinische Theologie in der Rezeption des Kolosser- und Epheserbriefes." In *Paulus in den neutestamentlichen Spätschriften,* 27–31. **Meyer, R. P.** *Kirche und Mission im Epheserbrief,* 58–60, 64–65. **Minear, P. S.** "The Vocation to Invisible Powers: Ephesians 3:8–10." In *To Die and to Live.* New York: Seabury, 1977, 89–106. **Mussner, F.** *Christus, das All und die Kirche,* 144–47. **Orbe, A.** "Una variante heterodoxa de Eph 3, 5a." *Greg* 37 (1956) 201–19. **Percy, E.** *Die Probleme der Kolosser- und Epheserbriefe,* 342–53. **Pesch, R.** "Das Mysterium Christi (Eph 3, 8–12, 14–19)." *Am Tisch des Wortes* 18 (1967) 11–17. **Ryrie, C. C.** "The Mystery in Ephesians 3." *BSac* 123 (1966) 24–31. **Thompson, G. H. P.** "Eph 3, 13 and 2 Tim 2, 10 in the Light of Col 1, 24." *ExpTim* 71 (1959–60) 187–89. **Wink, W.** *Naming the Powers.* Philadelphia: Fortress, 1984, 89–96.

Translation

¹*For this reason I, Paul, the prisoner of Christ Jesus for the sake of you Gentiles—* ²*assuming that you have of course heard about the stewardship of the grace of God which was given to me for you,* ³*that the mystery was made known to me according to revelation, as I have already written briefly.*[a] ⁴*In accordance with this you will be able, when you read, to perceive my insight into the mystery of Christ,* ⁵*which was not made known to people*[b] *in other generations as it has now been revealed to his holy apostles*[c] *and to prophets by the Spirit,* ⁶*and which involves the Gentiles' being joint heirs and joint members of the body and sharers in the promise in Christ Jesus through the gospel.* ⁷*Of this gospel I became a servant according to the gift of God's grace, which was given to me through the working of his power.* ⁸*To me, the very least of all the saints, this grace was given, to preach to the Gentiles the good news of the unsearchable riches of Christ,* ⁹*and to make plain to all*[d] *what is the administration of the mystery, which was hidden for ages in God who created all things,*[e] ¹⁰*in order that through the Church the manifold wisdom of God should*

now be made known to the principalities and authorities in the heavenly realms, ¹¹*according to the eternal purpose which he accomplished in Christ Jesus our Lord,* ¹²*in whom we have boldness and confident access through faith in him.* ¹³*I beg you, therefore, not to become discouraged because of my sufferings on your behalf, which are your glory.*

Notes

^a Verses 2–7 in the Greek form one sentence. This is not reflected in the translation.

^b Literally, "the sons of men."

^c In v 5 ἀποστόλοις is omitted by B Ambrosiaster, but the clear witness of all the other texts is to be followed. Presumably it was omitted in order to conform the wording to that of Col 1:26.

^d There is a textual question about the inclusion of πάντας, "all." φωτίσαι, "to make plain," without an object would be quite unusual. It could be argued that this is, therefore, the more difficult reading and original, but if it were, one would expect other variants as well as πάντας in an effort to make it easier. Since, also, the witnesses which have the object, P⁴⁶ ℵ^c B C D G K P Ψ it vg syr^{p, h} cop^{sa, bo} Marcion Tertullian, are weightier than those without it, ℵ* A 1739 Origen Augustine, πάντας is probably to be taken as original. Some who accept the shorter reading interpret the administration of the mystery as the object. But this ignores the pronoun τίς, "what," and the fact that οἰκονομία, "administration," is in the nominative case (cf. also Gaugler, 141; *pace* J. A. Robinson, 170; Gnilka, 171; Lindemann, *Aufhebung,* 222 n. 99; Schnackenburg, 139 n. 334).

^e In a number of texts, including D^c K L P many minuscules syr^{h**}, the phrase διὰ Ἰησοῦ Χριστοῦ, "through Jesus Christ," is added after κτίσαντι, "created." If the phrase was original, there appears to be no good explanation for its later omission. Since the external evidence clearly supports a reading without it (cf. P⁴⁶ ℵ A B C D* F G P 33 1319 most versions and patristic quotations), it is best to see the phrase as a later addition in line with Pauline thought about the role of Christ in creation.

Form/Structure/Setting

3:1–13 is formally a digression on Paul's apostolic ministry to the Gentiles and on the mystery which had been revealed to him and was at the heart of his ministry. The original intention of the thought begun in 3:1 is not completed, because the reference in it to Paul as a prisoner for the sake of the Gentiles leads to an expatiation on this theme. 3:1, then, is anacoluthic, and the repetition of the opening phrase τούτου χάριν, "for this reason," in 3:14 suggests that at that point the writer takes up again the intention with which he had started out in 3:1, which can now be seen to be to intercede on behalf of his Gentile Christian readers. In this case, the original τούτου χάριν of 3:1 provides a link with the thrust of the preceding pericope, 2:11–22, and particularly the last part, vv 18–22. If his Gentile Christian readers are no longer outside the scope of the history of salvation, but have been privileged to be part of God's new temple, then the writer sees them as in need of being empowered to fulfill their role in God's purposes, of being enabled to become what they are, and gives an account of his prayer to that effect. Since this intention begins in v 1 but is not taken up again until v 14, it is in fact, strictly speaking, vv 2–13 which form the digression on Paul's ministry to the Gentiles within the introduction to an intercessory prayer. In Paul's letters, connected with the thanksgiving period or its equivalent with its intercessory prayer-report concerned with the situation of the readers, there is often a statement focusing on the writer and his situation (cf. Rom 1:11–15; 2 Cor 1:8–14; Phil 1:12–26; Col 1:24–29; 1 Thess 2:1–12). In Ephesians the corresponding feature appears to be this digression, in which the ministry of the one in whose name the letter is written is the center of attention.

The digression falls into three sentences, two longer ones and then one short final sentence. The two longer sentences, vv 2–7 and vv 8–12, provide parallel statements about the mystery which is central to the gospel with which Paul was entrusted. The first statement is framed by references to Paul's apostleship in terms of grace and, in line with the reflections of 2:11–22, focuses on the mystery of the Gentiles' participation in God's people, the Church, while the second statement links the mystery with the Church's role in God's purposes for the cosmos and thereby recalls the earlier association of mystery with God's plan for the cosmos in 1:9, 10. In its talk of the recipients of the revelation of the mystery, the first statement speaks of Paul alongside the holy apostles and prophets, while in the second statement the focus narrows to Paul alone as the proclaimer of the mystery. The final sentence, v 13, rounds off the digression neatly by taking up from v 1, but in a different formulation, the notion of the suffering apostle for the Gentiles, which had caused the digression in the first place (cf. also Caragounis, *Mysterion,* 72–74; *contra* Gnilka, 179, who takes v 13 as part of the following pericope).

This pericope in particular highlights the pseudonymous form of the letter as a whole. In its thirteen verses we find in concentrated form the writer's identification with the apostle (cf. the discussion of this phenomenon in the *Introduction*). Through this follower of Paul the apostolic tradition is continued, and Paul speaks again to the churches of Asia Minor: "I, Paul, the prisoner of Christ Jesus" (v 1), "the administration . . . given to me" (v 2), "the mystery was made known to me," "as I have already written" (v 3), "my insight" (v 4), "I was made a minister," "God's grace which was given to me" (v 7), "to me who am the very least of all the saints" (v 8), "I beg," and "my sufferings" (v 13). The effect of the apostle speaking again to the churches is maintained also by the form of direct address to the Gentile Christian readers which continues from chap. 2, throughout which it has been dominant: "you Gentiles" (v 1), "assuming that you have indeed heard," "for you" (v 2), "you will be able, when you read" (v 4), "I beg you," "on your behalf," and "your glory" (v 13).

The style of the passage, like the rest of the letter to this point, involves the stringing together of relative clauses, repetition (cf. especially "the grace given to me" in vv 2, 7, 8, "mystery" in vv 3, 4, 9, and "to make known" in vv 3, 5, 10), and liturgical language (cf. especially vv 11, 12). This continuity in style, together with the points of continuity of substance with the earlier part of the letter, argues against the view that the digression was a later insertion into preformed liturgical material for the sake of conformity to epistolary style (*contra* Kirby, *Ephesians,* 129–32).

The pericope has a number of parallels with Col 1:23c–28 (cf. Merklein, *Das kirchliche Amt,* 160–71, for a detailed discussion of the literary relationship). The relation between the two passages can be set out in terms of wording and of themes.

(*i*) Wording:

	Colossians		Ephesians
1:23c	ἐγὼ Παῦλος διάκονος	3:1	ἐγὼ Παῦλος ὁ δέσμιος
1:24a	ὑπὲρ ὑμῶν	3:1	ὑπὲρ ὑμῶν
1:24b	τὰ ὑστερήματα τῶν θλίψεων τοῦ Χριστοῦ ἐν τῇ σαρκί μου ὑπὲρ τοῦ σώματος αὐτοῦ	3:13	ἐν ταῖς θλίψεσίν μου ὑπὲρ ὑμῶν
1:25a	ἧς ἐγενόμην ἐγὼ διάκονος	3:7a	οὗ ἐγενήθην διάκονος
1:25b	τὴν οἰκονομίαν τοῦ θεοῦ τὴν δοθεῖσάν μοι εἰς ὑμᾶς	3:2	τὴν οἰκονομίαν τῆς χάριτος τοῦ θεοῦ τῆς δοθείσης μοι εἰς ὑμᾶς
1:26a	τὸ μυστήριον τὸ ἀποκεκρυμμένον ἀπὸ τῶν αἰώνων καὶ ἀπὸ τῶν γενεῶν	3:4b, 5a	τῷ μυστηρίῳ τοῦ Χριστοῦ, ὃ ἑτέραις γενεαῖς οὐκ ἐγνωρίσθη
		3:9	τοῦ μυστηρίου τοῦ ἀποκεκρυμμένου ἀπὸ τῶν αἰώνων
1:26b	νῦν δὲ ἐφανερώθη τοῖς ἁγίοις αὐτοῦ	3:5b	νῦν ἀπεκαλύφθη τοῖς ἁγίοις ἀποστόλοις αὐτοῦ καὶ προφήταις
1:27, 28a	γνωρίσαι τί τὸ πλοῦτος τῆς δόξης τοῦ μυστηρίου τούτου ἐν τοῖς ἔθνεσιν, ὅ ἐστιν Χριστὸς ἐν ὑμῖν . . . ὃν ἡμεῖς καταγγέλλομεν	3:8b	τοῖς ἔθνεσιν εὐαγγελίσασθαι τὸ ἀνεξιχνίαστον πλοῦτος τοῦ Χριστοῦ
1:29b	κατὰ τὴν ἐνέργειαν αὐτοῦ τὴν ἐνεργουμένην ἐν ἐμοὶ ἐν δυνάμει	3:7c	κατὰ τὴν ἐνέργειαν τῆς δυνάμεως αὐτοῦ

(*ii*) Themes:

Col 1:23c	Introduction of Paul	Eph 3:1
Col 1:24	Suffering of Apostle	Eph 3:1, 13
Col 1:25	Office of Apostle	Eph 3:2
Col 1:26	Revelation of Hidden Mystery	Eph 3:4, 5, 9
Col 1:27	Content of Mystery	Eph 3:6
Col 1:28	Proclamation of Content	Eph 3:8, 9

As regards the themes, Ephesians can be seen to follow the same sequence as Colossians. Eph 3:1–13 appears clearly to be dependent on Col 1:23c–28 and to be an interpretation of it. The two major changes the writer has made in his use of Colossians are the focusing of the content of the mystery on Gentiles' membership in the Church composed of Jews and Gentiles, not just on Christ among the Gentiles (3:6; cf. Col 1:27), and the specifying, and thus narrowing down, of the recipients of the mystery to the holy apostles and prophets (3:5; cf. Col 1:26). Both reflect the distinctive emphasis of Ephesians on the Church and on the role of the apostles and prophets as its foundation. Ephesians' focus on the Church can at the same time allow a broadening of perspective in comparison with Colossians, for whereas in Col 1:26 the mystery is simply made known by God to believers, in the second statement about the mystery in Eph 3 it is made known by God through the Church to the principalities and authorities in the heavenly realms.

Ephesians' use of Colossians incorporates Colossians' own use of a "revelation schema" in Col 1:26, 27. Such a schema, in which a previously hidden mystery is said to be disclosed in the present, appears to have been fairly common in early Christianity's appropriation of terminology from the Jewish apocalypses. The motif first appears in 1 Cor 2:7–10, then in Col 1:26, 27, here in Eph 3:4, 5, 9, 10, and also in the non-Pauline doxology added to the end of Romans in Rom 16:25–27. The language of 2 Tim 1:9, 10; Titus 1:2, 3; 1 Pet 1:20 (cf. also 1 Tim 3:16) about present manifestation of that which existed previously may also be an echo of the same motif. (For discussion of the possible use of the revelation schema in early Christian proclamation, see N. A. Dahl, "Form-Critical Observations on Early Christian Preaching," in *Jesus in the Memory of the Early Church* (Minneapolis: Augsburg, 1976) 32–33; Lührmann, *Offenbarungsverständnis,* 124–33.) Whatever its origins, this schema appears to have become popular among Paul's disciples. The formulation of the schema in Ephesians is distinct from the other examples in the NT; it cannot therefore be traced to traditional material, but rather derives from the author's distinctive reworking of the Colossians passage (cf. also Merklein, *Das kirchliche Amt,* 165–70).

How does the material in this digression on the apostolic ministry relate to other parts of the first half of the letter? It is the immediately preceding section, 2:11–22, which feeds most directly into its depiction of Paul as the minister of the mystery of Gentiles having become part of the one body of the Church. Paul's ministry was only possible because Christ's work of reconciliation had first created that one body or one new person (2:15, 16). The new status which results for Gentile Christians is described by means of a συν- compound in 2:19 and by three such compounds in 3:6, while the access to God provided by Christ's reconciling activity (2:18) is celebrated again in the present pericope in 3:12. Both passages are addressed directly to the Gentile readers (2:11; 3:1), and both look back to the key role of apostles and prophets in God's purposes (2:20; 3:5).

In that Paul is seen as the vehicle of salvation for the Gentiles, it is not surprising that aspects of the blessings of that salvation mentioned in the eulogy of 1:3–14 are to be found again here in the digression. In particular, inheritance and promise figure in the formulation of 3:6 (cf. 1:13, 14), and "mystery" as a description of the salvation provided in Christ in 3:3, 4 has been preceded by the same designation in 1:10. The content of the earlier reference to mystery, the cosmic summing up in Christ, can in fact be seen to be anticipated in the one Church out of Jews and Gentiles, which is the content of the mystery in this digression. In both contexts, the relation of the mystery to God's eternal purpose, which centers in Christ, is very much to the fore (cf. 1:9, 10; 3:11).

In the thanksgiving period of 1:15–23 the writer had requested for all his readers the Spirit of wisdom and revelation in the knowledge of God (1:17) and knowledge of the working of God's mighty strength (1:19). But in 3:1–13 Paul as foundational apostle is seen as the one who has experienced par excellence such insight and revelation (cf. vv 3–5, 7–9) and such working of God's power (cf. v 7). As Paul's apostolic insight and revelation are passed on (vv 3, 4), the writer is instrumental in fulfilling his own request for his readers. It was in the intercessory prayer-report that the concepts of the Church and the Church as the body were first explicitly introduced, and these occur again in this pericope in 3:6 and 3:10. The relation of the Church to the cosmos and its powers, first treated in 1:21–23, is taken up again here in 3:10. In 1:1–10 the emphasis was on salvation as God's gift and all of grace; here in 3:1–13 this emphasis is carried over to the notion of Paul's apostleship, which is similarly seen as God's gift and all of grace (3:2, 7, 8).

As we have already noted, the passage is connected with the prayer which follows in 3:14–21 by the repetition of the opening phrase of 3:1 in 3:14. There are no specific points of contact between the content of the digression and the content of the prayer, which is finally reported after the digression has been brought to a conclusion, but there is a general link. The prayer shows the writer's concern that the apostolic roots of the gospel recalled in the digression be effectively appropriated by his readers. In addition, the digression functions as an elaboration on the person who prays (cf. also Caragounis, *Mysterion*, 55–56)—in this case the author, who has taken on the role of his master, Paul—and secondarily as an elaboration also on those for whom he prays—the Gentile readers. It also suggests the importance of the relationship between them. The digression is related in a similar way to the paraenesis of the second part of the letter. It supports the pseudonymous framework on which the paraenesis rests, so that 4:1 and 6:20 take up the notion of Paul as prisoner (cf. 3:1), and 6:19 takes up the language of "mystery" and "making known" with reference to Paul's ministry (cf. 3:3–5, 9, 10).

In discourses designed to persuade, the *digressio* was frequently found in association with the *narratio*, and could come at the beginning, in the middle, or at the end of the *narratio*. It was meant to treat a theme relevant, though not logically necessary, to the case being made, and to do so in such a way as to secure the audience's favor (cf. Quintilian 4.3.1, 14). Here, at the end, it increases the goodwill of the recipients by reminding them of the suffering apostle's ministry on their behalf. It underlines for the Gentile readers that they owe their participation in the salvation that had been promised, their membership in the same body as Jewish Christians, their part in the Church's cosmic role, and their access to God, to the gospel that was originally revealed to and proclaimed by Paul. Since the writer is addressing his readers in Paul's name, the *digressio* strengthens the bond between writer and readers, increasing the readers' willingness to accept the writer's authority and his extensive exhortations to appropriate conduct, which will follow in the second part of the letter.

In what setting was a digression to develop such an image of Paul necessary? The *Introduction*, which treats the general setting of the letter in more detail, is relevant to this question. Suffice it to say here that for the sake of his readers, the writer is concerned to strengthen the bonds between them and the Pauline tradition. In order to do so he builds on the prevailing positive image of Paul as the suffering imprisoned apostle on behalf of the Gentiles. Of course, Paul's apostleship to the Gentiles is clearly attested in his own writings (cf. Gal 1:16; 2:7–9; Rom 1:5, 13, 14; 11:13; 15:16, 18), as are his sufferings (cf. Gal 6:17; 1 Cor 4:9–13; 15:30–32; 2 Cor 1:3–11; 4:7–11; 6:3–10; 11:23–33; 12:7–10; Phil 3:7–10; Col 1:24), and his imprisonments (cf. 2 Cor 6:5; 11:23; Phil 1:7, 12–14, 17; Philem 1, 9, 10, 13, 23; Col 4:3, 10, 18) in the course of carrying out his apostolic ministry. But now this composite picture, a picture of one who was imprisoned and suffered as Christ's agent in bringing the gospel to the Gentiles, helps to enhance the authority of the apostolic tradition for the writer's Gentile readers.

It is Paul's distinctive contribution in the past that is in view. He is not being used as a model for the Church's missionary activity (*contra* Meyer, *Kirche und Mission*, 58–60), nor is the reference to his being the very least of all the saints (v 8) intended to make the point that his conversion is now paradigmatic for all believers (*contra* M. C. de Boer, "Images of Paul in the Post-Apostolic Period," *CBQ* 42 [1980] 374). Instead, to remember the distinctive work of Paul is to remember the unity and catholicity of the Church. As the previous pericope (2:11–22) demonstrated, the writer knows that ultimately the union of Jew and Gentile was effected by the reconciling work of Christ, so what are attributed to Paul are the insight into, and the proclamation of what had already been accomplished. His picture of Paul as the agent of an already-achieved unity gives no hint of the intense struggle over the issue with certain Jewish Christians, in which Paul was engaged until the end of his life. What is brought out, instead, by the stress on Paul as the recipient of revelation (vv 3, 5) and on the distinctive gracing of his ministry (vv 2, 7, 8) is the authoritative and revelatory status of the apostolic tradition, thereby underlining the notion of the apostolic foundation already introduced in 2:20. At the same time, to remember the work of the apostle to the Gentiles helps to reinforce the sense of identity of Gentile Christians. Setting Paul's work in the whole schema of revelation can reinforce their sense of identity in regard to the heritage of Judaism. Highlighting the cosmic scope of the mystery entrusted to Paul can reinforce that sense of identity in regard to the wider world in which Gentile Christians found themselves.

Comment

1 τούτου χάριν ἐγὼ Παῦλος ὁ δέσμιος τοῦ Χριστοῦ Ἰησοῦ ὑπὲρ ὑμῶν τῶν ἐθνῶν—, "for this reason I, Paul, the prisoner of Christ Jesus for the sake of you Gentiles—." This verse should not be made into a sentence by supplying εἰμί and treating ὁ δέσμιος as the predicate (*contra* the Peshitta; Chrysostom; Meyer, 153–54; and Houlden, 297). As noted in the previous section, this verse contains an incomplete statement and its thought is not taken up again until v 14. It appears to be the beginning of an account of a prayer asking that the Gentile Christian readers be enabled to live out their privileged role in God's purposes, a prayer in which the introductory phrase, "for this reason," refers back to the depiction of that role in 2:18–22 in particular. The incomplete sentence, with its emphasis on the person of Paul, "I, Paul," and its reference to him as Christ's prisoner on behalf of the Gentiles, in fact serves as the basis of the important digression on Paul's apostolic ministry which follows.

The phrase τούτου χάριν is not found in the major Paulines. Apart from its use in this verse and v 14, it occurs elsewhere in the NT only in Titus 1:5. ἐγὼ Παῦλος can be used by Paul himself (cf. 1 Thess 2:18; Gal 5:2; 2 Cor 10:1; Philem 19; cf. also Col 1:23), and so cannot in itself be held to suggest a magnified focus on the apostle typical of pseudonymity. But it is the combination of the emphatic self-reference with a further self-designation here, "the prisoner of Christ Jesus," which marks this reference off from the others and which justifies the claim that this is a "formal and somewhat magisterial" way of stating Paul's relation to Gentile Christians (cf. Houlden, 296).

"The prisoner of Christ Jesus" (cf. 4:1, "the prisoner in the Lord") has replaced Paul's description of himself as a minister or servant of the gospel in Col 1:23f, on which this passage is based. It takes up Paul's self-designation in Philem 1, 9, δέσμιος Χριστοῦ Ἰησοῦ, but adds to it the definite article and thereby heightens the distinctiveness of Paul's apostolic imprisonment (cf. also 2 Tim 1:8). The Philemon references and Phil 1:12–17, where his imprisonment is seen as ἐν Χριστῷ, show that Paul had already reflected on his captivity theologically. He can use the term "prisoner" in both a literal and metaphorical sense at the same time, so that his physical imprisonment can be seen as simply the consequence of his spiritual captivity to Christ. This latter metaphorical sense is similar to Paul's use of δοῦλος, "slave," to speak of his unconditional allegiance to his Lord.

There is a further theological significance attached to Paul's imprisonment. It can be said to be "for the sake of you Gentiles." ὑπὲρ ὑμῶν τῶν ἐθνῶν could in fact be taken as the part of the introduction to the interrupted prayer that designates those for whom the prayer is offered (cf., for example, Col 1:9, "we do not cease to pray for you [ὑπὲρ ὑμῶν]"). But it is probably preferable to take the phrase here as more closely related to its immediate antecedent, the notion of the apostle's imprisonment. Paul's imprisonment was integral to his special apostolic ministry of proclaiming the gospel to the Gentiles. Historically, his advocacy of a law-free Gentile mission was what provoked the opposition which led to his arrest and imprisonment. Now it is not just Gentiles in general, but the readers in particular, who are to see themselves as indebted to the sort of apostleship which would suffer in this way, as the form of direct address, "you Gentiles," is continued from the previous pericope.

2 εἴ γε ἠκούσατε τὴν οἰκονομίαν τῆς χάριτος τοῦ θεοῦ τῆς δοθείσης μοι εἰς ὑμᾶς, "assuming that you have of course heard about the stewardship of the grace of God which was given to me for you." The writer in his identification with Paul now begins his digression on Paul's ministry for the sake of the Gentile readers by capitalizing on their knowledge of the apostle's work. εἴ γε, which occurs elsewhere in the NT only in Eph 4:21; Gal 3:4; 2 Cor 6:3; and Col 1:23, introduces a statement which makes explicit an assumption lying behind a preceding assertion. It depends on the context whether such a strengthened "if" implies doubt or confident assumption (cf. BDF § 454 [2]; Moule, *Idiom-Book*, 164). Here the latter meaning is clear. A reference of this sort to the readers' knowledge of his apostolic work makes little sense in a letter from Paul himself to the church at Ephesus (*contra* Meyer, 154–55, who takes it as a delicate reference to Paul's earlier preaching to the readers). If Ephesians is held to be a circular letter from Paul written to churches in Asia Minor not known personally to him but founded by his co-workers, then sense can be made of the remark, although it still seems quite unnecessary and rather strange for Paul to have to speak of his ministry in this way. The remark becomes more understandable when it is seen as part of the device of pseudonymity.

The meaning of οἰκονομία is debated (cf. the earlier discussion of its use in 1:10). Here, rather than the actual act of administrating as in 1:10 (cf. also

3:9), or that which is administered (so Meyer, 155; Abbott, 79; Schlier, 148; Gnilka, 163; Merklein, *Das kirchliche Amt,* 173–74; Schnackenburg, 132), its specific connotation in connection with Paul's apostolic role may well be the office of administrating, i.e., the stewardship (cf. J. Reumann, *"Oikonomia =* 'Covenant': Terms for *Heilsgeschichte* in Early Christian Usage," *NovT* 3 (1959) 282; "Οἰκονομία-Terms in Paul in Comparison with Lukan *Heilsgeschichte,*" *NTS* 13 [1966–67] 147–49; Houlden, 297; Lindemann, *Aufhebung,* 79). This interpretation runs counter to the expectation of a unified usage of the term in Ephesians. Yet it should not be thought unusual for the writer to use the term in one way when it is more closely connected with God's activity (1:10; 3:9), and in another way when it is more closely connected with Paul's apostleship, especially when in the latter case he inherits a particular usage. That usage is found in the parallel passage in Colossians on which this verse is based. Col 1:25 has determined the connotation here in Eph 3:2 with its reversion to the earlier Pauline usage of 1 Cor 9:17 (cf. also 1 Cor 4:1, 2 where Paul uses οἰκονόμος of his apostleship).

In Col 1:25 Paul's ministry was described as "the stewardship of God which was given to me for you." But here it is "the stewardship of the grace of God" and in the Greek text "which was given to me for you" now modifies grace rather than stewardship. Grace has as its specific focus the special favor granted Paul in qualifying him to be apostle to the Gentiles (cf. also vv 7, 8). The slight change of emphasis from Col 1:25 is in line both with this writer's earlier general stress on God's grace (cf. 2:5–8) and with Paul's own particular association of that grace with his apostleship (cf. Gal 1:15; 2:9; 1 Cor 3:10; 15:10; Rom 1:5; 12:3; 15:15). As in v 1, the readers are explicitly related to Paul's apostleship. That apostleship mediates grace. The grace was given to Paul, but it was for the ultimate benefit of these Gentile Christians—"for you." This assertion underlines that the subject of the digression is not simply Paul himself, but his ministry for the Gentile readers.

Some commentators argue that the language of this verse suggests that teaching about Paul was already part of the instruction the readers had received. They point in support to the similar language about Christ in a context of instruction in 4:21 (cf. Schlier, 148; Gnilka, 163; Ernst, 327). But their inference about specific catechetical teaching is by no means a necessary one, and the writer's formulation makes just as good sense when taken as a reference to his readers' general knowledge of Paul.

3 ὅτι κατὰ ἀποκάλυψιν ἐγνωρίσθη μοι τὸ μυστήριον, καθὼς προέγραψα ἐν ὀλίγῳ, "that the mystery was made known to me according to revelation, as I have already written briefly." The special favor granted Paul in his office of apostle was that the mystery was made known to him. For the background and usage of the terminology "to make known a mystery," see the comments on 1:9, 10, where it was made clear that the secret God has disclosed to Paul has as its presupposition the fulfillment of God's plan of salvation in Christ. The comments on v 2 have already recalled the earlier use of the οἰκονομία word group in connection with Paul's apostleship in 1 Cor 4:1, 2, and in fact he speaks there of himself, Apollos, and Cephas as "stewards of the mysteries." Here, in all probability under the influence of Col 1:26, 27, the term "mystery" is in the singular, and, as becomes clear from v 6, it has as its specific focus the inclusion of the Gentiles in God's accomplishment of salvation in Christ. In Col 1:25 the stewardship received by Paul was spelled out in terms of his active proclamation of the gospel, but here in v 3 there is a different emphasis as it is elaborated instead in terms of his passive reception of revelation.

It is this notion of revelation which receives emphasis by the placing of the phrase κατὰ ἀποκάλυψιν, "according to revelation," at the beginning of the clause (cf. also the use of the verb in v 5), and by the way this placement reinforces the idea of disclosure already present in "was made known." κατὰ ἀποκάλυψιν should not simply be translated "by revelation," indicating the means by which the mystery was made known, as most commentators assume, since this is a meaning which is not attested for κατά with the accusative. Instead, this is an example of the use of κατά with the accusative to indicate the norm and, at the same time, the reason or ground (BAGD 407; cf. also Merklein, *Das kirchliche Amt,* 198). In Gal 1:12, 16, Paul had talked of "a revelation of Jesus Christ" in connection with his reception of the gospel and of the purpose of this revelation being the preaching of Christ among the Gentiles. Presumably it is this initial formative revelation on the Damascus road which provided the writer's inspiration for the link here with the disclosure of the mystery. At the same time, "revelation" appears to have become a more general concept for this writer, so that "in accordance with revelation" not only underlines Paul's role as the receptor of revelation but also indicates the normative status the writer attributes to Paul's interpretation of the gospel.

The last clause of v 3 has prompted speculation about the writer's reference. Among the more unlikely suggestions are that what has already been "written briefly" is a reference to Gal 1:12, 16 (Houlden, 298), that it is a reference to Rom 16:25–27, which also mentions the revelation of the mystery, and thus supports the claim that Romans 16 was originally addressed to Ephesus (Davies, *ExpTim* 46 [1934–35] 568), and that it is a reference to the other letters in the Pauline corpus and to be connected with the view that Ephesians is the introduction to the Pauline letter collection (Goodspeed, *Meaning,* 41–42, followed by Mitton, *Epistle,* 233–36). In regard to the last suggestion, it is difficult to see what is written in the rest of the Pauline corpus as "brief," a description which makes sense as a slightly depreciatory way of referring to what stands earlier in the same document (cf. 1 Pet 5:12; also Heb 13:22), but not as a reference to several documents. So, as the majority of commentators propose, the clause is best taken as a reference back to the earlier chapters of the present letter and, more specifically, 1:9, 10 and 2:11–22 with their discussions of the disclosure of the mystery and the inclusion of the Gentiles. Verse 3b indicates the writer's concern to preserve the formal features of a letter, and at the same time, suggests that he sees the sort of interpretation he has provided in 2:11–22 as part of the content of Pauline revelation (cf. Merklein, *Das kirchliche Amt,* 215–16).

4 πρὸς ὃ δύνασθε ἀναγινώσκοντες νοῆσαι τὴν σύνεσίν μου ἐν τῷ μυστηρίῳ τοῦ Χριστοῦ, "in accordance with which you will be able, when you read, to perceive my insight into the mystery of Christ." The readers are expected to recognize the writer's special insight from what he has already written earlier in the letter. πρός with the accusative can indicate a simple connection ("with regard to," "with reference to"), but it can also more specifically suggest a standard of evaluation or judgment ("in accordance with"), and the latter appears to be the case here (cf. BAGD 710[5d]; cf. also Gal 2:14; 2 Cor 5:10). The recipients of the letter are to make their judgment when they read, and in all probability it is the situation of the public reading of the letter in the assembly which is in view (cf. Col 4:16; *contra* Westcott, 45, who speaks of study of copies of the letter by individual Christians). What the writer expects to become clear from such a reading is his insight, his grasp of the significance of the secret which God has disclosed in Christ. The notion of insight into mysteries being given to those who have received revelations or visions is a frequent one in apocalyptic literature (cf. Dan 10:1; 4 Ezra 5:22; 14:40, 47; *T. Levi* 2.3; 18.1, 7). In addition, as, for example, K. G. Kuhn ("The Epistle to the Ephesians," 118–19) points out, the terminology in the Qumran hymns (cf. 1QH 2.13; 12.13) has strong parallels with that of Ephesians. The term σύνεσις was employed in Col 1:9; 2:2 as a quality which Paul desired for the whole community, and earlier in Ephesians itself, though with the use of synonyms (φρόνησις in 1:8 and ἐπίγνωσις in 1:17), the writer has emphasized such understanding as being for all believers. But now in Eph 3 there is a different focus, as the apostle himself is presented as the mediator of spiritual insight. This is not dissimilar to the role of the teacher of righteousness at Qumran, to whom insight was given which was for the benefit of the whole community (cf. 1QS 9.18). The insight for others with which the apostle is credited is insight into the mystery of Christ (cf. Col 4:3, also 1:27), the mystery of which the content is Christ. The particular aspect of what God has done in Christ which is in view becomes clear in v 6. It is how the Gentiles have become included in the disclosure of God's secret. Col 1:27 has again been influential in the development of the writer's thought about the mystery. Not only has Colossians already reduced the mysteries to one which centers in Christ, but it relates this to the Gentiles—Christ among the Gentiles. While the emphasis in Colossians is still on the Christological aspect of this statement, Eph 3 develops the latter, Gentile element in an ecclesiological direction.

The text's presentation of Paul as proclaiming his own insight raises the question of whether the genuine Paul would have boasted of his understanding in this way. On the one hand, it can be said that Paul was certainly not reticent about the special revelation of the gospel to him with its accompanying apostolic role (e.g., Gal 1 and 2) or about his spiritual authority as an apostle (e.g., 1 Cor 14:37, 38). Yet, on the other hand, Paul paraded his credentials only when under provocation or attack, and his reluctance to engage in such an enterprise is particularly clear in 2 Cor 10–13. This passage differs from others because its commendation of Paul's own insight is so unprovoked and unqualified. It is therefore best explained as further evidence of a pseudonymous writer looking back at the apostle's contribution and boosting the claims of his teaching authority for a later time. Yet, in some ways, the pseudonymity is at its most transparent here. The special insight attributed to Paul is that of the writer, and consists of his interpretation and development of Paul's thinking about the place of the Gentiles, as set out particularly in such letters as Galatians and Romans. This inspired insight, which builds on Paul and which has been seen particularly in 2:11–22, in all likelihood belongs to one whose role in the community is that of teacher (cf. 4:11), who looks back to the revelation given to the apostles and prophets as foundational, and who sees his own gift as perception of the significance of that revelation (cf. Merklein, *Das kirchliche Amt,* 218–20; Schnackenburg, 134). Since it is in close continuity with that original revelation, the writer can attribute his insight to the apostle himself, and in this way pseudonymity enables his interpretation of Paul to be authorized by Paul himself.

5 ὃ ἑτέραις γενεαῖς οὐκ ἐγνωρίσθη τοῖς υἱοῖς τῶν ἀνθρώπων ὡς νῦν ἀπεκαλύφθη τοῖς ἁγίοις ἀποστόλοις αὐτοῦ καὶ προφήταις ἐν πνεύματι, "which was not made known to people in other generations as it has now been revealed to his holy apostles and to prophets by the Spirit." Before the writer elaborates further on the content of the mystery, he sets it in the context of the revelation schema (discussed under *Form/Structure/Setting*), and he does this under the influence of Col 1:26 (*contra* Barth, 331, who, in taking this verse as a quotation from a hymn or confession, fails to take adequate account of these factors). Colossians and Ephesians have in common at this point the basic contrast between a period in which the mystery was not revealed and the present period of its revelation. But instead of "hidden for ages and generations" the writer of Ephesians has "was not made known in other generations," adds "to people" (literally, "to the sons of men") and does not use "hidden for ages" until v 9. In the second half of the contrast Ephesians adds ὡς, replaces φανεροῦν by ἀποκαλύπτειν, restricts τοῖς ἁγίοις αὐτοῦ with the addition of apostles and prophets, and includes a mention of the means of revelation, ἐν πνεύματι.

The contrast in the verse has three parts to it. The first and most basic focuses on the revelation of the mystery: "was not made known"/"has been revealed." The passives of the verbs are divine passives. His plan to have one Church out of Jews and Gentiles was something that had to be disclosed by God himself. In this formulation the contrast is a stark and absolute one. It is not as if previously there was a partial knowledge of God's plan. The writer's notion of "mystery" involves a hidden purpose of God that has only now been revealed and not before. Even the OT writers were ignorant of the sort of blessing that was to come to the Gentiles. Some commentators have attempted to weaken the force of such an assertion by suggesting that ὡς indicates a gradual comparison and that the thought is simply that in the past the mystery was not known as clearly as it is now (cf. Westcott, 45; Abbott, 82; Mare, *BETS* 8 [1965] 77–84; Caragounis, *Mysterion,* 102 and n. 24). But the ὡς does not indicate a relative difference or difference of degree; it marks the occurrence of something completely new (so also Schlier, 150; Steinmetz, *Protologische Heilszuversicht,* 58; Gaugler, 132; Ryrie, *BSac* 123 [1966] 24–31; Gnilka, 167; Merklein, *Das kirchliche Amt,* 166; Schnackenburg, 134). The clear distinction between past and present in the revelation schema of Col 1:26 has not been altered. For this writer some sort of participation of the nations in the salvation of the end-time, as foretold in the OT, does not amount to this new thing, the Church in which Gentiles and Jews are on equal footing on the basis of faith in Christ. It must be remembered from the discussion of 2:11–22 that for Ephesians there is a striking element of discontinuity between the Church and Israel, whereby the Church is a new creation which transcends the categories of Jew and Gentile. Barth is typical of those who have problems with this verse's perspective on the OT because they fail to bear this consideration in mind. He writes, "Verse 5 makes an affirmation which seems difficult to reconcile with the prophetic and Psalm quotations used in Ephesians: not even the elect men of Israel knew of the secret that is now revealed" (333), and, "If the author of Ephesians were pressed to say whether he really wanted to deny that the prophets and psalmists of Israel knew about the Gentiles' access to God and his people, he would probably refer to his OT allusion and quotation in 2:13, 17. For him Isa 57:19 predicted the approach of the nations" (334 n. 45; cf. also Schlier, 149–50; Caragounis, *Mysterion*, 102 n. 24). In the end, Barth has recourse to the hypothesis that the idiosyncracy of the subject matter of the verse derives from its being a quotation used by Paul. He has neglected to take account of Ephesians' perspective on the relation between the Church and Israel, and failed to recognize that this letter's use of quotations from the psalms and prophets, even the Isa 57:19 quotation, is not determined by a prediction and fulfillment schema. As an investigation of the writer's use of the OT shows, the thought of this verse and the letter's handling of Scripture are fully compatible (cf. Lincoln, *JSNT* 14 [1982] 16–57).

The second part of the verse's contrast makes the time element explicit: "in other generations"/"now." The dative ἑτέραις γενεαῖς is used here to specify a period of time (cf. 2:12; BDF § 200 [4]; J. H. Moulton and N. Turner, *A Grammar of New Testament Greek*, vol. 3 [Edinburgh: T. & T. Clark, 1963] 151–52). In the light of the discussion about the OT above, there is an interesting later textual variant, found in Hippolytus and in Gnostic texts cited by him, which replaces ἑτέραις by προτέραις, "earlier," in an attempt to make clear that the patriarchs and prophets and not just the Gentiles were in view and thereby to ensure support for their own notion of a total break between the OT and the NT (cf. Orbe, *Greg* 37 [1956] 201–19). But in the text we have, previous history can simply be described as "other generations" in contrast to the all-important "now," the decisive time after the death and resurrection of Christ, which is the period of the Church (cf. also Steinmetz, *Protologische Heilszuversicht*, 58; Gnilka, 166; Merklein, *Das kirchliche Amt*, 184–85).

The third and perhaps climactic part of the contrast, and that which most distinguishes this verse from Col 1:26, is that identifying the recipients of the revelation (or in the former case, potential recipients): "to the sons of men"/ "to his holy apostles and to prophets." The formulation of the first half of this contrast is of course a Hebraism for humans (e.g., LXX Gen 11:5; Pss 11:1, 8; 44:2; 48:2, and see Mark 3:28 for the only other NT example of the plural). Knowledge of God's purpose was previously inaccessible to humanity as such, but in the new period he chose a special group of people to be recipients of his disclosure, the apostles and prophets. The narrowing of the recipients of revelation from all believers in Col 1:26 to a particular group is striking and is clearly connected to the author's already expressed interest in the foundational role of the apostles and prophets in the Church (cf. 2:20). There are, however, questions of syntax and meaning which arise out of the writer's description of this group. First of all, what is the reference of αὐτοῦ, and do αὐτοῦ and ἁγίοις qualify only ἀποστόλοις or both ἀποστόλοις and προφήταις? It could be argued that the closest explicit antecedent of αὐτοῦ is Christ in v 4, and this reference fits the close relationship between Christ and his apostles (cf. Westcott, 46; Schnackenburg, 135). On the other hand, the passive form of the verb in this clause has as its implied subject God, and since this would also retain the original reference of αὐτοῦ from its source in Col 1:26, this interpretation may well be preferable (cf. also Meyer, 160). It is noticeable that the αὐτοῦ divides the phrase "apostles and prophets" instead of coming after it, which one might expect if it were meant to qualify both terms. This suggests, therefore, that both it and ἁγίοις modify only "apostles" rather than "apostles and prophets" (so Abbott, 82; Gaugler, 133; Merklein, *Das kirchliche Amt*, 187–88; Schnackenburg, 135; *contra* Schlier, 150). The syntax suggests, then, that in interpreting τοῖς ἁγίοις αὐτοῦ in Col 1:26 it is primarily the apostles that the writer has in mind as recipients of revelation and those who deserve to be designated as "holy." Then, as in 2:20, it becomes natural to include the prophets also because of their intimate connection with revelation. While the undisputed letters of Paul appear to distinguish between the revelation of the Christ-event to Paul and charismatic revelations to prophets, Ephesians brings both types together under the one rubric of revelation.

The designation of the apostles as "holy" has attracted considerable comment. The very fact that the term is used here of a restricted group marks it off from the general Pauline use of it of all believers as set apart for God (*pace* Abbott, 82; Schlier, 150; Caird, 65). It is the particular status of these individuals that is now in view. A number of factors contribute to this designation of the apostles as "holy." One is the writer's dependence on the source he is interpreting, Col 1:26. Next, "holy" in its use here must be seen as retaining its basic meaning of "set apart for God." It is simply that the context colors this so that the apostles are now characterized as specially set apart by God to receive revelation (cf. also Paul's self-description in Gal 1:15, 16; Rom 1:1; cf. Merklein, *Das kirchliche Amt*, 189–90). Yet, inevitably, the term also suggests reverence on the part of someone looking back at this privileged role played by the apostles, who were thereby set off from other believers (cf. also Ign. *Magn.* 3.1, which can speak of "the holy presbyters"; cf. Gnilka, 167).

It is not only the singling out of apostles as a holy group that makes the sentiments of this verse unlikely to have come from Paul himself, but also the willingness to attribute to the other apostles the reception of the distinctive revelation of the place of the Gentiles in the Church, which he regarded as his special commission. On both counts, a post-apostolic setting for Ephesians provides a better explanation.

What is the relation of the reception of the mystery by Paul to its reception by the holy apostles and the prophets? By the amount of space devoted to each, the writer makes clear that although he is concerned about the apostles and prophets as norms of revelation in the Church, he regards the revelation to Paul as having primacy (cf. vv 3, 4, 7, 8). It may well be that he is aware of two distinctive traditions about the revelation concerning the Gentiles, which are found elsewhere in the NT (on this, cf. Best, *JTS* 35 [1984] 1–31). There is the tradition about Paul's unique role as the apostle to the Gentiles and another tradition, which raises historical questions, about a commissioning of the Twelve to preach to the Gentiles (cf. Matt 28:19, 20; Luke 24:47; Acts 1:8). Ephesians appears simply to combine the two, while retaining Paul's predominant role. In fact, the insight of Paul about Gentiles being on equal footing with the Jews in the Church seems to have been accepted eventually by the other apostles, but only after some tensions and conflicts. Ephesians is unconcerned about this actual historical process and is content to attribute original revelation on this to those other apostles and prophets as well as Paul. There is no evidence for the speculative historical hypothesis of Caird (65) that "the revelation must have come to other apostles and prophets through an inspired utterance of the prophet Paul, which they were able to recognize as the guidance of the Spirit."

One final aspect of v 5 requires comment—the force of ἐν πνεύματι. Does this phrase qualify only the preceding noun "prophets," so that "prophets in the Spirit" corresponds to "holy apostles" (cf. Schlier, 150–51; Gaugler, 134; Merklein, *Das kirchliche Amt*, 189; Schnackenburg, 135)? There is clearly an intimate link between prophecy and the Spirit (cf. 1 Thess 5:19, 20; 1 Cor 12:9, 10), and yet this also tells against interpreting "prophets in the Spirit" as a unit, since it goes without saying that true prophets speak in the Spirit. The alternative is to take ἐν πνεύματι as qualifying the verb, so that the revelation to the apostles and prophets is said to have taken place through or by the Spirit (cf. Meyer, 160; J. A. Robinson, 78; Abbott, 83; Gnilka, 167; Mussner, 102). Eph 1:17 has already made a close connection between the Spirit and revelation (cf. also 1 Cor 2:10). It seems best to see that as in view here, though inevitably the phrase is likely to color particularly the term to which it is adjacent as well as to qualify the verb in the clause. It should be noted that this is exactly the way the writer used ἐν πνεύματι, when the phrase occurred at the end of 2:22.

6 εἶναι τὰ ἔθνη συγκληρονόμα καὶ σύσσωμα καὶ συμμέτοχα τῆς ἐπαγγελίας ἐν Χριστῷ Ἰησοῦ διὰ τοῦ εὐαγγελίου, "and which involves the Gentiles being joint heirs and joint members of the body and sharers in the promise in Christ Jesus through the gospel." The writer now comes to an explicit statement of the content of the mystery he has mentioned earlier (v 4). The infinitive εἶναι is epexegetical, clarifying what is meant by the mystery. What is concealed in English translation is that the content of the mystery, the full inclusion of the Gentiles in the Church, is described by means of three adjectives which each begin with the prefix συν-. As is likely to have been the case in 2:19 and was certainly the case in 2:21, 22, the συν- prefix has in view a relationship with other believers, but since the subject of the clause is τὰ ἔθνη, "the Gentiles," those other believers must primarily be those of Jewish birth. It is important to grasp rightly the writer's emphasis. He is not celebrating the relationship of Gentiles with Israel or the Jewish people as such (*contra* Barth, 337). With the terms he uses he directs attention to unity within the Church rather than unity with Israel and her past. For, as has already been observed from 2:11–22, the writer views the Church as a new entity which transcends old divisions and categories, and what for him is at the heart of God's disclosure is that the Gentiles are an essential constituent of this new entity.

This emerges particularly clearly from the second of the three adjectives, σύσσωμα, which is evidenced nowhere else in the literature of the time and might therefore be a term which the writer has coined for the occasion. The closest equivalent to be found is the use of the passive of the verb συσσωματοποιεῖν in Pseudo-Aristotle, *De mundo* 396a, 14. The best literal translation is " 'concorporate,' that is, sharers in the one Body" (J. A. Robinson, 78). The Gentiles have not been added to an already existing entity; they are fully equal joint members, totally necessary for the life of the body, which without them would not exist (cf. the notion of the one body in 2:16; 4:4, and the comments on the Church as Christ's body in 1:23). They have not only become joint members of the body with Jewish Christians but also συγκληρονόμα, "joint heirs." The inheritance in which they share is for Ephesians an image for the full salvation God has prepared for his people, which they have already begun to enjoy through the Spirit, who is the guarantee of complete future possession (cf. 1:14; 5:5, and note that in 1:18 κληρονομία is used of God's inheritance rather than that of believers). So, central to the mystery is the Gentiles' full and equal share in the inheritance of the blessings of salvation. συγκληρονόμος occurs elsewhere in the NT in Rom 8:17; Heb 11:9; and 1 Pet 3:7. The major difference from Paul's use in Rom 8:17 is that there the focus is Christological, believers as joint heirs with Christ, while here the focus is ecclesiological, Gentile Christians as joint heirs within the Church with those who were once Jews. συν- compounds can, however, be used with a Christological focus in Ephesians, as we have seen in 2:5, 6.

The third description, which makes a point similar to those which the first two have made, is συμμέτοχα τῆς ἐπαγγελίας, "sharers in the promise." Certainly for the writer there was a time when Israel possessed the promise through the covenant relationship with Yahweh (cf. 2:12). But as 2:11–22 makes clear, the way in which the promise was fulfilled and hope realized in Christ brought about an element of discontinuity with the past so that the fulfillment in Christ means that for the new community the promise now has its own distinctive Christian content, and, in this, Gentile Christians are participants together with Jewish Christians, with no difference between them.

ἐν Χριστῷ Ἰησοῦ is not to be related simply to the notion of promise but qualifies all three of the previous descriptions, characterizing the sphere in which Gentile incorporation takes place, and thus in which God's purpose is realized (cf. also 1:3, 9, 10) and salvation is accomplished (cf. also 2:6, 7). (Cf. Ernst, 330; Caragounis, *Mysterion*, 104; Schnackenburg, 136.) It is because of what has taken place in and through Christ (cf. 2:13, 18) that Gentile inclusion in the Church can be celebrated, but it is also because of the proclamation of this in the gospel, διὰ τοῦ εὐαγγελίου. As the Gentiles heard the gospel, God's purpose was being realized (cf. 1:13), and as the gospel is proclaimed further, that purpose continues to be accomplished (cf. 6:15, 19).

The content of the mystery which is revealed through the proclamation of the gospel, and which has been stated in 3:6, is not unrelated to the content of the mystery as expressed in 1:10 in terms of summing up all things in heaven and on earth in Christ. The former provides the model for the latter. In other words, the bringing together of the cosmos in Christ finds its present anticipation in the bringing together of humanity in Christ in the one Church out of Jews and Gentiles. This connection will be taken up in v 10.

7 οὗ ἐγενήθην διάκονος κατὰ τὴν δωρεὰν τῆς χάριτος τοῦ θεοῦ τῆς δοθείσης μοι κατὰ τὴν ἐνέργειαν τῆς δυνάμεως αὐτοῦ, "of this gospel I became a servant according to the gift of God's grace, which was given to me through the working of his power." The writer rounds off the first major statement about the mystery within the digression of 3:1–13 by returning to the thought and language with which he had begun it in vv 1, 2. With the mention of the gospel in the previous verse Paul can now be brought back to the fore as the servant of that gospel. This designation is taken up from Col 1:23 where Paul is also called a servant of the gospel (cf. also 1:25 where he is a servant of the Church). This exact terminology is not used by Paul in the undisputed letters, in which he does, however, draw an intimate connection between himself and the gospel (e.g., Rom 1:1: Gal 1:11) and does think of himself as a servant in the cause of the gospel (cf. 1 Cor 3:5; 2 Cor 3:6; 6:4; Rom 15:16). Ephesians sees Paul's service of proclamation of the gospel as decisive in God's revelation of the mystery. At the same time, it celebrates Paul not as a hero in himself, but as the instrument of God's grace. Preserving the perspective of Paul himself (e.g., 1 Cor 15:10), it sees him as exercising his ministry only through the gift of grace bestowed on him. κατὰ τὴν δωρεὰν τῆς χάριτος τοῦ θεοῦ τῆς δοθείσης μοι, "according to the gift of God's grace which was given to me," virtually repeats the language of v 2, which was in turn dependent on Col 1:25, with the simple exception of δωρεάν in place of οἰκονομίαν. We have already commented on the specific focus of χάρις in relation to Paul's apostleship in v 2. With the use of δωρεά (cf. also 4:7) God's graciousness is underlined. It is a term also employed by Paul to speak of the generosity of God's activity in Christ on behalf of humanity (cf. Rom 3:24; 5:15, 17; 2 Cor 9:15). The grace experienced by Paul in his ministry flowed out of the mighty power of God, κατὰ τὴν ἐνέργειαν τῆς δυνάμεως αὐτοῦ, "according to the working of his power." This phrase qualifies δοθείσης rather than being coordinate with the previous κατά clause and in direct relationship with ἐγενήθην διάκονος (*contra* Westcott, 47; Caragounis, *Mysterion,* 105). Both terms used for God's power are already present in the similar formulation Col 1:29 employs for the enabling of the apostolic ministry. They occur also earlier in Ephesians in 1:19 with its piling up of synonyms for God's power in connection with raising Christ from the dead. For the writer, the power of God which raised Christ from the dead and is at work in believers was also the power operative in conveying grace to the apostle. In this way the realization of the mystery concerning the Gentiles can also be traced back through Paul's apostleship to the power of God (cf. also Schlier, 151–52; Barth, 339).

8 ἐμοὶ τῷ ἐλαχιστοτέρῳ πάντων ἁγίων ἐδόθη ἡ χάρις αὕτη, τοῖς ἔθνεσιν εὐαγγελίσασθαι τὸ ἀνεξιχνίαστον πλοῦτος τοῦ Χριστοῦ, "to me, the very least of all the saints, this grace was given, to preach to the Gentiles the good news of the unsearchable riches of Christ." The first statement of the mystery proclaimed through Paul's apostleship began and ended with a reference to that apostleship in terms of grace (cf. vv 2, 7). Now the third reference to grace in the pericope introduces a further elucidation of the mystery with which Paul's apostleship was uniquely connected. "This grace" is in fact explained in what follows in terms of Paul's apostleship to the Gentiles. It consists in the preaching of the good news to them (cf. Gal 1:16).

Just as the emphasis on grace in regard to Paul's apostleship echoes the thought of 1 Cor 15:10, so the self-designation "the very least of all the saints" recalls that of 1 Cor 15:9, "the least of the apostles." The language of this self-evaluation has evoked quite diverse responses with respect to the issue of authenticity. Bruce (*Ephesians,* 53) can write, "to us the words are a very hallmark of apostolic authenticity. No disciple of Paul's would have dreamed of giving the apostle so low a place," while for Mitton (125) "this sounds a little like false modesty . . . artificial and exaggerated. The words are more easily understood as those of the later disciple who wished to make his master appear as excelling in penitence and humility as well as insight." Clearly, the impression conveyed by the words of this verse is an insufficient basis on which to draw conclusions about authorship. How the words are heard will, in any case, largely be determined by such conclusions which will already have been made on other grounds. Nevertheless, it can be pointed out that in relation to the words of Paul in 1 Cor 15:9, the formulation here in Ephesians involves both intensification and generalization. The intensification is twofold. Whereas in 1 Cor 15:9 Paul uses the superlative of himself, ἐλάχιστος, "least," here in Ephesians a superlative with a comparative ending is employed for greater emphasis, ἐλαχιστότερος, "very least" (cf. BDF § 60 [2]; 61 [2]). Again, whereas in 1 Cor 15:9 Paul compares himself with the other apostles, here the comparison is extended to one with all believers (*contra* Gaugler, 139 and Conzelmann, 103, who wish to restrict the reference of ἁγίων to those who are called "holy" in v 5, namely, the apostles and prophets). It should be noted that Ignatius is capable of similar sentiments: "Remember the church of Syria in your prayers. I am not worthy to be a member of it: I am the least of their number" (*Trall.* 13.1). But this intensification also fits the tendency of the post-apostolic churches to accentuate the unworthiness of the apostles in order to highlight the greatness of Christ's grace in their lives (cf. 1 Tim 1:15, where Paul now becomes not just the least worthy Christian, but the foremost of sinners; also *Barn.* 5.9: "But it was in his choice of the apostles, who were to preach his gospel, that he truly showed himself the Son of God; for those men were ruffians of the deepest dye, which proved that he came not to call saints but sinners"). The generalization in comparison with 1 Cor 15:9 can be seen in that here in Ephesians there is no mention of Paul's violent persecution of believers, which in 1 Cor is given as the specific reason for his talk of himself as the least of the apostles, which may also have been his taking up of the judgment of his critics (cf. also ἔκτρωμα, "prematurely born" or "abortion," in the previous verse). In Ephesians, the self-designation "the very least of all the saints" is quite unprovoked and stands in the context of a general reflection on the apostle's ministry. In its juxtaposition with "the unsearchable riches of Christ," it serves to give greater emphasis to the measure of God's grace with which Paul was endowed in order to be fitted to proclaim such wealth.

Although πλοῦτος is used elsewhere in Ephesians (1:7, 8; 2:7; 3:16), the particular phrase τὸ ἀνεξιχνίαστον πλοῦτος τοῦ Χριστοῦ, "the unsearchable riches of Christ," is unique to this verse. ἀνεξιχνίαστος "suggests the picture of a reservoir so deep that soundings cannot reach the bottom of it. No limit can, therefore, be put to its resources" (Mitton, 124). It is used in LXX Job 5:9; 9:10; 34:24 and in Rom 11:33 for the inscrutability of God's ways, but now the writer of Ephesians can employ the term in connection with Christ. "The riches of Christ" could be taken as a subjective genitive referring to the salvation of which Christ is the possessor and bestower (cf. Meyer, 164), but the other uses of πλοῦτος in Ephesians, and the writer's dependence on the thought of

Col 2:3, "in whom are hid all the treasures of wisdom and knowledge," and Col 1:27, "the riches of the glory of this mystery, which is Christ among you," make it far more likely that it is to be interpreted as an objective genitive. Christ himself constitutes the content of the riches of the gospel, and the wealth of the salvation to be found in him is unfathomable. Yet, for all the glory attributed to Christ by this formulation, in the context its thought is subordinated to the ministry of the apostle. It is to Paul that grace has been given to make these glorious riches of Christ available to the Gentiles.

9, 10 καὶ φωτίσαι πάντας τίς ἡ οἰκονομία τοῦ μυστηρίου, "and to make plain to all what is the administration of the mystery." The grace given to Paul equipped him not only to proclaim the unsearchable riches of Christ but also to enlighten all about how God has chosen to work out his secret purpose. On the inclusion of πάντας in the original text, see *Notes*. Its inclusion is also in line with the emphasis on the proclamation of the mystery to all in the Colossians passage which has so much influenced the digression (cf. Col 1:28). φωτίζειν, literally, "to enlighten," has been used earlier in the intercessory prayer-report (see *Comment* on 1:18). There the writer had prayed for his readers' enlightenment. Here it becomes evident that for the writer such enlightenment is inextricably linked with the apostle Paul's ministry, which was intended to produce this effect. His commission was to make plain to all what was involved in the administration of the mystery. The meaning of οἰκονομία has been discussed in the comments on 1:10 and 3:2. Here it refers to God's act of administering, how he has chosen to disclose and accomplish his purpose (*pace* NIV and Caragounis, 107, who take it to refer to Paul's administration). For the background and meaning of μυστήριον, see the comments on 1:9, 10 and 3:3. The particular cosmic aspect of the mystery which the writer has in view this time is set out in v 10.

τοῦ ἀποκεκρυμμένου ἀπὸ τῶν αἰώνων ἐν τῷ θεῷ τῷ τὰ πάντα κτίσαντι, "which was hidden for ages in God who created all things." As in v 5, the mystery is described in terms of a revelation schema (see the discussion of this under *Form/Structure/Setting*). The two descriptions run parallel and are both dependent on Col 1:26. "Hidden for ages" corresponds to "was not made known in other generations" (v 5) and takes up the actual wording of Col 1:26. The contrasting element "should now be made known" corresponds to "has now been revealed" (v 5), and its use of γνωρίζειν for the positive side of the contrast reflects its use in the elaboration on the Colossians schema in Col 1:27.

In the structure of the revelation schema ἀπὸ τῶν αἰώνων should be taken as contrasting with νῦν in v 10 (as also in Col 1:26; cf. Lohse, *Colossians*, 74; Schweizer, *Colossians*, 108; Gnilka, *Kolosserbrief*, 101; O'Brien, *Colossians*, 84) rather than as a contrasting parallel to ταῖς ἀρχαῖς καὶ ταῖς ἐξουσίαις as the recipients of revelation (cf. the force of "ages" in the revelation schemas of 1 Cor 2:7 and Rom 16:25). In other words, "ages" here, as in its earlier uses in 1:21; 2:2, 7, has temporal force and does not refer to personal powers. (Cf. the discussion of 2:2 and 2:7; so also Masson, 175 n. 3; Gaugler, 142; Mussner, *Christus*, 25–26; Gnilka, 172; Ernst, 332; Schnackenburg, 140; *contra* Schlier, 153–58; Beare, 670; Steinmetz, *Protologische Heilszuversicht*, 63–64; Lindemann, *Aufhebung*, 223. It is interesting to note, with R. McL. Wilson, "The Trimorphic Protennoia," in *Gnosis and Gnosticism*, ed. M. Krause [Leiden: E. J. Brill, 1977]

54 n. 13, that this Gnostic text also appears in fact to have taken the phrase "hidden from the ages" in a temporal sense.)

The mystery is described not only as hidden for ages, but also as hidden in God. As in Col 3:3, where it could be said of believers that their life is hidden with Christ in God, ἐν τῷ θεῷ has a locative sense. God has kept the mystery hidden in himself. This emphasis on its divine source suggests its security, both in terms of inaccessibility and of the certainty that accompanies its realization. That the mystery had its place from the beginning in God's creative plan is underlined by the following liturgical formula about God as creator of all. Previously, κτίζειν had been used by the writer to describe the new creation (cf. 2:10, 15), but in this traditional formulation the reference is clearly to the original creation. Similar formulations can be found in the wisdom literature (e.g., Wis 1:14; Sir 18:1; 24:8), in the worship of the Qumran community (e.g., 1QH 1.9–11; 16.8; 1QM 10.8) and in Christian liturgy (*Did.* 10.3; *1 Clem.* 60.1; cf. 19.2–20.12; 33.2–6). Certainly the thought of this verse, along with those of 3:15 and 4:6, makes clear that for the writer there is no cosmic dualism, but rather the God of creation and the God of salvation are one. But the clause is unlikely to be a consciously polemical aside (*pace* Schlier, 155; Houlden, 301). Rather, in the context of the ensuing mention of principalities and authorities, it functions as a reminder that God is able, because he is creator, to carry through his purpose of salvation as it affects all creation, including the rebellious powers.

ἵνα γνωρισθῇ νῦν ταῖς ἀρχαῖς καὶ ταῖς ἐξουσίαις ἐν τοῖς ἐπουρανίοις διὰ τῆς ἐκκλησίας ἡ πολυποίκιλος σοφία τοῦ θεοῦ, "in order that through the Church the manifold wisdom of God should now be made known to the principalities and authorities in the heavenly realms." This purpose clause beginning with ἵνα is best taken not so much as directly dependent on the first clause in the revelation schema, "which was hidden . . . in order that the manifold wisdom of God should be made known . . ." (cf. Meyer, 167; Abbott, 88; Westcott, 48), but as linked with the two previous infinitives, εὐαγγελίσασθαι and φωτίσαι, indicating the purpose of Paul's "preaching" and "making plain." In this way the purpose clause is ultimately dependent on ἐδόθη at the beginning of v 8. Grace was given to Paul to preach and to make plain the gospel, and the goal of such preaching and making plain was that the wisdom of God should be made known (cf. also Schlier, 153; Gaugler, 143; Gnilka, 174; Caragounis, *Mysterion,* 73, 108).

Whereas previously in this chapter the mystery can be said to have been made known to Paul (v 3) and to the apostles and prophets (v 5), and to have been proclaimed by Paul to the Gentiles (vv 8, 9), now the wisdom of God, which serves as a functional equivalent to mystery in v 9, is said to have as the recipients of its disclosure the principalities and authorities in the heavenly realms. For a discussion of the background of these terms and the hostile nature of the powers, see the comments on 1:20, 21. Mussner (105) connects the thought of this verse with that of 1 Pet 1:12, where more well-disposed angels are said to desire to look into the gospel, and claims that the mention of the principalities and authorities, therefore, serves simply to underline the significance of what God has done in the present time. But since other references make clear that for Ephesians the spiritual powers are evil forces who need to be subjected (cf. 2:2; 6:12), the notion of making known in relation to them has greater affinities with a passage such as 1 Pet 3:19–22, where the victory of Christ over such adversaries is proclaimed to them. Here, however, it is not the victory of Christ as such (cf. 1:20–23), but, as we shall see, the consequences of that victory in the bringing into existence of the Church that is the focus of the disclosure to the powers.

The principalities and authorities are located "in the heavenly realms." For a discussion of this phrase, see *Comment* on 1:3. That the writer can conceive of not only Christ and believers, but also hostile powers, in the heavenly realms is again to be explained against the background of the cosmic heavens in the OT and in the Jewish apocalypses, where angels and spirit powers were often represented as in heaven (e.g., Job 1:6; Dan 10:13, 21; 2 Macc 5:2; *1 Enoch* 61.10; 90.21, 24), a concept which was also developed in Philo (cf. *Spec.* 1.66; 2.45; *Plant.* 14; *Gig.* 6, 7). For Ephesians, God has placed in the heavenly realm creatures in family groupings, just as he has done on earth (cf. 3:15). Since, like Paul, the writer has inherited the two-age eschatological perspective often found in the apocalypses, a perspective which incorporated heaven and earth in each age, he could think of the present overlap of the ages, brought about by God's action in Christ, as a period in which heaven was still involved in the present evil age, so that though the powers had already been defeated, they would not be totally vanquished until the consummation.

The term νῦν, "now," is significant in this verse. Not until this particular time in the history of salvation has the mysterious plan of God been disclosed to the spiritual powers, and as in v 5, this "now" is clearly the period of the Church. In fact, the Church is the means by which God makes known his wisdom to the powers. This is only the second use of the actual term ἐκκλησία in the letter (see the discussion on its earlier use in 1:22). In the immediate context, its occurrence here recalls the ecclesiological content of the mystery from v 6, namely, Gentile Christians as fellow members of the same body with Jewish Christians. It is through this new entity, the one Church out of Jews and Gentiles, that the mystery is made known, as God's wisdom is demonstrated to the principalities and authorities. The writer does not spell out exactly how the Church makes known God's purpose to the powers. Conzelmann (104) claims that it is through the Church's preaching, and this same assumption misleads Wink (*Naming the Powers*, 89–96), who connects 3:10 with 3:8 and argues that the reference is to the preaching to the angels of the Gentile nations, which has to accompany the proclamation of the good news to the Gentiles. But the text does not mention preaching, and Wink's discussion ignores the function of the earlier reference to Paul's preaching the good news to the Gentiles and its relation to the thought of 3:6 that Gentiles have become joint members of the body. Wink also misses the fact that the Church is not the subject of the making known but the means through which it takes place, and fails to note that this undermines his suggested interpretation, because it is through the Church, made up of Jewish Christians and already-converted Gentiles, that the disclosure is made to the powers. Dahl ("Das Geheimnis," 73–74) suggests that the Church makes known God's purpose to the powers through its worship, in which the angels are present (cf. 1 Cor 11:10). But it is by no means clear that the angels present in worship can be identified with hostile powers.

The writer's thought is, therefore, best understood as being that by her very existence as a new humanity, in which the major division of the first-century world has been overcome, the Church reveals God's secret in action and heralds to the hostile heavenly powers the overcoming of cosmic divisions with their defeat (cf. also Minear, "The Vocation to Invisible Powers," 94–101). The syncretism combated in Colossians appears to have claimed that it was necessary for believers to placate the powers controlling the heavenly realm, in order to gain access to mysteries. The reflections of the writer to the Ephesians move in quite the reverse direction. The mystery is disclosed in the Church and through her is being made known to these very powers that their malign régime, particularly over that part of humanity, the Gentile world, thought to be especially under their sway, has come to an end.

In the Greek text the subject of the clause, indicating the content of the disclosure, the manifold wisdom of God, is delayed until the end for the sake of emphasis. God's administering of the mystery is seen in terms of his wisdom. As Caragounis (*Mysterion*, 108) remarks, "The *mysterion* is shaped by God's wisdom, it is a product of it. At the same time God's wisdom is reflected and revealed in the *mysterion*." This interconnection recalls 1 Cor 2:6–8, where Paul had linked the notion of the wisdom of God with that of mystery (σοφία ἐν μυστηρίῳ) and where this wisdom is said to have been hidden, to have been decreed by God before the ages, and not to be known by the rulers of this age. Earlier in Ephesians the writer has employed σοφία in connection with God's gift of wisdom to believers (cf. 1:8, 17), but his speaking of the wisdom of God itself in this verse has led some to see the Wisdom mythology of Hellenistic Judaism or Gnosticism as having influenced him (cf. Schlier, 159–66; U. Wilckens, "σοφία," *TDNT* 7 [1971] 465–76, 496–528, for discussion of such material). There is no need to posit a background in Gnostic thought, where Sophia, on her descent from the heavenly realm of light into the darkness and chaos of the material world, has to pass through intermediary powers and thereby becomes known to them. Motifs of hiddenness (cf. Job 28:12–22; Bar 3:9–4:4; 4 Ezra 5:9; *2 Apoc. Bar.* 48.36) and making known to specially chosen ones or to Israel (cf. Sir 4:11; 6:18, 19; 14:20–15:8; 24:8–23; Bar 3:9–4:4) are used of wisdom in the OT and Jewish literature. The accompanying adjective in Eph 3:10, πολυποίκιλος, is a *hapax legomenon* in the NT, but through it Schlier (159–66, followed less cautiously by Wilckens, *TDNT* 7 [1971] 524, and Conzelmann, 104) believes he can trace links with Hellenistic thought about Isis-Sophia, who constantly changes appearance and yet remains the same goddess. He holds that Jewish Gnostic interpretation of this Isis theology has influenced Ephesians, where God's wisdom is seen as having appeared in different forms and yet remaining one. But, against this, it has to be pointed out that Schlier gives no examples of the actual use of πολυποίκιλος of Isis or Sophia. His case depends instead on seeing this term as completely synonymous with πολυμόρφος, "multiform," and Dahl ("Das Geheimnis," 66–69) has exposed the problems of such an assumption. In addition, any notion of a sequence of different appearances of wisdom is foreign to Ephesians, which simply has in view the one wise purpose of God, which was once hidden but has now come to expression through the Church. (For further criticism of Schlier's hypothesis, cf. Dahl, "Das Geheimnis," 66–71; Schnackenburg, 141–42). Dahl

("Das Geheimnis," 69–70) suggests that πολυποίκιλος recalls the cosmic role of Wisdom as agent in creation and refers to the colorful splendor of Wisdom's ways in the created world, finding support in Theophilus, *Ad Autolycum* 1.6; 2.16 and pointing to other places in Ephesians where cosmological terminology has been given a soteriological or ecclesiological twist. But in all likelihood both Schlier and Dahl have attempted to build too much on this one term and to be too specific about the background of the phrase as a whole.

The phrase should be understood more generally, since in Ephesians the wisdom of God is not personified in the way it is in the wisdom literature or in Gnosticism. It is best taken as the wise divine purpose in the ordering of history. In this sense, it is analogous to the connotations of wisdom in the Qumran literature (cf. 1QS 4.18, 19, "But in the mysteries of his understanding, and in his glorious wisdom, God has ordained an end for falsehood, and at the time of the visitation He will destroy it for ever. Then truth, which has wallowed in the ways of wickedness during the dominion of falsehood until the appointed time of judgment, shall arise in the world for ever"), and more particularly to the wisdom which is praised by Paul, when in Romans 11 he reflects on the outworkings of God's plan of salvation in history for Jews and Gentiles (cf. Rom 11:33). As far as the term πολυποίκιλος is concerned, the prefix πολυ- merely intensifies what is meant by the simple ποικίλος ("diversified" or "many-colored"), and produces the sense of "richly diverse" or "multifaceted." As the description of it in Wis 7:22, which includes the word πολυμερές, makes clear, God's wisdom has a host of characteristics, and it is to this highly variegated splendor and gloriously intricate design of God's wise purpose in history that the writer of Ephesians draws attention.

Verses 9 and 10 are highly significant for the way in which they link the latter's ecclesiological and cosmic emphases. One can see why Caird (66) claims in regard to v 10, "It is hardly an exaggeration to say that any interpretation of Ephesians stands or falls with this verse." (Yet Caird is in danger of failing his own test when he reads into the verse a whole theology of the link between the powers and the state, and holds that the writer is saying "that even such structures of power and authority as the secular state are capable of being brought into harmony with the love of God" [67].) It is no accident that the terms used in these verses for the disclosure of the mystery—γνωρίζειν, οἰκονομία, μυστήριον—are those employed in the earlier discussion of the mystery in 1:9, 10, where its content was the summing up of all things in Christ, nor that the thought of these verses about the Church brings to mind the other discussion of the mystery in 3:3–6, where its content is the one Church out of Jews and Gentiles. The writer has reworked Col 1:26–28 in the light of these two earlier discussions, so that the existence of the Church, uniting hostile sections of humanity in one body, can be seen as proof to the powers that God is in fact summing up all things in Christ. This integration of cosmic and ecclesiological perspectives is reminiscent of the way the two were brought together earlier in 1:21–23, where Christ's lordship over the cosmos is shown to be on behalf of the Church and the Church has a special role as the medium of Christ's presence and rule in the cosmos. Here in 3:9, 10 also, we should understand that it is because the Church alone is Christ's body and fullness that only through the Church can the principalities and authorities be shown with clarity the claim of Christ's lordship.

11, 12 κατὰ πρόθεσιν τῶν αἰώνων ἣν ἐποίησεν ἐν τῷ Χριστῷ Ἰησοῦ τῷ κυρίῳ ἡμῶν, "according to the eternal purpose which he accomplished in Christ Jesus our Lord." These words should be connected with the whole of the previous clause, and, with v 12, add to the main thought about the content of the mystery the liturgical flourishes we have come to expect of this writer's style. In terms of style, the writer's designation of Christ involves an unusual combination, with the article before "Christ Jesus" and again before "Lord," which is followed by the possessive adjective. The closest equivalent is found in Col 2:6, where, however, there is no possessive adjective. What has been made known through the Church is tied to God's eternal purpose in the same way as the benefits of salvation were traced back to God's purposes throughout the eulogy of 1:3–14. In fact, the phrase κατὰ πρόθεσιν occurred earlier in that context in 1:11. In the expression πρόθεσιν τῶν αἰώνων, literally "purpose of the ages," "ages" should again be understood to have temporal force (*pace* Schlier, 157–58; Steinmetz, *Protologische Heilszuversicht*, 63–64; Lindemann, *Aufhebung*, 228, who understand the expression as an objective genitive meaning that God has included the personal aeons in his purpose). The meaning is not so much that God's purpose runs through the ages (*pace* Abbott, 89–90), as that it is before all time and eternal. In this way the expression is taken as a Hebraism in which the genitive functions as an adjective, here as the equivalent to αἰώνιος (cf. also 3:21; 1 Tim 1:17, and BDF § 165 [1]).

There is a further question of meaning in regard to the use of the verb ποιεῖν with πρόθεσιν. It could mean either to conceive or achieve a purpose. Some prefer the former, claiming that this would be more in line with the thought about the ultimate origins of the making known of the mystery in 1:9 and that one would expect a stronger term if the notion of achievement were in view. On this interpretation, Christ Jesus our Lord is understood as the preexistent mediator of the divine purpose (cf. Abbott, 90; J. A. Robinson, 171–172; Schmid, *Epheserbrief*, 232–33; Schlier, 157; Gaugler, 146; Gnilka, 177; Ernst, 334; Caragounis, *Mysterion,* 110; Mussner, 106). But the meaning of achievement or accomplishment seems to suit the context in this passage better, where the making known of the mystery has been described as realized through the existence of the Church, and where what follows will speak of that which has been accomplished in terms of access. The mention of Christ's lordship suggests the execution of God's purpose. κατὰ πρόθεσιν is connected with accomplishment in its earlier use in 1:11 ("according to the purpose of him who carries out all things . . ."). The usage of ποιεῖν elsewhere in Ephesians also supports this latter interpretation. In 2:3 ποιοῦντες τὰ θελήματα means "carrying out the wishes," and where there are periphrastic formulations with ποιεῖν, as in 1:16 and 4:16, they take the middle rather than the active form of the verb (cf. also Meyer, 170–71; Westcott, 49; Beare, 673; Barth, 346–47; Caird, 67; Mitton, 128; Schnackenburg, 143).

ἐν ᾧ ἔχομεν τὴν παρρησίαν καὶ προσαγωγὴν ἐν πεποιθήσει διὰ τῆς πίστεως αὐτοῦ, "in whom we have boldness and confident access through faith in him." Since the terms "boldness" and "access" are governed by one article in the Greek text, they may well form a hendiadys to emphasize the notion of bold access.

ἐν πεποιθήσει, "in confidence," which is to be taken with προσαγωγή, then bolsters this notion further to give the force of "the boldness of confident access." For discussion of the background and force of the imagery of access, see the comments on 2:18, where the term appeared earlier.

παρρησία, which occurs again in 6:19 and in the form of its verbal cognate in 6:20, was used originally in classical Greek for "freedom of speech," the democratic right "to say everything" one wished to say. It also took on connotations of openness and frankness in speech, a virtue that was highly valued in connection with friendship, and of boldness or courage in speech, which could sometimes turn into insolence. In Hellenistic Judaism the term also came to be used in the context of a person's relationship with God, especially in prayer (cf. LXX Job 22:26; 27:9, 10; Philo, *Spec.* 1.203, which speaks of the worshiper praying boldly from a pure conscience, as does Josephus, *Ant.* 2.4.4; cf. also *Ant.* 5.1.3). In the NT the two main connotations of the term are a similar joyful confidence before God, but now based on Christ's saving work, and a bold and open proclamation of the gospel. It is the former which is in view here, and it reflects the attitude of those who lack any fear or shame and have nothing to conceal, because they are assured of God's gracious disposition toward them in Christ. (For further discussion, cf. E. Peterson, "Zur Bedeutungsgeschichte von Παρρησία," in *Reinhold Seeberg Festschrift*, Vol. 1, ed. W. Koepp [Leipzig: D. Werner Scholl, 1929] 283–97; D. Smolders, "L'Audace de l'apôtre selon Saint Paul: Le thème de la parrésia," *Collectanea mechliniensia* 43 [1958] 16–30, 117–33; W. C. van Unnik, "The Christian's Freedom of Speech in the New Testament," and "The Semitic Background of ΠΑΡΡΗΣΙΑ in the New Testament," in *Sparsa Collecta,* Part 2 NovTSup 30 [Leiden: E. J. Brill, 1980] 269–89, 290–306; S. B. Marrow, "Parrhēsia and the New Testament," *CBQ* 44 [1982] 431–46.)

πεποίθησις, which occurs six times in the Pauline corpus (cf. also 2 Cor 1:15; 3:4; 8:22; 10:2; Phil 3:4), but nowhere else in the NT, intensifies the subjective element in the relationship with God through the notion of confidence. This newfound confidence through Christ was a strong note in Paul's faith and, if anything, the writer of Ephesians, with his alliterative heaping up of terms and combination of Pauline emphases from Rom 5:2 and 2 Cor 3:12, has increased its force. Since this attitude found particular expression in prayer, it is not surprising that almost immediately the writer will return to prayer in vv 14–21. A similar celebration of boldness of access into the very presence of God can be found in Heb 4:16; 10:19–22. The ἐν ᾧ phrase at the beginning of v 12 indicates the grounds for believers' confidence of access—it is because of the new situation God has brought about in and through Christ—while the phrase at the end of the verse, διὰ τῆς πίστεως αὐτοῦ, "through faith in him," indicates the means by which believers appropriate the new situation for themselves. Some take the latter phrase, along with similar ones in Paul, to refer to Christ's faith or faithfulness (cf. Barth, 347; Mitton, 128; G. E. Howard, "The 'Faith of Christ,' " *ExpTim* 85 [1973–74] 212–15). But the majority of commentators see rightly that it is faith in Christ which is in view. In Paul's treatment of access in Rom 5:2 it is a consequence of justification by faith, and the readers' faith has already been mentioned earlier in this letter in 1:13, 15, 19; and 2:8.

The function of this celebration of access to God in the writer's flow of thought is similar to that of its earlier treatment in 2:18. Both passages highlight the consequences of the outworking of God's salvific purposes for the present situation of believers, though in each case the context provides a distinctive nuance. While in 2:18 the access was the common access of two previously divided groups, here in 3:12 the access can be seen as one no longer impeded by the menace of hostile principalities and authorities (cf. also Schnackenburg, 143).

13 διὸ αἰτοῦμαι μὴ ἐγκακεῖν ἐν ταῖς θλίψεσίν μου ὑπὲρ ὑμῶν, ἥτις ἐστὶν δόξα ὑμῶν, "I beg you, therefore, not to become discouraged because of my sufferings on your behalf, which are your glory." διό refers back to all that has been said in vv 2–12, not just to v 12 (*contra* Bratcher and Nida, *Handbook*, 80). It is in the light of the significance of Paul's ministry as a whole that the readers are begged not to become disheartened. It is the readers of whom this request is made and not God (*pace* Barth, 348). The beginning of the prayer to God is marked clearly in v 14. This also rules out the possible interpretation that Paul is requesting God that he, Paul, should not become disheartened, which in any case would be out of line with the whole tenor of vv 2–12, and particularly the confident note struck in v 12 (*pace* Thompson, *ExpTim* 71 [1959–60] 188; N. Baumert, *Täglich Sterben und Auferstehen* [Munich: Kösel, 1973] 324–25). The verb ἐγκακεῖν occurs elsewhere in Paul's letters in 2 Cor 4:1, 16; Gal 6:9; and 2 Thess 3:13, where it has the connotations of either becoming discouraged or growing weary.

The possible cause of discouragement for the readers is Paul's sufferings on their behalf. Since it is unlikely that readers not known personally to Paul would actually need reassurance for their own faith because the apostle is suffering or had suffered, the request of this verse serves, rather, as an apologetic device to show how even Paul's sufferings and martyrdom are no cause for shame, but fit the magnificent scope of his apostolic ministry that has just been set forth (cf. also Gnilka, 180; Ernst, 335; Mussner, 106). His sufferings immediately receive an interpretation which reinforces for the readers the greatness of his apostleship: they are "for you" and indeed "your glory." Suffering, particularly apostolic suffering, is a significant topic in Paul's letters, and θλίψις is the term he most frequently uses in this connection. But it is in particular the thought of Col 1:24 which has influenced Eph 3:13. While Ephesians has ἐν ταῖς θλίψεσίν μου ὑπὲρ ὑμῶν, Colossians had ἐν τοῖς παθήμασιν ὑπὲρ ὑμῶν and employed the term θλίψις for Christ's afflictions which the apostolic suffering completed. The Ephesians formulation appears flatter and less dramatic because it omits this latter emphasis of Col 1:24b, "in my flesh I complete what is lacking in Christ's afflictions for the sake of his body, that is, the Church." Yet the dynamic of this notion may well lie behind the unusual way in which Ephesians states that the apostle's sufferings are the readers' glory, which is an additional statement not found in Colossians.

But this depends on how one interprets δόξα. As Caragounis (*Mysterion*, 112 n. 61) says, "The meaning of 'glory' has puzzled all interpreters." Even J. A. Robinson (80–81) contented himself with asserting that this verse contains "a logic which we can hardly analyze. . . . It is the language of the heart." Mitton (129) is unusual among modern commentators in that he believes the second clause in v 13 refers not just to the apostle's sufferings, but to the whole of the first clause, so that "for the readers to find courage rather than discouragement from the thought of Paul's ordeals, courage to be willing to share them . . . this is their glory . . . something of which they can be truly proud." Meyer (174) had long ago dismissed such an explanation as too general and commonplace. The writer's thought is indeed likely to be more profound than that Paul set an example which should stimulate others. It is certainly more natural to take the relative clause to refer to that which immediately precedes, Paul's sufferings. In this case, does "your glory" mean "for your honor or prestige"? Meyer (173) offered the interpretation that Paul's suffering for the readers redounded to their honor. But if the apostolic sufferings are held to be the cause for their prestige or glorying, one would expect the use of καύχημα rather than δόξα to express this, as in Phil 1:26. Could it be then that "your glory" simply means "for your benefit"? Abbott (92), following Chrysostom, espouses this line of thought; Paul's sufferings on his mission have all been in order that Gentile Christians might obtain the great blessings of salvation. It appears much more likely, however, that we should take our clue for the meaning of δόξα from the fact that when in Paul, as here, suffering and glory are juxtaposed, it is eschatological glory which is in view, the glorification of believers. (On this topic, cf. C. M. Smith, "Suffering and Glory: Studies in Paul's Use of the Motif in the Light of Its Early Jewish Background," Ph.D. dissertation, University of Sheffield, 1988.) In its appearances so far in Ephesians glory has been related to God rather than believers (cf. 1:6, 12, 14, 17, 18), but it is used in association with believers in Col 1:27 and 3:4, and in those cases also it denotes eschatological glory. In Paul's thought one of the relationships between suffering and glory is that the former is a precondition of the latter (cf. 2 Cor 4:17; Rom 8:17, 18). But the one who suffers is the one who is later glorified, while here in Eph 3:13 the one who suffers is Paul but those who are glorified are believers. Such a relationship, whereby apostolic suffering mediates salvation to others, is present in Paul's thought but expressed in different terms in 2 Cor 1:6 ("if we are afflicted, it is for your comfort and salvation") and 2 Cor 4:12 ("so death is at work in us, but life in you"). It is this concept of Paul's afflictions mediating the salvific benefits of Christ's sufferings to believers that is expressed here in Ephesians in terms of his sufferings and their glory. Suffering still must come before glory for the readers, but it is Paul who has fulfilled the condition of suffering for them, ὑπὲρ ὑμῶν. If this is the case, then the thought of this verse is similar to Col 1:24 after all, for Paul is seen as the one who contributes to making up the quota of messianic woes, of eschatological tribulation, prior to the consummation of salvation in glory (cf. O'Brien, *Colossians*, 75–81; but cf. also C. M. Smith, "Suffering and Glory," 193–209). It is in this way that Ephesians sees Paul's sufferings as bringing Gentile believers the experience of glory (cf. also Schlier, 166; Gnilka, 180; Caird, 67; Thompson, *ExpTim* 71 [1959–60] 187–89). A similar thought about Paul's ministry can be found in 2 Tim 2:10, "Therefore I endure everything for the sake of the elect, that they also may obtain salvation in Christ Jesus with its eternal glory." With v 13, this section of Ephesians ends as it began, by recalling for the Gentile Christian readers their intimate links with the apostle Paul. ὑπὲρ ὑμῶν here takes up the ὑπὲρ ὑμῶν τῶν ἐθνῶν of v 1 and the εἰς ὑμᾶς of v 2.

Explanation

In this reworking of material from Col 1:23c–28 the writer, after breaking off from the beginning of an intercessory prayer in v 1, depicts Paul's apostolic ministry to the Gentiles. In each of the two main sentences of what is strictly a digression, the apostolic ministry is linked with the making known of the mystery of Christ, and in each this mystery has its focus in the Church. The first time, the mystery, which was not even known to the OT prophets but was revealed to the apostles and prophets and particularly to Paul, is highlighted in terms of the Gentiles' becoming joint members of the body, the Church, on equal terms with Jewish Christians and joint heirs and sharers in the promise. The second time, the mystery involves the existence of the Church as in itself a disclosure of God's wise design to the principalities and authorities. There is also the reminder that God has accomplished his purpose in Christ and because of him believers can have confident access to God. The digression is rounded off with an exhortation not to lose heart, because the sufferings involved in Paul's apostolic ministry contribute to the Gentile Christian readers' glorification.

The digression functions not only to elaborate on the identity of the one who prays and his relationship to those for whom he prays (cf. 3:1, 14), a common feature in Paul's letters, but also to develop the device of pseudonymity on which this letter as a whole rests (cf. 1:1; 4:1). By speaking in the name of Paul and having Paul reflect on the significance of his ministry, the writer can develop his own understanding of the mystery of the Christ event and, at the same time, back his insights with the apostle's authority.

The features in the description of Paul that are relied on for such a treatment are his imprisonment for the sake of Christ (v 1), his Gentile mission (vv 1, 8), his imprisonment and suffering on behalf of the Gentiles (vv 1, 13), his special insight as a recipient of revelation (vv 3–5, 9), and his service in the cause of the gospel (v 7). These are of course general aspects of Paul's ministry and might have been expected in such a portrait. But three further elements emerge strongly and are emphasized by the writer in his identification with Paul. The first is Paul's indebtedness to the grace of God for his apostolic ministry (vv 2, 7, 8). Ephesians has already stressed that salvation is all of grace (2:8–10). Now it makes clear that the apostleship which was instrumental in bringing that salvation to the Gentiles was also all of grace. As the readers have been reminded in chap. 2 of what they have become through God's grace, so now in chap. 3 they are also reminded of what the apostle became through that same grace. The paradox of grace in his life was that to this one who had no claim to any but the lowest status among believers (v 8) was entrusted a great task of cosmic dimensions. The second element to be noted is the depiction of Paul as apostle and theologian of the Church. This ecclesiological context of Paul's work is clear from the fact that the mystery, which it is his task to make known, is twice explained as centering on the Church. It is this emphasis that also provides the reason for introducing the apostles and prophets alongside Paul in the first statement about the reception of the revelation of the mystery. Those whom the writer has already described as the foundation of the Church are mentioned in order to set Paul's ministry firmly in the context of the Church as a whole. Though Paul is quickly seen to be a far more dominant figure and, for this writer, the leading and normative interpreter of what God has done in Christ, he has now been established as a pillar of the Church, so that to remember the work of Paul is now also to remember the one Church, its coming into being and its role in the world. This brings us to the third noteworthy element in the depiction of Paul—his ministry takes on a cosmic significance. It is through the Church of Jews and Gentiles that God's wisdom is exhibited to the powers. Since Paul played such a prominent part in bringing this sort of Church into being, and since his task is also to make plain to all that this is God's way of working, his apostolic mission is seen to be caught up in the drama of God's cosmic purpose.

It is in vv 9, 10, with their talk of disclosure of the mystery to the principalities and authorities, that the two main aspects of the discussion of the mystery (and thus two of the major emphases of the first three chapters) come together. The elaboration on Paul's apostleship supplies the context for integrating the letter's ecclesiological and cosmic perspectives, explicitly brought together earlier only in 1:21–23. What now becomes clear is that the Church provides hostile cosmic powers with a tangible reminder that their authority has been decisively broken and that all things are subject to Christ. The overcoming of the barriers between Jews and Gentiles, as they are united through Christ in the Church, is a pledge of the overcoming of all divisions when the universe will be restored to harmony in Christ (cf. 1:10). In this way the Church as the focus of God's wise plan could give the readers an essential clue to the meaning of this world's history.

In comparison with the treatment of "mystery" in Colossians and with Paul's thought in general, in Ephesians the Church clearly has a far more prominent place. Yet this development from Paul is made in the midst of restatements of authentically Pauline emphases such as grace, Gentile inclusion through the gospel, boldness, access, faith, and apostolic sufferings.

Despite the concentrated attention paid to Paul's ministry and the tremendous significance attached to the Church, these human instruments have not taken over the writer's thought completely. Elements of the other dominant foci in the earlier sections of the letter, the Christological and the theological, still remain. The content of the mystery is spelled out in terms of its ecclesiological implications, but it remains the mystery of Christ (v 4) and God's purpose in his disclosure through the Church is, in fact, accomplished "in Christ Jesus our Lord" (v 11). Paul himself is subject to Christ as his prisoner (v 1), and the good news he preaches to the Gentiles is of "the unsearchable riches of Christ" (v 8). And though Paul is given so much credit for his insight into God's purposes in forming the Church, it should not be forgotten that the writer has already stated in 2:15 that it is Christ who is the creator of the Church. It is Christ also who provides the grounds for believers' confidence in the presence of God and is the object of their faith (v 12). Similarly, it is only because *God* chooses to reveal the mystery that it can be known by humanity (v 5). The mystery has its beginning and end in him. The ultimate source of its working out is God the Creator of all (v 9). It is in accordance with his eternal purpose, which he has accomplished (v 11), and it serves to exhibit the multifaceted splendor of his wisdom (v 10). The same goes for Paul's ministry, the vehicle for the disclosure of the mystery; it too is dependent through and through on God's grace and power (vv 2, 7, 8).

Explanation

This section on Paul as minister of the mystery to the Gentiles—with its ecclesiological focus, its cosmic backdrop, and its Christological and theological elements—is meant ultimately to strengthen the bonds between the letter's Gentile Christian readers and the Pauline tradition as the writer understands it. In order to effect this aim the readers are reminded that the revelation of the mystery of Christ and, as part of this, their own existence as the Church and the Church's role in the universe are inextricably bound up with the apostle Paul and the commission entrusted to him. They can verify from reading what has been written (cf. vv 3, 4) that Paul had indeed been given revelation and special insight for them. The "for you" at the beginning and end of the section drives this home. To the readers has been mediated, through Paul's apostleship, not only grace (v 2) but also glory (v 13).

Further Prayer—for the Completeness of the Readers' Experience of God— with Doxology (3:14–21)

Bibliography

Arnold, C. E. *Ephesians: Power and Magic,* 85–102. **Caragounis, C. C.** *The Ephesian Mysterion,* 74–77. **Dahl, N. A.** "Cosmic Dimensions and Religious Knowledge (Eph 3:18)." In *Jesus und Paulus,* ed. E. E. Ellis and E. Grässer. Göttingen: Vandenhoeck & Ruprecht, 1975, 57–75. **Deichgräber, R.** *Gotteshymnus und Christushymnus,* 25–40. **Dupont, J.** *Gnosis: La Connaissance religieuse dans les Épîtres de Saint Paul.* Paris: J. Gabalda, 1949, 476–528. **Ernst, J.** *Pleroma,* 120–35. **Feuillet, A.** *Le Christ, Sagesse de Dieu.* Paris: J. Gabalda, 1966, 307–19. "L'Église plérôme du Christ d'après Ephés., 1, 23," *NRT* 78 (1956) 593–610. **Milling, D. H.** "The Origin and Character of the NT Doxology." Ph.D. diss., Cambridge, 1972. **Mussner, F.** *Christus, das All und die Kirche,* 71–75. **Pesch, R.** "Das Mysterium Christi (Eph 3, 8–12, 14–19)." *Am Tisch des Wortes* 18 (1967) 11–17.

Translation

[14] *For this reason I kneel before the Father,*[a] [15] *from whom every family*[b] *in heaven and on earth derives its name,* [16] *in order that according to the riches of his glory he might grant you to be strengthened with power through his Spirit in the inner person,* [17] *that Christ might dwell in your hearts through faith, that you might be rooted and grounded in love,*[c] [18] *in order that you might be empowered to grasp with all the saints what is the breadth and length and height and depth,* [19] *and to know the love of Christ which surpasses knowledge, in order that you might be filled up to all the fullness of God.*[d]

[20] *Now to him who is able to do infinitely more abundantly above*[e] *all that we ask or think in accordance with the power which is at work within us,* [21] *to him belongs glory in the Church and*[f] *in Christ Jesus throughout all generations and for evermore. Amen.*

Notes

[a] Some manuscripts have the words τοῦ κυρίου ἡμῶν Ἰησοῦ Χριστοῦ, "of our Lord Jesus Christ," after πατέρα, "Father." They include ℵ^c D G K Ψ 88 it^{d, g} vg syr^{p, h}. But this is in all likelihood an addition in line with 1:3 and similar liturgical formulations. Since there would be no reason for omitting the words, it is all the more probable that the shorter text found in such weighty manuscripts as p⁴⁶ ℵ* A B C P 33 81 1739 syr^{pal} cop^{sa, boh} is the earlier.

[b] The Greek text has a play on words between πατριά, here rendered as "family" and πατέρα, "Father," in the previous verse, which an English translation is not able to capture.

[c] The position of the phrase "in love" in the Greek text is such that it could be connected with the clause that precedes it, "that Christ might dwell through faith in your hearts in love," or, as in our translation, with the clause that follows it, "that you might be rooted and grounded in love." With most commentators (*contra* J. A. Robinson, 85, 175; NEB) we have preferred the latter because the participles appear in need of qualification (cf. their use in Col 1:23 and 2:7).

[d] ℵ A C D G K P Ψ it vg syr^{p, h, pal} cop^{bo} goth all have πληρωθῆτε εἰς πᾶν τὸ πλήρωμα τοῦ θεοῦ, the reading reflected in the translation above, "(that) you might be filled up to all the fullness of

God." There is, however, a major variant, witnessed by p⁴⁶ B 462 cop^sa, which reads πληρωθῇ πᾶν τὸ πλήρωμα τοῦ θεοῦ, "(that) all the fullness of God may be filled up." Presumably this variant is the result of a desire to provide an easier syntactical construction or to avoid what were felt to be theological difficulties about humans possessing the total fullness of deity.

e Several witnesses, p⁴⁶ D E F G it^d,g vg Ambrosiaster, omit ὑπέρ, "above." Probably it was thought that ὑπέρ was redundant and that its omission would provide a smoother construction.

f The καί, "and," is witnessed by ℵ A B C vg, but some manuscripts omit it (D^c K L P), and others reverse the order of the Church and Christ so that Christ is given the priority (D* F G). Both variants are attempts to deal with what was perceived to be a theological difficulty, but the more difficult reading must be regarded as the original (*contra* Meyer, 152).

Form/Structure/Setting

In its form the whole passage is a prayer-report, which divides into two particular forms—an intercessory prayer-report (vv 14–19) and a doxology (vv 20, 21).

The intercessory prayer-report constitutes one long sentence in Greek. It has been possible to retain this feature in the translation without lapsing into incomprehensibility or too great an awkwardness of style. The style of the original contains many of the syntactical features already noted in connection with the earlier eulogy and thanksgiving period. The structure of thought in the intercessory prayer-report is as follows. Verses 14, 15 introduce the prayer and vv 16–19 relate its content. The content falls into three main requests, each of which is introduced by ἵνα. The first main request itself begins with ἵνα δῷ ὑμῖν, "that he might grant you . . . ," and this is followed by two parallel infinitive clauses and a participial clause. The first infinitive clause, with κραταιωθῆναι, elaborates that what the readers are to be granted is "to be strengthened with power through his Spirit in the inner man." The second, with κατοικῆσαι, provides a further equivalent, "that Christ might dwell in your hearts through faith." Verse 17b, with its two perfect passive participial forms, is best taken as a further subsidiary request, "that you might be rooted and grounded in love." It could be interpreted as a result clause, dependent on the two infinitives, which, in turn, provides the condition for the next request, i.e., "so that you, having been rooted and grounded in love, might be empowered" (so RSV, JB; also Caragounis, *Mysterion*, 75). But elsewhere in the NT, participles can function to express wishes or commands (cf. BDF § 468 [2]), and in the context of a prayer it is appropriate to understand them as having the force of a prayer-wish (so GNB; also Gaugler, 155; Gnilka, 185; Schnackenburg, 152; Bratcher and Nida, *Handbook*, 86). The second main request, with ἵνα, also asks for strengthening, this time using ἐξισχύσητε, "that you might be empowered." Again the ἵνα clause is followed by two infinitive clauses, which in all probability express parallel thoughts (see the comments on vv 18, 19). The empowerment is in order for the readers to grasp (καταλαβέσθαι) all the dimensions (of love) and to know (γνῶναι) the love of Christ which surpasses knowledge. By the time the third ἵνα clause has been reached, the prayer has gathered rhetorical momentum, and the final request becomes the climactic one—"that you might be filled up to all the fullness of God."

The formal features of an intercessory prayer-report have been considered earlier, in the discussion of 1:15–23 under *Form/Structure/Setting*. As one might expect, the report here in chap. 3, particularly when its introduction in v 1 is included, contains the following basic elements: (*i*) mention of the person who prays, "I, Paul, the prisoner of Christ Jesus" (v 1); (*ii*) the verb of praying, "I kneel" (v 14); (*iii*) mention of the person to whom prayer is made, "before the Father" (v 14), who is described further in v 15; (*iv*) mention of the persons for whom one prays, which is not found here with the verb of praying but becomes explicit with the ὑμῖν in v 16, "might grant you," which has earlier been elaborated as "you Gentiles" (v 1); and (*v*) the content of the prayer, which is often expressed by means of a final clause, here the ἵνα clauses of vv 16, 18, 19b. It differs from the earlier intercessory prayer-report in the thanksgiving period of 1:15–23 in that the verb for praying is not in participial form, there is no clear link with thanksgiving as in 1:16, 17, and there is no eschatological climax as in 1:21b.

The doxology also consists of one sentence. Verse 20 begins with the mention of the one to whom glory is ascribed, τῷ δὲ δυναμένῳ . . . , "now to the one who is able . . . ," but its elaboration on God's power becomes a lengthy one, making it necessary to begin the doxology again in v 21 with a repetition of the one to whom the praise is addressed, this time using the pronoun αὐτῷ. The link between the doxology and the preceding prayer-report is found in the thought of v 20 that God "is able to do infinitely more abundantly above all that we ask," which reflects the transition from request to praise. In an unusual formulation of the content of the praise, glory is ascribed to God in the Church and in Christ, and then two more usual features, an affirmation that such glory will last for ever and an Amen, round off the doxology.

In terms of form, doxology is being used here as the designation for ascriptions of some noble quality or qualities to God or Christ. The quality most frequently ascribed to God, particularly in the NT, is glory, hence the term doxology. But other words, synonyms for δόξα such as τιμή, "honor," or words for power, can also be used. There are two basic types of doxology: those which employ a verb of ascription, e.g., Ps 96:7, 8, "Ascribe to the Lord the glory due his name . . ." (cf. the NT terminology of "giving glory to God" using διδόναι in Luke 17:18; John 9:24; Acts 12:23; Rom 4:20; Rev 4:9; 11:13; 14:7; 16:9; 19:7), and those which simply employ a noun, e.g., 1 Chron 29:11, "Thine, O Lord, (is) the greatness, and the power, and the glory, and the victory, and the majesty." It is the latter type which is dominant in the NT, and of which Eph 3:20, 21 is an example. In this type, the quality ascribed is the subject of the sentence, the person addressed is usually in the dative case, the verb "to be" is generally omitted (occurring in the NT only in 1 Pet 4:11 and the variant reading of Matt 6:13), and the conclusion most frequently involves a formula for eternity and an Amen. The combination of a possessive dative with omission of the verb "to be" is rare in secular Greek. It reflects Hebrew usage, in which ל, *lĕ*, can be employed without a verb to express the fact that people, things, or qualities belong to God (cf. Deichgräber, *Gotteshymnus*, 25). In OT ascriptions which use this form and omit the verb, glory as the quality which is attributed to God occurs only once, in 1 Chron 29:11. In the NT, however, glory occurs in such ascriptions twenty-one times. Ascriptions of glory without a verb were becoming more frequent in Judaism (cf. 1 Esdr 4:59; Pr Man 15; 4 Macc 18:24; cf. also *2 Enoch* 67.3), and this factor, together

Form/Structure/Setting

with the influence of ascriptions of glory with a verb and the eschatological and Christological connotations of δόξα in early Christian usage, may help to explain the dominance of this particular attribute in the NT ascriptions which employ only a noun (cf. Milling, *Origin*, 146–47).

The formula for eternity, followed by Amen, occurs in only two types of praise, the eulogy and the doxology which simply employs a noun. The latter may well have taken over this feature from the former, for there are a number of OT blessings which have it (cf. 1 Chron 16:36; Pss 41:13; 72:19; 89:52; 106:48), but the ascriptions with it appear later (cf. Pr Man 15; 4 Macc 18:24; 2 *Enoch* 67.3). The feature occurs elsewhere in the NT, in ascriptions in Matt 6:13; Rom 11:36; 16:27; Gal 1:5; Phil 4:20; 1 Tim 1:17; 6:16; 2 Tim 4:18; Heb 13:21; 1 Pet 4:11; 5:11; 2 Pet 3:18; Jude 25; Rev 1:6; 5:13, 14; 7:12; 19:1–4. The standard formulation is εἰς τοὺς αἰῶνας. ἀμήν ("for ever. Amen.") or εἰς τοὺς αἰῶνας τῶν αἰώνων. ἀμήν ("for ever and ever. Amen."). It is unusual to diverge from these standard forms, and Eph 3:21 is unique in the NT in its inclusion of γενεά, "generation."

In Eph 3:21, the ascription of glory follows on from the intercessory prayer-report. Ascriptions at the end of various prayer forms can be found also in Pss 3:8; 68:34; Jonah 2:9; Pr Man 15; 1 Tim 1:17; Heb 13:20, 21; *Did.* 8.2; 9.2–4; 10.2–5; *1 Clem.* 64.

With its intercessory prayer-report and its doxology, this pericope combines formal features found separately in some Pauline letters. In terms of its contents, it has some similarities with the intercessory prayer-report of Phil 1:9–11, which emphasizes love as what is desired for the readers, but also mentions knowledge, being filled (with the fruit of righteousness), and God's glory. But again Colossians is the letter on which this writer is most dependent. In 3:1–13 he had employed Col 1:23c–28. Now he has in mind the last part of that passage, and what follows on from it in 1:29–2:10. The phrase τὸ πλοῦτος τῆς δόξης, "the riches of glory," in Col 1:27 appears in Eph 3:16, while Col 1:28c, "that we might present every man mature in Christ," can be seen as parallel to the goal of the whole prayer of Eph 3:14–19, although its terminology for maturity or completeness (τέλειος) is replaced here by "fullness" language, and τέλειος itself is not taken up until Eph 4:13. Col 1:29, κατὰ τὴν ἐνέργειαν αὐτοῦ τὴν ἐνεργουμένην ἐν ἐμοὶ ἐν δυνάμει, "in accordance with his energy which is at work in me in power," is echoed in the wording of Eph 3:20, κατὰ τὴν δύναμιν τὴν ἐνεργουμένην ἐν ἡμῖν, "in accordance with the power which is at work within us." From Col 2:2, αἱ καρδίαι αὐτῶν . . . ἐν ἀγάπῃ, "their hearts . . . in love," and εἰς ἐπίγνωσιν τοῦ μυστηρίου τοῦ θεοῦ, Χριστοῦ, "to the knowledge of God's mystery, Christ," may be reflected in Eph 3:17, ἐν ταῖς καρδίαις ὑμῶν, ἐν ἀγάπῃ . . . , "in your hearts, in love . . . ," and Eph 3:19, γνῶναί τε τὴν ὑπερβάλλουσαν τῆς γνώσεως ἀγάπην τοῦ Χριστοῦ, "to know the love of Christ which surpasses knowledge." The language of Col 2:7, ἐρριζωμένοι καὶ ἐποικοδομούμενοι ἐν αὐτῷ, "rooted and built up in him," combined with that of Col 1:23, τεθεμελιωμένοι, "grounded," has clearly influenced the formulation of Eph 3:17, ἐν ἀγάπῃ ἐρριζωμένοι καί τεθεμελιωμένοι, "rooted and grounded in love." Finally, the terminology of Col 2:9, 10—ἐν αὐτῷ κατοικεῖ πᾶν τὸ πλήρωμα τῆς θεότητος . . . καὶ ἐστὲ ἐν αὐτῷ πεπληρωμένοι, "in him the whole fullness of deity dwells . . . and you are filled in him" is picked up in two ways, in Eph

3:17, κατοικῆσαι τὸν Χριστόν, "that Christ might dwell," and in Eph 3:19, ἵνα πληρωθῆτε εἰς πᾶν τὸ πλήρωμα τοῦ θεοῦ, "that you might be filled up to all the fullness of God." In this way, language which is used in Colossians mainly in exhortations with a Christological focus is taken up again in Ephesians in the context of prayer with a theological framework.

The intercessory prayer-report and the doxology are liturgical elements which had their original setting in the prayer and praise of early Christian worship. In common with early Christian prayer in general, both the intercession and the doxology are addressed to God. Only a few examples of either prayer form are addressed to Christ. In both Jewish and early Christian worship, the eternity formula functioned as a vocal signal to which the Amen was the congregation's confirmatory response (cf. 1 Chron 16:36; Ps 106:48; cf. also 1 Cor 14:16). In their present setting in the letter, these elements from the early Church's worship function as the conclusion of the first part of the letter. As J. T. Sanders (*ZNW* 56 [1965] 214) asserts, ". . . the doxology at the end of ch. 3 is a *closing* liturgical element, just as the blessing and thanksgiving in ch. 1 are opening liturgical elements." Since Ephesians does not have the usual body of the Pauline letter, the intercessory prayer-report should not be classed as one within the body of the letter (*contra* G. P. Wiles, *Paul's Intercessory Prayers* [Cambridge: Cambridge University Press, 1974] 156 n. 3, 300) but as one within a thanksgiving period, in fact in continuity with the previous intercessory prayer-report of 1:15–23 within the extended thanksgiving period formed by the first three chapters.

In a rhetorical analysis of the letter, the intercessory prayer-report and the doxology can be seen as the *transitus* between the *narratio* of 2:11–22 and the *exhortatio* of 4:1–6:9, and as functioning as a new *exordium*. Again, the goodwill of the readers is maintained, as the emotive depiction of the writer kneeling in prayer on their behalf and the extravagance of the imagery and language of his prayer show his deep concern for their welfare. The doxology encourages them to identify with the praise of God's power in them and of his glory in the community, with the "Amen" in particular inviting their participation and assent. In terms of the letter's persuasive power, it is both crucial and effective for writer and readers to be in harmony at this high point of praise of God, before the writer moves on to make his appeal to the readers about how they are to conduct their lives.

In their content, the intercessory prayer-report and doxology hark back to some of the themes of 1:15–23, and do not reflect explicitly the major themes in the intervening material, though the notion of God's presence in believers through the Spirit (3:16) has surfaced previously in 2:22, and the privilege of being part of the Church has been elaborated on in chap. 2. The readers' relationship to "all the saints" is mentioned in 1:15 and in 3:18. The Father and glory are intimately linked in 1:17 and 3:16 (cf. also 3:21). Knowledge figures in 1:17 and 3:19, and the notion of naming heavenly powers occurs in 1:21 and 3:15. The language for God's power in believers (δύναμις, κράτος, ἐνέργεια) in 1:19 is recalled in 3:16, 20 (δύναμις, κραταιωθῆναι, ἐνεργουμένην), and, of course, πλήρωμα, "fullness," and its cognate verb are found in both 1:23 and 3:19. The earlier intercession for the readers emphasized their need for knowledge of God and of the blessings of salvation that were theirs, especially

God's power demonstrated in Christ's resurrection and exaltation and now made available for them. This pericope repeats the request for knowledge in 3:18, 19, though the formulation focuses on knowledge of the love of Christ, and is phrased more paradoxically, in that the object of the desired knowledge is, in fact, a quality which surpasses knowledge. The writer is also still concerned that believers experience God's power, now more specifically linked with the Spirit (3:16), and this concern surfaces again in the language of the doxology in 3:20. It is in the focus on love in 3:17–19 (though cf. the mention of the readers' love in the thanksgiving period in 1:15), and in the extravagant prayer for a total filling of believers by God, that the second intercessory prayer-report moves beyond the first.

If the writer's emphases in his prayer for his readers may be seen as to some extent reflecting by contrast the readers' needs as he perceives them, then this pericope reinforces the general view of the setting of the letter that has already emerged. The prayer for inner strength, roots, foundations, Christ dwelling in the heart, faith, knowledge, love, and complete experience of God, and the quite unusual stress on the Church in the doxology, suggest a variety of needs among the readers. There may well be tendencies to rootlessness and instability, to inferiority, or at least confusion, in the face of the claims of others to knowledge and fullness, to an insufficient sense of their identity as part of the Church, and to an inadequate appreciation of the power and love available to enable them to live as God's new people, the Church.

Comment

14, 15 Τούτου χάριν κάμπτω τὰ γόνατά μου πρὸς τὸν πατέρα, ἐξ οὗ πᾶσα πατριὰ ἐν οὐρανοῖς καὶ ἐπὶ γῆς ὀνομάζεται, "For this reason I kneel before the Father, from whom every family in heaven and on earth derives its name." Τούτου χάριν harks back to the use of the same phrase at the beginning of 3:1, where it had signaled the writer's intention of continuing to express his concern for his readers before God, having set out for them their privileges as a result of what God had done for them in Christ. Now that the intention is taken up, the following prayer for the enabling of the readers is inevitably colored by the digression of 3:2–13, with its statement of the readers' debt to Paul, containing further reminders of their part in the Church and the Church's part in God's cosmic plan.

The mention of the posture of kneeling in the terminology for prayer is significant, since the more usual Jewish and early Christian practice was to pray standing (cf. Mark 11:25; Luke 18:11, 13). Kneeling in the ancient world could signify subordination, servility, or worship, as well as being the posture of a suppliant before the gods. The last usage, as part of prayer, is attested more in Judaism than in Greco-Roman writings. Kneeling for prayer is found in the Greek versions of Dan 6:10 [11] Theod. (κάμπτειν ἐπὶ τὰ γόνατα), 3 Kgdms 8:54 LXX (ὀκλάζειν ἐπὶ τὰ γόνατα), and 1 Chr 29:20 LXX (κάμπτειν τὰ γόνατα), while in the NT references to kneeling and prayer occur mainly in Luke–Acts (Luke 22:41; Acts 7:60; 9:40; 20:36; 21:5, using τιθέναι τὰ γόνατα), but also in Mark 1:40; 10:17; Matt 17:14 (using γονυπετεῖν). Though used in the

LXX for prayer, the terminology here in Ephesians, κάμπτειν τὰ γόνατα, is used elsewhere in the NT to convey the notion of homage or worship. This occurs only in the Pauline corpus, and each time as part of an OT citation (cf. Rom 11:3 citing 1 Kgs 19:18, and Rom 14:11; Phil 2:10, both citing Isa 45:23). Intercessory prayer and worship are obviously not mutually exclusive activities, and it could well be that both connotations combine here in Eph 3:14 to suggest an attitude of deep reverence for God the Father, who is addressed. It could also be that describing the activity of prayer in terms of kneeling would have had more emotive force and conveyed a greater fervency of entreaty on the writer's part than the earlier reference to his praying in 1:16.

God, to whom the prayer is made, is described as the Father (cf. also 1:2, 3, 17; 2:18; 4:6; 5:20; 6:23). As in the earlier intercessory prayer-report in 1:17 ("Father of glory"), there is an expansion here on the notion of God's fatherhood in line with the letter's elaborate liturgical style. There has been much discussion of the meaning of the relative clause containing this expansion and of the play on words it introduces: πατριά, "family," relates back to πατήρ, "father." Sometimes the main point of the introduction of the clause, viz. that it is the writer's attempt to extol the fatherhood of God, is lost sight of in the discussion of the details. πατριά stands for a group derived from a single ancestor and in its use in the LXX can denote a family, one's father's house, a clan, a tribe, or even a nation. Elsewhere in the NT the term is employed only in Luke–Acts. In Luke 2:4 it is synonymous with οἶκος, "house," in the phrase "of the house and family (line) of David," while in Acts 3:25, quoting Gen 12:3, it is used of "all the families of the earth." It is best taken here in Ephesians as referring to every family or family grouping. πᾶσα πατριά is not to be interpreted as "the whole family." Normal Greek grammatical usage would require the article for such a meaning (cf. the discussion of this under 2:21). Nevertheless, Caird (69) seems to presuppose some such meaning, for he interprets every family on earth as the one household of faith, of which Jews and Gentiles have become members, and every family in heaven as the powers who have been reconciled. Mitton (131–32; *Epistle*, 237–39) similarly restricts the scope of this description to the realm of redemption. He attempts to do justice to the plurality of the families on earth, however, by seeing them as each local congregation within the family of the whole Church, yet still loses sight of the plurality of the families in heaven when he suggests that the reference is to the company of departed Christians. But these restrictions to redeemed families have to be read into the text.

"Every family in heaven," which is mentioned first, is best taken as referring to family groupings or classes of angels (see the discussion of angelic powers and references to their groupings under 1:21). This need not be taken to imply any notion of procreation among them (cf. Mark 12:25), though the phrase "sons or children of the angels" occurs in *1 Enoch* 69.3, 4; 71.1; 106.5, but simply that all such groupings have their origin in the One who created such beings and is their Father. It is not only good angels who are in view (*pace* Schnackenburg, 149). For this writer all such spirit powers, even the rebellious ones, owe their origin to God. The rabbis later could talk of the upper family and lower family, referring to the angels and Israel respectively, though God was seen more as the master of the house than as Father in regard to these families (cf. *b. Sanh.* 98b; also Str-B 1:744; 3:594). Here in Ephesians, "every family on earth" should be taken straightforwardly as a general reference to family groupings, and thus to the basic relationship structures of human existence.

The notion that all such family groupings, heavenly and earthly, derive their name from the Father not only underlines the play on words, but also evokes some of the OT connotations of "naming" in terms of exercising dominion over or even bringing into existence (cf. Eccl 6:10, "whatever has come to be has already been named," or Ps 147:4 and Isa 40:26, where God's calling the stars by name shows him as their Creator and Lord). The Father, then, is Creator and Lord of all family groupings; their existence and significance is dependent on him.

Some have attempted to push the thought of the verse further and to read it as an assertion that God is the archetype of all fatherhood, that human fatherhood is a more or less imperfect reflection of his perfect fatherhood, and that to call God Father is therefore not to project human language onto God but simply to acknowledge what he ultimately is in himself. This view can be found in Athanasius, who claims, "God as Father of the Son is the only true Father, and all created paternity is a shadow of the true" (*Orat. contra Arian.* 1.23, 24). J. A. Robinson (84) spells out the linguistic aspects of such a view: "So far from regarding the Divine fatherhood as a mode of speech in reference to the Godhead, derived by analogy from our conception of human fatherhood, the Apostle maintains that the very idea of fatherhood exists primarily in the Divine nature, and only by derivation in every other form of fatherhood, whether earthly or heavenly" (cf. also K. Barth, *Dogmatics in Outline* [London: SCM, 1949] 43; Bruce, 67; idem, "Name," *NIDNTT* 2 [1976] 655–56). But this interpretation moves far beyond the text on the basis of a mistaken rendering of πατριά as "fatherhood." The latter is an abstract concept which πατριά never denotes in the LXX. Even if πατριά could mean "fatherhood," what would be the meaning of "every fatherhood in heaven" (cf. also Meyer, 175)?

To extol God the Father as father of all family groupings in heaven and on earth is to set his fatherhood in the context of creation and of the cosmos. The idea of the cosmic father of all who is creator of all can be found elsewhere in, for example, Plato, *Timaeus* 28C, 37C, 41A; Philo, *Spec.* 2.165; 3.189; or *Corpus Hermeticum* 5.9; 11.6–8; 12.15b; 14.4. Explicit statements of God's universal fatherhood are not found elsewhere in the Pauline corpus, but a similar formulation occurs again later in this letter in 4:6, "one God and Father of all," and the thought has been prepared for by the reference in 3:9 to "God who created all things." It is certainly not surprising that it is Ephesians, which has already firmly set its Christology and its ecclesiology in a cosmic context, that also sets the fatherhood of God in such a context. God is not only Father as Redeemer but also as Creator. Yet the two notions cannot be held apart for the writer of Ephesians. The God who is Father of all families is the same God who is Father of Jesus Christ (cf. 1:3, 17) and who is at work to redeem a cosmos which has become alienated from him (cf. 1:10, 21, 22; 3:10). Some have seen the significance of the reference to God the Father as

Creator and Lord of all families at the beginning of this prayer-report in relation to the earlier theme of the inclusion of the Gentiles, suggesting that the universal scope of salvation is underlined, because God calls all families by their name, not just Israel (cf. Mussner, 109). But this is not a major concern of the prayer that follows, and if such a thought were in mind, there were certainly available much clearer ways of expressing it. Although by its relating of creation and redemption Ephesians leaves no room for cosmological dualism, there is no compelling reason for seeing this particular formulation as a deliberate corrective to Gnostic misunderstanding (*pace* Schlier, 168). Others have suggested that this reference is to be linked with the letter's mention of cosmic powers, a concern reflected more explicitly in Colossians (cf. Ernst, 336). There may be something to be said for this suggestion in that "every family in heaven" is mentioned first, and since just prior to this in 3:10 the Church's cosmic role as a witness to the powers has been asserted, it could well be that when the writer turns now to his prayer for this Church that cosmic context is still in mind. Probably the primary reason for this elaboration in the address to God, however, is simply that it serves to stress the Father's greatness. Elsewhere in the NT, Luke has the early Christians praying to God as Creator when they need to remind themselves that there is no opposing power that does not come under the superior sovereignty of its Creator (cf. Acts 4:24–30). Here too, where the writer is about to pray for the Church with its big role and intends to pray big prayers for its members (cf. vv 18, 19), he begins, as he ends in vv 20, 21, with a reminder in the address that he is praying to a big God, the scope of whose influence as Father extends over every grouping in the cosmos because he is the Creator and Lord of them all.

16, 17a ἵνα δῷ ὑμῖν κατὰ τὸ πλοῦτος τῆς δόξης αὐτοῦ, in order that according to the riches of his glory he might grant you. . . ." This first major request of the prayer-report recalls the language of the earlier prayer-report in chap. 1, especially 1:17, ἵνα . . . δώῃ ὑμῖν, "that . . . he may give you," and 1:18, ὁ πλοῦτος τῆς δόξης, "the wealth of the glory." Ephesians is fond of using πλοῦτος with a following genitive (cf. 1:7, 18; 2:7; 3:8) and, as in contemporary Greek usage, its gender alternates between masculine and neuter. The phrase "the riches of (his) glory" occurs in Paul in Rom 9:23 (cf. also Phil 4:19) and in Col 1:27. Glory can be synonymous with power (cf. Rom 6:4, where Christ is said to have been raised from the dead by the glory of the Father, and especially Col 1:11, which asks that the Colossians be empowered with all power according to the might of his glory). Here the term incorporates elements of both radiance and power as it conveys the perfection of God's activity. κατά, "according to," indicates the norm or measure of God's giving. For this writer, God's giving corresponds to the inexhaustible wealth of his radiance and power available to humanity, and that alone sets the limit for his prayer. In this way the writer's formulation of his request is meant to evoke further the confidence of the readers in God's ability to grant what is asked in a fashion more than adequate for their needs.

δυνάμει κραταιωθῆναι διὰ τοῦ πνεύματος αὐτοῦ εἰς τὸν ἔσω ἄνθρωπον, "to be strengthened with power through his Spirit in the inner person." The earlier prayer-report contained a reminder of the power available to believers, which was described as the same power with which God raised Christ from the dead (1:19). The apostle Paul's ministry is said to be energized by such power (3:7), and the writer will later exhort his readers to be strong in the battle against evil (6:10). Here there is a direct prayer for their strengthening, reminiscent of that in the thanksgiving period of Colossians (1:11). The tautologous style—"to be strengthened with power"—is again similar to that found in the Qumran writings (e.g., 1QH 7.17, 19; 12.35; 1QM 10.5; cf. also K. G. Kuhn, "The Epistle to the Ephesians," 117, 118). Power is to be mediated to believers by the Spirit, who has been previously mentioned as the one by whom believers are sealed, as the guarantee of the full salvation of the age to come (1:13, 14), and as the means by which God is present in the Church (2:22). Spirit and power were closely associated in Paul's writings (cf. 1 Thess 1:5; 1 Cor 2:4; 15:43, 44; 2 Cor 6:6, 7; Rom 1:4; 15:13), the Spirit being seen as the power of the age to come, and that association is continued here. The strengthening through the Spirit is to take place in "the inner person," a notion in popular use derived from Hellenistic anthropology of a dualistic variety. Plato had talked similarly of τοῦ ἀνθρώπου ὁ ἐντὸς ἄνθρωπος, "the person's inward person" (*Rep.* 9.589a), and Philo wrote also of ὁ ἄνθρωπος ἐν ἀνθρώπῳ, "the person within the person," which he equated with ὁ νοῦς, "the mind" (*Congr.* 97; cf. also *Plant.* 42; *Deter.* 23). In the *Corpus Hermeticum* this inner person is held to be imprisoned in Adam's earthly body (1:15; 9:5; 13:7, 14), while in later Gnostic anthropology, according to the church fathers, it is used as one of the terms for the divine spark within humanity (cf. Irenaeus, *Adv. Haer.* 1.21.4, 5; Hippolytus, *Ref.* 5.7.35, 36; cf. also K. Rudolph, *Gnosis*, tr. R. McL. Wilson [Edinburgh: T. & T. Clark, 1983] 88–113). The terminology is found in Paul in 2 Cor 4:16 and Rom 7:22, and R. Jewett (*Paul's Anthropological Terms* [Leiden: E. J. Brill, 1971] 391–401) has in fact argued that Paul took over the term from Corinthian Gnostics. It is just as likely, however, that he was familiar with the phrase "the inner person" from its popular usage and chose to use it for his own purposes—in 2 Cor 4:16 in connection with the believer, and in Rom 7:22 in connection with the Jew under the law. In 2 Cor 4:16, it stands for the inner part of a person's being, not accessible to sight, where the renovating power of the age to come is now in operation. It appears to be equivalent to the term "heart" used in the surrounding context in 2 Cor 4:6; 5:12. Elsewhere, in Rom 12:2, it is the mind, in particular, that is said to be renewed. In Rom 7:22, the inner person is equivalent to the mind (cf. vv 23, 25), and the focus is on the ability to make value judgments. Of course, context determines whether the use of such language conveys dualistic connotations. In Paul these are not present, for the inner person appears to bethat part of a person which is accessible to God but which, in the case of the person under the law, is ultimately in bondage to the powers of the flesh and sin, and, in the case of the believer, is being constantly renewed. Here in Ephesians the concept is used in a similar way. It is not to be equated with the new person or new humanity of Eph 4:24 (*contra* Schlier, 169), but is instead the base of operation at the center of a person's being where the Spirit does his strengthening and renovating work. In the parallel clause in v 17a its equivalent is again the heart, and in 4:23 it is the spirit of the mind which is said to be renewed. 1 Pet 3:4 has an interesting variation on this terminology when it speaks of ὁ κρυπτὸς τῆς καρδίας ἄνθρωπος, "the hidden person of the heart."

Barth (369, 391–93) translates the last part of this clause as "(to grow) toward the Inner Man," inserting the notion of growth from 2:21 and 4:15, 16, and arguing that this alone does justice to the force of the preposition εἰς, that Inner Man is a designation for Christ, who is the goal of believers' strength (cf. 4:15, 16), and that in the following parallel clause the reference to Christ is the explanatory equivalent of the Inner Man in this one. But in the next clause the heart, and not Christ, is the obvious functional equivalent to the inner person; nowhere else in the NT is a designation of this sort used for Christ; and within the NT εἰς frequently replaces ἐν in a local sense (cf. BDF para. 205), a fact which Barth himself admits (390). It appears that the primary motive behind such a novel and unfounded interpretation is Barth's desire to avoid finding any anthropology which might suggest openness to transcendence as a potential inherent within humanity. The prayer, however, is clearly one which asks God through the Spirit to vitalize and strengthen believers in that part of them which is not accessible to sight but which is open to his energizing influence.

κατοικῆσαι τὸν Χριστὸν διὰ τῆς πίστεως ἐν ταῖς καρδίαις ὑμῶν, "that Christ might dwell in your hearts through faith." In this second infinitive clause, which runs parallel to the preceding one and elaborates on what the writer desires his readers to be granted, not only is "in your hearts" equivalent to "in the inner person," but also Christ functions as equivalent to the role of the Spirit. This reflects the Pauline view in which in believers' present experience there is no real difference between Christ and the Spirit (cf. 1 Cor 15:45; 2 Cor 3:17; Rom 8:9, 10; also Gal 4:6). Believers do not experience Christ except as Spirit and do not experience the Spirit except as Christ. The implication, as far as this prayer is concerned, is that greater experience of the Spirit's power will mean the character of Christ increasingly becoming the hallmark of believers' lives.

The notion of "dwelling in," using οἰκεῖν, is in fact applied by Paul to the Spirit in relation to individual believers in Rom 8:9, 11 and in relation to the community in 1 Cor 3:16. Here Ephesians transfers this notion to Christ, using κατοικεῖν, which may well have been taken up from the passage in Colossians, 1:29–2:10, on which this section is most dependent, in particular from 2:9 (cf. 1:19). Ephesians has also earlier used κατοικητήριον in 2:22 for the Church as God's dwelling place in the Spirit. The verb indicates that the focus of the prayer request is not on an initial reception of Christ but on believers' experience of his constant presence.

This continuing presence of Christ is to be experienced "in your hearts." As in the OT, so in Paul and now here in Ephesians, the heart is understood as the center of the personality, the seat of the whole person's thinking, feeling, and willing. The writer has talked of believers' having the eyes of their hearts enlightened (1:18), and he will go on to speak of unbelievers' hardness of heart (4:18) (cf. also the references to the heart in 5:19; 6:5, 22).

Just as faith has played its part in believers' appropriation of the salvation (2:5, 8) and access to God (3:12) that have been accomplished for them, so also it is "through faith" that Christ's dwelling in the heart remains a reality for them. Faith involves a relationship of trust between two parties, and so there can be no implication that the notion of Christ living in the center of a believer's personality means the absorption of that individual personality or the dissolving of its responsibility. This is clear also from the original formulation of this sort of relationship by Paul himself in Gal 2:20, where, on the one hand, he can state, "It is no longer I who live, but Christ who lives in me," but, on the other, immediately explains this by saying, "and the life I now live in the flesh I live by faith in the Son of God, who loved me and gave himself for me." Just as Paul could talk both of believers as being in Christ and of Christ as being in believers (Gal 2:20; Rom 8:10), so this writer, before introducing the latter concept here, has already employed the former (see *Comment* on 1:3).

"Christ in the heart" is a popular notion in certain traditions of piety. It is interesting to note, therefore, that it is found in this particular formulation only here in the NT. What is its significance in the writer's prayer for his readers? Its force is that the character of Christ, the pattern of the Christ-event, should increasingly dominate and shape the whole orientation of their lives.

17b ἐν ἀγάπῃ ἐρριζωμένοι καὶ τεθεμελιωμένοι, "that you may be rooted and grounded in love." For reasons for construing "in love" with this clause, see under *Notes*, and for reasons for interpreting the clause as a further subsidiary request, see under *Form/Structure/Setting*. The participles "rooted" and "grounded," with their images of planting and building, are taken over from Col 2:7 and 1:23, passages where, in the face of false teaching, they are closely connected with "the faith." Here in Ephesians love is the soil in which believers are to be rooted and grow, the foundation on which they are to be built. There is debate among the commentators as to whether this love is God's love in Christ (e.g., Schnackenburg, 152) or believers' love (e.g., Meyer, 182; Abbott, 98, who speaks of "the grace of love in general as the 'fundamental' principle of the Christian character"; Gnilka, 185). In favor of the former is its support in Pauline thought, where it is God's love in Christ that provides the secure basis for Christian living (e.g., Rom 5:5, 8; 8:35–39). Also, here in Ephesians, stress has been placed on salvation's having its origin in God's great love (cf. 2:4, also 5:2, 25), and in the next part of this prayer the love of Christ will be specifically mentioned (v 19). In favor of the latter is the fact that one would normally expect a defining genitive if God's or Christ's love were in view, and yet this is absent. Also, elsewhere in the letter, there is the mention of believers' love (cf. 1:4, 15; 4:2, 16; 5:2; 6:24). It may well be a mistake, however, to draw such a sharp distinction between these two aspects of love (cf. also Ernst, 338). Love is the fundamental principle of the new age, of Christian existence in general and not just of Christian character. As in Paul's hymn to love in 1 Cor 13, love is to be seen as God's love embodied in Christ and mediated by the Spirit, but also as the power that moves believers to love others with no expectation of reward.

18, 19a ἵνα ἐξισχύσητε καταλαβέσθαι σὺν πᾶσιν τοῖς ἁγίοις τί τὸ πλάτος καὶ μῆκος καὶ ὕψος καὶ βάθος, "in order that you might be empowered to grasp with all the saints what is the breadth and length and height and depth." This second major request presupposes and builds upon the first. The empowering or enabling (and this is the only time this particular compound verb is found in the NT) necessary for comprehension is the sort which comes from being strengthened by the Spirit, indwelt by Christ, and rooted and grounded in love. καταλαβέσθαι, "to grasp, comprehend, perceive," is found elsewhere in the NT in Acts 4:13; 10:34; 25:25. Dupont (*Gnosis*, 501–21) argues that in other references it frequently occurs as part of philosophical terminology, denoting exact or certain knowledge, and was used by the Stoics in contexts similar to those in which they discussed the contemplation of the dimensions of the universe, while Feuillet (*NRT* 78 [1956] 598) points to its use in connection with Wisdom (cf. LXX Job 34:24; Sir 15:1, 7). But as the Acts references show, its use was by no means confined to such specific contexts.

In what is, for the modern interpreter, a puzzling formulation, the object of the comprehension desired for the readers is described simply in terms of the four dimensions. Is this a formula for the dimensions of the cosmos? Or do these dimensions merely stand for all the aspects, the inexhaustible greatness of some other object, and if so, which? Or has perhaps what was originally a formula for cosmic dimensions now been transferred to this other object? Scholars are in disarray as they attempt to answer such questions. Quite naturally, where the object does not appear to have been clearly spelled out, they have looked to material from the surrounding thought world—the OT, early Jewish literature, Hellenistic philosophy, Hermetic writings, magical papyri, and also later Christian authors—for clues to what the language of "breadth, length, height, and depth" might have meant for the writer and his readers. Valuable as such material is, it has not yet provided such clear parallels as to be decisive in the interpretation of this verse. Probably more determinative ultimately will be judgments about the context of the language here, and, in particular, the writer's sequence of thought.

Some of the attempts at interpretation, and the parallels adduced, will now be surveyed, beginning with those which seem less likely, and then interacting to a greater extent with the more probable options. The four dimensions have been equated with the four arms of Christ's cross, sometimes in association with the more general interpretation, which we shall consider below, of a reference to Christ's love, and sometimes in association with the interpretation which sees here a reference to the Gnostic Anthropos, Christ as world-encompassing Anthropos on a world-encompassing cross (cf. *Acts of Andrew* [*Martyrium Andreae prius*] 14; *Acts of Peter 9* [*Actus Vercellenses* 38]; *Acts of Philip* 140; Irenaeus, *Adv. Haer.* 5.17.14; Augustine, *Epist.* 112.14; 120.26, 36; *De Doctr. Christ.* 2.41; Schlier, 174; Houlden, 304–5). Although in Eph 2:14–16 Christ's reconciling death can be said to have both vertical and horizontal dimensions, in the one place the cross itself is mentioned (2:16) it is not treated as a symbol in its own right. It is unlikely that such highly developed symbolism would have attached itself to the cross by this stage and been readily understood by means of this cryptic allusion. And as for the association with the universal Anthropos, while, of course, cosmic Christology is a major facet of this writer's thinking, we have found no reason to believe that this is dependent on a Gnostic Anthropos myth.

Another symbol, more likely to have been available to the writer at this time, which is sometimes suggested as the reference here, is that of the heavenly

Jerusalem. In Rev 21:16 (cf. Ezek 48:16) its length, breadth, and height are mentioned, as the writer pictures the city in cubic form. When the same image is employed in Hermas, *Vis.* 3.2.5, it represents the Church in its ideal state. The earlier intercessory prayer-report did ask that believers might know the hope of their calling (1:18), but a specific reference to the heavenly Jerusalem seems unprepared for and out of place as the object of their knowledge in 3:18. If the image now stood for the Church, as in Hermas, it might be thought somewhat more appropriate. After all, the imagery of the city has been used in passing in connection with the Church in 2:19, the writer wants his readers to appreciate both their place in the Church and the Church's cosmic role, and the Church will have a prominent position in the doxology which follows. However, the ecclesiological element in this verse is supplied by the phrase "with all the saints," the imagery is not likely to have been widespread enough to have been understood simply through this language, and besides, the cubic form involves only three dimensions, not four.

The four dimensions do feature in magic texts, as is often pointed out by commentators. In these texts (cf. *PGM* 4:960–85), the cosmological connotations of the four dimensions have been put to use in spells, in which breadth, depth, length, and height are mentioned between light and brightness. Reitzenstein sees them as part of a formula intended to create a space of light into which to draw down the deity (cf. R. Reitzenstein, *Poimandres* [Leipzig: Teubner, 1904] 25–26). In his espousal of the view that these texts form the direct background to Eph 3:18, Arnold (*Ephesians,* 89–96) disputes Reitzenstein's interpretation and claims that in the magical papyri the dimensions are spiritual hypostases or expressions for power. He goes on to argue that they should, therefore, be understood in Ephesians as a reference to God's power. His strongest supporting argument from the context in the letter is that this would then provide a parallel structure to the first two petitions of 3:14–19. Both could now be seen as involving a request about power followed by a request about love. It should not be forgotten, however, that these magical texts are probably to be dated in the fourth century C.E. (cf. Preisendanz, in his introduction to *PGM* [64]). One's evaluation of this suggestion will also depend somewhat on the evaluation of Arnold's overall thesis about the relevance of magic practices as a background to the major concerns of the letter (on this, see Section 4 of the *Introduction*). This specific exegetical proposal depends on the readers' intimate knowledge of the magical formulae, but that also constitutes a problem for it. If the readers were as familiar with these magical traditions as Arnold supposes, then, because the dimensions in Ephesians have no qualifying object, the prayer could be readily interpreted as a request for the readers' knowledge of these spiritual hypostases. One would have expected the writer to signal in a much clearer way that although he has taken up such terms, they are no longer to have their original connotations but are now simply to be thought of as a general reference to God's power.

Gnilka (188) has offered a new interpretation that combines aspects of some of those already mentioned. Noting that in 2:14–17 the writer had taken a hymn about Christ uniting the cosmos in his own person and had corrected it with his emphases on the cross and the Church, he suggests that a similar process has been at work here. What were originally the dimensions of the cosmic Christ are now corrected by the focus in the context on the love of

Christ (shown in the cross) and by being interpreted as the space filled by this love of Christ, that is, as the Church. But Gnilka's interpretation must be judged as oversubtle, assuming an original use of this language and the readers' knowledge of it, for which there is no clear evidence. "That you might be empowered to grasp the Church as the space filled by the love of Christ" is hardly a straightforward reading of the text.

Another recent commentator, Mussner (112; also *Christus,* 71–74), argues that this clause is dependent both grammatically and for its meaning on the earlier infinitive clause, "that Christ might dwell in your hearts through faith." He claims, therefore, that the language of the four dimensions, a rhetorical formulation taken over from the OT and Stoicism, refers to Christ and to the whole fullness of salvation given in Christ. Mussner's argument about the grammar of the passage is not a decisive one, and reasons have already been given under *Form/Structure/Setting* for seeing the three ἵνα clauses as the main syntactical dividers, so there are no firm grounds for holding this particular ἵνα clause to be directly dependent on the earlier infinitive clause. Once the reference is broadened from Christ himself, however, and becomes the more general one of salvation in Christ, the interpretation becomes more plausible and finds other supporters (cf. Percy, *Probleme,* 310; Ernst, 339). It also becomes the equivalent of the view that the reference is to the mystery of Christ, for this is then frequently defined in terms of God's great plan of salvation (cf. Chrysostom; J. A. Robinson, 176; Gaugler, 157; Pesch, *Am Tische des Wortes* 18 [1967] 16; Schnackenburg, 154). In favor of these more general references is the fact that the writer has been wanting to instill in his readers an appreciation of the greatness of their salvation through the eulogy and thanksgiving period of chap. 1 and through the two major reminders that constitute chap. 2. Within that general purpose, knowledge of the mystery has been a specific factor that has been mentioned as recently as 3:9 (cf. also 1:9; 3:3, 4). What they fail to explain, however, is why this particular language of the four dimensions has been employed and why the writer did not find it necessary to write the genitive phrase "of salvation" or "of the mystery" in his formulation.

An explanation that does better justice to the language of the four dimensions is that which notes the frequent use of this terminology or similar terminology in cosmological contexts and claims that the dimensions should retain their cosmic connotations here (cf. Dupont, *Gnosis,* 476–93; Dahl, "Cosmic Dimensions," 57–75). Texts from the wisdom literature (Job 11:8, 9; Sir 1:3), from apocalyptic material (*1 Enoch* 60.11; 93.11–14), from Stoic philosophy, where the dimensions are associated with the motif of οὐρανοβατεῖν, walking in heaven in order to contemplate it and come to knowledge of God, since it is God whom one knows in understanding the universe filled by him (Seneca, *Nat. Quaest.* 1.12; Cicero, *Tusc.* 1.64; 5.69), from Plutarch (*Moral.* 939A), and from Gnostic thought (*Corpus Hermeticum* 10.25; 11.20; *Pistis Sophia* 133 cf. also 130, 148) can all be cited in this regard. For Dupont (*Gnosis,* 489, 497), the dimensions retain their cosmic reference for the author of Ephesians, whom he regards as Paul, but in this soteriological context they are now to be seen as the heavenly spheres to which Christ has been exalted. For Dahl, the writer mentions the cosmic dimensions as a preamble to his main point, as do some of the texts cited, and, like the apocalyptists and hermeticists, envisages them as a possible object of revealed knowledge. "He wants his readers to understand everything worth understanding, all mysteries, even the dimensions of the universe. But the one thing that matters is to know the love of Christ" ("Cosmic Dimensions," 75). This interpretation certainly has the merit of being consistent with the greatest number of parallels, and Dahl's version of it, in particular, underlines the preparatory role of the dimensions in the sequence of thought. The main problem with it, however, is in imagining the writer being concerned to pray for his readers' knowledge of the dimensions of the universe, even if this is preliminary to a greater concern. Nowhere else in this letter is he interested in the cosmos for its own sake. Such interests seem to have been a factor in leading the Colossians astray earlier. In fact, as we have seen earlier in this letter, in 2:14–16, the writer appears to have thought it appropriate to adapt a hymn with a mainly cosmic focus by emphasizing Christ's death in history and transferring it to the Jew-Gentile issue. Perhaps, then, this interpretation is concerned to pin down the reference of the four dimensions too precisely and fails to observe that the writer of Ephesians is often carried away in rhetorical flourishes. Might not this particular flourish simply be his expatiation on the vastness or greatness of an object in similar fashion to the tautologous expressions or piling up of synonyms we have noted earlier?

That object could well be the Wisdom of God. In fact, as Dahl himself concedes in his essay ("Cosmic Dimensions," 61, 73), in a number of the parallels cited the reference to the dimensions is rhetorical and serves to point up the real concern, which is an emphasis on Wisdom or the knowledge that God reveals. This can be seen in Job 11:5–9, one of the few parallel passages that actually mentions all four dimensions: "But oh, that God would speak, and open his lips to you, and that he would tell you the secrets of wisdom! For he is manifold in understanding. . . . Can you find out the deep things of God? Can you find out the limit of the Almighty? It is higher than heaven— what can you do? Deeper than Sheol—what can you know? Its measure is longer than the earth, and broader than the sea." The same holds true of Sir 1:3, "Who can find out the height of heaven, and the breadth of the earth, and the deep, and wisdom?" Cf. also Job 28:12–14, 21, 22; *1 Enoch* 93.11–14; *2 Apoc. Bar.* 54.1–4. The purpose of such texts is not to speak about the dimensions of the universe but to speak of the infinite dimensions of Wisdom. Feuillet (*NRT* 78 [1956] 600; *Christ Sagesse*, 310) asserts that whereas the Stoics would say that, in contemplating the universe, one knows God, these texts indicate that it is impossible to know the universe entirely, and even if one could, one would still not know Wisdom, whose dimensions are infinite. If the mention of the dimensions in such texts is meant to conjure up the vastness of God's Wisdom, might it not be that the writer of Ephesians has in view not actual cosmic dimensions but the metaphorical dimensions of the infinite Wisdom of God, which he has earlier in the chapter described as multifaceted (3:10)? We have already noted that this pericope is heavily dependent on Col 1:29–2:10, a passage which contains the wish that the readers might know Christ, "in whom are hid all the treasures of wisdom and knowledge" (Col 2:2, 3), and earlier in Ephesians wisdom has been seen both as a blessing already received (1:8) and as the object of prayer (1:17). Paul, in Rom 11:33– 36, had already spoken of the incomprehensibility of God's Wisdom, using the term βάθος, "depth," before breaking into a doxology, as the writer does here in vv 20, 21. Feuillet (*NRT* 78 [1956] 601; *Christ Sagesse*, 311) points out that such an interpretation fits the context here in Eph 3, since a number of elements with a Wisdom background occur. Not only is Wisdom itself mentioned (3:10), but also mentioned are the adjective ἀνεξιχνίαστος (3:8), which is found in LXX Job 5:9; 9:10; 34:24, and in Rom 11:33 for the inscrutability of God's Wisdom (cf. also the use of the verb ἐξιχνιάζειν in LXX Job 5:27; 8:8; 13:9; 28:27; Eccl 12:9; Wis 6:22; 9:16; Sir 1:3; 18:4, 6; 24:28), and the language of filling and fullness (3:19), which is partially derived from wisdom literature (cf. *Comment* on 1:23). If it is objected that in the wisdom literature the dimensions suggest the incomprehensibility of Wisdom, yet here the writer prays for the knowledge of these dimensions, it can be countered that the paradox of knowing what is too vast to know is found in that literature (e.g., Sir 24:28, 29) and is spelled out here in the next verse, v 19. But for this interpretation to be absolutely persuasive one might wish that in the background parallels cited, the link between the dimensions and Wisdom itself were more direct, instead of primarily preparatory.

Nevertheless, there is only one other interpretation that matches this last one for plausibility. It emphasizes that since the four dimensions are governed by only one article in the Greek they are to be treated as a unity, a totality which evokes the immensity of a particular object, and that object is not made explicit until the next and parallel clause, namely, the love of Christ (cf. NEB; NIV; Origen; Calvin; Meyer, 184; Abbott, 100; Roels, *God's Mission*, 176–78; Houlden, 304–5; van Roon, *Authenticity*, 262–66; Caird, 70; Mitton, 134; Caragounis, *Mysterion*, 75 n.7; Bratcher and Nida, *Handbook*, 87). So, on this view, the breadth and length and height and depth simply register the dimensions of the real object of comprehension. Instead of adding that object immediately by means of the genitive expression τῆς ἀγάπης τοῦ Χριστοῦ, "of the love of Christ," the writer has introduced a climactically parallel clause, which explains but also advances on the vaguer rhetorical language of this one. γνῶναι, "to know," corresponds to καταλαβέσθαι, "to grasp," but advances on it in that it can suggest not just intellectual apprehension but personal knowledge, while "which surpasses knowledge" is the more specific functional equivalent to the point made by the terminology of the four dimensions about immensity and incomprehensibility. The objection is sometimes leveled against this interpretation that one would normally expect the particle τε, in v 19, to introduce a new object of knowledge (cf. Feuillet, *Christ Sagesse*, 308). But this objection is unfounded. The paratactic conjunction simply indicates the close connection between the clauses it links (cf. BDF § 443). This interpretation that sees the all-embracing love of Christ as expressed by the four dimensions can claim some support from earlier Pauline material, since in Rom 8:35–39 two of the dimensions are mentioned in close association with the love of Christ. Its major advantage, however, is that it is able to provide an explanation from the immediate context which also clarifies the development of thought in the passage. The real object represented by the dimensions is immediately stated in the next clause but has already been prepared for by the emphasis on love in the preceding clause. In fact, on this interpretation the sequence, which moves from the notion of being rooted and grounded in love (v 17b), to that of being empowered to grasp (v 18a), to the vast dimensions and incomprehensibility of love (vv 18b, 19a), itself illustrates the all-encompassing nature of the love about which it speaks.

One is hard-pressed to choose between Wisdom and the love of Christ as the reference of the dimensions. Obviously, other commentators have felt this dilemma, since Westcott (52) interprets the dimensions to mean "the whole range of the sphere in which the Divine wisdom and love find exercise," and Barth, in one place, opts for a reference to the dimensions of Christ's love (373), yet, in another, supports the interpretation of the Wisdom of God (397). In the end, the choice depends on whether one places more weight on likely associations from the Wisdom background or on immediate contextual factors. How language functions in its present context is primarily determinative of its meaning, and on these grounds a reference to the love of Christ is probably to be preferred.

If the love of Christ is in view, it is not surprising that the grasping of his all-embracing love is an activity shared with other believers and that the context in which it takes place is, indeed, that of the whole Church, "with all the saints." ἅγιοι here refers to Christians, not angels (cf. 1:1, 15; 3:8; 6:18, and earlier discussions of 1:18 and 2:19; *pace* Dahl, "Cosmic Dimensions," 73). The comprehension the writer desires for his readers is not some esoteric knowledge on the part of individual initiates, not some isolated contemplation, but the shared insight gained from belonging to the community of believers. He will develop this thought further in 4:1–16, particularly in v 13, "until we all attain to the unity of the faith and of the knowledge of the Son of God."

γνῶναί τε τὴν ὑπερβάλλουσαν τῆς γνώσεως ἀγάπην τοῦ Χριστοῦ, "and to know the love of Christ which surpasses knowledge." The way in which this clause parallels but advances on the preceding one has already been treated in the discussion of the four dimensions, particularly in the exposition of the final option, which we preferred, of taking the dimensions to refer to the love of Christ. The implication of "which surpasses knowledge" being a more precise functional equivalent to the reference to the dimensions, in pointing to the immensity and incomprehensibility of Christ's love, is that it should not, therefore, be read as a polemical remark contrasting love and knowledge as ways to God in the face of Gnostic thinking (*contra* Houlden, 305; Ernst, 340). Instead the oxymoron of this clause should be taken seriously. Unlike 1 Cor 8:1–13 or 13:2, 9–13, where there is a contrast between believers' knowledge and their love, here any comparison is between believers' knowledge and Christ's love. This prayer in no way denigrates knowledge. As elsewhere in the letter (cf. 1:9, 17, 18; 3:3–5, 9; 4:13; 5:17), revealed knowledge is of utmost importance to the writer and it is something that he desires as a primary goal for his readers' growth, requesting it twice in this prayer (v 18 and v 19a). It is simply that the supreme object of Christian knowledge, Christ's love, is so profound that its depths will never be sounded and so vast that its extent will never be encompassed by the human mind. That which it is absolutely necessary to know, in fact, surpasses knowledge. There is a note of ultimate mystery about the divine intervention of which Christ's love is the manifestation, yet, as Caird (70) says, "the attempt to know the unknowable is a paradox which is at the heart of all true religion."

In Paul's thought God's love and Christ's love are two sides of the same coin, and in his great climax to Rom 8 he can ask, "Who shall separate us from the love of Christ?" (v 35) and reply that absolutely nothing "will be able to separate us from the love of God in Christ Jesus our Lord" (v 39). In two other places he focuses specifically on Christ's love: in Gal 2:20, "the Son of God who loved me and gave himself for me," and in 2 Cor 5:14, "for the love of Christ controls us." Here in Ephesians the writer's earlier emphasis has been on God's love in 2:4, but now the focus becomes the love of Christ (cf. also 5:2, 25). Just as in Paul's letters to know and love God is to be known by him (cf. Gal 4:9; 1 Cor 8:3), so in Ephesians to know the love of Christ involves being known by Christ and being controlled by his love. Later, the reflection or imitation of his love will be a significant motive to which appeal is made in the paraenesis (cf. 5:2).

19b ἵνα πληρωθῆτε εἰς πᾶν τὸ πλήρωμα τοῦ θεοῦ, "in order that you might be filled up to all the fullness of God." For discussion of the background and meaning of the term τὸ πλήρωμα, see *Comment* on 1:23. Here the language of filling and fullness forms the climax to the writer's intercessory prayer-report. In 1:23 the Church was said to be the fullness of Christ who fills the cosmos in every respect. Here, however, it is the fullness of God himself which is in view, and the prayer is that believers should attain to that fullness. εἰς does not so much signify that with which one is filled, as it conveys movement toward a goal, a being filled up to the measure of God's fullness (cf. also 4:13, which speaks of attaining to the stature of the fullness of Christ, and thus gives the thought a "teleological and eschatological" orientation; cf. Barth, 373). It is this eschatological perspective that explains how the Church, which is already the fullness (cf. 1:23; also Col 2:10), is still to be filled and to attain to the fullness (cf. also 4:13; 5:18). The relationship between what the Church is and what the Church is to become, like the relationship between the indicative and imperative, reflects ultimately the tension between the "already" and the "not yet" which this writer has inherited from Pauline eschatology. What the Church already is in principle, it is increasingly to realize in its experience.

Just as this pericope as a whole is dependent on Col 1:29–2:10, so this clause in particular is dependent on Col 2:9, 10. There the notion of the fullness of God, or rather of the fullness of deity (πᾶν τὸ πλήρωμα τῆς θεότητος), also occurs, as this is said to dwell in Christ and believers are said to be filled in him. The fullness of God, which is best explained as his presence and power, his life and rule, immanent in his creation, has been mediated to believers through Christ, in whom the fullness was present bodily. This pattern of thought is assumed as the writer now expresses his desire for his readers to be filled (*pace* Ernst, 340–41; *Pleroma*, 120–25, who wants to find an ecclesiological element in his definition of *pleroma* here in 3:19). It is expressed in the passive and in absolute form. Presumably this is a divine passive—they are to be filled by God—and presumably if they are to be filled up to the fullness of God, it is with this fullness that they are to be filled. What has come before in the prayer can be seen as giving further content to this thought. As believers are strengthened through the Spirit in the inner person, as they allow Christ to dwell in their hearts through faith, and as they know more of the love of Christ, so the process of being filled up to all the fullness of the life and power of God will take place. Response to the imperative of 5:18, "be filled with the Spirit," will also be part of the realization of this process.

This final clause of the writer's prayer is both bold and climactic. In his vision for his readers nothing can exceed attaining to the divine fullness. Indeed J. A. Robinson (89) could write, "No prayer that has ever been framed has uttered a bolder request. It is a noble example of παρρησία, of freedom of speech, of that 'boldness and access in confidence' of which he has spoken above." So bold is the request, in fact, that it might well leave the modern Christian asking whether there is any difference in kind between the fullness of deity that dwelt in Christ and that which is available to believers. Even though it is the eschatological goal of their existence, believers can become filled to capacity with all the divine fullness that can be communicated and that they can receive without ceasing to be human. Though θεότης, "deity, divine nature" (cf. Col 2:9), is not used in connection with believers, and though Christ is the supreme embodiment in history of this fullness and is its mediator to believers, is anything less involved in this vision of believers' potential than is involved in the case of Christ's relationship to the divine fullness? This sort of issue is one that could only arise after later dogmatic formulations. The need to make precise distinctions in this regard in his use of language would not have occurred to this writer, who would have believed, with Paul, that Christians are to be fully conformed to the image of Christ (cf. 2 Cor 3:18; Rom 8:29). The last part of his prayer is climactic also in moving from the thought of the love of Christ to that of the fullness of God as the goal of salvation. Once the love of Christ has mediated that which God has in store for humanity, the ultimate focus of attention can be on God himself (cf. 1 Cor 15:28; cf. also Gnilka, 190–91).

20, 21 τῷ δὲ δυναμένῳ ὑπὲρ πάντα ποιῆσαι ὑπερεκπερισσοῦ ὧν αἰτούμεθα ἢ νοοῦμεν κατὰ τὴν δύναμιν τὴν ἐνεργουμένην ἐν ἡμῖν, "now to him who is able to do infinitely more abundantly above all that we ask or think in accordance with the power which is at work within us." Other ascriptions of glory to God which begin with τῷ δὲ δυναμένῳ, "now to him who is able," can be found in Rom 16:25 (part of what is in all likelihood a post-Pauline addition to the letter); Jude 24, 25; and *Mart. Pol.* 20.2. The English translation obscures the link there is in the Greek text here in v 20 between this verbal form δυναμένῳ, "is able," and its cognate noun δύναμις, "power." The preceding prayer had asked that the readers be strengthened through the Spirit with power (v 16). Now the doxology praises the one who possesses this power that is already at work in them, and at work in a way that is far in excess of anything they could request in their prayers or could even imagine. Interestingly, it was at such a point, a description of God's power, that the writer's first intercessory prayer-report had begun to digress, "what is the surpassing greatness of his power toward us who believe, according to the working of his mighty strength" (1:19). Before returning to the theme of God's power in the second intercessory prayer-report and in this doxology, the writer has earlier declared how God has demonstrated that power in raising and exalting Christ, in doing the same for believers who were spiritually dead, in including Gentiles in his work of salvation, in creating one new humanity out of Jews and Gentiles in the Church, and in energizing the ministry of the apostle Paul, who proclaimed this accomplishment of God in Christ. Earlier, God's power, effective toward believers (1:19), was said to be actually at work (ἐνεργεῖν) within Christ (1:20). Now that language is used of believers—τὴν ἐνεργουμένην ἐν ἡμῖν, "which is at work within us." N. Baumert (*Täglich Sterben und Auferstehen* [Munich: Kösel, 1973] 276–79) has argued that this clause should be taken with "ask or think" rather than "do," so that the meaning would be that God is not even bound by the measure of his own power within us, by which we pray or think, but is able to do more. In addition to the proximity in word order, Baumert claims that the tautological nature of the usual interpretation, and the strangeness of the notion that God's power at work in *us* does more than *we* ask, favor his alternative. But these are weak arguments. In terms of syntax, it is more likely that "in accordance with the power which is at work within us" qualifies "is able to do"; tautologous expressions are quite usual in the rhetorical style of Ephesians; and it is not at all strange that God's power at work in believers retains a transcendent element and is not simply identified with believers themselves.

Whereas the prayer-report is expressed in the first person singular (cf. v 14), the doxology employs the first person plural in this clause. In this way, the readers are drawn further into sharing the writer's prayer concerns—"we ask"—and his praise. They are also drawn further into the breadth of his vision of God's power. Not even the boldness of his earlier petition comes near to taxing such power. Neither the boldest human prayer nor the greatest power of human imagination could circumscribe God's ability to act. Unlike God's ability to act, the writer's own rhetorical ability is stretched to breaking point as he attempts to express his vision. He gropes for the highest form of comparison available and finds the very rare compound adverb, ὑπερεκπερισσοῦ, used by Paul in 1 Thess 3:10; 5:13. Something of the force of the writer's rhetoric can be captured by showing the build-up of the thought reflected by his language. God is said to be able to do what believers ask in prayer; he is able to do what they might fail to ask but what they can think; he is able to do all (πάντα) they ask or think; he is able to do above all (ὑπὲρ πάντα) they ask or think; he is able to do abundantly above all (περισσοῦ ὑπὲρ πάντα) they ask or think; he is able to do more abundantly above all (ἐκπερισσοῦ ὑπὲρ πάντα) they ask or think; he is able to do infinitely more abundantly above all (ὑπερεκπερισσοῦ ὑπὲρ πάντα) they ask or think. And what is more, says the writer, this inexpressible power is at work within us!

αὐτῷ ἡ δόξα ἐν τῇ ἐκκλησίᾳ καὶ ἐν Χριστῷ Ἰησοῦ εἰς πάσας τὰς γενεὰς τοῦ αἰῶνος τῶν αἰώνων. ἀμήν, "To him belongs glory in the Church and in Christ Jesus throughout all generations and for evermore. Amen." After the rhetorical flourish that developed in describing the power of the one addressed, the introductory element of the doxology proper now has to be repeated by means of the pronoun αὐτῷ, "to him." For general discussion of the form of the doxology, see *Form/Structure/Setting*, and for textual issues raised by this verse, see *Notes*. Ascriptions of glory which simply employ a noun are best treated as predicative possessive statements rather than as wishes, so that the copula verb which is omitted should be thought of as in the indicative rather than the optative (cf. BDF § 128 [5]; A. Stuiber, "Doxologie," *RAC* 4:215; Milling, "Origin," 268–71; Gnilka, 192 n. 4; Schnackenburg, 159; *pace* Gaugler, 159, 283 n. 4; Deichgräber, *Gotteshymnus*, 30–32; Caragounis, *Mysterion*, 77). The doxology involves human acknowledgment and praise of that which properly belongs to God. In such ascriptions δόξα primarily denotes the splendor of God's exalted status or honor, but its other connotations of his radiance and power would not be entirely missing (cf. especially 1:17, "the Father of glory"; 3:16, "the riches of his glory").

What is so striking about this particular doxology is the way in which the writer's dominant interests have shaped it, so that it becomes the only doxology in the NT to include both a reference to the Church and the phrase "in Christ Jesus" (some have "through Jesus Christ"; cf. Rom 16:25–27; Jude 24, 25). Striking also, as the textual history witnesses, is the order in which the Church and Christ are mentioned. In line with the writer's earlier emphasis on the Church as the sphere of God's presence and rule (e.g., 1:22b, 23; 2:22; 3:10), his doxology sees the Church as the sphere in which God's glory is acknowledged. Glory is ascribed to God in the worship and praise of the redeemed community, but this will be not only in its cultic activity but also in the whole of its existence (cf. 1:6, 12, 14). There is an eschatological aspect to this, for God will only be perfectly glorified in the Church when it fully shares in his glory (cf. 3:13; 5:27). God's glory is also acknowledged in another locus, "in Christ Jesus." For discussion of this writer's use of "in Christ," see *Comment* on 1:3. Because believers have been incorporated into Christ, he can be seen as the sphere in which their glorification of God takes place. This is the writer's way of stressing that the Church's ascription of glory to God is dependent on Christ, both as the mediator of God's activity to humanity in the first place and as the mediator of humanity's response of praise to God (cf. also 5:20). As for the sequence in which the Church is mentioned before Christ, it is not unusual for this writer to move in his thought from the present visible sphere of God's activity on earth to that on which it is ultimately dependent (cf. especially 4:4–6, "one body . . . one Lord . . . one God and Father"). So here glory is ascribed to God in the Church, which is the body of Christ and the primary sphere of his present activity, and in Christ Jesus himself, who is the exalted Head of this Church and the one upon whom its activity and indeed its very existence depend.

There are other unique features of this doxology. It stands alone among the NT doxologies in its inclusion of the term γενεά, "generation," and in its combination of the singular and plural forms of αἰών. There are other early Christian doxologies which use some form of γενεά. *1 Clem.* 61.3 has εἰς γενεὰν γενεῶν καὶ εἰς τοὺς αἰῶνας τῶν αἰώνων. which is similar to the LXX idiom for "to all generations" (cf. LXX Isa 51:8; Joel 2:2; 3:20; Jdt 8:32; Sir 39:9), and *Mart. Pol.* 21 has ἀπὸ γενεᾶς εἰς γενεάν, another LXX idiom, "from generation to generation" (cf. LXX Ps 10:6; 85:5). The usual NT formulation, which repeats αἰών, combines two plurals, εἰς τοὺς αἰῶνας τῶν αἰώνων, but the combination of the singular with the plural does occur twice in the LXX (cf. LXX Dan 3:90; 7:18). As we have come to expect, Ephesians in its liturgical style shows a preference for the use of πᾶς, "all" (which is found in other doxologies in Jude 25; also LXX Tob 8:5, 15; 11:14; 13:4, 16; Dan 3:52), and for piling up synonyms. This particular instance appears to be the writer's own refinement of terminology derived from the LXX idiom εἰς πάσας τὰς γενεὰς τοῦ αἰῶνος (cf. LXX Tob 1:4; 13:10; 14:5) and the dominant early Christian formula for eternity εἰς τοὺς αἰῶνας τῶν αἰώνων. Its sonorous language is simply intended to underline the eternity of God's glory and should not be analyzed too precisely, as in interpretations which suggest that spiritual powers are in view or that the singular means that the present aeon encompasses all others (*pace* Schlier, 177; Ernst, 342). γενεά has been used earlier in the letter in 3:5 and αἰών in 1:21; 2:7; 3:9, 11, and in line with this earlier usage, the meaning here is that glory is due to God for generations to come and as one age follows on another into infinity.

That glory belongs to God in the Church and in Christ Jesus in history and on into eternity is to be confirmed by the readers with their "Amen." Originally Amen was not the ending for prayer or a way of strengthening one's own prayer, and in the NT ἀμήν is nearly always used after a doxology. When the pattern used here of intercessory prayer followed by doxology became the usual pattern for concluding prayer, then Amen occurred at the end of prayers and out of this came the custom of concluding every prayer with Amen. The first instance in early Christian usage of someone closing his own prayer with Amen is found in *Mart. Pol.* 15.1. This doxology with its Amen can be seen to be an entirely appropriate ending for the first part of the letter, as the writer encourages his readers yet again to share his vision of the God whose final goal in accomplishing salvation in history is his own eternal glorification, the same vision that had dominated the *berakah* with which the writer had begun in 1:3–14.

Explanation

The prayer-report in the name of Paul had begun in v 1 but had then been interrupted by the digression on the apostle's ministry; it is now carried through in two parts—an intercession (vv 14–19) and a doxology (vv 20, 21). Each part consists of one sentence and, not surprisingly in explicitly liturgical material, exhibits the same linguistic style we have noted throughout the first part of the letter, particularly in the earlier *berakah* and thanksgiving period. Just as the digression had been dependent on Col 1:23c–28, so now this prayer-report is dependent on the next section of that letter, Col 1:29–2:10.

The digression on the apostle's stewardship of the mystery had developed the notion of the Church as God's instrument for demonstrating to the powers his purpose of unifying the cosmos. The writer senses that if the Church is going to become in history an effective preview of God's purposes for the end of history, then God is going to have to help it in a big way. Adopting an attitude of deep reverence and fervent entreaty, he makes three major requests, with a subsidiary one between the first and second. As he begins the intercessory prayer-report, however, he first extols God the Father as the Creator and Lord of all family groupings in the cosmos and then, as he launches into the first request, reminds himself and his readers that this God's giving in response to supplication is in accord with the inexhaustible wealth of his glory, that is, of his radiance and power active on behalf of humanity. This first main request is that the readers should be strengthened through the Spirit in their inner persons, which need to be renewed constantly by the Spirit's energy. The request is then spelled out in different terms as the writer asks that Christ might take up permanent residence in their hearts, at the center of their personalities, so that through a relationship of faith Christ's character and the pattern of his death and resurrection increasingly shape their values and their living. A subsidiary prayer follows, which asks that the readers be rooted in the soil and built on the foundation of the love that is the principle of the new age.

The second major request concerns the readers' knowledge. The writer desires that, as they are strengthened, they will be enabled to grasp in company with the whole Church the vast dimensions of the all-embracing love of Christ and then, stating a similar wish, that, despite its ultimate incomprehensibility and mystery, they might know this love of Christ personally and in a way that controls their lives. The final and climactic request is that the recipients of the letter be filled up to all the fullness of God, that they experience to their capacity the life and power of God himself.

These are no small petitions; but both at the beginning of this section, in the address to God as cosmic Father, and now at the end, as he moves from intercession to doxology, the writer expresses his conviction that he has a great God. He ascribes glory throughout history and for evermore to the God whose power infinitely transcends all human praying or imagining. This is no merely theoretical statement about the omnipotence of God as an attribute, but an assertion of praise that springs from experience. For, as the writer says, this inexpressible power of God is the same power that believers know to be at work within them. The writer's own characteristic ecclesiological and Christological emphases mark off this doxology from any Jewish counterpart. Glory is due to God in the Church and in Christ Jesus. It belongs to God in the Church as Christ's body, the one new community out of Jew and Gentile, and it belongs to him in Christ Jesus as the Head, the one through whom this community came into being and on whom it depends for its life.

The major requests of the intercessory prayer-report can be seen as reflecting what the writer believes to be major needs of the churches to which he writes. His concern for their strengthening (v 16; cf. also v 18, "in order that you might be empowered") suggests some weakness or vacillation on their part (cf. also 4:14; 6:10). He wants to see instead vigorous Christians who are effective because of their quality of inner strength derived from the energizing of God's Spirit. His concern for their being rooted and grounded in love and for their knowledge of Christ's love suggests a lack of appreciation, on the part of the readers, of the significance of what is central to the gospel, resulting in an instability and in an insufficient sense of their identity and security. The writer wants to see, instead, Christians who in the company of fellow believers know themselves, because they know the all-encompassing love of Christ and have therefore been accepted and affirmed at the heart of reality. The concern that the readers be filled up to the fullness of God himself can be read as the writer's wish to compensate for any sense of inadequacy and insufficiency on their part, perhaps in the face of syncretistic claims to have penetrated to the *pleroma*. The writer wants to see, instead, Christians who, conscious of their significant role, have appropriated to their capacity all the resources of the fullness of God.

In many ways the substance of the different requests amounts to the same thing. To be strengthened through the Spirit, to be indwelt by Christ, to be rooted in love, to know the love of Christ, and to be filled to the fullness of God involve different aspects of the experience of the same reality. Perhaps the central part of the prayer, in which the quality of love dominates, indicates that here the writer sees that reality as best summed up in the costly, self-giving love of Christ.

Certainly it is the emphasis on love that is the most noticeable difference between this intercessory prayer-report and the earlier one in the thanksgiving period of 1:15–23. Both include a stress on knowledge and power. The first asked for greater knowledge, a part of which was to be knowledge of God's power. The second begins with the concern that believers be strengthened by power, and then indicates that it is this empowering that will enable comprehension. Clearly, the writer holds that the relationship between understanding and being strengthened works both ways, that intellectual knowledge and actual experience of God's power are mutually sustaining.

God, Christ, and the Spirit all receive mention in this section. In the one reference to the Spirit in v 16 it becomes clear that in the believer's present experience his role in the inner person is functionally equivalent to that of Christ in the heart. But, as in other sections of this first part of the letter, the triad that dominates the writer's perspective is that of God, Christ, and the Church. His intercessory prayer-report is on behalf of his readers as members of the Church, as those with its calling to fulfill, and they are explicitly reminded of that ecclesiological context through the phrase "with all the saints" in v 18. The Church will become more what it ought to be as it experiences more of the one who mediates God's purposes in salvation, more of Christ's presence through the Spirit, and more of his all-embracing love that surpasses knowledge. But the prayer is addressed to God the cosmic Father who is able to grant its requests and, despite the substantial similarity of the realities requested, the theocentric language of the final climactic petition is significant. Even greater than knowledge of the incomprehensible love of Christ, for which the writer can ask, is participation in the fullness of God himself. This pattern of relationship between God, Christ, and the Church is summed up by the doxology. How striking and how characteristic of this writer's belief in the importance of the Church that it should be mentioned in the doxology as the locus for God's glory! Yet the glorification of God in the Church is immediately said to be dependent on the glorification of God in Christ Jesus, and, of course, the doxology is addressed neither to the Church nor to Christ but to God. The theocentric perspective remains ultimate as the doxology underlines that what has happened in history for the salvation of the Church through Christ is for God's own glory and will redound to that glory throughout eternity.

In this way, the first part of the letter ends on the same note with which it had begun—a note of worship and praise of the God who is not only the initiator of salvation but also its final goal. The writer's major concerns in this half of the letter have been taken up into his prayer and praise. Just as the opening eulogy was meant to draw his readers into appreciation of a theological perspective that could be a vital inspiration to them, so also the closing doxology is intended to function in this fashion. In the second half of the letter he will exhort his readers to carry out their distinctive calling to be the Church in the world. He knows, however, that nothing short of an experience of the generous love of Christ, which roots and grounds them in love, will enable them to walk in the love to which he will exhort them (cf. 4:2, 15, 16; 5:2, 25, 28, 33; cf. also 6:23, 24). He knows also that nothing short of an experience of the greatness of the power of God at work within them and nothing short of a vision of the glory that belongs to God will sustain them in fulfilling the task to which God himself has called them. In other words, he has written to them in this particular way because he is aware that, ultimately, the profundity of their theological appreciation, appropriated in worship, will be far more effective in helping them to be what they were meant to be than merely piling moral exhortation upon moral exhortation.

The Church's Calling to Maintenance of the Unity It Already Possesses (4:1–16)

Bibliography

Barth, M. "Die Parusie im Epheserbrief, Eph 4, 13." In *Neues Testament und Geschichte.* FS O. Cullmann, ed. H. Baltensweiler and B. Reicke. Zürich: Zwingli, 1972, 239–50. **Benoit, P.** "Eph 4, 1–24: Exhortation à l'unité." *AsSeign* 71 (1963) 14–26. **Best, E.** *One Body in Christ,* 148–52. **Bieder, W.** *Die Vorstellung von der Höllenfahrt Jesu Christi.* Zürich: Zwingli, 1949, 81–90. **Bjerkelund, C. J.** *Parakalô.* Oslo: Universitetsforlaget, 1967. **Bony, P.** "L'épître aux Éphésiens." In *Le ministère et les ministères selon le Nouveau Testament,* ed. J. Delorme. Paris: Seuil, 1974, 74–92. **Caird, G. B.** "The Descent of Christ in Ephesians 4:7–11." *SE* 2. Tu 87 Berlin: Akademie, 1964, 535–45. **Cambier, J.** "La Signification Christologique d'Eph. 4:7–10." *NTS* 9 (1963) 262–75. **Dubois, J.-D.** "Ephesians IV 15: *alētheuontes de* or *alētheian de poiountes.* On the Use of Coptic Versions for New Testament Textual Criticism." *NovT* 16 (1974) 30–34. **Engelhardt, E.** "Der Gedankengang des Abschnittes Eph 4, 7–16." *TSK* 44 (1871) 107–45. **Ernst, J.** *Pleroma,* 135–49. **Fischer, K. M.** *Tendenz und Absicht,* 21–78, 137–39. **Fung, R.** "The Nature of the Ministry according to Paul." *EvQ* 54 (1982) 129–46. **Hadidian, D. Y.** "*Tous de euangelistas* in Eph. 4:11." *CBQ* 28 (1966) 317–21. **Halter, H.** *Taufe und Ethos,* 242–48. **Hamann, H. P.** "The Translation of Ephesians 4:12—A Necessary Revision." *Concordia Journal* 14 (1988) 42–49. **Hanson, A. T.** *The New Testament Interpretation of Scripture.* London: S.P.C.K., 1980, 135–50. **Hanson, S.** *The Unity of the Church,* 148–61. **Harris, W. H.** "The Descent of Christ in Ephesians 4:7–11: An Exegetical Investigation with Special Reference to the Influence of Traditions about Moses Associated with Psalm 68:19." Ph.D. diss., University of Sheffield, 1988. **Howard, G.** "Head/Body Metaphors of Ephesians." *NTS* 20 (1974) 354–55. **Käsemann, E.** "Epheser 4, 11–16." In *Exegetische Versuche und Besinnungen.* Vol. 1. Göttingen: Vandenhoeck & Ruprecht, 1970, 288–92. **Kirby, J. C.** *Ephesians: Baptism and Pentecost,* 61–69, 90–100, 138–46. **Klauck, H.-J.** "Das Amt in der Kirche nach Eph 4, 1–16." *Wissenschaft und Weisheit* 36 (1973) 81–110. **Lincoln, A. T.** *Paradise Now and Not Yet,* 155–63. ———. "The Use of the OT in Ephesians." *JSNT* 14 (1982) 18–25. **Lindars, B.** *New Testament Apologetic.* London: SCM, 1961, 51–59. **Martin, F.** "Pauline Trinitarian Formulae and Christian Unity." *CBQ* 30 (1968) 199–219. **Merklein, H.** *Das kirchliche Amt,* 57–117, 332–401. ———. "Eph 4, 1–5, 20 als Rezeption von Kol 3, 1–17." In *Kontinuität und Einheit,* ed. P. G. Müller and W. Stenger. Freiburg: Herder, 1981, 194–210. **Meyer, R. P.** *Kirche und Mission,* 65–77. **Moore, W. E.** "One Baptism." *NTS* 10 (1963–4) 504–16. **Peri, I.** "Gelangen zur Vollkommenheit. Zur lateinischen Interpretation von καταντράω in Eph 4, 13." *BZ* 23 (1979) 269–78. **Porter, C. H.** "The Descent of Christ: An Exegetical Study of Eph. 4:7–11." In *One Faith,* ed. R. L. Simpson. Oklahoma: Phillips University Press, 1966, 45–55. **Rubinkiewicz, R.** "PS. LXVIII 19 (=EPH. IV 8): Another Textual Tradition or Targum?" *NovT* 17 (1975) 219–24. **Schnackenburg, R.** "Christus, Geist und Gemeinde (Eph. 4:1–16)." In *Christ and Spirit in the New Testament,* ed. B. Lindars and S. Smalley. Cambridge: Cambridge University Press, 1973, 279–96. ———. "Er hat uns mitauferweckt." *Liturgisches Jahrbuch* 2 (1952) 159–82. **Smith, G. V.** "Paul's Use of Ps. 68:18 in Eph. 4:8." *JETS* 18 (1975) 181–89. **Steinmetz, F. J.** *Protologische Heilszuversicht,* 117–21. **Theron, F. T.** "Christus, die Gees, Kerk en Kosmos volgens Ef. 4:7–10." *Nederduitse Gereformeerde Teologiese Tydskrif* 14 (1973) 214–23. **Tromp, S.** "'Caput influit sensum et motum.' Col. 2, 19 et Eph. 4, 16 in luce traditionis." *Greg* 29 (1958) 353–66. **Warnach, V.** "Taufwirklichkeit und Taufbewusstsein nach dem Epheserbrief." *Liturgie und Mönch-*

tum 33/34 (1963/64) 36–51. **Wengst, K.** *Christologische Formeln und Lieder des Urchristentums.* Gütersloh: Mohn, 1972, 131–43. **Whitaker, G. H.** "συναρμολογούμενον καὶ συνβιβαζόμενον. Eph. iv. 16." *JTS* 31 (1930) 48–49. **White, L. M.** "Social Authority in the House Church Setting and Ephesians 4:1–16." *Restoration Quarterly* 29 (1987) 209–28. **Williams, R. R.** "Logic versus Experience in the Order of Credal Formulae." *NTS* 1 (1954–55) 42–44.

Translation

¹*I, the prisoner in the Lord, exhort you, therefore, to lead a life worthy of the calling with which you were called,* ²*with all humility and gentleness, with patience, bearing with one another in love,* ³*making every effort to maintain the unity of the Spirit by the bond of peace.* ⁴*There is*[a] *one body and one Spirit, just as you were also called to the one hope of your calling,* ⁵*one Lord, one faith, one baptism;* ⁶*one God and Father of all, who is above all and through all and in all.*[b]

⁷*To each one of us, however, grace has been given in the proportion allotted by Christ's giving.* ⁸*Therefore it says,*

"When he ascended on high, he led a host of prisoners captive, he gave[c] *gifts to men."*

⁹*Now, the expression "he ascended," what does it imply except that he also descended*[d] *to the lower regions,*[e] *to the earth?* ¹⁰*He who descended is himself the one who also ascended far above all the heavens in order that he might fill the cosmos.* ¹¹*And it was he who gave the apostles, the prophets, the evangelists, the pastors and teachers* ¹²*for bringing the saints to completion, for the work of service, for the building up of the body of Christ* ¹³*until we all attain to the unity of the faith and of the knowledge of the Son of God, to the mature person,*[f] *to the measure of the stature of the fullness of Christ,* ¹⁴*so that we may no longer be children, tossed back and forth by waves, and gusted here and there by every wind of teaching, by human cunning, by craftiness, in the scheming of error,* ¹⁵*but rather, speaking the truth in love, may grow up in every way to him who is the head, Christ,* ¹⁶*from whom the whole body, joined and brought together by every ligament which gives supply, makes bodily growth, according to the activity commensurate with each individual part, for the purpose of building itself up in love.*[g]

Notes

[a] The Greek formulation contains no verb and simply begins "one body and one Spirit. . . ." The words "there is" have been added for the sake of a smoother translation.

[b] One variant reading has ἡμῖν after πᾶσιν, "all of us," in line with the first person plural which follows in v 7; cf. D F G K L Ψ 181 326 917 920 it[d,g] vg syr[p,h] goth arm *al.* Another variant, preserved in the Textus Receptus, has ὑμῖν instead after πᾶσιν, "all of you," in line with the second person plural which has preceded in vv 1, 4; cf. 489 Chrysostom Theodoret *al.* But both are glosses restricting the reference of "all" to believers, and the reading which omits them has by far the strongest external support, including P⁴⁶ ℵ A B C P 082 33 88 104 cop[sa,bo] eth.

[c] Some texts, including ℵ[c] B C*,³ D[c] K P Ψ 81 104 181 326 330 436 syr[p,h] goth arm eth Origen Victorinus-Rome Chrysostom, have καὶ ἔδωκεν, "and he gave." But this looks like an attempt to improve the more difficult syntax of the reading without the καί, which is attested in such witnesses as P⁴⁶ ℵ* A C² D* G 33 88 it vg cop[sa,bo] Marcion Justin Irenaeus[lat] Tertullian.

[d] An important textual variant has πρῶτον after κατέβη, "he descended first," and has been influential in the history of interpretation of vv 9, 10. The variant is read in ℵ[c] B C[c] K P Ψ 88 104 181 614, the majority of the Latin manuscripts, and Ambrosiaster, and, via the Textus Receptus,

is reproduced in the KJV. It is omitted, however, in P[46] ℵ* A C* D G I[vid] 082 33 81 Irenaeus[lat] Clement Tertullian Origen, and thus on the weight of the manuscript evidence it is certainly not original. Evidently an early copyist felt it necessary to add this interpretative gloss because he wished to make clear that the descent preceded the ascent, whereas in the original the sequence of the ascent and descent could be taken either way. In a similar fashion the RSV translation of κατέβη as a pluperfect, "he had descended," is an interpretation which obscures the ambiguity of the original.

[e] μέρη is included after τὰ κατώτερα by ℵ A B C D[c] K L P vg arm Chrysostom Theodoret Augustine but omitted by P[46] D* E F G it syr[p,h] goth eth cop[sa] Irenaeus Theodotus Clement Origen. The latter reading could well be original (though Harris, "Descent," 59–64, considers it the result of accidental omission), but the variant here makes no substantial difference to the meaning, since some such term as μέρη needs to be supplied anyway.

[f] A literal translation of the Greek εἰς ἄνδρα τέλειον would be "to the mature man," but the emphasis of the phrase is not so much on the maleness, as such, as on becoming a mature person in contrast to the immature children mentioned in the following verse. For further discussion, see *Comment* on v 13.

[g] Vv 11–16 form one long sentence in Greek and this stylistic feature has been retained in the translation.

Form/Structure/Setting

This pericope begins the section of the letter which is one of the most extended pieces of paraenesis in any of the letters of the Pauline corpus. As has been noted in the *Introduction*, in Ephesians the paraenesis forms an *exhortatio*, which replaces the *argumentatio* found in most persuasive discourses. The various elements in the build-up of the rhetoric to this point—the *exordium*, the *narratio*, the *digressio*, and the *transitus*, which is a renewed *exordium*—all perform their own function in reminding the readers of who they are as the Church in Christ, but they also prepare most effectively for the *exhortatio* which now follows. They secure the audience's goodwill, inspire them, convince them of the rightness of the writer's perspective on their situation, and dispose them to carry out the specific injunctions of this *exhortatio*.

4:1–16 as a whole does not have a clearly defined form. It begins as a piece of paraenesis introduced by παρακαλῶ οὖν ὑμᾶς, "I exhort you therefore." The participial forms of the verbs which follow in vv 2b, 3 are also a common feature of paraenetic style. But, instead of continuing the paraenesis, the writer is led by his appeal for conduct characterized by harmony (vv 1–3) to expand on the theme of unity, first in terms of the realities on which the Church is based (vv 4–6) and then through depicting how the diversity of Christ's gifts to the Church provides for its building up and growth in love and unity (vv 7–16). This expansion means that the direct exhortation with which the passage began temporarily fades into the background to be replaced by theological assertion and has to be reintroduced in v 17 after this treatment of the Church's unity has been rounded off. A further indication of this transition in the form is the change from the second person plural of direct address (vv 1, 4) to the first person plural of the later statements (vv 7, 13–15). Although the form of direct paraenesis does not shape the whole passage, the writer's depiction of the goals of the Church's unity and maturity in vv 13–15 and of the proper functioning of the Church as a body in v 16 nevertheless constitutes an indirect

Form / Structure / Setting

appeal to the readers to play their part in enabling the Church to become what it should be. This combination of directly paraenetical elements and more discursive material was not unusual in epistolary paraenesis. Prescriptive and descriptive forms are, for example, often mixed in Seneca's epistles (cf. H. Cancik, *Untersuchungen zu Senecas Epistulae morales* [Hildesheim: Olms, 1967] 16–17).

The expansion on the theme of unity reflects, of course, this writer's distinctive interest in the topic of the Church. At the same time it exhibits elements of his distinctive style which pervaded the first part of the letter. Verses 11–16 in particular consist of one long overladen sentence in which prepositional phrase is piled upon prepositional phrase, clauses introduced by participles are intermingled with clauses introduced by conjunctions, and these all culminate in a complex relative clause, which itself contains two participles and five prepositional phrases.

In terms of its structure of thought, the passage falls into two main parts. The first part (vv 1–6) can itself be divided into two sections. It begins with the exhortation to the readers to live worthily of their calling, an exhortation grounded in the first part of the letter and one which soon focuses in the appeal to maintain the unity of the Spirit (vv 1–3). This leads on to an assertion of the unifying realities of the faith on which such an appeal is based (vv 4–6), which makes use of confessional material. These verses are also linked with the preceding ones through the writer's reference in v 4b back to the calling to which he had appealed in v 1. The beginning of the second part of the passage (vv 7–16) and of a distinct train of thought is marked by ἑνὶ δὲ ἑκάστῳ ἡμῶν. . . , "to each one of us, however, . . ." This introduces the note of diversity in the distribution of grace by Christ to each individual member of the Church. As becomes clear, this new note does not mean the abandonment of the earlier motif of unity. Instead, diversity is seen to contribute to unity, as the writer goes on to show that the purpose of the diverse gifts of Christ to the Church, particularly the gifts of apostles, prophets, evangelists, pastors, and teachers, is to build up the whole body, to enable it to attain maturity and unity (v 13), a unity in which there is still an integral role for the individual (cf. ἑκάστου again in v 16). As regards this flow of thought, v 11 would follow on quite naturally from v 7, as it takes up the concept of giving and elaborates on the variety in Christ's gift. Verses 8–10 appear to complicate the argument unnecessarily. How then do they fit into its structure? Verse 8, with its citation of Ps 68:18, functions as a scriptural confirmation of the notion of the exalted Christ giving gifts with ἀναβάς, "he ascended," and ἔδωκεν δόματα, "he gave gifts," as the key supporting terms from each line of the citation. There then follows an interpretation of each line. Verses 9, 10, which in many texts and translations are placed in parentheses and then treated by many commentators as a digression with little agreement about their purpose, provide a midrashic interpretation and identification of the psalm's words about the one who ascended. Possibly the most likely explanation for the details of the midrash is that, since the psalm mentions only an ascent in connection with giving gifts, the writer felt it necessary to show that the ascent also implies a descent in order to establish his point that the Christ who ascended is the giver of gifts in the Church (cf. *Comment* on vv 9, 10). In this way the midrash fulfills a typical function of Haggadah, filling out possible gaps in the meaning of a text. The identity of the ascender and the descender having been established, vv 11–16 can then interpret the second line of the citation in v 8, expanding first on the nature (v 11) and then on the purpose (vv 12–16) of the exalted Christ's gifts within the context of the whole Church. The gifts turn out to be a variety of particular people, all of whom have ministries involving some form of proclamation of the word. There are questions about the syntax of v 12 (cf. *Comment*), but its three prepositional phrases most likely describe three aspects of the purpose of such gifts—the equipping of others, service, and the building up of the Church. The temporal clause of v 13 further defines this last aspect in terms of all the Church's members attaining a goal, which again three prepositional phrases explain from three different angles—unity of faith and knowledge, maturity, and a maturity which is measured by the fullness of Christ. As if this were not enough, the purpose of the building up of the Church and of the gifts instrumental in this process is now elaborated negatively in v 14 by means of a ἵνα clause, which indicates the need to move away from a present immaturity in the readers' reception of teaching, and positively in v 15 through the addition of a participial clause, which speaks of their growing up into Christ who is the head. The concluding verse, v 16, consists of a relative clause, which recalls in summary fashion the already mentioned purposes of the growth and building up of the body, the Church, while underlining that these processes have their source in Christ and that they require the activity of each part of the body.

The paraenetic section of the letter is introduced in 4:1 by a particular form, the *parakalō* clause, characteristic of Paul's letters (cf. 1 Thess 4:1, 10; 5:14; 1 Cor 1:10; 4:16; 16:15; 2 Cor 2:8; 6:1; 10:1; Rom 12:1; 15:30; 16:17; Philem 8–10). It has been investigated extensively by Bjerkelund (*Parakalô*), although some of his analyses and conclusions are unsatisfactory (cf. also R. Hasenstab, *Modelle paulinischer Ethik* [Mainz: Grünewald, 1977] 73–80). He has isolated a pattern which predominates in Paul's usage, consisting of the verb in the first person singular or plural, followed by the conjunction οὖν, "therefore," or δέ, "but," by an object in the second person plural ὑμᾶς, "you," frequently in connection with the vocative ἀδελφοί, "brothers and sisters," by a prepositional phrase containing either διά, "through," with the genitive, or ἐν, "in," with the dative, and by the content of the exhortation expressed by means of an infinitive or an imperative or a ἵνα clause (*Parakalô*, 13–19). He has also shown that a similar formulation was not uncommon in Greek letters, particularly in official diplomatic letters where it indicated an issue of concern to the writer and sometimes followed an expression of thanksgiving for or praise of the addressee in regard to such an issue (cf. *Parakalô*, 34–74). As far as Paul's letters are concerned, Bjerkelund correctly notes that the *parakalō* clause marks the transition to a new section of the letter, which sets out a matter of some concern to the apostle but which is not necessarily the paraenetic section (cf. *Parakalô*, 112–90; cf. also T. Y. Mullins, "Petition as a Literary Form," *NovT* 5 [1962] 46–54).

The writer of Ephesians takes up the *parakalō* clause and employs it, as

Paul had done in 1 Thess 4:1 and Rom 12:1, to begin the major paraenesis of the letter (*pace* Bjerkelund, *Parakalô*, 140, 170, 189, who, on the basis of an artificial distinction, argues that the *parakalō* clauses in 1 Thess 4:1 and Rom 12:1 are purely formal epistolary transitions and not actually part of the new paraenetic sections which they mark; he therefore claims that Eph 4:1 departs from the earlier Pauline function of such clauses). There are two ways, however, in which the formulation in Eph 4:1 is dissimilar to the characteristic Pauline usage. First, unlike many of the Pauline references, this verse does not contain the vocative ἀδελφοί (cf. also Bjerkelund, *Parakalô*, 221 n 19; E. Schweizer ["Zur Frage der Echtheit des Kolosser—und des Epheserbriefes," *ZNW* 47 (1956) 287] has argued that the overall omission of this term in Colossians and Ephesians is one of the factors weighing against the authenticity of these letters). Second, unlike most of the uses of the clause by Paul, Eph 4:1 omits the accompanying prepositional phrase and instead has such a phrase, ἐν κυρίῳ, "in the Lord," in connection with the designation of the apostle—"I, the prisoner in the Lord"—where it underlines the apostolic authority behind the exhortation. Bjerkelund (*Parakalô*, 186) believes this to be a major departure from authentic Pauline usage, since he holds that in such usage the *parakalō* clause always assumes a relationship of intimacy and trust between Paul and his addressees and is not employed in a context in which apostolic authority has to be stressed. But the use at 2 Cor 10:1 with the emphatic self-designation αὐτὸς δὲ ἐγὼ Παῦλος, "But I, Paul, myself," demonstrates that such a generalization about the Pauline material will not hold. The formulation in Eph 4:1 can scarcely be said to betray an inadequate knowledge of the conventions of the Greek letter form (*pace* Bjerkelund, *Parakalô*, 187). Rather it exhibits both the continuities and the minor discontinuities one might expect from a follower of Paul, who wishes to retain a familiar feature from the paraenetic section of the apostolic letter as he starts his own paranaesis in the apostle's name.

In addition to retaining the Pauline *parakalō* formulation, the writer employs other traditional material, much of it Pauline, in 4:1–16. We shall examine this in the order in which it appears in this passage. The formulation of the initial major exhortation, to walk worthily of the calling to which the readers have been called, is dependent on the ideas and language of 1 Thess 2:11, 12, where Paul recalls his ministry among the Thessalonians in terms of exhorting, encouraging, and charging them to walk worthily of God who calls them into his kingdom and glory. παρακαλεῖν, "to exhort," ἀξίως περιπατεῖν, "to walk worthily," and καλεῖν, "to call," feature in both passages, but in Ephesians, in line with the earlier reference in 1:18, it is the call itself rather than the one who calls that receives the emphasis.

In specifying what living worthily of the call should mean for the community, the writer is, as earlier in the letter, heavily dependent on Colossians. Most recently he has made use of Col 1:23c–28 in 3:1–13 and of Col 1:29–2:10 in 3:14–21. Now the paraenesis of Eph 4:1–5:20 takes up that of Col 3:1–17 (cf. Merklein, "Eph 4, 1–5, 20," 194–210), and in particular vv 2–4 of this passage take up Col 3:12–15. The correspondence in the wording of the two passages can be shown as follows:

	Colossians		Ephesians
3:12	ταπεινοφροσύνην, πραΰτητα, μακροθυμίαν	4:2	μετὰ πάσης ταπεινοφροσύνης καὶ πραΰτητος, μετὰ μακροθυμίας
3:13	ἀνεχόμενοι ἀλλήλων	4:2	ἀνεχόμενοι ἀλλήλων
3:14	ἐπὶ πᾶσιν δὲ τούτοις τὴν ἀγάπην	4:2	ἐν ἀγάπῃ
3:14	ὅ ἐστιν σύνδεσμος τῆς τελειότητος	4:3	ἐν τῷ συνδέσμῳ τῆς εἰρήνης
3:15	ἡ εἰρήνη τοῦ Χριστοῦ	4:3	ἐν τῷ συνδέσμῳ τῆς εἰρήνης
3:15	εἰς ἣν καὶ ἐκλήθητε	4:4	καθὼς καὶ ἐκλήθητε (also 4:1, τῆς κλήσεως ἧς ἐκλήθητε)
3:15	ἐν ἑνὶ σώματι	4:4	ἕν σῶμα

The Colossians passage has been condensed and its key words taken over in this writer's own composition. It looks as though, through the notion of calling in v 1, the writer has fastened onto both the idea and the wording of Col 3:15, "you were called in the one body." Then, between v 1 and the introduction of "one body" and the repetition of the theme of calling in v 4, he has woven together the main terms from the preceding verses of Col 3 in the same sequence in which they are found there. This involves reducing the list of five virtues from Col 3:12 to the last three and omitting the exhortation about forgiveness from Col 3:13. The items omitted here are, however, drawn on later in the Ephesians paraenesis in 4:32. In the original Colossians paraenesis, Col 3:12–15 was dependent on the earlier major exhortation in Col 3:8–10 about putting off the old humanity and putting on the new. That Ephesians only later employs this passage, which had come earlier in Colossians (cf. especially Col 3:8–10 in Eph 4:22–24), and that before doing so it selects instead Colossians material about corporate harmony and then includes a passage about gifts of ministries, which is altogether lacking from Colossians, underlines its major concern with the Church and its unity.

There is discussion whether and to what extent traditional creedal formulations are quoted in vv 4–6. The oneness of the basic elements of the faith is set out in a series of acclamations, which at the same time serve as reminders to the readers of what they already know (cf. also Gnilka, 200). Despite the sevenfold nature of these acclamations, it is highly unlikely that vv 4–6 as a whole are a confession or hymn composed by the author (*pace* Barth, 429) or that they constituted an earlier unit which has simply been incorporated here. Although they are difficult to reconstruct with any certainty, it is more likely that behind the passage lie one or two pieces of creedal material that the writer has taken up in his own rhetorical stress on unity. Verse 4 appears to be the writer's own formulation. As we have seen, "one body" comes from the Colossians passage, on which vv 2–4 are dependent, and is a distinctive theme of the writer's, treated earlier in the letter (cf. 2:16). In that context, it was also associated closely with "one Spirit" (cf. 2:18), the phrase which follows in v 4. It is all the more natural for the writer's thought here to move from one body to one Spirit, since he has just mentioned the unity of the Spirit in v 3, and since one body and one Spirit complement each other in 1 Cor 12:11–13, a passage which will influence what follows in vv 7–16. The καθώς clause

Form / Structure / Setting

which concludes v 4 does not fit the style of creedal material (cf. also Wengst, *Christologische Formeln*, 141; Schnackenburg, 162), but is characteristic of the writer's own style earlier in the letter, and it treats the concepts of hope and calling which are again distinctive concerns of this writer (cf. 1:18; 2:12; 4:1). Verse 5, with its "one Lord, one faith, one baptism" and its alternation of expressions for "one"—εἷς, μία, ἕν—moves away from the more immediate concerns of the writer and reads much more like a traditional confessional acclamation which had its origin in a baptismal setting (cf. S. Hanson, *Unity*, 159–61; Moore, *NTS* 10 [1963–4] 514–5; Wengst, *Christologische Formeln*, 142; Schnackenburg, 162). The third part of the acclamation, "one baptism," suggests this setting, and in this light "one faith" is to be seen as the baptismal confession of faith in the one Lord. Confession is linked with the acclamation of Jesus as Lord and with faith in Rom 10:9, 10. So it is v 5 that contains most clearly traditional material, and it is likely that its form, that of acclamation, has influenced the writer's formulation in both v 4 and v 6, without his attempting to make these verses exact parallels (cf. Wengst, *Christologische Formeln*, 142). The formulation of v 6, with its description of God as one and its relating him to all things through prepositional phrases with πάντα, is reminiscent of other creedal or liturgical expressions such as 1 Cor 8:6 or Rom 11:36. It may have been one such tradition familiar to the churches of Asia Minor which has been used as the climax to this assertion of the unity of the faith. Yet it should not be forgotten that the writer of Ephesians is himself fond of expressions with πᾶς, and has already demonstrated his concern to relate Christ, the Church, and God to all things.

Verses 7–16, with their discussion of the diversity of gifts within the one body of the Church, immediately bring to mind the similar discussions by Paul in 1 Cor 12 and Rom 12. That both passages, in fact, influenced this writer seems clear from a comparison between their wording and that of vv 7, 11–16 in particular. We have already noted that παρακαλῶ οὖν ὑμᾶς, "I exhort you therefore," in Eph 4:1 occurs earlier in Rom 12:1, where Paul had gone on to speak of the one body in 12:4. Rom 12:3, which talks of each receiving the proportion of faith allotted by God, using ἕκαστος, "each," and μέτρον, "proportion or measure," and Rom 12:6, which mentions "gifts that differ according to the grace given to us," are both reflected in Eph 4:7, which speaks of grace being given to each one of us according to the proportion allotted by Christ's giving. Then, among the gifts listed in Rom 12:6–8 are prophecy, service (διακονία), and teaching (cf. Eph 4:11, 12). At this point, however, it is 1 Cor 12:28 that provides the closer parallel, since it talks of God placing in the Church not just activities but persons, "first apostles, second prophets, third teachers." We have already noted the terminology of one body and one Spirit earlier in the chapter (12:12, 13), and earlier still there has again been talk of different gifts (12:4), service (12:5), prophecy (12:10), and allotting to each one individually (12:11). Interestingly, Paul moves through the sequence, "the same Spirit," "the same Lord," "the same God" (12:4–6) in precisely the same order as that in which "one Spirit," "one Lord," "one God" are placed in Eph 4:4–6. Finally, in terms of similarities, all three passages put a stress on love in the context of their discussion of the diversity of gifts (cf. Rom 12:9, 10; 1 Cor 13; Eph 4:2, 15, 16).

While all three passages deal with both unity and diversity in the body, in 1 Cor 12 and Rom 12 it is on the diversity that Paul's main emphasis is placed, whereas in Eph 4 the diversity of gifts plays a subordinate role to the major theme of unity (cf. also Klauck, *Wissenschaft und Weisheit* 36 [1973] 105). Ephesians is also distinctive in that it does not employ the term χάρισμα, preferring χάρις, and in dependence on Ps 68, δόματα. Of the three passages, it is unique in applying the image of the body to the universal Church, in relating the concept of Christ as head to that of the Church as body, and in seeing specific ministers as gifts of the exalted Christ to the Church (contrast the formulation of 1 Cor 12:28 where *God places* such persons in the Church). The gifts listed in Rom 12 and 1 Cor 12 cover a broader range of activities, including administration, deeds of mercy, speaking in tongues, and working miracles, but, although Ephesians recognizes that all believers are gifted (vv 7, 16), it has narrowed its focus. In its concern for the establishment of doctrinal stability, it has placed greater emphasis on leaders who are ministers of the word and has extended this category by adding evangelists and pastors, who are not found in the other lists. Rather than being a specific gift, διακονία, "service," is now most probably a general description of the function of all the ministers mentioned. Whereas in Paul apostles and prophets are present in the churches, here it is likely that they are viewed as belonging to the foundational first generation of the Church. Unlike the Pauline passages, Ephesians also elaborates on the relation between the ministers it names and its vision for the Church as a whole.

Within this second major part of the passage there are further uses of traditional material. The citation of Ps 68:18 in v 8 is, of course, to be counted as such, but the midrash pesher rendering of the text and its Christological and ecclesiological exposition will be discussed in some detail under *Comment*. Although the content of the major section of this passage is not paralleled in Colossians, that letter has influenced the language here, particularly in v 16 but also in v 14. Behind the wording of v 14 lies Col 2:22, διδασκαλίας τῶν ἀνθρώπων, "human teaching"—to which Ephesians has added its own imagery and inserted a prepositional phrase, so that it now speaks of "every wind of teaching through human cunning," παντὶ ἀνέμῳ τῆς διδασκαλίας ἐν τῇ κυβείᾳ τῶν ἀνθρώπων. A much greater part in shaping the writer's formulation has been played by Col 2:19 in Eph 4:15, 16. Col 2:19 reads τὴν κεφαλήν, ἐξ οὗ πᾶν τὸ σῶμα διὰ τῶν ἁφῶν καὶ συνδέσμων ἐπιχορηγούμενον καὶ συμβιβαζόμενον αὔξει τὴν αὔξησιν τοῦ θεοῦ, "the head, from whom the whole body, supported and knit together through its ligaments and joints, grows with a growth that is from God." To this Ephesians has added the name Christ at the end of v 15 after κεφαλή, "head," and before the relative clause in v 16. In this clause it substitutes συναρμολογούμενον (cf. Eph 2:21) for ἐπιχορηγούμενον, using the latter's cognate noun with the phrase about ligaments, which it has modified by its characteristic preference for πᾶς with the singular form of the noun—διὰ πάσης ἁφῆς τῆς ἐπιχορηγίας, "by every supporting ligament." By means of such changes, and also by moving this phrase to a position after the two participles and omitting the accompanying reference to joints (σύνδεσμοι), Ephesians gives the phrase greater emphasis than in the Colossians original and makes likely the interpretation that links this particular image with the ministers named in v

11 (see *Comment* on v 16). Further elements in Ephesians' redaction of Colossians at this point are its use of ποιεῖν, "to make," with αὔξησις, "growth," instead of that noun's cognate verb and its addition of a number of prepositional phrases at the end, which round off the discussion by recalling the language and ideas of the preceding material in vv 7–15.

In regard to the setting of 4:1–16 in the letter, most commentators recognize that the οὖν, "therefore," of v 1 indicates that the paraenesis in general and this part of it in particular are based on what has preceded in the first half of the letter (*pace* Bjerkelund, *Parakalô*, 183, who denies any close connection between the two halves of the letter). It is not only this specific connective but also the concept of calling which points to this relationship. The paraenesis appeals to the readers to live worthily of their calling (4:1), and their understanding of aspects of that calling has already been a concern of the writer in the intercessory prayer-report (1:18). In fact, chaps. 1–3 as a whole can be seen as a thanksgiving for and reminder of the significance and privileges of their calling as part of the Church. Now the paraenesis spells out the way of life that is consistent with such a calling, the responsibilities that must accompany the privileges. Just as in Paul, where an ethical section of a letter often builds on earlier theological reflection (e.g., Rom 12:1), so here the ethical exhortation has its foundation in the earlier thanksgiving with its didactic function. The "walking," which is the common metaphor for this way of life used by the writer in v 1, has been anticipated by him earlier when he reminded his readers of the good works which God had prepared for them to walk in (2:10) and the contrast of these to the trespasses and sins in which they had previously walked (2:2). Numerous other links underline the way in which this first section of the paraenesis builds on the content of the earlier part of the letter. That love is to characterize believers' living (4:2, 15, 16) has already been made clear from 1:4, 15; 3:17, 19. The peace and unity expected from those who share the one Spirit in the one body (4:3, 4, 13) recalls the discussion and language of 2:14–18; 3:6. The language of the Church as body and Christ as head (4:12, 15, 16) takes up that of 1:22, 23. The interrelationship of the Church's members and its corporate growth (4:15, 16) have already been in view in 2:21, and the importance of its apostles and prophets (4:11) has been stressed earlier in 2:20; 3:5. The goal of knowledge (4:13) reflects the interests of 1:9, 17, 18; 3:18, 19, while "fill" and "fullness" language (4:10, 13) has been employed in 1:23; 3:19. The provision of grace for believers (4:7) has been a major emphasis earlier in 1:6, 7; 2:5, 7, 8, and their hope, which is made a focus of particular attention through its links with the terminology of calling repeated from the opening verse (4:4), has already been the object of similar reflection in 1:18; cf. also 1:12; 2:12. But, above all, its main theme of the Church's unity links this pericope with what has preceded. For the writer, as we have seen, the one Church out of Jews and Gentiles is both a pledge of the ultimate cosmic unity God will achieve and a witness to the hostile cosmic powers that God's cosmic purposes are already in the process of realization (cf. 3:9, 10). If the readers are to embody such a vision in their corporate life, then it is imperative that they maintain the unity that was inherent in the Church's creation. Despite these various links with the first half of the letter, the exhortation of the second half does not, however, for the most part, build directly or explicitly on what has come before. Rather, the writer relies primarily on the persuasive force of what has been said to this point, on the strength of the identification he has produced in his readers with his own perspective on their identity in Christ and their role as the Church, so that the ethical implications will now be accepted as flowing from this perspective as a whole.

The place of 4:1–16 in the letter is also significant in relation to the rest of the paraenesis. Major concepts are treated here which will be taken up again later. The exhortation to a "walk" that is appropriate to the readers' calling (4:1) has its negative counterpart in 4:17 in the appeal to cease an inappropriate walk, that of the Gentiles, and is repeated in 5:2, 8, 15, where the appropriate walk is associated respectively with love, light, and wisdom. The love to be practiced by all (4:2, 15, 16) reappears not only in the general context of the believer's walk in 5:2, but also in the more specific context of the household code as the appropriate attitude of a husband to his wife (cf. 5:25, 28, 33). It is also in this latter context in 5:23, 30 that the head/body imagery for the relationship between Christ and the Church (4:12, 15, 16) is reiterated. The image of the body from this earlier pericope has left its mark on the formulation in 4:25 about being "members one of another." The notion of truth (4:15) occurs again in 4:21, 24, 25; 5:9; 6:14, as does that of Christ as the measure or standard (4:13) in 4:20, 21. But in a fuller way than that which can be seen merely in the repetition of particular terms, 4:1–16 serves as an introductory framework for the rest of the paraenesis. The unity, stability, growth, and maturity within the Church, for which it calls, will provide major resources for the Church's attempt to live distinctively within society, which is the concern of the ethical exhortations that follow. The pericope's stress on the role of ministers of the word serves both to assert and to safeguard the authority of the Christian tradition, including its ethical teaching. Appeal will be made to this as a norm for the paraenesis in 4:20, 21.

There remains the issue whether any particular life-setting can be discerned behind the prominence given to this pericope at the beginning of the paraenesis. There is no clear polemical thrust that would enable us to identify specific opponents who threaten the Church. The reference to false teaching in 4:14 is much too general and principial to be used in this way. But two obvious questions still arise out of the text—why its emphasis on unity and why its underlining of the significance of the role of the ministers of the word named in v 11? The questions may be obvious, yet the amount of data, beyond the text itself, which is available for shaping the answers, is sparse. There is a danger of making such answers far more specific than the content of the text really warrants. Some scholars believe the cause of the exhortation to unity lies in a situation of disunity between Jewish Christians and Gentile Christians which the writer wishes to resolve. Fischer (*Tendenz*, 79–94, 201–2) claims that Gentile Christians are arrogantly disparaging Jewish Christians and no longer allowing them a place within the Church on their own terms, while Merklein ("Eph 4, 1–5, 20," 209) relates this problem more closely to the paraenesis and argues that Gentile Christian libertinism is constituting the threat to communal life with Jewish Christians. But we have already had cause to deny that a specific Jewish Christian–Gentile Christian problem lies behind the explicit discussion of Gentile Christians' relation to Israel earlier in the letter (see discussion of 2:11–22 under *Form/Structure/Setting*), and here there is not even any explicit mention of either Gentile or Jewish Christians. A call to unity between these ethnic groups simply has to be read into the text. Fischer (*Tendenz*, 21–39, 201–2) also has a very specific answer to our second question. According to him, the material about ministers has been written for a post-Pauline situation in which the attempt is being made to impose a hierarchical episcopal structure on the churches of the Pauline mission. The writer wishes to resist this move and to preserve instead the more charismatic ecclesiology of Paul's own time. For this reason he recognizes only apostles and prophets as the foundation of the Church and in this passage completely omits any mention of bishops, presbyters, or deacons. Even allowing for Fischer's insistence that the writer is concerned to be irenic rather than polemical in setting out his alternative, this hypothesis is highly implausible, since the pastors who are mentioned appear to be the equivalent to bishops or elders. Nowhere else in the letter is there the slightest trace of a tension between the ecclesiastical structures of the earlier Pauline mission and those of later episcopacy. The only evidence that can be marshalled in favor of it is this argument from silence from v 11.

To relate any response to the questions about life-setting to the more general situation of the Pauline churches of Asia Minor in the period after the death of the apostle is to be less adventurous but also to remain closer to plausibility. In this period the sort of cohesion produced by the presence and activities of the apostle and his co-workers is likely to have largely disappeared, and this has affected the sense of belonging together among the local Christian groups (cf. also Fischer, *Tendenz*, 42–46; Mussner, 116). So the issues of church life that the writer of Ephesians is addressing are how, without the apostle, the Pauline churches can remain unified and how, without the apostle, they can remain apostolic. His response reveals that to his mind the solutions to these issues are related. In response to the former, he exhorts his readers to unity as he reminds them of the givens of that unity (vv 1–6, cf. also 2:14–18; 3:6). In response to the latter issue, he underlines the significance of the bearers of the tradition of the Pauline gospel, who, along with the foundational apostles and prophets, now include evangelists, pastors, and teachers. These ministers are to be seen as no less than gifts of the exalted Christ to his Church, who will play a vital role both in the maintenance of its unity and in the preservation of its true teaching, the apostolic tradition of the gospel of Christ (vv 7–16, cf. also 4:20, 21). Since the writer of Ephesians himself attempts such a role, he presumably views himself as a teacher in the Church and the perspective of this passage would therefore also function, like the device of pseudonymity, to lend authority to his own application of the Pauline gospel (cf. also Merklein, *Das kirchliche Amt*, 395). Rather than taking his discussion of ministers as designed to combat episcopal developments, it should probably be seen as an exposition produced independently of such developments. Any structure of ministry it presupposes is somewhat more developed than that reflected in the Pauline homologoumena but not as regulated as that of Luke and the Pastorals with their elders/bishops (cf. Acts 14:23; 20:17, 28; 1 Tim 3:1, 2, 5; 4:14; 5:17, 19; Titus 1:5, 7), which led eventually to the monepiscopacy and the threefold order of bishop, presbyters, and deacons, first mentioned in the letters of Ignatius of Antioch (cf. also Klauck, *Wissenschaft und Weisheit* 36 [1973] 107–8).

Comment

1 παρακαλῶ οὖν ὑμᾶς, "I exhort you therefore. . . ." The verb παρακαλεῖν has three major senses in its NT usage. It can mean "to ask for help, beseech, entreat," "to comfort," or, as here, "to exhort" (cf. A. Grabner-Haider, *Paraklese und Eschatologie bei Paulus* [Münster: Aschendorff, 1968] 4–30; O. Schmitz and G. Stählin, "παρακαλέω," *TDNT* 5 [1967] 773–99). As noted under *Form/ Structure/Setting*, the *parakalō* clause with this last sense is a characteristic feature of Paul's letters and has been taken over with minor modifications here. It expresses a pastoral appeal to the readers' will and actions, and Paul often made clear that such an appeal derived from the content of his gospel (e.g., 2 Cor 5:20). The imperatives of ethical exhortation were based on the indicatives of the eschatological salvation inaugurated in Christ (cf. also V. P. Furnish, *Theology and Ethics in Paul* [Nashville: Abingdon, 1968] 224–27; A. Grabner-Haider, *Paraklese und Eschatologie bei Paulus;* H. Schlier, "Vom Wesen der apostolischen Ermahnung," in *Die Zeit der Kirche* [Freiburg: Herder, 1956] 74–89; idem, "Die Eigenart der christlichen Mahnung nach dem Apostel Paulus," in *Besinnung auf das Neue Testament* [Freiburg: Herder, 1964] 340–57). As in Rom 12:1, so here in Eph 4:1 the οὖν, "therefore," indicates that this ethical exhortation has its source in the earlier chapters' depiction of what God has done in Christ for human well-being.

ἐγὼ ὁ δέσμιος ἐν κυρίῳ, "I, the prisoner in the Lord" (cf. 3:1, "I, Paul, the prisoner of Christ Jesus," and see *Comment* on that verse and discussion of the image of Paul as imprisoned apostle under *Form/Structure/Setting* of 3:1– 13). A similar image is found elsewhere in post-Pauline writings (cf. 2 Tim 1:8; 2:9; also Acts 16:26; 20:23; 23:29; 26:29, 31). "The prisoner in the Lord" is a somewhat stylized expression but may still reflect the notion that, since for Paul the whole sphere of Christian living was "in the Lord," his imprisonment was to be seen as no exception. The phrase functions here to lend Paul's authority to the writer's pastoral appeal and to underline the seriousness with which it is intended. It should be noted that this explicit feature of pseudonymity begins and ends the paraenetical section of the letter (cf. 6:19, 20) but does not surface within it.

ἀξίως περιπατῆσαι τῆς κλήσεως ἧς ἐκλήθητε, "to lead a life worthy of the calling with which you were called." The relative pronoun in the last clause has been attracted to the case of its antecedent noun, and the use of a cognate noun and verb together continues a stylistic feature typical of the first part of the letter (cf. 1:3, 6, 19, 20, 23; 2:4; 3:19, 20). On περιπατεῖν for a "way of life," see also *Comment* on 2:2, 10. This is again characteristic Pauline terminology (cf. 1 Thess 2:12; 4:1, 12; Gal 5:16; Rom 6:4; 8:4; 13:13; 14:15; 1 Cor 3:3; 7:17; 2 Cor 4:2; 5:7; 10:2, 3; 12:18; Phil 3:17, 18; Col 1:10; 2:6; 3:7; 4:5). ἀξίως, "worthily," introduces the standard or criterion to which the readers' living is expected to conform (cf. Phil 1:27, "worthy of the gospel of Christ"; Col 1:10, "to lead a life worthy of the Lord"; and the reference closest to our verse in its wording, 1 Thess 2:12, "to lead a life worthy of the God who calls"). Here in Ephesians the criterion and the determining factor for believers' living is to be the call itself. The notion of this call (cf. also 1:18) is similar to that found in Paul, where it can be used, for example, for God's activity in making believers' predestination effective (cf. Rom 8:30) and in bringing them into the fellowship of his Son (1 Cor 1:9). Here the passive form of the verb is a "divine passive," underlining what is already inherent in the idea of the call: God's initiative in bringing humanity to the goal for which he intended it. The past tense looks back particularly to the readers' reception of the gospel and of the Spirit, referred to in 1:13. The use of the language of calling in the context of his ethical appeal indicates that for this writer God's sovereign initiative and human responsibility for living appropriately go hand in hand, so that he would not for one moment have expected his earlier stress on predestination and election (1:3, 4), and even on God's preparation of believers' good works ahead of time (2:10), to undermine the seriousness with which his exhortation was to be taken. The appeal to live worthily of God's calling presupposes that God's gracious initiative requires a continuous human response and that his call bestows both high privilege and high responsibility. (On the relation between the concept of calling and ethics in Paul's theology, see R. Hasenstab, *Modelle paulinischer Ethik* [Mainz: Grünewald, 1977] esp. 151–83.) The high privileges of the call have been delineated in the first part of the letter. Believers have been called into all the blessings of salvation and into experience of the power of the God who raised Christ from the dead and who brought them from death to life and to a share in Christ's reign in the heavenly realms. They have been called into the new humanity out of Jews and Gentiles, into the new temple, the one body (cf. Col 3:15, "called in the one body") of the Church, and thus called to be part of God's purposes for cosmic unity. In exhorting to a way of life that corresponds to such a calling, this first verse provides a framework designed to ensure that what follows will not be seen as mere moral advice but as an appeal to the readers' experience of the theological heart of the gospel.

2, 3 The exhortation continues with two prepositional phrases with μετά, "with," and two participial clauses with imperatival force. This is material which, as has been noted, builds on Col 3:12–15 and which spells out the qualities necessary for those called to be the one body that exhibits to the powers God's plan for the unity of the cosmos.

μετὰ πάσης ταπεινοφροσύνης καὶ πραΰτητος, μετὰ μακροθυμίας, "with all humility and gentleness, with patience." The πᾶς, "all," which qualifies the first two ethical qualities is characteristic of the writer's rhetorical style and functions to underscore the significance he attaches to these concepts. ταπεινοφροσύνη, "humility," is literally "lowliness of mind," and to be contrasted therefore with being high-minded or haughty (cf. ὑψηλὰ φρονεῖν in Rom 11:20; 12:16). As is frequently observed, humility was an attitude that was regarded primarily negatively in the Greco-Roman world and associated with contemptible servility (e.g., Josephus, *J.W.* 4.9.2 § 494; Epictetus, *Diss.* 1.9.10; 3.24.56). It takes on positive connotations in Jewish thought, however, where it is associated with the piety of the ʿănāwîm, the poor, and there are numerous OT references to God's activity in bringing down the proud and arrogant and exalting the humble.

A spirit of humility was also valued at Qumran, e.g., 1QS 4.2 (cf. also W. Grundmann, "ταπεινός," *TDNT* 8 [1972] 1–26). In Phil 2:3 Paul describes it further as the ability to count others as better than oneself and gives it a specifically Christian coloring when he illustrates this from the pattern of Christ's existence (cf. Phil 2:6–11). It should be clear that this virtue that is indispensable for Christian community (cf. also 1 Pet 5:5) assumes a proper sense of self-worth, not weakness of character, and that a proper evaluation of oneself is based on a realization of one's own dependence on the grace of God and on the worth of one's brothers and sisters in his eyes. πραΰτης, "gentleness," could be used in its adjectival form along with "humble" in the LXX translation of the category of the poor and oppressed in the OT, and again was a quality valued by the Qumran community, e.g., 1QS 2.24; 3.8; 5.3, 25; 11.1 (cf. also F. Hauck and S. Schulz, "πραΰς," *TDNT* 6 [1968] 645–51). It involves the courtesy, considerateness, and willingness to waive one's rights that come from seeking the common good without being concerned for personal reputation or gain. Paul recognizes it as a characteristic of Christ (2 Cor 10:1) and a fruit of the Spirit (Gal 5:23) and contrasts his coming to the Corinthians with a rod to his coming with love in a spirit of gentleness (1 Cor 4:21). The Pastorals also rate this quality highly as one which is to replace any tendency to quarrelsomeness in relationships with opponents (2 Tim 2:24, 25; Titus 3:2). It is worth noting that Matthew too expects both gentleness and humility from disciples (cf. 5:5; 18:4; 23:12) and sees these qualities embodied in Jesus himself, whose invitation is "Learn from me; for I am gentle and lowly in heart" (11:29).

μακροθυμία, "patience," is literally "long temper" in contrast to a short temper and can have the sense of steadfastness or forbearance. Since relationships with others are in view, it is the latter sense that is relevant here, as the following clause also makes clear. This ability to make allowance for others' shortcomings, this tolerance of others' exasperating behavior is a fruit of the Spirit (Gal 5:22) and again a quality essential for communal living (cf. 1 Thess 5:14; also 1 Cor 13:4; 2 Cor 6:6; Col 1:11). The three virtues singled out here have been taken from the list of five in Col 3:12, where they also functioned in the context of an appeal for peace and harmony in the community. The structure of the exhortation in Eph 4 means that these virtues are now subordinated more distinctively to the theme of the readers' calling to be the one body of the Church.

ἀνεχόμενοι ἀλλήλων ἐν ἀγάπῃ, "bearing with one another in love," is an amplification of what is meant by patience. When this verb has a personal object, that object is expressed in the genitive case—hence ἀλλήλων, "one another" (cf. BDF § 176 [1] on verbs of emotion). The writer knows that in the midst of tensions and conflicts the patience required will not be passive resignation but the positive attitude toward others that he will expand on later in 4:32. This type of ethical exhortation demonstrates that the writer's visionary conception of the Church and its role is accompanied by a realism about the problems of community life with its inevitable clashes of character, attitudes, and actions. To the straightforward "bear with one another" of Col 3:13 he has added "in love," a concept emphasized later and in a different way in Col 3:14, "And above all these put on love." Here in Eph 4:2 love is seen as the only means of Christian forbearance. Bearing with others means fully accepting them in their uniqueness, including their weaknesses and faults, and allowing them worth and space. It is only the love that is the power of the new age (cf. Gal 5:14, 22; 1 Cor 13), supplied by the Spirit of that age (cf. Rom 5:5), that can enable one to bear with others without expectation of reward so that their concerns weigh more heavily than one's own desires for personal fulfillment and peace of mind. Via the mention of love, the opening exhortation moves to the theme of unity that will dominate the rest of the passage. The transition is an appropriate one, for the absence of love always leads to the loss of unity.

σπουδάζοντες τηρεῖν τὴν ἑνότητα τοῦ πνεύματος ἐν τῷ συνδέσμῳ τῆς εἰρήνης, "making every effort to maintain the unity of the Spirit by the bond of peace." This clause is parallel to the previous one in that it too begins with a participle and ends with a prepositional phrase with ἐν. The unity of the Spirit involves not the human spirit but the Holy Spirit, as v 4 makes clear, and is a reference not to the congeniality of some social grouping but to the unity which God's Spirit gives and which is the ground of the Church's existence. The term ἑνότης, "unity," occurs in the NT only here and in v 13 but it becomes a basic Christian concept later in Ignatius (e.g., *Eph.* 4.2; 5.1; 14.1; *Phld.* 2.2; 3.2; 5.2; 8.1; 9.1). So whereas Col 3:14, 15 refer generally to love and peace, Ephesians distinctively and more specifically speaks of unity. Although this unity is already given and is not therefore the readers' own achievement, it must be preserved and protected. In fact, the force of the participle σπουδάζοντες suggests that the maintenance of the unity is to be a matter of the utmost importance and urgency—"Spare no effort; make it a priority for your corporate life to maintain the unity of the Spirit." Such an exhortation also makes plain that the unity of the Spirit is a reality that is to be demonstrated visibly.

In comparison with Col 3:14, 15, where love is the perfect bond and the peace of Christ is to rule, Ephesians speaks of "the bond of peace." The means of maintaining and demonstrating the unity of the Spirit is through peace, which has a bonding effect. Since Col 3 is the writer's source, it is highly unlikely that he has consciously transformed speculation about the Logos as cosmic bond from Philo (*pace* Gnilka, 199–200; Klauck, *Wissenschaft und Weisheit* 36 [1973] 88). Earlier Christ has been depicted as the personification of peace who brought reconciliation with God and reconciliation between Jew and Gentile (2:14–18), but now believers are to be agents of peace and reconciliation within the community in order to preserve its unity. Paul had treated this practice of peace as a fruit of the Spirit (Gal 5:22; cf. also Rom 8:6; 14:17; 15:13 for the relation between peace and the Spirit in Paul). The appropriate response to being called into the situation of peace and reconciliation created by the gospel is a life of peace and reconciliation. Living in this fashion binds believers together and thereby maintains the unity of the Spirit.

4–6 The Church's unity, already expressed in terms of the unity of the Spirit, is now asserted through a series of seven acclamations of oneness. These fall into two groups of three, plus a concluding acclamation of the one God with its own fourfold repetition of the word "all." For discussion of the use of traditional material here, see *Form/Structure/Setting*. The sequence of thought can be said to move from the Church, as the writer's most immediate concern, on to the Church's Lord and then on to God himself. This sequence corresponds to a number of the patterns of thought earlier in the letter. But the precise sequence is dictated more by compositional and rhetorical factors than by any deliberate preference for experiential rather than logical order in creedal formulation (*pace* Williams, *NTS* 1 [1954–55] 42–44). There is a Hellenistic Jewish background to formulations about oneness in general and formulations about the oneness of God (v 6) in particular. For example, *2 Apoc. Bar.* 85.14 can state, "Therefore, there is one law by One, one world and one end for all who exist," while Philo, *Spec.* 1.67, talks of there being one sanctuary because there is only one God. The oneness of God was, of course, a topic in Jewish diaspora propaganda (cf., e.g., 2 Macc 7:37; Philo, *Leg. Alleg.* 2.1; Josephus, *Ant.* 5.1. 25 § 97; 8.13.6 § 343; *Ag. Ap.* 2.23 § 193; *Sib. Or.* 3.11; 3.629; cf. also E. Peterson, ΈΙΣ ΘΕΟΣ [Göttingen: Vandenhoeck & Ruprecht, 1926] esp. 141–48, 254–56). Particularly interesting as parallels are passages which derive the unity of the Jewish people from the oneness of God. Philo, *Virt.* 7.35, asserts that "the highest and greatest source of this unanimity is their creed of a single God, through which, as from a fountain, they feel a love for each other, uniting them in an indissoluble bond" (cf. also *Spec.* 1.52; 4.159, and *2 Apoc. Bar.* 48.23, 24, which claims "we are all one people of the Name; we, who received one law from the One"). For the writer of Ephesians also there is a clear link between the unity of the Church and the various acclamations of oneness in vv 4–6. The behavior for which he has called, the maintenance of the unity of the Spirit, can now be seen to be the only consistent practical expression of the foundational unities he enumerates here. At the same time, by reminding his readers of these distinctive realities to which they are committed, he reinforces both the sense of cohesion he wants them to have as members of the Church and the sense of their distinctive identity vis-à-vis the surrounding society.

ἓν σῶμα καὶ ἓν πνεῦμα, καθὼς καὶ ἐκλήθητε ἐν μιᾷ ἐλπίδι τῆς κλήσεως ὑμῶν, "one body and one Spirit, just as you were also called to the one hope of your calling." It is not surprising that mention of the unity of the Spirit in v 3 should lead to the concept of the one Spirit in v 4. Col 3:15 refers to being called in the one body, while in 1 Cor 12:13 Paul had written of both one body and one Spirit. The traditional material associated with baptism in v 5 has probably suggested the acclamation form. It should be noted, however, that the writer has in any case already treated each of the unities in this first triad separately in the first part of the letter. Desiring to raise his readers' consciousness of belonging to the body of Christ and of participating in the Spirit, both of which are one and indivisible, he first recalls these realities. See *Comment* on 1:23 for the body imagery for the Church, on 2:14–16 for the notion of the one body out of the two former groupings of Jews and Gentiles, and on 2:18 for the one Spirit.

The clause "just as you were also called in the one hope of your calling" is clearly an important one for the writer, since it breaks up the form of the acclamations and repeats the idea of calling from v 1, where it provides the conceptual framework within which the rest of the paraenesis is to be understood. The hope of *his* calling earlier in the letter in 1:18 is a reference to the same reality as the hope of *your* calling here. It is simply that the former describes it in terms of the one who calls; the latter, in terms of those who are called. But what is the relation of calling, oneness, and hope presupposed by this clause? For the writer of Ephesians, when God calls believers, he calls them to a particular hope. Once his readers were separated from Christ and had no real hope (2:12), but now they can be described as those who have hoped in Christ (1:12) and have a hope that is certain because it rests on God's call, God's initiative (1:18). What that hope ultimately is can be expressed in traditional terms in 5:5 as "the kingdom of Christ and of God," but has been spelled out earlier in 1:9, 10 in this writer's own more distinctive terminology as "his good pleasure which he purposed in Christ for the administration of the fullness of time, to sum up all things in Christ, things in heaven and things on earth in him." The eschatological dimension to the call can now be seen to set the exhortation to unity in the Church in a broader context, since it recalls the cosmic unity which is the goal of the salvation God provides in Christ. The emphasis on realized eschatology in Ephesians has not meant a break with the "apocalyptic" hope of Paul's gospel. The one hope of Ephesians is not something individual and private but corporate and public, hope for a cosmos that is unified and reconciled, a world in which everything is brought together in harmony through that which God has done in Christ. This hope has already been related to the Church and its unity in 3:9, 10, where, as we have seen, the existence of the Church is God's announcement to the principalities and powers in the heavenly realms that he is going to make good on his multifaceted and wise plan for cosmic unity. The Church is depicted as providing the powers with a tangible reminder that their authority has been decisively broken and that everything is going to be united in Christ. It can play this role because it is the one new humanity in place of two (2:15) and the one body (2:16). For this writer the existence of the Church, in which the basic alienation between Jew and Gentile had been overcome, is a pledge that the one hope in its full cosmic scope will also be brought into being. The one hope is an appropriate reality with which to undergird the call to maintain unity, because it is hope which, in giving men and women a sense of expectancy, directs and unifies their actions. The writer recognizes that what his readers hope for in the end will determine what they practice in the present. The one hope of final cosmic unity is therefore meant to produce the urgent effort to maintain and demonstrate the anticipation of this in the Church.

εἷς κύριος, μία πίστις, ἓν βάπτισμα, "one Lord, one faith, one baptism." In the Greek there is a striking change from the masculine to the feminine to the neuter of the numeral one, which gives the whole triad a ringing quality. On an original baptismal association for this triad, see *Form/Structure/Setting*. "Lord" was a favorite title for Christ in Paul, who shared with the earliest Christians the affirmation of Jesus as Lord on the basis of his resurrection and by virtue of his exaltation (cf., e.g., 1 Cor 8:6; 12:3; Rom 10:9; 14:8, 9; Phil 2:9–11). The transfer of this title κύριος from Yahweh to Christ is likely to go back to Greek-speaking believers in earliest Palestinian Christianity (cf. especially J. A. Fitzmyer, "The Semitic Background of the New Testament *Kyrios*-Title," *A Wandering Aramean* [Missoula, MT: Scholars Press, 1979] 115–42; idem, "New Testament *Kyrios* and *Maranatha* and Their Aramaic Background," in *To Advance the Gospel* [New York: Crossroad, 1981] 218–35). For Ephesians, Christ is the one Lord who fills all things with his sovereign rule (1:23; 4:10) and who, as the head, has been given to the Church (1:22; 4:15, 16).

In connection with baptism, the "one faith" is likely to have in view the baptismal confession of Jesus as Lord, so that, as the majority of commentators hold, its primary reference would be to the content of faith, the unifying belief in the one Lord. Faith also has the meaning of that which is believed later in the passage in 4:13 (cf. also Col 1:23; 2:7). The "one baptism" is water baptism, the public rite of confession of the one faith in the one Lord. This baptism is one, not because it has a single form or is administered on only one occasion, but because it is the initiation into Christ, into the one body, which all have undergone and as such is a unifying factor. The connection between baptism and unity is also to be found in Paul (cf. Gal 3:27, 28; 1 Cor 12:13). The absence of the eucharist from this series of seven unifying factors is often noted. It is not particularly significant, since the writer was not attempting to be comprehensive, and mention of the eucharist neither formed part of the traditional material he uses nor fits the rhetorical pattern he builds up from that material.

εἷς θεὸς καὶ πατὴρ πάντων, ὁ ἐπὶ πάντων καὶ διὰ πάντων καὶ ἐν πᾶσιν, "one God and Father of all, who is above all and through all and in all." Behind this acclamation lies that of Paul in 1 Cor 8:6, which was in turn a Christian modification of the Shema of Deut 6:4. It contains the characteristically Christian way of speaking of the one God as Father (cf. also Gal 4:6; Rom 8:15). Here in Ephesians it is basically an affirmation of both God's supreme transcendence, "above all," and his pervasive immanence, "through all and in all." A number of scholars prefer to take the "all" references as masculine rather than neuter and therefore as denoting those in the Church, holding that the preceding context of a discussion of the Church's unity requires that any original cosmological meaning has now been transferred to believers (cf. Meyer, 201; Abbott, 109; S. Hanson, *Unity*, 155; Masson, 187; Schlier, 189; Ernst, 349; Mitton, 143; Mussner, 120; Schnackenburg, 170). But Ephesians does not completely collapse cosmological categories into ecclesiological ones, and it may well be better to take "all" as neuter and as continuing its cosmic connotations from 1:10, 22, 23; 3:9, which will also occur in 4:10 (cf. also J. A. Robinson, 93–94, 179; Houlden, 309; Gnilka, 204; Barth, 471). Formulations about God which use "all" have a cosmic reference in Paul (cf. 1 Cor 8:6; 15:28; Rom 11:36), and the elaboration on the universal fatherhood of God earlier in Eph 3:14, 15 surely tips the balances against restricting the scope of that fatherhood here. Formulations relating God to all things may well have been mediated to the Christian community via the Hellenistic synagogue from Stoicism (cf. Marcus Aurelius addressing Nature in *Medit.* 4.23, ἐκ σοῦ πάντα, ἐν σοὶ πάντα, εἰς σὲ πάντα, "All things are from you, all things are in you, all things are to you"; and for further discussion of the notion of God permeating all things, see *Comment* on 1:23). The God acclaimed by believers is the universal Father who is at work throughout his world. This confession of the one universal God means that, despite its distinctiveness from the world which will be stressed later in the paraenesis, the Church continues to exist for the world. The writer's primary purpose must, however, not be forgotten. The climactic acclamation of the one God in his universality is meant to provide the most profound ground for the Church's unity. Paul himself had reflected on the significance of God's oneness for the unity of Jew and Gentile in Rom 3:29, 30. As we noted above, this is similar to Jewish thought in which monotheism was seen as the source of Israel's unity (cf. S. Hanson, *Unity*, 5–23; W. A. Meeks, *The First Urban Christians* [New Haven: Yale University Press, 1983] 165–68). For Ephesians, it is no longer Israel, nor is it the world with its alienations and divisions, but it is the Church that is the expression of God's unity. There is an obvious corollary to such a notion. When the Church fails to maintain and express unity, it radically undermines the credibility of its belief in the one God.

7 Ἑνὶ δὲ ἑκάστῳ ἡμῶν ἐδόθη ἡ χάρις κατὰ τὸ μέτρον τῆς δωρεᾶς τοῦ Χριστοῦ, "To each one of us, however, grace has been given in the proportion allotted by Christ's giving." This verse begins the second part of the overall discussion on unity by sounding the note of diversity in Christ's distribution of grace. Whereas "one" had been used in vv 4–6 to signify unity, now it is employed to refer to the individuals who make up that unity. The verse also marks a change of style from the earlier direct address with "you" to the more inclusive "we," which, as previously, denotes the writer's identification with all his readers (*contra* Merklein, *Das kirchliche Amt*, 62, who holds that the writer is identifying himself with the ministers named in v 11). Perhaps the key concept in the flow of thought is that of giving. It is this which sparks off the Scripture citation and which provides the link between v 7 and v 11 (cf. "has been given," "Christ's giving" [v 7], "he gave gifts" [v 8], and "it was he who gave" [v 11]). The citation and the accompanying midrash in vv 9, 10 underline that it is Christ who is the giver of gifts, and vv 11–16 spell out the nature and role of those gifts. Since with his reference to grace here the writer has in view its outworking in a variety of ways in individual believers, it is equivalent to the use of χάρισμα in 1 Cor 12:4 and Rom 12:6. The unity of the Church, which has been prominent to this point, is now shown to be that of an organism in which Christ's sovereign distribution of grace produces the diversity. In the parallel passage in 1 Cor 12:4, the charismata are explicitly said to be from the Spirit. Elsewhere in the NT δωρεά, "gift," can refer to the Spirit (cf. Acts 2:38; 8:20; 10:45; 11:17). Yet here the term involves a more general reference to the exalted Christ's giving of grace, though this, of course, would not exclude the Spirit's agency. Previously, grace is said to have been given to the apostle for his ministry to the Gentiles (cf. 3:2, 7, 8), but now it can be said to be given to each individual believer, not simply for his or her own sake but for the good of the whole, as the passage will go on to show. The gifts in the form of ministers specified in v 11 illustrate the variety in Christ's giving and are accorded special significance. But despite the closely knit structure of the argument in vv 7–11, whereby v 11 interprets the scriptural citation which supports v 7, these ministers are not intended to delimit the reference to "each one of us" in v 7 (*contra* Engelhardt, *TSK* 44 [1871] 113; Schlier, 191; Merklein, *Das kirchliche Amt*, 59–60; Mussner, 122; Schnackenburg, "Christus," 290–91, though his later commentary, 177–78, reverses this position). The difference in emphasis between v 7 and v 11 is not to be ignored. In the former, grace is said to be given by Christ *to* each; in the latter, those named are themselves Christ's gifts to the Church. The variety of the operation of grace in individuals is to be traced to the sovereign way in which the exalted Christ apportions his giving—"in the proportion allotted by Christ's giving" (cf. the similar concepts in Rom 12:3 where God measures out different degrees of faith and 1 Cor 12:11 where it is the Spirit who sovereignly distributes the various charismata). That the differing proportions of grace are part of the overall purpose of enriching the whole body will be brought out in v 16, where the term μέτρος recurs and where growth is said to take place "according to the activity appropriate to each individual part."

8 διὸ λέγει, "therefore it says." The writer finds support for his statement about Christ's giving in Ps 68:18 (LXX 67:19; MT 68:19), which he introduces with this formula. The same introductory formula appears in 5:14 where it prepares for the citation from a hymn. λέγει is used elsewhere in the Pauline writings with scriptural citations in Gal 3:16 and Rom 15:10. The most likely implied subject is Scripture itself. The formula ἡ γραφὴ λέγει, "Scripture says," does occur six times in the Pauline corpus (Rom 4:3; 9:17; 10:11; 11:2; Gal 4:30; 1 Tim 5:18), although elsewhere God can be the subject (Rom 9:15; 2 Cor 6:2, 16) or a psalm can be introduced with "David says" (Rom 4:7, 8; 11:9, 10 which in fact cites Ps 68). In any case, in the Pauline writings "it says," "Scripture says," "God says," and "David says" are only different ways of saying the same thing, that is, that the quoted words have divine authority.

Ἀναβὰς εἰς ὕψος, "when he ascended on high." The Vaticanus text of the LXX already has the aorist participle instead of the second person singular of the aorist tense, and this more easily prepares the way for the alteration from the second person singular of the original to the third person in the rest of the citation. The original reference of the statement in the psalm was to Yahweh's triumphant ascent of Mount Zion after he had delivered his people. In the light of his earlier discussion of Christ's exaltation in 1:20–22, the writer can expect his readers to understand readily his Christological application of the psalm's language.

Once it is seen that the language of ascent is derived from the OT citation, it will be appreciated that this passage is not the most appropriate for ascertaining the writer's awareness of an ascension tradition in the sense of the Luke-Acts accounts, though he clearly held that the language of ascent could be applied to the resurrection-exaltation complex of events on which he focuses (cf. G. Lohfink, *Die Himmelfahrt Jesu* [Munich: Kösel, 1971] 87).

ᾐχμαλώτευσεν αἰχμαλωσίαν, "he led a host of prisoners captive." The person of the verb here has been changed from second to third in this cognate accusative expression. Since it is the triumphant ascent and the gifts which particularly interest the writer as parallels, he does not develop explicitly the concept of leading captive a host of prisoners. However, such a concept certainly fits the earlier depiction of Christ's exaltation over the powers in 1:21, 22, which these words from the psalm may well have conjured up again (cf. also Col 2:15).

ἔδωκεν δόματα τοῖς ἀνθρώποις, "he gave gifts to men." This is where the major modification of the LXX text has taken place so that in fact ἔλαβες, "you received," in the original has become ἔδωκεν, "he gave." It has been held that this modified form of the text closely follows the Syriac Peshitta, but the reading at this point in the Peshitta may be a corruption, which makes its value as evidence precarious (cf. Lindars, *Apologetic*, 52 n. 2). More significant, however, is the fact that in the Targum on the Psalms the concept of receiving has been changed to that of giving in the same way as in Eph 4:8—"You have ascended to heaven, that is, Moses the prophet; you have taken captivity captive, you have learnt the words of the Torah; you have given it as gifts to men." Since the Targum on the Psalms is a late work, it is probable that the writer has made use of an ancient rabbinic tradition which the Targum has also preserved (*pace* Rubinkiewicz, *NovT* 17 [1975] 219–24, who argues for direct use of an original shorter version of the Targum, but whose evidence for this from *T. Dan* 5.10, 11 will not bear the weight he places on it). It is also probable that this tradition has interpreted the Hebrew לקח, *lāqaḥ*, "to take," rather than reflected a variant textual tradition which had חלק, *ḥālaq*, "to distribute." (For a careful examination of the likely date of the tradition preserved in the Targum, see Harris, "Descent," 92–194.) The tradition has been taken over by this writer and incorporated into a midrash pesher rendering of the text in which he integrates his exposition of its meaning in the light of fulfillment in Christ into the actual quotation, a procedure which is, of course, not unusual in the contemporary Jewish exegetical techniques or elsewhere in the use of the OT in the NT (cf. also Lindars, *Apologetic*, 53; Ellis, *Paul's Use of the OT*, 144; *pace* Mitton, 145–46, who surprisingly finds it hard to believe a Christian writer would deliberately change a text of Scripture to support his own contention).

This use of Ps 68:18 in regard to Christ is in contrast to the use made of it in rabbinic tradition where it could refer to an ascension to heaven by Moses (cf. the Targum; *Midr. Tĕhillîm* on Ps. 68.11; *ʾAbot R. Nat.* 2.2a; and for an extensive discussion of the traditions of Moses' ascent in a variety of sources cf. also Harris, "Descent," 110–92). Ps 68:18 was linked with Moses going up Sinai and interpreted as an ascent to heaven to receive not only the Torah but also other heavenly secrets. The "Moses mysticism" with which this interpretation of the psalm is to be associated was widespread. It can be found elsewhere in the rabbinic writings (e.g., *Midr. Tĕhillîm* on Ps 24:1 and Ps 106:2; *b. Šabb.* 88b) and in Philo (e.g., *Quaest. Ex.* 2.40, 43; *Mos.* 1.158; *Poster.* 14; *Somn.* 1.186–88: cf. also W. Meeks, *The Prophet-King* [Leiden: E. J. Brill, 1967] 122–25, 205–9). Already Philo had used this tradition to speak to Hellenistic cosmological concerns, and it is possible that it was current in the religious syncretism of Asia Minor and used to support a penchant for heavenly visions. If this were the case, the writer might be relating Christ to the similar interests of his readers and in a "new Moses" typology showing that Christ has provided a link with the heavenly world that could not be matched by Moses (cf. J. Jeremias, "Μωϋσῆς," *TDNT* 4 [1967] 848–49; Cambier, *NTS* 9 [1963] 265; Ernst, 351; A. T. Hanson, *New Testament Interpretation*, 137). As a greater than Moses, Christ has ascended far above all heavens in order to fill all things (cf. v 10). His gift is not the Torah but his grace (v 7). Nor are his various special gifts heavenly secrets for the enlightenment of a few but people whose ministries will build up the whole body (vv 11–16).

The application of Ps 68:18 to Christ's ascent and his distribution of gifts by the Spirit may well have been aided by the psalm's association with Pentecost (cf. Caird, "Descent," 544; Kirby, *Ephesians*, 138–39, 146; Harris, "Descent," 195–234, who provides the most thorough evaluation of the evidence). As we have seen, the psalm citation was connected with Moses and the giving of the law, and Pentecost, besides celebrating harvest, was more and more coming to be regarded as the feast which commemorated the law-giving at Sinai. There is good reason to believe that this association existed from the middle of the second century B.C.E. The *Book of Jubilees*, which is usually dated between 135 and 105 B.C.E., makes Pentecost or the Feast of Weeks the most important of the annual festivals in the Jewish liturgical year, associating it with the institution of the various covenants in Israel's history but above all with the covenant at Sinai (cf. 1.5; 6.11, 17; 15.1–24). The Qumran community followed the calendar of the *Book of Jubilees* and celebrated an annual renewal of the covenant, in all probability combining it with the annual renewal of the members' own oath of entry into the community which took place at Pentecost (cf. 1QS 1.7–2:19; cf. also J. van Goudoever, *Biblical Calendars* [Leiden: E. J. Brill, 1959] 139–44; B. Noack, "The Day of Pentecost in Jubilees, Qumran and Acts," *ASTI* 1 [1962] 73–95; Kirby, *Ephesians*, 61–69). Additional evidence is available from the synagogue liturgy, which *may* have been in existence at the time of the writing of Ephesians. In the triennial cycle of readings, both Exod 19, 20 and Num 17, 18 were read at Pentecost, while according to the *Megilla* (*b. Meg.* 31a), representing the tradition which replaced the triennial cycle, the psalms for the day were 29 and 68 (cf. Goudoever, *Biblical Calendars*, 201; Caird, "Descent," 54 n. 1; Kirby, *Ephesians*, 92–94). Together with these factors, the two central themes of the Christian interpretation of the psalm citation, the exaltation of Christ and his distribution of gifts, suggest that Pentecost lies in the background of the citation's use here. It is also worth noting that a number of scholars hold that Ps 68:18 lies behind Acts 2:33 (cf., e.g., H. J. Cadbury, "The Speeches in Acts," in *The Beginnings of Christianity*, vol. 5, ed. F. J. Foakes Jackson and K. Lake [London: Macmillan, 1933] 408–9; G. Kretschmar, "Himmelfahrt und Pfingsten," *ZKG* 66 [1954–55] 209–53; Lindars, *New Testament Apologetic*, 42–45; J. Dupont, "Ascension du Christ et don de l'Esprit d'après Actes 2:33," *Christ and Spirit in the New Testament*, ed. B. Lindars and S. S. Smalley [Cambridge: CUP, 1973] 219–28; Harris, "Descent," 219–33).

9, 10 τὸ δὲ Ἀνέβη τί ἐστιν εἰ μὴ ὅτι καὶ κατέβη εἰς τὰ κατώτερα τῆς γῆς, "Now, the expression 'he ascended,' what does it imply except that he also descended to the lower regions, to the earth?" Whether the Christological midrash of these verses fits the argument or whether it is to be judged merely as an interruption or digression depends on how its details are interpreted and in particular on the reference of the descent which is introduced into the discussion. As can be seen from the discussion of the text under *Notes*, this question of the reference of the descent can be approached without prejudice about its temporal relation to an ascent (*contra* Lindemann, *Aufhebung*, 85 n. 110). A good case can be made for each of three main interpretations—a descent into Hades, the descent of the preexistent Christ in his incarnation, and the descent of the exalted Christ in the Spirit. (On the history of interpretation of the descent, see Harris, "Descent," 4–48.)

(1) A descent into Hades (Englehardt, *TSK* 44 [1871] 128; Meyer, 213–14; J. A. Robinson, 180; Benoit, *RB* 46 [1937] 348; F. Büchsel, "κάτω," *TDNT* 3 [1965] 641–42; Odeberg, *View of the Universe*, 17, 18; Schneider, "μέρος," *TDNT* 4 [1967] 597–98, who was convinced by Büchsel's article and changed the view he had expressed in "ἀναβαίνω," *TDNT* 1 [1964] 521–22; J. D. G. Dunn, *Christology in the Making* [London: SCM, 1980] 186–87; A. T. Hanson, *New Testament Interpretation*, 135–50). This interpretation is sometimes associated with the traditional doctrine of a *descensus ad inferos* or sometimes, as in the

more appealing case made by Büchsel, seen simply as a reference to Christ's death. It is held by some that if τὰ κατώτερα τῆς γῆς, "the lower regions [of] the earth," is to be in genuine contrast with ὑπεράνω πάντων τῶν οὐρανῶν, "far above all the heavens," this requires a reference to an underworld. But the contrast in these verses appears to be between an ascent to heaven and a descent from heaven, while the descent involved in the traditional view of a descent into Hades is not so much from heaven but from earth to the underworld or the realm of the dead. Besides, if the writer had had three levels in mind and meant that Christ descended to the deepest level just as he ascended to the greatest height, he would have been more likely to have used a superlative than a comparative. In fact, the psalm passages (63:9 and 139:15) which talk about the underworld as the depths of the earth are translated in the LXX by the superlative τὰ κατώτατα τῆς γῆς, not by the comparative. In addition, a three-story cosmology does not fit the worldview we encounter elsewhere in Ephesians, where the cosmos is seen as simply having two main parts—heaven and earth. This interpretation can however appeal to a Pauline passage, Rom 10:6, 7, where ascent into heaven is contrasted with descent into the abyss, which is explicitly said to be bringing Christ up from the dead. In the Romans passage, Paul's interpretation of the OT also has similarities with a Targum on the passage, which speaks about Moses ascending to heaven to receive the law. But while the use of καταβαίνειν, "to descend," in Rom 10:6, 7 demands a reference to Christ's death, this is by no means true of Eph 4:9, 10 (cf. also 1 Thess 4:16 where the verb refers to Christ's parousia). In fact, it is quite difficult to see how such a descent into Hades could be logically deduced from Christ's ascent, which, after all, appears to be the force of the argument here. If the midrash has any particular reason for stressing the identity of the descender and the ascender, again on this interpretation it is hard to see what that is.

The objections to this interpretation constitute some of the reasons why many scholars have held that it is preferable to take τῆς γῆς, "the earth," as a genitive of apposition which further defines the preceding noun. This grammatical feature occurs a number of times in Ephesians (cf. 2:14, 15, 20; 6:14, 16, 17). On this view the lower regions are not the lower parts of the earth but rather the lower parts of the cosmos, that is, the earth, and the writer is speaking of a descent to the earth. Those who agree with this point can support either of the following views, which differ not on the local but the temporal reference of the descent. (For a fuller discussion of the syntax of the genitive phrase, see Harris, "Descent," 65–78.)

(2) The descent of the incarnation (cf. Percy, *Probleme*, 273–74; Cambier, *NTS* 9 [1963] 262–75; Schlier, 192–93; Gaugler, 172; H. Traub, "οὐρανός," *TDNT* 5 [1967] 525; Klauck, *Wissenschaft und Weisheit* 36 [1974] 94–95; Gnilka, 209; Merklein, *Das kirchliche Amt*, 68–69; Ernst, 352; Mitton, 147–48; Lindemann, *Aufhebung*, 84–86, 218–21; Mussner, 123; *Christus*, 28, 41–44; Schnackenburg, 180–81; idem, "Christus," 288–89; while Bieder, *Vorstellung*, 89; and Barth, 433–34, want to include a reference to the crucifixion within this interpretation). The interpretation which takes the reference of the descent to be a prior descent in the incarnation has the advantage of following the order in the original meaning of the psalm. The descent to be inferred from the ascent

of Yahweh to Mount Zion would be that of his first descent to deliver his people and triumph over his enemies before going up to his dwelling place. On this view, the passage can be seen as a typical instance of a descent-ascent Christology to be found elsewhere in the NT, especially in the Fourth Gospel (cf. John 3:13; 6:62), but also represented in Paul by the humiliation-exaltation motif of the hymn in Phil 2:6–11. When asserted of Christ, "he ascended" could certainly imply a previous descent, yet it is hard to see what the writer's point in stressing this would be—"the expression 'he ascended,' what does it imply except that he also descended?" This stress could be nothing more than a convenient rhetorical way of introducing the descent, which, since the psalm does not explicitly mention the Messiah, will help to identify its subject as Christ. Yet this identification seems to be an obvious one presupposed by the very use of the citation. It appears strange to have to spell it out in this rather tortuous fashion, though, as we have seen, this writer is not the most economical with words. This explanation also presupposes that the reference of the descent will be obvious to the readers and will help them to identify the less obvious ascent. But is this the case? Does not the wording of v 9 suggest that the ascent is the known factor from which the descent, as a less obvious element, is to be inferred?

(3) The descent in the Spirit (cf. H. von Soden, *Der Brief an die Epheser* [Freiburg, 1891] 132; Abbott, 116; Roels, *God's Mission*, 162–63; J. J. Meuzelaar, *Der Leib des Messias* [Assen: Van Gorcum, 1961] 136–37; Caird, 73–75; idem, "Descent," 536–43; Porter, "Descent," 47; Kirby, *Ephesians*, 187 n. 51; Houlden, 310–11; Martin, "Ephesians," 156; Harris, "Descent," 235–65). On this interpretation, which takes the descent as subsequent to the ascent and thus as a descent in the Spirit, it is argued that the ascent and the giving of gifts can maintain their central function in the passage. The descent fits easily between the two and is seen to be a necessary and logical deduction in connecting the one who ascended to heaven with the gifts he has given to his Church on earth. In other words, it is suggested, the movement of thought from Christ's ascent to his gifts in the Church requires a descent in the Spirit. It would be natural that the writer, having spoken of the Spirit's work in the unifying of the body in vv 3, 4, in arguing from Christ's gift via his ascent to the gifts he has given to help maintain unity, should include the vital connecting link of the coming of the Spirit. That κατέβη, "he descended," is preceded by καί, "also," in v 9 may indicate, though it obviously does not necessitate, that the chronological order of an ascent and then also a descent was in view. It is this order which is followed in the exegetical tradition which applied the psalm to Moses and which is in the background here. After Moses ascended he would have to descend before being able to give the law (cf. Exod 19:3, 14; 19:20, 25; 24:18 and 32:15; 34:4, 29). It is interesting that Philo also used Moses' ascent followed by a descent at Sinai to suggest the necessity of a subsequent descent after the ascent of a mystical experience (cf. *Quaest. Gen.* 4.29). Caird holds that for the author of Ephesians Ps 68 is no longer to be viewed as a Jewish Pentecostal psalm concerning Moses but as "a Christian Pentecostal psalm, celebrating the ascension of Christ and his subsequent descent at Pentecost to bestow spiritual gifts upon the church" ("Descent," 541; cf. also the discussion of the probable role of Ps 68:18 in the formation of the theologoumenon "the gift

of the Spirit" in Lindars, *Apologetic,* 51–59). This descent of Christ in the Spirit to give gifts would be in line with one of the writer's sources, 1 Cor 12, where, in regard to the variety of gifts within the one body, the Spirit is most prominent in their distribution (vv 4, 7, 8, 11, 13). The main difficulty of this third interpretation, however, is that it is unusual for the Pentecostal event to be thought of as a descent of *Christ* (cf. Mitton, 148; Schnackenburg, "Christus," 287; J. D. G. Dunn, *Christology in the Making* [London: SCM, 1980] 331 n. 89). Yet a close association, and indeed virtual interchange, between Christ and the Spirit is evidenced elsewhere in Ephesians. In 1:13 the believer is sealed in Christ with the Spirit, while in 4:30 he or she is said to be sealed in the Spirit. In 3:16 the Spirit is in the "inner person," while in the following verse, 3:17, Christ dwells in the heart. In 1:23 the Church is the fullness of Christ, while in 5:18 believers can be exhorted to be filled with the Spirit. In Paul, in 1 Cor 15:45 the last Adam is said to become life-giving Spirit, and in Rom 8:9–11 Christ and Spirit are used interchangeably (cf. also the more disputed 2 Cor 3:17). Another objection to this third view is that the climactic statement in v 10 to the effect that the ascent is in order to fill all things rules out the thought of a subsequent descent being in the writer's mind (cf. Schnackenburg, "Christus," 287). But to this it can be replied that, once the inference of a subsequent descent has been made, the author returns to the ascent as his main notion and the one explicit in the psalm. In addition, the assertion of v 10b no more rules out a subsequent descent than it rules out a subsequent giving of gifts.

It is difficult to choose between the second and third interpretations. The incarnation provides what is on the surface the most obvious reference for the descent; but the descent in the Spirit, although it is still the minority view, may well be preferable if, as seems to be the case, the midrash is making a more complex point. It would explain why the inference of a descent from an ascent is necessary in the flow of the writer's argument and better fits the probable background and associations of the psalm citation. Whichever interpretation one takes, however, the real stress in the progress of thought is on the ascent. The concept of a descent, though it inevitably attracts so much discussion in an exegesis of the passage, was only brought in by the writer to help make his point about Christ's ascent in the context of his giving of gifts.

ὁ καταβὰς αὐτός ἐστιν καὶ ὁ ἀναβάς, "he who descended is himself the one who also ascended." Some who hold to the second interpretation of the descent have suggested that the reason for emphasizing the identity of descender and ascender is to guard against Docetism, but traces of such a notion are not reflected elsewhere in this letter. It is better on this interpretation to take the clause as simply underlining that the psalm citation applies to Christ, the one who descended and ascended, and to note that the writer often labors points unnecessarily. On the third interpretation of the descent, to which we are inclined, the identity would be a matter for emphasis, since it would bring home to the readers once more the Church's link with its exalted Lord. The one who by his Spirit is active in giving gifts to the Church and equipping it for its role is the same one who by virtue of his ascent became cosmic Lord. As Käsemann points out in regard to the writer's discussion of gifts, "the presupposition of this chain of reasoning is the principle . . . that the Giver is not to be separated from his gift but is really present in it" ("Ministry and Community in the NT," in *Essays on NT Themes* [London: SCM, 1964] 74). As over against any cosmological dualism on which the writer may have an eye, for the Church there can be no chasm between heaven and earth, because the Christ who has been exalted to heaven is integrally linked with his Church on earth through the Spirit in whom he has descended.

ὑπεράνω πάντων τῶν οὐρανῶν, "far above all the heavens." This phrase in the application corresponds to εἰς ὕψος, "on high," in the citation. Frequently in the NT the plural of οὐρανός, "heaven," can be explained on the basis of the translation of the Hebrew plural. "All," however, indicates that a number of heavens are in view here. Whether his readers think there are three, seven, or more heavens (for discussion of the number of heavens in first-century cosmologies, see my *Paradise*, 78–80), the writer asserts that Christ is above them all. The unique status ascribed to Yahweh in the OT and here in v 6 ("above all") as the high God whom the heavens cannot contain is now ascribed to the exalted Christ. It is interesting to note the paradoxical language used of Christ's exaltation in Ephesians. He can be viewed both locally as in heaven (cf. 1:20; 6:9) and at the same time as above the heavens, beyond that which can be conceived in terms of created reality.

ἵνα πληρώσῃ τὰ πάντα, "in order that he might fill the cosmos." Many scholars link this clause with both the descent and ascent in order to argue that, by having Christ descend to the lower parts of the cosmos and then ascend to heaven, the requirements for filling the universe are met. In this way they interpret the filling in a quasi-physical sense. Strictly speaking, however, the ἵνα clause is connected to the statement about Christ's ascent and not to both the descent and the ascent. Noting this enables one not to be misled by the concept of filling and to see the parallel with 1:22, 23, where it is by virtue of his exaltation that Christ can be said to fill the universe in every respect as he pervades it with his rule (cf. *Comment* on 1:23 for discussion of this meaning of "to fill").

11, 12 καὶ αὐτὸς ἔδωκεν, "and it was he who gave." The αὐτός picks up the αὐτός of v 10, making plain that he of whom the psalm said "he gave gifts to men" is the exalted Christ who fills the universe. The psalm citation with its reinterpretation continues to dominate the passage, for the gifts are now explained as the ministers whom the writer lists. They are seen as the royal largesse which Christ distributes from his position of cosmic lordship after his triumphant ascent. In fact Christ has given these ministers as part of the overall purpose for which he ascended—that his work of filling all things might be brought to completion. The link with the previous verse indicates that in the writer's vision Christ's giving of ministers of the word to build up the whole body into his fullness is interwoven with the goal of his pervading the cosmos with his presence and rule. This underlines the point the writer has already made in 1:22, 23. God *gives* Christ as head over all to the Church, and it becomes his instrument in carrying out his purposes for the cosmos. The readers are to see themselves as part of this Church which has a universal role and which is to be a pledge of the universe's ultimate unity in Christ. Now, the one who has been given to the Church as cosmic Lord, himself gives to the Church to equip it fully for its cosmic task. And to assert that the ministers are gifts of the exalted Christ, rather than merely officers created by the Church, is clearly meant to enhance their significance in the eyes of the readers. As in 1:22, the verb διδόγαι retains its general sense of "to give" rather than "to appoint" (see *Comment* on 1:22).

τοὺς μὲν ἀποστόλους, τοὺς δὲ προφήτας, τοὺς δὲ εὐαγγελιστάς, τοὺς δὲ ποιμένας καὶ διδασκάλους, "the apostles, the prophets, the evangelists, the pastors and teachers." As our translation indicates, in the expression τοὺς μὲν . . . τοὺς δὲ . . . , since it comes with a list of differing nouns, the article is most probably to be interpreted as simply an article which belongs directly with the following nouns and not as a substantive used absolutely with the nouns serving as predicates. In other words, the better translation is "it was he who gave, on the one hand, the apostles, on the other, the prophets" or simply, as above, "it was he who gave the apostles, the prophets," rather than, as in most versions, "it was he who gave some to be apostles, some to be prophets." The preferred translation is in line with the most frequent force of the article with μὲν . . . δὲ . . . in the NT and means that the writer's main concern is with listing the nouns themselves (cf. the full discussion of this grammatical point in Merklein, *Das kirchliche Amt*, 73–75; also Schnackenburg, 183). What does the exalted Christ give to the Church? He gives people, these particular people who proclaim the word and lead. In relation to vv 7, 8b, he gives not just grace to people, but he gives specific people to people. In Rom 12 gifts were ministries or functions and this is the way the term had been employed in 1 Cor 12, though in the latter passage in vv 28, 29 Paul could also speak of God appointing ministers as well as giving ministries. In contrast to both passages, here in Eph 4 the focus is narrowed to particular ministers of the word (as we shall see, even "pastors" cannot be completely separated from such proclamation of the word).

The first two groups of ministers listed, the apostles and the prophets, also appear first in Paul's list in 1 Cor 12:28 and have already been singled out as the object of the writer's reflection in Eph 2:20 and 3:5 (see *Comment* on 2:20 and 3:5 for a discussion of their identity and their foundational role as recipients and proclaimers of revelation). In these earlier references the apostles, as divinely commissioned missionaries and planters of churches, and the prophets, as specialists in mediating divine revelation, were viewed as norms from the past. It is likely that the same perspective is at work here. Drawing conclusions about the historical conditions of the churches in Asia Minor from the writer's theological reflections is a hazardous enterprise. So whether there were still prophets operating in the churches to which he writes cannot be ascertained with any certainty (*pace* Klauck, *Wissenschaft und Weisheit* 36 [1973] 96, 97 and Schnackenburg, 185, who state rather categorically that both apostles and prophets would have been no longer active). But even if the writer is aware of prophets still exercising their gifts (cf. *Did.* 11–13; 15:1, 2; Herm., *Man.* 11), it appears that for him the period of their significance was in the past, and the development whereby prophets became increasingly marginalized in the Christian movement as their leadership role was taken over by the more stable teaching and ruling ministries is one that fits in with the theological emphasis of this passage. (On the relation of prophets to other leaders cf. also Merklein, *Das kirchliche Amt*, 350–61; D. E. Aune, *Prophecy in Early Christianity* [Grand Rapids: Eerdmans, 1983] esp. 203–11).

It has been suggested that the triad of apostles, prophets, and teachers, enumerated by Paul in 1 Cor 12:28 by means of "first . . . second . . . third . . . ," represents a tradition about church leadership which can be traced back beyond Paul to the Antioch church through the sources behind Acts 13:1–3; 14:4, 14 (cf. Merklein, *Das kirchliche Amt*, 249–87), but it is unlikely that the meager evidence will support such a hypothesis (cf. the reservations of F. Hahn in his review of Merklein's work in *TRev* 72 [1976] 281–86 and the objections of H. Schürmann, "'. . . und Lehrer,'" *Orientierungen am Neuen Testament* [Düsseldorf: Patmos, 1978] 135 n. 90). In any case, to this group the writer of Ephesians has added two further categories of ministers, the evangelists and the pastors. In the post-apostolic period it is the evangelists who continue to carry out many of the activities of the apostles and it is the pastors who now exercise the leadership role, alongside the teachers, previously held by the prophets (cf. also Klauck, *Wissenschaft und Weisheit* 36 [1973] 97). As the name suggests, evangelists were involved in the proclamation of the gospel. The term is used of Philip in Acts 21:8 in the context of mission (cf. also Acts 8:14–17 where Luke depicts Philip's missionary activities as dependent on the apostles). It is used also in 2 Tim 4:5, where it may well be intended to be seen as part of the work of a church leader. Since the term "pastors" covers church leadership in Eph 4, it is likely that here "evangelists" are to be seen as those engaged in mission and the founding of churches and, therefore, as having responsibilities beyond the local congregation. A further reason for their mention here could be that the churches in Asia Minor, which are being addressed, were not founded directly by Paul but by just such people, co-workers and followers of Paul who continued his type of missionary activity (cf. also Schlier, 196; Ernst, 354). It is in this sense that the term is used much later by Eusebius, *Hist. Eccl.* 3.37.2 3; 5.10.2. The view, first proposed by Oecumenius, that the reference in Eph 4:11 is to "the office of gospel writer" (cf. Hadidian, *CBQ* 28 [1966] 317–21) is quite improbable.

The definite article, which has been employed for each of the three categories mentioned so far, is repeated before "pastors" but omitted before "teachers." What significance should be attached to this? Some have claimed that it indicates that the two groups are in fact identical (e.g., Barth, 438–39, who holds that one ministry only is being described, that of "teaching shepherds"). In Acts 13:1 those designated "teachers" in Antioch are shown exercising leadership, while in the Pastorals teaching is a major role of the church leader (cf. 1 Tim 3:2; 5:17; Titus 1:9). But it is doubtful whether this is enough to demonstrate that the two ministries were always exercised by the same people. It is more likely that they were overlapping functions, but that while almost all pastors were also teachers, not all teachers were also pastors. Whether the two functions were performed by a single individual within a particular local situation may well have depended on what gifted persons were present in that situation. The one definite article is therefore best taken as suggesting this close association of functions between two types of ministers who both operate within the local congregation (cf. also J. Jeremias, "ποιμήν," *TDNT* 6 [1968] 497; Merklein, *Das kirchliche Amt*, 362–65).

Though the noun ποιμήν, "shepherd, pastor," is used of Christ himself in John 10:11, 14; Heb 13:20; 1 Pet 2:25, it is employed for church leaders only here in the NT. The cognate verb does, however, describe their function in Acts 20:28 and 1 Pet 5:1–4 and Peter's activity in regard to the Church in John 21:16. It suggests the exercise of leadership through nurture, care, and guidance. Significantly, the concept of the shepherd and tending the flock is often found in association with that of the bishop or overseer and overseeing (cf. Jer 23:2; Ezek 34:11; Zech 11:16; CD 13.7–11, where the *měbaqqēr*, "guardian, overseer," in the Qumran community is likened to a shepherd with his flock; Acts 20:28, where those appointed bishops of the church at Ephesus are to shepherd the church of God; 1 Pet 2:25; 5:2; Ign. *Rom.* 9.1; *Phil.* 2.1, where the bishop is also called a pastor). It is probable, then, that the pastor of Eph 4:11 fulfills the functions denoted in Paul's writings by such terms as προΐστημι, "to rule, manage" (1 Thess 5:12; Rom 12:8), κυβέρνησις, "administration" (1 Cor 12:28), and ἐπίσκοπος, "bishop, overseer" (Phil 1:1). ἐπίσκοπος was a term taken from the Hellenistic world, but because the general notion of overseeing had close associations with the shepherd in Jewish thought, it is understandable that the term "pastor" could become interchangeable with "bishop" in the Christian movement. It is the equivalent to πρεσβύτερος, "elder," of Acts 14:23; 20:17; 1 Tim 4:14; 5:17, 19; Titus 1:5; 1 Pet 5:1, 5; Jas 5:14 (see Merklein, *Das kirchliche Amt*, 362–78, for an extended discussion). That bishops and deacons are not mentioned here, though they are in Phil 1:1; *Did.* 15.1; Herm. *Vis.* 3.5.1; *Mart. Pol.* 16.2, illustrates the variety of structures in the early church and the difficulty of obtaining any clear overall picture. But it justifies neither the assertion that "the churches here addressed had not yet reached that stage of development reflected in Phil 1:1" (*pace* Caird, 76) nor the speculation that the writer is opposed to these particular structures (*pace* Fischer, *Tendenz*, 21–39, 201–2, and see the discussion under *Form/Structure/Setting*).

The teachers, with whom the pastors are so closely associated, already had a special role in Paul's time (cf. 1 Cor 12:28, 29; 14:26; Rom 12:7) and are mentioned specifically elsewhere in early Christian writings (cf. Heb 5:12; Jas 3:1; Acts 13:1; 1 Tim 3:2; 4:11, 13, 16; 5:17; 2 Tim 2:2, 24; 3:16; 4:2, 3; Titus 1:9; 2:1, 7; *Did.* 13.2; 15.1, 2). Their function appears to have been preserving, transmitting, expounding, interpreting, and applying the apostolic gospel and tradition along with the Jewish Scripture. They were specialists in the inculcation of Christian norms and values and the conduct appropriate to them, and in this way became particularly associated with the qualities of wisdom and knowledge. (For a discussion of the teaching ministry in the early church, see F. V. Filson, "The Christian Teacher in the First Century," *JBL* 60 [1941] 317–28; H. Schürmann, "'. . . und Lehrer,'" 116–56.) Wisdom and knowledge are qualities which this writer has desired for his readers in the intercessory prayer-reports (cf. 1:17, 18; 3:18, 19), and knowledge of the Son of God forms part of the goal of the Church's existence here in 4:13. Teachers, then, are instrumental in the Church's growth in these qualities. That teachers instructed in practical Christian living is also clear from the immediate context in Eph 4:20, 21. In Colossians, over against the syncretistic philosophy, the importance of the apostolic tradition of teaching (1:5–7, 23; 2:6, 7) and its mediation through such people as Epaphras (1:7; 4:12), Tychicus (4:7), and Archippus (4:17) had been emphasized. Now in Ephesians also, the writer stresses the vital significance of such ministers in building up the body of Christ, a significance that is underlined in relation to the false teaching which he mentions in v 14. In this passage the writer's major concern is with the unity and maturity of the Church. So, of the ministers listed whom Christ has given to the Church, it is particularly the pastors and teachers active in his own day whose worth he wishes to assert. This could be seen as self-serving, for the writer himself is surely to be regarded as a gifted teacher who transmits and interprets the Pauline tradition on the basis of his own special insights (cf. also Merklein, *Das kirchliche Amt,* 351; Schürmann, "'. . . und Lehrer,'" 151). But the context makes clear that he is not out to promote his own position or that of any particular individuals. His burden is for the well-being of the Church as a whole. He genuinely believes that the preservation of the apostolic tradition is essential for such well-being and that pastors and teachers are the Christ-given means for accomplishing it. Because of the special foundational place given by this writer to the apostles and prophets, in effect a new triad of ministers, in comparison with the triad of 1 Cor 12:28, emerges as active in the churches of his time—evangelists, pastors, and teachers. Interestingly, it is the teachers who retain their place. While the evangelists carry on the missionary activity of the apostles and the pastors take over the earlier leadership functions of the prophets, evidently the role of the teachers has been consolidated as they provide the major element of continuity in ministry, the bridge between the apostolic and post-apostolic periods.

It is often asked whether functions or offices are involved in the list of 4:11. The superficial answer is neither. The writer talks about groups of persons, not about either their activities or their positions. But obviously the question can then be pursued. Do these persons receive the name they have been given simply because they perform certain functions from time to time or also because they occupy some clearly defined position within their communities? The discussion of this question has often been plagued by imposing on the evidence false dichotomies between "dynamic" and "static" categories, between charisma and institution, between ministry as event and ministry as office. The answers given are highly disputed, and it may simply be the case that a question is being asked of the text for which there is neither enough data in the text nor sufficient knowledge of church organization at this time and in this area to provide a convincing answer. But perhaps a number of general points can be established. On the one hand, there is no hint in Ephesians of ordination to office or of the sort of legitimation of office by the church which is reflected in the Pastorals. On the other hand, evangelists, pastors, and teachers were so called because they regularly exercised their ministries, and such ministries would have required acceptance and recognition by their churches, for even in Paul's time the exercise of charismata required evaluation and recognition on the part of the congregation, and certain congregations recognized clearly defined leaders (cf. the bishops and deacons of Phil 1:1). So, if the ordered regular nature of a ministry and its recognition by a local church makes it an office, then the ministers in 4:11 who are active in the writer's own day are officers. If, in addition, an office has to be constitutive for the life of the Church, then in this writer's theological perspective the ministers he lists fall into this category, since they are seen as the representatives and guarantors of the apostolic revelation and tradition which provide the norms for the Church's existence (*pace* Schweizer, who in his comment as a Protestant within

Schnackenburg's EKK commentary [195] and in his own commentary on Colossians [164 n. 41] plays down the extent to which these ministers are singled out in v 11 and in a minimalist interpretation claims they *only* provide examples of gifts given to every member of the community). Whether in the churches to which he wrote there were explicit ecclesiastical structures which corresponded to his theological vision and what sort of institutions had been developed for the acceptance and recognition of regular ministries are questions to which we do not know the answer. (For an extensive discussion of these and related issues, see Merklein, *Das kirchliche Amt,* 79–80, 348–92.)

πρὸς τὸν καταρτισμὸν τῶν ἁγίων εἰς ἔργον διακονίας εἰς οἰκοδομὴν τοῦ σώματος τοῦ χριστοῦ, "for bringing the saints to completion, for the work of service, for the building up of the body of Christ." Why does the exalted Christ give the apostles, the prophets, the evangelists, the pastors and teachers? Three reasons follow, each of which has a slightly different focus. Before we pursue the different nuances of each, we should note that this exegesis has not been univerally accepted by scholars and that there is an issue surrounding the intended relationship of the three prepositional phrases and, therefore, the punctuation of any translation. The view has become popular that the second prepositional phrase is not to be seen as distinct from the first and that the two taken together contain one idea, namely that the ministers have been given to equip the saints to carry out their service. In carrying out their service, the saints play their part in building up the body—the force of the third prepositional phrase. In support of this view, appeal is made to the change in preposition from πρός to εἰς between the first and second phrases, as a sign that the phrases are not coordinate, to v 7 with its notion that all have received grace for service, and to v 16 with its emphasis that building up the body is the work of all believers (cf. Westcott, 62–63; J. A. Robinson, 98–99; Roels, *God's Mission,* 192; Bruce, 86; Käsemann, "Epheser 4, 11–16," 290; Gnilka, 213; Klauck, *Wissenschaft und Weisheit* 36 [1973] 100; Barth, 439, 479–81; Caird, 76; Mitton, 151; Mussner, 127; Bratcher and Nida, *Handbook,* 102). However, the change of preposition cannot bear the weight of such an argument, and there are, in fact, no grammatical or linguistic grounds for making a specific link between the first and second phrases. An active role for all believers is safeguarded by vv 7, 16, but the primary context here in v 12 is the function and role of Christ's specific gifts, the ministers, not that of all the saints. In line with this, as we shall see, καταρτισμός, "completion," has a meaning which does not require supplementing by a further phrase, and διακονία, "service," is more likely to refer to the *ministry* of the *ministers* just named. What is more, to string together a number of prepositional phrases, all dependent on the main verb and coordinate with each other, is a characteristic feature of this writer's style. Three such phrases are found in 1:3; 1:20, 21; 2:7 and, significantly, in the following verses here, 4:13 and 4:14, as well as four in 6:12 and five in 1:5, 6. It is certainly preferable, therefore, to see the three prepositional phrases here as each dependent on the notion of the giving of ministers, and hard to avoid the suspicion that opting for the other view is too often motivated by a zeal to avoid clericalism and to support a "democratic" model of the Church (cf. also Abbott, 119; Dibelius, 82; S. Hanson, *Unity,* 157; Masson, 192–93; Schlier,

198–99; Ernst, 356; Merklein, *Das kirchliche Amt*, 76; Schnackenburg, 186; "Christus," 295; Hamann, *Concordia Journal* 14 [1988] 42–49). There is no reason, however, for making a distinction between the pastors and teachers and the other three groups of ministers and deciding either that the first two prepositional phrases relate only to the pastors and teachers, while the third applies to the task of all five types of ministers (Dibelius, 82), or that the last two phrases describe the role of all the ministers, while the first relates only to the pastors and teachers (Masson, 192–93). The writer is taking a general view of all the ministers given by Christ and describes the activity such ministers were intended to perform in three different ways, with the change from πρός to εἰς in the introductory preposition most likely being simply a variation in style.

They are to bring the saints to completion. On the term ἅγιοι, "saints," see the earlier discussion of 1:1, 15, 18; 2:19; 3:8. The noun καταρτισμός occurs only here in the NT. The verb καταρτίζειν is found in Paul, however, in 1 Thess 3:10; Gal 6:1; 1 Cor 1:10; 2 Cor 13:11; Rom 9:22 (cf. also Heb 13:21; 1 Pet 5:10) where its range of meaning includes "to complete," "to restore," and "to prepare." It is the notion of making complete, which can include making complete by restoring or training, that best fits the context, where, in the next verse, different images for the Church's completion will be used. The use of the noun in this sense is evidenced later in Clement, *Strom.* 4.26; Basil, *Hex.* 9.1; Ammonius, *Ac.* 18.25; and Chrysostom, Hom. 2.1 in Tit. Interestingly, the verb is used of the task of the philosopher or educator in the Hellenistic world (cf. Plutarch, *Cato Minor* 65.5; *Alex.* 7.1; *Them.* 2.5–6; Epictetus, *Diss.* 3.20.10; 4.9.16). All believers are to be brought to a state of completion, and it is the ministers Christ has given who are the means to this end as they exercise their ministries of proclamation, teaching, and leadership. These officers are Christ's gifts to the Church, but again it becomes clear that such a perspective on their role should never lead to self-glorification. They have been given to carry out the work of service, and it is service which provides the framework for understanding any ministerial function or office (cf. also Mark 9:35; 10:42–45, where service is a basic requirement of discipleship). In Rom 12:7 service is a particular charisma, while in 1 Cor 12:5 the term has a more general reference, as "varieties of service" stand parallel to "varieties of charismata." Here in Ephesians, the ministers named are seen as engaged in διακονία in this more general sense. There is precedent in Paul's writings for an association between specific leaders, not simply all believers, and διακονία. The term is used of the ministry of Paul himself in 2 Cor 3:8, 9; 4:1; 5:18; 6:3; Rom 11:13 and of that of his co-workers in 1 Cor 16:15, where Stephanas and his household are said to have devoted themselves to the service of the saints, and in Col 4:17 with reference to Archippus. The primary focus of this service for the ministers of Eph 4:11 has already been expressed in the preceding phrase—bringing the saints to completion. Like that of Stephanas and his household, their leadership in the various communities will be characterized by devotion to the service of the saints. The reason for the giving of ministers can also be summed up as "for the building up of the body of Christ," a phrase that combines body and building imagery. The writer had employed the biological imagery of growth when talking of the Church as a building in

2:21; now he employs building imagery when talking of the Church as a body. On the Church as the body of Christ, see v 4 earlier in this pericope and the extended *Comment* on 1:23. The notion of building up or edifying the body had been a major criterion in Paul's evaluation of various ministries (cf. 1 Cor 14:3–5, 12, 26). Now this is seen as the goal for which the ministers of the word were given to the Church. Although this building up is also the task of all the members of the body (v 16), the ministers have a distinctive and particularly significant role to play in it. Their transmission and interpretation of the apostolic gospel and tradition are what will prove especially constructive for the rest of the body.

13 μέχρι καταντήσωμεν οἱ πάντες εἰς ἑνότητα τῆς πίστεως καὶ τῆς ἐπιγνώσεως τοῦ υἱοῦ τοῦ θεοῦ, "until we all attain to the unity of the faith and of the knowledge of the Son of God." To the setting out of three purposes for which the ministers were given is now added a statement which incorporates a threefold description of the goal of the Church's existence. The first part of this description features the unity of the Church's faith and knowledge. μέχρι, "until," has both a prospective and a final force (cf. BDF § 383[2]). The ministers are to carry out their task both until the whole Church reaches this goal and in order that it might reach this goal. They are seen in the context of the entire Church ("we all"; cf. also 3:18, where it was stressed that growth in comprehension takes place in the company of all God's people), and this Church is depicted as on the way to its goal (cf. also the use of καταντᾶν, "to come to, attain to," in Phil 3:11). Barth (484–96, "Die Parusie," 248–49) has an unusual interpretation of this verse in which he claims to find a reference to believers going out to meet Christ at his parousia as king and bridegroom. But although the related substantives ὑπάντησις and ἀπάντησις can mean a procession to meet someone (cf. Matt 25:1, 6; 1 Thess 4:17), such a meaning is not in view with the use of the verb here and has to be read into it. Besides, although this meaning would fit with his interpretation of the second prepositional phrase as a reference to Christ as the "perfect man," it makes no sense at all to speak of processing to meet the unity of the faith and knowledge of the Son of God.

As in v 12, the three prepositional phrases in this verse are all dependent on the verb rather than on each other. The first one takes up again the theme of unity from the earlier part of the pericope. There we have already seen that the unity given still has to be maintained, and here we discover that the unity given is also still to be attained. This is particularly clear in the case of the first element of this unity—faith. In v 5 "one faith" was spoken of as a given, but now the writer's thought appears to be that the full appropriation of that oneness of the faith lies in the future. As in v 5, πίστις, "faith," used here in the context of an emphasis on the teaching ministry and the mention of false teaching, is likely to have an objective connotation. In other words, it is not primarily believers' exercise of faith that is in view but rather the content of that faith (cf. also Col 1:23; 2:7). The idea is of the whole Church moving toward the appropriation of all that is contained in its one faith. Similarly, attaining to the unity of the knowledge of the Son of God is likely to mean appropriating all that is involved in the salvation which centers in Christ (cf. Col 2:2, 3, which speaks of the knowledge of Christ in whom are hid all the treasures of wisdom and knowledge), and since there is one Lord (v 5), full knowledge of what is given in him will also have the quality of oneness. Earlier in his two intercessory prayers, the writer has spelled out a number of aspects of this one knowledge that he desires his readers to possess (cf. 1:17–19; 3:16–19). In the earlier passages such knowledge was regarded primarily as a gift to be received, but now it is also viewed as a goal to be reached.

Syntactically, the Son of God is likely to be the object of knowledge only and not also of faith, because the definite article is repeated before ἐπίγνωσις, "knowledge." This particular Christological title, Son of God, occurs nowhere else in Ephesians, but too much should not be read into this. It is more likely that the writer has simply taken up a traditional Pauline Christological title (cf. 1 Thess 1:10; Gal 1:16; 2:20; 4:4, 6; 1 Cor 1:9; 2 Cor 1:19; Rom 1:3, 4, 9; 5:10; 8:3, 29; Col 1:13) than that there were divergent views about Christ's divine sonship troubling his readers (*pace* Mussner, 128). Nevertheless, the unity of Christian faith and knowledge does provide a contrast to the mention of diverse winds of teaching in the next verse, and it is the task of the pastors and teachers, who are Christ's gifts to his Church, to ensure that there is a progressive movement toward the goal of full appropriation of the one faith and of the one knowledge of Christ (cf. also Meyer, 222; S. Hanson, *Unity*, 161; Merklein, *Das kirchliche Amt*, 103). It is worth noting that what emerges from the writer's treatment of the unity of faith and knowledge here is a version of the Pauline eschatological tension between the "already" and the "not yet" applied to the life of the Church. The unity of faith and knowledge is already possessed in Christ, but at the same time it still remains to be attained, and to be attained through the effective utilization of the gifts that are an element of that which is already possessed.

εἰς ἄνδρα τέλειον, εἰς μέτρον ἡλικίας τοῦ πληρώματος τοῦ Χριστοῦ, "to the mature person, to the measure of the stature of the fullness of Christ." These last two goals to which all believers are to attain are expressed in terms which describe the Church in its completed state. The Church in this state is seen as a corporate entity, not as disparate individuals. A comparison with Col 1:28 is instructive at this point. There the apostle's aim is "that we may present every person mature in Christ," and the focus is clearly on each individual. Here in Ephesians the focus has shifted onto the whole Church seen as a unified entity. "We all" are to move toward "the mature person" (*pace* Mitton, 154, and Mussner, 129, who hold that the individual believer is in view with this latter term; Bratcher and Nida, *Handbook*, 103–4, who recognize the corporate element but misleadingly still wish to translate as "we shall become mature people"). Some scholars have thought to find affinities between this term understood as "the perfect man" and the Gnostic Anthropos figure (cf. P. Vielhauer, *Oikodome*, 135–36; Pokorný, *Epheserbrief*, 78; Schlier, 200–201), but the expression is quite explicable without recourse to this speculation and in any case employs ἀνήρ rather than ἄνθρωπος. τέλειος has the nuance of mature rather than perfect (cf. also 1 Cor 2:6; 14:20; Heb 5:14), while ἀνήρ denotes here an adult male, a full-grown man. The emphasis is on the mature adulthood of this person in contrast with the children to be mentioned in the next verse. The Church, which has already been depicted as one new person (ἄνθρωπος) in Christ (2:15), is to attain to what in principle it already has in him—maturity and completeness.

This pattern of thought also helps to explain the language in which the third goal is depicted. The goal is not so much Christ himself in his perfect qualities (*pace* Mitton, 154–55; Mussner, 129) as the Church as his fullness. Both the mature person and the fullness of Christ are primarily terms for the Church, yet neither can be totally separated from Christ, since for this writer the Church is always seen as incorporated in him. The writer has already described the Church as the fullness of Christ (see *Comment* on 1:23), and now the same expression can also serve in this portrayal of the Church's goal. As Best puts it, "what in 1:23 was a statement of fact is now a standard of attainment" and "the Church is the dwelling place of Christ's attributes and powers and yet must seek more and more to give room for those very attributes and powers to dwell in it" (*One Body*, 141 and n. 2). This goal can also be compared with that which the writer had expressed in his prayer for his readers in 3:19, "that you might be filled up to all the fullness of God." The full description is introduced by the phrase "to the measure of the stature." There is some debate about whether to take ἡλικία as a reference to age or to bodily size, as it can denote either aspect of matured growth. Since the context contains the contrast between children and adults, some interpret it in terms of age as a further part of this contrast and as an explanation of what was meant by the "mature person" (cf. Abbott, 120; BAGD, 345; Percy, *Probleme*, 321; Mussner, 129). It seems preferable, however, to treat this third depiction as introducing a new image of completion and to recognize that πλήρωμα, "fullness," more naturally has spatial connotations, so that "stature" is probably the more appropriate interpretation (cf. S. Hanson, *Unity*, 160; Schlier, 201; Gnilka, 215; Ernst, 357; Merklein, *Das kirchliche Amt*, 106; Klauck, *Wissenschaft und Weisheit* 36 [1973] 101). The standard for believers' attainment is the mature proportions that befit the Church as the fullness of Christ. Again, we should recall that this is a continuation of the discussion of Christ's gifts and that it is through his gifts of ministers that Christ enables the Church to attain to the complete realization of what it already is. Ministers are important for the period of the "not yet," in which the Church has to be helped to progress toward the eschatological goals of unity and maturity.

14 ἵνα μηκέτι ὦμεν νήπιοι, κλυδωνιζόμενοι καὶ περιφερόμενοι παντὶ ἀνέμῳ τῆς διδασκαλίας, "so that we may no longer be children, tossed back and forth by waves, and gusted here and there by every wind of teaching." With a mixture of metaphors the writer now illuminates by negative contrast the significance of Christ's giving of gifts to the Church and the progress toward its goals that these gifts enable it to make. Through the building up and bringing to completion that the gifts effect, immaturity and instability can increasingly be left behind. νήπιοι, "children," contains a double contrast to "the mature person." Not only do silly infants contrast with the mature adult (cf. 1 Cor 2:6; 3:1; Heb 5:13, 14), but the plural of "children" also contrasts with the singular of "the mature person," individualism being a sign of childishness, unity a sign of maturity (cf. also Best, *One Body*, 148). For this writer immaturity is evidenced in instability, rootlessness, lack of direction, and susceptibility to manipulation and error. κλύδων denotes rough water or waves, and the passive participle of the cognate verb means "tossed by waves." So the picture conjured up by the two participles is of a little storm-tossed boat or of swirling flotsam and jetsam entirely at the mercy of the waves and the wind. In either case, the confusion and lack of direction evoked contrasts strongly with the goal-oriented language of the previous verse. The use of the imagery of wind and waves for instability was common and is found elsewhere in the NT in Jas 1:6, where it depicts the instability of doubt. But the sort of vocabulary contained in this passage is also employed in warnings against false teachers in Jude 12, 13 and Heb 13:9. Here in Ephesians, it is every wind of teaching that is pictured as gusting immature believers about. The use of the singular of διδασκαλία, "teaching," and of the definite article with it, has been seen as an indication that it is the Christian teaching that is in view, though this teaching is being used for perverted ends (cf. Merklein, *Das kirchliche Amt*, 107, followed by Schnackenburg, 189). It is true that the singular is employed when Christian teaching is under discussion in Rom 12:7; 15:4 and becomes almost a technical term in the Pastorals, though frequently accompanied by the adjective "sound" (cf. 1 Tim 1:10; 4:6, 13, 16; 5:17; 6:1; 2 Tim 3:16; 4:3; Titus 1:9; 2:1, 7), whereas the plural is used of false teaching in Matt 15:9; Mark 7:7; Col 2:22; and 1 Tim 4:1. But this does not sufficiently take into consideration the influence of Col 2:22 on the wording of Eph 4:14 (see above under *Form/Structure/ Setting*) and ignores the force of the adjective "every" in the phrase "every wind of teaching," which suggests any and all kinds of teaching in contrast to the unity of faith and knowledge of which the writer has spoken. It is better, therefore, with the majority of commentators to take this as a reference to false teaching in the guise of the various religious philosophies which threatened to assimilate, and thereby dilute or undermine, the Pauline gospel. The only other clue in the letter about the nature of this teaching, the warning of 5:6–13, suggests that the writer was perhaps more worried about its ethical consequences than anything else. The lack of specificity about such teaching does not mean that it was thought of as only a remote possibility. It is more likely that the writer deemed it a constant general threat. After all, he knew what had happened in the case of the Colossian church. Indeed, the warnings of Acts 20:29, 30; 1 Tim 1:3, 4; 6:3–5, 20 attest to problems with false teaching in the churches of this area in the post-apostolic period.

ἐν τῇ κυβείᾳ τῶν ἀνθρώπων ἐν πανουργίᾳ πρὸς τὴν μεθοδείαν τῆς πλάνης, "by human cunning, by craftiness, in the scheming of error." This further sequence of three prepositional phrases asserts that behind the threatening teachings, making them so dangerous, are deceitful people, ready to manipulate and take advantage of immature and unstable believers. κυβεία, translated here as cunning, literally meant the throw of the dice. In the ancient world dice-playing frequently had negative connotations of trickery, and the player was thought of as a wily and cunning customer (e.g., Epictetus, *Diss.* 2.19.28). "Human" here also has negative connotations as that which is purely human and opposed to that which is in Christ. The writer had found such a contrast already in Col 2:8 ("according to human tradition . . . and not according to Christ") and 2:20–22 ("with Christ . . . =according to human commandments and teachings"). Here human cunning can be seen as opposed to the fullness of Christ (4:13) or the truth in Jesus (4:21). πανουργία is the craftiness or unscrupulousness by which false teachers pursue their ends of leading the immature astray. Interestingly, this vice heads a massive list in Philo, *Sacrif.* 32, and in

2 Corinthians Paul had contrasted his apostolic ministry with the practice of cunning (4:2) and attributed the latter to the serpent in his deception of Eve (11:3). The noun μεθοδεία, "scheming," occurs elsewhere in the NT only in this letter—in 6:11 in connection with the devil. Its force can be ascertained from the cognate verb μεθοδεύειν, "to devise or scheme (evil)" (cf., e.g., LXX 2 Sam 19:27; Ign., *Phil.* 7.1). For this writer, such scheming produces error. Again, Paul had placed the vice of πλάνη, "error or deceit," in contrast to his apostolic practice in 1 Thess 2:3 and more generally in contrast to the truth in 2 Thess 2:11, 12. Here also in Eph 4:14 there is a contrast to the reference to truth in the following verse. "Error" is frequently used of false teaching (cf. Jude 11; 1 John 4:6; 2 Pet 2:18; 3:17). These parallel references prompt the reflection that the attitude to false teaching reflected here in Ephesians is similar to that found in the so-called Catholic epistles and in the Pastorals. A clear-cut difference between the apostolic tradition and all other teachings is assumed. There is no attempt to interact with or even to refute the content of any of these teachings, as had taken place in Colossians. Instead, attack is deemed the best form of defense, and the proponents of other teachings are accused of evil intentions and of being ready to manipulate the weaknesses of believers to their own erroneous ends (cf. also esp. 2 Tim 3:1–9; Titus 1:10–16; 2 Pet 2:10–22).

In the context of 4:7–16 this negative picture of v 14 is meant to underline the importance of Christ's giving of ministers to the Church. Immaturity on the part of believers cannot be treated as a neutral state which will be outgrown in due course. It is a highly dangerous condition because it lays them open to manipulation by cunning people and the forces of error. But it is for precisely such a situation that pastors and teachers have been provided—to prevent believers in their immaturity from falling prey to false teaching and to lead them from the instability which ends in error to the stability of the truth.

15a, b ἀληθεύοντες δὲ ἐν ἀγάπῃ, "but rather, speaking the truth in love." The writer returns to the positive side of his portrayal of the Church's movement toward its goals. He describes growth instead of immaturity, a growth which takes place as believers speak the truth in love instead of being taken in by those who propagate error through their unscrupulous craftiness. This contrast between the first part of v 15 and the last part of v 14 can be seen to have a chiastic structure with ἀληθεύοντες, "speaking the truth," in opposition to τῆς πλάνης, "of error," and ἐν ἀγάπῃ, "in love," in opposition to ἐν πανουργίᾳ, "by craftiness" (cf. also Schnackenburg, 190). Some argue that ἀληθεύειν refers not simply to speaking the truth but to doing the truth or living according to the truth (cf. Abbott, 123; Westcott, 64; J. A. Robinson, 185; Mitton, 156; Bratcher and Nida, *Handbook,* 105). There is in fact a textual variant ἀλήθειαν δὲ ποιοῦντες "rather doing the truth" (championed by Dubois, *NovT* 16 [1974] 30–34), although the manuscript evidence for it is very weak (FG). But ἀληθεύειν is used consistently in the LXX (cf. Gen 20:16; 42:16; Prov 21:3; Isa 44:26; Sir 31:4) and in Philo (cf. *Mos.* 2.177; *Ios.* 95; *Abr.* 107; *Decal.* 84) with a verbal connotation, meaning "to speak the truth," and that is its most likely force here in Ephesians (cf. also Schlier, 205; Gnilka, 217; Barth, 444; Schnackenburg, 190). Just as in Galatians Paul's claim to be telling the truth to his readers (4:16) is inextricably bound up with his proclamation of the truth of the gospel (2:5, 14), so in Eph 4:15 the Church's speaking the truth is determined by that word of truth which is the gospel of salvation (1:13; cf. also 6:14). In line with this, believers cannot make use of the same means of manipulation and deceit as those who are ready to lead believers astray. Instead, they proclaim the truth by means of love.

The phrase ἐν ἀγάπῃ, "in love," which occurs six times in this letter, has been connected syntactically by a few scholars (e.g., Meyer, 230) with the following verb αὐξήσωμεν, "we may grow up in love," and thereby paralleled with the notion of growth in love in v 16. But the majority of commentators connect the phrase with the preceding verse. The chiastic structure of the contrast to the end of v 15, which, as has been noted above, this clause then provides, adds to the likelihood that this is the right construal. A conceptual link with the notion of growth is to be found here in any case, since the whole clause, "speaking the truth in love," should be understood as the means of the Church's growth. The association of truth and love in this clause is a significant one. Any claim to loyalty to truth which results in lack of love to those perceived to be disloyal stands as much condemned as any claim to all-embracing love which is indifferent to truth. But it is not as if two competing claims or two quite different qualities have to be held in balance. Ultimately, at the heart of the proclamation of the truth is love, and a life of love is the embodiment of the truth. The Church reflects this relationship when its witness to the truth has love as its style and as its power (cf. also Schnackenburg, 191).

αὐξήσωμεν εἰς αὐτὸν τὰ πάντα, "may grow up in every way to him." Some scholars understand the syntax of this clause differently, taking the verb in a transitive sense, which it has for example in 1 Cor 3:9 or 2 Cor 9:10, and seeing τὰ πάντα, interpreted as the cosmos, as the verb's object (cf. Schlier, 205–7; Steinmetz, *Protologische Heilszuversicht*, 120; Ernst, 358–59; Howard, *NTS* 20 [1974] 355–56; Meyer, *Kirche und Mission*, 72–76). The verse would then be translated "but rather, speaking the truth in love, we may let the cosmos grow up or cause the cosmos to grow up to him who is its head" and would speak of the Church's role in bringing the cosmos to God's purposes for it in Christ. As Schlier ("κεφαλή," *TDNT* 3 [1965] 681) puts it, "When as the risen Lord He takes control of the world in His body, He is simply actualizing His real power over creation. . . . Hence, the Church as His body, when it relates the world to itself, is simply in process of taking over what truly belongs to it." In favor of such an interpretation are the predominant use of τὰ πάντα as the cosmos elsewhere in the letter, the fact that the letter's earlier reference to Christ as head is most immediately in relation to the cosmos (1:22), and the writer's concern with the Church's cosmic role. But whether the rest of the letter's teaching about the Church's cosmic role is rightly described in these terms and whether this role is in view at all here is highly questionable. Nowhere else in Ephesians is there talk of the Church's active influence on the cosmos, and nowhere else is the cosmos said to grow up to Christ (cf. also Merklein, *Das kirchliche Amt*, 111; Schnackenburg, 191). In fact, growth is posited only of the Church, not of the cosmos. In this context the preceding verses have been about the Church growing to maturity, and the following verse will discuss the growth of the body, so everything points to the growth in this verse being that of the Church. As in 2:21, the verb should therefore be taken intransitively rather than transitively (cf. BDF § 101, 309 [2]; BAGD 121), and τὰ πάντα should be understood as an adverbial accusative, meaning "in every way" and having the same force as the dative expression ἐν πᾶσιν in 1:23 (cf. BDF § 160; BAGD 633).

So Christ's giving of gifts to the Church is to enable the Church to move toward its goals, and that movement is seen in terms of believers' growth toward Christ. In Paul's letters, believers' faith can be said to grow (cf. 2 Cor 10:15; 2 Thess 1:3), and growth is used of the development of the local Corinthian church and credited to God in 1 Cor 3:6, 7. The concept occurs more often in Colossians, where it is employed of the work of the gospel itself in 1:6, of believers' knowledge of God in 1:10, and of the whole body of the Church, which is said in 2:19, the verse on which Eph 4:15, 16 is modeled, to "grow with a growth that is from God." Here in Ephesians, then, the notion of the Church's growth is elaborated, and 4:15 has affinities with 2:20, 21 where, as we have seen, Christ is presented as the keystone of a building in the process of growth. The earlier statements of the Church's goals in 4:13 were primarily descriptions of the Church itself in its state of completion, but now it is specifically Christ who is the standard of maturity, indicating again that for this writer ecclesiology remains determined and measured by Christology. The Church is in Christ and has to grow up toward him. This underlines that the Church's growth is not being thought of in terms of quantity, a numerical expansion of its membership, but in terms of quality, an increasing approximation of believers to Christ. In the face of the scheming of error, believers are not only to stand firm, as will be emphasized in 6:13, 14, but also to make progress. That proper growth and progress is to take place in every way, that is, in every aspect of the Church's life and particularly in those aspects singled out earlier, in unity, in knowledge, and in speaking the truth in love. While Ephesians makes reference to an end of history (e.g., 4:30; 5:5; 6:13), the imminence of that end is not in view in the same way as it is in some of Paul's letters. These notions of movement toward a goal, of progress, of maturing, and of growth may well function as Ephesians' equivalent to some of the future elements in Paul's eschatology (cf. also Steinmetz, *Protologische Heilszuversicht*, 114–21). They certainly suggest that the Church's future in history is being taken seriously.

15c, 16 ὅς ἐστιν ἡ κεφαλή, Χριστός, ἐξ οὗ πᾶν τὸ σῶμα . . . τὴν αὔξησιν τοῦ σώματος ποιεῖται, "who is the head, Christ, from whom the whole body . . . makes bodily growth." In 1:22, 23 the writer had already spoken of Christ as head over all things for the Church, described as his body. Implicit was the idea that he was also head over the Church. Now this relationship is made explicit, as the one toward whom believers grow is identified as Christ, the head. The terminology of Col 2:19 is taken up so that Christ, the head, can be seen as both the goal and the source of the Church's growth. The focus is more exclusively on Christ as the source of growth than in Colossians, since Colossians had also included a reference to the growth coming from God, but this writer omits τοῦ θεοῦ, "of God," after the noun "growth." In fact, he reworks Col 2:19 in such a way as to convey and summarize some of his own emphases from earlier in the pericope. This has resulted in an overloading of the relative clause in v 16 and explains the awkward syntax with its five prepositional phrases. The reason for the redundant genitive τοῦ σώματος, "of the body" or "bodily," as part of the verbal expression "makes bodily growth," is its distance from the first mention of "body" as the subject of the clause (cf. also J. A. Robinson, 188). For further discussion of the dependence on modification of Col 2:19 in Eph 4:15c, 16 see *Form/Structure/Setting*.

The metaphor of Christ as head was originally independent of the metaphor of the Church as body, but the two are brought together in Colossians and Ephesians, where the Church as body is seen as receiving its life from Christ and Christ's headship is understood in the sense of both rule and origin. For more extensive discussion of the likelihood of the writer having taken up Colossians' fusion of two separate metaphors, for which Hellenistic thought about the cosmos provided the catalyst (e.g., Philo, *Praem*. 125, "the virtuous one . . . will be the head of the human race and all the others like the members of a body which are animated by the powers in the head and above"), and for treatment of the development of thought, whereby growth can be said to come from the head because of the connotations of κεφαλή as determinative source, see *Comment* on 1:22b, 23. "Body" imagery for the Church has been employed already in this passage in vv 4, 12. Here in v 16, in comparison with its use by Paul in 1 Cor 12 and Rom 12, which also talk about the mutual contributions of the body's members, the writer's emphasis is on the necessity for corporate growth rather than on interdependence itself. Through the proper functioning of the parts, the whole body is to be active in promoting its own growth, although ultimately it is Christ who is seen as providing the means for the body to carry out such activity. From this perspective, relating Christ as head to the Church as his body becomes an appropriate way to sum up the main thrust of vv 7–16. As the one who has been exalted to sovereign rule over all things, Christ is in the position and has the power to supply his Church with the leadership, the life, and the love that are the requisites for its growth.

συναρμολογούμενον καὶ συμβιβαζόμενον διὰ πάσης ἁφῆς τῆς ἐπιχορηγίας, "joined and brought together by every ligament which gives supply." The first participle, συναρμολογούμενον, "joined together," has been used by this writer earlier in 2:21 as part of his architectural imagery for the Church's life, while the second, συμβιβαζόμενον, "brought together," has been taken over from Col 2:19 (cf. also Col 2:2) and is a term that was frequently employed in a context of reconciliation (cf. Herodotus 1.74.3; Thucydides 2.29.6; Plato, *Prot*. 337E). The two present participles are virtually synonymous (*pace* Whitaker, *JTS* 31 [1930] 48–49, who claimed, "the first participle speaks of position, the second of movement; the first of relation to Christ, the second of that relation in action"), and, taken together, underline forcefully that for the unified growth of the body its members have to be involved in a process of continual mutual adjustment. This interaction of the members is assisted "by every ligament which gives supply." ἁφή has been interpreted as sense or sensation (cf. Meyer, 234), contact (cf. Abbott, 126; Barth, 449), and joint or ligament (cf. most commentators). The last interpretation is almost certainly the right one, since in Col 2:19 ἁφή is linked through the use of a common article with σύνδεσμος, which had a recognized physiological connotation as a joint, and since it is also employed in this way in Aristotle for the connection between parts of the body (cf. *Metaph.* 4.4; 10.3; *Phys. Ausc.* 4.6; *De Gen. et Corr.* 1.6, 8; *De Caelo* 1.11; cf. also esp. Lightfoot, *St. Paul's Epistles to the Colossians and to Philemon,* 196–97, who concludes that the term refers to "the joinings, the junctures. When applied to the human body they would be 'joints,' provided that we use the word accurately of the relations between contiguous links, and not loosely [as it is often used] of the parts of the limbs themselves in the neighbourhood of the contact"). Each ligament is seen as a means of support or supply for the other parts of the body. ἐπιχορηγία occurs elsewhere in the NT only in Phil 1:19, where it means "help," "supply," or "support." But the cognate verb, in addition to its participial form in Col 2:19, is found in Paul's writings in Gal 3:5 and 2 Cor 9:10, where it is best translated as "to supply." Here the genitive phrase τῆς ἐπιχορηγίας, literally "of supply," should be understood in an active sense, referring to the ligaments giving supply rather than their being supplied to the body (cf. also Schlier, 208; Gnilka, 219; Klauck, *Wissenschaft und Weisheit* 36 [1973] 103; Schnackenburg, 192). In this way, the writer pictures the ligaments functioning to provide the connections between the various parts and thereby mediating life and energizing power throughout the body. In the light of the earlier part of the pericope, this is to be seen as an image of the ministers who have been given to help maintain unity and enable growth to maturity (cf. also Schlier, 207–8; Masson, 199; Gnilka, 220; Klauck, *Wissenschaft und Weisheit* 36 [1973] 103; Merklein, *Das kirchliche Amt,* 114–15; Schnackenburg, 193; Mussner, 131). It is true that ministers are unlikely to be the reference of the joints and ligaments of Col 2:19 (cf. Schweizer, *Colossians,* 164; O'Brien, *Colossians,* 147). But the writer of Ephesians has placed much greater emphasis on this aspect of the body metaphor by adding πᾶς, "every" or "each," by moving this prepositional phrase to a position after the two participles and immediately before the verbal expression, "makes bodily growth," by omitting the accompanying reference to joints, and by underlining the mediating function of the ligaments through the addition of the substantive expression "of supply" in comparison with the cognate participial formulation of Col 2:19. These modifications and the context in Eph 4 make it highly probable that what is being highlighted is the role of the ministers in the whole body ruled and nourished by Christ and that, just as in v 11 the giving of Christ was embodied in particular persons, so here in v 16 the growth from Christ is mediated by particular persons.

κατ' ἐνέργειαν ἐν μέτρῳ ἑνὸς ἑκάστου μέρους, "according to the activity commensurate with each individual part." These two prepositional phrases are part of the writer's additions to Col 2:19 and recall both the phrase κατὰ τὴν ἐνέργειαν in 1:19 and 3:7, where God's power which raised Christ was said to be operative in believers and in the apostle Paul, and the terminology of the earlier part of the pericope in v 7 (cf. κατὰ τὸ μέτρον and ἑνὶ δὲ ἑκάστῳ). So in this summarizing picture of v 16 both particular ministers and every member find a place. Each part of the body receives the energizing power it needs, and the proper growth of the whole body is in proportion to and adapted to each part. Each member has his or her distinct role in the well-being of the whole, and the unity in diversity depicted earlier in the passage is seen to be essential for the proper growth of the Church.

εἰς οἰκοδομὴν ἑαυτοῦ ἐν ἀγάπῃ, "for the purpose of building itself up in love."

On the notion of the building up of the body, see *Comment* on its earlier occurrence in this passage in v 12, where the ministers were understood as having been given for the edification of the Church. It now becomes clear that, however significant the writer deems their role to be in this regard, ministers do not have exclusive claims to this function. In the building up of itself the whole body is involved. The ἑαυτοῦ, "of itself," adds to the previous reference the note of the Church's active participation and is in line with the earlier emphasis of the verb on the Church's promotion of its own growth, though ultimately the source of that growth is Christ, the head. The final prepositional phrase of the pericope—"in love"—recalls its opening exhortation, particularly the clause in v 2—"bearing with one another in love" (cf. also v 15a). If any corporate growth or building up is to take place, love is the indispensable means. The climactic stress on this performs a function here similar to that of Paul's hymn to love in the midst of his discussion of the proper working of the body of Christ in 1 Cor 12–14. Love is the lifeblood of this body, and, therefore, the ultimate criterion for the assessment of the Church's growth will be how far it is characterized by love.

Explanation

This passage stands at the fore of the second, explicitly paraenetic half of the letter. As v 1 indicates, its ethical exhortation is based on the first half's thanksgiving for and reminder of the readers' calling, a calling which has at its heart membership of the one body of Christ, the Church. In this opening to the letter's second half, through a mixture of direct exhortation and theological assertion, the writer appeals to his readers to play their part in enabling the Church to attain to the unity and maturity which rightly belong to it. The appeal stresses the part all members must play and the necessity of love if they are to function in harmony, but it singles out in particular the vital role of the ministers of the word in bringing about unity and maturity.

4:1–16 consists of two main sections—vv 1–6 and vv 7–16. The first section is a call to unity. Using the Pauline formula of appeal, "I exhort . . . ," with minor modifications and taking up material from Col 3:12–15 in such a way as to underline his distinctive concern for the Church and its unity, the writer appeals to the recipients that, as a matter of the utmost urgency, they make every effort to preserve the unity already given by the Spirit. If they are to maintain and demonstrate this unity and be bound together as agents of peace and reconciliation, the qualities the readers will need to display are the humility which springs from a realization of their own dependence on God's grace and the worth of their fellow believers, the gentleness which issues in consideration of the needs of others, and the patience which is tolerant of the shortcomings of others. What will be necessary, in short, is a mutual forbearance that is only possible through the power of love. This ethical exhortation to show the virtues required for unity is given a theological framework and thereby linked to the first part of the letter through the introductory appeal to live worthily of their calling from God. Lives which contribute to the unity of the Church are, therefore, seen as the only appropriate response to the divine initiative in accomplishing all the blessings of salvation and to the divine purpose for cosmic unity which has its present focus in the Church. Further theological undergirding of the call to unity is provided as the writer shifts from direct appeal to assertion and, in a series of seven acclamations, reminds his readers of the fundamental unities on which the existence of the Church depends. He builds around traditional confessional material associated with baptism, as he moves from the oneness of the Church through the oneness of its Lord to the oneness of its God. As the letter has already made clear, the Church is one body out of Jews and Gentiles (cf. 2:16; 3:6), and in that one body lives and works the one Spirit by whom all were initiated into the body and are given access to the Father (cf. 1:13; 2:18). In a similar way, the reminder of the one hope of the readers' calling takes up not only the emphasis on God's calling from earlier in this passage but also the notion of hope from earlier in the letter (cf. 1:18). The calling to live lives that contribute to the unity of the Church can be seen to correspond to the one hope for a unified and reconciled cosmos (cf. 1:9, 10) which is anticipated in the existence of a unified Church (cf. 3:9, 10). The series of fundamental unities continues as believers are reminded that they acknowledged one Lord of the Church and cosmos when they confessed their one faith in Christ in the unifying initiation rite of the one baptism. These unities, which form the grounds for the initial appeal for the practice of unity, climax in the acclamation of the oneness of the God who in his supreme transcendence and pervasive immanence is the universal Father. The Church is to be the embodiment not only of the final cosmic unity planned by God but also of the unity of this God himself.

The second section of the passage, vv 7–16, indicates how the diversity of Christ's giving of grace, and particularly his gifts of various ministers of the word, is meant to contribute to the unity and maturity of the Church. In developing this point, the writer cites and expounds Ps 68:18 in the light of what he wants to say about Christ and the Church and employs for his own ends material from 1 Cor 12, Rom 12, and Col 2:19. Although it functions as an indirect appeal to the readers, the section continues with theological assertions and, not surprisingly, takes on the characteristic style of the first half of the letter, particularly in the long overladen sentence of vv 11–16.

To each individual who belongs to the Church Christ has given grace in various proportions. This notion of giving sets the direction for the rest of the passage, as first it is supported by Scripture, next the identity of the giver is underlined, and then the nature and purposes of the gifts are set out. Ps 68:18, which may well have had associations with Moses and the giving of the law, is now seen to speak of Christ's triumphant ascent, which results not in receiving, as in the original, but in giving gifts. In a midrashic exposition the writer goes on to show that an ascent also implies a descent, either the prior descent of the incarnation or, perhaps more likely, a subsequent descent in the Spirit to give the gifts. The identity of the giver is thus established. It is the ascended Lord, whose rule pervades the universe, who by his Spirit is active in the Church, giving it the necessary gifts to equip it for its task of being the pledge of the universe's ultimate unity in him. The specific gifts of the exalted Christ mentioned in the psalm citation are now identified as particular people—the apostles, the prophets, the evangelists, and the pastors and teachers. The apostles and prophets are again in a foundational role, and the evangelists carry on the work of missionary proclamation and founding of churches in the post-apostolic period, while the pastors and teachers pass on the apostolic tradition in such a way as to preserve the unity and promote the maturity of the Church. The responsibilities of pastors and teachers overlap, but are not identical. Pastors, as equivalents to those elsewhere designated bishops or elders, exercise leadership through nurture and guidance, and teachers, as they expound the apostolic traditions and the Scriptures, contribute to the Church's growth in wisdom and knowledge.

The writer has underlined the significance of these ministers by describing them as gifts of the exalted Christ. He now explains that significance further by asserting that they have been given to bring individual believers to a state of completion and to build up the whole body of Christ. These are the major aspects of the work of service they are to carry out until the Church reaches its goal and in order that it might reach its goal. The goal is depicted in three ways: (*i*) as appropriating the unity contained in its one faith and in its one knowledge of Christ, the divine Son, (*ii*) as becoming the mature person, reaching a full adulthood which is not individual but corporate, and (*iii*) as conforming to the measure of the stature of the fullness of Christ, taking on the mature proportions that befit the Church as the place of Christ's presence and rule. As they help the Church to attain to the complete realization of that which it already is, the ministers of the word enable believers to leave behind the immaturity of those who are children and the instability of those who are tossed to and fro by false teaching and are susceptible to the unscrupulousness and scheming of error of its proponents. Growth toward the Church's goal will instead be characterized by the proclamation of the truth which is embodied in a life of love. The final depiction of the Church's goal in this passage makes clear that the standard of completeness toward which it is to move is not just some potential inherent in its own existence but is Christ himself, the Church's head. In a summary of the passage's emphases on unity in diversity and on a growth in love, in which not only each believer in general but also ministers in particular have a part to play, the writer returns at the end to the body imagery for the Church. The whole body is to be active in promoting its own building up and growth in the quality of its life, as every part of the organism functions in harmony through a process of continual mutual adjustment. But the ligaments in particular, representing the role of the ministers, will provide connections between the other parts and mediate energizing power. The growth of the body is characterized by love, the body's lifeblood. Christ is not only the goal of the growth but also its ultimate source, supplying all that is necessary for the body's well-being.

It is often pointed out that in the acclamations of oneness in vv 4–6, "one God and Father," "one Lord," and "one Spirit" in close juxtaposition provide the elements of later trinitarian teaching. But it was not the writer's intention to relate these three unities in any confessional formulation. In fact, his emphasis in the series of seven unities falls more on "one body," "one Lord," and "one God and Father." This corresponds with earlier sections of the letter in which the three dominant foci have tended to be God, Christ, and the Church. However in the passage as a whole it is not surprising that, as the writer begins to direct his attention more specifically to his readers' lives and interrelationships, it is the Church in particular that dominates. But the Church has not become the exclusive focus. The exalted Christ in his relation to the Church also remains very much to the fore in the writer's perspective. The role of the Spirit is subordinated to that of the Church and of Christ. The unity of the Church that is to be maintained can be called the unity of the Spirit (v 3), and the one Spirit is linked to the one body (v 4). The role the Spirit had in the giving of gifts, according to 1 Cor 12, is now taken by Christ (vv 7, 11), and the Spirit's descent upon the Church may well have to be presupposed as lying behind the notion of Christ's descent (vv 9, 10). Similarly, God's initiative in salvation and in the bringing into being of the Church, stressed in the first half of the letter, is now presupposed rather than made explicit, except in connection with the notion of calling (vv 1, 4), where the passive form of the verbs indicates that God is the one who calls. The mention of God's universal fatherhood in v 6 is primarily to provide the climactic ground for the appeal for the Church's unity.

So Eph 4:1–16 concentrates heavily on the Church. In fact, no other section of the letter is so directly and intensively devoted to the Church's life and purpose. The Church is the sphere into which the readers have entered through their faith and their baptism, the context in which they live out their calling. The major image for this community, as earlier in the letter, is that of the body (vv 4, 12, 16) and, as earlier, this image can be combined with the language of building (vv 12, 16). The Church is also the fullness of Christ (v 13), again taking up an earlier description, and in its final state can be seen as "the mature person." All this is part of a dynamic picture of a corporate entity which grows as its individual members are involved in a continual process of mutual adjustment and which is on the move toward unity, completeness, maturity, and conformity to Christ. The unity of this society (vv 2–6, 13, 16) and, closely linked with this, its maturity (vv 12–16) are clearly the writer's major concerns. The Church is not a chance collection of individuals; it has a unity already given by God's Spirit, and the top priority on its agenda must be to preserve this. But at the same time, this unity is not a monochrome uniformity; the variety in Christ's distribution of grace to all ensures its rich diversity. As long as there is mutual forbearance, this differentiation can be a factor that promotes rather than hinders unity. As the writer stresses, both at the beginning (v 2) and at the end (vv 15, 16) of the passage, the essential ingredient for the achievement of the harmony of unity in diversity is love. Love is the energizing power behind the community's drive to maintain unity, at the heart of its proclamation of truth and all the way through its process of corporate growth.

This passage's distinctive contribution to the notion of the unity in diversity of the Church as the body of Christ is its emphasis on a structured unity, which can contain the diversity of the essential contributions of each individual member (vv 7, 16) while highlighting the particularly significant role of certain people—the apostles, prophets, evangelists, pastors, and teachers (vv 11–16). The importance and authority of these leaders and ministers of the word are underscored as they are depicted as the bounty which flows to the Church as the result of the triumph of its ascended Lord. The position of the evangelists, pastors, and teachers of the writer's own time is also strengthened by their being listed alongside the foundational apostles and prophets. In this writer's perspective, the gifts of the exalted Christ come in the form of particular people, and these ministers are Christ's means of equipping the Church to attain to its goals of unity and maturity. They are to bring both individual believers and the entire Church to a state of completion. As ligaments in the body, they play a vital, cohesive role in the Church's growth. Their ministries are viewed not simply as spontaneous and haphazard functions but more as offices that are constitutive for the life of a Church on the move toward becoming what it already is as the fullness of Christ. These offices are, above all, characterized by service which unifies, which builds up, which stabilizes, and which enables growth toward Christ. Evangelists, pastors, and teachers produce unity and maturity as they proclaim, preserve, and apply the apostolic tradition. The writer is particularly concerned with the part they have to play in contributing to the unity of faith and knowledge, in providing an antidote to false teaching, and in bringing about a community that proclaims the truth in love.

Although the Church is at the forefront of the writer's thought in this passage, it should again be clear that ecclesiology has not swallowed up Christology. Christ remains the one Lord of the one Church (v 5), who from his exalted position of cosmic Lordship gives both grace to individuals and ministers of the word to the Church. The Church is his fullness (v 13) and his body (v 12) and as its head Christ is both its beginning and its end, the source and the goal of its growth (vv 15, 16). In this way we see again that for the writer to the Ephesians the Church could never be thought of simply as a new religious cult or social grouping, and that its real character could only be appreciated when it was contemplated from the perspective of its relationship to its Lord.

The Church's confession of one universal God (v 6) means that it continues to exist for his one world. But it is the Church's relationship to its cosmic Lord that determines the shape of this relationship to the cosmos. The focus of the passage is on the Church's inner growth rather than on its mission, but the quality of its corporate life has everything to do with the Church's fulfilling its role in the world. The writer's belief is that Christ's ascension far above all the heavens was in order that he might fill the cosmos with his sovereign rule and that his work in his Church is part of the carrying out of that rule (vv 10, 11). Christ has been exalted to fill the cosmos, but at present only the Church *is* his fullness. So where the Church is increasingly appropriating what it is and attaining to the measure of the stature of the fullness of Christ (v 13), it is allowing Christ to take more and more possession of the world over which he is Lord. In particular, as it embodies the unity it already possesses, the Church fulfills its calling to be the paradigm of future cosmic unity (cf. vv 1, 4). Unity in the Church is a statement to the rest of the cosmos and its powers of God's purpose for his world.

Final cosmic harmony and the Church's unity as a pledge of this are what is involved in this passage's emphasis on the one hope of believers' calling (v 4). This notion of hope reflects an eschatological perspective which looks beyond the Church to the cosmos (cf. 1:9, 10). But it is not simply that the Church constitutes the realized element in the writer's eschatology; there are both an "already" and a "not yet" to the Church's own existence. If in the first half of the letter the realized eschatology was such that it might have appeared that the Church already possessed full salvation, it now becomes clear that appropriating what has already been provided is a continual process. In fact, in the latter part of this passage, it is the Church's final state of completion that occupies the future horizon. This goal can be pictured in terms of growing up toward Christ himself (v 15), but as the Church becomes what it already is in Christ, the end is viewed primarily in terms of the attainment of its unity and maturity rather than in the characteristically Pauline terms of the parousia of Christ. Growth is the major image for this eschatological perspective, which takes seriously the Church's future in history and which arises from the need to supply a vision of its continuing task and goals.

As a teacher in the generation after the death of Paul, the writer believes that the Pauline churches of Asia Minor need to regain a sense of cohesion and purpose. His appeal to them to maintain the Church's essential unity and to progress to maturity and his vision of the Church's calling on which this appeal is based are intended to achieve this end. Vital to the actual attainment of such unity and maturity, he is convinced, will be the role of other ministers like himself in faithfully and creatively transmitting the apostolic message in a post-apostolic situation. The priority of this concern about the Church's consciousness of its calling and of its unity as paramount within that calling and the continuity of this concern with that of the first half of the letter account for the focus on ecclesiology at the outset of the paraenetical section. The continued concentration on the overall picture of the Church's calling precedes further practical exhortation, as the corporate dimension of believers' existence is made foundational to their living in the world. Clearly in the view of this writer, Christian ethics is first of all a call to participate in a distinctive community, the Church. Unity, stability and progress toward maturity within the Church are necessities if this Church is to provide the responsible witness to the surrounding society for which the rest of the paraenesis will ask. But even after beginning his ethical appeal, the writer is constrained to show that the exalted Christ has in fact supplied what is necessary for the Church to become what it is meant to be. His vision of the Church and of its calling in the world is not to be thought of as a totally impossible ideal. He maintains that the resources have been given for the Church to be able to demonstrate its unity, to proclaim the truth in love, and to attain to completeness in Christ.

Exhortation to Live According to the New Humanity Rather Than the Old (4:17–24)

Bibliography

Benoit, P. "Eph 4, 1–24: Exhortation à l'unité." *AsSeign* 71 (1963) 14–26. **Coune, M.** "Revêtir l'homme nouveau (Ep 4, 23–28)." *AsSeign* 74 (1963) 16–32. **Fischer, K. M.** *Tendenz und Absicht,* 147–50, 152–61. **Gnilka, J.** "Paränetische Traditionen im Epheserbrief." In *Mélanges Bibliques.* FS B. *Rigaux,* ed. A. Descamps and A. de Halleux. Gembloux: Duculot, 1970, 397–410. **Halter, H.** *Taufe und Ethos,* 248–56. **Jervell, J.** *Imago Dei.* Göttingen: Vandenhoeck & Ruprecht, 1960, 236–56, 288–92. **Larsson, E.** *Christus als Vorbild: Eine Untersuchung zu den paulinischen Tauf- und Eikontexten.* Uppsala: Almquist & Wiksells, 1962, 223–30. **Merklein, H.** "Eph 4, 1–5, 20 als Rezeption von Kol 3, 1–17." In *Kontinuität und Einheit,* ed. P. G. Müller and W. Stenger. Freiburg: Herder, 1981, 194–210. **Potterie, I. de al.** "Jésus et la verité d'après Eph 4, 21." *AnBib* 18 (1963) 45–57. **Wegenast, K.** *Das Verständnis der Tradition bei Paulus und in den Deuteropaulinen.* Neukirchen: Neukirchener Verlag, 1961, 131–32. **Wild, R. A.** " 'Be Imitators of God': Discipleship in the Letter to the Ephesians." In *Discipleship in the New Testament,* ed. F. F. Segovia. Philadelphia: Fortress, 1985, 127–43.

Translation

[17] *This, then, I solemnly declare*[a] *in the Lord, that you are no longer to lead your lives as do the Gentiles,*[b] *in the futility of their minds,* [18] *being darkened in their thinking, separated from the life of God because of the ignorance that is in them, because of the hardening of their hearts.*[c] [19] *Their moral sensitivity having become dulled,*[d] *they indeed have given themselves over to debauchery in order to pursue every kind of impurity with covetousness.*[e] [20] *But that is not the way you learned Christ—*[21] *assuming that you have heard of him and were taught in him, as the truth is in Jesus,* [22] *that, as regards your former way of life, you should put off*[f] *the old person who is being corrupted because of the desires which come from deceit,*[g] [23] *that you should be renewed as regards the spirit of your mind*[h] [24] *and that you should put on the new person who is created in God's likeness*[i] *in the righteousness and holiness which come from the truth.*

Notes

[a] A literal translation of the Greek text, which contains two verbs, would be "I say and testify," but the function of the latter verb is to emphasize the importance to be attached to the former.

[b] There is a variant reading τὰ λοιπὰ ἔθνη, "the other Gentiles," in ℵc Db,c K L P Ψ syrp goth arm. λοιπά appears to be an interpretative intrusion which weakens the force of the designation that omits it. The latter is the more difficult reading and has the clear external support of p46 ℵ* A B D* F G 082 33 88 255 256 263 itd,g vg copsa,bo eth (*contra* Meyer, 191–92).

[c] The Greek text of this pericope contains two sentences—vv 17–19 and vv 20–24. In the *Translation* the former has been broken up, although in the Greek v 19 continues with the relative pronoun οἵτινες, "who indeed."

[d] D F G P 1241 it syrp goth arm eth Irenaeus have ἀπηλπικότες, "despairing," instead of ἀπηλγηκότες, lit. "having ceased to feel pain, become callous," which has the far stronger support of p46 ℵ A B syrh copsa,bo Clement Origen. The former is probably a straightforward scribal error because of the similarity of the words, although it might also be an interpretation of the original, possibly under the influence of the description of the Gentiles in 2:12.

ᵉ ἐν πλεονεξίᾳ, "with covetousness," could be taken as qualifying εἰς ἐργασίαν, "in order to practice, pursue," i.e., "in order to pursue with an insatiable desire." But in view of the later relationship of πλεονεξία to ἀκαθαρσία, "impurity," in 5:3 (cf. also 5:5) and the way the term is used in Col 3:5, to which this passage is also related, it has been construed here as an independent accompanying object of the pursuit. For this use of ἐν with the force of καί as part of the writer's characteristic Semitic style, see K. G. Kuhn, "The Epistle to the Ephesians," 120.

ᶠ There is much dispute about how the three infinitives in vv 22–24 should be construed and translated. This translation takes them as infinitives of content qualifying ἐδιδάχθητε, "you were taught," rather than as imperatives, though even on this construction they retain something of an imperatival force. For fuller discussion of the syntax, see under *Comment* on v 22. In fact, in the case of the second infinitive, the imperative ἀνανεοῦσθε can be found in the inferior variant of P⁴⁶ D K 33 69 it syrP. Similarly, in the case of the third infinitive, the imperative ἐνδύσασθε is found in some manuscripts (P⁴⁶ ℵ B* K it syr).

ᵍ τῆς ἀπάτης has been taken as a genitive of origin, "the desires which come from deceit," rather than as a genitive of quality, "the deceitful desires." Such a translation also brings out the contrast of this expression with the genitive τῆς ἀληθείας in the depiction of the new person in v 24, which involves "the righteousness and holiness which come from the truth" (cf. esp. Murphy-O'Connor, "Truth: Paul and Qumran," 207–10).

ʰ The Greek expression here is τῷ πνεύματι not ἐν τῷ πνεύματι as found in P⁴⁹ B 33 1175 1739 1835 1881, and is taken as a dative of respect rather than an instrumental dative.

ⁱ κατὰ θεόν, lit. "in accordance with God," could mean "according to God's will" or "similar to God, like God." For discussion of this, and justification for preferring the latter force, see *Comment* on v 24.

Form/Structure/Setting

In terms of its structure and sequence this pericope has two parts—the exhortation not to live like the Gentiles (vv 17–19) and a more positive counterpart setting out the type of life that is in accord with the Christian tradition (vv 21–24). Each part can be further divided into two subsections. The basic exhortation, no longer to live as the Gentiles, is expressed in a formulation indicating the importance, urgency, and authority the writer attaches to his exhortation (v 17ab). This is followed by an extended negative depiction of Gentile thinking and conduct, in which the writer, in characteristic fashion, strings together participial clauses, prepositional phrases, and a relative clause (vv 17c–19). Distinctively Christian thinking and conduct is first encouraged by contrast and in terms of tradition—"But that is not the way you learned Christ"—where Christ stands for the Christian tradition in which the readers were taught (vv 20, 21). That tradition in its ethical aspects is then spelled out through the use of three infinitives, the first again emphasizing the difference from the readers' previous way of life and involving putting off the old person, the second and third finally expressing the writer's positive expectations and involving being renewed and putting on the new person characterized by righteousness and holiness (vv 22–24).

This pericope is similar to other paraenetical material which defines a community by marking it off from other groups. The main formal characteristics of such material include explicit prohibitions or other negative assertions with hortatory force and the setting out of the relation between the addressees and outsiders in antithetical formulations which may include mention of virtues and vices or of a temporal relationship (e.g., once/now; no longer) or take the form "*not* this, *but* that." Here in 4:17–24 we find the prohibition "you are not to lead your lives . . ." (v 17), the contrast between believers and the

Gentiles (v 17), the negative picture of the Gentiles and their vices (vv 17–19) which is set over against "learning Christ" and "the truth in Jesus" (vv 20, 21), the temporal references "no longer" (v 17) and "your former way of life" (v 22), and the antitheses between putting off the old person (v 22) and putting on the new person (v 24), and between "the desires which come from deceit" (v 22) and "the righteousness and holiness which come from the truth" (v 24). Eph 5:3–14 and 5:15–20 also contain this type of material, as do 1 Thess 4:3–8 and 5:1–11. There are also parallels in the paraenesis of Hellenistic philosophical literature, e.g., *The Epistles of Crates* 6, 7, 18, 19, 21 (cf. K. Berger, "Hellenistische Gattungen im Neuen Testament," *ANRW* 2.25.2 [1984] 1340–41).

But there are not only analogies with Hellenistic ethical exhortation. The notion that the people of God are to "walk" differently from the surrounding nations was central to Judaism (cf., e.g., the Holiness Code of Leviticus, esp. 18:1–5, 24–30; 20:23). Because of the contrast between two ways of life, there are also inevitably affinities with other early Christian catechetical material which uses this motif and with its Jewish antecedents. This contrast between two ways of life occurs, for example, in Matt 7:13, 14 and in the "Two Ways" of *Did.* 1–5 and *Barn.* 18–20 (cf. also Herm. *Man.* 6.1; Ign. *Magn.* 5; *2 Clem.* 4), and again has its background in the OT and Jewish literature (cf., e.g., Ps 1; Deut 11:26–28; 30:15–20; Jer 21:8; *T. Ash.* 1.3, 5; 1QS 3, 4). It may well also be the case that the passage reflects three features from an underlying early Christian baptismal catechesis. They are (*i*) imagery of the new life entered upon through conversion and baptism, here as new person and new creation in v 24 (cf. also Rom 6:4; Gal 6:15; 2 Cor 5:17; Col 3:10; Titus 3:5; 1 Pet 1:22; 2:2; Jas 1:18), in close connection with (*ii*) a statement of the need to abandon the characteristics of the old life using the verb ἀποτίθεσθαι "to put away, put off," here in v 22 (cf. also Rom 13:12; Col 3:8; 1 Pet 2:1; Jas 1:21), and also accompanied by (*iii*) the mention of vices to be put away and virtues to be acquired, which are found more extensively in Col 3:5–12 but also here, vices in vv 19, 22 and virtues in v 24 (cf. P. Carrington, *The Primitive Christian Catechism* [Cambridge: CUP, 1940] 31–65; E. G. Selwyn, *The First Epistle of St. Peter* [London: Macmillan, 1946] 384–461; King, *ExpTim* 63 [1952] 275–76; E. Kamlah, *Die Form der katalogischen Paränese im Neuen Testament* [Tübingen: Mohr, 1964] 34–38, 183–89; on catalogues of virtues and vices, see further the discussion under *Form/Structure/Setting* for 4:25–5:2). In considering the relation of this passage to such material, as well as to the traditional baptismal imagery of "putting off" and "putting on" (cf. 1 Thess 5:8; Gal 3:27; Rom 13:12–14; Col 3:8–12), its dependence on Col 3:5–11, where these features are also found, must be borne in mind. It is necessary to reckon both with the primary mediation of such paraenetical topics through Colossians (see below) and with the writer's awareness and use of elements common to early Christian catechesis and found elsewhere than in Colossians (*pace* Jervell, *Imago Dei*, 239, who finds no dependence of Ephesians on Colossians here, but only dependence of both on earlier catechetical material). The characterization of Gentile lifestyle and its vices in vv 17–19, for example, has parallels with Col 3:5 and, in common with Col 3:5, with 1 Thess 4, but also independently of Colossians with Rom 1, 1 Peter, and earlier Jewish literature, such as the *Testa-*

ments of the Twelve Patriarchs and the Qumran literature (see *Comment* on vv 17–19 for details).

In this section of the letter, just as in the previous sections, there are a number of similarities to the thought and language of the earlier Paulines. The most striking is that of vv 17–19 to Rom 1:21, 24, which can be set out as follows:

Romans		Ephesians	
1:21	ἐματαιώθησαν ἐν τοῖς διαλογισμοῖς αὐτῶν	4:17c	ἐν ματαιότητι τοῦ νοὸς αὐτῶν
1:21	καὶ ἐσκοτίσθη ἡ ἀσύνετος αὐτῶν καρδία	4:18a	ἐσκοτωμένοι τῇ διανοίᾳ ὄντες
1:24	παρέδωκεν αὐτοὺς ὁ θεός . . . εἰς ἀκαθαρσίαν	4:19	ἑαυτοὺς παρέδωκαν . . . εἰς ἐργασίαν ἀκαθαρσίας πάσης

For further analysis of this relationship, see *Comment* on vv 17c–19.

As has been indicated, it is again Colossians, and in particular Col 3:5–11, on which the writer is most dependent. The earlier paraenesis of 4:2–4 has already taken up Col 3:12–15. Now, after his own special emphasis on the Church's unity and maturity and the role of its teachers in ensuring their realization, the writer returns to use the preceding section of Col 3. The correspondence between the two letters at this point can be set out as follows:

Colossians		Ephesians	
3:5	πορνείαν, ἀκαθαρσίαν, πάθος, ἐπιθυμίαν κακήν, καὶ τὴν πλεονεξίαν ἥτις ἐστὶν εἰδωλολατρία	4:19	εἰς ἐργασίαν ἀκαθαρσίας πάσης ἐν πλεονεξίᾳ (cf. also 5:3, 5)
		4:22	κατὰ τὰς ἐπιθυμίας τῆς ἀπάτης
3:7	ἐν οἷς καὶ ὑμεῖς περιεπατήσατέ ποτε	4:17	μηκέτι ὑμᾶς περιπατεῖν καθὼς καὶ τὰ ἔθνη περιπατεῖ
3:8	νυνὶ δὲ ἀπόθεσθε καὶ ὑμεῖς . . .	4:22	ἀποθέσθαι ὑμᾶς κατὰ τὴν προτέραν ἀναστροφὴν τὸν παλαιὸν ἄνθρωπον
3:9	ἀπεκδυσάμενοι τὸν παλαιὸν ἄνθρωπον σὺν ταῖς πράξεσιν . . .		
3:10	καὶ ἐνδυσάμενοι τὸν νέον	4:24	καὶ ἐνδύσασθαι τὸν καινὸν ἄνθρωπον
3:10	τὸν ἀνακαινούμενον εἰς ἐπίγνωσιν	4:23	ἀνανεοῦσθαι δὲ τῷ πνεύματι τοῦ νοὸς ὑμῶν
3:10	κατ' εἰκόνα τοῦ κτίσαντος αὐτόν	4:24	τὸν κατὰ θεὸν κτισθέντα

As can be seen, the prohibition against living any longer in the manner of the Gentiles in v 17 is reminiscent of Col 3:7, while the last part of the characterization of that previous way of living in v 19 takes over the vices of ἀκαθαρσία, "impurity," and πλεονεξία, "covetousness," from the list in Col 3:5. In describing the content of the Christian tradition as putting off the old person in v 22, the writer makes use of this designation from Col 3:9, but substitutes ἀποτίθεσθαι from Col 3:8 for ἀπεκδύεσθαι in 3:9. Whereas Col 3:9 talks in general terms of the practices of the old person, v 22 gives a more colorful description which draws on the term ἐπιθυμία found in Col 3:5. In speaking of being renewed and of the new person in vv 23, 24, the writer provides a variation in the use of καινός and νέος and their cognate verbs, reversing that found in Col 3:10, so that where Colossians has νέος for the new person and ἀνακαινοῦν for "to renew," Ephesians has καινός for the adjective and ἀνανεοῦν for the verb. Finally, v 24 expresses slightly differently the notion of the new person's creation in relation to God, the more cryptic κατὰ θεόν, lit. "according to God," replacing κατ' εἰκόνα, "according to the image" from Col 3:10.

Two further observations should be made about the relation of this passage to Colossians. The use of the participle ἀπηλλοτριωμένοι, "separated, alienated," in the depiction of the Gentiles in v 18 has more in common with the use of the same participle in describing the Colossians' former way of life in relation to God in Col 1:21 than it does with its earlier use in relation to the people of God in Eph 2:12. Then the material which has no parallel in Col 3:5–11, the discussion in vv 20, 21 about learning and being taught in the Christian tradition, where the tradition is seen as summed up in Christ and as significant for the Christian "walk," in fact owes much to the thought of Col 2:6, 7. "Received Christ Jesus," where παραλαμβάνειν is the semitechnical term for receiving something delivered by tradition, is the equivalent of "learned Christ" here in Eph 4. This tradition is related to Christian conduct—"as you received Christ Jesus the Lord, so walk in him"—and the verb ἐδιδάχθητε, "you were taught," is employed in 2:7 (cf. Eph 4:21).

It can now be seen that the overall effect of the writer's reworking of the paraenetical material of Col 3:5–11 is to replace its original framework of the contrast between heavenly and earthly life, where it illustrated the ethical consequences of true heavenly-mindedness (cf. Lincoln, *Paradise Now*, 122–31), with that of a sharp contrast between Gentile life and life in accordance with the Christian tradition (cf. also Merklein, "Eph 4:1–5:20," 202–4). It is through the initial prohibition in v 17ab, and then the addition both of material about the Gentiles in vv 17c–19a and of the formulations about the tradition in vv 20, 21, that the writer gives his paraenesis its distinctive framework and emphasis.

This stress on the tradition which the readers need to remember provides one of the major links with the preceding pericope of 4:1–16. The significance attached there to the ministers and their role in passing on the apostolic tradition, and thereby contributing to the building up and maturing of the body of Christ, can now be seen to be preparing for the reminder of that tradition which will be the vehicle for the writer's paraenesis. Attaining to the unity of the knowledge of the Son of God (4:13) and growing into Christ (4:15) involve learning Christ and the truth in Jesus (vv 20, 21). The other major link with the preceding pericope is through the notion of "walking." The direct appeal to the readers to live a life appropriate to their calling begun in 4:1–3 had led into the material on the unity of the Church and the gift of ministers to enable it to achieve its goals. Only now in v 17 does the paraenesis return to the form of direct address, as it is made clear that the style of living appropriate to the readers' calling is not that of the Gentiles.

The notion of "walking" also provides the main link between this pericope and the next three sections of paraenesis—4:25–5:2 (cf. 5:2), 5:3–14 (cf. 5:8), and 5:15–20 (cf. 5:15). 4:25–5:2 will illustrate more specifically what it means to put away the vices of the old person and put on the new person, while 5:3–14 and 5:15–20 will explicitly repeat the need for differentiation from the conduct of outsiders. The theme of darkness from v 18 recurs in 5:8, 11 and later in 6:12, and that of deceit from v 22 in 5:6. The vices of impurity and covetousness in v 19 are mentioned again in 5:3, 5, and the virtues of righteousness and truth in v 24 are taken up again in 5:9 and later in 6:14. More fundamentally, 4:17–24 should be seen as providing, along with 4:1–16 and its emphasis on the Church, the basic framework for the rest of the letter's paraenesis.

In relation to the first part of the letter, 4:17–24 has most in common with 2:1–10 and 2:11–22, and can be seen as an ethical version of the contrast in both of those passages between the readers' present privileges and their Gentile past. In fact, 2:1–10 has already expressed the contrast in terms of two different walks (cf. vv 2 and 10). The Gentile past is described in terms of death in 2:1, 5 and being without God in 2:12, conditions which are summed up in the phrase "separated from the life of God" in 4:18. Both in 2:3 and in 4:22 evil desires characterize this former manner of life. The Christian present is seen in terms of a new creation in 2:10, 15 and here in 4:24, while the terminology of καινὸς ἄνθρωπος, "new person," found with a corporate connotation in 2:15, returns in 4:24. Anticipations of the thought and language of 4:17–24 can also be found back in the eulogy of 1:3–14. There the goal of the election of believers is seen as holiness (1:4; cf. 4:24), and they are described as those who have heard the word of truth (1:13; cf. 4:22).

These, then, are the main features of the setting of 4:17–24 in the letter as a whole. But can the thought of this pericope shed any light on the readers' setting? Recently Merklein ("Eph 4:1–5:20," 208) has argued that the emphases of both 2:11–22 and 4:17–24 have a common denominator—the misunderstanding of Paul's law-free gospel on the part of post-Pauline Christians, which has resulted in the downplaying of the significance of Israel on the one hand and in the danger of ethical libertinism on the other. But this hypothesis goes far beyond any clear evidence from the letter itself. It fails to convince about 2:11–22, where the stress on the Gentiles' heritage in relation to Israel is more likely meant to deal with Gentile Christians' ignorance of their religious roots than to be specifically connected with an erroneous view of the law. In any case, to go beyond Paul and talk of "abolishing the law" (2:15) seems a strange way to correct attitudes based on drawing too radical consequences from Paul's teaching on the law. Then, there is no hint in the paraenesis, with the possible exception of 6:3, that a wrong attitude to the law has provoked the writer's extended exhortations. Paraenesis in Paul's letters tends to be the more traditional and more general material, used in support of and adapted to Paul's situational and contextual focus in other parts of the letter. It is somewhat hazardous, therefore, to use the more general part of what is already a fairly general letter from a follower of Paul to draw very specific conclusions about the situation of the addressees. Probably the most that can be ascertained from the writer's emphases here is that, along with the danger of forgetting their status and privileges as members of the Church, there is the danger of the assimilation of the readers to the surrounding world in their manner of life. The stress on the Christian tradition is meant to remind these readers of the distinctive ethical implications of their conversion and baptism.

Comment

17ab Τοῦτο οὖν λέγω καὶ μαρτύρομαι ἐν κυρίῳ, "This, then, I solemnly declare in the Lord." The οὖν, "therefore," has resumptive force, as the writer takes up again from 4:1–3 his direct exhortation of the readers. μαρτύρομαι, "I testify," does not have here the specific connotation of bearing witness or of speaking under oath, but in its more general force of "I affirm, declare" still attaches a sense of solemnity and significance to what is to be stated. Used here in conjunction with λέγω, "I say," it serves to strengthen the importance and urgency of the exhortation (cf. 1 Thess 2:12; also Jdt 7:28; Josephus, *Ant.* 10.7.2 § 104). ἐν κυρίῳ, "in the Lord," also functions to lend authority to the exhortation. The writer exhorts with Christ's authority in the same way that Paul had done (cf. 1 Thess 4:1; also earlier in this chapter in 4:1—"the prisoner in the Lord"). The initial τοῦτο, "this," has reference to the content of the exhortation which is to follow.

μηκέτι ὑμᾶς περιπατεῖν καθὼς καὶ τὰ ἔθνη περιπατεῖ, "that you are no longer to lead your lives as do the Gentiles." On περιπατεῖν, "to walk, lead a life," see the earlier discussion of its usage in 2:2, 10; 4:1. The infinitive with the accusative is employed here for the imperative in indirect speech (cf. also Acts 21:2, 4). This prohibition, which differentiates sharply between the way of life of the readers and that of the members of the surrounding society, underlines the distinctive quality necessary to any living that is to be worthy of believers' calling (cf. 4:1). The μηκέτι, "no longer," reminds one of the temporal ποτέ . . . νῦν, "once . . . now," contrast schema in both parts of chap. 2. The change of status for the Gentile readers, which was indicated there, has to be accompanied by a change of "walk" (cf. also 2:2, 10). They cannot continue in their actual conduct as they had done in the past and as though none of the immense changes the writer has recalled in chap. 2 had taken place. Continual effort, and therefore continued exhortation, is needed if they are to appropriate the effects of those changes. The prohibition is couched in terms of not living like the Gentiles, τὰ ἔθνη. This is an interesting formulation, since earlier the writer has called the readers simply "you Gentiles" (3:1) but also "you Gentiles in the flesh" (2:11), denoting an ethnic distinction which no longer counts as religiously significant. The latter perspective is apparent here, where the designation, "the Gentiles," stands for non-Jewish outsiders to the Christian community and where Christians who are ethnic Gentiles are exhorted not to live like Gentiles. This underscores the "third race" mentality of this writer, which emerged from 2:11–22 where the Church was depicted as a new creation, as one new person replacing the two old ethnic entities of Israel and the Gentiles (cf. also 1 Cor 10:32, where Paul himself could divide humanity into three groups—Jews, Greeks, and the church of God).

17c–19 The picture of the Gentiles style of life is painted in the blackest colors. The writer is not interested in a balanced analysis that would point out positive features of Gentile life, nor is his purpose to enable his readers to feel superior. Instead he wants to provide decisive reasons why they should be distinctively Christian, and the more drastic the contrast, the more effective is his exhortation likely to be. In this sort of characterization he is in line with traditional Jewish apologetic (cf. Wis 12–15; 18:10–19; *Ep. Arist.* 140, 277; *Sib. Or.* 3.220–35), which was taken over by other early Christians, including Paul himself in Rom 1. The elements in the characterization are strung together by the writer in the style typical of the earlier part of the letter, mixing prepositional phrases with participial and relative clauses. It is beside the point to attempt to work out a logically subordinate relationship for each part of the syntax (*pace* Schlier, 213; Mussner, 134–35). With the exception of the two διά, "because of," phrases, each of which provides the reason for the immediately preceding part of the description, the other elements of the syntax should be treated as coordinates. There is, however, an overall movement of thought which first treats the Gentiles' thinking and inner disposition before dealing with their conduct. It is worth noting that this movement is repeated on the positive side when mention of renewal as it affects the mind (v 23) precedes any delineation of the virtues (v 24).

ἐν ματαιότητι τοῦ νοὸς αὐτῶν, "in the futility of their minds." ματαιότης denotes not merely finitude or transitoriness but the emptiness, folly, and ultimate pointlessness that has affected the Gentiles' faculty of intellectual and moral perception. In Rom 1:21 Paul had talked of humans' becoming futile in their thinking because of their refusal to acknowledge God. Here too this condition of futility of mind is inevitably connected with that later described as being "separated from the life of God." Rom 1:21 is itself dependent on Wis 13:1 (cf. also Ps 94:11; Jer 2:5; 1QS 5.19). Elsewhere in early Christianity believers' former manner of life is characterized as futile in 1 Pet 1:18 (cf also *Did.* 5.2; *Barn.* 4.10; 20.2; *1 Clem.* 7.2; Herm. *Man.* 9.4; 11.8; 12.6; Ign. *Trall.* 8.2). So, because it lacks the right relationship to God, Gentile thinking suffers from a fatal flaw. It has lost its grasp on reality and fallen prey to folly.

Another way of describing this condition is ἐσκοτωμένοι τῇ διανοίᾳ ὄντες, "being darkened in their thinking." The rarer verb σκοτοῦν is employed here rather than σκοτίζειν. It is found elsewhere in the NT only in Rev 9:2; 16:10. διάνοια, "thinking, mind," is often interchangeable with καρδία, "heart," in the LXX for the center of human perception and is found as a translation of the Hebrew where one might have expected the latter (cf., e.g., Gen 8:21; 17:17; 24:45; 27:41; Exod 28:3). The light has gone out in the seat of Gentiles' understanding so that they are no longer capable of apprehending ultimate truth. There is a clear contrast with believers, who have been given knowledge and the eyes of whose hearts have been enlightened; (1:17, 18; cf. also the sustained contrast between darkness and light in 5:8–14). Again Rom 1:21, "their senseless hearts were darkened," provides the immediate background for the formulation here. (For the use of this imagery elsewhere in Judaism, cf. *T. Reub.* 3.8; *T. Gad* 6.2; *T. Dan* 2.4; *T. Levi* 14.4; Josephus, *Ant.* 9.4.3; 1QS 3.3.)

ἀπηλλοτριωμένοι τῆς ζωῆς τοῦ θεοῦ, "separated from the life of God." The flawed perception of reality that has been described accompanies a broken relation to the source of that reality, God. On ἀπηλλοτριοῦν, see *Comment* on 2:12 and note the use of the term in Col 1:21, where it also describes alienation from God. "The life of God is that life which answers to the nature of God and which he communicates to his children" (Westcott, 66). "Separated from the life of God" is, of course, equivalent to the earlier description of the readers' former condition as "dead" (2:1, 5) and "without God" (2:12). Loss of light can now be seen to amount to the same thing as loss of life (cf. also John 1:4; 8:12).

The reason for the Gentiles' estrangement from the life of God is now indicated. It is διὰ τὴν ἄγνοιαν τὴν οὖσαν ἐν αὐτοῖς, "because of the ignorance that is in them." This ignorance does not provide an excuse for the broken relationship with God. In the tradition of Jewish apologetic of which it is a part (cf. Wis 13:1, 8, 9; *T. Gad* 5.7), Gentile ignorance is viewed as culpable, and elsewhere in Jewish thought ignorance is linked with sin (cf. Sir 23:3; 28:7, 8). This is certainly also the perspective of the more extended and profound analysis of Rom 1:18–23, where knowledge of God becomes futility and folly and therefore, in effect, ignorance, because of a failure to honor God as God. Here in Ephesians, the Gentiles' responsibility for their own ignorance comes out more explicitly in the following characterizations, but is perhaps hinted at in the formulation "the ignorance that is in them." The ignorance cannot be blamed on other factors; it has its roots within them (cf. also Barth, 501; *pace* Caird, 79, who takes the meaning as "prevailing among them"). Elsewhere in the NT 1 Pet 1:14 describes the pre-Christian lives of its recipients in terms of "the passions of your former ignorance" (cf. also Acts 17:30).

διὰ τὴν πώρωσιν τῆς καρδίας αὐτῶν, "because of the hardening of their hearts." This prepositional phrase now makes clear that the Gentiles' ignorance is culpable. At the center of their thinking, feeling, and volition, they have hardened themselves to God and to the knowledge of him that was available to them. The connection with the immediately preceding statement is more likely than that with the participial clause about separation because of the preceding τὴν οὖσαν ἐν αὐτοῖς, "that is in them," instead of the simple αὐτῶν, "their" (cf. also Meyer, 240). πώρωσις (or the verb πωροῦν) is found in connection with the heart elsewhere in the NT in Mark 3:5; 6:52; 8:17; John 12:40 (cf. also Rom 11:7, 25; 2 Cor 3:14), and is most frequently used of Jewish response to the gospel. Here it is seen to be a concept equally applicable in a more general sense to Gentiles. The notion of hardening is, of course, employed frequently in the OT and Judaism, e.g., Exod 4:21; 7:3; 9:12; Ps 95:8; Isa 6:10; 63:17; *T. Levi* 13.7; 1QS 1.6; 2.14, 26; 3.3; 5.4; CD 2.17, 18; 3.5, 11; 8.8. Its focus is on a progressive insensitivity and obtuseness in relation to God. J. A. Robinson, in an extended note (264–74), attempts to argue for the meaning of blindness rather than hardening, but in the various uses of the term it is difficult to exclude the note of willful obstinacy from its connotations.

The portrayal of the Gentiles' lifestyle concludes by stressing the moral bankruptcy that accompanies their lack of true insight. The relative pronoun οἵτινες, "being those indeed who . . . ," may well have the function of emphasizing a characteristic quality which confirms a preceding statement (cf. BAGD, 587). The idea of insensitivity or callousness involved in "the hardening of their hearts" is continued in the use of the perfect participle ἀπηλγηκότες, lit. "having ceased to feel pain" and therefore in this context "their moral sensitivity having become dulled." This is the only use of this verb in the NT (cf. Thucydides

2.61; Polybius 1.35.5; 9.40.4). In this depiction, the lack of moral feeling and discernment on the part of the Gentiles means an inability to exercise any restraint in their plunge into degrading activities. Their part in actively pursuing and seeking out evil is brought out in both εἰς ἐργασίαν, "for the practice, pursuit," and ἑαυτοὺς παρέδωκαν, "they have given themselves over." Whereas Rom 1:24–32 emphasizes God's continued involvement in humanity's turning away from him with its threefold "God gave them over," in accord with the needs of paraenesis this verse stresses the moral responsibility of the Gentiles. The evil that characterizes their conduct is not some dark fate that has overtaken them without their consent. This evil is typified through the use of three terms that occur frequently in catalogues of vices. ἀσέλγεια, "debauchery, licentiousness," occurs in Mark 7:22; Rom 13:13; 1 Pet 4:3; Herm. *Vis.* 2.2.2; 3.7.2, and with ἀκαθαρσία, "impurity," in 2 Cor 12:21; Gal 5:19. It is also used in polemic against false teachers in 2 Pet 2:2, 7; Jude 4. The term encompasses generally riotous and excessive living, but frequently has unrestrained sexual behaviour in view. As in Rom 1:24–32, the abuse of sexuality is highlighted in illustrating the degradation resulting from failure to acknowledge the Creator. For the use of the term in Jewish literature, cf. Wis 14:26; 3 Macc 2:26; *T. Jud.* 23.1; Josephus, *Ant.* 4.6.12 § 151; 8.10.2 § 252; 8.13.1 § 318; 20.5.3 § 112; Philo, *De Vit. Mos.* 1.305. ἀκαθαρσία, "impurity, immorality," features again in 5:3 (cf. also Wis 2:16; 3 Macc 2:17; *T. Levi* 15.1; *T. Jud.* 14.5; 1QS 4.9–11; Rom 1:24; 2 Cor 12:21; Gal 5:19; 1 Thess 2:3; 4:7; Col 3:5). Sexual immorality may well be primarily in view, but again the reference is not limited to this; ἀκαθαρσίας πάσης, "all kinds of impurity," are included. πλεονεξία, "covetousness," the vice which Dio Chrysostom, *Or.* 67.6, 8, calls both the greatest cause of evils and the greatest evil, concludes v 19. It is mentioned frequently in the OT and in Jewish literature (cf., e.g., Ps 119:36; Jer 22:17; Ezek 22:27; Hab 2:9; 2 Macc 4:50; 1QS 4.10, 11; Philo, *De Spec. Leg.* 4.5; *De Vit. Mos.* 2.186), and appears also in NT and early Christian lists (cf. Mark 7:22; 1 Cor 5:10, 11; Rom 1:29; Col 3:5; 2 Pet 2:3; *Did.* 5.1; *1 Clem.* 35.5; *Barn.* 20.1; Herm. *Man.* 6.2, 5; 8.5). Later in Ephesians, the term is again associated with ἀκαθαρσία (5:3; cf. also 5:5) and is related to idolatry (cf. 5:5; Col 3:5, and see *Comment* on 5:5). Its use here suggests that Gentiles out of proper relationship to God live in excess but can never be satisfied. Their insatiable greed makes them oblivious of the needs of others and of the consequences for others.

20, 21 ὑμεῖς δὲ οὐχ οὕτως ἐμάθετε τὸν Χριστόν, "But that is not the way you learned Christ." The contrast to the readers' previous Gentile lifestyle begins forcefully—ὑμεῖς δὲ οὐχ . . . , lit. "but you not. . . ." Yet the immediate contrast that follows is made not through an equivalent depiction of Christian conduct but through a reminder of the readers' instruction in that conduct. The first formulation of the reminder in terms of learning Christ (μανθάνειν with a personal object) is without parallel. Significantly, it is Col 2:6, 7, where παρελάβετε τὸν Χριστὸν Ἰησοῦν means "you received the tradition about Christ Jesus," that provides the closest approximation. In both passages Christ stands for the tradition about him and is brought into direct relation with Christian conduct, and in both passages these notions are associated with being taught (*pace* Wegenast, *Das Verständnis der Tradition*, 131–32, who sees no notion of instruction in tradition in these passages). Learning Christ is, in fact, being on the receiving end of the process that in Acts 5:42 can be spoken of as teaching Christ. Elsewhere, μανθάνειν is used for learning the gospel tradition—in Col 1:6, 7 in connection with ἀκούειν, "to hear," and ἀλήθεια, "truth," two terms also used here in vv 20, 21; in Phil 4:9 in connection with παραλαμβάνειν and ἀκούειν; and in Rom 16:17 and 2 Tim 3:14. Just as a Jew learned Torah, so now a Christian can be said to learn Christ. But the personal object in the latter case does make a difference. Since Christians believed that Christ was a living person whose presence was mediated by the proclamation and teaching about him, learning Christ involved not only learning about, but also being shaped by, the risen Christ who was the source of a new way of life as well as of a new relationship with God.

εἴ γε αὐτὸν ἠκούσατε καὶ ἐν αὐτῷ ἐδιδάχθητε, "assuming that you have heard of him and were taught in him." The introductory εἴ γε implies confident assumption (see the discussion of the similar use in 3:2), while the concepts of hearing of Christ and being taught in him further explain the learning Christ of the previous verse. Being taught in him, i.e., about him, is, as we have seen, the other side of learning about him and involves receiving instruction in the gospel tradition (cf. also Larsson, *Christus*, 224–25). In regard to hearing of Christ, in the Greek text the pronoun for Christ is in the accusative with ἀκούειν, "to hear." With ἀκούειν, the person whose words one hears stands in the genitive, the person about whom one hears stands in the accusative (cf. BDF § 173). So to hear about Christ is to be on the receiving end of the proclamation about Christ (cf. 1 Cor 1:23; 2 Cor 1:19; Gal 1:16; Phil 1:15; Col 1:28). The reference is primarily to the readers' initial reception of this message (cf. 1:13, "having heard the word of truth, the gospel of your salvation"; also Rom 10:14; 15:21; Col 1:6, 23). Earlier there has been emphasis on the apostolic tradition and its transmission by evangelists, pastors, and teachers (cf. 2:20; 3:5; 4:11). Now, in a context where in particular the ethical aspects of the tradition are in view, "hearing" draws attention primarily to the first stage of its transmission, while "being taught" highlights the further stage of catechesis.

καθώς ἐστιν ἀλήθεια ἐν τῷ Ἰησοῦ, "as the truth is in Jesus." Because of the anarthrous ἀλήθεια, the use of the name Jesus, and questions about the relation of καθώς to what precedes, scholars have made heavy weather of the syntax and interpretation of this clause (cf., e.g., the spirited correspondence about it between Westcott and Hort, reproduced in the former's commentary [70–71], where Hort felt forced to propose an emendation; the article by I. de la Potterie in *AnBib* 18 [1963] 45–67, which provides discussion of some of the issues; and Barth, 505, 533–36, who resorts to taking καθώς as an introductory formula for a citation which begins, "Truth in Jesus!" and includes vv 22–24, apparently ignoring the dependence of these verses on Colossians). The translation given above—"as the truth is in Jesus"—appears to be the most straightforward and to make the most sense (cf. also AV, RSV). Other major translations sense rightly that the gist of the clause is about the content of Christian truth being summed up in Jesus. But from the translations which make the truth the direct object of "were taught" and drop "in him" from the previous clause (cf. NEB, "were . . . taught the truth as it is in Jesus"; JB, "were taught what the truth is in Jesus"; GNB, "were taught the truth that is in Jesus"), the reader would never suppose that the original contained the adverb καθώς. The objection that is often raised against our translation, however, is that since ἀλήθεια is without an article it cannot be the subject of the clause but has to be the predicate (cf. de la Potterie, *AnBib* 18 [1963] 48; Gnilka, 228 n. 3; Caird, 80). Certainly, one of the major reasons for ἀλήθεια being anarthrous here could be that it forms the predicate, but if so a subject needs to be supplied. The only real options for this clause would be "as he is truth in Jesus," referring back to the "him," i.e., Christ, of the preceding clause, or the more general "as there is truth in Jesus." The meaning "as Christ is truth in Jesus," despite its support from de la Potterie (*AnBib* 18 [1963] 48) and possibly Schlier (216) is barely intelligible, even on what we shall see is their unlikely assumption that this is a polemical statement against a Gnostic Christology. It is made more unlikely still when de la Potterie has to introduce a comma after "truth" to achieve his proposed meaning of "in the way that Christ is truth, namely in Jesus." The meaning of "as there is truth in Jesus" (cf. Westcott, 67, 70) is clear; the problem with it is that it seems to be too indefinite an assertion to have been intended here, "a strange understatement," as Hort puts it (Westcott, 71).

Given the unconvincing nature of these alternatives, it becomes necessary to look again at the issue of the anarthrous ἀλήθεια and to ask whether any explanations of it other than as a predicate are possible. It then becomes clear that the objection to our translation has been stated too strongly. ἀλήθεια, like other nouns, can be used anarthrously in the Pauline corpus for a number of different reasons—as a predicate (2 Cor 7:14c), with a verb of speaking (Eph 4:25; Rom 9:1; 2 Cor 12:6; 1 Tim 2:7b), after a preposition (Eph 5:9; 6:14; Rom 2:2; 2 Cor 7:14; Col 1:6; 1 Tim 2:7c), in genitive constructions (Rom 15:8; 1 Cor 5:8; 2 Cor 6:7; 11:10; 2 Thess 2:13; 1 Tim 2:4; 2 Tim 2:25; 3:7; Titus 1:1), with adverbial force (Phil 1:18), and, apparently, simply because it is an abstract noun (Gal 5:7). It is this last usage which is most instructive for discussion of the syntax of Eph 4:21. Paul frequently omits the article with abstract nouns such as "sin" or "grace" (cf. BDF § 258), and the writer of Ephesians can, for example, alternate between the anarthrous and the arthrous use of χάρις in 2:5, 8. There is, therefore, no decisive grammatical reason why ἀλήθεια in Eph 4:21 should not be seen as an instance of this sort of usage and be treated as the subject of the clause (cf. also Moule, *Idiom-Book*, 111–12, who concludes that "in such instances it is hard to avoid the impression that usage [i.e., of the article] is arbitrary" and finds no objection to construing ἀλήθεια in Eph 4:21 as though it had been ἡ ἀλήθεια).

Similarly, too much should not be made of the use of the name Jesus. It is likely to be a stylistic variation and should not immediately be assumed to have major theological significance. To hold such a view is to swim against the stream of recent scholarship. It is usually asserted that since this is the only instance of the name Jesus by itself in Ephesians, the writer's change to this appellation must not only be deliberate but also theologically significant. There are two views of what this significance is. The first has been mentioned already. It argues that the clause is aimed at Gnostic teaching that made a sharp divide between the heavenly Christ and the earthly Jesus (cf. Schlier, 217; de la Potterie, *AnBib* 18 [1963] 53; Gnilka, 228). That some such Christological point needed to be made in some contexts in the first century is possible (cf. 1 John 2:22; 4:3), but whether the teaching it would be aimed at is best described as Gnostic is another matter. It is also another matter whether such a polemical point is likely in a letter which nowhere else appears to combat Gnosticism, in a context where the emphasis is not Christological but paraenetic, and where there is no indication that Gentile attraction to the immorality described in vv 17–19 is because of some mistaken Christology. It is also in a form so cryptic as to make one wonder whether the original readers would have caught its force. The second view also argues that the change to the name Jesus is to draw attention to the earthly Jesus rather than the risen Christ, but that the point being made is that the truth of the tradition, and particularly its ethical aspects, is not just determined by the idea of Christ but has its roots in the life and death of the historical Jesus or contains teaching from the historical Jesus (cf. Larsson, *Christus,* 226 n. 2; Ernst, 363; Mitton, 163; Schnackenburg, 203; Mussner, 136). (Caird, 80, has his own version of a reference to the historical Jesus, arguing that the writer's point is that the teaching about putting off the old person and putting on the new first took place literally in the death and resurrection of Jesus—"just as was literally true in the case of Jesus." But Caird's interpretation requires far too much eisegesis, and the syntax will simply not support it.) If there were to be any significance at all to the variation in name, then this latter view would be preferable, although some versions of it are in danger of reading back too much of the modern debate about the historical Jesus. But although this is the only occasion on which the simple name Jesus appears by itself in Ephesians (but cf. "Lord Jesus" in 1:15), it must be doubted whether the variation is in fact capable of bearing this weight. In Paul the simple name Jesus appears in 1 Thess 1:10; 4:14; Gal 6:17; 1 Cor 12:3; 2 Cor 4:5, 10, 11, 14; 11:4; Rom 3:26; 8:11; Phil 2:10. In some of these texts it is clear that Paul is drawing on a traditional formulation, but despite various scholarly assertions to the contrary (e.g., Schlier, 217 n. 3; de la Potterie, *AnBib* 18 [1963] 53), in the others and particularly in 2 Cor 4 there is no clearcut theological reason for the shift between Christ and Jesus. Nor for that matter is there any special significance in the shift between either of these and Christ Jesus or Jesus Christ. The best explanation for the variation in Paul as well as here in Eph 4:20, 21 is stylistic (cf. also Bruce, *Epistles,* 357: "it is difficult to discern any distinction in emphasis between 'in Christ' and 'in Jesus' "). Having described the tradition in which the readers were taught in terms of Christ (vv 20, 21a), the writer can now also talk of that same tradition as summed up in Jesus (v 21b). In other words, to learn the gospel tradition is to be taught in Christ or to be taught the truth in Jesus.

Probably more significant than the use of the name Jesus is the introduction of the concept of truth in this context. As has been noted, ἀλήθεια occurred earlier in connection with ἀκούειν in 1:13, "having heard the word of truth," where this word of truth was immediately explained as "the gospel of your salvation" (cf. also Col 1:5, 6), and "truth" has this same force in Paul in Gal 2:5, 14; 5:7; 2 Thess 2:10, 12, 13. Truth as the content of the gospel and of the apostolic tradition through which that gospel is transmitted becomes the main focus of ἀλήθεια as that term is used in the Pastorals (cf. 1 Tim 2:4, 7;

3:15; 4:3; 6:5; 2 Tim 2:15, 18, 25; 3:7, 8; 4:4; Titus 1:1, 14). From the surrounding context in Eph 4:17–24, it becomes clear that the truth of the gospel tradition that can be summed up in Jesus, according to v 21, controls the whole of believers' lives and includes the ethical implications of the gospel as they had been developed in the Church's catechesis. (See *Comment* on 4:15 about believers proclaiming this truth instead of being taken in by those who propagate error, and on the notion of truth here compare also E. Hoskyns and F. N. Davey, *The Riddle of the New Testament* [London: Faber and Faber, 1931] 26–31; R. Bultmann, "ἀλήθεια," *TDNT* 1 [1964] 238–47; Murphy-O'Connor, "Truth: Paul and Qumran," 179–230; A. C. Thiselton, "Truth," *NIDNTT* 3 [1978] 874–901.)

It remains to note that καθώς in this clause functions syntactically to qualify the preceding clause and to indicate a comparison. It suggests, therefore, that the truth of the gospel tradition, as summed up in Jesus, was the norm in accord with which the readers had heard of Christ and been taught in him (cf. also NIV, "in accordance with the truth that is in Jesus"). In terms of the writer's train of thought, this clause contrasts with the οὐχ οὕτως, lit. "not thus," of v 20. He asserts that his readers had not been instructed in the Christian tradition falsely according to the Gentile pattern of life he has depicted in vv 17–19 but had been instructed according to the proper content of that tradition, that is, the truth in Jesus.

22 ἀποθέσθαι ὑμᾶς κατὰ τὴν προτέραν ἀναστροφὴν τὸν παλαιὸν ἄνθρωπον τὸν φθειρόμενον κατὰ τὰς ἐπιθυμίας τῆς ἀπάτης, "that, as regards your former way of life, you should put off the old person who is being corrupted because of the desires which come from deceit." The writer is dependent on Col 3:8–10 for his paraenetic material here in vv 22–24 (see *Form/Structure/Setting*), but among the differences from that passage is the syntax. ἀποθέσθαι, "to put off," is the first of the three infinitives of vv 22–24. Before any comment can be made on the content of the verses, a decision about the place of these infinitives in the syntax must be made. There are four main options. (*a*) The infinitives can simply be taken as imperatives. The infinitive can occasionally function as an imperative in the NT (e.g., Rom 12:15; Phil 3:16), and D. Daube has argued that a variety of imperatival forms, including participles and infinitives, is typical of Hebrew ethical codes ("Participle and Imperative in 1 Peter," in E. G. Selwyn, *The First Epistle of St. Peter* [London: Macmillan, 1946] esp. 480–81). The infinitive as imperative is also a common feature of Pseudo-Phocylides. What makes such a grammatical feature less likely here, however, is that v 22 contains not a simple infinitive but an infinitive plus an accusative—ὑμᾶς, "you" (cf. also BDF § 389). (*b*) The accusative and infinitive could be part of a final clause, indicating purpose and dependent on ἐδιδάχθητε, "you were taught." The readers were taught in order that they might put off the old person and put on the new. (*c*) Another possibility is that the accusative and infinitive form part of a consecutive or result clause. The readers were taught with the result that they have, in fact, put off the old person, are being renewed, and have put on the new (cf. J. Murray, *Principles of Conduct* [Grand Rapids: Eerdmans, 1957] 214–19). (*d*) The fourth main option is that the infinitive accompanied by the accusative is epexegetic, explaining the content of the teaching mentioned in v 21 (cf. also J. A. Robinson, 190; Moule, *Idiom-Book*, 127, 139;

Houlden, 318; Caird, 80; Bruce, *Epistles,* 358 n. 127). Any of the last three options is possible, but one would have thought that if the writer had wanted to make clear that the teaching had already resulted in a definitive putting on and off in the past, he would have done so by using ὥστε, "so that." As it is, the fact that the καθώς clause, "as the truth is in Jesus," already qualifies and defines "you were taught," makes it most likely that the infinitives are to be taken as a further explanation of the content of the teaching. Some make the infinitives directly dependent on the καθώς clause (cf. Meyer, 244–46; Gnilka, 229). This would make very little difference to the sense, but it is less natural syntactically than relating them to the major verb "were taught." Because of their context in what is a piece of paraenesis, these infinitives do take on some imperatival force (cf. also Schnackenburg, 203).

The readers had been taught that becoming believers involves a radical break with the past, the putting off of the old person. The imagery of putting off the old person and putting on the new is that of decisive change. Its meaning can be compared to that of the Synoptic language of repenting because of the coming of the kingdom (e.g., Mark 1:15). ἀποτίθεσθαι is employed in relation to a variety of sins in Rom 13:12; Col 3:8; Eph 4:25; Heb 12:1; Jas 1:21; and 1 Pet 2:1. But here it is not just particular vices that are to be put off but the whole old person who was leading a life dominated by sin.

The background for the "putting off" can be treated together with that for the "putting on" language. The connection of this imagery with the notion of the old or new person can then also be explored. Behind the language and concepts of this passage lies Col 3:8–10 (Ephesians, however, has replaced the ἀπεκδύεσθαι of 3:9 with the ἀποτίθεσθαι of 3:8), and behind that lies a cluster of passages in the undisputed Paulines. "Putting off" is, as we have seen, found in Rom 13:12 where it is in close juxtaposition with "putting on the Lord Jesus Christ" in Rom 13:14. "Putting on" is again employed in an exhortation in 1 Thess 5:8, while in Gal 3:27 to have put on Christ is equated with to have been baptized into Christ. Nowhere in the undisputed Paulines is this clothing imagery linked with the notion of the old or new person. In fact, the only occurrence of that notion is in Rom 6:6 where it is said that the believer's old person was crucified with Christ. It is frequently asserted that the language of putting off the old person and putting on the new derives from the practice of the removal of clothing before entering the water in baptism and the subsequent reclothing in a new garment (e.g., W. A. Meeks, *The First Urban Christians* [New Haven: Yale University Press, 1983] 155). This may have been the case, but the evidence is by no means decisive. Obviously, the clothing imagery cannot be confined to a baptismal context. In the OT there is the idea of being clothed with salvation (2 Chr 6:41) or with moral qualities (e.g., righteousness in Job 29:14; Ps 132:9). The picture of putting off vices is widespread in Greek writers (e.g., Demosthenes) 8.46; Lucian, *Dial. Mort.* 10.8, 9; *Ep. Arist.* 122; Plutarch, *Cor.* 19.4) as is that of putting on virtues (e.g., Philo, *De Conf. Ling.* 31; *Corpus Hermeticum* 13:8, 9). In addition, in the mystery religions the initiate can be described as becoming clothed with the powers of the cosmos and the divine life (cf. Apuleius, *Metamorph.* 11.24). But there is no exact parallel to the language of putting off the old person and putting on the new, which is first found in Colossians (cf. the discussion in Jervell, *Imago Dei*, 240–48). P. W. van der Horst ("Observations on a Pauline Expression," *NTS* 19 [1972–73] 181–87) has drawn attention to what is probably the closest linguistic usage in a fragment of Antigonus of Corystus about Pyrrho of Elis, preserved in Eusebius, *Praep. Evang.* 14.18.26, and Diogenes Laertius 9.66. Pyrrho, under attack from a dog, adopts normal patterns of behavior and seeks refuge, but this is inconsistent with his present philosophical convictions, and when he is mocked about this, he claims χαλεπόν ἐστιν τὸν ἄνθρωπον ἐκδῦναι, "it is difficult to put off the person." Although this tradition can be dated early enough, it is not easy to imagine that it had any decisive influence on the formulation found in Colossians, which appears instead to have been a combining of two images that had earlier functioned independently for Paul. Since both had had clear baptismal associations (cf. Gal 3:27; Rom 6:6), it could well be that it was the actual practice of baptism that was the catalyst in this new usage. But since our evidence that early Christian baptismal practice included derobing and then robing in a new garment afterward can be dated no earlier than the second century C.E., it is probably safer to say that this imagery is entirely appropriate to what we know of later baptismal rites. If, as is argued by J. Z. Smith ("The Garments of Shame," *HR* 5 [1965] 217–38), *Gos. Thom.* 37 contains an allusion to Christian baptismal practice, then this would be the earliest evidence, possibly from the first half of the second century C.E. Of other relevant material, *Gos. Phil.* 101 is dated between the second half of the second century and the second half of the third, Hippolytus' *Apostolic Tradition* reflects Roman practice at the end of the second century, and Cyril of Jerusalem's *Mystagogical Catechesis* II, which contains a reference to the practice, is dated c. 350 C.E., while the Syriac *Acts of John* in which the rite is found goes back only to the end of the fourth or beginning of the fifth century C.E. (cf. A. F. J. Klijn, "An Ancient Syriac Baptismal Liturgy in the Syriac Acts of John," in ΧΑΡΙΣ ΚΑΙ ΣΟΦΙΑ, FS K. H. Rengstorf, ed. U. Luck [Leiden: E. J. Brill, 1964] 216–28).

The change of clothing imagery signifies an exchange of identities, and the concepts of the old and the new persons reinforce this. These old and new persons are not simply Adam and Christ as representatives of the old and new orders (*pace* Barth, 539), nor more specifically Adam in the inner person and Christ in the inner person (*pace* Jervell, *Imago Dei*, 240–48). They are individuals, as those individuals are identified either with the old or with the new order of existence. The old person is the person living under the dominion of the present evil age and its powers, and this previous identity has to be dealt with decisively. If, as we have argued, the epexegetic infinitive has some hortatory force here, then there is a slight shift of emphasis between Ephesians and earlier references to the old person. Whereas both Rom 6:6 and Col 3:9 (cf. O'Brien, *Colossians*, 188–89) assert that the definitive break with the old person has been made in the past, Ephesians extends the tension between the indicative and the imperative to the notion of putting off the old person. Putting off the old person has already taken place through baptism, which transferred believers to the new order. This injunction is not an exhortation to believers to repeat that event but to continue to live out its significance by giving up on that old person that they no longer are. They are new people who must become in practice what God has already made them, and that involves the resolve to put off the old way of life as it attempts to impinge. This is made clear by the qualifying phrase which precedes the mention of the old person—"as regards your former way of life." The use of ἀναστροφή, "way of life," recalls the use of the cognate verb in the earlier depiction of the Gentile readers' past in 2:3. It should now be plain to them that learning Christ means giving up that Gentile past and its practices.

It makes no sense to continue with that former way of life, since it has no future. As opposed to the new person, who is in a process of renewal, the old person is in a process of moral corruption (cf. also the use of the noun φθορά in Rom 8:21; Gal 6:8), a rottenness and decay which will end in the final destruction of death (cf. also 1 Cor 3:17b; 2 Pet 2:12). The old way of life has already been described as one of death in 2:1, 5. 2 Pet 1:4 links the corruption in the world with ἐπιθυμία, "desire." The same link is found here in v 22 as the old person is depicted as being corrupted because of the desires which come from deceit. Again, there is a reminiscence of the earlier portrayal of the Gentile past in 2:3, where it is the desires of the flesh that characterize the old life (for ἐπιθυμία with negative force cf. also Col 3:5; Rom 1:24; 6:12; 7:7, 8; 13:14; Gal 5:16, 24; 1 Thess 4:5). ἀπάτη, "deceit," is found elsewhere in the Pauline corpus only in 2 Thess 2:10, where it stands in opposition to the truth, and in Col 2:8, where as part of the false philosophy ensnaring some. It can also be seen as in contrast to the gospel as the word of truth (cf. 1:5; for other uses cf. Mark 4:19; Matt 13:22; Heb 3:13; 2 Pet 2:13; *2 Clem.* 6.4; Herm. *Man.* 8.5; 11.12; Herm. *Sim.* 6.2.1; 6.3.3; 6.4.4; while in *Cebes Tablet* 23–24 deceit dominates the catalogue of vices, and in 1QS 4.2–26 it plays a significant role in the discussion of the two spirits). A false perspective on reality generates a confusion of desires which can never be satisfied because they have lost touch with what is true. Such desires serve the power of deceit, and so are themselves ultimately illusory and contribute to the ruin of the old person.

23 ἀνανεοῦσθαι δὲ τῷ πνεύματι τοῦ νοὸς ὑμῶν, "that you should be renewed as regards the spirit of your mind." By making the notion of renewal an independent element in the discussion in contrast to its function in Col 3:10, the writer highlights the aspect of continual challenge for the believer and in this regard brings the thought more into line with the exhortation of Rom 12:2, "Be transformed by the renewal of your mind." Elsewhere, ἀνακαινοῦσθαι or its cognate noun is employed for the process of renewal—in Col 3:10 (of the new person), in 2 Cor 4:16 (of the inner person), and in Rom 12:2 (of the mind). Here, ἀνανεοῦσθαι is used for renewal and καινός for the new person. Abbott (138) and Schnackenburg (204) argue for a deliberate distinction whereby the new person is καινός, qualitatively different and requiring the divine initiative to create, while the process of renewal employs a cognate of νέος, involving rejuvenation and encompassing human activity. But R. A. Harrisville ("The Concept of Newness in the New Testament," *JBL* 74 [1955] 69–79) shows the synonymity of these words for newness, both of which can have either qualitative or temporal connotations; thus the variation here is merely stylistic (cf. also Bruce, *Epistles*, 358 n. 126).

The renewal is to take place "in the spirit of your mind." The double expression τῷ πνεύματι τοῦ νοὸς ὑμῶν has generated much discussion. The majority of recent commentators (cf. Schlier, 220; Gnilka, 230; Houlden, 319; Halter, *Taufe*, 254–55; Ernst, 365; Schnackenburg, 204; Mussner, 137) opt for a reference to the divine Spirit on the grounds that nowhere else in Ephesians does πνεῦμα refer to the human spirit, and elsewhere in the letter it is the Spirit who controls believers (cf. 1:17; 3:16; 4:3; 5:18; 6:18). Also in Titus 3:5 the Holy Spirit is the explicit agent of renewal. Houlden (319) even translates the verse "Be renewed by the Spirit in your mind." But this is not what the Greek text says. It speaks about the spirit *of* your mind. Since this is so, we must agree that "it is improbable that God's Spirit would be described as 'of your mind'" (Mitton, 165). The Spirit can be said to be "of Christ" or "of God," but nowhere else is the divine Spirit depicted as belonging to a human being or to part of a human being. In Ephesians' characteristic style of pleonastic accumulation of synonyms, both spirit and mind are employed to designate a person's innermost being (cf. also Meyer, 249; Abbott, 137; J. A. Robinson, 191; Westcott, 68; Barth, 508; Mitton, 165; Bratcher and Nida, *Handbook*, 114–15; RSV; NEB). In this way, the reference is similar to that of 3:16 to the inner person. In Philo "the person within the person" is identified with the νοῦς (cf. *De Congress. quaer. erud. grat.* 97). So the new person is not yet totally new. The present tense of this infinitive underlines the continuous nature of the renewal that is still required, and the passive voice suggests that this takes place as believers allow themselves to be renewed. In line with Paul's thought, the present focus for renewal is not the body but the inner person, the mind, although as the next verse makes clear, this has consequences for external actions. The idea here is functionally equivalent to that of Col 3:10, which speaks of "being renewed in knowledge." There is to be a constant development of believers' perception which will result, in practice, in their ability to choose the good.

24 καὶ ἐνδύσασθαι τὸν καινὸν ἄνθρωπον τὸν κατὰ θεὸν κτισθέντα ἐν δικαιοσύνῃ καὶ ὁσιότητι τῆς ἀληθείας, "and that you should put on the new person who is created in God's likeness in the righteousness and holiness which come from the truth." For this writer, the notion of "the new person" has both corporate and individual connotations. The corporate aspect of the new humanity has been seen in 2:15, where the one new person replaces the two separate entities of Jews and Gentiles. But this new humanity also comes to expression individually. Just as the old person is the person under the dominion of this present age, so the new person is the person under the dominion of the new creation and its life. On the basis of what God has accomplished in Christ, this new identity must be appropriated—"put on"—in such a way that its ethical dimensions become apparent. The notion of the new creation is explicit in the description of the new person as "created in God's likeness." τὸν κατὰ θεὸν κτισθέντα, lit. "created like God," is Ephesians' version of Col 3:10, κατ' εἰκόνα τοῦ κτίσαντος αὐτόν, "according to the image of the one who created it," with its allusion to the language of Gen 1:26. The reference in Ephesians also shares these connotations of the motif of the new Adam in whom the image of God is restored, but as the following phrase, which is an addition to Colossians, shows, its focus is more on the new creation as involving a life which is patterned after God's (cf. also 5:1), an existence in conformity to the divine will. The goal of conduct could be formulated as living κατὰ θεόν in Josephus, *Ant.* 4.6.10,

143 (cf. also *Sentences of Sextus* 201, 216, 399; Wild, "'Be Imitators,'" 135). The believer is already in principle, and is becoming in practice, part of God's new creation (cf. 2:10, 15; cf. also 2 Cor 5:17; Gal 6:15). Here, the language reflects a perspective in which there is a combination of God's gracious initiative and human responsibility, as it is made clear that the new person is created by God but must be put on by the believer.

The new humanity has been created by God to be like him "in the righteousness and holiness which come from the truth." This latter phrase in the Greek text immediately follows the adjectival participle κτισθέντα, "created," and this makes it highly likely that the writer intended the virtues he mentions to be thought of primarily as God's creation (cf. also Schnackenburg, 205). The thought recalls his earlier formulation in 2:10, where believers are said to be "created for good works which God prepared beforehand." At the same time, as we have already seen, the mention of the virtues here in 4:24 is in an overall paraenetical context, in which it is made clear that believers must appropriate the new humanity and its ethical qualities. The choice of righteousness and holiness as the ethical qualities that are specified underlines the point that the new humanity has been recreated to be like God, because both are characteristics of God in LXX Ps 144:17 and Deut 32:4 (cf. also Rev 16:5). As the new creation in God's likeness, believers are to be righteous as he is righteous and holy as he is holy. ὁσιότης, "holiness," occurs elsewhere in the NT only in Luke 1:75 where it is again in conjunction with δικαιοσύνη, "righteousness." The latter term denotes in Ephesians not God's putting humanity in a right relationship with himself nor that right relationship itself, the characteristic Pauline usages, but an ethical virtue (cf. also 5:9; 6:14). Schlier (221–22) opts for the distinction already found in Plato, *Gorgias* 507B, and Philo, *De Abr.* 208, whereby righteousness is doing right in relation to humanity, while holiness is being right in relation to God. Such a distinction is an overdrawn one for NT usage where each term has both moral and religious connotations. It is probably best to see the two terms used together as "a summary of human virtue" (cf. Abbott, 139), as in Wis 9:3 and Luke 1:75 (cf. also the use of the cognate adverbs in 1 Thess 2:10 and adjectives in Titus 1:8). Further support is lent to this interpretation by the fact that most frequently in Plato (*Apology* 35D; *Crito* 54B; *Theatetus* 172B, 176B) and in Philo (*De Sacr.* 57; *De Spec. Leg.* 1.304; 2.180; *De Virt.* 50) both the adjectival and nominal forms of the two terms are employed together to denote virtuous living in general. It is also significant that in Plato's *Theatetus* 176B and its citation in Philo, *De Fug.* 63, this paired expression explains what it means to become like God. Here too in Ephesians, the new humanity displays these qualities that belong to God, because it has been recreated to be like God (cf. Wild, "'Be Imitators,'" 134–35).

The evil desires which characterized the old person sprang from deceit (v 22). Now, by contrast, the virtues which characterize the new person can be said to come from the truth. This truth is ultimately divine reality which has been disclosed in the gospel and the apostolic tradition (cf. 1:13; 4:21). By its very nature it gives rise to such virtues as righteousness and holiness. In the Qumran literature, truth is frequently contrasted with deceit or falsehood (e.g., 1QS 5.10; 1QH 1.26, 27, 30), and in 1QS 4.2–26 this contrast forms part of the discussion of the two spirits and their two ways, as it does in *T. Jud.* 20.1–3 (cf. also *T. Jud.* 14.1). Also in the Qumran material, the lives of the "sons of truth" can be said to be characterized by ways of righteousness of truth (1QS 4.2; cf. also Murphy-O'Connor, "Truth: Paul and Qumran," 208–10). Here in 4:24, the portrait of the new person as created in God's likeness in the righteousness and holiness which come from the truth functions as a challenge to the readers to enter into and to live out that which through their baptism they already know themselves to be. In this way, it is made clear to them that God has not accomplished some instant or total transformation but has made it possible for them to participate in the truth and thereby produce those ethical qualities appropriate to being like God.

Explanation

This passage, as a piece of direct exhortation about both what is inappropriate and what is appropriate to the believer's calling, continues the address to the readers begun in 4:1–3. God's calling of these particular readers has taken them out of their previous situation as Gentiles, with all the negative connotations the writer has attached to that identification, into a new creation in which ethnic differences are no longer the significant factor, into a body which transcends the Jew-Gentile divide (cf. chap. 2). Now they must walk worthily of such a calling by no longer living as they did before the call took effect, by no longer living as Gentiles. The positive side of the writer's exhortation to appropriate conduct appeals to the tradition of teaching the readers have received, and particularly those aspects of the tradition that have ethical implications. This concern has been prepared for in the preceding passage, not only through the notion of living worthily of the calling but also through the importance attached to those ministers whose task is to pass on the apostolic tradition and thereby enable the Church to grow into maturity.

The form the exhortation takes, with its denunciation of the readers' former way of life, which is at the same time a denunciation of the present way of life of outsiders to the Church, and its continual contrasts between such conduct and that which should characterize those who have been taught the Christian tradition, has certain parallels with both Jewish and Hellenistic ethical material. The content of the exhortation owes something to early Christian baptismal catechesis, but more immediately is dependent on Col 3:5–11. Whereas in Colossians the ethical appeal supported the contrast between heavenly and earthly life and the comparison with the readers' former lifestyle was secondary (cf. 3:7, 8), in Ephesians it is the latter contrast which gives the writer's adaptation of the material its distinctive shape and force.

So he begins in vv 17–19 with the strong insistence that his readers are not to fall back into the patterns of thinking and resultant behavior which characterize the surrounding Gentile world. In line with traditional Jewish apologetic, he draws a drastic contrast between such thinking and living and that which God intended. What Gentile Christians should have left behind is an existence in which intellectual perception is totally distorted and, having lost its grip on reality, has become permeated by folly and futility. In such a state, in which the addressees' surrounding society still finds itself, people's thinking has become darkened so that they are blind to the true purpose of life and incapable of apprehending truth. Their relationship to the source of life, God himself, has become broken. This is on account of their culpable ignorance, their hardening of themselves to the sense of God available to them. Accompanying this lack of basic insight is a moral bankruptcy, since dullness of ethical sensitivity has in turn led to general debauchery and unrestrained sexual behaviour, to the active pursuit of all kinds of immorality, and to an insatiable greed which disregards the welfare of others.

The transition from this general denunciation of Gentile conduct to what is expected of Christian believers comes in vv 20, 21, as the readers are told in a striking turn of phrase that all this type of behavior certainly has nothing to do with how they "learned Christ." Between them and their former Gentile lifestyle stands the teaching which can be summed up in Christ, the instruction in the tradition through which the risen Christ shapes the character and lives of believers. The writer is assured that they have not been instructed falsely in such a way as would reproduce the Gentile pattern of life but according to the truth in Jesus, the norm which should call forth the desired quality of life. Three fundamental aspects of that life are set out in vv 22–24. First, it involves stripping off the rotting garment of the old humanity. The old person is in a process of decay which will lead to final ruin, a process brought about through the evil desires generated by deceit, by an ultimately illusory view of life. Believers must live out the significance of what has already taken place through baptism and abandon the old person that they no longer are. Second, since they are not yet completely new, they must allow themselves to be continually renewed in the inner person, particularly in the mind. Third, this restoration to right thinking will result in right conduct, because the readers are to put on the fresh clean clothing of the new humanity with its just and holy living. The new identity, already achieved for believers, has to be appropriated so that its distinctive ethical qualities will become evident. The new person is created to be like God, and this likeness is exhibited in the righteousness and holiness that epitomize a life in a right relationship to God and humanity and also recall characteristics of this God himself. The existence of the new person is ultimately related to the truth of the gospel and of the apostolic tradition, a moral truth able to give rise to the virtues of righteousness and holiness in those who receive it.

Naturally, because of both the form and content of the passage as an ethical exhortation, believers and their lives are the focus of the writer's attention. In both their previous and their present state it is their relationship to God that is emphasized—separated from the life of God in the former case and created in God's likeness in the latter. In the writer's discussion of the existence of the new person, divine initiative and human responsibility go hand in hand. The decisive transference from the old humanity to the new has already been accomplished by God's action, but believers must appropriate this for themselves by abandoning the old person, taking on the new and its activities, and allowing themselves to be renewed. A Christological element is not absent from this section, since it is through Christ or, more precisely, through the catechetical tradition which can be summed up in Christ or in Jesus that the pattern of life of the new creation is passed on.

There are a number of other significant aspects of the thought of this passage. Outsiders to the Gentile Christian membership of the Church are designated Gentiles, which reinforces the impression already gained from earlier in the letter, and particularly from 2:11–22, that the writer himself is a Jewish Christian. This Jewish Christian is impressed by the way in which thinking leads to doing in both negative and positive contexts, by the power of ignorance of God in producing moral corruption, and by the power of a mind renewed in the truth in generating virtue. He also places great importance on the role of Christian tradition and of instruction in that tradition in effecting appropriate Christian conduct. Clearest of all is his conviction that being a Christian means having undergone a radical change—from the old person to the new, from futility of mind to renewal of mind, from the service of deceit to the service of truth, from a process of corruption to one of renewal, from a life of unrestrained passions to one of righteousness and holiness. This stress on the change of identity from the old to the new person is in line with Colossians and with earlier Pauline thought but may well introduce a variation. Here only is the tension between indicative and imperative extended to the terminology of the old and new persons, so that believers can be exhorted to put off the old person that they no longer are and to put on the new person that they already are.

Obviously, hortatory material is intended to effect a particular pattern of life in those to whom it is addressed. Here, the denunciation of Gentile lifestyle, the appeal to Christian catechetical tradition, and the antithetical formulations which characterize the passage are all meant to reinforce the new identity of believers, which is foundational to their new lifestyle, and to guard against their becoming conformed to the ethos of the surrounding society. The use of traditional material means that instruction about the distinctive ethical implications of the new identity can take place by way of reminder of what the readers should already know. This passage lays the essential groundwork on which the more detailed and specific ethical exhortations that follow in the next section, 4:25–5:2, depend. Only from these will it become clear how far and in what ways the conduct advocated by this writer really is new and distinctive in relation to ethical attitudes and behavior in the surrounding society.

Practical Injunctions About the Old and New Life (4:25–5:2)

Bibliography

Agrell, G. *Work, Toil and Sustenance.* Verbum: Hakan Ohlssons, 1976, 126–32. **Coune, M.** "Revêtir l'homme nouveau (Ep 4,23–28)." *AsSeign* 74 (1963) 16–32. **Findlay, J. A.** "Ephesians 4.29." *ExpTim* 46 (1934–35) 429. **Halter, H.** *Taufe und Ethos,* 256–69. **Merklein, H.** "Eph 4,1–5,20 als Rezeption von Kol 3,1–17." In *Kontinuität und Einheit,* ed. P. G. Müller and W. Stenger. Freiburg: Herder, 1981, 194–210. **Sampley, J. P.** "Scripture and Tradition in the Community as Seen in Eph 4:25 ff." *ST* 26 (1972) 101–9. **Schweizer, E.** "Gottesgerechtigkeit und Lasterkataloge bei Paulus (inkl. Kol und Eph)." In *Rechtfertigung.* FS E. Käsemann, ed. J. Friedrich, W. Pöhlmann, and P. Stuhlmacher. Tübingen: Mohr, 1976, 461–77. **Wild, R. A.** "'Be Imitators of God': Discipleship in the Letter to the Ephesians." In *Discipleship in the New Testament,* ed. F. F. Segovia. Philadelphia: Fortress, 1985, 127–43.

Translation

[25] *Therefore, put off falsehood and let each one speak the truth with his neighbor, for we are members of one another.* [26] *If you are angry,*[a] *do not sin; do not let the sun go down on your anger* [27] *and do not give an opportunity to the devil.* [28] *Let the thief no longer steal, but rather let him work hard, doing good with his own hands,*[b] *so that he might have something to share with the person in need.* [29] *Do not let any evil talk come out of your mouth, but whatever is good for building up as the need arises,*[c] *so that it may benefit those who hear.* [30] *And do not grieve the holy Spirit of God, in whom you were sealed for the day of redemption.* [31] *Let all bitterness and rage and anger and shouting and slander be removed from you along with all malice.* [32] *Be kind to one another, compassionate, forgiving one another, just as God in Christ forgave you.*[d] [5:1] *Be imitators of God, therefore, as dearly loved children,* [2] *and live in love, just as Christ loved us*[e] *and gave himself up for us as a fragrant offering*[f] *and sacrifice to God.*

Notes

[a] A literal translation would be "Be angry and do not sin," but the first imperative can have concessive force. See *Comment* on v 26.

[b] Of the numerous textual variants for this clause, six main ones should be noted. The two fullest readings are ταῖς ἰδίαις χερσὶν τὸ ἀγαθόν (ℵ* A D G 81 104 it[c,d,f] vg[cl] syr[p] goth arm eth), and, with the two parts in reverse order, τὸ ἀγαθὸν ταῖς ἰδίαις χερσίν (K 436 1877 syr[h] Theodoret). Then there are readings which have both of these sequences but omit ἰδίαις in each case: ταῖς χερσὶν τὸ ἀγαθόν (p[46,49vid] ℵ[c] B it[ar,e,x] vg[ww] cop[sa ms,bo]) and τὸ ἀγαθὸν ταῖς χερσίν (Ψ 88 326 614 Chrysostom). Finally, there are variants which omit one of the elements of these last two readings, where either τὸ ἀγαθόν stands by itself (P 33 1739 it[m] Clement) or ταῖς χερσίν is found alone (cop[sa] Tertullian). These shortest texts could well have come about as a result of the belief that manual labor and achieving good simply do not belong together. Of the other readings, the sequence in which τὸ ἀγαθόν appears second has by far the stronger support from the external evidence. If a scribe had wanted to change the order, he is more likely to have moved τὸ ἀγαθόν closer to the participle than further away from it. What is not so clear, however, is whether ἰδίαις is likely to be original or an interpolation on the basis of 1 Cor 4:12. Because Ephesians, in any

case, uses phrases from the Pauline letters, because it would be natural to omit ἰδίαις as superfluous, and because it has fairly strong external support, ταῖς ἰδίαις χερσὶν τὸ ἀγαθόν should probably be preferred as the original reading.

c A later copyist (D* F G 181 it vg cl Tertullian Cyprian Ambrosiaster) has changed the original strange combination of words (lit.—"for building up of need") to the expression "for the building up of faith (πίστεως)." See *Comment* below.

d Should the final pronoun of this verse be ὑμῖν, "you," or ἡμῖν, "us"? The former has the support of p46א A G P 81 326 614 *al* it cop sa,bo goth eth Clement Tertullian. Also in its favor is the fact that the second person plural has been used consistently from v 29 onward and continues into 5:1. The latter is read in p49vid B Dgr K Ψ 33 88 630 1739 syr p,h arm Origen. Since it interrupts the flow of the second person plurals, ἡμῖν is the more difficult reading, and it is possible that this clause reflects the "we"-style of traditional formulations. But a traditional formulation is more clearly in view in the two clauses of 5:2 (see *Notes* e and f). Because Col 3:13b, on which this passage appears dependent, reads ἐχαρίσατο ὑμῖν and the writer of Ephesians would have no cause to alter the pronoun in this context, and because ὑμῖν has strong external support and better fits the imperative style of the surrounding paraenesis, it has been preferred.

e There is again a textual question about the person of the plural pronoun at this point. Consideration of the question will also need to take into account the next, and related, textual issue in the same verse. ἡμᾶς, "us," has the slightly stronger external evidence (p46 אc D G K Ψ 33 88 614 630 1739 majority of it syr p,h goth arm Aphraates). Since it can be explained as part of the "we"-style of the traditional formulation that probably continues as far as τῷ θεῷ, and since it is in such close connection with ἡμῶν in the same formulation, which has by far the stronger support in comparison to its variant, it should be preferred to ὑμᾶς, "you" (א* A B P 81 few Old Latin cop sa,bo eth).

f Some manuscripts transpose the word order. Instead of ὑπὲρ ἡμῶν προσφορὰν καὶ θυσίαν, "for us as an offering and sacrifice," א has ὑπὲρ ἡμῶν θυσίαν καὶ προσφορὰν and D 1984 1985 have προσφορὰν ὑπὲρ ἡμῶν καὶ θυσίαν. The reading of 1241, ὑπὲρ ἡμῶν ἐν φθορᾷ, is the result of a transcriptional error. On the issue of whether ὑμῶν, "you," (B 31 69 442 it m,mon cop sa,bo eth Origen) should be read instead of ἡμῶν, "us," the decision is fairly clear-cut. The latter better suits the style of a traditional formulation and has much superior attestation (p46,49 א A D F G K L P Ψ 33 81 614 1739 it d,g vg syr p,h goth arm Clement Aphraates).

Form / Structure / Setting

Having laid the groundwork about the distinction between the way of life of the old humanity and that of the new in 4:17–24, the writer now provides specific injunctions which illustrate this distinction. The first group of these consists of the material in 4:25–5:2, and its structure can be analyzed as follows. First, four distinct and undesirable aspects of behavior are treated—lying (4:25), anger (4:26, 27), stealing (4:28), and evil talk (4:29). In each case a course of action is advocated and then supported by a motivating clause. With the first, third, and fourth of these topics, the course of action is expressed first in negative terms and then in positive. In the case of anger there are two prohibitions before the motivating clause, which is also framed negatively as a prohibition. The other motivating clauses are expressed positively. 4:25 has a causal clause with ὅτι, while 4:28, 29 have purpose clauses with ἵνα. After the fourth injunction a further prohibition follows in 4:30, "And do not grieve the holy Spirit of God." The pattern of exhortation followed by motivation suggests that this prohibition may also serve as a major motivation for all the preceding injunctions, though it is most closely associated with the immediately preceding advice about speech. It parallels the motivating element in 4:27, 28 which also took the form of a prohibition. The pattern which we have observed continues into 4:31, 32, where the removal of a list of negative features associated with anger and their replacement by positive qualities necessary for forgiveness is called for. This is followed by a motivating clause in which the comparative καθώς has causal force—"just as God in Christ forgave you." Some commentators (e.g., Gnilka, 233, 242; Barth, 525, 555; Ernst, 370; Mussner, 138–41) suggest that this first unit of more specific paraenesis ends in fact at 4:32. But rather than marking a new beginning, γίνεσθε οὖν, "Be . . . therefore," in 5:1 draws out the consequences of the exhortation of 4:32 with its opening γίνεσθε. If the recipients of the letter are to forgive one another just as God in Christ forgave them, that means, as 5:1 elaborates, that they are to be imitators of God. The unit ends on a positive note as 5:1, 2 contain two positive exhortations followed by a motivating clause similar to that of 4:32 expressed in positive terms and with an introductory καθώς, "just as Christ loved us and gave himself up for us." The second exhortation, to live in love (5:2), can now be seen as a general summary of the more specific admonitions which have preceded. Its motivating clause about Christ's death with its traditional formulation and cultic imagery provides a rhetorical climax for the pericope. It is only in 5:3, with its change of subject matter to sexual morality and its adversative δέ, that the beginning of a new series of injunctions is marked (cf. also Schnackenburg, 208).

It has become common among NT scholars to classify as *topoi* the individual stereotyped ethical motifs in such series of loosely connected paraenetical material. D. G. Bradley defined the *topos* as "the treatment in independent form of the topic of a proper thought or action, or of a virtue or a vice, etc." and held that it functioned as a general answer to recurring ethical problems (cf. "The *Topos* as a Form in the Pauline Paraenesis," *JBL* 72 [1953] 240; cf. also T. Y. Mullins, "Topos as a New Testament Form," *JBL* 99 [1980] 541–47). There are however three major problems in the discussion to date. Is the *topos* really a paraenetical *form*? Should it be assumed that the *topos* only gives general advice and never addresses specific situations? And is not *topos* a confusing term to use for the phenomenon under discussion anyway? Apart from the matter of independence of treatment, Bradley (*JBL* 72[1953] 238–46) had in fact worked in terms of content more than form and had adduced material from Isocrates, Marcus Aurelius, and the *Testament of Judah* as parallels. Mullins (*JBL* 99 [1980] 541–47) noted the problem about form and attempted to solve it by analyzing Bradley's parallels in order to isolate those which had the same form. He thereby reduced the material to be included under this category to that which has three essential features—an injunction, a reason for the injunction, and a discussion of its consequences. On this definition, none of the topics treated in Eph 4:25–5:2 would qualify as a *topos*, because none of them contains a discussion of the consequences of the injunction. Though Mullins isolated one particular form that paraenetical material can take, his sampling of ethical material was somewhat limited, and he gave no reason why the material which has his three essential features should be designated by the term *topos*, nor why only that material and not other forms of paraenesis could be involved in the treatment of a *topos*. More recently J. C. Brunt ("More on the *topos* as a New Testament Form," *JBL* 104 [1985] 495–500) has argued convincingly that it is invalid to claim that the *topos* phenomenon as such shows that advice is not directed to a specific situation. He also argues that, in fact, in ancient classical rhetoric the term *topos* had a different and more specialized meaning. It was used of the stereotyped lines of argument that could be applied to specific courtroom cases. Brunt claims that, because of the disparity between its ancient and modern usage, the choice of this term for the phenomenon Bradley wished to isolate is unfortunate. This latter point is not so convincing, however, since Brunt does not do justice to the fact that in ancient rhetoric *topos* was used in both a broader and a narrower sense to denote both a common theme employed in a variety of forms and a line of argumentation (cf. Aristotle, *Rhetoric* 1.4–15; 2.22–23; Quintilian 5.10.20; 10.5.12; cf. also D. E. Aune, *The New Testament in Its Literary Environment* [Philadelphia: Westminster, 1987] 172–74,189).

In this light, if the term *topos* is employed of paraenetic material, it would appear wise to restrict its use to the designation of the treatment of an independent general ethical theme and to avoid both applying it to any particular formal characteristics of such treatment and making assumptions about the generality or specificity of its function in a given context. It may well be better, however, to see the material in 4:25–5:2 as a collection of *sententiae*, sentences, frequently in the form of imperatives, which give a rule for conduct in daily life (cf. K. Berger, "Hellenistische Gattungen im Neuen Testament," *ANRW* 2.25.2 [1984] 1049–74; H. Lausberg, *Handbuch der literarischen Rhetorik* [Munich: Max Hueber, 1960] §§ 872–79; cf. also H. D. Betz, *Galatians* [Philadelphia: Fortress, 1979] 291–93). Composition of such ethical sentences was common among Hellenistic philosophers, such as Democritos, Isocrates, Ps.-Isocrates, Diogenes Laertius, and Seneca, and had been adopted by Hellenistic Judaism. If, then, we talk about 4:25–5:2 as epistolary paraenesis carried out by means of sentences on various topics, the type and form of each sentence can be analyzed in its own right. As we have seen from our discussion of structure above, this pericope has seven sentences, and five of those seven sentences (4:25; 4:26, 27; 4:28; 4:31, 32; 5:1, 2) take the form of two exhortations followed by a motivating clause. It could be argued that a sixth sentence (4:29) also takes this form, since although its exhortation only has one verb, a second exhortation is implied. In four of these sentences (4:25; 4:28; 4:29; 4:31, 32), an exhortation with negative form or content is followed by one with positive form or content before the motivation is supplied. In 4:28 the contrast is marked by μηκέτι . . . μᾶλλον δέ, and in 4:29 by μή . . . ἀλλά, while in 4:31, 32 it is carried through by means of a variation on the form of a series of vices followed by a series of virtues. In 4:26, 27 the exhortations are both prohibitions, as is the motivating clause, and in 5:1, 2 the exhortations are both expressed positively. The sentence in 4:30, like a number of the earlier imperatives, takes the form of a prohibition.

As has already been mentioned, the contrast of the sentences in 4:31, 32 makes use of what is a common form in paraenesis—the catalogue of vices and virtues. In fact, as we shall note below, the writer is dependent for his use of this form on Col 3:8, 12. In both sentences the writer has changed the verb from that found in Colossians. But of the five vices in Col 3:8 four appear here in Eph 4:31. Only αἰσχρολογία, "foul talk," is missing (but cf. Eph 5:4), and Ephesians has added πικρία, "bitterness," and κραυγή, "shouting." With the virtues in 4:32, Ephesians has reduced the five nouns of Col 3:12 to two and given them an adjectival form before going on to take up one of the participles of Col 3:13. The other nouns and participle from Col 3:12, 13 have already been employed in Eph 4:2. Although what we have in Eph 4:31, 32 is clearly a variation on a form mediated by Colossians and although a catalogue of vices will appear again in this letter in 5:3–5 and virtues will be mentioned in 5:9, the close juxtaposition of elements of both a vice list and a virtue list here make this an appropriate point at which to discuss briefly this phenomenon, on which a number of scholars have written (cf. Barth, 550–53; K. Berger, "Hellenistische Gattungen im Neuen Testament," *ANRW* 2.25.2 [1984] 1088–92, 1201–4; J. Bergman, "Zum Zwei-Wege-Motiv: Religionsgeschichtliche und exegetische Bemerkungen," *SEÅ* 41/42 [1976–77] 27–56; H. D. Betz, *Lukian von Samosata und das Neue Testament* [Berlin: Akademie-Verlag, 1961] 185–94, 206–11; G. E. Cannon, *The Use of Traditional Materials in Colossians* [Macon, GA: Mercer University Press, 1983] 51–94; P. Carrington, *The Primitive Christian Catechism* [Cambridge: CUP, 1940]; B. S. Easton, "New Testament Ethical Lists," *JBL* 51 [1932] 1–12; E. Kamlah, *Die Form der katalogischen Paränese im Neuen Testament* [Tübingen: Mohr, 1964]; G. Klein, *Der älteste christliche Katechismus und die jüdische Propaganda-Literatur* [Berlin: G. Reimer, 1909]; N. J. McEleney, "The Vice Lists of the Pastoral Epistles," *CBQ* 36 [1974] 203–19; O'Brien, *Colossians*, 179–81; E. Schweizer, "Gottesgerechtigkeit und Lasterkataloge bei Paulus [inkl. Kol und Eph],"in *Rechtfertigung,* ed. J. Friedrich, W. Pöhlmann, and P. Stuhlmacher [Göttingen: Vandenhoeck & Ruprecht, 1976] 461–77; E. Schweizer, "Traditional Ethical Patterns in the Pauline and Post-Pauline Letters and Their Development [lists of vices and house-tables]," in *Text and Interpretation,* ed. E. Best and R. McL. Wilson. [Cambridge: CUP, 1979] 195–209; M. J. Suggs, "The Christian Two Way Tradition: Its Antiquity, Form, and Function," in *Studies in New Testament and Early Christian Literature,* ed. D. E. Aune [Leiden: E. J. Brill, 1972] 60–74; J. Thomas, "Formgesetze des Begriffs-Katalogs im N.T.," *TZ* 24 [1968] 15–28; A Vögtle, *Die Tugend- und Lasterkataloge im Neuen Testament* [Münster: Aschendorff, 1936]; S. Wibbing, *Die Tugend- und Lasterkataloge im Neuen Testament* [Berlin: A. Töpelmann, 1959]). There are two main ways in which the lists appear in the NT. Vices or virtues can be part of a descriptive list which functions in an apologetic or paraenetic context (cf. Matt 15:19; Mark 7:21, 22; Rom 1:29–31; 1 Cor 5:10, 11; 6:9, 10; 2 Cor 6:6, 7; 12:20, 21; Gal 5:19–23; 1 Tim 1:9, 10; 3:2, 3; 6:4, 5; 2 Tim 3:2–5; Titus 1:7, 8; 3:3; Jas 3:17; 1 Pet 4:3; Rev 21:8; 22:15), or they can be part of an actual exhortation, as here in 4:31, 32 (cf. also 5:3, 4; Col 3:5, 8, 12; Rom 13:13; Phil 4:8; 1 Tim 6:11; 1 Pet 2:1; 3:8; 2 Pet 1:5–7). It is frequently and quite plausibly suggested that much of this widespread early Christian use of ethical lists is likely to have originated in baptismal catechesis. Particularly when such lists are linked with the language of "putting off the old person" and "putting on the new," as in Col 3:8, 12 and here in Eph 4:31, 32 with its connection with 4:22–24, a reminder of the significance of the readers' baptism may well be in view.

The ultimate origin of lists of virtues and vices and the route by which they entered into Christian usage are more debated issues. Numerous analogies can be found in both Jewish and Greco-Roman literature, but as yet no hypothesis about a single source or about the tradition history of the material has won the day. Some hold the primary influence to be the OT (e.g., the Holiness Code of Lev 18, 19 or the lists of blessings and curses in Deut 27–30) and the Two Ways pattern in Judaism (cf. Carrington, Cannon). Some wish to emphasize, in particular, Jewish proselyte catechisms, which they have attempted to reconstruct (cf. Klein, Carrington). For others, the Dead Sea Scrolls (e.g., 1QS 3.13–4.26) deserve to be recognized as an especially influential source within Judaism (cf. Wibbing, Kamlah), which, it is claimed, had in its turn been affected by the dualistic cosmology of Iranian religion (cf. Kamlah). Others still have found parallels in Stoicism and popular Greco-Roman philosophy to be the closest (cf. Easton, Vögtle, Betz, Berger), while it can also be pointed out that such material had already influenced Hellenistic Judaism, for example in Wis 14:25, 26 and Philo, *De Sacrif.* 20–45 (cf. Easton, Wibbing, Kamlah, Berger).

What is more important for our present purpose, however, is the use to which Paul and the writer of Ephesians put these ethical lists. Generally in Paul, these typical and somewhat random lists are not changed to represent ethical values that could be considered distinctively Christian. In this regard, they reflect his assumption that the behavior of believers should at least match that enjoined by the conventional ethical wisdom of his day. As in the case of the taking over of other types of traditional material, the expectation that these standards will receive general consent adds to the persuasiveness of Paul's appeal. The distinctive aspect of their use comes from the overall context in which they are placed, a context which brings them into relation with the eschatological and Christological dimensions of Paul's gospel. Consequently, on the one hand, the vices are seen as the manifestations of the old sinful order and, on the other, the virtues are produced by the new spiritual order inaugurated through Christ. In this way, they provide inclusive and concrete norms, which do not merely await achievement but whose accomplishment has already been set in motion because of believers' new situation in Christ. From what has already been seen of the ethical groundwork the writer to the Ephesians has laid in 4:17–24, it is clear that the same general considerations apply to his variation on the lists of vices and virtues from Colossians in this passage. More specifically, and in keeping with the letter's concern for the unity and edification of the Church, the vices and virtues selected are those which will either disrupt or enhance the life of a community. The lists also suggest an abundance, though not a completeness, of similar characteristics and would appeal to a writer whose pleonastic style has dominated the first part of the letter.

This pericope continues the pattern of dependence on Colossians that was noted in the previous section and in earlier passages of the letter. Eph 4:17–24 had been dependent on material from Col 3:5–11, and earlier 4:2–4 had drawn on Col 3:12–15. Now the writer returns to other elements in these sections (Col 3:8, 9a, 12–14a) as the main source of his paraenesis. The extent of the relationship can be set out as follows:

Ephesians		Colossians
4:25 διὸ ἀποθέμενοι τὸ ψεῦδος	3:8a	νυνὶ δὲ ἀπόθεσθε καὶ ὑμεῖς τὰ πάντα
	3:9a	μὴ ψεύδεσθε εἰς ἀλλήλους
4:26 ὀργίζεσθε καὶ μὴ ἁμαρτάνετε	3:8b	ὀργήν
4:29 πᾶς λόγος σαπρὸς ἐκ τοῦ στόματος ὑμῶν μὴ ἐκπορευέσθω	3:8b	αἰσχρολογίαν ἐκ τοῦ στόματος ὑμῶν
4:31 πᾶσα πικρία καὶ θυμὸς καὶ ὀργὴ καὶ κραυγὴ καὶ βλασφημία ἀρθήτω ἀφ' ὑμῶν σὺν πάσῃ κακίᾳ	3:8b	ὀργήν, θυμόν, κακίαν, βλασφημίαν
4:32 γίνεσθε εἰς ἀλλήλους χρηστοί, εὔσπλαγχνοι, χαριζόμενοι ἑαυτοῖς καθὼς καὶ ὁ θεὸς ἐν Χριστῷ ἐχαρίσατο ὑμῖν	3:12	ἐνδύσασθε . . . σπλάγχνα οἰκτιρμοῦ, χρηστότητα
	3:13	χαριζόμενοι ἑαυτοῖς . . . καθὼς καὶ ὁ κύριος ἐχαρίσατο ὑμῖν οὕτως καὶ ὑμεῖς
5:1 ὡς τέκνα ἀγαπητά	3:12	ὡς ἐκλεκτοὶ τοῦ θεοῦ, ἅγιοι καὶ ἠγαπημένοι
5:2 καὶ περιπατεῖτε ἐν ἀγάπῃ	3:14a	ἐπὶ πᾶσιν δὲ τούτοις τὴν ἀγάπην

As can be seen, Eph 4:25 takes up the notions of putting off and lying or falsehood from Col 3:8, 9a. The injunction about anger in 4:26 can be linked with the noun "anger" in Col 3:8b. "Evil talk out of your mouth" in 4:29 employs the thought and some of the language of the same verse in Colossians, and four of the six vices in 4:31 are also listed in Col 3:8b. The virtues of kindness and compassion expressed in adjectival form in 4:32 are found in nominal form in Col 3:12, and "forgiving one another, just as God in Christ forgave you" is Ephesians' version of "forgiving one another . . . , just as the Lord forgave you, so also should you forgive" in Col 3:13. "As dearly loved children" in Eph 5:1 replaces "as God's chosen ones, holy and dearly loved" in Col 3:12, while the emphasis on living in love in Eph 5:2 recalls the similar emphasis of Col 3:14a.

In line with the primarily traditional and unoriginal nature of paraenesis in Hellenistic writings, the writer not only relies on Colossians but also fills out his exhortation with additional traditional material. In 4:25, 26 this includes OT material, LXX Zech 8:16 and LXX Ps 4:5, in all probability mediated through Jewish paraenetic tradition (see *Comment* on these verses; cf. also Lincoln, "The Use of the OT in Ephesians," *JSNT* 14 [1982] 42, 43). 4:30 may well contain an allusion to Isa 63:10. The notion of the imitation of God found in 5:1 was traditional in Hellenistic Judaism (cf. *T. Ash.* 4.3; Philo, *De Sacr.* 68; *De Spec. Leg.* 4.73; *De Virt.* 168). The language and imagery of sacrifice in 5:2 also recall scriptural terminology—προσφορὰ καὶ θυσία (cf. LXX Ps 39:6) and εἰς ὀσμὴν εὐωδίας (cf., e.g., LXX Exod 29:18; Ezek 20:41), though the latter had already been employed by Paul in Phil 4:18 (cf. also 2 Cor 2:14–16). Language from other Pauline letters also forms part of the writer's traditional material. The last part of 4:25 takes up the phrase ἀλλήλων μέλη, "members of one another," found in Rom 12:5. The notions of working hard and doing something with one's own hands in 4:28b take up the terminology of 1 Cor 4:12 (cf. also 1 Thess 4:11). The formulation in 5:2, "Christ loved us and gave himself up for us," recalls the similar wording of Gal 2:20.

When connections are sought between this pericope and the rest of the letter, then clearly the closest links are with the immediately preceding pericope, 4:17–24. The negative and positive injunctions and motivating statements can all be related to the two basic notions which carry over from 4:22–24—the negative one of "putting off the old person" and the positive one of "putting on the new person." In fact 4:25, with its ἀποτίθεσθαι, "to put off" (cf. 4:22), and ἀλήθεια, "truth" (cf. 4:24), has specific verbal links with both these notions. In addition, the call to be imitators of God in 5:1 is inherent in the thought that the life of the new creation is one that is patterned after God's (cf. 4:24). The foundations for this pericope's emphasis on living in love, as 5:2 summarizes it, have been laid in 4:1–16, where love itself has been seen to be the essential ingredient in the life of the Church (cf. 4:2, 15, 16), where the notion of the body and the interdependence necessary for its growth (cf. 4:16) prepares for the thought of being members of one another in 4:25, and where the stress on building up others (cf. 4:12, 16) anticipates its mention in 4:29. Several concepts in 4:25–5:2 take us all the way back to the opening *berakah:* sealing, the Spirit, and redemption in 4:30 take up the terminology of 1:13, 14, while God's forgiveness mentioned in 4:32 may recall 1:7. Looking ahead to what follows in the rest of the paraenesis, we see that exhortation by means of contrasting patterns of behavior continues throughout 5:3–20. The language of "walking" for this behavior in 5:2 will be taken up again in 5:8, 15; the appeal to the example of Christ's love in 5:2 will feature again in the passage on marriage (cf. 5:25–28); and the devil mentioned in 4:27 will be given prominence again in the discussion of believers' spiritual battle (cf. 6:11; also 2:2; 6:16).

The nature of the pericope's paraenesis, with its traditional material of general applicability, means that inferences which move directly from individual exhortations to the supposed setting of the recipients are to be avoided. It should not be assumed, for example, on the basis of 4:25, 28 that the writer knows specifically that there are thieves and liars amongst his readers who need to be confronted. Nor does the basic nature of such paraenesis mean that it is being addressed to those who are newly baptized or converted (cf. also Schlier, 223; Gnilka, 234; idem, "Paränetische Traditionen," 400–401, 405; Halter, *Taufe,* 257). The links of some of the material with baptism, noted above, are far more indirect. What the addressees are being told would not have been new to them. Early Christian paraenesis often consists of reminders to believers, through selected examples, of what they had learned at the time of their baptism and of the sort of behavior expected of them as new persons. The fact that both this passage and 5:3–20 are given over to this sort of reminder does suggest, however, that the writer was less than satisfied with the general level of ethical attainment of his Gentile Christian readers and wanted them not only to be more aware of their responsibilities but also to carry them out more effectively. In particular, his choice and grouping of issues such as speaking the truth, dealing with anger, hard work and sharing, edifying speech, kindness, and love, show, as we know already from 4:1–16, how concerned this writer is with the Church's demonstration of its unity in love and the practical actions necessary for the realization of this ideal.

Comment

25 Διὸ ἀποθέμενοι τὸ ψεῦδος λαλεῖτε ἀλήθειαν ἕκαστος μετὰ τοῦ πλησίον αὐτοῦ, ὅτι ἐσμὲν ἀλλήλων μέλη, "Therefore put off falsehood, and let each one speak the truth with his neighbor, for we are members of one another." The opening διό marks both the link with the preceding pericope and a move from the more general to the more specific, as the deeds appropriate to those newly created in God's likeness are outlined. The link is both verbal (cf. "put off" in v 22 and "truth" in v 24) and conceptual. To put off the old person, corrupted by the desires born of deceit, is to put off falsehood. Since the new person is created in the righteousness and holiness which come from truth, it is speaking the truth that must take the place of lying. The aorist participle ἀποθέμενοι could be translated as a participle—"having put off falsehood, let each one speak the truth"—or be taken as above (cf. also Schnackenburg, 210) as one of the NT instances of the use of the participle for the imperative. In Col 3:9 the prohibition against lying had been based on the indicative (in the form of an aorist participle) of having put off the old person. Does "having put off lying" now form a similar indicative here? What tells against this in the context of Ephesians is that the notion of putting off the old person has already been discussed by this writer, and, as we have seen, the infinitive form in which it occurred in 4:22 had imperatival force. This suggests that the specific act of doing away with lying may also be seen by the writer not so much as one which has already been accomplished but more as one which is still incumbent on his readers. It is held by some (e.g., Mussner, 139) that the singular τὸ ψεῦδος refers to deception as a way of life. But both the dependence on Col 3:8, 9 and the fact that this singular is frequently used collectively for "lies" tells against such an interpretation. The exhortation not to lie does not occur in the undisputed Pauline letters but is found elsewhere in early Christian literature in *Did.* 3.5.

Speaking the truth with one's neighbor is to be cultivated in place of the old negative action of lying. This positive injunction is framed in the words of Zech 8:16, though the LXX has πρὸς τὸν πλησίον instead of μετὰ τοῦ πλησίον. Sampley (*ST* 26 [1972] 107–9) has argued that the original context in Zech 8 has influenced the form of this pericope in Ephesians. But the parallels he adduces are very strained, and he has failed to convince others (cf. also Agrell, *Work*, 215 n. 25; Halter, *Taufe*, 634 n. 5). It must even be doubtful whether the writer has made direct use of the OT at all. It may well be that, instead, he is dependent on Jewish ethical tradition which had already taken up the OT wording in its formulation (cf. Gnilka, 234; Ernst, 367). Indeed, in *T. Dan* 5.2 the precise LXX wording of Zech 8:16 is found in conjunction with a warning about anger and lying, as here in Ephesians (cf. also *T. Benj.* 10.3, "Do the truth each of you to his neighbor," which has μετά plus the genitive). The tradition conveys the message that one's neighbor has a right to the truth. It can also be said that to rob one's neighbor of that right, and there by of the freedom to respond to the real situation, is to dehumanize him or her.

The exhortation to tell the truth rather than lies is backed by an appeal to solidarity in terms of being members of one another. Clearly this assumes the notion of the Church as the body of Christ which has been employed earlier in the letter, though its implications for the mutual dependence of the members of the body, central to Paul's use of the image in 1 Cor 12:12–27 and Rom 12:4, 5, were not exploited until 4:15, 16, and the terms "members" and "body" will not be brought together in Ephesians until 5:30. The neighbor of the exhortation, who in Judaism would have been a companion in the covenant, now takes on the specific shape of a fellow member of the body of Christ. In this body, which is a paradigm of harmonious human relationships, there is no room for lies which poison communication and breed suspicion instead of mutual trust. As Mackay (*God's Order*, 185) puts it graphically, "a lie is a stab into the very vitals of the body of Christ." The point has already been established a little earlier in 4:15, where the writer insists that the essential means of building up the body of Christ is speaking the truth in love.

26, 27 ὀργίζεσθε καὶ μὴ ἁμαρτάνετε, "If you are angry, do not sin." This exhortation is in the words of LXX Ps 4:5 (ET Ps 4:4). The original Hebrew text, with its injunction about an attitude toward God, may well speak of trembling rather than anger, but this is irrelevant to the use of the Greek version by the writer to the Ephesians. It is in any case difficult to tell whether his use of the LXX is a direct or an indirect one. Since the juxtaposition of injunctions about lying and anger formed part of paraenetic tradition (cf. *T. Dan* 5.2), it could well be that, like Zech 8:16 in 4:25, this scriptural wording was also current in Christian paraenesis which drew on both Jewish and Hellenistic sources.

It is usually agreed that the first imperative in this formulation should be construed as having concessive force and that, in the syntax, parataxis is employed instead of a subordinate concessive clause (cf. BDF § 387 [1]; Schlier, 224 n. 3). It is important, however, to be clear about the force of this construction. It is not granting permission to be angry. Although v 26b recognizes that anger will occur, v 27 indicates how dangerous it is and v 31 repudiates all anger (cf. also 6:4). The focus of v 26a, then, is on not sinning by indulging in anger. Its paradoxical formulation was not meant to encourage speculation about what types of anger might be permissible. Whatever the merits of the traditional notion of righteous anger at injustice or the modern notion of the healthiness of expressing rather than suppressing anger, they should not be thought to have support in the concessive aspect of this prohibition. Its force may be conveyed by a paraphrase, "Anger is to be avoided at all costs, but if, for whatever reason, you do get angry, then refuse to indulge such anger so that you do not sin." In this way, the exhortation is very much in line with the view of anger elsewhere in the NT. Jas 1:19, 20 has similar force, "Let every man . . . be slow to anger; for the anger of man does not work the righteousness of God" (cf. also Matt 5:22; Gal 5:20; Col 3:8; 1 Tim 2:8; Titus 1:7). There is also an overwhelmingly negative evaluation of anger in wisdom sentences from a variety of sources (cf. Prov 15:1, 18; 22:24; 29:8, 11; Eccl 7:9, "Be not quick to anger, for anger lodges in the bosom of fools"; Sir 1:22; 27:30; *T. Dan* 2.1–5.1; Lucian, *Dem.* 51; Seneca, *De Ira;* Dio, *Orat.* 32; Ps-Phocylides 63–64; *Did.* 3.2, "Never give way to anger, for anger leads to murder"; *b. Ber.* 29b, "Do not flare up, so that you do not sin"). For Ephesians, anger and the estrangement which accompanies it, both as cause and result, are incompatible with the new relationships of those who are members of one another in the body of Christ (cf. v 25).

ὁ ἥλιος μὴ ἐπιδυέτω ἐπὶ παροργισμῷ ὑμῶν, "do not let the sun go down on your anger." παροργισμός is a *hapax legomenon* in the NT. Elsewhere, it is used most frequently to refer to provocation to anger, but here, as in LXX Jer 21:5, it has passive force and denotes the anger that has been provoked. Stylistic variation accounts for the use of this term, and no real difference of meaning from ὀργή should be read into it. If there is any connotation of less permanent anger or irritation, that comes from the context rather than the term itself (*pace* Meyer, 255; Abbott, 140; Barth, 514). Sunset was thought of as the time limit for a number of activities (cf., e.g., Deut 24:15) and is the time limit for dealing with anger in a formulation that had become associated with the Pythagoreans, but which may well have been commonplace. Plutarch says, "We should next pattern ourselves after the Pythagoreans, who, though related not at all by birth, yet sharing a common discipline, if ever they were led by anger into recrimination, never let the sun go down before they joined right hands, embraced each other, and were reconciled" (*Moralia* 488c). A similar practice is enjoined on the Essenes in the Damascus Rule—"They shall rebuke each man his brother according to the commandment and shall bear no rancor from one day to the next" (CD 7.2, 3). So the second prohibition reinforces the first. Sin is to be avoided by ensuring that anger, if it occurs, is brief and is expelled immediately. It so easily becomes destructive of harmony that it certainly must not be allowed to smolder overnight.

On the basis of similarities with texts from the Qumran literature like the one quoted above (cf. CD 7.2, 3; 9.6; 1QS 5.26–6:1), Gnilka (235–36) argues that the primary reference of vv 26, 27 is to anger against an erring member of the community and that in fact the verses function as a positive reminder of believers' responsibilities toward others in the community. He is followed by Agrell (*Work*, 129), who finds a connection with the exhortation of v 28 about work and thence also with 2 Thess 3:15 and its discussion of the disciplining of those who will not work, yet in such a way as to treat them not as enemies but as brothers. Certainly these verses would be applicable to dealing with anger against an erring brother or sister, and it is interesting that Eph 4:26 is quoted in the context of a discussion of discipline in Pol. *Phil.* 12.1. But to narrow the reference of the prohibitions to anger in disciplinary cases is unwarranted. There would surely have had to be far more indications from the context for the readers to have taken this as the meaning (cf. also Ernst, 367; Schnackenburg, 211 n. 499).

μηδὲ δίδοτε τόπον τῷ διαβόλῳ, "and do not give an opportunity to the devil." This third prohibition provides a motivation for the preceding two (*pace* Ernst, 368, and Mussner, 139, who wish to treat it independently of the topic of anger). Before the quotation of Zech 8:16 in *T. Dan* 5.2, which we have already noted, anger is associated not only with lying but also with the devil. "Avoid wrath, and hate lying, in order that the Lord may dwell among you, and Beliar may flee from you. . . . Anger and falsehood together are a double-edged evil, and work together to perturb the reason. And when the soul is continually perturbed, the Lord withdraws from it and Beliar rules it" (*T. Dan* 4.7–5.1, cf. also 1.7, 8; 3.6). A similar association can be found later in *Herm. Man.* 5.1.3, "For the Lord dwells in long-suffering and the devil dwells in ill temper." Here in Ephesians also, indulgence in anger is seen as giving free scope to the devil. The writer thinks in terms of a personal power of evil, which is pictured as lurking around angry people ready to exploit the situation (cf. also 1 Tim 3:7; 2 Tim 2:26; 1 Pet 5:8). Despite what he has said about believers having been seated with Christ in the heavenly realm, he deems it necessary for them to be on their guard against the devil (cf. also 6:11). In particular, anger in the community is "a kind of 'fifth-column' available for cooperation with the enemy" (Mitton, 169). In 2 Cor 2:11 Paul in a similar vein had claimed that forgiveness prevents a designing Satan from gaining the advantage over believers. It is noticeable that the undisputed Paulines speak only of Satan (cf. also Rom 16:20; 1 Cor 5:5; 7:5; 2 Cor 11:14; 12:7; 1 Thess 2:18), while the term "the devil" occurs in Ephesians (cf. also 6:11), as well as in the LXX and later NT and early Christian writings (cf. 1 Tim 3:7; 2 Tim 2:26; Jas 4:7; 1 Pet 5:8; *Mart. Pol.* 3.1; *2 Clem.* 18.2; Ign. *Eph.* 10.3; *Smyrn.* 9.1).

28 ὁ κλέπτων μηκέτι κλεπτέτω, μᾶλλον δὲ κοπιάτω ἐργαζόμενος ταῖς ἰδίαις χερσὶν τὸ ἀγαθόν, ἵνα ἔχῃ μεταδιδόναι τῷ χρείαν ἔχοντι, "Let the thief no longer steal, but rather let him work hard, doing good with his own hands, so that he might have something to share with the person in need." It is sometimes claimed that the present participle κλέπτων represents action preceding the main verb which has frequentative or durative force and can be translated as an imperfect, "he who used to steal" (cf. BDF § 339 [3]; Moule, *Idiom-Book*, 206). A better explanation, however, is that with the definite article the present participle virtually becomes a noun and has a timeless force (cf. Moulton, *Grammar* 1:126–27; Schlier, 225 n. 6; Agrell, *Work*, 215 n. 36). Injunctions against theft are of course found in the Decalogue (Exod 20:15; Deut 5:19) and the Holiness Code (Lev 19:11) and are repeated in the NT summaries of the law (Mark 10:19; Rom 13:9). Theft would not have been uncommon among slaves, in particular, in first-century society (cf. Gnilka, 271), and it could well be that Philem 18 indicates that Onesimus was guilty of it. But the main reason for its mention here is that it was a traditional topic in paraenetic material and could serve as another typical activity of the old sinful humanity which the readers are to put off (cf. also Rom 2:21; 1 Cor 6:10; 1 Pet 4:15; *Did.* 3.5).

Stealing is to be replaced by hard work. A similar relationship between these two topics can be found in a number of places, e.g., Ps-Phocylides 153–54, "Work hard so that you can live from your own means; for every idle man lives from what his hands can steal"; and *b. Qidd.* 29a, "R. Judah [c. 150 C.E.] said: He who does not teach his son a craft teaches him to be a robber." The high value placed on work in this exhortation was shared by a variety of ethical traditions with which the writer and his readers may have been familiar (cf. Exod 20:9; Sir 7:15; Epictetus, *Diss.* 1.16.16–17; 3.26.6–7; Ps-Phocylides 153–74; Dio, *Orat.* 7.112, 124–25, who recommends the urban poor to work with their hands). For a study of work in the NT and a comparison with OT and early Jewish material, see G. Agrell, *Work, Toil and Sustenance*, and for insight into Paul's own attitudes to work, see R. F. Hock, *The Social Context of Paul's Ministry* (Philadelphia: Fortress, 1980). It had been Paul's policy to support his missionary activity by his work as an artisan, making tents from leather, and he exhorted his congregations also to work with their hands (1 Thess

4:11, 12; cf. also 2 Thess 3:6–12). The formulation here in Ephesians combines expressions from 1 Cor 4:12 ("we work hard with our own hands") and Gal 6:10 ("let us do good"). In its present setting the emphasis on working with one's hands also plays its part in the contrast with theft which is accomplished with one's hands (cf. the citation above from Ps-Phocylides 153–54).

Paul had employed the verb κοπιᾶν and its cognate noun in his depiction of his apostolic sufferings in the end-times (cf. 1 Cor 4:12; 2 Cor 6:5; 11:23, 27). The taking up of this verb here enables the effort, the toil, and the trouble of work to be highlighted and suggests that, despite its predominantly realized eschatology, this letter has not lost sight of the struggle and the laborious aspect of work (cf. also Agrell, *Work*, 132). The expression "to do good" had been used in Gal 6:10 in the general sense of that which is morally worthy and beneficial to others. Agrell (*Work*, 129) argues, however, that since in Eph 4:29 ἐργάζεσθαι is complemented by the phrase "with his own hands" and the last clause suggests that the results of such work are to be shared, ἐργάζεσθαι τὸ ἀγαθόν should be understood as "to make a good product." But it is probable that this is too narrow an interpretation, for in the very next verse and later in Eph 6:8 and then elsewhere in the Pauline corpus in the various formulations in which believers are exhorted to do good (e.g., 1 Thess 5:15; 2 Thess 2:17; 2 Cor 9:8; Col 1:10; 1 Tim 6:18), "the good" has the same more general sense as in Gal 6:10, and in some contexts that can include the generous giving of material resources. Here also, working hard with one's hands is thought of as doing something good, because it produces that which becomes the means of sharing.

This is the explicit motivation provided for work in the last part of the verse. It is the medium for caring for the needy person. Exhortations to share with the poor and needy are not uncommon in early Jewish and early Christian literature (e.g., *T. Iss.* 7.5; *T. Zeb.* 6.1–8; Ps-Phocylides 22; 1 Tim 6:18; *Did.* 4.5–8). In Rom 12:13 Paul had urged, "Contribute to the needs of the saints" (cf. also 2 Cor 8, 9). Given the context, the needy person here in Eph 4 is also likely to have been thought of primarily, though not necessarily exclusively, as within the Church (cf. v 25). So "theft and indolence cause damage to Christ and his body, whereas work, by enabling the worker to aid the needy, builds up the body of Christ" (Agrell, *Work*, 128). The motive for work is not individual profit but rather communal well-being. This is different from the explicit reasons given for working in the discussions in 1 and 2 Thessalonians, namely to retain the respect of outsiders and not to become dependent on others, and is perhaps more directly related to the ideal of Christian love.

When this ethical sentence is taken as a whole, it illustrates beautifully the radical change involved in the call to put off the old humanity and put on the new. The thief is to become a philanthropist, as the illegal taking of the old way of life is replaced by the generous giving of the new.

It is becoming common to contrast the view of work in Ephesians as part of the unqualified positive approach of the deutero-Pauline material (cf. also 2 Thess 3:10; Acts 20:34–35) with the more ambiguous perspective on work of Paul himself (cf. Agrell, *Work*, 104, 115, followed by Hock, *The Social Context of Paul's Ministry*, 17). Sometimes, however, this contrast is taken too far. It is true that in 1 Thessalonians and in 1 Corinthians Paul treats work as a necessary element in a Christian existence conditioned by an imminent eschatological hope, and that such imminence has receded in Ephesians, so that despite the recognition of the negative aspect of toil, there is nothing in this letter that corresponds to "Let those who buy live as though they had no goods, and those who deal with the world as though they had no dealings with it" in 1 Cor 7:30, 31. But to argue that Paul never expressly says that work is God's will and shows no positive interest in work as a socially vital element and a prerequisite for generosity (cf. Agrell, *Work*, 105, 216 n. 53) evidences an atomistic and dogmatic approach to the letters that fails to do justice to the connection between 1 Thess 4:11, 12 and the preceding material in 4:1, 2, 9, 10a. It likewise fails to account for passages such as Rom 12:3 and 2 Cor 8, 9 and presses occasional paraenetical texts for a whole theology of work which they are incapable of providing.

29 πᾶς λόγος σαπρὸς ἐκ τοῦ στόματος ὑμῶν μὴ ἐκπορευέσθω, ἀλλὰ εἴ τις ἀγαθὸς πρὸς οἰκοδομὴν τῆς χρείας, ἵνα δῷ χάριν τοῖς ἀκούουσιν, "Do not let any evil talk come out of your mouth, but whatever is good for building up as the need arises, so that it may benefit those who hear." The contrasting middle section of this sentence, in fact, serves as a second exhortation once the verb from the initial prohibition is supplied. With its motivating purpose clause, following two clauses with hortatory force, this sentence can then be seen to be following the dominant pattern we have observed for the pericope—two exhortations followed by a motivating clause. The Semitisms of the Greek, including the use of πᾶς together with οὐ or μή (cf. Eph 5:5; John 3:16; 6:39; 12:46; Acts 10:14; Rom 3:20; 1 Cor 1:29; cf. also Moulton, *Grammar* 3:196–97), the traditional language of "proceed out of the mouth" (e.g., LXX Num 32:34; Deut 8:3; Jer 17:16; cf. also Matt 4:4; Luke 4:22; Jas 3:10), and the topic of speech found so frequently in Jewish wisdom literature (e.g., Prov 10:31, 32; 12:17–19; 15:2, 4; Sir 5:10–14; 18:15–19; 21:25, 26; cf. also 1QS 7.9; CD 10.17, 18) suggest that here again the writer may well have taken over traditional Jewish paraenetical material (cf. also *T. Isaac* 4.14, 17—"Be careful that an evil word does not come forth from your mouth. . . . See that you do not make sport with your tongue lest an evil word come forth from your mouth").

The term σαπρός is employed elsewhere in the NT in its literal sense of "rotten" or "decaying"—of a tree and in contrast to ἀγαθός in Matt 7:17, 18 (cf. also Matt 12:33, 34) and of fish and in contrast to καλός in Matt 13:48 (cf. C. Lindhagen, "Die Wurzel ΣΑΠ- im NT und AT," *UUA* 40 [1950] 27–69, on such contrasting word-groups). Here, however, it is likely to have its more general figurative sense of evil or unwholesome, unless the force of the salt imagery in "speech . . . seasoned with salt" in Col 4:6 is as a preservative and the writer has that text in mind. What is prohibited under the category of evil talk (cf. Col 3:8; Eph 5:4) includes obscenity, abusive language, and spreading malicious gossip. The focus is on the destructive power of words and the harm they can produce in communal life.

What is required instead is the use of words in a constructive fashion—that which is good for building up. Just as the ministers of the word and the whole Church have building up as their goal (cf. 4:12, 16), so individual believers must make this the aim of their communication with each other. In terms of speech, that which is morally good (cf. the use of ἀγαθός in the previous verse and ἀγαθωσύνη in 5:9) is that which builds up others rather than tears them down. This includes not only the addressing of one another in psalms and hymns and spiritual songs mentioned in 5:19, but also any words that build the confidence of one's sisters and brothers, encourage them in their tasks, and create goodwill. The additional phrase τῆς χρείας, which presumably came to the writer's mind as a result of the use of the same noun in the previous sentence, is difficult to classify grammatically. A later copyist alleviated the difficulty by substituting πίστεως for χρείας (see *Note* c). As it stands, the phrase could be an objective genitive—for the building up of what is needed or what is lacking (cf. Abbott, 143; BAGD, 885; Gnilka, 238)—or a genitive of quality, where the noun supplies an attributive that would ordinarily be provided by an adjective—for the needed building up (cf. Schlier, 226; Barth, 519). Our translation—"for building up as the need arises"—is meant to convey this latter sense. Findlay (*ExpTim* 46 [1934–35] 429) takes a quite different line, arguing for χρεία in the sense used by the rhetoricians of "pointed saying" or "good story," and translates, "Let no unclean speech issue from your lips, but such witty talk as is useful for edification." But attractive as such a sentiment might be, the suggestion involves taking τῆς χρείας with λόγος, and they are too far apart for this to be possible.

The motivating purpose clause, "so that it may benefit those who hear," reinforces the exhortation but is strictly speaking redundant, since what builds up others will be of benefit to them. The force of χάριν διδόναι is "to do a favor" or "to confer a benefit." Instead of harming others with their words, believers are to ensure that their language has a beneficial effect on their listeners. Human words can be vehicles of divine grace, but it should not be assumed on the basis of the use of the term χάρις that the writer has such a thought in mind here.

It can now be seen that the sentence of v 29 has links with that of v 28. ἀγαθός and χρεία function as catchword links: the contrast between evil and good is repeated but now associated with speech rather than action, with the mouth rather than the hands, and in both cases the well-being of others is the goal. So with their mouths as well as with their hands believers are to accomplish what is good, and what is good is what is beneficial to others.

30 καὶ μὴ λυπεῖτε τὸ πνεῦμα τὸ ἅγιον τοῦ θεοῦ, ἐν ᾧ ἐσφραγίσθητε εἰς ἡμέραν ἀπολυτρώσεως, "And do not grieve the holy Spirit of God, in whom you were sealed for the day of redemption." The Damascus Document contains the notion of defiling one's holy spirit (CD 5.11; 7.2); Paul exhorts believers not to quench the Spirit (1 Thess 5:18) and not to disregard God who gives his Holy Spirit (1 Thess 4:8), while Acts speaks of resisting the Holy Spirit (7:51). But this strikingly phrased prohibition, unique to Ephesians in the NT, appears to take up the thought of Isa 63:10, "But they rebelled and grieved his holy Spirit." It is closer to the MT, which uses the verb עצב ‘āṣab, "to hurt, pain, grieve," than to the LXX, which has παροξύνειν, "to provoke to wrath, irritate" (cf. also Sampley, *ST* 26 [1972] 104 n. 13). The closest LXX wording is to be found in 2 Sam [2 Kgdms] 13:21, which says that David did not grieve the spirit (οὐκ ἐλύπησεν τὸ πνεῦμα) of his son Amnon. The language of grieving the holy Spirit is found later in Herm. *Man.* 10.2.4; 10.3.2; *T. Isaac* 4.40, "But you shall take care and be alert that you do not grieve the Spirit of the Lord"; and in an agraphon preserved in Ps-Cyprian, *De Aleat.* 3, "Do not grieve the Holy Spirit who is in you, and do not extinguish the light which has been lit in you." Not only does the language of saddening or disappointing the Spirit by one's wayward actions provide a powerful personal metaphor, but the identity of the one offended is also underlined forcefully. The one who is grieved is the holy Spirit of God—that Spirit who is characterized by holiness and who is God himself at work in believers. It is not a question of some offense aimed directly at the Spirit but rather that believers by committing the sort of sins that have been mentioned in the earlier sentences, sins which disrupt communal life, are thereby disrupting and opposing the work of the Spirit in building up the Church (cf. 2:22; 4:3, 4; cf. also Halter, *Taufe*, 261). When believers act in a way that harms their brothers and sisters, God is hurt. Barth (548) is quick to point out the obvious theological implication— "the God proclaimed in Ephesians is not an unmoved mover."

Believers' sinful words and deeds are all the more grievous to the Spirit because they have been sealed in the Spirit for the day of redemption. On the notion of sealing, see *Comment* on 1:13, and on that of redemption, see *Comment* on 1:7 and 1:14. Through their reception of the Spirit, associated with their baptism, believers are those who have been stamped with the holy character of their owner. This is a guarantee of his taking final and full possession of them (cf. 1:14). The reference to "the day of redemption" is unique to Ephesians. In Rom 2:5 (cf. 2:16) Paul had spoken of the day of wrath and in Rom 13:11, 12 of the day, i.e. of salvation, but his more usual formulation for the last day and its accompanying consummation of salvation and judgment was "the day of the Lord" (cf. 1 Thess 5:2; 2 Thess 2:2; 1 Cor 1:8; 5:5; 2 Cor 1:14) or "the day of Christ" (cf. Phil 1:6, 10; 2:16). The writer to the Ephesians avoids these phrases, but the term "day" retains its temporal force as a reference to the goal of history (*pace* Mitton, 172, who holds that since there is no expectation of an imminent parousia in Ephesians, this is simply a reference to the fullness of life which awaits the believer in heaven, and Lindemann, *Aufhebung*, 230–32, who recognizes the future reference but attempts to play down any notion of a final redemption which involves more than the believer already enjoys) and as such takes its place alongside other references to the future in 1:14; 2:7; 5:5, 27; 6:8, 13. Believers' present experience of redemption involves the forgiveness of sins (1:7), but the future day of redemption will presumably include, as it did for Paul in Rom 8:23, the redemption of their bodies. Despite the future perspective which emerges in the last part of this verse, the emphasis is, in fact, on believers' present relationship to the Spirit, who guarantees their future and whom they should therefore not grieve.

In this way the prohibition functions as a strong Christian motivation for believers. But what is its connection with the surrounding verses? Is it to be associated with any of the other exhortations in particular? Ernst (368–69) sees no immediate links and holds that this sentence must be treated in its own right. Others believe that its closest relationship is to the verse that follows and that it is such vices as bitterness and wrath that grieve the Spirit and disrupt harmony (cf. Schlier, 228; Mitton, 172; Mussner, 140). But the loose connective καί at the beginning of the prohibition makes it more likely that those who see a relationship to the preceding verses and to v 29, in particular, are right (cf. Abbott, 143; J. A. Robinson, 113; Gnilka, 238; Schnackenburg, 214; Bruce, *Epistles*, 363). In CD 5.11, 12 defiling one's holy spirit is connected with sins of the mouth—"they defile their holy spirit and open their mouth with a blaspheming tongue against the laws of the covenant of God"—and both 1 Thess 5:18, 19 and Ephesians itself (in 5:18, 19 and 6:17) reflect the intimate link between speech and the Spirit. J. A. Robinson (113) is correct, therefore, when he claims, "The misuse of the organ of speech is accordingly a wrong done to, and felt by, the Spirit who claims to control it." Using hateful words against one's sisters and brothers in the community of faith distresses the Spirit who binds that community together. In this way, v 30 can be seen to stand in the same reinforcing relationship to v 29 as the motivation about giving no opportunity to the devil in v 27 stands in to the prohibition against anger of v 26.

31, 32 Verses 31 and 32, which, as we saw under *Form/Structure/Setting*, are dependent on Col 3:8, 12, 13, should be taken together, because in line with the dominant tripartite pattern observed in this pericope they contain an exhortation framed in negative terms (the call for the removal of vices), an exhortation expressed positively (the appeal for certain virtues), and a concluding motivating clause.

πᾶσα πικρία καὶ θυμὸς καὶ ὀργὴ καὶ κραυγὴ καὶ βλασφημία ἀρθήτω ἀφ᾽ ὑμῶν σὺν πάσῃ κακίᾳ, "Let all bitterness and rage and anger and shouting and slander be removed from you along with all malice." The writer returns to the topic of anger he has already introduced in v 26. Although two of the vices listed show anger in expression in speech, the exhortation is not a continuation of the emphasis on speech in vv 29, 30, providing a further description of evil talk (*pace* Bruce, *Epistles*, 364). Instead, the dangers of anger are now underlined in a fresh and decisive fashion. It is to be comprehensively rooted out of the readers' lives. Five different aspects of anger and "all malice," the generalizing addition at the end (note also the πᾶσα at the beginning of the list), are to be removed. αἴρειν, "to remove," is used by Paul in his exhortation to the Corinthians in 1 Cor 5:2 (cf. also its later use in paraenetic material in Herm. *Vis*. 2.2.4; Herm. *Man*. 10.1.1; 10.2.5; *Barn*. 21.4). Here in Eph 4:31 it has similar force to the earlier use of ἀποτίθεσθαι, "to put off, put away," in 4:22, 25. The passive form of the imperative is not a divine passive, to make the point that the activity required is God's rather than humanity's (*pace* Barth, 522), but is simply a stylistic variation. The first on the list of vices to be removed is πικρία, "bitterness," which indicates the hard-heartedness that harbors resentment about the past (cf. Diog. Laert. 4.46; Rom 3:14; Acts 8:23; Heb 12:15; cf. also Jas 3:14, ζῆλος πικρός, "bitter jealousy"). The cognate verb πικραίνειν is employed in Col 3:19, where husbands are exhorted not to be embittered against their wives. θυμός, "rage" (cf. also 2 Cor 12:20; Gal 5:20) and ὀργή, "anger" (cf. also 1 Tim 2:8; Jas 1:19, 20) were distinguished by the Stoics (cf., e.g., Diog. Laert. 7.114; Seneca, *De Ira* 2.36), the former denoting an initial explosion of rage and the latter a more settled feeling of gnawing hostility. But the two terms could also be used synonymously, as in Col 3:8 where they occur in reverse order. If the writer's listing of the various aspects of anger is meant to evoke intensification (see the discussion below), then it could well be that the change of order from Colossians is significant and the Stoic distinction is to be retained here. κραυγή, "shouting," is used only here in the NT to indicate a vice, though it occurs with different connotations in Matt 25:6; Luke 1:42; Acts 23:9; Heb 5:7; and Rev 21:4. It suggests the lack of restraint which erupts in angry yelling, while βλασφημία, "slander," indicates the more specific form this can take, namely the abuse and vilifying of others (cf. Col 3:8; Mark 7:22; 1 Tim 6:4; cf. also 2 Tim 3:2). The summarizing term κακία, "malice" (cf. Col 3:8; Rom 1:29; 1 Cor 5:8; 14:20; Titus 3:3; 1 Pet 2:1, 16; Jas 1:21), takes in any attitude or action which intends harm to one's neighbor.

A listing of vices associated with anger can be found in Philo, *De Ebr.* 223, but reflection on the different forms anger can take is most characteristic of Stoicism (cf. esp. Chrysippus, *frag.* 395; Seneca, *De Ira* 1.4). Here the writer makes use of this sort of tradition in his comprehensive indictment of anger as a major characteristic of the old person which is to be shunned. It may well be, as a number of commentators have suggested (cf. Westcott, 74; Schlier, 228; Barth, 521; Schnackenburg, 215), that his indictment had added rhetorical force, because within the comprehensive listing there is also a progression from anger's inner center (πικρία) through its initial eruption (θυμός) and steady festering (ὀργή) to its external expression (κραυγή) and damaging of others (βλασφημία). Certainly, a little later in early Christian paraenesis, this notion of the intensification in the varieties of anger had become explicit (cf. Herm. *Man.* 5.2.4, ". . . then from silliness comes bitterness [πικρία], from bitterness wrath [θυμός] from wrath rage [ὀργή], and from rage fury [μῆνις]; then fury, being compounded of such great evils, becomes great and inexpiable sin").

γίνεσθε εἰς ἀλλήλους χρηστοί, εὔσπλαγχνοι, χαριζόμενοι ἑαυτοῖς, "Be kind to one another, compassionate, forgiving one another." In formulating the virtues that are to replace the preceding vices, the writer has reduced the five nouns of Col 3:12 to two and given them adjectival form and then taken up one of the participles of Col 3:13. In line with these changes, the metaphor of putting on from Col 3:12 has been abandoned for the straightforward imperative "be" or "become." In contrast to the vices so destructive of harmonious relationships, the qualities now enjoined are those conducive to communal living. The use of ἀλλήλους, "one another," and the stylistic variation on this with ἑαυτοῖς (cf. Col 3:13; 1 Pet 4:9, 10; cf. also BDF § 287) underline the corporate dimension of the exhortation. Kindness has been attributed to God in 2:7, and the consideration of the needs and interests of others that it entails is now required of humans (cf. also Col 3:12; Gal 5:22; 2 Cor 6:6). Being sympathetic to others' needs is also the essence of compassion, which together with mercy and kindness is frequently held up as an exemplary virtue in the *Testaments of the Twelve Patriarchs* (e.g., *T. Zeb.* 5.1; 7.2; 8.1; *T. Sim.* 4.4) and in addition to Col 3:12 occurs elsewhere in the NT in the list of virtues in 1 Pet 3:8. χαριζόμενοι has the specific force of "forgiving" rather than the more general meaning of "granting favors" (cf. Col 2:13; 3:12; 2 Cor 2:7, 10; 12:13).

καθὼς καὶ ὁ θεὸς ἐν Χριστῷ ἐχαρίσατο ὑμῖν, "just as God in Christ forgave you." In Jewish and early Christian paraenesis the motivation for humans being compassionate and forgiving could be in order that God might forgive them (e.g., *T. Zeb.* 8.1; Matt 6:14; Mark 11:25) or because God had forgiven them (e.g., *T. Zeb.* 7.2; 1 John 4:11). Here the motivating clause takes the latter form. Such statements introduced by καθὼς καί have been called "the conformity pattern" and function within exhortations to show Christ's or God's saving activity as prototypical for believers' conduct (cf. N. A. Dahl, "Form-Critical Observations on Early Christian Preaching," in *Jesus in the Memory of the Early Church* [Minneapolis: Augsburg, 1976] 34). Here, as in later instances in 5:2, 25, 29, καθώς has both comparative and causal force. What God has done in Christ for believers, which has been the theme of the first half of the letter, now provides both the norm and the grounds for believers' own behavior. God's forgiveness of them becomes the paradigm for their mutual forgiveness. Whereas in the similar statement of Col 3:13 it is ὁ κύριος who has forgiven the readers, and the Lord is almost certainly Christ, here in Eph 4:32 it is God in Christ who has brought about the forgiveness that must now be worked out in believers' relationships.

5:1, 2 As has been noted earlier, the pericope as a whole ends on a positive note with two exhortations formulated in positive terms and a motivating clause similar in form to the one in 4:32 which has just been examined.

γίνεσθε οὖν μιμηταὶ τοῦ θεοῦ, ὡς τέκνα ἀγαπητά, "Be imitators of God, therefore, as dearly loved children." Both the οὖν, "therefore," and the repetition of the same imperative γίνεσθε, "be," from 4:32, make clear that this exhortation is drawing out the consequences of the previous one. The readers' forgiving of one another, just as God in Christ forgave them, entails their becoming imitators of God. They are to make God's activity the pattern for their lives. Their depiction as God's dearly loved children makes clear the basis on which the demand for imitation is made (cf. also Meyer, 263–64; Schlier, 230; Mitton, 175; Halter, *Taufe*, 266; Schnackenburg, 216; Wild, " 'Be Imitators,' " 143 n. 60). Believers have been adopted into God's family (cf. 1:5) and should exhibit the family resemblance. It would be incongruous to be God's dearly loved child and not to want to become like one's loving Father. In fact, the new child-Father relationship not only requires but also enables imitation to take place, as the children live their lives out of the love they have already experienced from their Father.

A frequent feature in ancient paraenesis was the provision of models for imitation (cf., e.g., Seneca, *Epp.* 6.5, 6; 11.9, 10; 95.72; Ps-Isocrates, *Demonicus* 11.36; *T. Benj.* 3.1; 4.1; Pliny, *Ep.* 8.13). The writer of Ephesians chooses the highest model possible and in so doing supplies the only passage in the NT where the explicit language of imitation of God is employed. (On the idea of imitation in the NT cf. E. Schweizer, *Lordship and Discipleship* [London: SCM, 1960]; A. Schulz, *Nachfolgen und Nachahmen* [Munich: Kösel-Verlag, 1962]; H. D. Betz, *Nachfolge und Nachahmung Jesu Christi im Neuen Testament* [Tübingen: Mohr, 1967]. B. Lindars' article, "Imitation of God and Imitation of Christ," *Theology* 76 [1973] 394–402, which asserts that the idea of the imitation of God "is neither biblical nor true to the ethical position of Jesus and the early Church, in so far as these can be recovered from the New Testament" does not take into account the language of Eph 5:1.) Paul, of course, urges his churches to imitate other churches (cf. 1 Thess 2:14), to imitate him (cf. 1 Cor 4:16, where he uses the father-child imagery in connection with this imitation; 1 Cor 11:1; Phil 3:17; 1 Thess 1:6; 2 Thess 3:7, 9), and to imitate Christ (1 Thess 1:6), but not to imitate God. This language occurs elsewhere in early Christian literature only later (cf. Ign. *Eph.* 1.1; Ign. *Trall.* 1.2; *Diogn.* 10.4–6). The actual language of imitation is very rare in the LXX (cf. Wis 4:2; 9:8; 15:9; 4 Macc 9:23; 13:9) and never used with reference to imitation of God. There are, however, functionally equivalent notions in the OT such as following Yahweh (e.g., Num 14:24; 32:11, 12; Josh 14:8, 9, 14; 1 Sam 12:14; 1 Kgs 11:6; 14:8) or the theme found frequently in the Holiness Code, e.g., Lev 19:2, "You shall be holy, for I the Lord your God am holy." Similarly, there are functional equivalents in the NT. In terms of content, the closest parallel is with Luke 6:35, 36 (cf. also Matt 5:44–48), where God's kindness and mercy are made the norm for human conduct. But whereas in Luke the eschatological reward for imitating these divine qualities will be to become sons of the Most High, in Ephesians this relationship has already been given and is what enables the imitation to take place.

For instances of the use of the actual language of imitating God one must turn to Hellenistic Jewish writings where this notion was traditional (cf. *T. Ash.* 4.3; Philo, *De Sacr.* 68; *De Spec. Leg.* 4.73, 187–88; *De Virt.* 168; cf. also Gnilka, 243; Barth, 556 n. 10, 588–92; and esp. Wild, "'Be Imitators,'" 128–33; *pace* Fischer, *Tendenz,* 140, who strangely claims that there is no mention of imitation of God even in Hellenistic Judaism). *De Virt.* 168 shows that Philo equated imitation of God with the ethical goal of assimilation to God (ὁμοίωσις θεῷ), a phrase which in Middle Platonism was seen as *the* statement of the purpose of human existence (cf. J. Dillon, *The Middle Platonists* [London: Duckworth, 1977] 44, 122, 145, 192, 299). In *De Fug.* 63 Philo cites Plato's *Theatetus* 176A-B on this: "Therefore we ought to flee from earth to heaven as quickly as we can. This flight means to become like God as far as is possible. In turn this becoming like him means with the help of insight to become just and holy [ὁμοίωσις δὲ δίκαιον καὶ ὅσιον μετὰ φρονήσεως γενέσθαι]." We have already noted that Eph 4:24 also holds that being in conformity to God (κατὰ θεόν) involves justice and holiness. The likelihood that the writer is familiar with similar traditions to those used by Philo is increased when it is observed that in *De Spec. Leg.* 4.72–73, as here in Eph 4:32–5:1, imitating God is seen in terms of showing kindness and forgiving. The tradition of the imitation of God has been made to serve the writer's perspective, in which a new relationship with God is needed for this imitation to be accomplished, and that relationship is based on God's saving activity in Christ.

καὶ περιπατεῖτε ἐν ἀγάπῃ, καθὼς καὶ ὁ Χριστὸς ἠγάπησεν ἡμᾶς καὶ παρέδωκεν ἑαυτὸν ὑπὲρ ἡμῶν προσφορὰν καὶ θυσίαν τῷ θεῷ εἰς ὀσμὴν εὐωδίας, "and live in love, just as Christ loved us and gave himself up for us as a fragrant offering and sacrifice to God." The idea of the imitation of God in 5:1 is defined both by what precedes (God's activity in forgiveness) and by what follows (his love, the essential characteristic of his activity in Christ). In fact, the imitation of God turns out to be the imitation of Christ, as in the motivating clause it is the latter's love and self-giving that are the ground and the norm for the behavior required of believers (see the discussion of 4:32 for the force of καθὼς καί and the "conformity pattern"). The sudden change of focus from God in 5:1 to Christ in 5:2 should be seen in the light of the dual reference to God's activity in Christ in the motivating clause of 4:32, although its immediate cause may well be simply that Christ was the subject in the traditional formulation which came to the writer's mind (cf. Gnilka, 244). The love involved in the events of salvation can be attributed both to God, as it is in 2:4, and to Christ, as it is here. The imperative that believers should live in love is grounded in the indicative of Christ's costly self-giving, which is the historical manifestation of the love of God. The imperative employs the verb περιπατεῖν, lit. "to walk" (see the discussion of the earlier use of this term in 2:2, 10; 4:1), which is found in each section of the paraenesis until the household code—4:1 in 4:1–16, 4:17 in 4:17–24, 5:2 in 4:25–5:2, 5:8 in 5:3–14, and 5:15 in 5:15–20. The language of walking in love had been used by Paul in his exhortation in Rom 14:15. Here, walking in love is the way in which one imitates God. The stress on the necessity of love is similar to that at the beginning of the paraenesis in 4:2, 15, 16 and reflects the emphasis it is given in Col 3:12–14, the text on which the writer draws. Certainly the sacrifice of one's own interests out of concern for the welfare of others is the quality above all that fosters harmony in the community.

The description of Christ's love is in traditional language, which gives the pericope a concluding rhetorical flourish. The combination of verbs in the assertion that Christ loved believers and gave himself up for them occurs later in 5:25, had been employed by Paul in Gal 2:20, and may have links with formulations in the earliest community about Christ giving himself up (cf. Mark 9:31; 10:33; 14:41). Though the language is likely to be traditional, there is no compelling reason for assigning it to a hymn (*pace* Barth, 557). The formulation states that Christ gave himself up ὑπὲρ ἡμῶν, "for us," on behalf of believers. He did this as their representative, and sometimes the notion of representation involves that of substitution (cf. also Gal 3:13; 2 Cor 5:14, 21). Certainly the sacrificial nature of Christ's death becomes explicit in the liturgical turns of phrase that now feature in this writer's effusive style. προσφορὰ καὶ θυσία (cf. LXX Ps 39:6) is a hendiadys employing two general terms, both of which included all kinds of sacrifices, grain and animal, while εἰς ὀσμὴν εὐωδίας utilizes the frequent LXX metaphor for a sacrifice which was particularly pleasing to God (e.g., Exod 29:18; Lev 2:9, 12; Ezek 20:41). Some commentators (cf. Schlier, 232; Gnilka, 245 n. 6) connect τῷ θεῷ with the latter rather than the former phrase, but because of its place in the sentence this is not as likely a construction (cf. also Meyer, 264; Abbott, 147). The imagery performs a doxological function at the end of the sentence, as through it the writer indicates that Christ's sacrifice of love was supremely pleasing and glorifying to God. But the rhetoric still serves the paraenesis, and the readers are reminded that Christ's sacrificial love should find a response in analogous acts of love toward each other. It is significant that Paul, in Phil 4:18, could in fact speak of the Philippians' sacrificial love for him in the same terms that this writer uses for Christ's sacrifice, "a fragrant offering, a sacrifice acceptable and pleasing to God."

Explanation

The preceding section of the letter had dealt with the distinctive conduct required of Christian believers in strong but general terms, choosing to underline the change from their previous behavior and their identity as new people, an identity which must be continually appropriated ethically. Now, by means of a series of hortatory sentences on a number of topics, the writer states more specifically what this involves. All but one of the seven sentences take the form of two exhortations followed by a motivating clause (a second exhortation is implicit in 4:29), and the remaining fifth sentence of 4:30 functions as a summarizing motivating clause for what has preceded. Colossians (3:8b, 9a, 12–14) again serves as the basic source for the content of five of the seven sentences but has been elaborated on by means of other traditional material from the LXX, Hellenistic Judaism, Stoicism, and Paul.

The exhortation of the first ethical sentence in v 25 follows up the writer's talk of putting off the old person and putting on the new person, whose way of life is derived from the truth, by an appeal to put off the lying characteristic of the old life and instead to speak the truth. The grounds for this appeal are then stated—believers are fellow members of the body of Christ. Their solidarity requires the mutual trust engendered by truthful communication. Not only lying, but also anger, presents an obstacle to harmonious relationships, and the second sentence takes up this topic in vv 26, 27. The readers are to avoid anger at all costs, and if they do become angry, they are not to indulge their anger, and thereby sin, but are instead to expel it immediately. The reason given for this counsel is that anger which is indulged gives the devil opportunity to exploit its effects.

Verse 28 treats a third topic that is illustrative of the change from the old to the new way of living. Instead of using their hands to steal, believers will use them to work hard and produce the resources to do good. The motive to which appeal is made in this call to engage in the toil and struggle of work is the well-being of others in the community. The hard worker will have something to share with those in need. The fourth sentence of v 29 returns to the topic of speech but this time employs the categories of good (taken up from the preceding sentence) and evil instead of truth and falsehood. What is prohibited is the use of words in an unwholesome and destructive fashion, and what is encouraged is their constructive use whenever the need for building up another person arises. The motivation and criterion for the right use of language is to be its beneficial effect. In v 30 the readers, who have been stamped with the holy character of the Spirit of God and guaranteed the future aspect of their redemption, are urged to do nothing to distress the Spirit. This fifth sentence functions as a further motivation supporting the preceding exhortations. There is a particular link with the immediately preceding topic, since the Spirit who binds the community together is especially grieved when words are used in a way that is detrimental to his work.

Just as the fourth sentence returned to the topic of the first, so now the sixth sentence in vv 31, 32 returns to the topic of the second—anger. Various vices associated with anger, and which may well progress from its inner core of bitterness through its initial eruption and steady festering to its external expression in yelling and the vilification of others, are all to be removed. In their place is to come the practice of the virtues of kindness, compassion, and forgiveness. A motivation for such action is attached to the last of these qualities and directs the readers' attention to the heart of their experience of salvation, namely that God in Christ has already forgiven them. The concluding sentence in 5:1, 2 exhorts the readers to be imitators of God in the activities described primarily in 4:32 but then also in 5:2—forgiveness and love. The general call to live in love can be seen as a positive summary of the passage's earlier admonitions. Walking in love includes thinking, talking, and working in love. Costly, sacrificial love is to become the distinguishing mark of the readers' lives because, as the traditional formulation embellished by the writer's rhetorical flourish puts it, Christ loved them and gave himself up for them as a fragrant offering and sacrifice to God.

The earlier part of the letter has reinforced for the readers their identity as part of a movement that is the focus within history of a new reality with cosmic dimensions. Now the attempt is made to show how this body of Christ comes to concrete expression and what exactly is required of its members in their daily living. Because of its general nature, the material in this passage can provide no clues to the specific circumstances of the letter's recipients. Clearly, however, the writer considers that his Gentile Christian readers need a reminder of some of the basic attitudes and actions necessary if they are to play their part in the Church's growth in unity and love. The topics chosen are illustrative of conduct befitting harmonious relationships. The function of the traditional material in the exhortations, and particularly of the motivating clauses, is to foster the desired conduct by appealing to various assumptions that the writer and his readers have in common as a result of their allegiance to the apostolic gospel and tradition.

What the writer in this passage expects of his readers' practical conduct can now be summed up. Negatively, the lives of the Gentile Christians of the Pauline churches in Asia Minor will be characterized by the absence of lying, destructive talk, stealing, and indulgence of anger or any of its associated vices. Positively, they will be marked by truthful and edifying speech, hard work enabling them to do good deeds, kindness, compassion, forgiveness, and love. The values and beliefs which are to sustain this quality of life emerge from the writer's motivating clauses. Prominent among these is a profound respect for the corporate nature of Christian existence which derives from his earlier vision of a unified Church; believers are members of one another (4:25), who are concerned about sharing with those of their number in need (4:28) and about the beneficial effect of their words on the rest of the community (4:29). Also involved are beliefs about the roles of God, Christ, the Spirit, and the devil in their lives. The experiential knowledge of God's forgiveness of them in Christ (4:32), of Christ's sacrificial love for them (5:2), and of the Spirit's sealing of them and personal involvement in their communal life (4:30) and the awareness of a personal power of evil able to exploit sinful situations (4:27) are all invoked to shape the response required of the readers in their everyday living.

Earlier in the letter, the writer has depicted the contrast between his readers' previous way of life in the surrounding society and their present existence as Christians in black and white terms. But how different from the surrounding mores are the standards proposed in this passage? Many of the moralists of his own day would have concurred with the writer's assessment and advice. Just as the form of the writer's exhortations—the use of ethical sentences, contrasting negative and positive injunctions, lists of vices and virtues, motivating clauses—can be found in Greco-Roman and Hellenistic Jewish literature, so also the content in regard to the specific behavior advocated can be found in that literature. In particular, similarities with the Stoics, Philo, and the *Testaments of the Twelve Patriarchs* have figured prominently in the detailed discussion of the sentences. How many people lived up to the aspirations of the moralists and whether Christians, in fact, achieved any greater success in this regard are questions which do not admit of easy answers. Two points are clear, however. It is the framework of motivations supplied by his gospel that makes this writer's ethical teaching coherent and distinctively Christian. He, at least, is convinced that the power at work in the apostolic gospel should enable his readers to fulfill his aspirations for them, resulting in qualitatively different lives.

Because of the nature of the hortatory material, in this section as in the previous one, the focus of attention is on the readers and their actions. The ecclesiological perspective dominates the early sentences, since three of the first four motivating clauses have in view the well-being of the Christian community. In the other motivating clauses attention is drawn first to the devil and then to the Spirit. With the exhortation of 5:1 to be imitators of God and with the motivations supplied in 4:32 and 5:2, the last part of the section shows that even in his ethical instruction the writer has not lost his theological and Christological perspectives. Indeed, if the command to love can be said to sum up the other injunctions, then the notion of the imitation of God which accompanies it can also stand as an encapsulation of the theocentric focus of the writer's ethical thinking. As elsewhere in the letter the theological and the Christological go hand in hand, for the God of whom the writer speaks is the God who has acted to forgive humanity in and through the love of Christ whose sacrifice was supremely pleasing to him. In this way, for believers, imitation of God also turns out to be imitation of Christ in his sacrificial love.

The concerns of this passage about both the words and deeds of the readers continue into the next section of exhortation where they focus on sexual morality in particular and are related to the images of light and darkness. The awareness of what is necessary for communal life will come to the fore again in the last part of 5:15–20, and the theme on which the pericope closes, human love as a reflection of Christ's love, will be taken up and elaborated in a striking fashion when the writer addresses wives and husbands in 5:21–33.

From Darkness to Light   (5:3–14)

Bibliography

Casel, O. "Εὐχαριστία—εὐχαριτία (Eph. 5, 3 f)." *BZ* 18 (1929) 84–85. **Dahl, N. A.** "Der Epheserbrief und der verlorene erste Brief des Paulus an die Korinther." In *Abraham unser Vater*. FS O. Michel, ed. O. Betz, M. Hengel, and P. Schmidt. Leiden: E. J. Brill, 1963, 65–77. **Dölger, F. J.** *Sol Salutis: Gebet und Gesang im christlichen Altertum*. Münster: Aschendorff, 1925, 364–410. **Engberg-Pedersen, T.** "Ephesians 5, 12–13: ἐλέγχειν and Conversion in the New Testament." *ZNW* 80 (1989) 89–110. **Fischer, K. M.** *Tendenz und Absicht*, 140–46. **Giblet, J.** "Les fruits de la lumière (Eph 5, 1–9)." *AsSeign* 80 (1964) 18–25. **Halter, H.** *Taufe und Ethos*, 269–81. **Horst, P. W. van der.** "Is Wittiness Unchristian? A Note on εὐτραπελία in Eph. v. 4." In *Miscellanea Neotestamentica*. Vol. 2, ed. T. Baarda, A. F. J. Klijn, and W. C. van Unnik. Leiden: E. J. Brill, 1978, 163–77. **Kuhn, K. G.** "The Epistle to the Ephesians in the Light of the Qumran Texts." In *Paul and Qumran*, 115–31. **Merklein, H.** "Eph 4, 1–5, 20 als Rezeption von Kol 3, 1–17." In *Kontinuität und Einheit*, ed. P. G. Müller and W. Stenger. Freiburg: Herder, 1981, 194–210. **Noack, B.** "Das Zitat in Eph 5, 14." *ST* 5 (1952) 52–64. **Schille, G.** *Frühchristliche Hymnen*, 94–101. **Schnackenburg, R.** "'Er hat uns mitauferweckt.' Zur Tauflehre des Epheserbriefes." *Liturgisches Jahrbuch* 2 (1952) 160–66. **Siber, P.** *Mit Christus leben*. Zürich: Theologischer Verlag, 1971, 200–205.

Translation

³*But fornication and every kind of impurity or covetousness should not even be mentioned among you, as befits saints,* ⁴*nor obscenity, foolish talk, or coarse joking, which are not fitting,*[a] *but rather thanksgiving.* ⁵*For be very sure of this,*[b] *no fornicator or impure or covetous person (such a person is an idolater)*[c] *has any inheritance in the kingdom of Christ and of God.*[d]
⁶*Let no one deceive you with empty words, for because of these things the wrath of God comes upon those who are disobedient.*[e] ⁷*Therefore do not become partners with them;* ⁸*for once you were darkness, but now you are light in the Lord; live as children of light* ⁹*—for the fruit of light*[f] *consists*[g] *in all goodness, righteousness, and truth—*¹⁰*discovering what is pleasing to the Lord.* ¹¹*And do not take part in the fruitless deeds of darkness, but rather expose them,* ¹²*for it is shameful even to speak of what is done by them in secret.* ¹³*But everything exposed becomes illumined*[h] *by the light,* ¹⁴*for everything that becomes illumined is light. Therefore it is said, "Awake, O sleeper, and rise from the dead, and Christ will shine upon you."*[i]

Notes

[a] The verb in Greek, ἀνῆκεν, is in the imperfect tense, but in expressions of necessity, obligation, or what is proper the imperfect could be used for assertions about the present (cf. also Col 3:18; cf. BDF § 358(2); Moulton, *Grammar* 3:90–91).

[b] This clause in Greek has two verbs of knowing—ἴστε, the imperative from οἶδα, and γινώσκοντες, the present participle from γινώσκω. It has been taken as a Hebraism (cf. also LXX 1 Kgs [3 Kgdms] 20:3; *Hexapla* Jer 49:22; *1 Clem.* 12.5) which reinforces the idea of the verb, and has therefore been translated in such a way as to convey emphasis (cf. BAGD 556; BDF § 422; Moulton, *Grammar* 3:156–57).

[c] Behind this parenthetical clause lie both a textual question and a syntactical question. Some texts (A D K L P and most minuscules) have ὅς ἐστιν instead of ὅ ἐστιν, but this appears to be a

later scribal attempt to be more accurate and to make the relative pronoun agree with the preceding noun, which it qualifies. In fact, the latter reading with the neuter ὅ has far stronger support (P46 ℵ B F G Ψ 33 81 it vg goth) and the neuter could be used where strictly a masculine or feminine was required (cf. BDF § 132 [2]). However, this does not necessarily mean that the reference of the neuter here is to the whole of the preceding clause rather than to its single antecedent (cf. BDF § 132 [2]; *pace* Moule, *Idiom-Book*, 130–31). The similar relationship between covetousness and idolatry in Col 3:5, on which Ephesians is dependent, supports the view that here too it is the covetous person who is seen as an idolater.

d This unusual double expression about the kingdom is clearly the original reading, although it gave rise to a number of variants. P46 1245 2147 read simply θεοῦ, possibly as a result of scribal oversight, but more probably under the influence of the more usual phrase "kingdom of God" (cf. Metzger, *Textual Commentary*, 607). Others have reversed the order under the same influence and read τοῦ θεοῦ καὶ Χριστοῦ (F gr G it g Ambrosiaster) or make the idea singular by substituting the definite article for καί: τοῦ Χριστοῦ τοῦ θεοῦ (1739* eth Theodoret).

e A literal translation of the Greek phrase would be "sons of disobedience" (cf. 2:2).

f There is a variant which reads πνεύματος instead of φωτός at this point and which finds support in P46 Dc K Ψ 88 104 614 1739mg. But φωτός, which fits the context better (note especially the contrast with τοῖς ἔργοις τοῖς ἀκάρποις τοῦ σκότους, "the fruitless deeds of darkness," in v 11), has stronger attestation (cf. P49 ℵ A B D* G P 33 81 1739* it vg syr p,pal cop sa,bo goth arm eth Origen). The variant is likely to have entered the textual tradition because of the phrase in Gal 5:22.

g There is no verb in the original. A functional equivalent for the verb "to be" has been supplied in translation.

h The passive form of the verb φανεροῦν would be translated literally as "to be revealed, become visible, appear." Because of its relation in this context to the term "light," what is meant is "to become visible through being lit up," i.e., "to become illumined" (cf. also NEB; *pace* Schnackenburg, 232).

i The translation follows what is clearly the best-attested text, but there is an early, weakly attested variant (D* it b Victorinus-Rome Ambrosiaster Jerome) ἐπιψαύσεις τοῦ Χριστοῦ, "you will attain to Christ, have a part in Christ."

Form/Structure/Setting

After the discrete ethical sentences of 4:25–5:2, which culminate in the positive exhortation to love, there is a change of style and of content in this pericope. 5:3–14 forms far more of a connected argument and begins by reverting to a negative note as it introduces the topic of sexual immorality. The verb περιπατεῖν, "to walk, live," which marks each section of the paraenesis up to the household code, occurs here in the imperative in 5:8.

The exhortation, which draws out the ethical consequences of belonging to the Christian community, proceeds in two main stages—vv 3–6 with their prohibition of talk about sexual vices and their warning about those who practice such vices, and vv 7–14 with their dominant imagery of light and darkness. Verse 7 provides the connection between the two parts. The opening exhortation of vv 3, 4, in fact, has an antithetical form—μηδέ . . . ἀλλὰ μᾶλλον . . .—but reads predominantly like a prohibition, because two sets of three vices are listed before the one contrasting virtue is set over against them. Verses 5, 6 add to the primarily negative atmosphere of the first half of the pericope by underlining the prohibition aspect of vv 3, 4 (cf. the γάρ at the beginning of v 5) with their two severe warnings about the consequences for those who are immoral and disobedient—exclusion from the kingdom of Christ and of God and experience of the wrath of God. A new prohibition is introduced in v 7, but it is linked to the preceding material through οὖν, "therefore." Since the consequences for those who indulge in sexual immorality are so dire, believers are not to join in with them. A further warrant for this prohibition is provided in v 8a (cf. the connective γάρ) by means of the ποτέ . . . νῦν contrast schema which introduces the images of light and darkness. The exhortation of vv 8b–10 makes use of the image of light in a positive fashion. The readers are to live as children of light. What this involves is illustrated in the parenthetical statement of v 9, with its triad of virtues, and the participial clause of v 10 about discovering what is pleasing to the Lord. The hortatory sentence which follows in vv 11, 12 again has an antithetical form (μή . . . μᾶλλον . . .). While reinforcing the earlier prohibition against participating in immoral activities, it also moves the exhortation on with its positive command to expose such deeds of darkness. Both parts of the main clause are given further warrant through the explanatory clause with γάρ in v 12. Verses 13, 14 round off the pericope by elaborating on the notion of exposure and linking it with the effect of light. The citation of the hymn or hymnic fragment in v 14b both provides support for this statement and returns the reader to the Christological basis for the writer's use of the image of light from v 8 onwards.

Within this paraenesis the writer employs three particular forms to which attention should be drawn. (*i*) There are lists of vices (cf. vv 3–5) and virtues (cf. v 9). For discussion of such lists, see under *Form/Structure/Setting* for 4:25– 5:2. (*ii*) There is the ποτέ . . . νῦν contrast (cf. v 8a). For discussion of this "once . . . now" schema, its likely origin and its function earlier in the letter, see under *Form/Structure/Setting* for 2:1–10 and 2:11–22. (*iii*) There is also the citation introduced by the formula διὸ λέγει, "therefore it says," in v 14b. A brief discussion of its form will follow here. More on the background of its ideas and the meaning and function of the material in its present context in the paraenesis will be found under *Comment* on v 14. The quotation is a rhythmic tristich which uses the rhetorical device of the first two lines having similar sounding endings. It has a Semitic style with the verbs at the beginning of the lines, the two imperatives linked by καί, and then the καί leading into the future tense of the third line (cf. also Gnilka, 260). The first two lines of synthetic parallelism constitute a summons to ethical awareness, while the last line offers the promise of Christ's aid.

It is much easier to describe the form these three lines take than to say with any certainty what their origin was. The difficulties become apparent when one looks at the attempts of the church fathers. Three main options soon emerged. Because Eph 4:8 uses the introductory formula found here with a scriptural citation, some attempted to trace the lines to the OT (e.g., Hippolytus). Others looked further afield to apocryphal writings (e.g., Epiphanius), while for others still (e.g., Origen, Severian, Theodoret) an early Christian hymn seemed the most likely option. When the attempt is made to find the origin of the citation in the OT, the most likely candidate is Isa 60:1, possibly in a mixed quotation with Isa 26:19. But at best the lines in Ephesians would provide only an indirect allusion to such passages. An allusion to Jonah 1:5, 6 and a *descensus ad inferos* (adduced by A. T. Hanson, *The New Testament Interpretation of Scripture,* London: S.P.C.K., 1980, 142–43) appears even less likely. If the lines were from an apocryphal scripture, it would have to be one which is now unknown to us. Epiphanius (*Haer.* 42.12.3) ascribed the lines to the *Apocalypse of Elijah,* but the closest passage is 3:3—"The whole world will behold him like the sun which shines from the eastern horizon to the western"—and is quite remote from the language of Eph 5:14. Clement of Alexandria (*Protr.* 9.84.2) is exceptional in suggesting that the passage is a word of the Lord and in providing a further three lines—"The sun of resurrection,/Begotten before the day-star,/Who has given life with his own beams." The additional lines presumably owe their origin to him (cf. also Schnackenburg, 233 n. 571), but they do raise the question whether the three lines in Ephesians are in fact part of an original larger whole. As the majority of modern commentators suggest, the most likely hypothesis is that the citation is of an early Christian hymn or hymnic fragment that would have been familiar to the readers. Because of their content, these lines came in all probability from an early Christian baptismal liturgy. Their wording might, of course, have been influenced by Isa 60:1 or have involved a reworking of it. They are formed not as praise of God or Christ but as a challenge and promise to the believer. Their language of exhortation and combination of the metaphors of sleep, death, and light applied to the life of the believer would have formed an appropriate chant with which the congregation could greet the newly baptized convert. There are possible associations between light and a baptismal setting in Col 1:12, 13; Heb 6:4; 10:32 and clear links in Justin, *Apol.* 61.12, 13; 65.1 and in the Syrian *Didascalia Apostolorum* 21, a baptismal text which speaks of Christ as the light that has shone on believers (cf. Dölger, *Sol Salutis*, 366–67). Noack (*ST* 5 [1952] esp. 62–64) argues that the three lines were originally an eschatological hymn which referred to the resurrection of the dead at the Parousia but which later had a secondary application in a baptismal context. But is not a call to awaken at the Parousia far more likely to have been in the plural, and what sort of purpose would have been served in the community's gathering for worship by the singing of such a hymn (cf. also Gnilka, 260 n. 3)? Noack's view simply involves one problematic and unnecessary hypothetical reconstruction too many.

The previous pericope, Eph 4:25–5:2, had been dependent on Col 3:8–14a. The early part of this pericope is dependent on the immediately preceding material in Colossians 3:5–8.

Ephesians		*Colossians*	
5:3 πορνεία δὲ καὶ ἀκαθαρσία πᾶσα ἢ πλεονεξία		3:5	πορνείαν, ἀκαθαρσίαν . . . καὶ τὴν πλεονεξίαν
5:4 καὶ αἰσχρότης		3:8	αἰσχρολογίαν
5:5 πλεονέκτης, ὅ ἐστιν εἰδωλολάτρης		3:5	καὶ τὴν πλεονεξίαν ἥτις ἐστὶν εἰδωλολατρία
5:6 διὰ ταῦτα γὰρ ἔρχεται ἡ ὀργὴ τοῦ θεοῦ		3:6	δι' ἃ ἔρχεται ἡ ὀργὴ τοῦ θεοῦ
5:8 ποτε . . . νῦν		3:7, 8	ποτε . . . νυνί

As can be seen, the writer of Ephesians takes up a number of vices from the lists in Colossians. There is a stylistic difference in that he prefers groups of three terms (cf. vv 3, 4, 5; cf. also the three virtues in v 9). There is also a shift of emphasis in the depiction. In Colossians, the vices were previously believers' own and now must be put away from them. In Ephesians, these vices belong characteristically to those outside, with whom there must be no partnership, although in v 8 the emphasis of Col 3 is retained temporarily in the "once . . . now" contrast which is adapted from Col 3:7, 8. The actual content of the contrast which is introduced—the opposition between light and darkness—has, however, no parallel in the equivalent section of Colossians (though cf. Col 1:12, 13). The motivating clause about the wrath of God in Eph 5:6 is similar to that in Col 3:6. (On the relation between Ephesians and Colossians at this point cf. also Merklein, "Eph 4, 1–5, 20," 206–7; Mitton, *Epistle*, 304–5.)

Other material in this passage is dependent on formulations from elsewhere in Colossians and the Pauline letters. The language of not inheriting the kingdom of God in 5:5 occurs after a similar list of vices or those who commit them in Gal 5:19–21 and 1 Cor 6:9. The fornicator, the covetous person, and the idolater are also included in the lists of 1 Cor 5:9–11. The notion of thanksgiving which is underlined in 5:4 has a similar centrality in Col 2:7, while the warning about being deceived through empty words in 5:6a recalls the language of Col 2:8 (cf. also Col 2:4). The exhortation of 5:7, 8, which prohibits partnership with the disobedient and then elaborates on this in terms of darkness and light, picks up on the language and thought of 1 Thess 5:5 and 2 Cor 6:14. Goodness is amongst the fruit of the Spirit in Gal 5:22, and here in Ephesians it is amongst the fruit of light (5:9). The formulation "discovering what is pleasing to the Lord" (5:10) appears to combine turns of phrase from Rom 12:2 and Col 3:20, while the phrase "deeds of darkness" (5:11) is found earlier in the Pauline corpus in Rom 13:12. The idea of exposing and making visible what is hidden in relation to unbelievers in 5:11–13 is anticipated in 1 Cor 14:24, 25.

On the basis of the similarities between this pericope and 1 Cor 5 and 6, Dahl has argued that it contains in only slightly modified form what must have been in Paul's first lost letter to the Corinthians. Both represent reworkings of the same original piece of Pauline catechesis (cf. "Der Epheserbrief," 70). It is certainly possible that the lost letter to the Corinthians contained advice something like that in this passage, which was misinterpreted by the Corinthians, but the inevitably speculative nature of any reconstruction of such advice tells against using the hypothesis to argue against any literary dependence of Eph 5:3–14 on Col 3:5–8. It remains most likely that the writer has supplemented his dependence on Colossians with his knowledge of paraenetical traditions current in the Pauline communities and reflected in some of the Pauline letters (*pace* Dahl, "Der Epheserbrief," 71–72).

In its setting in the letter, this passage, not surprisingly, has most links with the surrounding paraenetic material, especially 4:17–24. There is a similar black and white contrast between the ethical behavior of believers and that of outsiders in 4:17–21, in which the pairing of impurity and covetousness has already featured (4:19; cf. 5:3). In 4:22–24 this contrast had given way to that between the old and new humanities. Here in 5:3–14, an equivalent contrast is that between the disobedient or those who belong to the dark and the children of light. In fact, 4:18 had described Gentile outsiders in terms of "being darkened in their thinking." On the positive side, righteousness and truth figure in the triad of virtues in 4:24 as well as here in 5:9. The concern with speaking about sexual vices in 5:3–14 has links with the exhortations about sins of speech which featured so prominently in 4:25–5:2, while the mention of thanksgiving (5:4) will be developed in the following pericope, 5:15–20. The writer's underlying motivation in this type of paraenesis, that the Church should be holy, becomes explicit later in 5:27, as it had also been earlier in 1:4 and 2:21. Light imagery had been used of believers in 1:18. But the major connection with the early part of the letter is with 2:1–10 and its comparison between the believer's past and present. The connection can be seen in that passage's use of the contrast schema with ποτέ, its use of the phrase "sons of disobedience" (2:2; cf. 5:6), its mention of good works (2:10; cf. 5:9), and its death and resurrection metaphors for salvation from sin (2:1, 5, 6; cf. 5:14).

To talk about the pericope's setting in the letter is one thing; to assign it a specific setting in life is another. As was the case with 4:25–5:2, this pericope contains general ethical material, much of which serves as a reminder of the baptismal paraenesis the readers will have received at some earlier stage. The writer's use of it now to underline the necessity of believers' lives being morally distinctive simply shows that he recognizes that there was a constant temptation for Gentile Christians to lapse into moral laxity, especially in matters of sexuality, under pressure from the mores of the surrounding society.

Comment

3, 4 πορνεία δὲ καὶ ἀκαθαρσία πᾶσα ἢ πλεονεξία μηδὲ ὀνομαζέσθω ἐν ὑμῖν, καθὼς πρέπει ἁγίοις, "But fornication and every kind of impurity or covetousness should not even be mentioned among you, as befits saints." The adversative δέ marks the move from the topic of self-sacrificial love to that of self-indulgent sensuality. Sexual sins now dominate the vices mentioned in vv 3–5 and are primarily what is meant by the language of "deeds of darkness" and "what is done in secret" in vv 11, 12. With this prohibition, the writer also returns to the theme of the contrast between the Christian community and outsiders found earlier in the paraenesis in 4:17–24. Indeed, two of the triad of vices listed here—ἀκαθαρσία, "impurity," and πλεονεξία, "covetousness"—are contained in the earlier triad in 4:19. (For discussion of these terms, the *Comment* on 4:19 should be consulted.) ἀσέλγεια, "debauchery," at the beginning of the triad has here been replaced by πορνεία, "fornication," in line with Col 3:5. πορνεία is a broad term, signifying general sexual immorality but especially adultery and intercourse with prostitutes (cf. F. Hauck and S. Schulz, "πορνή," *TDNT* 6 [1968] 579–95; the discussion in B. Malina, "Does *Porneia* Mean Fornication?" *NovT* 14 [1972] 10–17; and J. Jensen, "Does *Porneia* Mean Fornication? A Critique of Bruce Malina," *NovT* 20 [1978] 161–84). Fornication of various sorts is condemned in the OT and in Hellenistic Judaism (cf. Sir 23:16–27; *T. Reub.* 1.6; 2.1; 3.3; 4.6; 5.1, 3; 6.1; *T. Sim.* 5.3; *T. Iss.* 7.2; Philo, *De Spec. Leg.* 3.51), and Paul himself had warned believers, especially the Corinthians, about indulging in it (cf. 1 Cor 5:1; 6:12–20; 7:2; 10:8; 2 Cor 12:21; Gal 5:19; 1 Thess 4:3; cf. also Col 3:5). The exhortation here in Ephesians has no specific situation in view but generalizes about "all impurity." ἀκαθαρσία is usually associated with sexual sin, and four of the above references have the term in combination with πορνεία (cf. 1 Thess 4:3, 7; Gal 5:19; 2 Cor 12:21;

Col 3:5). Because of the context, πλεονεξία, "covetousness," should also be taken as the sort of unrestrained sexual greed whereby a person assumes that others exist for his or her own gratification. The tenth commandment contains the injunction against coveting one's neighbor's wife; the combination of the ideas of covetousness and fornication is found in *T. Levi* 14.5, 6; *T. Jud.* 18.2; 1QS 4.9, 10; CD 4.17, 18; and the cognate verb πλεονεκτεῖν has sexual connotations in 1 Thess 4:6.

The writer wishes to stop such vices before they gain access to the communities to which he writes, and so he asserts that they must not even be named. It is sometimes claimed (e.g., Schlier, 233; Bratcher and Nida, *Handbook*, 125–26) that the prohibition is not to be taken literally and simply means that the vices are not to occur. But the use of the emphatic μηδέ and, in particular, the repetition of this notion in v 12—"it is shameful even to speak of what is done by them in secret"—suggest that the writer actually meant that these sins should not even be talked about. Believers' distancing from such vices must extend to their conversation. Presumably, the assumption behind this prohibition is that thinking and talking about sexual sins creates an atmosphere in which they are tolerated and which can indirectly even promote their practice. It would not occur to the writer, as it might to us, that strictly speaking he is breaking his own prohibition by mentioning these sins in his letter! What he is really attempting to discourage is sexual sin becoming the object of interest in conversation.

The motivation to which the writer appeals for the avoidance of such conversation is what is fitting for saints. πρέπει, "befits," is employed in similar formulations in 1 Tim 2:10; Titus 2:1; and *Barn.* 4.9, while in v 4 a similar motivation uses ἀνῆκεν. This appeal to what is fitting was a feature of Stoic ethics and mediated to early Christianity through Hellenistic Judaism (cf. M. Pohlenz, "Τὸ Πρέπον," *Nachrichten von der Gesellschaft der Wissenschaften in Göttingen, Philol.-Historische Klasse 1933*, vol. 1 [Berlin: Weidmann, 1933] 53–92; H. Schlier, "ἀνήκει," *TDNT* 1 [1964] 360; idem, "καθήκω," *TDNT* 3 [1965] 437–40). The absence of the article with ἁγίοις, "saints," places stress on the qualitative dimensions of the term, the holiness of those set apart for God, and serves as a reminder of believers' calling as that is depicted in 1:4. Paul's paraenesis in 1 Thess 4:3–7 had also explicitly linked the call to holiness with sexual morality.

καὶ αἰσχρότης καὶ μωρολογία ἢ εὐτραπελία, ἃ οὐκ ἀνῆκεν, ἀλλὰ μᾶλλον εὐχαριστία, "nor obscenity, foolish talk, or coarse joking, which are not fitting, but rather thanksgiving." Some commentators (e.g., Schlier, 233; Gnilka, 247; Schnackenburg, 223) argue that the verb from the previous verse does not govern these new vices and that one should supply "there should not be," because now types of speech themselves become the subject of being named. But this is to demand a precision of thought and style on the part of the writer that may well be alien to him. The new triad of vices should be seen as simply continuing the thought of the previous verse by making explicit the sort of naming of sexual sins that is being forbidden. The contrasting "thanksgiving" at the end of the verse can also still be seen to be governed by the earlier verb (with NIV; *contra* RSV, NEB). The thought of the verse is a variant on 4:29, "Do not let any evil talk come out of your mouth, but whatever is good for building up." The three terms for sinful speech in 5:4, which are *hapax legomena* in the NT, elaborate on "evil talk," and "thanksgiving" now substitutes as the positive element in the exhortation. The first and the last two terms in the triad are mutually illuminating. That the last two terms involve speech indicate that the first αἰσχρότης is not just obscenity or shamefulness in general but obscene speech. The Colossians passage (αἰσχρολογία, Col 3:8) also suggests that this is the connotation the writer has in mind. Similarly, the notion of obscenity colors the other two terms, so that it is foolish talk and coarse joking about sex that are in view. There were rigorous regulations about uncontrolled speech at Qumran with various penances attached: "whoever has spoken foolishly: three months . . . whoever has guffawed foolishly shall do penance for thirty days" (1QS 7.14–18). In fact 1QS 10.21–23 provides a close parallel to both the negative and positive elements of Eph 5:4: "In my mouth shall be heard no folly. . . . The fruit of holiness shall be on my tongue and no abominations shall be found upon it. I will open my mouth in songs of thanksgiving."

The last of the vices listed, εὐτραπελία, has occasioned much discussion, not least because Aristotle treats it as a virtue, as the ready wit which is essential to social flexibility. In *Eth. Eud.* 3.7.1234a.4–23 he talks of this wittiness as "a middle state, and the witty man as midway between the boorish or stiff man and the buffoon." What prompted the different evaluation of wittiness on the part of the writer to the Ephesians? Or did εὐτραπελία undergo a shift of meaning from an original earlier sense of "ready wit" with favorable connotations to a later sense of suggestive ribald jesting? In a fascinating address to the Eton Literary Society, Matthew Arnold used his analysis of this term's history as a springboard for a survey of Greek culture with application to education in nineteenth-century British society. He claimed that the Athenian genius for flexibility gradually lost its grasp on moral ideas, and "then the new and reforming spirit, the Christian spirit, which was rising in the world, turned sternly upon this gracious flexibility, changed the sense of its name, branded it with infamy, and classed it, along with 'filthiness and foolish talking,' among 'things which are not convenient' " ("A Speech at Eton," in *Irish Essays and Others* [London: Smith, Elder, and Co., 1891[2]] 148). Whatever the merits of Arnold's opinions about Greek culture, his brief analysis of the history of usage of εὐτραπελία is rather misleading. A much more reliable guide to its usage is provided by van der Horst ("Is Wittiness Unchristian?" 163–77). He shows that even Aristotle is aware that the term also has negative connotations (cf. *Eth. Nic.* 4.8.1128a.14–15; *Rhet.* 2.12.1389b.10–12, where it is listed among the excesses of youth), that in Isocrates it has both a negative (*Areop.* 49) and a positive meaning (*Antid.* 296), and that from the fifth century B.C.E. onward positive and negative meanings can be found side by side, though the positive predominates. In connection with conversation the negative connotation "may be buffoonery or some kind of inhumane or degrading jesting" ("Is Wittiness Unchristian?" 175). Van der Horst admits that, although there is no clear instance of this force elsewhere, the context of the use in Eph 5:4 suggests the meaning of "dirty jokes." He does point out, however, that there is one place in Aristotle which hints that the witty man is characterized by his innuendo, his insinuations in the direction of shameful things (cf. *Eth. Nic.* 4.8.1128a.23–24). So in Ephesians, the coarse joking prohibited may well involve the use of suggestive language and double entendres. Again, such conversation is described as not fitting (see above), and again, for this writer, the reason appears to be that to treat sexual matters as a topic of amusement is not to take them seriously enough and is likely to lead to an atmosphere in which the actual practice of sexual vices is also accepted too easily.

What is to replace the six vices and to be at the heart of Christian speech is thanksgiving, which appears like an oasis in a desert of negatives. There is no need to find this strange and, with Origen and Jerome in their commentaries on this text (followed by Casel, *BZ* 18 [1929] 84–85), to opt instead for εὐχαριτία, "graciousness," as a coined expression (cf. J. A. Robinson, 198–99). εὐχαριστία is chosen as the virtue not only because of its play on words with εὐτραπελία but also because it was a traditional contrast (cf. 1QS 10.21–23) and one which expressed a profound difference between values. As Houlden (*Paul's Letters*, 324) puts it, "whereas sexual impurity and covetousness both express self-centered acquisitiveness, thanksgiving is the exact opposite, and so the antidote required; it is the recognition of God's generosity." Philo saw thanksgiving as a preeminent virtue which could encapsulate the whole of a person's religious obligation (cf. *De Plant.* 126, 131), and in Paul's writings too (cf. 1 Thess 5:18; 1 Cor 10:30; 14:16, 17; 2 Cor 4:15; 9:11, 12; Rom 1:21; 14:6; Phil 4:6; cf. also Col 1:12; 2:7; 3:17; 4:2) "thanksgiving was almost a synonym for the Christian life" (cf. P. T. O'Brien, "Thanksgiving in Pauline Theology," in *Pauline Studies*, ed. D. A. Hagner and M. J. Harris [Grand Rapids: Eerdmans, 1980] 62). Behind the contrast of Eph 5:3, 4 lies a fundamental issue. What is acknowledged as ultimate—God or some aspect of being in the world, such as sexuality or sensual gratification (cf. also Rom 1:21)? For this writer and for the Judeo-Christian tradition, thanksgiving is an essential aspect of the faith that acknowledges God as the ultimate source of all that is, the creator, sustainer, and redeemer of life. The writer will elaborate on the need for thanksgiving in 5:20, but it has already become clear from the opening *berakah* (1:3–14) and thanksgiving section (1:15–23) that he believes this to be the proper response of those who have experienced the grace of God in Christ.

5 τοῦτο γὰρ ἴστε γινώσκοντες ὅτι πᾶς πόρνος ἢ ἀκάθαρτος ἢ πλεονέκτης, ὅ ἐστιν εἰδωλολάτρης, οὐκ ἔχει κληρονομίαν ἐν τῇ βασιλείᾳ τοῦ Χριστοῦ καὶ θεοῦ, "For be very sure of this, no fornicator or impure or covetous person (such a person is an idolater) has any inheritance in the kingdom of Christ and of God." There follows this solemn warning about the dire consequences for those who practice the vices listed in v 3. This time there is the additional thought that the person who is characterized by unrestrained sexual greed is, in fact, an idolater (cf. the link between covetousness and idolatry in Col 3:5). In Judaism *T. Jud.* 19.1 had linked covetousness with idolatry (cf. also Philo, *De Spec. Leg.* 1.23, 25), while fornication and sexual lust are associated with it in Wis 14:12; *T. Reub.* 4.6; *T. Jud.* 23.1. As L. T. Johnson (*Sharing Possessions* [Philadelphia: Fortress, 1981] 52, 55) says, "The important idolatries have always centered on those forces which have enough specious power to be truly counterfeit, and therefore truly dangerous: sexuality (fertility), riches, and power (glory). . . . All idolatry is a form of covetousness, for by refusing to acknowledge life and worth as a gift from the Creator, it seeks to seize them from the creation as booty." Sexual lust elevates the desired object, whether a person's own gratification or another person, to the center of life and is antithetical to the thanksgiving which recognizes God at the center.

Those who are idolaters of this sort will not inherit the kingdom of Christ and of God. Assurance about believers' future inheritance had been given in 1:14, 18, but now exclusion from the kingdom, which is mentioned in Pauline paraenesis in 1 Cor 6:9, 10 and Gal 5:21 and in a different context in 1 Cor 15:50, is held out as a threat to this particular class of people. The fornicator, the covetous person, and the idolater are also mentioned in the lists in 1 Cor 5:9–11 and 6:9, 10. This particular double formulation about the kingdom is unique in the NT (though cf. Rev 11:15). The kingdom is linked with Christ in 2 Tim 4:1, 18 and 2 Pet 1:11 (cf. also 2 *Apoc. Bar.* 39:7), and in some places the kingdom of Christ represents the present aspect of God's rule (cf. 1 Cor 15:24–28; Col 1:13; cf. also Eph 2:6). But the notion of two successive forms of God's rule should not be read into Eph 5:5 from 1 Cor 15:24–28. Instead, there is here an identity of the two kingdoms in terms of their time and their nature (cf. also Gnilka, 249; Barth, 564; *pace* Caird, *Paul's Letters*, 85). The kingdom of Christ is the kingdom of God and has both present and future aspects from which the fornicators and the impure and covetous persons are excluded. Those in bondage to their sexual appetites are not those over whom Christ and God rule.

The writer assumes that his readers are not among such people. To describe this verse, therefore, as a warning to believers that they can lose their salvation (cf. Ernst, 372) does not do justice to its function in the context. It provides a further motivation for the readers not even to mention these vices, namely, that those who actually perpetrate them are in a realm totally antithetical to the kingdom of Christ and God (*contra* Barth, 564, who takes the passage to be referring to church discipline and claims, "The immoral persons mentioned in 5:3 ff. are members of the congregation, not people outside the Church").

6 μηδεὶς ὑμᾶς ἀπατάτω κενοῖς λόγοις, διὰ ταῦτα γὰρ ἔρχεται ἡ ὀργὴ τοῦ θεοῦ ἐπὶ τοὺς υἱοὺς τῆς ἀπειθείας, "Let no one deceive you with empty words, for because of these things the wrath of God comes upon those who are disobedient." The motivation of v 5 is now underlined. Believers are not even to mention the vices listed previously, because they are so serious that on account of them Gentile outsiders will not only be excluded from the kingdom but will also experience the wrath of God. Those upon whom this wrath will come are the disobedient, the unbelieving Gentiles from amongst whom the readers have been saved (cf. 2:2, 3; 5:7, 8). The readers are not to be led astray by anyone who asserts that there will be no judgment on sin. The words of such a person are empty, devoid of truth (cf. Col 2:4, 8; cf. also LXX Exod 5:9; Deut 32:47; *T. Naph.* 3.1). In Colossians similar language had been used of those promulgating the false teaching, but here the reference is far more general. If any group is particularly in view, it is not so much likely to be Christians with a libertine or gnosticizing tendency (*pace* Abbott, 152; Schlier, 236; Barth, 565–66; Mitton, 181; Mussner, 143) as unbelieving Gentiles who claimed they had no need to worry and attempted to justify their vices as matters of indifference (cf. Meyer, 269; Westcott, 77; Schnackenburg, 225). This interpretation also maintains the insider/outsider contrast that runs throughout the passage. God's wrath, his holy anger against sin and the judgment that results from it, is real, and it is coming on the disobedient. The present tense of ἔρχεσθαι often has a future meaning, and that is most probably the case here. Most commentators allow for both present and future aspects of wrath in 5:5 (cf. Abbott, 152; Schlier, 236; Barth, 566; Ernst, 374; Schnackenburg, 226; Mussner, 144), but Meyer (270) may well be right to insist on the future aspect. Elsewhere, traditional formulations about the coming of wrath have a future reference (cf. 1 Thess 1:10; 5:9; Col 3:6). The children of wrath in 2:3 are those doomed to experience God's wrath on the day of judgment, and Ephesians shows no interest in developing any present aspects of wrath in the manner of Rom 1:18–32.

7 μὴ οὖν γίνεσθε συμμέτοχοι αὐτῶν, "therefore do not become partners with them." The content of this fresh prohibition makes explicit the assumption behind the preceding verses, namely, that the antithesis between the believing readers and immoral persons around them is one which must remain. By means of the οὖν, "therefore," the prohibition also builds on vv 5, 6. Since the consequences for the immoral are so severe, the readers are not to become partners with them. αὐτῶν, "with them," is to be taken as a reference to people rather than vices (cf. Meyer, 270; Abbott, 152; Schlier, 236; Schnackenburg, 226; *contra* Gnilka, 250; Ernst, 374, is undecided), and "the disobedient" is the most immediate antecedent (*contra* Bratcher and Nida, *Handbook,* 129, who opt for those attempting to deceive the readers, and Barth, 567, who thinks erring church members are involved). συμμέτοχος occurs in the NT only here and in 3:6, and in both places has the connotation of intimate involvement and participation with the other party. It is not possible for the readers to be sharers with Jewish Christians in the promise in Christ Jesus through the gospel (cf. 3:6) and at the same time to be sharers with immoral Gentiles (cf. also J. A. Robinson, 200; Bruce, *Epistles,* 373). How far is the separation urged upon the readers to be taken? Should it lead to the radical separatism on the part of the community reflected in the Qumran writings (cf. 1QS 1.4, 5; 5.10, 11; CD 6.14, 15)? The closest parallel in the Pauline corpus is 2 Cor 6:14–7:1, which has links with the Qumran material but which is suspected of being an interpolation and non-Pauline (on these issues, see most recently V. P. Furnish, *2 Corinthians* [New York: Doubleday, 1984] 371–83; R. P. Martin, *2 Corinthians* [Waco, TX: Word, 1986] 190–95). The context here in Ephesians makes clear that what is involved is not a general distancing from all aspects of life in the Gentile world but in particular a separation from its immoral aspects. The readers are not to become partners with disobedient Gentiles in their sins and thereby also in the judgment that will come on them.

8–10 ἦτε γάρ ποτε σκότος, νῦν δὲ φῶς ἐν κυρίῳ· ὡς τέκνα φωτὸς περιπατεῖτε, "for once you were darkness, but now you are light in the Lord; live as children of light." A more positive reason for not joining in with the disobedient is now adduced—the change that took place in the readers because of their conversion-initiation. The connecting γάρ grounds the previous prohibition but also introduces the imagery which dominates the rest of the pericope. The combination of the ποτέ . . . νῦν contrast schema (cf. 2:1–10; 2:11–22) and the imagery of darkness and light suggest that baptismal paraenesis is being employed, which at the same time as reminding the readers of their conversion also draws implications for their present attitude to the world. Images of darkness and light occur frequently in connection with conversion (e.g., *Joseph and Asenath* 8.10; 15.13; Philo, *De Virt.* 179; Acts 26:18; Col 1:12, 13; 1 Pet 2:9; *Odes Sol.* 14.18, 19; cf. also Heb 6:4; 10:32). Already in the OT, light can stand for the life of God and the salvation that comes from God (e.g., Ps 27:1; Isa 9:2; 10:17; 42:6, 16; 49:6; 51:4; 60:1), while darkness stands for death, Sheol, and God's judgment (e.g., Ps 49:19; Isa 5:30; 9:2; 47:5; 59:9; 60:2). In the Qumran literature, of course, this imagery is frequent and depicts two ways of life in relationship to God, not only in 1QM with its "War of the Sons of Light against the Sons of Darkness" (cf. 1.1–16; 3.6, 9; 13.16; 14.17) but also in 1QS 1.9, 10; 3.13, 19–21, 24, 25 (cf. K. G. Kuhn, "The Epistle to the Ephesians," esp. 122–24). A similar ethical dualism of light and darkness is found in *The Testaments of the Twelve Patriarchs* ("Choose for yourselves light or darkness, the law of the Lord or the works of Beliar," *T. Levi* 19.1; cf. also 14.4; *T. Benj.* 5.3). In the NT, the Johannine writings make particular use of this imagery (cf. 1:4, 5, 7–9; 3:19–21; 8:12; 9:5; 12:35, 36, 46; 1 John 1:5; 2:8), while in Paul it occurs in 1 Thess 5:5; 2 Cor 4:4, 6; 6:14; Rom 13:12, 13 and Col 1:12, 13. (For further discussion cf. S. Aalen, *Die Begriffe 'Licht' und 'Finsternis' im Alten Testament, im Spätjudentum und in Rabbinismus* [Oslo: I. Kommisjon Hos Jacob Dybwad, 1951]; R. Bultmann, "Zur Geschichte der Lichtsymbolik im Altertum," *Philologus* 97 [1948] 1–36; L. R. Stachiowak, "Die Antithese Licht-Finsternis: Ein Thema der paulinischen Paränese," *TQ* 143 [1963] 385–421.) Ideas and formulations from Qumran may well have influenced Christian baptismal paraenesis at an early stage, and paraenesis colored in this way appears to have been taken up in 2 Cor 6:14–7:1 and here in Ephesians. In Ephesians, darkness already represents ignorance (cf. 4:18), and now in this context it represents the immorality that has just been described, while light represents truth and knowledge (cf. 1:18) and now holiness. But what is striking is that people are not merely depicted as being in the realms of darkness or light but as themselves actually being darkness or light. Those governed by the dominion of darkness or light represent that dominion in their own persons (*pace* Engberg-Pedersen, *ZNW* 80 [1989] 102, there is no reason, however, to identify darkness and light with inner mental attitudes). So the readers are not just surrounded by the light but are identified with it. They have become identified with the light because of their identification with Christ. In the Qumran writings, a rigorous acceptance of the law separated the sons of light from the sons of darkness. In Ephesians, it is being "in the Lord" (cf. also 2:21; 4:1, 17; 6:1, 10) that distinguishes light from darkness. Elsewhere in the Pauline corpus there is a general tendency for ἐν κυρίῳ, in comparison with ἐν Χριστῷ, to be used in paraenetic contexts to refer to what believers are to become or to do in relationship to Christ (cf. M. Bouttier, *En Christ* [Paris: Presses Universitaires, 1962] 54–61; C. F. D. Moule, *The Origin of Christology* [Cambridge: CUP, 1977] 58–60). Here, though in a paraenetic context, it refers to the indicative of what believers are in relation to Christ. The imperative follows in the next clause. If the readers are light, then they are to walk or live (cf. 2:2, 10; 4:1, 17; 5:2) as children of light, a designation which contrasts with "the sons of disobedience" in v 6. Their behavior is to conform to their identity. As at Qumran, the light-darkness dualism in Ephesians concerns two ways of life and differs from the substantial dualism of later Gnosticism with its notion of the return of the soul to its original existence in the transcendental realm of light.

ὁ γὰρ καρπὸς τοῦ φωτὸς ἐν πάσῃ ἀγαθωσύνῃ καὶ δικαιοσύνῃ καὶ ἀληθείᾳ, "for the fruit of light consists in all goodness, righteousness, and truth." This parenthesis of v 9 with its triad of general virtues elaborates on what it means to live as children of light. Light is seen as a fertile power which produces fruit. The fruit of light is the equivalent to what Gal 5:22 calls the fruit of the Spirit (cf. also Phil 1:11—the fruit of righteousness) and stands over against the fruitless deeds or works of darkness of v 11, as the fruit of the Spirit stands over against the works of the flesh in Gal 5:19. The list of the three virtues which make up the fruit of light has some parallels in the OT and in the Qumran writings. 2 Chron 31:20 describes Hezekiah as doing "what was good and right and faithful before the Lord his God"; Mic 6:8 talks of doing good, justice, and steadfast love; and 1QS 1.5 has the wording "that they may . . . hold fast to all good; that they may practice truth, righteousness, and justice upon earth" (cf. also 1QS 8.2). Moral goodness can be described as virtue in general by Philo (cf. *Leg. Alleg.* 1.163) and is listed by Paul as among the fruit of the Spirit in Gal 5:22 (cf. also Rom 15:14; 2 Thess 1:11). Col 1:10 spoke about "bearing fruit in every good work," while earlier in Ephesians there has been mention of the good works for which believers have been created in Christ Jesus (2:10). Righteousness involves doing right in relation to both God and humanity (see *Comment* on 4:24; cf. also 6:14). Truth has been mentioned with a broad meaning in 4:21, 24 and in a reference to speaking the truth in 4:25. Here, in the light of the OT parallels to the triad and of the Qumran background, it may well have the force that אמת, *'emet,* frequently has, namely, "faithfulness" or "loyalty" (cf. also J. Murphy-O'Connor, "Truth: Paul and Qumran," in *Paul and Qumran,* 202–5). Each of these three virtues is very general in its range and could in fact stand for the whole of the Christian life (cf. J. Thomas, "Formgesetze des Begriffs-Katalogs im NT," *TZ* 24 [1968] 18–19).

δοκιμάζοντες τί ἐστιν εὐάρεστον τῷ κυρίῳ, "discovering what is pleasing to the Lord." δοκιμάζοντες, "discovering," is taken in this translation as a participle which further defines the walking as children of light called for in v 8, rather than as a separate imperative. The verb δοκιμάζειν has the force of testing or finding out in the circumstances the ethically right course of action. It was an important term in Stoic ethics, where the testing was according to reason (cf. esp. Epictetus, *Diss.* 1.20.7; 2.23.6, 8; 4.5.16; 4.6.13; 4.7.40). In Paul, the term is found in 1 Thess 5:21; Phil 1:9, 10; and Rom 12:2, which has other linguistic links with this passage—"discovering what is the will of God, what is good [τὸ ἀγαθόν], and acceptable or pleasing [εὐάρεστον]." Previously, in Rom 2:18, Paul had spoken of the Jews as knowing God's will and approving or discovering what is excellent because of their instruction in the law. When the Qumran literature mentions seeking God's will, it refers to returning to every commandment of the law of Moses (cf. 1QS 5.9). But Paul holds that believers are able to discover the will of God in the concrete situations they face, as they place their whole beings at God's disposal. Cullmann (*Christ and Time* [London: SCM, 1962] 228–29) stresses the significance of this term: "The working of the Holy Spirit shows itself in the testing (δοκιμάζειν), that is in the capacity of forming the correct Christian ethical judgment at each given moment. . . . This 'testing' is the key of all New Testament ethics." In the Pauline tradition, then, the testing is according to the will of God, now revealed most fully in Christ. Here, that notion is formulated in terms of "what is pleasing to the Lord."

Because the readers are light in the Lord, they will want to discover what pleases their Lord. The idea of pleasing God or the Lord is found frequently in the LXX (e.g., Gen 5:22, 24; 6:9; Sir 44:16) and as the goal and motivation of Christian living in Paul (cf. Rom 12:2; 14:18; 2 Cor 5:9; Phil 4:18; Col 3:20). If the readers' motivation is to please their Lord, then living as children of light will involve exercising a responsible freedom and developing an intuitive sense about how to act in a given situation.

11, 12 καὶ μὴ συγκοινωνεῖτε τοῖς ἔργοις τοῖς ἀκάρποις τοῦ σκότους, μᾶλλον δὲ καὶ ἐλέγχετε, "And do not take part in the fruitless deeds of darkness, but rather expose them." It is now underlined that living as children of light (v 8) not only involves producing the fruit of light (v 9) but also, since light and darkness are incompatible, inevitably excludes participation in the fruitless deeds of darkness. It also becomes clear that "do not become partners with them" in v 7 refers to taking part in the vices of the disobedient. By naming these vices "fruitless deeds of darkness" (cf. also Rom 13:12) in contrast to the virtues which are the fruit of light, the writer shows his awareness that darkness also produces, but produces only "works" (ἔργα; cf. Gal 5:19, "works of the flesh") which are sterile, lacking direction, and futile (cf. Mark 4:19; Titus 3:14; 2 Pet 1:8; Jude 12). In other words, darkness spreads only darkness. It could be that just as the reference of light alternates between the sphere of power and those who represent it, so also darkness here stands not merely for the realm but also for those who represent it and who perform the fruitless deeds. After all, the writer has previously said that the readers were darkness (cf. the observations above about the personal focus of the imagery of v 8) and will go on to speak in personal terms in v 12 of what is done by *them* (cf. Schnackenburg, 230). In any case, the readers are not to engage in deeds of darkness but are to expose them.

Of the range of meanings that ἐλέγχειν can have, such as "to convict," "to reprove," "to discipline," in this sentence it is the meaning of "to expose" that is most appropriate (cf. BAGD 249). Engberg-Pedersen (*ZNW* 80 [1989] 95–101) criticizes Bauer for placing this meaning first on his list, although he admits that it is a sense that ἐλέγχειν acquired. Engberg-Pedersen prefers to emphasize the core meaning of the verb as "confronting somebody or something with the aim of showing him or it to be, in some determinate respect, at fault." He claims that the two crucial factors in its use are "that there is a question as to whether some person or thing conforms to some standard of rightness and wrongness and that the person or thing is being directly confronted (as opposed to being allowed to pass unnoticed) by some other person or thing in such a way that the answer to the question becomes clear." In this context, however, where the object of the verb is not named in the Greek text but should be assumed to be the deeds mentioned in the previous clause, and where these deeds will be said to have been done in secret, to confront them in such a way as to show their wrongness is the same as to expose them. That the object of the verb is the fruitless deeds of darkness also makes it less likely that ἐλέγχειν should be taken as a reference to verbal reproof or rebuke on analogy with LXX Lev 19:17; Sir 19:13–17 and passages in the Qumran literature such as 1QS 5.24, 26; CD 7.2; 9.8; 20.4 which speak of reproving a neighbor or member of the community. Because of the Qumran texts and because the imperative of ἐλέγχειν is frequently used in the NT for admonishing members of the Christian community (cf. Matt 18:15–17; 1 Tim 5:20; 2 Tim 4:2; Titus 1:9, 13; Rev 3:19), Gnilka (255–56, followed by Halter, *Taufe*, 276) claims that the reference here is to the correction and rebuke of fellow believers who fall into sin. But this does not fit the use of the darkness imagery and the argument of the passage to this point, which has been with reference to the sins of outsiders (cf. also Ernst, 375–76; Schnackenburg, 230 n. 559; Engberg-Pedersen *ZNW* 80 [1989] 90–91). Paul's discussion in 1 Cor 14:24, 25, which uses vocabulary similar to that employed here in order to speak about someone who is convicted and whose secrets become illumined or revealed, refers to an outsider, and in John 16:8 it is the unbelieving world that the Paraclete convicts about sin. K. G. Kuhn ("The Epistle to the Ephesians," 124–31) takes Eph 5:11 as requiring a verbal summons to the sinner to be converted. But Prov 9:7; 15:12; 1QS 9.16 warn against verbal correction of outsiders. As we have seen, it is more likely that ἐλέγχειν refers to exposure of the sinner's deeds, and that, since v 12 discourages even speaking about such deeds, this exposure is meant to take place through the readers' behavior. As they refuse to join in evil actions and display a different quality of life, they cast their illuminating beam into the dark recesses of the surrounding society and will invariably show up its immoral practices for what they are.

τὰ γὰρ κρυφῇ γινόμενα ὑπ' αὐτῶν αἰσχρόν ἐστιν καὶ λέγειν, "for it is shameful even to speak of what is done by them in secret." A further reason is given (cf. γάρ) for both the positive and the negative aspects of the previous exhortation of v 11. The deeds of darkness are so abhorrent that it is shameful even to speak of them. They are described as "what is done in secret." This refers to the same sexual vices that have been discussed earlier, and there is no reason for thinking that the expression has some special connection with libertine rites at mystery cults (*pace* Schlier, 239). ὑπ' αὐτῶν, "by them," is to be understood in terms of those who belong to the darkness that has been mentioned in v 11 (cf. also BDF § 282 [2]), who are the same as the disobedient of vv 6, 7. Their activities are not even to be mentioned (cf. v 3; cf. also Philo, *De Op. Mund.* 80, for a similar way of underlining wickedness). Instead, the light must simply be allowed to have its effect of exposure and illumination. There is no need to import into the argument at this point the notion that the hidden deeds retain a dangerous attraction for believers (*pace* Engberg-Pedersen, *ZNW* 80 [1989] 102). The focus of the passage is on what light does to the dark deeds of unbelievers, not on how it can fortify believers against their inner inclination toward such deeds (*pace* Engberg-Pedersen, *ZNW* 80 [1989] 103).

13, 14a τὰ δὲ πάντα ἐλεγχόμενα ὑπὸ τοῦ φωτὸς φανεροῦται, πᾶν γὰρ τὸ φανερούμενον φῶς ἐστιν, "But everything exposed becomes illumined by the light, for everything that becomes illumined is light." The force of these assertions in support of the writer's exhortation is not immediately obvious, and they have given rise to a number of different interpretations. Some clarity is achieved, however, if it is seen that the movement of thought progresses from the notion of exposure, taken up from v 11, through that of illumination by the light to a concentration on the light itself. ὑπὸ τοῦ φωτός, "by the light," could be taken either with ἐλεγχόμενα, "exposed" (cf. Abbott, 155; J. A. Robinson, 201; Westcott, 79; Gnilka, 258 n. 1; Bratcher and Nida, *Handbook*, 132), or φανεροῦται, "becomes illumined" (cf. Meyer, 275; Schlier, 239; Barth, 572; Ernst, 376; Mussner, 145; Schnackenburg, 231). This makes little substantial difference to the sense, but it may well be that since light is not explicitly mentioned with the notion of exposure in v 11, it does not accompany that idea when it is found again in v 13 but awaits the introduction of the concept of becoming visible or illumined. On this construction also, a move is more easily made from light as a reference to believers, which it has been up to this point in the passage, to light as a reference to Christ, which it becomes in v 14b. CD 20.3–5 combines the notions of being exposed and being revealed, as does John 3:19–21, which talks, on the one hand, of the failure of the person in darkness to come to the light lest his deeds be exposed (ἵνα μὴ ἐλεγχθῇ τὰ ἔργα αὐτοῦ) but, on the other, of the one who does the truth coming to the light in order that his deeds might be revealed for what they are (ἵνα φανερωθῇ αὐτοῦ τὰ ἔργα). Light in this latter passage has both negative and positive effects. Negatively, it exposes evil, and positively, it illumines good. Similarly, in regard to v 13 here, J. A. Robinson (200–201) argues that "since ἐλέγχεσθαι and φανεροῦσθαι are appropriate respectively to the evil and the good . . . , the transformation of the one into the other is marked by the change of the verbs." The process by which darkness is transformed into light is spelled out. As the children of light expose the deeds of darkness by their living, so what is exposed itself becomes illumined by the sphere of light. In fact, as the further explanation asserts, whatever becomes illumined in this way is then itself part of the sphere of light. The participle φανερούμενον is taken as passive in line with the verb in the first clause, rather than as middle with active force. The force of the middle, an assertion that "whatever reveals or illumines is light" (cf. Abbott, 156), would be, as Moule (*Idiom-Book*, 25) says, "a not very illuminating remark!" The exposure carried out through believers' lives enables others to see the nature of their deeds and respond to the light in such a way that they are themselves light (cf. Schlier, 239–40; *pace* Schnackenburg, 232, who holds that this is an overinterpretation of v 14a). This is a transformation the readers had themselves experienced. As v 8 put it, "once you were darkness, but now you are light in the Lord." J. B. Phillips' version brings out this force well: "It is even possible (after all, it happened with you!) for light to turn the thing it shines upon into light also." The citation that follows reminds the readers of their experience.

14b διὸ λέγει, Ἔγειρε, ὁ καθεύδων, καὶ ἀνάστα ἐκ τῶν νεκρῶν, καὶ ἐπιφαύσει σοι ὁ Χριστός, "Therefore it is said, 'Awake, O sleeper, and rise from the dead, and Christ will shine upon you.'" The lines from the baptismal hymn remind the readers of the summons and promise they received at baptism. On the form and origin of these lines, see the discussion under *Form/Structure/Setting*. The introductory formula διὸ λέγει, "therefore it is said," is used with a Scripture citation in Eph 4:8 (cf. also Jas 4:6). Its employment here presumably indicates that for the writer the Christian liturgical material, from which his citation was in all probability taken, was also an authoritative tradition which could provide forceful support for his exhortation. The διό, "therefore," provides a link most immediately with v 14a but also with v 8, which began the writer's train of thought here. Attempts have been made to explain the contents of the lines from a number of possible backgrounds. Some look to the mystery religions, where there was often a call to awaken issued to the initiate (cf. Aristophanes, *Ranae* 340–42; *Orph. Hymn.* 50.90; cf., e.g., Fischer, *Tendenz*, 142–44, who has to attempt a hypothetical reconstruction of initiation in a mystery cult in order to provide the analogy according to which the baptismal call here in Ephesians would have been formed). Others have claimed the hymnic fragment is to be understood in the light of Gnostic thought, instancing the second strophe of a Zarathustra song in a Turfan fragment and the "Hymn of the Pearl" in *Acts of Thomas* 110.43–48 (cf. R. Reitzenstein, *Hellenistic Mystery-Religions*, tr. J. E. Steely [Pittsburgh: Pickwick Press, 1978] 58; Pokorný, *Der Epheserbrief*, 119; Lindemann, *Aufhebung*, 234 n. 167). But nothing in the three lines demands that their framework be the call for the spark of light in the soul to awaken out of its drunken sleep of being in the material world and to remember its immortal heavenly home. It is early Christianity's heritage in the OT and early Judaism that, in fact, provides the background for understanding not only this image but also the other major aspects of the citation. 1QH 3.19–21 contains imagery about being rescued from the death of sin. Sleep was of course a euphemistic image for physical death (e.g., Job 14:12), and in *Pss. Sol.* 16.1–4 both sleep and death stand for sin and its consequences (cf. also K. G. Kuhn, "The Epistle to the Ephesians," 126–30). This is true in Paul also, where sleep is the condition of forgetfulness and drunkenness which is part of belonging to the sinful darkness (cf. 1 Thess 5:5–8; Rom 13:11–14) and where baptism is a rising from the death of sin (Rom 6:13; cf. 6:4). Ephesians' own perspective on the imagery of death as humanity's situation of sin (cf. 2:1, 5; cf. also Col 2:13) should surely be decisive in favor of this sort of interpretation. The association of Christ with a shining light can be seen to have its background in the use of this image for Yahweh coming to save or help his people (cf. Deut 33:2; Ps 50:2; 80:1–3, 7, 19—the repetition of "let your face shine, that we may be saved!"; 1QH 4.5, 6, 23; 9.31; CD 20.25, 26; *T. Zeb.* 9.8) and in its application to the Messiah (cf. *T. Levi* 18.2–4; *T. Jud.* 24.1). Christ is depicted as a shining light elsewhere in the NT (e.g., Luke 2:32; John 1:4, 5, 9; 3:19–21; 8:12; 9:5; 12:46; Rev 1:16) and in early Christianity (cf. esp. *Odes Sol.* 15.2, "Because he is my sun, and his rays have restored me; and his light has dismissed all darkness from my face"; for extensive discussion of the symbol of light with reference to Christ in early Christianity, see Dölger, *Sol Salutis*, 342–410).

These words heard at their baptism function now to remind the readers of the power of the light, of the transformation to their new status that has taken place, and of its ethical implications. Given the writer's earlier emphasis in this letter on God's gracious sovereignty in the accomplishment of salvation, it may well be that the call of the first two lines should now be understood not simply as issuing from the congregation to the newly baptized convert but as echoing God's call. Their baptism, then, signified a movement from the sleep of spiritual death into the light of life in response to the divine call. Both divine initiative and human effort are represented in their conversion-initiation according to these lines. There was the call that broke in upon them in the first place, demanding a response (cf. also 1:18; 4:1); there was the response of turning away from the sleep and death of the old life; and there was the gracious and powerful light of Christ that came to them in that response.

Explanation 333

Perhaps in relation to the previous verses, the first two aspects are what takes place as the light does its work of exposure, while the third corresponds to its work of illumination. In any case, in rounding off this section of exhortation, the lines are meant to have the effect of strengthening the readers' confidence in the power of the light and their determination to live out of that power.

Explanation

The previous section of the letter had singled out seven topics on which to exhort the readers about how the difference between the old life and the new should come to expression in their speech and conduct. Now the contrast is not so much between the old and the new as, in similar fashion to 4:17–21, between the believing community and sinful outsiders. The stark contrast has to do first with matters of sexual morality. Then its black and white nature is appropriately represented in the symbols of darkness and light.

The paraenesis falls into two parts. Verses 3–6, which make use of lists of vices and those who perpetrate them, are primarily dark in tone, dominated by prohibitions and warnings of judgment. Though v 7 makes the bridge into the second part with another prohibition, drawing out the consequences of the previous verses, vv 7–14 as a whole with their contrast schema, list of virtues, and citation of a hymn fragment become more and more positive, so that their dominant tone is light. The first part is primarily dependent on Col 3:5–8, while the contrast between light and darkness of the second part develops more extensively imagery Paul had already employed in his ethical exhortations.

In vv 3, 4 the writer stresses that sexual immorality is totally alien to the Christian way of life by prohibiting even the mention of any form of impurity. For those who are called to be holy, what is appropriate is a radical distancing from the gross sensuality and sexual greed of the surrounding world. Their conversation is to be distinctive and to avoid obscenity and foolish talk and coarse joking about sex. The one positive note in these verses is struck at the end, where thanksgiving is contrasted with the preceding vices and enjoined as the essential characteristic of Christian speech. Instead of the self-centeredness which characterizes sexual impurity, thanksgiving embodies a recognition of the Creator and his goodness. Two warnings, which are meant to provide motivation to take note of the prohibitions, follow in vv 5, 6. Fornicators and impure and covetous persons are excluded from the kingdom of Christ and God. In fact, such disobedient outsiders will also experience the wrath of God. No one, therefore, should be misled by those who claim that one's sexual activities are a matter of indifference. Such a claim could not be further from the truth, for God's judgment will fall on all sinful conduct. In v 5 in line with traditional Jewish thought, the sexually covetous person is deemed an idolater. This underlines why thanksgiving has been presented as the contrasting virtue. Instead of the latter's recognition of the Creator at the center of life, the idolatry of sexual lust makes some other desired object supreme.

The writer sums up the significance of his prohibitions and of the implications of his warnings as he urges his readers not to become partners with disobedient Gentile outsiders in their sinful activities (v 7). This time the prohibition is backed by a reminder of the change that has taken place in the readers' lives (v 8). Once they were identified with the dominion of darkness, but now through their relationship to their Lord they have become identified with that of the light. To become involved in immorality would be a total contradiction of everything the readers now are because of their baptism. The implication of this change of identity is now put positively. If the readers are light, then they are to live as children of light. What that involves is first indicated in v 9 by means of a triad of virtues—goodness, righteousness, and truth—which are depicted as light's fruit, the ethical outcome of its power. But since the change in the readers' identity was also a change of dominions (they became light *in the Lord*), living as children of light will also mean discovering in the specific situations they face what pleases their Lord (v 10). The old dominion of darkness was sterile in its effects, and so what is absolutely clear is that living as children of light will exclude participation in the fruitless deeds of darkness. Instead, and more positively, it will mean exposing by a contrasting quality of life such secretly executed deeds, of which it is shameful even to speak (vv 11, 12). What is exposed in this fashion, in fact, becomes illumined by the light of the Christian sphere of living. What is more, whatever becomes revealed or lit up is then part of the realm of light (vv 13, 14a). The readers ought to know this, because, as the writer now reminds them by his citation from a baptismal hymn (v 14b), they themselves had experienced the light in just such a way. Baptism had involved their waking out of the sleep of the old life, their rising from the death of sin, as the light of Christ shone on them. They should be assured that the light that had transformed their darkness had lost none of its power.

What specifically constitutes Christian behavior according to this passage? Negatively, it will be characterized by the absence of any talk about fornication or sexual impurity, any dirty jokes or sexual innuendo, let alone any participation in immoral acts. Positively, it will mean thanksgiving, goodness, righteousness, truth, discovering what is pleasing to the Lord, and exposing sinful activity. The warrants for exhortation to this pattern of life can be as general as "what is fitting" (v 4), but this should be interpreted in the light of the more specifically Christian motivation, "as befits saints," to be what is appropriate for those called to be holy (v 3). Other aspects of the framework of motivations include judgment (exclusion from the kingdom of Christ and God and experience of the wrath of God), believers' change of status through their conversion-initiation and the ethical implications this carries, and assurance about the power of the light and its source, Christ.

It can be seen that Eph 5:3–14 reflects the early Christian concern about the use of language that has already been prominent in 4:25–5:2. That sexual immorality should not even be a subject of conversation among believers is asserted twice (cf. vv 3, 12). In fact, in vv 3, 4 sexual vices are condemned and the virtue of thanksgiving is recommended, but all at one remove through the topic of speech about these matters. The writer attaches significance to the spoken word as a key element in the sequence—thought, speech, action—believing that talking about sexual sins promotes an ethos which will be tolerant of their practice. For the contemporary reader, however, not even mentioning sexual vices might well be thought prudish and at odds with the honesty and openness about sexual matters that are nowadays considered virtues.

But the light and darkness imagery suggest the uncompromising nature of this writer's ethical demands. There appears to be no room for shady gray areas. The different references of his use of the image of light in this passage can perhaps be combined in an overall picture. Christ, as the center of God's sphere of influence, beams out its light on the darkness of this world, like a spotlight playing on the stage of a darkened theater. Believers stand in the beam and become identified with and live in its light. As they do so, the light is reflected off them, showing up the darkness around. As they see the light reflected, some who sit in darkness choose to enter the light. In this way, the beam of light extends its influence, but the edge of its circle of light remains clearly defined. The drawing of specific boundaries between the Church and the world is a task that each generation of Christians has to perform for its own time and place, but if continuity with the perspective of this writer is to be retained, the light of the gospel of Christ, rather than the gloom of the world's values, will always be made the determinative factor in such an endeavor.

Again believers and their conduct, this time especially vis-à-vis the outside world, are the center of attention in the section. But the writer's theological and Christological perspectives on human action are not to be missed. It is the theological that predominates in the first part of the passage, where the contrast between thanksgiving, on the one hand, and covetousness or idolatry, on the other, recalls the basic structures of the Creator-creature relationship, and where the notion of God's judgment on disobedience is invoked. Even here, however, the kingdom from which immoral people will be excluded is said to be that of both Christ and God. In the second part of the section, with its darkness and light imagery, it is the Christological that is to the fore. Christ as Lord is at the center of the dominion of light. He can be seen as the source of its light—"Christ will shine upon you." It is he who determines believers' status—they are "light in the Lord"—and it is what meets with his approval that determines their conduct—"what is pleasing to the Lord."

This paraenetic material functions primarily to give the readers a clearer sense of their own identity by drawing sharply defined boundaries, especially in regard to sexual purity, between their life and behavior and those of the surrounding society. The writer wants his readers to realize that the Church is to live by values as radically opposed to that society's values as light is opposed to and incompatible with darkness. Yet it is interesting to note that this clear sense of being different from others is not meant to lead the Church into isolationism or defeatism in relation to the world. Rather than being corrupted by the surrounding darkness, believers are urged to exercise their influence on it. The readers are to be nothing less than a community whose conduct shines as a beacon to others, illuminating how life should be lived. Indeed, the writer suggests in vv 11–14 that as the Church in the midst of society is true to its own distinct identity as the light, so that light is able to transform the darkness around it. In its conflict with the light, the darkness cannot ultimately prevail, since the light has the risen Christ as its source. This optimistic note is in line with the letter's universal hopes. Yet if the Church has some sort of missionary role in this passage, it is not through proclamation by word but through its very existence as the sphere of light (cf. also 3:10).

The conflict between light and darkness will emerge again later as believers are depicted in battle against the powers of darkness (6:12), and in that same section of exhortation the qualities of truth and righteousness will again be singled out, this time as part of the believer's armor for the battle (6:14). More immediately, however, in the next section of the letter the notions of doing what the Lord wishes (5:17; cf. v 10) and of thanksgiving (5:20; cf. v 4) provide a continuity, while the focus of the exhortation shifts to the corporate dimension of Spirit-filled living.

Wise and Spirit-Filled Living (5:15–20)

Bibliography

Adai, J. *Der heilige Geist als Gegenwart Gottes*, 217–31. **Hengel, M.** "Hymns and Christology." In *Between Jesus and Paul*. London: SCM, 1983, 78–96. **Lindemann, A.** *Die Aufhebung der Zeit*, 232–34. **Martin, R. P.** *Worship in the Early Church*. London: Marshall, Morgan and Scott, 1964, 39–52. **Rogers, C. L.** "The Dionysian Background of Ephesians 5:18." *BSac* 136 (1979) 249–57.

Translation

[15] *Pay careful attention then to how* [a] *you live, not as unwise people but as wise,* [16] *making the most of the time, because the days are evil.* [17] *Therefore do not be foolish, but understand what the will of the Lord is.* [18] *And do not get drunk with wine, leading to* [b] *dissipation, but be filled with the Spirit,* [19] *speaking to one another in psalms and hymns and songs inspired by the Spirit,* [c] *singing and making music to the Lord in your heart,* [20] *always giving thanks for everything in the name of our Lord Jesus Christ to our God and Father.* [d]

Notes

[a] Some texts read πῶς ἀκριβῶς, which would associate the adverb "carefully" with "walking" rather than "watching" (cf. D^gr G K P Ψ 88 181 it^f,g,mon syr^p,h,pal arm Ambrosiaster Victorinus-Rome). The external evidence for ἀκριβῶς πῶς, the reading reflected in the translation, is, however, stronger (cf. p^46 ℵ* B 33 81 104 cop^sa Origen Chrysostom). Metzger (*Textual Commentary*, 608) suggests that πῶς may well have been omitted after -βῶς and then reinserted in the wrong place. There are also less well attested variants of both sequences containing the term ἀδελφοί, "brothers and sisters." It is highly unlikely that this was original, since apart from the poor manuscript support, there is no obvious reason for the omission of the term.

[b] The literal translation of this clause would be "in which is dissipation." The thought is that to become drunk involves one in an action which is characteristic of a dissipated life.

[c] πνευματικαῖς, "spiritual, inspired by the Spirit," is omitted in p^46 B it^d,e Ambrosiaster, and it is disputed whether this reading is to be preferred or not. J. K. Elliott, "The United Bible Societies' Textual Commentary Evaluated," *NovT* 17 (1975) 145, argues for the shorter text and holds that the longer reading found in ℵ D^gr G K P Ψ 33 81 88 it^ar,c,dem,f,g,mon,x,z vg syr^p,h,pal cop^sa,bo goth arm has been added through assimilation to Col 3:16. Certainly the even longer reading, unique to A, with ἐν χάριτι after πνευματικαῖς, is an assimilation to the Colossians parallel. But Metzger, *Textual Commentary*, 608, and J. R. Royse, "The Treatment of Scribal Leaps in Metzger's *Textual Commentary*," *NTS* 29 (1983) 539–44, who claims "the longer text . . . is 'virtually certain,'" argue that πνευματικαῖς was accidentally omitted because of homoeoteleuton. This scribal error of leaping from -αῖς to -αῖς may well be the more likely occurrence in this case.

[d] The translation of this last phrase reflects the presence of καί between θεῷ and πατρί in the Greek text, where, in the light of the earlier references in the letter in which καί is used to link these two nouns (1:3; 4:6), it may well have more emphasis than a simply epexegetical καί (cf. also J. A. Robinson, 122–23; NEB). There is also a textual question at this point, since some witnesses read θεῷ καὶ πατρί (ℵ A B D^b I K P Ψ 33 81 614 vg syr^p,h cop^sa,bo), while others reverse the nouns and have πατρὶ καὶ θεῷ (p^46 D*,c G it^d,g syr^pal goth arm). While the latter could be considered the more difficult reading, the former is more widely supported and follows the sequence found elsewhere in the letter (cf. 1:3; 4:6; also 1:2, 17; 6:23).

Form/Structure/Setting

The citation of hymnic material rounded off the preceding section of paraenesis with its use of the darkness and light symbolism to draw the ethical contrast between believers and the surrounding world. A new pericope is also signaled by yet another use of the verb περιπατεῖν, "to walk, live," in the opening exhortation (cf. its use in each of the earlier sections—4:1, 17; 5:2, 8). This time the readers are called upon to live wisely, and then the focus of the paraenesis moves to life within the community and in particular its worship. But where does this section end? In terms of content, the focus on life within the community continues throughout the household code. In terms of syntax, the participial clause of v 21, on which the exhortation to wives and husbands in vv 22–33 depends, is itself, in fact, dependent on the main verb πληροῦσθε, "be filled," in v 18. There is a strong case, therefore, for seeing this particular exhortation about conduct, "walking wisely," as including the household code and extending from 5:15 to 6:9 (cf. also Schlier, 242; Gnilka, 264–65). In terms of the structure of the letter, 5:15–6:9 is the next overall unit. But for convenience of analysis in this commentary, such a large unit needs to be divided. This division is being made primarily according to the topics treated, although there are also structural indicators. This still leaves a question about v 21. It is certainly transitional, but in comparison with vv 19, 20 it contains a new topic which has the same subject matter as the verses which follow—submission. For our purposes, then, what tells against making v 21 part of this section rather than the following one is the fact that without it the exhortation to wives in v 22 would lack any verb. In addition, the formulation "in the name of our Lord Jesus Christ to our God and Father" can be seen as providing a fitting rhetorical conclusion to this section, while the notion of fear frames vv 21–33, being found in both the opening and the closing verses.

It is noticeable that each of the three main exhortations in the pericope contains a μή . . . ἀλλά contrast. In v 15 this is added after the exhortation to the readers to pay attention to how they live—not as unwise people but as wise, while in vv 17, 18 the exhortations themselves have two parts—a negative with μή and a positive which follows after ἀλλά.

The section can be seen to fall into three parts grouped around these three main exhortations. In vv 15, 16 the call to a wise walk is followed, as we have noted, by the μή . . . ἀλλά phrase which is dependent on it, as is the participial clause of v 16a which spells out what wise living means in regard to the attitude to time. This clause is in turn followed by the motivating clause of v 16b about the days being evil. Verse 17 provides a fresh generalizing exhortation but one which is based on vv 15, 16 (cf. διὰ τοῦτο and the notion of folly). It has negative ("do not be foolish") and positive ("but understand what the will of the Lord is") halves. The third part, vv 18–20, begins with the prohibition against getting drunk, which is followed by a motivating clause elaborating on the vice involved. "Be filled with the Spirit," the exhortation which contrasts with the initial prohibition, then determines the rest of the passage, as what this involves is indicated by the four participles or three participial clauses which follow. As we have seen, when the transitional v 21 is brought into the picture, the number of participles and participial clauses dependent on πληροῦσθε, "be filled," becomes five and four respectively.

This section of Ephesians is dependent on Col 3:16, 17; 4:5, as is set out below:

	Ephesians		Colossians
5:15	... πῶς περιπατεῖτε, μὴ ὡς ἄσοφοι ἀλλ' ὡς σοφοί	4:5	ἐν σοφίᾳ περιπατεῖτε πρὸς τοὺς ἔξω
		3:16b	ἐν πάσῃ σοφίᾳ
5:16	ἐξαγοραζόμενοι τὸν καιρόν ...	4:5	τὸν καιρὸν ἐξαγοραζόμενοι
5:19a	λαλοῦντες ἑαυτοῖς ἐν ψαλμοῖς καὶ ὕμνοις καὶ ᾠδαῖς πνευματικαῖς	3:16b	... διδάσκοντες καὶ νουθετοῦντες ἑαυτοὺς ψαλμοῖς, ὕμνοις, ᾠδαῖς πνευματικαῖς
5:19b	ᾄδοντες καὶ ψάλλοντες τῇ καρδίᾳ ὑμῶν τῷ κυρίῳ	3:16c	ἐν χάριτι ᾄδοντες ἐν ταῖς καρδίαις ὑμῶν τῷ θεῷ
5:20	εὐχαριστοῦντες πάντοτε ὑπὲρ πάντων ἐν ὀνόματι τοῦ κυρίου ἡμῶν Ἰησοῦ Χριστοῦ τῷ θεῷ καὶ πατρί	3:17	ποιῆτε ... πάντα ἐν ὀνόματι κυρίου Ἰησοῦ, εὐχαριστοῦντες τῷ θεῷ πατρὶ δι' αὐτοῦ

The exhortation with which the pericope begins is based on Col 4:5. But whereas Colossians has in view believers' relationship to outsiders, this aspect of wise behavior is no longer explicit in Ephesians, where, as we have observed, the writer's attention is now moving more toward relationships within the community. He does, however, keep one eye on the outside world in his reformulation of the phrase "in wisdom" in terms of a comparison between the unwise and the wise. What wise behavior means in regard to attitude to time is expressed in the same way in both passages. Ephesians simply inverts the word order in the participial clause from Colossians and adds a motivating clause. It may well be the notion of wisdom that led the writer to think of taking up Col 3:16, 17 after adding independent material in vv 17, 18, since "in all wisdom" introduces the Colossians exhortation about psalms, hymns, and spiritual songs. When it employs this exhortation, Ephesians omits the second reference to wisdom, however, and changes "teaching and admonishing one another" to "speaking to one another." The writer then makes minor modifications to the following participial clause from Col 3:16c. He omits the introductory ἐν χάριτι, "with thankfulness," to ᾄδοντες, "singing," adds a second participle ψάλλοντες, "making music," uses the dative singular of καρδία instead of ἐν plus the dative plural, and makes the one to whom worship is addressed "the Lord" instead of "God." Eph 5:20 has then taken the participle εὐχαριστοῦντες, "giving thanks," from the second half of Col 3:17, but to this it has added the phrase "in the name of our Lord Jesus Christ," which is its version of "in the name of the Lord Jesus," from the first half of Col 3:17, where it had been associated not with giving thanks but with doing all things. The "all things" from Colossians has also been transferred to the clause about giving thanks, where it is reflected in the terminology πάντοτε ὑπὲρ πάντων, "always for all things." Mitton (*The Epistle to the Ephesians*, 246) describes the use of Colossians in Eph 5:20 as "a curious instance of the merely accidental association of words prevailing over the meaning which they were originally used to convey." This prompts him to ask (81), "Is this mechanical reproduction of words, in violation of their original sense, what we should expect of Paul in a second letter closely modelled on an earlier one and written immediately after it? ... Is it not, on the other hand, just the kind of phenomenon that betrays the hand of an imitator ... ?"

Of the material in Ephesians not adapted from Colossians, v 17 with its "understand what the will of the Lord is" is reminiscent of Rom 12:2 and its "prove what the will of God is," while v 18 with its contrast between drunkenness and being filled with the Spirit recalls the language of Luke's Pentecost (Acts 2:4, 15). But in neither case is the corrrespondence close enough to suggest literary dependence. The wording of the first part of the exhortation of v 18, "Do not get drunk with wine," is held by many commentators to be a citation of Prov 23:31 (e.g., J. A. Robinson, 121; Houlden, *Paul's Letters*, 238; Bruce, *Epistles*, 379), though Lindemann (*Die Aufhebung der Zeit*, 82) contends that the exhortation is an everyday one and the agreement is coincidental. The most likely view, however, is that the use of Prov 23:31 is indirect and has been mediated through Jewish ethical traditions (cf. also Gnilka, 28, 269). It is the *Testaments of the Twelve Patriarchs* which provide a parallel, because there, as here in Eph 5:18, warnings against drunkenness are closely linked with warnings against debauchery (cf. *T. Iss.* 7.2, 3; *T. Jud.* 11.2; 12.3; 13.6; 16.1). The warning in *T. Jud.* 14.1 has exactly the same wording as that of Ephesians, μὴ μεθύσκεσθε οἴνῳ, in agreement with the A text of LXX Prov 23:31, rather than the B text with ἐν οἴνοις, or the א text with οἴνοις.

An exhortation concerning worship follows earlier exhortations about renouncing the old life and precedes the household code both here in Ephesians and in Colossians. But there is no clear evidence that there is a dependence of both on an original early Christian holiness code, in which the three elements were always in this sequence (*pace* A. C. King, "Ephesians in the Light of Form Criticism," *ExpTim* 63 [1952] 276, who follows E. G. Selwyn, *The First Epistle of St. Peter* [London: Macmillan, 1946] 400–406). Jas 1:27 and 1 Pet 2:4–9, which are cited as the parallel sections of the sequence in other NT letters, scarcely count as equivalent instructions about the church's worship. So one is simply left with the dependence of Ephesians on Colossians for such a sequence. The material in 5:15–20, however, is general in nature and on that account likely to be typical of early Christian paraenesis. No conclusions can be drawn from its contents about, for example, the readers of this letter having specific problems of sloth or drunkenness.

In its setting in the letter, this pericope has links both with what precedes and with what follows. Living as wise people (5:15) follows from living as children of light (5:8) and living in love (5:2). The contrast between wise and unwise or foolish people is consistent with the thought of the earlier part of the letter, where believers are described as having wisdom bestowed on them (1:9, 17) and pagan Gentiles as futile in their thinking and ignorant (4:17, 18). The motivation for the exhortation to make the most of the time speaks of the days being evil (5:16), while the later passage about the Christian's armor will mention an evil day that has to be faced (6:13). The necessity of thanksgiving (5:20) has already been highlighted in the immediately preceding pericope (5:4; cf. also 1:16). At the heart of this passage stands the exhortation to be filled with the Spirit, and this can be seen as taking up an emphasis on the believer's relationship to the Spirit which is pervasive in this letter (cf. 1:3, 13, 14, 17; 2:18, 22; 3:16; 4:30; 6:17, 18). It is also, of course, on this exhortation about the Spirit that the key transitional verse about mutual submission, which introduces the immediately following household code, depends (cf. 5:21).

Comment

15, 16 βλέπετε οὖν ἀκριβῶς πῶς περιπατεῖτε, μὴ ὡς ἄσοφοι ἀλλ᾽ ὡς σοφοί, "Pay careful attention then to how you live, not as unwise people but as wise." The οὖν, "therefore," links the new instruction in a general way with the previous overall exhortation to walk as children of light and to expose the works of darkness. This can only be obeyed if believers take care that their conduct is characterized by wisdom. The new exhortation is not simply "walk/live as wise people," but its importance and urgency are reinforced by the use of both βλέπετε, "watch," and ἀκριβῶς, "carefully." As has been noted, the notion of "walking wisely" has been taken over and generalized from Col 4:5, where it had specific reference to believers' behavior in relation to outsiders. The contrast between the walk of wise people and that of unwise people has its roots, of course, in the wisdom tradition with its contrast of two ways and of the wise person and the fool (cf., for example, Prov 4:10–14; 9; 10:8, 14). In the Qumran literature, those who have been contrasted as the sons of light and the sons of darkness in 1QS 3.19–25 are then said to walk in wisdom on the one hand and walk in foolishness on the other in 1QS 4.24 (cf. also K. G. Kuhn, "The Epistle to the Ephesians," 125–26). To live as a wise person is not just to have knowledge but to have skill in living, to have the sort of perception that authenticates itself in practice. This requires ethical insight into God's will. Whereas for the Jewish wisdom tradition such wise living was living in accordance with Torah (cf. *T. Naph.* 8.10, "So be wise in the Lord and discerning, knowing the order of his commandments, what is ordained for every act"), now in Ephesians it is a living informed by an understanding of the will of the Lord (cf. v 17), meaning the will of Christ, and this is something no longer identical with Torah.

ἐξαγοραζόμενοι τὸν καιρόν, ὅτι αἱ ἡμέραι πονηραί εἰσιν, "making the most of the time, because the days are evil." Those who have insight will have the right attitude to time, using it to discover and practice the will of the Lord. But it is disputed what exactly this right attitude to time is. LXX Dan 2:8 has a similar clause—καιρὸν ὑμεῖς ἐξαγοράζετε, "you are buying time," i.e., "you are attempting to gain time." It is just possible that the words have a similar meaning in Ephesians. The force would be that because they are living in the last days, which are both evil and short, believers should attempt to gain time in order to be able to continue to do what is good and right and true (cf. v 9). On the basis of *Mart. Pol.* 2.3 and its use of the middle of the verb in the sense of "to buy off," BAGD (271) suggests as a possible meaning that time presents wrathful demands (cf. 1 Cor 7:29–32) which must be satisfied or bought off. In Gal 3:13 and 4:5 the verb is used of Christ's act of redemption, and some hold that it retains that force here (e.g., J. A. Robinson, 201–2— "ransom the time from its evil bondage"; Barth, 578). But as C. F. D. Moule (*The Epistles to the Colossians and to Philemon,* 134) says, "It seems, however, slightly bizarre to treat ὁ καιρός as a person needing help . . . and it is perhaps more natural, after all, to treat it as a commodity to be eagerly bought." This latter meaning is the one favored by the majority of commentators (cf. also R. M. Pope, "Studies in Pauline Vocabulary: Redeeming the Time," *ExpTim* 22 [1910–11] 552–54; F. Büchsel, "ἀγοράζω, ἐξαγοράζω," *TDNT* 1 [1964] 124–

28, who defines the force of the verb as "an intensive buying, a buying which exhausts the possibilities available"). The usage is that of the commercial language of the market place, and the prefix ἐκ- intensifies the force of the verb. So καιρός here refers to time in the sense of the opportunities it offers, each of which is to be capitalized upon, to be exploited (cf. also Gal 6:10, "So then, as we have opportunity [καιρός], let us do good").

The motivation for the exhortation to make the most of the time is that the days are evil. In Jewish and early Christian tradition evil was seen as characteristic of the last days in general (e.g., *T. Dan* 5.4; *T. Zeb.* 9.5, 6; 2 Tim 3:1; 2 Pet 3:3). It is possible that for some of its force the notion of evil days here retains the implications of its use in the apocalyptic tradition, where these evil days are the last days, are precarious, and will only endure for a limited period. This would produce a sense of urgency about the remaining present and its opportunities. However, this interpretation may sound a note of the imminence of the end which would be atypical for Ephesians. It is more likely that for this writer the notion has a more general, though still eschatologically oriented, force. For him, from one perspective the present is still under the control of the prince of the power of the air (2:2) and part of this evil age (cf. Gal 1:4). Therefore, believers still have to live out the life of the age to come, which they already enjoy, in a surrounding moral climate which is predominantly evil. From another perspective, however, the present is the time of opportunity for believers—the acceptable time of salvation and of response to that salvation (cf. 2 Cor 6:2), the time in which to produce the good works (cf. 2:10) to counteract the evil around them. Making the most of the time to do good in the midst of evil would then be parallel to the notion of the preceding pericope about the positive effects of living as light in the midst of darkness. It makes it all the more imperative to exploit every present opportunity for good, if the evil days in which believers live are going to increase in intensity and culminate in a climactic evil day (cf. 6:13). As Abbott (160) paraphrases this verse, "The moments for sowing on receptive soil in such evil days being few, seize them when they offer themselves." It is the overall eschatological perspective on the flow of history in God's purpose in Christ which undergirds the wise use of daily opportunities and which distinguishes this writer's exhortation from general maxims such as Seneca's "gather and save your time" (*Epist.* 1.1). According to this explanation, καιρός is a neutral term and not to be equated with the evil days, which are part of the eschatological explanation for the exhortation (cf. also Gnilka, 267–68; *pace* Lindemann, *Aufhebung*, 232–33, who equates the two in a rather forced explanation that the wise person does not have to show respect to time, if it is evil, and can therefore exploit it to the full; for Mussner [148] the clear temporal connotations of the motivation of this verse shows the absurdity of Lindemann's desire to talk about *die Aufhebung der Zeit*, "the abrogation of temporal categories," in Ephesians).

17 διὰ τοῦτο μὴ γίνεσθε ἄφρονες, ἀλλὰ συνίετε τί τὸ θέλημα τοῦ κυρίου, "Therefore do not be foolish, but understand what the will of the Lord is." Those who have already been exhorted not to live as unwise people in v 15 are now again warned not to succumb to folly. ἄφρων, frequently used in the LXX for the fool as a denier of God (cf. G. Bertram, "φρήν κτλ.," *TDNT* 9 [1974] 220–35), is a variation on ἄσοφος of v 15. The contrast between wise and unwise is now replaced by that between being foolish and having understanding. Just as the children of light will learn what is pleasing to the Lord (5:10), so those who are wise will understand what the will of the Lord is. Indeed, understanding the will of the Lord is the heart of wisdom (cf. also Col 1:9, "filled with the knowledge of his will in all spiritual wisdom and understanding"). For believers, wise living involves a practical perception dependent on the direction of their Lord. Understanding τί τὸ θέλημα τοῦ κυρίου, "what is the will of the Lord," here can be compared with discovering τί τὸ θέλημα τοῦ θεοῦ, "what is the will of God," in Rom 12:2, although κύριος in Ephesians always refers to Christ rather than God (*pace* Mitton, 188). What the will of Christ entails, the readers have already been taught (cf. 4:20, 21) and the writer himself is in the midst of elaborating. Most immediately (cf. διὰ τοῦτο, "therefore"), understanding the Lord's will for the present time and avoiding folly means recognizing the nature of the times in which one lives and making the most of opportunities for good in the overlap of the ages.

18 καὶ μὴ μεθύσκεσθε οἴνῳ, ἐν ᾧ ἐστιν ἀσωτία, ἀλλὰ πληροῦσθε ἐν πνεύματι, "And do not get drunk with wine, leading to dissipation, but be filled with the Spirit." This is the final imperative in the series with its μὴ . . . ἀλλά contrast and leads into the chain of participles which are all subordinate to its second half. The relationship of the wording of its first half to Prov 23:31 and to the *Testaments of the Twelve Patriarchs* has been discussed under *Form/Structure/Setting*. Its more specific force introduces a change from the general nature of the preceding exhortations which at first appears quite surprising. Is there some particular reason for the prohibition of drunkenness, or is it simply included as part of a general paraenetic tradition and because it provides a neat contrast with the positive imperative about being filled with the Spirit? Some suggest that it is directed against misconduct in the assembly, such as that indicated in 1 Cor 11:21 (cf. Schlier, 246; Gnilka, 269; Houlden, 328; J. D. G. Dunn, *Jesus and the Spirit* [London: SCM, 1975] 238; Adai, *Der heilige Geist*, 223, 226). It is true that this passage goes on to deal with worship in the assembly, but there is no evidence at all that the earlier problems in Corinth were being duplicated in the churches which this letter is addressing, and the prohibition's supporting clause seems too weak and inappropriate for such an offense (cf. also Meyer, 284; Abbott, 161; Schnackenburg, 241). Others hold that the injunction has in view the pagan mystery cult celebrations in which some of the Gentile Christian readers would previously have indulged (cf. Ernst, 379; Mussner, 148), and some (cf. Rogers, *BSac* 136 [1979] 249–57; M. Hengel, *Between Jesus and Paul*, 188 n. 7) suggest the Dionysian cult is particularly in view. But although such cults were widespread, there is again no clear evidence that they had a continuing negative influence on the churches of Asia Minor. Others still attempt to link the prohibition with the earlier thought of v 16 and claim that the writer is saying that drunkenness is no solution to the difficulties of living in evil days and that it is only the Spirit that enables a person to cope (cf. Barth, 581; Mitton, 188–89; Adai, *Der heilige Geist*, 223, 230). It is far more likely, however, that any link with the surrounding material is first with the basic contrast between folly and wisdom and beyond that with the earlier contrast between darkness and light found in the immediately preceding section of paraenesis. In both 1 Thess 5 and Rom 13, which lay behind that contrast, Paul had talked of drunkenness as a prime characteristic of the darkness. In 1 Thess 5:6–8, sobriety by contrast is seen as a quality of the light. In Rom 13:12, 13, drunkenness, as here in Eph 5, is associated with debauchery. It looks, then, as though the writer may well have gone back to these sources, as he will do again later in 6:11–17 for his imagery of the believer's armor, and have drawn on them to continue the contrast from the beginning of this section between the foolish behavior of unbelievers and the wise conduct of believers. Other references in the NT to drunkenness include Matt 24:49; Luke 12:45; 1 Cor 5:11; 6:10; 1 Tim 3:8; Titus 2:3; and 1 Pet 4:3. Here in Eph 5:18, drunkenness is said to lead to dissipation, that is, to sexual excess and debauchery. ἀσωτία is used elsewhere in the NT only in Titus 1:6 and 1 Pet 4:4, where it is in close association with the mention of drunkenness in the preceding verse, while the cognate adverb is used to describe the way of life of the prodigal son in Luke 15:13. The use of the term here reminds one of the writer's earlier sweeping condemnation of non-Christian Gentile lifestyle in 4:19, where the synonym ἀσέλγεια, "debauchery," was employed. Again there is no need, with Rogers (*BSac* 136 [1979] 256, followed by Adai, *Der heilige Geist*, 223, 225), to be too precise and connect this vice specifically with the Dionysian cult.

The shift from the notion of drunkenness to that of being filled with the Spirit is not as abrupt as it may appear at first sight. The former represents folly; the latter is the prerequisite for wisdom. Both involve the self coming under the control of an external power, and the states of alcoholic and of religious intoxication were often compared. Luke's Pentecost narrative, where the earliest believers' experience of being filled with the Spirit is mistaken for drunkenness (cf. Acts 2:4, 13, 15), is frequently cited in this connection, although there is no evidence that the writer of Ephesians is actually drawing on the Acts passage (*pace* Mitton, *Epistle*, 205–6). But Philo's reflections on drunkenness are equally illuminating. Not only does he identify drunkenness with spiritual folly (cf. *De Ebr.* 11, 95, 125–26, 154), but he also sees a comparison between it and being possessed by God: "Now when grace fills the soul, that soul thereby rejoices and smiles and dances, for it is possessed and inspired, so that to many of the unenlightened it may seem to be drunken, crazy, and beside itself. . . . For with the God-possessed not only is the soul wont to be stirred and goaded as it were into ecstasy but the body also is flushed and fiery . . . and thus many of the foolish are deceived and suppose that the sober are drunk . . . and it is true that these sober ones are drunk in a sense" (*De Ebr.* 146–48). In all probability, it is this sort of comparison that lies behind Ephesians' contrast between drunkenness and being possessed by the Spirit of God.

The imperative is in the present tense, indicating that believers' experience of the Spirit's fullness is to be a continuing one. The use of ἐν with πληροῦσθαι in an instrumental sense is unusual (cf. also Abbott, 161–62; J. A. Robinson, 204; Schnackenburg, 242 and n. 598). Believers are to be filled by the Spirit and thus also filled with the Spirit. The idea of being filled with the Spirit recalls that of being filled up to all the fullness of God in 3:19 and that of the Church as the fullness of Christ in 1:23 (cf. also 4:13). Clearly, the Spirit mediates the fullness of God and of Christ to the believer. The command to be filled with the Spirit stands in the center of the passage and has links with what precedes—wisdom—as well as with what follows—worship. The Spirit provides the power for both aspects of Christian living. Believers, who have already been reminded of their sealing by the Spirit (1:13; 4:30) and enjoined not to grieve the Spirit (4:30), are now exhorted to allow the Spirit to have the fullest control that they are conscious of in their lives and to open themselves continually to the one who can enable them to walk wisely and to understand Christ's will and who can inspire their worship and thanksgiving. The power of the Spirit in the inner person has already been mentioned in 3:16, and earlier still, in the letter in the intercessory prayer report in 1:17, the Spirit has been linked to wisdom. The connection between being filled with the Spirit and worship, which emerges through the subordinate participles of vv 19, 20, should not be interpreted as meaning that participation in the church's liturgy is what produces the experience of the fullness of the Spirit (*pace* Adai, *Der heilige Geist*, 225–26, who reads a particular theology into the text). The following participles are best interpreted as the consequences of the experience rather than its means.

19, 20 λαλοῦντες ἑαυτοῖς ἐν ψαλμοῖς καὶ ὕμνοις καὶ ᾠδαῖς πνευματικαῖς, ᾄδοντες καὶ ψάλλοντες τῇ καρδίᾳ ὑμῶν τῷ κυρίῳ, εὐχαριστοῦντες πάντοτε ὑπὲρ πάντων ἐν ὀνόματι τοῦ κυρίου ἡμῶν Ἰησοῦ Χριστοῦ τῷ θεῷ καὶ πατρί, "speaking to one another in psalms and hymns and songs inspired by the Spirit, singing and making music to the Lord in your heart, always giving thanks for everything in the name of our Lord Jesus Christ to our God and Father." Drunkenness leads to disorderly and dissolute behavior, but being filled with the Spirit produces very different results—praise, thanksgiving, and, when the participle of v 21 is also included, mutual submission.

Although the first participial clause mentions hymns, its focus in fact is not on praise of God. The psalms, hymns, and spiritual songs are part of believers' addressing of one another in the assembly, serving as a means of edification, instruction, and exhortation (cf. also Col 3:16, "teaching and admonishing one another"). In this regard, it is significant that much of what is taken to be hymnic in the Pauline corpus has a didactic and paraenetic function in its present form and context (e.g., Phil 2:6–11; Col 1:15–20; 1 Tim 3:16). As most scholars hold, it is difficult to draw any hard and fast distinctions among the three categories of psalms, hymns, and spiritual songs mentioned both here and in the material in Col 3:16 from which this writer draws. Apart from these two passages, ψαλμός, "psalm," is used elsewhere in the NT to refer to OT psalms in Luke 20:42; 24:44; Acts 1:20; 13:33, and in all probability to a Christian song in 1 Cor 14:26; ὕμνος, "hymn," is used nowhere else, though the cognate verb is found in Mark 14:26; Matt 26:30; Acts 16:25; Heb 2:12; and ᾠδή, "song," is employed for the songs of heavenly worship in Rev 5:9; 14:3; 15:3. Some have made an attempt to distinguish between them. R. P. Martin (*Worship in the Early Church* [London: Marshall, Morgan and Scott, 1964] 47 [though cf. Martin, *Colossians*, 115–16, for a different view]; cf. also Mitton, 191; Bruce, *Epistles*, 158–59, for a similar classification) suggests that the "psalms" may refer to Christian odes patterned on the OT psalter, "hymns" to longer compositions, parts of which are actually cited in the NT, and "spiritual songs" to snatches of spontaneous praise prompted by the Spirit. J. D. G. Dunn (*Jesus and the Spirit* [London: SCM, 1975] 238–39) thinks that all three categories probably refer to charismatic hymnody and that even if "spiritual" refers only to "songs," the distinction between psalms and hymns, on the one hand, and spiritual songs, on the other, is not between established liturgical forms and spontaneous song, but between spontaneous singing of intelligible words or familiar verses and spontaneous singing in tongues. In fact, the three terms used here are best seen as another example of this writer's fondness for piling up synonyms, which in this case he has been able to take over from Colossians. They are the three most common terms in the LXX for religious songs and occur there interchangeably in the titles of the psalms. Elsewhere, Josephus associates ὕμνοι, "hymns," with ψαλμοί, "psalms," in *Ant.* 12.7.7 § 323 and with ᾠδαί, "songs," in *Ant.* 7.12.3 § 305. Their synonymity makes it all the more likely that the adjective πνευματικαῖς, "spiritual," although agreeing in gender with only the last in the series, embraces all three terms (cf. BDF § 135 [3]). The songs which believers sing to each other are spiritual because they are inspired by the Spirit and manifest the life of the Spirit. But spirituality should not necessarily be identified with spontaneity, and all forms of Christian hymnody found in the early church are likely to have been in view, from liturgical pieces that had already established themselves in the churches' worship, of which Phil 2:6–11; Col 1:15–20; Eph 5:14; 1 Tim 3:16 may provide some examples which have found their way into the NT, to snatches of song freshly created in the assembly. Given that these songs are described as being addressed by believers to one another, it is likely, however, that it is intelligible singing rather than singing in tongues that is in view (cf. 1 Cor 14:15 where Paul contrasts singing with the Spirit, probably singing in tongues, with singing with the mind, i.e., with intelligible words).

The second participial clause builds up the sentence in the writer's characteristic style by employing the verbal forms of two of the previous nouns—ᾠδή, "song," and ψαλμός, "psalm." Although its original meaning involved plucking a stringed instrument, ψάλλω here means to make music by singing (cf. also 1 Cor 14:15; Jas 5:13), so that there is no reference in this verse to instrumental accompaniment (cf. the discussion in BAGD 891; *pace* Barth, 584). If the singing involved in the first participial clause has a horizontal and corporate dimension, that of the second clause has a more vertical and individual focus. The singing is now directed to the Lord, who, as in v 17, is Christ (a change from Col 3:16 where the singing had been addressed to God). Pliny's account (*Epistles* 10.96.7) of Christians who "recited to one another in turns a hymn to Christ as to God" is often cited in connection with these songs directed to Christ. Believers who are filled with the Spirit delight to sing the praise of Christ, and such praise comes not just from the lips but from the individual's innermost being, from the heart, where the Spirit himself resides (cf. 3:16, 17, where the Spirit in the inner person is equivalent to Christ in the heart).

In addition, believers who are filled with the Spirit will give thanks. The writer still has in view primarily thanksgiving in public worship (cf. also 1 Cor 14:16, 17), which, as well as spiritual songs, could well include material like that found in his opening *berakah*. But the attitude of thanksgiving that is expressed in their worship will also be one that permeates believers' whole lives. They will give thanks not just sometimes for some things but always for everything (cf. also 1 Thess 5:18). And this time their thanks is directed to the ultimate giver of all good things, to the one who is both God and Father, and offered in the name of the Lord Jesus Christ—a formulaic expression with liturgical connections (cf. 1 Cor 5:4; Phil 2:10; 2 Thess 3:6) but one whose significance goes beyond such settings. So the Spirit inspires thanksgiving to God the Father, and everything for which there is cause for thanks is summed up in and mediated through Christ. For further discussion of the profound importance of thanksgiving, see *Comment* on 5:4 (cf. also Col 3:15–17, where the need for thankfulness is stressed three times). The use of the participle εὐχαριστοῦντες is in a general, not a technical, sense, such as is found in *Did.* 9.2, 3; 10.1–4 or Justin, *Apol.* 67.5, and is not a sufficient reason for holding that the specific worship setting in view in these verses is the celebration of the eucharist. Nor, as we have seen, does connecting the prohibition against drunkenness with the misuse of the *agapē* meal add anything substantial to this supposition (*pace* Schlier, 248, 250; Adai, *Der heilige Geist*, 226–28).

Explanation

This section of paraenesis continues the contrast of 5:3–14 between the behavior of the believing community and that of unbelieving outsiders. Whereas the previous section had carried this out in terms of sexual morality and the antithesis between light and darkness, 5:15–20 begins with the contrast between wisdom and folly. Wise living is then shown to be Spirit-filled living, which is described primarily in terms of its consequences for the community's corporate worship.

The section is organized around three main exhortations—vv 15, 16; v 17; vv 18–20—each of which contains a contrast between negative and positive behavior. In the last, the positive element is predominant and is spelled out by means of three (or four, if the transitional v 21 is included) participial clauses. The first exhortation urges the readers to take care that they live as wise rather than unwise people. It explains that this will involve a wise attitude to time, which does not idle it away but makes the most of the opportunities it offers to do good, thereby counteracting the evil moral climate of the present age. The second exhortation continues but varies the contrast of the first, as the readers are told this time not to be foolish but to gain practical understanding of what their Lord requires. The third admonition, not to be drunk but to be filled with the Spirit, is another variation on the same theme, since traditionally drunkenness was associated with folly and the Spirit was seen as the mediator of wisdom. The joyful celebration that is to characterize the lives of believers will come not from an excess of wine but from their continual openness to the influence of the Spirit. This Spirit-filled living will manifest itself in their corporate worship, as they address and edify one another by means of all the types of songs that the Spirit inspires, as they sing their praise of Christ from the heart, and as they in Christ's name offer thanksgiving to their God and Father for all the blessings he has bestowed upon them. In terms of both the structure and the content of the passage as a whole, v 18, with its contrast between being drunk with wine and being filled with the Spirit, can be seen to be at the center, providing the link between the wisdom/folly contrast of the first part and the focus on worship of the last part.

In developing his exhortation, the writer has adapted traditional material to fit his own emphasis on the necessity of the community's experience of the Spirit. Here, as elsewhere, he draws primarily on Colossians (3:16, 17; 4:5). He is also dependent on the wisdom tradition's contrast between two ways, and his prohibition against drunkenness in v 18 draws on Prov 23:31, as mediated in Jewish ethical traditions (cf. also *T. Jud.* 14.1), and is influenced by Paul's treatment of this topic in 1 Thess 5:6–8 and Rom 13:12, 13.

The focus of the passage is again on believers and the conduct that is required of them if they are to be distinct from the surrounding society. This conduct can be summed up in terms of a wise living that discerns the times and the Lord's will, an openness to and appropriation of the power of the Spirit, and a participation in corporate worship that is full of song, praise, and thanksgiving. The explicit emphasis on the Church's joyful celebration in worship in vv 19, 20 is distinctive to this section of the letter. The three participial clauses incorporate several aspects of worship, highlighting the importance of song, indicating the role this can play in corporate edification ("speaking to one another . . ."), stressing the need for worship to come from the individual's heart, telling of praise addressed to Christ and thanksgiving directed to God, and above all making clear the indispensable function of the Spirit. The mention of "speaking to one another" in v 19 recalls this writer's concern in earlier sections to contrast outsiders' sinful speech with believers' edifying discourse. As opposed to the coarse and empty words of outsiders (5:4, 6), believers' speech is characterized by the psalms, hymns, and songs the Spirit puts in their mouths.

A "trinitarian" dimension to the community's consciousness of the transcendent emerges clearly. Christ's divine status is implicit. He is the Lord whose will the community is to understand (v 17), and to him worship is directed (v 19). Yet, at the same time, he is the mediator between God the Father and believers, as thanksgiving is offered in his name to the one who is the ultimate source of all goodness and salvation (v 20). Even more central to the passage is the Spirit's mediation of the divine power and presence. It is the Spirit who produces the wisdom and understanding called for in the first two exhortations, and it is the Spirit who prompts and pervades the worship elaborated on in the third, so much so that the very songs believers sing can be called spiritual. It is no wonder then that the central call of the passage is for believers to be continually filled with this Spirit, the motivating force for their distinctive life of wise conduct and glad worship.

Being filled with the Spirit is the functional equivalent of what the writer elsewhere thinks of as being filled with Christ (cf. 1:23; 4:13) or being filled with God (cf. 3:19). As we have seen, fullness was a notion prominent in Hellenistic syncretism. Readers of this letter are being reminded in a number of ways that the fullness of the presence of God is not something to which they have to penetrate through visionary experience or ascetic techniques, but is part of their Christian experience to be appropriated. Being filled with the Spirit involves not simply private mystical experiences but corporate worship and relationships. The singing prompted by the Spirit is an addressing of fellow believers, and the mutual submission of v 21 is also a manifestation of the Spirit's fullness. Thus believers' being filled with the Spirit means, on the one hand, their praising Christ and thanking the Father together and, on the other, their speaking and submitting to one another. According to this writer's perspective, therefore, the fullness of the Spirit can only be properly experienced in community.

Again, a primary purpose of this paraenetic material is to give the readers a clearer sense of their distinctive identity by contrasting the qualities which should characterize their conduct with the folly and drunkenness of the world. The Spirit-filled worship which the writer enjoins also contributes to the community's sense of identity and cohesion that he is attempting to foster. The spiritual songs, the praise, and the thanksgiving all help to shape believers' attitudes and to form the community's ethos. The development of the argument in this section suggests, however, that the emphasis on the experience of the Spirit and on the community's worship is not intended by the writer to lead to an obsession with religious enthusiasm for its own sake or to an absorption by the community in its own life and a corresponding retreat from the world. On the contrary, as has been noted, the passage links Spirit-led worship with the wisdom required for living in this present evil age. It is precisely the experience of being filled with the Spirit that gives believers understanding of their Lord's will, and it is the spiritual songs that are a means of promoting the knowledge of that will. In this way the community's worship can be seen to make a vital contribution to its wise living in the world.

This wise and Spirit-filled living in the world will be further elaborated in the relationships of the household code that follow in 5:21–6:9. The writer's treatment of the Christian warfare against the powers of evil in 6:10–20 provides another indication that withdrawal from the world is not part of his vision and at the same time takes up the notions of believers' relationship to the Spirit (6:17, 18) and the evil nature of the end-time (6:13; cf. 5:16).

Household Relationships—Wives and Husbands (5:21–33)

Bibliography

Baltensweiler, H. *Die Ehe im Neuen Testament.* Zürich: Zwingli, 1967, 218–35. **Batey, R.** " 'Jewish Gnosticism' and the 'Hieros Gamos' of Eph. v. 21–33." *NTS* 10 (1963) 12–27. ———. "The μία σάρξ Union of Christ and the Church," *NTS* 13 (1966–67) 270–81. ———. *New Testament Nuptial Imagery.* Leiden: Brill, 1971, 20–37. **Best, E.** *One Body in Christ,* 169–83. **Bouwman, G.** "Eph V 28—Versuch einer Übersetzung." In *Miscellanea Neotestamentica.* Vol. 2, ed. T. Baarda, A. F. J. Klijn, and W. C. van Unnik. Leiden: Brill, 1978, 179–90. **Cambier, J.** "Le Grand Mystère concernant le Christ et son Église: Eph. 5:22–33." *Bib* 47 (1966) 43–90, 223–42. ———. "Doctrine paulinienne du marriage chrétien: Étude critique de 1 Cor 7 et d'Eph 5:21–33 et essai de leur tradition actuelle." *Église et théologie* 10 (1979) 13–59. **Chavasse, C.** *The Bride of Christ.* London: Faber, 1940. **Clark, S. B.** *Man and Woman in Christ.* Ann Arbor: Servant Books, 1980, 71–87. **Fennema, D.** "Unity in Marriage: Ephesians 5, 21–33." *Reformed Review* 25 (1971) 62–71. **Feuillet, A.** "La dignité et le rôle de la femme d'après quelques textes pauliniens." *NTS* 21 (1975) 157–91. **Fischer, K. M.** *Tendenz und Absicht,* 176–200. **Greeven, H.** "Der Mann ist des Weibes Haupt." *Die neue Furche* 6 (1952) 99–109. **Hahn, F.** "Die christologische Begründung urchristlicher Paränese." *ZNW* 72 (1981) 88–99. **Halter, H.** *Taufe und Ethos,* 281–86. **Howard, G. E.** "The Head/Body Metaphors of Ephesians." *NTS* 20 (1975) 350–56. **Kahler, E.** *Die Frau in den paulinischen Briefen.* Zürich: Gotthelf, 1960, 88–140. **Kamlah, E.** "Ὑποτάσσεσθαι in den neutestamentlichen 'Haustafeln.' " In *Verborum Veritas.* FS G. Stählin, ed. O. Bocher and K. Haacker. Wuppertal: Brockhaus, 1970, 237–43. **Lincoln, A. T.** "The Use of the OT in Ephesians." *JSNT* 14 (1982) 16–57. **Maillet, H.** "Alla . . . plēn." *ETR* 55 (1980) 566–74. **Meeks, W. A.** "The Image of the Androgyne: Some Uses of a Symbol in Earliest Christianity." *History of Religions* 13 (1974) 165–208. **Miletic, S. F.** *"One Flesh": Eph. 5.22–24, 5.31: Marriage and the New Creation.* Rome: Pontifical Biblical Institute, 1988. **Muirhead, I. A.** "The Bride of Christ." *SJT* 5 (1952) 175–87. **Munro, W.** "Col. iii.18–iv.1 and Eph. v.21–vi.9: Evidence of a Late Literary Stratum?" *NTS* 18 (1972) 434–47. **Mussner, F.** *Christus, das All und die Kirche,* 147–60. **Neuhausler, E.** "Das Geheimnis ist gross: Einführung in die Grundbegriffe der Eheperikope Eph 5, 22–29." *BibLeb* 4 (1963) 155–67. **Pagels, E.** "Adam and Eve: Christ and the Church." In *The New Testament and Gnosis.* FS R. McL. Wilson, ed. A. H. B. Logan and A. J. M. Wedderburn. Edinburgh: T. & T. Clark, 1983, 146–75. **Perkins, P.** "Marriage in the New Testament and Its World." In *Commitment to Partnership,* ed. W. Roberts. New York: Paulist, 1987, 5–30. **Rengstorf, K. H.** "Die neutestamentlichen Mahnungen an die Frau, sich dem Manne unterzuordnen." In *Verbum Dei.* FS O. Schmitz. Witten: Luther Verlag, 1953, 131–45. **Sampley, J. P.** *"And the Two Shall Become One Flesh": A Study of Traditions in Eph 5:21–33.* Cambridge: CUP, 1971. **Schnackenburg, R.** " 'Er hat uns mitauferweckt.' " *LJ* 2 (1952) 178–83. **Schüssler, Fiorenza E.** *In Memory of Her: A Feminist Theological Reconstruction of Christian Origins.* New York: Crossroad, 1983, 266–70. **Small, D. H.** *Marriage as Equal Partnership.* Grand Rapids: Baker, 1980. **Terrien, S.** *Till the Heart Sings.* Philadelphia: Fortress, 184–88. **Walker, W. O., Jr.** "The 'Theology of Woman's Place' and the 'Paulinist' Tradition." *Semeia* 28 (1983) 101–12. **Wall, R. W.** "Wifely Submission in the Context of Ephesians." *Christian Scholar's Review* 17 (1988) 272–85. **Witherington, B.** *Women in the Earliest Churches.* Cambridge: CUP, 1988, 54–61.

Translation

²¹ *Submit to one another in the fear of Christ.* ²² *Wives, submit*[a] *to your husbands as to the Lord,* ²³ *for the husband is the head of the wife as Christ also is the head of the church and is himself*[b] *the Savior of the body.* ²⁴ *But as the church submits to Christ, so also should wives submit to their husbands in everything.* ²⁵ *Husbands, love your wives, as Christ also loved the church and gave himself up for her,* ²⁶ *in order that he might sanctify her, cleansing her by washing in water*[c] *through the word,* ²⁷ *in order that he might present the church to himself in splendor, without spot or wrinkle or any such thing, but rather that she might be holy and blameless.* ²⁸ *In the same way husbands also should love their wives as their own bodies. He who loves his wife loves himself,* ²⁹ *for no one ever hated his own flesh, but nourishes it and cherishes it, as Christ also does the church,* ³⁰ *since we are members of his body.*[d] ³¹ *"For this reason a man shall leave his father and his mother and be joined to his wife, and the two shall become one flesh."*[e] ³² *This mystery is great, but I am speaking about Christ and about the church.* ³³ *In any case, let each one of you also so love his wife as he loves himself, and let the wife fear her husband.*

Notes

[a] Although the verb "submit" has been supplied for the sake of the English translation, it is most likely that the best Greek text has no verb and was dependent for its sense on the participle in the previous verse. This is the reading found in P⁴⁶ B Clement ¹/² Greek mss ᵃᶜᶜ· ᵗᵒ ᴶᵉʳᵒᵐᵉ Jerome Theodore. Other traditions actually supply some form of ὑποτάσσειν, "to submit," after either γυναῖκες, "wives," or ἀνδράσιν, "husbands." The second person plural imperative ὑποτάσσεσθε is placed after γυναῖκες in D G 1985 lect⁵⁵ it ᵈ,ᵉ and after ἀνδράσιν in K 181 326 614 629 630 1984 syr ᵖ,ʰ Chrysostom, while the third person plural form ὑποτασσέσθωσαν is placed after γυναῖκες in Ψ cop ˢᵃ,ᵇᵒ and after ἀνδράσιν in ℵ A I P 33 81 88 104 330 436 451 it ᵃʳ,ᶜ,ᵈᵉᵐ,ᶠ vg syr ᵖᵃˡ goth arm eth Clement ¹/² Origen. But these longer readings are all best explained as scribal additions for the sake of clarity.

[b] A similar consideration applies here. For the sake of smooth translation a conjunction and verb have been supplied in English. The best Greek texts simply have αὐτὸς σωτὴρ τοῦ σώματος, lit. "himself Savior of the body," after the previous clause. The alternative reading with καί and ἐστίν in ℵᶜ Dᵇ syr arm goth Basil Chrysostom should again be seen as a later expansion for the sake of clarity and style.

[c] In the Greek text this phrase is preceded by the definite article—τῷ λουτρῷ τοῦ ὕδατος, lit. "by the washing of water."

[d] The best-attested text ends at this point before the quotation of Gen 2:24 in the next verse (cf. P⁴⁶ ℵ* A B 048 33 81 1739* 1881 cop ˢᵃ,ᵇᵒ eth Origen ˡᵃᵗ Methodius Euthalius Ps-Jerome), but there are variants which expand the verse and which appear to have been formulated in the light of Gen 2:23. The most popular of these is ἐκ τῆς σαρκὸς αὐτοῦ καὶ ἐκ τῶν ὀστέων αὐτοῦ, "of his flesh and of his bones," found in ℵᶜ D G P Ψ 88 104 181 326 330 436 451 614 630 it vg syr ᵖ,ʰ arm Irenaeus ᵍʳ,ˡᵃᵗ Ambrosiaster Victorinus-Rome Chrysostom Jerome. It is possible that the shorter reading could have come about through homoeoteleuton with a scribe moving from αὐτοῦ to αὐτοῦ. But this ending has stronger external support and is favored by the internal evidence, since the longer reading raises problems for the consistency of the use of "body" imagery in the letter as well as problems of sense (what does it mean to be members of Christ's bones?). The longer reading is most plausibly explained as a later addition under the influence of the OT citation in v 31. Irenaeus shows knowledge of it in a context in which he deals with Gnostic opponents of the real physical existence of Christ and of the bodily resurrection (*Adv. Haer.* 5.2.3), and it could be that anti-docetic convictions prompted the expansion in the first place (cf. also Schlier, 261 n. 1; Gnilka, 286).

[e] There are variant readings of the OT quotation. Marcion Origen Cyprian omit the clause

καὶ προσκολληθήσεται πρὸς τὴν γυναῖκα αὐτοῦ, "and be joined to his wife." This could have resulted from haplography, from a desire to get straight to the point of the quotation or from the influence of Mark 10:7, where the best-attested reading (א B Ψ 892* lect⁴⁸ syrˢ goth) also omits this clause from its citation of Gen 2:24. Among those texts which do contain the clause, there is also a variation in the wording which reflects variation in the LXX texts. Some have πρὸς τὴν γυναῖκα, "to his wife," while others simply have the dative τῇ γυναικί. It could be that the latter, which agrees with the Alexandrian Codex of the LXX and with the citation of Gen 2:24 in Matt 19:5 and is supported here by P⁴⁶ א* A D* G 31 33 462 Chrysostom, is in fact the better-attested reading for Ephesians. The decision does not, however, affect the meaning.

Form/Structure/Setting

5:21–33 can be seen as a unit. Its first verse acts as a link, completing the thought of 5:18–20 about being filled with the Spirit and at the same time introducing a new topic, submission, which is to be developed in the rest of the passage. Its introductory function is twofold. Not only does the admonition of v 22 depend on the participle of v 21 for its sense, but the notion of fear in the latter verse also provides the opening element of an *inclusio* which will be completed in v 33.

The writer's exhortations to marriage partners are closely related to what he has said earlier in the letter about the relationship of Christ and the Church and about the Church's calling in the world. It is not surprising that his vision of the exalted Christ's relationship to the Church, portrayed particularly powerfully in 1:20–23, colors his perspective on human relationships. To be sure, his primary aim in the pericope is to give instructions about marriage, but he bases these on assertions about the relationship of the heavenly bridegroom, Christ, to his bride, the Church. Throughout the passage there is this interplay between the two relationships. It is indicated by the use of comparative particles—ὡς (vv 23, 24), οὕτως (vv 24, 28), and καθώς (vv 25, 29). Although, as we shall see, this does not do adequate justice to the syntactical structure of the pericope, one way of viewing its argument is to note the movements back and forth between marriage and Christ and the Church (cf. also Sampley, *"And the Two,"* 103–8). The wife-husband relationship is set out in vv 22, 23a and supported by exposition of the Christ-Church relationship in vv 23b, 24a. Human marriage is the focus of vv 24b, 25a, and Christ and the Church again provide a warrant in vv 25b–27. What is said about this relationship in turn supplies the model for the attitude of the husband to his wife called for in vv 28, 29a, which is compared once more in vv 29b, 30 to the way in which Christ and the Church relate. The two relationships are brought together in vv 31, 32 via the reference to Gen 2:24, and the writer finally underlines his main purpose by summarizing his instructions on marriage in v 33.

This perspective on the pericope makes clear that, while the two relationships are inextricably interwoven in the argument, and although the union of human marriage can be seen as pointing to the union between Christ and the Church in vv 31, 32, the standard and prototype for the writer's instructions about human marriage is the bond between the heavenly bridegroom and his bride (cf. also Miletic, *"One Flesh,"* 27, who suggests the Christ-Church relationship is "analogically prior" to the husband-wife relationship). Chavasse (*The Bride of Christ,* 77) rightly observes, "He is arguing from the Heavenly Marriage to human marriages, not vice versa; he is seeing the human in the light of the heavenly, and therefore will have the human model itself on the heavenly." But he is certainly not correct in concluding from this that "his thought is not primarily of men and women in their earthly marriages. These are only shadows of the one great archetypal Marriage." Goodspeed (*Meaning*, 60–62) draws a similarly mistaken conclusion when he claims that the writer is not so much interested in the marriage relationship as he is in the union between Christ and the Church, and that he is more concerned about marriage as a symbol than he is about right relationships in marriage. After all, this passage begins and ends with exhortations to husbands and wives; it is part of the household code; and it is in the midst of the letter's serious paraenesis about believers' behavior in the world.

Although there are no excessively long sentences in this pericope, the interweaving of perspectives means that it is not always easy to unravel the thread of the writer's argument. To obtain a clear view of the structure, it is best to see the paraenesis as falling into four main parts. There is first of all in 5:21 the exhortation to all believers to submit to one another in the fear of Christ. This is then followed in 5:22–24 by the exhortation to wives to submit to their husbands as to the Lord. Verse 22 contains the initial exhortation, which is supported by the warrant of v 23 (cf. ὅτι, "for") that the husband is head of the wife, as Christ is head of the Church and himself the Savior of the body. The exhortation is repeated in v 24 and reinforced with ἐν παντί, "in everything," but this time the sequence of thought is reversed. The element from the analogy is given first, "as the Church is subject to Christ," and this leads into "so wives should be subject to their husbands in everything."

The third main section of the argument, and the longest one, is the exhortation to husbands in 5:25–32, which itself has two parts. In vv 25–27 the writer exhorts husbands to love their wives as Christ loved the Church. The actual exhortation is found in v 25a. The analogy of Christ's love for the Church functions as the warrant in vv 25b–27, which depict Christ's love in terms of his sacrificial death. Three final clauses with ἵνα (v 26, to sanctify her; v 27a, to present her to himself in splendor; v 27c, to enable her to be holy and blameless) spell out the purpose of this sacrificial love as the Church's holiness, the notion repeated in the first and third clauses. The second part of this section, vv 28–32, reiterates the exhortation to husbands to love their wives. This time the warrant comes in a combination of the analogies of a person's love for himself and Christ's love for the Church. Verse 28a states husbands' obligation to love their wives, and v 28b supports this by a comparison with their love for their own bodies. The use of σῶμα, "body," here suggests that the comparison might well already be associated in the writer's mind with his major analogy of Christ's love for his *body*, the Church (cf. vv 23, 30). However, most immediately in vv 28c–29b the comparison is elaborated on by the statement that "he who loves his wife loves himself" and the further supporting assertion (cf. γάρ in v 29a) that no one hates his own body (this time σάρξ, "flesh"), but instead nourishes and cherishes it. This prompts a return in vv 29c, 30 to the analogy of Christ and the Church, as Christ also is said to nourish and cherish the Church. In v 30 a supporting statement (ὅτι, "because, since") is added, which includes writer and readers in its scope, "since we are members of his body." In this way a person's loving his own body is now explicitly related to Christ's treatment of his body. Verses 31, 32, with their quotation and interpretation of Gen 2:24, are sometimes seen as a separate stage in the argument, but they are best taken as providing a further justification (the ἀντὶ τούτου, "for this reason," of the quotation offering an appropriate link) for the appeal to husbands to love their wives as their own bodies. There is a sense in which wives are their husbands' bodies, since Gen 2:24 declares that marriage makes husband and wife one body. σάρξ, "flesh," is the term used, but σάρξ and σῶμα, "body," are interchangeable here (cf. the shift between the two in vv 28, 29). This leads the writer to assert that basing his paraenesis about marriage on the relationship between Christ and the Church is entirely appropriate, because he interprets Gen 2:24 as a reference to the profound mystery of the union between Christ and the Church.

The fourth and final section of the argument is constituted by 5:33. The previous thought could lead the writer beyond his immediate objective, and so he breaks off and concludes with a summarizing rehearsal (indicated by the introductory πλήν, "however, in any case") of his basic exhortations to both husbands and wives. This time, following on the immediately preceding discussion of vv 25–32, husbands are addressed first, "Let each one of you also so love his wife as he loves himself." The thought has been set out in vv 28, 29, but now the wording is varied and is reminiscent of the command to love one's neighbor as oneself in Lev 19:18. The wording of the exhortation to the wife is also different. She is to fear her husband. The use of the verb "to fear" rather than "to submit" enables the writer to round off the passage with an *inclusio,* because the notion of fear, fear of Christ, was the motivation in the opening appeal to mutual submission back in v 21. In this way, vv 21 and 33 provide the frame for this pericope's marriage paraenesis.

The previous section of Ephesians, 5:15–20, had made use of Col 3:16, 17 in conjunction with Col 4:5. Now Eph 5:21–6:9 uses the next section of Colossians, its household code, from 3:18–4:1. The treatment of the same three pairs of household relationships follows the same basic sequence and has the same basic content, though, as we shall see, the writer to the Ephesians has expanded on this material in his own creative fashion. Whereas Colossians puts its emphasis on the last pair, the slave-master relationship, Ephesians concentrates most attention on the first, the wife-husband relationship. Eph 5:21–33, in particular, is dependent on Col 3:18, 19, and as in Colossians this topic follows on from exhortations about singing and giving thanks. (There is little to be said in favor of W. Munro's complicated hypothesis [*NTS* 18 (1972) 434–47] that, although Ephesians as a whole is dependent on Colossians, the household code in Colossians is dependent on that in Ephesians.) Like Colossians, Ephesians has the appeal to wives before that to husbands. Col 3:18 reads αἱ γυναῖκες, ὑποτάσσεσθε τοῖς ἀνδράσιν, ὡς ἀνῆκεν ἐν κυρίῳ, "Wives, submit to your husbands, as is fitting in the Lord." In comparison with this, in Eph 5:21–24 the writer has added the exhortation to mutual submission in v 21, which immediately gives the passage a different flavor, because in the Colossians original the notion of submission is only applied to the wives. Also, in his address to the wives, he omits the verb so that the notion of submission has to be carried over from the present participle of the previous clause. He then adds ἰδίοις, "own," before ἀνδράσιν, "husbands," and instead of ὡς ἀνῆκεν ἐν κυρίῳ, "as is fitting in the Lord," has the more direct ὡς τῷ κυρίῳ, "as to the Lord." The force of the additional ἰδίοις, "own," need not be emphatic. The adjective often functions in the same way as a personal pronoun, here substituting for ὑμῶν, "your," or it could be seen as the equivalent of ἑαυτῶν, "their" (cf. v 28). While in Colossians the Christian warrant for wives' submission is simply that this is fitting in the Lord, the rest of the exhortation in Ephesians spells out how this is fitting in terms of the Church's relation to Christ, and in so doing expands the original from one verse (Col 3:18) to three and a half (Eph 5:22–24, 33b) or from nine to forty-seven words in Greek. It should also be noted that in the repetition of the exhortation in v 24b the writer adds ἐν παντί, "in everything," to the Colossian original. Colossians does not have an absolutizing of its exhortation to wives but has this phenomenon instead in its appeal to children and slaves (cf. κατὰ πάντα in 3:20, 22).

In the appeal to husbands, Col 3:19 has οἱ ἄνδρες, ἀγαπᾶτε τὰς γυναῖκας καὶ μὴ πικραίνεσθε πρὸς αὐτάς, "husbands, love your wives and do not be embittered with them." In Eph 5:25 the first five words are repeated, but the injunction against bitterness is omitted (the writer has, however, listed πικρία, "bitterness," as a vice in 4:31). Instead, what it means to love is elaborated on in terms of the analogies with Christ's love for the Church and one's love for oneself (vv 25b–33a). Ten words addressed to husbands in Colossians become one hundred forty-three in Ephesians. So while in Colossians equal weight is placed on the duties of wives and husbands, the writer to the Ephesians addresses over three times as much of his appeal to husbands, the dominant partners, as to wives, the subordinate ones. There are other reminiscences of Colossians in the writer's expansion of the original, but these are instances where he has already made use of the language and concepts earlier in his letter. 5:23, which depicts Christ as head and the Church as his body, recalls Col 1:18, "He is the head of the body, the church," but this has already been developed in Eph 1:22, 23 and 4:15, 16. Col 1:22 speaks of "presenting" the readers "holy and blameless," and these terms are taken up separately in Eph 5:27, although the latter pair of adjectives has already been employed in Eph 1:4. All in all, this writer's treatment of the first part of the household code should probably be judged as more thoroughly Christian than that of Colossians (but see the *Explanation* for an evaluation of it in its own right). It is true that Colossians sets the relationship "in the Lord" and requires husbands to love, but Ephesians adds explicitly the qualifying notion of mutual submission and reinforces the sacrificial and demanding nature of the love required of husbands through its Christological analogy.

As we have seen, the major element in the form of this pericope (and of the material in 6:1–9)—a household code—is taken over from Colossians and adapted. For an overview of some of the earlier discussion of the background of the household code and the occasion of its use in Colossians, see the Word Biblical Commentary on Colossians (P. T. O'Brien, *Colossians, Philemon* [Waco, TX: Word, 1982] 214–19). For further, more detailed discussion of household codes and of their use in the NT, see the following:

Balch, D. L. *Let Wives Be Submissive: The Domestic Code in 1 Peter.* Chico, CA: Scholars Press, 1981. ———. "Household Codes." In *Greco-Roman Literature and the New Testament,* ed. D. E. Aune. Atlanta, GA: Scholars Press, 1988, 25–50. **Berger, K.** *Formgeschichte des Neuen Testaments.* Heidelberg: Quelle & Meyer, 1984, 135–41. **Cannon, G. E.** *The Use of Traditional Materials in Colossians.* Macon, GA: Mercer University Press, 1983, 95–131. **Carrington, P.** *The Primitive Christian Catechism.* Cambridge: CUP, 1940. **Crouch, J. E.** *The Origin and Intention of the Colossian Haustafel.* Göttingen: Vandenhoeck & Ruprecht, 1972. **Elliott, J. H.** *A Home for the Homeless.* Philadelphia: Fortress, 1981, 165–266. **Fiedler, P.** "Haustafel." *RAC* 13 (1986) 1063–73. **Gnilka, J.** *Der Kolosserbrief.* Freiburg: Herder, 1980, 205–16. **Goppelt, L.** "Jesus und die 'Haustafel'-Tradition." In *Orientierung an Jesus.* FS J. Schmid, ed. P. Hoffmann. Freiburg: Herder, 1973, 93–106. **Hartman, L.** "Code and Context: A Few Reflections on the Paraenesis of Col 3:6–4:1." In *Tradition and Interpretation in the New Testament.* FS E. Earle Ellis, ed. G. F. Hawthorne and O. Betz. Grand Rapids: Eerdmans, 1987, 237–47. **Hunter, A. M.** *Paul and His Predecessors.* London: SCM, 1962, 52–57, 128–31. **Kamlah, E.** "Ὑποτάσσεσθαι in den neutestamentlichen Haustafeln." *Verborum Veritas.* FS G. Stählin, ed. O. Böcher and K. Haacker. Wuppertal: Brockhaus, 1970, 237–43. **Lillie, W.** "The Pauline House-Tables." *ExpTim* 86 (1975) 179–83. **Lohse, E.** *Colossians and Philemon.* Philadelphia: Fortress, 1971, 154–57. **Lührmann, D.** "Neutestamentliche Haustafeln und antike Ökonomie." *NTS* 27 (1980) 83–97. **MacDonald, M.** *The Pauline Churches.* Cambridge: CUP, 1988, 102–22. **Martin, R. P.** "Haustafeln." *NIDNTT* 3 (1975) 928–32. **Müller, K.-H.** "Die Haustafel des Kolosserbriefes und das antike Frauenthema: Eine kritische Rückschau auf alte Ergebnisse." In *Die Frau im Urchristentum,* ed. G. Dautzenberg et al. Freiburg: Herder, 1983, 263–319. **Rengstorf, K. H.** "Die neutestamentlichen Mahnungen an die Frau, sich dem Manne unterzuordnen." In *Verborum Dei.* FS O. Schmitz. Witten: Luther Verlag, 1953, 131–45. **Sampley, J. P.** *"And the Two Shall Become One Flesh."* Cambridge: CUP, 1971, 17–30. **Schrage, W.** "Zur Ethik der neutestamentlichen Haustafeln." *NTS* 21 (1975) 1–22. **Schroeder, D.** "Die Haustafeln des Neuen Testaments." Dissertation, Hamburg, 1959. **Schweizer, E.** "Die Weltlichkeit des Neuen Testaments—die Haustafeln." In *Beiträge zur alttestamentlichen Theologie.* FS W. Zimmerli, ed. H. Donner, R. Hanhart and R. Smend. Göttingen: Vandenhoeck & Ruprecht, 1977, 397–413. ———. *The Letter to the Colossians.* London: S.P.C.K., 1982, 213–220. ———. "Traditional Ethical Patterns in the Pauline and Post-Pauline Letters and Their Development (lists of vices and house-tables)." In *Text and Interpretation.* FS M. Black, ed. E. Best and R. McL. Wilson. Cambridge: CUP, 1979, 195–209. **Selwyn, E. G.** *The First Epistle of St. Peter.* London: Macmillan, 1946, 419–39. **Strobel, A.** "Der Begriff des 'Hauses' im griechischen und römischen Privatrecht." *ZNW* 56 (1965) 91–100. **Thraede, K.** "Zum historischen Hintergrund der 'Haustafeln' des Neuen Testaments." In *Pietas.* FS B. Kötting, ed. E. Dassmann. Münster: Aschendorff, 1980, 359–68. **Verner, D. C.** *The Household of God: The Social World of the Pastoral Epistles.* Chico, CA: Scholars Press, 1983. **Weidinger, K.** *Die Haustafeln: Ein Stück urchristlicher Paränese.* Leipzig: J. C. Hinrichs, 1928. **Wendland, H.-D.** "Zur sozialethischen Bedeutung der neutestamentlichen Haustafeln." In *Botschaft an die soziale Welt.* Hamburg: Furche, 1959, 104–14. **Wicker, K. O.** "First Century Marriage Ethics: A Comparative Study of the Household Codes and Plutarch's Conjugal Precepts." In *No Famine in the Land.* FS J. L. McKenzie, ed. J. W. Flanagan and A. W. Robinson. Missoula, MT: Scholars Press, 1975, 141–53. **Yoder, J.** *The Politics of Jesus.* Grand Rapids: Eerdmans, 1972, 163–92.

For our purposes of setting this writer's exhortations in their contemporary context, we shall focus attention briefly on some of the conclusions of more recent discussion about the background of this form and its use in early Christianity. We shall then return at the end of this section, in our treatment of the life-setting of 5:21–33, to what was said about marriage relationships in such household codes and more broadly in the ancient world.

With the work of Crouch as its most detailed exposition, a consensus (cf. also Lohse, Martin, O'Brien, Schrage, Schweizer) prevailed in study of the origins of the household code that maintained that its immediate source was not Stoic moral philosophy (*pace* Dibelius, Weidinger) nor was it a Christian creation (*pace* Rengstorf, Schroeder, Goppelt) but that instead it was mediated to early Christianity from Hellenistic Judaism. Under the influence of the Hellenistic tradition of "unwritten laws" and in an attempt to show that there were Jewish laws which were equally valid for Gentiles, Jewish propagandists such as Philo (*Hypothetica* 7.1–14; *De Decal.* 165–67; *De Post. Caini* 181), Josephus (*c. Ap.* 2.22–28 §§ 190–210), and Ps.-Phocylides (175–227) were able to show links between the social duties of Judaism, with their special interest in wives, children, and slaves, and Hellenism as represented by popular Stoic philosophy. In all probability, this type of Hellenistic Jewish material was mediated to early Christianity via the Hellenistic synagogues (cf. Crouch, *Origins*, 95–101). In the early church the catalyst for its use was a response in the Pauline churches to enthusiastic excesses on the part of some women and slaves which appealed to the sort of baptismal formulation found in Gal 3:28. The household code of Colossians could then be seen as confirming qualifications that Paul had already made in 1 Corinthians and as safeguarding good order in his churches (cf. Crouch, *Origins*, 120–51).

More recently, however, it has been argued convincingly, especially by Balch (cf. also Thraede, Verner, Lührmann, Elliott, but for a different hypothesis, see Berger), that this sort of analysis does not do enough justice to the important influence of the discussion about the topic of household management in the ancient world. This discussion, which treats husband-wife, parent-child, and master-slave relationships, focuses on authority and subordination within these relationships, and relates the topic of the household to the larger topic of the state, can be found as early as the classical Greek philosophers (cf. Plato, *Leges* 3.690A-D; 6.771E—7.824C; Aristotle, *Pol.* 1.1253b, 1259a). It is worth noting how Aristotle introduces his discussion of the topic: "Now that it is clear what are the component parts of the state, we have first of all to discuss household management; for every state is composed of households. . . . The investigation of everything should begin with the smallest parts, and the primary and smallest parts of the household are master and slave, husband and wife, father and children; we ought therefore to examine the proper constitution and character of each of these three relationships, I mean that of mastership, that of marriage . . . , and thirdly the progenitive relationship" (*Pol.* 1.1253b). The continuity of the discussion of household management, retaining its Aristotelian outline down into the later Roman period, is demonstrated by its use, for example, in the Peripatetic *Magna Moralia*, by Aerius Didymus, Dio Chrysostom, Ariston, Hecaton, Seneca, Hierocles, and Dionysius of Halicarnassus, and by Neopythagoreans such as Bryson and Callicratidas. Philo and Josephus also adapted Aristotle's outline of household subordination in their interpretation and praise of Mosaic law (cf. Balch, *Wives*, 23–62). Josephus could write, "The woman, it [the Law] says, is in all things inferior to the man. Let her accordingly be obedient, not for her humiliation, but that she may be directed; for God has given authority to the man" (*c. Ap.* 2.24 § 199), while Philo instructs, "Wives must be in servitude to their husbands, a servitude not imposed by violent ill-treatment but promoting obedience in all things" (*Hyp.* 7.3). Typical of the content of all these discussions is the notion that the man is intended by nature to rule as husband, father, and master, and that not to adhere to this proper hierarchy is detrimental not only to the household but also to the life of the state.

The reminder of the links between discussion of the household and discussion of the state in the Greco-Roman world, whereby the household was viewed as the foundation of the state, is extremely significant for interpretation of the early Christian use of household codes. It reveals that proper household management was generally regarded as a matter of crucial social and political concern and that any upsetting of the traditional hierarchical order of the household could be considered a potential threat to the order of society as a whole.

The religious dimension of this situation was also crucial. In Greco-Roman culture, wives, children, and slaves were expected to accept the religion of the male head of the household, the *paterfamilias,* and so religious groups that attracted women and slaves were particularly seen as potentially subversive of societal stability. Writers in Greco-Roman society singled out the cults of Dionysus and Isis, which attracted women devotees, and also Judaism, since Jewish slaves rejected the worship of their Roman masters' gods, for stereotyped criticism on grounds of producing immorality and sedition. Dionysius of Halicarnassus, criticizing foreign mystery cults and supporting Roman virtues, praised Roman household relationships with their insistence on the obedience of wives, children, and slaves (*Rom. Ant.* 2.24.3–2.27.4). And in response to slanders about the Jews, Josephus' apology in *c. Ap.* 2.24, 27, 30 §§ 199, 206, 216 (cf. also Philo, *Hyp.* 7.3.5) stresses subordination within the three household relationships to show that Judaism did, in fact, accept the ethic demanded by Greco-Roman society and was not subversive of it (cf. Balch, *Wives,* 63–80).

As Christianity spread in the Roman world and women and slaves converted to this new religion, it too became the object of similar suspicion and criticism. Social tensions between Christians and the rest of society, as well as tensions within the early Christian movement, need, therefore, to be given their due in any account of the emergence of Christian household codes. It may well have been external factors, the need to respond to accusations from outsiders and to set standards in line with common notions of propriety, as much as internal ones, the need to respond to enthusiastic demands for freedom on the part of believers, that led Christians to take up the household code. It can be shown that 1 Peter in its particular use of the household code, set in an apologetic framework (cf. 1 Pet 2:12; 3:15, 16), insists that despite their conversion to a new religion, Christian wives and slaves should still be subordinate and thereby silence criticisms (cf. Balch, *Wives,* 81–116). What is certainly a factor by the time of the code's use in 1 Peter may also have been an element in its emergence within early Christianity in the first place. However, the precise reason for early Christians' taking up this topic originally and the exact relation between inner and outer social tensions in such a move must remain matters of conjecture. Colossians contains the first extant Christian household code, and, in its setting in that letter, neither the attempt to combat gnosticizing enthusiasm based on an over-realized eschatology nor an apology in the face of society's criticisms is the prime factor in its use. Over-realized eschatology was not an element in the beliefs the letter is combating, and although the paraenesis does later have an eye on relationships with outsiders (cf. 4:5), this is not a motivation directly connected with the household code. Instead, its introduction is appropriate, because devotees of the false teaching, with its stress on asceticism and visionary experiences, needed to be recalled to the significance of earthly life with its domestic duties. For the author of Colossians these are integral to the ethical consequences of true heavenly-mindedness and an appreciation of Christ's lordship (cf. Lincoln, *Paradise*, 130–31; Schweizer, *Text*, 204; Hartman, "Code and Context," 243).

Whatever the original reason for the introduction of the code into a letter like Colossians, it remains true that, given the dominant ethos about the household in the Greco-Roman world, the specific content assigned to the domestic duties would be bound to have a bearing on believers' relationship to the norms in their surrounding society. The same holds true for Ephesians, where there is no mention of relationships with outsiders in connection with the household code itself, but the writer does see its injunctions as part of believers' wise conduct in the world, which makes the most of opportunities for good and understands the will of the Lord for present circumstances (cf. 5:15–17). Some (e.g., Thraede, Müller) have claimed that the early Christian codes take a moderate, progressively conservative position between two more extreme options, the egalitarianism of Musonius and Plutarch, on the one hand, and the unqualified patriarchy of Philo and the Neopythagoreans, on the other. But this involves a misrepresentation of these other views, all of which contained much more of a mixture of patriarchal and egalitarian elements (cf. esp. Balch, "Household Codes," 29–33; *Wives*, 139–49, who points out that the significant social contrasts are not within Greco-Roman society but between that society and foreign Egyptian patterns and between its codes and the earlier Jesus movement in Palestine). Musonius' ideal for marriage is often quoted, and it does appear more egalitarian than that of Ephesians: "But in marriage there must be above all perfect companionship and mutual love of husband and wife, both in health and sickness and under all conditions, since it was with desire for this as well as for having children that both entered upon marriage. Where, then, this love for each other is perfect and the two share it completely, each striving to outdo the other in devotion, the marriage is ideal and worthy of envy, for such a union is beautiful" (Musonius Rufus, *Or*. XIIIA; C. Lutz, *Musonius Rufus* [New Haven: Yale University Press, 1947] 89). But it needs to be remembered that this stands alongside material which argues that men should work outside the house and women inside (*Or*. IV), which assumes that men are the rulers and superior while women are the ruled and inferior (*Or*. XII), and which refers to the wife as a great help, who must be willing to serve her husband with her own hands (*Or*. III; cf. also O. L. Yarbrough, *Not Like the Gentiles* [Atlanta, GA: Scholars Press, 1985] 55–56). The early Christian codes, despite their distinctive Christian motivations, turn out in practice to be in line with the variety within the consistent patriarchal pattern throughout Greco-Roman society, where subordination of wives to husbands, children to parents, and slaves to masters was the overarching norm (cf. also Verner, *Household*, 27–81, who notes some differences in the legal status of women under Greek, Roman, and Jewish law but concludes that in both Greece and Rome "the household was conceived as a patriarchal institution, whose male head . . . exercised sweeping, although not entirely unrestricted authority over the other members" and that "from the social structure alone, one would have a difficult time distinguishing pagan from Jewish households in the cities of Hellenistic-Roman Diaspora" [79–80]). They reflect a stage in which Christians were conscious of criticisms of subverting society and of the need to adjust to living in the Greco-Roman world without unnecessarily disrupting the status quo.

The household codes of Colossians and Ephesians can be seen as part of the process of stabilizing communal relations in the Pauline churches (cf. esp. MacDonald, *The Pauline Churches*, 102–22). In so doing, they continue the "love-patriarchalism" of the early Pauline movement (cf. G. Theissen, *The Social Setting of Pauline Christianity: Essays on Corinth* [Philadelphia: Fortress, 1982] esp. 107). As MacDonald (*The Pauline Churches*, 102–3) observes, "On the one hand, the rule-like statements reflect a more conservative attitude toward the role of subordinate members of the household; they leave much less room for ambiguity and, consequently, for exceptional activity on the part of certain members. On the other hand, the instructions are not incompatible with Paul's own teaching about women and slaves (cf. 1 Cor 11:2–16; 1 Cor 14:34–36; 1 Cor 7:20–24; Philem 10–20)." Despite the Christian modifications he provides for conduct within the household, which at times produce tensions with the notion of patriarchal domination (see *Comment* on v 25), and despite what he has said earlier about the radical contrast between believers and unbelievers, the writer of Ephesians, like the writers of other early Christian household codes, assumes that in this area the basic pattern of Christian conduct will have the same hierarchical structure as that prevailing in society as a whole. The death of the apostle Paul and the delay of the parousia would both have been factors contributing to Pauline Christians taking a long-term perspective on their churches' need to assimilate to life in society while preserving their essential identity. The form the code takes in Ephesians reflects its writer's attempt to contribute to this process.

Although discussions of the traditional topic of household management influenced the early Christians' taking up of this topic, there is of course no one model from the Greco-Roman world, including the adaptation of the household code in Hellenistic Judaism, on which Christian codes are directly dependent. Apart from the examples in Colossians and Ephesians, other early Christian codes that focus specifically on the household, though not addressing each member of all three pairs, can be found in 1 Pet 2:18–3:7; 1 Tim 6:1, 2; Titus 2:1–10; *Did.* 4.9–11; *Barn.* 19.5–7; *1 Clem.* 21.6–9; Ign. *Pol.* 4.1–6:1; Pol. *Phil.* 4.2–6:3. Despite their variations, these early Christian codes share a particular pattern or schema, over and above any distinctive Christian content. There are four major elements in this schema: an address to a particular social group, an imperative that is often accompanied by an appropriate object, an amplification of the imperative that often takes the form of a prepositional phrase, and a reason clause providing motivation or theological warrant (cf. esp. Verner, *Household*, 86–87). Verner (*Household*, 86–87) may have overstated the distinctiveness of this schema. Balch ("Household Codes," 36–40) offers some criticisms, not all equally telling ones, of Verner's discussion, and provides some parallels to the form of the individual exhortations in the codes. The closest parallel is what is stated about masters and slaves in Philo, *De Spec. Leg.* 2.67–68. But what appears to remain distinctive in Christian usage is the application of this schema in a *series* of exhortations to *different groups* within the household. Although there is direct literary dependence only between the Ephesians and the Colossians code within early Christianity, it appears that, once it had developed, the same basic pattern was taken up and applied differently for different situations. If the Colossians code is close to the earliest form, then later users of the pattern felt free to adapt and develop it by singling out particular groups for treatment, by expanding the amplification and reason sections, by sandwiching other types of exhortation between that addressed to the particular household groups, and, especially in the later examples, by merging household concerns with those of church organization (cf. also Verner, *Household*, 89, 92–107).

Apart from its use of Colossians and its household code, Eph 5:21–33 draws on other traditions. Sampley's monograph *"And the Two Shall Become One Flesh"* is, as its subtitle indicates, "a study of traditions in Ephesians 5:21–33" and should be consulted critically for a fuller treatment of some of the issues (cf. esp. 16–85, 158–62). The formulation of v 25, that Christ "loved the church and gave himself up for her," takes over via its earlier use in 5:2 the combination of the same verbs from Gal 2:20, where Paul had spoken of "the Son of God, who loved me and gave himself for me." The terminology in v 27 about the Church being holy and blameless has also been used earlier in 1:4. It reflects Paul's concerns for the purity of his churches (cf., e.g., 1 Thess 4:3–8; 1 Cor 7:14; 2 Cor 6:14–7:1; 11:2), which in turn reflects concerns for holiness prevalent in the OT and Judaism, where the language of cultic purity, that demanded of the priests and the sacrifices, could also be applied to Israel as a whole. The imagery of headship, as applied to the husband's relationship to his wife (v 23), recalls Paul's discussion in 1 Cor 11:3, while the terminology of body and members of the body, as applied to believers (vv 28–30), not only recalls the earlier statements of 1:23; 3:6; 4:16, 25 but also is reminiscent of Paul's language in 1 Cor 12:27 and Rom 12:4, 5. A major piece of tradition found in our passage is LXX Gen 2:24, cited in v 31 and underlying the exhortation of vv 28–30, a text used rather differently by Paul in 1 Cor 6:16 (cf. Lincoln, *JSNT* 14 [1982] 30–36, and *Comment* for fuller discussion). Both Sampley (*"And the Two,"* 51–61, 96–102, 110–14) and Miletic (*"One Flesh,"* 18–22, 47–66, 112–14) overestimate the extent of the influence of Gen 2:24 on the writer's argument. Miletic (esp. 48) misunderstands my earlier discussion. I do not assume that subordination has nothing to do with mutuality, nor dispute that the two notions can be combined theologically, nor deny that the writer holds them both together in this passage. I simply dispute that the quotation from Gen 2:24 performs this function in the writer's argument. Instead, it functions in a more limited way and is brought in to make his point about only one of these notions—the mutual "one flesh" relationship. Another OT text which has influenced the writer's formulation in v 33, "let each one of you also so love his wife as he loves himself," is Lev 19:18, "you shall love your neighbor as yourself." Its influence on the writer's language is clear here, but not in v 28 (*pace* Sampley, *"And the Two,"* 32–34, 139–42).

Finally, Eph 5:21–33 takes up what are known as *hieros gamos* or "sacred marriage" traditions. The term is used to cover a range of diverse relationships—the union between divine or celestial beings, the union betweeen a divine being and an earthly one, the union of the representatives of the divine and the earthly, or the ritual enactment of the union of celestial beings in the sexual union of two humans. A sacred marriage between a divine being and an earthly one is the imagery in which Yahweh's covenant relationship with Israel is sometimes depicted by the prophets (e.g., Isa 54:1, 5, 6; 62:4, 5; Jer 2:2, 3, 32; Ezek 16; 23; Hos 2:19, 20; Mal 2:14). In Ephesians, the imagery is used of the exalted Christ, now a heavenly being, and his relationship with the Church, to which believers on earth belong, although because of its relationship to Christ this Church has heavenly connections (cf. esp. 2:6). In Ephesians this union between Christ, the bridegroom, and the Church, his bride, is also seen as the archetype for human marriage, the "one flesh" relationship between husband and wife. Some scholars have correctly observed that because of this latter element, Ephesians' use of the sacred marriage imagery goes beyond that of its OT antecedents. They have gone on to claim that in this regard its writer has been influenced by ideas from a Gnostic thought world. (Cf. Schlier's lengthy excursus, 264–76, which concludes that the ideas that form the background to Ephesians "come mostly from the environment of a Gnosis connected with hellenistic Judaism" [275]. Batey, *NTS* 10 [1963] 121–27, claims more specifically that Ephesians was written in a milieu influenced by Jewish Gnosticism like that found in Justin the Gnostic's *Baruch*, where the marriage between Elohim and Eden serves as a pattern for human marriage relationships; Fischer, *Tendenz*, 181–200, adds to the material cited by Schlier Nag Hammadi texts such as *Exeg. Soul* 132–34; *Gos. Phil.* 64–72, 76, and concludes that while in Gnosticism the union between the Savior and Sophia serves ascetic tendencies, Eph 5 can be understood as a correction of the Gnostic mystery [195]. However, both these texts are dependent on Ephesians.) That the writer of Ephesians knew some earlier form of a Gnostic Sophia myth that related heavenly syzygies to human sexual relationships has, however, not been demonstrated by such scholars (cf. also Gnilka, 290–94). There is nothing that parallels the conception in Philo's writings either. The closest similarity is a discussion of taking Abraham and Sarah allegorically to stand for the union between the good mind or soul and virtue, a union which, however, is then sharply contrasted with physical marriage (cf. *De Abr.* 99–102; *De Somn.* 1.200). It is of course possible that the writer had some general knowledge of the links that were made between marriages of the gods and human marriages in the mystery religions, where, for example, the marriage of Zeus and Hera was thought of as a pattern for human marriage in terms of procreation and fecundity, and where the sacred marriage could be enacted in a human ritual (cf., e.g., W. K. C. Guthrie, *The Greeks and Their Gods* [London: Methuen, 1950] 53–73). It is also often observed that in the Villa Item the wedding of Dionysus and Ariadne may well be represented as a model for the future marriage of devotees (cf. E. Stauffer, "γαμέω," *TDNT* 1 [1964] 653).

What can be said more definitely is this. The writer has adapted Paul's picture of the Corinthian church as a pure bride for Christ from 2 Cor 11:2 with its language of presentation and applied it to Christ's relationship to the universal Church. This is related to other NT nuptial imagery, which portrays the salvation of the end-time as a marriage feast or more specifically as a marriage between Christ and the Church depicted as the heavenly Jerusalem (cf. Mark 2:18–22; Matt 22:1–14; 25:1–13; Rev 19:7–9; 21:2, 9; 22:17). This imagery has parallels in Jewish apocalyptic material (cf. 4 Ezra 9:26–10:59). Characteristically, in Ephesians, with its more realized eschatology, the marriage between Christ and the Church is now viewed as a present relationship. In depicting this union, the writer in vv 26, 27 also draws on the prophetic picture of Yahweh's marriage to Israel in Ezek 16:8–14 with its notions of cleansing, bathing with water, and the splendor of the bride (cf. also Sampley, "*And the Two,*" 38–43; Canticles and Ps 45 are, however, not direct sources for Ephesians' depiction, *pace* Sampley, "*And the Two,*" 45–51). The application of "sacred marriage" imagery to paraenesis about marriage appears to be this writer's distinctive contribution to the tradition. It is possible that he knew of ascetic tendencies in the churches of Asia Minor (cf. Col 2:18, 20–23 and *Comment* on Eph 5:29, 31, 32) and that this was the catalyst that led to this new direction of thought. But making the marriage of Christ and the Church the archetype for Christian marriage has no antecedent and is Ephesians' unique addition to the early Christian household code tradition.

As such, it is also a major contribution to the whole process of the "sacralizing" of marriage. It needs to be remembered that within the world of the first century C.E. marriage was primarily a contractual relationship. Although usually accompanied by some form of feast, it was a contractual agreement, and not any further legal or religious ceremony, that constituted a marriage. Within Judaism, of course, it was presumed that the permanence of the relationship was God's intention, that marriage would be within the Jewish community and not with Gentiles, and that it would be within the permitted degree of kinship. Ephesians, though it does not talk of marriage as a "sacrament" as did later Christian theology, does introduce a perspective on the relationship quite distinct from other contemporary views by linking it so closely to the mystery of Christ and the Church and giving it so prominent a place in the outworking of salvation (cf. esp. Perkins, "Marriage," 6–11, 23). As Perkins ("Marriage," 26) puts it, "the incorporation of the household code into a larger vision of the Church as the 'beloved' bride/body of Christ in Ephesians opens up the door for a qualitatively new perception of marriage. It participates in and reflects the new reality of grace which is at the heart of salvation."

As we have noted, in its setting in the letter this exhortation to wives and husbands is linked via the introductory exhortation about mutual submission to the previous pericope (5:15–20), so that its injunctions are to be seen as specific examples of the wise living in the fullness of the Spirit that this writer requires of believers. The formulations and themes of 5:21–33 also have links with the writer's earlier discussion. The exhortation to mutual submission is a further variation on previous calls to bear with one another in love (4:2), to be kind and forgiving to one another, and to walk in love (4:32–5:2). The "one flesh" unity of the marriage relationship is a further instance of the unity motif that has previously been expressed in regard to the cosmos (1:10) and the Church (2:14–18; 4:1–16). The analogy to human marriage of Christ's relationship to the Church, where he is the head and the Church is the body, recalls the writer's earlier use of this imagery in 1:22, 23 and 4:15, 16 (cf. also 2:16; 3:6), and when believers are said to be members of his body (v 30), this is language that has already been used of them in 4:25. Christ's unity with his Church is called a "mystery" (v 32). Other aspects of God's hidden purpose have already been expounded as mysteries in 1:9; 3:3, 4, 9, and the term will be taken up again with reference to the gospel in 6:19. The writer's depiction of Christ's love and self-giving for the Church (v 25) employs a formulation encountered earlier in 5:2. The depiction of the results of that love in terms of the Church's sanctification and glory repeats the notions of 1:4 "that we should be holy and blameless," and of 1:18 and 3:21, which speak of the glory involved in God's possession of his people and in the Church. Providing a motivation for household relationships where both parties are to carry out their responsibilities as part of their obedience to Christ will, of course, continue to be the focus of the writer's concern in the remainder of the household code in 6:1–9.

Why has this writer placed such a heavy stress on the marriage relationship, and why has he done so from the distinctive perspective found in this passage? As with other such issues in Ephesians, there are frustratingly few clues about any actual life-setting for such an exposition. There are three possible ways in which marriage might not have been held in the regard which this writer thought was its due. It could simply be that, as with other aspects of their conduct, the readers were not realizing the importance of living out their distinctive calling and that some of the married members of the churches addressed were not relating this area of their lives to their faith, but viewing marriage simply as a natural relationship and treating it no differently from the way that their non-Christian neighbors treated it (cf. Mussner, 156). For this reason, the writer would be at pains to relate it to the heart of his interpretation of the Christian message and to emphasize the distinctiveness produced by Christian motivation. It could also be that the sexual immorality inveighed against in 4:19; 5:3–6, 12, 18 was seen by the writer as a real threat and that, therefore, the stress on the special status of Christian marriage was a further means of combating such a menace. On the other hand—and this is probably the most likely of the three options, since we know of ascetic tendencies that had to be combated in Colossians (cf. 2:16–23), of ascetic interpretations of Gen 2:24 that might have been current (see *Comment* on vv 31, 32), and of the continuing attraction of Christian asceticism in Asia Minor (cf. 1 Tim 4:1–3 and *Acts of Paul and Thecla*)—this passage's extolling of marriage could have been in the face of its denigration through such attitudes (cf. MacDonald, *The Pauline Churches*, 118–19). Having said all this, it may yet also be the case that the writer needed no particular occasion or difficulty about marriage to cause him to elaborate in this way. His vision of life in the world is one which is particularly concerned with unity—the ultimate unity of the cosmos in Christ and the present anticipation of that in the unity of the Church. An essential aspect of unity in the Church is harmony in the Christian household, and the pairing within the household that lends itself most to the exposition of unity is clearly that of husband and wife. There may also be an equivalent here in Ephesians to the link between household and state in traditional discussions, where the household was seen as a subunit or microcosm of the *polis*.

Now the household is regarded as the subunit or microcosm of Christian society, the Church, which this writer has described as God's household (2:19). In Ephesians, then, marital unity serves as an instance of Church unity, and Church unity serves as an instance of ultimate cosmic unity. As Sampley ("*And the Two*," 149) puts it, "for the author of Ephesians, the marriage relationship is transparent to God's purposes on a larger scale . . . no other relationship within the family so fully mirrors God's purposes in the universe." For this writer, not only can marriage provide a superb example of the mutual submission that is necessary for harmony in the Church, but also, through its specific roles of loving headship and voluntary submission, it can reflect the way another major unity, the fundamental unity between Christ and his Church, is expressed. As we have seen, this pattern of Christian marriage would not have been viewed as strange or upsetting within the cities of Asia Minor. Despite its distinctively Christian elements, in terms of the actual roles it enjoins it falls well within normal expectations about the patriarchal household in the Greco-Roman world.

Comment

21 ὑποτασσόμενοι ἀλλήλοις ἐν φόβῳ Χριστοῦ, "Submit to one another in the fear of Christ." As has already been pointed out, this verse is transitional, completing the series of participles which are dependent on the verb πληροῦσθε, "be filled," from v 18, while itself providing the verbal form on which the first injunction in the following household code is dependent. This enables it to be the appropriate link between the writer's appeal to the whole community and his advice to specific groups within it. If believers are filled with the Spirit, this should manifest itself in their mutual submission. There are similarities with the earlier paraenesis in 4:2, 3, where "bearing with one another in love" stands parallel to "making every effort to maintain the unity of the Spirit," and in 4:30, where it is clear from the context that what grieves the Spirit are the words and deeds of believers that are disruptive of communal life. The call to mutual submission "demands readiness to renounce one's own will for the sake of others, i.e., ἀγάπη, and to give precedence to others" (G. Delling, "ὑποτάσσω," *TDNT* 8 [1972] 45). It is significant that although, as we shall see, there are similar injunctions in the writings of Paul, only here in the Pauline corpus is the actual verb "to submit" employed for mutual relationships among believers. Elsewhere the notion of submission is only used for the attitude of specific groups—women (1 Cor 14:34; Col 3:18; 1 Tim 2:11; Titus 2:5), children (1 Tim 3:4), and slaves (Titus 2:9)—or for the attitude of believers to the state (Rom 13:1, 5; Titus 3:1).

But how does the injunction to mutual submission relate to what follows? On the one hand, it is possible to take it as a general heading for what follows. In other words, there is to be subjection to one another, and then the specific subjection meant is spelled out as wives to husbands, children to parents, and slaves to masters (cf. Clark, *Man and Woman*, 74–76, who holds that there is, therefore, no appeal for mutual subordination and that what is meant is "let each of you subordinate himself or herself to the one he or she should be subordinate to"). But this does not do enough justice to the force of this verse.

On the other hand, it is possible so to emphasize this verse that it is then understood as completely relativizing what follows. Sampley (*"And the Two,"* 117), for example, goes too far in asserting that it is a critique of the rest of the passage and that the ensuing household code contains a viewpoint with which the writer does not entirely agree. Yet if he disagreed with it, why would the writer have made such extended use of it as is made in this letter? Justice has to be done *both* to the force of v 21 *and* to the force of the specific types of submission in the household code. Modern interpreters might perceive the first admonition as undermining or deconstructing the others, but clearly the original writer did not find them incompatible. There is an interesting parallel in 1 Pet 5:5, where the exhortation "you that are younger be subject to the elders" is followed immediately by the further appeal "clothe yourselves, all of you, with humility toward one another." The latter admonition was not meant to cancel out the former. Rather, the writer holds that there is a general sense in which elders are to serve their flock, including its younger element, in a submissive attitude, but that mutuality goes along with a hierarchical view of roles. Thus there is a specific sense in which the flock in general and the younger in particular are to be obedient to the elders. Similarly, here in Ephesians mutual submission coexists with a hierarchy of roles within the household. Believers should not insist on getting their own way, so there is a general sense in which husbands are to have a submissive attitude to wives, putting their wives' interests before their own, and similarly parents to children and masters to slaves. But this does not eliminate the more specific roles in which wives are to submit to husbands, children to parents, and slaves to masters. As Schüssler Fiorenza (*Memory*, 269) correctly notes, "The general injunction for all members of the Christian community, 'Be subject to one another in the fear of Christ,' is clearly spelled out for the Christian wife as requiring submission and inequality."

Paul had called for mutual submission and service in such passages as Gal 5:13b and Phil 2:3, 4. In fact, in the latter passage, the qualities of selflessness and a regard for others that does not insist on one's own rights that the apostle desires to see are linked to the heart of his gospel by being grounded on the pattern of Christ's life. He did not insist on the equality with God that was his by rights but became a servant. And in the light of this, the Philippians are exhorted to live out that sort of pattern of salvation in fear and trembling in the face of God's activity among them (cf. Phil 2:5–13). Here in Ephesians, the ground and motivation for believers' mutual submission, the placing of themselves at one another's disposal for which the writer calls, is more specifically the fear of Christ. Barth (608, 662–68) is right to insist that translations should not tone down φόβος to the weaker notion of respect. "Fear" need not involve fright or terror but conveys a more serious sense of reverence and obligation than "respect." In the OT, the fear of the Lord was the appropriate attitude of a creature to the Creator, producing obedience to his will (cf. also H. R. Balz, "φόβος," *TDNT* 9 [1974] 189–219). In Paul's writings "fear of the Lord" or "fear of Christ" is virtually interchangeable with "fear of God." 2 Cor 5:11 sounds an eschatological note, "knowing the fear of the Lord, we persuade people," while 2 Cor 7:1 exhorts that holiness should be made perfect in the fear of God (cf. also Phil 2:12). Col 3:22 had talked about "fearing the Lord" as a motivation for slaves, but here it is the attitude all believers are to have.

Just as in the OT the guiding principle for wise living within the covenant was the fear of Yahweh, so now the writer of Ephesians indicates that the overriding motivation for wise living (cf. v 15) and relationships within the new community must be the fear of Christ. This is an attitude that looks to Christ in awe at his overwhelming love and at his power and that also lives in the light of his sovereign claim and righteous judgment (cf. also 6:8, 9). The mutual submission required depends on all parties' having this attitude to Christ, and the specific relationships within marriage that are set out are also to flow from and be an expression of such fear (cf. also the later references to the wife's fear and to slaves' fear and trembling in 5:33 and 6:5).

22 Αἱ γυναῖκες τοῖς ἰδίοις ἀνδράσιν ὡς τῷ κυρίῳ, "Wives, submit to your husbands as to the Lord." Within the marriage relationship, wives are addressed first. It should be noted that in this household code those who are to be subordinate, wives, children, and slaves, are addressed as moral agents. Although some elements of the Pauline gospel (cf. Gal 3:28) might have led women and slaves in the Pauline churches to different conclusions about their roles in the church and in society, this writer asks wives voluntarily to subordinate themselves to their husbands. It is of course noteworthy, as we have already seen, that this verse does not actually contain the verb ὑποτάσσεσθαι, "to be subordinate." Nor for that matter does the syntax of v 24b apply the verb directly to the wife. But in both cases, this is so clearly to be understood from the preceding clauses that it is doubtful whether any theological significance should be read into its omission. The writer's theological framework can be discerned from what he says explicitly and does not need to be inferred from an ellipsis (*pace* Miletic, "One Flesh," 7, 17, 27–30, 99–101). ὑποτάσσεσθαι means to take a subordinate role in relation to that of another (cf. Delling, "ὑποτάσσω," *TDNT* 8 [1972] 39–46; Kamlah, "ὑποτάσσεσθαι," 239–40). What it involves more specifically will depend on the relationship to which it is applied and the social expectations attached to that relationship. In other words, in its concrete manifestation, subordination takes a particular shape in the relation of citizens to the state, another in the relation of slaves to masters, and yet another in the relationship of wives to husbands. In the NT, the term is used of this last relationship in Col 3:18; Titus 2:5; 1 Pet 3:1. Outside the NT, there are, however, only two examples of the use of the actual verb ὑποτάσσεσθαι for the wife's attitude toward her husband, Plutarch, *Conj. Praec.* 33 (*Moralia* 142e), and Ps-Callisthenes, *Hist. Alex. Magni* 1.22.4 (cf. Rengstorf, "Die neutestamentlichen Mahnungen," 132), though the call for wives to obey husbands was common in Hellenistic Judaism (cf., e.g., Philo, *Hyp.* 7.3; Josephus, *c. Ap.* 2.24 § 201).

But does the fact that there are varieties of subordination and that the subordination is willing mean that a distinction should be made, as is done by some (e.g., Barth, 714), between subordination and obedience? In support of such a distinction, it is pointed out that the verb used for the attitude required from wives is ὑποτάσσεσθαι, "to submit, be subordinate," while that employed in the case of children and slaves is ὑπακούειν, "to obey." But this is to drive a wedge between terms that are frequently synonymous. To be sure, "to submit" is the broader term, but to subordinate oneself to another may well entail being willing to obey that person, and such obedience would certainly have been seen as part of a wife's role in relation to her husband in most parts of the ancient world. Certainly also, the Church's subordination to Christ, on which the wife's subordination to her husband is based in v 24, would be seen as involving glad obedience (cf. also Clark, *Man and Woman*, 82). There is obviously a difference between willing submission and imposed obedience but hardly a major distinction between voluntary subordination and voluntary obedience. Here the obedience of children and slaves is to be seen as part of the mutual subordination enjoined in v 21. Elsewhere in the NT, in 1 Pet 3:5, 6, submission of wives to husbands and obedience of wives to husbands are explicitly paralleled.

The wife is to be subject to her husband as to the Lord. Her subordination is called for not just because it is the role society has allotted her but because this is the way she can serve her Lord (cf. also Caird, *Paul's Letters*, 88). The "Lord" is not a direct reference, as some have suggested, to the husband as lord of the wife in line with 1 Pet 3:6, "Sarah obeyed Abraham, calling him lord" (*pace* Mussner, 156; idem, *Christus*, 148; Gaugler, 207–8; Sampley, "*And the Two*," 112, 122, holds that the writer is being deliberately ambiguous in his use of κύριος). Greek grammar would demand the plural "as to their lords" instead of the singular ὡς τῷ κυρίῳ. As the next verse will explain, what is involved here is that in voluntarily subordinating herself to her husband the wife is to see this as done in subordination to the Lord, because in the marriage relationship her husband reflects the Lord while she reflects the Church. Fear of Christ (v 21) becomes in the concrete marriage situation submission to the husband, even fear of the husband (v 33). But in this specific situation the same motivation is to be maintained as in the general admonition of v 21; that is, submission is to be practiced as if to the Lord himself. As Schüssler Fiorenza (*Memory*, 269) observes, "The instruction to the wives clearly reinforces the patriarchal marriage pattern and justifies it christologically" (*contra* Wall, *CSR* 17 [1988] 280, who claims, "The spiritual hierarchy in effect dismantles the social hierarchy").

23 ὅτι ἀνήρ ἐστιν κεφαλὴ τῆς γυναικὸς ὡς καὶ ὁ Χριστὸς κεφαλὴ τῆς ἐκκλησίας, "for the husband is the head of the wife as Christ also is the head of the church." In the flow of the argument this statement provides the reason for the wife's submission. The ὅτι, "for," is to be noted. This link suggests fairly clearly, therefore, that for the writer the husband's headship, especially when seen in the light of the analogy with Christ's headship in the second half of the statement, involves a role of authority. Although the meaning would correspond with the thrust of the passage, it is doubtful that the actual words ὡς καί, "as also," have the force of "only in the same way that" and indicate that the husband's headship is to be limited by the way in which Christ exercised his (*pace* Barth, 613–14). Rather, they simply have comparative force and serve to introduce the analogy. The analogy takes up a concept the writer has already employed earlier in the letter. As we have seen, in 1:22 κεφαλή, "head," is used with the significance of leader or ruler, which it sometimes has in the LXX, to express Christ's supremacy and authority over the cosmos. This headship is thought of as a position of power which he now exercises on behalf of the Church (cf. also Col 1:18; 2:10). In its LXX usage, where it translated the Hebrew ראשׁ, *rō'š*, κεφαλή also took on at times the further connotations of that Hebrew term and had the force of determinative source or origin. This connotation to a large extent explains the writer's reference in 4:15 (cf. also Col 2:19), where Christ as the Church's head is also viewed as the source of its life. The apostle Paul had made use of the concept of headship in 1 Cor 11:3, where, in the context of a response to a problem about women participating in worship with their heads uncovered, he set out an order of headship—God as head of Christ, Christ as head of man, and man as head of woman. Whether the apostle employed κεφαλή there to mean ruler or source or, more likely, a mixture of both is still highly disputed. (For some recent discussion of the term, cf. W. Grudem, "Does κεφαλή ('Head') Mean 'Source' or 'Authority over' in Greek Literature? A Survey of 2,336 Examples," *Trinity Journal* 6 [1985] 38–59; G. D. Fee, *The First Epistle to the Corinthians* [Grand Rapids: Eerdmans, 1987] 502–5; C. C. Kroeger, "The Classical Concept of *Head* as 'Source,'" in G. G. Hull, *Equal to Serve* [Old Tappan, NJ: Revell, 1987] 267–83.) Here there can be little doubt, in light of the usage in 1:22, of the general context of the authority structure of the Greco-Roman household (see *Form/Structure/Setting* on the household code), and of the specific context of the submission of wife to husband within marriage in vv 22–24, that the writer has the role of leader or ruler and with that the notion of authority in view in his use of the term "head" (*pace*, e.g., Wall, *CSR* 17 [1988] 281). This perspective is no different from what would have been the dominant expectation about the role of the *paterfamilias* in the ancient world (cf. Aristotle, *Pol.* 1255b, "The rule of the household is a monarchy, for every house is under one head"; cf. also Plutarch, *Moralia* 142e). Despite the fact that by the time of the early empire most marriages in Rome took place *sine manu* (without power transferred to the husband), and that Greek women also had greater legal independence, writings about the household retained this patriarchal structure as necessary for the stability of society (cf. also, e.g., Verner, *Household*, 27–81; *pace* Kroeger, "The Classical Concept," 280–82, there are no reasons for seeing *sine manu* marriage as leading to nonhierarchical definitions of headship and submission in the early Christian codes). In light of the other earlier reference to Christ's headship of the Church in association with his being the source of its life and growth (cf. 4:15, 16), the connotation of source might also in theory be included here as part of what is involved in the husband's headship of the wife. One could certainly talk in a general way about the husband's providing for his wife's well-being, but it is difficult to see what it could mean to say that the husband is the source of the wife's life, particularly when at this point the background of Eve coming into being through Adam in the creation story is not part of the argument, as it had been in 1 Cor 11. It is not at all clear that one should read into the use of "head" here in 5:23 all of Paul's argument from creation in 1 Cor 11. The writer is not arguing from the creation story but from the relationship of Christ to the Church. To be sure, he later brings Gen 2:24 into his paraenesis, but to make a different point (*pace* Miletic, "*One Flesh*," esp. 67–79). It should also not be supposed that, just because the writer has applied the term "head" to Christ in Eph 1:22b after an Adamic allusion through the quotation of Ps 8:6 in 1:22a, "Adamic" connotations can be read into the term when it is employed in the different context of Eph 5:23 (*pace* Miletic, "*One Flesh*," 79–87). The writer's point is this: the husband's headship or authority, which the wife is to recognize, is one that is patterned on the unique character of Christ's headship over the Church, and, as the rest of the passage will make clear, that sort of headship included Christ's giving his life for the Church.

αὐτὸς σωτὴρ τοῦ σώματος, "and is himself the Savior of the body." There is a question whether this latter part of v 23 refers solely to the relationship between Christ and the Church (cf., e.g., Abbott, 166; Dibelius, 93; Barth, 614–17; Schnackenburg, 252; Miletic, "*One Flesh*," 40, 102) or is also part of the analogy with the husband and wife, so that the husband is even to be understood as in some sense the savior of his wife as Christ is the Savior of the body (cf., e.g., J. A. Robinson, 124; W. Foerster, "σωτήρ," *TDNT* 7 [1971] 1016; Hendriksen, 248–49; Wall, *CSR* 17 [1988] 281–82; Bruce, *Epistles*, 385, who allows that this may be "a reference to the husband's role as his wife's protector"). The only other place in the NT where the concept of salvation is used of the husband's relation to the wife is in 1 Cor 7:16, where, if a believing husband stays in a marriage with an unbelieving wife, he may save his wife. But this reference is of no help, since the context shows that this salvation is in terms of evangelization, the same is said of a believing wife's relation to an unbelieving husband, and here in Ephesians it is clear that both husband and wife are assumed to be believers. Tobit 6:18 reports Raphael as saying that Tobias' marriage to Sarah will save her. But again there is a specific context which disqualifies this as in any way an analogous concept, for Tobias at the same time as he marries Sarah saves or rescues her from the power of a demon (cf. also Bruce, *Epistles*, 385). What arguments, then, can be adduced in favor of this latter interpretation? It can be claimed that "Savior" should be taken in the general sense of protector or provider for welfare and order in the way it would have been applied to the emperor in its Hellenistic usage. This would suit the close conjunction with κεφαλή, "head," for earlier in 4:15, 16 Christ as head had been depicted as providing for the nourishment and welfare of the body. This more general sense could include connotations of rule, which would also suit the main point of this part of the analogy. It can be argued further that later in the passage the wife is in fact seen as the husband's body (vv 28–30), and this is explicitly paralleled to Christ's relationship to his body, the Church. So if Christ is Savior of his body, should not the analogy hold at this earlier point also and the husband be seen as the savior of his body, the wife? The writer might well have been willing to accept this extension of his analogy, but the syntax suggests that this is not the specific point he is making at this stage of his discussion. On introducing his analogy between Christ and the husband, he has primarily had the notion of "headship" in mind and then as an additional thought has provided a further description which applies to Christ as head of the Church. The place and force of αὐτός, "himself," in this additional statement indicate that Christ is the focus of attention and that the writer did not intend this description to serve also as a model for the husband's role in marriage. This conclusion is reinforced by the fact that the adversative ἀλλά, "but" (see *Comment* on v 24), precedes the reintroduction of the analogy between the Church's relationship to Christ and the wife's relationship to her husband in the next sentence and by the specifically redemptive connotations that adhere to the notion of salvation earlier in the letter in 1:13 and 2:5, 8 and later in 6:17.

There is little to be said for the rather startling claim of Miletic (*"One Flesh,"* 43–45) that v 23c "is both the structural core and theological center of the address to the wives." The structural elements to which he appeals can equally well be explained on the supposition that v 23c is an additional thought that disturbs the flow of the argument, and the theological center of the appeal is surely the analogy with Christ and the Church in terms of submission and headship. Once the purpose of this latter part of v 23 is seen to be simply to provide an additional description of Christ's relationship to the Church, there is also no need to claim that it functions as a deliberate qualification of the husband's authority (*pace* Sampley, "And the Two," 125–26).

The concept of Christ as "Savior of the body" is found nowhere else in the NT. This has prompted some scholars to suggest that it is dependent on Gnostic thought, in which there can be found variations on the theme of a preexistent Sophia falling and being saved through union with the Redeemer in a heavenly syzygy (cf. Schlier, 266–76; Fischer, *Tendenz,* 176, 194). But the alternation between bride and body as images of the Church in relation to its head cannot be clearly derived from such material. Fischer (*Tendenz,* 186–94), who finds strong similarities between 5:21–33 and the *Exeg. Soul* in its bridal imagery, has to admit that there is no parallel to the head-body language in that document. The only other place in which the two images of bride and body are juxtaposed is *2 Clem.* 14, which may well be dependent on Ephesians for this combination. In addition, it must be noted that there is no clear parallel in Ephesians to the notion of the preexistence of the redeemed bride (see *Comment* on 1:4). The emphasis in this letter is more on the Church's being created through Christ's reconciling death (cf. 2:15). To call Christ the Savior of the body does not necessarily imply that the latter was in existence before its salvation (*pace* Schlier, 255). It need mean no more than that those who at present make up that body were at one time in a situation from which they needed to be saved (cf. 2:1–5).

It makes more sense, therefore, to see the writer as simply combining the title "Savior" for Christ with his own characteristic term "body" for the Church. "Savior" as a title for Christ occurs in Paul in Phil 3:20 (*pace* Mitton, 200, who asserts it is not found in the genuine Paul). There is an element of similarity in that there it is used in conjunction with another title of rule, κύριος, "lord," which features here also in Eph 5:22. But there is also an element of difference in that in Phil 3:20 the focus is on Christ's activity at the Parousia whereas here, in line with Ephesians' characteristic realized eschatology, Christ is already the Church's Savior. The use of the title Savior for Christ increased toward the end of the first century (cf. 2 Tim 1:10; Titus 1:4; 2:13; 3:6; 2 Pet 1:1, 11; 2:20; 3:2, 18), possibly as part of Christians' stance toward its free application to emperors. Nevertheless, its roots are in the OT conception of Yahweh as the Savior or Deliverer of his people (cf., e.g., LXX Deut 32:15; 1 Sam 10:19; Ps 24:5; Isa 12:2; 45:15; 62:11; Mic 7:7; Hab 3:18). What it means for Christ to be Savior has been seen in the depiction in 2:1–10 of the divine act of deliverance in which Christ is the agent, and is spelled out further in vv 25–27. It involves his sacrificial death (cf. also 5:2) that enables him to make the Church holy. Miletic (*"One Flesh,"* 53–66) is not content with such an explanation and claims that the notion of Christ as Savior is "Adamic" and should be interpreted in the light of what is said of Christ's death in 2:14–18. That passage illuminates the salvation brought by Christ in a general way, but in it Christ in his reconciling death is seen as Creator, "Adamic" language is used of the Church ("one new person") and not of Christ, and what his death creates is not a new Eve (*pace* Miletic, *"One Flesh,"* 53) but a new Adam! For Christ in his saving death to be the Creator and the new Adam at the same time would be a strange and awkward mingling of images, even for Ephesians (*pace* Miletic, *"One Flesh,"* 66).

24 ἀλλὰ ὡς ἡ ἐκκλησία ὑποτάσσεται τῷ Χριστῷ, οὕτως καὶ αἱ γυναῖκες τοῖς ἀνδράσιν ἐν παντί, "But as the Church submits to Christ, so also should wives submit to their husbands in everything." As has been suggested above, ἀλλά, "but," is best taken as an adversative, providing a contrast with the immediately preceding words in v 23c. In relation to their additional distinctive thought about Christ, it provides the link back to the main analogy and has the force of "notwithstanding the difference" (cf. Abbott, 166; Barth, 619; Maillet, *ETR* 55 [1980] 570; *pace* J. A. Robinson, 124, 205, who claims it simply has a resumptive force, focusing on the main aspect of the previous argument, and Miletic, *"One Flesh,"* 102 n. 6, who holds it has consecutive force).

So v 24 restates, and in the process reinforces, the exhortation and its warrant in the analogy of Christ and the Church that has preceded in vv 22, 23. In the new formulation, the analogy is stated first and in a way that corresponds to the role of wives, "as the Church submits to Christ, so. . . ." The Church's submission to Christ is certainly willing and free rather than coerced and therefore underlines what has been said about the wife's submission as voluntary in the comments on v 22. If one asks what the writer thinks is involved in the Church's subordination to Christ, one can look for an answer to the way in which he depicts the Church's relation to Christ in the rest of the letter. The Church receives God's gift of Christ as head over all on its behalf (1:22). In the building imagery of 2:20, 21 the Church looks to Christ as the crowning stone of its structure and the one who holds it all together. It opens itself to his constant presence (3:17) and comes to know his all-encompassing love (3:19). The Church receives his gift of grace (4:7) and his gifts of ministers for its own upbuilding (4:11, 12). It grows toward its head and receives from him all that is necessary for such growth (4:15, 16), including teaching about him (4:20, 21). The Church imitates Christ's love (5:2) and tries to learn what is pleasing to him (5:10) and to understand his will (5:17). It sings praises to him (5:19) and lives in fear of him (5:21). The Church's subordination, then, means looking to its head for his beneficial rule, living by his norms, experiencing his presence and love, receiving from him gifts that will enable growth to maturity, and responding to him in gratitude and awe. It is such attitudes that the wife is being encouraged to develop in relation to her husband. Miletic (*"One Flesh,"* 43) sums up the way in which the analogy grounds the exhortation in his assertion that "the Christ/church relationship provides direction ('to the Lord'), perception (husband as 'head' as Christ is 'head') and example (church as paradigm) for the wife's act of subordination."

It is an interesting theological idea that the Church is depicted as showing to Christ the subordination which, according to 1 Cor 15:28, Christ will show to God, but it is unlikely that the writer has deliberately transferred the Pauline notion of Christ's subordination to God to what he now sees required of the

Church (*pace* Miletic, "*One Flesh*," 88–94). It is far more likely that the notion of submission suggested itself to the writer for his depiction of the Church's attitude to its head because this was the term found in the household code in Col 3:18 on which he is dependent, the term which he has already taken up in 5:21, and the term on which the exhortation to wives in 5:22 is dependent.

The element of reinforcement in the new formulation of the exhortation to wives is provided by the concluding phrase ἐν παντί, "in everything." Although the writer has just made an assertion distinctive of Christ, this does not at all qualify his basic exhortation to wives (*pace* Sampley, "*And the Two*," 125–26). Instead, full and complete subordination is required. It is noteworthy that Ephesians calls for complete submission of wives to husbands, whereas Colossians, with its use of κατὰ πάντα in 3:20, 22, had called for complete obedience of children to parents and slaves to masters (cf. also Schüssler Fiorenza, *Memory*, 269). There is to be no limit to the submission expected of wives, just as there is no limit to the Church's obedient service of Christ. In this ideal picture of Christian marriage, the possibility is not even considered that wives' submission to their husbands might conflict with their submission to Christ. On the other hand, it must be said that in Ephesians the Church's submission to Christ is for the Church's benefit, enabling its growth, unity, and maturity, so that the wife's subordination to her husband also presupposes that it is part of a relationship in which the husband has her welfare constantly in view. As the following verses will make explicit, full and complete commitment of the husband to his particular role of loving is also required (cf. also Schlier, 254; Gnilka, 277; Schnackenburg, 252–53; Miletic, "*One Flesh*," 105, "subordination is to selfless love—expressed through the husband's headship—and not to the whims of the husband"). So in this writer's vision of Christian marriage what is called for from wives is complete subordination to complete love (cf. also Miletic, "*One Flesh*," 111, "both roles demand total self-renunciation").

Certainly in this exhortation to wives the writer has no intention of doing away with the hierarchical structure of family life in the ancient world, and it looks at this point as if the analogy with Christ and the Church, although offering a distinctive motivation, is simply being used to reinforce the conventional social mores (cf. also Schüssler Fiorenza, *Memory*, 269). But whether this can stand as a judgment about the entire passage will need to be reexamined later, since the exhortation to husbands suggests that the relation between the writer's ideals for Christian behavior and conventional marital expectations may be not quite so clearcut as this. In that light, does wifely submission have different overtones when it is regarded as voluntarily serving a partner who in turn gives himself in loving service?

25 Οἱ ἄνδρες, ἀγαπᾶτε τὰς γυναῖκας, καθὼς καὶ ὁ Χριστὸς ἠγάπησεν τὴν ἐκκλησίαν καὶ ἑαυτὸν παρέδωκεν ὑπὲρ αὐτῆς, "Husbands, love your wives, as Christ also loved the Church and gave himself up for her." After the exhortation to wives to submit, with its depiction of husbands as heads, what might well have been expected by contemporary readers would be an exhortation to husbands to rule their wives (cf. Schrage, *NTS* 21 [1975] 13). Instead the exhortation is for husbands to love their wives. This takes up the first five words of Col 3:19, omitting the injunction "do not be embittered with them" and replacing this with a Christological grounding and a further lengthy elaboration, in the course of which the exhortation to love occurs twice more. There is no contrast with the Colossians passage, where "masculine love is an emotion of inner attitude" and "men are invited to feel love," while Ephesians calls for a different quality of love (*pace* Terrien, *Till the Heart Sings*, 185). Rather both passages see the love required as involving an act of the will (cf. also Col 3:12–14). It is simply that Ephesians reinforces this by showing the radical extent of that love through its analogy with Christ's love for the Church.

Elsewhere in the letter, love has been seen as an essential quality in Christian living (cf. 1:4; 3:17; 4:2, 15, 16). Significantly, the call to all to loving sacrifice for one another in 5:1, 2 takes a similar form to that directed to husbands here in 5:25, since in both places the analogy with Christ's own self-sacrificing love provides the warrant for the appeal. The exhortation to sacrifice one's own interests for the welfare of others, which is so necessary for the harmony of the community, now finds a more specific application in the husband's role in contributing to marital harmony. Husbands are asked to exercise the self-giving love that has as its goal only their wives' good and that will care for their wives without the expectation of reward. It can now be seen clearly that for this writer the exhortation to wives to submit is not to be separated from this call to husbands to give themselves in love and that any exercise of headship on the part of husbands will not be through self-assertion but through self-sacrifice (cf. also Gnilka, 279). The parallel to the love of Christ for the Church means, of course, that the husband's love is one that will make even the ultimate sacrifice of life itself. In the marriage relationship this love demanded in terms of the most profound self-sacrifice is not separate from, but takes place in and through, natural affection and sexual love.

Exhortations to husbands to love their wives are found outside the NT, but they are fairly infrequent (Ps.-Phocylides 195–97 uses the verb στέργω in commanding husbands to love their own wives, while in the rabbinic tradition *b. Yeb.* 62b is "concerning a man who loves his wife as himself"). It is noteworthy, however, that ἀγαπᾶν does not occur in Greco-Roman household codes in setting out the husband's duties. So in terms of contemporary instructions on marriage, this writer's exhortation to husbands is by no means conventional or matter of course. In any case, he makes it distinctive by radicalizing the love for which he calls, as he models it on that of Christ for the Church. Schüssler Fiorenza (*In Memory of Her*, 269–70) can, therefore, rightly assert, "the patriarchal-societal code is theologically modified in the exhortation to the husband. . . . Patriarchal domination is thus radically questioned with reference to the paradigmatic love relationship of Christ to the church."

The analogy with Christ's love for the Church is introduced by καθώς, which in addition to its primary comparative force also has causal connotations. Christ's love for the Church not only presents the model but also provides the grounds for the husband's love for his wife. On the traditional formulation of the language of Christ's loving and self-giving, see *Comment* on 5:2. What is unique about its use here in 5:25 is that the recipient is the Church as a corporate whole. That the Church can be linked to Christ's death in this way does not mean that the writer believed it to have been already in existence when Christ died (*pace* Schlier, 255–56). This is a retrospective way of talking about the significance of Christ's death for the present Church (cf. also Schnackenburg,

"Er hat uns auferweckt," *LJ* 2 [1952] 178). Christ's death is seen as the particular point in history at which his love for the Church was demonstrated and at which his loving relationship with her began (cf. also 2:13–16). For the writer to the Ephesians, this love of Christ for the Church should find its reflection within the Christian community, particularly in the love of husbands for their wives.

26 ἵνα αὐτὴν ἁγιάσῃ καθαρίσας τῷ λουτρῷ τοῦ ὕδατος ἐν ῥήματι, "in order that he might sanctify her, cleansing her by washing in water through the word." The writer now elaborates on the goal of Christ's love for the Church in three ἵνα clauses. In this first one, the purpose of that love is seen as the Church's sanctification. As Westcott (85) put it, "Christ loved the Church not because it was perfectly lovable, but in order to make it such." Sanctification in the light of its OT cultic background involves a setting apart to effect a state and condition of moral purity. Through Christ's death on their behalf, believers have been separated from the sinful world and transferred to the sphere of God's holiness. The writer has repeatedly drawn attention to this aspect of the readers' identity through his use of the term ἅγιος, "holy" (cf. 1:1, 4, 15, 18; 2:19; 3:18; 4:12; 5:3). Sampley (*"And the Two,"* 42–43, 129) makes the interesting observation that in rabbinic literature the Hebrew term for "to sanctify," קדשׁ, *qādaš*, can mean "to espouse a wife," but this specific denotation is not the force of ἁγιάζειν, "to sanctify," here, nor likely to have been in the writer's mind as a secondary allusion in terms of marital imagery.

Instead, sanctification is explained as a cleansing that takes place through washing with water. The action of the aorist participle, καθαρίσας, "cleansing," is best taken as coincident with that of the main verb, ἁγιάσῃ, "sanctify"; hence the translation "cleansing" rather than "having cleansed." The definite article (lit., "*the* washing in water") may well indicate a specific event, and the readers are scarcely likely to have taken this as anything other than a reference to their experience of baptism. In 1 Cor 6:11 washing and sanctifying occur together as metaphors of salvation, with an allusion to baptism highly probable. But here, the explicit mention of water suggests not simply an extended metaphor for salvation (*pace* Barth, 691–99) but a direct reference to water baptism (cf. also Acts 22:16; Heb 10:22), not to baptism by the Spirit (*pace* J. D. G. Dunn, *Baptism in the Holy Spirit* [London: SCM, 1970] 163; Barth, 698). Sanctification and cleansing had also been linked with ritual washing at Qumran (cf. 1QS 3.4, 8–10; 1QH 11.10–12). Again, in line with the writer's perspective in this passage, the Church as a whole, and not merely individual believers, can be seen as having been sanctified through baptism as a washing. If Christ's death is the point in history at which his love was demonstrated, baptism is the point at which the Church experiences Christ's continuing purifying love for her as his bride. Indeed, the language of "the washing with water" is likely to have as a secondary connotation the notion of the bridal bath. This would reflect both Jewish marital customs with their prenuptial bath and the marital imagery of Ezek 16:8–14 which stands behind this passage. In Ezek 16:9 Yahweh, in entering his marriage covenant with Jerusalem, is said to have bathed her with water and washed off the blood from her. (Among those who support an allusion to the bridal bath here are Meyer, 295, 298; Abbott, 168–69; O. Casel, "Die Taufe als Brautbad der Kirche," *Jahrbuch für Liturgie und Wissenschaft*

5 [1925] 144–47; Dunn, *Baptism*, 162–63; Bruce, *Epistles*, 387; Halter, *Taufe*, 282.)

The Church's sanctification takes place not only through a cleansing involving a washing in water but also ἐν ῥήματι, "through the word." It is difficult to decide whether this phrase is meant to be taken as linked closely to the washing of water and related specifically to baptism, or as connected with the aorist participle καθαρίσας, "cleansing" (this is more likely than a connection with ἁγιάσῃ, "sanctify"; *pace* TEV; Meyer, 295; Cambier, *Bib* 47 [1966] 75; Schnackenburg, 255) and having instrumental force. If it is the former, as the majority of commentators hold, and is taken as signifying accompanying or attendant circumstances, then ῥῆμα is best understood not as a reference to the baptismal confession of faith (*pace* Westcott, 84; Bruce, *Ephesians*, 116; idem, *Epistles*, 388; Kirby, *Ephesians: Baptism and Pentecost*, 152; Mitton, 203) but as a reference to the baptismal formula pronounced over the candidate (cf. Abbott, 169; J. A. Robinson, 125, 206–7; Schlier, 257; Sampley, *"And the Two,"* 132; Gnilka, 282; Halter, *Taufe*, 284; Mussner, 158). This would have included a reference to the name of Christ (cf. Acts 2:38; Jas 2:7) and thus to what had been achieved through him on behalf of believers. If "through the word" is to be taken more closely with "cleansing," then ῥῆμα could have the more general sense of the gospel message (cf. also Meyer, 295; Batey, *New Testament Nuptial Imagery*, 28; Caird, *Paul's Letters*, 89; Hendriksen, 252). This is the way the term is employed elsewhere in Ephesians in 6:17, where it is the preached word of the gospel that the Spirit uses as his sword (cf. also Rom 10:8, 17; Heb 6:5; 1 Pet 1:25). The writer would then be saying that, as well as being cleansed through baptism, the Church is cleansed through the purifying word of the gospel (cf. also John 15:3; 17:17 for notions of being cleansed and sanctified through the word). On either of these interpretations, this writer sees the Church's cleansing from the moral pollution of sin being carried out not through baptism only but through baptism accompanied by the word which points to Christ. Sanctification takes place through both water and the word.

27 ἵνα παραστήσῃ αὐτὸς ἑαυτῷ ἐνδοξον τὴν ἐκκλησίαν, μὴ ἔχουσαν σπίλον ἢ ῥυτίδα ἤ τι τῶν τοιούτων, ἀλλ' ἵνα ᾖ ἁγία καὶ ἄμωμος, "in order that he might present the church to himself in splendor, without spot or wrinkle or any such thing, but rather that she might be holy and blameless." Christ's giving of himself in love for the Church has as its further goal his presentation of this Church to himself as his pure bride. At this point in the depiction of the relationship between Christ and the Church, the bridal imagery for the Church comes much more to the fore. On possible backgrounds for the idea of a marriage between Christ and the Church, see *Form/Structure/Setting*. What is important to note here is that the writer takes up the more general notion of presenting believers holy and blameless from Col 1:22 and combines it with the presentation language that had a specific marital context in Paul's use in 2 Cor 11:2. There, Paul asserted that he had betrothed the local Corinthian church to Christ in order to present her to her one husband as a pure virgin or bride (παρθένον ἁγνὴν παραστῆσαι) and saw his own role as either that of the bride's father or that of the escort friend of the groom (cf. also John 3:29). In Ephesians, however, the bride is the universal Church, and Christ as the bridegroom does not need someone else to present his bride; he does so himself.

He presents his bride to himself ἔνδοξον, "in splendor, glorious." The imagery may well again reflect Ezek 16 where in vv 10–14 Yahweh decks out his bride in magnificent clothing and jewelry, so that she displays regal beauty and perfect splendor (cf. כָּלִיל בַּהֲדָרִי, *kālîl bahădārî*, "perfect by my splendor," Ezek 16:14). Elsewhere in Ephesians, the Church is seen as God's glorious inheritance (1:18) and the sphere in which his glory is acknowledged (3:21). Here, the glory with which the Church as the bride is adorned will be elaborated on in terms of her moral perfection. The bride's beauty is to be all-encompassing and is not to be spoiled by anything, by the least spot or wrinkle. σπίλος could mean a stain or defect of any sort, but together with ῥυτίς, which denotes a wrinkle in the skin, may well refer to a spot on the body or a physical defect (cf. also BAGD 762). These terms fit not so much with the notion of purifying (after all, spots and wrinkles do not wash off!) but with the image of a young and lovely bride. The picture is of Christ preparing a bride for himself that has no physical blemish. But it then becomes crystal clear from the final ἵνα clause that this bride's beauty is moral. She is to be holy and blameless, the two terms found so frequently in OT contexts of cultic and ethical purity, used with the language of presentation in Col 1:22, and already taken up earlier in this letter in 1:4, where the display of such holiness and blamelessness is seen as the purpose of God's election of believers from before the foundation of the world. Impurity is what characterizes outsiders (cf. 4:19; 5:3); purity is the distinguishing mark of Christ's Church.

There are no grounds for deducing from the wording of this verse that Christ's presentation of his pure bride to himself awaits the parousia, though many commentators have assumed this (e.g., Meyer, 297; Bruce, *Epistles*, 389; Hendriksen, 252–53; Barth, 628, 669, 678). Muirhead (*SJT* 5 [1952] 184) is wrong to claim, "It is only in the End that the Church becomes the Bride. . . . We cannot correctly speak of the Church being now the Bride; rather is it what she shall be." This ignores the fact that later in v 32 the "one flesh" marriage union is applied to the present relationship between Christ and the Church and that throughout the passage the past and present relationship between Christ and his Church is the model for husbands and wives to follow in their marriages. Here, in line with this writer's more realized eschatology, glory and holiness are seen as present attributes of the Church, and Christ's activity of endowing the Church with these qualities is a present and continuing one (cf. also Schlier, 258; Schnackenburg, 256). After all, in 1:4 holiness and blamelessness, along with love, are present aspects of Christian existence. His loving and sanctifying have already secured for Christ a completely glorious and pure bride, and his continuing care will maintain her moral beauty. In this way, the perspective on the Church is similar to that of 4:1–16, where the Church is already the fullness of Christ and already one, yet is also to grow into completeness and unity.

What is important for the paraenesis to husbands, as the return to the notion of love in v 28 will confirm, is the stress on Christ's love in v 25. Just as the writer had earlier, in v 23, elaborated on Christ's headship with an additional statement about his being the Savior of the body, so here, in vv 26, 27, he has elaborated on Christ's love with additional statements about his work of sanctification. The depiction of his sanctifying activity has illustrated the nature of his love but, as we concluded also in the case of v 23c, was probably not intended by the writer to apply to the husband's responsibility for his wife (*pace* Mussner, 158, who claims that the husband's love for his wife also serves her sanctification). The fact that vv 25–27 go beyond the strict requirements of the paraenesis and contain some traditional language is not sufficient evidence that the writer is quoting a hymn at this point (*pace* Barth, 622–23).

28a οὕτως ὀφείλουσιν καὶ οἱ ἄνδρες ἀγαπᾶν τὰς ἑαυτῶν γυναῖκας ὡς τὰ ἑαυτῶν σώματα, "In the same way husbands also should love their wives as their own bodies." Christ's love for the Church set out in vv 25–27 now serves as the model (cf. οὕτως, "in the same way") for the writer's second assertion of husbands' obligation to love their wives. The earlier use of οὕτως in v 24, its place here at the beginning of the sentence, and the passage's constant links between its paraenesis and the underlying analogy, all suggest that οὕτως in this verse has reference to what precedes rather than simply being taken as part of the sentence's later comparison in a οὕτως . . . ὡς construction, as in v 33a where the order of the syntax is, however, different (*pace* Schlier, 260; Schnackenburg, 257; although Cambier, *Bib* 47 [1966] 60–61, and Bouwman, "Eph. V 26," 179–90, can even argue in support of the reference of οὕτως to what precedes that it functions as the apodosis to the καθώς of v 25b). The writer varies this second assertion by introducing the thought that husbands' love for their wives should be as their love for their own bodies. Just as a husband cares for his body's needs, so his love for his wife should be of the sort that cares for her needs and facilitates her growth and development. Some (e.g., Meyer, 300; Abbott, 170–71; Westcott, 85; Barth, 629–30; Mussner, 159) object to this explanation as too banal or demeaning to wives in its comparison and argue that, instead, the Greek means that husbands should love their wives "as being their own bodies." But there is little to be said for this objection, since ὡς τὰ ἑαυτῶν σώματα, "as their own bodies," is equivalent to ὡς ἑαυτόν, "as himself," in v 33a. In the latter instance, as we shall note, the language reflects that of Lev 19:18, "you shall love your neighbor as yourself," so that the phrase with ὡς must mean "as you love yourself" not "as being yourself" (cf. also Bratcher and Nida, *Handbook*, 178 n. 74). In fact, vv 28, 29 are able to bring together both a more mundane and pragmatic warrant for the exhortation to love and the profound one of Christ's love for the Church. The notion of husbands loving their wives as their own bodies reflects the fact that in the Christological model Christ's love for the Church can also be seen as his love for his body (cf. v 23 and also v 30). It also anticipates and is dependent on the idea spelled out more fully later in the writer's citation of Gen 2:24 in v 31. It is because of the claim of the Genesis text that the act of marriage makes husband and wife one flesh that he can make the comparison of the wives to their husbands' bodies. The quotation in v 31 has the term σάρξ, "flesh," but σάρξ and σῶμα, "body," are equivalent in the writer's purposes here, as the shift to σάρξ in v 29a before the citation indicates (cf. also the interchangeable relation between these two terms when Paul cites Gen 2:24 in 1 Cor 6:16). Since from the Gen 2 perspective marriage declares that husband and wife are, in fact, one body, the husband can be said to be under the obligation to love his wife as his own body.

Plutarch (*Praec. Conjug.* 142E) has a somewhat similar comparison of the wife to the body, when he says, "The husband, however, should rule his wife, not as a master his property, but as the soul the body. . . ." It should, of course, be noted that, unlike Ephesians, this is dependent on the soul-body distinction and is part of an instruction to the husband to rule, not to love, his wife. It has been argued (cf. Sampley, *"And the Two,"* 32–34, 139–42) that Lev 19:18, "you shall love your neighbor as yourself," has influenced the writer's thought in both parts of v 28, but such an allusion is not necessary for understanding the flow of the argument at this point and becomes more appropriate as an explanation for the formulation of v 33a, "let each . . . love his wife as himself" (cf. also Schnackenburg, 258).

28b–30 ὁ ἀγαπῶν τὴν ἑαυτοῦ γυναῖκα ἑαυτὸν ἀγαπᾷ, οὐδεὶς γάρ ποτε τὴν ἑαυτοῦ σάρκα ἐμίσησεν, ἀλλὰ ἐκτρέφει καὶ θάλπει αὐτήν, καθὼς καὶ ὁ Χριστὸς τὴν ἐκκλησίαν, ὅτι μέλη ἐσμὲν τοῦ σώματος αὐτοῦ, "He who loves his wife loves himself, for no one ever hated his own flesh, but nourishes it and cherishes it, as Christ also does the church, since we are members of his body." In line with his adoption of the Gen 2 perspective, where husbands and wives can be seen as a single entity, one person, the writer continues his argument by asserting that he who loves his wife loves himself. Again, he combines this thought with a more mundane observation. Everyday experience should show, he claims, that ordinarily no man hates himself, that is, his own flesh (the change to σάρξ is now in preparation for the citation in v 31). On the contrary, he nourishes and cherishes it. It is possible that in making this observation the writer also has an eye on ascetic tendencies (cf. Pagels, "Adam and Eve, Christ and the Church," 150; MacDonald, *The Pauline Churches,* 119, who see it as a direct response to ascetic extremism), but the primary force of this point, although its explicit statement will be delayed until v 33a while the analogy to Christ and the Church is resumed, is that, therefore, there is every reason for a husband to love his wife as himself.

In the resumed analogy, Christ is said also to nourish and cherish the Church, and in the clause of v 30 the readers are now explicitly reminded that the Church is Christ's body, of which they with all believers are members (cf. 1:23; 3:6; 4:16, 25; for the language of being members of the body in Paul, cf. Rom 12:4, 5; 1 Cor 12:27). At this point, two of the writer's major images for the Church—the body and the bride—are explicitly brought together. The verb ἐκτρέφειν, "to nourish," occurs again within the household code in 6:4, where it is used of the bringing up of children, and the verb θάλπειν, "to cherish," was used by Paul in 1 Thess 2:7 of a nurse's care of children. Although these verbs (ἐκ)τρέφειν and θάλπειν can be closely associated with children, outside the NT they are used in a variety of contexts (cf. the combination τρέφει καὶ θάλπει in *Vit. Aesopi* 1, c.9 [BAGD 246]). It is a distortion of the writer's analogy to suggest that believers are being thought of as the offspring of the marriage between Christ and the Church (*pace* Best, *One Body,* 178 n. 1, 181 n. 1). It might remain closer to the analogy to consider the Church as a child-bride who is being brought to maturity by the bridegroom's care. Most relevant to Eph 5:29, however, is the appearance of the two verbs in reverse order to set out the husband's duties to his wife in a marriage contract, θάλπειν καὶ τρέφειν καὶ ἱματίζειν αὐτήν, "to cherish and nourish and clothe her" (Preisigke-Kiessling,

Wörterbuch der griechischen Papyrusurkunden, 1:460; cf. Gnilka, 285). In any case, the imagery as applied to Christ's treatment of the Church is meant to recall his constant provision for and building up of his body (cf. 4:11–16) and his sanctifying and cleansing it through baptism and the word (cf. 5:26). It is unlikely that the language also alludes to the eucharist (*pace* Mussner, *Christus*, 154; Schlier, 261).

The introduction of the first person plural into the discussion in v 30 with ἐσμέν, "we are," may well be intended to underline for the letter's recipients their own participation in the reality of Christ's loving care for his body and to emphasize that what has been said in the preceding argument about the Church applies to them, because they are, in fact, members of this privileged community, Christ's body (cf. also Sampley, "And the Two," 146; Schnackenburg, 259). Under *Notes*, we have already concluded that the addition to v 30 found in some manuscripts, "flesh of his flesh, bone of his bone," is to be rejected, and so there are no grounds for finding in this verse a reference to the Church as the second Eve deriving her being from the second Adam (*pace* S. Bedale, "The Theology of the Church," in *Studies in Ephesians*, 72).

31, 32 ἀντὶ τούτου καταλείψει ἄνθρωπος τὸν πατέρα καὶ τὴν μητέρα καὶ προσκολληθήσεται πρὸς τὴν γυναῖκα αὐτοῦ, καὶ ἔσονται οἱ δύο εἰς σάρκα μίαν. τὸ μυστήριον τοῦτο μέγα ἐστίν, ἐγὼ δὲ λέγω εἰς Χριστὸν καὶ εἰς τὴν ἐκκλησίαν, "For this reason a man shall leave his father and his mother and be joined to his wife, and the two shall become one flesh. This mystery is great, but I am speaking about Christ and about the church." Gen 2:24, which has influenced the writer's argument from v 28, is now quoted without any introductory formula, possibly because the opening phrase of the citation itself provides an introductory link. The wording differs at only two insignificant points from that of the LXX. ἀντὶ τούτου, "for this reason," replaces ἕνεκεν τούτου, "for this reason," and the possessive pronoun αὐτοῦ, "his," is omitted after πατέρα, "father," and μητέρα, "mother." The writer asserts that he refers this citation to Christ and the Church (for parallels to the somewhat unusual use of εἰς, "about, with reference to," with λέγειν, "to say," cf. Acts 2:25). He does not mean that every part of the citation applies to Christ and the Church. All allegorizing interpretation to the effect that Christ left his heavenly Father and his mother, seen as either the heavenly Jerusalem or Mary at the cross, in order to cleave to his Church is out of place (*pace* W. L. Knox, *St. Paul and the Church of the Gentiles* [Cambridge: CUP, 1939] 200; J. Jeremias, "νύμφη," *TDNT* 4 [1967] 1104–5). Because the writer is concerned with the union between Christ and the Church, it is only the latter part of the quotation, καὶ ἔσονται οἱ δύο εἰς σάρκα μίαν, "and the two shall become one flesh," that serves his purpose here. The future tense does not mean that the union between Christ and the Church is seen as happening in the future, at the parousia (*pace* Meyer, 304–8), but instead is either a gnomic future (cf. BDF § 349[1]; also Barth, 639) or reflects the way categorical injunctions or statements of what should be the case are sometimes rendered in the LXX (cf. BDF § 362).

Of the statement in v 31, it is then claimed in v 32 that "this mystery is great," with μέγα, "great," indicating the mystery's significance and profundity. There is much discussion, however, whether μυστήριον, "mystery," has a meaning distinct from its other uses in this letter. Some hold that it is a reference to marriage as such from which mystical and symbolic truth is to be drawn (cf.

W. L. Knox, *St. Paul and the Church of the Gentiles* [Cambridge: CUP, 1939] 183–84; Mitton, 207–8). Along similar lines, the Latin Vulgate interpreted this as a reference to marriage and used the translation *sacramentum*, which led to this verse being employed as scriptural support for the doctrine that marriage is a sacrament. But the reference of "mystery" is not to marriage but to the Christ-Church relationship. There can therefore be no question of a sacramental interpretation as the original meaning of the text, but there do remain questions about the special relationship between human marriage and the redemptive sphere of Christ's relationship with his Church, which some Catholic theologians wish to formulate in sacramental terms (cf. the discussion in Gnilka, 289; Barth, 344–53; Schnackenburg, 261–62; 346–49, who prefer, however, covenantal rather than sacramental categories for a theological interpretation of marriage). Others take the term simply as a reference to a deeper meaning of the Scripture passage (cf. Meyer, 308; G. Bornkamm, "μυστήριον," *TDNT* 4 [1967] 823; R. E. Brown, *The Semitic Background of the Term 'Mystery' in the New Testament* [Philadelphia: Fortress, 1968] 65–66; Mussner, 160; idem, *Christus*, 152; Barth, 642–44; Caird, *Paul's Letters*, 89; Bruce, *Epistles*, 394), but this sense would be unparalleled not only in Ephesians but also in the NT, although it can be found at Qumran (cf. the use of רז, *rāz*, "mystery") and in some second-century Christian writings, including Justin. In the other five occurrences of the term in Ephesians (cf. 1:9; 3:3, 4, 9; 6:19), "mystery" has reference to the once-hidden purpose of God which has now been revealed in Christ. Different aspects of this mystery can be highlighted according to the context (cf. C. C. Caragounis, *The Ephesian 'Mysterion'* [Lund: Gleerup, 1977] esp. 136–46, for a fuller discussion, though he believes 5:32 to contain a special usage referring simply to the incomprehensibility of the union of the Church and Christ; cf. 59 n. 15), and in chap. 3 it has a particular focus in the coming together in Christ of Jews and Gentiles in the one Church. It is most likely, then, that here in 5:32 the term has the same Christ-event in view, highlighting the aspect of it which has been central in this passage, namely the intimate union between Christ and his Church (cf. also J. Coppens, " 'Mystery' in the Theology of St. Paul and Its Parallels at Qumran," in *Paul and Qumran*, 147; Schlier, 262–63; Cambier, *Bib* 47 [1966] 84–89; Sampley, *"And the Two,"* 90–96; Gnilka, 287–88). Both the OT passage and the marriage relationship of which it speaks are connected with the mystery, but their connection is that they point to the secret that has now been revealed, that of the relationship between Christ and the Church. "Mystery," therefore, is not *any* deeper meaning of an OT text but precisely *this* meaning of Christ and the Church posited by this writer. Similarly, the mystery is not any marriage or marriage itself, but the special marriage relationship of Christ and the Church. This is not a denial of the straightforward reference of Gen 2:24 by any means. Indeed, as we have seen, that interpretation of Gen 2:24 underlies the exhortation to husbands in vv 28–30. But even that use of Gen 2:24 depended for its force on the ultimate reference the writer believed it had to the archetypal union between Christ and the Church (for fuller discussion of the extent and nature of the use of the Genesis text in this passage, see Lincoln, *JSNT* 14 [1982] 30–36). It was because the Church was Christ's body which was one with him, a relationship which was the model for human marriage, that wives could be seen in terms of their husbands' bodies.

The emphatic ἐγώ and the particle δέ in v 32b make clear that the writer is stressing that this particular interpretation of Gen 2:24 as a reference to the profound mystery of the union between Christ and the Church is his own. If, in fact, it also originated with him, then presumably he reached it through a typological exegesis, resting on a correspondence between creation (Gen 2:24) and redemption (Christ and the Church). Christ has already been seen in Adamic terms in Eph 1:22 (the Church is his body), and so a text that refers to Adam's bodily union can now be claimed for Christ's union with the Church. ἐγὼ δὲ λέγω, "but I am speaking," occurs also in the antitheses of the Sermon on the Mount in Matthew 5, where it serves to introduce an interpretation contrary to the generally accepted interpretation of the Scripture passage in view. Here also it sets the typological exegesis of Gen 2:24 which is offered over against other interpretations. But does it simply set the writer's interpretation over against that which limits the meaning of Gen 2:24 to the physical union between a man and a woman, as in Mark 10:7; Matt 19:5; 1 Cor 6:16 (cf. R. E. Brown, *The Semitic Background of the Term 'Mystery' in the New Testament* [Philadelphia: Fortress, 1968] 65 n. 190)? Does it show that the writer is aware of a variety of other interpretations which were current (Dibelius, 95; Gnilka, 288, 294; Barth, 735; Schnackenburg, 261)? Or does it have more polemical overtones and show that the writer was opposed to some particular interpretations of Gen 2:24 (cf. G. Bornkamm, "μυστήριον," *TDNT* 4 [1967] 823; Schlier, 262; Sampley, *"And the Two,"* 52, 87–89)? It is difficult to decide this question.

Certainly, there were interpretations of Gen 2:24 which could have been current in the syncretistic religious environment of Asia Minor and associated with mysteries other than the one this writer is advocating. In Gnostic and Encratite circles in the second and third centuries, the human plight was seen in terms of the differentiation of the sexes, and correspondingly salvation involved the restoration of the original androgynous unity. Not surprisingly, Gen 2 figured prominently in the elaboration of this pattern of salvation (for an illuminating survey of second-century controversies concerning marriage and their use of Genesis 1 and 2, see E. H. Pagels, "Adam and Eve, Christ and the Church," in *The New Testament and Gnosis,* ed. A. H. B. Logan and A. J. M. Wedderburn [Edinburgh: T. & T. Clark, 1983] 146–75). A number of the documents in the Nag Hammadi library, including the *Gospel of Thomas,* the *Gospel of Philip,* the *Hypostasis of the Archons,* and the *Exegesis on the Soul,* reflect this schema (for a discussion of ethical implications drawn from Genesis 1 and 2 in some of the Nag Hammadi documents, see E. H. Pagels, "Exegesis and Exposition of the Genesis Creation Accounts in Selected Texts from Nag Hammadi," in *Nag Hammadi, Gnosticism, and Early Christianity,* ed. C. W. Hedrick and R. Hodgson, Jr. [Peabody, MA: Hendrickson, 1986] 257–85). In *Gospel of Philip* 70 it is said, "Because of this Christ came to repair the separation which was from the beginning and again unite the two. . . . But the woman is united to her husband in the bridal chamber. Indeed those who have united in the bridal chamber will no longer be separated. Thus Eve separated from Adam because she was never united with him in the bridal chamber" (cf. J. M. Robinson, ed., *The Nag Hammadi Library* [Leiden: Brill, 1977] 141–42). "Great is the mystery of marriage," says *Gospel of Philip* 64. The spiritual, sacramental union in the bridal chamber is also called a mystery in *Gospel of Philip* 67, 71 and has its archetype in the union of the Savior with Sophia. Through it, also, the Gnostic receives a foretaste and assurance of ultimate union with an angelic heavenly counterpart. There is some debate about whether this Valentinian Gnosticism involved an acting out of the sacred marriage in a ritual of sexual intercourse, although the early church fathers believed that it did (cf. Irenaeus, *Adv. Haer.* 1.6.3, 4; Clement of Alexandria, *Strom.* 3.1.1; 3.5.1; Tertullian, *De Jejun.* 17; cf. Meeks, *History of Religions* 13 [1974] 191; Batey, *NTS* 13 [1966–67] 276; Barth, 729 and n. 462; Fischer, *Tendenz*, 192; Pagels, "Adam and Eve, Christ and the Church," 169). The *Gospel of Philip* probably dates from the second half of the third century, but the notion of the restoration of the androgynous image can be found earlier in the *Gospel of Thomas*, usually dated around the middle of the second century and associated with the Encratite Christianity of eastern Syria. In logion 22 of the *Gospel of Thomas* one of the mysteries Jesus utters is, "When you make the two one, and when you make the inside like the outside and the outside like the inside and the above like the below, and when you make the male and the female one and the same, so that the male not be male nor the female female . . . then will you enter the Kingdom" (cf. J. M. Robinson, ed., *The Nag Hammadi Library*, 121). In Encratite circles this union of male and female represents a renunciation and neutralization of sexuality (cf. Meeks, *History of Religions* 13 [1974] 193–97; Fischer, *Tendenz*, 192–93; Pagels, "Adam and Eve, Christ and the Church," 151–52). This sort of notion of the unification of male and female may be traced further back to Christians in Corinth, where a "realized eschatology" probably suggested to the Corinthian pneumatics that they were already enjoying resurrection existence and were thus equal to the angels who neither marry nor are given in marriage (cf. Luke 20:34–36). Many interpreters hold that such a view lies behind the sexual libertinism, the sexual asceticism, and the confusion about the role of women reflected in 1 Corinthians (cf. Meeks, *History of Religions* 13 [1974] 199–204). It can also be argued that Paul himself in Gal 3:28 used a baptismal reunification formula which reverses the "male and female" distinction of Gen 1:27 (cf. Meeks, *History of Religions* 13 [1974] 180–86; H. D. Betz, *Galatians* [Philadelphia: Fortress, 1979] 195–200). An androgynous interpretation of Genesis—whereby the "man" in Gen 1 was bisexual, was then divided into two when his rib was taken and Eve was formed, and was finally reunited into "one flesh" by God when he led the woman to the man in Gen 2:24—can also be found in Philo (cf. *Leg. Alleg.* 2.13, 19–50; *Quis Div. Her.* 164; *Quaest. in Gen.* 1.25). Given the early existence of such androgynous interpretations of Genesis and the ethical implications that were drawn from them, and given the likelihood that some had found their way into the Pauline communities, it could well be the case that the writer to the Ephesians is at least asserting his own interpretation of Gen 2:24 in the face of interpretations which linked this text with other types of spiritual union and/or drew from it implications which he deemed were detrimental to a proper regard for marriage.

It is also worth noting that in so doing this writer's interpretation of Gen 2:24 as a reference to a spiritual as well as a sexual union is quite different from that of Paul in 1 Cor 6:16–17. There, the apostle had contrasted the sexual "one flesh" relationship with the union between Christ and believers, which he talks of instead as ἓν πνεῦμα, "one spirit" (cf. further Lincoln, *JSNT* 14 [1982] 36).

33 πλὴν καὶ ὑμεῖς οἱ καθ᾽ ἕνα ἕκαστος τὴν ἑαυτοῦ γυναῖκα οὕτως ἀγαπάτω ὡς ἑαυτόν, ἡ δὲ γυνὴ ἵνα φοβῆται τὸν ἄνδρα, "In any case, let each one of you also so love his wife as he loves himself, and let the wife fear her husband." With the πλήν at the beginning of this sentence, the writer brings his readers back to the gist of his exhortation on marriage. πλήν can be adversative ("but," "however") or, as here, be used to round off a discussion and accentuate its main point ("now," "in any case"; cf. also 1 Cor 11:11; Phil 3:16; 4:14; cf. BDF § 449[2]; Sampley *"And the Two,"* 106; Maillet, *ETR* 55 [1980] 570). In this way, the writer reminds his readers that the exalted depiction of marriage in the light of the relationship of Christ and the Church is meant to serve the purpose of practical exhortation. In doing so, this time he addresses the husbands first and directly, "let each one of *you*," an emphatic inclusion of every husband, and the wives second and only indirectly, "let *the* wife." The literary unity of the passage can be seen in that it contains a broad chiasmus. There is an exhortation to wives (vv 22–24), an exhortation to husbands (vv 25–32), an exhortation to husbands again (v 33a), and a second exhortation to wives (v 33b; cf. also Sampley, *"And the Two,"* 147). The unity is reinforced through the literary device of *inclusio* with the mention of fear in v 21 and in v 33.

The injunction to husbands to love their wives as themselves not only summarizes the line of argument from v 28 in terms of loving wives as their own bodies but also incorporates the argument from v 25 about loving wives as Christ loved the Church. The writer has now shown explicitly in vv 31, 32 that Christ's love for the Church involves the Church's becoming one body with him, so that Christ can be seen as loving the Church as himself. He can conclude therefore by telling the husband to love his wife as himself. At this point the language clearly reflects that of Lev 19:18 with its command to love one's neighbor as oneself (cf. also Sampley, *"And the Two,"* 30; Barth, 704–5). The additional οὕτως is part of a οὕτως . . . ὡς construction which reinforces the comparison (cf. also 1 Cor 4:1; 9:26a, b; Jas 2:12; cf. BAGD 598). Neither the command to love one's neighbor as oneself nor the command to love one's wife as oneself involves a further command, namely, to love one's self. Therefore, neither anticipates modern psychological theories that people must first learn to accept themselves in order to be able to accept others. Both simply assume that love of self is present in all (cf. v 29) and then demand that this be transcended by a love that is directed to another in the same way. Here, the wife is the special instance of the neighbor. As Barth (719) puts it, "the special form of agape between husband and wife flourishes within the framework of a general love for neighbors and enemies, is the school and test case of the latter, and publicizes its reality and power. The wife is the husband's primary and exemplary neighbor."

In the writer's summary of the wife's duties, the construction with ἵνα and the subjunctive replaces a command or imperative (*pace* Barth, 648, who claims it functions as a wish rather than as an imperative). Many translators and interpreters attempt to make the writer less patriarchal and more palatable to modern readers by substituting "respect" for "fear" in the command to wives (cf. Barth, 648, 662). As in the earlier instructions, the wife's attitude to her husband is to be modeled on the Church's attitude to Christ. Her fear of her husband reflects the fear of all believers for Christ (cf. v 21). This fear certainly includes having respect, but is stronger than this, though not the fear of a slave (cf. J. A. Robinson, 127 "the fear of the Church for Christ—which is the pattern of the fear of the wife for her husband—is no slavish fear, but a fear of reverence"). In the case of human relations, as we noted with the notion of subordination also, fear involves observance of the appropriate authority structures, whether of citizens toward the state (cf. Rom 13:3, 4, 7), children to parents (*Barn.* 19.5; *Did.* 4.9), slaves to masters (Eph 6:5; 1 Pet 2:18; *Did.* 4.11), or, as here, wives to husbands (cf. also 1 Pet 3:2). As Balz ("φόβος," *TDNT* 9 [1974] 217–8) observes, "fear can denote the obedience demanded by the superior authority of masters or husbands as lords" and "has a settled place in household tables." Since the fear of Christ (v 21) is believers' appropriate response to his overwhelming love and power, the wife's fear is her appropriate response to her husband's headship exercised in self-sacrificial love.

The summarizing exhortations in v 33 indicate the high status this writer accords to marriage. Through the love, on the one hand, and the fear, on the other, which marriage involves, husband and wife are to mirror the great mystery itself, the union between Christ and his Church. At the same time, for the modern reader the form and content of this verse underline the passage's masculine perspective and its acceptance of a patriarchal structure, and yet they retain within them the radical emphasis on the husband's love with its potential for their transformation.

Explanation

In this letter the writer's exhortations about household relationships form the major part of the paraenesis about wise living which begins at 5:15. The primary resource for such living is the Spirit, with whom believers are to be filled, resulting in mutual edification, worship, constant thanksgiving, and mutual submission. The exhortation to mutual submission forms a transition between the preceding injunctions in 5:15–20 and the instructions to wives and husbands in 5:22–33. Its participle is dependent on the main verb of 5:18, "be filled," and, in turn, the exhortation to wives in 5:22 is dependent on this participle for its sense, since it contains no verb. These intricate syntactical links suggest a close conceptual connection between the two sections of paraenesis. For this writer, not only should the wise living that comes from being filled with the Spirit work itself out within the structures of the household, but also both the communal worship, which, of course, took place in houses, and the attitude of thanksgiving, flowing from the Spirit, should be seen to have their effects on all the other relationships occurring in such houses.

The exhortation to *all* the members of the household to submit to one another (v 21) is this writer's distinctive introduction to the specific duties of the household code which follow. It is a reminder that, whatever roles are appropriate because of the structures imposed by the household, there remains the overarching demand that in all lowliness and meekness with patience believers should bear with one another in love (cf. 4:2). For the writer of Ephesians, this powerful initial appeal to all, whatever their status in the household, to display the selfless regard for others which puts oneself at their disposal, sits perfectly compatibly with the requirements for particular subordination that he goes on to make. The introductory injunction also sets the tone for the ensuing household code through its Christological motivation. Each group within the household will be encouraged to fulfill its role as part of its relationship to Christ, and here the all-embracing claim upon them for mutual submission has as its motivation "the fear of Christ," a living in awe at both his sovereignty and his overwhelming love.

In taking up the specifics of the household code, Ephesians is directly dependent on Col 3:18–4:1, which was, in turn, influenced by a tradition of discussions of household management in Greco-Roman writings, stemming from Aristotle. In such discussions, the three pairs—husband-wife, parent-child, and master-slave—were treated, with, as might be expected, the former member being given the authoritative and the latter the subordinate role. This patriarchal and hierarchical conception of household management was seen as crucial for the stability of society as a whole. Whereas in its adaptation of this discussion Colossians devotes most attention to the master-slave relationship, Ephesians' unique contribution to early Christian household codes is in its sustained treatment of the husband-wife relationship, which it compares to the relationship between Christ and his Church. Just as earlier in the letter believers' lives and humanity as a whole are to be viewed from the vantage point of what God has done in Christ, so now the same holds true for the marriage relationship. The analogy between human marriage and Christ's relationship to his Church, in which the latter provides the archetype for the former, dominates the paraenesis of 5:22–33 with the movement of thought continually shifting between the two relationships before they are brought together in the quotation and interpretation of Gen 2:24 in vv 31, 32.

In the marriage paraenesis, wives are addressed first in vv 22–24. As responsible moral agents, they are asked by means of two exhortations, the second of which (v 24) intensifies the first (v 22), to subordinate themselves to their husbands in everything. Submission is called for in this code not simply because it is the conventional role allotted to wives in society, but because in voluntarily subordinating themselves to their husbands wives are to see this as part of their subordination to their Lord. In the warrant for this exhortation, the analogy with Christ and the Church is introduced in v 23 and then becomes the basis for the repetition of the exhortation in v 24. In the application to human marriage, the husband takes the role of Christ and the wife the role of the Church. So the husband is the head of the wife, as Christ is the head of the Church, and the wife submits to the husband, as the Church submits to Christ. Discussion of both Christ's and the husband's "headship" has in view primarily their authority, as the readers would have expected, although, of course, the writer will also indicate in the appeal to husbands that it is an authority that expresses itself in self-giving love. Complete submission by both the Church and the wife involves willing obedience. In this writer's ideal depiction, just as the Church's subordination to Christ is to a beneficial and loving rule that enables growth, so the wife's subordination to her husband is thought of as taking place in the context of a similar rule. The writer's analogy to the relation of Christ to the Church leads him in v 23 to an additional thought that applies to Christ but not to the husband. Employing a title used by Paul in Phil 3:20 and which was becoming increasingly prominent in the early church,

Explanation

the writer sees Christ as "himself the Savior of the body" as well as the head. He occupies his position as head uniquely as a result of having rescued those who constitute his body, the Church, from a previous situation of death, sin, and alienation (cf. 2:1–10; 2:14–18; 5:2).

It is the role of husbands to which the writer devotes the major part of his attention in the marriage paraenesis. He does so in two stages—vv 25–27 and vv 28–32. In both stages the exhortation is for husbands to love their wives, and in both the warrant involves Christ's love for the Church. It is significant that following on the admonition to wives to submit, the corresponding admonition to husbands is not to rule but to love their wives (v 25). What has previously been seen as an essential quality in the lives of all believers (cf. 1:4; 3:17; 4:2, 15, 16; 5:2) is now required specifically of husbands in relation to their wives. They are asked to exercise the self-giving love that acts for the good of their wives without the expectation of reward. Just as in 5:2 Christ's self-giving love provided the model in the appeal to all believers to live in love, so here in vv 25b–27 Christ's love and self-giving for the Church forms the model and the grounds for the appeal to husbands to love their wives. This time, not content with a bare statement about Christ's love, the writer goes on to elaborate on its purpose. The purpose of Christ's sacrificial death, in which his love for the Church was demonstrated, was that that Church might be holy. Taking up imagery from both Ezek 16:8–14, which depicts Yahweh's relationship with Jerusalem in marital terms, and from Paul in 2 Cor 11:2, where the Corinthian church is to be presented to Christ as a pure bride, the writer explains that Christ's love for his bride, the Church, was intended to sanctify her through a washing of water so that he might present her to himself in glory and moral perfection. The language of washing with water evokes not only bridal bath imagery but also primarily believers' experience of baptism. Their transference into the sphere of God's holiness has taken place through both water, baptism, and the word, the purifying message of the gospel. The bride Christ presents to himself is depicted in terms of a beauty unmarred by any physical defect. This beauty, the writer immediately indicates, is to be seen as the moral purity and blamelessness of the Church produced by Christ's sanctifying activity. The elaboration on this sanctifying activity has illustrated the nature of Christ's love, but it is that love itself which has all the import for the paraenesis to husbands. It has the radicalizing force of indicating that the husband's love for his wife should also be of the sort that is willing to go to the ultimate extent of laying down his life for her.

Christ's love for the Church portrayed in vv 25–27 serves as the model at the beginning of the second stage of the writer's exhortation to husbands with its further assertion of husbands' obligation to love their wives (cf. "in the same way," v 28a). As this section (vv 28–32) progresses, the warrant changes to what might at first appear to be a more mundane analogy of husbands' love for their own bodies (vv 28, 29a) before returning to the profound one of Christ's love for his body, the Church (vv 29b, 30). Both analogies are closely associated in the writer's mind, as both the "body" terminology in each case and the "flesh" language for each relationship (cf. vv 29, 31) indicate. Just as husbands care for all their own bodies' needs, so their love for their wives should be of the sort that cares for all their needs. The comparison becomes an extended one with two further assertions: first, that the person who loves his wife loves himself, and, second, in a formulation that would leave no room for ascetic extremism, that no one ever hated his own flesh but instead nourishes and cherishes it. This prompts the explicit return to the analogy of Christ and the Church. The readers are reminded that the body of which they are members can also be said to be nourished and cherished by Christ, as he lovingly provides for its growth and sanctifies and cleanses it. The various threads of the second stage of the exhortation to husbands are brought together in the citation and interpretation of Gen 2:24 in vv 31, 32, which constitute a final justification for the appeal that husbands should love their wives as their own bodies. For this writer the perspective of Gen 2:24, which has shaped his thought from v 28 onwards, suggests, first of all, that there is a sense in which wives are their husbands' bodies, since husband and wife are "one flesh." But more than that, basing his paraenesis about marriage on the relationship between Christ and the Church has been entirely appropriate, because he, in the face of other current interpretations which may have drawn quite different implications from it, interprets Gen 2:24 as referring to the profound mystery that God has now revealed in Christ, namely, the union between Christ and the Church.

The marriage paraenesis can now be rounded off in v 33 with the summarizing exhortations, which, in line with the recent sequence of thought, this time address husbands first and then wives. Despite the extended expositions of the analogy with Christ and the Church, there can be no doubt for the reader that ultimately their point has been to drive home the duties of husbands and wives. Taking up the language of Lev 19:18 and building on the argument of vv 28–32, the writer calls on the husband to love his wife as himself. His concluding appeal to the wife involves a variation on the earlier language of subordination. Just as elsewhere in early Christian paraenesis citizens are to fear the state, children their parents, and slaves their masters, the wife's appropriate response to her husband's authority exercised in love should be fear of her husband. By means of this formulation the writer provides an *inclusio* with his introductory exhortation to mutual submission in v 21, which had "fear of Christ" as its motivation.

So in this distinctive piece of teaching about Christian marriage, the writer has creatively combined the theological and the ethical concerns evidenced in the letter as a whole, as he makes the union between Christ and the Church the prototype for the relationship of believing husbands and wives. In the process he builds on what has been said earlier in the letter about Christ and about the Church. Here, as earlier, Christ is the exalted head (cf. 1:22; 4:15). He is the one who loves and gives himself for believers (cf. 3:19; 5:2), who brings the Church into being by his saving death (cf. 1:7, 13; 2:5, 6; 2:14–18), who cares for its needs and growth (cf. 4:11, 16), who is intimately related to the Church as he fills it, dwells in believers' hearts, and is the source of their life (cf. 1:23; 2:21; 3:17; 4:15, 16). But now these elements are given a new focus as Christ is specifically called Savior (v 23), as his care for the Church is talked of in terms of nourishing and cherishing it (v 29), as his sanctifying activity is elaborated (vv 26, 27), and as he is seen as the bridegroom whose concern is for his bride's glory and purity (v 27) and whose relation to his Church can be depicted as a spiritual marriage union (vv 31, 32). Here, as earlier, the Church is Christ's body (cf. 1:23; 2:16; 3:6; 4:4, 12, 16), is associated with glory (cf. 1:6, 12, 14, 18; 3:21), and is to be holy and blameless (cf. 1:4; 2:21; 4:24; 5:3–14). What had been assumed previously in depicting Christ as head and in talking of learning Christ (cf. 4:20, 21) is now expressed explicitly—the Church is subject to Christ (v 24). As with Christ's side of their intimate relationship, so with the Church's—the marital imagery adds a new focus. The Church is now to be seen as the bride who is not only subordinate to Christ but in union with him (vv 31, 32). In line with the letter's earlier perspective on believers' salvation and its view of the Church as already being Christ's fullness and yet needing to attain to that fullness, of already having unity and yet still needing to realize it completely, there is an "already" and a "not yet" to the image of the Church as bride, with the stress on the former aspect, as the "one flesh" marriage union is applied to the present relationship between Christ and his Church.

The writer's thoughts about the two relationships—Christ and the Church, husband and wife—have influenced each other. The formulations about each are part of this two-way process. But paraenesis is his primary concern, and in the end the Christological and ecclesiological formulations serve that purpose. The focus of the pericope is believers' conduct. Although all is under the banner of mutual submission, the specific conduct required can be summed up for the wife as submitting to and fearing her husband's loving headship and for the husband as treating his wife with the same care that he expends on himself and, even more, with the quality of love that would enable him to sacrifice his life for her. For both partners there is a Christological motivation which comes mainly through the analogy with Christ and the Church but is also formulated in other ways. The wife is to view her husband's headship in the light of Christ's headship of the Church (v 23). In addition she is to submit "in the fear of Christ" (v 21) and "as to the Lord" (v 22). The husband is also to submit "in the fear of Christ" (v 21), while his self-giving love is to be modeled on that of Christ for the Church (v 25), and his nourishing and cherishing love for his wife as for his own body will reflect the love of Christ for his body, the Church (v 29).

The new element in this passage's exposition of the roles of Christ and of the Church is its striking emphasis on their unity, brought out by the quotation of Gen 2:24 and the depiction of the union as a profound mystery. Earlier in the letter, the language of mystery had also been applied to the notion of unity: to cosmic unity in Christ (1:9, 10), to the unity of Jew and Gentile in the one body, the Church (3:3–6), and to the way in which the latter unity acts as an announcement about the former (3:9, 10). Now not only do believers form a unity in Christ, but as the Church their relationship to Christ is one of unity. Just as other aspects of the relation between Christ and the Church form a prototype for believers' marriages, so does this fundamental aspect of unity. It is because a husband and wife are one flesh or one body that the husband can be urged to love his wife as his own body. In this way, the unity of Christ and the Church can be employed to underline the unity of husband and wife, and marital unity within the household can be seen to be an essential part of the expression of the unity of God's household, the Church. Again, if the Church's display of unity is to act as a pledge of God's purposes of unity for the cosmos, then marital unity in particular will also be a reflection of God's cosmic purposes. Just as maintenance of the Church's unity encompasses a diversity of gifts and roles in love, so the maintenance of marital unity involves diversity of roles—loving headship and fearing subordination—within mutual submission.

Whether it is because of its value as a further expression of the Church's unity for which he is so concerned, or whether it is also because of actual threats to the status of marriage within the churches he addresses, such as its disparagement by those attracted by ascetic teachings, the writer of Ephesians has chosen to provide his major elaboration on the household code of Colossians in regard to this relationship. The way in which he does so underlines its profound significance. This constitutes a quite different perspective on marriage from that of 1 Cor 7, where, although both husbands and wives have conjugal rights, because of the imminence of the parousia and because of the need to give undivided devotion to the Lord, Paul makes clear that the preferred state is celibacy and that those who have wives should live as though they had none. With a different perception of the Church's stage in history, the writer of Ephesians does not treat marriage as a second-best option but instead, by relating it so intimately to Christ's union with his Church, gives it an exalted status and lays the foundation for the development of the Christian "sacralizing" of the relationship.

For the readers, this analogy which serves as a prototype would have been thought of neither as an abstract illustration nor as mere theological rhetoric, but as a reality which was part of their experience. Christ's love was for a Church of which they were a part, his giving of himself for them had taken place on a cross in relatively recent history, and they were enjoying the privileges of experiencing the continuing love of their exalted Lord as he cared for them by dwelling in their hearts, giving gifts of ministry, and providing resources of life, love, and power. The other side of this prototype relationship was equally real for them as they attempted to submit to their head by learning what actions pleased him, by being thankful, by conducting themselves blamelessly, and by living in awe of him. Since they were participating in the reality of this relationship, the writer's appeal to them to model their marriages on it, so that those marriages would be an equally real reflection of its dynamic, would have had a powerful effect.

In terms of external roles and duties, the marriages of those who accepted this writer's invitation would have looked no different from those of the majority of people in the Greco-Roman world. So from one angle the analogy with Christ and the Church can be seen as simply reinforcing the traditional hierarchical pattern of marriage of the patriarchal household. The household codes of both Colossians and Ephesians do reflect a stage in the life of the Pauline churches in which they were coming to terms with their continuing existence over an extended period in society and accommodating to the structures that were held to provide the stability of their society. They reflect not only an external accommodation but also, as part of the same process, the internal stabilizing of the structures of community life which would aid the churches' coexistence with other members of society. But the acculturation of minority

Pauline churches to the dominant Greco-Roman society was not simply a oneway process. The writer of Ephesians brings a distinctive vision of marriage to the process, and, although the roles and duties of believers who shared this vision would from the outside have been hard to distinguish from those in other marriages, the internal ethos and dynamic of such marriages would have felt quite different. To have fulfilled one's role and carried out one's duties under the guidelines of mutual submission, and as a wife to have subordinated oneself voluntarily to a husband who cherishes one with a self-sacrificial love, would have been to experience a very different reality than that suggested by the traditional discussions of household management.

While there may have been gains for some women from this writer's vision of marriage, one of its consequences was losses for others. Although there is some continuity in this household code with Paul's instructions about women in relation to men in their conduct in the Corinthian assembly (cf. 1 Cor 11 and 14), there is evidence from Paul's letters of some women having leadership roles. But the instructions about subordination in the household code would have had implications for the role of women in the general life of the churches and have contributed to the identification of positions with any authority as male prerogatives, making it harder for the acceptance of the leadership abilities of exceptional women (cf. also MacDonald, *The Pauline Churches*, 119–20). The results of this can be seen already in the Pastorals, where, as the household becomes the dominant model for the Church, women are excluded from authoritative teaching roles (cf. 1 Tim 2:8–3:15; cf. also Wall, *CSR* 17 [1988] 273, "within the Pauline corpus the Ephesians handling of the tension between gender differentiation and equality occupies a mediating point somewhere between Galatians 3:28 and the Pastorals").

Although Greek religion could link marriage between gods and human sexual union, the use of "sacred marriage" imagery as an archetype in paraenesis about human marriage appears to be the distinctive contribution of Ephesians. Commentators have, however, differed widely in their assessment of the effectiveness and success of this contribution as a whole. Barth, for example, who devotes 147 pages of his commentary to this passage, can claim that "a greater, wiser and more positive description of marriage has not yet been found in Christian literature" and "this chapter belongs among the outstanding literary documents that provide a charter of liberty and responsibility to both partners in marriage, based upon the dignity, peace and unity given to them by God through Jesus Christ" (715, 753). On the other hand, Mitton, for example, holds that despite the rhetoric of the passage, "if it is studied in detail, it is found to be lacking in systematic construction and in strong internal connexions" and its use of traditional materials "is not one of the more successful parts of the letter" (210). In reply to Mitton, it must be said that our detailed study has revealed a piece of exhortation which is remarkably creative in its use of the analogy of Christ and the Church as the motivation and grounds for the conduct of husbands and wives and that this creativity is combined with a thoroughly coherent argument (cf. also Sampley, *"And the Two,"* 163: "Eph 5:21–33 is indeed an elaborate passage, but not labored. The author pursues very carefully and judiciously an intricate train of thought, with careful literary balance and structure from beginning to end"). Barth's assessment, however, takes us well beyond descriptive exegesis and calls for a somewhat more extended response. There are obviously questions about how all the message of Ephesians is to be appropriated (see the brief discussion in the *Introduction* under *Theology and Impact*), but since, on the one hand, this passage has served and still serves for many, such as Barth, as the model for Christian marriages, while, on the other hand, in the egalitarian and feminist climate of contemporary society it provides for others a source of some embarrassment or offense, it would be remiss of a commentator in this series not to reveal at least briefly his or her own evaluation of this particular passage and how it might be appropriated in an overall theology of Christian marriage.

Seen within its own setting, this creative paraenesis provides at one and the same time an acceptance of the basic framework of the traditional codes' treatment of marriage and yet a distinctive Christian modification of it. Both the writer's call to mutual submission and his depiction of the husband's exercise of headship in terms of loving sacrifice give the traditional roles a quite different dynamic (cf. also Miletic, *"One Flesh,"* 116: "The patriarchal structure remains intact [i.e., the wife is subordinate to the husband], but the dynamics within that structure are radically refocused on the wife's well-being"). Implicitly, our exegesis has indicated that nothing is to be gained by a revisionist and anachronistic interpretation of the passage which attempts to conform it to modern sensitivities and to make the writer an egalitarian before his time, either by treating the injunction to mutual submission as a radical critique of all that follows, or by emptying the concept of headship of all suggestions of authority, or by redefining subordination to the husband to mean "identification with" him. On the other hand, nothing is to be gained by pretending that the analogy with Christ and the Church makes this piece of paraenesis a timeless and universal prescription for marriage through the ages. For a start, this idealized picture of marriage, even within its own time, is limited in its scope and does not address important practical questions. It assumes that both partners have the same Christian commitment and depends on a mutual acceptance of the roles it requires. There is no advice about what to do when this is not the case: when mutuality breaks down or when the wife is faced with a husband who does not exercise his headship in the way Christ treats the Church in love. By building so exclusively on the model of Christ's relationship with the Church, not enough account can be taken of the sinful reality in which all human relationships are caught up and which can be experienced particularly intensely in the most intimate relationship of marriage. More importantly, from the perspective of the modern reader, the writer's use of the analogy of Christ and the Church reveals that the point of view of the passage is pervasively androcentric. Why should it simply be assumed that the model of Christ is for the husband and the model of the Church for the wife? Why should not a wife be able to take Christ as her model for marriage, and why should love only be expected of the husband and not of the wife? Why should the wife be likened to her husband's body and the husband not also be thought of as his wife's body?

It is best, then, to see this vision of marriage for what it is—conditioned by the cultural assumptions of its time—and to appreciate what it attempts to accomplish in its own setting—bringing its interpretation of the Pauline gospel to bear on the household structures of its society to produce a distinctive adaptation of those structures. Contemporary Christians can best appropriate it by realizing that they are to attempt to do something similar in their own setting—to bring to bear what they hold to be the heart of the Christian message on the marriage conventions of their time. Those who consider love and justice to be the central thrust of the Bible's ethical teaching will, therefore, want to work out a view of marriage where both partners are held in equal regard, where justice will require that traditional male dominance cannot be tolerated (cf. also Miletic, *"One Flesh,"* 116–20, who argues that since the text challenges male domination *even* in its own androcentric setting, it can continue to speak powerfully to the temptation to domination in contemporary marriage), and where love will ensure that the relationship does not degenerate into a sterile battle over each partner's rights to his or her own fulfillment.

By candidly acknowledging one's own contemporary Christian perspective, one is free not to allow the writer's analogy with Christ and the Church, which was illuminating and to some extent liberating in its application to the hierarchical patterns of his time, to straitjacket subsequent reflection on the passage, but instead to decide which elements of his vision might remain of value and which are now outmoded. An appropriation of the text which respects historical exegesis, but is not bound by it, might well reject the hierarchical elements in the exhortation about roles and the corresponding application of the hierarchical elements of the relationship between Christ and the Church to marriage and instead ponder the implications of the concept of union which is so important in this writer's overall concerns. The permanent "one flesh" union of Gen 2:24 which underlies the writer's exhortation to husbands, as well as being the vehicle for his distinctive interpretation of Christ and the Church, will remain the Christian ideal for marriage, providing the secure context for commitment, trust, and growth, and challenging the notion that relationships exist for personal profit and can be discarded when they fail to yield enough. Such an ideal for marriage can still be seen to be a reflection of the reality of the union between Christ and the Church and thus to have a "sacramental" dimension. In continuity with Ephesians, marriage can be exalted, not because it is so different from the rest of life but because in the midst of everyday life it provides a special focus for demonstrating the sort of unity that is at the center of God's purposes for all humanity and the cosmos, that at present is realized in the union between Christ and his Church, and that for its outworking in the relationship between a husband and a wife needs the support of the Pauline gospel of grace.

Instead of assigning love to the husband and submission to the wife, a contemporary appropriation of Ephesians will build on this passage's own introductory exhortation (v 21) and see a mutual loving submission as the way in which the unity of the marriage relationship is demonstrated. Indeed, Ephesians itself elsewhere asks both love (cf. 5:2) and submission (cf. 4:2) of all. Both wife and husband can look to Christ as the model for the sacrificial kind of love required (cf. 5:2). In this way, submission and love can be seen as two sides of the same coin—selfless service of one's marriage partner. What is required of both partners is costly care and commitment, thereby challenging other assumptions about love as purely a romantic feeling or ecstatic experience.

What is required of both partners is the submissive attitude that, presupposing the freedom and dignity of both, will voluntarily subordinate their own interests to those of the other, thereby challenging other assumptions that result in relationships of self-centered competition for control. A contemporary reading of Eph 5:21–33 cannot afford to ignore what this passage sees as the necessary motivation for mutual submission—"the fear of Christ"—and will want to stress that the encouragement for working toward the Christian ideal for marriage comes from looking to Christ's overwhelming love, drawing resources from his and the Spirit's power (cf. also 5:18), and, particularly when falling short of the ideal, relying on his cleansing and sanctifying activity.

Household Relationships—Children and Parents (6:1–4)

Bibliography

Gärtner, M. *Die Familienerziehung in der alten Kirche.* Cologne: Bohlau, 1985, 32–38.
Lincoln, A. T. "The Use of the OT in Ephesians." *JSNT* 14 (1982) 37–40.

Translation

¹Children, obey your parents in the Lord,[a] *for this is right. ² "Honor your father and mother"—which is the first commandment with a promise—³ "that it may go well with you and that you may live long on the earth." ⁴And fathers, do not make your children angry, but bring them up in the training and admonition of the Lord.*

Notes

[a] Some weighty witnesses (B D* G it d,e,f,g Marcion Clement Tertullian Cyprian Ambrosiaster [Pelagius]) omit the phrase ἐν κυρίῳ, "in the Lord," and a few interpreters (e.g., NEB; Caird, *Paul's Letters,* 89–90) believe this shorter reading to be original. Others (e.g., Schlier, 281–82; Houlden, *Paul's Letters,* 336; Mussner, 162; Bruce, *Epistles,* 397) are not so decisive and simply consider the authenticity of the phrase to be quite doubtful. It could be argued that the words were inserted later to conform to 5:22 and 6:5, so that each injunction to the subordinate party had a Christological motivation. But in that case, why was it not ὡς τῷ κυρίῳ or ὡς τῷ Χριστῷ that was added, as in these other two instances? An alternative explanation would be that the phrase was added in assimilation to the wording of Col 3:20. But in Col 3:20 ἐν κυρίῳ comes at the end of the warrant for the exhortation to children, "for this is pleasing in the Lord," and so one would have expected such a scribal addition here in Ephesians to have come at the end of the verse—"for this is right in the Lord." In addition, it is possible that Marcion, the earliest witness to the omission, may have found the link between the Christological motivation and the warrant from the OT commandment inappropriate and emended his text accordingly (cf. Gnilka, 295). B, which omits this phrase, also omits ἐστίν from the original of v 2. The evidence for the longer reading is widespread and also includes early and strong testimony—p⁴⁶ ℵ A Bᶜ K P Ψ 33 81 88 104 181 it ar,c,dem,mon,x,z vg syr p,h cop sa,bo arm eth Origen Ambrosiaster Basil Chrysostom Jerome. On internal grounds, one would expect a Christological motivation for the exhortation, and this reading provides it in a stylistic variation from both 5:22 and 6:5 that is most likely the writer's intentional adaptation of his Colossian source. Since, as has been noted, the explanations for a later addition are not compelling, this reading with ἐν κυρίῳ is to be preferred as the original (cf. also Meyer, 311; Abbott, 176; Metzger, *Textual Commentary,* 609; Barth, 654 n. 194, 755; Mitton, 210–11; Gnilka, 295; Schnackenburg, 267).

Form/Structure/Setting

Following on from the exhortations to wives and husbands in 5:22–33, the next groups within the household to be addressed are children and parents. It should be remembered that the instructions given are to be seen both as part of the wise and Spirit-filled living that the writer had discussed in 5:15–20 and as coming under the umbrella of the exhortation to mutual submission that had introduced the household code in 5:21.

As in the earlier part of the code, the subordinate group, here the children, is addressed first. The structure of the exhortation in v 1 follows the pattern that we have seen to be dominant in these early Christian codes. There is first the address to the particular group, "children," then follows an imperative with the appropriate object, "obey your parents," and then the amplification of the imperative with a prepositional phrase, "in the Lord." This is followed by a reason clause providing the motivation or warrant, "for this is right." The quotation in vv 2, 3 functions in two ways. It provides a further motivation or warrant from Scripture, and this is underlined by the inserted comment in v 2 that it is the first commandment in the decalogue that contains a promise. Yet at the same time, the actual wording of Scripture contains a second exhortation to the children, "honor your father and mother," and two motivating clauses introduced by the single ἵνα, "that it may go well with you and that you may live long on the earth." When the writer appeals to the parents, it is simply the fathers who are singled out for address in v 4, and the instructions are much briefer, with a straightforward exhortation. This exhortation is in two parts with a negative imperative, "do not make your children angry," followed by a positive one, "but bring them up in the training and admonition of the Lord," in a μή . . . ἀλλά construction (cf. also 4:29; 5:17, 18). It is not amplified by a prepositional phrase or a motivating clause.

In his paraenesis in these verses, the writer is again dependent on the form of the household code as mediated by Colossians. On the household code and its origins, see under *Form/Structure/Setting* on 5:21–33. Again, Ephesians works creatively with its original in Col 3:20, 21 (*pace* Schlier, 280, who unconvincingly argues that the differences rule out imitation or literary dependence). In the exhortation to children, the address, and basic imperative have the same wording. However, Ephesians omits κατὰ πάντα, "in everything," from Col 3:20, adds the possessive adjective ὑμῶν, "your," to "parents," and moves ἐν κυρίῳ, "in the Lord," from the motivating clause in Col 3:20 to make it the prepositional phrase that elaborates on the imperative. The motivating clause in Eph 6:1 is τοῦτο γάρ ἐστιν δίκαιον, "for this is right," instead of Colossians' τοῦτο γὰρ εὐάρεστόν ἐστιν ἐν κυρίῳ, "for this is pleasing in the Lord." This reworking of Colossians is a far more likely explanation than Col 3:20 being a conflation of Eph 5:10 with 6:1 (*pace* W. Munro, *Authority in Paul and Peter* [Cambridge: CUP, 1983] 31). Just as Ephesians' expansion on the paraenesis to wives and husbands had contained an OT quotation (Gen 2:24) with brief comments on it, so its distinctive expansion on the instructions to children contains an OT quotation (Exod 20:12) with brief comment on its significance. Ephesians connects the exhortation to fathers more closely to that to children by adding καί, "and," before the address and changes the negative imperative from μή ἐρεθίζετε, "do not irritate" (Col 3:21), to μὴ παροργίζετε, "do not make angry." Whereas the negative imperative in Colossians is continued by the clause ἵνα μὴ ἀθυμῶσιν, "lest they become discouraged," in Ephesians it is followed by the positive exhortation ἀλλὰ ἐκτρέφετε αὐτὰ ἐν παιδείᾳ καὶ νουθεσίᾳ κυρίου, "but bring them up in the training and admonition of the Lord." It can be seen, therefore, that as in its use of the paraenesis for wives and husbands in Colossians, Ephesians expands on its Colossians original. In so doing, it strengthens the Christianizing of the material by moving "in the Lord" to link it with the imperative to children to obey and by adding something specifically Christian to the exhortation to fathers, a feature missing in Colossians, namely, the mention of "the training and admonition of the Lord."

Apart from its use of Colossians, this pericope in Ephesians employs another major piece of tradition, a commandment from the decalogue. Scholars have differed about which version of the fifth commandment the writer quotes. E. E. Ellis (*Paul's Use of the Old Testament* [Edinburgh: Oliver & Boyd, 1957] 152, 185) and Bruce (*Epistles,* 298), for example, believe Deut 5:16 to be in view, while Martin ("Ephesians," 171) considers the citation to be a complex conflation of Exod 20:12; Deut 5:16; and Deut 22:7. It is true that the clause "that it may go well with you" is not found in the Massoretic text of Exod 20:12, whereas it is in Deut 5:16 and 22:7. However, this clause is found in LXX Exod 20:12. The citation in Eph 6:2, 3, therefore, stands very close to the LXX version of Exod 20:12. It is closer to this text than to LXX Deut 5:16. In the case of both texts, Ephesians would have replaced ἵνα, "that," and γένῃ, "may be," in the clause about living in the land with ἔσῃ, "may be," and omitted the specific description of the land after τῆς γῆς, "the land." But in the case of LXX Deut 5:16, it would have had to make further alterations, omitting the σοῦ, "your," after μητέρα, "mother" (this is only in the B text of LXX Exod 20:12) and also dropping the clause ὃν τρόπον ἐνετείλατό σοι κύριος ὁ θεός σου, "as the Lord your God commanded you," after μητέρα σου. The text in Eph 6:2, 3 is, therefore, a modified citation of LXX Exod 20:12. As has been noted, the citation omits the specific description of the land as that "which the Lord your God gives you," which tied the original promise to the land of Canaan. This omission was common in Jewish tradition once the question of the promised land was no longer a current one (cf. Str-B 3:614), but this is not sufficient evidence for the view that Ephesians' use of the OT at this point is not a direct one and that the writer is simply taking up general Jewish Christian tradition (*pace* Lindemann, *Aufhebung,* 87).

As has been noted, the most immediate ties of this passage to its setting in the letter as a whole are to 5:15–20 and 5:21, but there are other links with the surrounding paraenesis. The injunction to children to obey anticipates the same command to slaves in 6:5. The Christological motivation for this through the phrase "in the Lord" is similar to the Christological motivation used for the wives' subordination, "as to the Lord" (5:22), and the slaves' obedience, "as to Christ" (6:5). The general warrant of v 1, "for this is right," has some similarity with the earlier general appeal to what is or is not fitting in 5:4, although there the writer had made this criterion more specifically Christian by talking of what was fitting for saints in 5:3. The use of OT material as support in the paraenesis is found elsewhere in 4:25, 26; 5:18; 5:31, 32; and 6:14–17. The writer's exhortation to fathers not to make their children angry echoes his earlier concern about anger in 4:26, 27, 31, and the positive instructions about bringing children up in the training and admonition of the Lord recall his earlier emphasis on learning the tradition of Christian teaching in 4:20, 21.

There is nothing specific in the situation of the churches to which Ephesians is addressed that prompted this advice to children and parents. It is included, in dependence on Colossians, because it is one of the three basic household relationships treated in the discussion of household management in the Aristotelian tradition. We noted previously (see under *Form/Structure/Setting* on 5:21–33) apologetic factors at work in the code's use in Hellenistic Judaism and in its possible original adoption by early Christians. These apply also to this particular relationship. Tacitus (*Hist.* 5.5) attacked the Jews as a subversive threat, saying, "Those who converted to their ways follow the same practice, and the earliest lesson they receive is to despise the gods, to disown their country, and to regard their parents, children, and brothers as of little account." When he makes the point that the Jews are not impious, Philo (*Hyp.* 7.14) can say, "Any of them whom you attack with inquiries about their ancestral institutions can answer you rapidly and easily. The husband seems competent to transmit knowledge of the laws to his wife, the father to his children, the master to his slaves." Attacks on Christians also talked of their subversion of children. It is worth noting the later variant readings of Luke 23:2 where Jesus is indicted for "leading astray both women and children." Although there are gospel traditions which point out that some Pharisaic traditions obscure the fifth commandment and which place great value on children (cf., e.g., Mark 7:9–13; 10:13–16), the radical demands of discipleship in the Jesus movement had also cut across the normal obligations of family life (cf., e.g., Mark 3:31–35; 10:29, 30; 13:12; Luke 9:59–62; 14:26). But, as with the use of the code as a whole, Eph 6:1–4 reflects the stage of the stabilizing of communal relations in the Pauline churches and the accompanying accommodation to some of the basic traditional structures of surrounding society. The undisputed Pauline letters have scarcely anything to say directly about the relationship between parents and children. In 1 Cor 7:14 the apostle had made it clear that he took for granted that the children of a marriage between a believer and an unbeliever were not unclean but holy. In Rom 1:30 he lists disobedience to parents as one of the signs of Gentiles' lack of acknowledgment of their Creator. But his main interest in the father-child relationship is its use as a metaphor for his own relationship to believers in the churches he had founded. Paul's use of this metaphor reflects the usual assumptions of his day about the father's authority and the need for the father to admonish his children and correct them with the rod as well as about parents' love and provision for their children (cf., e.g., 1 Cor 4:14, 15, 21; 2 Cor 12:14, 15). Some of these assumptions in the ancient world about parents and children and children's upbringing can be sketched further as the background against which the instructions here in Ephesians can be seen.

Barclay, W. *Educational Ideals in the Ancient World.* London: Collins, 1959. **Bertram, G.** "παιδεύω κτλ." *TDNT* 5 (1967) 596–625. **Blomenkamp, P.** "Erziehung." *RAC* 6 (1966) 502–59. **Bonner, S. F.** *Education in Ancient Rome.* London: Methuen, 1977. **Gärtner, M.** *Die Familienerziehung in der alten Kirche.* Cologne: Bohlau, 1985. **Jentsch, W.** *Urchristliches Erziehungsdenken: Die Paideia Kyriou im Rahmen der hellenistisch-jüdischen Welt.* Gütersloh: G. Mohn, 1951. **Lacey, W. K.** *The Family in Classical Greece.* London: Thames & Hudson, 1968. **Marrou, H. I.** *A History of Education in Antiquity.* London: Sheed & Ward, 1956. **Oepke, A.** "παῖς κτλ." *TDNT* 5 (1967) 636–54. **Schrenk, G.** "πατήρ κτλ." *TDNT* 5 (1967) 945–1022.

By the first century C.E., Greco-Roman society had become heavily influenced by traditional Roman notions of family life and education. The almost absolute legal power of the father, the *patria potestas*, is a well-known feature. Dionysius of Halicarnassus (*Rom. Ant.* 2.26.4) could write in praise of it, "The law-giver of the Romans gave virtually full power to the father over his son, whether he thought proper to imprison him, to scourge him, to put him in chains, and keep him at work in the fields, or to put him to death; and this even though the son were already engaged in public affairs, though he were numbered among the highest magistrates, and though he were celebrated for his zeal for the commonwealth." The father functioned as a magistrate within the family, able to impose these various penalties. The *paterfamilias* also had the authority to decide on the life and death of his newborn children. Weak and deformed children could be killed, usually by drowning, and unwanted daughters were often exposed or sold. All his children were reckoned to be under his control, not only those living with him, and also the children of his sons. The mother, on the other hand, had no legal power. The father's power also carried responsibility, since he was legally liable for the actions of members of his household. The jurist Gaius could write, "The power which we have over our children is peculiar to Roman citizens and is found in no other nation" (*Inst.* 1.55). The extent of the father's powers was laid down clearly in the formulae of adoption which spoke of his powers of life and death over the son (cf. Cicero, *De Domo* 29.77). In Rome the father's power ended with his death. In Greece, when he reached the age of about sixty, he usually handed over authority to his eldest married son.

Fathers often remarried, in which case the children of their various wives grew up in the same household, since by law, both in the case of divorce or the death of a wife, fathers retained the children. Their own children were often brought up with the slave children in the household. It is worth noting that a Roman master could only sell a slave once, but if a Roman father sold his child and the child became free at a later stage, the father could sell the child again. As Dionysius says, Roman law gave "greater power to the father over his son than to the master over his slaves" (*Rom. Ant.* 2.27.1).

It is, of course, important to distinguish between these legal powers and the extent to which they were actually employed in everyday life. It is clear that on some occasions the most extreme punishments were carried out, and Dionysius could note that Roman fathers were at times so severe that "Greeks regarded the Romans as cruel and harsh" (*Rom. Ant.* 2.27.1). But with the passage of time public opinion became hostile to excessive severity. Terence's comedy *Adelphoe* has as a major element the conflict between fathers and sons and whether Demea's severe disciplinary methods or Micio's more liberal attitude is more likely to achieve the desired results with one's sons. Pseudo-Plutarch (*De Lib. Educ.* 12) advocated the use of praise and blame and other verbal means of instruction rather than beatings, and one of the most popular debates in rhetorical education became how far a father's legal powers could reasonably extend in practice (cf. Quintilian 7.4.27).

Hellenistic Judaism also stressed the status and authority of parents. Philo talks of parents as belonging to the superior class which comprises seniors, rulers, benefactors, and masters, while children occupy the inferior position with juniors, subjects, receivers of benefits, and slaves (cf. *De Decal.* 165–67; *De Spec. Leg.* 2.227). Parents are in fact like gods to their children: "Parents, in my opinion, are to their children what God is to the world, since just as He achieved existence for the non-existent, so they in imitation of His power, as far as they are capable, immortalize the race. And a father and mother deserve honour, not only on this account, but for many other reasons" (*De Spec. Leg.* 2.225, 226; cf. also *De Decal.* 119, 120). The OT had legislated the death penalty for the dishonoring of parents (cf. Lev 20:9; Deut 21:18–21), and this was reemphasized as a punishment for children who failed to demonstrate thoroughgoing obedience to their parents: "A father is empowered to upbraid or beat his children, to impose harsh punishments on them and keep them locked up. But in case the children nevertheless remain obdurate . . . the Law has even authorized parents to go so far as to impose the death penalty" (Philo, *De Spec. Leg.* 2.232; cf. also *Hyp.* 7.2); "honour to parents the Law ranks second only to honour to God, and if a son does not respond to the benefits received from them—for the slightest failure in his duty towards them—it hands him over to be stoned" (Josephus, *c. Ap.* 2.27 § 206; cf. also *Ant.* 4.8.24 § 264). Again, there are questions about the relation of such statements to actual practice, and, again, voices were raised occasionally against too severe use of force by fathers (cf. Ps.-Phocylides 207–9: "Do not be harsh with your children, but be gentle. And if a child offends against you, let the mother cut her son down to size, or else the elders of the family or the chiefs of the people"). Of course, within Judaism, where children were seen as gifts from God, a father had no rights over the lives of newborn children, and the pagan practices of abortion and exposure were attacked (cf. Philo, *De Spec. Leg.* 3.108–19; *Hyp.* 7.7; Josephus, *c. Ap.* 2.24 § 202; Ps.-Phocylides 184–85).

In Roman society, as far as the bringing up and the education of children were concerned, the father's influence was paramount. Although the mother was the main influence on a son for his first seven years, the father, particularly in the early days of the empire, then took over as his teacher and close companion (cf. the depiction of Cato as a good father in Plutarch, *Cato Maior* 20). This continued until the boy was about sixteen, when he was placed in the charge of some distinguished or trusted friend for a year or two. Even later when, under the Greek influence, it became the general practice for children to go to school from the age of seven and to be accompanied by a pedagogue, the father was still considered to be the child's real teacher, and an important part of education was the *praecepta paterna*, "paternal precepts." In Greco-Roman society, such education included ethical and religious instruction. First through the women of the household and then under the charge of the father, children listened to stories of the gods and learned the proper cultic procedures in worship devoted to the household gods, especially in regard to practices associated with meals (cf., e.g., Prudentius, *C. Symm.* 1.197–214). That parents sometimes failed to live up to these ideals for the upbringing of their children can be seen from the way in which Tacitus bemoans the current situation in comparison with the good old days: "The parents themselves make no effort to train their little ones in goodness and self-control; they grow up in an atmosphere of laxity and pertness, in which they come gradually to lose all sense of shame, and all respect both for themselves and other people" (*Dial.* 29.1–3).

Within Judaism the emphasis was heavily on the religious upbringing of children, and this was seen as ultimately the responsibility of the father. Again, children were taken to school by their fathers from the age of seven, but ideally the real center of education remained the home. At the heart of the instruction was the Torah, which itself enjoined the teaching of the commandments to children (cf. Deut 4:9; 6:7; 11:19; 32:46). The duty of parents to instruct and particularly to discipline their children features prominently in the wisdom literature: "Train up a child in the way he should go, and when he is old he will not depart from it" (Prov 22:6). Severe discipline (with παιδεύειν used in this sense in the LXX) and beatings were seen as part of an upbringing that had the child's ultimate moral well-being at heart: "He who spares the rod hates his son, but he who loves him is diligent to discipline [παιδεύει] him" (LXX Prov 13:24); "Do not withhold discipline [παιδεύειν] from a child; if you beat him with a rod, he will not die. If you beat him with the rod, you will save his life from Sheol" (LXX Prov 23:13, 14; cf. also 19:18; 29:15, 17; Sir 7:23). In an extended passage, Sir 30:1–13 contends that a loving upbringing of a son should involve severe discipline, including whipping, rather than pampering or playing and laughing with him. Later, Hellenistic Judaism continued to stress the importance of the education of children. Philo could write, "Since Jews esteem their laws as divine revelations, and are instructed in the knowledge of them from their earliest youth, they bear the image of the Law in their souls. . . . They are taught, so to speak, from their swaddling-clothes by their parents, by their teachers, and by those who bring them up, even before instruction in the sacred laws and the unwritten customs, to believe in God, the One Father and Creator of the world" (*Leg. ad Gaium* 31; cf. also *De Spec. Leg.* 2.228; *Hyp.* 7.14). Josephus could say, "Our ground is good, and we work it to the utmost, but our chief ambition is for the education of our children. . . . We take most pains of all with the instruction of children, and esteem the observation of the laws, and the piety corresponding with them, the most important affair of our whole life" (*c. Ap.* 1.12 § 60; cf. 2.18 § 178; 2.25 § 204). As noted earlier in discussing the father's authority, severe discipline continued to be seen as an essential part of such instruction (cf. Philo, *De Spec. Leg.* 2.232; *Hyp.* 7.2; Josephus, *c. Ap.* 2.27 § 206; *Ant.* 4.8.24 § 264).

Certainly the main practical effect of the Roman *patria potestas* was that children took it for granted that they should do what they were told by their father. An emphasis on children's obligations toward their parents was widespread in the Greco-Roman world. Most commonly, this was spoken of in terms of honoring parents, although honoring was assumed to include obeying. So, for example, according to Dionysius (*Rom. Ant.* 2.26.1–4), children are to honor and obey parents in all things. Honoring parents is found alongside honoring the gods as chief among the virtues in the "unwritten laws" (cf. the fragment of Euripides preserved in Stobaeus, *Anth.* 3.1.80; Xenophon, *Mem.* 4.4.19, 20; Plato, *Resp.* 4.425b). Hierocles in "How to Conduct Oneself towards Parents" instructs that parents are to be honored as earthly gods and that the duty to parents includes all other duties, because they are the images of the gods, benefactors, relatives, masters, and friends (Stobaeus, *Anth.* 4.25.53; cf. also Cicero, *De Offic.* 1.58; Diogenes Laertius 7.108, 120; Epictetus, *Diss.* 2.17.31; 3.7.26). Philo (*De Spec. Leg.* 2.236) states that children should be willing to obey parents in everything that is just and profitable, and within Judaism the duty of honoring one's parents, embodied in the fifth commandment (Exod 20:12; Deut 5:16) and underlined in a variety of ways in the wisdom literature (cf., e.g., Prov 19:26; 20:20; Sir 3:1–16; 7:27, 28), is repeated frequently (cf., e.g., Tob 4:3, 4; *Ep. Arist.* 228; *Jub.* 7.20; Philo, *De Ebr.* 17; *De Mut. Nom.* 40; *De Vit. Mos.* 2.198; *De Post. Caini* 181, where among "the best things in the world" is listed first "honour paid to parents"; Josephus, *c. Ap.* 2.27 § 206).

It can be seen that Ephesians upholds the authority structure of the family but makes this subservient to the overall obedience to Christ as Lord of both children and parents and, even more strikingly, to some sort of mutual submission of both groups in the fear of Christ (cf. 5:21). It treats children as those who in their own right have a relationship with this Lord which both transcends and includes the duty to their parents. Along with both the Greco-Roman world and Judaism, it makes fathers ultimately responsible for the religious upbringing of their children. In its exhortation to fathers, Ephesians provides restraints on paternal authority, guarding against its abuse, and focuses instead on the Christian training fathers are to provide. It is worth noting that this emphasis is different from that of the later Pastoral Epistles, where, although slaves are given duties (cf. 1 Tim 6:1, 2), children are not, but appear instead as the objects of discipline (cf. 1 Tim 3:4, 5, where a bishop "must manage his own household well, keeping his children submissive and respectful in every way"; cf. also 3:12; Titus 1:6). Ephesians' emphasis on the need for Christian training for children can be found in other early Christian writings (cf. *1 Clem.* 21; Pol. *Phil.* 4:2; Herm. *Vis.* 1.3.1, 2; 2.3.1).

Comment

1 Τὰ τέκνα, ὑπακούετε τοῖς γονεῦσιν ὑμῶν ἐν κυρίῳ, "Children, obey your parents in the Lord." Addressing instructions to children is not in itself unusual, but it is distinctive in relation to discussions of household management in the Greco-Roman world, where it was the male adult free person who was addressed rather than the subordinate parties. Children's duty to obey parents was, as we have seen under *Form/Structure/Setting,* taken for granted throughout the ancient world. Elsewhere in the Pauline corpus, disobedience to parents is considered a sign of Gentile depravity (Rom 1:30) or a sign of the evil of the last days (2 Tim 3:2). Here in Ephesians, the duty of obedience is owed to both parents, despite 6:4 being addressed to fathers only. Whereas Col 3:20 asks for obedience to parents in everything (κατὰ πάντα) without qualification, Ephesians calls for an obedience "in the Lord" (for the use of this phrase elsewhere in the letter cf. 2:21; 4:1, 17; 5:8; 6:10, 21). This has similar force to the motivation attached to the wives' subordination and to the slaves' obedience; it is to be carried out not simply because the other party has superior authority and status but as part of their Christian discipleship and therefore "as to the Lord" or "as to Christ" (cf. 5:22; 6:5). Their relationship to their parents presents children with a sphere in which to carry out obedience to their Lord. As was argued earlier (see *Comment* on 5:22), it is doubtful whether any major implications can be drawn from positing a substantial distinction between obedience enjoined on children (and slaves) and subordination enjoined on wives (*contra* Caird, *Paul's Letters,* 89–90, who uses this and the claim that "in the Lord" was not in the original text to argue that the subjection of children to parents was seen as part of the natural order, whereas the subordination of wife to husband was not, and that this suggests Paul's progressive views on women's equality).

In Judaism, children's attitude to their parents was often set alongside and seen as part of their relationship to God. *Sib. Or.* 3.593 says of the Jews, "they honor only the Immortal who always rules, and then their parents," while Ps.-Phocylides 8 exhorts, "Honor God foremost, and afterward your parents" (cf. also Philo, *De Spec. Leg.* 2.224–25; 2.235-36; Josephus, *c. Ap.* 2.27 § 206; Tob 4:3–5; *T. Reub.* 3.8). Now for Christian children there is a similar juxtaposition between obedience to parents and obedience to the Lord. It is unlikely, however, that Ephesians has in view the response to pagan parents of Christian children, who may need to be reminded to put obedience to Christ before obedience to parents (*pace* Mitton, 210–11). It should be assumed that the parents are Christian parents (cf. also Gnilka, 295–96; Bruce, *Epistles,* 397) and that the exhortation is making clear that the relationship to parents is as much a part of submitting to one another in the fear of Christ (5:21) and of obedience to the Lord as any other relationship or conduct.

So these children are seen as fully part of the Christian community, able to exercise their Christian obedience in this way and to view their conduct as determined not just by social convention but in the light of their Lord's will (cf. also 5:10, 17). They are addressed as among those who would hear the letter as it was read at meetings of believers for worship in various households. The text is, however, irrelevant for discussion of the issue of whether infants were baptized as part of households in the early church (cf. also Meyer, 314; Abbott, 176; Gnilka, 295 n. 6). τέκνον, "child," primarily denotes relationship rather than age and can be used of adults as well as small children. From the context, the children in view here have to be old enough to be conscious of a relationship to their Lord and to be appealed to on the basis of it, but young enough still to be in the process of being brought up (cf. 6:4). As Mitton (211) puts it, this exhortation "could only refer to older children (perhaps what we should call teenagers) who were of an age to make a personal commitment to Christ, but still young enough to be living at home with their parents" (cf. also Gärtner, *Die Familienerziehung,* 36–37, who maintains, however, that Col 3:20 has adult children in view).

τοῦτο γάρ ἐστιν δίκαιον, "for this is right." The children are appealed to not only on the basis of their Christian commitment but also on the basis of what is right or just. Such a motivation replaces "for this is pleasing in the Lord" from Col 3:20. This writer had already talked of discovering what is pleasing to the Lord in the general paraenesis in 5:10. He had also used righteousness in 4:24 as a virtue that is part of the new humanity's having been created in God's likeness, but this specifically Christian connotation to the notion does not carry over to the adjective here (*pace* Mussner, 162, who interprets "this is right" as "this is appropriate to the proper Christian ordering of the community"). The appeal to what is generally held to be right or just was common. It is found, for example, in Stoic teaching (cf. Epictetus, *Diss.* 1.22.1; 2.17.6) and elsewhere in the NT in Luke 12:57; Phil 4:8; and Col 4:1. Josephus defined the right as obedience to God's commandments (cf. *Ant.* 6.8.1 § 165; 8.7.7 § 208; 9.4.3 § 58). This, together with the citation of the commandment in the following verse, has led some to claim that "this is right" means this "corresponds to the righteous divine order enjoined by the commandment" (cf. G. Schrenk, "δίκαιος," *TDNT* 2 [1964] 188; cf. also J. A. Robinson, 127). But from what we know of the universality with which the obedience of children to parents was upheld, it is far more likely that the writer's appeal is to this general sense of what was fitting and right, to which he then gives further biblical support in vv 2, 3.

2, 3 τίμα τὸν πατέρα σου καὶ τὴν μητέρα, ἥτις ἐστὶν ἐντολὴ πρώτη ἐν ἐπαγγελίᾳ, ἵνα εὖ σοι γένηται καὶ ἔσῃ μακροχρόνιος ἐπὶ τῆς γῆς, "Honor your father and mother"—which is the first commandment with a promise—"that it may go well with you and that you may live long on the earth." So far the motivation for children's obedience toward their parents has been twofold; it is part of their Christian commitment, "in the Lord," and it is generally the right and proper thing to do. Now a third justification is provided by the citation of LXX Exod 20:12. As we have noted under *Comment* on v 1, making an association between what is right and what is in the law would have been in line with Hellenistic Jewish thinking (cf. also Schnackenburg, 267). Obedience to parents is a scriptural injunction. What is more, a fourth reason, although it is a subdivision of the third, is that this is a particularly important scriptural injunction, since it is the first commandment with a promise.

This description inserted into the citation has puzzled commentators. How can the fifth commandment be said to be the first commandment with a promise, when the second commandment in Exod 20:4–6 also appears to include a promise about God showing steadfast love to those who love him and keep his commandments? Some suggest that the writer must view the fifth commandment as the first after the four chief commandments which deal with a person's relationship to God, pointing to a similar view in Philo (*De Spec. Leg.* 2.261, although *De Decal.* 121 treats the fifth commandment as the last of those concerned with specific duties toward God; cf., e.g., Gnilka, 297, who claims that what is meant is that the commandment stands in the first place in regard to duties toward other humans and it possesses a promise). Others (e.g., Schlier, 281 n. 3; Ernst, 393) argue that "first" should not be understood numerically but in terms of the importance or difficulty of the commandment (cf. the use in Mark 12:28, 29, though with reference to a different commandment). They also draw attention to the rabbinic tradition preserved in *Deut. Rab.* 6 on Deut 22:6, which holds that God has provided the most difficult and the easiest commandments with a promise. The most difficult is said to be the fifth commandment, and the easiest is said to be Deut 22:7, which states that if one comes across a bird's nest with both mother and young in it, one is to let the mother go but may keep the young. Both commandments have the same promise attached, "that it may go well with you, and that you may live long." Neither of these explanations is compelling, and it may be best to question the assumption that has led to their having been produced, namely, that the second commandment has a promise attached. Strictly speaking, the words "but showing steadfast love to thousands of those who love me and keep my commandments" in Exod 20:16 are not a promise connected with "you shall not make for yourself a graven image" in Exod 20:4, but are the positive side of the description of Yahweh as a jealous God which follows in Exod 20:5. It is not surprising, therefore, for Exod 20:12 to be thought of as the first commandment with a promise. If it is objected that this would make the fifth commandment not simply the first but the only commandment with a promise, it must be replied that the writer views the decalogue as but the beginning of the many commandments contained in the Torah (cf. also Meyer, 314; J. A. Robinson, 210; Dibelius-Greeven, 95; Caird, *Paul's Letters,* 90; Mitton, 211–12).

As does the injunction of the household code itself in v 1, so the fifth commandment lays an obligation on children toward both parents. They are to honor and respect (τιμᾶν) father and mother. As we have noted (see *Form/Structure/Setting*), this was the most common formulation of the obligation in both Jewish, presumably influenced by the wording of the commandment, and Greco-Roman writings. It was understood as involving not only a respectful attitude but also care for the parents' physical needs when they became old. So for children still in the father's house it would mean obedience to parents, and for those who had left home it would mean continued deference to and care for aging parents.

This commandment is found elsewhere in the NT in Matt 15:4; 19:19; Mark 7:10; 10:19; Luke 18:20, but only here in Eph 6:2, 3 is the attached promise also cited. The writer's wording of the promise omits the clause "which the Lord your God gives you" from LXX Exod 20:12, which linked the original promise to the land of Canaan. This omission, of course, has the effect of making the promise more generally applicable. The promise is now of well-being and long life on the earth. But this raises further questions. Has the promise merely been included to emphasize the importance of the commandment (so Gnilka, 297; Schnackenburg, 268)? Or does the writer expect his readers to apply it to themselves? The actual citation of this part of the verse and its modification in the direction of general applicability (although as noted under *Form/Structure/Setting* the latter was fairly common in Judaism) certainly allow for the writer intending it still to have force for his readers. But if so, what is that force? Philo (*De Spec. Leg.* 2.262) had spiritualized the promise by taking "well with you" to be the virtue a person possesses through obeying the commandments and "live long" to be immortality. But there is no hint of such a meaning being intended here. In Paul's writings, the OT promises about the seed and the land are seen as fulfilled in the salvation provided in Christ and the inheritance which that provides (cf. Gal 3 and 4; Rom 4 and 8), and earlier in Ephesians the notion of inheritance has been interpreted in a similar way (cf. 1:14; 3:6). So some commentators (e.g., Schlier, 282) have tied the promise to this soteriological interpretation of inheritance. But unlike the writer's reinterpretation of Gen 2:24 in 5:31, 32, there is no indication from 6:3 or its immediate context that he has imposed such a Christian perspective on this text. It probably does more justice to this verse to take it at its face value as promising well-being and long life on the earth and to judge that, since it had been introduced to reinforce the commandment, the writer may not have integrated its Jewish this-worldly perspective consistently with his interpretation of inheritance in the first half of the letter. The use of the OT to support earthly rewards for Christian obedience seems foreign to Paul, who, when he does employ talk of rewards as part of his ethical motivation, has in view a future life after the judgment (cf. 1 Cor 3:12–15; 2 Cor 5:10). It is closer to the perspective of the Pastorals, where godliness can be said to be "of value in every way, as it holds promise for the present life and also for the life to come" (1 Tim 4:8). To take the promise in a communal sense to mean that a society in which the aged are respected and cared for by their children is a healthy and stable one is a modern reinterpretation (as Mitton, 213, who suggests this, acknowledges). In the passage itself, the rewards of well-being and long life are held out to individual children who honor their parents. It is also worth noting that not only the promise of earthly reward but also the specific content of that reward, long life on earth, would be alien to the Paul who expected an imminent parousia, even if this Paul had come to terms with his own death before that event. It is more likely to have been penned by a Jewish Christian follower of the apostle who has become more acclimatized to a longer period of the church's existence on earth before the parousia.

4 Καὶ οἱ πατέρες μὴ παροργίζετε τὰ τέκνα ὑμῶν, ἀλλὰ ἐκτρέφετε αὐτὰ ἐν παιδείᾳ καὶ νουθεσίᾳ κυρίου, "And fathers, do not make your children angry, but bring them up in the training and admonition of the Lord." The link between the exhortations to both halves of the pairing, children and fathers, is underlined by the καί, "and," at the beginning of v 4. Both groups, not just the subordinate one, have obligations. The plural οἱ πατέρες, "fathers," can refer to parents in general and not just fathers (cf. Heb 11:23), and some suggest that this may be the meaning here (cf., e.g., BAGD 635; Schnackenburg, 268). But the change of wording from γονεῖς, "parents," in v 1, the omission of the mention of mothers after this has been explicit in the commandment of v 2, and the fact (as we have observed under *Form/Structure/Setting*) that in the ancient world in both Greco-Roman and Jewish writings it is fathers in particular who are held responsible for the education of the children, make it far more likely that Ephesians is in conformity with this way of thinking and is addressing male heads of households in their role as fathers. In later Judaism this point was made expressly: "All the obligations of a father toward his son enjoined in the Law are incumbent on men but not on women, and all obligations of a son toward his father enjoined in the Law are incumbent both on men and on women" (*m. Qidd.* 1.7).

The exhortation to fathers in Col 3:21 remained in the negative, "Do not provoke (embitter) your children, lest they become discouraged," and the first part of Eph 6:4 is similar in thought but employs different terminology. "Do not make your children angry" continues this writer's concern with anger from earlier in the paraenesis. The verb παροργίζειν is used elsewhere in the NT only in Rom 10:19 of God making Israel angry, but the noun παροργισμός occurs earlier in this letter in 4:26, where it denotes anger that has been provoked and that can give the devil opportunity if it is not dealt with quickly. Fathers are made responsible for ensuring that they do not provoke anger in their children. This involves avoiding attitudes, words, and actions which would drive a child to angry exasperation or resentment and thus rules out excessively severe discipline, unreasonably harsh demands, abuse of authority, arbitrariness, unfairness, constant nagging and condemnation, subjecting a child to humiliation, and all forms of gross insensitivity to a child's needs and sensibilities. The sentiments of Ephesians are in line with such advocates of moderation as Menander—whose sayings (e.g., "a father who is always threatening does not receive much reverence" or "one should correct a child not by hurting him but by persuading him") are preserved in the section "How Fathers Ought to Behave to Their Children" in Stobaeus, *Anth.* 4.26.7, 13—and Ps.-Phocylides 207, "Do not be harsh with your children but be gentle." So this writer does not exhort fathers to exercise their authority. Instead, he presupposes that authority and then sets the bounds for its use. He also presupposes that children are not just property over whom the father has legal rights. They are owed dignity as human beings in their own right.

In the positive addition to its Colossians counterpart, Ephesians also calls on fathers to bring up their children in a distinctively Christian way. The verb ἐκτρέφειν had been used earlier in 5:29 with the force of "to nourish," but here it has the more general sense of "to rear, bring up." In fact, with his fondness for similar terms, the writer employs here three closely related words. The verb ἐκτρέφειν with παιδεία, "training, upbringing," is virtually tautological—"bring up your children in the upbringing"—and some scholars (e.g., Bertram, *TDNT* 5 [1967] 624) consider παιδεία and νουθεσία, "admonition," a hendiadys. The latter two terms are used together elsewhere (cf., e.g., Philo, *Quod Deus* 54, where it is said that anthropomorphisms used of God are "for training and admonition," or *De Spec. Leg.* 2.239, where the cognate verbs occur together of children who "are subject to instruction and admonition"; cf. also 4.96), but it is probable that here they have slightly different nuances. Although in their broader Greek usage they referred to education in general and to its goal of culture, in the LXX, παιδεία and its cognates acquired the sense of discipline and chastisement. As we have seen from the sketch of views of education under *Form/Structure/Setting*, these words were used of the training of children, either through instruction or frequently through correction or punishment. At the same time, in the LXX wisdom literature παιδεία is often linked with σοφία, "wisdom" (cf., e.g., Sir 1:27, "For the fear of the Lord is wisdom and instruction"; 23:2, "O that whips were set over my thoughts, and the discipline of wisdom over my mind!"; cf. also Bertram, *TDNT* 5 [1967] 608–12). For both Philo and Josephus, the παιδεία word group continues to have the sense of education, which can involve discipline, and is one of the concepts which forms a bridge between the law and Greek culture (cf. Bertram, *TDNT* 5 [1967] 612–17). In the NT also, the word group can have both the more comprehensive meaning of education or training (cf. Acts 7:22; 22:3; 2 Tim 3:16; Titus 2:12) and the more specific sense of discipline or chastisement (cf. 1 Cor 11:32; 2 Cor 6:9; Heb 12:5, 7, 8, 11). Here in Eph 6:4, it is most likely that the general sense is in view and that νουθεσία then denotes the more specific aspect of this training that takes place through verbal admonition or correction (cf. also Abbott, 178; Gnilka, 298; Schnackenburg, 268; Gärtner, *Die Familienerzeihung*, 38; for an older discussion of the relation between these two terms cf. also R. C. Trench, *Synonyms of the New Testament* [Cambridge: Macmillan, 1854] 125–29). Admonition is seen as an essential part of a father's training of his children in the LXX (cf. Wis 11:10; 12:25, 26; 1 Sam 3:13, where Eli is said to have failed in this respect with his sons). The noun νουθεσία occurs elsewhere in the NT only in 1 Cor 10:11 and Titus 3:10, while the verb νουθετεῖν, "to admonish," is found more frequently. In 1 Cor 4:14 Paul states that he is writing to admonish the Corinthians as his beloved children, and in Col 1:28 admonishing and teaching are seen as central to his ministry. This is also an activity that believers engage in with one another (cf. Rom 15:14; Col 3:16, where the verb again occurs with διδάσκειν, "to teach"). The activity of admonishing can take place through encouragement or reproof but usually implies that there is some difficulty or problem in the attitude or behavior of those receiving the admonition that needs to be resolved or some opposition to be overcome. As H. Cremer said of νουθεσία, "Its fundamental idea is the well-intentioned seriousness with which one would influence the mind and disposition of another by advice, admonition, warning, putting right according to circumstances" (*Biblico-Theological Lexicon of New Testament Greek* [Edinburgh: T. & T. Clark, 1895] 442; cf. also J. Behm, "νουθετέω, νουθεσία," *TDNT* 4 [1967] 1019–22).

The training and admonition to be given by fathers is described further as "of the Lord" (κυρίου). Some (cf. Meyer, 318; Bertram, *TDNT* 5 [1967] 624; Mussner, 163) see this as a subjective genitive referring to what the Lord does through the fathers as his representatives. This interpretation would also reflect the force of παιδεία κυρίου, "discipline of the Lord," in LXX Prov 3:11, where the Lord's discipline is the discipline he exercises. But we have already claimed that the sense of παιδεία here in Ephesians is broader than discipline, and it is more likely that the genitive is a genitive of quality, indicating that the training and admonition is that which is in the sphere of the Lord or has the Lord as its reference point, i.e., Christian instruction (cf. Mitton, 213, "truly Christian, compatible with loyalty to Christ as Lord"; cf. also Schlier, 283; Gnilka, 298–99; Gärtner, *Die Familienerziehung*, 38). The phrase ἐν Χριστῷ, "in Christ," functions in a similar way in *1 Clem.* 21.8, which states that children are "to participate in Christian instruction" (τῆς ἐν Χριστῷ παιδείας μεταλαμβάνειν). By specifying that the various forms of instruction are to be "of the Lord," the writer underlines that the education that goes on in the household has a new orientation. The learning Christ and being taught in him spoken of in 4:20, 21 is to be an activity that takes place not only in the Christian community in general but also specifically in the family, with the fathers as those who teach their children the apostolic tradition about Christ and help to shape their lives in accordance with it.

Explanation

The second section of Ephesians' household code, after that dealing with the marriage relationship, treats the second pairing often found in discussions of household management in the ancient world, that of parents and children. The writer is again reliant on the form of the household code mediated by Colossians (cf. Col 3:20, 21), and, as with the material on wives and husbands, he changes and expands his Colossian original, in particular by adding the OT citation and his comment on it in his exhortation to the children in 6:2, 3.

Just as previously the writer had addressed the subordinate group, the wives, first, so here again he follows a similar pattern, appealing first to the children to obey their parents. They are to do this, because it is part of their commitment to the Lord, because such behavior is generally held to be right, and because honoring father and mother is enjoined on children by the fifth commandment. Additionally this commandment is the first in the law that has a promise attached to it. The promise, whose wording the writer then cites after the first part of the commandment from LXX Exod 20:12 and to which a generalized force is given through the omission of the original reference to the land of Canaan, holds out well-being and long life on earth for those who honor their parents.

The writer's briefer exhortation to parents continues the androcentric perspective of the code, since it is not addressed to both parents but to fathers only, and reminds them not of their authority but of their responsibility, which is linked to their Christian faith. This responsibility is expressed both negatively and positively. They are not to abuse their authority by making their children angry. Instead, their rearing of their offspring should be marked by the sort of training and verbal admonition that is determined by their relationship to their Lord and that educates their children in the tradition about this Lord.

The advice the writer gives remains general, but is more elaborate, more positive, and more distinctively Christian than in the parallel passage in Colossians. The authority structure of the ancient household is maintained. But children are not seen as totally subject to the power of their parents. It is significant that the writer treats them as responsible moral agents to whom appeal needs to be made and that they are given four reasons for submitting to their parents in obedience. The primary one is that such behavior is appropriate to their ultimate allegiance to their Lord. The writer is, however, eclectic in his choice of warrants. After the first Christological one, he adds the appeal to "natural law," to what was seen to be fitting in the ancient world, and then the appeal to the Jewish law. In his appeal to fathers, paternal authority is assumed, but what is stressed is not fathers' rights or powers but the need to have regard for the dignity of the children by not making them angry through excessive harshness. Here, the Christological motivation is contained in the reference to the Lord in the second half of the exhortation about bringing up children in the training and admonition of the Lord. Corporal punishment is not mentioned, as it would have been in much contemporary advice from Greco-Roman and Hellenistic Jewish writers about the rearing of children. Instead, what is called for is teaching and correcting of children through practical example and through words that are aimed at producing lives shaped by the tradition about Christ the Lord.

As in the exhortation about marriage, this Christian paraenesis both adapts to and modifies the values of the surrounding society. It adapts to the patriarchal household, and the specific behavior enjoined, which balances obedience on the part of children with the restraint of harsh paternal authority, would have been the moderate line endorsed by many outside the churches. But the nature of the teaching to be given by fathers and the overriding Christological motivation would have given the relationship between Christian children and parents a distinctive ethos, particularly when it is remembered that, from this writer's perspective in 5:21, the relationship was to be seen as a specific case of the mutual submission of believers to each other, which should characterize the Christian community as a whole.

The writer wants his readers to realize that the child-parent relationship provides another specific sphere in which their obedience to their Lord is to be lived out in a society with varying ideals of what this relationship should entail and varying levels of attainment to those ideals. As we have seen with the previous section of the household code about marriage, the specifics of the code are tied to their own time and social setting. But again, the writer's creative stance can be suggestive for contemporary Christian families as they attempt to express and live out the mutual honor, respect, and loving admonition at the heart of the Christian message in a world where, on the one hand, parental power can be frequently abused, including even the sexual abuse of children, and, on the other hand, attempts to exercise moral discipline or correction of a child can frequently be denounced in the name of a child's freedom or autonomy.

Household Relationships—Slaves and Masters (6:5–9)

Translation

⁵ *Slaves, obey your earthly*[a] *masters with fear and trembling in singleness of heart, as you would obey Christ,*[b] ⁶ *not to catch their eye*[c] *as those who please men,*[d] *but as slaves of Christ doing the will of God wholeheartedly,*[e] ⁷ *serving with enthusiasm, as you would the Lord and not men,*[f] ⁸ *knowing that each person, if he does something good, will be recompensed for this by the Lord, whether he is a slave or free.* ⁹ *And masters, do the same to them, abandoning the use of threats, knowing that both their and your Master*[g] *is in heaven, and there is no partiality with him.*

Notes

[a] The Greek text describes the masters as κατὰ σάρκα, "according to the flesh." This sets up an implicit contrast with another sort of relationship to a master, and since in v 9 that other Master will be described as in heaven, "earthly" becomes an appropriate translation for the phrase used of the relationship to human masters.

[b] This clause provides a smoother translation of the Greek phrase ὡς τῷ Χριστῷ than the literal "as Christ."

[c] This translates the Greek phrase κατ᾽ ὀφθαλμοδουλίαν, literally, "according to eyeservice."

[d] ἄνθρωπος and its compound ἀνθρωπάρεσκοι need not be translated specifically as masculine terms, but the perspective of the passage is androcentric and those that the slaves would be pleasing are the masters, the male heads of households.

[e] The phrase in Greek is ἐκ ψυχῆς, literally, "from the soul."

[f] See *Note* d.

[g] The Greek text has κύριος in this reference to Christ. It would normally be translated as "Lord" but is here translated as "Master" to bring out the deliberate contrast with earthly masters (κύριοι). See also *Note* a.

Form/Structure/Setting

The third pairing in the household code is that of masters and slaves. Again, it should be remembered that the paraenesis of this part of the code is intended as part of the instruction about wise and Spirit-filled living (cf. 5:15–20) and is a specific instance of the mutual submission that is a consequence of being filled with the Spirit (cf. 5:21).

The outline of the formal structure of the paraenesis is similar to that noted in the earlier sections of the code, with the most variation occurring in the section of amplification on the imperative. Again, the subordinate group, here the slaves, is addressed first (v 5a). This is followed by the imperative and its appropriate object (here in the dative case after the verb ὑπακούειν, "obey your earthly masters"—v 5b). The amplification of the exhortation begins in v 5cd with two prepositional phrases, "with fear and trembling" and "in singleness of heart," and is followed by the comparative expression "as Christ," which introduces the note of Christological motivation (v 5e). This is explained negatively ("not to catch their eye as those who please men," v 6a) and positively ("but as slaves of Christ," v 6b) and then with the help of two participial clauses, "doing the will of God wholeheartedly" (v 6c) and "serving with enthusiasm as you would the Lord and not men" (v 7), of which the latter one repeats the motivation of vv 5e, 6ab. Finally, a reason clause beginning with εἰδότες ὅτι, "knowing that," introduces the warrant in v 8, which is "each person, if he does something good, will be recompensed for this by the Lord, whether he is a slave or free." The mention of "free" provides the transition to the advice to masters which now follows. This exhortation to the superior social grouping is similar, with an address, "and masters" (v 9a), an imperative with πρὸς αὐτούς, "to them," functioning as the indirect object in reference to the slaves, "do the same to them" (v 9b), amplification of this by means of a participial clause, "abandoning the use of threats" (v 9c), and a warrant, again introduced by εἰδότες ὅτι, "knowing that," which is formulated as "both their and your Master is in heaven, and there is no partiality with him" (v 9de).

This section of the household code, like the other two, is dependent on the form of the code mediated by Colossians. On the household code in general and its origins in particular, see under *Form/Structure/Setting* on 5:21–33. As in the case of the other two sections, the writer of Ephesians again adapts his source material creatively, here from Col 3:22–4:1.

Ephesians	*Colossians*
6:5 οἱ δοῦλοι, ὑπακούετε	3:22a οἱ δοῦλοι, ὑπακούετε κατὰ πάντα
τοῖς κατὰ σάρκα κυρίοις	3:22b τοῖς κατὰ σάρκα κυρίοις
μετὰ φόβου καὶ τρόμου	3:22e φοβούμενοι τὸν κύριον
ἐν ἁπλότητι τῆς καρδίας ὑμῶν ὡς τῷ Χριστῷ	3:22d ἀλλ᾽ ἐν ἁπλότητι καρδίας
6:6 μὴ κατ᾽ ὀφθαλμοδουλίαν ὡς ἀνθρωπάρεσκοι	3:22c μὴ ἐν ὀφθαλμοδουλίᾳ ὡς ἀνθρωπάρεσκοι
ἀλλ᾽ ὡς δοῦλοι Χριστοῦ ποιοῦντες τὸ θέλημα τοῦ θεοῦ ἐκ ψυχῆς	3:23a ὃ ἐὰν ποιῆτε, 3:23b ἐκ ψυχῆς ἐργάζεσθε,
6:7 μετ᾽ εὐνοίας δουλεύοντες, ὡς τῷ κυρίῳ καὶ οὐκ ἀνθρώποις	3:23c ὡς τῷ κυρίῳ καὶ οὐκ ἀνθρώποις,
6:8 εἰδότες ὅτι ἕκαστος,	3:24a εἰδότες ὅτι ἀπὸ κυρίου ἀπολήμψεσθε τὴν ἀνταπόδοσιν τῆς κληρονομίας
	3:24b τῷ κυρίῳ Χριστῷ δουλεύετε
ἐάν τι ποιήσῃ ἀγαθόν, τοῦτο κομίσεται παρὰ κυρίου, εἴτε δοῦλος εἴτε ἐλεύθερος.	3:25a ὁ γὰρ ἀδικῶν κομίσεται ὃ ἠδίκησεν, 3:25b καὶ οὐκ ἔστιν προσωπολημψία.
6:9 καὶ οἱ κύριοι, τὰ αὐτὰ ποιεῖτε πρὸς αὐτούς, ἀνιέντες τὴν ἀπειλήν, εἰδότες ὅτι	4:1a οἱ κύριοι, τὸ δίκαιον καὶ τὴν ἰσότητα τοῖς δούλοις παρέχεσθε, 4:1b εἰδότες ὅτι
καὶ αὐτῶν καὶ ὑμῶν ὁ κύριός ἐστιν ἐν οὐρανοῖς, καὶ προσωπολημψία οὐκ ἔστιν παρ᾽ αὐτῷ.	καὶ ὑμεῖς ἔχετε κύριον ἐν οὐρανῷ. 3:25b καὶ οὐκ ἔστιν προσωπολημψία.

The address to slaves, the imperative, and the description of masters as κατὰ σάρκα, "earthly," in Eph 6:5 are taken over from Col 3:22ab, but κατὰ

Form / Structure / Setting

πάντα, "in everything," is omitted. Ephesians then has the prepositional phrase "with fear and trembling," which appears to be an adaptation of the participial clause "fearing the Lord" from Col 3:22e. In Col 3:22 "but with singleness of heart" had followed on as a contrast to "not to catch their eye as those who please men," but in Eph 6:5 the former phrase is introduced first in its own right with the addition of the definite article (τῆς) before and the second person plural possessive adjective (ὑμῶν) after καρδίας, "heart." The Christological reference of Col 3:22e in terms of "the Lord" is then taken up at the end of Eph 6:5 in "as Christ." At this point, in 6:6, the writer of Ephesians brings in the expression "not to catch their eye as those who please men," which had appeared earlier in the Colossians paraenesis in 3:22c. He also introduces a slight variation in wording with κατ' ὀφθαλμοδουλίαν, "to catch their eye," replacing ἐν ὀφθαλμοδουλίᾳ, "by catching their eye." Whereas in Colossians the contrast to this expression had been "but in singleness of heart" (3:22d), in Eph 6:6 the contrast is ἀλλ' ὡς δοῦλοι Χριστοῦ, "but as slaves of Christ," terminology distinctive to the Ephesians' paraenesis but clearly building on the clause found later in the Colossians' pericope in 3:24b, τῷ κυρίῳ Χριστῷ δουλεύετε, "you are serving the Lord Christ." Col 3:23ab had exhorted slaves ὃ ἐὰν ποιῆτε, ἐκ ψυχῆς ἐργάζεσθε, "whatever you do, work wholeheartedly," and Eph 6:6 elaborates on what it means to be slaves of Christ by turning the Colossians' exhortation into a participial clause which relates the work of slaves to the will of God, ποιοῦντες τὸ θέλημα τοῦ θεοῦ ἐκ ψυχῆς, "doing the will of God wholeheartedly." Whereas Col 3:23c immediately states that the slaves' work is to be done "as to the Lord and not to men," Eph 6:7 adds another participial clause before repeating this same wording. That clause, μετ' εὐνοίας δουλεύοντες, "serving with enthusiasm," is distinctive to the passage in Ephesians but can again be related to Col 3:24b, "you are serving the Lord Christ." When it comes to the major warrant for the exhortation to slaves, both Eph 6:8 and Col 3:24a introduce this in the same way, εἰδότες ὅτι, "knowing that," and the central concept is the same, that of being recompensed by the Lord. Colossians puts this both positively (ἀπὸ κυρίου ἀπολήμψεσθε τὴν ἀνταπόδοσιν τῆς κληρονομίας, "from the Lord you will receive the reward of inheritance," 3:24a) and negatively (ὁ γὰρ ἀδικῶν κομίσεται ὃ ἠδίκησεν, "for he who does wrong will be recompensed for the wrong he has done," 3:25a), while Eph 6:8 simply has a more basic positive statement, ἕκαστος, ἐάν τι ποιήσῃ ἀγαθόν, τοῦτο κομίσεται παρὰ κυρίου, "each person, if he does something good, will be recompensed for this by the Lord." It omits Col 3:24b, "you are serving the Lord Christ," having already made this point in a different way, and replaces Col 3:25b, "and there is no partiality," which it will use in its exhortation to masters, with a similar thought that the principle of recompense applies "whether a person is a slave or free" (εἴτε δοῦλος εἴτε ἐλεύθερος). This last phrase of Eph 6:8 may well take up the language of Col 3:11 where it is said that in the new humanity, amongst various other categories, δοῦλος, "slave," and ἐλεύθερος, "free," no longer count, but instead Christ is all in all.

There is a similar relationship of dependence and modification in the exhortation to masters in the two letters. Eph 6:9 underlines the link with the exhortation to slaves both by the addition of καί, "and," in the address and by formulating its main imperative as "do the same to them" instead of the stronger imperative in Col 4:1a, "show justice and fairness to your slaves." Ephesians is, however, more specific in its instruction to masters in the participial phrase "abandoning the use of threats" (ἀνιέντες τὴν ἀπειλήν). Again, the warrants for the exhortations to masters are introduced in the same fashion by εἰδότες ὅτι, "knowing that" (Eph 6:9 and Col 4:1b), and both contain the same concept, that the masters have their own Lord or Master in heaven. But while Col 4:1b has the basic assertion καὶ ὑμεῖς ἔχετε κύριον ἐν οὐρανῷ, "you also have a Master in heaven," Eph 6:9 varies this with the plural expression ἐν οὐρανοῖς, lit. "in the heavens." Ephesians also strengthens the notes of mutual relationship and joint accountability in the slave-master pairing by describing the Master in heaven as καὶ αὐτῶν καὶ ὑμῶν ὁ κύριος, "both their and your Master," and adding "and there is no partiality with him," a formulation virtually the same as that which had been employed in the warrant to slaves in Col 3:25b.

This pericope also contains ideas and wording reminiscent of the undisputed Pauline letters. The additional phrase "with fear and trembling" in 6:5 is found in 2 Cor 7:15 (cf. also 1 Cor 2:3) and Phil 2:12, and in the latter instance also modifies the verb "to obey" (ὑπακούειν). The terminology "slaves of Christ" is used of Paul in Rom 1:1 and of Paul and Timothy in Phil 1:1. In addition, when Paul calls himself a slave of Christ in Gal 1:10, he contrasts this with the notion of pleasing people, as does the writer here in 6:6. In the discussion of the situations of slave and free in 1 Cor 7, the person who was free when called is said to be a slave of Christ, and both groups are called on not to become slaves of men (cf. 7:22, 23). The belief that each person will be recompensed for the good he or she has done is found in both 2 Cor 5:10, where the verb κομίζειν also occurs, and in Rom 2:6–11. In the latter case there is also the wording "for there is no partiality with God," which, mediated via Col 3:25b, is now applied to Christ in the exhortation to masters in 6:9. The language "whether he is a slave or free" of 6:8, as has been noted, takes up most immediately the variation on the baptismal formulation of Gal 3:28 in Col 3:11, but it matches more exactly the variation on that formulation in 1 Cor 12:13. In each case, this occurrence of additional Pauline terminology from the undisputed Pauline corpus is best explained by the hypothesis of Ephesians' expansion of material from Colossians, rather than finding in Col 3:22–4:1 an edited version of Eph 6:5–9 (*pace* W. Munro, *Authority in Paul and Peter* [Cambridge: CUP, 1983] 27–29).

As is to be expected, 6:5–9 has its closest ties within the letter to the surrounding paraenesis, although there are also one or two links with the first part of the letter. The notion of the subordinate group within the household obeying the group with superior status (6:5) has already been encountered in the case of children's attitude to parents in 6:1, and the response of fear (6:5) has also been met already in the case of wives' attitudes to husbands (5:33; cf. also 5:21). The motivation "as Christ" (6:5) corresponds to the earlier motivation in the code "as to the Lord" (5:22) and "in the Lord" (6:1). "Doing the will of God" (6:6) is reminiscent of the exhortation in 5:17 about understanding the will of the Lord and of the talk of God's will in the address (1:1) and in the opening eulogy (1:5, 9, 11). Again, the idea of doing good (6:8) reminds one of the exhortation to the erstwhile thief in 4:28 to do good with his own hands and of the earlier emphasis on good works (2:10) and what is good

(5:9). Finally, when masters are told that both they and their slaves have a Master in heaven (6:9), this can be seen as in continuity with the letter's cosmic perspective in which attention has been focused on Christ as the heavenly Lord (cf. 1:20; 2:6; 4:10).

The paraenesis to slaves and masters clearly has a general setting in life in the institution of slavery in the first-century Greco-Roman world. There are questions about the more specific setting of the early Christians' relation to this institution and the conditions that may have called forth the emphases of the household codes of both Colossians and Ephesians. Only a few of the salient features of first-century slavery can be described here, and for this purpose S. S. Bartchy's monograph has proved particularly helpful. (For other discussions see the following works.)

Bartchy, S. S. *ΜΑΛΛΟΝ ΧΡΗΣΑΙ: First-Century Slavery and the Interpretation of 1 Corinthians 7:21*. Missoula, MT: Scholars, 1973. **Buckland, W. W.** *The Roman Law of Slavery*. Cambridge: C.U.P., 1970. **Finley, M. I.,** ed. *Slavery in Classical Antiquity*. Cambridge: W. Heffer, 1960. **Gayer, R.** *Die Stellung des Sklaven in den paulinischen Gemeinden und bei Paulus*. Bern: H. Lang, 1976. **Gülzow, H.** *Christentum und Sklaverei in den ersten drei Jahrhunderten*. Bonn: R. Habelt, 1969. **Laub, F.** *Die Begegnung des frühen Christentums mit der antiken Sklaverei*. Stuttgart: Katholisches Bibelwerk, 1982. **Schweizer, E.** "Zum Sklavenproblem im Neuen Testament." *EvT* 32 (1972) 502–6. **Stuhlmacher, P.** *Der Brief an Philemon*. Zürich: Benzinger, 1975, esp. 42–48. **Urbach, E. E.** "The Laws Regarding Slavery as a Source for Social History of the Period of the Second Temple, the Mishnah and Talmud." *Papers of the Institute of Jewish Studies* (London), ed. J. G. Weiss. Jerusalem, 1964, 1:1–94. **Vogt, J.** "The Structure of Ancient Slave Wars." *Ancient Slavery and the Ideal of Man*. Tr. T. Wiedemann. Cambridge, MA: Harvard, 1975, 39–102. **Westermann, W. L.** *The Slave Systems of Greek and Roman Antiquity*. 3rd Edition. Philadelphia: American Philosophical Society, 1964. **Wiedemann, T.** *Greek and Roman Slavery*. London: Croom Helm, 1981. **Zeitlin, S.** "Slavery during the Second Commonwealth and the Tannaitic Period." *JQR* 53 (1962–63) 185–218.

The early Christians' apparent indifference to the institution of slavery has to be seen in the light of the prevailing attitudes to slavery. Hardly anyone considered the system optional or thought of an alternative. In fact, although there were debates about how slaves should be treated (e.g., Seneca, *Ep.* 47), slavery as a social, legal, and economic phenomenon seldom became the object of reflection at all. No ancient government thought of abolishing the institution, and none of the slave rebellions had as its goal the abolition of slavery as such (cf. Bartchy, *First-Century Slavery*, 63, 116–17). "The institution of slavery was a fact of Mediterranean economic life so completely accepted as a part of the labour structure of the time that one cannot correctly speak of the slave 'problem' in antiquity" (Westermann, *Slave Systems*, 215).

As we have seen, the master-slave relationship was mentioned in the traditional discussions of household management where the focus was on how a master should rule his slaves. Aristotle (*Pol.* 1.1253b–1254a) deals with this relationship at greater length than with the other two, and Philodemus (*Concerning Household Management* 30.18–31.2) is fairly typical with his advice that slaves' work, food, and punishment should be kept moderate. Elsewhere, Aristotle expounds his view that the relationship between master and slave in the household is one in which it is inappropriate to talk about justice, because there can be no injustice in relating to things that are one's own, and a slave is a man's chattel (cf. *Eth. Nic.* 5.1134b). He can say, "for where there is nothing common to ruler and ruled, there is not friendship either, since there is not justice; e.g., between craftsman and tool, soul and body, master and slave; the latter in each case is benefited by that which uses it, but there is no friendship nor justice towards lifeless things. . . . For there is nothing common to the two parties; the slave is a living tool and the tool a lifeless slave" (*Eth. Nic.* 8.1161ab). Later Stoic views were, however, much more humanitarian. Seneca (*Ep.* 47) provides the most well-known discourse on treating slaves as human beings: " 'These people are slaves.' No: they are human beings. 'These people are slaves.' No: they are those with whom you share your roof. 'These people are slaves.' No: when you consider how much power Chance can exert over you both, they are fellow-slaves." Seneca goes on: "I don't want to let myself go on this vast topic, and give you a homily on how to treat your slaves: we behave toward them in a proud, cruel and insulting fashion. The sum of what I wish to preach is this: treat those whose status is inferior to your own in the same manner as you would wish your own superior to treat you." Impressive as this rhetoric is, Seneca did nothing to try to change the actual institution of slavery, and Wiedemann's comment (*Greek and Roman Slavery*, 233) is that in practice "Seneca is much more interested in writing exciting Latin than in improving the conditions of his readers' slaves." Palestinian Judaism accepted the institution of slavery, with slaves being viewed as the property of their masters. According to Philo, the Therapeutae and the Essenes rejected it (cf. Philo, *Quod Omnis* 79; *De Vita Cont.* 70). As far as the Essenes are concerned, this attitude to slavery probably holds only for the core community in the desert and not for any Essenes who, like the early Christians, continued to live in society, since the Damascus Rule contains instructions on the treatment of slaves (cf. CD 11.12; 12.10–12; cf. also Stuhlmacher, *Philemon*, 47). Although Josephus (*c. Ap.* 2.3 § 215–17) can call for slaves to receive severe punishments for their offenses, in general Hellenistic Jewish writings reflect contemporary Hellenistic appeals to masters to treat their slaves reasonably (cf. Sir 4:30; 7:20, 21; 33:31; Philo, *De Spec. Leg.* 2.66–68, 89–91; 3.137–43; Ps.-Phocylides 224). Philo saw slaves as indispensable, "for the course of life contains a vast number of circumstances which demand the ministrations of slaves" (*De Spec. Leg.* 2.123). Although he does not address slaves directly, he talks of instructions given "to servants on rendering an affectionate loyalty to their masters, to masters on showing the gentleness and kindness by which inequality is equalized" (*De Decal.* 167).

Modern readers need to free themselves from a number of assumptions about first-century slavery, including the assumptions that there was a wide separation between the status of slave and freedperson, that all slaves were badly treated, and that all who were enslaved were trying to free themselves from this bondage. It is true that Roman *law* distinguished sharply between the status of slave and free in terms of the legal powerlessness of the slave, but in *practice* there was a broad continuum of statuses between slave and free in both Roman and Greek society. For example, slaves of Greek owners could own property, including their own slaves, and could obtain permission to take other employment in addition to their duties as slaves. Greek law defined four elements of freedom—freedom to act as one's own legal person, freedom from being seized as property, freedom to earn a living in the way one wanted, and freedom of movement, including the right to live where one wished. But to establish freedperson status only the granting of the first of these was necessary. In practice any other aspects of freedom were often greatly curtailed in favor of the former slave owner, because before slaves were manumitted they had to sign a contract which could require them to make a regular payment and provide various services to their previous owners and which would specify what would happen to them and their property if they failed to do so. Slaves of Roman masters also continued to have specific obligations to their patrons after manumission, and so the step from the status of slave to freedperson was often a very small one in practice (cf. Bartchy, *First-Century Slavery*, 40–44, 73–74, 115). The change in legal status was, however, an important one for most people, affecting their own sense of social identity and the perception of their social status by others, and so many slaves did work hard to achieve manumission. During the first century c.e. there was an increase in the ease and frequency of manumission, and this relieved the sort of pressures that might have provoked slave revolts. Domestic and urban slaves could expect to be manumitted as a reward for hard work after serving their owners for ten to twenty years. It was also frequently in the owners' own interests to manumit their slaves, since their labor could be obtained more cheaply if they were freedpersons. It should be noted, however, that while there were a number of ways in which slaves could encourage owners to manumit them, there were no ways in which they could refuse freedperson status if owners decided to manumit them, since they had no legal rights (cf. Bartchy, *First-Century Slavery*, 98, 104, 118–19). Despite the general picture of increasing manumission in the first-century Greco-Roman world, it seems to have taken place less frequently in Asia Minor, in whose cities freedpersons would have been a smaller proportion of the population than, for example, in Rome (cf. Verner, *Household of God*, 44, 63).

Although the Roman *"paterfamilias* had complete control over all slaves owned in his *familia,* the power of punishment by whipping and by confinement in the *ergastulum,* and the right of execution of the death penalty" (Westermann, *Slave Systems,* 76), daily life was usually much better than this legal situation might suggest, especially for domestic slaves. Inevitably, a person's experience as a slave depended primarily on the character and social status of his or her master. But in general slaves were treated reasonably well, if only because their masters recognized that this was the way to get the best out of them. An owner's treatment of his slaves was frequently similar to his treatment of his children, and the master who was considerate toward his children would behave similarly toward his slaves. This is not, of course, to paint a picture of paradise as descriptive of the domestic slave's situation. There were undoubtedly far too many cases of cruelty, brutality, and injustice, but there was no general climate of unrest among slaves (cf. Bartchy, *First-Century Slavery,* 85–87, 115).

One-third of the population of Greece and Italy was enslaved. The work of these slaves covered the whole range of activities in the ancient world—from privileged positions in the household of the emperor to working in the mines. In between came such work as the civil service, medical care, teaching, accountancy, business, domestic work, and agricultural employment. By the first century C.E., the main supply of slaves was no longer through war or piracy but rather through birth in the house of a slave owner. This produced a different social climate, as Bartchy notes: "These house-born slaves were given training for a wide variety of domestic, industrial and public tasks of increasing importance and sensitivity. Roman legal practice kept pace with this development by guaranteeing to those in slavery more humane treatment" (*First-Century Slavery*, 117). Many slaves in the Greco-Roman world enjoyed more favorable living conditions than many free laborers. Contrary to the supposition that everyone was trying to avoid slavery at all costs, it is clear that some people actually sold themselves into slavery in order to climb socially, to obtain particular employment open only to slaves, and to enjoy a better standard of living than they had experienced as free persons. Being a slave had the benefit of providing a certain personal and social security (cf. Bartchy, *First-Century Slavery*, 46, 116).

Some scholars (e.g., Crouch, *Origins*, 126–27; Schüssler Fiorenza, *Memory*, 214–18) have argued that Christian talk of "freedom" and the baptismal formulation represented in Gal 3:28 would have aroused expectations of manumission in the minds of slaves and that the paraenesis about the slave-master relationship in the household codes should therefore be viewed as a reaction against such unrest among Christian slaves. But as has been said, there was no general desire to obtain manumission at all costs. In a situation where the majority of slaves were born in the house of their owners, talk of freedom in the sense of an inner or spiritual freedom could receive a sympathetic hearing. Stoics had already been teaching that true freedom was dependent on one's inner attitude rather than outward circumstances (cf., e.g., Epictetus, *Diss.* 4.1; cf. also Bartchy, *First-Century Slavery*, 65–67, 117). It may well be that Gal 3:28 was understood by the Corinthian *women* in terms of an emancipation in their social roles. It is certainly significant that Paul does not include the male-female pairing in the variation on the traditional formula in 1 Cor 12:13. But there is no evidence that the formula was understood in a similar way by slaves. In fact, Paul was able to employ the circumcision-uncircumcision and slave-free pairings as illustrations of his main point in 1 Cor 7:17–24, precisely because these were not the source of problems in Corinth. As Balch (*Wives*, 107) observes, "If Gal 3:28 was not understood by the Corinthian slaves as modifying their social role, the assumption that this baptismal formula stimulated such 'unrest' among slaves that it formed the background against which the household code must be understood is without foundation" (cf. also MacDonald, *Pauline Churches*, 112).

Christian slaves posed no direct political threat to society by calling for emancipation, but there was one major area in which there was potential for causing offense. Domestic slaves were considered part of the household and, therefore, were generally expected to share the religion of the *paterfamilias*. But those slaves who converted to Christianity refused to participate in the worship of the traditional gods. Balch (*Wives*, 90) claims, "In this sense Christianity, following Jewish precedent, brought a new understanding of personhood to slaves by teaching that they had a right to choose their own God." This may, however, be an overstatement of the case, since under the principate Romans, in fact, became more tolerant about slaves' participation in other cults, and there was considerable freedom for slaves to practice their own religion (cf. Laub, *Begegnung,* 56–62).

Paul had treated the distinction between slave and free as irrelevant for life in the new community (cf. Gal 3:28; 1 Cor 12:13). He recognized some advantages in manumission and advised slaves whose masters set them free to make use of this new opportunity (1 Cor 7:21), but if there was no chance of such freedom this did not matter, since "he who was called in the Lord as a slave is a freedman of the Lord. Likewise, he who was free when called is a slave of Christ" (1 Cor 7:22). In the church, slaves were to be seen as full brothers and sisters in the Lord, and masters were to accept them in this way (cf. Philemon). Colossians continues with a similar emphasis. Col 3:11 repeats the notion of there being no distinction between slave and free in the new community, while the Colossian household code makes clear that the writer saw a difference between status in the church and roles in the Christian household, where the hierarchical social structures still pertain. What is perhaps most striking about the codes of Colossians and Ephesians, however, is that slaves are addressed not simply as members of the household but as full members of the church. Nor is it simply, as in some other societies or cults, that there was no distinction between masters and slaves in the ritual activities, but these codes reflect the life of a community in which, despite the differences in their duties, both slaves and free can equally fully practice their faith in everyday life. Virtues are encouraged in slaves not only, as in the traditional discussions of household management, because these will enhance the well-being of the household and its head, but because slaves are valued as persons whose obedience to Christ is as important as that of other social groups in the church into which they have been fully integrated (cf. also Laub, *Begegnung,* 91–93).

There has been discussion about why in the Colossian code so great a proportion of the paraenesis is addressed to slaves as compared with that addressed to masters. Some have attempted to relate this phenomenon to the case of Onesimus (cf. esp. J. Knox, *Philemon among the Letters of Paul* [Chicago: Chicago University Press, 1935] 13–24; but against this cf., e.g., Crouch, *Origins,* 11). But it may be that it reflects the social composition of the church addressed, which contained more slaves than slave owners. Alternatively, it may be that the code reflects the perspective of the leaders of the community, "and the ethos of the leaders is rather more that of the owners than of the slaves" (W. Meeks, *The First Urban Christians* [New Haven: Yale University Press, 1983] 64). MacDonald (*Pauline Churches,* 114–15) also argues that this emphasis in Colossians may represent a tightening of organizational structures in the post-Pauline churches, restricting any leadership on the part of slaves and putting power more firmly in the hands of masters. However, this view may blur too much the distinction these Pauline churches still seem to have been able to make between what went on in the community's gatherings for worship and what went on in the everyday life of the household in closer contact with the surrounding society (cf. also Meeks, *First Urban Christians,* 161–62, on the ambiguity of the relation between the reality presented in Christian ritual and everyday reality). In devoting more attention to slaves, Ephesians is simply following the precedent of Colossians, in which also four verses are addressed to slaves and one to masters. In terms of reciprocity, both Colossians and Ephesians fare better than the later Pastorals (cf. 1 Tim 6:1, 2; Titus 2:9–10), where masters are not addressed at all about their duties toward slaves, where the author clearly writes from the perspective of the householder, and where the church itself is now understood on the model of the patriarchal household.

Comment

5 οἱ δοῦλοι, ὑπακούετε τοῖς κατὰ σάρκα κυρίοις μετὰ φόβου καὶ τρόμου ἐν ἁπλότητι τῆς καρδίας ὑμῶν ὡς τῷ Χριστῷ, "Slaves, obey your earthly masters with fear and trembling in singleness of heart, as you would obey Christ." As has been noted, advice about how slaves should conduct themselves can be found elsewhere, but what does seem to be unprecedented about the advice to slaves in the Pauline corpus is its direct address to the slaves themselves (cf. also 1 Cor 7:21; Col 3:22). In this version of the household code, the writer makes clear that he views slaves as ethically responsible agents and appeals to them to obey their earthly masters. The designation "earthly masters" points to the play on the terms κύριος, "lord, master," and δοῦλος, "slave," that runs through the pericope. Those addressed, who are literally slaves (v 5), are also asked to see themselves as metaphorically slaves of Christ (v 6), and their obedience to their literal masters (v 5) is to be seen as part of their obedience to the true Lord (vv 7, 8). In fact, the contrast between the fleshly or earthly masters (v 5) and the Lord or Master in heaven (v 9) ties the passage together. For Christian slaves there was ultimately only one κύριος, and reminding them of this by calling their masters κατὰ σάρκα in distinction from the Master in heaven immediately sets the social structures of the household in a Christian perspective and limits their significance. Despite this relativizing of the relationship, slaves' obedience to their master is to be thoroughgoing. What is involved in such obedience will be explained positively (v 5b), negatively (v 6a), and then positively again (vv 6b, 7). It is to be carried out not just with fear, the attitude required of wives in relation to their husbands in 5:33 and 1 Pet 3:2, or of citizens in relation to the state in Rom 13:7, or elsewhere of slaves in relation to their masters in 1 Pet 2:18, *Did.* 4.11 and *Barn.* 19.7, but "with fear and trembling," a phrase found frequently in the LXX (e.g., Gen 9:2; Exod 15:16; Deut 2:25; Ps 2:11; Isa 19:16), three times in Paul (1 Cor 2:3; 2 Cor 7:15; Phil 2:12), and in a verbal form in Mark 5:33, and which functions here to intensify the attitude of respect for the authority of masters. It emphasizes the obedience owed to human masters, not to God or Christ (*pace* Caird, 90, who reads Col 3:22, "fearing the Lord," into Eph 6:5). Proper obedience will also be carried out "in singleness of heart," a phrase which underlines the purity of motivation which should characterize slaves' relationship to their masters. The heart, seen as the inner center which determines attitudes and actions, is to have integrity and singleness of purpose. For this virtue of uprightness or integrity of heart, the "simple goodness, which gives itself without reserve" (BAGD 86) see, e.g., 1 Chr 29:17; Wis 1:1; 1 Macc 2:37; *T. Iss.* 3.1–6; 4.1–6:1; *T. Reub.* 4.1;

T. Sim. 4.5; 2 Cor 11:3; Col 3:22. This sort of inner commitment is made possible by slaves seeing in their obedience to their masters obedience to Christ, the heavenly Master. This perspective does not mean that earthly masters stand in Christ's stead as his representatives, as in *Did.* 4.11 (*pace* Schlier, 284). Rather, in their service to their masters, slaves are to see the opportunity to serve Christ and to perform their work as if they were doing it for Christ. This Christological motivation is a major factor in the paraenesis to slaves and is found not only here in ὡς τῷ Χριστῷ, "as to Christ," but also in ὡς δοῦλοι Χριστοῦ, "as slaves of Christ" (v 6), ὡς τῷ κυρίῳ, "as to the Lord" (v 7), and παρὰ κυρίου, "by the Lord" (v 8). In this way, everyday work is related to the lordship of Christ, and the instructions provide a specific application of the exhortation found in Col 3:17, "Whatever you do, in word or deed, do everything in the name of the Lord Jesus."

6, 7 μὴ κατ᾽ ὀφθαλμοδουλίαν ὡς ἀνθρωπάρεσκοι, "not to catch their eye as those who please men." The integrity called for will exclude the dissimulation and fawning referred to in terms of trying to catch their masters' eye or to find approval with them. ὀφθαλμοδουλία, literally "eyeservice," is a word not attested earlier than its two NT occurrences, here and in Col 3:22. In context here it indicates the sort of service carried out by slaves in order to attract their masters' attention. It could also refer to doing only what the masters can see and, therefore, acting differently and cutting corners when their backs are turned (cf. C. F. D. Moule, "A Note on ὀφθαλμοδουλία," *ExpTim* 59 [1947–48] 250). The expression "as those who please men" continues the notion of currying favor with the masters, and this idea of pleasing men is found elsewhere (e.g., Ps 52:6; *Pss. Sol.* 4.7, 8, 19; Gal 1:10; 1 Thess 2:4; Col 3:22; 2 *Clem.* 13.1; Ign. *Rom.* 2.1; Justin, *Apol.* 1.2).

ἀλλ᾽ ὡς δοῦλοι Χριστοῦ ποιοῦντες τὸ θέλημα τοῦ θεοῦ ἐκ ψυχῆς, "but as slaves of Christ doing the will of God wholeheartedly." Those who are simply out to please their masters are slaves of men, but the writer wants his addressees to see themselves primarily as slaves of Christ. Their allegiance lies ultimately not to other people but to Christ, and their aim should be not to please men but "to learn what is pleasing to the Lord" (cf. 5:10). The designation "slaves of Christ" intensifies the idea of carrying out obedience to masters as part of obedience to Christ from 6:5. This way of speaking can be compared with Paul's relativizing of the social status of slave and free in 1 Cor 7:20–22, where he calls the free man a slave of Christ. Here the writer does not explicitly call slave owners slaves of Christ, although this is implicit in the reminder that will come to them that they have a Master in heaven. Believing slaves who perform their household duties as slaves of Christ will also be doing the will of God, since that will has been expressed supremely in Christ. For this writer, the will of God which has its focus in Christ is concerned not only with his plan for salvation and the cosmos (cf. 1:5, 9, 11) but also with the everyday life of household work and duties. Those who see themselves as slaves of Christ will carry out God's will in the sphere of the household ἐκ ψυχῆς, lit. "from the soul" (cf. similar expressions in *T. Gad* 2.1; *T. Benj.* 1.5). There is a shift from the mention of the heart in the previous verse to the soul as the inner center. The two terms are virtually synonymous in the LXX version of the great commandment in Deut 6:5, "you shall love the Lord your God with all your heart, and with all your soul, and with all your might" (cf. also Mark 12:30 and pars.). Again the emphasis is on an inner motivation that is wholehearted and unreserved and that contrasts with the earlier "eyeservice" motivated by external considerations. For slaves to have their hearts and souls in doing the will of God in their work would make possible an experience of inner independence within their situation.

μετ' εὐνοίας δουλεύοντες, ὡς τῷ κυρίῳ καὶ οὐκ ἀνθρώποις, "serving with enthusiasm, as you would the Lord and not men." This clause underlines the points the writer has already made in his paraenesis. Slaves' service is to be done not just for their masters but instead is to be determined by their obedience to the one Lord. This will mean that their service is performed enthusiastically rather than grudgingly or out of sheer necessity. εὔνοια, "good will, enthusiasm, zeal," is seen as a virtue of slaves in Lucian, *Bis Accus.* 16; Ecclus, *On Justice* 78.10–11; and POxy 494.6, a papyrus dated 156 C.E. in which in a master's will a number of slaves are to be set free because of their enthusiasm and affection (κατ' εὔνοιαν καὶ φιλοστοργίαν) in serving their master (for a translation of this will, cf. Wiedemann, *Greek and Roman Slavery*, 101).

8 εἰδότες ὅτι ἕκαστος, ἐάν τι ποιήσῃ ἀγαθόν, τοῦτο κομίσεται παρὰ κυρίου, εἴτε δοῦλος εἴτε ἐλεύθερος, "knowing that each person, if he does something good, will be recompensed for this by the Lord, whether he is a slave or free." The preceding participles and the whole exhortation to obedience are grounded in the reminder that the Lord will reward each one for the good that he does. Some discussions of household management recommended motivating slaves by holding out various rewards, for example, more praise, more food, better clothing, and shoes (cf. Xenophon, *Oec.* 13.9–12). This code attempts to motivate Christian slaves by holding before them the prospect of eschatological reward: no good deed will go unrecompensed (on κομίζεσθαι and the writer's use of the idea of the connection between deed and reward to underline the relationship between a way of life and its ultimate outcome, see S. H. Travis, *Christ and the Judgment of God* [London: Marshall Pickering, 1966] 110–113). Even if work seems to go unrecognized by earthly masters, this is no reason to start trying to catch their eye, because the heavenly Master sees all that is done and will respond accordingly. This latter thought holds for both slave and free. In regard to reward from the heavenly Master, earthly social status makes no difference. The concept of reward, particularly at the final judgment, was a common one in Judaism and is taken over in the NT. In the light of the allusion in the next verse (via Col 3:25) to the impartiality of God in Rom 2:11, it may well be that the thought of Rom 2:6–10 about reward for the one who does good has also been an influence here (cf. also 2 Cor 5:10). It is surprising, however, in light of its use earlier in this letter (cf. 1:14, 18; 5:5) that the writer does not take over the notion from Col 3:24 of the reward as "the inheritance." It is noteworthy that when the concept of reward becomes more specific in the parallel passage in Col 3:25, the focus is on the negative and it functions as a threat, "for the wrongdoer will be paid back for the wrong he has done." But here in Ephesians the positive formulation of being recompensed for doing something good acts as an encouragement. However, the emphasis is not just on reward at the final judgment as consolation for slaves. The stress in v 8 is on "each one," and reward for good applies equally

to both slave and free (cf. also Gnilka, 301). The expression "whether slave or free" may well allude to the early Christian baptismal tradition which pronounced that there was no distinction between slave and free in Christ (cf. the formulations in Col 3:11; 1 Cor 12:13, where this expression is found in the plural; and Gal 3:28). In this application of the tradition to the household, the emphasis is on the equal standing of slave and free at the future judgment. The Christian household retains the distinctive social statuses of slave and free, but in light of the coming judgment they are ultimately insignificant.

9 καὶ οἱ κύριοι, τὰ αὐτὰ ποιεῖτε πρὸς αὐτούς, ἀνιέντες τὴν ἀπειλήν, εἰδότες ὅτι καὶ αὐτῶν καὶ ὑμῶν ὁ κύριός ἐστιν ἐν οὐρανοῖς, καὶ προσωπολημψία οὐκ ἔστιν παρ' αὐτῷ, "And masters, do the same to them, abandoning the use of threats, knowing that both their and your Master is in heaven, and there is no partiality with him." By means of both the mention of the free at the end of the previous verse and the connective καί, "and," the writer ties the paraenesis to slaves and that to masters closely together. The link is strengthened further by the main imperative to masters being framed as "do the same to them." In comparison to the equivalent imperative in Col 4:1, this imperative seems rather colorless, but the writer's main concern is to foster a sense of reciprocity and in his paraenesis to place the two groups as nearly as possible on the same footing. "Do the same" does not refer specifically to doing good in v 8, but rather to having a corresponding attitude to that required of the slaves, namely, making their service of the one heavenly Master determinative for their actions. Both masters and slaves have the same Lord, and, therefore, both have the same standard of conduct in their relationship to each other. Whereas Seneca (*Ep.* 47; see under *Form/Structure/Setting* for this quotation) had reminded masters that they were under the same power, Chance, and were therefore fellow slaves, this writer reminds Christian masters that they are under the same Lord, Christ, as their slaves, and are, therefore, his fellow slaves. If masters realize this, it will mean that, although they have power, they will not abuse it by heavy-handed threats of punishment, treating their slaves as property on whom they can arbitrarily work out their frustrations (Seneca's comments on the importance of masters' controlling their anger illustrate the vulnerability of slaves to their masters' moods; cf. *De Ira* 3.24.2; 3.32.1, and Wiedemann, *Greek and Roman Slavery*, 179–80). Angry threatening would simply humiliate slaves and would at best produce "eyeservice." It would not encourage obedience from the heart or serving with enthusiasm. The mutual relationship of master and slave before their Lord (cf. 5:21) is stressed twice more, and each time the insistence on this is much more explicit than the equivalent paraenesis in Colossians. First, the writer reminds masters that "both their and your Master is in heaven," whereas Col 4:1 simply has "you also have a Master in heaven." Then he adds "and there is no partiality with him." This thought has now been employed in connection with both groups in Ephesians (cf. the equivalent "whether slave or free" in v 8) in contrast to Colossians, where it is only used in regard to slaves. Mitton (217) notes the appropriateness of the emphasis on impartiality being used in the address to masters rather than to slaves, since the higher up in social status people feel themselves to be, the more likely they are to expect to be accorded special consideration.

The noun προσωπολημψία, "partiality" (cf. Col 3:25; Rom 2:11), comes from the Hebraistic verbal expression πρόσωπον λαμβάνειν, "to show partiality, to judge purely at face value or on the basis of external factors" (cf. Lev 19:15; Deut 10:17; Sir 4:22, 27; 1 Esd 4:39; Luke 20:21; Gal 2:6; *Barn.* 19.4; *Did.* 4.3). In the OT and Jewish writings, impartiality in judgment is attributed to God (cf. esp. Sir 35:11–13; *Jub.* 5.15–19; *Pss. Sol.* 2.18; cf. also Rom 2:11; 1 Pet 1:17), but here and in Colossians this is transferred to Christ as Lord. In Rom 2:11, the notion of there being no partiality with God is associated explicitly with the last judgment. This association may be implicit here, but the assertion of Christ's impartiality functions more to make masters conscious of their present accountability, which they share equally with their slaves, to their heavenly Lord (*pace* Schüsser Fiorenza, *In Memory of Her*, 268, it cannot be stated in an unqualified fashion that "while the author insists on the mutuality, unity and equality of uncircumcised and circumcised here and now, he maintains such equality for slaves and freeborn only for the eschatological future"). In *Divine Impartiality: Paul and a Theological Axiom* (Chico, CA: Scholars Press, 1982, esp. 178–83), J. M. Bassler analyzes the way in which Paul adapted the tradition about God's impartiality and made it the theological axiom behind his advocacy of the equality of Jew and Gentile in the church. She also notes correctly that the apostle's vision of impartiality was reapplied in the household code in a way that was not foreign to his own statement in Gal 3:28: "If social conditions did not permit or encourage at that time a full emancipation movement to realize in history the programmatic 'neither slave nor free,' yet it is clear that there was within the Christian communities a movement, apparently rather widespread, to relax the distinction between master and slave and to ameliorate the conditions of servitude" (ibid., 183). This attitude reflected in the codes could also appeal to the divine impartiality which now has Christ as its agent. In Eph 6:9, the assertion of Christ's impartiality is part of the warrant that grounds the exhortation to masters, reminding them that their higher social status gives them no advantage in Christ's eyes and that they are to treat their slaves in this light as fellow servants of the heavenly Master (cf. also Gnilka, 302; Bassler, *Divine Impartiality*, 178).

Explanation

What is true of the household code as a whole, namely that its injunctions are to be seen as illustrating the wise living and mutual submission of those who are filled with the Spirit (cf. 5:15, 21), needs to be kept in mind in considering its third and final part, the exhortations to slaves and masters. For this section, the writer again adapts the equivalent part of the Colossians code (3:22–4:1). He adds some expressions familiar from the undisputed Pauline letters, and in the process he develops his own distinctive advice.

As in the previous two pairings, the subordinate group is addressed first. In a fashion unprecedented in the traditional discussions of household management, slaves are appealed to directly. They are treated as ethically responsible persons who are as fully members of the Christian community as their masters. In line with the expectations of the traditional household code, they are exhorted in v 5 to obey their masters and to carry out their obedience both with deep respect for the masters and with a commitment characterized by integrity and singleness of purpose. The Christian perspective of this paraenesis emerges clearly through the reminder that their masters are earthly (in comparison with the Master in heaven, v 9) and through the appeal to carry out the obedience as obedience to Christ. The writer elaborates further on the call to obedience with integrity in v 6 by pointing out, on the negative side, that this should not involve a superficial working aimed only at attracting the attention of masters and gaining their favor and, on the positive side, that it will instead mean performing their duties in the light of their ultimate allegiance to Christ, as they see themselves as Christ's slaves who are out to please him by doing God's will wholeheartedly and unreservedly. The same basic points are underscored in v 7, as slaves are exhorted to serve enthusiastically and in a way that shows they are ultimately serving not human masters but the one Lord or Master. Finally, in v 8 these appeals are grounded in the reminder that slaves will be recompensed for the good that they do, not by earthly masters offering praise, material benefits, or even manumission but by *the* Master rewarding their good service at the final judgment. The encouragement to wholehearted service, which this thought offers, applies, however, not only to slaves but also to freedpersons and masters. In the light of the future judgment and its rewards, both slave and free stand on equal footing.

This notion also provides a neat transition to the appeal to masters which follows more briefly in v 9. There is a striking note of reciprocity in the call to masters to do the same to slaves as slaves are to do to them. In other words, their attitudes and actions, like those of the slaves, are to be determined by their relationship to the heavenly Lord they have in common. A specific consequence of this will be the abandoning of any attempts to manipulate, demean, or scare their slaves by threats. The warrant on which these appeals to masters are grounded is twofold. First, they are reminded that the one who is both the slaves' Master and their own Master is in heaven, so that as fellow slaves both groups are equally accountable to him. Second, they are to remember that this heavenly Master is impartial, so that in his eyes their higher social status gives them no advantage and they should expect to receive no special consideration in comparison with their slaves.

As regards actual practice in the household, the writer's advice remains general. Slaves are enjoined to obey their masters and to serve with the proper attitudes of fear, integrity, wholeheartedness, and enthusiasm. Because of the vagueness of the imperative, "do the same to them," what is asked of masters is a mixture of the even more general treatment of slaves with a corresponding Christian attitude, and the very specific abandonment of threats. In itself and apart from the very significant fact that slaves are appealed to directly, what is called for here does not differ substantially from the practice expected in other appeals in the ancient world for moderation in the master-slave relationship. Again, it is, of course, the motivations for such behavior which give the paraenesis its distinctiveness and which alter the whole dynamic of the relationship. A Christological motivation is pervasive, and the phrases or clauses which express this are "as you would obey Christ" (v 5), "as slaves of Christ" (v 6), "as you would the Lord" (v 7), "by the Lord" (v 8), "both their and your Master" (v 9), and "no partiality with him" (v 9). This Christological emphasis brings to the fore the question of one's ultimate allegiance. For both slaves and masters, this allegiance is to Christ as the true Lord or Master. Relating to the other party becomes an opportunity for serving him. Slaves need to be conscious of both his present lordship and his lordship at the future judgment, when he will reward the good that they do. Concentration on this ultimate allegiance also produces a motivation that is determined by inner commitment rather than by external factors, obedience that is rooted in the heart, and devotion to God's will that is "from the soul" rather than service that is out to catch the eye of masters and please them at any cost. Masters too should bear this future lordship in mind; it is relevant to slave and free. They should also be conscious that at present they have an impartial heavenly Master.

As in the equivalent Colossians passage, here too the focus on Christ as Lord relativizes the social distinction between slaves and masters. This is made explicit by the contrast which frames the passage between human or earthly masters (v 5) and the Master in heaven (v 9). The fact that the same word κύριος is used for the master as for Christ as Lord means that there is a play on words in the background when the Lord, i.e., the true Master, is mentioned in vv 7, 8. Asking slaves to see themselves as slaves of Christ (v 6), a designation which Paul had used of himself, produces a similar relativizing effect and intensifies this emphasis which had already been present in Colossians. Ephesians also intensifies the note of reciprocity. Focusing on Christ as Lord or Master puts slaves and masters on equal footing in relation to him, and the writer reflects this as he links the two groups in a variety of formulations. He points out that the notion of reward for good holds for both slave and free, adds "and" in the address to masters, makes his main imperative to masters "do the same to them", tells them in regard to their slaves that "both their and your Master is in heaven," and underlines that this Master makes no partial judgments on the basis of social distinctions.

This part of the household code indicates that not only marriage and family life but also other household relationships and the sphere of work come within the scope of Christ's lordship and are thereby related to God's good will. This perspective was meant to give Christian slaves in their work, as well as Christian masters in their management of the household, the opportunity of turning their duties into acts of faith and worship by doing them for the true Master. It could produce also for slaves a sense of inner freedom in the midst of their particular social circumstances. But unlike the inner freedom advocated by many Stoics, which was aimed at liberating people from all ties and producing an indifference to social conditions, this freedom paradoxically comes from an enslavement to Christ, which enables slaves to give full weight to external ties and indeed to throw themselves wholeheartedly and enthusiastically into honoring their relationship with their masters.

What strikes most modern readers about this part of the code is its reinforcement of the subordination of slaves within the household. But perhaps most striking to contemporary readers in a setting where there was no questioning of such social structures was the writer's address to slaves as full members of the Christian community who are seen as equally responsible with their masters to their common Lord. Not just while engaged in cultic rituals, but in everyday life in society, both groups are to live out this responsibility, in different social roles to be sure, but fundamentally as fellow slaves of the same heavenly Master.

The mutual subordination called for earlier in 5:21 is effectively reinforced in such paraenesis. In this way, this part of the code, like the two preceding sections, both accommodates to and modifies the Greco-Roman patriarchal household. The household relationships of those who lived out its specific instructions might not differ very much externally from those in non-Christian households run by the more humane masters, but again the ethos of the Christian households would be likely to be quite different. It is the ethos of "love-patriarchalism" which allows social differences to stand but transforms the relationships within them according to the new life in Christ. The writer of Ephesians has in view Christian households, where those who model being a good servant through enthusiastic service and being a good master through the nonthreatening exercise of authority do this because they also treat each other as brothers and sisters in Christ, as fully accountable fellow servants of the same Lord.

The "love-patriarchalism" of this passage, which recognizes yet transcends the existing social structures, continues the perspective that Paul himself had brought to bear on the topic of slavery. The disproportionate amount of advice offered to slaves in comparison with that offered to masters in this code, as in Colossians, may well reflect the point of view of someone who is socially more aligned with the masters than with the slaves. But the writer's determined effort to emphasize the reciprocity of the relationship makes it hard to believe that he would sanction any exclusion of slaves from positions of responsibility in the church, including pastors and teachers (cf. 4:11). Nevertheless, this may have been one of the unforeseen later consequences of the household groupings being taken over into the paraenesis for the Christian community. By the time of the Pastoral Epistles, in which the view of the Church and the model of the household have become more fully identified, the perspectives of the church leaders and masters of households have also become closely identified. Consequently, the note of reciprocity is absent, as it is only slaves and not masters who are exhorted about their duties.

In the exhortations to slaves and masters, the more relevant the writer's specific instructions are to his readers' first-century social setting, the less relevant they are to that of contemporary Christian readers. Such readers need to avoid two different tendencies. The first is to try to rescue the passage for today by ignoring the distance between the situation of masters and slaves in the Greco-Roman world and employers and employees, management and labor, in more democratic societies of the present day. The second is to dismiss the passage out of hand on the basis of the totally unrealistic expectation that the early Christians should have overthrown the existing structures of their society by attempting to abolish the whole system of slavery. But once these tendencies are set aside, the general thrust of the writer's argument remains to be appropriated. Like Paul, this writer still argues from elements at the center of his gospel, here particularly the lordship of Christ, and applies them in a way that neither immediately demolishes nor baptizes as Christian the social structures of his time but rather transforms them from within. The Ephesians household code, and particularly this part of it, serves as a reminder that Christians will always need to bring to bear the lordship of Christ on their everyday life in its social and economic concreteness, even though specific expressions of this will become obsolete as social conditions change and new forms of obedience need to be found. Recognizing that Christ's lordship molds a community in which all believers, regardless of social status, are fully members and equally responsible to him will mean that Christians will, however, always be part of a movement away from owner-slave economies, whatever form they take, toward free and equal human community. As part of this movement, they will also attempt to make their employment and the social structures in which they find themselves opportunities for serving their Lord and to play their role in ensuring that the relationships within their churches embody their Lord's ultimate disregard for any distinctions based on social status.

Concluding Appeal to Stand Firm in the Battle Against Spiritual Powers (6:10–20)

Bibliography

Adai, J. *Der Heilige Geist,* 134–46; 231–43; 260–72. **Arnold, C. E.** *Ephesians: Power and Magic,* 103–22. ———. "The 'Exorcism' of Ephesians 6:12 in Recent Research." *JSNT* 30 (1987) 71–87. **Carr, W.** *Angels and Principalities.* Cambridge: CUP, 1981, 93–111. **Fischer, K.-M.** *Tendenz und Absicht,* 165–72. **Harnack, A.** *Militia Christi.* Tr. D. Gracie. Philadelphia: Fortress, 1981, 27–64. **Jones, P. R.** "La Prière par l'Esprit. Ephésiens 6:18." *RevRef* 27 (1976) 128–39. **Kamlah, E.** *Die Form der katalogischen Paränese im Neuen Testament.* Tübingen: Mohr, 1964, 189–96. **Lash, C. J. A.** "Where Do Devils Live? A Problem in the Textual Criticism of Ephesians 6.12." *VigChr* 30 (1976) 160–74. **Lincoln, A. T.** *Paradise Now and Not Yet,* 164–66. ———. "A Re-Examination of 'the Heavenlies' in Ephesians." *NTS* 19 (1972–73) 468–83. ———. "The Use of the OT in Ephesians." *JSNT* 14 (1982) 42–43. **Lindemann, A.** *Die Aufhebung der Zeit,* 63–66, 235–36. **Lövestam, E.** *Spiritual Wakefulness in the New Testament.* Lund: Gleerup, 1963, 64–77. **O'Brien, P. T.** "Principalities and Powers: Opponents of the Church." In *Biblical Interpretation and the Church,* ed. D. A. Carson. Exeter: Paternoster, 1984, 110–50. **Oepke, A.** "ὅπλον κτλ." *TDNT* 5 (1967) 292–315. **Pfitzner, V.** *Paul and the Agon Motif.* Leiden: Brill, 1967, 157–64. **Pierrou, J.** "Être armés pour le combat chrétien (Eph 6, 10–17)." *AsSeign* 76 (1964) 14–28. **Whiteley, D. E. H.** "Expository Problems: Eph 6:12: Evil Powers." *ExpTim* 68 (1957) 100–103. **Wild, R. A.** "The Warrior and the Prisoner: Some Reflections on Ephesians 6:10–20." *CBQ* 46 (1984) 284–98. **Wink, W.** *Naming the Powers.* Philadelphia: Fortress, 1984, 84–89.

Translation

> [10] *Finally, be strong in the Lord and in his mighty strength.* [11] *Put on the full armor of God in order that you may be able to stand against the schemes of the devil:* [12] *for our* [a] *battle is not against flesh and blood,* [b] *but against the principalities, against the authorities, against the world rulers of this darkness, against the spiritual forces of evil in the heavenly realms.* [c] [13] *Therefore take up God's full armor, so that you may be able to withstand on the evil day, and having accomplished everything, to stand.* [14] *Stand therefore, having fastened the belt of truth around your waist,* [d] *and having put on the breastplate of righteousness,* [15] *and having fitted your feet with the readiness of the gospel of peace;* [16] *besides all these having taken up the shield of faith, with which you will be able to extinguish all the burning arrows of the evil one.* [17] *And receive the helmet of salvation, and the sword of the Spirit, which is the word of God,* [18] *through every prayer and petition, praying at all times in the Spirit, and to this end keeping alert in all perseverance and petition for all the saints,* [19] *and for me, that when I open my mouth the word may be given to me, to make known boldly and openly* [e] *the mystery of the gospel,* [f] [20] *for which I am an ambassador in chains, that I may talk of it boldly and openly as I ought to speak.*

Notes

[a] There is weak evidence (cop^sa Origen^lat) for the omission of the personal pronoun, but strong external evidence (P46 B D* G Ψ 81 several Old Latin mss syr^p, pal goth eth Ambrosiaster Lucifer

Ephraem Priscillian) for ὑμῶν ἡ πάλη, "your battle." There is also good evidence (א A Dc I K P 0230 33 88 104 181 several Old Latin mss vg syrh copbo arm Clement Tertullian Origengr, lat Cyprian Methodius Eusebius) for ἡμῶν ἡ πάλη, "our battle." Since the rest of the paraenesis in this section is in the second person plural, this last reading could be judged the more difficult, and for the same reason it is more likely that scribes would have altered ἡμῶν, "our," to ὑμῶν, "your," than vice versa.

b The Greek text has this phrase in the reverse order—"blood and flesh."

c Lash (*VigChr* 30 [1976] 161–74) draws attention to an early Syrian alternative tradition (though this had already been noted at the turn of the century by J. A. Robinson, 214). The tradition reflects a Greek reading ἐν τοῖς ὑπουρανίοις, "in the realms under the heavens," which would fit the idea of 2:2 but is clearly a scribal emendation designed to explain the difficult notion of evil powers in the heavens. A similar motive accounts for the omission of the phrase ἐν τοῖς ἐπουρανίοις, "in the heavenly realms," in P46.

d A literal translation would be "having belted your waist with truth."

e The Greek text reads ἐν παρρησίᾳ and this has been translated by two adverbs to give the connotations of the Greek term. The same has been done for the cognate verb in v 20. See *Comment* on v 19.

f It could be argued that the reading which omits τοῦ εὐαγγελίου, "of the gospel" (B G itg, mon Tertullian Ambrosiastercomm Victorinus-Rome Ephraem) is more likely to be original and that these words are a scribal gloss. However, the evidence for their inclusion is strong and widespread (א A D I K P Ψ 33 81 88 104 181 various Old Latin mss vg syrp, h copsa, bo goth arm Ambrosiastertxt Chrysostom Jerome), and as Metzger (*Textual Commentary*, 610) also points out, there are no other variant readings, such as τοῦ Χριστοῦ, "of Christ," or τοῦ θεοῦ, "of God," as in Col 2:2, which might have been expected if the longer reading were a copyist's addition. It is, therefore, quite likely that in this case the longer reading is original and that the omission was made in the light of Eph 3:3, 9, where "mystery" can stand by itself because the surrounding context explains its content.

Form/Structure/Setting

From 5:15, the appeal to the readers to conduct themselves in the world in a way that is worthy of their calling has been in terms of living wisely in their household relationships. Now in conclusion, the appeal is for believers to preserve and appropriate all that has been done for their salvation and their conduct by God in Christ, and to do so in the face of evil, seen from the perspective of its ultimate transcendent source. This is not, of course, the language the writer himself uses. Instead, he pictures this appropriate Christian living in terms of a battle against cosmic spiritual powers in which believers must put on the armor which God supplies in order to withstand and prevail.

The pericope of 6:10–20 falls into three subsections: (*i*) vv 10–13 which stress the necessity of putting on God's full armor in order to be strong and to stand in the battle against the spiritual powers; (*ii*) vv 14–17 which detail the pieces of the armor that must be put on; (*iii*) vv 18–20 which emphasize in addition the need for constant prayer and watchfulness, the prayer including intercession for all believers but especially for the imprisoned apostle's bold proclamation of the mystery.

As regards content, vv 10–17 of this passage, with their treatment of the equipping of believers for battle, seem to form a unit in themselves, while vv 18–20, which take over material from Colossians, move on to the different topic of prayer. But as regards syntax, vv 18–20 are clearly joined to what has preceded through the two participial clauses of v 18. This makes clear that the themes of spiritual warfare and watching and praying are in fact closely connected. There is a further conceptual link between the two units through the notion of the Spirit, which forms a bridge between v 17 and v 18.

The transition to the concluding part of the paraenesis is made through τοῦ λοιποῦ, "finally," which introduces the first imperative ἐνδυναμοῦσθε, "be strong," which is then followed by a combination of two prepositional phrases indicating the source of the strength, ἐν κυρίῳ, "in the Lord," and, in the by now familiar style of synonyms linked in a genitive construction, ἐν τῷ κράτει τῆς ἰσχύος αὐτοῦ, "in his mighty power." How the first imperative is to be carried out is explained in v 11 by a second imperative, ἐνδύσασθε τὴν πανοπλίαν τοῦ θεοῦ, "put on the full armor of God." The purpose of donning the armor is delineated by means of an accusative and infinitive construction introduced by πρός, "in order that you may be able to stand against the schemes of the devil." The reason for putting on the armor is further underlined by the ὅτι clause of v 12, which makes clear that the battle in which believers are engaged is not one against human foes but one against spiritual cosmic powers. Verse 12 does not function as the central element in 6:10–20, as Wild (*CBQ* 46 [1984] 285–86) claims. Rather, it has a supportive role, explaining the exhortation to put on the full armor of God in order to stand (cf. also Arnold, *Ephesians*, 105, 202 n. 8). The paraenesis progresses in a circular fashion. The imperative to put on God's armor has been justified in vv 11b, 12, and now that justification serves as the grounds (διὰ τοῦτο, "therefore," v 13) on which the earlier imperative is repeated in a different form, ἀναλάβετε τὴν πανοπλίαν τοῦ θεοῦ, "take up the full armor of God." Again, the purpose of this is that the readers may be able to stand, but the second time around this thought is expressed by means of a ἵνα clause and in a more emphatic fashion with both ἀντιστῆναι, "to withstand," and στῆναι, "to stand."

The writer builds on the repeated call to put on God's armor in order to stand (cf. οὖν, "therefore," in v 14) and moves on to describe various pieces of this armor. So far, the idea of standing has figured as part of purpose clauses, but now it is expressed as an imperative, στῆτε, "stand," which represents the main thrust of the pericope's exhortation. It is followed in vv 14–16 by four clauses with aorist participles. These state the actions believers need to have taken if they are to stand, but because of the context, they could also be taken as participles with imperatival force. The first three clauses are linked by καί, "and," and the fourth is introduced by ἐν πᾶσιν, "besides all these." They talk of "having fastened the belt of truth around your waist," "having put on the breastplate of righteousness," "having fitted your feet with the readiness of the gospel of peace," and "having taken up the shield of faith." In regard to the last, a relative clause explains that this shield enables believers to extinguish the burning arrows of the evil one. Still in connection with the pieces of armor, a new imperative, parallel to the preceding participles and linked by a καί, "and," is introduced in v 17, δέξασθε, "receive." The two further pieces of armor to be received are the helmet of salvation and the sword of the Spirit, which is identified as the word of God. Following directly in v 18, but more loosely connected with what immediately precedes (they may well relate back to the main imperative στῆτε, "stand," in v 14 rather than to δέξασθε, "receive," in v 17), are two clauses with present participles surrounded by prepositional phrases. These stress the need for continual praying in the Spirit and for keeping alert with perseverance and petition. There is a question of whether the first prepositional phrase in v 18 διὰ πάσης προσευχῆς καὶ δεήσεως, "through every prayer and petition," should be associated syntactically more closely with v 17 and, therefore, be seen either as the means of receiving the helmet of salvation and the sword of the Spirit or as the accompanying circumstances of their reception. But given this writer's style, which has earlier combined cognate nouns and verbs (cf. 1:6, 23; 3:19; 4:1) and tends toward the tautological, it is more likely that this phrase goes with the following participle προσευχόμενοι, "praying." The prepositional phrase at the end of v 18 speaks of petition being made for all believers, and v 19 adds that it should also be made for the writer. Two ἵνα clauses then indicate the content of such a prayer. It is that the writer may be given the word to enable him to make known the mystery of the gospel boldly. The stress on boldness and openness despite his imprisonment is underscored by the purpose clause at the end of v 20, "that I may talk of it boldly and openly as I ought to speak."

6:10–20 is both the concluding element of the paraenesis which had begun in 4:1 and the concluding section of the main part of the letter as a whole. In terms of a rhetorical analysis of the letter as a persuasive communication that would be read out loud to its recipients, this section functions as the *peroratio*. In the *peroratio* (cf. Quintilian 6.1.1) an author not only sought to bring his address to an appropriate conclusion but also to do so in a way which would arouse the audience's emotions. According to Aristotle (*Rhet.* 3.19) the *epilogos*—his equivalent term—had four parts: making the audience well-disposed toward the speaker and ill-disposed toward any opposition, magnifying or minimizing leading facts, exciting the required kind of emotion in the hearers, and refreshing their memories by means of recapitulation. There is no particular reason why *all* these factors should be found in this conclusion, but they can provide a convenient point of comparison, and the writer does appear to have fashioned his own version of them.

This is especially clear in the case of the third factor, an appeal to the readers' wills via their imaginations and emotions. Appeals to be strong, stand firm, pray, and be alert can be found in Paul's writings (e.g., 1 Thess 5:6–8; 1 Cor 15:58; 16:13; Rom 13:11–14), but here they are more elaborate and intense. Houlden (*Paul's Letters*, 337) has noted that the writer's "words form an inspiring exhortation . . . they help to put Ephesians into the category of liturgy or oratory." The passage is a rousing call to the readers to summon all their energies in firm resolve to live out the sort of Christian existence in the world to which the whole letter has pointed. The battle imagery arouses a sense of urgency and intensity. At the same time, the passage does not provoke any feeling of panic or fear but conveys the sense of confidence and security that the readers can have in the midst of a bitter combat. For those familiar with the Scriptures, the passage's OT allusions would lend it both added authority and effect.

In this *peroratio*, the readers are made ill-disposed not toward any particular human opposition but toward the spiritual forces that are at the source of all opposition, toward the ultimate enemy. They are made well disposed toward the author, as he takes on the identity of the apostle imprisoned for the cause of the gospel which has changed their lives, and who, though in chains, desires to proclaim that gospel boldly and openly. This portrait of Paul arouses both sympathy and admiration.

Recapitulation takes place as various concerns, themes, and terminology from earlier in the letter are taken up. It is not so much that assertions or exhortations are restated but that they recur in a different form. The same issues—believers' identity, their relation to Christ and to the resources of power in him and in God, their need both to appropriate salvation from God and to live a righteous life in the world, the cosmic opposition to God's purposes for human well-being—appear again but now under new imagery (for more detailed discussion see below on the setting of the passage in the letter). Through their recapitulation in this guise, these leading themes of the letter are magnified.

This particular *peroratio* takes the form of a call to battle or, to be more precise, a call both to be ready for battle and to stand firm in the battle that is already in progress. As such, it also, not surprisingly, has features in common with speeches of generals before battle, urging their armies to deeds of valor in face of the impending dangers of war. These hortatory speeches, called παραίνεσις, "paraenesis," or προτρεπτικὸς λόγος, "advisory word or speech," can be found frequently in Greek literature, and were considered part of the epideictic genre of rhetoric (cf. esp. T. C. Burgess, "Epideictic Literature," *Studies in Classical Philology* 3 [1902] 209–14, 231–33). Representative of the range of these military speeches are those of Phormio in Thucydides 2.89, Cyrus in Xenophon, *Cyrop.* 1.4, Hannibal and Scipio in Polybius 3.63, Postumius in Dionysius of Halicarnassus 6.6, Nicius in Diodorus Siculus 18.15, Alexander in Arrian, *De Ex. Alex.* 2.83, Caesar in Dio Cassius 38.36–46, Antony and Augustus Caesar in Dio Cassius 50.16–30, and Severus in Herodianus 3.6 (cf. Burgess, "Epideictic Literature," 212–13). Among the topics dwelt on in these speeches are the soldiers' heritage, including their glorious achievements in the past, an exhortation not to disgrace this heritage by suffering defeat, a comparison with enemy forces with a reminder that it is ultimately valor and not numbers that will prevail, a detailing of the prizes that await the victors, a pointing to favorable auspices and to the gods as allies, an appeal to patriotism, a reminder that this enemy has been conquered before, a depicting of the wrongs inflicted by the enemy, and praise of the commander as superior to the leaders of the opposing forces. Such speeches in the various histories were well known as places where writers indulged their rhetorical powers, sometimes to excess. Plutarch (*Praec. Ger. Reip.* 6.7.803B) remarks of some of them, "but as for the rhetorical orations and periods of Ephorus, Theopompus, and Anaximenes, which they made after they had armed and arranged their armies, one may say: 'None talk so foolishly so near the sword.'"

Seen in this light, the writer's combination and adaptation of OT traditions (see below) takes as its overall shape what also turns out to be an adaptation of a well-known hortatory form. He has thereby created an extremely effective *peroratio*. It too dwells on the need for valor with its exhortations to be strong, prepared and alert, and to stand firm. It points out the dangers and strengths of the enemy. It braces its soldiers for a successful outcome of the battle by reminding them of the superior strength, resources, and equipment they possess. It makes clear not only that they have God on their side but also that he has put his own full armor at their disposal. It gives them a model for triumph in an embattled situation by bringing to their consciousness the boldness and freedom of proclamation of the imprisoned apostle. This battle speech has rhetorical force but is restrained rather than overindulgent. Among its rhetorical features are: the combination of synonyms in a genitive construction for emphasis (v 10); repetition of the verb "to stand" (vv 11, 13, 14), including the effective sequence of vv 13b, 14, "so that you may be able to withstand on the evil day, and having accomplished everything, to stand. Stand therefore . . ."; repetition of ἡ πανοπλία τοῦ θεοῦ, "the full armor of God" (vv 11, 13), and of the verb δύνασθαι, "to be able to" (vv 11, 13, 16); the build-up in the depiction of the enemy forces with its repetition of πρός, "against" (vv 11b, 12); the powerful cumulative effect of the metaphors linking the individual pieces of armor with gifts of salvation or Christian virtues (vv 14–17); the plerophory through the fourfold use of πᾶς, "all" (v 18); the alliteration of words beginning with π- (v 18), to which both the plerophory and combination of cognate noun and verb contribute; and the pathos and encouragement of the vision of the triumphant ministry of the imprisoned apostle (vv 19, 20).

The employment of extended battle imagery in an appeal to his readers to stand firm is the distinctive contribution of the writer of Ephesians. It stands out as unique in comparison with his model in Colossians, although the opening exhortation of 6:10, ἐνδυναμοῦσθε . . . ἐν τῷ κράτει τῆς ἰσχύος αὐτοῦ, "be strong in the strength of his might," has some similarities with Col 1:11, ἐν πάσῃ δυνάμει δυναμούμενοι κατὰ τὸ κράτος τῆς δόξης αὐτοῦ, "being strengthened with all power according to the strength of his glory." His instructions to the members of the household had been based on Col 3:22–4:1, but whereas Colossians immediately moves on to a call to prayer in general, and prayer for the apostle and his co-workers in particular in 4:2–4, Ephesians only takes up a similar call at the end of this passage in vv 18–20. At this point, there are again striking similarities with, as well as some divergences from, the Colossians original. Both use the noun and the verbal form for prayer in close juxtaposition—τῇ προσευχῇ . . . προσευχόμενοι, "in prayer . . . praying" (Col 4:2, 3), and διὰ πάσης προσευχῆς . . . προσευχόμενοι, "through every prayer . . . praying" (Eph 6:18). But whereas Colossians links this with the notion of thanksgiving which had preceded its household code in 3:16, 17, Ephesians associates it with the Spirit, who has been mentioned in the preceding verse at the end of the elaboration on the believer's armor. Ephesians also adds in 6:18 that prayer is to be offered for all God's people, all the saints (cf. also 3:18). Both passages mention perseverance and vigilance together. In Col 4:2 this is done through an imperative followed by a participle: προσκαρτερεῖτε γρηγοροῦντες, "persevere, being watchful." In Eph 6:18 the order of the two concepts is reversed, the synonymous participle ἀγρυπνοῦντες, "keeping alert," replaces γρηγοροῦντες, "being watchful," and the cognate noun replaces the imperative in the case of perseverance: ἀγρυπνοῦντες ἐν πάσῃ προσκαρτερήσει, "keeping alert in all perseverance." When it comes to the appeal to pray for the apostle, Colossians includes Paul's co-workers (cf. ἡμῶν . . . ἡμῖν, v 3) in addition to Paul himself. In Ephesians, the focus is exclusively on the apostle. But the content of what is to be requested for them is virtually the same in each letter, although the expression varies. From Col 4:3 "that God may open to us a door for the word," the terms for "opening" and "the word" are taken over, but the whole now becomes "that when I open my mouth the word may be given to me" (Eph 6:19). In both cases, what is to be prayed for is the declaration of the mystery, the mystery for the sake of which Paul is imprisoned. In Col 4:3, 4 the former notion is expressed as λαλῆσαι τὸ μυστήριον τοῦ Χριστοῦ . . . ἵνα φανερώσω αὐτό, "to speak the mystery of Christ . . . that I may make it clear," while Eph 6:19, 20 varies the verbs, makes the mystery the mystery of the gospel, and adds the distinctive note of boldness or openness—ἐν παρρησίᾳ γνωρίσαι τὸ μυστήριον τοῦ εὐαγγελίου . . . ἵνα ἐν αὐτῷ παρρησιάσωμαι, "to make known boldly the mystery of the gospel . . . that I may talk of it boldly." Eph 6:20 repeats verbatim from Col 4:4 the notion that this is how the apostle believes he ought to speak—ὡς δεῖ με λαλῆσαι, "as I ought to speak." Paul's imprisonment for the sake of the mystery is expressed in Col 4:3 by δι' ὃ καὶ δέδεμαι, "on account of which I am bound," and in Eph 6:20 by ὑπὲρ οὗ πρεσβεύω ἐν ἁλύσει, "for which I am an ambassador in chains."

For his discussion of the Christian warfare, where he has moved away from Colossians, the writer is dependent for the idea of associating pieces of armor with aspects of Christian existence primarily on inspiration from Paul, and he elaborates on this with allusions to the armor of God and his Messiah in OT passages from Isaiah. There is, of course, more general background in ancient mythologies and religions (particularly Babylonian and Iranian) for the concepts of the representation of the gods as warriors and of wise or righteous people participating in battles as soldiers of the gods (cf. Dibelius-Greeven, 96–97; Oepke, *TDNT* 5 [1967] 296–98; Kamlah, *Form,* 85–92, 102), but any influence from such sources on this writer has already been mediated by the OT and Hellenistic Judaism. Eschatological strands in the literature of Second-Temple Judaism depicted an end-time war with extreme tribulation for the faithful but ultimate victory in God's hand (cf., e.g., *T. Sim.* 5.5; *T. Dan* 5.10, 11; *1 Enoch* 55.3–57.3; *4 Ezra* 13:1–13; 1QM; 1QH 3.24–39; 6.28–35), but again this notion would have been mediated via Paul. Paul's use of military imagery for the Christian life can be found in 1 Thess 5:8; 2 Cor 6:7; 10:3, 4; Rom 6:13, 23; 13:12, and the first and last of these references are in the context of an imminent expectation of the end. The appeal of 1 Cor 16:13, "Be watchful, stand firm in your faith, be courageous, be strong," and the brief detailing of the believer's armor in 1 Thess 5:8, "put on the breastplate of faith and love, and for a helmet the hope of salvation," may well have given this writer the ideas for his expanded and more elaborate appeal.

Some (e.g., Oepke, *TDNT* 5 [1967] 301) claim that in his elaboration the writer is guided first and foremost by what he knows about the armor of the Roman legionary. Polybius 6.23.2 lists as belonging to this equipment the shield (θυρεός), the sword (μάχαιρα), the helmet (περικεφαλαία), two spears or javelins (ὑσσοί), greaves or armor for below the knees (προκνημίς), and the breastplate (καρδιοφύλαξ) or, for the more wealthy, the coat of mail (ἁλυσιδωτὸς θώραξ) (cf. also Diodorus Siculus 20.84.3). Ephesians in comparison opts for the term θώραξ for breastplate, omits greaves and javelins, and adds the military belt and sandals, both of which were probably part of the general clothing of the soldier and not peculiar to the heavily armed soldier, the ὁπλίτης. Certainly the term πανοπλία, "full armor," would have brought to mind for Gentile readers in western Asia Minor the suit of armor of the Roman soldier. But the writer is not concerned with an accurate or detailed description of such armor. As we have seen, he omits some key items and includes other more general equipment, and in this his ultimate focus is on the Christian realities to which he desires to point. For this purpose he is aided more by his knowledge of OT imagery than by his observation of Roman soldiers (cf. also J. A. Robinson, 133).

As far as the OT is concerned, traditions that picture Yahweh as a warrior (e.g., Isa 42:13; Hab 3:8, 9; Ps 35:1–3) and his agents as in need of his strength or power for their battles (e.g., Ps 18:1, 2, 32, 39 [LXX 17:1, ἰσχύς; 17:32, 39, δύναμις]; 28:7; 59:11, 16, 17; 68:35; 89:21; 118:14; Isa 52:1) may well stand in the background, but it is the depictions of the armor of Yahweh and his Messiah in Isa 11:4, 5 and Isa 59:17 that are in the foreground for the writer. The former passage (according to the LXX) declares of the Messiah, "he shall smite the earth with the word [τῷ λόγῳ] of his mouth, and with the breath [ἐν πνεύματι] through his lips he shall slay the ungodly. With righteousness shall he be girded around his waist [δικαιοσύνη ἐζωσμένος τὴν ὀσφὺν αὐτοῦ], and with truth [ἀληθείᾳ] bound around his sides." The latter passage (according to the LXX) states of Yahweh, "He put on righteousness as a breastplate [ἐνεδύσατο δικαιοσύνην ὡς θώρακα], and he placed a helmet of salvation [περικεφαλαίαν σωτηρίου] upon his head, and he put on a cloak of vengeance and the covering." The two passages can account for Ephesians' mention of having the belt of truth around the waist, the breastplate of righteousness, the helmet of salvation, the word, and the Spirit. In addition, LXX Isa 49:2, which says of the servant, "he made my mouth like a sharp sword [ὡς μάχαιραν ὀξεῖαν]," may provide via the mention of the mouth the link with Isa 11:4 and the association of word and Spirit with the sword. Wis 5:17–20a, which is already dependent on Isa 59:17, states that "the Lord will take his zeal as his whole armor [πανοπλίαν], and will arm all creation to repel his enemies; he will put on righteousness as a breastplate, and wear impartial justice as a helmet; he will take holiness as an invincible shield [ἀσπίδα], and sharpen stern wrath as a sword." This text would supply for Ephesians the term πανοπλία, which does not appear in the Isaiah passages, and the idea of the shield, although it uses a different term, ἀσπίς, denoting the smaller rather than the larger shield, θυρεός. The only remaining part of the equipment in Ephesians to be accounted for is the footwear. Here another text from Isaiah comes into play. LXX Isa 52:7 mentions both feet and the gospel of peace—ὡς πόδες εὐαγγελιζομένου ἀκοὴν εἰρήνης, "as the feet of one preaching the good news of a report of peace." Lindemann's claim (*Aufhebung*, 89) that there are no conscious reminiscences of OT texts or formulations in this passage seems clearly wrong, but there is no consensus among scholars about the exact relationship of the material in Ephesians to these texts. While some argue that the use of the OT is indirect by way of traditions (e.g., Gnilka, 28, 310), others claim that the writer is actually citing Isa 11:4, 5 and 59:17 (e.g., Barth, 788 n. 175). More likely to be right are those who suggest conscious allusion or inexact recollection rather than actual citation (e.g., Schlier, 294–97; Caird, *Paul's Letters*, 93; Mitton, 224; Schnackenburg, 283). If Paul in 1 Thess 5:8 also had Isa 59:17 in mind, he did not transfer the divine armor directly to believers but found corresponding human qualities—the triad of faith, love, and hope. Ephesians makes a much closer identification of the divine armor and believers' equipment (cf. also Kamlah, *Form*, 190–91). The OT allusions function as scriptural confirmation for the writer's contention that believers have at their disposal not just any armor or weapons but those of God himself (cf. also Schnackenburg, 283).

It has sometimes been suggested that Eph 6:10–20 is dependent for its battle imagery on similar ideas in Stoicism or in the Qumran literature. Although there can be no question of any direct dependency, the comparison with this material remains worthwhile. Military imagery was used in a transferred sense by philosophers, adherents of the mystery cults, and orators (cf. H. Emonds, "Geistlicher Kriegsdienst: Der Topos der 'Militia spiritualis' in der antiken Philosophie," in *Heilige Überlieferung*, FS I. Herwegen, ed. O. Casel [Münster: Aschendorff, 1938] 21–50; J. Leipoldt, "Das Bild vom Kriege in der griechischen Welt," in *Gott und die Götter*, FS E. Fascher, ed. G. Delling [Berlin: Evangelische Verlagsanstalt, 1958] 16–30; A. J. Malherbe, "Antisthenes and Odysseus, and Paul at War," *HTR* 76 [1983] 143–74). Its use to describe the life of the wise man was especially popular among the Stoics. It is encapsulated in the dictum of Seneca—*vivere militare est*, "life is a battle" (*Ep*. 96.5; cf. also *Ep*. 107.9). Seneca was confident that the wise man could withstand every attack and not be injured (*De Const. Sap*. 3.4–5). Bravery is his fortress, and surrounded by it he can use his own strength as his weapons (*Ep*. 113.27–28). If his inner defenses are strengthened, he may be attacked but will not be captured, especially if he employs reason as a weapon (*Ep*. 74.19–21). Protected by philosophy, he stands on unassailable ground (*Ep*. 82.5). The following excerpts from Epictetus (*Diss*. 3.24, 25) also provide points of comparison with Ephesians' elaboration of the metaphor:

> Do you not know that human life is a warfare? that one man must keep watch, another must go out as a spy, and a third must fight? . . . Every man's life is a kind of warfare, and it is long and diversified. You must observe the duty of a soldier and do everything at the nod of the general; if it is possible, divining what his wishes are: for there is no resemblance between that general and this, neither in strength nor in superiority of character. . . . Being appointed to such a service, do I still care about the place in which I am, or with whom I am, or what men say about me? and do I not entirely direct my thoughts to God and to His instructions and commands? Having these things always in hand, and exercising them by yourself, and keeping them in readiness, you will never be in want of one to comfort you and strengthen you. . . . For we must not shrink when we are engaged in the greatest combat, but we must even take blows. For the combat before us is not in wrestling and the Pancration . . . but the combat is for good fortune and happiness themselves.

While for many Stoics the philosopher's armor was reason, virtue, or wise words, more rigorous Cynics claimed that their characteristic dress of the threadbare cloak worn without a tunic and with a staff and a wallet was the armament that they had received from the gods (cf. Ps.-Crates, *Epp*. 19, 23; Ps.-Diog. *Ep*. 10.1). Not surprisingly, given the common use of the military metaphor, a number of the individual motifs overlap with those in Ephesians, but whereas the predominant emphasis in the Stoic-Cynic material is on the self-sufficiency of the wise man, in Ephesians it is on the sufficiency that derives from dependence on divine resources that are at the disposal of all believers.

The Qumran texts also depict a whole community's role in the world in terms of battle imagery and make clear that for the community all power and help come from God (cf. esp. 1QM; 1QH 3.24–39; 6.28–35). However, although the battle envisaged in the Qumran literature has angels fighting on either side, it is an actual one with real weapons fought against human enemies, whereas Ephesians treats the weapons metaphorically and spiritually. Also for the Qumran community the battle lies in the future still, while for Ephesians it is already taking place and the decisive victory has already been won by Christ.

In its setting in the letter, this pericope concludes the paraenesis. The focus of the paraenesis began with life in the Church (4:1–16), moved out to living the life of the new humanity in society (4:17–5:14), then back into the worship and household living of the community (5:15–6:9), and now out again to Christian existence in the face of the powers of evil (6:10–20). Believers and the Church have been placed in a cosmic setting and related to the cosmic powers in the first half of the letter, but this is the first time the paraenesis is related to this setting in any extended fashion (but cf. 4:27). At first sight, Mitton's remarks (218–19) appear apposite: "This striking portrayal of the Christian life as a continuing struggle . . . seems to break upon the reader without much warning. . . . There is little to prepare us for the sudden rousing call to preparedness." Although he is right about the change of mood of this exhortation with its increase in intensity, further reflection on its content reveals substantial continuity with what has come before.

The pericope's place in the letter is obviously related to its function as a *peroratio*, whereby it sums up some of the broad themes of the letter in effective fashion under new imagery. These have been suggested in our earlier discussion, and now more specific links can be detailed. The imperative to be strong (6:10) with its indication of the resources for strength—in the Lord and his power—recalls the stress on the availability for believers of God's power manifested in Christ's resurrection and exaltation (1:19, 20), the relating of that power to Paul's apostleship (3:7), the connection of believers' strengthening with the Spirit (3:16), and the praise of God's power at work among believers (3:20). Earlier emphasis on all that has been achieved for believers, on the Church, and on the life of the new humanity had not been totally triumphalist or utopian but had recognized that this life of the new age was being experienced in the midst of the continuation of the present evil age and the powers behind it. Christ has triumphed over the powers, but they still exist (1:21; 3:10); indeed, the ruler of the realm of the air is at present at work in those who are disobedient (2:2), and the new life of believers is frequently contrasted with the surrounding darkness, alienation, and immorality of Gentile life in the evil days of the present throughout 4:17–5:14. Now the fact that Christian existence takes place on a battleground between the old age and the new, between darkness and light, between evil and good, is brought more explicitly to the fore, but the accent remains on believers' participation in the victory, on their prevailing in the battle. Some of the depiction of the opposition to be faced is familiar from earlier in the letter. The readers have been warned about scheming against them in 4:14, but there it was human scheming; here it is the schemes of the devil (6:11), who was singled out for mention previously in 4:27. Of the cosmic spirit forces listed in 6:12, the principalities and the authorities have appeared earlier in 1:21 and 3:10, and the sphere in which they operate is described as the heavenly realms both here in 6:12 and in 3:10 (cf. also "the air" of 2:2). The present age over which they hold sway is depicted in terms of darkness in 6:12, but also previously in 5:8, 11 (cf. also 4:18). Earlier this present age was seen in terms of evil days (5:16), and here it is conceived of as culminating in "the evil day" (6:13).

The realities represented by the pieces of armor have already been drawn to the readers' attention. The term "truth" has occurred in 4:25 and 5:9 (cf. also the use of the verb in 4:16 and the use of the noun with a different connotation in 1:13; 4:21, 24), and "righteousness" in 4:24 and 5:9. "The readiness of the gospel of peace" recalls the peace greeting in 1:2, the discussion of peace and reconciliation in 2:14–18, and the mention of "the bond of peace" in 4:3. The notion of peace will be evoked again in the wish of peace in 6:23. The readers' "faith" (6:16) has frequently been in view (cf. 1:1, 13, 15, 19; 2:8; 3:12; 4:5, 13) and will be mentioned again in connection with the peace wish of 6:23. "Salvation" here in 6:17 is τὸ σωτήριον in the Greek text, but the cognate nouns and verb (σωτηρία, σωτήρ, and σῴζειν) have featured before in the letter in 1:13; 2:5, 8; and 5:23. The designation of the gospel as ῥῆμα θεοῦ, "the word of God," would remind the readers of the mention of ῥῆμα in 5:26, where it probably has the same force, and also of the description of the gospel as "the word of truth" (ὁ λόγος τῆς ἀληθείας) in 1:13.

Again, in the call to prayer in 6:18–20, some of the terminology has already been employed in earlier contexts: the language of "prayer" itself was used in the writer's intercessory prayer-report in 1:16; the notion of belonging to "all the saints" occurred in 3:18; the term "mystery" has of course been prominent in 1:9; 3:3, 4, 9; and 5:32; the notion of "boldness" was employed in the context of believers' relationship to God in 3:12; and Paul's imprisonment has been alluded to in different terms in 3:1 and 4:1.

It is worth noting that a good number of the links in theme and terminology are with chap. 1 and its eulogy and thanksgiving section. There is a correspondence between the beginning and end of the letter in that what God has been praised for and asked for is now to be preserved by believers against all opposition. The attitude of prayer which frames the first half of the letter is now underlined by the call to constant prayer at the end. Not only are there links with what has preceded through the restatement of main themes and the explicit repetition of terminology, but there is also a more implicit connection with the paraenetical section of which this pericope forms the conclusion. The appeals for unity and maturity, for living out the life of the new humanity, for truthful and edifying talk, for honest work, for love, for purity in word and deed, and for wise and Spirit-filled living in marriage, family, and work all depend on believers appropriating the resources they have in God and Christ and resisting the forces that pull in the opposing direction. Behind all such forces stands the superhuman power of the devil (cf. 2:1–3; 4:27). Wild (*CBQ* 46 [1984] 298) is quite right, therefore, in suggesting that for the writer of Ephesians "the individual who engages in productive work or who speaks the truth or who loves his wife is successfully resisting and standing his ground in the fight against the powers."

A number of settings in life have been suggested for this concluding call to stand firm in the battle. Some see a baptismal situation, pointing to the language of "putting on" the armor as parallel to that of "putting on" the new humanity (cf. 4:24) and designating the pericope as "baptismal paraenesis" (e.g., Kamlah, *Form*, 192; Gnilka, 305). No doubt the pericope could form an appropriate part of a homily to baptismal candidates, but there are no particularly compelling reasons for thinking that it is such people who are being addressed by the material in its present form and position in the letter. There are others who speculate that some of the material may have come originally from baptismal catechesis. Fischer (*Tendenz*, 165–66) makes too much of a tension between two different eschatological perspectives in the pericope and argues from this tension that the more apocalyptic material originated in baptismal catechesis in which baptism was viewed as armor to protect believers in the end-time battle. Carrington (*The Primitive Christian Catechism* [Cambridge: CUP, 1940] 31–57) believed he had found a common pattern in the paraenesis of Colossians, Ephesians, 1 Peter, and James, centering on the imperatives "put off," "be subject," "watch," and "resist," which were used to catechize baptismal candidates. Apart from the fact, which Carrington concedes, that Colossians does not contain the last of these imperatives, there may be some value in this hypothesis. Yet at best it leads one back to an original setting for the calls to watch and to resist, and cannot adequately explain the reason for this writer's distinctive and creative elaboration on these basic appeals.

One explanation for this is to posit a persecution setting. The need to stand firm and the mention of the evil one's flaming arrows might suggest that the readers were facing persecution, but these would be the only such hints in the letter. There is no clear evidence for this setting (*pace* Lindemann, "Bemerkungen zu den Adressaten und zum Anlass des Epheserbriefes," *ZNW* 67 [1976] 242–43, who holds that the readers were in a situation of persecution under Domitian in 96 C.E.).

The stress on the nature of the opposition as evil spiritual powers reflects a lively awareness of these forces on the part of both writer and readers. But whereas in Colossians, on which this letter is based, these powers had played a specific role in the false teaching addressed, here there is no such controversy in view. The significant part which the powers played in the consciousness of the Gentile readers and in particular their continuing malevolent influence is simply assumed. Whether the attention given to these evil powers indicates that the passage is addressed to readers who can be specifically identified as those who had participated in the Artemis cult and practiced magic, as Arnold (*Ephesians*, 122) holds, must be considered far more doubtful.

What can be said without indulging in too much speculation is that this pericope, like the letter as a whole (see also *Introduction* on "The Purposes and Setting of Ephesians"), reflects the writer's response to what he perceives to be a crisis of confidence on the part of his readers. Through his distinctive use of military imagery and the emphasis on the resources of power, armament, and prevailing in the battle, the writer is concerned to bolster his readers' confidence by reminding them again of their identity and what this means for being enabled to maintain an appropriate lifestyle in the midst of an alien society and in the face of the powerful forces that lie behind it. What is necessary is that the readers should be strengthened in their resolve, and for this they are pointed to God's power which stands at their disposal. In addition, the portrait of Paul with his desire to proclaim the gospel boldly and openly even in the adversity of imprisonment reflects what the writer wishes for both himself and his readers—the fearless living out of Christian existence in the midst of a hostile world.

Comment

10 Τοῦ λοιποῦ ἐνδυναμοῦσθε ἐν κυρίῳ καὶ ἐν τῷ κράτει τῆς ἰσχύος αὐτοῦ, "Finally, be strong in the Lord and in his mighty strength." This verse with its call for valor and firm resolve and its indication of the resources available for exercising these qualities introduces the theme and sets the tone for the rest of the pericope. The battle is yet to be depicted, but the opening exhortation encourages the readers to be strong by reminding them of their position of strength—in the Lord—and their source of strength—his power.

τοῦ λοιποῦ, "finally," marks this as the concluding section of the writer's exhortation to his readers. The phrase more usually has temporal force—"from now on, in the future" (cf. Gal 6:17)—and some commentators opt for this meaning here, believing that the strength needed is for future conflict, an impending crisis (cf. Westcott, 92; Schlier, 289; Barth, 759–60; Caird, *Paul's Letters*, 92). τὸ λοιπόν, "finally," which might have been expected here (cf. Phil 4:8; 2 Cor 13:11; 1 Thess 4:1; 2 Thess 3:1), can itself sometimes have a future force (cf. 1 Cor 7:29; Heb 10:13) and so appears to be interchangeable with τοῦ λοιποῦ. Although the battle will become even fiercer, it is taking place now and the need for strength is a present one. It therefore seems more likely that τοῦ λοιποῦ has the sense of "finally" in this context (cf. also BAGD 480; Gnilka, 304; Schnackenburg, 277 n. 694).

The call to "be strong" in the context of battle is reminiscent of similar calls to, for example, Joshua—"Be strong and of good courage" (Josh 1:6, 7, 9)— or the Qumran community—"Be strong and valiant; be warriors! . . . Do not fall back" (1QM 15.6–8). Paul also had appealed at the close of 1 Corinthians for the readers to be strong (cf. 1 Cor 16:13, κραταιοῦσθε). Although the imperative could be construed as a middle (cf. Bruce, *Epistles*, 403), it is more likely that it should be taken as a passive with the sense of "be strengthened, be empowered," reinforcing the notion that the strength is to be drawn from an external source and corresponding to the passive in the prayer of 3:16, δυνάμει κραταιωθῆναι, "to be strengthened with might." Here the external source is "the Lord," and the wording is again reminiscent of the OT (cf. 1 Sam 30:6, "David strengthened himself in the Lord his God"; Zech 10:12, "I will make them strong in the Lord"). Now, however, the Lord is Christ. The relationship to him is described in terms of ἐν κυρίῳ, "in the Lord" (cf. also 2:21; 4:17; 5:8; 6:1, 21), which conforms to the overall tendency in this letter for what believers are in relation to Christ to be expressed in terms of ἐν Χριστῷ, "in Christ," and what they are to become or to do in relation to him to be expressed in terms of ἐν κυρίῳ, "in the Lord" (see *Comment* on 2:21). Believers' relationship to Christ gives them access to his power. The exhortation takes up the language of the intercessory prayer-report of Col 1:11, "being strengthened with all power according to the might of his glory." But it recalls also the ideas of this letter's earlier prayer-reports about the experience of the power of God operative in Christ's resurrection and exaltation and in the rescue of believers from the death and bondage of the past (cf. 1:19–2:10 with its earlier combination in 1:19 of the same synonyms in a genitive construction, "the strength of his might") and about strengthening through the Spirit (cf. 3:16). Now this final reminder is of the need to appropriate and rely on Christ's power.

11 ἐνδύσασθε τὴν πανοπλίαν τοῦ θεοῦ πρὸς τὸ δύνασθαι ὑμᾶς στῆναι πρὸς τὰς μεθοδείας τοῦ διαβόλου, "Put on the full armor of God in order that you may be able to stand against the schemes of the devil." It now becomes clear that the readers need to be strong because they are in a battle whose ultimate antagonists are God and the devil (cf. the implicit contrast between the armor of God and the schemes of the devil). If they are to prevail in the face of the devil's attacks, they must put on God's "full armor." The notion of putting on the armor is the functional equivalent of putting on the new humanity (cf. 4:24). From 4:25 onward, the writer had elaborated on putting off the old humanity, and now the detailing of the armor to be worn can be seen as the writer's development of the idea of putting on the new. πανοπλία, "full armor," is the term used for the full equipment, both defensive and offensive, of the heavily armed foot soldier (cf. also Polybius 6.23; Thucydides 3.114; Jdt 14:3; 2 Macc 3:25; Luke 11:22). Despite the fact that not every piece of the armor will be listed, the emphasis is on the full protection it provides rather than on its adornment or splendor (*pace* Barth, 793–95). The genitive "of God" certainly indicates that the armor is supplied by God, but in view of the OT passages which depict Yahweh as a warrior in similar armor (see under *Form/Structure/Setting*), it is hard to avoid the impression that more is intended and that the armor given by God to believers is in some sense his own. This would underline both the serious nature of the battle and the writer's belief that believers are only able to prevail through the protection and power of God himself. The point is similar to that of Paul in 2 Cor 10:4, "the weapons of our warfare are not fleshly but have divine power."

What has been described here in terms of being able to prevail is, of course, spoken of in the text as being "able to stand." δύνασθαι, "to be able to," recurs in vv 13, 16, and the notion of ability or enablement is related to those of strength and power, but it is auxiliary to infinitives of main verbs and should not be overinterpreted (*pace* Arnold, *Ephesians*, 107, who claims it "bears the full significance of δύναμις"). Mention of the need to stand also recurs twice (cf. vv 13, 14) and can be seen as summing up the main thrust of this pericope's exhortations. It involves standing firm, holding one's position, resisting, not surrendering to the opposition but prevailing against it. It is a mistake to interpret the call to stand as implying that the battle is open-ended and its result in doubt. Lindemann (*Aufhebung*, 65) is right to insist that victory is assured, over against Schlier (294), but not to see all temporal assumptions about the battle as being done away with and believers having no historical responsibilities because victory is automatic. The decisive victory has already been won by God in Christ, and the task of believers is not to win but to stand, that is, to preserve and maintain what has been won. It is because this victory has been won that believers are involved in the battle at all. They are in a decisively new situation in contrast to their previous condition described in 2:2, 3, where there could be no battle or resistance because they were in total bondage to the enemy. So the call to the readers to stand against the powers is also a reminder of their liberation from the tyranny of these powers. The major victory has been achieved, but the eschatological tension with its indicative and imperative characteristic of Paul's thought remains. Believers must appropriate what has already been gained for them and do so against continuing assaults, and this is not automatic. Indeed there may be minor defeats along the way; hence the urgency of the imperatives. The writer's focus, however, is not on the possibility of such minor defeats but on the ability of his readers to make the assured outcome of the overall battle their own by standing and maintaining the ground that has been won.

The rest of the verse begins the depiction of the enemy that believers are up against. Here "the devil" is singled out as the primary enemy, the chief of the opposing army, so that the forces of evil which lie behind human activity are seen as having a personal center. The power of evil is operative through human beings (cf. 2:2; 4:14) but cannot be reduced to or explained solely in terms of their activities. On the use of "devil" as opposed to "Satan," the dominant term in Paul, see *Comment* on 4:27 (for other depictions of the devil as the enemy who wages war on God's people, see, e.g., 1 Pet 5:8; Rev 12, esp. v 17). In 4:14 human scheming had been mentioned; here it is the schemes of the devil against which believers have to stand. This language makes clear that the devil does not always attack through obvious head-on assaults but employs cunning and wily stratagems designed to catch believers unawares. The writer has already mentioned one such ploy in 4:27—exploiting anger in order to sow disruption in the community.

12 ὅτι οὐκ ἔστιν ἡμῖν ἡ πάλη πρὸς αἷμα καὶ σάρκα, ἀλλὰ πρὸς τὰς ἀρχάς . . . ἐν τοῖς ἐπουρανίοις, "for our battle is not against flesh and blood, but against the principalities . . . in the heavenly realms." This verse, which sets out the nature of the enemy, explains further why it is that believers need the divine armor if they are to stand. The spiritual and cosmic nature of the opposition makes such armor absolutely necessary. This is the only place in the Pauline corpus where believers are explicitly said to be in a battle against evil spirit powers. But its uniqueness does not mean that the verse can or should be treated as an interpolation (*pace* Carr, *Angels and Principalities*, 104–10). There is no manuscript evidence at all for its omission, and its view of the powers as evil is not out of line with the rest of the letter or the Pauline corpus (cf. Arnold, *JSNT* 30 [1987] 71–87, for a thoroughgoing critique of Carr's theory, and for further discussion of the nature and interpretation of the powers, see under *Comment* on 1:20, 21). In conformity with the contemporary worldview, the writer depicts human existence as under the influence of powers that work evil. Others tried to deal with these powers in various ways that included resignation to fate, magical practices, and initiation into mystery cults. But this writer sees them as having been defeated by Christ, yet still attempting to make inroads into the lives of believers and to thwart the advance of the gospel before their final subjugation.

The term πάλη, "battle," usually denotes a wrestling match, and some have suggested that it should retain that force here, so that the writer would be saying, "Our battle against the powers of darkness is not like the contest of the wrestler, for he can easily come to grips with his opponent" (cf. Pfitzner, *Paul,* 159). However, the contrast is not between a battle and a wrestling match but between human and spiritual opposition. The athletic term could in any case be transferred to military contexts and could stand for any contest or battle (cf. Euripides, *Heracl.* 159; Philo, *De Abr.* 243; 2 Macc 10:28; 14:18; 15:9), and this is most likely the force of the term here. The Christian's battle is not ultimately "against flesh and blood." As in Heb 2:14, the terms are in the reverse order—blood and flesh—but the meaning is the same as the more usual phrase, viz., humanity in its weakness and transitoriness (cf., e.g., Sir 14:18; 17:31; Matt 16:17; Gal 1:16; 1 Cor 15:50). The real enemy is not so easily resisted and disposed of as such human opposition.

The evil powers, who are opposing believers and who are listed in this verse, appear to be subject to the devil (v 11), to the ruler of the realm of the air (2:2). They include the "principalities" and "authorities" already mentioned in 1:21 (cf. also 3:10) as those over whom Christ rules not only in this age but also in the age to come. Because this age continues and believers live in it as well as enjoying the benefits of the age to come, these powers are still able to threaten and menace them. Also listed are "the world rulers of this darkness." The term κοσμοκράτορες, "world rulers," originated in astrological discussion where it referred to the planets and their determination of human fate and world affairs. The sun in the magical papyri and other planets in later Mandaean Gnosticism (cf. *Ginza* 99.15–32; 104.5, 6; 105.24–33) are described in this way. Also in the magical papyri, gods such as Sarapis and Hermes are called world rulers, and the use of this term for evil spirit powers here may indicate that the writer shares the view of Paul in 1 Cor 10:20 that pagan gods are closely linked with demonic forces (cf. Arnold, *Ephesians,* 65–67). The second-century C.E. *Testament of Solomon* also employs this term for evil spirit powers. In it the demons introduce themselves to Solomon in 8.2 as *stoicheia* who are world rulers and in 18.2 (probably under the influence of the language of Ephesians) call themselves "the world rulers of the darkness of this age." In Ephesians, darkness has already been associated with the past from which believers have been delivered, with the life of outsiders (5:8, 11), with those who are under the sway of this world-age (cf. 2:2). "This darkness" therefore has reference to this present age, this world (cf. also Col 1:13, "the dominion of darkness"). Personal powers of evil are also associated with such a sphere of darkness in the Qumran literature, where the community will be in an end-time battle against the angel of darkness and his hosts (cf. esp. 1QM 13; 16.11–16; 17.5–9) and where it is said that "all the children of falsehood are ruled by the Angel of Darkness and walk in the ways of darkness" (1QS 3.20, 21).

The last grouping in the list of opponents, τὰ πνευματικὰ τῆς πονηρίας ἐν τοῖς ἐπουρανίοις, "the spiritual forces of evil in the heavenly realms," serves not so much to designate a separate class of cosmic powers but as a general term for all such powers and an indication of their locality. It is equivalent to the term "evil spirits" found, for example, in *Jub.* 10.3, 5, 13; 11.4, 5; 12.20; *1 Enoch* 15.8–12; *T. Sim.* 4.9; 6.6; *T. Levi* 18.12. The writer has listed different groups of evil forces not for the sake of some schematic classification or completeness, but in order to bring home to the consciousness of his readers the variety and comprehensiveness of the power the enemy has at his disposal. The phrase "in the heavenly realms" refers primarily to the sphere of the evil powers and not to that in which believers are fighting (cf. also Percy, *Probleme*, 182). However, the statement that the fighting is not against flesh and blood indicates not only the spiritual nature of the adversary but also the spiritual character of believers' combat. On the relationship between the heavenly realms and the air (2:2) as the location of the malevolent agencies and the Jewish background for the idea of hostile angelic or spiritual powers in heaven, see *Comment* on 2:2 (cf. also Lincoln, *NTS* 19 [1973] 475–76). Although the opposing forces are formidable, the fact that they are in the heavenly realms need no longer pose a threat to believers, because they are not fighting to break through the hold of such powers and penetrate to the heavenly realm themselves, as some in Colossae attempted, but are to see themselves as fighting from a position of victory, having already been seated with Christ in the heavenly realms (cf. 2:6).

13 διὰ τοῦτο ἀναλάβετε τὴν πανοπλίαν τοῦ θεοῦ, ἵνα δυνηθῆτε ἀντιστῆναι ἐν τῇ ἡμέρᾳ τῇ πονηρᾷ καὶ ἅπαντα κατεργασάμενοι στῆναι, "Therefore take up God's full armor, so that you may be able to withstand on the evil day, and having accomplished everything, to stand." The readers have now been warned about the fierce opposition they face. Earlier in the letter, the writer had dispelled any need for them to fear such an enemy by reminding them of their relationship to Christ and his all-powerful rule, of the benefits of their salvation, and of their part in the Church, all of which have removed them from the dominion of this present age and its spirit rulers. It has become clear, however, that he does not want them to be complacent in the face of the threats of evil powers. They are to take them seriously because such powers still need to be resisted. But even here in the paraenesis, the earlier note of assurance is sounded. All the resources are available for a successful resistance. These resources are divine and are summed up as the "full armor" of God, which is mentioned for the second time (cf. v 11). All that believers need to do is to "take up" the armor to appropriate the resources.

"To withstand" (ἀντιστῆναι; cf. the calls to resist the devil in Jas 4:7; 1 Pet 5:9) will be especially necessary "on the evil day." The reference of this phrase, "the evil day," is disputed, and there are four main competing interpretations. (*i*) Some hold that the reference is to a particular time of special tribulation immediately preceding the end of the world. Meyer (331) claims that the emphatic designation could suggest to the readers only a single evil day well known to them, and that is shortly before the parousia, "the day in which the Satanic power . . . puts forth its last and greatest outbreak" (cf. also Dibelius-Greeven, 98; Schlier, 292–93; Kirby, *Ephesians*, 144; Houlden, *Paul's Letters*, 339; Caird, *Paul's Letters*, 92). (*ii*) Others believe any time of crisis or special temptation is in view (cf. Abbott, 184; Percy, *Probleme*, 259; Mitton, 223). (*iii*) Still others see the terminology as a reference to the whole of the present age (cf. Mussner, 168; Bruce, *Epistles*, 406; Arnold, *Ephesians*, 114, who treats it as synonymous with "the evil days" of 5:16; and Lindemann, *Aufhebung*, 64, 235–36, who, in a strange argument, disputes that "the evil day" is a recognized concept in apocalyptic writings but then claims the writer has taken a traditional eschatological concept and made it a present reality). (*iv*) A fourth position attempts to do justice to the strengths of the first and third interpretations and is to be preferred. It recognizes that the terminology would carry clear connotations of a final time of evil at the end of history. Jer 17:7, 8 talks of "the day of evil" that is to come, Amos 5:18–20 of the day of the Lord bringing with it darkness and judgment, Dan 12:1 of a time of trouble before a time of deliverance, *1 Enoch* in a variety of ways of a day of tribulation (cf. 50.2; 55.3; 63.8; 96.2; 99.4), *Jub.* 23.16–25 of a final generation of great evil before the time of salvation, *T. Dan* 5.4–6 of the evil and apostasy of the last days, *T. Lev.* 5.5 of the day of tribulation, *2 Apoc. Bar.* 48.31 of a time of affliction, and *Apoc. Abr.* 29.9 of the twelfth hour of impiety. Particularly significant is the combination of the language of a final time of evil with that of battle in 1QM 1.10–13: "for that shall be the day appointed from ancient times for the battle of destruction of the sons of darkness. . . . On the day of calamity, the sons of light shall battle with the company of darkness amid the shouts of a mighty multitude and the clamour of gods and men to (make manifest) the might of God. And it shall be a time of (great) tribulation for the people which God shall redeem; of all its afflictions none shall be as this, from its sudden beginning to its end in eternal redemption." Paul also talks of a time of distress (1 Cor 7:26) and of the day of the Lord bringing with it sudden destruction (1 Thess 5:2–4; cf. also 2 Thess 2:3–12 with its time of rebellion and lawlessness before the day of the Lord). Yet at the same time as the terminology of Ephesians carrying these overtones, the call to put on the armor of God and the orientation of the battle are present. The two perspectives of present and future overlap. The readers are to realize that they are already in the evil days (cf. 5:16), but that these will culminate in a climactic evil day, when resistance will be especially necessary (cf. also Gnilka, 308; Barth, 804–5; *pace* Schnackenburg, 282, who opts for a combination of present and indefinite future). Just as redemption is already experienced but there will be a final day of redemption (1:7 and 4:30), so evil is already present but there will also be a final day of evil. The writer's point should not be forgotten in the debate about the time reference. It is to underline the efficacy of God's armor, and he does so with particular reference to the future. The armor is the only thing that enables believers to prevail both now and when the final evil day arrives.

What is all-important it that believers should stand firm. Every action should be geared toward this end. κατεργάζεσθαι most frequently means "to do" or "to accomplish," but in some contexts it can mean "to overpower" or "to overcome." Some commentators believe that the latter is its force here. Meyer (331–32) claims that the picture is of "the victor, who, after the fight is finished, is not laid prostrate, or put to flight, but stands" (cf. also Schlier, 293; Mitton, 223). But since the verb is used twenty-one times in the Pauline corpus and all with the former meaning, and since this makes good sense here, it is to be preferred (cf. also Westcott, 95; Abbott, 184; J. A. Robinson, 214; Gnilka, 309; Schnackenburg, 282). Having accomplished all that is necessary in preparation for the battle and being fully armed, believers are to stand firm. "To stand" does not refer to receiving God's approval at the judgment (*pace* Schlier,

293). In the contexts in which the verb has this force, it is followed by a prepositional phrase which makes such a connotation clear (e.g., 1QS 11.16, 17; 1QH 4.21; Luke 21:36; Rom 14:4; cf. also Schnackenburg, 282).

14 στῆτε οὖν περιζωσάμενοι τὴν ὀσφὺν ὑμῶν ἐν ἀληθείᾳ, καὶ ἐνδυσάμενοι τὸν θώρακα τῆς δικαιοσύνης, "Stand therefore, having fastened the belt of truth around your waist, and having put on the breastplate of righteousness." The exhortation about the need to "stand" is reiterated (cf. vv 11, 13c and also "to withstand" in v 13b), but this time it takes the form of an imperative. The verb has the same force throughout (cf. also Gnilka, 310; *pace* Meyer, 333), suggesting the stance of the soldier in combat, standing firm, resisting, and prevailing against the enemy. It is clearly a vital notion for the writer, and it is worth noting that it was also important in Paul's writings. 1 Thess 3:8 speaks of standing fast in the Lord, while 2 Thess 2:15 exhorts "stand firm" and Gal 5:1 "stand fast therefore." In 1 Corinthians Paul speaks of some who think they stand needing to take heed lest they fall (10:12) and of the gospel in which the Corinthians stand (15:1), and exhorts them to stand firm in their faith (16:13; cf. also 2 Cor 1:24). In Romans he talks of "this grace in which we stand" (5:2) and warns Gentile Christians that they "stand fast only through faith . . . stand in awe" (11:20). In Philippians the apostle wants to know that his readers stand firm in one spirit, not frightened by their opponents (1:27, 28), and exhorts them to stand firm in the Lord (4:1). In Col 4:12 Epaphras' prayer for the Colossians is that they may stand mature and fully assured in all the will of God. Here in Ephesians, the thought also is of the readers taking up by faith and occupying steadfastly the position which is theirs through their experience of the gospel of God's grace in Christ.

The discussion of the different parts of the believer's armor which now follows is illustrative of the writer's main point about the total equipment provided by God, shows what it means to have accomplished everything necessary for battle, and explains how it is that one stands. The first action necessary is fastening "the belt of truth around your waist." To fasten clothing securely around the waist made rapid movement easier and was vital preparation for any vigorous activity. In Luke 12:35, 37; 17:8, for example, girding one's loins is a sign of readiness for service. As we have seen under *Form/Structure/Setting*, the primary influence on the writer's choice of terminology at this point is LXX Isa 11:5, where the Messiah-King is said to have righteousness girding his loins and truth clothing his sides. If the Roman soldier is also specifically in view, then, since it is the first item of equipment mentioned, the girdle will not be the metal-studded belt worn over the armor or the sword-belt, but rather the leather apron worn under the armor like breeches (cf. Oepke, *TDNT* 5 [1967] 303, 307). Other metaphorical uses of the terminology in the OT include Yahweh being girded with might (Ps 65:6) and Yahweh girding the psalmist with strength for battle (Ps 18:32, 39), and in the NT the awkward mixed metaphor of 1 Pet 1:13 about girding up the loins of one's mind. E. Levine ("The Wrestling-Belt Legacy in the New Testament," *NTS* 28 [1982] 560–64) claims that all such references still carry allusions to the belt-wrestling practices of the ancient Near East and that the wrestling belt became symbolic of soldiers ready for battle. Here in Ephesians, the belt which provides support and braces the soldier ready for action is truth. Since in LXX Isa 11:5 truth referred to faithfulness and loyalty and what was said there of the Messiah is now applied to believers, it is likely that that is also the force of "truth" in this verse. The qualities to which the various pieces of armor point are used rather generally and loosely and cannot always be pinned down precisely. The interpreter has to attempt to discover an acceptable range of meaning from the context and the use of the terms elsewhere in the letter. Since the next three qualities mentioned all appear to be those that the believer must exercise, it is probable that truth here refers to an element of character and activity to be demonstrated by the readers (cf. 4:25; 5:9; cf. also Meyer, 333; Westcott, 95; Abbott, 185) rather than the truth of the gospel (cf. 1:13; 4:21, 24; *pace* Schlier, 295; Oepke, *TDNT* 5 [1967] 307–8), though to be sure the moral rectitude and faithfulness demanded by the gospel is also made available through that gospel.

"The breastplate of righteousness" was part of Yahweh's armor in the depictions found in Isa 59:17 and Wis 5:18 (cf. also Isa 11:5, where righteousness is the Messiah's girdle). The righteousness or justice of Yahweh is an attribute that it is now essential for the believer to display. This is not the justifying righteousness of Rom 3:21–26 (*pace* Barth, 796; Oepke, *TDNT* 5 [1967] 310) but an ethical quality (cf. the earlier use of the term in 4:24; 5:9 and δίκαιος in 6:1; cf. also Meyer, 334; Westcott, 96; Abbott, 185; Schnackenburg, 284). In terms of the armor of the Roman soldier, the θώραξ was the frontal metal piece vital for the protection of chest, lungs, and heart. Doing right and practicing justice is equally vital for the Christian soldier in his or her battle against the powers of evil. In 1 Thess 5:8 Paul had made the virtues of faith and love the Christian's breastplate, but he also depicted righteousness as necessary for the battle when he spoke of "the weapons of righteousness for the right hand and the left" in 2 Cor 6:7.

15 καὶ ὑποδησάμενοι τοὺς πόδας ἐν ἑτοιμασίᾳ τοῦ εὐαγγελίου τῆς εἰρήνης, "and having fitted your feet with the readiness of the gospel of peace." Proper footwear is required if the soldier is to be ready for combat. ὑποδήματα, "sandals," could be used of military sandals (cf. Xenophon, *Anab.* 4.5.14; Josephus, *J.W.* 6.1.8), and the Roman soldier frequently wore the *caliga*, a half-boot, which was part of the equipment for long marches and which could be studded with sharp nails to enable a firm grip. But it is significant that the writer does not refer directly to the footwear and instead talks of the feet being fitted or shod, showing again that he is primarily influenced by the language of an OT passage which mentions feet in connection with proclaiming the gospel of peace. The text in question is LXX Isa 52:7, "as the feet of one preaching glad tidings of peace" (cf. also Nah 1:15). Paul had used this verse in connection with the preacher of the gospel in Rom 10:15, but this writer links the equipping of the feet not with the proclamation of the gospel of peace but with the ἑτοιμασία, "readiness," of the gospel of peace. The force of this term is disputed. Some (e.g., A. F. Buscarlet, "The 'Preparation' of the Gospel of Peace," *ExpTim* 9 [1897] 38–40, followed by E. H. Blakeney, *ExpTim* 55 [1944] 138; J. A. F. Gregg, *ExpTim* 56 [1944] 54; Barth, 797–99) link it with one of the connotations it has in the LXX of a prepared or solid foundation (cf. LXX Ps 88:14; Ezra 2:68) and transfer it to mean "firm footing" or "steadfastness." In this way, a connection can be made with the overall exhortation to stand. But the term nowhere actually means "firm footing," and its more usual sense is readiness, preparedness, or preparation (cf., e.g., LXX Ps 9:17; Wis 13:12; *Ep. Arist.* 182; Josephus, *Ant.* 10.1.2 § 9 *v.l.*). The reference is, therefore, not to readiness to proclaim the gospel (*pace* Schlier, 296; Oepke, *TDNT* 5 [1967] 312; Gnilka, 311–12; Ernst, 400) but to the readiness or preparedness for combat and for standing in the battle that is bestowed by the gospel of peace (cf. also Meyer, 334–35; Abbott, 185; Hendriksen, 277). The writer's emphasis is paradoxical. It is the appropriation of the gospel of peace that makes one ready for war. As we have seen from 2:14–18, the gospel of peace is embodied in Christ who "is our peace," and this is a peace with both vertical and horizontal axes: peace with God the Father and peace between human beings, Jews and Gentiles, who were formerly at enmity. Since such peace is the pledge of future cosmic harmony (cf. 1:10; 3:10), its realization in the Church not only sounds the death knell for opposing cosmic powers but also, in the meantime, leads to the intensification of their opposition. A continuing preservation and appropriation of the gospel of peace is, therefore, necessary if the powers are to be resisted and if believers are to be ready to make their stand in the world, the stand that is in line with their calling. Believers' preparation for standing firm and prevailing against the alienating and fragmenting powers of evil is the harmony produced by the gospel.

16 ἐν πᾶσιν ἀναλαβόντες τὸν θυρεὸν τῆς πίστεως, ἐν ᾧ δυνήσεσθε πάντα τὰ βέλη τοῦ πονηροῦ τὰ πεπυρωμένα σβέσαι, "besides all these, having taken up the shield of faith, with which you will be able to extinguish all the burning arrows of the evil one." Further armor is necessary. Although ἐν πᾶσιν could mean "in all circumstances," it more probably has the force of "besides or in addition to all (these)." The last of the pieces of spiritual armor, which are virtues or attitudes to be practiced by the believer, is "the shield of faith." In the OT, the shield was used as an image for God's protection of his people (cf., e.g., Gen 15:1; Pss 5:2; 18:2, 30, 35; 28:7; 33:20; 35:2; 59:11; 91:4; 115:9–11; 144:1). Here the term employed is θυρεός or *scutum*, the large shield, four feet in length and two and a half feet in width, which is described by Polybius 6.23.2 as the first part of the Roman πανοπλία and which protected the whole body. This Roman shield was generally made of wood with a thick coating of leather (cf. also Homer, *Il.* 5.452; Herodotus 7.91; Pliny 8.39). It is to be distinguished from the ἀσπίς or *clipeus*, a small round buckler, which is the term found in the depiction of Yahweh's armor in LXX Wis 5:19. Faith is mentioned throughout the letter (cf. 1:13, 15; 2:8; 3:12, 17; 4:5, 13; 6:23), and in this context it is the confident trust in and receptiveness to Christ and his power that protects the whole person (*pace* Oepke, *TDNT* 5 [1967] 314, who claims it is "an objective, divinely given reality"). Faith takes hold of God's resources in the midst of the onslaughts of evil and produces the firm resolve which douses anything the enemy throws at the believer (cf. also 1 Thess 5:8, where faith is part of the breastplate, and 1 Pet 5:8, 9, where firm faith is necessary for resisting the devil).

Faith will enable the believer "to extinguish all the burning arrows of the evil one." The future δυνήσεσθε, "you will be able," relates to the effect of taking up the shield and does not indicate that the conflict itself is future (*pace* Meyer, 337). "The evil one" is a title for the enemy which is not found elsewhere in the Pauline corpus (though perhaps it is in view in 2 Thess 3:3), but occurs in Matt 13:19; John 17:15; 1 John 2:13, 14; 5:18, 19. "Burning arrows" feature in the OT in Ps 7:13 and Prov 26:18 and are elsewhere called βέλη πυρφόρα (Diodorus 20.96) or πυρφόροι ὀϊστοί (Thucydides 2.75.4). They are the *malleoli*, arrows tipped with inflammable tow or pitch and shot off after being lit. Livy (*Hist.* 21.8) graphically describes how these arrows, even when not hitting the body but caught by the shield, caused panic because they blazed fiercely and tempted soldiers to throw down their burning shields and become vulnerable to the spears of their enemies. Some writers (e.g., Oepke, *TDNT* 5 [1967] 314; Schnackenburg, 285) claim that the shields could not deal effectively with the burning arrows and that this is a place where the writer's metaphorical language breaks with reality. But in Thucydides 2.75.5 skins and hides were used to protect workmen from incendiary arrows, and the leather coating of each shield was soaked in water before battle. This meant that the wood of the shield was not set on fire and the destructive power of the arrows was neutralized. Here the burning arrows represent every type of assault devised by the evil one, not just temptation to impure or unloving conduct but also false teaching, persecution, doubt, and despair. Faith is the power which enables believers to resist and triumph over such attacks.

17 καὶ τὴν περικεφαλαίαν τοῦ σωτηρίου δέξασθε, καὶ τὴν μάχαιραν τοῦ πνεύματος, ὅ ἐστιν ῥῆμα θεοῦ, "And receive the helmet of salvation, and the sword of the Spirit, which is the word of God." Believers are to "receive," i.e., from God (v 13) who offers them, "the helmet" and "the sword." Wild (*CBQ* 46 [1984] 297) is right to claim that "the shift from the string of participles in 6:14–16 to *dexasthe* in 6:17a is meant to signal a shift from a listing of virtues in a somewhat conventional sense as qualities which involve a certain degree of human effort to objects which are gifts in the purest sense, 'salvation' and 'the word of God.' " The order of this verse, with the helmet being received before the sword, makes good sense, because the soldier who is being depicted already grasps the shield with his left hand. If he had taken the sword first, there would be no hand free to receive and put on the helmet (cf. also Meyer, 338). The helmet, which for the Roman soldier was made of bronze and had cheek pieces, provided protection for another vital part, the head. The language of "the helmet of salvation" alludes again to LXX Isa 59:17 (cf. "the breastplate of righteousness" in v 14). It is this allusion that explains the use of σωτήριον rather than σωτηρία. The former term, which was employed frequently in the LXX for salvation, occurs nowhere else in the Pauline corpus (but cf. Luke 2:30; 3:6; Acts 28:28). In the OT God is himself salvation and deliverance for those oppressed (cf. also, e.g., Pss 18:2, 46–48; 35:3; 37:39, 40; 65:5; 70:4, 5; Isa 33:2, 6; 45:17; 46:13; 51:5, 6; Jer 31:33), and here in Ephesians believers are to receive the divine salvation. Paul in 1 Thess 5:8 had talked of the helmet as the hope of salvation, but in line with his more realized eschatology this writer again thinks of salvation as a present reality (cf. esp. 2:5, 8; *pace* Schlier, 297, who reads the idea of hope into 6:17, and Barth, 776, who claims that a decision between present and future salvation cannot be made). For him, what ultimately protects believers is that God has already rescued them from bondage to the prince of the realm of the air and seated them with

Christ in the heavenly realms (cf. 2:1–10). By appropriating this salvation as their helmet, believers have every reason to be confident of the outcome of the battle.

With the final piece of equipment, the writer's emphasis shifts from the defensive to the offensive. The sharp short sword (μάχαιρα as opposed to ῥομφαία, the long sword) was the crucial offensive weapon in close combat. There is a corresponding stylistic shift. Whereas with the breastplate of righteousness, the shield of faith, or the helmet of salvation, the former element represents the latter, this is not the case with "the sword of the Spirit." The sword stands not for the Spirit but for "the word of God." In fact, the relative pronoun ὅ in the following clause, "which is the word of God," refers back to the whole phrase "the sword of the Spirit." The Spirit is not so much the one who supplies the sword (*pace* Meyer, 339)—both the helmet and the sword are to be received from God—but the one who gives it its effectiveness, its cutting edge (cf. also Schnackenburg, 286). Since the writer has already drawn on Isa 11:5 for v 14, he may well have been influenced in this verse by the imagery and language of LXX Isa 11:4, where the Spirit of God rests on the Messiah who "shall smite the earth with the word [λόγος] of his mouth, and with the breath [πνεῦμα] through his lips shall he destroy the ungodly." If this is so, an assertion about the Messiah would again be transferred to the Christian. Isa 11:4 is also taken up in 2 Thess 2:8, where the Lord Jesus will slay the lawless one with the breath of his mouth. In Revelation Christ wages war with the sword of his mouth, and his word reveals people's deeds for what they are (cf. 1:16; 2:12, 16; 19:13, 15). In Ephesians, however, when the Christian solider wields the sword of the word, it is not first of all the word of judgment but the good news of salvation. ῥῆμα here, not λόγος, refers to the gospel (cf. also 5:26; Rom 10:18; 1 Pet 1:25). This is "the word of truth, the gospel of your salvation" (1:13), "the gospel of peace" (6:15). This form of the word of God is also a sharp sword (cf. Heb 4:12), and the Spirit gives it its power and penetration (cf. 1 Thess 1:5). As believers take hold of and proclaim the gospel, they are enabled to overcome in the battle. And as regards the powers, that gospel does sound a note of judgment, for it announces their defeat. The paradox again is that it is the gospel of peace and reconciliation that is the sword that enables the *militia Christi* to advance. As the Church continues to be the reconciled and reconciling community, the gospel conquers the alienating hostile powers and brings about God's saving purposes.

18 διὰ πάσης προσευχῆς καὶ δεήσεως προσευχόμενοι ἐν παντὶ καιρῷ ἐν πνεύματι, καὶ εἰς αὐτὸ ἀγρυπνοῦντες ἐν πάσῃ προσκαρτερήσει καὶ δεήσει περὶ πάντων τῶν ἁγίων, "through every prayer and petition, praying at all times in the Spirit, and to this end keeping alert in all perseverance and petition for all the saints." Standing ready for combat is to be combined with prayer. The participles "praying" and "keeping alert" are probably to be connected with the verb of the main exhortation in v 14, στῆτε οὖν, "stand therefore," rather than with the intervening δέξασθε, "receive," in v 17, which should be seen as subordinate to στῆτε (cf. also Meyer, 341; Abbott, 187). But prayer is not the seventh piece of spiritual armor as some claim (*pace* Schlier, 298, 300; Gaugler, 228). The military metaphors are limited to vv 14–17. Instead, the close link between the material on prayer and what has preceded, through the participles and διά, "through," underlines the spiritual nature of believers' combat. This is more than a worldly or a human conflict. The writer has taken over material from Col 4:2–4 and employed it differently as an elaboration on what it means for the Christian soldier to stand firm and be strong in the Lord. Putting on, taking up, and receiving God's armor all require an attitude of dependence on God. Prayer for strengthening from God can be seen as a major way in which believers appropriate the divine armor and are enabled to stand. The expression for prayer is a double one, using the two terms προσευχή and δέησις. Paul had also used this twofold expression in Phil 4:6, "in everything by prayer and petition with thanksgiving let your requests be made known to God" (cf. also LXX 3 Kgdms 8:45; 2 Chron 6:19 [twice]; 1 Tim 2:1; 5:5; Ign. *Magn.* 7.1). They are employed together here primarily for the sake of intensification, but usually the former term has a more general and comprehensive reference, while the latter indicates more specifically the request or petition aspect of prayer. In this verse, the two elements are taken up separately: first, "praying at all times in the Spirit," and then "to this end keeping alert in all perseverance and petition for all the saints."

The need to pray "at all times" is a theme found frequently in the Pauline writings, though the expression may vary (cf. πάντοτε, "always," in Phil 1:4; Col 1:3; 4:12; 2 Thess 1:11, and ἀδιαλείπτως, "unceasingly," in 1 Thess 5:17; Rom 1:9, 10). Earlier in Eph 5:20, giving thanks is also an activity which is to take place always (πάντοτε). The writer has demonstrated the importance he attaches to prayer, and particularly prayer for awareness of divine power and strengthening through that power, in his own prayers for the readers reported in 1:15–23 and 3:14–21. The immediate context of the battle against evil powers only makes all the clearer the constant need for calling on divine aid.

Praying "in the Spirit" has reference to the Holy Spirit (cf. also Jude 20, "Pray in the Holy Spirit") rather than to the human spirit (*pace* Westcott, 97). In Paul's thought, the Spirit is intimately involved in believers' prayers (Rom 8:15, 16) and enables them to repeat the prayer of Jesus to the Father, "Abba" (Gal 4:6; Rom 8:15, 16). Jones (*RevRel* 27 [1976] 128–39) rightly sees a connection with 2:18 and access to the Father in the one Spirit, but pushes this too far when he interprets 6:18 as also about unity between Jew and Gentile because of its association with the preceding allusion to Isa 59:17, which in its context is tied to the notion of God's salvation of the nations (cf. also Schnackenburg, 288 n. 740). The writer is calling for prayer inspired, guided, and made effective through the Spirit. Those who are united in their access to the Father through the Spirit (2:18), who are built into God's dwelling place in the Spirit (2:22), and who are being filled with the Spirit (5:18) can and should pray constantly in and through this Spirit (for further discussion of "prayer in the Spirit," see Adai, *Der Heilige Geist,* 237–43).

To give oneself to this sort of prayer, it is essential to keep alert. This is underlined by the prepositional phrases which surround ἀγρυπνοῦντες, "keeping alert." The preceding εἰς αὐτό, "to this end," stresses that the purpose of keeping alert is to pray constantly, and the following ἐν πάσῃ προσκαρτερήσει καὶ δεήσει makes clear that this watchfulness is to be accompanied by perseverance and prayer. The exhortation to watch and pray was part of early Christian paraenetic tradition, and either ἀγρυπνεῖν or γρηγορεῖν, which are found as synonyms in the LXX and the NT, can be employed for the former concept. In Mark 14:38 Jesus in Gethsemane tells the sleeping Peter to watch (γρηγορεῖν) and pray. This had been preceded by the threefold call to the disciples to watch (once with ἀγρυπνεῖν and twice with γρηγορεῖν) in Mark 13:33–37. Luke makes this watching a constant activity and links it with prayer for strengthening: "But watch [ἀγρυπνεῖν] at all times, praying that you may have strength" (Luke 21:36). (On this traditional association of watching and praying, see further E. Lövestam, *Spiritual Wakefulness in the New Testament* [Lund: Gleerup, 1963] 64–77.) To be alert involves renouncing the spiritual sleep of the darkness of this age (cf. also 1 Pet 4:7). As Lövestam (*Spiritual Wakefulness*, 75) observes: "For the one who fails to keep awake . . . but is entangled and absorbed in this world and age, this becomes hindering and devastating for the prayer life." The notions of perseverance and prayer come together elsewhere, although Eph 6:18 is the only place in the NT that the noun προσκαρτέρησις, "perseverance," is used rather than the cognate verb (cf. the exhortations to persevere in prayer in Rom 12:12 and Col 4:2; cf. also Acts 1:14; 2:42; 6:4). If earlier in the passage much emphasis has been given to God's provision of resources, there is now also stress on the need for effort and self-discipline on the part of believers, in order to avoid spiritual complacency and fatigue and pursue a life of prayer.

The petitions believers offer as part of this life of prayer are to be "for all the saints." The writer has earlier reminded his readers of their links with all the saints (cf. 1:15; 3:18), and this consciousness of fellowship with all believers, of being part of a universal Church, which he has attempted to instill should bear fruit in the breadth of their concerns and prayers. The fourfold use of πᾶς, "all," in this verse is both typical of the writer's plerophory of style and indicative of the significance he attaches to prayer. As Barth (778) comments, "Nothing less is suggested than that the life and strife of the saints be one great prayer to God, that this prayer be offered in ever new forms, however good or bad the circumstances, and that this prayer not be self-centered but express the need and hope of all the saints."

19, 20 καὶ ὑπὲρ ἐμοῦ . . . ἵνα ἐν αὐτῷ παρρησιάσωμαι ὡς δεῖ με λαλῆσαι, "and for me . . . that I may talk of it boldly and openly as I ought to speak." In addition to calling for prayer for all believers, the writer, having taken on the persona of Paul as part of the device of pseudonymity, appeals for prayer especially for himself. This appeal is an adaptation of material from Col 4:3, 4, but with the focus on Paul himself, not his co-workers as well. Elsewhere in the Pauline writings the apostle requests prayer for himself or assumes his readers are praying for him. Sometimes this is in relation to a specific situation or need (cf. Rom 15:30–32; Phil 1:19; Philem 22) and sometimes it is more generally for himself and his ministry (cf. 1 Thess 5:25; 2 Cor 1:11; 2 Thess 3:1, 2). This call for prayer comes into the latter category.

Prayer is asked for the apostle's ministry, which is described in terms familiar from earlier in the letter—making known the mystery of the gospel. God has made known to all believers the mystery of his will (1:9, 10). In particular, he has made it known to Paul, who in turn has a mission to enlighten all about this mystery (3:3–6, 9). In addition, the Church has a crucial role in making it known (3:10). The gospel can be identified with this mystery. Since at the heart of making known the mystery is the reconciliation of Jews and Gentiles in the one body of the Church, it is natural for the gospel to be called elsewhere in relation to the Gentile readers "the gospel of your salvation" (1:13) and "the gospel of peace" (6:15). As has been emphasized earlier, making known the mystery of the gospel is not a purely human effort but relies on God's grace (cf. 3:2, 7, 8). Here this is underlined through the notion of the word being given. The apostle is dependent on God not only for the revelation of the mystery but also for its proclamation.

Some hold that this emphasis is continued through the words ἐν ἀνοίξει τοῦ στόματός μου, "in opening my mouth," which would refer to the opening of the mouth by God and "complete from the subjective side what is expressed on the objective side in δοθῇ λόγος ["the word may be given"]" (Abbott, 189; cf. also J. A. Robinson, 136; Schlier, 303). In Col 4:3, which is the point of departure for the language of opening, the opening is done by God, though it is not of the mouth but of a door for the word. In the wisdom literature Wisdom is said to open the mouth of the righteous (cf. Wis 10:21; Sir 15:5). This way of construing the request, with both the giving of the word and the opening of the mouth being done by God, is certainly possible. But it is more likely that the majority of the commentators are right in taking it as a request that when the apostle opens his mouth ("when I open my mouth") God will fill it with the appropriate utterance. Opening the mouth is a common biblical expression for proclaiming God's word (cf. Ps 78:2; Ezek 3:27; 33:22; Dan 10:16).

The gospel which it is the apostle's mission to proclaim is one for which he is "an ambassador in chains." This notion of being an ambassador picks up on Paul's self-understanding in 2 Cor 5:20 and Philem 9 (on this latter disputed reference, see O'Brien, *Colossians, Philemon* [WBC 44] 290). The term was used of the emperor's legates, who were empowered to be official representatives of his government. Likewise, Paul in his mission to the Gentiles was acting as the authorized representative of the gospel (cf. also 3:7, 8). Through the concept of authorized representation there are clear overlaps between ambassadorship and apostleship. Here the depiction of the imprisoned apostle continues (cf. also 3:1; 4:1). ἅλυσις, "chain," is used in the portrayal of Paul's imprisonment in Acts 28:20 and 2 Tim 1:16. To talk of an ambassador in chains is to employ an oxymoron. Normally an ambassador had diplomatic immunity and could not be imprisoned by those to whom he was sent, but prison chains now become the appropriate insignia for representing the gospel, the mark of the suffering apostle (cf. also Barth, 782).

One of the writer's distinctive additions to the material from Col 4:3, 4 is his emphasis on boldness and openness (cf. ἐν παρρησίᾳ, v 19, and παρρησιάσωμαι, v 20). Earlier he has used the noun παρρησία, "boldness," to refer to the believer's direct and bold access to God (cf. 3:12; for fuller discussion and reference to the literature, see *Comment* on this verse). Elsewhere in Greek literature the term primarily refers to freedom of speech, the sort of speech appropriate to a free human being. Boldness and freedom were supposed to characterize the speaking of a true philosopher, demonstrating that he had found genuine personal freedom and on the basis of this could expose the shortcomings of others in an attempt to educate them. Dio Chrysostom describes the ideal Cynic as "a man who with purity and without guile speaks with a philosopher's boldness" (*Orat.* 32.11; cf. also Epictetus, *Diss.* 3.22.19; Lucian, *Demonax* 3).

In the NT the verb is frequently used of Paul's bold proclamation of the gospel (cf. 1 Thess 2:2; Acts 9:27, 29; 13;46; 19:8; 26:26). In both Phil 1:20 and Philem 8 Paul the prisoner talks about his freedom or boldness. Here too the picture is of the ambassador who continues to pass on his message freely and openly even while he is in chains. Since that message is also called the mystery, there is a further connotation of παρρησία. That which was hidden, but is now revealed openly, is also to be proclaimed openly.

These verses obviously raise the question of how they were meant to be taken if, as we have argued, the letter was not written by Paul himself but by a follower writing in his name. On such a reading, they form part of the literary device of pseudonymity through which the message is conveyed. As part of such a device which aimed at verisimilitude, there is no difference in principle between having the apostle ask for prayer for himself toward the end of the letter, although he is in fact deceased, and simply claiming the name of the deceased apostle at the beginning. But these verses are more than merely a literary device. Through them the recipients of the letter are being presented with the paradoxical image of Paul the imprisoned apostle proclaiming the gospel freely and openly. There is a similar picture of Paul in 2 Tim 2:9, and it is striking that Luke's picture of the imprisoned Paul at the end of the Acts has the same features—he preaches and teaches μετὰ πάσης παρρησίας ἀκωλύτως, "with all openness, unhindered" (Acts 28:31; cf. also Wild, *CBQ* 46 [1984] 292 n. 31). The impression to be conveyed is of the untrammeled triumph of the gospel despite opposition and extreme adversity. Here also, then, the readers' prayers are to be for the triumph of the apostolic gospel that is summed up by this image. Since the writer considers himself a representative of Paul, the request can also be understood as his appeal for prayer for his own bold proclamation of the Pauline gospel (see also *Comment* on 3:4). The readers' intercession will demonstrate their own solidarity with this apostolic gospel. At the same time, this image of Paul encourages and braces them in their own Christian witness. If, as they know, Paul proclaimed the gospel boldly even in prison, whatever the difficulties of their circumstances they have no reason to be ashamed of and every reason for confidence in his gospel, to which they owe their Christian existence. They are not to think of themselves as a little group that needs to hide away. Rather, they have a gospel that is to be announced freely and openly in the midst of the surrounding world. Wild (*CBQ* 46 [1984] 294) is right to claim that "6:19–20 presents us with a typological model of Christian existence in the world" but wrong in his explanation of this. It is not that Christians are also prisoners, apparently in bondage to the demonic powers, yet not prisoners because of Christ. Nowhere does Ephesians indicate any such control, even apparent, of the powers over believers' lives. The model is more indirect and general—boldness and openness in the midst of opposition and adversity. For *Paul*, this adversity and opposition meant imprisonment, but this is not the case for the readers, even metaphorically.

Explanation

After the writer's ethical exhortations to his readers have taken him into the details of household living, he now steps back. In his concluding appeal in 6:10–20, he looks at their task of living in the world from a broader and more general perspective. He sets the task in a cosmic context and under the sustained new imagery of a spiritual battle urges the readers to stand firm against the evil powers that are arrayed against them. Battle imagery had been used extensively in the Qumran literature to depict the community's role in the world and was employed in a transferred sense in Stoic writings to expound the attitudes and conduct of the wise man. This passage is both the conclusion of the paraenesis and the final major section of the letter as a whole. As such, in rhetorical terms it is the *peroratio,* the closing part of an address that sums up its main themes in a way that evokes the appropriate emotional response in the audience. In regard to both form and content, the exhortation has features in common with the speeches in Greek literature of generals rallying their troops to do battle against daunting enemies. The main sources for the writer's inspiration, however, are the brief exhortations in various places in Paul's letters to stand, to be strong, and to put on faith and love as a breastplate and the hope of salvation as a helmet, and the language of a number of passages in Isaiah, two of which depict the armor of Yahweh and his Messiah (cf. Isa 11:4, 5; 59:17; cf. also Wis 5:17–20a) and two of which provide further motifs through the mention of sword and feet (cf. Isa 49:2; 52:7). The resulting picture of the believer's armor does have a correspondence to that of a heavily armed Roman legionary, but this is not the writer's primary point of departure. The call to stand firm in the battle is his distinctive addition to the material in Colossians, which has provided the source for the letter as a whole. He only returns to adapt and modify this source at the end of the passage with the exhortation to prayer based on Col 4:2–4.

The passage has three main parts: vv 10–13, vv 14–17, and vv 18–20. In the first part, the readers are exhorted to be strong and reminded that they derive such strength from their Lord and his power. The context for this call to strength and courage soon becomes clear. It is a spiritual battle in which the readers are on the side of God against the devil. If they are to stand firm in the face of the cunning stratagems with which the devil attacks them, then in order to be strong they will need divine protection and equipping. For this reason, the writer urges them to put on the full armor of God. The necessity of God supplying believers with his own armor is further underlined as the writer goes on to depict the nature of the battle and the strength of the opposing forces. The battle is not against a human enemy, but, seen from a cosmic perspective, is against spiritual powers, designated in the terminology of the time as principalities and authorities and the world rulers of this darkness. These powers, under the leadership of the devil, dominate the present evil age and are summed up by the writer as "the spiritual forces of evil." In common with both Jewish and Hellenistic thought, the writer sees these hostile powers as located in the heavenly realms. Thus, in line with Paul, he conceives of the "already" and the "not yet," the overlap between the present age and the age to come produced by what has happened in Christ, culminating in his exaltation, as involving both heaven and earth. In the time between the decisive defeat of the powers by Christ and their ultimate submission, the powers of evil are still active, and so believers cannot afford to be complacent. So for the second time (v 13), the readers are urged to take up God's full armor, and are thereby reminded that they have all the resources necessary for successful resistance of any inroads into their lives that the hostile powers attempt to make. Appropriating the divine resources for living is not only essential now but will be especially crucial when the present age culminates in a climactic time of evil. Accordingly, having fully equipped themselves for battle, the readers must concentrate all their resources on standing firm.

The second part of the passage (vv 14–17) begins with the imperative "stand," summing up the main thrust of the writer's appeal to his readers to occupy steadfastly the position in the battle against the powers that is theirs in Christ. This time the writer spells out some of the specific pieces of armor they need to have put on if they are to stand firm. The first four items are the belt of truth, the breastplate of righteousness, the sandals of the readiness of the gospel of peace, and the shield of faith. Truthfulness and moral integrity will provide support and brace the believer. Doing right and practicing justice will give essential protection. Being in a state of readiness by living out the peace produced by the gospel is paradoxically but appropriately the best preparation for combat against powers out to produce disunity. Confident trust in and constant openness to God's resources in Christ will offer further full protection against every type of assualt rained upon believers by the evil one. In v 17 the syntax changes from a series of participles to a new imperative, "receive," and this signals a change in the nature of the two final pieces of armor. The helmet of salvation and the sword of the Spirit are no longer subjective qualities required of the believer but objective gifts from God. Of course, for this writer there is no ultimate distinction, and both ethical qualities of the new humanity and soteriological benefits have their source in God (cf. 2:8–10; 4:24). Here the allusions to OT language about the armor of Yahweh and his Messiah are a constant reminder that all the pieces of armor are part of God's full armor that he is giving to believers. Through the last two pieces of armor, believers are being told that they are protected in the battle by the present reality of salvation, through which they have been delivered from the dominion of the ruler of darkness, and that they can move on to the offensive against the forces of evil by wielding the word of the gospel, which is given its penetration and power by the Spirit.

The third section of the letter's final exhortation (vv 18–20) is closely related to what has preceded through its participial constructions, making clear that appropriating the divine armor and standing firm in the battle require a life of dependence on God in prayer. Believers are to pray at all times, and their prayers are to be inspired and guided by the Spirit through whom they have confident access to God the Father. For such a life of prayer they need the alertness which keeps at bay spiritual sleep and complacency and the perseverance which overcomes fatigue and discouragement. Their prayer will not only involve dependence on God for their own strengthening but will also include petitioning on behalf of all believers and, more specifically, on behalf of the apostle that, in the midst of his imprisonment for the sake of the gospel, he may be given the words to proclaim boldly and openly the mystery that is at the heart of his gospel. By addressing them in the name of the apostle who is an ambassador in chains and asking prayer for the free and open proclamation of the apostolic gospel despite Paul's imprisonment, the writer is asking for prayer both for his own ministry in continuity with that of Paul and for the triumph of the apostolic gospel despite opposition and adversity. In asking the readers to demonstrate their solidarity with Paul's gospel in this way, the writer, through this portrait of Paul, is at the same time indirectly providing them with a model for their own task of living in the world. Their witness too is to be bold and open, whatever the difficulties and however formidable the opposition that they face.

Since this passage concludes the letter's ethical exhortations, its focus, like that of the preceding material in this half of the letter, is on believers and their situation. This situation is not simply one of relating to the surrounding society and its values in a distinctive fashion but one which has a cosmic dimension. In their situation, believers must reckon with superhuman agencies. The point is driven home that the world in which they live out their Christian existence is not neutral territory but a battleground. On their side, believers relate to God (vv 11, 13, 17), Christ (v 10), and the Spirit (vv 17, 18). On the other side, they are up against the devil or evil one (vv 11, 16) and his spiritual forces (v 12). The perspective of the letter as a whole indicates, however, that this dualism is only a temporary one and that the two sides are not equally matched. God's purpose is to bring the whole cosmos into harmony in Christ (1:10), and the opposition has already been defeated (1:20–22; 4:8–10). In the meantime, while history as the readers know it continues, the remainder of the battle must be fought to a conclusion. Although it is God's purpose to sum up all things in Christ and in the process to create a new reconciled people who live together in harmony and lead a holy and righteous life in the world, the defeated powers of evil attempt to do their utmost to thwart this plan. It is striking that a letter which in its first half depicts the peace produced by the gospel should in its second half conclude with an emphasis on war. But this only underlines that God's purposes are not yet complete and that the powers that are hostile to the well-being of believers, to the existence of the Church, and to the advance of the gospel have not yet given up their ultimately futile opposition. In this way, the readers are given a realistic perspective on Christian existence and disabused of any naïve notion that living out their calling in the world will be an effortless or trouble-free assignment.

The writer has not, however, suddenly forgotten all that he has said in the first part of the letter about the whole range of the benefits of salvation that the readers enjoy in Christ, including participation in his exaltation and victory (cf. 2:6). On the contrary, the very depiction of their situation in its cosmic context as a battle against the powers underlines its newness. Previously, the readers were totally under the control of the prince of the realm of the air (2:2). Now, because of their share in Christ's decisive victory, they are in a position to be able to resist the devil and his cohorts. All they have to do is continue to appropriate the resources of strength that are theirs in Christ. If they were to be left to themselves or to depend on their own resources, there would be no contest and they would be back in their former bondage, darkness and death. But as it is, the full armor of God provides all that is needed to prevail.

This passage with its call to stand firm provides an appropriate conclusion not only to the ethical exhortations but to the letter as a whole. In the first part of the letter the readers have been reinforced in their identity as Christian believers by being reminded of their relationship to Christ, of the benefits of the salvation they have received, and of their part in the one Church that has been created out of Jews and Gentiles. In the second half they have been exhorted to live out their new life as the Church in the world. They are to become what they already are. All that has been said about what God has accomplished for believers and about the Church's role in the world has been set against a cosmic backdrop. Now in conclusion, the cosmic dimension of the drama of salvation comes to the fore and colors the way the writer takes up again both the issue of believers' identity and that of their task in the world. As regards their identity, believers are to see themselves as Christian soldiers fitted out in God's full armor. Interpreters have long disputed whether the pieces of armor are to be taken as objective or subjective, as soteriological benefits or ethical qualities. But the mixture of the two, with the first four as activities or attitudes to be demonstrated by believers and the last two as gifts from God, is entirely appropriate for a concluding appeal which combines both the letter's more recent concerns about the life of the new humanity that is to be appropriated and lived out and its earlier emphasis on a salvation that has been given. As regards the Church's role in the world, the readers are made aware that the opposition they run up against in living out the life of the new humanity has as its source the supernatural powers of evil. The Church's witness poses a threat to these powers by reminding them of their ultimate defeat, and so they attempt to retaliate with all the means at their disposal. But, as we have seen, as well as being made aware of the opposition to their task, the readers are made equally aware of the totally adequate resources available both for the defensive and the offensive aspects of their role. The emphases of this passage provide an effective conclusion to the preceding exhortations about the Church's role in the world. Maintaining the unity of the Spirit, attaining to maturity and building up the body of Christ in the face of false teaching, living lives of righteousness, holiness, and truth, dealing with anger, cultivating edifying talk, loving others, valuing words and conduct that are free from sexual impurity, worshiping and giving thanks, submitting and loving in marriage, obeying and avoiding provocation in child-parent relationships, and obeying and abstaining from threatening in slave-master relationships can now all be seen to be part of resisting the powers of evil and to depend on appropriating Christ's strength. The Church that lives out the ethical exhortations of the letter is the *militia Christi* that has put on the divine armor and is standing its ground in the battle with evil in all its manifestations.

At the same time, Christian soldiers are to be on constant prayer alert as they perform their task, interceding in the Spirit not only for divine aid for themselves but for the whole Church and for the advance of the apostolic gospel in the world. The letter's earlier reminders of the readers' communal identity and of the debt that they owe to Paul's proclamation of the mystery have not been forgotten. The emphasis on prayer has also been pervasive in the first part of the letter, which began with a prayer of blessing and praise, continued with a prayer that the readers might know the greatness of God's power in Christ, and ended with a further prayer for their strengthening through the Spirit. Now at the end of the letter as a whole, believers' own praying ensures that their living in the world retains an awareness of its transcendent dimension and can be seen as the means by which they appropriate the divine resources of strength for the battle.

The exhortation to stand, which sums up the main thrust of the appeal to the readers in this passage, has reference to their holding their position as they live out their life in the world. Popular expositions which summarize the message of the letter in terms of the three verbs "sit," "walk," and "stand" have caught the significance of its progression of thought. The first part of the letter has dealt with believers' identity in terms of their status and position. Their participation in Christ's victory over the powers is expressed most strikingly in the assertion that they have been seated with Christ in the heavenly realms. The second part of the letter with its repeated use of the verb "to walk" in all its sections appeals to them to live out their status and calling in the world. Now the concluding exhortation to stand combines both of these earlier emphases in its call to believers to maintain and appropriate their position of strength and victory as they live out their lives in the world in the face of the opposition of evil cosmic powers.

In this way, the letter's final appeal is admirably suited to its writer's purpose of reminding his readers of their distinctive calling as members of the Church in the world. Its battle imagery recapitulates his earlier exposition in a new and powerful fashion. It enables him to convey the urgency and challenge of their task as he calls for courage, firm resolve, prayerfulness, alertness, and perseverance. At the same time, his focus on Christ's strength and God's full armor enables him to leave them with a sense of security and confidence. Their confidence and firm resolve are further strengthened by his parting picture of the open proclamation of the gospel by the imprisoned apostle to whom, humanly speaking, they owe their Christian existence and who now serves as a model for their own bold witness in the world in the face of intense opposition.

Postscript (6:21–24)

Translation

²¹*Now in order that you also may know my circumstances, how I am getting along,*ᵃ *Tychicus, the dear brother and faithful servant in the Lord, will tell you everything.*ᵇ ²²*I am sending him to you for this very purpose, that you may know how we are and that he may encourage your hearts.*
²³*Peace be to the brothers and sisters,*ᶜ *and love with faith from God the Father and the Lord Jesus Christ.* ²⁴*Grace be with all who love our Lord Jesus Christ, grace and immortality.*ᵈᵉ

Notes

ᵃ A literal translation of this clause would be "what I am doing" but it was frequently employed more idiomatically (cf. BAGD 698).

ᵇ In the Greek text the sentence does not end at this point but continues with a relative clause "whom I am sending to you. . . ."

ᶜ τοῖς ἀδελφοῖς means literally "to the brothers," but the plural ἀδελφοί can include both brothers and sisters (cf. BAGD 16), and undoubtedly both men and women would have been among the intended recipients.

ᵈ For justification for linking the final phrase ἐν ἀφθαρσίᾳ with "grace" in this way, see *Comment* on v 24.

ᵉ There is a variant reading which has an additional ἀμήν, "Amen," at the end of the verse and which would bring the ending into conformity with the liturgical close of the first half of the letter in 3:21 (cf. ℵᶜ D K L P most minuscules syrᵖ·ʰ goth ethᵖᵖ). But the evidence for its omission (p⁴⁶ ℵ* A B F G 33 copˢᵃ·ᵇᵒ·ᶠᵃʸ arm ethʳᵒ) is far superior.

Form/Structure/Setting

In the final part of the paraenesis the readers had been asked to pray for Paul's bold proclamation of the mystery of the gospel and had been reminded of his situation of imprisonment. It is a natural progression to mention in conclusion that Tychicus is being sent to provide the readers with further information about Paul's welfare and circumstances. The concluding postscript has two sections—the recommendation of Tychicus and explanation of his task as apostolic emissary in vv 21, 22—and then two common features of the Pauline letter-ending—the wish of peace and the grace-benediction in vv 23, 24. In vv 21, 22 two purpose clauses surround the central statement of Tychicus' task and the description of him. The central assertion is that "Tychicus will tell you everything." He is described as "the dear brother and faithful servant in the Lord, whom I am sending to you." Preceding the assertion is a ἵνα clause which explains that the sending of Tychicus is in order that the readers may know how the apostle is doing. Following it, added on to the relative clause and underlining the notion of purpose through both εἰς αὐτὸ τοῦτο, "for this very purpose," and ἵνα, is the repeated explanation that this is in order that the readers "may know how we are" together with a new element—that Tychicus might encourage their hearts. In the two closing epistolary elements of vv 23, 24, the accent falls on the first words of each: εἰρήνη, "peace," and ἡ χάρις, "grace." In neither are the readers addressed directly in the second person plural, as is more common in the undisputed Pauline letters, but the recipients of the wish of peace and the blessing of grace are designated in the third person: "the brothers and sisters" for the former and "all who love our Lord Jesus Christ" for the latter. To the wish of peace is added the wish of love with faith, and all three benefits are said to come "from God the Father and the Lord Jesus Christ." There is also a distinctive addition to the grace-benediction in the final phrase, ἐν ἀφθαρσίᾳ, "in immortality," which confers immortality along with grace on the readers.

As is well known, Eph 6:21, 22 provides the longest example of exact repetition of the wording of Colossians to be found in the letter. The final epistolary features of 6:23, 24, however, are quite different from those in Colossians. The long personal greetings section of Col 4:10–17 is omitted, as is the note of greeting in Paul's own hand, which also asks the readers to remember his fetters (Col 4:18ab). Schnackenburg (294 n. 750) suggests that the writer does not repeat the autograph because he may believe Colossians to be a genuine Pauline letter. Colossians has no wish of peace, but does conclude with a brief grace-benediction (4:18c), though this bears little resemblance to that of Eph 6:24.

As regards the relation between Eph 6:21, 22 and Col 4:7, 8, the writer of Ephesians reproduces in total thirty-two words found in the same sequence as in Colossians. The twenty-nine words from πάντα γνωρίσει, "will tell everything," to τὰς καρδίας ὑμῶν, "your hearts," are all taken from Colossians. So what the writer of Ephesians has done is to add before τὰ κατ' ἐμέ, "my circumstances, affairs," which he takes over from Colossians, the clause ἵνα δὲ καὶ ὑμεῖς εἰδῆτε, "now in order that you also may know," and to add after it τί πράσσω, "how I am getting along." The rest of vv 21, 22 are exactly the same as what follows in Col 4:7, 8 with the one exception that Ephesians omits καὶ σύνδουλος, "and fellow slave," from the description of Tychicus in Col 4:7. Such a description had closely associated Tychicus with Paul's ministry and self-designation, and its omission in Ephesians has the effect of maintaining the rest of the letter's more exclusive focus on the apostolic ministry of Paul himself. Col 4:9 had gone on in the same sentence to link Onesimus with Tychicus and to restate the intention behind sending these two, namely that they will tell the Colossians everything about what is happening in the place of the letter's provenance. All of this is omitted in Ephesians.

One feature of 6:22 in particular may betray the origin of the material elsewhere. It is that the writer has transferred the first person plural reference, ἵνα γνῶτε τὰ περὶ ἡμῶν, "that you may know how *we* are." That made good sense in Col 4:8, where earlier in the prescript Paul and Timothy are named as co-senders of the letter and where in 4:9–14 several other co-workers who are with Paul are mentioned. In Eph 6:22 it makes sense. After all, Tychicus is to be envisaged as with the apostle at the time of writing, but it is out of keeping with the consistent emphasis of the letter as a whole on Paul alone (cf., e.g., 1:1; 3:1–4, 7, 8, 13, 14; 4:1).

In comparison with Paul's letters, Ephesians has reduced the closing elements to a minimum. Elsewhere, there may be a commendation of an emissary, hortatory remarks, notices about Paul's visits, requests for prayer, a wish of peace, greetings, a command for the recipients to greet one another with a holy kiss, a personal autograph, and a grace-benediction. Here the request for prayer has already been made part of the final section of paraenesis, and so there are simply the commendation of Tychicus, the wish of peace, and the grace-benediction. In Pauline conclusions there is, however, a set sequence of the major items—hortatory remarks, wish of peace, greetings, and grace-benediction. Whatever elements may be added or omitted, this sequence does not vary. Primarily because of the absence of greetings, Ephesians is the only letter where the wish of peace and the grace-benediction come together, but they remain in the Pauline sequence (*contra* Abbott, 190, who is simply incorrect in his claims that elsewhere the grace-benediction is first and the wish of peace last and that their different order here argues for the genuineness of the letter and against an imitation). The commendation of an emissary may be compared not only with Col 4:7–9 but also with Rom 16:1 and 1 Cor 16:10. The wish of peace occurs elsewhere in different formulations and is absent only from 1 Corinthians, Philemon, and Colossians. In Rom 15:33 it is "the God of peace be with you all," in 2 Cor 13:11b "the God of love and peace will be with you," in Phil 4:7 "the peace of God . . . will keep your hearts and your minds in Christ Jesus," in Phil 4:9 "the God of peace will be with you," in 1 Thess 5:23 "may the God of peace himself sanctify you wholly," and in 2 Thess 3:16 "may the Lord of peace himself give you peace at all times in all ways." Because the recipients of the wish are not addressed directly in the second person plural in Ephesians, its wish of peace has most in common with that in Gal 6:16, "peace and mercy be upon all who walk by this rule, upon the Israel of God." But the addition of love and faith to the wish in Ephesians means that it remains unique among the wishes of peace in the Pauline corpus. Similarly, all the other grace-benedictions in the Pauline corpus confer grace directly on the recipients, addressing them in the second person plural. They declare "the grace of our Lord Jesus Christ be with you" (Rom 16:20; 1 Thess 5:28), "be with you all" (Rom 16:24; 2 Thess 3:18), "be with your spirit" (Gal 6:18; Phil 4:23), "the grace of the Lord Jesus be with you" (1 Cor 16:23), "the grace of the Lord Jesus Christ and the love of God and the fellowship of the Holy Spirit be with you all" (2 Cor 13:14), or simply "grace be with you" (Col 4:18; cf. also 1 Tim 6:21; 2 Tim 4:22). Ephesians is unique in its third-person designation of the recipients of the blessing as "all who love our Lord Jesus Christ" and in its addition of immortality to grace in the content of the blessing.

Both parts of the postscript are discrete elements with little relationship to the rest of the letter. The only link between 6:21, 22 and what has preceded is through the literary convention of pseudonymity which it rounds off (cf. 1:1; 3:1–13; 4:1). The wish of peace and the grace-benediction in 6:23, 24 are conventional formulae, but at the same time they do recall the letter's opening salutation in 1:2, where they occurred in the reverse order and where both God the Father and the Lord Jesus Christ were named as the source. In this way, the postscript refers back to the prescript and can also evoke the other places in the letter where peace (cf. 2:14–18; 4:3; 6:15) and grace (1:6, 7; 2:5, 7, 8; 3:2, 7, 8; 4:7, 29) are emphasized. Similarly, love and faith (6:23) were mentioned together in connection with believers, but in the reverse order in 1:15 and 3:17. Elsewhere their love, which will be stressed again in 6:24, is featured in 1:4; 4:2, 15, 16; 5:2, 25, 28, 33 and their faith in 1:1, 13, 19; 2:8; 3:12; 6:16.

How the postscript contributes to the discussion of the letter's life-setting is determined by one's views about the letter's authenticity. If Ephesians was written by Paul himself, then Tychicus, who also carried the letter addressed to the specific problems of the Colossian Christians, was the bearer of this general letter. But if, as has been suggested throughout this commentary, the letter is not by the apostle himself, then the commendation of Tychicus is part of the device of pseudonymity, adding a further note of verisimilitude to the letter, as the writer takes up the role of Paul in order to present his message for a new situation. The personal note in this postscript is however kept to a minimum. There is no fiction about the apostle's plans for the future or impending visits. The person of Paul is now mediated through the Pauline circle or school, and so one of his co-workers and followers who is known to believers in Asia Minor is mentioned. Mitton (230) suggests that Tychicus could have been the writer of the letter and that he used the passage from Colossians about himself to remind the readers of the trust which Paul had placed in him. This is of course possible, but it is difficult to explain, if this is the case, why he should have omitted the designation "and fellow slave" from this description of himself. The absence of greetings indicates that even a pseudonymous letter was not originally intended for Ephesus, because a Pauline follower would have realized that Paul had worked there for an extended period and knew many Christians personally. But the reference to Tychicus, who was from Asia Minor, confirms that the letter was in all probability written to Christians in that area.

Comment

21, 22 Ἵνα δὲ καὶ ὑμεῖς εἰδῆτε τὰ κατ' ἐμέ . . . καὶ παρακαλέσῃ τὰς καρδίας ὑμῶν, "Now in order that you also may know my circumstances . . . and that he may encourage your hearts." The phrase καὶ ὑμεῖς, "you also," has provoked considerable interest among commentators. Some see in it an implicit but conscious reference to the Colossians and Tychicus' mission to them according to Col 4:7, 8. He is to inform not only them but also the recipients of this letter about Paul's circumstances (cf. Meyer, 22, 348; Schlier, 305–6). This could be the case, whether the letter was genuinely sent along with the one to the Colossians or whether this was part of the verisimilitude of the device of pseudonymity (cf. Ochel, *Bearbeitung*, 4, 5). Abbott (190) argues that such a reference to the Colossians seems forced, because this significance of καί could hardly occur to the readers. But this is to discount their knowledge of Tychicus' mission. In any case such a reference would be natural for the writer, whether Paul or a follower dependent on Colossians. Abbott's own suggestion is that the reference is a general one. The readers of this letter, like other believers, are to receive news of the apostle's situation (cf. also Barth, 809). Others take καί as more loosely attached to the whole sentence with the meaning being that Tychicus is beng sent so that, in addition to their learning the contents of the letter, the readers might also learn something about Paul's situation (cf. Dibelius-Greeven, 99; Gnilka, 321). All of these suggestions may, however, be attempts to read too much into καί, and it may well be more likely that it is being employed very loosely to emphasize the following pronoun ὑμεῖς and is not making any further point (cf. the earlier use of κἀγώ in 1:15, where there is no need to assume that others apart from the writer are giving thanks and interceding on the addressees' behalf; cf. also Ernst, 403; Schnackenburg, 295).

As we have seen, this recommendation of Tychicus repeats almost verbatim that found in Col 4:7, 8. It functions as part of the framework through which the writer presents his message as a personal letter from Paul. By means of this device, the writer is able to avoid having to say anything more specific about Paul's situation and can instead simply point the readers to Tychicus. Some advocates of the letter's pseudonymity would go further and suggest that this amounts to a thinly veiled self-recommendation on the part of the writer himself, conveniently taken from Colossians with which he was closely associated (cf. W. L. Knox, *St. Paul and the Church of the Gentiles* [Cambridge: CUP, 1939] 203; Mitton, *Epistle,* 268; Thompson, 18–19). Tychicus features elsewhere in the NT as one of Paul's co-workers, who is particularly associated with Asia Minor. In Acts 20:4 he is one of the representatives from the province of Asia who accompanies Paul on his visit to Jerusalem, while in the Pastorals he is said to have been sent on missions to both Ephesus and Crete (cf. 2 Tim 4:12; Titus 3:12). He is likely to have been known to the recipients of the letter as one of the leading representatives of the Pauline mission. The designation of him as a "dear brother and faithful servant in the Lord" reinforces his intimate relationship with Paul and his proven record of reliable ministry in the cause of Christ. These are excellent qualifications for the tasks with which he is entrusted—to pass on information about Paul's situation and to encourage the hearts of the letter's recipients. The latter task would be accomplished not only by Tychicus conveying news about Paul but also through his own strengthening and exhorting of the readers in a ministry in line with what have been the writer's concerns in this letter.

ἔπεμψα, "I have sent" (v 22), is an epistolary aorist, whereby the sender of the letter adopts the point of view of the recipients. From his own standpoint at the time of writing the postscript, of course, the sending of the bearer of the letter is an event that is still about to happen.

23 Εἰρήνη τοῖς ἀδελφοῖς καὶ ἀγάπη μετὰ πίστεως ἀπὸ θεοῦ πατρὸς καὶ κυρίου Ἰησοῦ Χριστοῦ, "Peace be to the brothers and sisters, and love with faith from God the Father and the Lord Jesus Christ." The letter began with a salutation of grace and peace which served as a prayer-wish (1:2), and it now closes with similar elements but in reverse order—a wish of peace followed by a blessing of grace. As has been noted, this wish of "peace" is unlike those in the rest of the Pauline corpus, with the exception of Gal 6:16, in that it does not address the readers directly. Instead, peace is wished on the brothers and sisters, a designation which reflects the common Pauline view of all believers as members of God's family in Christ. Interestingly, however, although believers are seen as members of God's household in 2:19, this is the only place in this letter where the readers are described with this familial term. In contrast to the frequent practice of the undisputed Paulines, it is never used to address them. This third person formulation of the wish of peace, as of the grace-benediction which follows, may be a further indication that the letter was intended as a general one with more than one church in view as the readership (cf. also 1 Pet 5:9 which speaks of "your brotherhood throughout the world").

Although the wish of peace was a conventional element of the Pauline letter's closure, at this stage of this particular letter the notion of peace takes on connotations beyond that of general Christian well-being. It inevitably recalls the earlier emphasis on that peace which is God's gift to a divided humanity of reconciliation with himself and with one another, a gift which is embodied in Christ and is to be appropriated and maintained by believers (cf. 2:14–18; 4:3; 6:15). The writer wishes not only this peace but also "love" and "faith" to be conferred on the readers. The phrase μετὰ πίστεως, "with faith," does not give special emphasis or priority to faith (*pace* Barth, 811, who translates "and above all, faith"). Believers' faith and love have been mentioned together earlier in 1:15 and 3:17, and for this writer peace is realized among believers through mutual love (cf. 4:2, 3). Such love presupposes a common and lively faith (cf. 1:15; 4:5). All three qualities, peace, love, and faith, have their source in and flow from both God and Christ.

24 ἡ χάρις μετὰ πάντων τῶν ἀγαπώντων τὸν κύριον ἡμῶν Ἰησοῦν Χριστὸν ἐν ἀφθαρσίᾳ, "Grace be with all who love our Lord Jesus Christ, grace and immortality." Again, although the grace-benediction is the conventional ending for the Pauline letter, this one would be likely to strike its recipients as highly appropriate for a letter which had earlier laid so much stress on all that they owed to the undeserved favor of God and Christ (cf. 1:6, 7; 2:5, 7, 8; 4:7). As has been noted, this particular grace-benediction is unique among the closing benedictions in the Pauline corpus because it changes the usual second person plural address—"with you" or "with your spirit"—to a third person plural formulation—"with all who love our Lord Jesus Christ." The prayer-wish of v 23 had spoken of love coming from God and Christ, and now the blessing in v 24 confers grace on all those who respond in love for Christ. This is a Christological adaptation of the common expression "those who love God," found in the OT, Second Temple Judaism, and the NT (cf., e.g., Exod 20:6; Deut 5:10; 7:9; *Pss. Sol.* 4.25; 6.6; *T. Sim.* 3.6; *1 Enoch* 108.8; Rom 8:28; 1 Cor 2:9; 8:3; Jas 1:12; 2:5). Elsewhere the letter has referred to God's love for believers (cf. 2:4) and Christ's love for them (cf. 3:19; 5:2, 25), to believers' love for one another (cf. 1:15; 4:2), to believing husbands' love for their wives (cf. 5:25, 28, 33), and to believers' love in general (cf. 1:4; 3:17; 4:15, 16; 5:2; 6:23), but this is the only place where their love for Christ is made explicit. In this way, the letter closes with a stress on believers' personal relationship and commitment to Christ. For this writer, it is important not only that his readers are aware of the objective benefits of the great salvation God has provided in Christ but also that they have made their subjective response. And what is significant about their response of allegiance is that it is not merely to the apostolic teaching or to the Pauline gospel but to the one to whom these bear witness, the Lord Jesus Christ who loved them and gave himself for them. There is a negative equivalent in the postscript of 1 Corinthians, "if any one has no love for the Lord, let him be accursed" (16:22). Here, those who, like the readers of 1 Peter, "without having seen him . . . love him" (1:8) receive a blessing of grace.

The final words of the letter, ἐν ἀφθαρσίᾳ, "in immortality," provide a closing rhetorical flourish similar to those with which the readers had become acquainted through the style of the first part of the letter. It is, however, a flourish that has caused the commentators consternation in regard to its meaning.

The meaning of the noun ἀφθαρσία itself is clear. It refers to immortality in the sense of imperishability or incorruptibility, and in Paul this quality primarily characterizes the life of the resurrection (cf. Wis 2:23; 6:18, 19; 4 Macc 9:22; 17:12; 1 Cor 15:42, 50, 52–54; Rom 2:7; 2 Tim 1:10). Two recent suggestions for the interpretation of the phrase in which it stands seem unlikely. Caird (94) claims that a complex idea has become compressed into the brevity of a benediction and that the blessing is for "those who love our Lord Jesus Christ and share in his undying life." But this writer is not known for his brevity of expression and has shown himself quite capable of expanding both the conventional wish of peace and the grace-benediction in order to convey his own meaning. Caird's suggestion involves having to read far too much into the final two words. The other recent distinctive suggestion is that of Barth (812–14), who argues, on the one hand, that the phrase is loosely attached to all the earlier elements in the blessing but also, on the other hand, that it should be separated from the rest of the sentence and translated as "in eternity" so that the letter ends with praise of the "eternal." But it is improbable both that the last two words have no specific syntactical relationship to the rest of the sentence and that in this formulation, whose function is meant to be the conferring of a blessing on believers, the writer would be intending a doxology to the quality of the eternal. More serious attention should be given to the three standard alternative explanations, each of which links "in immortality" to a particular aspect of the preceding sentence. Some (e.g., Dibelius-Greeven, 100; Martin, "Ephesians," 177) connect it with the immediately preceding "our Lord Jesus Christ," who is, therefore, described as in immortality. They appeal for support to 1 Tim 1:17, where the adjective "immortal" is used of Christ, or more broadly to Jas 2:1, where he is described as "our Lord Jesus Christ of glory," and argue that the letter has previously associated Christ with the heavenly realm and that now this is being recalled in different terminology. Against this interpretation, however, is the fact that ἀφθαρσία is not employed locally elsewhere. Some (e.g., RSV; NIV; Meyer, 351–53; Abbott, 191; Westcott, 100; J. A. Robinson, 138, 220; Houlden, *Paul's Letters*, 341) make the connection not with Christ but with the preceding participle ἀγαπώντων, so that the blessing is conferred on all those who love our Lord Jesus Christ with an undying love or a love that is free from corruption. Imperishability, it is claimed, is the characteristic of the life of the new age and, therefore, of believers' love which belongs to that age. Appeal is sometimes made to the similar syntax of Titus 3:15 which exhorts: "Greet those who love [φιλοῦντας] us in the faith [ἐν πίστει]." This view is certainly a plausible one, though on the face of it one might have expected this writer to have linked immortality more closely with God or one of his benefits than with the quality of believers' love. This is why a third interpretation, which is probably the majority one (cf. NEB; Schlier, 311–12; Gnilka, 325–26; Mitton, 232; Ernst, 405; Schnackenburg, 297–98; Mussner, 174; Bruce, *Epistles*, 416), is more attractive. This view associates "in immortality" with the preceding noun "grace," although it is further removed in the syntax. ἐν is used as a connective between nouns earlier in the letter (cf. 2:7, where the first noun is "grace"; 3:12; 6:2). So just as "and love with faith" is an addition to peace in 6:23, "in immortality" is an addition to grace here in 6:24. Both grace and immortality are seen as blessings from

God that the writer desires to be conferred on his readers. The combination of grace with immortality is an appropriate one, allowing for each notion to color the other. God's grace, emphasized throughout the letter, can be seen to be imperishable, not subject to corruption, while immortality can be seen as the result of God's undeserved favor, the immeasurable riches of which are to be shown in the coming ages (cf. 2:7).

Explanation

The writer concludes his letter with the most extensive piece of direct borrowing from Colossians (cf. Col 4:7, 8) in the letter. In it Tychicus is recommended as Paul's emissary who will tell the readers all they need to know about the apostle's situation and who will encourage them. In this way, the postscript completes the literary device of pseudonymity which frames the letter (cf. also 3:1–13; 4:1). The two final epistolary elements—the wish of peace and the grace-benediction—correspond to the opening salutation of grace and peace (1:2). They come in the same order in which they are found in the closures of the undisputed Pauline letters, but are distinctive because they are formulated in the third person plural rather than the second and because they add further blessings. The readers are described for the first time in the letter as the brothers and sisters and as all who love our Lord Jesus Christ. The wish of peace is expanded to a wish of peace, love, and faith, and the blessing of grace becomes a blessing of grace and immortality. In continuity with the contents of the letter as a whole, 6:23, 24 speak of both the gifts believers receive from God and Christ, namely peace, love, faith, grace, and immortality, and the response they make to Christ, namely love. The common factor of love highlights what has been a consistent emphasis of the writer: what is required of believers is already given by God.

Through thanksgiving and paraenesis the writer has been concerned to reinforce his readers' sense of their calling in Christ, to remind them of the privileges of salvation that are theirs, and to encourage them in the light of these to lead a distinctive life in the world. In such a letter, which has attempted to make Paul's gospel speak again to a new situation among some of the churches of the Pauline mission in Asia Minor, the final grace-benediction is particularly appropriate. The blessing of grace, which was a liturgical form before it was an epistolary form, recalls the language of worship and the liturgical forms which frame the first half of the letter. It also recalls through its content two of the great themes of the first half—that all the privileges of salvation believers enjoy are theirs through God's grace, which has been lavished on them in Christ, and that one of the greatest of those privileges is their share in Christ's resurrection and exaltation, which they experience now but which they will continue to experience in the coming ages. Having exhorted his readers in the second half of the letter to maintain the Church's unity and participate in its growth and to demonstrate the life of the new humanity in society, and having braced them for the battle against the powers of evil which this will involve, the writer comes full circle, as he once again points the readers back to the divine resources that are available and calls on God to bestow his abundant grace and glorious immortality upon them.

Index of Principal Subjects

Access 149–50, 189–91
Administration liii, 31–32, 173–74, 184
Adoption 25–26
Advice xli
Anamnesis remembering, reminder xxxvi–xxxvii, xl–xli, 132, 135
Anger 301–2, 308–9, 406–7
Apostles lxiv, lxxi, 153–54, 178–80, 249–50
Apostleship lxii–lxxiii, 5–6, 182–83
Armour 435–37, 439, 442, 447–51
Authorship of Ephesians lix–lxxii, 52
Asia Minor lxxii, lxxx–lxxxv, 464, 465

Baptism xl, lxxix, 18, 39–40, 58, 90–91, 130–31, 228–29, 240, 272, 284–85, 296, 326, 331–33, 375–76, 440
Battle lxxxvii–lxxxviii, 109, 429–60
Berakah, blessing, eulogy xxxvii, 8–44
Blood 28, 139
Boasting 113
Body liii, xciv, 67–72, 80, 180–81, 189–90, 238, 254–55, 261–63, 370–72, 378–80
Body of letter xxxviii–xxxix
Boldness 454–55
Bride xciv, 352–53, 362–63, 376–77

Calling xxxvi, 59, 231, 234–35, 238–39
Canon lxxii, xcvi,
Children and parents lxiv, 395–410
Christ lxiv–lxv, xc–xcii, 6, 43, 119, 136–37, 140, 160–61, 183–84, 206–7, 209–10, 239, 256, 268, 279–83, 311–12, 315, 325, 368, 369–73, 379–83, 388–90, 401, 408, 420–24, 426
 Ascent of 242–43, 247–48
 Cosmic Christ lvi, xc–xcii, 18, 32–33, 65–70, 77–78, 128–30, 209–10, 247–48, 415
 Death of lxiii–xiv, xciv, 142, 146, 148–49, 161–62, 374–75
 Descent of 244–48
 Exaltation of lxiii, xci, xcvii, 22, 34, 61–62, 108–9, 154, 155
 Headship of xci, 67–70, 261–62, 368–70
 "in Christ" 6, 11, 21–22, 26–27, 34, 44, 105, 138, 157, 181, 217, 326–27, 395, 402, 441
 Love of 212–14, 219–20, 373–78
 Pre-existence of 22, 24
 Resurrection of lxiii, xcvii, 61, 101–2, 105–6, 108–9
 "with Christ" 101–2, 105
Church lxiv, xciv–xcv, 66–68, 79–82, 156, 161–63, 186, 188–89, 193–94, 217, 220, 257, 264–69, 315, 372–83, 388–90
Colossians, relation to xlvii–xlviii, lxvi–lxviii, lxxv, 69, 71, 73–75, 89–90, 93, 105–7, 128–30, 135, 168–70, 174, 177, 199–200, 214, 228–31, 273–74, 295–96, 298, 319–20, 339, 354–55, 396–97, 412–14, 419–20, 434–35, 462

Conduct xxxvii
Congratulation xl–xli
Cosmos xcv–xcvi, 33–34, 65–70, 77, 128–30, 188–89, 203–4, 210–11, 239, 248, 268–69, 458
Covetousness 279, 321, 324
Cross lvii, xc–xci, 146

Darkness 58, 277, 326–27, 329, 334–35, 444
Date of Ephesians lxiii–lxxiii
Death xxxi, 85–86, 92–93, 286
Deliberative genre xli–xlii, lxxv
Devil 302, 443
Digressio xliii–xliv, 168, 171
Doxology xxx, 198–201, 216–18

Election 17, 22–25, 35–36
Ephesus lxxx–lxxxi, 1–4
Epideictic genre xli–xlii, lxxv
Eschatology lxxxix–xc, 14, 21, 37, 41, 65, 97, 186, 268–69, 342, 442–43
 realized xiv, xc, 34–35, 66, 92–93, 105–6, 108, 450
 future xc, 65, 261, 422–24, 446
Evil 95, 342, 444–46, 450
Exhortatio xliii, xliv, 224
Exordium xliii–xliv, 53–54

Faith 5–6, 39, 46, 54–55, 111–12, 190, 206–7, 239–40, 256, 449–50, 465–66
Family xciv, 152, 196, 202–4
Fear 354, 366–67, 384–85, 420
Flesh 97–98, 124, 135, 142, 362, 378–83, 411, 420, 444
Forgiveness 28–29, 309–10
Fullness liii–liv, lxiv, xciv, 32, 72–78, 80–81, 214–15, 247, 344–45

Gentiles xxxvi–xxxvii, lxiii, lxxxiv, 88, 92, 132–34, 135–36, 142, 150–51, 162–65, 173, 180–81, 274, 276–79, 289, 326
Glory 59–60, 191–92, 198–99, 204, 216–18, 377
Gnosticism lxxix, lxxxii–lxxxiii, 58, 68–71, 73–74, 92–93, 107, 130, 157, 185, 187, 205, 208, 331–32, 362, 382–83, 444–45
God 25, 42–43, 56, 81, 119, 138, 194, 220–21, 240–41, 288, 310–11, 315, 325–26, 461
 As Father 6–7, 10, 56, 149–50, 202–4, 240
 Glory of 26, 36, 42, 44, 56
 Love of 100–101
 Mercy of 100
 Power of 60–61, 79, 85–86, 182, 215–16
 Will of 5, 23, 26, 30–31, 36, 328–29, 415, 421
Grace xcii, 6–7, 26, 29, 100, 102–4, 109–10, 116, 118, 119–21, 181–82, 241–42, 461–68
Grace benediction xxxviii, 461–64, 466–68

Growth 157, 260–64, 266–67
Guarantee 40–41

Heart 58, 205–7, 278, 346, 420–21
Heaven, heavenly realms lxiii, 19–21, 34, 62, 95–96, 106–9, 186, 248, 423–24, 445
Holiness xcv, 5–6, 24–25, 288, 375–78
Homily, sermon xl
Hope 36–37, 59, 137–38, 238–39
Household code lxiv, xcv, 350–428
Hymn 13–14, 50, 127–31, 318–19, 331, 345–46, 378

Identity lxxxvi–lxxxvii, 81–82, 201, 219, 291, 335–36, 349, 440–41, 458–60
Idolatry 279, 325
Imitation 310–11
Implied author lx–lxii, lxxv–lxxxvi
Implied readers lxxv–lxxxvii
Impurity 278–79, 321–22, 324
Inheritance 40–41, 59–60, 181, 324–25
Intercessory prayer report xxxvi, lxxviii, 49–51, 197–201
Israel xxxvi, lxiii, xciii, 132–34, 136–37, 162–64, 362–63

Judaism lxxix, xciii–xciv
 Hellenistic Judaism lxxxiii, 42, 70, 130, 237–38, 297, 321, 357, 399–401, 416
Justification lxii–lxiii, xcii, 104

Knowledge 57–58, 78–79, 212–13, 255–56

Law lxiii, xciii–xciv, 112–13, 142–43, 275, 404–5
Letter form xxxvii–xliii, lxx–lxxi, 4–5, 52–53, 225–27
Life xxxvi–xxxvii, 101–2, 277–78
Light 58–59, 184, 326–28, 330–33, 334–36
Liturgy, liturgical forms xxxvi, xxxvii, 10–12, 50–52, 88–89, 200–201, 331–32
Love 17, 24–25, 54–55, 196–97, 207, 219–20, 236–37, 260–61, 263–64, 311–12, 373–74, 378–79, 384–85, 394, 465–68

Magic lxxxi, 209, 440, 443–44
Marriage liv, xcvi, 350–94
Midrash lviii, 127–28, 225, 244–48
Ministers xciv, 232–34, 448–55
Mystery xxxvi, liv–lv, 30–31, 35, 174–76, 180, 184–85, 193–95, 380–84, 453–54

Narratio xliii–xliv, 91, 131–32
New creation 113–14, 143–44, 287–88
New humanity, new person xxxvi–xxxvii, 116–17, 143–44, 273–74, 285–91

Old humanity, old person 116–17, 213–14, 284–86, 290–91

Index of Principal Subjects

"Once-now" contrast 86–88, 124–26, 130, 138–39, 318, 326

Paranaesis xxxvii, xxxix, xli, 224, 231–32, 271–73, 275, 294–97, 299, 314–15, 320–21, 430–31, 438
Parousia lxiv, 360, 377, 390, 406
Paul lvi–lxx, xcvi–xcvii, 4–7, 54, 71–72, 118–19, 133–34, 143, 152–54, 171–73, 176–77, 182–83, 191–94, 229–30, 234–35, 304–5, 390, 398, 414, 419, 433, 435–36, 453–55, 464
  Death of lxxix, lxxxv, 7, 233, 269, 360, 406
Pauline corpus, relation to lvi–lviii
Pauline school lxx–lxxii
Peace xliv, 6, 140–41, 146–49, 161–62, 237, 448–49, 465–66
Pentecost lxxix, 243–44, 340, 344
Peroratio xliii–xliv, lxxv, 432–34, 438–39
Postscript xxxvii–xxxviii, 461–68
Power lxxx, 204–5, 215–16, 441–42
Powers lxiv, lxxx–lxxxi, 35–36, 62–65, 94–97, 108–10, 185–86, 440–41, 443–45, 461
Praise 44, 345–46
Prayer 55–56, 201–2, 218–20, 434, 451–53, 461
Prescript xxxvii–xxxviii, 1–7
Promise 39–40, 137, 181, 405–6
Prophets lxiv, 153–54, 178–80, 249–50
Proselytes 138–39, 143–44, 146–47, 297
Pseudonymity, lix–lxxii, 7, 168–69, 176–77, 453–55, 463–65
Purpose lxix, lxxiii–lxxxvii

Qumran lxxx, 58, 92, 107–8, 114, 156, 185, 187, 205, 297, 302, 326–27, 341, 381, 416, 438, 441, 444, 446

Reconciliation xciii, 144–46, 161–62
Redemption 27–28, 41–42, 307–8
Revelation 57, 170, 175, 184–85
Rhetoric xxxvii–xxxviii, xli–xliv, lxxiv–lxxix, 15, 18, 53–54, 86, 91, 131–32, 200, 295, 432–34
Righteousness 288–89, 328, 403, 448

Saints 5–6, 55, 59–60, 150–52, 213, 253–54, 453
Salvation lxiv, xcii–xciii, 38, 104–5, 118, 450
Sealing 39–40, 307
Setting lxxiii–lxxxvii
Sins 29, 93, 99–100
Slaves and masters 411–28
Speech 305–8, 322–23, 325, 329–30, 334, 348, 453–54
Spirit 19, 39–42, 56–57, 96–97, 149–50, 158–59, 180, 204–6, 237–38, 246–47, 286–87, 306–8, 340, 343–45, 348–49, 451–52
Stand, withstand 442–43, 445–47, 459–60
Style xliv–xlvi, xcvi, 11–12
Submission 351, 365–68, 372–73, 393
Suffering xcvii, 191–92

Temple xxxvi, xciv, 141–42, 152–59
Thanksgiving 55, 324–25, 346–47

Thanksgiving period xxxvi–xxxix, 19, 45–82
Topos 294–95
Tradition lxx, lxxii–lxxiii, 271, 274, 279–80, 282–83
Traditional material xlvii–xlviii, 13–14, 126–31, 227–31, 298–99, 361–62, 397, 435–38
Transitus liii–xliv, 200
Trinitarian pattern 13, 43–44, 80–81, 160, 266, 348
Truth 38–39, 259–60, 280–83, 288–89, 300–301, 328, 448

Unity xxxvi, lxxx, xcv, xcvi–xcvii, 140–41, 162, 164–65, 222–69, 363–64, 389–90, 393–94

Vices and virtues 272, 278–79, 295–98, 308–12, 318

Walk xxxvi, 94, 116, 234–35, 274–76, 338, 341
Wisdom 17–18, 29–30, 56, 74–75, 187–88, 211–12, 340–43
Wish of peace xxxvii–xxxviii, 461–63, 465–66
Wives and husbands 350–94
Work 303–5
Works lxiii, xcii–xciii, 112–16
World xciv–xcv, 80, 95, 138, 268–69, 276, 348–49, 458
Worship 44, 220–21, 345–48
Wrath 98, 325–26

Index of Authors Cited

Aalen, S. 327
Abbott, T. K. xxix, 2, 9, 17, 20, 28, 32, 37, 39, 41, 47, 54, 57, 60, 66, 75, 77, 95, 101, 105, 112, 115, 135, 141, 148, 150, 156, 174, 177, 179, 180, 185, 189, 192, 212, 240, 246, 253, 257, 259, 262, 287–88, 302, 306–7, 312, 325–26, 330–31, 342–44, 370, 372, 375–76, 378, 395, 403, 407, 445–46, 448–49, 451, 454, 463–64, 467
Adai, J. xxx, lxix, lxxxviii, 337, 343–45, 347, 429, 452
Agrell, G. 292, 300, 302–5
Ahern, B. 8
Aland, K. lix, lxxi
Albani, J. xxx
Alexander, N. xxx
Alexander, P. S. xxxv, xxxix, lxxi
Allan, J. A. xxix, xxx, 8, 22, 105
Allen, T. G. 45, 83
Arnold, C. E. xxx, lxxii, lxxix, lxxxi, lxxxv, lxxxviii, 65, 196, 209, 429, 431, 440, 442, 444–45
Arnold, M. 323
Audet, J. P. xxxv, xxxvii, 48, 429
Aune, D. E. xxxv, xxxvii, xlii, 249, 295

Bailey, K. E. 126
Baker, N. L. xxx
Balch, D. L. 355, 357–60, 418
Baltensweiler, H. 350
Balz, H. R. lix, lxxii, 366, 385
Banks, R. 27, 67
Barclay, W. 122, 398
Barker, G. W. xxxv
Barr, J. 32, 33
Bartchy, S. S. 415, 417, 418
Barth, C. 92
Barth, K. 116, 207
Barth, M. xxix–xxx, xlvii, lxii, lxix, lxxiii, lxxxviii, 2, 9, 17, 20, 24, 29, 32–33, 37, 40, 47–48, 51, 57–58, 60, 64–66, 68, 73, 75, 77, 88–89, 91–94, 97, 99, 101, 110, 115–16, 122, 127–28, 135–38, 142, 144–46, 148, 150, 152, 154, 157, 177–78, 182, 189–91, 203, 206, 213–14, 222, 228, 240, 245, 250, 253, 255, 259, 262, 278, 280, 285, 287, 294, 296, 302, 306–9, 312, 325–26, 331, 341, 343, 346, 366–68, 370, 372, 375, 377–78, 380–84, 391–92, 395, 436, 441–42, 446, 448, 450, 453–54, 464, 467
Bassler, J. M. 424
Batey, R. I. 350, 362, 376, 383
Bauckham, R. J. lix, lxxi–lxxii
Bauer, W. (Also Arndt, W. F., Gingrich, F. W. and Danker, F. W.) lxxxiii–lxxxiv, 36, 77, 99, 175–76, 256, 259, 278, 306, 329, 341, 346, 378, 406, 441, 461
Baumert, N. 191, 216
Baur, F. C. lix, lxii
Bean, G. E. lxxxiii

Beare, F. W. xxix, 2, 46, 57, 75, 135, 184, 189
Beasley-Murray, G. R. 40, 91, 106
Bedale, S. 45, 67–68, 70, 380
Beet, J. A. xxix
Behm, J. 28, 408
Beker, J. C. 35
Bengel, J. A. xxix
Benoit, P. xxix–xxx, xlvii, lxxxviii, 45, 68, 72–73, 76–77, 83, 222, 244, 270
Berger, K. xxxv, xxxviii, xli–xlii, lxx, 67, 103, 272, 295–97, 356–57
Bergman, J. 296
Bertram, G. 342, 398, 407–8
Best, E. xxx, lxxiii, lxxxi, 1–4, 8, 21, 45, 68, 71–72, 75–76, 83, 90, 92–93, 101, 145, 154, 166, 179, 222, 257, 350, 379
Betz, H. D. 295–97, 310, 383
Bieder, W. xxx, 222, 245
Billerbeck, P. (See Strack, H. L.)
Bjerkelund, C. J. xxxv, xxxviii, 222, 226–27, 231
Black, M. 45
Blakeney, E. H. 448
Blass, F. (Debrunner, A. and Funk, R. W.) 2, 17, 26, 77, 96, 124, 173, 177, 183, 189, 197, 206, 212, 236, 246, 260, 280–81, 283, 300, 303, 309, 317–18, 330, 345, 380, 383
Bloch, R. lviii
Blomenkamp, P. 398
de Boer, M. C. 172
Bogdasovich, M. 45
Bonhoffer, A. 99
Bonner, S. F. 398
Bony, P. 222
Borland, A. xxx
Bornkamm, G. 31, 381–82
Bouttier, M. xxx, lxxxviii, 21, 327
Bouwman, G. 350, 378
Bowman, J. W. xxxi
Bradley, D. G. 294–95
Bratcher, R. G. xxxi, 73, 77, 148, 150, 191, 197, 212, 253, 256, 259, 287, 322, 326, 330, 378
Brown, R. E. lxxxviii, 17, 30–31, 35, 166, 381–82
Brox, N. lix
Bruce, F. F. xxix, xxxi, lxii, lxxix, 27, 39, 47, 112, 154, 182, 203, 253, 282, 284, 286, 307–8, 326, 340, 345, 370, 376–77, 381, 395–96, 403, 441, 445, 467
Brunt, J. C. 294–95
Büchsel, F. 21, 28, 244–45, 341
Buckland, W. W. 415
Bujard, W. xlviii, lxvi
Bultmann, R. 98, 103, 113, 283, 327
Burger, C. xxxi, 122, 128–30, 148
Burgess, T. C. xiv, xxxv, xlii, xliv, 433
Buscarlet, A. 448

Cadbury, H. J. xxxi, lix, 244
Caird, G. B. xxix, lxii, lxviii–lxix, 17, 20, 28, 33, 37, 55, 57, 60, 64–65, 73, 95–97, 141, 145, 148, 150, 154, 179, 188–89, 192, 212, 222, 243–44, 246, 251, 253, 278, 281–82, 284, 325, 368, 376, 402, 404, 436, 441, 445, 467
Caldwell, E. C. xxxi
Calvin, J. xxix, 212
Cambier, J. xxxi, 8–9, 13–15, 37, 41, 222, 243, 245, 350, 376, 378, 381
Cancik, H. 225
Cannon, G. E. 296–97, 356
Caragounis, C. C. xxxi, 8–9, 12, 17, 20–22, 30–31, 35, 166, 168, 171, 178, 181–82, 185, 187, 189, 191, 196–97, 212, 216, 381
Carr, W. xxxi, 21, 45, 63–64, 83, 95, 429, 443
Carrington, P. 272, 324, 375
Casel, O. 316, 324, 375
Cerfaux, L. xxxi
Chadwick, H. xxix, xxxi, lxxiii, lxxx
Chavasse, C. 350, 352
Childs, B. S. xxxv
Clark, S. B. 350, 365, 368
Coggan, F. D. 122
Coleridge, S. T. x
Colpe, C. xxxi, 45, 69, 71
Conzelmann, H. xxix, xxxviii, lix, lxx, lxxiv, 20, 103, 154, 183, 187
Coppens, J. 31, 166, 381
Corley, B. xxxi, lxxxviii
Coune, M. 8, 270, 292
Countess, R. H. 83
Coutts, J. xxxi, xl, xlvii, li, lxxix, 8, 13, 18, 37
Cranfield, C. E. B. 5, 106
Cremer, H. 408
Cross, F. L. xxxi
Crouch, J. E. 356–357, 418–19
Crowther, C. 83
Cullmann, O. ix, 328
Culpepper, R. A. lxx

Dahl, N. A. xxix, xxxi, xxxv, xl, xlvii, l, lviii, lx, lxiii, lxxix, lxxxiv, lxxxviii, 1, 4, 8, 11, 17–19, 37–38, 114, 144, 166, 170, 187–89, 196, 210–11, 213, 309, 316, 320
Dale, R. W. xxix
Danker, F. W. xxxi, 11
Daube, D. 283
Dautzenberg, G. xxxi, lxxxviii
Davey, F. N. 283
Davies, L. 166, 175
Davies, W. D. xxxi, 34, 71
Debrunner, A. 8, 13
Deichgraber, R. xxxi, 8, 11–15, 18–19, 45, 51, 90, 122, 127, 196, 198, 216
Deissman, A. 21
Delling, G. 45, 75, 365, 367
Denton, D. R. 8, 41
Dibelius, M. ix, xxix, xlvii, liii, 141, 154, 253, 357, 370, 382, 404, 435, 445, 464, 467
Dickey, S. lxxxiii
Dillon, J. 311
Dodd, C. H. x
Dölger, F. J. 316, 319, 332

Index of Authors Cited

Donelson, L. R. lix, lxxi–lxxii
Donfried, K. P. 5
Doty, W. ix, xxxv, xxxviii, 4
Doughty, D. J. 103
Drago, A. 8
Dreyfus, F. 8, 36
Dubois, J.-D. 222, 259
Duling, D. C. xxxv
Dunn, J. D. G. lix, lxx–lxxii, 24, 39, 91, 244, 247, 343, 345, 375–76
Dupont, J. 45, 108, 145, 196, 210, 244

Eadie, J. A. xxix
Easton, B. S. 296, 297
Efird, J. M. xxxi
Elliger, W. lxxxiii
Elliott, J. H. lxxxiii, 356–57
Elliott, J. K. 337
Ellis, E. E. lxx, 243, 396
Emonds, H. 437
Engberg-Pedersen, T. 316, 327, 329–30
Engelhardt, E. 222, 241, 244
Erasmus, lix, lxii
Ernst, J. xxix, xxxi, xlviii, l, liii, lxviii, 9, 14, 17, 22, 37, 39, 45, 54, 60, 73, 75–76, 88, 91, 95–96, 110, 115, 128, 135, 150, 174, 181, 184, 189, 191, 196, 203, 207, 210, 213–14, 222, 240, 243, 245, 250, 254, 257, 260, 282, 287, 294, 300, 302, 307, 325–26, 330–31, 343, 404, 449, 467
Evanson, E. lix, lxii
Ewald, P. xxix

Fee, G. D. 369
Fendt, L. xxxi, lxxxviii
Fennema, D. 350
Fenton, J. C. lix
Feuillet, A. 45, 73, 75–76, 196, 208, 212, 350
Fiedler, P. 356
Filson, F. V. 251
Findeis, H.-J. xxxi
Findlay, J. A. 292, 306
Finley, M. I. 415
Fischer, K. M. xxxi, xxxv, xxxviii, xlvii, lix, lxxiii, lxxx, 8, 13, 14, 45, 50–51, 83, 89, 122, 128–30, 133, 148, 166, 222, 232–33, 251, 270, 311, 316, 332, 350, 362, 371, 383, 429, 440
Fitzmyer, J. A. 146, 239
Flowers, H. J. 25, 45, 57
Foakes-Jackson, F. J. (and Lake, K.) 2
Foerster, W. 370
Foulkes, F. xxix
Fowler, R. 45
Francis, F. O. 52–53
Fuller, R. H. xxv, xxxviii
Fung, R. xxxi, 222
Furnish, V. P. xxix, xxxvi, 234, 326

Gamble, H. 4–5
Gärtner, B. 122, 150, 157
Gärtner, M. 398, 403, 407–8
Gaugler, E. xxix, xxxvi, 50, 54, 57, 59–60, 73, 77, 95, 110, 112, 124, 144, 146, 150, 167, 177, 180, 183, 184–85, 189, 197, 210, 216, 245, 368, 451
Gavin, F. xl
Gayer, R. 415
Gewiess, J. xxxi, 45, 75, 77
Giavini, G. 122, 126
Gibbs, J. G. 8

Giblet, J. 316
Gnilka, J. xi, xxix, xxxi, xxxix, xlvii, liii, lv, lxvi, lxx, lxxii, lxxxiii, lxxxv, lxxxviii, 2, 9, 12, 14–18, 22, 28, 30–35, 37–39, 41, 47, 51, 54, 57, 59, 64, 66, 73, 75, 77, 88, 91, 93–94, 96, 99, 105, 110, 112, 122, 128, 130, 137–138, 141, 145–46, 148, 150, 154, 157, 166–68, 174, 177–80, 184–85, 189, 191–92, 197, 207, 209–10, 215–16, 228, 237, 240, 245, 253, 257, 259, 263, 270, 281, 285, 287, 294, 299–300, 302–3, 306–7, 311–12, 318–19, 322, 325–26, 330, 338, 340, 342–43, 356, 362, 373–74, 376, 380–82, 395, 403–5, 407–8, 424, 436, 440–41, 446–47, 449, 464, 467
Goguel, M. xxxi
Goodspeed, E. J. x, xxxi, lvi, lviii–lix, lxix, lxxix, 175, 353
Goppelt, L. 356–57
Gore, C. xxxi
van Goudoever, J. 244
Grabner-Haider, A. 234
Greeven, H. (see also under Dibelius, M.) 350
Gregg, J. A. F. xxxi, 2, 448
Grob, F. xxxi
Grudem, W. 369
Grundmann, W. 102, 236
Gulzow, H. 415
Gundry, R. H. 45, 72
Guthrie, D. xxxv, liii, lix, lxii, lxviii, lxxii
Guthrie, W. C. 362

Hadidian, D. Y. 222
Hahn, F. 250, 691
Halter, H. xxxii, lxxxviii, 37–39, 83, 87–88, 90–91, 94, 110, 115, 222, 270, 287, 292, 299–300, 307, 310, 316, 330, 350, 376
Hamann, H. P. 222, 254
Hamerton-Kelly, R. 22, 24, 115
Hammer, P. L. 8, 41
Hanson, A. T. 222, 244, 318
Hanson, S. xxxii, lxxxviii, 33–34, 45, 75, 77, 122, 141, 150, 154, 157, 222, 229, 240–41, 243, 253, 256–57
Harnack, A. 1, 3, 429
Harris, W. H. 222, 224, 243–46
Harrison, P. N. lix
Harrisville, R. 286
Hartin, P. J. 8
Hartman, L. xl, 356, 359
Harvey, A. E. 30–31
Hasenstab, H. 226, 235
Hauck, F. 236, 321
Haupt, E. xxix
Hay, D. M. 62
Headlam, A. x, lxv
Hegermann, H. 45, 69–70, 110, 157
Hemer, C. J. lxxxiii–lxxxiv
Hendriksen, W. xxix, 142, 370, 376–77, 449
Hengel, M. lix, 337, 343
Henle, F. A. xxix
Hester, J. D. 41
Hill, D. 28, 41, 153
Hitchcock, A. E. M. 45, 73
Hock, R. F. 303–4
Hodge, C. xxix
Hofius, O. 8, 23–24, 145
Holtzmann, H. J. xxxii, l
van der Horst, P. W. 285, 316, 323

Hort, F. J. A. xxxii, 280–81
Hoskyns, E. 282
Houlden, J. L. xxix, xxxii, lxxxviii, 3, 39, 41, 58–61, 65, 104, 115, 141, 150, 154, 172–75, 185, 208, 212–13, 240, 246, 283, 287, 324, 340, 343, 395, 432, 445, 467
Howard, G. E. xxxii, 45, 66, 68, 77, 190, 222, 260, 350
Howard, J. E. 122
Hugedé, N. xxix
Hunter, A. M. 356

Innitzer, T. 8, 13

Jankowski, A. 8, 37
Jayne, D. 8, 38
Jeal, R. R. xxxii, xli
Jensen, J. 321
Jentsch, W. 398
Jeremias, J. 122, 154, 243, 250, 380
Jervell, J. 270, 284–85
Jewett, R. xxxv, xxxviii, 98, 205
Johanson, B. C. xxxv, xli
Johnson, L. T. xxxv, lxii, 324
Johnson, S. E. lxxxiii
Johnston, G. xxix
Jones, A. H. M. lxxxiii
Jones, P. R. 429, 452
Jülicher, A. lxix

Kahler, E. 350
Kamlah, E. 272, 296–97, 350, 356, 367, 429, 435, 437, 440
Käsemann, E. x, xxxii, xxxviii, lxxx, lxxxviii, 20, 45, 68, 105, 122, 133, 247, 253
Keck, L. E. xxxv–xxxvi
Kennedy, G. A. xxxv, xli, lxxvii
Kessler, P. D. 8
Kim, S. 166
King, A. C. xxxii, xlvii, 272, 340
Kirby, J. C. xxxii, xxxix, xl, lxxix, 2, 39, 52, 91, 126, 139, 168, 222, 243–44, 246, 376, 445
Klauck, H.-J. 222, 230, 234, 237, 245, 249–50, 253, 257, 263
Klein, G. 166, 296–97
Klijn, A. F. J. 285
Klinzing, G. 122, 150
Knoch, O. xxxii, lxxxviii
Knox, W. L. 380–81, 419, 465
Koester, H. xxxv, lxxxiii
Kraemer, H. 8–9, 13–18, 37
Kroeger, C. C. 369
Kruse, C. 8
Kuhn, H.-W. 30, 92, 107
Kuhn, K. G. xxxii, xlv, lxvi, 12, 30, 114, 176, 205, 316, 327, 330, 332, 341
Kümmel, W. G. xxxv, xxxviii, xl, lxviii, lxxiii, 2
Küng, H. xcvi

Lacey, W. K. 398
Lampe, G. W. H. 39, 40
Lane, W. L. xxxv
Lang, F. 8, 11, 14, 17–18
Larsson, E. 83, 270, 280, 282
Lash, C. J. A. 429–30
Laub, F. lix, lxxii, 405, 419
Lausberg, H. xxxv, xli, xliv, xlvi, lxx, 295
Leipoldt, J. 437
Lemmer, H. R. 100
Levine, E. 447

Index of Authors Cited

Lightfoot, J. B. xxix, xxxii, lxvii, 1, 3, 8–9, 17, 45, 74–75, 262
Lillie, W. 356
Lincoln, A. T. xxxii, xlvii, lv, lx, lxxxiv, lxxxviii, 8, 14, 21, 35, 60, 63, 65–66, 83, 106, 108, 122, 174, 178, 198, 222, 350, 359, 362, 381, 383, 398, 429, 445
Lindars, B. 222, 242–44, 247, 310
Lindemann, A. xxix, xxxii, xxxviii, lxxiii, lxxix, lxxx, lxxxiii–lxxxiv, lxxxviii, 1–2, 32–34, 37–38, 45, 51, 65, 73, 77, 83, 88, 94, 98, 104–5, 110, 122, 127–29, 148, 150, 154, 166–67, 174, 184, 189, 244–45, 307, 332, 337, 340, 342, 397, 429, 436, 440, 442, 445
Lindhagen, C. 305
Loader, J. A. 139
Loader, W. R. 62
Lock, W. xxix
Lohfink, G. 242
Lohmeyer, E. 8, 13, 16, 102
Lohse, E. xxix, liii, lxvi, 27, 40, 47, 55, 58, 60, 69, 74, 90, 105, 130, 184, 356–57
Lona, H. E. xxxii, lxxiii, lxxvi, lxxxiv, lxxxviii
Lövestam, E. 429, 453
Lührmann, D. 146, 166, 170, 356–57
Lutz, C. 359
Luz, U. 83, 88, 90, 110
Lyall, F. 25, 122
Lyonnet, S. 8, 10, 17, 37
Lyons, G. xli

MacDonald, M. Y. xxxii, lxxiii, lxxxviii, 356, 360, 364, 379, 391, 418–19
Mackay, J. A. xxxii, 301
MacPhail, J. R. xxxii
MacRae, G. W. 69
Magie, D. lxxxiii
Maillet, H. 350, 372, 384
Malherbe, A. J. xxxv, xl–xli, 437
Malina, B. 321
Mare, W. H. 166, 177
Marrou, H. I. 398
Marrow, S. 190
Marshall, I. H. 27, 41, 46
Martin, F. 222
Martin, R. P. xxix, xxxii, xxxv, lxvi, lxix, lxxiii, lxxxiv, lxxxviii, 40–41, 60, 122, 128, 133, 135, 139, 141, 147, 246, 326, 337, 345, 356–57, 397, 467
Marxsen, W. xxxv
Masson, C. xxix, 11, 13, 184, 240, 253–54, 263
Maurer, C. 8, 14, 17–18, 37
McEleney, N. J. 122, 294
McGlashan, A. R. 45, 73
McHugh, J. 8, 33
McKelvey, R. J. 122, 141, 154–55, 157
McNicol, J. 8
Meade, D. G. lvii, lix, lxviii, lxx, lxxii–lxxiv, lxxxv
Meeks, W. A. xxxii, lxxiv, lxxxiii, lxxxviii, 122, 241, 243, 284, 350, 383, 419
Mehlmann, J. 83, 99
Meinardus, O. F. A. lxxxiii
Meinertz, M. xxix
Meritan, J. xxxii
Merkel, H. xxxii, lxxxii, lxxxviii
Merklein, H. xxxii, xlvii–xlviii, l, liii–lv, lviii–lix, lxvii–lxviii, lxx, lxxiii, lxxxviii, 83, 122, 128, 130–33, 140, 144, 148–50, 152, 154, 166, 168, 170, 174–75, 177–80, 222, 227, 232–33, 241, 245, 250–54, 256–57, 260, 263, 270, 274–75, 292, 316, 320
Metzger, B. M. xxxii, lix, 47, 124, 317, 337, 395, 427
Meuzelaar, J. J. 45, 68, 71, 124, 139, 150, 246
Meyer, H. A. W. xxix, 1, 96, 101, 112, 115, 138, 141, 145–46, 150, 152, 156, 172–74, 179, 180, 183, 185, 189, 192, 197, 207, 212, 240, 244, 256, 260, 262, 270, 278, 284, 287, 302, 310, 312, 325–26, 331, 343, 375–78, 380–81, 395, 403–4, 408, 445, 447–51, 467
Meyer, R. P. xxxii, lxxxix, 45, 77, 166, 172, 222, 261
Michaels, J. R. xxxv
Michel, O. 122
Miletic, S. F. 350, 352, 361, 367, 369–73, 392–93
Milling, D. H. 196, 198, 216
Miltner, F. lxxxiii
Minear, P. S. 166, 187
Mitton, C. L. xxix, xxxii, xlvii, xlviii, li–lvi, lviii–lix, lxii, lxvi–lxix, lxxix, lxxxiv, 14, 17, 27, 34, 37, 52, 57, 59–60, 65, 72, 79, 95, 109, 112, 132, 137, 141, 145, 148, 150, 154, 156–57, 175, 183, 189–91, 202, 212, 240, 243, 245, 247, 253, 256–57, 259, 282, 287, 303, 307, 310, 320, 325, 339, 343–45, 371, 376, 381, 391, 395, 403–4, 408, 423, 436, 438, 445–46, 464–65, 467
Moffatt, J. xxxv, lxvi, lxviii
Moir, I. A. xxxii
Montagnini, F. 8, 27
Moody, D. xxxii
Mooney, C. F. xxxii
Moore, M. S. 122
Moore, W. E. 222, 229
Morris, L. 27–28
Moule, C. F. D. xxix, xxxii, 22, 34, 40, 45, 47, 55, 73, 77, 156–57, 173, 281, 303, 317, 327, 331, 341, 421
Moule, H. C. G. xxxiii
Moulton, H. K. xxix
Moulton, J. H. 2, 178, 303, 306, 316
Muirhead, I. A. 350, 377
Müller, K. H. 356, 359
Mullins, T. Y. 226, 294
Munro, W. 350, 354, 414
Murphy-O'Connor, J. xxxiii, 31, 38, 271, 283, 289, 328
Murray, J. 283
Mussner, F. xxx, xxxiii, xl, lx, lxviii, lxxix, 8, 15, 31, 33–34, 37, 45, 59, 67, 71, 73, 75, 77, 83, 92, 95, 107, 110, 112, 122, 128, 138, 141, 148, 150, 152, 153–54, 157, 166, 180, 184–85, 189, 191, 196, 204, 210, 233, 240–41, 245, 253, 256–57, 263, 287, 294, 300, 302, 307, 325–26, 331, 342–43, 350, 364, 368, 376, 378, 380–81, 395, 403, 408, 445, 467

Nauck, W. 123, 130–31
Neudecker, F. 2
Neugebauer, F. 21
Neuhausler, E. 350

Nida, E. A. (see under Brachter, R.)
Nineham, D. E. lix, lxvii, lxix
Noack, B. 244, 316, 319
Nock, A. D. 94, 197
Norden, E. 11
Norris, F. W. lxxxiii

O'Brien, P. T. xxx, xxxv, xxxviii, xlvii, lxvi, 8, 14, 18–19, 45, 48–49, 52, 55, 64, 184, 263, 285, 296, 323, 355, 357, 429, 454
Ochel, W. xxxiii, xlvii, liii, lv–lvi, lxviii, 464
Odeberg, H. xxxiii, lxxxix, 8, 20, 244, 464
Oepke, A. 398, 429, 435, 447–50
Olbrechts-Tyteca, L. xxxv, xli
Ollrogg, W.-H. lxx
Olshausen, H. xxx
Orbe, A. 166, 178
Oster, R. E. lxxxiii
Overfield, P. D. 45, 74–76

Pagels, E. 350, 379, 382–83
Patzia, A. G. xxx, xxxvi, lix, lxx
Pelletier, A. lx
Percy, E. xxxiii, xlvi–xlvii, liii, lix, lxii, lxviii–lxix, lxxix, 1, 3–4, 17, 21–22, 37, 45, 72, 95, 98, 123, 145, 154, 166, 210, 245, 257, 445
Perelman, Ch. xxxv, xli–xlii, xlv
Perels, O. xxxiii, lxxxix
Peri, I. 222
Perkins, P. 350, 363
Perrin, N. xxxv
Pesch, R. 166, 196, 210
Peterson, E. 190, 238
Pfammatter, J. xxx, 123, 150, 153–54
Pfitzner, V. 429, 444
Pierrou, J. 429
Pohlenz, M. 322
Pokorný, P. xxxiii, xl, lxxx, 45, 68, 133, 256, 332
Polhill, J. B. xxxiii, xlvii, l
Pope, R. M. 341
Porter, C. H. 222, 246
de la Potterie, I. 45, 73, 270, 280–82
Preisendanz, K. 209
Proksch, O. 150

Rader, W. 123, 130, 134
Ramaroson, L. 46, 83–84, 97, 101, 123
Ramsay, W. R. lxxxiii
Reitzenstein, R. 332, 409
Rengstorf, K. H. 153, 285, 350, 356–57, 367
Rese, M. 123, 137
Reumann, J. H. P. 32, 174
Reuss, J. xxxiii
Ridderbos, H. xxxiii, lxxxix, 35, 46, 68, 75, 77, 98
Riensche, R. 83
Rist, M. lix
Robbins, C. J. 9, 15
Roberts, J. H. xxxv, xxxviii
Robinson, J. A. xi, xxx, 3, 17, 26, 28, 31, 36–37, 41, 47, 59, 75–76, 84, 86, 88, 95–97, 99, 105, 124, 136, 138, 141, 150, 157, 167, 180, 189, 196, 203, 210, 215, 244, 253, 259, 262, 278, 283, 287, 307–8, 324, 326, 330–31, 339–41, 344, 370, 372, 376, 382–84, 403–4, 430, 436, 446, 454, 467
Robinson, J. A. T. 46, 68, 72, 75–76

Robinson, J. M. 48
Robinson, T. A. lxxxiv
Roels, E. xxxiii, lxxxix, 46, 77–78, 150, 212, 246, 253
Roetzel, C. J. xxxv–xxxvi, xxxix, 123, 132, 142
Rogers, C. L. 337, 343–44
Roller, O. 3
Romaniuk, K. 83
van Roon, A. viii, xxx, xxxiii, xlv–xlvii, l–li, lv, lviii–lix, lxii, lxvi, lxxiii, 1, 3–4, 12–13, 20, 212
Rowston, D. J. xxxiii
Royse, J. R. 337
Rubinkiewicz, R. 222, 243
Rudolph, K. 205
Russell, W. H. 25
Ryrie, C. C. 166, 177

Sahlin, H. 123, 138, 153
Salmond, S. D. F. xxx
Sampley, J. P. xxxiii, 292, 300, 306, 350, 352, 356, 361–63, 365–66, 368, 371, 375–76, 379–82, 384, 391
Sand, A. 98
Sanday, A. x, lxv
Sanders, E. P. xxxiii, 28, 103
Sanders, J. N. lix, lxvii, lxxiii
Sanders, J. T. xxxiii, xxxv–xxxvi, xxxix, xlvii, 9, 14–15, 46, 50–51, 83, 89–90, 123, 127–28, 200
Santer, M. 1, 3
Sasse, H. 94–95, 110
Schäfer, K. T. 123, 154
Schattenmann, J. 9, 13
Schenk, W. 1–2, 6
Schenke, H.-M. xxxv, xxxviii, lix, lxx, 46, 69, 71
Schille, G. xxxiii, lix, 9, 13, 34, 50, 83, 87–89, 123, 127–28, 148, 316
Schlatter, A. xxx
Schlier, H. xxx, xxxiii, lx, lxii, lxxix, lxxxix, 4, 9, 14, 17, 20, 22, 24, 26, 30–33, 35, 37, 41, 46, 54, 58–60, 64–65, 68, 73, 75, 77, 88, 91, 94, 96–97, 99, 105, 110, 112, 115, 127–29, 141–42, 145, 148, 150, 154, 156–57, 174, 177–80, 182, 184–85, 187–89, 192, 203, 205, 208, 234, 240–41, 245, 250, 253, 257, 259–60, 263, 277, 281–82, 287–88, 299, 301, 303, 306–7, 309–10, 312, 322, 326, 330–31, 338, 343, 347, 351, 362, 371, 373–74, 376–78, 380–81, 383, 395–96, 404, 408, 421, 436, 441–42, 445–46, 448–50, 454, 464, 467
Schmid, J. xxxiii, xlvi–xlvii, l, lxvii, lxxi, lxxxix, 1, 3, 18
Schmitz, O. 234
Schnackenburg, R. xi, xxx, xxxiii, xl, lx, lxvi–lxviii, lxxiv, lxxx, lxxxix, xcvii, 2, 9, 14–17, 34, 37, 46, 51, 59, 65, 73, 75, 77, 83, 88, 91, 94, 105, 110, 112, 115, 123, 127–28, 145, 154, 157, 167, 174, 177–81, 184, 187, 189, 191, 197, 202, 207, 210, 216, 222, 229, 240–41, 245, 247, 249, 253–54, 256, 259, 260, 263, 282, 285, 287–88, 294, 300, 302, 307, 309–10, 316–17, 319, 322, 325–26, 329–31, 343–44, 350, 370, 373–74,
376, 378–82, 395, 404–7, 436, 441, 446–48, 450–52, 462, 467
Schneider, G. 244
Schoenberg, M. W. 25
Schrage, W. 356–57, 373
Schrenk, G. 398, 403
Schroeder, D. 356–57
Schubert, P. xxxv, xxxviii–xxxix, 19, 46–50, 52
Schulz, A. 310
Schulz, S. 236, 321
Schürmann, H. 250–52
Schüssler Fiorenza, E. lxxv, 350, 366, 368, 373–74, 418, 424
Schweizer, E. xxx, xxxiii, liv, lix, lxvi, lxviii, 25, 46, 69, 71, 74, 77, 90, 102–3, 130, 184, 227, 253, 263, 292, 296, 310, 356–57, 359, 415
Scott, E. F. xxx
Seebass, H. 98
Selwyn, E. G. 272, 283, 340, 356
Siber, P. 102, 316
Simpson, E. K. xxx
Sint, J. A. lix, lxxi
Small, D. H. 350
Smalley, S. S. xxxiii
Smith, C. M. 192
Smith, D. C. xxxiii, lxxiv, lxxx, 123, 147
Smith, G. V. 222
Smith, J. Z. 285
Smolders, D. 190
von Soden, H. 246
Souter, A. 4
Speyer, W. lix
Staab, K. xxx
Stachiowak, L. R. 327
Stagg, F. 18
Stählin, G. 234
Stauffer, E. 362
Stegemann, E. 123
Steinmetz, F.-J. xxxiii, lxxxix, 83, 88, 91, 94, 150, 177–78, 184, 189, 222, 260, 261
Stott, J. R. W. xxxiii
Stowers, S. K. xxxv
Strack, H. L. 140, 142, 147, 202, 390
Strobel, A. 356
Stuhlmacher, P. 123, 127, 138, 140, 146, 148, 415–16
Stuiber, A. 216
Suggs, M. J. 296
Summers, R. xxxiii
Swain, L. xxx
Synge, F. C. xxx

Tachau, P. xxxiii, 83, 86–88, 91, 123, 125, 128, 138
Tannehill, R. C. 102
Taylor, V. 145
Taylor, W. F. xxx
Terrien, S. 350, 374
Theissen, G. 360
Theron, D. J. 25
Theron, F. T. 222
Thiselton, A. C. 98, 283
Thomas, J. 296, 328
Thompson, G. H. P. xxx, 166, 191–92, 465
Thraede, K. 356–57, 359
Thrall, M. E. 53
Thüsing, W. 9
Thyen, H. xxxvi, xxxix

Tooley, W. 32
Traub, H. 245
Travis, S. H. 422
Trench, R. C. 407
Trinidad, J. T. 9
Tromp, S. 222
Turner, N. 2, 178

van Unnik, W. C. 190
Urbach, E. E. 415
Usami, K. xxxiii, lxxxix
Ussher, J. 3
Usteri, L. lix, lxii

Vanhoye, A. xxxiii
Vermes, G. 139
Verner, D. 356–57, 359–61, 369, 417
Vielhauer, P. 123, 150, 154, 157, 256
Vogt, J. 415
Vögtle, A. 296–97

Walker, W. O. 350
Wall, R. W. 350, 368–70, 391
Warnach, V. xxxiii, 222
Wedderburn, A. J. M. 46, 71, 382
Wegenast, K. 270, 279
Weidinger, K. 356–57
Weiss, H.-F. xxxiii
Wendland, H.-D. 356
Wengst, K. 89, 123, 128–29, 223, 229
Westcott, B. F. xxx, 9, 47, 176–78, 182, 185, 189, 213, 253, 259, 278, 280–81, 309, 325, 330, 375–76, 378, 441, 446, 448, 452, 462
Westermann, C. 10
Westermann, W. L. 415, 417
de Wette, W. M. L. xxx, lx, lxii
Wetter, G. P. 103
Whitaker, G. H. 223, 262
White, J. L. ix, xxxvi, xxxviii
White, L. M. 223
Whiteley, D. E. H. 429
Wibbing, S. 296–97
Wicker, K. O. 356
Wiedemann, T. 415–16, 422–23
Wikenhauser, A. xxxv, 46
Wilckens, U. 187
Wild, R. A. xxxiii, lxxxix, 270, 288, 292, 310–11, 429, 431, 439, 450, 455
Wiles, G. P. 50, 200
Wilhelmi, G. 123
Williams, R. R. xl, 223, 238
Williamson, L. xxxiv
Wilson, R. A. xxxiv, 9, 38
Wilson, R. McL. 184, 205
Wink, W. xxxiv, 46, 63–64, 96, 166, 186, 429
Witherington, B. 350
Wobbe, J. 103
Wolter, M. 123, 127, 148

Yamauchi, E. lxxxiv, 69
Yarbrough, O. L. 359
Yates, R. xxxiv, 46, 75–76
Yoder, J. 356

Zeitlin, S. 415
Zepf, M. 94
Zerwick, M. xxx
Zimmerli, W. 103
Zuntz, G. 3
de Zwaan, J. xxxiv, xxxvi, xlv

Index of Biblical and Other Ancient Sources

A. The Old Testament

Genesis
1:1	34
1:26–28	66
1:26	287
1:27	383
2:23	351
2:24	lvii, 694, 352, 354, 361, 369, 378, 380, 381, 382, 383, 388–389, 393
8:21	277
9:2	420
11:5	178
12:3	21, 202
14:20	10
15:1	449
15:6	143
15:7–21	137
17:1–21	137
17:17	277
20:16	259
21:12	21
24:27	10
24:45	277
26:2–5	137
27:41	277
28:13–15	137
28:17	157
38:17–20	40
42:16	259

Exodus
3:14	2
4:21	278
7:3	278
9:12	278
12:14	135
15:6	62
15:16	420
19, 20	244
19:3	246
19:5	42
19:6	6
19:14	246
19:20	246
19:25	246
20:6	466
20:9	303
20:12	lxiv, 396, 397, 404–5
20:15	303
24:1–8	137
24:18	246
28:3	56, 277
29:18	298, 312
29:37	24
31:3	56
32:15	246
33:19	103
34:4	246
34:6	100
34:29	246
35:31	56

Leviticus
1:3	149
2:9	312
2:12	312
3:3	149
4:14	149
18–19	297
18:1–5	272
18:24–30	272
19:2	311
19:11	303
19:17	329
19:18	361, 378, 379, 384, 388
20:9	399
20:23	272

Numbers
6:14	21
15:39	98
17, 18	244
19:2	24
26:55, 56	36

Deuteronomy
	xl
2:25	420
4:9	400
4:20	59
5:10	103, 466
5:16	396, 401
5:19	303
6:4	240
6:5	421
6:7	400
7:6–8	23
7:8	27
7:9	103, 466
7:12	103
9:26	59, 27
9:29	59, 36
11:19	400
11:26–28	272
13:5	27
14:2	42, 23
15:15	27
21:18–21	399
22:7	397, 404
24:15	302
24:18	27
26:18	42
27–30	297
28:13	67
28:49	138
29:22	138
30:15–20	272
32:4	288
32:8, 9	36
32:15	26
32:17	63
32:46	400
33:2	332
33:5	26
33:12	27
33:26	26
34:9	56

Joshua
1:6, 7	441
1:9	441

Judges
10:18	67
11:11	67

1 Samuel
26:16	98

2 Samuel
7	137
12:5	98
13:21	306
19:27	259
21:3	59
22:44	67

1 Kings
5:7	11
8:13	158
8:15	10
8:39	158
8:41–43	149
8:41	138
8:43	158
8:49	158
8:51	59
8:53	59
8:56	10
18:24	65
19:18	202

2 Kings
6:17	34
21:14	59
25:17	154

1 Chronicles
16:36	200, 199
17:21	27
22:12	29
28:8	156
29:11	198
29:20	201

2 Chronicles

1:10–12	29
2:11, 12	11
6:41	289
31:20	328

Job

1:6	34, 96, 186
5:9	183, 212
5:27	212
8:8	212
9:10	183, 212
11:5–9	211
11:8, 9	210
13:9	212
14:12	332
15:15	60, 151
22:26	190
27:9, 10	190
28:12–22	190, 211
28:27	212
29:14	284
34:24	183, 208, 212

Psalms

1	272
3:8	199
4:5	298, 301
5:2	449
7:13	450
8:6	xci, 51, 64, 65, 66, 79, 369
9	50
9:17	449
10:6	217
11:1	178
11:8	178
13:1–3	92
14:2	24
17:24	24
18:1, 2	436
18:2	449
18:32	436, 447
18:39	436, 447
18:46–48	450
20:6	62
23:1	75
27:1	327
28:9	59
29	50, 247
30:3	92
31:12	92
33:12	59
35:1–3	436
39:6	312, 298
41:13	10, 199
44:2	178
44:3	62
45	363
48:2	178
48:10	62
49:19	326
50:2	332
59	50
63:9	245
65:5	450
65:6	447
68	xci, 230
68:9	59
68:18	463, 242–47, 493
68:34	199
69	50
72:18, 19	10
72:19	73, 199
77:22	55
78:2	454
78:62	59
78:71	59
80:1–3	332
80:7	332
80:18	62
80:19	332
85:5	217
88:3–6	92
88:6	60
88:8	60
89:5, 6	154
89:13	62
89:28	103
89:52	10, 199
91:4	114, 449
94:11	277
94:14	59
95:8	278
96:7, 8	198
100:3	109
102:20	98
106:5	59
106:40	59
106:48	10, 199–200
110:1	xci, 51, 61, 62, 64, 66, 79
115:9–11	449
118:22	154, 155
119:36	279
132:9	284
139:15	245
142:5	114
143:3	92
144:17	288
145:8	100
147:4	203
148:14	139

Proverbs

1:2	29
1:14	36
3:11	408
3:19	29
4:10–14	341
8:1	29
9	674, 341
9:7	330
10:8	341
10:14	341
10:23	29
10:31, 32	305
12:17–19	305
13:24	401
15:1	301
15:2	305
15:4	305
15:12	330
15:18	301
19:18	401
21:3	259
22:6	400
22:24	301
23:13, 14	401
23:31	340
26:18	450
29:8	301
29:11	301
29:15	401
29:17	401

Ecclesiastes

6:10	203
7:9	301
12:9	212

Isaiah

2:2–4	140
5:1	27
5:7	27
5:26	138
5:30	327
6:1	75
6:3	73
6:10	278
7:8, 9	67
9:2	327
9:5, 6	127
9:6	140
10:17	327
11:2	56, 29, 436
11:4, 5	436, 456
11:4	451
11:5	447, 448
19:25	59
26:19	318
28:16	154, 155
40:26	203
41:10	62
42:6	327
42:13	436
42:16	327
43:7	36
43:21	36
44:2	26
44:26	251
45:23	409
47:5	327
47:6	59
48:9–11	36
48:13	62
49:6	327
51:4	327
51:6	20
51:8	217
52:1	436
52:7	126, 131, 148, 147, 159, 160, 436, 448
54:8–10	103
56:6–8	149
56:6, 7	156
57:15	60
57:19	126, 127, 128, 131, 146, 147, 148, 159, 178
59:9	327
59:17	436, 448, 450
60:1	318, 319, 327
60:2	327
63:10	306
63:17	59, 278
65:17	20
66:22	20

Jeremiah

2:5	277
5:15	139
10:12	29
10:16	59
11:15	27
12:6	55
12:7	27
13:11	36
17:7, 8	446
21:5	302
21:8	272
22:17	279
22:24	62
23:2	251
23:23, 24	73
23:24	77

Index of Biblical and Other Ancient Sources

31:33		450	7:18		217	Jonah	
51:19		59	7:22		107		
			7:27		107	1:5, 6	318
Ezekiel			8:13		60	2:6	92
			10:1		176	2:9	199
3:27		454	10:13		96, 186		
9:4–6		39	10:16		454	Micah	
16:8–14		763, 375, 387	10:20		63		
16:10–14		377	10:21		96, 186	4:1–4	140
20:41		298, 312	12:1		446	6:8	328
22:27		279					
33:22		454				Habakkuk	
34:11		251	Hosea				
43:5		75				2:9	279
44:4		75	13:14		92		
48:16		209				Haggai	
			Joel			2:6	20
Daniel						2:7	75
2:8		341	2:2		217	Zechariah	
2:18		30	2:28–32		40		
2:19		30	3:20		217	3:1	34
2:20–23		53				8:16	298, 300–302
2:21		29				8:20–23	149
2:27–30		30				11:16	251
2:47		30	Amos				
3:52		217				Malachi	
3:90		217	3:1		156		
4:34		27, 28	4:2		60	3:17	42
6:10		201	5:18–20		446		

B. The New Testament

Matthew			5:34	104	11:22	110, 442	
			6:52	278	12:57	403	
5:5		236	7:7	258	14:26	398	
5:22		301	7:9–13	398	15:13	344	
6:13		198, 199	7:10	405	15:24	93	
7:13, 14		272	7:21, 22	296	15:32	93	
7:17, 18		305	7:22	579	17:18	198	
8:22		93	8:17	278	17:19	104	
9:16		75	8:20	75	18:11	201	
11:29		236	9:35	254	18:13	201	
12:32		65, 110	10:7	352	18:20	405	
12:33, 34		305	10:13–16	398	18:30	110	
13:19		450	10:17	201	20:13	27	
13:22		286	10:19	303, 405	20:17, 18	155	
13:48		305	10:29, 30	398	20:34–36	383	
15:4		405	10:30	110	20:42	345	
15:9		258	10:42–45	254	21:28	28	
15:19		296	10:52	104	21:36	453	
16:18		154	11:10	46	22:41	201	
17:14		201	11:25	201	23:2	398	
18:4		236	12:10	155	24:44	345	
18:15–17		330	12:25	202	24:47	179	
19:5		352	13:12	398			
19:19		405	13:33–37	453	John		
19:28		107	14:26	345			
23:12		236	14:38	453	1:4	278, 321	
23:15		99	14:58	136	1:5	327	
25:1		255			1:7–9	327	
25:6		255			3:13	246	
26:30		345	Luke		3:19–21	656, 327	
28:19, 20		179			5:24, 25	93	
			1:28	26	6:62	246	
Mark			1:68–75	10	7:8	32	
			1:75	288	8:12	278, 327	
1:15		71, 284	2:4	202	9:5	327	
1:40		201	2:30	450	9:24	198	
3:5		278	3:6	450	10:11	250	
3:28		178	6:35, 36	311	10:14	250	
3:31–35		398	7:50	104	12:31	94	
4:19		286	9:59–62	398	12:35, 36	321	
5:33		420	9:60	93			

12:40	278	20:29, 30	250	3:27			112
15:3	376	20:32	60	3:29, 30			240
16:11	94	20:36	201	3:30			111
17:15	450	21:2	276	3:31		lxxxviii, xciii, 143
17:17	376	21:4	276	4			xciv, 143
21:16	251	21:5	201	4:2		lvii, 104, 112, 113
		21:8	250	4:3			112, 242
Acts	lxxxii	21:9, 10	153	4:4			113
		22:3	407	4:5			112
1:7	32	22:16	375	4:6			112
1:8	179	22:28	32, 137	4:7, 8			242
1:20	345	23:29	234	4:11			39
2:4	340, 344	25:25	208	4:13, 14			41
2:13	344	26:18	60, 326	4:15			98
2:15	340, 344	26:26	455	4:17			102
2:17	40	26:29	234	4:20			198
2:32, 33	61	26:31	234	4:25			29
2:33	244	28:20	454	5–7			93
2:34	62	28:28	450	5:1, 2			149
2:36	156	28:31	455	5:1			104, 140
2:37–39	39			5:2, 3			113
2:37	38	Romans	xxxix, lxiii, lxiv, lxvi, lxvii, xcv, cxxx,	5:2		lvii, 104, 128, 190, 447
2:38	18, 241			5:5			100, 420, 237
3:25	202			5:8–11			86–87
4:11	155	1	272, 277	5:8			87, 100, 207
4:13	208	1:1–15	5	5:9, 10			87, 100, 207
4:24–30	204	1:1	5, 179, 182	5:9			87, 98, 104, 286
5:17	2	1:3	256	5:10			145–146, 256
5:42	280	1:4	61, 205, 256	5:11			lxv, 113, 145
7:2	56	1:5	liv, 171, 174	5:12–21		71, 93, 99, 102, 104
7:22	401	1:7	3, 4, 6	5:15			29, 112, 182
7:48	136	1:8	54	5:16			29, 93
7:60	201	1:9, 10	49	5:17			112, 182
8:12–17	39	1:9	49, 56, 256	5:20, 21			103
8:14–17	250	1:11–15	168	5:20			29
8:17, 18	40	1:13, 14	171	6			236
8:20	241	1:13	31	6:1–11			105
9:27	455	1:15	4	6:1–4			91
9:29	455	1:16	39	6:1			103
9:36	115	1:18–3:20	99	6:4		56, 102, 235, 272
9:40	201	1:18–32	325	6:5			102, 219
10:34	208	1:18–23	278	6:6		211, 284–285, 569
10:44–46	40	1:18	98	6:7			104
10:45	241	1:20	114	6:8			101–2, 105
11:17	241	1:21	lvii, 273, 277, 273, 324	6:10, 11			105
11:27	153	1:24–32	279	6:12			286
12:23	198	1:24	lvvii, 273, 279, 286	6:13			93, 435
13:1–3	153, 250	1:26	99	6:14			103, 143
13:1, 2	153	1:29–31	276	6:15–23			86
13:1	2, 250–51	1:29	279	6:16–18			87
13:7	38	1:30	398, 402	6:16			87
13:33	345	2:2	281	6:20			87
13:44	38	2:4	110	6:21			87
13:46	455	2:5	98, 307	6:22, 23			87
14:4	250	2:6–11	414	6:23			87, 92–93, 435
14:13	2	2:6–10	422	7:4–6			143
14:14	250	2:7	115, 467	7:4			142
14:23	233, 251	2:8	98	7:5, 6			86–87
15:11	104	2:11	lvii, 423, 424	7:5		29, 87, 93, 97
15:32	153	2:13	104	7:6			87, 143
16:25	345	2:14, 15	99	7:7–25			146, 164
16:26	234	2:18	328	7:7, 8			286
17:26	156	2:21	303	7:9			93
17:30	278	2:27	99	7:10			93
18:19–21	1	2:28, 29	136	7:13			93
19:1–20:1	1	3:5	98	7:22			205
19:2	39	3:19, 20	146, 164	7:23			205
19:5, 6	39, 40	3:20	156	7:25			205
19:6	40, 153	3:22–25	111	8:1			22
19:8	455	3:22	54	8:3			256
19:10	38	3:24–28	lvii, xcii, 119	8:4			234
20:4	cxxiii, 465	3:24	104, 112, 182	8:5–7			98
20:17–38	1	3:25, 26	111	8:6			237
20:17	233, 251	3:25	54, 139	8:8			98
20:23	234	3:26	282	8:9–11			247
20:28	42, 233, 251	3:27, 28	111	8:9, 10			206

8:9	206	12:5	lvii, 71, 298	1:31	113
8:10	207	12:6–8	229	2:1	31
8:11	102, 206, 282	12:6	153, 229, 241	2:3	414, 420
8:14, 15	25	12:7	251, 254, 258	2:4	205
8:15, 16	149, 452	12:8	251	2:6–16	57
8:15	lv, 25, 57, 240	12:9, 10	229	2:6–8	187
8:16	57	12:12	453	2:6	65, 94–95, 256–57
8:17, 18	192	12:13	304	2:7–10	170
8:17	lvii, 41, 102, 101, 107, 181	12:15	283	2:7	25, 31, 184
8:18–23	33	12:16	235	2:8	65, 94, 95
8:21	286	12:19	98	2:9	466
8:23	lvi, 25, 28, 307	13:1	365	2:10–13	57
8:24	104	13:3	115, 385	2:10	180
8:28–30	23	13:4	385	2:12	97
8:28	36, 80, 466	13:4, 5	98	3:1	257
8:29	lvi, 23, 25, 215, 256	13:5	365	3:3	234
8:30	25, 235	13:7	385	3:5	182
8:34	61, 62	13:8–10	143	3:6, 7	261
8:35	214	13:9	33, 303	3:6	lvii
8:35–39	207, 212	13:10	74	3:9–17	152
8:38	63	13:11–14	432	3:9–12	lvii
8:39	100, 214	13:11, 12	307	3:9	72, 156, 260
9–11	xciv, 134, 137, 164	13:11	104	3:10, 11	154–55
9:1	281	13:12–14	272	3:10	liv, 103, 152, 174
9:4, 5	137	13:12, 13	326–27, 344	3:11	lxiv, 152–53, 155
9:4	24, 137	13:12	lvii, 272, 284–84, 329, 435	3:12	152
9:11	36, 112	13:13	279, 234, 296	3:14	152
9:13	24	13:14	97, 284, 286	3:15	104
9:15, 16	100	14:8, 9	239	3:16, 17	156
9:15	242	14:11	202	3:16	lvii, 152, 158, 206
9:16	112	14:15	234, 312	3:17	152
9:17	242	14:17	237	3:18, 19	95
9:18	24, 100	14:18	329	3:18	65
9:22	24, 98, 109, 254	14:20	114	4:1, 2	174
9:23	100, 115, 204	14:23	4	4:1	31–32
9:25	27	15	xciv	4:7	113
9:26	25	15:4	258	4:9–13	171
9:30–10:4	146, 164	15:8	281	4:12	292, 298, 304
9:32	112	15:10	242	4:14	lvii, 407
10:3	112	15:13	237	4:16	lvii, 226
10:4	143	15:14	650	4:21	236
10:6, 7	245	15:15	174	5:1	321
10:9, 10	229	15:16	171, 182	5:5	lxv, 104, 303
10:9	104, 239	15:18	171	5:8	309
10:10	104	15:21	280	5:9–11	320, 325
10:11	242	15:25–31	2	5:10, 11	279, 296
10:13	104	15:25	151	6:2	107
10:14–17	38	15:26	151	6:9–11	86–87
10:14	280	15:29	74	6:9, 10	lvii, 41, 296, 325
10:15	448	15:30	226	6:9	320
11	xciii, 185	15:31	151	6:10	303
11:2	242	15:33	4, 463	6:11	375
11:3	202	16	13	6:12–20	321
11:6	112	16:1	463	6:14	56, 61
11:7	278	16:17	226, 280	6:15, 16	lvii
11:9, 10	242	16:20	lxv, 303, 463	6:16	361, 378, 382
11:12	74	16:24	463	6:19	156
11:13	171, 254	16:25–27	170, 175, 217	6:20	28
11:15	145	16:25	31, 184, 215	7	lxiv, xcv, 390
11:13–32	133	16:27	199	7:2	321
11:20	235, 447			7:5	lxv, 303
11:22	110	*1 Corinthians*	xciv	7:7–14	418
11:25–27	34			7:14	398
11:25	31, 74, 75, 278	1:1	5, 15	7:16	370
11:26	156	1:2	4	7:17	234
11:30–32	86–87, 100, 125	1:3	6	7:20–22	421
11:33–36	211	1:4	54–55	7:21	419–20
11:33	lvii, 183, 188, 212	1:9	235	7:22, 23	414
11:36	199, 240, 229	1:10	226, 254	7:22	419
12	xciv, 71, 230, 249 262	1:18	39, 104	7:23	28
12:1	lxxiv, 226–27, 229, 231, 234	1:20	65, 95	7:26	446
12:2	lvii, 65, 416, 286, 571, 320, 329, 340, 343	1:21	104	7:29–32	341
		1:23	280	7:30, 31	305
12:3	lvii, liv, 174, 229, 242	1:27, 28	140	8:3	214, 466
12:4, 5	71, 301, 713	1:28–31	119	8:5, 6	138
12:4	229	1:30	140	8:6	229, 237, 240

480 INDEX OF BIBLICAL AND OTHER ANCIENT SOURCES

9:17	32, 174	15:32	lxxxi	6:4			182
10:4	137	15:42	467	6:5			171, 304
10:8	321	15:43, 44	205	6:6, 7			205, 296
10:11	65, 407	15:44–49	20, 71	6:6			236
10:12	447	15:44	40	6:7		85, 281, 435, 448
10:16, 17	71	15:45–49	143	6:14–7:1		326, 327
10:16	139	15:45	102, 206, 247	6:15			6
10:20	444	15:47–49	108	6:16			156, 242
10:26	74–75	15:50	41, 325, 444, 467	6:18			25
10:32	xciv, 67, 144, 276	15:51	31	7:1			366
11	153, 369	15:52–54	467	7:14			281
11:3	lvii, 67, 361, 369	15:56	93	7:15			414, 420
11:10	186	15:58	432	8:4			151
11:14	99	16:1	309	8:22			190
11:21	343	16:8	cxxiii	9:1			151
11:23–32	71	16:10	463	9:8			29, 115, 304
11:25	135, 139	16:13	432, 435, 441, 447	9:10			260, 263
12–14	264	16:15	226	9:12			151
12	xciv, 71, 229–30, 247, 249, 262	16:22	466	9:14			110
12:3	237, 282	16:23	463	9:15			112, 182
12:4–13	150			10–13			176
12:4–6	229	*2 Corinthians*		10:1		172, 226–27, 236
12:4	229, 241, 247			10:2, 3			234
12:5	229, 254	1:1	3, 5	10:2			190
12:6	36, 76	1:2	6	10:3, 4			435
12:7, 8	247	1:3–11	53, 171	10:4			442
12:9, 10	180	1:3, 4	11	10:15			261
12:10	229	1:3	lvi	10:17			113
12:11–13	228	1:6	192	11:2			376, 387
12:11	229, 242	1:8–14	168	11:3			259
12:12–27	71, 301	1:11	453	11:4			282
12:12, 13	71, 143, 229	1:15	190	11:10			281
12:13	238, 240, 247, 414, 418, 423, 818	1:19	256, 280	11:14			lxv, 303
		1:22	lvi, 86, 89	11:23–33			171
12:27	71, 361	2:8	226	11:23			171, 304
12:28, 29	251	2:11	lxv, 303	11:27			304
12:28	lvii, lxiv–lxv, xciv, 67, 153, 229, 230, 249–51, 252	2:14–17	53	11:30			113
		2:14–16	298	12:2–4			108
13	207, 229, 237	2:15	104	12:6			281
13:2	31, 213	3:4	190	12:7–10			171
13:4	236	3:6	102, 182	12:7			lxv
13:9–13	213	3:7–11	146, 164	12:9			113
13:12	58	3:8, 9	254	12:18			234
14	57, 153	3:12	190	12:20, 21			296
14:2	31	3:14	278	12:21			279
14:3–5	255	3:17	206, 247	13:4			61, 102, 106
14:6	57	3:18	215	13:11			254, 463
14:12	255	4:1	191, 254	13:14			463
14:15	324	4:2	85, 234, 259				
14:16, 17	324	4:4	56, 65, 94, 95, 327				
14:16	xxxix, 200	4:5	282	*Galatians*		*lxxxviii, xciv, xcv*
14:20	256	4:6	56, 205, 327				
14:24, 25	330	4:7–11	171	1–2			176
14:26	57, 251, 255, 345	4:10	282	1:1			61
14:30	57	4:11	282	1:3			6
14:34	365	4:12	192	1:4			29, 65
14:36	38	4:14	101, 282	1:5			199
14:37, 38	176	4:16	191, 205, 286	1:10			lvii, 414, 421
15:2	104	4:17	192	1:11			182
15:3	29, 61	5:1	lxv	1:12			175
15:7	29	5:5	40	1:13			lxiv, xciv, 67
15:9, 10	lvii	5:7	234	1:15, 16			179
15:9	lxiii–lxiv, xciv, 67, 182	5:10	115, 176, 405, 414	1:15			103, 174
15:10	103, 174, 182	5:11	366	1:16		171, 175, 182, 256, 280, 444
15:19	37	5:12	205	1:23			86
15:20–22	71	5:14	214	2:5			38, 260, 282
15:22, 23	101	5:17	49, 114, 144, 272	2:7–9			171
15:22	21, 143	5:18–21	146	2:9			103, 174
15:24–28	51, 66, 77, 325	5:18, 19	lxv, 145	2:14		38, 176, 260, 282
15:24–27	51	5:18	254, 297	2:15			99
15:24–26	64	5:19	29, 38	2:16			54, 119
15:24	lvi, 63	5:20	lvii, 145, 234, 454	2:19			102, 143
15:25–27	xci	6:1	226	2:20		lvii, 54, 207, 214, 256, 298, 361
15:27	lvi, 66	6:2	104, 242	2:21			103
15:28	76, 77, 215, 240, 372	6:3–10	171	3–4			xciv
15:30–32	171	6:3	173, 254	3:2–5			112

Index of Biblical and Other Ancient Sources

3:3	98	1:3–12	lxi	1:23	xlvi, liv, lxxxix, lxiv, xciv, 35, 72, 92, 128, 142, 155, 180, 212, 214, 231, 238, 239–40, 247, 249, 254, 257, 344
3:4	173	1:3–11	xlv		
3:5	263	1:3, 4	235		
3:9, 10	112	1:3	lxiv, lxv, xc, 6, 19, 19–22, 34, 56, 72, 86, 150, 158, 181, 203, 207, 217, 253, 340		
3:9	6			2	lxiv, lxxv, 19
3:10–22	146, 164			2:1–22	l, lxi, lxxvii, 86
3:13	28, 142, 312	1:4	lii, lxv, xcv, 6, 22–25, 59, 86, 115–16, 207, 231	2:1–10	xxxvi, xxxvi, xlvii, li, xcii, 84–121, 131, 165, 275, 326
3:14	lvi, 20, 23, 40–41				
3:16–22	137	1:5, 6	xlvi, 25–27, 253	2:1–7	xlv, lxvi, 88
3:16	23, 242	1:5	xlvi, lvi, lxxvi, 19, 36, 59, 95, 115, 149	2:1–3	lxxvii, 34, 102, 104
3:18	41			2:1, 2	116
3:19	29	1:6, 7	lii, 6, 104	2:1	xxxvi, xxxviii, xlv, lxv, 90, 91–93, 278
3:22	54	1:6	lxxvi, 72, 100, 109, 192, 217		
3:24, 25	143	1:7, 8	27–30, 183	2:2, 3	25
3:26	25, 55	1:7	xlv–xlvi, xlviii, lxiii, lxv, lxxvi, xci, 42, 50, 86, 109, 139, 146, 204	2:2	xc, lxv, cxxxix, 35, 64, 89, 93–97, 108–9, 138, 184–85, 231, 234, 276, 312, 445
3:27, 28	143, 240				
3:27	272, 284–85	1:8	xlv, lii, lxxvi, 18, 50, 57, 176, 187, 211		
3:28	xcv, 134, 161, 163, 383, 418, 419, 423, 424			2:3–7	lxi
		1:9, 10	liv, 19, 30–35, 114, 167, 170, 174–75, 184, 188, 239, 268	2:3	lvii, lxv, 90, 97–99, 104, 135, 146, 189, 286, 326
3:29	23, 41				
4:1	41	1:9	lxv, 19, 25, 35, 50–51, 181, 194, 210, 213	2:4–10	87
4:3–7	86–87			2:4–8	xlv
4:4, 5	32	1:10	lii–liii, lv, lxv, xci, xcv, 18–19, 59, 65, 74, 77, 132, 144, 161, 164, 173–74, 181, 184, 194, 203, 241	2:4	26, 99–100, 138, 207, 214
4:4	lvi, 25, 256			2:5–8	174
4:5	25, 28, 341			2:5, 6	lxxvi, 61, 91, 100–109, 146, 180
4:6	149, 206, 240, 256, 452	1:11–13	88		
4:7	41	1:11, 12	35–37, 86	2:5	liii, lxxvi, xci, 6, 19, 26, 39, 89, 206, 275, 281, 450
4:8–10	86	1:11	xlv, lxv, 19, 59, 95, 115, 189		
4:8	99, 138	1:12	26, 50, 55, 59, 109, 115, 192, 217, 239	2:6, 7	19, 181
4:9	58, 214			2:6	lxiv, lxv, xc, 19, 22, 34, 41, 62, 90, 151, 154
4:16	259	1:13, 14	lvi, 19, 37–42, 131, 158, 170, 205, 340		
4:25–27	134			2:7–9	104
4:26	108, 151	1:13	lii, lx, lxv, lxxvi, 19, 54, 88, 104, 137, 181, 190, 234, 247, 260, 280	2:7	xlvi, xcii, 6, 19, 29, 64–65, 94, 109–11, 183–84, 204, 218, 253
4:30	41, 242				
5:1	447	1:14	lix, lxi, xci, 19, 26, 28, 50, 59, 65, 108–9, 181, 192, 217	2:8–10	lxiv, 193
5:2	33			2:8, 9	lvii, xcii, 90, 111–13
5:4	103	1:15–23	xxxvi, xlv, lxi, lxvi, 38, 46–83, 131, 165, 170, 197–99, 220	2:8	lxxvi, xci, 6, 19, 26, 39, 190, 206, 281, 449
5:5	104, 320				
5:6	58, 114	1:15–17	li	2:10	lxi, lxxvi, lxxxvi, 109, 113–16, 143, 184, 231, 234, 276, 288, 312
5:7	38, 281, 282	1:15, 16	lxi, lx, 54–56		
5:13	366	1:15	lxv, lxxvii, lxxxivl, 2, 6, 17, 132, 151, 190, 200, 207, 213, 231, 254, 282	2:11–22	xxxvii, xlvii, l, lxiii, lxv, xciii, 85, 91, 124–64, 170, 172, 176, 177, 181, 200, 232, 276, 275
5:14	237				
5:16	97, 234, 286				
5:19–23	296	1:16–19	lxxvii, 49	2:11–18	lxi
5:19–21	320	1:16, 17	55–58, 198	2:11–16	li
5:19	279, 321, 329, 557	1:16	189	2:11–13	lxxvii, 125, 130, 140
5:20	301	1:17–19	lxvii, 256	2:11, 12	c, 139
5:21	41	1:17, 18	xlv, 213, 251, 277	2:11	xxxvii, lxi, lxxvi, 38, 91, 97, 101, 134–36, 149, 276
5:22	236–237, 320, 328	1:17	lxv, 57, 66, 150, 176, 368, 187, 192, 200, 203, 205, 428, 217, 287, 340		
5:23	236			2:12	lvii, lxv, 59, 136–38, 150, 178, 181, 229, 239, 277
5:24	97, 286				
6:1	57, 254	1:18, 19	58–61	2:13	xci, 139, 148, 181
6:8	286	1:18	xxxvi, xlvi, lii, lxxvi, 37, 41, 138, 151, 181, 184, 192, 204, 206, 209, 213, 229, 231, 234, 238–39, 254	2:14–18	xlv, lxxvi, 125, 126–30, 132, 146, 231–32, 371, 449
6:9	191				
6:10	114, 152, 304, 342			2:14–17	209
6:13	113	1:19–23	146	2:14–16	xlvii, lxi, lxxvii, 139–46, 148, 208, 211, 238
6:14	113	1:19, 20	xlv, liii, 26, 100		
6:15, 16	163	1:19	xlv, lxi, lxv, 66, 73, 85, 95, 110, 114, 182, 190, 205, 215, 263	2:14, 15	xciii, 124
6:15	114, 144, 272			2:14	6, 97, 245
6:16	134, 463, 465			2:15, 16	170
6:17	171, 282, 441	1:20–23	xlvii–xlviii, lxi, xci, 34, 47, 51, 153, 186	2:15	lxiii, xciii, xcv, 6, 112, 114, 133, 184, 239, 245, 256, 275, 287–88
6:18	463				
		1:20–22	xci, 51, 108, 242		
		1:20, 21	61–65, 85, 185, 250	2:16	lxiii, lxv, lxxvi, xci, xciii, xcv, 71, 146, 150, 181, 228, 239
Ephesians		1:20	xlvii, lxv, xc, 19, 21–22, 26, 86, 97, 105, 107, 109, 216, 248		
1–3	xxxvi, xlii, 231			2:17, 18	xciii
1	xxxiv, xci	1:21–23	188, 194	2:17	xlvii, cxii, xciv, 6, 146–149
1:1, 2	xxxvii, xlviii, 1–7	1:21, 22	lvi, 203, 242	2:18–22	172
1:1	lx, lxxvi, 54–55, 60, 151, 213, 254	1:21	lii, xc, 21, 34–35, 47, 121, 94, 95, 110, 184, 198, 200, 411, 218	2:18	lvii, lxi, 149–50, 158, 170, 181, 189–91, 202, 228, 478, 340
1:2	202				
1:3–3:21	xxxvi, xxxvii, 51	1:22, 23	xxxviii, lxi, lxiv, xclv, xcv, 19, 66–78, 130, 217, 231, 241, 248, 261	2:19–22	130–31
1:3–2:10	xxxvi			2:19	lxxvi, xciv, 60, 126, 132, 146, 150–52, 170, 180, 209, 213, 254, 265
1:3–14	xxxvi, xlvii, xliv, liii, lvi, lxi, lxvi, lxxvii, lxxx, 8–44, 54, 109, 170, 189, 218, 275				
		1:22	xlvii, liii, lix, lxiv, xci, 34–35, 65–66, 77, 186, 186, 249, 260, 368, 733, 770	2:20–22	lxii, xciv, 127, 140, 149, 152–59
				2:20, 21	261

Index of Biblical and Other Ancient Sources

2:20	lv, lxi, lxiv, xci, xcv, 57, 151, 170, 179, 231, 245 249, 280	4:1	xxxvi, xxxvii, xlix, lvii, lx, lx, lxxii, lxxvi, xci, 5, 19, 26, 54, 59, 94, 100, 109, 173, 227, 229, 234–35, 238, 276, 312	5:2	xxxvii, xlvii, lvii, lxi, lxi, lxxvi, cxi, 17, 94, 100, 109, 146, 207, 214, 221, 232, 313, 310
2:21, 22	75, 151, 180			5:3–14	xxxvii, lvii, xcv, xcv, 272, 274, 316–336
2:21	xcv, 206, 230–31, 255, 524				
2:22	lxv, 180, 205–6, 217, 340	4:2–4	liii, 227	5:3–5	lii
3	xxxix, xl, liv, 19	4:2, 3	235–37	5:3, 4	xlvii, 296, 321–324
3:1, 14–19	xxxvii, 50, 180	4:2	17, 207, 221, 229, 264	5:3	lxv, 151, 271, 279
3:1–13	xxxvi, xlix, li, lvii, lxii, lxxvii, lxxv, lxxix, lxxvii xcv, 132, 166, 167–95, 233	4:3–5	132	5:4	305
		4:3, 4	158, 246	5:5	lxii, lxiv, xcii, 19, 41, 65, 108, 181, 239, 261, 271, 279, 325–26
		4:3	xliii, lxv, 6, 19, 132, 161, 287		
3:1–7	xlv, lxvi	4:4–6	xlvii, 150, 217, 237–41, 266	5:6	lii, 98, 325–26
3:1	lxxiv, lx, lxxi, lxxvi, 5, 53, 135, 172–73, 190, 198, 201, 214	4:4	lxii, lxiv, lxxvii, xcv, 37, 129, 71, 138, 144, 150, 181	5:7–14	80
				5:7–13	lxvii
3:2–13	xxxvii, xliv, lxxvii	4:5	lxxix, 255	5:7–10	88
3:2–12	191	4:6	19, 184, 202, 204, 248	5:7	326
3:2–6	lxi	4:7–16	155, 221, 233	5:8–14	l, 227
3:2–4	32	4:7	lxi, xciv, 6, 19, 66, 112, 181, 241–42, 263	5:8–10	326–29
3:2	xlviii, li, liv, lx, lxxvii, 2, 6, 19, 32, 66, 173–74, 184, 241, 280, 392			5:8	xxxvii, lii, lvii, lxxvi, xci, 86, 94, 109, 232, 312
		4:8–10	lx, lxxvi, 34, 154		
3:3–10	31, 35	4:8	xlvii, lxi, lxv, 66, 242–44	5:9	xlvii, 232, 281, 305
3:3–6	liv, 34	4:9, 10	224, 244–48	5:10	lxiii
3:3–5	19, 213	4:10	xci, 19, 35, 62, 77, 239, 240	5:11, 12	329–30
3:3, 4	210	4:11–16	xlv, lxvi, xciv, 224	5:11	lvii, lxv
3:3	lxxvii, 31, 56, 57, 153, 174–75, 184	4:11, 12	lxiii, 248–55	5:13, 14	330–31
		4:11	lvii, lxv, 66, 153, 176, 241, 263, 280	5:13	lxv
3:4	lxiv, 31, 165, 175–77			5:14	xlvii, lxi, lxv, lxxvi, 58, 90, 93, 242, 331–33
3:5, 6	132	4:12	xlvi, 71, 132, 151, 156, 264		
3:5	liv, lxi, lxiii, xciv, xciv, 56, 57, 150, 153, 177–80, 183, 184, 218, 231, 249, 280	4:13–15	lxi	5:15–6:9	xliv, 337, 438
		4:13	liv, xciv, 58, 74, 155, 199, 214, 240, 253, 258, 344	5:15–20	xxxvii, lii, 272, 275, 321, 337–49
3:6	lvii, lxiii, lxxvii, 71, 135, 137, 151, 180–81, 186, 231, 232	4:14	lxxxiii, 38, 154, 219, 253, 257–59	5:15, 16	341–42
				5:15	xxxvii, lxv, xci, 57, 94, 109, 232, 312
3:7–13	lxi	4:15, 16	liii, xci, xciv, 68, 71, 132, 155, 157, 206, 229, 237, 261, 301, 369, 370		
3:7	xlv, lxi, lxxvi, 6, 19, 60, 61, 66, 112, 181–82, 241, 262			5:16	445–46
		4:15	lxv, 17, 19, 39, 68, 77, 221, 261–269, 283 369	5:17	lviii, 19, 213, 342–43
3:8	xlvi, lvii, lxiii, lxi, xxxvi, 6, 19, 60, 66, 135, 151, 182–84, 204, 212, 213, 241, 259			5:18, 19	307
		4:16	xlviii, lxxvi, xciv, 17, 71, 156, 158, 189, 207, 221, 242	5:18	xlvii, 19, 214, 247, 287, 343–45
				5:19, 20	345–47
3:9, 10	liv, xcvi, 19, 34, 132, 184–89, 231, 239, 265	4:17–5:20	l, 438	5:19	20, 206, 306
		4:17–24	xxxvii, li, xcv, 81, 82, 88, 132, 270–91, 321	5:20	lii, lxvii, 202, 217, 324, 452
3:9	xlviii, liii, 19, 31–32, 34, 94, 174, 177, 210, 213, 218, 240			5:21–6:9	xxxvii, xlvii, lii, xcv
		4:17–19	lvii, xcv, 273, 276–79, 282	5:21–33	xlvi, l, 350–95
3:10	lxi, lix, lxv, lxiv, 19, 20, 24, 56–57, 63, 67, 78, 95, 110, 161, 203, 211, 217	4:17	xxxvii, lxi, lxxvi, xci, 94, 109, 135, 232, 276, 312	5:21	338, 365–67, 384
				5:22	367–68
		4:18	58, 93, 131, 206	5:23–33	xciv
3:11, 12	189–91	4:19	444	5:23–25	lxiv
3:11	lxv, 170, 218	4:20–24	lxvi, lxxvii	5:23	lviii, lxxvii, xci, 39, 67, 68, 71, 232, 368–72
3:12	lvii, lxi, lxxvi, 111, 132, 149, 206	4:20, 21	xlii, 232–33, 251, 279–83		
3:13	lx, lxxii, lxxvi, 191–93, 217	4:20	lxv	5:24	67, 372–73
3:14–21	xxxvi, xliv, xlix, liii, lvii, lxi, 166, 171, 190, 196–221	4:21	lxv, 1, 2, 19, 38, 173–74, 232, 250	5:25–27	xcv, 371
				5:25	xlvii, lvii, lxiii, lxxvi, cxl, 17, 67, 100, 146, 207, 214, 221, 232, 310, 373–75
3:14–19	lxvi, lxxvii, l	4:22–24	xlvii, 227, 271		
3:14, 15	201–204, 240	4:22	97, 283–86		
3:15	185	4:23	lxv, 57, 205, 286–87	5:26, 27	lxiv, 6
3:16–19	256	4:24	lxv, xcv, 114, 205, 232, 287–91, 448	5:26	375–76
3:16, 17	204–7			5:27	lxiv, lxxvii, 60, 65, 67, 108, 157, 217, 376–78
3:16	xlvi, liii, 66, 183, 216, 217, 247, 287, 345, 441	4:25–5:20	xlvii		
		4:25–5:14	li	5:28–30	379–80
3:17	liii, 17, 111, 152, 207, 231, 247	4:25–5:2	xxxvii, lvii, 275, 291–315, 319, 321	5:28	17, 221, 232, 378–79
3:18, 19	xlv, 207–215, 231, 251			5:29	lxv, 67, 71, 97
3:18	lxxvi, 55, 255	4:25, 26	xlvii	5:30, 31	lviii
3:19	liii, liv, 58, 73, 74, 76, 135, 155, 214–15, 231, 257, 344	4:25	lvi, lxxi, lxxvii, 19, 466, 281, 300–301, 448	5:30	301, 432
				5:31, 32	xlvii, 380–83
3:20, 21	xxxvi, 215–18, 435–40	4:26, 27	301–303	5:31	97
3:20	liii, lxi, 61	4:26	406	5:32	liv, lxiv, lxiv, 31, 34, 68
3:21	xli, lxi, lxxxiii, lxiv, 60, 67, 110, 189	4:27	lxv, 66, 95, 97, 438, 439, 443	5:33	17, 221, 232, 383–85
		4:28	lvii, 303–5	6:1–4	395–428
4–6	xxxvi	4:29	6, 19, 66, 156, 305–6, 322	6:1	402–3
4	xxxvii, xci, xc, 236	4:30	lvii, lxiv, lxiv, xcv, 19, 28, 39, 42, 65, 108, 247, 261, 306–8, 345	6:2, 3	xlvii, lxiii, xciii, 404–6
4:1–6:20	xxxvi, xxxix			6:2	143
4:1–6:9	200	4:31, 32	xlvii, lii, 293, 308–10	6:3	275
4:1–5:20	227	4:32	lxv, lxxvi, 228, 236	6:4	379, 406–8
4:1–16	xxxvii, xliii, xlvi, liii, lxi, lxxvii, xciv, xcv, 213, 222–69, 274	5	lxiv, xcv	6:5–9	411–428
		5:1, 2	310–12, 373	6:5, 6	liv
4:1–6	lxvi, 225, 232	5:1	lvii, lxv, lxxvi	6:5	97, 206, 385, 411, 420–21
4:1–3	274				

Index of Biblical and Other Ancient Sources

6:6, 7	421–22	3:3	113	1:28	29, 189, 256, 280, 408		
6:6	19, 411	3:4	190	1:29–2:10	l, 199, 206, 214, 218, 227		
6:7	lxv	3:6	xciv, 67	1:29	liii, 182		
6:8	xci, 65, 108, 307, 422–23	3:7–10	171	2:1–3	3		
6:9	lvi, 62, 248, 423–24	3:9	22, 54, 112	2:1	5		
6:10–20	xxxvii, xlii, xlvi, lviii, lxxv, lxxvii, lxxviii, lxxx, 97, 430–460	3:10	61, 102	2:2, 3	212, 255		
		3:11	255	2:2	liv, 34, 58, 176, 262		
		3:16	283	2:3	29, 184		
6:10–18	39	3:17, 18	234	2:4	325		
6:10–17	xlii, l	3:20	108, 151, 371	2:5	54		
6:10	xlv, 60, 205, 219, 441–42	3:21	66, 72	2:6, 7	250, 274, 279		
6:11–16	xci, 109	4:1	447	2:6	189, 234		
6:11	lxv, 94, 95, 259, 303, 442–43	4:6	lvii, 324, 452	2:7	liii, lv, lxiv, 152, 240, 320, 324		
6:12	lxi, lxiii, lxv, lxxvi, 19–21, 35, 63, 64, 96–97, 185, 253, 443–45	4:7	463	2:8	63, 74, 258, 286, 320, 325		
		4:8	296, 403, 441	2:9, 10	lii, 73, 75, 214		
6:13, 14	261	4:9	463, 558	2:9	liv, 73, 74, 76, 215		
6:13	lxiv, xci, 65, 108, 261, 342, 445–47	4:18	lvii, 298, 312	2:10–13	89		
		4:19	204	2:10	liii, liv, 63, 67, 74, 214		
6:14–20	xlv, lxvi	4:20	199	2:11	li, 40, 102, 106, 135, 136, 139		
6:14–17	xlvii	4:23	463	2:12–15	89		
6:14–16	xlv, lvi			2:12	liii, 50, 61, 91, 102, 105, 106		
6:14	19, 232, 245, 260, 281, 447–48			2:13	liii, 85–87, 89, 92–93, 101–102, 135		
6:15	6, 132, 147, 161, 181, 448–49	Colossians	lvi–lxxii, lii, xxvii, xciii–xcvii, cxxiv				
6:16	94, 95, 245, 449–50			2:14	li, 142		
6:17, 18	340			2:15	63, 66, 242		
6:17	19, 245, 308, 376, 450–51	1:1, 2	xlvii	2:18	98, 363		
6:18–20	lii, lvii, 439	1:1	5	2:19	xlviii, liii, 68, 71, 157, 230, 260, 261, 262, 263, 265		
6:18	lxxvi, 19, 55, 151, 212, 287, 451–53	1:2	5–6				
		1:3, 4	52, 55	2:20–23	363		
6:19, 20	lxi, 234, 453–55	1:3	48, 54–55	2:20–22	258		
6:19	lxxvii, 19, 31, 34, 57, 66, 181, 190	1:4, 5	55	2:20	63, 102, 106, 142		
		1:4	li, 5, 17, 48, 49, 50, 54–55	2:22	230, 258		
6:20	lxxii, lxxvii, 171, 190	1:5–7	250	2:23	29		
6:21–24	xxxviii, 461–68	1:5, 6	282	3:1–17	227		
6:21, 22	xlviii, l, lii, liii, lxi, cxii, 2, 3, 464–65	1:5	lii, lxv, 37–38, 59, 286	3:1–3	xc, 111		
		1:6, 7	280	3:1	22, 61, 62, 102, 105, 106		
6:22	206	1:6	77, 261, 280–81	3:1, 2	106, 119		
6:23, 24	6, 17, 221	1:7	250	3:3, 4	106, 111		
6:23	lxv, 202, 465–66	1:8	17	3:3	106, 185		
6:24	lxv, 19, 55, 207, 466–68	1:9–12	52	3:4	lxiv, 101, 140, 192		
		1:9, 10	55	3:5–17	1		
Philippians	*lviii*	1:9	li, lii, 20, 48–49, 56–57, 173, 176, 343	3:5–12	272		
				3:5–11	li, lii, 272–274		
1:1	3, 5, 251, 252	1:10	58, 77, 115, 234, 261, 328	3:5–8	320		
1:2	6	1:11	133, 204–5, 236, 442	3:5, 6	98		
1:3	48, 54	1:12, 13	52, 58, 319, 326–27	3:5	lii, lvii, 87, 270, 272, 279, 286, 296, 321, 324		
1:4	48, 49, 55, 452	1:12	34, 59, 152, 324				
1:6	48, 114, 307	1:13, 14	l, lii, 27	3:6	lii, 87, 326		
1:7	171	1:13	18, 27, 95, 256, 325	3:7, 8	lii, 86		
1:9–11	199	1:14	xlviii, 18, 26, 28, 93	3:7	87, 90, 93, 234		
1:9, 10	17, 24, 328	1:15–20	xlviii, li, 50, 71, 128, 129	3:8–14	319		
1:9	48	1:15, 16	24	3:8–12	272		
1:10	307	1:16	lii, liii, lxv, 34, 64, 114	3:8–10	227, 282, 283		
1:11	26	1:18	liii, liii, xciv, 50, 67, 69, 71, 128, 144	3:8, 9	300		
1:12–26	168			3:8	xliv, 566, 284, 295, 296, 297, 305, 308, 309, 323		
1:12–17	173	1:19	liii, 20, 73, 74, 76				
1:12–14	171	1:20	lii, lxiii, lxiv, lxv, 27, 33–34, 140, 144–45, 146	3:9	285, 300, 566		
1:15	280			3:10, 11	143		
1:17	171	1:21–23	xlvii, l, 125, 130	3:10	58, 272, 286, 287, 337		
1:19	263	1:21, 22	li, 86, 129	3:11	76, 142, 161, 413, 414, 419, 423		
1:20	455	1:21	lix, lvii, 136, 274, 277	3:12–15	liii, 227, 235		
1:23	101	1:22	liii, 24, 143, 145, 146, 376, 377	3:12–14	lii, 313		
1:26	192	1:23–28	l, 168, 199	3:12	lii, 27, 236, 295, 296, 308, 309		
1:27, 28	447	1:23	xlviii, liii, 58, 152, 172, 182, 207, 240, 250, 255, 280, 173	3:13	liii, 236, 293, 308, 310, 309		
1:27	234			3:14, 15	236, 237		
2:3, 4	366	1:24–29	li, 169, 170	3:14	236		
2:3	236	1:24	xciv, 66, 69, 71, 171, 191, 192	3:15	71, 235, 238		
2:6–11	51, 236, 246	1:25–27	32	3:16, 17	lii, 348		
2:8	146	1:25	xlviii, li, liv, 32, 174, 175, 182	3:16	20, 38, 339, 341, 407		
2:9–11	65, 239	1:26–28	188	3:17	lii, lxvii, 324, 421		
2:9	61	1:26, 27	liv, 34, 174	3:18–4:1	lii, 354–55		
2:10, 11	66	1:26	xlviii, lv, 29, 57, 167, 177, 177, 178, 179, 184	3:18, 19	l		
2:10	202, 282			3:18	lvii, 364, 367, 373		
2:12	104, 414, 420	1:27–2:10	liii	3:19	308, 373		
2:16	38, 307	1:27	liii, liii, 34, 58, 138, 176, 184, 190, 204	3:21, 21	732, 396		
3:2, 3	136			3:20	296, 297, 320, 402, 403		

3:21	396, 406	5:2	307	4:3	283		
3:22–4:1	412–14	5:5–8	332	4:6	258		
3:22	lvii, 366, 419, 420, 421	5:5–7	lvii	4:8	405		
3:24	41, 422	5:5	320	4:10	6		
3:25	lvii, 422	5:6–8	344, 432	4:11	251		
4:1	403, 423, 424	5:8	lvii, 272, 284, 435–36, 448–49, 450	4:12	6		
4:2–4	lii, lvii, 434, 452			4:13	251, 258		
4:2	453	5:10	101	4:14	233, 251		
4:3, 4	453, 454	5:12	251	4:16	251, 258		
4:3	liv, 34, 171, 176, 454	5:13	216	5:6	93		
4:5, 6	li	5:14	226, 236	5:8	152		
4:5	lii, 234, 339, 348	5:15	114, 303	5:10	115		
4:6	305	5:18, 19	308	5:16	6		
4:7–17	li	5:18	306, 324, 347	5:17	233, 250, 251, 258		
4:7–9	463	5:19, 20	180	5:18	242		
4:7, 8	xxxvlii, x, lii, lxxxii, 3, 462, 464, 465, 468	5:20	153	5:19	233, 251		
		5:21	328	5:25	115		
4:7	250	5:23	463	6:1, 2	360, 420		
4:10–17	li, 462	5:25	453	6:1	258		
4:10	171	5:28	463	6:2	6		
4:12	250, 447			6:3–5	258		
4:13	lxxxiv, 3, 5			6:4, 5	296		
4:15, 16	xciv, 66	*2 Thessalonians*	*lxxvi*	6:5	283		
4:16	176			6:11	296		
4:17	250, 254	1:2	6	6:15	32		
4:18	171, 462, 463	1:3	52, 54–55, 55, 261	6:16	199		
		1:7	60, 151	6:18	115, 304		
		1:10	60, 151	6:20	258		
1 Thessalonians	*xxxviii, xl,*	2:2	307				
		2:3–12	446				
1:1	6	2:7	31	*2 Timothy*			
1:2–3:13	xxxviii	2:8	451				
1:2–5	xxxviii	2:9	lxv	1:8	173, 234		
1:2	48, 55, 56	2:10	286	1:9, 10	170		
1:3, 4	48	2:11, 12	259	1:9	23, 104, 112		
1:3	54, 55	2:12	282	1:10	371, 467		
1:4	24, 27	2:13	23, 27, 52, 55, 281–82	1:13	55		
1:5	205, 451	2:15	447	1:16	454		
1:6–3:13	xxxviii	2:17	115, 304	2:2	251		
1:6	310	3:1, 2	453	2:9	234, 455		
1:8	38	3:2	85	2:10	192		
1:10	61, 256, 282	3:3	450	2:15	283		
2:1–12	160	3:6–12	304	2:18	283		
2:2	455	3:13	151, 191	2:24, 25	236		
2:3	259, 279	3:15	302	2:24	251		
2:7	379	3:16	463	2:25	281, 283		
2:11, 12	227	3:18	463	2:26	303		
2:12	lvii, 276			3:1–9	259		
2:13	24, 38, 48, 52			3:1	342		
2:14	310	*1 Timothy*		3:2–5	296		
2:18	lxv, 172, 303			3:7, 8	283		
3:8	443	1:3, 4	258	3:7	281		
3:9	52	1:9, 10	296	3:14	280		
3:10	216, 254	1:10	258	3:15	55		
3:12, 13	17, 24	1:13, 14	86–87	3:16	251, 407		
3:13	60, 151	1:13	100	4:2, 3	251		
4	272	1:14	55, 87	4:3	250		
4:1	226, 227, 276	1:15	55, 183	4:4	283		
4:3–8	272	1:17	50, 181, 199, 467	4:5	250		
4:3–7	321	2:4	281, 282	4:12	lxxxii, 465		
4:3	321	2:7	281, 282	4:18	199		
4:5	138	2:8–3:15	391				
4:6	322	2:8	301				
4:7	279, 322	2:10	115, 322	*Titus*			
4:8	306	2:11	365				
4:10	226	3:1, 2	233	1:1	281, 283		
4:11, 12	303	3:2, 3	296	1:2, 3	170		
4:11	298	3:2	250, 251	1:4	371		
4:13	lvii, 137	3:4, 5	402	1:5	172, 233, 251		
4:14	101, 282	3:4	365	1:6	6, 344		
4:16	245	3:5	233	1:7, 8	296		
4:17	101, 255	3:7	303	1:7	233, 301		
5:1–11	272	3:13	55	1:9	250, 251, 258		
5:1	32	3:15	283	1:10–16	259		
5:2–4	446	3:16	51, 170	1:14	283		
		4:1–3	364	2:1–10	360		

Index of Biblical and Other Ancient Sources

2:1	251, 258, 322	*James*		3:2	371		
2:5	365, 367	1:6	258	3:3	342		
2:7	115, 251, 258	1:12	466	3:17	259		
2:9, 10	420	1:18	272	3:18	199, 371		
2:9	365	1:19, 20	301, 308				
2:12	407	1:21	272, 284	*1 John*			
2:13	371	1:27	340				
2:14	115	2:1	467	1:5	327		
3:1	365	2:5	466	2:8	327		
3:2	236	3:1	251	2:13, 14	450		
3:3–7	86, 88, 91	3:17	296	2:22	282		
3:3–5	87, 100	4:7	303, 445	3:14	93		
3:3	87, 296	5:13	341	4:3	282		
3:4	87, 110	5:14	251	4:6	259		
3:5	87, 112, 236, 272, 287			4:11	309		
3:6	371	*1 Peter*	lxxxiv, 272	5:18, 19	450		
3:7	87	1:3–12	11				
3:8	115	1:3–9	38	*2 John*			
3:10	407	1:8	466				
3:12	465	1:12	185	*3 John*	50		
3:14	115, 329	1:13	448				
3:15	467	1:14	278	*Jude*	xlviii		
		1:20	23, 170				
Philemon		1:22	272	4	279		
1	lvii, 171, 173	2:1	272, 284, 296	11	259		
3	6	2:2	272	12, 13	258		
4, 5	lvi	2:4–9	340	12	329		
4	48, 49, 54, 55, 56	2:5	158	20	452		
5	47, 48, 54, 55	2:6–8	155	24, 25	215, 217		
6	48	2:9	42, 326	25	199		
8–10	226	2:10	86, 87, 100				
8	455	2:12	358	*Revelation*	lxxx		
9	lvii, 171, 173, 454	2:18–3:7	360				
10	171	2:18	385, 420	1:3	153		
11	86	2:25	86, 87, 250	1:6	199		
13	171	3:1	367	1:16	451		
18	303	3:2	385	2:12	451		
19	172	3:4	206	2:16	451		
23	171	3:5, 6	368	3	lxxxiv		
		3:7	181	3:1	93		
Hebrews		3:8	296	3:14–17	3		
1:3	20, 66	3:15, 16	358	3:21	xc, 107		
1:13	66	3:18	101	4:9	198		
2:5–8	66	3:19–22	186	5:9	345		
2:8	115	3:22	66	5:13, 14	199		
2:12	345	4:3	279, 296	7:1–8	39		
2:14	444	4:4	344	7:12	199		
4:12	451	4:7	453	9:2	277		
4:16	190	4:11	198, 199	9:4	39		
5:12	251	4:15	303	10:11	153		
5:13, 14	251	5:1–4	251	11:13	198		
5:14	256	5:1	251	14:3	345		
6:4	320, 319	5:2	251	14:7	198		
6:5	110	5:5	236, 251, 366	15:3	345		
8:1	32, 62	5:8, 9	449	16:5	288		
9:11	136	5:8	302	16:6	153		
9:24	136	5:9	445, 465	16:9	198		
10:19–22	190	5:10	254	16:10	277		
10:22	375	5:11	199	18:2	158		
10:24	115	5:12	175	18:20	153		
10:32	314, 320			18:24	153		
11:9	181	*2 Peter*	xlvii, lxxi	19:1–4	199		
11:23	406			19:7	198		
12:1	284	1:1	371	19:10	153		
12:5	407	1:5–7	296	19:13	879		
12:7	407	1:8	329	19:15	879		
12:8	407	1:11	371	20:4	107		
12:11	407	2:2	279	21:8	296		
12:22	151	2:3	279	21:14	154		
13:9	258	2:7	279	21:16	209		
13:20	250	2:10–22	259	22:6–10	153		
13:21	199, 254	2:18	259	22:15	296		
13:22	175	2:20	371	22:18, 19	153		

C. Old Testament Apocrypha and Pseudepigrapha

Apocalypse of Abraham

| 22 | 115 |
| 29:9 | 446 |

Apocalypse of Elijah

| 37:3, 4 | 107 |

Apocalypse of Moses

| 3 | 98 |

Ascension of Isaiah

7:9	96
7:10	157
9:18	107
10:29	96
11:23	96

Baruch

| 3:9–4:4 | 187 |

2 Baruch xxxix

4:2–6	157
21:12	21
40:30	32
48:23, 24	238
48:31	446
48:36	187
48:49	21
52:7	21
54:1–4	211
78–87	lxxi
78:2	6
81:4	30
85:14	238

3 Baruch

| 2:1, 2 | 129 |

1 Enoch

5:4–8	103
9:6	30
14:9	129
15:8–12	444
16:1–4	21
21:1–16	21
49:3	56
50:2	446
51:3	30
55:3–57:3	435
55:3	446
60:11, 12	63
60:11	210
61:10	63, 96, 186
63:8	446
69:3, 4	202
71:1	202
89:59, 60	21
90:21	96, 186
90:24	96, 186
90:29	157
91:16	21
92–105	lxxi
93:11–14	210, 211

96:2	446
99:4	446
99:13	103
103:2	30
104:10	30
106:5	202
108:8	466
108:12	107

2 Enoch

20–22	63
29:4, 5	96
67:3	199

1 Esdras

| 4:59 | 198 |

4 Ezra

4:37	32
5:9	187
5:22	176
6:5	39
7:14	21
7:83	21
9:26–10:59	363
13:1–13	435
13:18	21
14:5	30
14:40	176
14:47	176

Epistle of Jeremiah lxxi

Joseph and Asenath

8:9	23
8:10	326
15:13	326
61:4, 5	144

Jubilees

1:5	244
2:2	63
6:11	244
6:17	244
7:20	401
10:3	444
10:5	444
10:13	444
11:4, 5	444
12:20	444
15:1–24	244
22:6–9	53
23:16–25	446

Judith

7:28	276
8:32	217
14:3	442

Letter of Aristeas lvi, lix, lxxi

122	284
139	141
140	277

142	141
182	448
228	401
277	277

1 Maccabees lxxi

2:37	420
12:6–18	49
12:11	56

2 Maccabees lxxi

1:1–10	49
1:10–2:18	53
3:24	63
3:25	442
4:11	137
4:50	279
5:2	96, 186
7:37	238
8:17	137
10:28	444
14:18	444
15:9	444

3 Maccabees

| 2:17 | 279 |
| 2:26 | 279 |

4 Maccabees

1:18	29
9:22	467
9:23	310
13:9	310
17:12	467
18:24	199

Odes of Solomon

7:11	74
7:13	74
14:18, 19	326
15	58
15:2	279
17:7	74
19:5	74
26:7	74
35:6	74
36:1, 2	74
36:6	74
41:13	74

Prayer of Manasseh

| 15 | 199 |

Psalms of Solomon

4:7, 8	421
4:19	421
4:25	465, 466
6:6	465
16:1–4	332

Pseudo-Phocylides

| 8 | 402 |
| 22 | 304 |

Index of Biblical and Other Ancient Sources

63–64	301	4:1	420	5:10, 11	243, 435
153–74	303	4:6	321, 324	5:12, 13	157
153–54	306	5:1	321		
175–227	357	5:3	321	*Testament of Naphtali*	
184–85	400	6:1	321		
195–97	374			3:1	325
207–9	400	*Testament of Simeon*		8:10	361
207	406				
224	416	3:6	466	*Testament of Gad*	
		4:4	309		
Sibylline Oracles		4:5	421	2:1	421
		4:9	444	5:7	277, 278
3.11	238	5:3	321	6:2	277
3.220–35	277	5:5	435		
3.629	238	6:6	444	*Testament of Asher*	
Sirach		*Testament of Levi*		4:3	311
1:3	210, 212, 428	2:3	176	*Testament of Benjamin*	
1:22	301	2:7	129		
1.27	407	3	67	1:5	421
3:1–16	401	5:5	446	3:1	310
4:11	187	13:7	278	3:4	96
4:30	416	14:4	277, 327	4:1	310
5:10–14	305	14:5, 6	322	5:3	327
6:18, 19	187	15:1	279	10:3	300
7:15	303	18:1	176		
7:20, 21	416	18:2–4	332	*Tobit*	
7:23	401	18:7	176		
7:27, 28	401	18:12	444	1:4	217
14:18	444	19:1	327	4:3, 4	401, 403
14:20–15:8	187			6:18	370
15:1	208	*Testament of Judah*		8:5	217
15:5	454			8:15	217
15:7	208	11:2	340	11:14	217
17:31	444	12:3	340	13:4	217
18:1	185	13:6	340	13:10	217
18:4	212	14:1	289, 348	13:16	217
18:6	212	14:5	279	14:5	32, 217
18:15–19	305	16:1	340		
19:13–17	329	18:2	322	*Wisdom*	
21:25, 26	305	19:1	324		
23:1	407	20:1–3	289	1:7	73
23:3	278	23:1	279, 324	1:14	185
23:16–27	321	24:1	332	2:9	36
24:8–23	187			2:16	279
24:8	185	*Testament of Issachar*		2:23	467
24:28, 29	212			3:8	107
24:28	212	3:1–6	420	3:9	103
27:30	301	4:1–6:1	420	4:2	310
28:7, 8	278	7:2, 3	340	4:14, 15	103
30:1–13	401	7:2	321	5:5	36, 60
31:4	259	7:5	304	5:15, 16	107
33:31	416			5:17–20	45
39:9	217	*Testament of Zebulun*		5:18	448
				5:19	449
Testament of Isaac		5:1	309	6:18, 19	467
		6:1–8	304	6:22	212
4:14	305	7:2	309	7:22	188
4:17	305	8:1	309	9:3	288
4:40	306	9:5, 6	342	9:8	157, 310
		9:8	332	9:16	212
Testament of Job				10:21	454
		Testament of Dan		12–15	277
33:3–5	107			13:1	277, 278
		1:7, 8	302	13:8	278
Testament of the Twelve Patriarchs		2:1–5:1	301	13:9	278
		2:4	277	13:12	449
Testament of Reuben		3:6	302	14:12	324
		4:7–5:1	302	14:25, 26	297
1:6	321	5:2	300, 301, 302	14:26	279
2:1	321	5:4–6	446	15:9	310
3:3	321	5:4	342	18:10–19	277
3:8	277, 403				

D. Dead Sea Scrolls

CD

2:17, 18	278
3:5	278
3:11	278
3:15	26
4:17, 18	322
5:11, 12	307
5:11	306
6:14, 15	320
7:2, 3	302
7:2	306, 329
8:8	278
9:6	302
9:8	329
10:17, 18	305
13:7–11	251
20:3–5	331
20:4	329
20:25, 26	332

1QH

	xlvi, lxvi, 109
1:9–11	185
1:26, 27	288
1:30	288
2:13	176
3:7	30
3:19–22	107
3:19–21	332
3:19	92
3:21–23	151
3:22	36
3:24–39	435, 438
4:5, 6	332
4:23	332
4:30–32	114
5:20	10
6:7	151
6:10–14	151
6:28–35	435, 438
7:17	205
7:19	205
7:27	30
9:31	332
10:4	30
10:14	10
11:7, 8	60
11:9	30
11:10–14	92
11:10–12	107, 375
11:16	30
11:27	10
11:29	10
11:32	10
11:33	10
12:13	176
12:35	415
14:14	139
15:13–22	25
16–18	50
16:8	10, 185

1QM

	435, 438
1:1–16	327
1:10–13	446
3:6	327
3:8	30
3:9	327
10:5	205
10:8	185
12:1, 2	151
13	444
13:16	327
14:14	32
14:17	327
15:6–8	441
16:9	30
16:11–16	444
17:5–9	444

1QS

1:4, 5	326
1:5	328
1:6	278
1:7–2:19	244
1:9, 10	327
2:3	58
2:14	278
2:24	236
2:26	278
3–4	272
3:3	277, 278
3:4	375
3:8–10	375
3:8	236
3:13–4:26	97, 297
3:13	327
3:19–25	341
3:19–21	327
3:20, 21	444
3:21–23	30
3:24, 25	327
4:2–26	288
4:2	236, 288, 289
4:3–5	56
4:9–11	279
4:9, 10	322
4:18, 19	188
4:18	30, 32
4:24	341
4:26	36
5:3	236
5:4	278
5:6	155
5:9	328
5:10, 11	320
5:10	288
5:19	277
5:24	329
5:25	236
5:26–6:1	302
5:26	329
6:16	139
6:22	139
7:9	305
7:14–18	233
8:2	328
8:4–10	156
8:4, 5	155
8:5, 6	151
8:18	139
9:5, 6	156
9:15, 16	139
9:16	330
9:18	176
10:21–23	323, 324
11:1	236
11:3–6	58
11:7, 8	60, 151, 157
11:7	36
11:15	10
11:34	30

1QpHab

7:2	32
7:4	30
7:8	30
7:13	30, 32

4QFlor

1:6, 7	156

E. Philo

De Abr.

99–102	362
107	259
208	288
243	444

De Conf. Ling.

31	284
78	151

De Congress.

97	205, 572

De Decal.

84	259
119, 120	399
121	404
165–67	357, 399

De Ebr.

11	344
17	401
95	344
125–26	344
146–48	344
154	341
223	308

De Fug.

63	280

De Gig.

6, 7	96, 186
47	77

Hypothetica

7.1–14	357
7.2	400, 401
7.3	358, 367
7.7	400
7.14	397, 401

Index of Biblical and Other Ancient Sources

De Jos.		*Quaest. in Gen.*		1.210	70
95	257	1.25	383	1.272	75
		4.29	249	1.304	288
Leg. ad Gaium				2.45	186
31	401	*Quaest. in Exod.*		2.66–68	416
		2.40, 43	243	2.67, 68	361
Leg. Alleg.		2.117	69	2.89–91	416
1.4	77			2.123	416
1.163	328	*Quis Div. Her.*		2.165	203
2.1	238	164	383	2.180	574
2.13	383			2.224–225	403
2.19–50	383	*Quod Det. Pot. Ins.*		2.225, 226	399
3.4	73	23	205	2.227	399
				2.228	401
De Migr. Abr.		*Quod Deus*		2.232	400–401
220	70	54	407	2.235–236	403
				2.236	401
De Mut. Nom.		*Quod. Omn. Prob. Lib.*		2.239	407
40	401	41	75	2.261	404
		79	416	2.262	405
De Op. Mundi				3.51	321
80	330	*De Sacrif.*		3.108–19	400
82	70	20–45	297	3.131	70
		57	288	3.137–143	416
De Plant.		67–68	77	3.189	203
7	70	67	73	4.159	238
14	96, 186	68	311	4.5	279
42	205			4.72–73	311
126	324	*De Sacrif. Abel. et Cain.*		4.73	311
131	324	32	258	4.96	407
				4.187–88	311
De Post. Caini		*De Somn.*			
14	243	1.128	69	*De Virt.*	
30	77	1.186–88	243	7.35	238
181	357, 401	1.200	362	50	288
				168	311
De Praem. et Poen.		*De Spec. Leg.*		179	326
65	75	1.23	324		
109	75	1.25	324	*De Vita Cont.*	
114	125	1.52	238	70	416
125	125, 262	1.66	96, 186		
		1.96	70	*De Vit. Mos.*	
		1.203	190	1.158	243
				1.305	279
				2.127	70
				2.133, 134	70
				2.177	259
				2.186	279
				2.198	401
				2.238	73, 77

F. Josephus

Antiquities		8.318	279	2.190–210	357
2.4.4	190	8.343	238	2.193	230
4.6.10	287	9.4.3	277	2.199	358
4.6.143	288	9.58	403	2.201	367
4.151	279	10.9	449	2.202	400
4.264	400–401	10.104	276	2.204	401
5.1.3	190	12.3.1	137	2.206	400–401, 403
5.97	238	12.12–118	lv	2.216	358
5.195	110	12.323	341		
6.23	110	15.11	141		
6.165	403	20.112	279		
7.305	341			*Jewish War*	
8.50–54	lxxi, 53	*Contra Apionem*		4.494	235
8.53	11	1.12	401	5.5	141
8.208	403	2.18	401	6.1.8	448
8.252	279				

G. Rabbinic Writings

Mishnah

Aboth

1:1, 2	141
3:18	141

Eduyyot

5.2	92

Tosephta Berakoth

7.13	39

Babylonian Talmud

Berakoth

18a	92
29b	301
34b	147

Megilla

31a	244

Qiddusin

29a	303

Sanhedrin

98b	203

Shabbat

88b	243

Yebamoth

62b	374

Yoma

54b	151

Palestinian Talmud

Berakoth

2.4	92

Qiddusin

1.7	406

Midrash

Genesis Rabbah

1.5	24
4.2	157
39.7	92
39:14	144
68.12	157

Exodus Rabbah

40.3	71

Numbers Rabbah

8.4	139, 147
11.7	147
12.4	157

Deuteronomy Rabbah

6	404

Midrash on Psalms

74.1	24
93.3	

Midrash Qoheleth

9.5	92

Midrash Samuel

28.6	147

Midrash Tehillim

Ps 24:1	243
Ps 106:2	243

Mekilta Exodus

18:5	139
20:25	147

Aboth R. Nathan

2.2a	243

Pesikta Rabbati

35	147

Pirke Aboth

2.9	114

Pirke R. Eliezer

32:35	157

Shemoneh Esreh 25, 50

Yalkut Genesis

120	157

Targums

Targum of Job

5:7	96

Targum on the Psalms

68:18	242–43

H. Apostolic Fathers

Barnabas lxxi

3:6	26
4:3	26
4:8	26
4:9	322
4:10	277
5:9	183
9:6	39
18–20	272
19:5–7	360
19:5	385
19:7	420
20:1	279
20:2	277
21:4	308

1 Clement

5:2	lxxi
7:2	272
12:5	316
19:2–20:12	185

21	402
21:6–9	360
21:8	408
32:3	112
33:2–6	185
35:5	279
36:2	58
42:1–5	lxxi
44:1, 2	lxxi
59:3	58, 128
60:1	185
61:3	217

2 Clement

4	272
6:4	286
7:6	39
8:6	39
13:1	421
14	371
14:1	24

Didache

1–5	543
3:2	301
3:5	300, 303
4:9–11	360
4:9	385
4:11	385, 421
5:1	279
5:2	277
9:2, 3	347
10:1–4	347
10:3	184
11–13	153, 249
13:2	251
15:1, 2	251, 499
15:1	251

Diognetus

5:9	151
10:4–6	310

Index of Biblical and Other Ancient Sources

Hermas, Shepherd of Mandates		2.3.1	402	Polycarp	
5.1	302	2.4.1	24	4:1–6:1	360
5.2.4	309	3.2.5	209	5:1	lxxii
6.1	272	3.5.1	251		
6.2	279	3.7.2	279	Romans	
6.5	279	4.3	110	2:1	421
8.5	279, 286	4.5	110	9:1	251
9.4	277				
10.1.1	308	Ignatius		Smyrneans	
10.2.4	306			inscr.	24
10.2.5	308	Ephesians		1:1	lxxii
10.3.2	306	1:1	310	9:1	303
11	249	4:2	237		
11.8	277	5:1	237	Trallians	
11.12	286	10:3	303	1:2	617
12.6	277	14:1	237	8:2	277
				13:1	183
Similitudes		Magnesians			
4.8	110	5	272	Martyrdom of Polycarp	
6.2.1	286	7:1	452	2:3	341
6.3.3	286			3:1	303
6.4.4	286	Philadelphians		15:1	218
8.6.3	39			16:2	251
9.16.3–6	40, 93	2:1	251	20:2	215
9.17.4	40	2:2	237	21	217
		3:2	237		
Visions		5:2	237	Polycarp's Letter to the Philippians	
1.1.6	24	7:1	259		
1.3.1, 2	402	8:1	237	4:2–6:3	360
2.2.2	279	9:1	237	12:1	302
2.2.4	308				

I. Other Early Christian and Gnostic Writings

Acts of Andrew		Epist.		Corpus Hermeticum	
14	208	112.14	208	1:2, 3	70
		120.26	208	1:15	205
Acts of Paul and Thecla	364	120.36	208	4:2	70
				4:11	58
Acts of Peter		De Doctr. Christ.		5:9	203, 205
9	208	2.41	208	6:4	74, 75
				7:1	58
Acts of Philip		Basil		9:5	205
140	208			10:12	70
		Hex.		10:25	210
Acts of Thomas		9.1	254	11:6–8	203
110.43–48	332			11:20	210
131	40	Chrysostom		12:15	74, 203
				13:7	205
Ammonius		Hom. 2.1 in Tit.	254	13:8, 9	567
				13:14	205
Ac.		Clement		14:4	203
18.25	508			16:3	74
		Protr.			
Aphraates		9.84.2	319	Didascalia Apostolorum	
				21	319
Hom.		Strom.			
1:6, 7	159	3.1.1	383	Epiphanius	
Athanasius		3.5.1	383	Haer.	
Orat. contra Arian.		4.26	254	42.12.3	318
1.23, 24	203				
		3 Corinthians	lxxi	Epistle to the Laodiceans	xxi
Augustine					
				Eusebius	

Index of Biblical and Other Ancient Sources

Historia Ecclesiastica

3.37.2, 3	250
5.10.2	250

Praeparatio Evangelica

9.34	27, 53
14.18.26	285

Exegesis on the Soul

132–34	371
	162

Ginza

99:15–32	444
104:5, 6	444
105:24–33	444

Gospel of Philip

64–72	562
67	282
70	282
70:10–17	93
71	282
76	362
101	285

Gospel of Thomas

22	282
37	285

Gospel of Truth

16	74
22, 38–23, 1	110
27, 5–7	110
34–36	74
41	74

Hippolytus

Elench.

5:7	154
5:35	154

Ref.

1.21.5	73
5.7.35, 36	205
6.29–34	74
6.35.6	93

Irenaeus

Adversus haereses

1.1–5	74
1.6.3, 4	383
1.11.1	74
1.11.3	74
1.11.5	74
1.21.4, 5	205
3.11.1	74
3.18.1	33
5.2.3	351
5.17.14	208
5.29.2	33

Justin

Apology

1:2	421
61:12, 13	319
61:12	58
65:1	58, 319
67:5	319

Dialogue with Trypho

39.2	58
122.1, 2	58
122.6	58

Origen

De Principiis

2.8.4–8	33
3.6.6	33

Pistis Sophia

130	210
133	210
148	210

Pseudo-Cyprian

De Aleat.

3	306

Tertullian

Adv. Marc.

3:7	145
4.5	lxxii
5.11	4
5.17	4

Dejejun.

17	383

Testament of Solomon

8:2	444
18:2	444
22:7–23:3	154

Theophilus

Ad Autolycum

1.6	188
2.16	188

Treatise on Resurrection

44	74
45	107
46	74
49	74

Trimorphic Protennoia 378

Tripartite Tractate

70	74
75	74
77	74
78	74
80	74
86	74
90	74
93–95	74
97	74
122–25	74
136	74

J. Other Ancient and Classical Texts

Aeschines

3.150	137

Apuleius

Metamorph.

11:24	284

Aristides

Or.

45.21, 24	73

Aristophanes

Ranae

340–42	657

Aristotle

De Caelo

1.11	263

Eth. Eud.

3.7.1234a. 4–23	323

Eth. Nic.

4.8.1128a.14–15	323
4.8.1128a.23–24	323
5.1134b	416
6.6.7	29
8.1161ab	416

Fragments

123	33

De Gen. et Corr.

1.6, 8	263

Metaph.

4.4	263
10.3	263

Phys. Ausc.

4.6	263

Pol.

1.1, 2	70
1.1253b–1254a	415
1.1253b	357
1.1255b	369
1.1259a	357
3.6.1278b–1279a	137

Rhet.

2.12.1389b.10–12	232
3.6.1–11	cliv
3.14.11	42
3.19	432

Arrian

De Ex. Alex.

2.83	433

Cebes Tablet

23–24	286

Chrysippus

Frag.

395	309

Cicero

De Domo

29.77	399

Nat. Deor.

1.35	70
3.9	70

De Off.

1.25	70
1.58	401
1.85	70

Phil.

8.5, 16	70

Tusc.

1.64	210
5.69	210

Index of Biblical and Other Ancient Sources

Epistles of Crates		Gaius		Pliny	
6	272	Inst.		Ep.	
7	272	1.55	399	8.13	310
18	272	Herodianus		8.39	441
19	272	3.6	433	Plutarch	
21	272	Herodotus		Alcibiades	
Curtius Rufus		1.74.3	262	35.6	76
Historiae Alexandri Magni		7.91	449	Cato Maior	
Macedonensis		Homer		20	400
10.9.1	67	Il.		Cor.	
Demosthenes		5.452	449	19.4	284
8.46	284	Isaeus		Praec. Ger. Reip.	
Dexippus		Orat.		6.7.803B	433
Hist.		11.48	76	Polybius	
32	37	Isocrates		1.35.5	279
Gal.		Antid.		3.63	433
16,822	37	296	323	6.23.2	435, 449
Dio Cassius		Areop.		9.40.4	279
38.36–46	433	49	323	Posidippus	
50.16–30	433	Livy		27.8	37
Dio Chrysostom		2.32.8–12	70	Pseudo-Callisthenes	
Or.		21.8	450	Hist. Alex. Magni	
7.112	303	26.16.19	70	1.22.4	368
7.124–25	303	Lucian		Pseudo-Diogenes	
32.11	454	Bis Accus.		Ep.	
67.6, 8	557	16	422	10.1	437
Diodorus Siculus		Dem.		Pseudo-Isocrates	
18.15	433	3	454	Demonicus	
20.84.3	435	51	301	11.36	310
20.96	430	Dial. Mort.		Pseudo-Plutarch	
Diogenes Laertius		10.8, 9	284	De Lib. Educ.	
4.46	308	M. Ant. (Marcus Aurelius)		12	399
7.108	401	Meditations		Quintilian	
7.114	308	2.12.1	92	3.6.47	cliv
7.120	401	4.23	240	3.8.7	xliv, 42
7.138	70	12.33.2	92	4.1.5	xliv, 42
7.142, 143	70	Musonius Rufus		4.2.1	xliv
7.147	70	Or.		4.3.1	xliv, 171
9.66	568	3	359	4.3.9	xliv
Dionysius of Halicarnassus		12	359	4.3.14	171
Rom. Ant.		13A	358	5.10.20	587
2.24.3–2.27.4	358	Orphic Fragments		6.1	33
2.26.1–4	401	168	69	6.1.1	432
2.26.4	378	Orphic Hymns		Seneca	
2.27.1	399	50.9	331	De Benefic.	
Eccelus		Philodemus		4.8.2	
On Justice		Concerning Household		De Clem.	
78.10–11	422	Management		1.5.1	70
Epictetus		30.18–31.2	415	De Const. Sap.	
Diss.		Plato		3.4–5	437
1.3.3	92	Apology		Ep.	
1.9.10	235	35D	288	1.1	343
1.16.16–17	303	Crito		6.5, 6	309
1.20.7	328	54B	288	11.9, 10	309
2.17.6	403	Gorgias		Sextus	
2.17.31	401	493E	76	Sentences	
2.19.27	92	507B	288	201	288
2.19.28	258	Leges		216	288
2.23.6, 8	328	3.690A–D	357	399	288
3.7.26	401	6.771E–7.824C	357	Stobaeus	
3.20.10	251	Prot.		Anth.	
3.22.19	454	337E	262	3.1.80	401
3.24,25		Resp.		4.25.53	401
3.24.56	35	4.425B	401	4.26.7	401
3.26.6–7	303	5.464B	70	4.26.13	401
4.1	418	9.589A	205	Tacitus	
4.5.16	328	10.619C	137	Annals	
4.6.13	328	Theatetus		1.12, 13	69
4.7.40	328	172B	288	Dial.	
4.9.16	251	176AB	34	29.1–3	400
Euripides		176B	288	Hist.	
Heracl.		Tim.		5.1–13	141
159	444	28C	203	5.5	397

494   Index of Biblical and Other Ancient Sources

Thucydides		*Xenophon*		*Mem.*	
1.127.3	137	*Anab.*		4.4.19, 20	401
2.29.6	262	*Cyr.*		*Oec.*	
2.61	278–279	7.5.45	149	13.9–12	422
Vit. Aesopi		*Hellenica*			
1.c.9	379	5.4.56	76		

K. Papyri and Inscriptions

PGM		POxy.		Preisigke	
4.960–85		494.6	422	1.460	379